W9-CTY-820

GROLIER

NEW WEBSTER'S DICTIONARY

GROLIER
NEW WEBSTER'S DICTIONARY

Grolier Incorporated
Danbury, Connecticut

ISBN 0-7172-5321-X

Printed and manufactured in the United States of America.

10 9 8 7 6 5 4 3

Contents

Guide to the Use of the Dictionary

1. ENTRY WORDS AND PHRASES

A. The Main Entry

Main entry words and phrases are set in boldface type and indented from the lefthand margin. Main entry words are syllabicated, with boldface center· periods between the syllables: **bal·le·ri·na, Bot·swa·na.** Main entry words are not syllabicated, nor are they pronounced, if the form has already been so treated: **barrow** in the sense of "grave mound" follows **bar·row** "wheeled handcart".

Main entry phrases are not syllabicated if each word in the phrase is syllabicated in its own main entry position: **barrel organ.** If any word of a main entry phrase is not entered in its normal alphabetical place, it is syllabicated at the phrasal main entry: **bar mitz·vah.**

Certain main entry phrases are inverted so that the most logical reference word may be consulted at its alphabetical place. These entries are mainly surnames, geographical names, or the names of historical events or periods. Surnames are syllabicated and pronounced, with given names following in Roman (ordinary text type): **An·der·son** (ændərs'n), Carl David. The key or reference word of a geographical or historical main entry phrase is syllabicated, followed by the beginning of the phrase in main-entry boldface: **A·zov, Sea of; Bau·tzen, Battle of.** Such surnames or reference words are not syllabicated and pronounced, however, if they have already been so treated previously: **Buenos Aires, Lake** occurs after the syllabicated and pronounced entry for the city of Buenos Aires.

B. Variant Forms

Spelling variants are given, separated by commas, in the main entries: **adze, adz; As·wan Dam, As·suan Dam.** The first form is regarded as the more common. If the variation represents a difference between American and British spelling conventions, this is noted, with the American form listed first: **balloon tire,** *Br.* **balloon tyre.**

Spelling variants are treated in the same manner when they occur within the definition block itself as a variant of a subentry: **ac·knowl·edg·ment, ac·knowl·edge·ment.**

For other variants reflecting British usage, see *Usage Labels* below.

C. Inflected Forms

The spellings of plurals (when these are not simply formed by the addition of -s or -es), of participial and past tense forms of verbs, and of comparative and superlative forms of adjectives and adverbs are given in a boldface slightly smaller than the main-entry face and identified by abbreviated italicized labels: **bus·by** . . . *pl.* **bus·bies; brakes·man** . . . *pl.* **brakes·men; ar·tic·u·late** . . . *pres. part.* **ar·tic·u·lat·ing** *past* and *past part.* **ar·tic·u·lat·ed; brave** . . . *comp.* **brav·er** *superl.* **brav·est.**

D. Derivatives and Compounds

When a word is formed by the affixing of a derivational suffix or a compounding word to a base form, the derivative or compound may be entered, and when necessary defined, within the definition block for the base form, rather than treated separately as a main entry: **blame·a·ble, blame·less,** and **blame·wor·thy** appear as derivatives within the definition block of the verb **blame; bounc·er** is entered within the definition block of **bounce; af·fix·a·tion** and **af·fix·ture** are entered in the main entry for the verb **af·fix.**

Such subentries are made when the editor judges that the derivative term within the definition block will be both readily and logically located by the reader. If the derivative is of great currency or is otherwise regarded as sufficiently prominent for separate main entry status, it appears in its own alphabetical place: **bot·a·nist** is a main entry and not a subentry under **bot·a·ny.** Occasionally a less common derivative is entered as a sort of variant in the definition block of a more common form: **brach·y·ceph·a·lous** is entered under main entry **brach·y·ceph·al·ic.**

This dictionary does not attempt to enter all possible derivatives. For instance the regular agent nouns in -er and the very numerous nouns formed with -ment are not entered unless the derivative differs in meaning from what is predictable from the use of the suffix. "Bouncer" above is a case where the sense is not predictable from the meaning of "bounce" plus -er.

Pronunciations are given for derivatives and compounds if these are not readily inferrable from the main entry. Even if the pronunciation is not shown, derivatives and compounds are syllabicated and stresses are marked: under **bu·reauc·ra·cy,** the derivative **bu·reau·crat** is pronounced because two of the vowels have altered sounds, but the additional derivatives **bu·reau·crát·ic** and **bu·reau·crát·i·cal·ly** are marked for primary stress only.

E. Run-in Phrasal Entries

The English language is rich in set phrases, especially in idiomatic phrases whose meaning cannot readily be inferred from the meanings of the separate words, and in phrases consisting of verbs plus adverbs or particles, which are used and understood as if they were linguistic units rather than combinations of units. When a word, especially a verb, enters into many of these phrases, they are "run in" under the main entry for the key word. Under **break,** for instance, the dictionary defines **to break a record, to break away, to break down, to break in,** and ten other such phrases, showing variants where they exist: **to break loose** (or **free**). In a related sort of run-in phrasal entry, **the blind** is entered and defined under the main entry **blind.**

2. PRONUNCIATION

The respelling system of this dictionary is based upon the International Phonetic Alphabet, a scientific notation devised by phoneticians for recording every possible speech sound. It therefore will require, for most persons, a little effort of memory to retain and use the symbols. This system will repay such effort, since it is superior in precision and accuracy over any other system based on "natural" spelling, where in English especially one letter or group of letters may have many pronunciations. The complete respelling system and pronunciation guide will be found inside the front and rear covers and opposite the first page of the dictionary. For the user's convenience, a brief version of the respelling system is printed at the bottom of each page.

This dictionary does not attempt the enormous and probably impossible task of transcribing the pronunciation variants of all the American (and British) dialects, but it does show variant pronunciations that occur within the "General American" (something like educated Northern or North Midwestern) patterns taken here as the standard. For example, **bear** is given only the pronunciation including -r, which does not represent the "-r-less" speech of Southern and Northeastern Americans, whereas words like **a·de·nine** and **a·dieu** show pronunciations that might be heard among educated speakers of the adopted standard. The variant given first is not meant to be "preferred to" or "more correct than" those given second or third.

When the pronunciation of a word changes to indicate a change in part of speech, this is indicated by showing the altered pronunciation at the beginning of the appropriate definition:**ab·stract** (æbstrækt) for the adjective and noun senses, and (æbstrǽkt) for one verb sense and (æbstrǽkt) for another as the situation requires; differing pronunciations are similarly recorded for the verb, adjective, and noun senses of **ag·gre·gate.**

Foreign words, which are especially frequent among the encyclopedic entries, are not always shown as they would be pronounced in the source language, but rather as they would be spoken and recognized by educated American speakers. In practice this means that when a word or name is well "naturalized" in English, it is respelled with a normal English sound (see **Ab·bas**), but when the word still feels foreign, or is new to most American ears, it is given the proper foreign-language pronunciation (see **A·bruz·zi e Mo·li·se**). In the intermediate case, the word or name is often given both an English and a foreign-language pronunciation (see **Ar·a·gon**).

3. DEFINITIONS

The generic-word definitions of this dictionary aim above all to be brief and to be clear. They are designed to be substitutable for the word defined. The encyclopedic "definitions," or descriptions, interspersed with the generic ones aim to give the appropriate information briefly and clearly. The dictionary conforms to the best practices of those dictionaries—more common in American lexicography than in European—that do not puristically rule factual information out of lexicography, but treat word-information and thing-information as equally valid and equally deserving of space in a useful reference work.

The initial words of definitions are not capitalized. If the definition requires more than one sentence, the first word of the subsequent sentence is capitalized in the customary way.

A. The Definition Block

The definitions are organized in three kinds for ready and easy consultation. First, when a word or phrase has one or more senses and only one part of speech, it is written as a single block with the senses introduced by a single italicized part-of-speech label (see the list of abbreviations for these), and the various senses are then separated by double bars (‖). See, for example, the entry at **ba·cil·lus.**

Second, when the term has several definitions in several parts of speech, all senses in one part of speech are introduced by a boldface numeral, and then separated again from one another by double bars. See the entry at **bal·loon.**

Third, when the word or phrase is defined in several parts of speech and many senses, but one part of speech is not dominant over another, or is not clearly the source of another, the definition is divided among two or more main entries and definition blocks. See, for example, the entries at **bal·ance.**

These slightly varying styles of definition block contribute not only to simplicity of use but to a grasp of the particular semantics of the term.

Within the definition block, senses are ordered logically by frequency of use and by apparent semantic derivation. For example, under **busi·ness**, the first sense is the basic occupational one, and the more specialized or transferred senses follow; under **butch·er,** the noun is defined before the verb, and so on.

B. Examples

The examples in this dictionary are brief and precise, with the aim not merely of showing the term in a possible or random context but also in one where the sense distinction becomes sharper. For instance, the examples under **burn** set the word or phrase in precise contexts where the particular sense is both illustrated and required: *to burn a hole, the pepper burned her throat, the fire is burning brightly, to burn with shame, to burn into one's memory, her burst of energy soon burned out.*

Examples are printed in italics, as here, and their initial words are not capitalized.

C. Cross-references

Cross-references are printed in small capital letters and are preceded by an asterisk or by an abbreviated label in Roman (ordinary text) type.

They are used most commonly to refer the reader to a related word or phrase that supplements or complements the definition at hand: under **ac·count·ant** cross-reference is made to *CERTIFIED PUBLIC ACCOUNTANT and to *CHARTERED ACCOUNTANT; under **ac·ti·nide series** cross-reference is made to *PERIODIC TABLE; under **accrued dividend** the cross-reference is cf. CUMULATED DIVIDEND: under **ac·i·do·sis** it is opp. ALKALOSIS. Such cross-references enrich the semantic field of the term being defined.

Cross-references are also used as a form of quick definition that refers the user from one main entry to another that is synonymous and is judged to be the more current and "normal" term: the main entry **action painting** is defined by the cross-reference *ABSTRACT EXPRESSIONISM.

4. RESTRICTIVE LABELS

Restrictive labels are of several sorts, and all aim to narrow, specify, modify, or otherwise restrict the term and distinguish it from or within current educated standard American English. Labels are printed in italics within parentheses. All labels are simple and self-explanatory, though the user may need to consult the table of abbreviations from time to time.

A. Field Labels

Field labels indicate, often with an abbreviation, the occupational, technical, or other specialized use of the term at hand: one sense under **ac·tion** is labeled *(horol.)*; one sense under **ag·ate** is labeled *(games)*; one sense under **a·pron** is labeled *(theater)*.

B. Usage Labels

Usage labels indicate the relation of the word or phrase to the dictionary's target language, current educated standard American English. Such labels most often either show a regional or geographical peculiarity of the word or phrase, or they indicate how it differs from strict and accurate standard speech: under **a·gree** two verb senses are labeled (Br.), British use; under **al·so-ran** one sense is labeled *(loosely)*; under **an·te** one sense is labeled *(pop.)*; at **belle** the label *(old fash.)* is used, and so on.

5. ETYMOLOGIES

Etymological derivations are shown at the end of the definition block and within square brackets. The names of source languages or language families are usually abbreviated and are printed in Roman type.

When the word or phrase has simply been borrowed from the source language without change of form or meaning, the etymology shows only the language of origin: under **ab·do·men** the etymology is [L.].

When the English word or phrase differs in form but not in meaning from the source term, only the language of origin and the source form are shown: under **ace** the etymology is [O.F. *as*].

When the word or phrase is an English translation or version of the foreign source, the etymology shows the language of origin, and then the English gloss after the equal sign: under **aard·wolf** the etymology is [Du.=earth wolf].

In the most common case, the language of origin and the cognate form are shown, with the form in italics and the meaning of the form is shown in Roman, following a comma: under **ac·count** the etymology is [O.F. *aconter*, to count].

When the source word appears in a form that does not closely resemble the English word, as often happens in the case of derivatives from Greek or Latin, the basic source (usually an infinitive or a noun in the nominative case) will be supplemented with the immediate source (often a noun in the accusative case): under **a·tro·cious** the etymology is [fr. L. *atrox (atrocis)*, cruel].

When the source term itself is derived from another language, this is shown by the abbreviation "fr.": under **ap·sis** the etymology is [L.=arch fr. Gk]; under **bail·iff** the etymology is [M.E. *baillif, custodian* fr. O.F.].

When the actual source of the word or phrase is not entirely certain, a range of related possible source words may be given: under **ba·bel** the etymology is [Heb. *bábel,* Assyrian-Babylonian *Báb-ilu,* Babylon (Gate of God)].

When the elements of a compound word or a phrase, or the base of a derivative, are entered elsewhere in the dictionary, and the etymologies are given at those main entries, the etymology is in effect a cross-reference printed in small capitals directing the user to look in those places for a full etymology: under **ac·et·al·de·hyde** the etymology is [ACETYL + ALDEHYDE].

ROBERT L. CHAPMAN
Professor Emeritus, Drew University

Dictionary Usage Guide

Guide words showing the alphabetical range of entries on the page

abnegate

Syllabicated main entry See Part 1A.

Usage labels See Part 4B.

Derivative forms See Part 1D.

Encyclopedic entry See Part 3.

Plural form See Part 1C.

Pronounced derivative See Part 1D.

Multiple definitions in single part of speech See Part 3A.

ab·ne·gate (ǽbnigeit) *pres. part.* **ab·ne·gat·ing** *past* and *past part.* **ab·ne·gat·ed** *v.t.* to renounce, give up (a right etc.) [fr. L. *abnegare* *(abnegatus)*, to deny]

ab·ne·ga·tion (æbnigéiʃən) *n.* renunciation, denial [fr. L. *abnegatio (abnegationis)*]

ab·nor·mal (æbnɔ́rməl) *adj.* different from the norm or average, unusual ‖ pertaining to that which is not normal, *abnormal psychology* **ab·nor·mal·i·ty** (æbnɔrmǽliti:) *pl.* **ab·nor·mal·i·ties** *n.* [fr. F. *anormal* and L. *abnormis*]

ABO a classification of blood groups (A, B, AB or O) with regard to their use in transfusion

a·board (əbɔ́rd, əbóurd) 1. *adj.* and *adv.* on or into a ship, plane, train etc. 2. *prep.* on board, *aboard the last ship*

a·bode (əbóud) *n.* *(old-fash., rhet.)* the place someone lives in *(old-fash., rhet.)* residence, *he took up his abode at the east gate of the city* [fr. ABIDE]

abode alt. *past* and *past part.* of ABIDE

ab·ohm (æbóum) *n.* the cgs electromagnetic unit of resistance equal to 10^{-9} ohm

a·bol·ish (əbɔ́liʃ) *v.t.* to do away with completely, put an end to (laws, customs, taxes, privileges etc.) [F. *abolir (aboliss-)*]

ab·o·li·tion (æbəlíʃən) *n.* the act of abolishing ‖ *(esp. hist.)* the movement against slavery **ab·o·li·tion·ism, ab·o·li·tion·ist** *ns* [F. or fr. L. *abolitio (abolitionis)*] —The movement to abolish the international slave trade and the institution of chattel slavery was largely religious. It centered in Great Britain, the U.S.A. and western Europe, between c. 1783 and 1888. Following the pioneer work of Granville Sharp, the struggle was led by the Quakers, who had outlawed slavery in Pennsylvania as early as 1675. Under the leadership of William Wilberforce they obtained, almost single!handedly, the abolition of the slave trade in the British Empire and the U.S.A. by acts of Parliament and Congress in 1808. In England the struggle then became one for emancipation, while in the U.S.A. the act of Congress was blatantly defied. The U.S. movement, led chiefly by William Llyod Garrison, Theodore Dwight Weld, and Frederick Douglass, was obstructed by the U.S. Constitution's toleration of slavery and by the South's economic defense of it. Only after the Civil War could the 13th amendment outlawing slavery be enacted. In 1862 the U.S.A. adhered to an international agreement reached in 1842 affording the reciprocal right of search, which thereafter put an end to the slave trade

ab·o·ma·sum (æbəméisəm) *pl.* **ab·o·ma·sa** (æbəméisə) *n.* the fourth chamber of the stomach of a ruminant [Mod. L. fr. *ab*, from + *omasum*, bullock's tripe]

A-bomb (éibɒm) *n.* atomic bomb

a·bom·i·na·ble (əbɔ́minəb'l) *adj.* causing intense disgust, *an abominable crime* [F.]

abominable snowman a bearlike creature said to inhabit the high Himalayas

a·bom·i·na·bly (əbɔ́minəbli:) *adv.* in an abominable way

a·bom·i·nate (əbɔ́mineit) *pres. part.* **a·bom·i·nat·ing** *past* and *past part.* **a·bom·i·nat·ed** *v.t.* *(rhet.)* to detest [fr. L. *abominari (abominatus)*]

a·bom·i·na·tion (əbɒminéiʃən) *n.* disgust ‖ a loathsome act or thing [F.]

ab·o·rig·i·nal (æbəridʒinəl) 1. *adj.* existing from the earliest times ‖ pertaining to aborigines 2. *n.* an aborigine **ab·o·rig·i·nal·i·ty** (æbəridʒinælíti:) *n.* [fr. L. *ab origine*, from the beginning]

ab·o·rig·i·ne (æbəridʒíni:) *n.* a native inhabitant of a country, esp. before colonization. *an Australian aborigine* ‖ *(pl.)* the native plants and animals of a region [fr. L. *aborigines* pl. n., inhabitants from the beginning]

a·bort (əbɔ́rt) *v.i.* *(med.)* to give birth to a fetus before it is viable ‖ *(biol.)* to become arrested in development ‖ to come to nothing, *their plans aborted* ‖ *(space, of a missile)* to stop before completion of the scheduled flight ‖ *v.t.* *(space)* to bring (a missile flight) to an end before completion of schedule [fr. L. *aboriri (abortus)*, to die, to abort]

a·bor·ti·fa·cient (əbɔrtiféiʃənt) 1. *n.* something which produces an abortion 2. *adj.* producing an abortion [fr. L. *aboriri (abortus)*, to abort + *faciens (facientis)*, causing]

a·bor·tion (əbɔ́rʃən) *n.* the spontaneous or induced expulsion from the womb of a nonviable human fetus ‖ a monstrous person or thing ‖ the failure of a project or attempt **a·bór·tion·ist** *n.* a

ab·ro·ga·tion (æbrəgéiʃən) n. the act of abrogating (e.g. a law) [fr. L. abrogatio (abrogationis)]

ab·rupt (əbrʌ́pt) adj. sudden, unexpected, an abrupt halt ‖ steep, precipitous ‖ rough, brusque in manner ‖ disconnected, an abrupt style [fr. L. abrumpere (abruptus), to break away]

A·bruz·zi e Mo·li·se (ɑbrúːttsi:emɔ́liːze) a region (area 5,954 sq. miles, pop. 1,221,900) in central Italy, formed of the provinces of Aquila, Campobasso, Chieti, Pescara and Teramo, lying in the highest and wildest part of the Apennines (Gran Sasso d'Italia, 9,560 ft), and bounded on the east by the Adriatic: olives, vines, almonds, sheep, hydroelectric power, oil

Ab·sa·lom (æbsələm) the third and best-loved son of David, king of Judah (11 Samuel xiii–xix)

ABSCAM (æbskæm) an investigation conducted by the Federal Bureau of Investigation in 1978–80. Seven U.S. Congressmen and various state and local officials were convicted of bribery, conspiracy, and related charges after FBI agents impersonating an Arab sheikh and his associates had videotaped government officials accepting bribes. Critics accused the FBI of entrapment, but the courts ruled that the FBI acted within legal limits

ab·scess (æbses) n. a localized collection of pus occurring anywhere in the body **ab·scessed** adj. [fr. L. abscessus, a going away]

ab·scis·sa (æbsísə) n. (math.) the horizontal or x-coordinate in a plane coordinate system [L. = (part) cut off]

ab·scis·sion (æbsíʒən) n. a cutting off [fr. L. abscissio (abscissionis)]

ab·scond (æbskɔ́nd) v.i. to flee secretly, esp. to escape the law [fr. L. abscondere, to hide]

ab·sence (æbsəns) n. a being away ‖ a failure to be present ‖ lack, absence of proof [F.]

absence of mind inattention, mental abstraction

ab·sent (æbsənt) adj. away, not present ‖ abstracted, an absent air [F.]

ab·sent (æbsént) v. refl. to keep (oneself) away, to absent oneself from a meeting **ab·sen·tee** (æbsəntíː) n. a person who is absent **ab·sen·tée·ism** n. persistent absence from work, usually without good reason [F. absenter]

absentee landlord a proprietor who does not live on his estate and care for his tenants but merely exploits his property

ab·sent·ly (æbsəntli:) adv. in an absent way, inattentively

ab·sent·mind·ed (æbsəntmáindid) adj. preoccupied and for that reason not paying attention to what one is doing

ab·sinthe, ab·sinth (æbsinθ) n. the plant wormwood ‖ a strongly alcoholic liqueur made from high-proof brandy, wormwood and other aromatics [F.]

ab·sis·sic acid (æbsísik) (chem.) [$C_{15}H_{20}O_4$] organic inhibitor of plant growth marketed as Dormin. abbr **ABA**

ab·so·lute (æbsəluːt) 1. adj. whole, complete ‖ pure, absolute alcohol ‖ having unrestricted power, an absolute ruler ‖ not conditioned by, or dependent upon, anything else ‖ (gram.) of a case not determined by any other word in the sentence [*ABLATIVE] ‖ (philos.) existing independently of any cause outside itself and of our sense perceptions 2. n. something that is absolute **the Absolute** the self-existent, the First Cause, God [F. absolut]

absolute address location of stored information in a digital computer

absolute alcohol ethyl alcohol containing not less than 99% pure ethyl alcohol by weight

absolute altimeter radio or similar apparatus designed to indicate the true vertical height of an aircraft above the terrain

absolute code (computer) code for an absolute address

absolute dud (mil.) a nuclear weapon that fails to explode when launched at, or emplaced on, a target

absolute expansion the true expansion of a liquid irrespective of the expansion of the containing vessel

absolute film *ABSTRACT FILM

absolute humidity the humidity of the air measured by the number of grams of water vapor present in one cubic meter of the air

absolute music music which does not illustrate or depict (in contrast to program music)

absolute pitch the pitch of a note as determined by a simple frequency, not a combination

---

Guide words showing the alphabetical range of entries on the page

Pronunciation respelling
See Part 2.

Foreign pronunciation
See Part 2.

Etymology
See Part 5.

Field label
See Part 4A.

Stress-marked derivative
See Part 1D.

Unsyllabicated main entry
See Part 1A.

Spelling variants
See Part 1B.

Multiple definitions in several parts of speech
See Part 3A.

Cross-reference to related term
See Part 3C.

Defining cross-reference
See Part 3C.

Editorial Abbreviations

Å	Angstrom unit	comp.	comparative	Gk	Greek
abbr.	abbreviation, abbreviated	conj.	conjunction	gm	gram
A.C.	alternating current	contr.	contraction	Gmc	Germanic
A.D.	anno domini	Copt.	Coptic	gram.	grammar
adj.	adjective	Corn.	Cornish	Heb.	Hebrew
adv.	adverb	Corp.	Corporation	Hind.	Hindustani
aeron.	aeronautics	corrup.	corruption	hist.	history
A.F.	Anglo-French	craniol.	craniology	H.M.	Her (His) Majesty('s)
Afrik.	Afrikaans	crystall.	crystallography	hort.	horticulture
agglom.	agglomeration	cu.	cubic	hr, hrs	hour, hours
agric.	agriculture	Czech.	Czechoslovakian	Hung.	Hungarian
alt.	alternative	d.	died	I.	Island
Am.	American	Dan.	Danish	Icel.	Icelandic
anat.	anatomy	Dec.	December	i.e.	id est, that is to say
Anglo-L.	Anglo-Latin	Dept.	Department	imit.	imitative
anthrop.	anthropology	dial.	dialectal	imper.	imperative
Antiq.	Antiquity	dim.	diminutive	impers.	impersonal
approx.	approximately	Du.	Dutch	in., ins	inch, inches
Apr.	April	dynam.	dynamics	incl.	including
Arab.	Arabic	E.	East	indef.	indefinite
Aram.	Aramaic	eccles.	ecclesiastical	infin.	infinitive
archaeol.	archaeology	econ.	economics	infl.	influenced
archit.	architecture	ed.	edition	interj.	interjection
A.S.S.R	Autonomous Soviet Socialist Republic	e.g.	exempli gratia, for example	internat.	international
		Egypt.	Egyptian	Ir.	Irish
astron.	astronomy	elec.	electricity	Is	Islands
at.	atomic	embry.	embryology	Ital.	Italian
attrib.	attributive, attributively	Eng.	English	Jan.	January
Aug.	August	engin.	engineering	Jap.	Japanese
Austral.	Australian	entom.	entomology	kc.	kilocycle, kilocycles
b.	born	Esk.	Eskimo	kg.	kilogram, kilograms
bacteriol.	bacteriology	esp.	especially	km.	kilometer, kilometers
B.C.	Before Christ	etc.	et cetera	kv.	kilovolt, kilovolts
Belg.	Belgian	ethnol.	ethnology	kw.	kilowatt, kilowatts
biochem.	biochemistry	etym.	etymology	L.	Latin
biol.	biology	Eur.	Europe, European	lb., lbs	pound, pounds
bot.	botany	eV	electron volt, electron volts	L.G.	Low German
Br.	British	excl.	excluding	L. Gk	Late Greek
Braz.	Brazilian	F.	French; Fahrenheit	lit.	literally
Bulg.	Bulgarian	fam.	family	L.L.	Late Latin
C.	Centigrade	Feb.	February	m.	meter, meters
c.	century; circa	fem.	feminine	mach.	machinery
Canad.	Canadian	ff.	and following	mag.	magnetism
Capt.	Captain	fig.	figuratively	Malay.	Malayalam
Carib.	Caribbean	Fin.	Finnish	Mar.	March
cc.	centuries	fl.	fluid	math.	mathematics
c.c.	cubic centimeter	Flem.	Flemish	mc.	megacycle, megacycles
Celt.	Celtic	fr.	from	M. Du.	Middle Dutch
cf.	confer	ft	foot, feet	M.E.	Middle English
c.g.s.	centimeter/gram/second	G.	German	mech.	mechanics
chem.	chemistry	Gael.	Gaelic	med.	medicine
Chin.	Chinese	gen.	genitive	metall.	metallurgy
cm.	centimeter, centimeters	Gen.	general	meteor.	meteorology
Co.	Company, County	geog.	geography	Mex.	Mexican
collect.	collective, collectively	geol.	geology	M.F.	Middle French
comb.	combined, combining	geom.	geometry	mil.	military

min., mins	minute, minutes	*part.*	participle	*Sept.*	September
mineral.	mineralogy	*pass.*	passive	*sing.*	singular
mistrans.	mistranslation	*perh.*	perhaps	*Skr.*	Sanskrit
M.L.	Medieval Latin	*Pers.*	Persian	*Span.*	Spanish
M.L.G.	Middle Low German	*Peruv.*	Peruvian	*specif.*	specifically
mm.	millimeter, millimeters	*petrog.*	petrography	*sp. gr.*	specific gravity
Mod.	Modern	*pharm.*	pharmacy	*sq.*	square
M.P.	Member of Parliament	*philos.*	philosophy	*S.S.R.*	Soviet Socialist Republic
m.p.h.	miles per hour	*phon.*	phonology	*st.*	stone, stones
Mt	Mount	*photog.*	photography	*St*	Saint
Mtns	Mountains	*phys.*	physics	*Sta*	Santa
mus.	music	*physiol.*	physiology	*superl.*	superlative
mythol.	mythology	*pl.*	plural	*surg.*	surgery
N.	North	*pop.*	popular; population	*survey.*	surveying
n.	noun	*Port.*	Portuguese	*S.W.*	southwest
naut.	nautical	*pred.*	predicate	*Swed.*	Sweden, Swedish
N.E.	northeast	*prep.*	preposition	*telecomm.*	telecommunications
neg.	negative	*pres.*	present	*theol.*	theology
N.F.	Northern French	*Pres.*	President	*trans.*	translation
no.	number	*prob.*	probably	*Turk.*	Turkish
Norw.	Norwegian	*pron.*	pronoun	*T.V.*	television
Nov.	November	*Prov.*	Provençal	*U.K.*	United Kingdom
N.W.	northwest	*psychoanal.*	psychoanalysis	*ult.*	ultimately
N.Y.	New York	*psychol.*	psychology	*univ.*	university
O. Arab.	Old Arabic	*R.*	river	*U.S.*	American
obs.	obsolete	*rail.*	railroad, railroads	*U.S.A.*	United States of America
Oct.	October	*redupl.*	reduplication	*U.S.S.R.*	Union of Soviet Socialist
O.E.	Old English	*refl.*	reflective		Republics
O.F.	Old French	*rel.*	related	*v.*	volt, volts
O.H.G.	Old High German	*rhet.*	rhetorical	*var.*	variant
O. Ir.	Old Irish	*Rom.*	Roman	*vet.*	veterinary
old-fash.	old-fashioned	*Rum.*	Rumanian	*v.i.*	verb intransitive
O.L.G.	Old Low German	*R.S.F.S.R.*	Russian Soviet Federal	*vol., vols*	volume, volumes (of a book)
O.N.	Old Norse		Socialist Republic	*v.t.*	verb transitive
O.N.F.	Old Northern French	*Russ.*	Russian	*W.*	West
O. Pers.	Old Persian	*S.*	South, *(Ital.)* Santo	*wd*	word
opp.	opposite of, opposed to	*Scand.*	Scandinavian	*wt*	weight
orig.	originally	*Scot.*	Scottish	*yd, yds*	yard, yards
O. Scand.	Old Scandinavian	*S.E.*	southeast	*zool.*	zoology
oz.	ounce, ounces	*sec., secs*	second, seconds		
p.a.	per annum	*Sem.*	Semitic		

Pronunciation Key

ə	adjust, bacillus, colony	l	life, lily, dull	əː	bird, learn
æ	cat, apple, laugh	'l	rabble, trouble	u	bull, cushion, book
ɑ	father, guitar, art	m	moon, lemon, dam	uə	poor, sewer
ɛə	bear, aerial	n	night, train, canal	uː	food, true
ei	snake, alien, parade	'n	redden	juː	unite, confuse
b	banana, rebel, ebb	ŋ	bring, wearing	v	verb, over, wave
tʃ	charm, fetch, ratchet	ɒ	lock, rotten	w	well, waver
d	dog, elder, feed	ɔ	fawn, court	x	loch
e	egg, exit, request	ou	vote, elope, low	j	youth, yellow
iː	even, relief, sneeze	au	cow, round	z	zoom, rose
iə	fear, career, earring	ɔi	void, royal		
f	fee, effort, rough	p	pack, slipper, wrap		
g	goat, hog, bigger	r	rise, errand, paper	**Foreign Sounds**	
h	house, behind	s	silly, whisper, juice		
i	fish, kitten, corrosive	ʃ	fish, action, fission	y	lune
ai	tiger, bright	t	time, wet, letter	ɔ̃	bon
dʒ	general, legend, dodge	θ	thick, truth	ɑ̃	an
ʒ	leisure, corsage	ð	mother, though	ɛ̃	vin
k	kill, luck, vacation	ʌ	duck, tough, rudder	œ̃	brun

Stress ′ over the sign (or first sign of a diphthong) indicates primary stress,   under the sign indicates secondary stress.
Derived words in black type show primary stress only, the stress mark being incorporated in the word (though the word is never written in this way) where no change of vowel sound from that shown at the headword is involved.

COMMON ABBREVIATIONS

ABBREVIATIONS, ə-brē-vē-ā′shᵊnz, are letter symbols or contractions used as shortened forms of words and phrases to facilitate writing and to save space. The practice of abbreviating goes back to antiquity; early examples of abbreviation have survived on coins and inscriptions, where lack of space made the shortening of words necessary. With the development of papyrus and, later, of parchment, writing increased and abbreviations were adopted by copyists to save labor.

In modern times the rapid growth of the sciences, technology, and business, and the increase of governmental agencies have produced a vastly increased vocabulary of abbreviations for use in some fields, symbols other than letters are employed, as in physics and mathematics. The following list of abbreviations often used in printing or writing includes only letter symbols or contractions, in the Roman alphabet.

A

A.—absolute (temperature)
A., Å., A—angstrom unit
a.—about; acre(s)
AA—Alcoholics Anonymous
A.A.—Associate in Arts
AAA—Agricultural Adjustment Administration; Amateur Athletic Association; American Automobile Association; anti-aircraft artillery
AAAL—American Academy of Arts and Letters
AAAS—American Association for the Advancement of Science
AAU—Amateur Athletic Union
AAUP—American Association of University Professors
A.B.—Artium Baccalaureus (Lat.), Bachelor of Arts
A.B., a.b.—able-bodied (seaman); airborne
ABA—American Bar Association
abbr., abbrev.—abbreviation; abbreviated
ABC—American Broadcasting Company
abp.—archbishop
abr.—abridged; abridgment
ABS—American Bible Society
AC—Air Corps; Army Corps; Athletic Club
AC, A.C., a.c., a-c—alternating current
A/C, a/c, ac.—account
Ac—actinium
ac—acre(s)
acad.—academic; academy
accel.—accelerando (It.), more quickly (music)
acct.—account; accountant
ACDA—Arms Control and Disarmament Agency
ACLS—American Council of Learned Societies
ACLU—American Civil Liberties Union
ACP—American College of Physicians
ACS—American Chemical Society; American College of Surgeons
ACTH—adrenocorticotropic hormone
A.D.—anno Domini (Lat.), in the year of our Lord
ADA—American Dental Association; Americans for Democratic Action
adag.—adagio (It.), slowly (music)
ADC, a.d.c.—aide-de-camp
add.—addenda; addendum; addition; additional; address
adj.—adjacent; adjective; adjourned; adjustment; adjutant
ad lib., ad libit.—ad libitum (Lat.), at one's pleasure

adm.—administration; administrative; admiral
adv.—adverb; adversus; advertisement; advocate
ad val.—ad valorem (Lat.), according to the value
ae., aet., adtat.—aetatis (Lat.), of age, aged
AEC—Atomic Energy Commission
AEF—American Expeditionary Force
aero.—aeronautics
AF—Air Force; audio frequency
AFAM—Ancient Free and Accepted Masons
AFB—Air Force Base
AFC—automatic frequency control
AFL-CIO—American Federation of Labor-Congress of Industrial Organizations
AFTRA—American Federation of Television and Radio Artists
Ag—argentum (Lat.), silver
agr., agri., agric.—agricultural; agriculture
agt.—agent
A.H.—anno Hegirae (Lat.), in the year of Hegira (Mohammedan era)
AHA—American Historical Association
AIA—American Institute of Architects
A.I.Ch.E.—American Institute of Chemical Engineers
AID—Agency for International Development
AIEE—American Institute of Electrical Engineers
AKC—American Kennel Club
Al—aluminum
ALA—American Library Association
Ala.—Alabama
Alas.—Alaska
Alba.—Alberta
alg.—algebra
alt.—alternate; alternating; altitude; alto
Alta.—Alberta
AM—amplitude modulation
A.M., A.M., a.m.—ante meridiem (Lat.), before midday
A.M.—Artium Magister (Lat.), Master of Arts
Am—americium
AMA—American Medical Association
amb.—ambassador
A.M.E.—African Methodist Episcopal
amp.—amperage; ampere
AMS—Agricultural Marketing Service
amt.—amount
AMVETS—American Veterans (of World War II and Korea)
AN, AN.—Anglo-Norman

ANA—American Nurses Association
anal.—analogy, analysis; analytic
ANC—Army Nurse Corps
and.—andante (It.), slowly (music)
anon.—anonymous
ant.—antenna; antonym
anthrop., anthropol.—anthropological; anthropologist; anthropology
antiq.—antiquarian; antiquary
ANZAC—Australian and New Zealand Army Corps
AOH—Ancient Order of Hiberians
AP—Associated Press
APA—American Philological Association
APO—Army Post Office
app.—apparent; appended; appendix; appointed; apprentice
approx.—approximately
Apr., Apr—April
apt.—apartment
AQ—accomplishment quotient; achievement quotient
aq.—aqua; aqueous
Ar—argon
Ar.—Arabian; Arabic; Aramaic
ARA—Agricultural Research Administration; American Railway Association
A.R.A.—Associate of the Royal Academy
Arab.—Arabian; Arabic
ARC—American Red Cross
arch.—archaic; archbishop; archery; archipelago; architect; architecture
archaeol.—archaeological; archaeology
archd.—archduke
arith.—arithmetic
Ariz.—Arizona
Ark.—Arkansas
ARS—Agricultural Research Service
AS, AS.—Anglo-Saxon
As—arsenic
ASCAP—American Society of Composers, Authors and Publishers
ASCE—American Society of Civil Engineers
ASME—American Society of Mechanical Engineers
ASPCA—American Society for the Prevention of Cruelty to Animals
assn., assoc.—association
ASSR—Autonomous Soviet Socialist Republic
asst.—assistant
ASTM—American Society for Testing Materials
ASTP—Army Secialized Training Program
astrol.—astrologer; astrological; astrology

TWO-LETTER GEOGRAPHICAL ABBREVIATIONS RECOMMENDED BY THE UNITED STATES POSTAL SERVICE

ALABAMA	AL	GEORGIA	GA	MARYLAND	MD	NEW MEXICO	NM	SOUTH DAKOTA	SD
ALASKA	AK	GUAM	GU	MASSACHUSETTS	MA	NEW YORK	NY	TENNESSEE	TN
ARIZONA	AZ	HAWAII	HI	MICHIGAN	MI	NORTH CAROLINA	NC	TEXAS	TX
ARKANSAS	AR	IDAHO	ID	MINNESOTA	MN	NORTH DAKOTA	ND	UTAH	UT
CALIFORNIA	CA	ILLINOIS	IL	MISSISSIPPI	MS	OHIO	OH	VERMONT	VT
CANAL ZONE	CZ	INDIANA	IN	MISSOURI	MO	OKLAHOMA	OK	VIRGINIA	VA
COLORADO	CO	IOWA	IA	MONTANA	MT	OREGON	OR	VIRGIN ISLANDS	VI
CONNECTICUT	CT	KANSAS	KS	NEBRASKA	NE	PENNSYLVANIA	PA	WASHINGTON	WA
DELAWARE	DE	KENTUCKY	KY	NEVADA	NV	PUERTO RICO	PR	WEST VIRGINIA	WV
D. OF C.	DC	LOUISIANA	LA	NEW HAMPSHIRE	NH	RHODE ISLAND	RI	WISCONSIN	WI
FLORIDA	FL	MAINE	ME	NEW JERSEY	NJ	SOUTH CAROLINA	SC	WYOMING	WY

astron.—astronomer; astronomical; astronomy
ASV—American Standard Version
ATC—Air Transport Command
at. no.—atomic number
ATP—adenosine triphosphate
ATS—Army Transport Service
attn.—attention
atty.—attorney
atty. gen.—attorney general
at. wt.—atomic weight
A.U., A.U., a.u., a.u.—angstrom unit
Au—aurum (Lat.), gold
Aug., Aug—August
AUS—Army of the United States
aux.—auxiliary
A.V.—Authorized Version (Bible)
av.—avenue; average; avoirdupois
AVC—American Veterans Committee; automatic volume control
advp.—avoirdupois
ave.—avenue
avoir—avoirdupois
AWOL—absent without leave

B

B—bishop (chess); boron
b.—base; bass; bat; battery; bay; book; born; brother
B.A.—Baccalaureus Artium (Lat.), Bachelor of Arts; British Association (for the Advancement of Science); Buenos Aires
Ba—barium
bact.—bacteria; bacteriology
Bap., Bapt.—Baptist
bap.—baptized
B.Ar., B. Arch.—Bachelor of Architecture
Bart.—Baronet
B.B.A.—Bachelor of Business Administration
BBB—Better Business Bureau
BBC—British Broadcasting Corporation
bbl—barrel, barrels
B.C.—before Christ; British Columbia
B.C.E.—Bachelor of Civil Engineering
B.Ch.E.—Bachelor of Chemical Engineering
B.C.L.—Bachelor of Civil Law
B.D.—Bachelor of Divinity
BSDA—Business and Defense Services Administration
B.E.—Bachelor of Engineering; Bachelor of Education
Be—beryllium
Bé.—Baumé
B.Ed.—Bachelor of Education
BEF—British Expeditionary Force(s)
B.E.M.—British Empire Medal
BEV, bev—billion electron volts
bf.—boldface
Bi—bismuth
bib.—Bible; biblical
bibliog.—bibliography
biochem.—biochemistry
biog.—biographer; biographical; biography
biol.—biology
B.I.S.—Bank for International Settlements; British Information Service
Bk—berkelium
bk.—bank; block; book
bkg.—banking
B.L.—Baccalaureus Legum (Lat.), Bachelor of Laws
bldg.—building
B.Lit(t).—Baccalaureus Lit(t)erarum (Lat.), Bachelor of Literature (or Letters)
BLS—Bureau of Labor Statistics
B.L.S.—Bachelor of Library Science
blvd.—boulevard
BM—basal metabolism
B.M.—Baccalaureus Medicinae (Lat.), Bachelor of Medicine; British Museum
B.Mus.—Baccalaureus Musicae (Lat.), Bachelor of Music
BOAC—British Overseas Airways Corporation
bor.—borough

bot.—botanical, botany
bp.—bishop
b.p.—boiling point
BPOE—Benevolent and Protective Order of Elks
Br—bromine
brig.—brigade; brigadier
brig. gen.—brigadier general
bro.—brother
B.S.—Bachelor of Science
BSA—Boy Scouts of America
B.S.A.—Bachelor of Science in Agriculture
B.Sc.—Baccalaureus Scientiae (Lat.), Bachelor of Science
B.T., B.Th.—Baccalaureus Theologiae (Lat.), Bachelor of Theology
B.T.U., Btu, b.t.u., btu—British thermal unit
bu—bushel
bur.—bureau
B.V.M.—Blessed Virgin Mary

C

C—carbon
C., c.—candle; capacitance; cape; carat; cathode; cent; center; century; chapter; circa, about; cirrus (meteor.); copyright; cubic; cup; current; cycle
C., C̄, c., c̄—centigrade; centimeter
CA—chronological age; Coast Artillery
Ca—calcium
c.a.—chartered accountant; chief accountant; commercial agent; consular agent; controller of accounts
CAA—Civil Aeronautics Administration (or Authority)
CAB—Civil Aeronautics Board; Consumers' Advisory Board
Cal.—California; large calorie
cal.—calendar; caliber; small calorie
Calif.—California
Cant.—Canticles
CAP—Civil Air Patrol
cap.—capital; capitalize
capt.—captain
CAR—Civil Air Regulations
CARE—Cooperative for American Remittances to Everywhere
Cath.—Catholic
cath.—cathedral
CAVU—ceiling and visibility unlimited
C.B.—Chirurgiae Baccalaureus (Lat.), Bachelor of Surgery; Companion of the Bath
Cb—columbium
CBC—Canadian Broadcasting Corporation
C.B.E.—Commander (of the Order) of the British Empire
CBS—Columbia Broadcasting System
cc, cc., c.c.—cubic centimeters
CCC—Commodity Credit Corporation
CCS—Combined Chiefs of Staff
Cd—cadmium
CE—Chemical Engineer; Chief Engineer; Civil Engineer; Church of England; Christian Endeavor
Ce—cerium
CEA—Council of Economic Advisers
CED—Committee for Economic Development
CEF—Canadian Expeditionary Force(s)
Celt.—Celtic
CEMA—Council for Mutual Economic Assistance
cent.—centigrade; centimeter; central; century
CENTO—Central Treaty Organization
Cf—californium
cf.—confer (Lat.), compare
CG—center of gravity; Coast Guard; commanding general; consul general
cg, cgm—centigram
cgs—centimeter-gram-second
CGT—Confédération Générale du Travail (Fr.), General Confederation of Labor

CH—clearing house; courthouse; customhouse
C.H.—Companion of Honor
ch.—chaplain; chapter; check (chess); chief; child; children; chirurgia (Lat.), surgery; church
chan.—channel
chap.—chaplain; chapter
Ch.E.—Chemical Engineer
chem.—chemical; chemist; chemistry
chm.—checkmate
Chr.—Christ; Christian
Chron.—Chronicles
chron.—chronology
CIA—Central Intelligence Agency
C.I.E.—Companion (of the Order) of the Indian Empire
CIF—cost, insurance, freight
C. in C.—Commander in Chief
CIO—Congress of (formerly Committee for) Industrial Organizations
cir., circ.—circular; circa (Lat.), about
cit.—citation; cited; citizen
civ.—civil; civilian
Cl—chlorine
clk.—clerk
C.M.—Chirurgiae Magister (Lat.), Master in Surgery
Cm—curium
cm, cm.—centimeter(s)
C.M.G.—Companion (of the Order) of St. Michael and St. George
CO—Commanding Officer; conscientious objector
Co—cobalt
co.—company; county
c.o., c/o—care of; carried over
COD, c.o.d.—cash on delivery; collect on delivery
C. of C.—Chamber of Commerce
C. of S.—Chief of Staff
Col.—Colorado; Colossians
col.—collected; collector; college; colonel; colonial; colony; column
colloq.—colloquial; colloquialism
Colo.—Colorado
Coloss.—Colossians
com.—comedy; command; commandant; commerce; commercial; commission(er); committee; commodore; common; communication; community
comdr.—commander
COMECON—Council for Mutual Economic Assistance
comr.—commissioner
con.—concerto; consolidated; consul
conf.—conference
confed.—confederate
Cong.—Congregational
cong.—congress
conj.—conjugation; conjunction
Conn.—Connecticut
consol.—consolidated
constr.—construction
cont.—containing; contents; continent; continental; continue(d)
Cor.—Corinthians
CORE—Congress of Racial Equality
corp.—corporal; corporation
cos—cosine
CP—candlepower; chemically pure; command post; Communist Party
cp.—candlepower; compare
CPA—Certified Public Accountant
cpl.—corporal
CPO—chief petty officer
Cr—chromium
cr.—credit; creditor; creek
cres., cresc.—crescendo (It.), increasingly loud (music)
crit.—criticism
CS—civil service
C.S.—Christian Science
Cs—cesium
CSA—Confederate States of America
C.S.B.—Bachelor of Christian Science
CSC—Civil Service Commission

C.S.I.—Companion of (the Order of) the Star of India
CST—Central Standard Time
ct.—carat; cent; court
Cu—cuprum (Lat.), copper
cu—cubic
CWA—Civil Works Administration
cwt—hundredweight
CYO—Catholic Youth Organization

D

D—deuterium
D., d.—dam (in pedigrees); date; daughter; day(s); dead; democrat; density; diameter; died
d.—pence, penny
D.A.—delayed action; district attorney
DAB—Dictionary of American Biography
Dan., Danl.—Daniel
DAR—Daughters of the American Revolution
DAV—Disabled American Veterans
D.B.E.—Dame Commander (of the Order of) British Empire
D. Bib.—Douay Bible
DC, D.C., d.c., d-c—direct current
D.C.—da capo (Lat.), repeat (music); District of Columbia; Doctor of Chiropractic
D.C.L.—Doctor of Civil Law
D.C.M.—Distinguished Conduct Medal (Brit. Army)
D.C.T.—Doctor of Christian Theology
D.D.—Divinitatis Doctor (Lat.), Doctor of Divinity
D.D.S.—Doctor of Dental Surgery
Dec., Dec—December
dec.—deceased; declaration; declension; declination; decrease; decrescendo (It.), decreasing in loudness (music)
deg.—degree(s)
Del.—Delaware
Dem.—Democrat; Democratic
D.Eng.—Doctor of Engineering
dep.—department; departure; deposit; depot; deputy
dept.—department; deputy
der., deriv.—derivation; derivative
dermatol.—dermatology
Deut.—Deuteronomy
DEW—distant early warning
DFC—Distinguished Flying Cross
diag.—diagram
dial.—dialect
dict.—dictionary
dim.—diminuendo (It.), diminishing in loudness (music)
dipl.—diplomat; diplomatic
dir.—director
disc.—discount; discovered
dist.—distinguished; district
div.—dividend; division; divorced
D.Lit., D.Litt.—Doctor Lit(t)erarum (Lat.), Doctor of Literature (or, Letters)
D.L.S.—Doctor of Library Science
dm, dm.—decameter; decimeter
D.M.D.—Doctor of Medical Dentistry
D.Mus.—Doctor of Music
DNA—deoxyribonucleic acid
DNB—Dictionary of National Biography (Brit.)
D.O.—Doctor of Optometry; Doctor of Osteopathy
do.—ditto (It.), the same
DOA—dead on arrival
doc.—document
doz.—dozen
DP—degree of polymerization; diametrical pitch; displaced person
dpt.—department
D.R., D/R, d.r.—dead reckoning; deposit receipt
Dr.—doctor
dr.—debit; debtor; drachma; dram
D.S., D.Sc.—Doctor of Science
DSC—Distinguished Service Cross

DSM—Distinguished Service Medal
DSO—Distinguished Service Order
DST—Daylight Saving Time
d.t.—delirium tremens; double time
dup., dupl.—duplicate
D.V.—Deo volente (Lat.), God willing; Douay Version
D.V.M.—Doctor of Veterinary Medicine
dwt—pennyweight
Dy—dysprosium

E

E, E., e.—east, eastern
e., e—erg: errors (baseball)
ea.—each
ECA—Economic Cooperation Administration
eccl., eccles.—ecclesiastical
Eccles., Eccl.—Ecclesiastes
Ecclus.—Ecclesiasticus
ECG—electrocardiogram
ecol.—ecology
econ.—economic; economics; economy
ECSC—European Coal and Steel Community
ed.—edited; editor; edition
EDC—European Defense Community
Ed.D.—Doctor of Education
EDT—Eastern Daylight Time
EEC—European Economic Community
EEG—electroencephalogram
EFTA—European Free Trade Association
e.g.—exempli gratia (Lat.), for example
Egyptol.—Egyptology
EHF, e.h.f.—extremely high frequency
EIB—Export-Import Bank
EKG—electrocardiogram
elec., elect.—electric(al); electrician; electricity
elev.—elevation
Eliz.—Elizabeth; Elizabethan
E.M.—Engineer of Mines
EMF, e.m.f., emf.—electromotive force
emp.—emperor; empire; empress
e.m.u.—electromagnetic unit
enc.—enclosed
ency., encyc., encycl.—encyclopedia
eng.—engineer; engineering; engraved
ens.—ensign
entom., entomol.—entomologist; entomology
Eph., Ephes.—Ephesians
Epis., Episc.—**Episcopal**
Er—erbium
ERA—Emergency Relief Administration
ERP—European Recovery Program
Es—einsteinium
ESB—Economic Stabilization Board
ESC—Economic and Social Council (United Nations)
Esk.—Eskimo
ESP—extrasensory perception
Esq., Esqr.—Esquire
EST—Eastern Standard Time
est.,—established; estimate
Esth.—Esther
et al.—et alii (Lat.), and elsewhere; et alii (Lat.), and others
etc.—et cetera (Lat.), and so forth
ETO—European Theater of Operations
et seq.—et sequens (Lat.), and the following; et sequentes or seqentia (Lat.), and those that follow
Eu—europium
Ex.—Exodus
ex.—examined; example
exch.—exchange; exchequer
exec.—executive; executor
ex lib.—ex libris (Lat.), from the books of
Exod.—Exodus
Ez., Ezr.—Ezra
Ezek.—Ezekiel

F

F—Fahrenheit; farad; fathom; fluorine; function (math.)

F.—Fahrenheit; Fellow; Friday
f—forte (It.), loud (music)
f.—farad; father; farthing; fathom; feminine; fluid (ounce); folio; following; franc; frequency
FAA—Federal Aviation Agency
fac.—facsimile
Fahr.—Fahrenheit
FAO—Food and Agricultural Organization of the United Nations
FBI—Federal Bureau of Investigation
FCA—Farm Credit Administration
FCC—Federal Communications Commission
FCIC—Federal Crop Insurance Corporation
FDA—Food and Drug Administration
FDIC—Federal Deposit Insurance Corporation
Fe—ferrum (Lat.), iron
Feb., Feb—February
fec.—fecit (Lat.), he (she) did, *or* made, it
fed.—federal; federated; federation
fem.—female; feminine
FEPC—Fair Employment Practice Committee
ff—fortissimo (It.), very loud (music)
ff.—folios; following
FFA—Future Farmers of America
FHA—Farmers Home Administration; Federal Housing Administration; Future Homemakers of America
FICA—Federal Insurance Contributions Act
fig.—figure
fin.—finance
fl.—florin; flourished; fluid
Fla., Flor.—Florida
F.L.S.—Fellow of the Linnaean Society
FM—frequency modulation
Fm—fermium
FMB—Federal Maritime Board
FMCS—Federal Mediation and Conciliation Service
fn.—footnote
FOB, f.o.b.—free on board
FOE—Fraternal Order of Eagles
fol.—folio; following
F.P., f.p.—foot pound; freezing point
FPC—Federal Power Commission
FPHA—Federal Public Housing Authority
FPO—Fleet Post Office
fps—feet per second
Fr.—francium
Fr.—Father (eccl.); Frater (Lat.), brother; Friar; Friday
fr.—fragment; franc; from
F.R.A.S.—Fellow of the Royal Astronomical Society
F.R.C.P.—Fellow of the Royal College of Physicians
F.R.C.S.—Fellow of the Royal College of Surgeons
F.R.G.S.—Fellow of the Royal Geographical Society
F.R.Hist.S.—Fellow of the Royal Historical Society
Fri.—Friday
F.R.I.B.A.—Fellow of the Royal Institution of British Architects
front.—frontispiece
FRS—Federal Reserve System
F.R.S.—Fellow of the Royal Society
F.R.S.C.—Fellow of the Royal Society of Canada
F.R.S.E.—Fellow of the Royal Society, Edinburgh
F.R.S.L.—Fellow of the Royal Society of Literature; Fellow of the Royal Society, London
FSA—Farm Security Administration; Federal Security Agency
F.S.A.—Fellow of the Society of Antiquaries, or Arts
FSCC—Federal Surplus Commodities Corporation
FSH—follicle-stimulating hormone

F.S.A.—Fellow of the Society of Antiquaries, or Arts
FSCC—Federal Surplus Commodities Corporation
FSH—follicle-stimulating hormone
F.S.S.—Fellow of the (Royal) Statistical Society
ft—feet; foot
ft.—fort
FTC—Federal Trade Commission
F.Z.S.—Fellow of the Zoological Society

G

G., g.—conductance; gauge; grain; gravity; guinea; gulf
g., g—gram
GA—general agent; General Assembly
Ga.—gallium
Ga.—Gallic; Georgia
Gael.—Gaelic
Gal.—Galatians; Galen
gal, gall.—gallon
GAO—General Accounting Office
GAR—Grand Army of the Republic
GATT—General Agreement on Tariffs and Trade
gaz.—gazette; gazetteer
G.B.E.—Grand (Cross, Order) of the British Empire
GCA—ground-controlled approach
G.C.B.—(Knight) Grand Cross of the Bath
GCI—ground-controlled interceptor
G.C.I.E.—(Knight) Grand Commander (of the Order) of the Indian Empire
G.C.L.H.—Grand Cross of the Legion of Honor
G.C.M.G.—(Knight of the) Grand Cross (of the Order) of St. Michael and St. George
G.C.S.I.—(Knight) Grand Commander (of the Order) of the Star of India
GCT—Greenwich civil time
G.C.V.O.—(Knight) Grand Cross of the (Royal) Victorian Order
Gd—gadolinium
Ge—germanium
Gen.—Genesis
gen.—gender; genera; general; genus
geod.—geodesy; geodetic
geog.—geographer; geographical; geography
geol.—geologic; geologist; geology
geom.—geometric; geometry
ger.—gerund
GHA—Greenwich hour angle
GHQ—General Headquarters
GI—general issue, or government issue (U.S. Army)
GI, g.i.—gastrointestinal
gloss.—glossary
GM—General Manager; George Medal (Brit.); Grand Master; guided missiles
gm—gram
GMT—Greenwich mean time
GNP—gross national product
GOP—Grand Old Party (Republican)
Goth.—Gothic
gov.—governor
govt.—government
GP—general practitioner
GPO—General Post Office; Government Printing Office
gr—grain(s); gram(s)
gram.—grammar; grammarian
GS—General Staff
GSA—General Services Administration; Girl Scouts of America
GSC—General Staff Corps

H

H—henry (elec.); hydrogen; intensity of magnetic field
h.—hard; hardness; high; hits (baseball); husband
Hab.—Habakkuk
hab. corp.—habeas corpus (Lat.), that you have the body

Hag.—Haggai
Hal.—halogen
Haw.—Hawaii
Hb—hemoglobin
H.B.M.—His (Her) Britannic Majesty
H.C.—House of Commons
H.C.M.—His (Her) Catholic Majesty
H.E.—His Eminence; His Excellency
He—helium
Heb., Hebr.—Hebrew(s)
her.—heraldry
HF—high frequency
Hf—hafnium
Hg—hydrargyrum (Lat.), mercury
H.H.—His (Her) Highness; His Holiness (the Pope)
HHFA—Housing and Home Finance Agency
HIFI—high fidelity
H.I.H.—His (Her) Imperial Highness
hist.—historical; historian; history
H.J.S.—hic jacet sepultus (Lat.), here lies buried
H.L.—House of Lords
H.M.—His (Her) Majesty
H.M.S.—His Majesty's Service, Ship, or Steamer
Ho—holmium
Hon.—Honorable
hort.—horticultural; horticulture
Hos.—Hosea
H.P., HP, h.p., hp—high pressure; horsepower
HQ, H.Q., hq, h.q.—headquarters
H.R.—Home Rule; House of Representatives
hr—hour(s)
H.R.H.—His (Her) Royal Highness
H.R.I.P.—hic requiescit in pace (Lat.), here rests in peace
H.S.H.—His (Her) Serene Highness
ht.—height

I

I—iodine
I.—Island; Isle
Ia.—Iowa (not official)
IADB—Inter-American Defense Board
ib., ibid.—ibidem (Lat.), in the same place
IBRD—International Bank for Reconstruction and Development
ICAO—International Civil Aviation Organization
ICBM—intercontinental ballistic missile
ICC—Interstate Commerce Commission; Indian Claims Commission
ichth.—ichthyology
ICJ—International Court of Justice
Id.—Idaho (not official)
id.—idem (Lat.), the same
i.e.—id est (Lat.), that is
IFC—International Finance Corporation
IGY—International Geophysical Year
IHS—the first three letters of the Greek word for Jesus
ILA—International Longshoremen's Association
ILGWU—International Ladies' Garment Workers' Union
Ill.—Illinois
ILO—International Labor Organization
I.L.P.—Independent Labour Party
IMF—International Monetary Fund
imp.—imperative; imperial; imports; imprimatur (Lat.), let it be printed
In—indium
in.—inch; inches
inc.—including; income; incorporated
Ind.—Indian; Indiana
Inf.—infantry
in loc. cit.—in loco citato (Lat.), in the place cited
INRI—Iesus Nazarenus, Rex Iudaeorum (Lat.), Jesus of Nazareth, King of the Jews
INS—International News Service

ins.—inches; insurance
inst.—instant, the present month; institute
introd.—introduction
IOF—Independent Order of Foresters
IOOF—Independent Order of Odd Fellows
IOU—I owe you
IQ—intelligence quotient
Ir—iridium
IRA—Irish Republican Army
IRO—International Refugee Organization
IRS—Internal Revenue Service
Is., is.—island(s); isle
Isa.—Isaiah
ITO—International Trade Organization
ITU—International Telecommunications Union
IU—international unit
IWW—Industrial Workers of the World

J

J—joule
J.—Justice; Judge
JA—Judge Advocate
Jan., Jan—January
Jas.—James
JCC—Junior Chamber of Commerce
J.C.D.—Juris Civilis Doctor (Lat.), Doctor of Civil Law
J.D.—Juris Doctor (Lat.), Doctor of Law
Jer.—Jeremiah
j.g.—junior grade
Jno.—John
Josh.—Joshua
jour.—journal
J.P.—Justice of the Peace
Jr., jr—junior
J.U.D.—Juris Utriusque Doctor (Lat.), doctor of both laws (canon and civil)
jud.—judicial
Judg.—Judges (Bible)

K

K—kalium (Lat.), potassium; king (chess)
K, k.—kilogram; king
K.—Kelvin
k.—kilo, thousand
ka—kathode *or* cathode
Kan., Kans., Kas.—Kansas
KB—king's bishop (chess)
K.B.—King's Bench; Knight Bachelor; Knight of the Bath
K.B.E.—Knight (Commander of the Order) of the British Empire
KBP—king's bishop's pawn (chess)
K.C.—King's Counsel; Knights of Columbus
kc—kilocycle
K.C.B.—Knight Commander of the Bath
K.C.I.E.—Knight Commander (of the Order) of the Indian Empire
K.C.M.G.—Knight Commander of St. Michael and St. George
K.C.S.I.—Knight Commander of the Star of India
K.C.V.O.—Knight Commander of the Victorian Order
KEV, Kev—thousand electron volts
K.G.—Knight of the Garter
kg—kilogram
Ki.—Kings (Bible)
kilo.—kilogram; kilometer
KKK—Ku Klux Klan
K Kt—king's knight (chess)
K Kt P—king's knight's pawn (chess)
KLM—Royal Dutch Airlines
km—kilometer
KO—knockout
K. of P.—Knights of Pythias
KP—king's pawn (chess); kitchen police, assistants to cooks
K.P.—Knight of St. Patrick; Knights of Pythias
KR—king's rook (chess)
Kr—krypton
KRP—king's rook's pawn (chess)

K.T.—Knight of the Thistle; Knight Templar
Kt.—Knight
kt.—carat
kv.—kilovolt
kw.—kilowatt
K.W.H., kw-h, kw-hr—kilowatt-hour
Ky.—Kentucky

L

£, L, l.—libra (Lat.), pound
L., l.—lake; left; length; liber (Lat.), book; lira
l., l—liter
l., ll.—line; lines
La—lanthanum
La.—Louisiana
Lab.—Labrador
lab.—laboratory
Lam.—Lamentations
lang.—language
Lat.—Latin
lat.—latitude
lb—libra (Lat.), pound
LC—landing craft (following letter specifies type, for example, LCI Landing Craft Infantry)
L.C.—Library of Congress
l.c.—loco citato (Lat.), in the place cited; lower case (print.)
LD—lethal dose; Low Dutch
leg.—legal; legend; legato (It.), in a smooth manner (music); legislative; legislature
legis.—legislation; legislative; legislature
Lev.—Leviticus
LG—Low German
LH—luteinizing hormone
L.H.D.—lit(t)erarum Humaniorum Doctor, or In Litteris Humanioribus Doctor (Lat.), Doctor of Humanities
L.I.—Long Island
Li—lithium
lib.—liberal; librarian; library
lieut.—lieutenant
ling.—linguistics
Linn.—Linnaeus; Linnaean
liq.—liquid; liquidation; liquor
lit.—literally; literary; literature
Lit.B., Litt.B.—Lit(t)erarum Baccalaureus (Lat), Bachelor of Letters or Literature
Lit.D., Litt.D.—Lit(t)erarum Doctor (Lat.); Doctor of Literature
LL—Late Latin; Low Latin
LL.B.—Legum Baccalaureus (Lat.), Bachelor of Laws
LL.D.—Legum Doctor (Lat.), Doctor of Laws
LL.M.—Legum Magister (Lat.), Master of Laws
loc. cit.—lococitato (Lat.), in the place cited
log.—logarithm
Lon., Lond.—London
lon., long.—longitude
LOOM—Loyal Order of Moose
loq.—loquitur (Lat.), he, or she, speaks
L.R.A.M.—Licentiate of the Royal Academy of Music
L.R.C.P.—Licentiate of the Royal College of Physicians
L.R.C.S.—Licentiate of the Royal College of Surgeons
LS—landing ship (following letter specifies type, for example, LST, Landing Ship Tank)
l.s.—locus sigilli (Lat.), place of the seal
L.S.A.—Licentiate of the Society of Apothecaries
LSD—lysergic acid diethylamide
L.S.D., ls.d., l.s.d.—librae, solidi, denarii (Lat.), pounds, shillings, and pence
lt.—lieutenant
Ltd., ltd.—limited
Lu—lutetium
Luth.—Lutheran
Lw—lawrencium

M

M—magnitude; thousand
M.—Majesty; Monsieur (Fr.), miter
m.—male; mark (German money); married; meridian; meridies (Lat.), noon; meter; mile; minute; month
MA—Maritime Administration; mental age
M.A.—Magister Artium (Lat.), Master of Arts
ma, ma., mA—milliampere
Mac., Macc.—Maccabees
Maced.—Macedonia(n)
mach.—machine; machinist
maj.—major
Mal.—Malachi
Man.—Manitoba
MAP—Military Assistance Program
Mar., Mar—March
mas., masc.—masculine
Mass.—Massachusetts
math.—mathematician; mathematics
MATS—Military Air Transport Service
Matt.—Matthew
M.B.—Medicinae Baccalaureus (Lat.), Bachelor of Medicine
M.B.A.—Master of Business Administration
MBS—Mutual Broadcasting System
M.C.—Medical Corps; Master of Ceremonies; Member of Congress
mc—megacycle
M.D.—Medicinae Doctor (Lat.), Doctor of Medicine; Medical Department
Md—mendelevium
Md.—Maryland
M.D.S.—Master of Dental Surgery
mdse.—merchandise
ME, ME., M.E.—Middle English
M.E.—Methodist Episcopal; mining or mechanical, engineer
Me.—Maine
mech.—mechanical; mechanics
med.—medical; medicine; medieval
Medit.—Mediterranean
M.E.E.—Master of Electrical Engineering
mem.—memento (Lat.), remember, memorandum
mep—mean effective pressure
Messrs.—Messieurs (Fr.), gentlemen
metal.—metallurgy
meteorol.—meteorology
Meth.—Methodist
MEV, Mev—million electron volts
mf—mezzo forte (It.), moderately loud (music); millifarad
mf, mfd—microfarad
M.F.A.—Master of Fine Arts
mfg.—manufacturing
mfr.—manufacture; manufacturer
MG—Military Government
Mg—magnesium
mg, mg., mgm—milligram
MGB—Ministerstvo Gosudarstvennoi Bezopasnosti (from the Russian), the Soviet Ministry of State Security
mgr.—manager; monsignor
MHG, M.H.G.—Middle High German
M.I.—Military intelligence
mi—mile; mill
Mic.—Micah
Mich.—Michigan
M.I.E.E.—Member of the Institution of Electrical Engineers
mil., milit.—militia; military
M.I.Mech.E.—Member of the Institution of Mechanical Engineers
M.I.Min.E., M.I.M.E.—Member of the Institution of Mining Engineers
min—Minute(s)
min.—mineralogy; minimum; mining
Minn.—Minnesota
M.Inst.C.E.—Member of the Institution of Civil Engineers
misc.—miscellaneous
Miss.—Mississippi

M.I.T.—Massachusetts Institute of Technology
ML, M.L.—Medieval, or Middle, Latin
M.L.—Magister Legum (Lat.), Master of Laws; Medieval, or Middle, Latin
ml, ml.—milliliter
MLA—Modern Language Association
MLG, M.L.G.—Middle Low German
M. Lit(t).—Magister Lit(t)erarum (Lat.), Master of Letters
Mlle.—Mademoiselle (Fr.), Miss
MM—Messieurs (Fr.), gentlemen; (Their) Majesties
mm—millimeter(s); millia (Lat.), thousands
M.M.E.—Master of Mining, or Mechanical, Engineering
Mme.—Madame (Fr.), Madam
Mn—manganese
MO, m.o.—medical officer; money order
Mo—molybdenum
Mo.—Missouri
mo.—month(s)
mod.—moderate
Moham.—Mohammedan
Mon.—Monday; Monsignor
Mont.—Montana
MOS—military occupational specialty (duty classification by serial number)
MP—military police
M.P.—Member of Parliament
mp—mezzo piano (It.), moderately soft (music)
MPH, mph—miles per hour
Mr., Mr—Mister
MRA—Moral Re-Armament
MRP—Mouvement Républicain Populaire (Fr.), Popular Republican Movement
Mrs.—Mistress
MS, Ms, ms, ms.—manuscript
M.S., M.Sc.—Master of Science
msgr.—monsignor
m.s.l.—mean sea level
MSS, MSS., mss, mss.—manuscripts
MST—Mountain Standard Time
M.S.W.—Master of Social Work
mt.—mount; mountain
MTO—Mediterranean Theater of Operations
Mt. Rev.—Most Reverend
mts.—mountains
mu—micron
mus.—museum; music; musician
Mus.B., Mus.Bac.—Musicae Baccalaureus (Lat.), Bachelor of Music
Mus. D.—Musicae Doctor (Lat.), Doctor of Music
MVA—Missouri Valley Authority
MVD—Ministerstvo Vnutrennikh Del (from the Russian), the Soviet Ministry of Internal Affairs
M.V.O.—Member of the (Royal) Victorian Order
myth., mythol.—mythology

N

N—nitrogen
N, N., n—north, northern
N., n.—navy; noon; normal (solution)
n.—natus (Lat.), born; neuter; note; noun
Na—natrium (Lat.), sodium
NAACP—National Association for the Advancement of Colored People
NAB—National Association of Broadcasters
NAD—National Academy of Design
Nah.—Nahum
NAM—National Association of Manufacturers
NAS—National Academy of Sciences
NASA—National Aeronautics and Space Administration
nat.—national; native; natural
natl.—National
NATO—North Atlantic Treaty Organization
NATS—Naval Air Transport Service

naut.—nautical
nav.—naval; navigation
N.B.—New Brunswick
N.B., n.b.—nota bene (Lat.), mark well, take notice
Nb—niobium
NBA—National Basketball Association; National Boxing Association
NBC—National Broadcasting Company
NBS—National Bureau of Standards
NC—Nurse Corps
N.C.—North Carolina
NCAA—National Collegiate Athletic Association
NCCJ—National Conference of Christians and Jews
NCO, n.c.o.—noncommissioned officer
N.D.—North Dakota
N.D., n.d.—no date
Nd—neodymium
N.Dak.—North Dakota
N.E.—New England
NEA—National Education Association
Neb., Nebr.—Nebraska
NED—New English Dictionary (the Oxford English Dictionary)
neg.—negative
Neh.—Nehemiah
neur., neurol.—neurology
Nev.—Nevada
Newf.—Newfoundland
New M.—New Mexico
New Test.—New Testament
N.F.—Newfoundland; Norman French
NFL—National Football League
Nfld.—Newfoundland
NG—National Guard
N.G., n.g.—No good
N.H.—New Hampshire
NHA—National Housing Administration
NHG, O.H.G., H.H.G.—New High German
Ni—nickel
NIH—National Institutes of Health
NIRA—National Industrial Recovery Administration
N.J.—New Jersey
NKVD—from the Russian for People's Commissariat for Internal Affairs, the secret police succeeding OGPU
NL, N.L.—New Latin
n.l.—new line (print.); non licet (Lat.), it is not permitted or it is not lawful; non liquet (Lat.), it is not clear
NLRB—National Labor Relations Board
N.M., N.Mex.—New Mexico
NMU—National Maritime Union
No—nobelium
No.—north; northern
No., no.—numero (Lat.), number
noncom.—noncommissioned officer
non obst.—non obstante (Lat.), notwithstanding
non pros.—non prosequitur (Lat.), he does not prosecute
non seq.—non sequitur (Lat.), it does not follow
Nor.—Norman; North
NORAD—North American Air Defense Command
Nov., Nov—November
N.P.—nisi prius (Lat.), no protest (banking); Notary Public
Np—neptunium
n.p. or d.—no place or date
NRA—National Recovery Administration
NRAB—National Railroad Adjustment Board
N.S.—New Style (calendar); Nova Scotia
NSC—National Security Council
NSF—National Science Foundation
NSPCA—National Society for the Prevention of Cruelty to Animals
NSPCC—National Society for the Prevention of Cruelty to Children
NT., N.T.—New Testament
Num., Numb.—Numbers (Bible)
NWLB—National War Labor Board

N.W.T.—Northwest Territories
N.Y.—New York
NYA—National Youth Administration
N.Y.C.—New York City

O

O—oxygen
o—ohm
o.—ocean; order
OAS—Organization of American States
Obad.—Obadiah
O.B.E.—Officer (of the Order) of the British Empire
obit.—obituary
obj.—object, objective
obs.—observation; obsolete
OCD—Office of Civilian Defense
OCDM—Office of Civil and Defense Mobilization
OCS—Officer Candidate School
Oct., Oct—October
oct., 8vo.—octavo (print.)
O.D.—Officer of the Day; ordinary seaman; overdraft or overdrawn
ODT—Office of Defense Transportation
OE, O.E.—Old English
OECD—Organization for Economic Co-operation and Development
OED—Oxford English Dictionary
OEO—Office of Economic Opportunity
OES—Office of Economic Stabilization
O.E.S.—Order of the Eastern Star
OF, O.F.—Old French
O.F.M.—Order of Friars Minor
OHG, O.H.G.—Old High German
O.H.M.S.—On His (Her) Majesty's Service
O.K., OK—correct or approved
Okla.—Oklahoma
Old Test.—Old Testament
O.M.—Order of Merit
ON, O.N.—Old Norse
Ont.—Ontario
O.P.—Order of Preachers (Dominicans)
op. cit.—opere citato (Lat.), in the work cited
Ore., Oreg.—Oregon
orig.—original; originally
ornith.—ornithology
OS, O.S.—Old Saxon
O.S.—Old Style (calendar)
Os—osmium
O.S.A.—Order of St. Augustine
O.S.B.—Order of St. Benedict
O.S.F.—Order of St. Francis (Franciscan, or Capuchin, Order)
OSRD—Office of Scientific Research and Development
OSS—Office of Strategic Services
O.T.—Old Testament
OTS, O.T.S.—Officers' Training School
oz.—ounce (It. abbrev. of onza)

P

P—phosphorus
P., p.—pater (Lat.), father; pawn (chess); père (Fr.) father; post (Lat.), after; president; priest; prince
p—piano (It.), softly (music)
p,—page; part; participle; penny; per (Lat.), by
PA—public address (system); power of attorney
Pa—protactinium
Pa.—Pennsylvania
PAC—Political Action Committee
Pac., Pacif.—Pacific
PAL—Police Athletic League
paleon.—paleontology
par.—paragraph; parallel
parl.—parliamentary
pat., patd.—patent; patented
Pat. Off.—Patent Office
path., pathol.—pathology
PAU—Pan American Union
Pb—plumbum (Lat.), lead
PBS—Public Buildings Service

PBX—private branch exchange
PC—Preparatory Commission
P.C.—Police Constable; Privy Council; Privy Councilor
PCA—Progressive Citizens of America
pct.—percent
P.D.—Police Department
Pd—palladium
Pd.—paid
p.d.—per diem (Lat.), by the day
P.E.N.—Poets, Playwrights, Editors, Essayists and Novelists (International Association of)
pen.—peninsula
Penn., Penna.—Pennsylvania
per an.—per annum (Lat.), by the year
pers.—person; personal
Pet.—Peter
pfc, pfc.—private first class
PGA—Professional Golfers Association
*p*H—(not an abbrev.) a symbol indicating the negative logarithm of the hydrogen ion concentration.
Ph—phenyl
PHA—Public Housing Administration
phar., pharm.—pharmaceutical; pharmacology; pharmacopoeia; pharmacy
Ph.B.—Philosophiae Baccalaureus (Lat.), Bachelor of Philosophy
Ph.C.—Pharmaceutical Chemist
Ph.D.—Philosophiae Doctor (Lat.), Doctor of Philosophy
Phil.—Philemon
Phila.—Philadelphia
Philem.—Philemon
philol.—philologist; philology
philos.—philosopher; philosophy
phon.—phonetics
PHS—Public Health Service
phys.—physical; physician; physicist; physics
pizz.—pizzicato (It.), plucked (music)
pl.—plural
P.M.—Past Master; Police Magistrate; Postmaster
P.M., P.M., p.m.—post meridiem (Lat.), after noon
Pm—promethium
P.M.G.—Paymaster General; Postmaster General
Po—polonium
po.—putouts (baseball)
p.o.—petty officer; postal order; post office
POE—Port of Embarkation
pop.—population
POW, P.O.W., POWs, P.O.W.'s—prisoner(s) of war
P.P., p.p.—parcel post; parish priest; postpaid
pp—pianissimo (It.), very soft (music)
pp.—pages
P.P.C.—pour prendre congé (Fr.), to take leave
ppd.—postpaid; prepaid
P.Q.—Province of Quebec
p.q.—previous question
P.R.—Puerto Rico; proportional representation
Pr—praseodymium
PRA—Public Roads Administration
prep.—preparation; preparatory; preposition
pres.—president
Presb.—Presbyterian
prin.—principal; principle
PRO—public relations officer
proc.—proceedings; process
prod.—production
Prof., prof.—professor
prom.—promontory
pron.—pronoun; pronunciation
Prot.—Protestant
pro tem.—pro tempore (Lat.), for the time being
Prov.—Provençal; Proverbs
prov.—province; provisional; provost
prox.—proximo mense (Lat.), next month
Prus.—Prussia(n)

P.S.—Privy Seal; Public School
P.S., p.s.—post scriptum (Lat.), postscript
Ps.—Psalm(s)
pseud.—pseudonym
psi—pounds per square inch
PST—Pacific Standard Time
psychol., psych.—psychological; psychologist; psychology
Pt—platinum
pt—pint
pt.—part; payment; point; port
PTA—Parent-Teacher Association
PT boat—patrol torpedo boat
P.T.O.—please turn over
Pu—plutonium
pub.—public; published; publisher; publication
pvt.—private
PW—Prisoner of War
PWA—Public Works Administration
PWD—Public Works Department
pwt—pennyweight
PX—Post Exchange

Q

Q—Queen (chess)
Q—quasi (Lat.), as it were, almost; Quebec; queen; query; question
q.—quarto; question
QB—queen's bishop (chess)
Q.B.—Queen's Bench
QBP—queen's bishop's pawn (chess)
Q.C.—Quartermaster Corps; Queen's Counsel
Q.E.D.—quod erat demonstrandum (Lat.), which was to be proved
Q.E.F.—quod erat faciendum (Lat.), which was to be done
QKT—queen's knight (chess)
QM, Q.M.—quartermaster
QMG—quartermaster-general
QP—queen's pawn (chess)
Q.P., q.pl.—quantum placet (Lat.), as much as you please
qq.v.—quae vide (Lat.), which see (plural)
QR—queen's rook (chess)
qr.—quarter
QRP—queen's rook's pawn (chess)
qs—quantum sufficit (Lat.), as much as may suffice
qt—quart
q.t.—quiet (slang)
Que.—Quebec
ques.—question
quot.—quotation
q.v.—quod vide (Lat.), which, or whom, see

R

R—radical (hydrocarbon radical, chem.); radius; rates (math.); rook (chess)
R, r—resistance (elec.); royal; ruble
R.—Reaumur
R., r.—rabbi; rector; regina; river; road; royal; rupee
r.—radius; reigned; runs (baseball)
R.A.—Rear Admiral; Royal Academy, or Academician; Royal Artillery
Ra—radium
RAAF—Royal Australian Air Force
RAF—Royal Air Force
R.A.M.—Royal Academy of Music; Royal Arch Mason
Rb—rubidium
RBC—red blood cells; red blood count
r.b.i., rbi, RBI—run(s) batted in (baseball)
R.C.—Red Cross; Reserve Corps; Roman Catholic
RCAF—Royal Canadian Air Force
RCMP—Royal Canadian Mounted Police
R.D.—Rural Delivery
Rd., rd.—road
R.E.—real estate; Reformed Episcopal; Right Excellent; Royal Engineers
Re—rhenium
REA—Rural Electrification Administration
rec.—receipt; recipe; record; recorded

rect.—receipt; rector
ref.—referee; reference; reformed
Ref. Ch.—Reformed Church
reg.—regent; regiment; region; register; registrar; regular; regulation
Rep., Repub.—Republic; Republican
Rev.—Revelation (Bible); Reverend
Rev. Ver.—Revised Version (Bible)
RF—radio frequency
RFC—Reconstruction Finance Corporation
R.F.D.—Rural Free Delivery
Rh—rhodium
Rh factor—Rhesus factor (agglutinogen often present in human blood, biochem.)
R.I.—Rhode Island
RIBA—Royal Institute of British Architects
R.I.P.—requiescat in pace (Lat.), let him, or her, rest in peace
rit., ritard.—ritardando (It.), more slowly (music)
riv.—river
R.M.S.—Railway Mail Service
R.N.—Registered Nurse; Royal Navy
Rn—radon
RNA—ribonucleic acid
R.N.R.—Royal Naval Reserve
R.N.V.R.—Royal Naval Volunteer Reserve
Rom.—Roman; Romans (Bible)
ROTC—Reserve Officers Training Corps
R.P.—Regius Professor (Lat.), Royal Professor; Reformed Presbyterian
RPF—Rassemblement du Peuple Français (Fr.), Reunion of the French People
rpm—revolutions per minute
rps—revolutions per second
R.R.—Railroad; Right Reverend
RRB—Railroad Retirement Board
R.S.A.—Royal Society for Antiquarians; Royal Scottish Academy
RSFSR—Russian Socialist Federated Soviet Republic
RSV—Revised Standard Version (Bible)
R.S.V.P., r.s.v.p.—répondez s'il vous plait (Fr.), answer if you please
Rt. Hon.—Right Honorable
Rt. Rev.—Right Reverend
Ru—ruthenium
R.V.—Revised Version (Bible)
Ry.—Railway

S

S—sulfur
S, S., s.—south
S.—Sabbath; Samuel (Bible); Saturday; Saxon; Seaman; September; Signor; Sunday
S., s.—saint, soprano; southern
s.—second; semi-; shilling; silver; sire; solo; son
S.A.—Salvation Army
SAC—Strategic Air Command
Sam., Saml.—Samuel
Sans., Sansk.—Sanskrit
SAR—Sons of the American Revolution
S.A.S.—Societatis Antiquariorum Socius (Lat.), Fellow of the Society of Antiquaries
Sask.—Saskatchewan
Sat.—Saturday; Saturn
S.B.—Scientiae Baccalaureus (Lat.), Bachelor of Science
Sb—stibium (Lat.), antimony
SBA—Small Business Administration
SC—Security Council (United Nations)
S.S.—Sanitary Corps; Signal Corps; South Carolina; Supreme Court
Sc—scandium
Sc.—science; Scotch; Scots; Scottish
sc.—scale; scene; science; screw
s.c.—small capitals (print.)
Scan., Scand.—Scandinavia(n)
SCAP—Supreme Commander Allied Powers
Sc.B.—Scientiae Baccalaureus (Lat.), Bachelor of Science

Sc.D.—Scientiae Doctor (Lat.), Doctor of Science
sch.—school
sci.—science; scientific; scientist
Sc.M.—Scientiae Magister (Lat.), Master of Science
Scot.—Scotch; Scotland; Scottish
scr.—scruple (pharm.)
Script.—Scripture
sculp., sculp.—sculptor; sculptural; sculpture
S.C.V.—Sons of Confederate Veterans
s.d.—sine die (Lat.), without day or without appointing a day
S.Dak.—South Dakota
Se—selenium
SEATO—Southeast Asia Treaty Organization
SEC—Securities and Exchange Commission
sec—secant; second(s)
sec.—secretary
sect.—section
secy.—secretary
sen.—senate; senator
Sep.—Septuagint
Sept., Sept.—September
seq., seqq.—sequentia (Lat.), following
serg., sergt.—sergeant
sf., sfz.—sforzando (It.), sudden strong accent (music)
SFSR—Soviet Federated Socialist Republic
sg, s.g.—senior grade
s.g.—specific gravity
sgt.—sergeant
SHAEF—Supreme Headquarters, Allied Expeditionary Forces
SHAPE—Supreme Headquarters Allied Powers (Europe)
Si—silicon
Sig., sig.—signature; signor (It.), mister
sin—sine
sing.—singular
S.J.—Society of Jesus
S.J.D.—Scientiae Juridicae Doctor (Lat.), Doctor of Juridical Science
Slav.—Slavic; Slavonian; Slavonic
S.M.—Scientiae Magister (Lat.), Master of Science; Sergeant Major; Soldier's Medal; State Militia
Sm—samarium
Sn—stannum (Lat.), tin
So.—South; Southern
soc.—society
S. of Sol.—Song of Solomon
sol.—solicitor
sop.—soprano
SOS—Service of Supply; the signal of distress is not an abbreviation but a prescribed code
SP—shore patrol or shore police (U.S. Navy)
sp.—special; species; specific; specimen; spelling; spirit
s.p.—sine prole (Lat.), without issue
SPARS—Women's Coast Guard Reserves (from the Coast Guard motto, "Semper Paratus—Always Ready")
SPCA—Society for the Prevention of Cruelty to Animals
spec.—special
sp gr—specific gravity
sp ht—specific heat
SPR—Society for Psychical Research
Sq.—Squadron
sq.—square; sequence
SR—Sons of the Revolution
Sr—strontium
Sr.—Senior; Señor; Sir
SRO—standing room only
SS, S.S.—Schutzstaffel (Ger.), protective force (a military unit of the Nazis)
SS, S.S., S/S—Steamship
SS.—Saints
S.S.—Sunday School
SSA—Social Security Administration

SSR—Soviet Socialist Republic
SSS—Selective Service System
St.—saint; strait; street
stacc.—staccato (It.), detached (music)
S.T.B.—Sacrae Theologiae Baccalaureus (Lat.), Bachelor of Sacred Theology
S.T.B.—Sacrae Theologiae Doctor (Lat.), Doctor of Sacred Theology
Ste.—Sainte (Fr., fem. of saint)
ster., stg.—sterling
St. Ex.—Stock Exchange
sub.—submarine; substitute; suburb
subj.—subject; subjective; subjunctive
Sun., Sund.—Sunday
sup.—superior; supplement; supply; supra (Lat.), above; supreme
supp., suppl.—supplement
supt.—superintendent
surg.—surgeon; surgery
sym.—symbol; symphony
syn.—synonym; synonymous

T

T—tantalum; temperature (absolute scale); (surface) tension; tritium
T.—Testament; Tuesday
t.—temperature; tempo; tempore (Lat.), in the time of; tenor; tense (gram.); territory; time; ton(s); town; transitive; troy (wt.)
Ta—tantalum
TAC—tactical air command
tan—tangent
TASS—Telegraphnoye Argentstvo Sovyetskovo Soyuza (Russ.), the Soviet News Agency
T.B., Tb., Tb, t.b.—tubercle bacillus; tuberculosis
Tb—terbium
tbs., tbsp.—tablespoon
TC—Trusteeship Council (United Nations); teachers college
Tc—technetium
Te—tellurium
tech.—technical; technology
tel.—telegram; telephone; telegraph
temp.—temperature; temporary
ten.—tenor; tenuto
Tenn.—Tennessee
terr., terr.—territory
Test.—Testament
Teut.—Teuton(ic)
Tex.—Texas
TF—Task Force
Th—thorium
Th.D.—Theologiae Doctor (Lat.), Doctor of Theology
theol.—theologian; theological; theology
Thess.—Thessalonians
Thur., Thurs.—Thursday
Ti—titanium
Tim.—Timothy
Tit.—Titus
TKO—technical knockout
Tl—thallium
Tm—thulium
TNT, T.N.T.—trinotrotoluene; trinitrotoluol
Tob.—Tobias
topog.—topography; topographical
tox.—toxicology
tr.—transitive; translated; translation; translator; transpose
trag.—tragedy; tragic
trans.—transaction; translation; translator; transportation
treas.—treasurer; treasury
trem.—tremolo, wavering, trembling (music)
trig., trigon.—trigonometric; trigonometry
tsp.—teaspoon
Tu., Tues.—Tuesday
TV—television; terminal velocity
TVA—Tennessee Valley Authority
TWA—Trans World Airlines
twp.—township

TWU—Transport Workers Union
typ.—typographer; typographical; typical

U

U—uranium
UAR—United Arab Republic
UAW—United Automobile Workers
U.B.—United Brethren
UDC—United Daughters of the Confederacy
UFO—unidentified flying objects
UHF—ultrahigh frequency
UK—United Kingdom
ult.—ultimate
UMT—Universal Military Training
UMW—United Mine Workers
UN, U.N.—United Nations
UNESCO—United Nations Educational, Scientific and Cultural Organization
UNICEF—United Nations Children's Fund
Unit.—Unitarian
Univ.—Universalists
univ.—universal; university
UNRRA—United Nations Relief and Rehabilitation Administration
UPI—United Press International
UPU—Universal Postal Union
U.S., US—United States
U.S.A., USA—United States Army; United States of America
USAF—United States Air Force
USCG—United States Coast Guard
USDA—United States Department of Agriculture
USES—United States Employment Service
USIA—United States Information Agency
USM—United States Mail; United States Mint
USMA—United States Military Academy
USMC—United States Marine Corps; United States Maritime Commission
USN—United States Navy
USNA—United States Naval Academy
USNG—United States National Guard
USNR—United States Naval Reserve
USO—United Service Organizations
USP—United States Pharmacopoeia
USPHS—United States Public Health Service
USS—United States Ship *or* Steamer
USSR—Union of Soviet Socialist Republics
U.S.W.A.—United Steel Workers of America
U.S.W.V.—United Spanish War Veterans
Ut.—Utah (not official)
U.T.W.A.—United Textile Workers of America
uv—ultraviolet

V

V—vanadium; vector (math.); velocity; victory
v.—verb; verse; versus; vide (Lat.), see; voltage; von (in German names)
VA—Veterans Administration
Va.—Virginia
VAR—visual-aural range
Vat.—Vatican
V.C.—Veterinary Corps; Vice-Chancellor; Victoria Cross
VD—venereal disease
ven.—venerable
vet.—veteran; veterinary
VFW—Veterans of Foreign Wars
V.G.—Vicar General
VHF—very high frequency
vid.—vide (Lat.), see
VIP—very important person
VISTA—Volunteers in Service to America
viz.—videlicet (Lat.), namely
V.M.D.—Veterinariae Medicinae Doctor (Lat.), Doctor of Veterinary Medicine
VNA—Visiting Nurse Association
vol.—volcano; volume
VOR—very high frequency omnirange

vox pop.—vox populi (Lat.), voice of the people
v.p.—vice president
V.R.—Victoria Regina (Lat.), Queen Victoria
V. Rev.—Very Reverend
V.S.—Veterinary Surgeon
vs.—versus (Lat.), against
vs., vss.—verse, verses
v.s.—vide supra (Lat.), see above
VSS—versions
Vt.—Vermont
VTOL—vertical take off and landing
Vulg., Vul.—Vulgate (Bible)

W

W—wolfram (Ger.), tungsten
W, W., w—watt; west
W.—Wales; Wednesday; Welsh
w., w.—width; work (physics)
WAAF—Women's Auxiliary Air Force (Brit.)
WAAS—Women's Auxiliary Army Service (Brit.)
WAC—Women's Army Corps (U.S.)
WAF—Women in the Air Force (U.S.)
Wash.—Washington
WASP—Women's Air Force Service Pilots
WAVES—Women Accepted for Volunteer Emergency Service (U.S. Navy)
WBC—white blood cells; white blood count
WCTU—Women's Christian Temperance Union
WD, W.D.—War Department
Wed.—Wednesday
w.f.—wrong font (print.)
WFU—World Federation of Trade Unions
WHO—World Health Organization (United Nations)
Wis., Wisc.—Wisconsin
WMO—World Meteorological Organization (United Nations)
WO—warrant officer
WPA—Works Projects Administration
wpm—words per minute
WRENS, W.R.N.S.—Women's Royal Naval Service (Brit.)
wt—weight
W.Va.—West Virginia
WVS—Women's Voluntary Service (Brit.)
WW—world war
Wyo., Wy.—Wyoming

X

X—Christ; Christian
x—an abscissa (math.); an unknown quantity
Xe—xenon
Xmas—Christmas

Y

Y—yttrium
Y.—Young Men's (Women's) Christian Association
y—an ordinate (math.); an unknown quantity
Yb—ytterbium
yd—yards(s)
YMCA—Young Men's Christian Association
YMHA—Young Men's Hebrew Association
yrbk.—yearbook
yr—year(s)
YWCA—Young Women's Christian Association
YWHA—Young Women's Hebrew Association

Z

Z—atomic number; zenith distance
z—an unknown quantity
Zech.—Zechariah
zn—zinc
Z.O.A.—zoological; zoology
Zr—zirconium

A

A, a (ei) the first letter in the English alphabet

a (ə *or, with emphasis,* ei) *adj.* the singular indefinite article, one ‖ any, each one of a kind ‖ denoting an apparent plural. Before vowels and a silent h, 'an' replaces 'a'

a- (ə) *prefix* on ‖ in ‖ at

a- (ei) *prefix* not, without. It changes to 'an-' before vowels and usually before h

aard·vark (árdvɑrk) *n. Oryctheropus afer,* an African anteater

aard·wolf (árdwụlf) *pl.* ˈaard·wolves (árdwụlvz) *n.* a carnivorous, burrowing animal of S. Africa

AB a blood group

A.B. Bachelor of Arts ‖ ablebodied seaman

ab- *prefix* from ‖ away, outside of

a·back (əbæk) *adv. (naut.)* with sails pressed back against the mast by head winds **taken aback** disagreeably astonished

ab·a·cus (æbəkəs) *pl.* **ab·a·ci** (æbəsai), **ab·a·cus·es** *n.* a calculating instrument consisting of a frame with beads on rods or wires

a·ban·don (əbændən) *n.* lighthearted yielding to impulse, letting go of restraint

abandon *v.t.* to give up ‖ to forsake ‖ to yield (oneself) **a·ban·doned** *adj.* forsaken, *an abandoned wife* ‖ dissolute

a·ban·don·ment (əbændənmənt) *n.* the act of abandoning

a·base (əbéis) *pres. part.* **a·bas·ing** *past and past part.* **a·based** *v.t.* to degrade, to humiliate **a·based** *adj.* humiliated **a·base·ment** *n.*

a·bash (əbæʃ) *v.t.* to cause a slight feeling of embarrassment to, disconcert **a·bash·ment** *n.*

a·bate (əbéit) *pres. part.* **a·bat·ing** *past and past part.* **a·bat·ed** *v.t.* to reduce, do away with ‖ *v.i.* to grow less **a·bate·ment** *n.*

ab·at·toir (æbətwar) *n.* a slaughterhouse

ab·bess (æbis) *n.* the woman superior of a nunnery or convent

ab·bey (æbi:) *n.* a monastery under an abbot or convent under an abbess

ab·bot (æbət) *n.* the superior of the community of an abbey **ab·bot·cy, ab·bot·ship** *ns*

ab·bre·vi·ate (əbri:vi:eit) *pres. part.* **ab·bre·vi·at·ing** *past and past part.* **ab·bre·vi·at·ed** *v.t.* to shorten (usually, a word) ‖ to reduce in extent

ab·bre·vi·a·tion (əbri:vi:éiʃən) *n.* the act or result of abbreviating a word

ABC (éibí:sí:) *n.* the alphabet ‖ the first principles of a subject

ab·di·cate (æbdikeit) *pres. part.* **ab·di·cat·ing** *past and past part.* **ab·di·cat·ed** *v.t.* to give up (a throne, position or responsibility ‖ *v.i.* to resign from power

ab·di·ca·tion (æbdikéiʃən) *n.* the renouncing of power or high office, esp. of kingship

ab·do·men (æbdəmən, æbdóumən) *n.* that part of the human body below the diaphragm containing the major organs of digestion and reproduction ‖ *zool.* the hind part of insects, spiders etc. **ab·dom·i·nal** (æbdómin'l) *adj.*

ab·duct (æbdʌkt) *v.t.* to kidnap, take away (esp. a woman or child) by force ‖ *(med.)* to draw (a part of the body) away from the midline

ab·duc·tion (æbdʌkʃən) *n.* the act of kidnapping, of forcibly taking away

ab·duc·tor (æbdʌktər) *n.* a person who kidnaps or takes away forcibly

a·ber·rant (əbérənt) *adj.* straying from normal standards ‖ *(biol.)* deviating from the normal type

ab·er·ra·tion (æbəréiʃən) *n.* a deviation from right or normal standards

a·bet (əbét) *pres. part.* **a·bet·ting** *past and past part.* **a·bet·ted** *v.t.* to encourage, support (someone) in wrongdoing **a·bét·ment, a·bét·ter** *(law),* **a·bét·tor** *ns*

a·bey·ance (əbéiəns) *n.* temporary suspension, usually of a custom, rule or law

ab·hor (æbhɔ́r) *pres. part.* **ab·hor·ring** *past and past part.* **ab·horred** *v.t.* to detest, regard with horror or disgust

ab·hor·rence (æbhɔ́rəns, æbhɔ́rəns) *n.* detestation, horror

ab·hor·rent (æbhɔ́rənt, æbhɔ́rənt) *adj.* arousing detestation, horror or disgust

a·bid·ance (əbáid'ns) *n.* (with 'by') compliance, *strict abidance by the rules*

a·bide (əbáid) *pres. part.* **a·bid·ing** *past and past part.* **a·bode** (əbóud), **a·bid·ed** *v.t.* to bear patiently, tolerate (used negatively and interrogatively) ‖ *v.i.* to continue in being, remain **to abide by** to accept (rules or a ruling), to stick to (one's decision) **a·bíd·ing** *adj.* constant, enduring

a·bil·i·ty (əbíliti:) *pl.* **a·bil·i·ties** *n.* skill or power in sufficient quantity, the *ability to see a job through* ‖ (often *pl.*) cleverness, talent

ab·ject (æbdʒekt) *adj.* despicable ‖ very humble ‖ without any moral resource ‖ servile ‖ wretched

ab·jec·tion (æbdʒékʃən) *n.* the state of being abject

ab·ju·ra·tion (æbdʒuréiʃən) *n.* a formal renunciation

ab·jure (æbdʒúər) *pres. part.* **ab·jur·ing** *past and past part.* **ab·jured** *v.t.* to renounce, give up solemnly, repudiate

ab·late (æbléit) *pres. part.* **ab·lat·ing** *past and past part.* **ab·lat·ed** *v.t.* *(space)* to remove by ablation ‖ *v.i.* *(space)* to undergo ablation

ab·la·tion (æbléiʃən) *n.* the removal of part of the body by surgery ‖ *(space)* the burning away of parts of a nose cone by the heat generated when a missile reenters the earth's atmosphere

a·blaze (əbléiz) *pred. adj. and adv.* on fire ‖ (fig.) lit up

a·ble (éib'l) *adj.* clever, competent, skilled

a·ble-bod·ied (éib'lbódi:d) *adj.* robust and in good health

ab·ne·gate (æbnigeit) *pres. part.* **ab·ne·gat·ing** *past and past part.* **ab·ne·gat·ed** *v.t.* to renounce, give up (a right etc.)

ab·ne·ga·tion (æbnigéiʃən) *n.* renunciation, denial

ab·nor·mal (æbnɔ́rməl) *adj.* different from the norm or average, unusual **ab·nor·mal·i·ty** (æbnɔrmǽliti:) *pl.* **ab·nor·mal·i·ties** *n.*

ABO a classification of blood groups with regard to their use in transfusion

a·board (əbɔ́rd, əbóurd) **1.** *adj. and adv.* on or into a ship, plane, train etc. **2.** *prep.* on board

a·bode (əbóud) *n.* *(old-fash., rhet.)* the place someone lives in ‖ *(old-fash., rhet.)* residence

a·bol·ish (əbɔ́liʃ) *v.t.* to do away with completely, put an end to

ab·o·li·tion (æbəliʃən) *n.* the act of abolishing ‖ (esp. *hist.*) the movement against slavery **ab·o·li·tion·ism, ab·o·li·tion·ist** *ns*

A-bomb (éibɒm) *n.* atomic bomb

a·bom·i·na·ble (əbóm' inəb'l) *adj.* causing intense disgust, *an abominable crime*

(a) æ, cat; ɑ, car; ɔ fawn; ei, snake. **(e)** e, hen; i:, sheep; iə, deer; ɛə, bear. **(i)** i, fish; ai, tiger; ə:, bird. **(o)** o, ox; au, cow; ou, goat; u, poor; ɔi, royal. **(u)** ʌ, duck; u, bull; u:, goose; ə, bacillus; ju:, cube. x, loch; θ, think; ð, bother; z, Zen; ʒ, corsage; dʒ, savage; ŋ, orangutang; j, yak; ʃ, fish; tʃ, fetch; 'l, rabble; 'n, redden. Complete pronunciation key appears inside front cover.

a·bom·i·na·bly (əbɔ́mɪnəbli:) *adv.* in an abominable way

a·bom·i·nate (əbɔ́mineit) *pres. part.* **a·bom·i·nat·ing** *past and past part.* **a·bom·i·nat·ed** *v.t. (rhet.)* to detest

a·bom·i·na·tion (əbɔ̩minéiʃən) *n.* disgust ‖ a loathsome act or thing

ab·o·rig·i·nal (æbəridʒinəl) **1.** *adj.* existing from the earliest times ‖ pertaining to aborigines **2.** *n.* an aborigine **ab·o·rig·i·nal·i·ty** (æbəridʒinǽliti:) *n.*

ab·o·rig·i·ne (æbəridʒini:) *n.* a native inhabitant of a country, esp. before colonization

a·bort (əbɔ́rt) *v.i. (med.)* to give birth to a fetus before it is viable ‖ *(biol.)* to become arrested in development ‖ *v.t. (space)* to bring (a missile flight) to an end before completion of schedule

a·bor·tion (əbɔ́rʃən) *n.* the spontaneous or induced expulsion from the womb of a nonviable human fetus **a·bór·tion·ist** *n.* a doctor or other person who induces abortions

a·bor·tive (əbɔ́rtiv) *adj.* of premature birth ‖ ending in failure

a·bound (əbáund) *v.i.* to be abundant

a·bout (əbáut) **1.** *adv.* all around ‖ here and there ‖ in the opposite direction **about to (do something)** on the point of (doing something) **to come about** to happen **2.** *prep.* concerning, in connection with ‖ approximately

a·bove (əbʌ́w) **1.** *adj.* preceding, just mentioned **2.** *adv.* higher up, overhead ‖ earlier (in a book) **3.** *prep.* higher than ‖ beyond ‖ more than (in number or quantity) **above all** more than anything else **over and above** in addition to

a·brade (əbréid) *pres. part.* **a·brad·ing** *past* and *past part.* **a·brad·ed** *v.t.* to roughen or wear away the surface of by rubbing or scraping

a·bra·sion (əbréiʒən) *n.* the action of wearing by friction, esp. of grazing the skin ‖ the result of rubbing

a·breast (əbrést) *adv.* side by side and facing in the same direction **to keep abreast of** to keep oneself informed about

a·bridge (əbrídʒ) *pres. part.* **a·bridg·ing** *past* and *past part.* **a·bridged** *v.t.* to shorten ‖ to curtail

a·bridg·ment, a·bridge·ment (əbridʒmənt) *n.* the act of shortening or curtailing

a·broad (əbrɔ́d) *adv.* in a foreign land

ab·ro·gate (æbrəgeit) *pres. part.* **ab·ro·gat·ing** *past* and *past part.* **ab·ro·gat·ed** *v.t.* to cancel, repeal, annul, *to abrogate a law*

ab·rupt (əbrʌ́pt) *adj.* sudden, unexpected ‖ steep, precipitous ‖ rough, brusque in manner ‖ disconnected

ab·scess (æbses) *n.* a localized collection of pus occurring anywhere in the body **áb·scessed** *adj.*

ab·scond (æbskɔ́nd) *v.i.* to flee secretly, esp. to escape the law

ab·sence (æbsəns) *n.* a being away ‖ a failure to be present ‖ lack, *absence of proof*

ab·sent (æbsənt) *adj.* away, not present ‖ abstracted, *an absent air*

ab·sent (æbsént) *v. refl.* to keep (oneself) away **ab·sen·tee** (æbsənti:) *n.* a person who is absent **ab·sen·tée·ism** *n.* persistent absence from work

ab·sent·ly (æbsəntli:) *adv.* in an absent way, inattentively

ab·sent·mind·ed (æbsəntmáindid) *adj.* preoccupied and for that reason not paying attention to what one is doing

ab·so·lute (æbsəlu:t) **1.** *adj.* whole, complete ‖ pure ‖ having unrestricted power ‖ not conditioned by, or dependent upon, anything else **2.** *n.* something that is absolute **the Absolute** the self-existent, the First Cause, God

absolute pitch the pitch of a note as determined by a simple frequency, not a combination of frequencies ‖ the ability to identify a note sounded in isolation

ab·so·lu·tion (æbsəlú:ʃən) *n.* the forgiveness of sin, setting free from guilt

ab·so·lut·ism (æbsəlu:tĭzəm) *n.* autocratic government unrestrained by law

ab·solve (æbzɔ́lv, æbsɔ́lv) *pres. part.* **ab·solv·ing** *past*

and *past part.* **ab·solved** *v.t.* to set free from obligation, guilt or sin ‖ to remit (a sin) by absolution ‖ to acquit

ab·sorb (æbsɔ́rb, æbzɔ́rb) *v.t.* to take up (a substance) into or throughout a system by physical or chemical means ‖ to take in as if by swallowing or sucking ‖ to assimilate, receive without adverse effects ‖ to interest profoundly, occupy completely

ab·sorb·en·cy (æbsɔ́rbənsi:, æbzɔ́rbənsi:) *n.* the state or quality of being absorbent

ab·sorb·ent (æbsɔ́rbənt, æbzɔ́rbənt) **1.** *adj.* having the ability, capacity or tendency to absorb **2.** *n.* a substance having this ability, capacity or tendency

ab·sorp·tion (æbsɔ́rpʃən, æbzɔ́rpʃən) *n.* an absorbing or being absorbed

ab·stain (æbstéin) *v.i.* (with 'from') to choose not to participate ‖ (with 'from') to choose not to indulge oneself

ab·sten·tion (æbsténʃən) *n.* the act or practice of abstaining

ab·sti·nence (æbstinəns) *n.* refraining from, or doing without, food, drink or pleasure

ab·sti·nent (æbstinənt) *adj.* practicing abstinence

ab·stract (æbstrækt) **1.** *adj.* considered apart from perception or any concrete object, idealized ‖ theoretical **2.** *n.* a summary ‖ a short version of a piece of writing, report etc. **the abstract** (æbstrǽkt) the ideal **3.** (æbstrǽkt) *v.t.* to take out, remove ‖ to steal ‖ (æbstrækt) to make a written summary of

ab·strac·tion (æbstrǽkʃən) *n.* the act of taking away, abstracting ‖ formation of an idea apart from concrete things, situations etc.

ab·struse (æbstrú:s) *adj.* not easy to understand

ab·surd (æbsɔ́:rd, æbzɔ́:rd) *adj.* foolishly contrary to reason ‖ ridiculous

ab·surd·i·ty (æbsɔ́:rditi:, æbzɔ́:rditi:) *pl.* **ab·surd·i·ties** *n.* the state or quality of being absurd ‖ something absurd

a·bun·dance (əbʌ́ndəns) *n.* richness, plenty

a·bun·dant (əbʌ́ndənt) *adj.* plentiful, copious

a·buse (əbjú:z) *pres. part.* **a·bus·ing** *past* and *past part.* **a·bused** *v.t.* to use badly or wrongly ‖ to ill-treat, injure ‖ to call (somebody) foul names

a·buse (əbjú:s) *n.* misuse ‖ ill-treatment ‖ an instance of injustice or corruption

a·bu·sive (əbjú:siv) *adj.* characterized by abuse ‖ (of language) vituperative

a·but (əbʌ́t) *pres. part.* **a·but·ting** *past* and *past part.* **a·but·ted** *v.i.* (with 'on' or 'against') to border, to have a common boundary or frontier ‖ to end or lean for support **a·bút·ment** *n.* the place where one thing abuts on another

a·byss (əbís) *n.* a chasm, deep gorge **a·byss·al** (əbisəl) *adj.* of the lower depths of the sea

ac·a·dem·ic (ækədémik) **1.** *adj.* scholarly ‖ related to a school, college or university ‖ of theoretical interest rather than practical value **2.** *n.* a member of a university

ac·a·dem·i·cal (ækədémik'l) *adj.* of or pertaining to a college or university **ac·a·dém·i·cals** *pl. n.* academic costume (cap and gown, hood)

a·cad·e·my (əkǽdəmi:) *pl.* **a·cad·e·mies** *n.* a school devoted to specialized training, *a military academy, an academy of art* ‖ a society of scholars or artists

a cap·pel·la (ɑkəpélə) (of choral music) unaccompanied instrumentally

ac·cede (æksí:d) *pres. part.* **ac·ced·ing** *past* and *past part.* **ac·ced·ed** *v.i.* to agree ‖ (with 'to') to come to (the throne), become invested with (an office), attain (some honor)

ac·cel·er·ate (ækséləreit) *pres. part.* **ac·cel·er·at·ing** *past* and *past part.* **ac·cel·er·at·ed** *v.i.* to go faster ‖ *v.t.* to make (something) go faster

ac·cel·er·a·tion (æksɛləréiʃən) *n.* an increase of speed or velocity

ac·cel·er·a·tor (æksélərɛitər) *n.* a device for increasing speed, e.g. in a car

ac·cent (ǽksent) *n.* the emphasis by stress or pitch on a word or syllable, specifically in poetic rhythms ‖ the mark used to indicate such a stress ‖ a local or national quality in pronunciation ‖ (*loosely*) emphasis of any kind

ac·cent (ǽksent, æksént) *v.t.* to pronounce with emphasis ‖ to emphasize

ac·cen·tu·al (ækséntʃuːəl) *adj.* characterized by accent, having rhythm based on stress

ac·cen·tu·ate (ækséntʃuːeit) *pres. part.* **ac·cen·tu·at·ing** *past* and *past part.* **ac·cen·tu·at·ed** *v.t.* to emphasize, attribute special importance to

ac·cen·tu·a·tion (æksentʃuːéiʃən) *n.* an accentuating or accenting

ac·cept (æksépt) *v.t.* to take (something offered) ‖ to admit the truth or correctness of ‖ to agree to meet (an obligation) ‖ to take on the responsibility of (an office) ‖ to give an affirmative answer to (an invitation)

ac·cept·a·bil·i·ty (ækseptəbíliti:) *n.* the state or quality of being acceptable

ac·cept·a·ble (ækséptəb'l) *adj.* agreeable, satisfactory ‖ worth accepting ‖ welcome ‖ barely satisfactory **ac·cépt·a·bly** *adv.*

ac·cept·ance (ækséptəns) *n.* a taking or consenting to take something offered ‖ approval ‖ agreement to meet an obligation

ac·cess (ǽkses) *n.* way of approach ‖ right of approach

ac·ces·si·bil·i·ty (æksesəbiliti:) *n.* the state or quality of being accessible

ac·ces·si·ble (æksésəb'l) *adj.* easy to approach ‖ able to be reached ‖ able to be influenced, open **ac·cés·si·bly** *adv.*

ac·ces·so·ry, ac·ces·sa·ry (æksésəri:) **1.** *n. pl.* **ac·ces·so·ries, ac·ces·sa·ries** (usually *pl.*) something added for more convenience or usefulness ‖ (*pl.*) accompanying items for a woman's dress, such as handbag, shoes, gloves etc. **2.** *adj.* additional ‖ (*law*) concerned in a crime without being the chief protagonist

ac·ci·dent (ǽksidənt) *n.* a mishap ‖ a chance event commonly involving catastrophe, suffering or damage

ac·ci·den·tal (æksidént'l) *adj.* happening by chance, fortuitous

ac·claim (əkléim) **1.** *v.t.* to applaud by shouting, hail enthusiastically **2.** *n.* loud applause, vociferous welcome ‖ enthusiastic praise

ac·cla·ma·tion (ækləméiʃən) *n.* a shouting of assent

ac·cli·mate (əkláimət, ǽkləmeit) *pres. part.* **ac·cli·mat·ing** *past* and *past part.* **ac·cli·mat·ed** *v.t.* to acclimatize

ac·cli·ma·ti·za·tion (əklaimətizéiʃən, əklaimətaizéiʃən) *n.* the process by which plants and animals can live and reproduce in an environment different from their native one

ac·cli·ma·tize (əkláimətaiz) *pres. part.* **ac·cli·ma·tiz·ing** *past* and *past part.* **ac·cli·ma·tized** *v.t.* to accustom to a new climate or to new conditions ‖ *v.i.* to become accustomed to a new climate or to new conditions

ac·co·lade (ǽkəleid) *n.* any solemn recognition of merit

ac·com·mo·date (əkɔ́mədeit) *pres. part.* **ac·com·mo·dat·ing** *past* and *past part.* **ac·com·mo·dat·ed** *v.t.* to provide lodging for ‖ to hold, have space enough for ‖ to oblige, esp. with a loan of money ‖ to adapt, adjust ‖ to settle (a difference) **ac·cóm·mo·dat·ing** *adj.* obliging, willing to adapt oneself to other people's convenience

ac·com·mo·da·tion (əkɔmədéiʃən) *n.* (*Am. pl., Br. sing.*) lodgings ‖ space, capacity to receive people ‖ a loan of money ‖ a settlement or agreement ‖ something designed for convenience

ac·com·pa·ni·ment (əkʌ́mpəniːmənt) *n.* a thing which goes naturally or inevitably with something ‖ (*mus.*) an instrumental part which supports a solo instrument or singer

ac·com·pa·nist (əkʌ́mpənist) *n.* (*mus.*) someone who plays an accompaniment for a performer

ac·com·pa·ny (əkʌ́mpəni:) *pres. part.* **ac·com·pa·ny·ing** *past* and *past part.* **ac·com·pa·nied** *v.t.* to go out with (someone), to escort ‖ to cause something specified to be done, uttered etc. conjointly with (something) ‖ (*mus.*) to play an accompaniment for or to ‖ *v.i.* (*mus.*) to play in accompaniment

ac·com·plice (əkɔ́mplis) *n.* an active partner in a misdemeanor or crime

ac·com·plish (əkɔ́mpliʃ) *v.t.* to bring to a successful conclusion, fulfil **ac·cóm·plished** *adj.* proficient ‖ competent in the social graces

ac·com·plish·ment (əkɔ́mpliʃment) *n.* a superficial rather than a thorough skill ‖ a feat ‖ a bringing to completion ‖ a social grace

ac·cord (əkɔ́rd) *n.* an agreement ‖ harmony, esp. of tone, color, sounds etc. **of one's own accord** willingly, without constraint

ac·cor·dance (əkɔ́rd'ns) *n.* agreement, conformity

ac·cor·dant (əkɔ́rd'nt) *adj.* in harmony, in agreement

ac·cord·ing·ly (əkɔ́rdiŋli:) *adv.* therefore, in consequence ‖ in accordance with the circumstances

ac·cor·di·on (əkɔ́rdi:ən) *n.* a small wind instrument **ac·cór·di·on·ist** *n.*

accordion pleats narrow pleats used in dressmaking, lampshade making etc.

ac·cost (əkɔ́st, əkɔ́st) *v.t.* to approach and start a conversation with ‖ (of a prostitute) to solicit

ac·count (əkáunt) *v.t.* to consider, believe to be **to account for** to explain, answer for ‖ to render an explanatory statement for (expenses etc.)

account *n.* a statement of income and expenditure ‖ a bill for work done or services rendered ‖ a statement, description, explanation **of no (some, any, little) account** of no (some etc.) value, importance **on account** in part payment of a sum owed or as an advance payment of earnings **on account of** because of **on any account** for any reason **on one's own account** in one's own interest **to give a good account of oneself** to perform well **to square accounts** to settle what is owing ‖ to redress a grievance **to take into account, to take account of** to take into consideration (when coming to a decision) **to turn to account** to put to advantageous use

ac·count·a·bil·i·ty (əkauntəbiliti:) *n.* the quality or state of being accountable

ac·count·a·ble (əkáuntəb'l) *adj.* answerable, bound to give an explanation ‖ able to be explained, explicable **ac·cóunt·a·bly** *adv.*

ac·count·ant (əkáuntənt) *n.* a person skilled in keeping accounts, or someone who examines or inspects the accounts of a business or company

ac·cred·it (əkrédit) *v.t.* to cause (an ambassador, envoy etc.) to be officially recognized ‖ to recognize (an educational institution) as meeting defined standards **ac·cred·i·tá·tion** *n.* **ac·créd·it·ed** *adj.* officially recognized

ac·cre·tion (əkriːʃən) *n.* growth, esp. organic growth ‖ an adhesion of things usually separate ‖ the act of accreting ‖ the result of this act

ac·cru·al (əkrúːəl) *n.* something which has accrued ‖ the process of accruing

ac·crue (əkrúː) *pres. part.* **ac·cru·ing** *past* and *past part.* **ac·crued** *v.i.* to come about as a natural consequence ‖ (of interest on investments) to accumulate

---

ac·cu·mu·late (əkjú:mjəleit) *pres. part.* **ac·cu·mu·lat·ing** *past* and *past part.* **ac·cu·mu·lat·ed** *v.t.* to gather together in large numbers or quantity, amass ‖ *v.i.* to increase in number or quantity

ac·cu·mu·la·tion (əkjumjəléiʃən) *n.* an accumulating or being accumulated ‖ something accumulated ‖ increase of money by the addition of interest

ac·cu·ra·cy (ǽkjərəsi) *n.* the quality of being accurate, precision

ac·cu·rate (ǽkjərit) *adj.* precise, exact

ac·cu·sa·tion (ækjuzéiʃən) *n.* a charge of having done wrong ‖ an indictment **to bring an accusation against** to charge with doing wrong

ac·cuse (əkjú:z) *pres. part.* **ac·cus·ing** *past* and *past part.* **ac·cused** *v.t.* to charge with doing wrong ‖ to blame **the accused** the person or persons charged in a court of law

ac·cus·tom (əkʌstəm) *v.t.* (esp. *refl.* and *pass.*) to get used ‖ to habituate **ac·cús·tomed** *adj.* usual, habitual

a·cer·bic (əsə́:rbik) *adj.* bitter, sour ‖ (of wit etc.) edged with harshness

ac·e·tate (ǽsiteit) *n.* a salt or ester of acetic acid ‖ a synthetic fabric or yarn derived from the acetic ester of cellulose

a·ce·tic (əsí:tik) *adj.* relating to vinegar

ac·e·tone (ǽsitoun) *n.* a colorless volatile inflammable liquid commonly used as a solvent for organic compounds **ac·e·ton·ic** (æsitónik) *adj.*

a·cet·y·lene (əsét'li:n) *n.* a colorless inflammable gas. It is a highly unsaturated compound of carbon and hydrogen

ache (eik) **1.** *n.* a continuous dull pain as opposed to a sharp, sudden pain **2.** *v.i. pres. part.* **ach·ing** *past* and *past part.* **ached** to suffer continuous dull pain ‖ to have painful yearnings

a·chiev·a·ble (ətʃí:vəb'l) *adj.* able to be achieved

a·chieve (ətʃí:v) *pres. part.* **a·chiev·ing** *past* and *past part.* **a·chieved** *v.t.* to carry out successfully ‖ to attain ‖ *v.i.* (*Am.*) to reach a required standard of performance

a·chieve·ment (ətʃí:vmənt) *n.* something carried out successfully ‖ the act of achieving

A·chil·les heel (əkíli:z) a vulnerable spot

Achilles' tendon a tendon joining the calf muscles to the bone in the heel

ac·id (ǽsid) *adj.* having a sour, sharp taste, like a lemon ‖ relating to or having the characteristics of an acid ‖ acidproducing ‖ looking or sounding bitter or sour, *an acid remark* ‖ (*slang*) LSD or d-lysergic acid diethylamide, an hallucinogenic drug

a·cid·ic (əsídik) *adj.* acid-forming ‖ acid

a·cid·i·fy (əsídifai) *pres. part.* **a·cid·i·fy·ing** *past* and *past part.* **a·cid·i·fied** *v.t.* to make sour ‖ (*chem.*) to make acid ‖ *v.i.* to become sour

a·cid·i·ty (əsíditi:) *pl.* **a·cid·i·ties** *n.* the state or quality of being acid ‖ an acid remark

a·cid·ly (ǽsidli:) *adv.* (of a manner of speaking) bitterly

ac·knowl·edge (əknólidʒ) *pres. part.* **ac·knowl·edg·ing** *past* and *past part.* **ac·knowl·edged** *v.t.* to recognize as a fact, admit the truth of ‖ to report the receipt of ‖ to recognize in a legal form ‖ to recognize and answer (a greeting, nod etc.) **ac·knówl·edg·ment, ac·knówl·edge·ment** *n.* the act of acknowledging ‖ a receipt for something given **in acknowledgment of** in gratitude for, in recognition of

ac·me (ǽkmi:) *n.* the highest point, peak of perfection

ac·ne (ǽkni:) *n.* a skin disease caused by chronic inflammation of the sebaceous glands

ac·o·lyte (ǽkəlait) *n.* a person who assists a priest at Mass ‖ an admiring follower

a·cous·tic (əkú:stik) *adj.* pertaining to sound ‖ pertaining to acoustics ‖ designed to improve hearing **a·cóus·ti·cal** *adj.*

a·cous·tics (əkú:stiks) *n.* the science of sound waves and their production, transmission, reception and control ‖ the study of hearing ‖ the acoustic properties, e.g. of an auditorium

ac·quaint (əkwéint) *v.t.* to familiarize, inform **to be acquainted with** to know (a person or thing)

ac·quaint·ance (əkwéintəns) *n.* someone whom one knows only slightly ‖ knowledge of something **ac·quáint·ance·ship** *n.*

ac·qui·esce (ækwi:és) *pres. part.* **ac·qui·esc·ing** *past* and *past part.* **ac·qui·esced** *v.i.* to agree, sometimes reluctantly, to a decision made by others ‖ to concur in an arrangement, suggestion etc.

ac·qui·es·cence (ækwi:és'ns) *n.* the act of acquiescing

ac·qui·es·cent (ækwi:és'nt) *n.* acquiescing ‖ submissive, compliant by nature

ac·quire (əkwáiər) *pres. part.* **ac·quir·ing** *past* and *past part.* **ac·quired** *v.t.* to gain for oneself, to come to have

ac·quire·ment (əkwáiərmənt) *n.* the act of acquiring ‖ a skill acquired or mental attainment

ac·qui·si·tion (ækwiziʃən) *n.* the gaining of something for oneself, act of acquiring ‖ the thing gained or acquired

ac·quis·i·tive (əkwízitiv) *adj.* very anxious to acquire

ac·quit (əkwít) *pres. part.* **ac·quit·ting** *past* and *past part.* **ac·quit·ted** *v.t.* to declare (a person) not guilty of an offense ‖ to settle (a debt) ‖ to discharge from responsibility **to acquit oneself** to conduct oneself, esp. to show one's quality **ac·quít·tal** *n.*

ac·quit·tance (əkwít'ns) *n.* full payment of a debt

a·cre (éikər) *n.* a measure of land, 4,840 sq. yds. or approx. 4,000 sq. meters

a·cre·age (éikəridʒ) *n.* the area of land in acres ‖ acres collectively

ac·rid (ǽkrid) *adj.* bitter to the smell or taste

a·crid·i·ty (əkríditi:) *n.* the state or quality of being acrid

ac·ri·mo·ni·ous (ækrəmóuni:əs) *adj.* harsh, bitter, *an acrimonious quarrel*

ac·ri·mo·ny (ǽkrəmouni:) *pl.* **ac·ri·mo·nies** *n.* harshness or bitterness of temper or manner ‖ an instance of this

ac·ro·bat (ǽkrəbæt) *n.* someone who performs gymnastic feats **ac·ro·bát·ic** *adj.* **ac·ro·bát·i·cal·ly** *adv.* **ac·ro·bát·ics** *pl. n.* feats performed by acrobats

ac·ro·nym (ǽkrənim) *n.* a name made up of the initial letters of an official title. e.g. UNESCO

a·cross (əkrós, əkrɔ́s) **1.** *adv.* crosswise ‖ from side to side ‖ to or on the other side **2.** *prep.* on the other side of ‖ from one side to the other side of **to come across** to meet or find by chance ‖ (*pop.*) to pay out money ‖ (*pop.*)to give out information

a·cros·tic (əkró́stik, əkró́stik) *n.* a composition, usually in verse, in which the initial, final or other prearranged letters in each line when taken together spell out a word

act (ækt) *n.* a deed ‖ the doing of a deed ‖ one of the main divisions of a play ‖ a feature in a variety show, circus etc. ‖ a law passed by a legislative body

act *v.t.* to perform (a play or a part in a play) ‖ to play the part of ‖ *v.i.* to behave in a certain way ‖ to fulfil a particular function ‖ to intervene effectively ‖ to produce an effect, *the acid acts on the metal* **to act for** to represent with full authority

act·ing (ǽktiŋ) **1.** *adj.* doing temporary duty for someone else, *the acting mayor* **2.** *n.* the art of performing in plays or films ‖ this as a profession

ac·tion (ǽkʃən) *n.* the process of doing, acting ‖ something done, a deed ‖ effective intervention ‖ the working of one thing on another ‖ enterprise, deeds as compared with words ‖ a bodily movement performed repeatedly ‖ the series of events in a play or novel ‖ (*law*) a proceeding in a court of law where someone seeks to enforce his rights **to take action** to begin to be effective ‖ (*pop.*) goings on, *where the action is* ‖ to initiate practical measures **ác·tion·a·ble** *adj.* giving ground for an action at law **ác·tion·a·bly** *adv.*

ac·ti·vate (ǽktiveit) *pres. part.* **ac·ti·vat·ing** *past* and *past part.* **ac·ti·vat·ed** *v.t.* to make particularly active, esp. by chemical reaction

ac·ti·va·tion (æktivéiʃən) *n.* the act or process of

activating

ac·ti·va·tor (ǽktiveitər) *n.* a substance which activates

ac·tive (ǽktiv) *adj.* busy, energetic, *active in local politics* ‖ (of a volcano) erupting from time to time ‖ *(commerce)* productive, bearing interest, *active assets* ‖ *(gram.)* descriptive of a voice or form of the verb which shows the subject as performer of the action of the verb

ac·tiv·ism (ǽktivizəm) *n.* a theory that calls for militant propaganda action by individuals or the practice (esp. political) of such action

ac·tiv·ist (ǽktivist) *n.* someone who takes militant action in the service of a party or doctrine

ac·tiv·i·ty (æktíviti:) *pl.* **ac·tiv·i·ties** *n.* the state of being active ‖ capacity for being active ‖ *(pl.)* ways in which people use their energies, *social and cultural activities*

ac·tu·al (ǽktʃuːəl) *adj.* existing as a fact of experience, real as opposed to potential

ac·tu·al·i·ty (æktʃuːǽliti:) *pl.* **ac·tu·al·i·ties** *n.* reality ‖ *(pl.)* realities, things having existence

ac·tu·al·ly (ǽktʃuːəli:) *adv.* in fact, really, *he pretended to be deaf but actually he was not* ‖ at this moment

ac·tu·ar·y (ǽktʃuːeri:) *pl.* **ac·tu·ar·ies** *n.* a statistician who estimates risks and probabilities, particularly in insurance, lotteries etc.

ac·tu·ate (ǽktʃuːeit) *pres. part.* **ac·tu·at·ing** *past* and *past part.* **ac·tu·at·ed** *v.t.* to put into action or motion ‖ to motivate the actions of (a person) **ac·tu·a·tion** *n.*

a·cu·i·ty (əkjúːiti:) *n.* shrewdness, acuteness of perception

a·cu·men (əkjúːmən, ǽkjumən) *n.* keen insight or perceptiveness, *financial acumen*

a·cute (əkjúːt) *adj.* penetrating, perceptive ‖ severe, sharp, *acute pain* ‖ crucial, critical ‖ (of the senses) keen, *acute hearing* ‖ *(med.)* beginning suddenly, developing rapidly and not prolonged

A.D. *ANNO DOMINI

ad·age (ǽdidʒ) *n.* an ancient piece of popular wisdom, a saw or saying

a·da·gio (ədáːdʒou) **1.** *adv.* and *adj. (mus.)* in slow tempo (as an instruction for the execution of a musical piece) **2.** *n.* a slow piece or a slow movement

ad·a·mant (ǽdəmənt) **1.** *n.* a substance of utmost hardness **2.** *adj.* (of a person), unyielding **ad·a·man·tine** (ædəmǽntain, ædəmǽnti:n) *adj.*

a·dapt (ədǽpt) *v.t.* to put (oneself) in harmony with changed circumstances ‖ to make more suitable by altering **a·dapt·a·bil·i·ty** *n.* **a·dápt·a·ble** *adj.*

ad·ap·ta·tion (ædæptéiʃən) *n.* the act or process of adapting ‖ the condition of being adapted ‖ *(biol.)* an inherited or acquired structure or function serving to fit a plant or animal for its environment ‖ something adapted, *a screen adaptation of a play*

a·dapt·er (ədǽptər) *n.* a device for connecting two pieces of apparatus, esp. in electrical equipment

a·dap·tive (ədǽptiv) *adj.* tending or able to adapt ‖ showing adaptation

add (æd) *v.t.* to join, unite or combine (something) with something else so as to increase in size, number or quantity ‖ to add up, *add 6 and 4* ‖ *v.i.* to do addition **to add in** to include, *add this in with the rest* **to add to** to increase, *losing the rope added to our difficulties* **to add up** to find the sum of (two or more numbers) ‖ to make sense, bear close inspection, *his story doesn't add up* ‖ (with 'to') to reach a specified total

ad·den·dum (ədéndəm) *pl.* **ad·den·da** (ədéndə) *n.* something to be added ‖ a supplementary part or appendix of a book

ad·der (ǽdər) *n.* a small poisonous snake

ad·dict (ədíkt) **1.** *v.t.* to habituate, esp. **to be** (or **become**) **addicted to** to have given oneself up to (a practice or habit, usually bad) and be or become unduly dependent upon (it) **2.** (ǽdikt) *n.* a person addicted to something harmful, usually a drug ‖ *(loosely)* someone inordinately fond of something not harmful, *a jazz addict*

ad·dic·tion (ədíkʃən) *n.* the state of being addicted

ad·dic·tive (ədíktiv) *adj.* causing addiction

ad·di·tion (ədíʃən) *n.* the process of adding ‖ an arithmetic sum ‖ an increase, something extra **in addition to** as well as **ad·dí·tion·al** *adj.* extra

ad·di·tive (ǽditiv) *n.* something added to a food product to give it color, make it keep etc. ‖ something added to a substance (e.g. paint) to give it a desired quality

ad·dress (ədrés) **1.** *v.t.* to make a speech or deliver a sermon to ‖ to speak or write formally to ‖ to write the destination on (a letter, parcel etc.) **2.** (ədrés, ǽdres) *n.* the place where a person lives ‖ the written direction on a letter, parcel etc. **ad·dress·ee** (ædresíː) *n.* the person to whom a letter, parcel etc. is addressed

ad·e·noid (ǽdnɔid) *adj.* of or resembling a lymphoid tissue **ad·e·nóid·al** *adj.* of or relating to the adenoids **ád·e·noids** *pl.* a soft mass of lymphoid tissue at the back of the nose and throat

ad·ept (ədépt) **1.** *adj.* clever, particularly proficient **2.** *n.* (ǽdept, ədépt) someone thoroughly clever or skilled in anything, an expert

ad·e·qua·cy (ǽdikwəsi:) *n.* the state of being adequate

ad·e·quate (ǽdikwit) *adj.* equal to or sufficient for a special requirement

ad·here (ædhíər) *pres. part.* **ad·her·ing** *past* and *past part.* **ad·hered** *v.i.* to cling, cleave, stick fast (to a thing, a person or an idea)

ad·her·ence (ædhíərəns) *n.* the action of adhering, attachment

ad·her·ent (ædhíərənt) **1.** *adj.* clinging, sticking **2.** *n.* a follower, supporter

ad·he·sion (ædhíːʒən) *n.* the act or condition of adhering ‖ *(phys.)* intermolecular attraction holding together surfaces in contact

ad·he·sive (ædhíːsiv) **1.** *adj.* sticky, able to stick fast **2.** *n.* a substance used to stick two surfaces together

ad hoc (ædhók) exclusively for some understood special purpose

ad·ja·cen·cy (ədʒéisənsi:) *pl.* **ad·ja·cen·cies** *n.* the condition of being adjacent

ad·ja·cent (ədʒéisənt) *adj.* near, nearby ‖ next, bordering

ad·jec·tive (ǽdʒiktiv) *n. (gram.)* a part of speech used to qualify, define or limit a substantive

ad·join (ədʒɔ́in) *v.t.* to lie next to, be adjacent to ‖ *v.i.* to be immediately next to another

ad·journ (ədʒə́ːrn) *v.t.* to suspend, defer (a meeting etc.) with a view to later resumption ‖ *v.i.* to suspend or defer a meeting etc. **ad·jóurn·ment** *n.*

ad·judge (ədʒʌ́dʒ) *pres. part.* **ad·judg·ing** *past* and *past part.* **ad·judged** *v.t.* to judge or declare after careful consideration ‖ *(law)* to find, *adjudged guilty* ‖ *(law)* to award, *the estate was adjudged to the claimant*

ad·junct (ǽdʒʌŋkt) *n.* something added or extra but subordinate ‖ *(gram.)* a word or phrase added to another with the purpose of qualifying or defining it ‖ *(logic)* a nonessential quality **ad·junc·tive** (ədʒʌ́ŋktiv) *adj.*

ad·ju·ra·tion (ædʒuréiʃən) *n.* earnest command, entreaty

ad·jure (ədʒúər) *pres. part.* **ad·jur·ing** *past* and *past part.* **ad·jured** *v.t.* to charge (a person) to do something as though on oath ‖ *(rhet.)* to beseech

ad·just (ədʒʌ́st) *v.t.* to set right, make orderly ‖ to regulate for proper use ‖ to adapt (oneself) **ad·júst·er, ad·jús·tor** *n.* someone who, or something which adjusts (machines or equipment) **ad·júst·ment** *n.* the act of adjusting ‖ a settlement

ad·lib (ædlíb) *pres. part.* **ad·lib·bing** *past* and *past part.* **ad·libbed** *v.i.* to speak or perform without preparation ‖ *v.t.* to improvise (a speech, performance etc.) **ad lib** *adv.* in unrestricted plenty

ad·min·is·ter (ædmínistər) *v.t.* to manage, direct (business affairs, an estate etc.) ‖ to serve out, dispense ‖ to give, provide ‖ to tender (the oath) to someone ‖ *v.i.* to act as administrator

ad·min·is·tra·tion (ædmịnistréiʃən) *n.* the act of administering ‖ the art or practice of carrying out a policy in government, business or public affairs ‖ the act of administering a sacrament, oath, remedy, punishment etc. ‖ *(law)* management of a dead person's property

ad·min·is·tra·tive (ædmínistreịtiv, ædmínistrətiv) *adj.* concerned with administration

ad·mi·ra·ble (ædmərəb'l) *adj.* worthy of admiration ‖ excellent **ad·mi·ra·bly** *adv.*

ad·mi·ra·tion (ædməréiʃən) *n.* a delighted contemplation of something worthy or beautiful ‖ esteem, respect

ad·mire (ædmáiər) *pres. part.* **ad·mir·ing** *past* and *past part.* **ad·mired** *v.t.* to contemplate or consider with pleasure or respect ‖ to express admiration for **ad·mir·er** *n.* someone who admires ‖ *(old-fash.)* a lover

ad·mis·si·ble (ædmísəb'l) *adj.* (of ideas or propositions) that may be allowed or conceded ‖ able to be admitted to a post or office ‖ *(law)* allowable as evidence or judicial proof **ad·mis·si·bly** *adv.*

ad·mis·sion (ædmíʃən) *n.* the action of admitting, of giving access or entrance ‖ the price of admission ‖ entry into an office or status ‖ acknowledgment of the truth of a fact or statement

ad·mis·sive (ædmísiv) *adj.* tending to admit, allowing admission or inclusion

ad·mit (ædmít) *pres. part.* **ad·mit·ting** *past* and *past part.* **ad·mit·ted** *v.t.* to allow to enter or have access to a place ‖ to recognize as true ‖ to acknowledge ‖ (of an enclosed space) to have room for ‖ *v.i.* (with 'to') to make an acknowledgment ‖ *(rhet.)* to give entrance **to admit of** to allow as a possibility **ad·mit·tance** *n.* the act of admitting ‖ right of entry **ad·mit·ted·ly** *adv.* as is generally admitted ‖ as I am willing to admit

ad·mon·ish (ædmóniʃ) *v.t.* to reprove mildly ‖ to warn ‖ to urge, exhort **ad·món·ish·ment** *n.*

ad·mo·ni·tion (ædməníʃən) *n.* warning ‖ rebuke

a·do·be (ədóubi:) *n.* sun-dried brick, not fired in a kiln ‖ a building made of such bricks

ad·o·les·cence (æd'lésəns) *n.* that period of life in which the child changes into the adult

ad·o·les·cent (æd'lésənt) **1.** *n.* a person who is no longer a child but is not fully adult **2.** *adj.* of, belonging to or characteristic of such a person

a·dopt (ədópt) *v.t.* to make one's own (an idea, belief, custom etc. that belongs to or comes from someone else) ‖ to become the legal parent of (a child not one's own) ‖ to accept

a·dop·tion (ədópʃən) *n.* an adopting or being adopted

a·dop·tive (ədóptiv) *adj.* of a relationship acquired by adoption, *an adoptive father, an adoptive country*

a·dor·a·ble (ədɔ́rəb'l, ədóurəb'l) *adj.* worthy of adoration ‖ lovable (often in trivial contexts), *an adorable puppy* **a·dór·a·bly** *adv.*

ad·o·ra·tion (ædəréiʃən) *n.* the act of adoring, worshiping

a·dore (ədɔ́r, ədóur) *pres. part.* **a·dor·ing** *past* and *past part.* **a·dored** *v.t.* to worship, venerate ‖ to love ‖ (in trivial contexts) to live very much **a·dór·ing** *adj.*

a·dorn (ədɔ́rn) *v.t.* to add beauty or splendor to (something) by decoration **a·dórn·ment** *n.* the act of adorning ‖ something which adorns

a·dren·al·in, a·dren·a·line (ədrén'lin) *n.* a pair of hormones produced by the medulla of the adrenal glands that prepares the organism for emotional stress

a·drift (ədríft) *pred. adj.* and *adv.* afloat without control, at the mercy of wind and sea ‖ at the mercy of circumstances

a·droit (ədrɔ́it) *adj.* dextrous, nimble ‖ lively and resourceful in dealing with difficult situations or people

ad·sorb (ædsɔ́rb, ædzɔ́rb) *v.t.* to retain by adsorption **ad·sórb·ate** *n.* an adsorbed substance **ad·sórb·ent 1.** *adj.* having the tendency or capacity to adsorb **2.** *n.* an agent with this property **ad·sórp·tion** *n.* a process by which molecules are taken up on the surface of a solid by chemical or physical action **ad·sórp·tive** *adj.* and *n.*

ad·u·late (ædʒəleit) *pres. part.* **ad·u·lat·ing** *past* and *past part.* **ad·u·lat·ed** *v.t.* *(rhet.)* to praise fulsomely ‖ to admire to excess

ad·u·la·tion ('ædʒəléiʃən) *n.* fulsome flattery ‖ excessive admiration

ad·u·la·tor (ædʒəl'eitər) *n.* a person who adulates

ad·u·la·to·ry (ædʒələtɔ:ri:, ædʒələtouri:) *adj.* fulsomely flattering ‖ excessively admiring

a·dult (ædʌlt, ədʌ́lt) **1.** *n.* a mature, fully grown person, one who has passed adolescence ‖ *(law)* a person who has come of age ‖ a fully grown plant or animal **2.** *adj.* of, for, belonging to or characteristic of an adult

a·dul·ter·er (ədʌ́ltərər) *n.* a man who commits adultery **a·dul·ter·ess** (ədʌ́ltəris) *n.* a woman who commits adultery

a·dul·ter·ous (ədʌ́ltərəs) *adj.* of or characterized by adultery

a·dul·ter·y (ədʌ́ltəri:) *n.* voluntary sexual intercourse of a married man with a woman other than his wife or of a married woman with a man other than her husband

ad·vance (ædvǽns, ædváns) **1.** *v. pres. part.* **ad·vanc·ing** *past* and *past part.* **ad·vanced** *v.i.* to go forward ‖ to progress, move towards completion ‖ to go up in rank, status etc. ‖ *v.t.* to move forward ‖ to cause (an event) to happen sooner than planned or expected or to bring forward in time ‖ to pay over (money) before the date when it is due **2.** *n.* a moving forward, progress ‖ an improvement in knowledge, technique etc. ‖ a payment of money before it is due ‖ *(pl.)* attempts to make one's personal relations with someone intimate **in advance** beforehand ‖ in front **ad·vánced** *adj.* (of ideas etc.) progressive, in front of most other people's ‖ far developed ‖ (of knowledge) developed beyond the ordinary or elementary level **of advanced years** old

ad·van·tage (ædvǽntidʒ, ædvántidʒ) *n.* a condition or position conferring superiority ‖ a condition or set of circumstances which helps one to reach a desired end ‖ something which gives benefit or profit **to advantage** in a favorable way **to take advantage of (someone)** to mislead or trick (someone) **to take advantage of (something)** to make the most of, profit by (an opportunity etc.) **ad·van·ta·geous** (ædvəntéidʒəs) *adj.*

ad·ven·ture (ædvéntʃər) *n.* a dangerous or exciting incident, or a hazardous enterprise ‖ a delightful experience

ad·ven·tur·er (ædvéntʃərər) *n.* someone who lives by his wits ‖ an unscrupulous speculator ‖ any seeker after adventure

ad·ven·ture·some (ædvéntʃərsəm) *adj.* *(rhet.)* venturesome

ad·ven·tur·ess (ædvéntʃəris) *n.* a woman out to get money or social position by guile and charm

ad·ven·tur·ous (ædvéntʃərəs) *adj.* enterprising, liable to take risks ‖ requiring courage, fraught with danger

ad·verb (ædvə:rb) *n.* *(gram.)* a part of speech which modifies or limits a verb, an adjective, or another adverb **ad·ver·bi·al** (ædvɔ́:rbi:əl) *adj.*

ad·ver·sa·ry (ædvərseri:) *pl.* **ad·ver·sa·ries** *n.* opponent, enemy

ad·verse (ædvə:rs, ædvɔ́:rs) *adj.* contrary, opposing ‖ unfavorable, unpropitious

ad·ver·si·ty (ædvɔ́:rsiti:) *pl.* **ad·ver·si·ties** *n.* misfortune, trouble, affliction ‖ a misfortune

ad·ver·tise, ad·ver·tize (ædvərtaiz) *pres. part.* **ad·ver·tis·ing, ad·ver·tiz·ing** *past* and *past part.* **ad·ver·tised, ad·ver·tized** *v.t.* to make known, proclaim publicly, esp. in order to promote sales ‖ to draw attention to, make conspicuous ‖ *v.i.* to publish an advertisement **to advertise for** to ask for (someone or something) by public notice **ad·ver·tise·ment, ad·ver·tize·ment** (ædvərtáizmənt, advɔ́:rtismənt) *n.* public notice or announcement, usually offering goods or services for sale **ád·ver·tis·ing, ád·ver·tiz·ing** *n.*

ad·vice (ædváis) *n.* a stated opinion meant to help to determine correct action or conduct ‖ *(commerce)* a notification of a transaction ‖ *(pl.)* information sent by an agent or agency **to take advice** to consult the opinion of a specialist ‖ to do what one has been advised to do

ad·vis·a·bil·i·ty (ædvaizəbíliti:) *n.* the quality of being advisable

ad·vis·a·ble (ædváizəb'l) *adj.* prudent, expedient ‖ to be recommended **ad·vis·a·bly** *adv.*

ad·vise (ædváiz) *pres. part.* **ad·vis·ing** *past and past part.* **ad·vised** *v.t.* to give advice to, recommend a course of action to ‖ *(commerce)* to notify ‖ *v.i.* to give advise **ad·vis·ed·ly** (ædváizidli:) *adv.* with due deliberation **ad·vís·er, ad·ví·sor** *n.* someone who gives advice **ad·vi·so·ry** (ædváizəri:) *adj.* having the power to advise ‖ consisting of advice

ad·vo·cate (ǽdvəkit, ǽdvəkeit) *n.* a person who pleads on behalf of another, esp. in a court of law ‖ a person who speaks or writes in support of some cause, argument or proposal

ad·gis, e·gis (í:dʒis) *n.* patronage, sponsorship ‖ direction, control

aer·ate (ɛ́əreit, éiəreit) *pres. part.* **aer·at·ing** *past and past part.* **aer·at·ed** *v.t.* to impregnate with air ‖ to charge (a liquid) with gas or air **aer·á·tion** *n.*

aer·i·al (ɛ́əri:əl) **1.** *adj.* of the air or atmosphere ‖ existing or moving in the air ‖ thin as air ‖ overhead, in the air, *an aerial railway* **2.** *n.* an antenna

aer·i·al·ist (ɛ́əri:əlist) *n.* an acrobat who performs feats in the air

aer·o·bics (ɛəroubiks) system of exercise based on increasing oxygen intake to stimulate heart and lung activity

aer·o·dy·nam·ic (ɛ̀əroudainǽmik) *adj.* of or relating to aerodynamics

aer·o·dy·nam·ics (ɛ̀əroudainǽmiks) *n.* the science of air flow, particularly the study of the motion of solid bodies through air, and their control and stability

aer·o·naut·ics (ɛ̀ərɔnɔ́tiks, ɛ̀ərənɔ́tiks) *n.* the science and practice of flight by aircraft

aer·o·space (ɛ́ərəspeis) **1.** *n.* the earth's atmosphere together with cosmis space beyond **2.** *adj.* of or pertaining to the technology of flight or ballistics in aerospace

aes·thete (ésθi:t, *Br.* i:sθi:t) *n.* a person who professes to put beauty before other considerations

aes·thet·ic (esθétik, *Br.* i:sθétik) *adj.* concerning appreciation of the beautiful, esp. in the arts ‖ (of persons) appreciative of the beautiful **aes·thét·i·cal** *adj.* **aes·the·ti·cian** *n.* a person devoted to, or professionally occupied with, aesthetics **aes·thét·i·cism** *n.* **aes·thét·ics** *n.* the part of philosophy which deals with the perception of the beautiful as distinguished from the moral or the useful

a·far (əfár) *adv.* far off, at a distance **from afar** from a distance

af·fa·ble (ǽfəb'l) *adj.* easy to talk to, good-natured, courteous ‖ mild, not aggressive, *an affable reply* **áf·fa·bly** *adv.*

af·fair (əfɛ́ər) *n.* concern, business ‖ *(pl.)* daily concerns of a business organization or government ‖ (intentionally vague) an incident, *an unfortunate affair* ‖ a love affair

af·fect (əfékt) *v.t.* to make an impression on, move ‖ to have an effect on (something) ‖ to have a hurtful effect on ‖ (of a disease etc.) to attack, cause a particular condition in

affect *v.t.* to pretend, feign, *to affect indifference* ‖ to make a whimsical or ostentatious display of

af·fec·ta·tion (æfektéiʃən) *n.* a pretense made for effect ‖ studied artificiality in behavior and speaking

af·fec·tion (əfékʃən) *n.* fondness, tender feelings ‖ friendly feelings of attachment ‖ an illness, disease

af·fec·tion·ate (əfékʃənit) *adj.* showing fondness, tenderness, affection

af·fi·da·vit (æfidéivit) *n.* a written statement, sworn on oath to be true, esp. one signed in the presence of a notary

af·fil·i·ate (əfíli:eit) **1.** *v. pres. part.* **af·fil·i·at·ing** *past and past part.* **af·fil·i·at·ed** *v.i.* (usually of societies, institutions etc., with 'with' or 'to') to enter into association ‖ *v.t.* to add as an associate **2.** (əfíli:it, əfíli:eit) *n.* an associate, a person affiliated to something ‖ a subsidiary organization

af·fil·i·a·tion (əfili:éiʃən) *n.* an affiliating or being affiliated

af·fin·i·ty (əfíniti:) *pl.* **af·fin·i·ties** *n.* any close link or connection ‖ a strong liking or attraction between one person and another ‖ relationship by marriage ‖ *(biol.)* relationship between species which indicates a common origin

af·firm (əfə́:rm) *v.t.* to state positively, with conviction ‖ *v.i. (law)* to make a declaration of truthfulness (in place of the oath) ‖ to make a statement in the affirmative

af·fir·ma·tion (æfərméiʃən) *n.* an assertion, a positive statement ‖ *(law)* a solemn declaration

af·firm·a·tive (əfə́:rmətiv) **1.** *adj.* asserting that a fact is so, affirming by answering 'yes' **2.** *n.* the affirmative mode upholding a proposition ‖ an affirmative word or expression

af·fix (ǽfiks) *n.* something affixed, an appendage ‖ *(gram.)* a prefix, infix or suffix

af·fix (əfíks) *v.t.* to fasten ‖ to attach ‖ to append (usually a signature) ‖ to ascribe (censure, a salary etc.) **ad·fix·a·tion** (æfikséiʃən) *n.* the act or process of affixing ‖ the use of an affix **af·fix·ture** (əfíkstʃər) *n.* the state of being affixed

af·flict (əflíkt) *v.t.* to trouble or distress ‖ to inflict grievous physical or mental suffering on

af·flic·tion (əflíkʃən) *n.* something which causes trouble or distress ‖ physical or mental suffering

af·flu·ence (ǽflu:əns) *n.* wealth ‖ *(rhet.)* profusion

af·flu·ent (ǽflu:ənt) **1.** *adj.* rich **2.** *n.* a tributary stream

af·ford (əfɔ́rd, əfóurd) *v.t.* (with 'can' or 'be able to') to be in a position (to do something) ‖ (with 'can') to be able to buy (something) ‖ to give, provide

af·front (əfrʌ́nt) **1.** *v.t.* to insult, cause offense to **2.** *n.* an insult, deliberate act of disrespect

a·fire (əfáiər) *pred. adj.* and *adv.* on fire

a·flame (əfléim) *pred. adj.* and *adv.* in flames, burning ‖ glowing as though on fire

a·float (əflóut) *pred. adj.* and *adv.* floating ‖ not aground ‖ flooded, nearly submerged in water ‖ *(fig.)* in circulation, *rumors are afloat that he will resign* ‖ free of debt, solvent

a·foot (əfút) *pred. adj.* and *adv.* walking, on foot ‖ beginning to make progress

a·fraid (əfréid) *adj.* frightened, *snakes are afraid of people* ‖ apprehensive, fearful, *afraid of the consequences* ‖ *(loosely)* regretful

a·fresh (əfréʃ) *adv.* anew, again, *to start afresh*

af·ter (ǽftər, áftər) **1.** *prep.* in search of, in pursuit of ‖ later than, subsequent to, following in time ‖ in

---

(a) æ, c*a*t; ɑ, c*ar*; ɔ f*aw*n; ei, sn*a*ke. **(e)** e, h*e*n; i:, sh*ee*p; iə, d*ee*r; ɛə, b*ear*. **(i)** i, f*i*sh; ai, t*i*ger; ə:, b*ir*d. **(o)** o, *o*x; au, c*ow*; ou, g*oa*t; u, p*oor*; ɔi, r*oy*al. **(u)** ʌ, d*u*ck; u, b*u*ll; u:, g*oo*se; ə, b*a*cill*u*s; ju:, c*u*be. x, lo*ch*; θ, *th*ink; ð, bo*th*er; z, *Z*en; ʒ, cor*s*a*ge*; dʒ, sa*v*a*ge*; ŋ, oranguta*ng*; j, *y*ak; ʃ, *fi*sh; tʃ, fe*tch*; 'l, rabb*le*; 'n, redd*en*. Complete pronunciation key appears inside front cover.

spite of ‖ in imitation of, in the manner of **to be** (or **get**, etc.) **after** to be in angry pursuit of **to be named after someone** to be given someone's name **to look after** to take care of **to take after** to be like in looks or character **2.** *adv.* behind in time or place, later **3.** *conj.* subsequently to the time when

af·ter·birth (ǽftərbə:rθ, ɑ́ftərbə:rθ) *n.* the placenta, tissue connected with the fetus in the womb

af·ter·burn·er (ǽftərbə:rnər) *n.* device for destroying (usually by burning) carbon wastes, e.g., from the engine of a motor vehicle to reduce air pollution — **afterburn** *v.*

af·ter·math (ǽftərmæθ, ɑ́ftərmæθ) *n.* outcome, consequence (usually of a disastrous nature)

af·ter·noon (æftərnú:n, ɑftərnú:n) *n.* the time of day between midday and evening

a·gain (əgén) *adv.* once more ‖ furthermore, in addition **again and again** very often **as many** (or **much**) **again** the same quantity in addition **over again** once more

a·gainst (əgénst) *prep.* opposite to, contrary to ‖ in contrast to ‖ in anticipation of ‖ into contact with ‖ in exchange for ‖ in the opposite direction to ‖ to be charged to or deducted from (an account, or something thought of as an account) ‖ next to

a·gape (əgéip) *pred. adj.* openmouthed with surprise

age (eidʒ) **1.** *n.* the length of time that a person or thing has lived or existed ‖ the time of life when one is legally, socially, physically or mentally qualified for a particular purpose ‖ old age ‖ a generation ‖ an epoch ‖ a great period of time distinguished from others by its special characteristics. *Middle Ages* ‖ *(geol.)* a subdivision of an epoch ‖ *(pop., often pl.)* a very long time **2.** *v. pres. part.* **ag·ing, age·ing** *past* and *past part.* **aged** *v.t.* to make older ‖ *v.i.* to become perceptibly older ‖ to mellow **a·ged** (éidʒid) *adj.* old, showing visible signs of old age ‖ (éidʒd) of the age of

age·less (éidʒlis) *adj.* not affected by age or time

a·gen·cy (éidʒensi:) *pl.* **a·gen·cies** *n.* an organization (or its building) existing to promote the exchange of goods and services ‖ the profession of being an agent

a·gen·da (ədʒéndə) *n.* (construed as *pl.*) things to be done ‖ (construed as *sing.*) a list of things to be discussed at a business meeting ‖ a memorandum book

a·gent (éidʒənt) *n.* someone who represents a person or a firm in business ‖ an intermediary

ag·glom·er·ate (əglɔ́məreit) **1.** *v. pres. part.* **ag·glom·er·at·ing** *past* and *past part.* **ag·glom·er·at·ed** *v.t.* to gather into a ball or mass ‖ *v.i.* to grow into a ball or mass **2.** *adj.* (əglɔ́mərit) collected into, forming, growing into a ball or mass **3.** *n.* (əglɔ́mərit) a mass, collection **ag·glom·er·a·tion** *n.* a cohesive mass, e.g. a town's suburbs **ag·glom·er·a·tive** (əglɔ́məreitiv, əglɔ́mərətiv) *adj.*

ag·gran·dize (əgrǽndaiz, ǽgrəndaiz) *pres. part.* **ag·gran·diz·ing** *past* and *past part.* **ag·gran·dized** *v.t.* to make (a person or nation) greater in power, rank, prestige or wealth ‖ to exaggerate, to give the appearance of greatness to **ag·gran·dize·ment** (əgrǽndizmənt) *n.*

ag·gra·vate (ǽgrəveit) *pres. part.* **ag·gra·vat·ing** *past* and *past part.* **ag·gra·vat·ed** *v.t.* to make (an existing trouble) more serious ‖ *(pop.)* to irritate **ag·gra·va·tion** *n.*

ag·gre·gate (ǽgrigeit) **1.** *v. pres. part.* **ag·gre·gat·ing** *past* and *past part.* **ag·gre·gat·ed** *v.t.* to collect together into a mass ‖ to total ‖ *v.i.* to come together in a mass **2.** (ǽgrigit) *adj.* formed of parts making a collection, massed together ‖ total, collective ‖ *(geol.)* made up of different mineral crystals **3.** (ǽgrigit) *n.* a total derived by addition **in the aggregate** collectively **ag·gre·ga·tion** *n.*

ag·gres·sion (əgréʃən) *n.* a deliberate, unprovoked attack by one country or group on another

ag·gres·sive (əgrésiv) *adj.* wanting to dominate by attacking, domineering ‖ involving attack ‖ enterprising

and forceful

ag·gres·sor (əgrésər) *n.* a person, nation etc. making a deliberate attack

ag·grieved (əgrí:vd) *adj.* having a grievance

a·ghast (əgǽst, əgɑ́st) *pred. adj.* filled with terror or amazement or both

ag·ile (ǽdʒil, esp. *Br.* ǽdʒail) *adj.* quick moving, nimble, active in body or mind **a·gil·i·ty** (ədʒíliti:) *n.*

ag·i·tate (ǽdʒiteit) *pres. part.* **ag·i·tat·ing** *past* and *past part.* **ag·i·tat·ed** *v.t.* to shake, stir up ‖ to upset (feelings, people) ‖ *v.i. (politics)* to stir up the public by means of slogans, demonstrations etc. either to produce disorder or to secure reform

ag·i·ta·tion (ædʒitéiʃən) *n.* a disturbance, mental or physical, esp. worry ‖ public disturbance on a large scale, or the process of creating it

ag·i·ta·tor (ǽdʒiteitər) *n.* a person who provokes social, political or religious disaffection

a·glow (əglóu) *adv.* and *pred. adj.* in a glow

ag·nos·tic (ægnɔ́stik) **1.** *n.* a person who thinks that nothing can be known about the existence or nature of God ‖ a person who thinks that knowledge of all matters is relative **2.** *adj.* referring to agnosticism **ag·nós·ti·cal·ly** *adv.* **ag·nos·ti·cism** (ægnɔ́stisizəm) *n.*

ag·o·nize (ǽgənaiz) *pres. part.* **ag·o·niz·ing** *past* and *past part.* **ag·o·nized** *v.t.* to cause intense suffering in mind or body to ‖ *v.i.* to suffer intensely in mind or body, writhe with pain

ag·o·ny (ǽgəni:) *pl.* **ag·o·nies** *n.* intense mental or physical suffering ‖ an intense feeling ‖ *pl., loosely)* a hard struggle **last agony** the pangs of death

a·grar·i·an (əgréəri:ən) *adj.* relating to land or its management or distribution

a·gree (əgri:) *pres. part.* **a·gree·ing** *past* and *past part.* **a·greed** *v.i.* to assent ‖ to be in harmony ‖ to be suitable (as regards one's tastes, health etc.) ‖ *v.t.* to consent

a·gree·a·bil·i·ty (əgri:əbíliti:) *n.* the state or quality of being agreeable

a·gree·a·ble (əgri:əb'l) *adj.* pleasant ‖ prepared **a·grée·a·bly** *adv.*

a·gree·ment (əgrí:mənt) *n.* the act of agreeing ‖ the state of agreeing ‖ *(law)* a contract legally binding the contracting parties

ag·ri·cul·tur·al (ægrikʌ́ltʃərəl) *adj.* related to or characteristic of agriculture

ag·ri·cul·tur·al·ist (ægrikʌ́ltʃərəlist) *n.* a person competent in farming theory

ag·ri·cul·ture (ǽgrikʌltʃər) *n.* the science or practice of large-scale soil cultivation

ag·ri·cul·tur·ist (ægrikʌ́ltʃərist) *n.* an agriculturalist

a·gron·o·mist (əgrɔ́nəmist) *n.* someone who specializes in agronomy

a·gron·o·my (əgrɔ́nəmi:) *n.* the theory and practice of crop production and soil science

a·ground (əgráund) *adv.* and *pred. adj.* (of a ship) touching the bottom in shallow water

a·head (əhéd) **1.** *adj.* in front, in advance ‖ forward **2.** *adv.* in or to the front ‖ forward **ahead of** in front of ‖ before **to get ahead** to be successful

aid (eid) **1.** *n.* help, assistance ‖ someone who helps or something which helps **2.** *v.t.* and *i.* to help

ail (eil) *v.i.* to be slightly ill ‖ *v.t. (rhet.)* to trouble, afflict

ail·ment (éilmənt) *n.* an illness of a trivial nature

aim (eim) **1.** *v.t.* to direct (a missile, blow, gun etc. or a remark, purpose etc.) at an objective ‖ *v.i.* to take aim, direct a weapon or missile ‖ to direct efforts, purposes etc. **2.** *n.* the action of aiming ‖ a purpose, intention **to take aim** to aim **áim·less** *adj.* without purpose

air (ɛər) **1.** *n.* the atmosphere, the mixture of gases surrounding the earth which all people and land animals breathe ‖ the space above us ‖ a melody ‖ appearance, manner ‖ *(pl.)* affectations of superiority **by air** in an airplane **in the air** unsettled, uncertain ‖ prevalent, circulating, *rumors are in the air* **on the**

air in or by means of a radio broadcast **to give (someone) the air** to send away or dismiss (someone) **to walk on air** to be light-headed with happiness **up in the air** vague || not yet decided 2. *v.t.* to expose to fresh air, ventilate

air·bag (ɛ́ərbæg) *n.* plastic bag for automobile dashboard, designed to inflate upon collision to form a protective cushion

air·borne (ɛ́ərbɔ́rn, ɛ́ərbǫurn) *adj.* carried by air || in the air

air·con·di·tion (ɛ́ərkəndíʃən) *v.t.* to equip (a building) with air-conditioning apparatus

air conditioner an air-conditioning device

air conditioning a process by which air is purified and its temperature and humidity are regulated before it enters a room or building

air·craft (ɛ́ərkræft, ɛ́ərkrǫft) *sing.* and *pl. n.* any flying machine: an airplane, airship, glider or balloon

air·frame (ɛ́ərfreim) *n.* the body of an aircraft without the engines || the framework, envelope, and cabin of an airship || the assembled principal structural components of a missile

air·i·ly (ɛ́ərili:) *adv.* in an airy manner, gaily || unconcernedly, jauntily

air·i·ness (ɛ́əri:nis) *n.* the state or quality of being airy || lack of concern

air·less (ɛ́ərlis) *adj.* stuffy, oppressive, without movement of air

air·lift (ɛ́ərlíft) *n.* a large-scale system of replacing sea or land transport of goods or men by air in an emergency

air·line (ɛ́ərlain) *n.* a regular air service for the transport of goods and passengers || the route covered by such a service

air·mail (ɛ́ərmeil) *n.* letters and parcels, carried by air || the system for transporting such letters and parcels

air·plane (ɛ́ərplein) *n.* a heavier-than-air flying machine powered by motors or jets

air pocket a condition in the atmosphere, usually a partial vacuum, which causes an aircraft in flight to drop suddenly

air·port (ɛ́ərpɔ̨rt, ɛ́ərpǫurt) *n.* an expanse of level ground (or water) with control buildings, hangars, workshops etc., equipped to deal with aircraft passengers, refueling and repair of aircraft etc.

air raid an attack by aircraft

air·sick (ɛ́ərsik) *adj.* afflicted with nausea, vomiting etc. when (and as a result of) flying in an aircraft

air·space (ɛ́ərspeis) *n.* the part of space immediately over some specified territory or area, esp. with regard to jurisdiction

air·tight (ɛ́ərtait) *adj.* closed tightly so that air cannot get in or out || watertight, sure, certain

air·wor·thi·ness (ɛ́ərwə̨ːrðɨ:nis) *n.* the condition of being airworthy

air·wor·thy (ɛ́ərwə̨ːrðɨ:) *adj.* (of aircraft) in suitable condition for flying

air·y (ɛ́əri:) *adj.* open to the air || light-hearted, cheerful || self-complacent || graceful, delicate, moving freely as the air || immaterial, without reality

aisle (ail) *n.* (*archit.*) a side division of a church, flanking the nave || the passage between rows of seats in a church, theater etc. **aisled** (aild) *adj.*

a·jar (ədʒáɾ) *pred. adj.* and *adv.* (of doors and gates) slightly open

a·kin (əkín) *adj.* related by blood || or similar nature or character

al·a·bas·ter (ǽləbǽstər, ǽləbǫstər) *n.* a translucent, fine-grained variety of gypsum

a·lac·ri·ty (əlǽkriti:) *n.* briskness || eager readiness

a·larm (əláɾm) **1.** *n.* a signal warning of danger || an

excited, frightened anticipation of danger 2. *v.t.* to inspire with fear

alarm clock a clock with a device which rings at a previously set time

a·las (əlǽs) *interj.* expressing grief, regret, pity, concern

al·ba·tross (ǽlbətrɔs, ǽlbətrɒs) *pl.* **al·ba·tross·es al·ba·tross** *n.* a bird of the genus *Diomedea*, the largest seabird

al·be·it (ɔlbíːit) **1.** *conj.* (*rhet.*) even if, although **2.** *adv.* (*rhet.*) although, *he went, albeit unwillingly*

al·bi·nism (ǽlbinizəm) *n.* the state or quality of being an albino

al·bi·no (ælbáinou, esp. *Br.* ælbíːnou) *n.* a person with a congenital deficiency of pigment in the skin and hair, which are white, and in the eyes, which have a deep red pupil and pink or blue iris and are unable to bear ordinary light || any animal or plant similarly deficient in coloring pigment

al·bu·men (ælbjúːmən, ǽlbjumən) *n.* the white of an egg || (*biochem.*) albumin **al·bú·men·ize** *pres. part.* **al·bu·men·iz·ing** *past* and *past part.* **al·bu·men·ized** *v.t.* (*photog.*) to coat with an albuminous solution

al·bu·min (ælbjúːmən, ǽlbjumən) *n.* (*biochem.*) one of a group of heat coagulable colloidal proteins, soluble in water, and occurring in egg white, blood plasma or serum, milk and many animal and vegetable tissues

al·bu·min·ous (ælbjúːmənəs) *adj.* having the properties of albumen or albumin

al·che·mist (ǽlkəmist) *n.* a person who studied or practiced alchemy

al·che·my (ǽlkəmi:) *pl.* **al·che·mies** *n.* a medieval chemical art whose principal objectives were to find the panacea, and to transmute base metals into gold

al·co·hol (ǽlkəhɔl, ǽlkəhɒl) *n.* a colorless, volatile, intoxicating, inflammable liquid, ethyl alcohol, obtained commercially by distilling wine or other fermented liquors and by the hydration of ethylene || (*chem.*) a class of organic chemicals regarded as arising from the hydrocarbons by replacing one or more hydrogen atoms with hydroxyl (-OH) groups **al·co·hól·ic 1.** *adj.* of alcohol || containing or using alcohol || caused by alcohol **2.** *n.* a person who is addicted to alcohol **al·co·hól·i·cal·ly** *adv.*

al·co·hol·ism (ǽlkəhɔlizəm, ǽlkəhɒlizəm) *n.* dipsomania || the action of alcohol on the human system

al·cove (ǽlkouv) *n.* a recess in the wall of a room

ale (eil) *n.* alcoholic beverage brewed from an infusion of malt and flavored with hops, sugar etc., often stronger in alcohol and heavier in body than beer

a·lert (əlɔ́ːrt) **1.** *adj.* watchful, vigilant || brisk, nimble **2.** *n.* a warning, alarm, esp. of an air raid **on the alert** tensely watchful **3.** *v.t.* to warn, put on guard, call to a state of readiness

al·fal·fa (ælfǽlfə) *n.* a perennial hay crop of the highest quality grown widely in the U.S.A.

al·ga (ǽlgə) *pl.* **al·gae** (ǽldʒiː), **al·gas** *n.* a member of a larger group of nonvascular plants belonging to any of seven phyla of thallophytes **ál·gal** *adj.*

al·ge·bra (ǽldʒəbrə) *n.* a branch of mathematics in which symbols are used to represent numbers, variables or entities, either as means of expressing general relationships or to indicate quantities satisfying particular conditions **al·ge·bra·ic** (ǽldʒəbréiik), **al·ge·brá·i·cal** *adjs.* **al·ge·brá·i·cal·ly** *adv.* **al·ge·brá·ist** *n.*

a·li·as (éili:əs) *pl.* **a·li·as·es 1.** *adv.* otherwise called **2.** *n.* an assumed name

al·i·bi (ǽləbai) *pl.* **al·i·bis** *n.* (*law*) the plea of having been somewhere else at the time of a crime || (*pop.*) an excuse

al·ien (éiljən, éili:ən) **1.** *adj.* belonging to another country, foreign || (with 'from') differing in character ||

(with 'to') opposed in nature **2.** *n.* a non-naturalized foreigner, someone living in a country of which he is not a citizen || intelligent extraterrestrial being come to earth

al·ien·a·ble (éiljənəb'l, éili:ənəb'l) *adj.* capable of being alienated

al·ien·ate (éiljəneit, éili:əneit) *pres. part.* **al·ien·at·ing** *past* and *past part.* **al·ien·at·ed** *v.t.* to cause (affection) to be withdrawn || to cause (someone) to withdraw affection || to lose or give up (some natural right) **al·ien·á·tion** *n.*

a·light (əláit) *pres. part.* **a·light·ing** *past* and *past part.* **a·light·ed,** *rarely* **a·lit** (əlít) *v.i.* to get down from a vehicle || to come to rest after flight

a·lign, a·line (əláin) *pres. part.* **a·lign·ing, a·lin·ing** *past* and *past part.* **a·ligned, a·lined** *v.t.* to line up || to bring into line or into correct relative position || to join in sympathy || *v.i.* to be in proper line **a·lign·ment, a·line·ment** *n.* being in line, being in correct relative position to something else

a·like (əláik) **1.** *adv.* in the same manner **2.** *pred. adj.* similar, like each other

al·i·ment (ǽləmənt) **1.** *n.* food for body or mind **2.** (ǽləment) *v.t.* to provide with the means of support **al·i·mén·tal** *adj.*

al·i·men·ta·ry (ǽləméntəri:) *adj.* of or relating to the function of nutrition

al·i·mo·ny (ǽləmouni:) *pl.* **al·i·mo·nies** *n.* money payable on a judge's order by a man to his wife or former wife, or (sometimes) by a woman to her husband or former husband, for maintenance after separation or divorce

a·live (əláiv) *pred. adj.* and *adv.* living || brisk, lively || (with 'to') alert || in existence || (with 'with') swarming, *his coat was alive with fleas*

al·ka·li (ǽlkəlai) *pl.* **al·ka·lis, al·ka·lies** *n.* a usually soluble hydroxide or carbonate of the alkali metals, or less often of the alkaline earth metals **al·ka·li·fy** (ǽlkəlifai) *pres. part.* **al·ka·li·fy·ing** *past* and *past part.* **al·ka·li·fied** *v.t.* to make alkaline || *v.i.* to become alkaline

al·ka·line (ǽlkəlain) *adj.* having the properties of an alkali

all (ɔl) **1.** *adj.* the whole quantity of || the whole sum or number of || any whatever || everyone of || the greatest possible **2.** *pron.* everyone **3.** *n.* everything, one's total possessions **in all** in total **4.** *adv.* entirely, completely **all at once** suddenly **all but** very nearly **all in** exhausted **all in all** on balance, having considered every aspect of the question **all the better** better still **all told** counting everything **all very well** used to express discontent **at all** in any way whatever **for good and all** for ever, finally **not at all** used as a polite disclaimer of thanks or priase **not at all bad** used as an understatement for something rather good

all-a·round (ɔ́lərạund) *adj.* general, *a good all-around education*

al·lay (əléi) *v.t.* to make less, alleviate || to put at rest, make calm

al·le·ga·tion (ǽligéiʃən) *n.* an assertion or statement yet to be proved

al·lege (əlédʒ) *pres. part.* **al·leg·ing** *past* and *past part.* **al·leged** *v.t.* to affirm without necessarily being able to prove **al·leg·ed·ly** (əlédʒidli:) *adv.*

al·le·giance (əlí:dʒəns) *n.* devotion, loyalty || the duty of a subject to his sovereign, his rulers or his country

al·le·gor·ic (ǽligɔ́rik, ǽligɔ́rik) *adj.* containing, of the nature of, allegory **al·le·gór·i·cal** *adj.*

al·le·go·ry (ǽligɔri:, ǽligɔuri:) *pl.* **al·le·go·ries** *n.* a work of art in which a deeper meaning underlies the superficial or literal meaning || the carrying of one meaning by another in this way

al·le·gro (əléigrou) **1.** *adv.* and *adj.* (*mus.*) rather fast (as an instruction for the execution of a musical piece) **2.** *n.* a lively piece or movement

al·ler·gic (əlɔ́:rdʒik) *adj.* caused by, of the nature of, an allergy || (with 'to') having an allergy or allergies

al·ler·gist (ǽlərdʒist) *n.* a doctor specializing in the treatment of allergies

al·ler·gy (ǽlərdʒi:) *pl.* **al·ler·gies** *n.* an exaggerated and specific antigen-antibody reaction marked by sneezing, difficulty in breathing, swelling, itching, rash or other symptoms

al·le·vi·ate (əli:vi:eit) *pres. part.* **al·le·vi·at·ing** *past* and *past part.* **al·le·vi·at·ed** *v.t.* to lessen, relieve (esp. pain) || to make lighter, mitigate, moderate **al·le·vi·a·tion** *n.* **al·lé·vi·a·tive** *adj.* and *n.* **al·lé·vi·a·to·ry** *adj.*

al·ley (ǽli:) *n.* a narrow lane between buildings, esp. in a city || a wide path in a garden or park || an enclosure for bowling games **up** (or **down**) **one's alley** just what one likes best or does best or is most interested in

al·ley·way (ǽli:wẹi) *n.* a narrow passage for pedestrians between buildings

al·li·ance (əláiəns) *n.* a treaty between governments || the relationship formed by it between nations || the state of being allied || a uniting of qualities in a perceived relationship

al·li·ga·tor (ǽligeitər) *n.* a genus of large reptiles of the crocodile family || the leather made from its hide

all in all 1. *n.* the person or thing one loves best or sets most store by **2.** *adv.* all things being considered, on the whole || altogether

al·lit·er·ate (əlítəreit) *pres. part.* **al·lit·er·at·ing** *past* and *past part.* **al·lit·er·at·ed** *v.i.* to write or speak in words beginning with the same letter || to constitute alliteration **al·lit·er·á·tion** *n.* the repetition of the same initial letter (usually a consonant) in a group of words, e.g. 'a deep, dark ditch' **al·lit·er·a·tive** (əlítərəitiv, əlítərətiv) *adj.* of or characterized by alliteration

al·lo·cate (ǽləkeit) *pres. part.* **al·lo·cat·ing** *past* and *past part.* **al·lo·cat·ed** *v.t.* to distribute, share out || to assign, earmark

al·lo·ca·tion (ǽləkéiʃən) *n.* the act of allocating || the amount allocated || something allocated

al·lo·cu·tion (ǽləkjú:ʃən) *n.* a formal speech of some gravity

al·lot (əlɔ́t) *pres. part.* **al·lot·ting** *past* and *past part.* **al·lot·ted** *v.t.* to assign in portions || to distribute by lot

al·lot·ment (əlɔ́tmənt) *n.* the share of something allotted to a person || the act of allotting

al·low (əláu) *v.t.* to permit, let || to permit to have (something) || to admit as true or acceptable || to grant as a concession || to keep in hand as a working margin || *v.i.* (with 'for') to plan with an adequate margin, *to allow for unexpected expenses* || (with 'of') to admit, *the passage allows of only one interpretation* **al·lów·a·ble** *adj.* **al·lów·a·bly** *adv.*

al·low·ance (əláuəns) *n.* a regular periodical sum of money paid to a dependant || money granted for the performance of certain tasks, *traveling allowance* || permission **to make allowances for** to take (something) into account and so make a more lenient judgment

al·loy (əlɔ́i) *v.t.* to blend (metals) so as to form an alloy || to impair or debase through mingling, *public success alloyed with private failure*

al·loy (ǽlɔi, əlɔ́i) *n.* a metallic substance composed of two or more metals esp. in solid solution

al·lude (əlú:d) *pres. part.* **al·lud·ing** *past* and *past part.* **al·lud·ed** *v.i.* to refer briefly || to refer indirectly

al·lure (əlúər) **1.** *v.t. pres. part.* **al·lur·ing** *past* and *past part.* **al·lured** to attract, entice **2.** *n.* attraction, fascination **al·lure·ment** *n.*

al·lu·sion (əlú:ʒən) *n.* an indirect reference

al·lu·sive (əlú:siv) *adj.* containing an allusion or a great number of allusions

al·ly (əláy) **1.** *v.t. pres. part.* **al·ly·ing** *past* and *past part.* **al·lied** to unite in an alliance || to relate by certain similarities, *jazz is allied to primitive folk music* **2.** *n.* (ǽlai, əlái) *pl.* **al·lies** a country or person allied to another

al·ma ma·ter (ǽlməméitər, ǽlməmɒ́tər, úlməmɑ́tər) *n.* (*rhet.*) one's school or university

al·ma·nac (ɔ́lmənæk) *n.* a calendar of the year with information about the sun, moon, stars, tides, public holidays etc. ‖ a regular publication of a generally informative or statistical kind

al·might·y (ɔlmáiti:) **1.** *adj.* all-powerful **2.** *n.* **the Almighty** God

al·mond (úmənd) *n.* a small, pink-flowered tree ‖ the high-protein nut obtained from the stone (fruit) of this tree

al·most (ɔ́lmoust, ɔlmóust) *adv.* nearly, all but

alms (úmz) *sing.* and *pl. n.* money or goods given to the poor ‖ a charitable gift

a·loe (ǽlou) *n.* a member of *Aloe*, fam. *Liliaceae*, a genus of xerophytes having fleshy leaves with a waxy epidermis from which a juice is obtained. It is dried and used as a purgative ‖ (*pl.*) this drug **al·o·et·ic** (ǽlouétik) *adj.* (*med.*) containing aloes

a·loft (əlɔ́ft, əlɒ́ft) *adv.* and *pred. adj.* high up, in the air ‖ (*naut.*) among the top masts, in the upper rigging

a·lone (əlóun) **1.** *adj.* (usually follows the word it modifies) by oneself, away from all others, unaccompanied, solitary **2.** *adv.* only, solely, exclusively, *he alone knows why* **let alone** not considering, not taking into account **to leave alone** to leave unaccompanied ‖ to ignore, not touch or molest

a·long (əlɔ́ŋ, əlɒ́ŋ) **1.** *prep.* from one end to the other end of **2.** *adv.* with you (or with him, her etc.), *bring your bathing things along* ‖ onward, forward, *to stroll along* **all along** all the time **to get along with** to be on terms of tolerant understanding with ‖ to proceed with **to go along with** to have the same opinion as

a·loof (əlú:f) **1.** *adv.* away, at a physical or spiritual distance **2.** *adj.* reserved, cold in manner

a·loud (əláud) *adv.* in a normal speaking voice, so as to be heard, *read this story aloud* **to cry aloud for** to demand urgently

al·pac·a (ælpǽkə) *n.* a species of llama with fine woolly hair ‖ the hair itself, or the cloth made from it

al·pha (ǽlfə) *n.* the first letter (A, α = a) of the Greek alphabet ‖ (*astron.*) the brightest star in a constellation

al·pha·bet (ǽlfəbet) *n.* the letters or signs representing speech sounds used in writing a language, arranged in a conventional order **al·pha·bet·i·cal** *adj.* of or following the alphabet, *alphabetical order* **al·pha·bet·ize** *pres. part.* **al·pha·bet·iz·ing** *past* and *past part.* **al·pha·bet·ized** *v.t.* to arrange in alphabetical order

al·read·y (ɔlrédi:) *adv.* by this time, before a particular moment

al·right (ɔlráit) *adv.* all right (a commonly written form, still often held to be incorrect)

al·so (ɔ́lsou) *adv.* as well, in addition, besides

al·tar (ɔ́ltər) *n.* the structure on which bread and wine are consecrated in a Christian church ‖ any raised structure for offering sacrifices to a deity

al·ter (ɔ́ltər) *v.t.* to make different, modify, change ‖ to resew (a garment or parts of it) for a new fit or style ‖ *v.i.* to become different

al·ter·a·tion (ɔltəréiʃən) *n.* the act or result of altering

al·ter·cate (ɔ́ltərkeit) *pres. part.* **al·ter·cat·ing** *past* and *past part.* **al·ter·cat·ed** *v.i.* to dispute with anger or violence, wrangle

al·ter·ca·tion (ɔltərkéiʃən) *n.* a quarrel, angry dispute

al·ter e·go (ɔ́ltəríːgou) *pl.* **al·ter e·gos** someone so perfectly sharing the views, intentions, tastes etc. of another that he can be regarded as that other's second self ‖ an inseparable friend

al·ter·nate (ɔ́ltərnit, *Br.* ɔ:ltɔ́:nit) **1.** *adj.* (of things which

occur in series) every other ‖ (*bot.*) of leaves distributed at different heights on either side of a stem in turns **2.** *n.* a substitute **3.** (ɔ́ltərneit) *v. pres. part.* **al·ter·nat·ing** *past* and *past part.* **al·ter·nat·ed** *v.t.* to interchange (two things) by turns ‖ *v.i.* to take turns, happen by turns

al·ter·na·tion (ɔltərnéiʃən) *n.* an alternating, an occurrence of things by turns

al·ter·na·tive (ɔltɔ́:rnətiv) **1.** *adj.* offering a choice of two things, or (*loosely*) of several things **2.** *n.* one of two things which must be chosen, or (*loosely*) one of a number of things

al·though (ɔlðóu) *conj.* in spite of the fact that, though

al·ti·me·ter (æltímitər, ǽltəmí:tər) *n.* an instrument for measuring height

al·ti·tude (ǽltitu:d, ǽltitju:d) *n.* height above sea level ‖ (*pl.*) regions at a great height above sea level **al·ti·tú·di·nal** *adj.*

al·to (ǽltou) *n.* (esp. choral singing) the lowest female voice, contralto ‖ (esp. choral singing) the highest male voice, countertenor ‖ a singer with such a voice, esp. a contralto

al·to·geth·er (ɔltəgéðər, ɔ́ltəgeðər) *adv.* completely, thoroughly, *altogether in agreement* ‖ on the whole, all things considered

al·tru·ism (ǽltru:izəm) *n.* consideration for other people without any thought of self as a principle of conduct ‖ (*loosely*) unselfishness **ál·truist** *n.* **al·tru·ís·tic** *adj.* **al·tru·ís·ti·cal·ly** *adv.*

a·lu·mi·na (əlú:minə) *n.* aluminum oxide

a·lu·mi·num (əlú:minəm) *n.* (*Am.* = *Br.* aluminium) a light, silvery-white metallic element

a·lum·na (əlʌ́mnə) *pl.* **a·lum·nae** (əlʌ́mni:) *n.* a woman or girl who is a former student of a school, college or university

a·lum·nus (əlʌ́mnəs) *pl.* **a·lum·ni** (əlʌ́mnai) *n.* a man or boy who is a former student of a school, college or university

al·ways (ɔ́lweiz, ɔ́lwəz) *adv.* at all times, on all occasions ‖ invariably, without exception ‖ continually ‖ in any case, *we can always try again*

a.m., A.M. (éiém) *ANTE MERIDIEM

a·mal·gam (əmǽlgəm) *n.* an alloy of mercury ‖ a combination of characteristics, *an amalgam of pride and vanity*

a·mal·ga·mate (əmǽlgəmeit) *pres. part.* **a·mal·ga·mat·ing** *past* and *past part.* **a·mal·ga·mat·ed** *v.t.* (*chem., mining*) to alloy with mercury ‖ to join together, mix, unite (companies, movements, clubs, ideas etc.) ‖ *v.i.* (of companies etc.) to unite, join together **a·mal·ga·má·tion** *n.* **a·mál·ga·ma·tor** *n.* someone who amalgamates, or a machine which amalgamates

a·mass (əmǽs) *v.t.* to gather together, accumulate (esp. wealth)

am·a·teur (ǽmətə:r, ǽmətʃuər, ǽmətjuər) *n.* someone who cultivates an activity as a pastime rather than as a means of making money ‖ (*derogatory*) a dabbler, dilettante **am·a·téur·ish** *adj.* lacking proficiency, without professional finish **ám·a·teur·ism** *n.*

am·a·to·ry (ǽmətɔri:, ǽmətouri:) *adj.* dealing with or inducing love or sexual passion

a·maze (əméiz) *pres. part.* **a·maz·ing** *past* and *past part.* **a·mazed** *v.t.* to astonish, astound, overwhelm with wonder **a·máze·ment** *n.*

am·a·zon (ǽməzən, ǽməzɒn), *n.* a strong, manly woman, lacking feminine graces **am·a·zo·ni·an** (æməzóuni:ən) *adj.* of or like an amazon

am·bas·sa·dor (æmbǽsədər) *n.* an official of highest rank who represents his government in the capital of another country

---

(**a**) æ, c*a*t; ɑ, c*a*r; ɔ f*aw*n; ei, sn*a*ke. (**e**) e, h*e*n; i:, sh*ee*p; iə, d*ee*r; ɛə, b*ea*r. (**i**) i, f*i*sh; ai, t*i*ger; ə:, b*i*rd. (**o**) o, *o*x; au, c*ow*; ou, g*oa*t; u, p*oo*r; ɔi, r*oy*al. (**u**) ʌ, d*u*ck; u, b*u*ll; u:, g*oo*se; ə, b*a*cillus; ju:, c*u*be. x, lo*ch*; θ, *th*ink; ð, bo*th*er; z, *Z*en; ʒ, cor*s*age; dʒ, sava*g*e; ŋ, oranguta*ng*; j, *y*ak; ʃ, *fi*sh; tʃ, fe*tch*; 'l, rabb*le*; 'n, redd*en*. Complete pronunciation key appears inside front cover.

am·ber (ǽmbər) *n.* a fossilized form of resin, derived from certain extinct coniferous trees. It is yellowish in color and translucent ‖ the color of amber

am·bi·dex·ter·i·ty (æmbidekstériti:) *n.* the state of being ambidextrous

am·bi·dex·trous (æmbidékstrəs) *adj.* (of people) able to use both hands with equal ease ‖ two-faced, double-dealing, giving support to both sides in a quarrel

am·bi·ence (æmbi:əns) *n. (acoustics)* the total acoustic environment of a sound-reproducing system

am·bi·gu·i·ty (æmbigjú:iti:) *pl.* **am·bi·gu·i·ties** *n.* the quality of having more than one meaning ‖ an idea, statement or expression capable of being understood in more than one sense

am·big·u·ous (æmbígju:əs) *adj.* having more than one meaning or interpretation, equivocal ‖ doubtful, uncertain

am·bi·tion (æmbíʃən) *n.* eagerness to attain success, honor, power, fame etc. ‖ the object of a person's aspirations

am·bi·tious (æmbíʃəs) *adj.* full of ambition ‖ showing or requiring ambition, *an ambitious project*

am·biv·a·lence (æmbívələns) *n.* the state of being ambivalent

am·biv·a·lent (æmbívələnt) *adj.* having conflicting feelings about something or characterized by or expressing such feelings

am·ble (æmb'l) **1.** *v.i. pres. part.* **am·bling** *past* and *past part.* **am·bled** (of horses) to walk at an easy gait ‖ (of people) to stroll, walk in a leisurely manner **2.** *n.* an easy gait

am·bu·lance (æmbjuləns) *n.* a special vehicle for transporting sick or injured people

am·bu·la·to·ry (æmbjulətɔ:ri:, æmbjulətɔuri:) *adj.* of or concerning walking, adapted to walking, movable ‖ *(med.)* able to walk about, not confined to bed

am·bus·cade (æmbəskéid) *n.* an ambush, esp. by soldiers

am·bush (ǽmbuʃ) *n.* a hidden body of soldiers waiting to attack a passing enemy ‖ the place where they are hidden

ambush *v.t.* to attack from an ambush

ameba *AMOEBA

amebic *AMOEBIC

a·mel·io·rate (əmí:ljəreit) *pres. part.* **a·mel·io·rat·ing** *past* and *past part.* **a·mel·io·rat·ed** *v.t.* to improve, make better ‖ *v.i.* to become better **a·mel·io·ra·tion** *n.* **a·mel·io·ra·tive** (əmí:ljərɛitiv, əmi:ljərətiv) *adj.*

a·men (ámén, éimén) *interj.* so be it, truly it is so (used after a prayer)

a·me·na·bil·i·ty (əmi:nəbíliti:, əmɛnəbíliti:) *n.* the state or quality of being amenable

a·me·na·ble (əmí:nəb'l, əménəb'l) *adj.* responsive, *amenable to suggestion* ‖ answerable, responsible, *amenable to the law* ‖ able to submit to a test or to particular conditions **a·mé·na·bly** *adv.*

a·mend (əménd) *v.t.* to correct, free from faults ‖ *v.i.* to change for the better

a·mend·ment (əméndmənt) *n.* the act or result of amending ‖ a revision or change made in a law, bill etc. ‖ (in a public meeting or committee) a proposed modification (of a resolution) put forward for adoption ‖ a correction

a·mends (əméndz) *sing.* and *pl. n.* (only in) **to make amends** to make compensation, reparation or restitution (for loss or injury)

a·men·i·ty (əméniti:, əmí:niti:) *pl.* **a·men·i·ties** *n.* the quality of being pleasant ‖ something that tends to make life more comfortable, adds to the convenience of a place, increases the delightfulness of an area etc. **the amenities** courtesies, civilities

A·mer·i·can (əmérikən) **1.** *adj.* of or belonging to the American continent ‖ of, characteristic of, or belonging to the U.S.A. or its people etc. **2.** *n.* a person born in or inhabiting the American continent ‖ a citizen of the U.S.A. ‖ the English language as used in the U.S.A.

am·e·thyst (ǽmiθist) *n.* a precious stone (crystallized quartz), purple or violet in color **am·e·thys·tine** (æmiθístain) *adj.*

a·mi·a·bil·i·ty (ɛimi:əbíliti:) *n.* the quality of being amiable

a·mi·a·ble (éimi:əb'l) *adj.* good-natured, friendly **á·mi·a·bly** *adv.*

am·i·ca·bil·i·ty (æmikəbíliti:) *n.* the quality of being amicable

am·i·ca·ble (æmikəb'l) *adj.* friendly, peaceable **ám·i·ca·bly** *adv.*

a·mid (əmid) *prep.* in the midst of, among

a·mid·ship (əmídʃip) *adv.* amidships

a·mid·ships (əmídʃips) *adv. (naut.)* in the middle of a ship

a·midst (əmídst) *prep.* amid

a·mi·no acid (əmí:nou, ǽminou) one of a class of organic acids having amino groups in place of hydrogen atoms, in the hydrocarbon groups of fatty acids or other organic acids

a·miss (əmís) **1.** *pred. adj.* wrong, not as one would wish it to be **2.** *adv.* wrongly ‖ away from the mark **to come amiss** to happen at the wrong moment **to take amiss** to take offense at

am·me·ter (ǽmmi:tər) *n.* an instrument for measuring electric current

am·mo·nia (əmóunjə, əmóuni:ə) *n.* a gaseous compound of nitrogen and hydrogen having a pungent smell and very soluble in water to give an alkaline solution

am·mo·ni·ac (əmóuni:æk) *adj.* of the nature of, or having the properties of, ammonia **am·mo·ni·a·cal** (æmənáiək'l) *adj.*

am·mu·ni·tion (æmjuníʃən) *n.* everything (projectiles, charges, fuses etc.) necessary to feed guns or small arms

am·ne·sia (æmní:ʒə) *n.* loss of memory caused by shock, injury etc. **am·ne·sic** (æmní:zik) *adj.*

am·nes·ty (ǽmnisti:) **1.** *n. pl.* **am·nes·ties** an act of pardon by a legislative authority which effaces not merely a punishment inflicted but the cause of it as well, so that no fresh proceedings can be instituted **2.** *v.t. pres. part.* **am·nes·ty·ing** *past* and *past part.* **am·nes·tied** to grant an amnesty to, to pardon

am·ni·on (ǽmni:ɒn) *pl.* **am·ni·ons, am·ni·a** (ǽmni:ə) *n. (anat.)* a thin, membranous, fluid-filled sac enclosing the embryo of higher vertebrates

am·ni·os·co·py (æmni:ɒ́skəpi:) *n. (med.)* visual examination of uterine cavity of a pregnant female through surgically inserted optical instruments — **amnioscope** *n.* instrument for examining fetus within the uterus

am·ni·ot·ic fluid (æmni:ɒ́tik) the fluid in the amnion

a·moe·ba, a·me·ba (əmí:bə) *pl.* **a·moe·bae** (əmí:bi:), **a·moe·bas, a·me·bae, a·me·bas,** *n.* a microscopic, freshwater protozoan, the simplest form of animal, consisting of a naked mass of protoplasm **a·móe·bic, a·mé·bic** *adj.*

a·mok, a·muck (əmɒ́k, əmʌ́k) **1.** *n.* an outbreak of violent madness, occurring chiefly in S.E. Asia, in which the victim is liable to kill anyone in sight **2.** *adv.* (in the phrase) **to run amok** to be seized with this frenzy

a·mong (əmʌ́ŋ) *prep.* surrounded by, in the midst of ‖ in the company of ‖ in the class of, esp. outstanding in the class of, *a prince among princes* ‖ in or from the number of ‖ by the common or collective action of ‖ in relation to, with (each other), *they fought among themselves* ‖ with a share for each of, *divide it among them*

a·mongst (əmʌ́ŋst) *prep.* among

a·mor·al (eimɔ́rəl, eimɒ́rəl) *adj.* indifferent to morality **a·mo·ral·i·ty** (eimərǽliti:) *n.*

am·o·rous (ǽmərəs) *adj.* much given to making love ‖ concerned with love ‖ showing or betraying love

a·mor·phous (əmɔ́rfəs) *adj.* formless ‖ *(bot.)* not conforming to the normal structural organization ‖ *(geol.)* unstratified

am·or·ti·za·tion (æmərtizéiʃən, əmɔ́rtizéiʃən) *n.* the act or process of amortizing **am·or·tize** (æmərtaiz, əmɔ́rtaiz) *pres. part.* **am·or·tiz·ing** *past* and *past part.* **am·or·tized** *v.t.* to provide for paying off gradually (a large capital outlay or a debt)

a·mount (əmáunt) **1.** *n.* the sum total, *the full amount* ‖ a quantity, *a large amount of cement* **2.** *v.i.* (with 'to') to add up ‖ (with 'to') to be equivalent, *a statement amounting to libel*

amp (æmp) *n.* an ampere [shortening]

amp. ampere ‖ amperage

am·per·age (æmpəridʒ) *n.* the magnitude of an electric current expressed in amperes

am·pere (æmpiər) *n.* the mks unit of electric current, equivalent to a flow of one coulomb per second **am·pere-hour** (æmpiəráuər) *n.* a unit of electric charge, being the quantity of electricity transferred in one hour by a current of one ampere

am·per·sand (æmpərsænd) *n.* the sign &, symbol for 'and'

am·phib·i·an (æmfíbi:ən) **1.** *n.* (*biol.*) a member of *Amphibia*, a class of vertebrates intermediate between fish and reptiles **2.** *adj.* of or pertaining to one of the *Amphibia*

am·phib·i·ous (æmfíbi:əs) *adj.* able to live on land and in the water

am·phi·the·a·ter (æmfiθíətər) *n.* a round or oval arena enclosed by rising tiers of seats, used for games and other contests ‖ the gallery of a modern theater **am·phi·the·at·ri·cal** (æmfi·θi:ætrik'l) *adj.*

am·ple (æmp'l) *adj.* abundant, copious ‖ enough, easily sufficient

am·pli·fi·ca·tion (æmplifikéiʃən) *n.* an extension or enlargement of something ‖ an amplified statement

am·pli·fi·er (æmplifaiər) *n.* an apparatus used to increase the volume of sound

am·pli·fy (æmplifai) *pres. part.* **am·pli·fy·ing** *past* and *past part.* **am·pli·fied** *v.t.* to expand or enlarge, esp. by adding details to ‖ (*elec., radio*) to use (input of power, current, voltage) so as to increase the output ‖ *v.i.* to explain oneself in greater detail

am·pli·tude (æmplitu:d, æmplitju:d) *n.* largeness, breadth, extent

am·ply (æmpli) *adv.* in an ample way

am·pul·la (æmpúlə) *pl.* **am·pul·lae** (æmpúli:) *n.* an ancient Roman vase, with a globe-shaped body and two handles at the neck **am·pul·lar** *adj.*

am·pu·tate (æmpjuteit) *pres. part.* **am·pu·tat·ing** *past* and *past part.* **am·pu·tat·ed** *v.t.* to cut off, esp. in surgery **am·pu·ta·tion**, **ám·pu·ta·tor**, **am·pu·tée** *n.*

am·u·let (æmjulit) *n.* an ornament or gem worn on the body as a protection against evil spirits

a·muse (əmjú:z) *pres. part.* **a·mus·ing** *past* and *past part.* **a·mused** *v.t.* to cause to laugh or smile ‖ to divert pleasantly **a·muse·ment** *n.* pleasant diversion or entertainment

an (æn) *indef. art.* (the form used before a vowel or a silent 'h'), *an egg, an hour*

an- *prefix* (the form used before a vowel, and usually before 'h') not, without, as in 'anhydrous'

-an *suffix* of or pertaining to, as in 'Nigerian'

a·nach·ro·nism (ənækrənizəm) *n.* something which does not fit in with its context chronologically **a·nach·ro·nis·tic** *adj.*

an·a·con·da (ænəkόndə) *n. Eunectes murinus*, a large tree-climbing boa of tropical South America ‖ (*loosely*) any large snake that crushes its prey

an·a·gram (ænəgræm) *n.* a word or phrase made by changing the order of letters in another word or phrase, e.g. 'best in prayer' is an anagram of 'presbyterian'

an·a·gram·mat·ic (ænəgrəmætik), **an·a·gram·mát·i·cal** *adjs*

a·nal (éin'l) *adj.* related to, or situated near, the anus

an·al·ge·sia (æn'ldʒí:ʒə, æn'ldʒí:zi:ə) *n.* insensibility to pain **an·al·ge·sic** (æn'ldʒí:zik) **1.** *adj.* producing analgesia **2.** *n.* a drug which does this

a·nal·o·gize (ənælədʒaiz) *pres. part.* **a·nal·o·giz·ing** *past* and *past part.* **a·nal·o·gized** *v.i.* to use analogy ‖ *v.t.* to bring into analogy

a·nal·o·gous (ənæləgəs) *adj.* similar, corresponding in some respects

an·a·logue, an·a·log (æn'lɔg, æn'lɒg) *n.* a thing analogous to some other thing

a·nal·o·gy (ənælədʒi:) *pl.* **a·nal·o·gies** *n.* the relationship between two things which are similar in many, though not in all, respects ‖ (*biol.*) similarity of function between organs which are different in structure and development

analyse *ANALYZE

a·nal·y·sis (ənælisis) *pl.* **a·nal·y·ses** (ənælisi:z) *n.* the process of analyzing ‖ a document setting out the results of this process ‖ psychoanalysis

an·a·lyst (æn'list) *n.* someone skilled in analysis

an·a·lyst (æn'list) *n.* (*computer*) one skilled in defining problems and developing algorithms to solve them

an·a·lyt·ic (æn'litik) *adj.* pertaining to analysis ‖ given to the use of analysis **an·a·lýt·i·cal** *adj.*

an·a·lyze (æn'laiz) *pres. part.* **an·a·lyz·ing** *past* and *past part.* **an·a·lyzed** *v.t.* to study (a problem) in detail by breaking it down into various parts ‖ (*chem.*) to submit (a substance) to certain tests in order to identify its constituents ‖ to break up (a substance) into its simplest elements

an·ar·chism (ænərkizəm) *n.* the political theory that individual freedom should be absolute and that all government and law is evil

an·ar·chist (ænərkist) *n.* someone who believes in anarchism ‖ (*loosely*) a terrorist

an·ar·chy (ænərki:) *pl.* **an·ar·chies** *n.* the absence of law and order ‖ a general state of disorder and confusion

a·nath·e·ma (ənæθəmə) *n.* the gravest ecclesiastical censure. 'Let him be anathema' involves total expulsion from the Church and consignment to Satan ‖ (*loosely*) something intensely disliked **a·náth·e·ma·tize** *pres. part.* **a·nath·e·ma·tiz·ing** *past* and *past part.* **a·nath·e·ma·tized** *v.t.* to pronounce anathema against

an·a·tom·ic (ænətόmik) *adj.* pertaining to, or dealing with, anatomy **an·a·tóm·i·cal** *adj.*

a·nat·o·mist (ənætəmist) *n.* a specialist in anatomy

a·nat·o·mize (ənætəmaiz) *pres. part.* **a·nat·o·miz·ing** *past* and *past part.* **a·nat·o·mized** *v.t.* to dissect, esp. so as to reveal anatomical detail ‖ to analyze minutely

a·nat·o·my (ənætəmi:) *pl.* **a·nat·o·mies** *n.* the branch of morphology concerned with the structure of animals or plants ‖ the science of dissection ‖ the structure of an organism

an·ces·tor (ænsestər) *n.* a forefather, a person from whom one is descended ‖ (*biol.*) an earlier type of a species

an·ces·tral (ænséstrəl) *adj.* coming from, or belonging to, one's ancestors ‖ (*biol.*) relating to an original or earlier type of a species

an·ces·tress (ænsestris) *n.* a female ancestor

an·ces·try (ænsestri:) *pl.* **an·ces·tries** *n.* the line of descent from ancestors

an·chor (ænkər) *v.t.* to secure by an anchor ‖ *v.i.* to cast anchor

anchor *n.* a heavy iron instrument, consisting of a shank and two arms, which is lowered from a ship to grip the bottom and so hold her fast **to weigh anchor** to take up the anchor, to depart

an·chor·age (ǽŋkəridʒ) *n.* a place where ships may lie at anchor ‖ the fee for anchoring ‖ something that can be absolutely relied on

an·cho·vy (ǽntʃouvi:, ǽntʃəvi:) *pl.* **an·cho·vies** *n. Engraulis encrasicholus,* a small bony fish of the herring family

an·cient (éinʃənt) *adj.* belonging to times long past ‖ antique, old-fashioned ‖ *(loosely)* old, decrepit

an·cil·lar·y (ǽnsəleri, *Br.* esp. ænsíləri) *adj.* subordinate, subsidiary

and (ænd) *conj.* a joining word, used between two words, two phrases or two clauses, sometimes written & **and so forth, and so on** et cetera (etc.)

an·dan·te (ændǽnti:) **1.** *adj.* and *adv. (mus.)* at a moderate speed **2.** *n.* a piece or movement for andante performance

an·drog·y·nous (ændródʒinəs) *adj.* combining characteristics of both sexes, hermaphrodite ‖ *(bot.)* having stamens and pistils in the same flower or in the same inflorescence

an·ec·do·tal (ænikdóut'l) *adj.* relating to or characteristic of anecdotes

an·ec·dote (ǽnikdout) *n.* a short account of an interesting or amusing incident or event **an·ec·dot·ic** (ænikdótik), **an·ec·dót·i·cal** *adjs* **án·ec·dot·ism, án·ec·dot·ist** *ns*

a·ne·mi·a (əní:mi:ə) *n.* a reduction in the amount of hemoglobin or the number of red cells in the blood **a·né·mic** *adj.*

a·nem·o·ne (ənéməni:) *n.* a member of *Anemone,* fam. *Ranunculaceae,* a genus of plants bearing colorful flowers

an·es·the·sia (ænisθi:ʒə) *n. (med.)* loss of the normal perception of pain **an·es·thet·ic** (ænisθétik) **1.** *n.* a substance or gas which produces anesthesia **2.** *adj.* producing anesthesia ‖ relating to anesthesia **an·es·the·tist** (ənésθitist) *n.* someone who administers anesthetics **an·es·the·ti·za·tion** (ənesθitizéiʃən) *n.* **an·es·the·tize** (ənésθitaiz) *pres. part.* **an·es·the·tiz·ing** *past* and *past part.* **an·es·the·tized** *v.t.* to render insensible by the use of anesthetics

an·es·the·si·o·lo·gist (ænisθi:zi:ólədʒist) *n.* a specialist in anesthesiology

an·es·the·si·o·lo·gy (ænisθi:zi:ólədʒi:) *n.* the science of administering anesthetics

an·eu·rysm, an·eu·rism (ǽnjurizəm) *n. (med.)* the dilation of a section of an artery, due to weakness of the artery wall

a·new (ənjú:, ənú:) *adv.* again ‖ in a new form or way

an·gel (éindʒəl) *n.* a messenger of God ‖ a member of the lowest order in the celestial hierarchy ‖ a person of exceptional goodness or loveliness ‖ *(theater, pop.)* the financial backer of a theatrical production

angel dust *(slang)* phencyclidine hydrochloride, a highly dangerous animal tranquilizer sometimes smoked with marijuana to heighten hallucinogenic effects

an·gel·ic (ændʒélik) *adj.* belonging to, or characteristic of, angels ‖ of exceptional goodness or loveliness

an·ger (ǽŋgər) **1.** *n.* rage, passionate displeasure **2.** *v.t.* to make angry, to enrage

an·gi·na (ændʒáinə) *n. (med.)* inflammation of the throat, quinsy

angina pec·to·ris (péktəris) *n.* a disease of the heart causing momentary pain in the chest, sometimes spreading to the arms and neck

an·gle (ǽŋg'l) *n.* the difference in the direction of two intersecting lines or planes, measured in degrees, minutes and seconds ‖ a point of view, *our readers want the woman's angle on this*

angle *pres. part.* **an·gling** *past* and *past part.* **an·gled** *v.i.* to fish with line and hook, attracting the fish by bait

an·gled (ǽŋ'ld) *adj.* having an angle or angles ‖ being at an angle

an·gler (ǽŋglər) *n.* a person who fishes with rod and line

An·gli·can (ǽŋglikən) **1.** *adj.* of the Church of England or the Anglican Communion **2.** *n.* a member of the Church of England or the Anglican Communion

An·gli·cize (ǽŋglisaiz) *pres. part.* **An·gli·ciz·ing** *past* and *past part.* **An·gli·cized** *v.t.* to make English in form, character or pronunciation (esp. words and names)

An·glo-Sax·on (ǽŋglousǽksən) *n.* a person of English descent in any country ‖ Old English

an·go·ra (ǽŋgórə, æŋgóurə) *n.* a soft, fluffy fabric made from the hair of the angora goat or angora rabbit

Angora cat a variety of domestic cat with long silky hair

an·gri·ly (ǽŋgrili:) *adv.* in an angry way

an·gry (ǽŋgri:) *comp.* **an·gri·er** *superl.* **an·gri·est** *adj.* (with 'about', 'at' or 'with') feeling or showing anger ‖ *(rhet.)* menacing, stormy

an·guish (ǽŋgwiʃ) *n.* severe mental suffering, often involving anxiety

an·guished (ǽŋgwiʃt) *adj.* acutely distressed, suffering or expressing anguish

an·gu·lar (ǽŋgjulər) *adj.* having angles or sharp corners ‖ *(phys.)* measured in terms of angles ‖ (of people) bony, spare, scraggy ‖ stiff, ungracious in manner

an·gu·lar·i·ty (æŋgjulǽriti:) *n.* the quality of being angular

an·hy·drous (ænháidrəs) *adj. (chem.)* without water, esp. of crystallization

an·i·mal (ǽnəməl) **1.** *n.* any of various organisms of the kingdom *Animalia,* distinguished from plants by their voluntary movement, by their nonphotosynthetic methods of nutrition, by their usually requiring complex organic nutriments, by a more or less centralized nervous system, and by their noncellulose cell membrane ‖ such an animal other than man ‖ a man who behaves like a brute **2.** *adj.* like or relating to animals

an·i·mate (ǽnəmit) **1.** *adj.* living ‖ pertaining to animal as opposed to plant life **2.** (ǽnəmeit) *v.t. pres. part.* **an·i·mat·ing** *past* and *past part.* **an·i·mat·ed** to give life to ‖ to have a direct or inspiring influence upon, motivate **án·i·mat·ed** *adj.* (of a person) full of communicative liveliness ‖ (of a lecture, argument etc.) infused with the energy, enthusiasm etc. of the protagonist or protagonists

an·i·ma·tion (ænəméiʃən) *n.* the act of animating ‖ the state or quality of being animate or animated ‖ *(cinema)* the preparation of an animated cartoon

an·i·mos·i·ty (ænəmósiti:) *pl.* **an·i·mos·i·ties** *n.* a feeling of hatred or ill will, strong dislike

an·i·mus (ǽnəməs) *n. (sing. only)* animosity, hostility

an·ise (ǽnis) *n.* a plant native to the Mediterranean, cultivated widely

an·kle (ǽŋk'l) *n.* the joint between the foot and the leg ‖ the narrowest part of the leg

an·nal·ist (ǽn'list) *n.* a writer of annals **an·nal·is·tic** *adj.*

an·nals (ǽn'lz) *pl. n.* a year-by-year record of events, a chronicle ‖ *(fig.)* unwritten history

an·neal (əní:l) *v.t.* to improve the properties of by heating and then cooling

an·nex (ǽneks) *n.* a building attached to, or depending on, a larger building ‖ an appendix or supplement to a book or document

an·nex (ənéks) *v.t.* to take possession of (a territory etc.) and incorporate it ‖ to append

an·nex·a·tion (ænikséiʃən) *n.* an annexing or being annexed ‖ something annexed

an·ni·hi·late (ənáiəleit) *pres. part.* **an·ni·hi·lat·ing** *past* and *past part.* **an·ni·hi·lat·ed** *v.t.* to destroy completely, wipe out **an·ni·hi·la·tion** *n.*

an·ni·ver·sa·ry (ænivə́:rsəri:) *pl.* **an·ni·ver·sa·ries** *n.* the yearly return of the date of an event, or the particular day on which such a return is celebrated, *wedding anniversary*

an·no Dom·i·ni (ǽnoudómənai) *(abbr.* A.D.*)* in the year specified of the Christian era

an·no·tate (ǽnouteit) *pres. part.* **an·no·tat·ing** *past* and *past part.* **an·no·tat·ed** *v.t.* to write explanatory or critical notes on or for (a book or document) **an·no·ta·tion, án·no·ta·tor** *ns*

an·nounce (ənáuns) *pres. part.* **an·nounc·ing** *past* and *past part.* **an·nounced** *v.t.* to make known publicly or formally ‖ to introduce (a radio or television item) ‖ *v.i.* to be a radio or television announcer **an·nóunce·ment** *n.* **an·nóunc·er** *n.* someone who announces esp. on the radio or television

an·noy (ənói) *v.t.* to vex, irritate, trouble ‖ *v.i.* to have an annoying effect or behave in an annoying way

an·noy·ance (ənóiəns) *n.* the physical or mental discomfort caused by being annoyed ‖ something that vexes or irritates, a nuisance

an·noy·ing (ənóinŋ) *adj.* irritating, troublesome

an·nu·al (ǽnju:əl) **1.** *adj.* occurring regularly once a year ‖ measured by the year, *annual income* **2.** *n.* a yearly publication ‖ a plant which grows from seed, comes to maturity and dies within one year

an·nu·i·ty (ənú:iti:, ənjú:iti:) *pl.* **an·nu·i·ties** *n.* a fixed yearly payment or pension

an·nul (ənʌ́l) *pres. part.* **an·nul·ling** *past* and *past part.* **an·nulled** *v.t.* to make null and void

an·nul·ment (ənʌ́lmənt) *n.* an annulling or being annulled

an·nun·ci·ate (ənʌ́nsi:eit, ənʌ́nʃi:eit) *pres. part.* **an·nun·ci·at·ing** *past* and *past part.* **an·nun·ci·at·ed** *v.t. (rhet.)* to announce

an·nun·ci·a·tion (ənʌnsi:éiʃən, ənʌnʃi:éiʃən) *n. (rhet.)* an announcement **the An·nun·ci·a·tion** the announcement made by the Archangel Gabriel to the Virgin Mary that she was to be the mother of Christ

a·noint (ənóint) *v.t.* to apply oil or ointment to, either medically or sacramentally (as at the crowning of a sovereign) **a·nóint·ment** *n.*

a·nom·a·lis·tic (ənóməlístik) *adj.* characterized by anomaly

a·nom·a·lous (ənómələs) *adj.* not in conformity with what is usual or expected, often involving an apparent contradiction or paradox

a·nom·a·ly (ənóməli:) *pl.* **a·nom·a·lies** *n.* something contrary to the general rule or to what is expected

an·o·nym (ǽnənim) *n.* a person who conceals his name or whose name is not known ‖ a pseudonym **an·o·ným·i·ty** *n.* the state of being anonymous

a·non·y·mous (ənónəməs *(abbr.* anon.*) adj.* without a known or disclosed name ‖ written or given by a person whose name is not known or not disclosed

an·oth·er (ənʌ́ðər) **1.** *adj.* (not preceded by def. art.) additional, *another cup of tea* ‖ different ‖ the equal of **2.** *pron.* an additional one of the same kind ‖ a different one ‖ a similar thing, person etc. ‖ *(oldfash.)* somebody else, *he loves another*

an·swer (ǽnsər, ɑ́nsər) *v.t.* to reply to ‖ to defend oneself against ‖ to fit, agree with ‖ to correspond to ‖ *v.i.* to reply in words, actions etc. ‖ to act in response ‖ to correspond, *to answer to a description* ‖ to be suitable (to a purpose, need) **to answer back** to give a saucy answer when scolded **to answer for** to vouch or take responsibility for ‖ to be judged for, pay the penalty for, *to answer for one's actions*

answer *n.* a reply (in speech, writing, or action) ‖ a solution, *the answer to a sum, the answer is to try harder*

an·swer·a·ble (ǽnsərəb'l, ɑ́nsərəb'l) *adj.* responsible

ant (ænt) *n.* a small insect, related to bees and wasps

-ant *suffix* denoting an activity, as in 'consultant' ‖ equivalent to '-ing', as in 'expectant'

ant·ac·id (æntǽsid) **1.** *adj.* preventing or counteracting acidity, esp. in the stomach **2.** *n.* an agent which does this

an·tag·o·nism (æntǽgənizəm) *n.* open opposition or resistance, hostility

an·tag·o·nist (æntǽgənist) *n.* an open enemy, rival **an·tag·o·nis·tic** *adj.* **an·tag·o·nis·ti·cal·ly** *adv.*

an·tag·o·nize (æntǽgənaiz) *pres. part.* **an·tag·o·niz·ing** *past* and *past part.* **an·tag·o·nized** *v.t.* to provoke to enmity or hostility

Ant·arc·tic (æntɑ́rktik, æntɑ́rtik) **1.** *adj.* South polar **2.** *n.* **the Antarctic** the South polar regions

an·te·ced·ence (æntisí:d'ns) *n.* priority in time or in a sequence of cause and effect

an·te·ced·ent (æntisí:d'nt) **1.** *adj.* going before, in time or in any other sequence, preceding **2.** *n.* that which precedes ‖ an earlier type ‖ *(pl.)* a man's past life or origins ‖ *(pl.)* ancestors

an·te·date (ǽntideit) *pres. part.* **an·te·dat·ing** *past* and *past part.* **an·te·dat·ed** *v.t.* to predate

an·te·di·lu·vi·an (ænti:dilú:vi:ən) **1.** *n.* an antiquated person or thing **2.** *adj.* from before the Flood ‖ very old-fashioned or antiquated

an·te·lope (ǽnt'loup) *pl.* **an·te·lope, an·te·lopes** *n.* a deerlike ruminant mammal in Asia, in India and in North America ‖ their hide used as leather

an·te·me·rid·i·an (ænti:mərídi:ən) *adj.* before noon

an·te me·rid·i·em (ænti:mərídi:əm) *adj. (abbr.* a.m., A.M.*)* after midnight and before noon

an·ten·na (ænténə) *pl.* **an·ten·nae** (ænténi:), **an·ten·nas** *n.* the sensitive jointed feeler or horn of an insect or crustacean ‖ a device for converting electrical currents into electromagnetic waves, or vice versa

an·te·ri·or (æntíəri:ər) *adj.* nearer the front ‖ *(anat.)* toward or relating to the head ‖ earlier in time **an·te·ri·or·i·ty** (æntiəri:óriti:, ɒntiəri:ɒriti:) *n.*

an·them (ǽnθəm) *n.* a piece of choral music sung in church, often verses of scripture sung antiphonally ‖ a song of praise or joy, *national anthem*

an·thol·o·gist (ænθólədʒist) *n.* a person who compiles an anthology

an·thol·o·gy (ænθólədʒi:) *pl.* **an·thol·o·gies** *n.* a collection of poetry or prose chosen to represent the work of a particular writer, a literary school or a national literature

an·thra·cite (ǽnθrəsait) *n.* a form of coal which is hard and very rich in carbon. It burns slowly, and emits very little smoke **an·thra·cit·ic** (ænθrəsítik) *adj.*

an·thrax (ǽnθræks) *pl.* **an·thra·ces** (ǽnθrəsi:z) *n.* an infectious, often fatal disease in sheep and cattle ‖ a virulent infectious disease in man, contracted by exposure to infected animals or animal products

an·thro·poid (ǽnθrəpoid) **1.** *adj.* manlike in appearance ‖ of the anthropoid apes **2.** *n.* an anthropoid ape

an·thro·po·log·i·cal (ænθrəpəlódʒik'l) *adj.* of or pertaining to anthropology

an·thro·pol·o·gist (ænθrəpólədʒist) *n.* a specialist in anthropology

an·thro·pol·o·gy (ænθrəpólədʒi) *n.* the science which studies man both as an animal and as living in society, his origins, development, distribution, social habits, culture etc.

anti- (ǽnti:, ǽntai) *prefix* against, opposite, instead

an·ti (ǽnti:) **1.** *n. (pop.)* a person who opts against some action etc. **2.** *adj. (pop.)* against, opposed

an·ti·bi·ot·ic (ænti:baiótik) *n.* a substance usually produced by a microorganism (e.g. a fungus or a bacterium) that is used therapeutically to destroy or inhibit the growth of a pathogen (usually another bacterium or a virus)

an·ti·bod·y (ǽntibɒdi:, ǽnti:bɒdi:) *pl.* **an·ti·bod·ies** *n.* any of a group of proteins produced by the body of higher organisms in response to the presence of foreign substances called antigens. Antibodies possess the ability to render these foreign substances innocuous

an·tic (ǽntik) *n.* a caper, extravagant or grotesque gesture ‖ *(pl.)* foolish, annoying or irresponsible behavior

---

an·ti·ci·pate (æntísəpeit) *pres. part.* **an·ti·ci·pat·ing** *past and past part.* **an·ti·ci·pat·ed** *v.t.* to look forward to, feel in advance ‖ to assume, use or realize in advance ‖ to achieve before (another person) or happen before (another event) ‖ to meet in advance ‖ to prevent by prior action ‖ *(pop.)* to expect

an·ti·ci·pa·tion (æntisəpéiʃən) *n.* an anticipating or being anticipated

an·tic·i·pa·tor (æntísəpeitər) *n.* one who anticipates **an·tic·i·pa·to·ry** (æntísəpətɔri:, æntísəpətouri:) *adj.*

an·ti·cli·max (ænti:kláimæks) *n.* a disappointing or unimpressive end to what promised well

an·ti·dot·al (æntidout'l) *adj.* of or serving as an antidote

an·ti·dote (æntidout) *n.* a remedy counteracting a poison etc.

an·ti·his·ta·mine (ænti:hístəmi:n) *n.* one of a group of synthetic drugs used in the treatment of such allergic reactions as hay fever

an·ti·ma·cas·sar (ænti:məkǽsər) *n.* a covering to protect the back of an upholstered chair or sofa from dirty marks

an·ti·mat·ter (ænti:mætər) *n.* matter built up from antiparticles

an·ti·mis·sile (ænti:mísəl) *n.* a guided missile used for intercepting and destroying guided missiles

an·ti·pa·thet·ic (ænti:pəθétik) *adj.* feeling antipathy ‖ arousing antipathy **an·ti·pa·thét·i·cal** *adj.*

an·tip·a·thy (æntípəθi:) *pl.* **an·tip·a·thies** *n.* a strong hostility or lack of sympathy

an·tip·o·dal (æntípəd'l) *adj.* of the antipodes

an·ti·pode (æntipoud) *n.* an exact opposite

an·tip·o·des (æntípədi:z) *pl.* *n.* that part of the earth's surface which is diametrically opposite to one's position

an·ti·quat·ed (æntikweitid) *adj.* out-of-date, obsolete, ancient

an·tique (æntí:k) **1.** *adj.* old and precious ‖ belonging to or surviving from distant times ‖ antiquated, old-fashioned **2.** *n.* an object, often beautiful and valuable, surviving from the past **the antique** the classical style of Greek or Roman sculpture and architecture

an·tiqu·ing (æntí:ki:ŋ) *n.* *(slang or colloq.)* visiting antique shops

an·tiq·ui·ty (æntíkwiti:) *pl.* **an·tiq·ui·ties** *n.* the far-distant past ‖ great age ‖ the people who lived in the distant past ‖ *(pl.)* remains of ancient times and culture

an·ti-Sem·ite (ænti:sémait, *Br.* esp. æntisi:mait) *n.* someone who is prejudiced against Jews **an·ti-se·mit·ic** (ænti:səmítik) *adj.* **an·ti-Sem·i·tism** (ænti:sémitizəm) *n.*

an·ti·sep·sis (æntisépsis) *n.* an antiseptic condition ‖ the use of antiseptics

an·ti·sep·tic (æntiséptik) **1.** *adj.* counteracting the putrefying effect of bacteria in a wound or cut **2.** *n.* something which does this **an·ti·sep·ti·cize** (æntiséptisaiz) *pres. part.* **an·ti·sep·ti·ciz·ing** *past and past part.* **an·ti·sep·ti·cized** *v.t.* to make antiseptic

an·ti·so·cial (ænti:sóuʃəl) *adj.* contrary to the interests of society ‖ rejecting the laws on which the security of society depends ‖ disliking or disinclined for social intercourse

an·tith·e·sis (æntíθisis) *pl.* **an·tith·e·ses** (æntíθisi:z) *n.* a direct opposite (e.g. 'peace' to 'war', 'beautiful' to 'ugly') ‖ the statement opposed to the thesis of a syllogism

an·ti·thet·ic (æntiθétik) *adj.* contrasted, containing opposite ideas **an·ti·thét·i·cal** *adj.*

an·ti·tox·in (ænti:tóksin) *n.* a serum which counteracts the toxin of a particular disease

an·ti·trust (ænti:trʌst) *adj.* opposed to, or designed to prevent, the concentration of industry and commerce under the control of large combines

ant·ler (æntlər) *n.* the branched horn of animals of the deer family **ánt·lered** *adj.*

an·to·nym (æntənim) *n.* a word which means the exact contrary of another

a·nus (éinəs) *n.* the lower opening of the rectum

an·vil (ænvil) *n.* the iron block on which a smith hammers metal into shape ‖ the incus

anx·i·e·ty (æŋzáiiti:) *pl.* **anx·i·e·ties** *n.* intense dread, apprehension ‖ nagging worry or an instance of this ‖ eagerness

anx·ious (ǽŋkʃəs) *adj.* worried and uncertain ‖ causing worry and uncertainty ‖ eager

an·y (éni:) **1.** *adj.* one, one or more, some ‖ every, whichever you care to choose ‖ unlimited **2.** *sing. and pl. pron.* any person or thing, any persons or things **3.** *adv.* at all, to any degree

an·y·bod·y (éni:bɒdi:, éni:bʌdi:) **1.** *pron.* any person **2.** *n.* a person of importance

an·y·how (éni:hau) *adv.* carelessly, in a slapdash manner ‖ whatever may happen, in any event

an·y·one (éni:wʌn) *pron.* any person, anybody

an·y·thing (éni:θiŋ) **1.** *pron. and n.* any kind of thing ‖ something **2.** *adv.* in any degree or way

an·y·way (éni:wei) *adv.* anyhow

an·y·where (éni:hwɛər, eni:wɛər) *adv.* in, at or to any place

a·or·ta (eiɔ́rtə) *n.* the principal artery through which the blood leaves the heart and passes to the body **a·or·tal, a·or·tic** *adjs.*

a·part (əpárt) **1.** *pred. adj.* separate **2.** *adv.* in parts, in pieces **apart from** aside from, *apart from other issues* **to take apart** to separate (something) into its component parts ‖ to be able to be separated in this way

a·part·heid (əpártheit, əpárthait) *n.* the racial policy of the government of South Africa, under which white, African, Asiatic and Colored communities live separately, in principle so that each group may develop to the full its own society and culture

a·part·ment (əpártmənt) *n.* a set of rooms on one floor of a building used as a separate residence

ape (eip) **1.** *n.* an anthropoid ape ‖ a person who copies or mimics others in a way which makes him ridiculous **2.** *v.t. pres.* **ap·ing** *past and past part.* **aped** to copy or mimic in such a way as to make oneself ridiculous **3.** *adj.* *(slang)* beyond reason or restraint, *to go ape*

a·pé·ri·tif (ɑperití:f, əpériti:f) *n.* a short alcoholic drink taken before a meal to whet the appetite

ap·er·ture (ǽpərtʃər, ǽpərtiuər) *n.* an opening, space between two things ‖ an opening in an optical or other kind of instrument that controls the diameter of a beam of emitted or entering radiation or particles, e.g., the opening in a photographic lens

a·pex (éipeks) *pl.* **a·pex·es, a·pi·ces** (éipisi:z, ɑ́pisi:z) *n.* the topmost point, climax

a·pha·sia (əféiʒə) *n.* loss of the power to speak, through damage to the brain **a·pha·sic** (əféizik) *n.* and *adj.*

aph·o·rism (ǽfərizəm) *n.* a short, neatly expressed general truth **aph·o·ris·mic, aph·o·ris·tic** *adjs.* **aph·o·rís·ti·cal·ly** *adv.*

aph·ro·dis·i·ac (æfrədízi:æk) **1.** *adj.* increasing sexual desire **2.** *n.* a drug, food etc. which does this

a·pi·ar·y (éipi:eri:) *pl.* **a·pi·ar·ies** *n.* a place in which a number of beehives are kept

a·piece (əpí:s) *adv.* to or for each one of several, as each one's share

a·plomb (əplóm) *n.* self-assurance, self-possession

ap·o·gee (ǽpədʒi:) *n.* the point in the orbit of the moon, or in that of a planet round the sun, when it is farthest from the earth ‖ the farthest or highest point, climax

a·pol·o·get·ic (əpplədʒétik) **1.** *adj.* asking pardon, self-excusing **2.** *n.* (often *pl.*) a defense **a·pol·o·gét·i·cal** *adj.*

a·pol·o·gize (əpólədʒaiz) *pres. part.* **a·pol·o·giz·ing** *past and past part.* **a·pol·o·gized** *v.i.* to say that one is sorry

a·pol·o·gy (əpólədʒi:) *pl.* **a·pol·o·gies** *n.* an expression of regret for wrongdoing ‖ an excuse or defense

ap·o·plec·tic (æpəpléktik) **1.** *adj.* suffering or appearing to suffer from apoplexy ‖ liable to apoplexy ‖ causing apoplexy **2.** *n.* an apoplectic person **ap·o·pléc·ti·cal**

ap·o·plex·y (ǽpəplęksi:) *n.* *(med.)* a sudden and total loss of movement and consciousness, commonly called 'a stroke'

a·pos·ta·sy (əpóstəsi:) *pl.* **a·pos·ta·sies** *n.* the public abandoning of a religious faith, esp. Christianity, for another ‖ a similar abandoning of a doctrine or party

a·pos·tate (əpóstit, əpósteit) **1.** *n.* someone who abandons his religious faith (or party etc.) for another **2.** *adj.* guilty of doing this

a·pos·ta·tize (əpóstətaiz) *pres. part.* **a·pos·ta·tiz·ing** *past and past part.* **a·pos·ta·tized** *v.i.* to become an apostate

A·pos·tle (əpós'l) *n.* one of the 12 men chosen by Christ to preach the gospel, early missionaries **a·pós·tle** the first to introduce Christianity in a pagan land ‖ any early or prominent advocate of a belief

ap·os·tol·ic (ǽpəstólik) *adj.* of, like, or of the time of, the apostles ‖ papal, *an apostolic letter* **ap·os·tól·i·cal** *adj.*

a·pos·tro·phe (əpóstrəfi:) *n.* *(printing or writing)* a punctuation mark (') marking the omission of a letter or letters, the possessive case, or the plural of letters, e.g. can't (cannot), men's (of men)

a·poth·e·car·y (əpóθikeri) *pl.* **a·poth·e·car·ies** *n.* *(old-fash.)* a dispensing chemist, druggist

ap·pal, ap·pall (əpól) *pres. part.* **ap·pal·ling, ap·pall·ing** *past and past part.* **ap·palled** *v.t.* to shock with terror, horrify ‖ to fill with dismay

ap·pal·ling (əpóliŋ) *adj.* horrifying ‖ very bad in quality

ap·pa·ra·tus (ǽpərétəs, ǽpəréitəs) *pl.* **ap·pa·ra·tus, ap·pa·ra·tus·es** *n.* the equipment (material, tools etc.) needed for a certain task

ap·par·el (əpǽrəl **1.** *n.* *(rhet.)* clothes ‖ *(commerce)* clothing ‖ embroidery on certain church vestments **2.** *v.t. pres. part.* **ap·par·el·ing** *past and past part.* **ap·par·eled** *(rhet.)* to clothe, adorn

ap·par·ent (əpǽrənt, əpéərənt) *adj.* seeming, but not real ‖ real and evident, obvious

ap·par·ent·ly (əpǽrəntli:, əpéərəntli:) *adv.* seemingly ‖ clearly, obviously

ap·pa·ri·tion (ǽpəriʃən) *n.* an appearance, in particular of a being from another world ‖ an appearing, coming into sight ‖ the being or thing that appears, a ghost

ap·peal (əpí:l) *v.t.* *(law)* to call upon a higher authority to review (the decision of a lower) ‖ *v.i.* to address oneself to a higher authority ‖ to turn for an opinion or judgment ‖ to make an earnest request ‖ to ask for voluntary contributions ‖ to be pleasing **appeal** *n.* the act of appealing ‖ the right to appeal to a higher authority ‖ the power to arouse or stimulate desire

ap·peal·a·ble (əpí:ləb'l) *adj.* *(law,* of a case) that can be referred to a higher court

ap·peal·ing (əpí:liŋ) *adj.* moving, endearing ‖ beseeching ‖ pleasing

ap·pear (əpíər) *v.i.* to come in sight ‖ to be in sight ‖ to come on the scene, arrive ‖ to present oneself ‖ to act or perform in public ‖ to be published ‖ to seem or look what a person or thing is or is not ‖ to be evident or probable

ap·pear·ance (əpíərəns) *n.* the act of appearing ‖ looks ‖ dress and general bearing ‖ *(pl.)* outward or superficial evidence **to all appearances** so far as one can see or judge **to make an appearance** to put in an appearance ‖ to appear in public **to put in an ap-pearance** to be present for only a short time

ap·peas·a·ble (əpí:zəb'l) *adj.* capable of being appeased

ap·pease (əpí:z) *pres. part.* **ap·peas·ing** *past and past part.* **ap·peased** *v.t.* to calm or pacify, esp. by making concessions to ‖ to satisfy

ap·pease·ment (əpí:zmənt) *n.* the act of appeasing or being appeased

ap·pel·lant (əpélənt) **1.** *adj.* *(law)* appealing to a higher court **2.** *n.* someone who makes an appeal to a higher court

ap·pel·late (əpélit) *adj.* *(law)* hearing appeals, *appellate courts*

ap·pel·la·tive (əpélətiv) **1.** *n.* *(gram.)* a common as opposed to a proper noun **1.** *adj.* relating to a common noun

ap·pend (əpénd) *v.t.* to attach, add, esp. as an appendix

ap·pend·age (əpéndidʒ) *n.* *(biol.)* an external organ, e.g. a tail ‖ an adjunct or accompaniment

ap·pen·dec·to·my (æpəndéktəmi:) *n.* the surgical operation of removing the appendix

ap·pen·di·ci·tis (əpendisáitis) *n.* an inflammation of the appendix

ap·pen·dix (əpéndiks) *pl.* **ap·pen·dix·es, ap·pen·di·ces** (əpéndisi:z) *n.* an addition to a document or book (generally at the end) which supplements or illustrates the text ‖ the vermiform part of the intestinal canal in the lower right abdomen

ap·per·tain (æpərtéin) *v.i.* to belong by right or custom

ap·pe·tite (ǽpitait) *n.* a natural desire to satisfy hunger ‖ some other natural desire of the body, *sexual appetite* ‖ a strong desire which demands gratification, *appetite for power*

ap·pe·tiz·er (ǽpitaizər) *n.* a short drink or snack that whets the appetite

ap·pe·tiz·ing (ǽpitaiziŋ) *adj.* arousing appetite

ap·plaud (əplód) *v.i.* to show approval by clapping or cheering ‖ *v.t.* to demonstrate approval of by clapping or cheering

ap·plause (əplóz) *n.* approval shown by clapping or cheering ‖ *(rhet.)* praise

ap·ple (ǽp'l) *n.* a tree of the temperate regions bearing roundish, firm, juicy fruit ‖ the fruit (a pome) of this tree

ap·pli·ance (əpláiəns) *n.* a piece of apparatus for a particular use ‖ a fitting that can be put on a machine or tool to adapt it to a particular use ‖ a mechanical or electrical device using a power supply ‖ the act of applying

ap·pli·ca·bil·i·ty (æplikəbíliti:) *n.* the state or quality of being applicable

ap·pli·ca·ble (ǽplikəb'l) *adj.* capable of being applied, intended to apply ‖ suitable, appropriate

ap·pli·cant (ǽplikənt) *n.* someone making an application

ap·pli·ca·tion (æplikéiʃən) *n.* the act of applying ‖ a putting on to a part of the body ‖ a putting into effect of a general rule or principle ‖ a using of a force or a method ‖ a request, esp. to be considered as a candidate, made in person or in writing **on application** to anyone making the appropriate request, *available on application*

ap·plied (əpláid) *adj.* turned or related to practical use

ap·pli·que (æpli·kéi) *n.* a fabric decoration made by cutting out different materials and attaching them on another ‖ a comparable process in metalwork

ap·ply (əplái) *pres. part.* **ap·ply·ing** *past and past part.* **ap·plied** *v.t.* to put (something on another thing), to *apply polish to brasswork* ‖ to bring into use or action ‖ to devote so as to make specified use ‖ to use (a word or expression) in order to name or describe ‖ to devote attentively ‖ to use for a particular purpose ‖ *v.i.* to pertain, *this rule applies only to children* ‖ to make a request, *to apply for a job*

ap·point (əpóint) *v.t.* to select for an office or position ‖ to set, choose (a date, time, place etc.) **ap·póint·ed** *adj.* decided or determined before hand, *the ap-*

pointed time ‖ (combined with 'well-', 'ill-' etc.) fitted out, *a well-appointed ship*

ap·point·ment (əpóintmənt) *n.* a prearranged meeting, date ‖ a selecting for an office or position ‖ this office or position **to keep an appointment** to be present at the right time and place for a prearranged meeting **to make an appointment** to agree on a time and place to meet

ap·por·tion (əpórʃən, əpóurʃən) *v.t.* to share out, divide into shares **ap·pór·tion·ment** *n.* an apportioning or being apportioned

ap·po·si·tion (æpəzíʃən) *n.* an application, addition, e.g. of a seal or signature to a document ‖ the addition to a word of another word or words having the same grammatical function, by way of explanation or qualification, e.g. the words between commas in 'his health, never robust, grew worse' **in apposition** in the grammatical relationship of words so used **ap·po·sí·tion·al** *adj.*

ap·prais·al (əpréiz'l) *n.* the act of appraising ‖ a judgment formed by appraising

ap·praise (əpréiz) *pres. part.* **ap·prais·ing** *past* and *past part.* **ap·praised** *v.t.* to judge the quality of ‖ *(Am. = Br.* value) to give an expert opinion on the value or cost of

ap·prais·er (əpréizər) *n. (Am. = Br.* valuer) someone whose profession is to estimate the market value of something

ap·pre·cia·ble (əprí:ʃəb'l, əprí:ʃi:əb'l) *adj.* large or important enough to be taken into account or noticed **ap·pré·cia·bly** *adv.* noticeably

ap·pre·ci·ate (əprí:ʃi:eit) *pres. part.* **ap·pre·ci·at·ing** *past* and *past part.* **ap·pre·ci·at·ed** *v.t.* to perceive the nature and quality of ‖ to enjoy intelligently ‖ to be grateful for ‖ to have an estimate of ‖ to raise in value ‖ *v.i.* to rise in value

ap·pre·ci·a·tion (əprí:ʃi:éiʃən) *n.* understanding of the nature and quality of something ‖ intelligent enjoyment ‖ gratitude ‖ an increase in money value ‖ a critical estimate or judgment

ap·pre·hend (æprihénd) *v.t.* to arrest, capture ‖ to become aware of ‖ to understand ‖ to expect with anxiety

ap·pre·hen·si·ble (æprihénsəb'l) *adj.* capable of being apprehended by the mind or senses

ap·pre·hen·sion (æprihénʃən) *n.* anxious expectation ‖ capture, arrest ‖ mental perception, understanding

ap·pre·hen·sive (æprihénsiv) *adj.* anxious ‖ relating to or capable of apprehending, *apprehensive powers*

ap·pren·tice (əpréntis) **1.** *n.* someone learning a craft or trade from an employer to whom he is bound by legal agreement for a specified period ‖ a beginner **2.** *adj.* concerning apprenticeship ‖ made or done by a learner **3.** *v.t. pres. part.* **ap·pren·tic·ing** *past* and *past part.* **ap·pren·ticed** to bind as an apprentice **ap·prén·tice·ship** *n.* the state or period of being an apprentice

ap·prise, ap·prize (əpráiz) *pres. part.* **ap·pris·ing, ap·priz·ing** *past* and *past part.* **ap·prised, ap·prized** *v.t. (rhet.)* to inform

ap·proach (əpróutʃ) **1.** *v.i.* to come close or closer or go near or nearer ‖ *v.t.* to come close to ‖ to seek a way of dealing with ‖ to resemble somewhat, approximate to ‖ to address oneself **2.** *n.* the act of coming close or closer, or of going near or nearer ‖ a way by which one approaches ‖ the descent of an aircraft towards the landing area ‖ a method of beginning ‖ *(pl.)* efforts to establish personal or business relations **ap·proach·a·bíl·i·ty** *n.* **ap·próach·a·ble** *adj.* able to be approached ‖ (of a superior) easy to talk to, friendly

ap·pro·ba·tion (æprəbéiʃən) *n.* approval

ap·pro·pri·ate (əpróupri:eit) **1.** *v.t. pres. part.* **ap·pro·pri·at·ing** *past* and *past part.* **ap·pro·pri·at·ed** to take for one's own property ‖ to steal ‖ to set aside for a special purpose **2.** *adj.* (əpróupri:it) suitable

ap·pro·pri·a·tion (əproupri:éiʃən) *n.* the act of appropriating ‖ a sum of money devoted to a special purpose

ap·pro·pri·a·tive (əpróupri:ɛitiv, əpróupri:ətiv) *adj.* relating to appropriation

ap·pro·pri·a·tor (əpróupri:ɛitər) *n.* someone who appropriates

ap·prov·al (əprú:vəl) *n.* favorable opinion or judgment ‖ official recognition or sanction **on approval** (of goods ordered) to be sent back if not satisfactory

ap·prove (əprú:v) *pres. part.* **ap·prov·ing** *past* and *past part.* **ap·proved** *v.i.* to give or have a favorable opinion or judgment ‖ *v.t.* to give official agreement or sanction to ‖ to be favorably disposed towards, consider to be right, good, advantageous etc.

ap·prox·i·mal (əpróksəməl) *adj. (anat.)* touching, in contact with one another

ap·prox·i·mate (əpróksəmeit) **1.** *v. pres. part.* **ap·prox·i·mat·ing** *past* and *past part.* **ap·prox·i·mat·ed** *v.t.* to come close to, be almost the same as ‖ to give as roughly correct ‖ *v.i.* (with 'to') to be almost the same **2.** *adj.* (əpróksəmit) unverified but not far from being correct or exact **ap·prox·i·má·tion** *n.* the act or process of approximating ‖ the result of this process **ap·prox·i·ma·tive** (əpróksəmeitiv) *adj.*

a·pri·cot (éiprikɒt, æprikɒt) *n.* a fruit tree, native to China ‖ its round, yellowish-orange fruit (a drupe) ‖ the color of this fruit

a·pron (éiprən) *n.* a protection for the clothes, generally made of cloth, leather or canvas, worn in front, and tied around the waist ‖ anything like an apron either in shape or in purpose, e.g. a guard over the moving or vulnerable parts of a machine ‖ *(theater)* the part of the stage in front of the curtain ‖ the open space in front of the hangars on an airfield **tied to his mother's (wife's) apron strings** completely dependent on or dominated by his mother (wife)

ap·ro·pos (æprəpou, æprəpóu) **1.** *adj.* to the point **2.** *adv.* by the way ‖ fitly, suitably as regards time or circumstances **3.** *prep.* with reference to **apropos of** with reference to

apse (æps) *n.* the semicircular or many-sided end to the chancel, aisles or transepts

apt (æpt) *adj.* to the point, cleverly suited or timed ‖ liable or likely ‖ quick to understand or learn

ap·ti·tude (æptitu:d, æptitju:d) *n.* a natural talent, bent ‖ ability to learn easily and quickly ‖ *(psychol.)* a set of factors which can be assessed and which show what occupation a person is probably best suited to

a·quar·i·um (əkwɛəri:əm) *pl.* **a·quar·i·ums, a·quar·i·a** (əkwɛəri:ə) *n.* a tank (often of glass) or pond in which fishes, aquatic plants and animals are kept alive

a·quat·ic (əkwætik, əkwɒtik) **1.** *adj.* living or growing in or near water ‖ taking place on or in water, *aquatic sports* **2.** *n.* an aquatic plant or animal ‖ *(pl.)* water sports

aq·ue·duct (ækwidʌkt) *n.* a channel constructed to carry a supply of water by gravity from one place to another, esp. one carried on arches across a valley or river

a·que·ous (éikwi:əs, ækwi:əs) *adj.* watery, like water ‖ made with or from water ‖ *(geol.)* made by the action of water

aq·ui·line (ækwilain) *adj.* of or like an eagle ‖ (esp. of a nose) hooked like the beak of an eagle

Ar·ab (ærəb) **1.** *n.* one of the Semitic people inhabiting the Arabian peninsula **2.** *adj.* of, relating to or characteristic of the Arabs

ar·a·besque (ærəbésk) **1.** *n.* a complex intertwining design of geometric patterns, used decoratively in early Islamic architecture ‖ any elaborate or fantastic interlaced design, which may introduce natural objects and human figures ‖ *(ballet)* a position in which the dancer leans forward on one leg, the arm on the same side held forward horizontally, the other leg and arm held backward horizontally **2.** *adj.* showing an arabesque design

Ar·a·bic (ærəbik) **1.** *adj.* of the Arabs or their language **2.** *n.* the Arabic language

Arabic numerals the figures 1, 2, 3 etc., in common

use, as opposed to the Roman numerals I, II, III etc.

ar·a·ble (ǽrəb'l) **1.** *adj.* (of land) plowed or suited to plowing || produced from plowland, *arable crops* **2.** *n.* arable land, plowland

ar·bi·ter (árbitər) *n.* someone who decides what will or should be accepted || someone who controls

ar·bi·trage (ɑrbitráʒ) *n.* the buying of goods in one place in order to sell them immediately in another at a higher price

ar·bi·trar·y (árbitrεri:) *adj.* arrived at without allowing argument or objection || resulting from personal inclination entirely || decided by chance or whim || prejudiced, not based on reasoned examination || absolute, despotic

ar·bi·trate (árbitreit) *pres. part.* **ar·bi·trat·ing** *past* and *past part.* **ar·bi·trat·ed** *v.i.* to decide a dispute by arbitration || to act as an arbitrator || *v.t.* to settle (a dispute) by arbitration || to judge (a dispute) as an arbitrator

ar·bi·tra·tion (ɑrbitréiʃən) *n.* the settling of a dispute by an arbitrator or arbitrators

ar·bi·tra·tor (árbitreitər) *n.* an impartial judge, or one of a number, whose decision both parties to a dispute agree to accept

ar·bor (árbər) *n.* a pleasant shady spot in a garden or wood, either natural or made by training foliage over a framework

ar·bo·re·tum (ɑrbərí:təm) *pl.* **ar·bo·re·tums, ar·bo·re·ta** (ɑrbərí:tə) *n.* a collection of trees, usually of rare species, for display

arc (ɑrk) *n.* part of the circumference of a circle or part of any other curve || *(astron.)* part of the circle above the horizon (diurnal arc), or below the horizon (nocturnal arc), through which the sun or any other heavenly body appears to pass || *(phys.)* an electric arc, a sustained luminous electrical discharge between separated electrodes

ar·cade (ɑrkéid) *n.* a roofed-in passage, often with arches on one or both sides, and sometimes with shops or stalls || *(archit.)* a row of arches

arch (ɑrtʃ) *n.* a curved construction built to bridge a gap and support weight above it, or used ornamentally || a curve or curved shape

arch *v.t.* to span with, or as though with, an arch || to shape with or like an arch || *v.i.* to serve or appear as an arch **to arch one's eyebrows** to show surprise or disapproval by raising one's eyebrows

ar·chae·o·log·i·cal, ar·che·o·log·i·cal (ɑrki:əlɒ́dʒik'l) *adj.* of or pertaining to archaeology

ar·chae·ol·o·gist, ar·che·ol·o·gist (ɑrki:ɒ́lədʒist) *n.* a specialist in archaeology

ar·chae·ol·o·gy, ar·che·ol·o·gy (ɑrki:ɒ́lədʒi:) *n.* the study of prehistory and of ancient periods of history, based on the examination of their physical remains || the body of knowledge obtained from this

ar·cha·ic (ɑrkéiik) *adj.* belonging to ancient times || fallen into disuse **ar·chá·i·cal·ly** *adv.*

arch·bish·op (ɑrtʃbíʃəp) *n.* a bishop who has a certain limited authority and precedence in dignity over other bishops in an ecclesiastical province, a metropolitan || (in the Eastern Churches) a bishop who is directly beneath a patriarch but who has no suffragans

arch·bish·op·ric (ɑrtʃbíʃəprik) *n.* the diocese, or office, of an archbishop

arch·er (ártʃər) *n.* someone who shoots with a bow and arrow || **the Archer** the constellation Sagittarius

ar·cher·y (ártʃəri:) *n.* the sport of shooting arrows from varying distances at a target

ar·che·typ·al (ɑrkitáip'l) *adj.* pertaining to an archetype

ar·che·type (árkitaip) *n.* the model from which later examples are developed, or to which they conform, a prototype || the assumed exemplar or perfect model which inferior examples may resemble but never equal

ar·chi·pel·a·go (ɑrkəpéləgou, ɑrtʃəpéləgou) *pl.* **ar·chi·pel·a·goes, ar·chi·pel·a·gos** *n.* a group of islands || a sea with many islands **the Ar·chi·pel·a·go** the Aegean Sea, studded with islands, to which the name was first given

ar·chi·tect (árkitekt) *n.* someone whose profession is to design buildings etc., and to see that his plans are correctly followed by the builders

ar·chi·tec·tur·al (ɑrkitéktʃərəl) *adj.* of or pertaining to architecture || used in architecture

ar·chi·tec·ture (árkitektʃər) *n.* the art, science or profession of designing buildings || buildings with reference to their style

ar·chives (árkaivz) *pl. n.* a place in which are kept records of interest to a government, or to an institution, a firm, a family etc. || the records themselves

arch·way (ártʃwei) *n.* an arch under which people pass || a passage roofed by a vault held up by arches

Arc·tic (árktik, ártik) *adj.* near or relating to the North Pole **arc·tic** *(pop.)* intensely cold **the Arctic** the Arctic Regions

ar·dent (árd'nt) *adj.* passionate || eager

ar·dor (árdər) *n.* passion || eagerness, enthusiasm

ar·du·ous (árdʒuəs, esp. *Br.* árdjuəs) *adj.* steep, hard to climb || difficult, trying || strenuous

ar·e·a (έəri:ə) *n.* the extent of a surface as measured by the number of squares it contains each with side 1 unit long or by another standard measure (e.g. for a circle or triangle) when it cannot be so measured || a district or region, vicinity || a sphere of operation

a·re·na (ərí:nə) *n.* the open central area of the Roman amphitheater, in which games and fights between gladiators or wild animals took place || any large area, indoors or outdoors, used for sport, exhibitions, concerts etc.

ar·gon (árgɒn) *n.* an odorless, colorless, chemically inert gaseous element. It is used in electric bulbs and for fluorescent lighting

ar·got (árgou, árgɒt) *n.* the slang of a social group, e.g. thieves, students

ar·gu·a·ble (árgju:əb'l) *adj.* for which good, if not necessarily convincing, reasons may be found || open to doubt **ár·gu·a·bly** *adv.* not certainly, but reasonably held to be

ar·gue (árgju:) *pres. part.* **ar·gu·ing** *past* and *past part.* **ar·gued** *v.t.* to apply reason to (a problem) || to maintain (an opinion) || to persuade by talk || to be a sign of, to prove || *v.i.* to dispute || to wrangle

ar·gu·ment (árgjumənt) *n.* a reason put forward (for or against something) || a chain of reasoning || a discussion, debate || a dispute || a wrangling || a summary of the contents of a book

ar·gu·men·ta·tion (ɑrgjumentéiʃən) *n.* the mental process of constructing a chain of reasoning || its expression in words or writing || discussion

ar·gu·men·ta·tive (ɑrgjuméntətiv) *adj.* excessively fond of arguing or raising objections

a·ri·a (ári:ə) *n.* an air, melody, esp. in opera

ar·id (ǽrid) *adj.* dry, barren || dull, uninteresting

a·rid·i·ty (əríditi:) *n.* the state or quality of being arid

a·rise (əráiz) *pres. part.* **a·ris·ing** *past* **a·rose** (əróuz) *past part.* **a·ris·en** (əriz'n) *v.i.* to come into being, begin || to originate from a particular source or as a natural consequence || to come up for notice or into consideration

ar·is·toc·ra·cy (æristɒ́krɔsi:) *pl.* **ar·is·toc·ra·cies** *n.* government by a small, privileged, hereditary class, drawn from the leading families in the state ‖ a state so governed ‖ the members of such a governing class, in particular those who bear titles of nobility ‖ the best or most prominent of any class, *aristocracy of intellect*

a·ris·to·crat (ərístəkræt, ǽristəkræt) *n.* a member of the ruling class in an aristocracy ‖ a noble

a·ris·to·crat·ic (ərìstəkrǽtik, ǽristəkrǽtik) *adj.* of or pertaining to an aristocracy ‖ patrician (in origin, manners, taste etc.)

a·rith·me·tic (əríθmətik) **1.** *n.* the manipulation of numbers by addition, subtraction, multiplication, division **2.** (æriθmétik) *adj.* arithmetical

a·rith·me·ti·cian (ərìθmətíʃən) *n.* someone skilled in the science or practice of arithmetic

arm (ɑrm) *n.* the upper limb of the human body, from the shoulder to the hand ‖ a similar limb of an animal ‖ a part attached to or projecting from something, *an arm of the sea, the arm of a chair* ‖ a sleeve of a garment **the long arm of the law** the power of the police to arrest wrongdoers **with open arms** joyfully, *to welcome someone with open arms*

arm *n.* (often *pl.*) a weapon ‖ (*pl.*) the heraldic devices on the shield of a family, diocese, institution, state etc. **in arms** (*rhet.*) armed and ready for war **to bear arms** (*rhet.*) to serve actively as a soldier **to stand to arms** to come to a state of readiness to meet attack **to take up arms** (*rhet.*) to prepare for war or wage war **under arms** mobilized for war **up in arms** vexed and prepared to offer resistance

arm *v.t.* to provide with weapons, or other means of fighting or attacking ‖ to protect or defend ‖ to provide with what is needed ‖ to fit with some device, tool, or equipment ‖ *v.i.* to build up armaments

ar·ma·da (ɑrmádə) *n.* a fleet of warships ‖ any large fleet of ships or aircraft

ar·ma·dil·lo (ɑrmədílou) *n.* a member of *Dasypodidae,* a family of edentate mammals, allied to anteaters, but having some teeth. They inhabit Central and South America, and are characterized by an armor of horny scales covering the body

ar·ma·ment (ɑ́rməmənt) *n.* the weapons, guns, rockets etc. with which a ship, aircraft, army, fighting vehicle etc. is equipped ‖ (*pl.*) the weapons and munitions of war

arm·ful (ɑ́rmful) *pl.* **arm·fuls, arms·ful** *n.* the amount that can be held in both arms

ar·mi·stice (ɑ́rmistis) *n.* an agreement by which fighting is suspended while peace terms are negotiated

ar·mor (ɑ́rmər) *n.* (*hist.*) protection for the body worn in battle ‖ the steel protective skin of a battleship, tank etc. ‖ tanks, armored cars and other armored forces ‖ the protective covering of an animal

ar·mor·er (ɑ́rmərər) *n.* a maker of arms ‖ someone who looks after and repairs arms

ar·mor·y (ɑ́rməri) *n.* a place in which arms and ammunition are kept, a large building with offices, drill hall etc.

arm·pit (ɑ́rmpit) *n.* the hollow (axilla) under the joint of the shoulder and arm

ar·my (ɑ́rmi) *pl.* **ar·mies** *n.* a body of men (or women, or both) organized for war on land ‖ the whole of a nation's military force

a·ro·ma (əróumə) *n.* the characteristic, usually pleasant, odor given off by certain plants, spices etc.

ar·o·mat·ic (ærəmǽtik) **1.** *adj.* with a sharp, pleasant smell, like that of spices **2.** *n.* an aromatic plant or drug

a·round (əráund) **1.** *adv.* more or less in a circle, on all sides ‖ near, more or less in the vicinity **to have been around** to be worldly wise ‖ to have traveled widely **2.** *prep.* round about, encircling ‖ approximately ‖ within, in the area of

a·rous·al (əráuz'l) *n.* an arousing or being aroused

a·rouse (əráuz) *pres. part.* **a·rous·ing** *past* and *past part.* **a·roused** *v.t.* to excite, stir up ‖ (*old-fash., rhet.*) to wake up

ar·raign (əréin) *v.t.* to call before a court to answer a charge **ar·ráign·ment** *n.*

ar·range (əréindʒ) *pres. part.* **ar·rang·ing** *past* and *past part.* **ar·ranged** *v.t.* to put in order ‖ to dispose with taste ‖ to settle (a dispute etc.) ‖ to plan ‖ (*mus.*) to adapt (a composition) for voices or instruments for which it was not originally written ‖ *v.i.* to make arrangements

ar·range·ment (əréindʒmənt) *n.* the act of arranging ‖ the way in which arranging is done ‖ a settlement (of a dispute etc.) ‖ something decided in advance ‖ something made up from different things, or parts of things ‖ (*pl.*) plans, preparations

ar·ray (əréi) *v.t.* to arrange (troops etc.) in order ‖ to dress (oneself) magnificently ‖ (*law*) to impanel (a jury)

ar·rest (ərést) *v.t.* to seize and hold by legal authority or superior force ‖ to bring to a stop, check ‖ to attract and hold (one's sight or attention)

arrest *n.* seizure and imprisonment by legal authority or superior force ‖ a check, a stopping of forward movement or progress **under arrest** held in confinement, or prison **under house arrest** not allowed to leave one's house **under open arrest** (esp. *mil.*) not allowed to leave one's quarters

ar·ri·val (əráivəl) *n.* the act of arriving ‖ a person or thing that has arrived

ar·rive (əráiv) *pres. part.* **ar·riv·ing** *past* and *past part.* **ar·rived** *v.i.* to come to a place, reach a destination, end a journey ‖ to appear, come on the scene ‖ to win success, be recognized as successful **to arrive at** to gain (an object), reach (an end or state)

ar·ro·gance (ǽrəgəns) *n.* haughtiness, an overbearing manner

ar·ro·gan·cy (ǽrəgənsi:) *n.* arrogance

ar·ro·gant (ǽrəgənt) *adj.* haughty, having or showing too high an opinion of one's own position or rights, contemptuous of others

ar·ro·gate (ǽrəgeit) *pres. part.* **ar·ro·gat·ing** *past* and *past part.* **ar·ro·gat·ed** *v.t.* to claim for oneself improperly **ar·ro·gá·tion** *n.*

ar·row (ǽrou) *n.* the weapon shot from a bow with a pointed (often barbed) head, and slender shaft, to the end of which feathers are attached ‖ a directing sign (→)

arse (ɑrs) *ASS (buttocks)

ar·se·nal (ɑ́rsən'l) *n.* a place for the making and storing of weapons and munitions

ar·se·nic (ɑ́rsnik, ɑ́rsənik) **1.** *n.* a semimetallic element. Its compounds are highly poisonous and are used in pest control and in medicine **2.** (ɑrsénik) *adj.* (*chem.*) of a compound in which arsenic is pentavalent

ar·son (ɑ́rs'n) *n.* the crime of maliciously burning somebody else's building or property, or of burning one's own to get insurance money

art (ɑrt) *n.* the use of the imagination to make things of aesthetic significance ‖ the technique involved ‖ the theory involved ‖ objects made by creative artists ‖ a sphere in which creative skill is used ‖ one of the humanities (as distinct from a science) ‖ (*pl., old-fash.*) artifice, wiles ‖ one of the liberal arts

ar·te·ri·al (ɑrtíəri:əl) *adj.* (*anat.*) of, from or like an artery ‖ of or pertaining to an artery in a system of communication or transport

ar·te·ri·o·scle·ro·sis (ɑrtìəri:ouskləróusis) *n.* a chronic disease of the arteries characterized by the progressive hardening and thickening of the walls, leading to complete blockage and rupture

ar·ter·y (ɑ́rtəri:) *pl.* **ar·ter·ies** *n.* (*anat.*) one of the tubular, thick-walled, elastic vessels through which blood is pumped by the heart throughout the body (to return through the veins) ‖ an important channel (road, railway, river) in a system of communication and transport

art·ful (ɑ́rtfəl) *adj.* tricky, crafty

ar·thrit·ic (ɑrθrítik) *adj.* of or having arthritis

ar·thri·tis (ɑrθráitis) *n.* inflammation of a joint or joints

ar·thro·pod (ɑ́rθrəpɒd) *n.* (*zool.*) a member of *Arthro-*

poda, an animal phylum characterized by a segmented body, a chitinous exoskeleton, and jointed appendages, which are modified for feeling, feeding, walking etc. **ar·throp·o·dal** (ɑrθrópəd'l), **ar·throp·o·dous** (ɑrθrópədəs) *adjs*

ar·ti·choke (ɑ́rtitʃouk) *n. Helianthus tuberosus*, the Jerusalem artichoke, closely related to the sunflower. It is tall, with a yellow flower, and has edible tubers somewhat like potatoes in appearance ‖ *Cynara scolymus*, the globe artichoke, related to the thistle. It produces flower heads enclosed in an involucre of edible fleshy bracts. Span. fr. Arab. *al-karshuf*

ar·ti·cle (ɑ́rtik'l) **1.** *n.* a particular thing of a distinct class ‖ a particular piece of writing in a larger work ‖ a clause in a document ‖ a statement, regulation etc. ‖ *(gram.)* the words 'the', 'a', 'an' or analogous words in other languages, used as adjectives **2.** *v. pres. part.* **ar·ti·cling** *past* and *past part.* **ar·ti·cled** *v.t.* to bind by articles of apprenticeship ‖ to state (someone's offenses) in articles ‖ *v.i.* (with 'against') to bring charges

ar·tic·u·late (ɑrtíkjulit) **1.** *adj.* divided by joints ‖ (of speech) divided into distinct words and syllables ‖ intelligible, able to speak intelligibly ‖ able to speak with fluency ‖ clearly and distinctly arranged or expressed **2.** *v.* (ɑrtíkjuleit) *pres. part.* **ar·tic·u·lat·ing** *past* and *past part.* **ar·tic·u·lat·ed** *v.t.* to pronounce (words and syllables) clearly and distinctly ‖ (generally in passive) to join together in sections, to joint ‖ *v.i.* to pronounce sounds distinctly

ar·tic·u·la·tion (ɑrtíkjuléiʃən) *n.* the pronouncing of distinct sounds of speech ‖ (of man, animals, plants) the way in which different parts are joined together ‖ a joint

ar·ti·fi·cial (ɑrtifíʃəl) *adj.* man-made ‖ made to imitate a natural product ‖ synthetic ‖ insincere ‖ affected, *an artificial way of writing*

ar·til·ler·y (ɑrtíləri:) *n.* guns, cannon etc., as opposed to portable firearms ‖ the branch of the army equipped with such weapons

ar·ti·san (ɑ́rtiz'n) *n.* a trained craftsman

ar·tist (ɑ́rtist) *n.* a person who uses deliberate skill in making things of beauty, esp. *(pop.)* a painter ‖ a person who uses skill and taste in any activity

ar·tis·tic (ɑrtístik) *adj.* relating to the fine arts ‖ of or connected with artists ‖ made or done with taste and skill, with an eye to beauty ‖ proficient in, fond of, or appreciative of the fine arts **ar·tis·ti·cal·ly** *adv.*

as (æz, əz) **1.** *conj.* because ‖ at the time when ‖ in the way in which ‖ in accordance with that which, *as he predicted* ‖ though ‖ (often with a correlative 'so' or 'as') to the same amount or degree that ‖ (with a preceding 'so' or 'such') in such a way or to such an extent that **as it were** so to speak **as you were** *(mil.)* oral cancellation of a statement or order to troops **2.** *prep.* in the aspect, role, function, capacity of ‖ like **as a rule** usually **3.** *adv.* to the same amount or degree ‖ for example **as for** with reference to **as from** dating from ‖ written or sent as though from **as if** as it would if **as long as** provided that **as of** at or on (a specified time or date) **as regards** with reference to **as though** in a way that resembles **as to** with reference to **as well** also, in addition

as·bes·tos (æsbéstəs, æzbéstəs) **1.** *n.* fibrous silicate materials, chiefly calcium magnesium silicate, used in the manufacture of flameproof fabrics and building materials, and for heat insulation **2.** *adj.* made of or containing asbestos

as·cend (əsénd) *v.i.* to go or come up ‖ to rise ‖ to slope upwards ‖ (of sounds) to rise in pitch ‖ to rise from

a lower degree or level ‖ *v.t.* to climb ‖ *(rhet.)* to mount ‖ to go up towards the source of

as·cend·ance, as·cend·ence (əséndəns) *n.* ascendancy

as·cend·an·cy, as·cend·en·cy (əséndənsi:) *pl.* **as·cen·dan·cies, as·cen·den·cies** *n.* dominating influence or control

as·cend·ant, as·cend·ent (əséndənt) **1.** *adj. (astron.,* of a heavenly body) climbing towards the zenith, before beginning to set **2.** *n. (astrol.)* the point of the ecliptic that is rising above the eastern horizon at any given instant (believed to have a dominating influence)

as·cend·er (əséndər) *n. (printing)* the tall stroke of b, d, f, h, k, l, t

as·cend·ing (əséndiŋ) *adj.* rising, mounting ‖ *(bot.)* curving upwards

as·cent (əsént) *n.* the act of ascending ‖ a climbing ‖ a rising from a lower degree or level ‖ a way up ‖ an amount of upward slope ‖ a going back in time, e.g. in a genealogy

as·cer·tain (æsərtéin) *v.t.* to find out **as·cer·táin·a·ble** *adj.* **as·cer·táin·ment** *n.*

as·cet·ic (əsétik) **1.** *adj.* practicing self-discipline with a view to spiritual improvement, esp. by learning to do without things good in themselves (e.g. warmth, comfort) ‖ frugal, austere ‖ (of personal appearance) giving the impression of self-denial, gaunt, spare **2.** *n.* a person who practices asceticism ‖ a person who lives an austere life **as·cét·i·cal** *adj.* **as·cét·i·cal·ly** *adv.* **as·cét·i·cism** *n.*

as·cribe (əskráib) *pres. part.* **as·crib·ing** *past* and *past part.* **as·cribed** *v.t.* to assign to a cause or source ‖ to assign (to an author) as a conjecture, or from the available evidence ‖ to regard as belonging

as·crip·tion (əskrípʃən) *n.* a document or statement which ascribes ‖ an ascribing

a·sep·sis (eisépsis, əsépsis) *n.* freedom from bacteria ‖ the method or process of excluding bacteria, esp. in surgery

a·sep·tic (eiséptik, əséptik) **1.** *adj.* free from bacterial infection ‖ (or surgical instruments or materials) sterilized ‖ designed to exclude bacteria **2.** *n.* a self-sterilizing substance **a·sép·ti·cal·ly** *adv.*

a·sex·u·al (eisékʃu:əl) *adj.* without sex, sexless ‖ *(biol.,* of reproduction) by other than sexual action, without the union of male and female germ cells **a·sex·u·ál·i·ty** *n.* **a·séx·u·al·ly** *adv.*

ash (æʃ) *n.* the powder left when something has been burned, *wood ash*

ash *n.* a genus of trees of temperate regions with pinnate leaves and roughish gray-green bark ‖ the smooth-grained, springy wood of the ash, used for tool handles

a·shamed (əʃéimd) *adj.* feeling shame, dishonor or disgust, at one's own bad or unworthy behavior or because or on behalf of another ‖ refusing, or reluctant, to do something through pride or fear of ridicule

a·side (əsáid) **1.** *adv.* to or on one side ‖ out of the way ‖ apart, *joking aside* **2.** *n.* words spoken in a play which by convention are heard by the audience but not by the actors ‖ a digression

as·i·nine (æsinain) *adj.* stupid **as·i·nin·i·ty** (æsiníniti:) *pl.* **as·i·nin·i·ties** *n.* crass stupidity or an instance of this

ask (æsk, ɑsk) *v.t.* to request (something) of someone ‖ to inquire about ‖ to inquire of (someone) ‖ to demand (a price) ‖ to invite ‖ *v.i.* to make a request ‖ to inquire ‖ (with 'for') to necessitate **for the asking** simply by asking, without charge **to ask after someone** to ask for news of someone, esp. to inquire about his health **to ask for it** (or **trouble**) to behave in a way that will get one into trouble

---

a·skance (əskǽns) *adv.* (in the phrase) **to look askance at** to view with suspicion or disapproval

a·skew (əskjú:) *adv.* and *pred. adj.* crooked, out of line

ask out *v.* to withdraw

a·slant (əslǽnt, əslánt) **1.** *adv.* slantwise, across at an angle **2.** *prep.* obliquely across

a·sleep (əslí:p) **1.** *pred. adj.* sleeping ‖ numb, esp. through cramp **2.** *adv.* into a state of sleep **to fall asleep** to pass from waking to sleeping ‖ *(euphemistic)* to die

a·so·cial (eisóuʃəl) *adj.* tending to avoid social intercourse ‖ self-centered and indifferent to the social needs of others

asp (æsp) *n.* a small poisonous European snake

as·par·a·gus (əspǽrəgəs) *n.* a perennial plant native to the E. Mediterranean region. Each spring the plant (or 'crown') produces edible, leafless, thick green shoots

as·pect (ǽspekt) *n.* look, outward appearance ‖ the direction in which a thing faces ‖ the angle from which a thing may be regarded ‖ *(astron.)* the relative position of one planet to another, as seen from the earth, which astrologers held to influence human fortunes

as·per·i·ty (əspériti:) *pl.* **as·per·i·ties** *n.* (of the temper or the tongue) sharpness ‖ (of a surface) roughness, unevenness ‖ (of weather) severity

as·perse (əspɔ́:rs) *pres. part.* **as·pers·ing** *past* and *past part.* **as·persed** *v.t.* to malign, try to hurt the reputation of

as·per·sion (əspɔ́:rʒən, əspɔ́:rʃən) *n.* an oblique assault on a person's reputation ‖ a sprinkling with holy water

as·phalt (ǽsfɔlt, ǽsfælt) **1.** *n.* a bituminous derivative of petroleum occurring as an industrial residue or naturally, and containing varying proportions of other organic and mineral materials, used principally for surfacing roads and flat roofs **2.** *adj.* with a surface of asphalt **3.** *v.t.* to apply a surface of asphalt to

as·phyx·i·a (æsfíksi:ə) *n.* the condition in which a person is not able to get air into his lungs **as·phýx·i·ant 1.** *adj.* causing asphyzia or suffocation **2.** *n.* an agent with this property **as·phyx·i·ate** (æsfíksi:eit) *pres. part.* **as·phyx·i·at·ing** *past* and *past part.* **as·phyx·i·at·ed** *v.t.* to cause asphyxia in ‖ *v.i.* to be a victim of asphyxia **as·phyx·i·a·tion, as·phýx·i·á·tor** *ns*

as·pir·ant (əspáiərənt, ǽspərənt) *n.* a person anxious to win a desirable thing or position, *an aspirant to the priesthood*

as·pi·rate (ǽspəreit) **1.** *v.t. pres. part.* **as·pi·rat·ing** *past* and *past part.* **as·pi·rat·ed** to pronounce with an h sound ‖ *(med.)* to remove (fluid or gas) with an aspirator **2.** (ǽspərit) *n.* the sound represented by the letter h **3.** *adj.* pronounced as an aspirate ‖ *(phon.*, of a consonant) followed by a slight puff of breath

as·pi·ra·tion (æspəréiʃən) *n.* ambition or an ambition ‖ the pronunciation of an aspirate or the sign that marks one ‖ *(med.)* the action or use of an aspirator

as·pi·ra·tor (ǽspəreitər) *n.* a suction pump or similar device ‖ *(med.)* an instrument used to suck fluid or poison from the body

as·pire (əspáiər) *pres. part.* **as·pir·ing** *past* and *past part.* **as·pired** *v.i.* to be eager (to *win* something), to have an ambition (to achieve something desirable or lofty)

as·pi·rin (ǽspərin, ǽsprin) *n.* acetylsalicylic acid. It is widely used in powder or tablet form to relieve pain or reduce fever, and has a beneficial effect on certain forms of rheumatism

ass (æs) *n.* any of several mammals of the genus *Equus,* esp. *E. asinus,* the donkey ‖ a stupid person **to make an ass of oneself** to do something foolish

ass *n.* (*Am.* = *Br.* arse, not in polite usage) the buttocks

as·sail (əséil) *v.t.* to attack vigorously

as·sail·ant (əséilənt) *n.* an attacker

as·sas·sin (əsǽsin) *n.* a person who kills, or tries to kill, another by violent means

as·sas·si·nate (əsǽsineit) *pres. part.* **as·sas·si·nat·ing** *past* and *past part.* **as·sas·si·nat·ed** *v.t.* to kill as an as-sassin **as·sas·si·ná·tion** *n.* the act of an assassin ‖ death at the hands of an assassin

as·sault (əsɔ́lt) *n.* a vigorous armed attack ‖ a violent critical attack ‖ *(law)* an unlawful threat to use force against another person

assault *v.t.* to make an assault on ‖ *(law)* to use violence against

as·say (æsei, əséi) *n.* the determination of the proportion of a metal in an ore or alloy ‖ a sample of metal for such trial ‖ the result of the trial

as·sem·blage (əsémblidʒ) *n.* a number of persons or things gathered together ‖ an assembling ‖ art form or composition of scraps of various materials, e.g. cloth, hardware, paper

as·sem·ble (əsémb'l) *pres. part.* **as·sem·bling** *past* and *past part.* **as·sem·bled** *v.t.* to bring together ‖ to fit together ‖ *v.i.* to come together

as·sem·bly (əsémbli:) *pl.* **as·sem·blies** *n.* a gathering of people ‖ (of machines etc.) assemblage ‖ *(computer)* conversion of a source program to a machine language

as·sent (əsént) *n.* an acceptance (of a doctrine, statement, logical proposition etc.) as true

as·sent *v.i.* to give expressed or unexpressed mental acceptance to the truth or rightness of a doctrine, conclusion etc. ‖ to say yes

as·sert (əsɔ́:rt) *v.t.* to state as true ‖ to maintain, insist on ‖ to make effective, use with effect **to assert itself** to become active, make its effect felt **to assert oneself** to impose one's proper authority ‖ to be domineering

as·ser·tion (əsɔ́:rʃən) *n.* a positive statement ‖ the act of asserting

as·ser·tive (əsɔ́:rtiv) *adj.* dominating ‖ positive, allowing no denial or opposition

as·sess (əsés) *v.t.* to fix the value or amount of, esp. for the purpose of taxation ‖ to impose a charge for ‖ to judge the value or worth of (other than in money), to estimate **as·séss·a·ble** *adj.* **as·séss·ment** *n.* the amount assessed ‖ the act of assessing ‖ an estimate

as·ses·sor (əsésər) *n.* a person who assesses value for taxation, or apportions taxes, fines etc. ‖ *(insurance)* a person who estimates the value of property for which a claim is made and investigates the legality of the claim **as·ses·so·ri·al** (æsisɔ́ri:el, əsisóuri:əl) *adj.*

as·set (ǽset) *n.* anything one owns or any quality one has that is of value or use ‖ *(pl.)* the total property of a person, firm or institution ‖ *(pl.)* the positive items on a balance sheet

as·si·du·i·ty (æsidú:iti:, æsidjú:iti:) *n.* untiring diligence or attention

as·sid·u·ous (əsídʒuəs) *adj.* constant in working or giving attention

as·sign (əsáin) *n.* *(law)* a person to whom property or a right is legally assigned

assign *v.t.* to give as a share, allot, *to assign positions to people* ‖ to nominate, appoint, *to assign a person to a position* ‖ to give or make over (property or a right) ‖ to fix or determine (a day, time etc.) ‖ to ascribe to a given time, authorship, origin, class ‖ to give as a task

as·sig·na·tion (æsignéiʃən) *n.* a secret arrangement to meet, usually between lovers or conspirators ‖ an attribution of origin and esp. of date ‖ the act of assigning

as·sign·ee (æsiní:, əsainí:) *n.* *(law)* a person who has been given the right or duty of acting in place of another ‖ a person to whom property or a right has been legally assigned

as·sign·ment (əsáinmənt) *n.* the act of assigning ‖ the thing (task) assigned ‖ an attribution, assignation ‖ *(law)* transference of property or a right ‖ *(law)* the document by which this is done

as·sist (əsíst) **1.** *v.t.* to help (someone) ‖ *v.i.* to be of service **2.** *n.* (games) help given to another player

as·sis·tance (əsístəns) *n.* usefulness, service ‖ financial or other practical help

as·sis·tant (əsístənt) **1.** *n.* a helper ‖ a person holding a subordinate position **2.** *adj.* helping ‖ subordinate

as·so·ci·ate (əsóuʃiːit) **1.** *adj.* acting on equal terms || subordinate || accompanying, allied **2.** *n.* a fellow worker or partner || a subordinate || a person whom one is friendly with or much in company with || a member (of a society) with less than full rights **3.** *v.* (əsóuʃiːeit) *pres. part.* **as·so·ci·at·ing** *past* and *past part.* **as·so·ci·at·ed** *v.t.* to connect in one's mind || to cause to participate in some cooperative capacity || *v.i.* to join as companion etc. **to associate oneself with** to manifest publicly one's solidarity with (a corporate act of protest etc.) **as·só·ci·ate·ship** *n.* less than full membership

as·so·ci·a·tion (əsousi:éiʃən) *n.* the act of associating or being associated || an organized body of people with a common interest or object || an idea identified in one's mind with some object and recalled by it || companionship, social or business relationship

as·so·nance (ǽsənəns) *n.* a similarity of sound between words or syllables || the controlled repetition in verse of an accentuated vowel, but not of the consonants following, esp. in the last words of consecutive lines, e.g. pale/brave **ás·so·nant**

as·sort (əsórt) *v.t.* (*old-fash.*) to sort, classify; *v.i.* to harmonize, go together **as·sórt·ed** *adj.* classified || of various kinds, miscellaneous || (in combined words) matched

as·sort·ment (əsórtmənt) *n.* a mixture or collection made up of different things, or different kinds of the same thing

as·suage (əswéidʒ) *pres. part.* **as·suag·ing** *past* and *past part.* **as·suaged** *v.t.* to soothe, lessen || to satisfy **as·suáge·ment** *n.*

as·sume (əsúːm) *pres. part.* **as·sum·ing** *past* and *past part.* **as·sumed** *v.t.* to suppose, accept or believe (something) to be true || to suppose, believe or accept (someone) to be something || to put on as a pretense || to adopt (e.g. an attitude or role) || to manifest itself under || to begin effectively in (office) || to begin to exercise (control) **as·súmed** *adj.* accepted as, or believed to be true || pretended, false || taken as one's right **as·súm·ing** *adj.* proud, arrogant

as·sump·tion (əsʌmpʃən) *n.* the act of assuming || something taken for granted

as·sur·ance (əʃúərəns) *n.* something, e.g. a promise, pledge, convincing reason etc. on which one can rely as a guarantee of truth || certainty || self-confidence

as·sure (əʃúər) *pres. part.* **as·sur·ing** *past* and *past part.* **as·sured** *v.t.* to make certain || to tell as a certain fact || to insure **as·súred** *adj.* certain, safe || self-confident **as·sur·ed·ly** (əʃúəridli:) *adv.* certainly, emphatically yes **as·sur·ed·ness** (əʃúəridnis) *n.* certainty || self-confidence **as·súr·er** *n.* someone who assures **as·súr·or** *n.* (*law*) an underwriter || someone who insures his life

as·ter·isk (ǽstərisk) **1.** *n.* (in printing or writing) a mark like a star [*] which calls attention to a note, or distinguishes a word or words **2.** *v.t.* to mark with an asterisk

a·stern (əstə́ːrn) *adv.* (*naut.*) in, at, or towards the rear (of a vessel) || (*naut.*) backwards

as·ter·oid (ǽstərɔid) **1.** *n.* (*astron.*) one of the small planets occupying orbits mainly between those of Mars and Jupiter || (*zool.*) a starfish **2.** *adj.* like the conventional shape of a star **as·ter·óid·al** *adj.* **as·ter·ói·de·an** *adj.* and *n.*

asth·ma (ǽzmə, ǽsmə) *n.* a disease which causes wheezing and difficulty in breathing, due to swelling and congestion of the air passages in the lungs. This is the result of an allergic reaction to various substances

asth·mat·ic (æzmǽtik, æsmǽtik) **1.** *adj.* caused by asthma or affected with asthma **2.** *n.* someone who suffers from asthma **asth·mát·i·cal** *adj.*

as·tig·mat·ic (æstigmǽtik) *adj.* affected by astigmatism || (of a lens) correcting, or corrected for, this defect

a·stig·ma·tism (əstígmətiʒəm) *n.* (*phys.*) a defect of the eye, of a lens or of an image formed by either, the curvature of the refracting surface or surfaces being different in different planes

as·ton·ish (əstóniʃ) *v.t.* to strike with amazement or wonder || to shock **as·tón·ish·ing** *adj.* amazing, wonderful || shocking **as·tón·ish·ment** *n.* the state of being astonished || a cause for astonishment

as·tound (əstáund) *v.t.* to shock with fear. wonder or amazement || to surprise greatly **as·tóund·ing** *adj.*

a·stray (əstréi) *adv.* on the wrong road || wandering, lost || mistaken, wrong

a·stride (əstráid) **1.** *pred. adj.* and *adv.* with one leg on each side || in the position of striding **2.** *prep.* with one leg on each side of

a·strin·gen·cy (əstríndʒənsi:) *n.* the quality of being astringent

a·strin·gent (əstríndʒənt) **1.** *adj.* (of something acting on the tissues of the skin etc.) tightening || (of flavor) causing the mouth to feel dry and puckered || (of medicine) styptic || (of style or criticism) dry and sharply to the point **2.** *n.* an astringent agent

as·tro·labe (ǽstrəleib) *n.* a circular ring or metal disk on which the heavenly sphere was projected and used from early times to measure the altitudes of stars, but now replaced by the sextant

as·trol·o·ger (əstrólədʒər) *n.* a person who practices astrology

as·tro·log·i·cal (æstrəlódʒik'l) *adj.* pertaining to astrology or astrologers

as·trol·o·gy (əstrólədʒi:) *n.* the art of predicting or determining the influence of the planets and stars on human affairs

as·tro·naut (ǽstrənɔt, ǽstrənɒt) *n.* a space traveler

as·tro·nau·tics (æstrənɔ́tiks, æstrənɒ́tiks) *n.* the science of travel in outer space

as·tron·o·mer (əstrónəmər) *n.* a person skilled or learned in astronomy

as·tro·nom·ic (æstrənómik) *adj.* pertaining to astronomy || (*fig.*, of figures, quantity, distance) enormous **as·tro·nóm·i·cal** *adj.* **as·tro·nóm·i·cal·ly** *adv.*

as·tron·o·my (əstrónəmi:) *n.* the science of the heavenly bodies

as·tute (əstjúːt, əstúːt) *adj.* shrewd || ready-witted, clever, *an astute answer*

a·sun·der (əsʌ́ndər) *adv.* (*rhet.*) into two or more parts, into pieces, *torn asunder*

a·sy·lum (əsáiləm) *n.* a mental home, hospital for the mentally ill || (*rhet.*) a place affording safety from attack or shelter || refuge

a·sym·met·ric (eisimétrik, æsimétrik) *adj.* showing asymmetry **a·sym·mét·ri·cal** *adj.*

a·sym·me·try (eisímitri:, æsímitri:) *n.* lack of symmetry, uneven disposition on each side of an (imaginary) central line or point

at (æt) *prep.* expressing position || expressing place in time || expressing the direction or end of movement, or the end towards which action or will is directed || expressing manner of action or employment || expressing situation or condition || expressing cause or occasion of an action or state || expressing position in a scale that measures degree, amount, price etc. **at all** (in a question, or after a negative or a word implying a negative), to any degree

at·e·lier (ǽtəljei) *n.* an artist's studio || a workroom used for crafts, dressmaking etc.

---

a·the·ism (éiθi:izəm) *n.* the denial of the existence of God ‖ godlessness in belief or as a guide in conduct **á·the·ist** *n.* and *adj.* **a·the·is·tic** *adj.* **a·the·ís·ti·cal·ly** *adv.*

ath·lete (ǽθli:t) *n.* a person with the skill and training to be good at sports

athlete's foot a contagious skin disease, most common between the toes, a form of ringworm

ath·let·ic (æθlétik) *adj.* of or pertaining to athletes ‖ strong, fit and agile **ath·lét·ics** *n.* the sports practiced by athletes

a·thwart (əθwɔ́rt) **1.** *adv.* across the length of a ship or across her course **2.** *prep.* across the length of (a ship) or across (her course) **a·thwart·ships** (əθwɔ́rtʃips) *adv.* from side to side across a ship

at·las (ǽtləs) *n. (physiol.)* the first vertebra in the neck, which supports the head ‖ a book containing a collection of maps ‖ *pl.* **at·lan·tes** (ætlǽnti:z) a pillar in the form of a man, supporting a weight

at·mos·phere (ǽtməsfiər) *n.* the gases that surround the earth, divided into layers according to such criteria as rate of temperature change with increasing altitude, composition and electrical nature ‖ the air in any enclosed space with respect to its effects on people or things subjected to it ‖ a set of prevailing moral or mental influences on an institution, locality, group etc. ‖ a unit of pressure equal to that exerted by a column of mercury 76 cm high at 0°C and under standard gravity

at·mos·pher·ic (ætməsférik) *adj.* **at·mos·phér·i·cal** *adj.*

atmospheric pressure the pressure exerted by the earth's atmosphere

a·toll (ǽtɒl) *n.* a coral reef in the shape of a ring or horseshoe enclosing a lagoon

at·om (ǽtəm) *n.* the smallest portion of matter displaying the characteristic properties of a particular chemical element ‖ a very small quantity, *not an atom of truth in it*

a·tom·ic (ətómik) *adj.* of, related to, or characterized by atoms **a·tóm·i·cal·ly** *adv.*

atomic pile a nuclear reactor

at·om·ize (ǽtəmaiz) *pres. part.* **at·om·iz·ing** *past* and *past part.* **at·om·ized** *v.t.* to convert (a liquid, e.g. a perfume, insecticide or medicine) into very fine particles, generally as a spray forced through a nozzle **át·om·iz·er** *n.* a device for atomizing a liquid

a·tone (ətóun) *pres. part.* **a·ton·ing** *past* and *past part.* **a·toned 1.** *v.i.* to make amends **2.** *v.t.* (used only passively and with 'for') to make amends for

a·tone·ment (ətóunmənt) *n.* the act of atoning ‖ that which is done in order to atone

a·tri·um (éitri:əm) *pl.* **a·tri·a** (éitri:ə) *n.* the central hall of a Roman house, where the household gods were ‖ an open court with a covered passage on three or four sides leading e.g. to a basilica ‖ *(anat.)* a cavity in the body

a·tro·cious (ətróuʃəs) *adj.* shockingly cruel or wicked ‖ of very bad quality ‖ extremely painful ‖ very unpleasant

a·troc·i·ty (ətrósiti:) *pl.* **a·troc·i·ties** *n.* shocking cruelty or wickedness ‖ extreme painfulness ‖ an atrocious deed ‖ something atrocious or very bad of its kind

at·ro·phy (ǽtrəfi:) **1.** *n.* a wasting or withering away or failure to develop normally, from lack of food or use ‖ *(fig.)* loss of power or vigor **2.** *v. pres. part.* **at·ro·phy·ing** *past* and *past part.* **at·ro·phied** *v.t.* to cause atrophy in ‖ *v.i.* to suffer atrophy

at·tach (ətǽtʃ) *v.t.* to fasten, connect (one thing to another) ‖ to bind by love or esteem ‖ to appoint or assign in some added role ‖ *(mil.)* to place temporarily under the orders of some other unit for specified purposes ‖ *(law)* to seize (a person or property) by legal authority ‖ to attribute, *to attach blame* ‖ *v.i.* to be fastened in some specified way ‖ *(fig.)* to adhere

at·ta·che (ætəʃéi, *Br.* esp. ətǽʃei) *n.* a person attached to an embassy for some specific activity, *press attaché*

at·tach·ment (ətǽtʃmənt) *n.* the act of attaching one thing to another ‖ the device or method by which one object is attached to another ‖ the object attached ‖ a bond of affection or friendship ‖ *(law)* the legal seizure of persons or property

at·tack (ətǽk) *n.* the act of attacking ‖ a bout of illness ‖ *(mus.)* the action or manner of beginning a piece or phrase ‖ *(sport)* offensive rather than defensive play

attack *v.t.* to set upon, try to get the better of or destroy or win ‖ to assail in words or writing ‖ to start upon (a difficulty, task or occupation) ‖ to have a harmful or destructive effect on ‖ *v.i.* to make an attack

at·tain (ətéin) *v.t.* to arrive at, obtain, win **to attain to** to arrive at, *to attain to full maturity* **at·tain·a·bíl·i·ty** *n.* **at·táin·a·ble** *adj.*

at·tain·der (ətéindər) *n.* the loss of all rights as a citizen, part of the punishment of a person condemned to death or outlawry for treason or felony (now abolished)

at·tain·ment (ətéinmənt) *n.* the act of attaining ‖ an acquired personal skill

at·tempt (ətémpt) **1.** *v.t.* to try (to do something), to try or make trial of ‖ to try to achieve, *to attempt a rescue* **to attempt the life of** *(rhet.)* to try to kill **2.** *n.* the act of attempting, often unsuccessful ‖ a failed attack by a killer

at·tend (əténd) *v.t.* to be present at ‖ to go regularly to ‖ to visit and treat (as doctor, nurse etc.) ‖ to accompany as attendant ‖ to accompany (often as a result) **to attend to** to apply oneself to ‖ to care for, look after ‖ to wait upon, serve **to attend upon** to accompany for the purpose of giving service

at·tend·ance (əténdəns) *n.* the act or habitual practice of attending, being present ‖ those who are present or attend **to dance attendance on** to run about after (somebody) to do their least bidding

at·tend·ant (əténdənt) **1.** *n.* a servant, an employee in charge ‖ a companion, usually of lower rank ‖ *(rhet.)* an accompaniment

at·ten·tion (əténʃən) *n.* the giving of one's mind to something, mental concentration ‖ notice ‖ nursing, care, looking after ‖ a mending or overhauling ‖ service by a waiter etc. ‖ *(mil.)* the formal position of readiness on parade ‖ *(mil.)* the order to come to this position ‖ *(interj.)* used as a warning word before an important announcement to impress the need to listen ‖ *(pl.)* attentiveness, acts of politeness **to call attention to** to point out

at·ten·tive (əténtiv) *adj.* paying attention, giving one's mind to what is going on ‖ thoughtful for others

at·test (ətést) *v.t.* to bear witness to, esp. by signing (a statement) ‖ to confirm as authentic, *his secretary attests the truth of his statement* ‖ to administer an oath to ‖ *v.i.* to testify

at·test·ant (ətéstənt) **1.** *adj.* attesting **2.** *n.* someone who attests

at·tes·ta·tion (ætestéiʃən) *n.* the act of bearing witness ‖ the evidence given by a witness ‖ confirmation of truth or authenticity ‖ the administering of an oath

at·tic (ǽtik) *n.* a room just under the roof of a house

at·tire (ətáiər) **1.** *v.t. pres. part.* **at·tir·ing** *past* and *past part.* **at·tired** (usually very formal) to dress grandly **2.** *n.* fine clothing

at·ti·tude (ǽtitju:d, ǽtitu:d) *n.* posture ‖ a mental position ‖ **to strike an attitude** to assume a histrionic pose **at·ti·tú·di·nize** *pres. part.* **at·ti·tu·di·niz·ing** *past* and *past part.* **at·ti·tu·di·nized** *v.i.* to strike an attitude

at·tor·ney (ətɔ́:rni:) *n.* a person who has legal authority to act on behalf of another ‖ a legal agent qualified to act for someone engaged in legal proceedings

at·tract (ətrǽkt) *v.t.* to draw towards itself or oneself, cause to move towards itself ‖ to appear lovely or pleasing to the mind and senses ‖ to cause to center on itself, direct towards itself or oneself

at·trac·tion (ətrǽkʃən) *n.* the power or act of attracting ‖ a desirable or pleasant quality or thing ‖ *(phys.)* the force, due to gravitational, electric, magnetic or other effects, causing or tending to cause two bodies to

at·trac·tive (ətrǽktiv) *adj.* charming, good-looking ‖ pleasant, enticing, *an attractive idea*

at·tri·bute (ǽtribju:t) **1.** *n.* a quality proper to or characteristic of a person or thing ‖ a symbol often associated with a person of thing ‖ *(logic)* an essential quality ‖ *(gram.)* a word or phrase used adjectivally **2.** *v.t.* (ətríbju:t) *pres. part.* **at·trib·ut·ing** *past* and *past part.* **at·trib·ut·ed** to consider (something) as being proper to or belonging to a person or thing ‖ to consider (a thing) as being ascribable to a cause ‖ to consider (a thing) as having its origin in a certain time or place, or as being the work of a certain person or persons

at·tri·bu·tion (ætribjú:ʃən) *n.* the act of attributing ‖ the thing or quality attributed

at·trib·u·tive (ətríbju:tiv) **1.** *adj. (gram.),* of an adjective or other modifier) preceding the word it modifies, e.g. in 'a wrong answer', 'wrong' is attributive, but in 'your answer is wrong', 'wrong' is predicative **2.** *n.* an attributive word

at·tri·tion (ətríʃən) *n.* a wearing away by rubbing or friction ‖ exhaustion by a constant loss of strength or of resistance ‖ normal reduction, e.g. by death, retirement, graduation ‖ the reduction of the effectiveness of a force caused by loss of personnel and material

au·burn (ɔ́bərn) **1.** *adj.* reddish-brown (esp. of hair) **2.** *n.* the color auburn

auc·tion (ɔ́kʃən) **1.** *n.* a public sale at which the goods are sold to the highest bidder ‖ an offer to give something to whoever will pay the most **2.** *v.t.* to sell by auction

au·da·cious (ɔdéiʃəs) *adj.* daring, ready to take calculated risks ‖ too daring by conventional moral standards, *audacious language*

au·dac·i·ty (ɔdǽsiti:) *pl.* **au·dac·i·ties** *n.* boldness or an instance of it ‖ impudence, shamelessness, or an instance of it

au·di·bil·i·ty (ɔdəbíliti:) *n.* the ability to be heard

au·di·ble (ɔ́dəb'l) **1.** *n. (football)* a surprise substitute play or formation called at the scrimmage line **2.** *adj.* able to be heard **au·di·bly** *adv.*

au·di·ence (ɔ́di:əns) *n.* a group of persons assembled to listen to or watch something, esp. a public performance or speech ‖ those who read a publication or listen to a broadcast ‖ an official or formal interview, *a papal audience*

au·di·o (ɔ́di:ou) **1.** *adj.* or electronic apparatus using audio frequencies ‖ of or relating to sound broadcasting, or to sound transmission or reception in television **2.** *n.* the part of television, or of television equipment, concerned with sound ‖ sound transmission or reception in broadcasting

au·dit (ɔ́dit) **1.** *n.* a full check and examination of account books ‖ the final account after the examination **2.** *v.t.* to make such an examination of (accounts) ‖ *v.i.* to examine account books in such a way

au·di·tion (ɔdíʃən) **1.** *n.* a trial of talent in which a prospective employer assesses an actor, singer etc. ‖ the sense or act of hearing **2.** *v.t.* to submit (candidates) to an audition ‖ *v.i.* to compete in an audition

au·di·tor (ɔ́ditər) *n.* a person who makes an audit, either professionally or in an amateur, honorary capacity ‖ a listener, e.g. to a broadcast ‖ a person who attends a high school or college course without aiming to obtain the attached credit **au·di·to·ri·al** (ɔditɔ́ri:əl, ɔditóuri:əl) *adj.*

au·di·to·ri·um (ɔditɔ́ri:əm, ɔditóuri:əm) *n.* the part of a theater or movie theater etc. in which the audience sits ‖ a lecture hall or assembly room

au·di·to·ry (ɔ́ditɔri:, ɔ́ditouri:) *adj.* relating to the sense of hearing

auditory meatus the channel leading from the outer ear to the eardrum

au·ger (ɔ́gər) *n.* a tool, larger than a gimlet, for boring holes in wood ‖ any tool similar in shape and principle for boring holes or drilling

aught, ought (ɔt) *n. (archaic)* anything

aug·ment (ɔgmént) *v.t.* to add to ‖ *(mus.)* to increase (certain intervals) by sharpening the higher note ‖ *v.i.* to increase

aug·men·ta·tion (ɔgmentéiʃən) *n.* an increasing or being increased ‖ something which is an increase or addition ‖ *(mus.,* in counterpoint) the repeating of a phrase in notes longer than those first used

aunt (ænt, ɑnt) *n.* a sister of one's mother or father ‖ (by courtesy) the wife of one's uncle

au·ra (ɔ́rə) *n.* the atmosphere of a thing ‖ *(spiritualism)* a vague, luminous glow surrounding a figure or object **áu·ral** *adj.*

au·re·o·la (ɔrí:ələ) *n.* an aureole

au·re·ole (ɔ́ri:oul) *n.* the heavenly crown which is the symbolic reward of sanctity, often represented in art by a halo ‖ this halo ‖ the halo of light seen around a heavenly body or bright light in misty weather ‖ the clear space between the sun or moon and a surrounding halo or corona

au·re·o·my·cin (ɔri:oumáisin) *n.* the yellow crystalline 'broad-spectrum' antibiotic chlortetracycline, active against many organisms resistant to penicillin and streptomycin, and used to stimulate animal growth

au·ri·cle (ɔ́rik'l) *n. (anat.)* the external part of the ear ‖ the chamber or either of the two chambers in the heart connecting the veins with the ventricles ‖ *bot.)* an earlike growth

au·ro·ra (ɔrɔ́rə, ɔróurə) *n.* the redness of the sky just before sunrise ‖ the aurora australis or the aurora borealis

aurora aus·tra·lis (ɔstréilis) *n.* a phenomenon in the southern hemisphere analogous to the aurora borealis

aurora bo·re·al·is (bɔri:ǽlis, bɔuri:ǽlis) *n.* a colored glow visible at night in high latitudes. It has the appearance of a fan of ascending luminous streamers near the northern horizon, and is supposed to be of electrical origin

aus·pice (ɔ́spis) *n. (Rom. hist.)* the observation of the flight and behavior of birds, and observation of other animals, so as to learn whether the gods would be pleased or displeased by a proposed action ‖ a sign so observed **under the auspices of** under the patronage of, by care and favor of

aus·pi·cious (ɔspíʃəs) *adj.* giving promise of good fortune ‖ *(rhet.)* fortunate

aus·tere (ɔstíər) *adj.* stern and strict ‖ stern in appearance, grim ‖ simple and without decoration ‖ marked by the absence of comfort or luxury

aus·ter·i·ty (ɔstériti:) *pl.* **aus·ter·i·ties** *n.* the quality of being austere ‖ (esp. *pl.*) an austere habit or practice

au·tar·chic (ɔtárkik) *adj.* of or characteristic of an autarchy **au·tár·chi·cal** *adj.*

au·tar·chy (ɔ́tarki:) *pl.* **au·tar·chies** *n.* despotism, the rule of an autocrat ‖ a country under such rule

au·then·tic (ɔθéntik) *adj.* genuine ‖ true, reliable **au·thén·ti·cal·ly** *adv.*

au·then·ti·cate (ɔθéntikeit) *pres. part* **au·then·ti·cat·ing** *past* and *past part.* **au·then·ti·cat·ed** *v.t.* to prove the genuineness or truth of, *to authenticate a claim* **au·then·ti·cá·tion, au·thén·ti·cá·tor** *ns*

au·then·tic·i·ty (ɔθentísiti:) *n.* the quality of being authentic

au·thor (ɔ́θər) *n.* the writer of a book, article etc. ‖ a person whose profession is writing ‖ a maker, originator **au·tho·ri·al** (ɔθɔ́ri:əl) *adj.*

au·thor·i·tar·i·an (əθɔrité̞ɑri:ən, əθɔrité̞ɑri:ən) **1.** *adj.* favoring, or relating to, the theory that respect for authority is of greater importance than individual liberty ‖ domineering **2.** *n.* a person supporting this theory **au·thor·i·tár·i·an·ism** *n.*

au·thor·i·ta·tive (əθɔ́riṭeitiv, əθɔ́riṭeitiv) *adj.* coming from an official source or from an appropriate authority ‖ fully expert ‖ with an air of command

au·thor·i·ty (əθɔ́riti:, əθɔ́riti:) *pl.* **au·thor·i·ties** *n.* the right and power to command and be obeyed, or to do something ‖ such power, or proof of such power, entrusted to another ‖ an official body which controls a particular department or activity ‖ (esp. *pl.*) the government, those in charge ‖ someone whose knowledge and opinions command respect and belief ‖ the power of such knowledge ‖ a book or other writing which is trusted or quoted as evidence, or its author ‖ evidence, reasons for a statement

au·thor·i·za·tion (ɔθərizéiʃən) *n.* an authorizing or being authorized

au·thor·ize (ɔ́θəraiz) *pres. part.* **au·thor·iz·ing** *past* and *past part.* **au·thor·ized** *v.t.* to give legal power or right to ‖ to give permission for ‖ to delegate power to **áu·thor·ized** *adj.* officially approved or appointed, holding or done with the necessary rights or powers

au·thor·ship (ɔ́θərʃip) *n.* writing as an activity or profession ‖ the identity of the author of a literary work ‖ the source of an event or deed

au·to·bi·og·ra·pher (ɔtoubaiɔ́grəfər) *n.* a person who writes the story of his life

au·to·bi·o·graph·ic (ɔtoubai̞əgrǽfik) *adj.* relating to, consisting of or characterized by autobiography **au·to·bi·o·gráph·i·cal** *adj.*

au·to·bi·og·ra·phy (ɔtoubaiɔ́grəfi:) *pl.* **au·to·bi·og·ra·phies** *n.* a written account of one's own life ‖ autobiographical writing as a literary genre

au·to·bus (ɔ́toubʌs) *n.* a bus

au·toc·ra·cy (ɔtɔ́krəsi:) *pl.* **au·toc·ra·cies** *n.* government by a single absolute ruler ‖ a state so governed

au·to·crat (ɔ́tokræt) *n.* an absolute ruler, a despot ‖ someone who insists on his own way and will not defer to others **au·to·crát·ic, au·to·crát·i·cal** *adjs*

au·to·gi·ro, au·to·gy·ro (ɔtoudʒáirou) *n.* aircraft driven by a conventional propeller but with the wings wholly or partly replaced by a freely revolving horizontal rotor

au·to·graph (ɔ́təgræf, ɔ́təgrɒf) **1.** *n.* something written in a person's own handwriting, esp. his signature **2.** *v.t.* to sign with one's name **au·to·graph·ic** (ɔ́təgrǽfik), **au·to·gráph·i·cal** *adjs*

autogyro *AUTOGIRO

au·to·mat (ɔ́təmæt) *n.* a restaurant where prepared food is served in locked glass compartments ‖ an automatic device, e.g. one used in controlling machinery

au·to·mat·ic (ɔtəmǽtik) **1.** *adj.* mechanically self-acting ‖ *(firearms)* of a gun in which the spent cartridge is ejected, and the gun reloaded and fired ‖ not controlled by the will ‖ done or said without consideration or hesitation ‖ (of artistic creation) done unconsciously or subconsciously ‖ happening without the need for, or in spite of, some further action **2.** *n.* an automatic rifle, pistol etc. **au·to·mát·i·cal·ly** *adv.*

au·to·ma·tion (ɔtəméiʃən) *n.* a technique by which mechanical processes are subject to some degree of automatic control, without human intervention

au·to·mo·bile (ɔ́təməbi:l, ɔtəməbi:l, ɔtəmóubi:l) *n.* a (usually) four-wheeled vehicle which may seat from two to eight people, driven by an engine (gasoline, diesel, electric etc.)

au·ton·o·mous (ɔtɔ́nəməs) *adj.* self-governing (generally used not of a sovereign state or completely independent body but of one which, under the general control of a larger body, enjoys self-government in its internal affairs)

au·ton·o·my (ɔtɔ́nəmi:) *pl.* **au·ton·o·mies** *n.* self-government ‖ a self-governing political community

au·top·sy (ɔ́tɒpsi:) *pl.* **au·top·sies** *n.* the examination of a dead body to determine the cause of death

au·to·sug·ges·tion (ɔtousədʒéstʃən, ɔtousəgdʒéstʃən) *n.* the process of influencing one's conduct, or state of mind or body, by an idea which one keeps constantly in mind

au·tumn (ɔ́təm) *n.* the third season of the year in temperate zones, between summer and winter

au·tum·nal (ɔtʌ́mn'l) *adj.* of autumn, appearing in, or suggesting, autumn

aux·il·ia·ry (ɔgzíljəri:, ɔgzíləri:) **1.** *adj.* helping, providing additional help when needed ‖ supplementary **2.** *n. pl.* **aux·il·ia·ries** a supplementary group or organization ‖ an auxiliary verb

a·vail (əvéil) **1.** *v.t. (rhet.)* to help, be useful to ‖ *v.t.* to be effective **to avail oneself of** to put to good use, enjoy the benefit of **2.** *n.* use, benefit, advantage **a·vail·a·bíl·i·ty** *n.* **a·váil·a·ble** *adj.* ready or free for use, capable of being used

av·a·lanche (ǽvəlæntʃ, ǽvəlɒntʃ) *n.* a great mass of snow, ice, earth, rocks etc. which breaks away on a mountainside and pours down the slope ‖ any sudden flood or massive descent

a·vant-garde (ævɒ̃gærd, ɑvɑŋgárd) *n.* those who experiment boldly in the arts and are in advance of their time ‖ those who experiment in the arts without discipline and make a virtue of novelty

av·a·rice (ǽvəris) *n.* greed for money and abnormal hatred of parting with it

a·venge (əvéndʒ) *pres. part.* **a·veng·ing** *past* and *past part.* **a·venged** *v.t.* to inflict just punishment in return for an injury or wrong

av·e·nue (ǽvinju:, ǽvinu:) *n.* a formally designed or planted approach or road ‖ a wide street ‖ a road or path which leads to or through a place

a·ver (əvə́:r) *pres. part.* **a·ver·ring** *past* and *past part.* **a·verred** *v.t.* to assert, declare firmly

av·er·age (ǽvəridʒ) **1.** *n.* the arithmetic mean, the value arrived at by adding the quantities in a series and dividing the total by their number ‖ a common or usual standard ‖ the estimate of the loss involved in shipping damage and its division between those responsible ‖ *(insurance)* a less than total loss incurred by a ship or cargo ‖ expenses for damage at sea, generally shared by all concerned **2.** *adj.* worked out as a mathematical average ‖ undistinguished, ordinary **3.** *v. pres. part.* **av·er·ag·ing** *past* and *past part.* **av·er·aged** *v.t.* to work out the average of ‖ to divide as an average ‖ *v.i.* to be on average

a·verse (əvə́:rs) *adj.* opposed ‖ *(bot.)* turned away from the stem or axis

a·ver·sion (əvə́:rʒən, əvə́:rʃən) *n.* an active or pronounced dislike ‖ the object of such dislike

a·vert (əvə́:rt) *v.t.* to turn away or aside ‖ to prevent, ward off

a·vi·ar·y (éivi:eri) *pl.* **a·vi·ar·ies** *n.* an enclosure or cage for breeding and rearing birds

a·vi·a·tion (eivi:éiʃən) *n.* the science of flying aircraft ‖ aircraft manufacture

a·vi·a·tor (éivi:eitər) *n.* a pilot or member of an aircraft crew, in the early days of flying

av·id (ǽvid) *adj.* intensely eager, *avid for fame* ‖ very keen, *an avid reader*

av·o·ca·do (ævəkódou, ɑvəkádou) *pl.* **av·o·ca·dos, av·o·ca·does** *n.* the fruit (a drupe) of trees of the genus *Persea*, fam. *Lauraceae*, the alligator pear, native to tropical America

av·o·ca·tion (ævəkéiʃən) *n.* an occupation, esp. one followed for pleasure, or one of minor importance

a·void (əvɔ́id) *v.t.* to keep out of the way of ‖ to refrain from ‖ *(law)* to invalidate **a·vóid·a·ble** *adj.* **a·vóid·ance** *n.*

a·void·ance (əvɔ́idəns) *n.* *(psych.)* measures taken in advance to avoid an unpleasantness **avoidant** *adj.* of the avoidance behavior

av·oir·du·pois (ævərdəpɔ́iz) *(abbr.* avoir.*) n.* a system of reckoning weight in English-speaking countries based on the pound equal to 16 ounces ‖ *(pop.)* portliness

a·vow (əváu) *v.t.* to admit to be true, openly acknowledge **a·vów·al** *n.* open admission **a·vówed** *adj.* openly admitted ‖ declared **a·vow·ed·ly** (əváuidli:) *adv.*

a·wait (əwéit) *v.t.* to wait for, look out for ‖ to be in store for ‖ *v.i.* to wait ‖ to be in store as a future experience

a·wake (əwéik) *pres. part.* **a·wak·ing** *past* **a·woke** (əwóuk) *past part.* **a·wok·en** (əwóukən), **a·waked**, **a·wak·ened** (əwéikənd) *v.i.* to stop sleeping ‖ (with 'to') to realize ‖ *v.t.* to rouse from sleep, wake up ‖ *(fig.)* to stir up

awake *pred. adj.* not asleep ‖ with a full realization of ‖ alert

a·wak·en (əwéikən) *v.t.* to wake up (someone) ‖ *v.i.* to awake **a·wák·en·ing** *n.* the act of ceasing to sleep or rousing from sleep ‖ a realization of circumstances ‖ an arousal of interest or activity

a·ward (əwɔ́rd) *n.* a judicial decision, esp. after arbitration ‖ a prize, grant etc. won or given

award *v.t.* to give as a prize, reward, or judgment

a·ware (əwɛ́ər) *pred. adj.* conscious, informed

a·wash (əwɔ́ʃ, əwɒ́ʃ) *pred. adj.* and *adv.* just covered by water (e.g. of a ship's deck in a storm) ‖ (e.g. of flotsam) washing about in the sea ‖ *(colloq.)* inebriated

a·way (əwéi) **1.** *adv.* to, or at, a distance ‖ in a different direction ‖ at an end or to a weakened or lessened condition or degree ‖ continuously, steadily **far and away** beyond all doubt, *he is far and away the cleverest* **to do away with** to get rid of, murder or cause to be murdered **to fall away** to give up, fail or desert ‖ to work less well **to get away with** to succeed in stealing ‖ to escape with only ‖ to do or say with impunity **to take away** to detract ‖ to subtract **2.** *adj. (sports)* played on the ground of one's opponents ‖ absent ‖ at a distance (i.e. far ahead)

awe (ɔ) **1.** *n.* a feeling of deep wonder and respect for overpowering grandeur ‖ fear and respect **2.** *v.t. pres. part.* **aw·ing** *past* and *past part.* **awed** to fill with awe ‖ to subdue or overcome by so doing

aw·ful (ɔ́fəl) *adj.* very bad ‖ shocking, appalling ‖ inspiring awe ‖ *(pop.)* very great or large, extreme **áw·ful·ly** *adv.* very

a·while (əhwáil, əwáil) *adv.* for a while, for a short time

awk·ward (ɔ́kwərd) *adj.* not quite right, *an awkward fit* ‖ inconvenient ‖ difficult to deal with ‖ obstinate, unhelpful, unaccommodating ‖ clumsy, uncouth ‖ causing inconvenience or embarrassment

awl (ɔl) *n.* a short pointed tool used for making holes, esp. in leather by a shoemaker

awn·ing (ɔ́niŋ) *n.* a sheet of canvas, used chiefly to protect against strong sunlight or rain

A.W.O.L. *(mil.)* absent without leave (but not intending to desert)

a·wry (ərái) *adv.* and *adj.* crooked, not straight **to go awry** to go wrong, turn out badly

ax, axe (æks) **1.** *n.* a tool consisting of a wooden handle fitted with a steel cutting head (sometimes a double head), used for cutting down trees, or chopping, splitting or roughly shaping wood ‖ *(hist.)* such an ax used as a battle weapon, or by an executioner in beheadings ‖ drastic cutting of expenditure **to have an ax to grind** to have a personal interest at stake in something **2.** *v.t. pres. part.* **ax·ing** to shape with an ax ‖ to put an end to ‖ to reduce drastically

ax·i·al (æksi:əl) *adj.* of, or relating to, or like an axis, or relating to the central structure of an organism

ax·i·om (æksi:əm) *n. (logic* and *math.)* a self-evident truth or proposition ‖ an accepted principle ‖ a maxim or proverbial truth

ax·i·o·mat·ic (æksi:əmǽtik) *adj.* self-evident, obvious ‖ making use of axioms **ax·i·o·mát·i·cal·ly** *adv.*

ax·is (æksis) *pl.* **ax·es** (æksi:z) *n.* the line, real or imaginary, around which a thing rotates ‖ the central line around which a structure, pattern or figure is built or formed ‖ one of the reference lines in a coordinate system ‖ *(bot.)* a main stem or central cylinder ‖ *(zool.)* the central skeleton or nervous chord of an organism ‖ a structure at the base of an insect's wing ‖ *(anat.)* the vertebra in the neck on which the head turns ‖ an alliance between countries to ensure solidarity of foreign policy

ax·le (æksəl) *n.* the bar or pin on which the hub of a wheel turns or which turns with the wheel ‖ the arm or axletree joining two wheels of a vehicle

az·i·muth (æziməθ) *n. (astron., navigation, surveying)* the horizontal arc expressed as the clockwise angle between a fixed point (such as true north) and the vertical plane through the object ‖ a bearing, course or direction **az·i·muth·al** (æzimúθəl) *adj.*

az·ure (æʒər, éiʒər) **1.** *adj.* of a light, bright blue, sky-blue ‖ *(heraldry)* blue **2.** *n.* azure color

B

B, b (bi:) the second letter of the English alphabet

B.A. Bachelor of Arts

bab·ble (bǽb'l) *v. pres. part.* **bab·bling** *past* and *past part.* **bab·bled** *v.i.* to chatter idly or continuously ‖ (of a brook etc.) to murmur ‖ *v.t.* to utter confusedly or incoherently **bab·bler** (bǽblər) *n.* someone who chatters

ba·boon (bæbú:n, *esp. Br.* bəbú:n) *n.* large, ferocious, terrestrial, dog-faced monkeys of Africa and Arabia

ba·bush·ka (bəbú:ʃkə) *n.* a scarf worn by a woman over her hair and tied under the chin

ba·by (béibi:) **1.** *pl.* **ba·bies** *n.* an infant ‖ a young child ‖ the youngest member of a family ‖ a timorous person

2. *adj.* **3.** *pres. part.* **ba·by·ing** *past* and *past part.* **ba·bied** *v.t.* to treat with inordinate care or indulgence

ba·by·hood (béibi:hud) *n.* the state or age of being a baby

ba·by·ish (béibi:iʃ) *adj.* like a baby

bac·ca·lau·re·ate (bækəlɔ́ri:it) *n.* the bachelor's degree

bac·cha·nal (bǽkən'l) **1.** *n.* a drunken orgy ‖ a person taking part in such festivities **2.** *adj.* bacchanalian ‖ riotous

bach·e·lor (bǽtʃələr, bǽtʃlər) *n.* an unmarried man ‖ a man or woman who has taken the first university (or college or professional school) degree

ba·cil·lus (bəsíləs) *pl.* **ba·cil·li** (bəsílai) *n.* a large genus

---

of aerobic, rod-shaped bacteria which reproduce by endospores

back (bæk) **1.** *n.* the hinder part of the body, or, in most animals, the upper part from the neck to the end of the spine ‖ the less important side or surface of a thing, opposite the front ‖ the remoter part ‖ a defensive position in certain games **at the back of** (*fig.*) behind, in support of **behind one's back** without one's knowledge, deceitfully or treacherously **in back of** behind **to be on one's back** to be ill in bed **to be on someone's back** to harass someone with constant urgings and scoldings **to break one's back** to overwork **to break the back of a task** to achieve the greater or more difficult part of a task **to have one's back to the wall** to be hard pressed and fighting for survival **to put one's back into** to work very hard at **to put someone's back up** to irritate, offend, antagonize someone **to turn one's back on** to turn one's back on (someone) in order to snub him ‖ to go away from **2.** *v.t.* to give moral or material support to ‖ to support or line ‖ to cause to move backwards ‖ to furnish with a background or serve as a background to ‖ to bet on the success of ‖ *v.i.* to move backwards ‖ to retreat **to back down** to stop asserting something **to back out** to withdraw from an undertaking, contest etc. **to back up** to give moral support to **3.** *adj.* to the rear ‖ remote ‖ in arrears ‖ (of a magazine or journal) of an earlier date than the current issue **to take a back seat** to take a minor part in some activity **4.** *adv.* to the rear, backward, at a distance **to get back** to return ‖ to recover, *to get one's money back* **to get back at someone** to get even with someone **to give back** to restore (something borrowed or taken) **to go back on** to fail to keep (a promise, one's word etc.) **to keep back** to withhold ‖ to conceal (a fact etc.) **to pay back** to discharge (a debt), return in kind (something borrowed) **to pay someone back** to return a loan to someone ‖ to avenge oneself on somebody **to play back** to listen to (what one has recorded on tape or disk) **to take back** to return (something sold) to stock and refund the purchase money ‖ to retract, unsay

back·bone (bǽkboun) *n.* the spinal column ‖ courage, determination ‖ the spine of a book

back·drop (bǽkdrɒp) *n.* a painted cloth or drop curtain at the back of the stage

back·fire (bǽkfaiər) **1.** *n.* a premature explosion in the cylinder of an internal combustion engine, or in the breach of a gun **2.** *v.i. pres. part.* **back·fir·ing** *past* and *past part.* **back·fired** to explode in this way ‖ (*fig.*) to go wrong, esp. in such a way as to have the reverse effect of what was intended

back·ground (bǽkgraund) **1.** *n.* the part of a picture against which the principal figures are shown, or a surface on which there are patterns ‖ an inconspicuous position ‖ a person's past history, family circumstances and social class etc. ‖ music or sound effects to accompany e.g. a radio broadcast ‖ any accompanying noise **2.** *adj.* of an off-the-record, official, informal news conference designed to provide nonquotable information

back·hand (bǽkhænd) (*racket games,* of a stroke) *n.* a backhand stroke, or the capacity to play backhand strokes ‖ handwriting whose strokes slope to the left **báck·hánd·ed** *adj.* made with the back of the hand ‖ (of an apparent compliment) double-edged

back·side (bǽksaid) *n.* the buttocks

back·slide (bǽkslaid) *pres. part.* **back·slid·ing** *past* **back·slid** (bǽkslid) *past part.* **back·slid, back·slid·den** (bǽkslid'n) *v.i.* to fall away or lapse from former virtuous beliefs or conduct

back·stage (bǽkstéidʒ) **1.** *adv.* (*theater*) at or to a backstage area or position **2.** (bǽkstéidʒ) *adj.* (*theater*) of or relating to a backstage **3.** (bǽkstéidʒ) *n.* (*theater*) the stage area behind the proscenium, esp. the dressing rooms

back·ward (bǽkwərd) **1.** *adj.* turned or directed to the

back ‖ not progressing normally ‖ shy **2.** *adv.* backwards

back·woods (bǽkwudz) *pl. n.* the remote, sparsely settled areas of a country

ba·con (béikən) *n.* the flesh from a pig's back and sides, cured dry or in pickle and smoked

bac·te·ri·al (bæktíəri:əl) *adj.* of or resulting from bacteria

bac·te·ri·ol·o·gist (bæktɪəri:ɒ́lədʒist) *n.* someone who studies bacteriology

bac·te·ri·ol·o·gy (bæktɪəri:ɒ́lədʒi:) *n.* the scientific study of bacteria

bac·te·ri·um (bæktíəri:əm) *pl.* **bac·te·ri·a** (bæktíəri:ə) *n.* a member of *Schizomycophyta*, a large class of microscopic unicellular plants lacking chlorophyll and fully defined nuclei

bad (bæd) **1.** *adj. comp.* **worse** (wə:rs) *superl.* **worst** (wə:rst) wicked, evil ‖ defective, inadequate ‖ not prosperous ‖ decayed rotten ‖ severe ‖ serious ‖ faulty ‖ unwelcome, distressing ‖ disagreeable ‖ (*pop.*) distressed, upset ‖ harmful ‖ unskilled, not clever **to go bad** to decay **to go from bad to worse** to become more and more deplorable **2.** *n.* that which is bad ‖ misfortune **to go to the bad** to become criminal, corrupt etc. **3.** *adv.* (*substandard*) badly

badge (bædʒ) *n.* a distinctive device worn as a sign of office, employment or membership ‖ an award for attainment

badg·er (bǽdʒər) **1.** *n.* a burrowing, carnivorous, nocturnal mammal **2.** *v.t.* to nag with requests

bad·i·nage (bædinɒ́ʒ) *n.* playful teasing ‖ joking and repartee

bad·ly (bǽdli:) *comp.* **worse** (wə:rs) *superl.* **worst** (wə:rst) *adv.* not well (made, done etc.)

baf·fle (bǽfəl) **1.** *v.t. pres. part.* **baf·fling** *past* and *past part.* **baf·fled** to puzzle, perplex **2.** *n.* a device to direct or control the flow of a fluid or the propagation of light and sound waves

bag (bæg) **1.** *n.* a receptacle of leather, cloth, paper etc. often shaped like a sack and easily opened and closed ‖ loose, pouchy skin **a bag of bones** a thin, scrawny creature **bag and baggage** (with) all one's belongings **in the bag** as good as secured **in the bottom of the bag** to be used as a last resource **to be left holding the bag** to be left to take the blame for something or to assume an unwanted responsibility ‖ (*slang*) something one likes; one's way of life ; a packet of drugs **2.** *v. pres. part.* **bag·ging** *past* and *past part.* **bagged** *v.t.* to put into a bag or bags ‖ to kill or capture (game) ‖ *v.i.* to hang loosely

bag·gage (bǽgidʒ) *n.* personal luggage

bag·gy (bǽgi:) *comp.* **worse** (wə:rs) *superl.* **bag·gi·est** *adj.* stretched out of shape and hanging loosely

bag·pipe (bǽgpaip) *n.* (usually *pl.*) a musical wind instrument, very popular in Scotland **bag·pip·er** *n.*

bail (beil) *n.* a money or property security deposited to obtain a prisoner's freedom of movement, pledging that he will appear before the court when called **out on bail** having one's freedom on these conditions **to jump** (or **forfeit**) **one's bail** to fail to appear as pledged

bail, bale **1.** *n.* a vessel used to scoop water out of a boat, a bailer **2.** *v.t.* to scoop out (water) from inside a boat **to bail out** to bail ‖ to make a parachute jump esp. in an emergency

bail·iff (béilif) *n.* the agent or steward of an estate ‖ a court officer who keeps order in court

bait (beit) *v.t.* to put food on (a hook) or in (a trap) to lure a fish or animal ‖ to tease, provoke

bake (beik) *pres. part.* **bak·ing** *past* and *past part.* **baked** *v.t.* to cook (food) in dry heat, esp. in an oven ‖ to make hard by heating ‖ *v.i.* to bake bread etc. ‖ to become baked

bak·er (béikər) *n.* a professional breadmaker ‖ someone who sells bread and pastries

baker's dozen thirteen

bak·er·y (béikəri:) *pl.* **bak·er·ies** *n.* a place where bread is baked ‖ a baker's shop

bal·a·lai·ka (bæləláikə) *n.* a triangular, guitar-like musical instrument popular esp. in Russia

bal·ance (bǽləns) *pres. part.* **bal·anc·ing** *past* and *past part.* **bal·anced** *v.t.* to weigh in a balance ‖ to weigh by comparing (two arguments, advantages, choices etc.) ‖ to match, offset ‖ to keep in equilibrium ‖ to compare both sides of (an account) and make the entry needed to equalize them ‖ *v.i.* to remain in equilibrium ‖ (of account entries) to be equal on the credit and debit sides

balance *n.* an instrument for measuring the weight of a body ‖ the weighing of actions or opinions ‖ equilibrium ‖ mental or emotional stability ‖ a regulating mechanism in a clock or watch ‖ *(accounts)* the difference between the debit and credit sides ‖ the remainder **to hold the balance** to have the power to decide

bal·co·ny (bǽlkəni:) *pl.* **bal·co·nies** *n.* an accessible platform, usually with a safety rail or parapet, projecting outwards from the window or wall of a building ‖ *(theater)* a tier of seats

bald (bɔld) *adj.* without (or partly without) hair or fur, feathers etc., where these normally grow ‖ *(fig.)* unadorned ‖ featureless

bal·der·dash (bɔ́ldərdæʃ) *n.* nonsense, foolish talk

bale (beil) **1.** *n.* a quantity of cotton, wheat, straw etc., tightly bound for ease of handling **2.** *v.t. pres. part.* **bal·ing** *past* and *past part.* **baled** to make up (wheat etc., or merchandise) into such bundles

bale·ful (béilfəl) *adj.* willing evil ‖ causing evil

balk, baulk (bɔk) **1.** *n.* a hindrance or stumbling block ‖ *(baseball)* a foul by a pitcher ‖ a ridge of land left unplowed ‖ a roughly squared length of lumber ‖ the tie beam, or main horizontal beam, of a roof **2.** *v.t.* to hinder, thwart ‖ *v.i.* to pull up, refuse to proceed ‖ *(baseball)* to commit a balk

balk·y (bɔ́ki:) *comp.* **balk·i·er** *superl.* **balk·i·est** *adj.* given to balking

ball (bɔl) **1.** *n.* a spherical object of any size ‖ the object which is kicked, hit, thrown etc., in various sports ‖ *(baseball)* a ball pitched outside home plate at which the batter does not swing ‖ the rounded part of the foot near the base of the big toe ‖ the mound at the base of the thumb, set in the palm **on the ball** alert **to keep the ball rolling** to do one's share in conversation, or any activity **to play ball** to play a game in which a ball is thrown, kicked or hit ‖ to cooperate **to set** (or **start**) **the ball rolling** to start some cumulative action **2.** *v.t.* to wind up into a ball ‖ *v.i.* to form a ball **balled up** *(pop.)* confused, muddled

ball *n.* a formal assembly for social dancing **to give a ball** to invite people to such an assembly **to open the ball** to lead off the first dance

bal·lad (bǽləd) *n.* a narrative poem, usually in short stanzas, generally about heroic or tragic deeds, or love, often in vivid, unliterary language ‖ any simple song, esp. a romantic or sentimental one, having the same melody for each stanza

bal·last (bǽləst) **1.** *n.* any heavy substance placed in a ship's hold, or balloon basket, to improve stability **to be in ballast** (of a ship) to carry ballast but no goods **2.** *v.t.* to steady with ballast, stabilize ‖ to fill in with ballast

bal·le·ri·na (bæləri:nə) *n.* a female ballet dancer

bal·let (bǽlei, bæléi) *n.* a performance, usually by two or more dancers, in which music, movement and mime are combined

bal·lis·tics (bəlístiks) *n.* the scientific study of projectiles (shells, bombs, rockets), their ejection, flight through the air, and impact with the target

bal·loon (bəlú:n) **1.** *n.* an envelope of gasproof fabric distended by the pressure of a gas less dense than air

at ground level ‖ *(chem.)* a hollow glass sphere used in distillations ‖ something balloon-shaped ‖ a balloon sail ‖ (in a comic strip) the frame enclosing the words or written-out thoughts of the characters **2.** *v.i.* to go up in a balloon ‖ to swell out like a balloon

bal·lot (bǽlət) **1.** *n.* a paper used in secret voting ‖ a vote cast by this method ‖ the total votes cast at an election **2.** *v.i.* to vote by ballot papers

ball·room (bɔ́lru:m, bɔ́lrum) *n.* a large room for dancing

balm (bɑm) *n.* a genus of perennial fragrant herbs widely cultivated in temperate regions for the oil in the leaves, which is used for flavoring ‖ an aromatic and medicinal resin obtained from certain trees ‖ balsam ‖ *(loosely)* an ointment used for soothing and healing ‖ any calming or consoling influence

balm·i·ly (bɑ́mili:) *adv.* in a balmy manner

balm·i·ness (bɑ́mi:nis) *n.* the state or quality of being balmy

balm·y (bɑ́mi:) *comp.* **balm·i·er** *superl.* **balm·i·est** *adj.* of or like balm ‖ fragrant, gentle, refreshing ‖ *(pop.)* crazy, weak in the head

ba·lo·ney, bo·lo·ney (bəlóuni:) *n. (pop.)* bologna (sausage) ‖ *(slang)* nonsense, humbug

bal·sa (bɔ́lsə) *n.* an American tree ‖ the wood of this tree, which is lighter than cork and is used for rafts, floats etc.

bal·sam (bɔ́lsəm) *n.* a mixture of resins in volatile oils often used in medicines and perfumes ‖ any plant or tree yielding balsam

bal·us·ter (bǽləstər) *n.* one of the small pillars which support the railing of a staircase or balcony etc., a banister

bam·boo (bæmbú:) *n.* an arborescent grass grown in the tropics and subtropics

ban (bæn) *pres. part.* **ban·ning** *past* and *past part.* **banned** *v.t.* to prohibit, forbid

ban *n.* a formal prohibition ‖ *(eccles.)* a formal interdict

ba·nal (béin'l, bənǽl, bənɑ́l) *adj.* commonplace, flat

ba·nal·i·ty (bənǽliti:) *pl.* **ba·nal·i·ties** *n.* triteness ‖ something commonplace

ba·nan·a (bənǽnə) *n.* the edible fruit of a genus of plants cultivated widely in tropical and subtropical areas

band (bænd) *n.* a group of musicians playing together (usually percussion and brass or wind, never a symphonic or chamber group) ‖ an organized group of persons

band·age (bǽndidʒ) **1.** *n.* a strip of cloth used to protect or bind an injured part of the body **2.** *v.t. pres. part.* **band·ag·ing** *past* and *past part.* **band·aged** to tie up with a bandage

ban·dit (bǽndit) *n.* a robber, esp. one of a group roving in uninhabited districts

bane (bein) *n.* a cause of misery, worry, or anxiety ‖ a person who constantly gets on one's nerves **báne·ful** *adj.* harmful

bang (bæŋ) **1.** *v.t.* to strike suddenly and violently ‖ to cause to make a loud, sudden noise ‖ *v.i.* to make the sound of a blow or explosion **2.** *n.* a hard knock ‖ a loud, sudden noise ‖ *(pop.)* a thrill of pleasure **3.** *adv.* abruptly ‖ explosively

ban·ish (bǽniʃ) *v.t.* to compel (someone) to leave a country ‖ to drive away from home or an accustomed place ‖ to dismiss from one's presence or thoughts **bán·ish·ment** *n.*

ban·is·ter (bǽnistər) *n.* the upright support of a stair rail or handrail

ban·jo (bǽndʒou) *pl.* **ban·jos, ban·joes** *n.* a stringed musical instrument, strummed or plucked with the fingers **bán·jo·ist** *n.*

bank (bæŋk) **1.** *n.* a place where money is kept and

(a) æ, cat; ɑ, car; ɔ fawn; ei, snake. (e) e, hen; i:, sheep; iə, deer; ɛə, bear. (i) i, fish; ai, tiger; ə:, bird. (o) o, ox; au, cow; ou, goat; u, poor; ɔi, royal. (u) ʌ, duck; u, bull; u:, goose; ə, bacillus; ju:, cube. x, loch; θ, think; ð, bother; z, Zen; ʒ, corsage; dʒ, savage; ŋ, orangutang; j, yak; ʃ, fish; tʃ, fetch; 'l, rabble; 'n, redden. Complete pronunciation key appears inside front cover.

paid out, lent, borrowed, issued or exchanged ‖ *(gambling)* the fund of the keeper of the table ‖ a reserve supply of a thing, *blood bank* **2.** *v.t.* to deposit (money or valuables) at a bank ‖ *v.i.* to use the services of a bank **to bank on** to rely upon **bánk·a·ble** *adj.*

bank 1. *n.* the rising ground bordering a lake, river etc. ‖ earth raised above the ground, esp. to mark a dividing line ‖ an elevation of mud or sand etc., in a sea or river bed ‖ the cushion in billiards ‖ the tilting of an aircraft rounding a curve **2.** *v.t.* to raise or form in a bank, *to bank earth around a building* ‖ *v.i.* to tilt sideways when rounding a curve in flight ‖ (with ṵp') to pile up into a bank

bank·er (bǽŋkər) *n.* a person conducting the business of a bank

bank·ing (bǽŋkiŋ) *n.* the business of a banker

bank·rupt (bǽŋkrəpt) **1.** *n.* a person who cannot pay his debts ‖ *(law)* a person declared by a court unable to pay his debts and whose property will be administered by the court for the benefit of the creditors **2.** *adj.* insolvent, unable to pay one's debts **3.** *v.t.* to reduce to bankruptcy **bank·rupt·cy** (bǽŋkrəptsi:) *n.*

ban·ner (bǽnər) *n.* a cloth flag on a pole used as a military standard ‖ the flag of a country

ban·quet (bǽŋkwit) **1.** *n.* a feast ‖ an official celebration dinner with speeches **2.** *v.t.* to honor with a banquet ‖ *v.i.* to be a guest at a banquet

ban·tam (bǽntəm) *n.* a small variety of domestic fowl of which the cock is very aggressive ‖ a small but spirited person

ban·tam·weight (bǽntəmweit) *n.* a boxer whose weight does not exceed 118 lbs

ban·ter (bǽntər) **1.** *n.* playful teasing **2.** *v.t.* to make good-humored fun of ‖ *v.i.* to talk jokingly

bap·tism (bǽptizəm) *n.* the religious practice of sprinkling a person with water, or immersing him in it, to symbolize the washing away of sin ‖ the naming of church bells or ships ‖ an experience that initiates a new way of life **bap·tis·mal** (bæptízməl) *adj.*

bap·tis·try (bǽptistri:) *pl.* **bap·tis·tries** *n.* the part of a church (or formerly a separate building) used for baptism ‖ in a Baptist chapel, the tank used for immersion

bap·tize (bæptáiz, bǽptaiz) *pres. part.* **bap·tiz·ing** *past and past part.* **bap·tized** *v.t.* to administer baptism ‖ to give a name to ‖ to nickname ‖ *v.i.* to administer baptism

bar (bɑr) *n.* a long piece of wood, metal etc. used as a support, an obstruction or a lever ‖ a barrier of any kind ‖ a rectangular slab of rigid material ‖ a metal strip on the ribbon of a medal as an additional award ‖ a strip (of light or color) ‖ a straight line considerably longer than it is broad ‖ *(mus.)* a vertical line across a staff dividing it into equal measures of time ‖ a barrier in a law court where the prisoner stands ‖ any tribunal ‖ the legal profession ‖ a counter over which liquor and food may be served ‖ the space behind this counter ‖ the room containing it

bar 1. *v.t. pres. part.* **bar·ring** *past and past part.* **barred** to fasten, secure ‖ to obstruct ‖ to prohibit ‖ to exclude ‖ to mark with stripes **2.** *prep.* except, excluding

barb (bɑrb) **1.** *n.* the part of an arrow, fishhook, bee's sting etc., that points backwards and prevents or hinders removal ‖ the beardlike feelers of a barbed fish **2.** *v.t.* to supply (an arrow etc.) with barbs

bar·bar·i·an (bɑrbɛ́əri:ən) **1.** *n.* a savage, uncivilized person ‖ an uncultured person **2.** *adj.* of or like a barbarian

bar·bar·ic (bɑrbǽrik) *adj.* savage, *barbaric cruelty* ‖ utterly lacking in taste, breeding, etc. ‖ (of a work of art) having a rough or primitive quality, forceful and without finish **bar·bár·i·cal·ly** *adv.*

bar·bar·i·ty (bɑrbǽriti:) *pl.* **bar·bar·i·ties** *n.* savage cruelty ‖ barbaric taste or an object showing this

bar·bar·ous (bɑ́rbərəs) *adj.* uncivilized ‖ cruel ‖ uncouth

bar·be·cue (bɑ́rbikju:) **1.** *n.* an ox, hog etc. roasted whole (or slit) over a wood fire in a pit for a feast ‖

a feast at which a barbecue is served ‖ *(loosely)* any party where food is grilled on a metal frame over charcoal ‖ the grill itself ‖ the food cooked on the grill with a highly seasoned sauce **2.** *v.t. pres. part.* **bar·be·cu·ing** *past and past part.* **bar·be·cued** to roast over a barbecue pit or grill

barbed wire a steel wire to which pointed steel barbs are attached at close intervals

bar·ber (bɑ́rbər) *n.* a person whose business is cutting and dressing men's hair, shaving, etc.

bar·ber·shop (bɑ́rbərʃɒp) *n.* a barber's premises

bar·bi·tu·rate (bɑrbítʃurit, bɑrbítʃureit) *n.* one of a group of drugs derived from barbituric acid

bare (bɛ́ər) **1.** *adj.* uncovered, naked, *barefeet* ‖ without trees or any tall growth ‖ empty, *a bare cupboard* ‖ without decoration ‖ scant, meager ‖ plain, unconcealed ‖ very slight **2.** *v.t. pres. part.* **bar·ing** *past and past part.* **bared** to uncover ‖ to reveal (feelings)

bare·ly (bɛ́ərli:) *adv.* only just, merely ‖ scantily

bar·gain (bɑ́rgin) *n.* an agreement on terms of give and take ‖ something acquired or offered cheaply, or advantageously **into the bargain** in addition to the terms agreed, as well **to conclude** (or **drive** or **make** or **settle** or **strike**) **a bargain** to come to terms

barge (bɑrdʒ) **1.** *n.* a flat-bottomed freight boat without sails, chiefly used on rivers and canals ‖ a large, ornamental, oared boat for state occasions **2.** *v.i. pres. part.* **barg·ing** *past and past part.* **barged** to move about clumsily ‖ (with 'in', 'into') to intrude ‖ (with 'into') to collide (with someone)

bar·i·tone, bar·y·tone (bǽritoun) **1.** *n.* a male voice between tenor and bass ‖ a man having such a voice **2.** *adj.* having the range and quality of a baritone voice

bark (bɑrk) **1.** *n.* the tissue in woody stems and roots external to the cambium **2.** *v.t.* to strip or peel bark from (a tree)

bark 1. *v.i.* to make the sharp, explosive, vocal noise characteristic of dogs ‖ *v.t.* to snap out sharply and abruptly **to bark up the wrong tree** to misdirect one's attack, be on the wrong track **2.** *n.* the brief, explosive cry of esp. dogs and foxes ‖ any similar sound **his bark is worse than his bite** he speaks angrily but is really harmless

bar·ley (bɑ́rli:) *n.* a cereal grass of genus *Hordeum*

bar mitz·vah (bɑrmítsvə) *n.* the Jewish ceremony admitting a boy to adult membership of the Jewish community ‖ the boy himself **bas mitzvah** similar ceremony for a Jewish girl

barn (bɑrn) *n.* a farm building for storing grain, hay, farm implements etc. or for housing animals

bar·na·cle (bɑ́rnək'l) *n.* a goose of N. Europe ‖ a crustacean of the sub-class *Cirripedia*

ba·rom·e·ter (bərɒ́mitər) *n.* an instrument for measuring atmospheric pressures **bar·o·met·ric** (bærəmétrik), **bar·o·mét·ri·cal** *adjs* **ba·róm·e·try** *n.* the science of making barometric measurements

ba·ron (bǽrən) *n.* (*Br.*) a member of the lowest order of nobility (called Lord —, not Baron —) ‖ a great merchant in some particular commodity, *a beef baron*

ba·roque (bəróuk) *adj.* of painting and sculpture, architecture, literature and music of the late 16th and 17th cc.

bar·rack (bǽrək) **1.** *n.* (esp. *pl.*) a large building for lodging soldiers ‖ (esp. *pl.*) any large, drab building **2.** *v.t.* to place in barracks

bar·ra·cu·da (bærəkú:də) *pl.* **bar·ra·cu·da, bar·ra·cu·das** *n.* a member of fam. *Sphyraenidae*, predatory fishes found in warm seas

bar·rage (bərɑ́ʒ, esp. *Br.* bǽrɑʒ) *n.* the barring of a watercourse to increase its depth ‖ a barrier, esp. of artillery shellfire, to impede enemy action ‖ a formidable number (of questions, protests etc.) poured out in a rush

bar·rel (bǽrəl) **1.** *n.* a flat-ended, curved cylindrical container, usually made of wood hooped by metal bands, a cask ‖ the metal tube of a gun ‖ the case containing the mainspring of a clock or a watch ‖ the body of a capstan **2.** *v. pres. part.* **bar·rel·ing, bar·rel·ling** *past and past part.* **bar·reled, bar·relled** *v.t.* to put in barrels ‖ to cause to travel very fast ‖ *v.i.* to travel very fast

bar·ren (bǽrən) **1.** *adj.* sterile, incapable of bearing (children, fruit etc.) ‖ unprofitable, without result ‖ unable to produce new ideas, dull **2.** *n.* (esp. *pl.*) a tract of poor sandy country with little vegetation

bar·rette (bərét) *n.* a hinged clip shaped in the form of a short, slightly curved bar, for keeping a girl's hair in place

bar·ri·cade (bǽrikeid, bærikéid) **1.** *n.* a defense or obstruction, esp. one hastily made across a road or street **2.** *v.t. pres. part.* **bar·ri·cad·ing** *past and past part.* **bar·ri·cad·ed** to block with a barricade

bar·ri·er (bǽri:ər) *n.* an obstacle barring advance or access ‖ (*horse racing*) the movable gate at the starting line ‖ something that hinders progress ‖ a mental or emotional obstacle

bar·row (bǽrou) *n.* a small wheeled handcart ‖ a wheelbarrow

bar·tend·er (bártendər) *n.* an attendant at a bar serving alcoholic drinks

bar·ter (bártər) **1.** *v.t.* to exchange (goods or services against something else) without using money ‖ *v.i.* to engage in such trade **2.** *n.* trade by exchange ‖ the thing exchanged

ba·salt (bəsɔ́lt, bǽsɔlt) *n.* black or dark gray rock, chiefly sodium or potassium alumino-silicates, with some iron, basic in character, supposed to constitute the bulk of the earth beneath its solid crust, and found as intrusions at the surface in some places

base (beis) **1.** *n.* the bottom, the lowest part ‖ that on which something is mounted or to which it is fixed and on which it stands ‖ groundwork ‖ foundation ‖ the stem or root of a word, to which suffixes are added ‖ (*archit.*) the lower part of a column or wall when treated as a separate feature ‖ the place from which an army or military force starts and where its supplies are ‖ the essential ingredient of a mixture ‖ (*geom.*) the line or area on which a figure stands ‖ (*biol.*) that end of a part which is attached to the main portion ‖ (*survey.*) the precisely measured distance from which triangulation starts **off base** (*baseball*) not on one's base ‖ (*pop.*) wrong, mistaken **2.** *v.t. pres. part.* **bas·ing** *past and past part.* **based** to found

base·ball (béisbɔl) *n.* the national game of the U.S.A. ‖ the ball used

base·less (béislis) *adj.* groundless, without foundation

base·ment (béismənt) *n.* the story of a building below the ground floor

bash (bæʃ) **1.** *v.t.* (*pop.*) to strike violently ‖ (*pop.*) to smash or buckle ‖ *v.i.* to crash, collide **2.** *n.* (*pop.*) a violent blow

bash·ful (bǽʃfəl) *adj.* shy, self-conscious

ba·sic (béisik) *adj.* fundamental ‖ forming a basis

bas·il (bǽz'l) *n.* a genus of aromatic plants used as culinary herbs

ba·sin (béis'n) *n.* a hollow vessel for holding a liquid ‖ a dock, or group of docks ‖ a tract of land drained by a river and its tributaries

ba·sis (béisis) *pl.* **ba·ses** (béisi:z) *n.* a foundation, base ‖ an underlying principle ‖ the main ingredient in a mixture

bask (bæsk, bɑsk) *v.i.* to luxuriate in warmth and light, or in something compared with these

bas·ket (bǽskit, bɑ́skit) *n.* a vessel for containing shopping, laundry, wastepaper etc. ‖ the quantity contained in a basket ‖ the passenger part of a balloon ‖ a goal in basketball

bas·ket·ry (bǽskitri:, bɑ́skitri:) *n.* the art of making baskets ‖ things worked in cane, osiers etc.

bass (beis) **1.** *n.* the lowest part in harmonized music ‖ the lowest male singing voice ‖ a singer with such a voice **2.** *adj.* deep in tone or pitch

bas·set hound (bǽsit haund) a short-legged hunting dog of a breed used for digging out foxes and badgers

bas·so (bǽsou) *n.* a bass voice ‖ a bass singer

bas·soon (bəsú:n) *n.* a wooden musical instrument of the double reed type, the lowest of all the woodwind instruments in pitch except the double bassoon **bas·sóon·ist** *n.* a bassoon player

bas·tard (bǽstərd) **1.** *n.* an illegitimate child (used also as a term of abuse) ‖ something false or of questionable origin or departing from standard ‖ a hybrid **2.** *adj.* illegitimate ‖ not genuine, counterfeit

bas·tard·ize (bǽstərdaiz) *pres. part.* **bas·tard·iz·ing** *past and past part.* **bas·tard·ized** *v.t.* to declare to be illegitimate

baste (beist) *pres. part.* **bast·ing** *past and past part.* **bast·ed** *v.t.* to pour hot liquids over (esp. meat) during roasting to prevent its drying out ‖ (*pop.*) to thrash or batter (someone)

baste *pres. part.* **bast·ing** *past and past part.* **bast·ed** *v.t.* to stitch temporarily with large loose stitches

bast·ing (béistiŋ) *n.* a temporary stitching with large, loose stitches ‖ the thread used in basting

bas·tion (bǽstʃən, bǽsti:ən) *n.* part of a fortification, with two flanks, which juts out from the main defense work ‖ any strong defense

batch (bætʃ) *n.* a quantity (of loaves or cakes) produced at one baking ‖ a number or quantity of things produced at one time or to be taken together as a set

bath (bæθ, bɑθ) **1.** *n.* the immersion of the body or part of it in water to clean it, or as a minor pleasure ‖ (*pl.*) an indoor swimming pool, or public building where a person can go to wash himself ‖ exposure of the body to the sun, steam etc. **2.** *adj.* accessory to a bath, used for a bath

ba·ton (bətɔ́n, bǽt'n) *n.* (*mus.*) the stick with which the conductor beats time ‖ a staff which is a symbol of office ‖ the stick carried in a relay race ‖ the stick twirled by a drum majorette in a parade

bat·tal·ion (bətǽljən) *n.* (*mil.*) a unit of infantry consisting of a headquarters and two or more companies ‖ (*pl.*) a large fighting or warlike force, *battalions of ants*

bat·ter (bǽtər) **1.** *v.t.* to strike (something or someone) violently and often ‖ to beat out of shape ‖ to impair by hard usage ‖ *v.i.* to strike, heavily and often **2.** *n.* a semiliquid mixture, esp. of eggs, flour and milk beaten before cooking

bat·ter·y (bǽtəri:) *pl.* **bat·ter·ies** *n.* a battering ‖ a verbal attack ‖ (*mil.*) a unit of artillery ‖ the emplacement of a unit's guns and the men who use them ‖ a double row of cannon on a warship ‖ (*elec.*) a grouping of cells, condensers etc., for making electricity, esp. for a car, radio etc. ‖ (*baseball*) the pitcher and catcher together

bat·tle (bǽt'l) *n.* a fight between armies or forces ‖ a combat between two individuals **to do battle** (*rhet.*) to fight

battle *pres. part.* **bat·tling** *past and past part.* **bat·tled** *v.t.* to fight, *to battle one's way* ‖ *v.i.* to struggle

bau·ble (bɔ́b'l) *n.* a bright, showy trinket of no value

bawd (bɔd) *n.* a woman who keeps a brothel

bawd·i·ly (bɔ́dili:) *adv.* in a bawdy way

bawd·i·ness (bɔ́di:nis) *n.* the quality or state of being bawdy

bawd·y (bɔ́di:) *comp.* **bawd·i·er** *superl.* **bawd·i·est** *adj.* obscene, lewd

---

(**a**) æ, c*a*t; ɑ, c*ar*; ɔ f*aw*n; ei, sn*a*ke. (**e**) e, h*e*n; i:, sh*ee*p; iə, d*eer*; ɛə, b*ear*. (**i**) i, f*i*sh; ai, t*i*ger; ə:, b*ir*d. (**o**) o, *o*x; au, c*ow*; ou, g*oa*t; u, p*oor*; ɔi, r*oy*al. (**u**) ʌ, d*u*ck; u, b*u*ll; u:, g*oo*se; ə, b*a*cillus; ju:, c*u*be. x, lo*ch*; θ, *th*ink; ð, bo*th*er; z, *Z*en; ʒ, cor*sa*ge; dʒ, sa*va*ge; ŋ, oranguta*ng*; j, *y*ak; ʃ, *fi*sh; tʃ, fe*tch*; 'l, rabb*le*; 'n, redd*en*. Complete pronunciation key appears inside front cover.

bawl (bɔl) *v.t.* to shout, *to bawl curses* ‖ *v.i.* to cry loudly and without restraint

bay (bei) *n.* a wide inlet of the sea

bay 1. *adj.* (of a horse) reddish brown **2.** *n.* a reddish-brown horse

bay 1. *n.* the cry of hounds on the scent ‖ a dog's wail **at bay** (of an animal) forced to face its pursuers and defend itself **to bring to bay** to force (a quarry or victim) to turn and defend itself **to keep** (or **hold**) **at bay** to prevent from coming in to attack ‖ to ward off **2.** *v.i.* to bark (esp. during pursuit of a quarry) ‖ *v.t.* to bark at

bay·o·net (béiənit, béiənet) **1.** *n.* a dagger which can be attached to a rifle **2.** *v.t. pres. part.* **bay·o·net·ing, bay·o·net·ting** *past* and *past part.* **bay·o·net·ed, bay·o·net·ted** to stab with a bayonet ‖ to compel or coerce with or as if with a bayonet

bay·ou (báju:, báijou) *n. (Am.)* a marshy creek or tributary to another river (used of offshoots of the lower Mississippi basin and rivers in the Gulf coast region)

ba·zaar (bəzár) *n.* an Oriental marketplace or permanent market, where goods of all kinds are bought and sold ‖ a sale of goods donated by people in order to raise money for some charity etc.

ba·zoo·ka (bəzú:kə) *n. (mil.)* a portable antitank rocket launcher used in the 2nd world war

be (bi:) (*pres.* **I am, you are, he, she, it is, we, you, they are** *past* **I was, you were, he, she, it was, we, you, they were**) *pres. part.* **be·ing** *past part.* **been** (bin) *v.i.* used as a copulative or connective verb ‖ to equal ‖ to add up to ‖ to cost ‖ to become ‖ to exist ‖ to live ‖ to continue ‖ to remain ‖ (followed by the infinitive) used to express obligation ‖ used as an auxiliary verb with the past participle of transitive verbs to form the passive voice ‖ used with the present participle to form the continuous tenses (active and passive) **to be for** to be in favor of ‖ to wish or intend to partake of ‖ **to be the way to to be oneself** to be behaving in a normal or usual fashion ‖ to be in good health

beach (bi:tʃ) **1.** *n.* the shore of the sea or a lake washed by the water and covered by sand, shingle or larger rocks **2.** *v.t.* to draw (a boat) up on to the shore

bea·con (bí:kən) *n.* a fire or light used as a signal ‖ a lighthouse

bead (bi:d) **1.** *n.* a small ball pierced for threading and used with others for ornament ‖ a small round drop ‖ *(archit.)* a molding like a row of beads, beading ‖ that part of a tire which grips the rim of a wheel ‖ *(pl.)* a necklace ‖ *(pl.)* the rosary **2.** *v.t.* to supply or cover with beads or as if with beads ‖ to adorn with beading ‖ *v.i.* to form or grow into beads

beak (bi:k) *n.* the projecting jaws of a bird, made of hard material and differently adapted for ripping, striking etc. ‖ the similar curving mandible of certain other animals, e.g. the turtle ‖ a hooked nose ‖ any beaklike projection

beak·er (bí:kər) *n.* an antique drinking vessel ‖ a tumbler-shaped drinking mug in pottery, plastic etc. ‖ a deep, widemouthed, thin-walled, cylindrical vessel with a pouring lip for scientific experiments

beam (bi:m) **1.** *n.* a long, heavy piece of wood used with others in building for supporting a roof, ceiling etc. ‖ a ray of light ‖ a gleam ‖ a bright smile ‖ the bar of a balance from which the scales hang ‖ one of the horizontal timbers which join the two sides of a ship and support the deck ‖ a directional radio or other electromagnetic-radiation signal used to maintain aircraft on course **on the beam** on course ‖ functioning well **on the starboard** (**port**) **beam** on the right (left) side of a ship **to fly** (or **ride**) **the beam** to fly an aircraft on the course given by a radio beam **2.** *v.i.* to send forth rays of heat or light ‖ to smile broadly ‖ *v.t. (radio)* to aim (a broadcast) in a particular direction

bean (bi:n) *n.* one of the seeds from any of several climbing or erect leguminous plants ‖ a plant producing these seeds ‖ the edible pod of certain of these plants and the seeds in it ‖ any of several fruits or seeds that resemble beans, *coffee bean*

bear (béər) *n.* heavily built, thick-furred, plantigrade, carnivorous mammal found throughout all the northern hemisphere and some parts of the tropics ‖ a rough, ill-mannered person ‖ *(stock exchange)* someone who sells stock in the hope of buying it at a lower price later

bear *pres. part.* **bear·ing** *past* **bore** (bɔr, bour) *past part.* **born, borne** (bɔrn, bourn) *v.t.* to support ‖ to sustain ‖ to carry ‖ to be marked with ‖ to have and be known by ‖ to conduct ‖ to tolerate ‖ to admit of ‖ to be suitable for ‖ to give birth to ‖ to produce ‖ to carry or conduct (oneself) ‖ to give, offer ‖ *v.i.* to change direction by something less than a turn **to bear down** to press downwards **to bear down on** (or **upon**) to sail or move rapidly towards, esp. in a menacing way ‖ to be a burden on **to bear on** (or **upon**) to relate to **to bear out** to confirm **to bear up** to uphold ‖ to remain courageous **to bear with** to be patient with

beard (bíərd) **1.** *n.* the hair that grows on the lower part of men's faces ‖ the chin hair of a goat, or similar appendage of other animals ‖ the gills of an oyster ‖ the awns of grasses, e.g. barley **2.** *v.t.* to face up to (someone) boldly, to defy

bear·ing (béəriŋ) *n.* the action of carrying ‖ carriage, deportment ‖ relevancy ‖ endurance, the capacity to tolerate ‖ *(pl.)* position in relation to some reference point ‖ *(pl.)* grasp of one's situation ‖ a part of a machine that bears the friction set up by a moving part **to lose one's bearings** to be lost ‖ to be puzzled

beast (bi:st) *n.* any four-legged animal, esp. a wild one ‖ a farm animal ‖ a person with savage, brutal ways **beast·ly** *comp.* **beast·li·er** *superl.* **beast·li·est** *adj.* revolting to any of the senses ‖ (of a man) behaving like a beast

beat (bi:t) **1.** *v. pres. part.* **beat·ing** *past* **beat** *past part.* **beat·en** (bí:t'n) *v.t.* to strike deliberately and often ‖ to flap vigorously ‖ to strike repeatedly so as to whip or mix ‖ to strike with a cane etc. in punishment ‖ to work (metal) by hammering ‖ to clear (a path) by striking etc. ‖ to give the measure for (musical time) ‖ to baffle ‖ to surpass ‖ to strike the bushes etc. in (specified woods etc.) in order to make game leave cover ‖ *v.i.* to dash ‖ to throb ‖ to produce a noise by dealing blows **beat it!** *(pop.)* go away! **to beat about** *(naut.)* to tack against the wind **to beat about** (or **around**) **the bush** to approach a subject indirectly ‖ to avoid the main issue **to beat a retreat** to run away, withdraw to safety **to beat back** to repulse, fight off **to beat down** (of the sun) to be intensely hot without respite ‖ (of rain) to fall heavily and steadily or in a storm **to beat (someone) down** to force (a seller) to lower his price in bargaining **to beat the air** to fail to come to grips with a problem **to beat up** to knock (someone) about with great physical violence ‖ *(pop.)* to raise, muster **2.** *n.* a stroke (on a drum etc.) or the noise made ‖ a throb or pulsation ‖ the movement of a conductor's baton or hand ‖ a rhythmic pulse in music ‖ the stroke of a bird's wing ‖ a policeman's or watchman's round ‖ *(naut.)* a tack **3.** *adj.* exhausted

beat·en (bí:t'n) *adj.* defeated ‖ made smooth by constant treading ‖ shaped or made thin by hammering **off the beaten track** little-frequented ‖ aside from what is well known or familiar

beat·ing (bí:tiŋ) *n.* punishment by repeated striking ‖ a severe defeat

be·at·i·tude (bi:ǽtitju:d, bi:ǽtitu:d) *n.* blessedness ‖ bliss

beau·ti·ful (bjú:tifəl) **1.** *adj.* having beauty ‖ physically lovely ‖ morally or intellectually pleasing **2.** *n.* (with 'the') beauty in the abstract, the ideal to which all beautiful things are referred

beau·ti·fy (bjú:tifai) *pres. part.* **beau·ti·fy·ing** *past* and *past part.* **beau·ti·fied** *v.t.* to make beautiful, adorn

beau·ty (bjú:ti:) *pl.* **beau·ties** *n.* that which delights the senses or exalts the mind ‖ physical loveliness ‖ qualities pleasing to the moral sense ‖ *(pop.)* a particularly good example or specimen of a thing

bea·ver (bí:vər) *pl.* **bea·ver**, **bea·vers** *n.* a semiaquatic rodent having webbed hind feet and a very broad scaly tail ‖ its fur

be·cause (bikɔ́z, bikɔ́z, bikʌ́z) *conj.* for the reason that **because of** on account of

beck·on (békən) *v.t.* to summon ‖ *(fig.)* to invite ‖ *v.i.* to wave, nod or make some other gesture recognized as an invitation, summons or signal

be·come (bikʌ́m) *v. pres. part.* **be·com·ing** *past* **be·came** (bikéim) *past part.* **be·come** *v.i.* to come to be ‖ to be in process of change or development ‖ *v.t.* to suit, enhance the attractiveness of ‖ to be fitting or proper in **to become of** to happen to **be·cóm·ing 1.** *adj.* suitable, attractive **2.** *n.* *(philos.)* the state of undergoing development ‖ *(philos.)* a coming into being

bed (bed) *n.* a piece of furniture for sleeping in or resting on ‖ a resting place for animals ‖ the firm base on which something is supported ‖ the ground at the bottom of the sea or a river etc. ‖ a piece of ground prepared for plants etc. ‖ the ballast or foundation of a road or railroad ‖ the level surface of a printing press on which the type rests ‖ a layer or stratum of rock etc. **to get out of bed on the wrong side, get out of the wrong side of bed** to be in a bad temper for the day **to go to bed** to retire to one's bed ‖ *(of a newspaper etc.)* to go to press **to line on the bed one has made** to accept the consequences of one's actions **to make a bed** to arrange the bedclothes on a bed **to put to bed** to prepare for sleep and place in bed ‖ to work on (an edition of a newspaper) until it is ready to go to press **to take to one's bed** to go to bed and stay there because one is ill

bed *pres. part.* **bed·ding** *past* and *past part.* **bed·ded** *v.t.* to provide with a place to sleep ‖ to fix in a foundation ‖ to arrange or form in a bed or layer

be·dev·il (bidévəl) *pres. part.* **be·dev·il·ing**, *esp. Br.* **be·dev·il·ling** *past* and *past part.* **be·dev·iled**, *esp. Br.* **be·dev·illed** *v.t.* to interfere with and throw into confusion ‖ to pester **be·dév·il·ment** *n.* exasperating interference and trouble ‖ a pestering

bed·lam (bédləm) *n.* a scene of uproar

be·drag·gled (bidrǽg'ld) *adj.* with clothing, hair, fur etc. wet or hanging limply and unbecomingly

bed·rid·den (bédrid'n) *adj.* compelled to stay in bed because of illness or infirmity

bed·stead (bédsted) *n.* the framework of a bed supporting the springs and mattress

bee (bi:) *n.* a four-winged insect producing wax and honey ‖ a gathering of people for work or amusement, *sewing bee, spelling bee* **to have a bee in one's bonnet** to be obsessed about some matter, esp. a matter to which one is opposed

beef (bi:f) **1.** *n.* the flesh of a bull, cow or ox ‖ *(pl.* **beeves** (bi:vz), **beefs**, or collectively **beef)** a bull, cow or ox fully or nearly grown **2.** *v.i.* *(pop.)* to complain

bee·hive (bí:haiv) *n.* a hive

beer (bíər) *n.* an alcoholic drink brewed from fermented malt flavored with hops ‖ any of some other slightly fermented drinks

beet (bi:t) *n.* a genus of fleshy roots, used as a source of sugar (white or sugar beet) or (esp. *Am.* = *Br.* beetroot) in salads and cookery (red beet)

bee·tle (bí:t'l) **1.** *n.* an insect of the order *Coleoptera* ‖ any of various insects resembling the beetle, e.g. the cockroach **2.** *v.i. pres. part.* **bee·tling** *past* and *past part.* **bee·tled** to project, jut out as though menacing,

beetling cliffs

be·fall (bifɔ́l) *pres. part.* **be·fall·ing** *past* **be·fell** (bifél) *past part.* **be·fall·en** (bifɔ́lən) *v.t. (rhet.)* to happen to ‖ *v.i. (rhet.)* to come to pass

be·fit (bifít) *pres. part.* **be·fit·ting** *past* and *past part.* **be·fit·ted** *v.t.* to be suitable or proper for **be·fit·ting** *adj.*

be·fore (bifɔ́r, bifóur) **1.** *adv.* previously, already **2.** *prep.* in front of ‖ ahead of ‖ under the impulse of ‖ in or into the presence of ‖ which concerns and awaits ‖ earlier than ‖ higher in rank, nobility or worth ‖ rather than **3.** *conj.* sooner in time than

be·fore·hand (bifɔ́rhænd, bifóurhænd) *adv.* and *adj.* in advance

be·friend (bifrénd) *v.t.* to be helpful to with friendly sympathy

beg (beg) *pres. part.* **beg·ging** *past* and *past part.* **begged** *v.i.* to solicit money, clothing, food etc. for a living ‖ (of a holy person) to ask alms ‖ (of an animal) to express demands by making noises or assuming beseeching postures ‖ to ask earnestly ‖ *v.t.* to solicit as charity ‖ to ask for as a favor ‖ to ask earnestly **beg off** to back out of an undertaking and ask to be excused **to beg the question** to avoid the issue **to go begging** to be unwanted

be·gin (bigín) *pres. part.* **be·gin·ning** *past* **be·gan** (bigǽn) *past part.* **be·gun** (bigʌ́n) *v.t.* to start ‖ to come into existence ‖ *v.i.* to cause to start ‖ to commence **not to begin to** to be in in no position to ‖ not to manage in the last degree to **be·gin·ner** (bigínər) *n.* someone beginning, a novice **be·gin·ning** (bigíniŋ) *n.* a start ‖ the early part ‖ the time when life started ‖ origin ‖ *(pl.)* early stages

be·grudge (bigrʌ́dʒ) *pres. part.* **be·grudg·ing** *past* and *past part.* **be·grudged** *v.t.* to envy (someone something) ‖ to feel unwillingness or dissatisfaction at

be·guile (bigáil) *pres. part.* **be·guil·ing** *past* and *past part.* **be·guiled** *v.t.* (esp. with 'into', 'out of') to fool, deceive ‖ to charm ‖ to relieve the tedium of

be·half (bihǽf, biháf) *n.* (only in phrases) **in** (or **on**) **behalf of** in the interest of

be·have (bihéiv) *pres. part.* **be·hav·ing** *past* and *past part.* **be·haved** *v.t.* to conduct oneself

be·hav·ior (bihéivjər) *n.* manners, deportment ‖ moral conduct ‖ the way in which a machine, organ or organism works, with respect to its efficiency ‖ the way in which something reacts to environment **be·hav·ior·al** *adj.*

be·head (bihéd) *v.t.* to cut off the head of

be·hind (biháind) **1.** *adv.* in the rear ‖ in the past ‖ in a place where one is no longer ‖ in arrears **2.** *prep.* in back of ‖ in the past for ‖ remaining after when one has gone on ‖ in an inferior position to ‖ motivating but not disclosed or made evident by ‖ in support of ‖ running later than, progressing more slowly than **to put something behind one** to get over some past incident and concentrate on the future **3.** *n.* the buttocks

be·hold (bihóuld) *pres. part.* **be·hold·ing** *past* and *past part.* **be·held** (bihéld) *v.t. (rhet.)* to look at and consider ‖ *(Bible)* to see in a vision

be·hold·en (bihóuldən) *pred. adj.* under an obligation, bound in gratitude

beige (beiʒ) *n.* the color of natural wool

be·ing (bí:iŋ) **1.** *n.* existence, *to bring into being* ‖ the substance or essence of an existing person or thing ‖ one who exists, *a human being* **2.** *adj.* (in the phrase) **for the time being** for the present

be·la·bor (biléibər) *v.t. (rhet.)* to thrash ‖ to abuse with words

be·la·ted (biléitid) *adj.* late ‖ retarded

(a) æ, c*a*t; ɑ, c*ar*; ɔ *faw*n; ei, sn*a*ke. **(e)** e, h*e*n; i:, sh*ee*p; iə, d*eer*; ɛə, b*ear*. **(i)** i, f*i*sh; ai, t*i*ger; ə:, b*ir*d. **(o)** o, *o*x; au, c*ow*; ou, g*oa*t; u, p*oo*r; ɔi, r*oy*al. **(u)** ʌ, d*u*ck; u, b*u*ll; u:, g*oo*se; ə, b*a*cillus; ju:, c*u*be. x, lo*ch*; θ, *th*ink; ð, bo*th*er; z, *Z*en; ʒ, corsa*g*e; dʒ, sava*g*e; ŋ, oranguta*ng*; j, *y*ak; ʃ, fi*sh*; tʃ, fe*tch*; 'l, rabb*le*; 'n, redd*en*. Complete pronunciation key appears inside front cover.

be·lea·guer (bilí:gər) v.t. (rhet.) to besiege

bel·fry (bélfri:) pl. **bel·fries** n. a bell tower || the room in a tower where the bells hang

be·lie, be·ly (bilái) pres. part. **be·ly·ing** past and past part. **be·lied** v.t to give a false impression of, esp. by hiding || to fail to fulfil

be·lief (bilí:f) n. the conviction that something is true, esp. the teachings of a religion || the conviction that something exists, belief in fairies || the conviction that something is right, belief in a cause || something accepted as true || a religion or creed || an opinion **to the best of one's belief** as far as one knows

be·liev·a·ble (bilí:vəb'l) adj. able to be believed

be·lieve (bilí:v) pres. part. **be·liev·ing** past and past part. **be·lieved** v.t. to accept as true || to give credence to (a person) || to hold as one's opinion || v.i. to have religious faith **to believe in** to have confidence in the existence, truth or efficacy of

bell (bel) **1.** n. a hollow, usually cup-shaped instrument, widening at the lip, which makes a ringing sound when struck || an electric device sounding a note when made to do so || its sound || (naut.) a halfhourly division of the watch || something shaped like a bell, such as the corolla of certain flowers **sound as a bell** morally or physically in perfect condition || (of schemes, investments etc.) stable **2.** v.i. to take the form of a bell || v.t. to provide with a bell **to bell the cat** to undertake a risky venture, esp. on behalf of others

bell·boy (bélbɔi) n. a hotel or club page boy

bel·li·cose (bélikous) adj. warlike || aggressive || fond of fighting **bel·li·cos·i·ty** (belikósiti:) n.

bel·lig·er·ence (bəlídʒərəns) n. aggressiveness

bel·lig·er·en·cy (bəlídʒərənsi:) n. the state of being at war || belligerence

bel·lig·er·ent (bəlídʒərənt) **1.** adj. (internat. law) waging a war || (of international or personal relations) aggressive, hostile **2.** n. a nation at war

bel·low (bélou) **1.** v.i. (of a bull) to roar || (of guns, men in pain or anger, children in a temper etc.) to make a similar noise || to shout very loudly || v.t. to shout out, to bellow abuse **2.** n. the noise of a bull || any comparable noise

bel·lows (bélouz) pl. and sing. n. an instrument which, by expanding and collapsing, draws air in through a valve and forces it out, to give draft to a fire, cause organ pipes to sound etc. || the expanding part of a folding camera

bel·ly (béli:) **1.** n. pl. **bel·lies** the abdomen || the front part of the human body between the diaphragm and the thighs || the corresponding part of an animal || the stomach || anything resembling the rounded exterior of the belly || the lower or undersurface of anything, e.g. of a large piece of machinery standing off the ground **2.** v.t. pres. part. **bel·ly·ing** past and past part. **bel·lied** to cause to swell out || v.i. to become swollen out

be·long (bilɔ́ŋ, bilɔ́ŋ) v.i. to have a rightful place **to belong to** to be a possession of || to be a member of || to be classified with **be·lóng·ings** pl. n. possessions, property

be·loved (bilʌ́vd, bilʌ́vid) **1.** adj. much loved, favored **2.** (bilʌ́vid, bilʌ́vd) n. someone who is dearly loved

be·low (bilóu) **1.** adv. under, in a lower place || downstream || further down a page or further on in a book **2.** prep. lower than, under || lower in quality than || downstream from || unworthy of, not befitting the dignity of

belt (belt) **1.** n. a strip of fabric, leather etc., worn around the waist to support clothes or to draw them in || a strip of canvas, leather etc., worn over one shoulder and across to the opposite hip for carrying grenades, a sword etc. || a district characterized by certain physical or climatic conditions, or by the prevalence of a mineral, species, crop etc., cotton belt || (mech.) an endless band connecting wheels or pulleys **to tighten one's belt** to take austerity measures **2.**

v.t. to fasten with a belt || (pop., with 'out') to sing in a loud, coarse voice || (pop.) to thrash, esp. with a belt

be·mire (bimáiər) pres. part. **be·mir·ing** past and past part. **be·mired** v.t. (rhet.) to cover with mud

be·moan (bimóun) v.t. to moan over || to express deep sorrow or regret for

be·mused (bimjú:zd) adj. deep in thought || dazed

bench (bentʃ) **1.** n. a long wooden or stone seat for two or more people || a work table || a judge's seat or the office of judge or magistrate || judges or magistrates || a narrow shelf of ground, esp. a former shoreline of a river or lake || a raised shelf in a mine **2.** v.t. to send (a player in a game) to the bench, i.e. remove him from the game

bend (bend) **1.** v. pres. part. **bend·ing** past and past part. **bent** v.t. to make curved or crooked || to render (something curved or crooked) straight || to fold || to force to submit || v.i. to become curved or crooked || to change direction || to submit || to stoop **2.** n. a curve or turn || a part that is not straight **bénd·er** n. (pop.) a spree

be·neath (biní:θ) **1.** adv. under, in a lower place **2.** prep. under, at, in or to a position lower than || lower in amount, quality or rank than || unworthy of, not befitting **to marry beneath one** to marry a social inferior

ben·e·dic·tion (benidíkʃən) n. a blessing, esp. a formal prayer of blessing

ben·e·fac·tion (benifǽkʃən) n. a financial gift to a charity || a handsome donation or gift to an organization, club etc.

ben·e·fac·tor (bénifæktər, benifǽktər) n. someone who helps, esp. financially **ben·e·fac·tress** (bénifæktris, benifǽktris) n. a woman benefactor

be·nef·i·cence (bənéfisəns) n. kindness on a large scale || a particular instance of it **be·néf·i·cent** adj. actively good, producing good results

ben·e·fi·cial (benifíʃəl) adj. helpful, causing improvement || (law) receiving (property etc.) for one's own benefit or enjoyment

ben·e·fi·ci·ar·y (benifíʃi:ɛri:, benifíʃəri:) **1.** n. pl. **ben·e·fi·ci·ar·ies** someone receiving a benefit

ben·e·fit (bénifit) **1.** n. help, profit || advantage || an allowance, pension, etc. || a performance whose proceeds are given to a particular charity or person **2.** v.t. pres. part. **ben·e·fit·ting, ben·e·fit·ing** past and past part. **ben·e·fit·ted, ben·e·fit·ed** to do good to || v.i. to receive help or benefit

be·nev·o·lence (bənévələns) n. kindheartedness || generous giving

be·nev·o·lent (bənévələnt) adj. wellwishing, friendly || charitable

be·nign (bináin) adj. kind, well-disposed || (of diseases) not dangerous

be·nig·nan·cy (binígnənsi:) n. the state or quality of being benignant

be·nig·nant (binígnənt) adj. kind, gracious

be·nig·ni·ty (binígniti:) n. kindliness

bent (bent) past and past part. of BEND || **1.** adj. altered from a previous straight or even state || (with 'on' or upon) determined, resolved **2.** n. a mental inclination || a leaning, tendency **at the top of one's bent** in one's best form

be·queath (bikwí:ð, bikwí:θ) v.t. to will (money, possessions etc.) at one's death || to hand down (intangibles) to posterity

be·quest (bikwést) n. something that is left under a will

be·rate (biréit) pres. part. **be·rat·ing** past and past part. **be·rat·ed** v.t. to scold, chide

be·reave (birí:v) pres. part. **be·reav·ing** v.t. (past and past part. **be·reaved**) to leave desolate, esp. by death || (past and past part. **be·reft** (biréft)) to deprive **be·réave·ment** n.

be·ret (bəréi, bérei) n. a soft, round, flat woolen cap of Basque origin

ber·i·ber·i (béri:béri:) n. a disease due to deficiency of vitamin B₁

ber·ry (béri:) **1.** *n. pl.* **ber·ries** any small, juicy fruit with seeds ‖ (*bot.*) a many-seeded fleshy fruit **2.** *v.t. pres. part.* **ber·ry·ing** *past* and *past part.* **ber·ried** to bear berries ‖ to gather or look for berries

ber·serk (bəːrséːrk, bəːrzéːrk) *adj.* frenzied **to go berserk** to have a sudden fit of frenzy

berth (bəːrθ) **1.** *n.* a bunk in a ship or train ‖ a place at a wharf where a ship can lie at anchor ‖ an appointment, job **to give a wide berth to** to give (a ship) plenty of room to maneuver ‖ to take care to avoid **2.** *v.t.* to moor (a ship) at a suitable place ‖ to assign a berth to ‖ *v.i.* to take up moorings

be·seech (bisíːtʃ) *pres. part.* **be·seech·ing** *past* and *past part.* **be·sought** (bisɔ́t) *v.t.* to implore **be·séech·ing** *adj.*

be·set (bisét) *pres. part.* **be·set·ting** *past* and *past part.* **be·set** *v.t.* to surround, hem in ‖ to set upon, waylay **be·sét·ting** *adj.* continually harassing or assailing

be·side (bisáid) *prep.* by the side of, close to ‖ compared with **beside the point** irrelevant **to be beside oneself** to be overcome with worry, rage, joy

be·sides (bisáidz) **1.** *adv.* moreover ‖ also, in addition **2.** *prep.* in addition to

be·siege (bisíːdʒ) *pres. part.* **be·sieg·ing** *past* and *past part.* **be·sieged** *v.t.* to surround with armed forces, lay siege to ‖ to throng around ‖ to assail (with requests etc.)

be·smirch (bisméːrtʃ) *v.t.* to cast a slur on, sully

be·speak (bispíːk) *pres. part.* **be·speak·ing** *past* **be·spoke** (bispóuk) *past past.* **be·spoke, be·spoken** (bispóukən) *v.t.* to order in advance ‖ to indicate, show evidence of

best (best) **1.** *adj.* (*superl.* of GOOD) finest in quality ‖ most advantageous ‖ largest, *the best part of an hour* **2.** *n.* anything which is best ‖ greatest effort, utmost, *to try one's best* ‖ best clothes, *Sunday best* ‖ (*pl.*) persons superior in any category, *the best of the recruits* **it's all for the best** it will work out advantageously in the long run **to be at one's best** to be in one's best form or state **to get** (or **have**) **the best of** to dominate, have the advantage over or be the winner of, *he had the best of the argument* **to make the best of** to do as well as one can in (a difficult situation) **to the best of one's ability** as well as one can **to the best of one's belief** (or **knowledge**) as far as one knows **with the best** as well as anyone else, *he can dance with the best* **3.** *adv.* (*superl.* of WELL) most, *bears like honey best* ‖ in the most excellent way, *the engine runs best at night* **at best** in the most hopeful circumstances, *at best we can only hope to finish third* **had best** would find it wisest to, *he had best hurry up* **4.** *v.t.* to do better than, *she can best him at swimming* ‖ to get the better of

bes·tial (béstʃəl, bésti:əl) *adj.* of or like a beast ‖ vile ‖ obscene, lustful **bes·ti·ál·i·ty** *n.*

be·stow (bistóu) *v.t.* to confer, *to bestow a medal* ‖ to devote (thought, time)

bet (bet) **1.** *n.* a wager of money etc. against someone else's on the outcome of a doubtful event ‖ the money etc. that is staked ‖ the thing that is wagered upon **one's best bet** one's safest course of action **2.** *v. pres. part.* **bet·ting** *past* and *past part.* **bet, bet·ted** *v.t.* to wager (a sum etc.) ‖ *v.i.* to lay a bet ‖ to be in the practice of laying bets

be·ta (béitə, *Br.* bíːtə) *n.* the second letter (B, β = b) of the Greek alphabet ‖ the second brightest star in a constellation

be·tray (bitréi) *v.t.* to act treacherously towards ‖ to reveal treacherously ‖ to reveal accidentally ‖ to fail to justify ‖ to give evidence of **be·tráy·al** *n.*

be·troth (bitróuð, bitróθ) *v.t.* (*rhet.*) to affiance, promise in marriage **be·tróth·al** *n.* an engagement to marry **be·trothed 1.** *n.* the person to whom one is engaged **the betrothed** an engaged couple **2.** *adj.* engaged to be married

bet·ter (bétər) **1.** *adj.* (*comp.* of GOOD) having good qualities in a greater degree ‖ preferable ‖ improved ‖ improved in health ‖ larger, *the better part of a day* **better off** richer ‖ in a more satisfactory situation **no better than** just as bad as, virtually the same as, *he's no better than a thief* **to be better than one's word** to do what one promised and more besides **2.** *adv.* (*comp.* of WELL) in a more excellent manner, *he swims better than most* ‖ in a higher degree, *your efforts are better appreicated now* ‖ (of preference) more, *to like beer better than wine* **had better** would find it wiser, *you had better come early* **to know better** to be wiser (than to think or do a thing), *you should know better than to tease him* **to think better of it** to change one's mind **3.** *n.* someone superior in age, rank, knowledge etc. ‖ advantage, *to get the better of someone*

better *v.t.* to improve ‖ to surpass

bet·ter·ment (bétərmənt) *n.* improvement

bet·tor, bet·ter (bétər) *n.* a person who bets

be·tween (bitwíːn) **1.** *prep.* in the intervening space of ‖ within two limits of (distance, time or amount) ‖ intermediate in quality, degree etc. ‖ to and from ‖ common to ‖ distinguishing ‖ linking ‖ jointly among (two or more persons etc.) **between ourselves** in confidence **2.** *adv.* in an intermediate space ‖ in an interval of time

bev·er·age (bévəridʒ, bévridʒ) *n.* a drink

bev·y (bévi:) *pl.* **bev·ies** a group or company (correctly of women, quails, larks or roes)

be·ware (biwéər) *v.i.* (only *infin.* and *imper.*) to be careful, be on one's guard

be·wil·der (biwíldər) *v.t.* to throw into mental confusion ‖ *v.i.* to be a cause of mental confusion **be·wil·der·ment** *n.*

be·witch (biwítʃ) *v.t.* to fascinate or charm ‖ to affect by witchcraft **be·witch·ing** *adj.*

be·yond (bijónd, biːónd) **1.** *adv.* further **2.** *prep.* on the further side of ‖ later than ‖ past the comprehension of ‖ ahead of ‖ past **3.** *n.* **the beyond** what lies after death

bi·as (báiəs) **1.** *n.* a temperamental or emotional leaning to one side **2.** *v.t. pres. part.* **bi·as·ing** *past* and *past part.* **bi·ased** to cause to incline to one side ‖ to cause to be prejudiced in opinion, judgment etc.

bib (bib) *n.* a small piece of cloth placed under a child's chin at mealtimes to protect his clothes ‖ the top of an apron or overalls coming above the waist in front

Bi·ble (báib'l) *n.* the sacred writings of the Christian faith **bi·ble** the authoritative book on a subject

bib·li·cal (bíblik'l) *adj.* of or relating to the Bible

bib·li·og·ra·pher (bìbli:ógrəfər) *n.* someone who writes or compiles bibliographies ‖ someone who has a knowledge of bibliography

bib·li·o·graph·i·cal (bìbli:əgrǽfik'l) *adj.* of or relating to bibliography

bib·li·og·ra·phy (bìbli:ógrəfi:) *pl.* **bib·li·og·ra·phies** *n.* a complete list of a writer's work ‖ a list of books on a particular subject ‖ a list of references at the end of a book ‖ the history of books, authorship, editions etc. ‖ a book containing such information

bi·cen·ten·ni·al (bàisenténi:əl) **1.** *n.* a 200th anniversary or its celebration **2.** *adj.* occurring every 200 years ‖ lasting 200 years

bi·ceps (báiseps) *pl.* **bi·ceps, bi·ceps·es** (báisepsiz) *n.* a muscle with two heads or origins, two attachments

---

to the bone, esp. the large flexor muscle in the upper arm

bick·er (bíkər) **1.** *v.i.* to squabble ‖ to quarrel about trifles **2.** *n.* snappish quarrel of a not very serious kind

bi·cy·cle (báisik'l) **1.** *n.* a vehicle esp. for one person, consisting of two large, spoked, tandem wheels, a steering handle and a saddle on which the rider sits to work two pedals **2.** *v.i. pres. part.* **bi·cy·cling** *past and past part.* **bi·cy·cled** to cycle **bi·cy·clist** *n.* a cyclist

bid (bid) **1.** *v. pres. part.* **bid·ding** *past and past part.* **bid** *v.t.* to offer (a price), esp. at an auction sale ‖ *(card games)* to make (a bid) ‖ *(past also* **bade** (beid) *past part. also* **bid·den** (bid'n)) to command ‖ *v.i.* to make a bid in an auction, card games etc. **to bid fair** *(rhet.)* to promise favorably **2.** *n.* an offer of a price, esp. at a sale ‖ an offer to do a job etc. for a certain price **to make a bid for** to try to gain (e.g. freedom) **bid·der** *n.* someone who bids **bid·ding** *n.* a command or commands ‖ the offers made at an auction **to do someone's bidding** *(rhet.)* to obey someone

bide (baid) *pres. part.* **bid·ing** *past* **bid·ed, bode** (boud) *past part.* **bid·ed** *v.t.* (only in the phrase) **to bide one's time** to wait for the right opportunity

bi·en·ni·al (baiéni:əl) **1.** *adj.* lasting for two years ‖ occurring once every two years **2.** *n.* an event occurring once every two years ‖ *(bot.)* a plant which vegetates one year and flowers, fruits and dies in the second

bier (biər) *n.* the frame on which a coffin or corpse is taken to its burial

bi·fo·cal (baifóuk'l) *adj.* having two points of focus **bi·fó·cals** *pl. n.* bifocal spectacles

big (big) **1.** *adv. comp.* **big·ger** *superl.* **big·gest** large, *a big book* ‖ grown-up ‖ important ‖ boastful ‖ *(pop.)* magnanimous **2.** *adv.* boastfully

big·a·mist (bígəmist) *n.* a person who makes a second marriage illegally while the first marriage remains valid

big·a·mous (bígəməs) *adj.* guilty of bigamy ‖ involving bigamy

big·a·my (bígəmi:) *n.* illegally having two wives or husbands at the same time

big·ot (bígət) *n.* someone obstinately and intolerantly devoted to his own beliefs, creed or party **big·ot·ed** *adj.* narrow-minded, prejudiced **big·ot·ry** *n.* the mental attitude and behavior of a bigot, obstinate narrow-mindedness

bike (baik) **1.** *n. (pop.)* a bicycle **2.** *v.i. pres. part.* **bik·ing** *past and past part.* **biked** *(pop.)* to bicycle, cycle

bi·ki·ni (bikí:ni:) *n.* a woman's minimal two-piece bathing suit

bi·lat·er·al (bailǽtərəl) *adj.* affecting each of two sides or parties ‖ having two sides ‖ ranged upon two sides

bile (bail) *n.* a bitter, greenish-yellow alkaline fluid secreted by the liver of many vertebrates ‖ ill humor

bi·lev·el (bɒilévəl) *adj.* of a two-story dwelling, one partially below ground —**bilevel** *n.*

bilge (bildʒ) **1.** *n.* the bottom of a ship from the keel to where the sides begin to rise ‖ the swelling part of a barrel ‖ bilge water ‖ *(pop.)* foolishly mistaken ideas or remarks **2.** *v. pres. part.* **bilg·ing** *past and past part.* **bilged** *v.t.* to cause to fracture in the bilge ‖ *v.i.* to have a fracture in the bilge

bil·i·ar·y (bíli:ɛri:) *adj.* of or connected with the bile

bil·ious (bíljəs) *adj.* of or connected with the bile ‖ having or resulting from a liver or bile disorder ‖ ill-tempered ‖ sickly looking

bilk (bilk) *v.t.* to defraud (a creditor) by avoiding payment of one's debts ‖ to evade, give (someone) the slip

bill (bil) **1.** *n.* an account for goods sold or services rendered ‖ the draft of a law ‖ a poster ‖ a handbill or leaflet ‖ a concert or theater program ‖ a piece of paper money **2.** *v.t.* to charge (an account) for goods or services ‖ to announce by means of playbills

bill *n.* a beak ‖ a narrow promontory ‖ the end of an anchor fluke

bill·board (bílbɔrd, bílbourd) *n. (Am. = Br.* hoarding) a wall of planks etc. for the display of advertisement posters

bil·let (bílit) *n.* a section of a log split lengthwise (for firewood) ‖ a small bar of iron or steel

billet **1.** *n.* the quarters to which a soldier etc. is officially assigned **2.** *v.t.* to find or provide quarters for (soldiers, refugees etc.)

bill·fold (bílfould) *n.* a wallet for paper money

bil·liards (bíljərdz) *n.* any of several games played on a large, rectangular, cushioned, clothcovered table, ivory balls being driven by a tapering wooden cue

bil·lion (bíljən) *n.* *NUMBER TABLE

bil·lion·aire (biljənɛ́ər) *n.* someone whose posessions are worth a billion dollars (or pounds etc.)

bil·low (bílou) **1.** *n.* a large wave ‖ anything that sweeps along like a wave, *a billow of laughter* **2.** *v.i.* to roll along or rise and fall like a wave ‖ to bulge or swell **bil·low·y** *adj.*

bil·ly goat (bíli: gout) a male goat

bi·month·ly (baimánθli:) **1.** *adj.* happening every two months ‖ happening twice a month **2.** *n. pl.* **bi·month·lies** a bimonthly publication **3.** *adv.* once in two months ‖ twice a month

bin (bin) *n.* a receptacle for storing e.g. bread, coal or flour

bi·na·ry (báinəri:) *adj.* consisting of two

bind (baind) *pres. part.* **bind·ing** *past and past part.* **bound** (baund) *v.t.* to tie up ‖ to fasten together ‖ to bandage ‖ to provide a decorative or strengthening border for ‖ to place (someone) under an agreement or obligation ‖ to cause to cohere or adhere ‖ *v.i.* to stick together in a hard lump or cohesive mass ‖ to become jammed ‖ to be obligatory **to bind over** to impose a legal obligation on

bind·er (báindər) *n.* someone who binds, esp. a bookbinder ‖ the part of a reaping machine for binding sheaves, or the part of a harvester which binds the straw into bales ‖ a binding substance, e.g. tar ‖ a cover for fastening loose papers together

bind·er·y (báindəri:, báindri:) *pl.* **bind·er·ies** *n.* a factory or workshop where books are bound

bind·ing (báindiŋ) **1.** *n.* the action of someone who binds ‖ a bookcover ‖ material used to strengthen or decorate the edges e.g. of a blanket, mat or garment **2.** *adj.* involving moral obligation

binge (bindʒ) *n. (pop.)* a drinking spree

bin·go (bíŋgou) *n.* a gambling game in which each of several players has a numbered card on which he covers the numbers as they are called or indicated on a wheel

bin·oc·u·lar (binɒ́kjulər, bainɒ́kjulər) *adj.* having or requiring the use of two eyes **bin·óc·u·lars** *pl. n.* an optical instrument

bi·og·ra·pher (baiɒ́grəfər, bi:ɒ́grəfər) *n.* an author of a biography or biographies

bi·o·graph·ic (baiəgrǽfik) *adj.* of or relating to biography **bi·o·gráph·i·cal** *adj.*

bi·og·ra·phy (baiɒ́grəfi:, bi:ɒ́grəfi:) *pl.* **bi·og·ra·phies** *n.* a written account of a person's life ‖ biographical writing as a literary genre

bi·o·log·ic (baiəlɒ́dʒik) *adj.* of or relating to biology **bi·o·lóg·i·cal** *adj.*

bi·ol·o·gist (baiɒ́lədʒist) *n.* a specialist in biology

bi·ol·o·gy (baiɒ́lədʒi:) *n.* the science of life and all its manifestations: an area of study concerned with living organisms, their form and structure, their behavior, their function, their origin, development and growth and their relationship to their environment and to like and unlike organisms, both living and extinct ‖ the plant and animal life of a given region

bi·op·sy (báiɒpsi:) *pl.* **bi·op·sies** *n. (med.)* the examination of tissue taken from the living body

bi·par·ti·san (baipártizən) *adj.* of the two-party system in politics ‖ marked by the cooperation of both parties

bi·pár·ti·san·ship *n.*

bi·ped (báiped) **1.** *adj.* having two feet **2.** *n.* a two-footed animal, e.g. man

birch (bə:rtʃ) *n.* a deciduous forest tree of the temperate areas of the northern hemisphere

bird (bə:rd) *n.* a warm-blooded vertebrate of the class *Aves*, covered with feathers except for the legs and feet, which are scaly, and having the forelimbs converted into wings ‖ a game bird ‖ the shuttlecock in badminton **birds of a feather** people of similar character **to kill two birds with one stone** to achieve two aims simultaneously

bird·ie (bə́:rdi:) *n. (golf)* a score of one stroke under par in playing a hole

birth (bə:rθ) *n.* the event of being born ‖ the act of bringing forth young ‖ a coming into existence ‖ lineage, descent **to give birth to** to bring forth (young)

birth·day (bə́:rθdei) *n.* the day of one's birth or the anniversary of this day

birth·mark (bə́:rθmɑrk) *n.* a mark on the skin at birth

bis·cuit (bískit) **1.** *n.* a soft unsweetened roll or bun, usually eaten hot with butter ‖ pottery fired once before glazing and refiring ‖ a very light brown color **2.** *v.t.* to fire (raw pottery) without glaze

bi·sect (baisékt) *v.t.* to cut or divide into two equal parts ‖ to cut or divide into two parts (not necessarily equal) **bi·séc·tion** *n.* **bi·séc·tion·al** *adj.* **bi·séc·tor** *n.* a bisecting line

bi·sex·u·al (baisékʃu:əl) *adj.* of or relating to both sexes ‖ having both sexes

bish·op (bíʃəp) *n.* a member of the highest order in the Christian Church ‖ *(chess)* one of the two pieces which move only diagonally

bish·op·ric (bíʃəprik) *n.* the office of a bishop ‖ a diocese

bi·son (báis'n, báiz'n) *pl.* **bi·son, bi·sons** *n.* a genus of large, shaggy, bovine mammals, often called buffalo, having a large hump on the withers and back

bisque, bisk (bisk) *n.* a rich soup made from shellfish etc.

bit (bit) *n.* the metal bar of a bridle, which is put into the horse's mouth ‖ the part of a key which enters the lock and grips the lever ‖ the boring piece of a drill used in a brace ‖ the gripping part of pincers **to take the bit between the teeth** (of a horse) to run away, bolt ‖ (of a person) to reject control

bit by bit gradually, piecemeal

bitch (bitʃ) *n.* the female of the dog or other canine ‖ a spiteful, malicious woman ‖ a sexually promiscuous woman **bitch·y** *comp.* **bitch·i·er** *superl.* **bitch·i·est** *adj.*

bite (bait) **1.** *v. pres. part.* **bit·ing** *past* **bit** (bit) *past part.* **bit·ten** (bít'n, **bit** *v.t.* to seize and grip with the teeth ‖ to cut with the teeth ‖ to cut or pierce ‖ (of insects, snakes etc.) to sting ‖ to cause sharp pain to ‖ to corrode ‖ to grip ‖ *v.i.* to seize and grip something with the teeth ‖ to have a tendency to make attacks in this way ‖ to cause a biting sensation ‖ (of a fish) to take the bait **to bite off more than one can chew** to attempt more than one can manage **to bite the dust** *(rhet.)* to fall to the ground, esp. mortally wounded **2.** *n.* a biting ‖ the wound made by biting ‖ something bitten off ‖ a snack ‖ the nibbling or swallowing of bait by a fish ‖ sharp pain ‖ sharpness, pungency ‖ a grip or hold

bit·ter (bítər) **1.** *adj.* acrid-tasting, tart ‖ hard to bear ‖ caused by or expressing deep grief ‖ harsh, biting ‖ acrimonious, showing deep resentment **to the bitter end** to the very last, come what may **2.** *adv.* bitingly

bit·tern (bítərn) *n.* a genus of long-legged marsh birds allied to herons

bi·valve (báivælv) **1.** *n.* an animal that has a hinged double shell **2.** *adj.* having a shell consisting of two hinged valves, allowing the shell to open and close

biv·ou·ac (bívu:æk, bívwæk) **1.** *n.* a temporary camp without tents or with pup tents only ‖ a makeshift shelter **2.** *v.t. pres. part.* **biv·ou·ack·ing** *past* and *past part.* **biv·ou·acked** to spend the night in a bivouac

bi·zarre (bizár) *adj.* fantastic, strange (often with a suggestion of the ridiculous or the uncanny)

blab (blæb) **1.** *v. pres. part.* **blab·bing** *past* and *past part.* **blabbed** *v.i.* to give away secrets thoughtlessly, talk indiscreetly ‖ to chatter wearisomely ‖ *v.t.* to reveal (a secret etc.) thoughtlessly or indiscreetly **2.** *n.* vague, windy talk ‖ chatter

black (blæk) **1.** *adj.* without light, or not able to reflect it ‖ colorless, or so dark as to appear colorless ‖ the opposite of white ‖ not hopeful ‖ *(rhet.)* sad ‖ very dirty ‖ *(rhet.)* wicked ‖ evil ‖ darkskinned ‖ reflecting discredit ‖ illegal ‖ of the members of a religious order wearing a black habit ‖ of or concerning a black or blacks **2.** *n.* a black pigment, fabric etc. ‖ dirt, soot ‖ a person whose natural skin color is black **3.** *v.t.* to make black ‖ to polish with blacking ‖ *v.i.* to become black, blacken **to black out** to darken, cause to give out or receive no light ‖ to lose consciousness or memory, usually temporarily

black·ber·ry (blǽkbɛri:, blǽkbəri:) *pl.* **black·ber·ries** *n.* a genus of trailing or erect, usually prickly, bushes bearing edible berries ‖ one of the berries

black·bird (blǽkbə:rd) *n.* a thrush common throughout Europe and found in N. Africa ‖ any bird of fam. *Icteridae*, esp. *Agelaius phoeniceus*, the red-winged blackbird

black·board (blǽkbɔrd, blǽkbourd) *n.* a large piece of slate or painted wood with a dark smooth surface which can be written or drawn on with chalk

black·en (blǽkən) *v.t.* to make black or dark ‖ to speak ill of, defame ‖ *v.i.* to grow black or dark

black·guard (blǽgɑrd, blǽgərd) **1.** *n.* a scoundrel ‖ an utterly unscrupulous person **2.** *v.t.* to destroy the character of (someone) with false accusations

black·head (blǽkhed) *n.* any of several blackheaded birds, esp. gulls ‖ a plug of grease and dirt blocking a sebaceous gland duct

black·jack (blǽkdʒæk) **1.** *n.* a pirate flag ‖ a card game ‖ a small rubber club with lead in it and a flexible handle **2.** *v.t.* to strike or menace with this weapon

black magic magic used in the service of evil

black·mail (blǽkmeil) **1.** *n.* an attempt to extort money by threats, esp. of exposure ‖ the money extorted in this way **2.** *v.t.* to extort money from (someone) by intimidation, esp. by threats of exposure

black·out (blǽkaut) *n.* a preventing of lights inside a building from being seen outside ‖ a temporary loss of consciousness or memory

black·smith (blǽksmiθ) *n.* a man who works iron in a forge, shoes horses etc.

blad·der (blǽdər) *n. (anat.)* a membranous sac filled with fluid or air, esp. the musculo-membranous receptacle for urine

blade (bleid) *n.* the cutting part of a knife, sword ‖ a long slender leaf, esp. of grass ‖ *(bot.)* the outspread part of a leaf, excluding the stalk ‖ a thin flattened edge, e.g. of an oar or propeller ‖ a flattened bone, esp. the scapula or shoulder blade **in the blade** (of cereal crops) not yet having produced ears

blam·a·ble, blame·a·ble (bléiməb'l) *adj.* deserving blame

blame (bleim) **1.** *v.t. pres. part.* **blam·ing** *past* and *past part.* **blamed** to hold responsible ‖ to attribute the cause of **to be to blame** to be held responsible **2.** *n.*

---

censure, expression of disapproval ‖ responsibility for something wrong or unsatisfactory **to lay the blame on** to hold responsible **blá·me·a·ble** *adj.* **bláme·less** *adj.* free from fault or blame ‖ innocent **bláme·wor·thy** *adj.* deserving blame, at fault

blanch (blæntʃ, blɑntʃ) *v.t.* to make white or pale ‖ to make white by peeling away the skin of (almonds), by depriving (e.g. celery) of light, by scalding (meat) etc. ‖ to give a white luster to (silver coins, before stamping) ‖ to coat (sheet iron or steel) with tin ‖ *v.i.* to grow pale

bland (blænd) *n.* mild ‖ suave ‖ soothing and nonirritating

blan·dish (blǽndiʃ) *v.t.* to coax or flatter ‖ to tempt with flattering words **blán·dish·ment** *n.* (often *pl.*)

blank (blæŋk) **1.** *adj.* not written on ‖ expressionless ‖ empty, without incident ‖ unrelieved, without variety **2.** *n.* an empty space left in printed matter ‖ a void ‖ a blank cartridge ‖ a coin before stamping ‖ a key before the notches have been cut ‖ a raffle ticket which does not win a prize for its holder **to draw a blank** to be unsuccessful, e.g. in an inquiry or search **3.** *v.t.* (with 'out') to blot out

blan·ket (blǽŋkit) **1.** *n.* a warm covering used esp. on a bed ‖ any extended covering **2.** *v.t.* to cover as if with a blanket ‖ to stifle (noise, rumors, questions etc.) **3.** *adj.* applicable to all persons or in all circumstances

blare (bleər) **1.** *v. pres. part.* **blar·ing** *past* and *past part.* **blared** *v.i.* to make a loud, harsh sound ‖ *v.t.* to proclaim loudly **2.** *n.* any continuous, loud, harsh noise or trumpeting

blar·ney (blɑ́rniː) **1.** *n.* persuasive cajolery, wheedling talk **2.** *v.t.* to try to influence or persuade by blarney ‖ *v.i.* to talk blarney

bla·sé (blɑzéi, blɑ́zei) *adj.* satiated with pleasure and left without enthusiasm ‖ affectedly sophisticated in a world-weary way

blas·pheme (blæsfíːm) *pres. part.* **blas·phem·ing** *past* and *past part.* **blas·phemed** *v.t.* to speak impiously of (God and things regarded as sacred) ‖ *v.i.* to utter blasphemy **blas·phe·mous** (blǽsfəməs) *adj.*

blas·phe·my (blǽsfəmi) *pl.* **blas·phe·mies** *n.* contemptuous or irreverent speech about God or things regarded as sacred

blast (blæst, blɑst) **1.** *n.* a strong gust of wind ‖ a draft of air used to increase the heat of a furnace ‖ a wave of highly compressed air created by an explosion ‖ a ringing sound from a trumpet etc. **(at) full blast** at top capacity ‖ *(slang)* an exciting event **2.** *v.t.* to make by the use of explosives ‖ to shatter ‖ to attack violently ‖ *v.i.* (with 'off') to take off under selfpropulsion **3.** *interj.* an expletive expressing annoyance **blást·ed** *adj.* damnable, annoying

bla·tan·cy (bléit'nsi) *n.* the state or quality of being blatant

bla·tant (bléit'nt) *adj.* very obvious, *a blatant lie* ‖ (of voices, colors, clothes etc.) strident, harsh

bla·ther (blǽðər) **1.** *v.i.* to talk foolishly ‖ *v.t.* to utter foolishly **2.** *n.* foolish talk

blaze (bleiz) **1.** *n.* a bright fire ‖ an unintended fire ‖ a bright display (of color, light) ‖ an outburst ‖ full, direct light **2.** *v.i. pres. part.* **blaz·ing** *past* and *past part.* **blazed** to burn brightly ‖ to be bright with light or color ‖ to shine or glare fiercely ‖ to burst forth (with anger etc.) **to blaze away** to shoot or fire continuously or very frequently

bleach (bliːtʃ) **1.** *v.t.* to remove the color or stains from (something) ‖ to lighten the color of (hair) by hydrogen peroxide or other chemicals ‖ to lighten the color of, as if by chemical bleaching **2.** *n.* a chemical used in bleaching **bléach·er** *n.* someone who bleaches (clothes etc.) ‖ a machine or chemical used for bleaching ‖ *(pl.)* a section in a stadium etc. containing uncovered seats for spectators of outdoor sports

bleak (bliːk) *adj.* exposed, desolate ‖ cheerless ‖ cold, bitter

blear (bliər) **1.** *adj.* (of the eyes) bleary **2.** *v.t.* to blur

bléar·i·ness *n.* **bléar·y** *comp.* **blear·i·er** *superl.* **blear·i·est** *adj.* dim, misted, filmy

bleat (bliːt) **1.** *v.i.* (of a sheep or goat) to make its characteristic cry ‖ to speak plaintively ‖ *v.t.* to say in a bleating manner **2.** *n.* the cry of a sheep or goat

bleed (bliːd) *pres. part.* **bleed·ing** *past* and *past part.* **bled** (bled) *v.i.* to lose or emit blood ‖ (of plants) to lose sap ‖ *v.t.* to draw blood from (surgically) ‖ to take sap from ‖ to extort money from ‖ *(printing)* to cause (an illustration) to extend to the edge of a page without a margin **bléed·er** *n.* a hemophiliac

blem·ish (blémiʃ) **1.** *v.t.* to spoil or impair **2.** *n.* a physical or moral defect or flaw

blend (blend) **1.** *n.* a harmonious mixture **2.** *v. pres. part.* **blend·ing** *past* and *past part.* **blend·ed, blent** (blent) *v.t.* to mix together ‖ *v.i.* to merge harmoniously

bless (bles) *v.t. pres. part.* **bless·ing** *past* and *past part.* **blessed** (less frequently) **blest** (blest) to call down God's favor upon ‖ to consecrate ‖ to enrich ‖ to praise **to bless oneself** to make the sign of the cross over oneself

bless·ed (blésid) **1.** *adj.* holy, revered ‖ *(Roman Catholicism)* beatified, accorded the second of three degrees of sanctitiy ‖ (blest) lucky, favored ‖ *(ironic)* cursed **2.** *n.* **the bless·ed** (blésid) the souls in Heaven **bless·ed·ness** (blésidnis) *n.* a state of happiness, esp. through the enjoyment of God's favor

bless·ing (blésiŋ) *n.* divine favor or the invocation of it ‖ a source of consolation ‖ a piece of good fortune **a blessing in disguise** something unwelcome at first, which turns out to be fortunate

blight (blait) **1.** *n.* any plant disease or injury characterized by or resulting in withering, growth cessation, and a more or less general death of parts without rotting ‖ an organism which causes this ‖ something which spoils hope, plans, festivity etc. **2.** *v.t.* to wither ‖ to spoil, destroy ‖ to frustrate

blimp (blimp) *n.* a small, nonrigid dirigible used esp. for observation

blind (blaind) **1.** *adj.* without sight ‖ undiscerning or unwilling to judge ‖ without foresight or thought ‖ without seeing objects or facts ‖ having no outlet ‖ having no opening **2.** *n.* something which prevents strong light from coming through a window ‖ a coverup to conceal the truth ‖ *(Am. = Br.* hide) a concealed place for a hunter or observer of wildlife **3.** *v.t.* to deprive of the faculty of sight ‖ to dazzle

blind·fold (bláindfould) **1.** *v.t.* to cover the eyes of (someone) with a cloth **2.** *adj.* having the eyes covered to prevent vision **3.** *n.* a cloth tied around the eyes to prevent vision

blind·ly (bláindli) *adv.* not being able to distinguish objects, facts etc. ‖ without resisting or questioning

blink (bliŋk) **1.** *n.* a quick shutting and opening of the eyes ‖ a momentary glimmer **2.** *v.i.* to shut and open one's eyes quickly ‖ to shine with an unsteady light ‖ *v.t.* to shut and open (the eyes) quickly ‖ to make (eyes, light etc.) blink

bliss (blis) *n.* great but quiet enjoyment ‖ perfect happiness, heavenly joy **bliss·ful** *adj.*

blis·ter (blístər) **1.** *n.* a portion of skin raised by the pressure of fluid beneath it ‖ a portion of a surface similarly raised **2.** *v.t.* to cause blisters to form in or on ‖ to criticize (a person) harshly ‖ *v.i.* to become covered with blisters

blithe (blaið, blaiθ) *adj.* lightheartedly cheerful, happy

bliz·zard (blízərd) *n.* a blinding snowstorm accompanied by a strong wind

bloat (blout) **1.** *n.* *(vet.)* a windy swelling of the abdomen, esp. in cattle and horses, caused by eating too quickly **2.** *v.t.* to inflate with air or water ‖ to cause to swell with excessive pride, make vain ‖ *v.i.* to swell up

bloc (blɒk) *n.* a group of parties, governments etc. associating together to achieve (or prevent) something

block) *n.* a large solid piece of stone, wood etc. ‖ a wooden mold for shaping hats ‖ a pulley ‖ a piece of wood or metal engraved for use in printing ‖ a prepared piece of stone for building ‖ a large building consisting of offices, shops etc. ‖ an area in a city enclosed by four intersecting streets ‖ an obstruction ‖ *(psychol.)* a mental mechanism preventing a topic with unpleasant associations from being thought about ‖ a number of seats all together, e.g. in a theater ‖ a piece of wood or other material used in sets by children playing at building ‖ a large number of shares

block *v.t.* to cause obstruction in, prevent the passage of ‖ to make difficult or impossible, put obstacles in the way of ‖ *(med.)* to prevent sensation in (a nerve) by the use of a local anesthetic ‖ to shape (a knitted garment) or mold (a hat) on a block ‖ to stamp (a book cover) ‖ *(sports)* to obstruct (a player) ‖ *v.i.* to become blocked ‖ to cause a block **to block in** (or **out**) to mark out the general lines of (a drawing etc.) **to block in** (or **up**) to close off, seal

block·ade (blɒkéid) **1.** *n.* an attempted starving into surrender of an enemy by preventing goods from reaching or leaving him **to raise a blockade** to stop blockading **to run a blockade** to succeed in breaking through blockading forces, or attempt to do so **2.** *v.t. pres. part.* **block·ad·ing** *past* and *past part.* **block·ad·ed** to subject to blockade by surrounding with troops or warships etc.

blond, blonde (blɒnd) **1.** *adj.* (of hair) yellowish in color ‖ (of the complexion) pale **2.** *n.* (**blond** only) a boy or man with yellowish hair and fair skin ‖ (**blonde** only) a girl or woman with such hair and skin

blood (blʌd) *n.* a fluid circulating throughout the vertebrate body, carrying nutrients and oxygen to the tissues and removing wastes and carbon dioxide **in cold blood** deliberately, not in an excess of passion **in one's blood** as an inborn passion or natural capacity **to have blood on one's hands** to be guilty of having caused someone's death **to make one's blood boil** to make one passionately angry

blood·hound (blʌ́dhaund) *n.* a powerful dog with a keen sense of smell

blood·i·ly (blʌ́d'li:) *adv.* in a bloody manner

blood·i·ness (blʌ́di:nis) *n.* the state or quality of being bloody

blood·shed (blʌ́dʃed) *n.* violent death or injury as a phenomenon

blood·shot (blʌ́dʃɒt) *adj.* (of the eyes) suffused with blood

blood·y (blʌ́di:) *adj. comp.* **blood·i·er** *superl.* **blood·i·est** of the nature or appearance of blood ‖ stained with blood ‖ in which blood is shed ‖ concerned with bloodshed ‖ vicious, murderous

bloom (blu:m) **1.** *n.* the state of flowering ‖ a flower, blossom ‖ (of people) the time of physical perfection ‖ a flush or glow on the cheek ‖ a pleasing, glowing surface ‖ a kind of raisin ‖ a cloudy defect on a varnished surface **2.** *v.i.* to blossom, to be or come into flower ‖ to be in, or come into, fullness of beauty ‖ (of people) to look radiant

bloop·er (blú:pər) *n. (pop.)* a blunder

blos·som (blɒ́səm) *n.* a flower, usually of a fruit-producing tree or bush ‖ the mass of bloom on a fruit tree or bush ‖ a youthful, fresh stage of growth **blós·som·y** *adj.* full of blossoms ‖ resembling a blossom

blossom *v.i.* to open into flower ‖ to develop **to blossom out** to lose reserve, develop an attractive personality

blotch (blɒtʃ) **1.** *n.* a patch of ink or color ‖ a disfiguring spot on the skin **2.** *v.t.* to make a blotch on (something) ‖ *v.i.* to make a blotch **blotched** *adj.* **blótch·y** *comp.* **blotch·i·er** *superl.* **blotch·i·est** *adj.*

blot·ter (blɒ́tər) *n.* a piece or pad of blotting paper ‖ a book in which transactions, happenings etc. are noted before being permanently recorded elsewhere, *police blotter*

blouse (blaus, blauz) **1.** *n.* a woman's shirt ‖ a loose working garment **2.** *v. pres. part.* **blous·ing** *past* and *past part.* **bloused** *v.t.* to make (the bodice of a garment) fit loosely like a blouse ‖ *v.i.* to fit loosely like a blouse

blow (blou) **1.** *v. pres. part.* **blow·ing** *past* **blew** (blu:) *past part.* **blown** (bloun) *v.i.* (of the wind) to move ‖ to direct air from the mouth ‖ to sound when blown into ‖ to make a noise as of blowing ‖ (of whales) to eject air forcibly from the lungs through blowholes ‖ (of a fuse) to melt when overloaded with electric current ‖ to leave ‖ *v.t.* to cause (air, steam etc.) to move ‖ to direct (air) from the mouth at something ‖ to sound by blowing ‖ (of the wind) to buffet ‖ to clear (the nose) of mucus by forcing air through it ‖ to shape (molten glass) by forcing one's breath into it ‖ to work the bellows of (an organ) **to blow away** (of the wind) to carry away ‖ (of a thing) to be carried away by the wind **to blow hot and cold** to look on something favorably one moment and unfavorably the next **to blow one's top (off)** to lose one's temper **to blow out** to extinguish by blowing ‖ to become extinguished **to blow over** to die down, pass off **to blow up** to inflate (e.g. a balloon) ‖ to destroy by exploding ‖ to enlarge greatly ‖ to explode ‖ to lose one's temper **2.** *n.* a blowing of wind, esp. a gale ‖ a blast of air from the mouth or nose, or from an instrument or machine

blow *n.* a sudden vigorous stroke with the hand or an instrument ‖ a sudden shock ‖ a stroke of bad luck **at one blow** by a single action, in one go **to come to blows** to begin fighting

blow·er (blóuər) *n.* that which blows, e.g. something which increases the draft of air to a fire or supplies air to the bellows of an organ ‖ an escape of gas, or the opening giving vent to it

blow·up (blóuʌp) *n.* an explosion ‖ a violent quarrel or fit of temper ‖ a big photographic enlargement

blub·ber (blʌ́bər) **1.** *n.* fat from the whale or other marine mammal, from which oil is extracted ‖ noisy weeping and complaining **2.** *v.t.* to utter with gasping sobs ‖ *v.i.* to weep noisily and with choking sobs **blúb·ber·y** *adj.* having lots of blubber or (of people) loose fat

bludg·eon (blʌ́dʒən) **1.** *n.* a heavy stick or sticklike weapon, with one end weighted **2.** *v.t.* to hit repeatedly with such a weapon ‖ to force (someone into a course of action) by violent argument

blue (blu:) **1.** *adj.* of the color sensation stimulated by the wavelengths of light in that portion of the spectrum between green and violet, being the color of e.g. a cloudless sky ‖ having pallid skin due to cold or fear ‖ depressing in outlook ‖ unhappy, melancholy **2.** *n.* a blue color, pigment, fabric etc. **out of the blue** without any warning **3.** *pres. part.* **blue·ing, blu·ing** *past* and *past part.* **blued** *v.t.* to use bluing on ‖ to cause to become blue

blue·bell (blú:bel) *n.* a plant of the genus *Campanula* esp. the harebell

blue·bird (blú:bə:rd) *n.* a member of *Sialia*, a genus of American songbirds related to the robin

blue jay a crested jay of Eastern North America with bright blue feathers on its back

blue jeans blue work trousers of jean or denim

blue·print (blú:print) **1.** *n. (engin., archit.)* a copy of an original diagram or plan, used as a working draw-

---

(**a**) æ, cat; ɑ, car; ɔ fawn; ei, snake. (**e**) e, hen; i:, sheep; iə, deer; ɛə, bear. (**i**) i, fish; ai, tiger; ə:, bird. (**o**) o, ox; au, cow; ou, goat; u, poor; ɔi, royal. (**u**) ʌ, duck; u, bull; u:, goose; ə, bacillus; ju:, cube. x, loch; θ, think; ð, bother; z, Zen; ʒ, corsage; dʒ, savage; ŋ, orangutang; j, yak; ʃ, fish; tʃ, fetch; 'l, rabble; 'n, redden. Complete pronunciation key appears inside front cover.

ing ‖ a detailed plan for achieving some large undertaking 2. *v.t.* to make a blueprint of

blues (blu:z) *pl. n.* (with 'the') a mood of profound melancholy, depression ‖ a type of jazz

bluff (blʌf) 1. *v.t.* to mislead deliberately by pretending to be in a more favorable or advantageous position than one really is ‖ to intimidate by threats one cannot fulfill ‖ *v.i.* to use deception in these ways 2. *n.* a bluffer, a person who bluffs ‖ the act of bluffing ‖ a taking in by bluffing **to call someone's bluff** to make someone expose his real weakness

bluff 1. *adj.* hearty, blunt and direct but good-natured 2. *n.* a steep cliff or headland with a broad, rounded front

blu·ing, blue·ing (blú:iŋ) *n.* (*Am.* = *Br.* blue) a product used in laundering to make clothes white

blu·ish, blue·ish (blú:iʃ) *adj.* rather blue in color ‖ tinged with blue

blun·der (blʌ́ndər) 1. *n.* a crass, stupid mistake 2. *v.t.* (often with 'along', 'into', 'through') to move heavily and clumsily ‖ to make a crass mistake ‖ (with 'upon') to find by chance ‖ *v.t.* to make a clumsy failure of

blunt (blʌnt) 1. *adj.* having an edge or point that is not sharp ‖ (of wits) insensitive, unperceptive, slow in understanding ‖ (of manner or character) lacking in finesse, scorning tact 2. *v.i.* to become less sharp ‖ *v.t.* to make less sharp

blur (blə:r) 1. *n.* a confused visual impression ‖ a blemish or smudge ‖ indistinct appearance ‖ indistinct sound 2. *v. pres. part.* **blur·ring** *past* and *past part.* **blurred** *v.t.* to make indistinct ‖ *v.i.* to become spoiled by smudging etc. ‖ to become indistinct

blurb (blə:rb) *n.* a publisher's commendation of one of its books, usually printed ·on the wrapper or in advertising notices ‖ any similar sales copy or fulsome piece of publicizing

blur·ry (blə́:ri:) *comp.* **blur·ri·er** *superl.* **blur·ri·est** *adj.* marked by blurs ‖ indistinct

blurt (blə:rt) *v.t.* (with 'out') to say impulsively, or under pressure, *to blurt out the truth*

blush (blʌʃ) 1. *n.* a suffusion of the cheeks with red, from pleasure, shame, modesty etc. ‖ a rosy color, e.g. of a peach or an apple **at first blush** at first glance 2. *v.i.* (esp. of the cheeks) to become red, esp. from pleasure, shame, modesty etc. ‖ (with 'for') to feel shame

blush·er (blʌ́ʃər) *n.* face rouge that creates a natural-seeming shining quality

blus·ter (blʌ́stər) 1. *n.* a loud, gusty wind ‖ noisy, ineffectual anger 2. *v.i.* (of wind) to blow violently and gustily ‖ (of weather) to be violently windy ‖ to talk with histrionic anger, usually so as to assert one's own importance ‖ *v.t.* to force by overbearing talk **blús·ter·ous, blús·ter·y** *adjs*

boar (bɔr, bour) *n.* the uncastrated male pig ‖ its flesh

board (bɔrd, bourd) 1. *n.* a piece of sawn lumber longer than it is broad ‖ a square or oblong piece of thin wood or other similar material used for a special purpose ‖ (*basketball*) the backboard behind the basket ‖ (*hockey*) the wall surrounding the ice ‖ (*surfing*) the buoyant surfboard ‖ a council or authoritative body ‖ daily meals served in exchange for payment or services **above board** openly, without deceit **on board** aboard a ship, train etc. **to sweep the board** (in gambling) to win all the stakes 2. *v.t.* (often with up') to cover with boards or planks, close up (an opening) with boards ‖ to provide with meals, and often ·with lodging ‖ to make one's way onto (a ship, train or aircraft) as a passenger ‖ *v.i.* (usually with at' or 'with') to be given meals at a fixed rate over a certain period of time **to board out** to have meals in a house other than the one where one sleeps ‖ to place (children) in families for meals **bóard·er** *n.* a person who is given food and lodging by someone in exchange for a fee

boast (boust) 1. *n.* a claim about oneself, or something

connected with oneself, whether made with proper pride or with inordinate pride ‖ something one is proud of 2. *v.i.* to brag, make an exaggerated claim ‖ *v.t.* to be justly proud of **bóast·ful** *adj.*

boat (bout) 1. *n.* any small open vessel propelled by oars, sail, an engine, or paddles ‖ any ship from a liner to a dinghy ‖ a boat-shaped vessel for the table **in the same boat** running the same risks or sharing the same misfortunes 2. *v.i.* to go out rowing in a small boat for amusement

boat·swain (bóus'n, bóutswein) *n.* a ship's officer who calls men on duty

bob (bɒb) 1. *v. pres. part.* **bob·bing** *past* and *past part.* **bobbed** *v.t.* to lower and quickly raise again ‖ to perform with a quick jerky movement ‖ *v.i.* to move up and down in quick jerky movements ‖ to curtsy 2. *n.* a short, bouncing or jerky movement ‖ a curtsy

bob 1. *n.* a short, straight hair style for women ‖ the docked tail of a horse 2. *v.t. pres. part.* **bob·bing** *past* and *past part.* **bobbed** to style (hair) short and straight ‖ to dock (a horse's tail)

bob·o·link (bɒ́bəliŋk) *n.* a North American migratory songbird

bob·sled (bɒ́bsled) 1. *n.* a long sled with independent runners at front and back 2. *v.i. pres. part.* **bob·sled·ding** *past* and *past part.* **bob·sled·ded** to ride on a bobsled

bob·white (bɒ́bhwáit, bɒ́bwáit) *n.* a North American game bird of the genus *Colinus*

bode (boud) *pres. part.* **bod·ing** *past* and *past part.* **bod·ed** *v.t.* to portend, indicate by signs (something to come) ‖ *v.i.* (with 'well' or 'ill') to be a (good or bad) omen **bóde·ful** *adj.* (*rhet.*) warning of evil to come

bod·ice (bɒ́dis) *n.* the top part of a woman's dress

bod·i·ly (bɒ́d'li:) 1. *adj.* pertaining to the body 2. *adv.* in person ‖ altogether

bod·y (bɒ́di:) *pl.* **bod·ies** *n.* the physical substance of a man or animal ‖ a corpse ‖ the main portion of an army, plant, building etc. ‖ the main part of a document or printed article ‖ a collective unit of people ‖ a mass (of facts, ideas etc.) ‖ a mass of matter ‖ a rich, full flavor in wine ‖ the quality in cloth which makes it firm and durable ‖ (*printing*) the block of metal supporting the typeface **in a body** (of people) as a single group **to keep body and soul together** to manage to stay alive

bod·y·guard (bɒ́di:gɑrd) *n.* a man or group of men guarding the safety of another

bog (bɔg, bɒg) 1. *n.* an area of ground saturated with water and decayed vegetation 2. *v. pres. part.* **bog·ging** *past* and *past part.* **bogged** *v.t.* (often with 'down') to submerge into or as if into a bog ‖ *v.i.* (usually with 'down') to become sucked into or as if into a bog

bo·gey (bóugi:) *pl.* **bo·geys, bo·gies** *n.* (*golf*) one over par

bo·gey, bo·gy (bóugi:) *pl.* **bo·geys, bo·gies** *n.* an imaginary source of fear, a bugbear ‖ an evil goblin

bog·gle (bɒ́g'l) *pres. part.* **bog·gling** *past* and *past part.* **bog·gled** *v.i.* to hesitate or hold back because one is startled or fearful

bo·gus (bóugəs) *adj.* sham

boil (bɔil) 1. *v.i.* (of a liquid) to bubble at a high temperature and give off vapor ‖ to be cooked in boiling liquid ‖ to seethe like a boiling liquid ‖ to be very agitated ‖ *v.t.* to cook in boiling liquid ‖ to heat to the boiling point ‖ to make or clean by boiling **to boil away** to evaporate **to boil down** to reduce by boiling ‖ to condense ‖ to simplify **to boil down to** to signify basically **to boil over** to overflow while boiling **to keep the pot boiling** to make sure one has enough of a thing (usually money) 2. *n.* the boiling point ‖ the state of boiling **to bring to a boil** to heat until the boiling point is reached

boil·er (bɔ́ilər) *n.* (*engin.*) a container in which water can be heated under pressure and converted into steam

‖ a stove which heats water for conveyance to a hot-water system

bois·ter·ous (bɔ́istərəs, bɔ́istrəs) *adj.* gusty ‖ agreeably rough ‖ cheerfully loud

bold (bould) *adj.* brave ‖ daring ‖ confidently original ‖ well defined ‖ strongly assertive ‖ impudent

boll (boul) *n.* a capsule, esp. of cotton or flax

boll weevil a small gray weevil which lays its eggs in the bolls and squares of the cotton plant, doing very great damage

bo·lo·gna (bəlóuni:) *n.* a seasoned, boiled and smoked sausage of ground beef, pork and veal

bol·ster (bóulstər) 1. *n.* a long cylindrical pillow stretching from one side of a bed to the other or an often wedge-shaped pillow along the back of a sofa etc. ‖ a support, bolsterlike in shape, in some machines or instruments ‖ (*archit.*) a support, e.g. the crosspiece capping a pillar under a beam 2. *v.t.* to support, prop

bolt (boult) 1. *n.* a sliding bar for keeping a door closed ‖ the sliding piece moved in a lock by the key ‖ a thick tight roll of cloth ‖ a roll of wallpaper of a certain length ‖ a thunderbolt ‖ a quick dash, esp. one made so as to flee **a bolt from the blue** an utter surprise, often disagreeable **to have shot one's bolt** to have taken a decisive action and be left with no possibility of turning back etc. **to make a bolt for it** to try to escape by running away 2. *v.t.* to secure (a door or window) with a bolt ‖ to fasten together with bolts ‖ to eat very quickly ‖ to break with, withdraw support from (a political party) ‖ *v.i.* to make off at a run ‖ to run away out of control ‖ to withdraw support from a political party

bomb (bɒm) 1. *n.* an explosive missile dropped from an aircraft, fired from a mortar or thrown by hand, which explodes on contact or by means of a time mechanism ‖ (*basketball*) a long shot ‖ (*football*) a long pass ‖ (*theater*) a flop 2. *v.t.* to drop bombs upon ‖ *v.i.* to drop bombs **to bomb out** to deprive (someone) of home, business premises etc. by bombing **to bomb up** to put bombs into (an aircraft) ‖ to take on a load of bombs ‖ (*colloq.*) to fail 3. *adj.* **bombed** drunk

bom·bard (bɒmbárd) *v.t.* to attack with big guns, hurl shells and bombs repeatedly at ‖ to pester (with questions, complaints etc.) ‖ (*phys.*) to subject (a substance) to rays or the impact of small particles

bom·bar·dier (bɒmbərdíər) *n.* that member of a bomber crew who aims the bombs at the target

bom·bard·ment (bɒmbárdmənt) *n.* a bombarding or being bombarded ‖ a bombarding attack

bom·bast (bɒ́mbæst) *n.* swollen rhetoric, pretentious language, hollow ranting **bom·bas·tic** *adj.* **bom·bas·ti·cal·ly** *adv.*

bo·nan·za (bənǽnzə) *n.* a very rich deposit of ore in veins of gold or silver ‖ something bringing profit or prosperity

bon·bon (bɒ́nbɒn, bɔ́bɔ̃) *pl.* **bon·bons** (bɒ́nbɒnz, bɔ́bɔ̃) *n.* a sweet candy

bond (bɒnd) 1. *n.* that which unites ‖ a written legal agreement by someone to pay money to another person ‖ a document issued by a government or a company recording money borrowed and the promise to pay back with interest to the holder ‖ bond paper ‖ (*chem.*) any of several mechanisms by which atoms, groups of atoms, or ions are held together in a molecular or crystal structure ‖ a method of laying bricks or stone to give strength and pleasing appearance ‖ (*rhet.*) a shackle **in bond** kept in charge of customs officers in a warehouse until the appropriate duty is paid **to take out of bond** to remove (goods) from

the customs warehouse after paying the duty 2. *v.t.* to place bricks in building (a structure) in such a way as to hold them firmly together ‖ to place (imported goods) in bond ‖ to mortgage

bond·age (bɒ́ndidʒ) *n.* (*hist.*) slavery ‖ (*rhet.*) subjection to the constraint of duty or of some strong desire etc.

bond·ed (bɒ́ndid) *adj.* (of goods) placed in bond ‖ (of a warehouse) under bond to pay duty on goods stored ‖ attached by adhesive to make a single product of two components

bone (boun) 1. *n.* one of the hard parts of the skeleton of a vertebrate animal ‖ the hard substance which composes it ‖ (*pl.*) the living body ‖ (*pl.*) the dead body **to feel in one's bones** to know intuitively **to have a bone to pick with someone** to have a reproach or complaint to make to someone **to make no bones about (something)** to be blunt about (a matter) 2. *v.t. pres. part.* **bon·ing** *past* and *past part.* **boned** to remove the bones from (fish, poultry)

bon·fire (bɒ́nfaiər) *n.* a fire built outdoors, for burning rubbish, for festivity or celebration, or sometimes as a signal

bon·net (bɒ́nit) *n.* a kind of hat worn mainly by babies, fastened under the chin with ribbons or strings ‖ (*hist.*) a woman's headdress fitting closely round the head ‖ a cap worn by Scotsmen ‖ a protective cover over parts of some machines

bo·nus (bóunəs) *pl.* **bo·nus·es** *n.* a grant of money as a gratuity to workers ‖ a special earned payment based e.g. on production ‖ an extra dividend or gift of stock or shares from a company to its shareholders ‖ anything welcome that one receives over and above what is expected or usual

bon·y (bóuni:) *comp.* **bon·i·er** *superl.* **bon·i·est** *adj.* (of persons) with large, prominent bones ‖ (of persons and animals) very thin ‖ full of bones ‖ like or consisting of bone or bones

boo (bu:) 1. *n.* a cry of contemptuous disapproval ‖ an interjection made suddenly and loudly to cause fright 2. *v. pres. part.* **boo·ing** *past* and *past part.* **booed** *v.t.* to shout contemptuous boos at ‖ *v.i.* to shout contemptuous boos

boo·by (bú:bi:) *pl.* **boo·bies** *n.* a stupid fool, a clumsy lout

booby trap a trap laid for the unwary as a practical joke, often humiliating ‖ (*mil.*) a harmless-looking object containing an explosive charge liable to go off when disturbed

book (buk) *n.* a number of printed pages fastened together and enclosed in a cover ‖ a literary composition ‖ a treatise ‖ one of the works which make up the Bible ‖ a libretto ‖ (*pl.*) business accounts ‖ a number of stamps, tickets, checks etc. fastened together as in a book ‖ (*betting*) a record of bets made by a bookmaker at a race, esp. a horserace, *to make book* **in someone's bad** (or **black**) **books** out of favor with someone **in someone's good books** in favor with someone **on the books** included in a list of members **to read someone like a book** to know by intuition what someone is thinking **to speak by the book** to speak authoritatively, with appropriate information **to take a leaf out of someone's book** to learn a lesson from someone and imitate him

book *v.t.* to reserve in advance ‖ to put down someone's name for or issue (such advance tickets) ‖ to enter (someone's name) on a reservation list ‖ to engage in advance (a speaker or performer) ‖ to record (an order)

book·bind·er (búkbaindər) *n.* someone who binds books

book·bind·ing (búkbaindiŋ) *n.* the craft of binding books

---

by hand or machine

book·ish (búkiʃ) *adj.* of or relating to books ‖ fond of reading and studying ‖ reflecting vicarious experience gathered from books, rather than practical experience

book·keep·ing (búkki:piŋ) *n.* the regular recording of the essential facts about the transactions of a business or enterprise

book·let (búklit) *n.* a book of not very many pages, usually in paper covers

boom (bu:m) **1.** *n.* a hollow-sounding roar, as of a distant explosion ‖ a sudden increase in a particular business or commodity etc., or in general prosperity ‖ a surge in popularity **2.** *v.i.* to make a hollow roar ‖ to be notably successful or prosperous or in demand ‖ *v.t.* to cause to boom

boom *n.* a long spar, usually of wood, with one end attached to the mast, used to stretch the sail foot ‖ a floating barrier, usually of wood or chain, across a harbor or river mouth, used to prevent the access of enemy ships, or to keep sawmill logs from floating away ‖ a mass of floating logs thus contained

boom·er·ang (bú:məræŋ) *n.* a curved or smoothly angular wooden missile used by Australian aborigines ‖ an argument or idea which rebounds and harms the originator

boon (bu:n) *n.* a blessing, something that comes as a help or comfort

boor (búər) *n.* an uncouth, insensitive, ill-bred person **bóor·ish** *adj.*

boost (bu:st) **1.** *n.* a lifting up ‖ something that gives an impetus or encouragement **2.** *v.t.* to push from below, hoist ‖ to increase the power, value etc., of (an industrial scheme, person etc.) ‖ to help, assist ‖ *(elec.)* to raise the voltage in (a battery, circuit etc.) **bóost·er** *n.* a substance which increases the efficiency of an immunizing agent, or a dose renewing it ‖ *(engin.)* a machine which increases pressure, voltage etc. ‖ *(rocketry)* the first stage of a multistage rocket, used to supply the main thrust for takeoff

boot (bu:t) **1.** *n.* an article of footwear coming to the ankle or higher ‖ the part of a reed pipe encasing the reed ‖ *(baseball)* a fielding error ‖ a naval or marine recruit in the first stage of training ‖ *(pop.)* dismissal **the boot** (or **shoe) is on the other foot** the precise opposite is the case **to have one's heart in one's boots** to feel sudden despairing apprehension **to lick someone's boots** to flatter someone in a servile way **2.** *v.t.* to kick

booth (bu:θ, *Br.* bu:ð) *pl.* **booths** (bu:θs, bu:ðz) *n.* a temporary structure of canvas and boards, esp. a covered stall in a fair or market ‖ a small permanent structure affording privacy

boot·leg (bú:tlɛg) **1.** *v.t. pres. part.* **boot·leg·ging** *past* and *past part.* **boot·legged** *(pop.)* to smuggle ‖ *(pop.)* to sell or make (alcoholic liquor) illegally **2.** *adj.* *(pop.)* illicit **bóot·leg·ger** *n.* a smuggler of liquor, esp. during Prohibition in America

boo·ty (bú:ti:) *pl.* **boo·ties** *n.* spoils taken in war, or by thieves ‖ any rich prize

booze (bu:z) **1.** *v.i. pres. part.* **booz·ing** *past* and *past part.* **boozed** *(pop.)* to drink alcoholic liquor to excess **2.** *n. (pop.)* alcoholic drink **booz·y** *comp.* **booz·i·er** *superl.* **booz·i·est** *adj.*

bor·der (bɔ́rdər) **1.** *n.* an edge, an outer side ‖ a frontier, a boundary between two countries ‖ the state between one condition and another ‖ a strip (often ornamental) around the edge of a handkerchief, dress etc. **2.** *v.t.* to put or be a border around ‖ *v.i.* (with 'on') to be in an adjoining position ‖ (with 'on' or 'upon') to come near to something specified

bore (bɔr, bour) **1.** *n.* a deep hole made by drilling in the ground to find oil etc. ‖ the internal cylinder of a gun barrel ‖ the gauge of a shotgun barrel ‖ the caliber of other gun barrels **2.** *v. pres. part.* **bor·ing** *past* and *past part.* **bored** *v.t.* to drill (a hole) ‖ to create by boring, *to bore a tunnel* ‖ to force (a way) as if by drilling ‖ *v.i.* to make a hole by drilling or

as if by drilling

bore·dom (bɔ́rdəm, bóurdəm) *n.* the state or quality of being bored, the condition of having one's interest either unaroused or extinguished

born (bɔrn) *past part.* of BEAR(to give birth) ‖ *adj.* having a certain natural characteristic **born of** *(rhet.)* arising from

bor·ough (bɔ́:rou, bárou) *n.* a municipal corporation resembling an incorporated town ‖ one of five political divisions of Greater New York ‖ a county in Alaska

bor·row (bɔ́rou, bárou) *v.t.* to take (something) on the understanding that it will be returned later ‖ to appropriate, to take and use (an idea etc.) not thought of by oneself ‖ when subtracting, to take 1 from a figure in the minuend in order to add 10 to the next lower denomination, when the latter is less than the corresponding figure in the subtrahend

bos·om (búzəm, bú:zəm) **1.** *n.* a human being's breast ‖ a woman's breasts ‖ something suggesting the human breast ‖ that part of a dress etc. covering the breast ‖ the space between this part of the dress and the body **2.** *adj.* intimate, beloved

boss (bɔs, bɒs) **1.** *n.* an employer ‖ a foreman ‖ a person in charge ‖ the professional manager of a political organization **2.** *v.t.* to direct or manage (a business, a show etc.) **to boss about** (or **around**) to order about in a domineeering way

bos·sy (bɔ́si:, bɒ́si:) *comp.* **bos·si·er** *superl.* **bos·si·est** *adj.* domineering, fond of giving orders

bo·tan·ic (bətǽnik) *adj.* botanical **bo·tán·i·cal** *adj.* of or pertaining to botany

bot·a·nist (bɒ́t'nist) *n.* a specialist in botany

bot·a·ny (bɒ́t'ni:) *n.* the branch of biology concerned with plant life and all its manifestations ‖ the plant life of a given region

botch (bɒtʃ) **1.** *n.* a badly done piece of work **2.** *v.t.* to bungle (a piece of work) **bótched** *adj.*

both (bouθ) **1.** *adj.* the two, each of two **2.** *pron.* the one and the other

both·er (bɒ́ðər) **1.** *n.* inconvenience ‖ a nuisance ‖ disturbance ‖ a fuss **2.** *v.t.* to worry persistently ‖ *v.i.* (with 'about' or 'with') to take trouble ‖ (with the infinitive) to take the trouble **3.** *interj.* an expression of impatience

both·er·some (bɒ́ðərsəm) *adj.* causing bother

bot·tle (bɒ́t'l) **1.** *n.* a narrow-necked vessel without a handle, usually of glass, for containing liquid ‖ the contents of a bottle ‖ the amount contained by a bottle **the bot·tle** alcoholic liquor **2.** *v.t. pres. part.* **bot·tling** *past* and *past part.* **bot·tled** to put into bottles ‖ to preserve in glass jars **to bottle up** to restrain (feelings etc.)

bot·tle·neck (bɒ́t'lnɛk) *n.* a narrowing in a road, where traffic may become congested ‖ any similar obstruction to flow

bot·tom (bɒ́təm) **1.** *adj.* lowest, last ‖ frequenting the bottom **to bet one's bottom dollar** to stake everything one has **2.** *n.* the lowest interior or exterior part of anything ‖ the seat (of a chair) ‖ the buttocks ‖ the bed of the sea, a lake, river, or pond ‖ the low land in a river basin ‖ any low-lying land ‖ the less exalted or distinguished end of a table, class etc. ‖ the basic facts, foundation, reality **at bottom** essentially **from the bottom of my heart** with deep feeling **to go to the bottom** (of a ship) to sink **to send to the bottom** to sink (a ship) **3.** *v.i.* to touch the bottom (of the sea etc.) ‖ *v.t.* to put a bottom on

bot·u·lism (bɒ́tʃələizəm) *n. (med.* and *vet.)* food poisoning

bou·doir (bú:dwɑr, bú:dwɔr) *n.* a lady's small private room

bough (bau) *n.* a branch of a tree, esp. a main branch

bouil·la·baisse (bu:jæbes, bu:ljəbéis) *n.* a Provençal dish containing various Mediterranean fish and shellfish cooked in water or white wine, with olive oil, garlic, tomato, saffron, and herbs

bouil·lon (búljɒn, búljən) *n.* a clear soup made esp.

from beef

boul·der (bóuldər) *n.* a large stone, or mass of rock, rounded and smoothed by water, ice or wind

boul·e·vard (búləvɑrd, bú:ləvɑrd) *n.* a broad street, usually with trees on either side or down the middle

bounce (bauns) **1.** *n.* a sudden rebound, e.g. of a rubber ball ‖ vitality **2.** *v. pres. part.* **bounc·ing** *past* and *past part.* **bounced** *v.t.* to cause to rebound ‖ *(pop.)* to throw out of a bar etc. ‖ *v.i.* to rebound ‖ to jump up ‖ *(pop., of a check)* to be refused by a bank because there is not enough money in the account to cover it **bóunc·er** *n.* an attendant employed to eject people who make themselves a nuisance in dance halls, nightclubs etc. **bóunc·ing** *adj.* full of health and vitality

bound (baund) *adj.* (often with 'for') making the trip to, on the way to ‖ going, *homeward bound*

bound 1. *n.* a limit of an estate etc. ‖ (usually *pl.*) restraining rules, laws or standards, *beyond the bounds of decency* **out of bounds** not to be entered **2.** *v.t.* to set limits to ‖ to set upper or lower permitted limits ‖ (esp. in passive, with 'by') to delimit by boundaries

bound·a·ry (báundəri:, báundri:) *pl.* **bound·a·ries** *n.* the real or undesrtood line marking a limit

boun·te·ous (báunti:əs) *adj. (old-fash.)* generously giving ‖ freely and generously given ‖ plentiful

boun·ti·ful (báuntifəl) *adj.* bounteous, freely giving ‖ *(old-fash.)* abundant

boun·ty (báunti:) *pl.* **boun·ties** *n.* liberality in giving, generosity ‖ a sum of money given as a subsidy or reward, esp. by a government

bou·quet (bu:kéi, boukéi) *n.* a bunch of flowers ‖ the distinctive perfume of a wine

bour·bon (bə́:rbən) *n.* a whiskey distilled from mainly corn mash

bour·geois (búərʒwɑ, burʒwá) **1.** *adj.* belonging to or typical of the middle classes ‖ having self-centered, materialistic and conformist ideas **2.** *n.* someone having such limited ideas ‖ a member of the middle classes

bour·geoi·sie (buərʒwɑzí:) *n.* the middle classes ‖ (in Marxist ideology) the capitalist class

bout (baut) *n.* a period (of work or other activity) ‖ a fit or period (of illness) ‖ a fight, trial of strength

bou·tique (bu:tí:k) *n.* a chic little store selling smart or fashionable clothes and accessories

bo·vine (bóuvain, bóuvin, bóuvi:n) *adj.* of or pertaining to an ox or a cow ‖ (of humans) cowlike

bow (bau) *n. (naut., often pl.)* the forepart of a ship ‖ the bow oar

bow (bou) **1.** *n.* a weapon made of a long strip of wood, tensely arched by means of a cord stretched between the ends, used for shooting arrows ‖ a strip of wood with horsehairs stretched between the ends, used in playing the violin and some other string instruments ‖ a stroke of such a bow ‖ a slipknot, often ornamental, formed by doubling a shoelace, ribbon, etc., into one or two loops **to have more than one string to one's bow** to have more than one plan or idea **2.** *v.t.* to use a bow on (a violin etc.) ‖ *v.i.* to use the bow on a violin etc. ‖ to curve in an arch

bow (bau) **1.** *n.* a bending of the head or body, in respect, greeting, assent etc. **2.** *v.t.* to cause to bend ‖ to express by bowing ‖ (with 'in' or 'out') to show (a person) in or out with a bow ‖ *v.i.* to submit or give in ‖ to bend the head or body in respect, greeting, politeness etc. **to bow one's knee** to genuflect

bow·el (báuəl, baul) *n.* (usually *pl.*) the intestine, the lower end of the alimentary canal ‖ entrails ‖ *(rhet.)* the innermost part

bowl (boul) **1.** *n.* a heavy wooden ball for rolling in the game of lawn bowling, esp. one shaped and weighted on one side to make it run a curved course **2.** *v.t.* to make (something, esp. a hoop) roll along the ground ‖ to score at bowling ‖ *v.i.* to play lawn bowling ‖ to go bowling ‖ to have a turn at bowling or lawn bowling ‖ to move smoothly and rapidly, esp. in a vehicle **to bowl over** to knock down ‖ to overwhelm

bowl *n.* a deep, round basin or dish for holding liquids, food etc. ‖ the contents of such a dish ‖ the bowl-shaped part of anything

bow·leg·ged (bóulegid, bóulegd) *adj.* with legs curved outwards

bowl·ing (bóuliŋ) *n.* any of several games in which pins are bowled at ‖ the activity of playing lawn bowling

bowling alley a long wooden lane for bowling ‖ the building containing the alleys

box (bɒks) **1.** *n.* a container, usually lidded, made of a stiff material such as pasteboard, wood, metal etc. ‖ the contents of a box ‖ the quantity a box will hold ‖ a small separate compartment in a theater ‖ a special compartment in a court of law ‖ a compartment in a stable for a horse ‖ *(baseball)* the space where the batter stands **2.** *v.t.* to enclose in a box, or a small space ‖ to divide off from other compartments **to box the compass** *(naut.)* to name the 32 points of the compass in their right order ‖ to turn in a circle in argument, etc. **to box up** to confine

box 1. *n.* a cuff or slap **2.** *v.i.* to fight with the fists covered in thickly padded gloves, in sport

box·car (bɒ́kskɑr) *n. (rail.)* a closed, roofed freight car

box·ing (bɒ́ksiŋ) *n.* the sport of fighting with the fists, in accordance with the rules laid down

boxing gloves heavily padded, laced leather mittens worn in boxing

box kite a kite of paper or canvas stretched over a light frame in two boxlike sections

box office the ticket office in a theater ‖ receipts from a play

box spring mattress a mattress consisting of a honeycomb arrangement of spiral springs which are prevented from buckling by being isolated from each other, in cloth compartments

boy (bɔi) *n.* a male child, till puberty or young manhood ‖ a son of any age

boy·cott (bɔ́ikɒt) **1.** *v.t.* to join with others in refusing to have any dealings with (some other individual or group) ‖ *(commerce)* to exclude (a product) from a market by united action **2.** *n.* the act of boycotting

boy·ish (bɔ́iiʃ) *adj.* characteristic of a boy

bra (brɑ) *n.* a brassiere

brace (breis) *n. (carpentry)* the tool into which a bit is inserted for boring holes ‖ *(engin.)* a rod, girder etc., used to strengthen a structure by its power to hold under tension ‖ (often *pl.*) a dental appliance worn to straighten crooked teeth ‖ a linking mark } in printing ‖ *(pl.* **brace**) a pair, couple, esp. of pistols and of certain game birds or hunted animals

brace *pres. part.* **brac·ing** *past* and *past part.* **braced** *v.t.* to fasten tightly ‖ to stretch into a state of tension ‖ to strengthen so as to resist pressure or weight, or to support ‖ to prepare to take a strain or a shock ‖ to stimulate ‖ *(naut.)* to move (a sail) by braces

brace·let (bréislit) *n.* an ornamental band or chain worn on the arm

brack·et (brǽkit) **1.** *n.* a right-angled piece of metal, wood, stone etc. of which one surface bears on the upright and so allows the other surface to form a support ‖ one of a pair of punctuation marks [] to isolate the words enclosed in them from the surrounding text ‖ a social classification, involving an upper and a lower limit **2.** *v.t.* to enclose within brackets,

---

esp. *(math.)* to enclose (certain figures) in brackets to establish a relationship with other figures ‖ to couple together to show some kind of equality

brack·ish (brǽkiʃ) *adj.* (of water) impure, slightly salt ‖ of unpleasant taste

brad (bræd) *n.* a thin, flat, slight-headed, short nail of uniform thickness, tapering in width

brag (bræg) **1.** *n.* a boast ‖ boasting talk ‖ that which is boasted about ‖ a card game like poker **2.** *v.i. pres. part.* **brag·ging** past and past part. **bragged** (often with 'of' or 'about') to boast

brag·gart (brǽgərt) *n.* someone who brags, a habitual boaster

braid (breid) *n.* a plait of hair made by weaving several strands together ‖ anything plaited ‖ silk etc. woven into an ornamental binding and used esp. on uniforms

braid *v.t.* to plait (esp. hair) ‖ to ornament or trim by binding with ribbon ‖ to edge with braid

Braille (breil) *n.* a system of representing letters and figures by raised dots, for use by the blind

brain (brein) **1.** *n.* that part of the central nervous system within the cranium that is the organ of thought, memory and emotion ‖ in invertebrates, the corresponding regulating ganglion ‖ *(loosely)* the intellect **to have** (or **get**) **something on the brain** to be (or become) obsessed by something **to pick someone's brain** (or **brains**) to find out and use another's ideas **to rack one's brain** (or **brains**) to think very hard **2.** *v.t.* to dash out the brains of

brain·y (bréini:) *comp.* **brain·i·er** superl. **brain·i·est** adj. *(pop.)* intelligent, clever above average

braise (breiz) *pres. part.* **brais·ing** past and past part. **braised** *v.t.* to cook slowly in fat and very little liquid in a tightly covered pan

brake (breik) **1.** *n.* a device for diminishing or preventing the motion of a body, usually by opposing a frictional force **2.** *v. pres. part.* **brak·ing** past and past part. **braked** *v.t.* to slow down (a moving body) ‖ *v.i.* to operate or apply a brake

bram·ble (brǽmb'l) *n.* a brier, any prickly bush or vine

bram·bly (brǽmbli:) *comp.* **bram·bli·er** superl. **bram·bli·est** adj. resembling or having brambles

bran (bræn) *n.* the broken husks of grain separated from the ears by threshing

branch (bræntʃ, brɑntʃ) **1.** *n.* a stem growing out from the trunk or from a bough of a tree ‖ a similar division ‖ a subunit **2.** *(computer)* leaving the normal sequence of instructions ‖ selection of one of several paths based on a standard branch instruction **3.** *v.i.* to put forth branches ‖ to subdivide ‖ (with 'out' or 'off') to spring as though in branches **to branch away** to diverge **to branch out** to expand in scope, enlarge one's activities

brand (brænd) **1.** *n.* a mark made by a hot iron, e.g. on cattle to identify ownership ‖ a trademark ‖ a proprietary make, blend etc. ‖ a piece of burning or charred wood ‖ an iron stamp for burning a mark ‖ a blight on leaves etc., characterized by a burnt look **2.** *v.t.* to mark (cattle etc.) with a hot iron ‖ to stigmatize morally

bran·died (brǽndi:d) *adj.* preserved in brandy

branding iron an implement of iron used to brand cattle etc.

bran·dish (brǽndiʃ) *v.t* to wave about or flourish (a weapon etc.), often menacingly

bran·dy (brǽndi:) *pl.* **bran·dies** *n.* a spirit distilled from wine ‖ a liquor distilled from fermented fruit juices

brash (bræʃ) *adj.* tiresomely self-satisfied and bragging, cocky ‖ reckless, foolhardy

brass (bræs, brɑs) *n.* a yellow alloy of copper and zinc ‖ the color of this alloy ‖ impudence ‖ *(pl.)* the brass ‖ *(pop.)* brass hats collectively **the brass** the brass wind instruments of an orchestra **to get down to brass tacks** to go to the (often financial) heart of a matter, and stop talking peripherally

bras·siere, bras·sière (brəzír) *n.* a light garment which supports a woman's breasts

brass·y (brǽsi:, brɑsi:) *comp.* **brass·i·er** superl. **brass·i·est** adj. of or like brass, esp. in color or sound ‖ (of a voice) harsh and suggesting self-satisfaction (of manner) ‖ cocksure

brat (bræt) *n.* (usually contemptuous or impatient) a child, esp. a bad-mannered or troublesome one

bra·va·do (brəvádou) *n.* a bold front, a pretense of indifference to risk or misfortune

brave (breiv) **1.** *comp.* **brav·er** superl. **brav·est** adj. bold, courageous, mastering fear ‖ testifying to this quality ‖ displaying well **2.** *n.* a North American Indian warrior **3.** *v.t. pres. part.* **brav·ing** past and past part. **braved** to face the risk of **to brave it out** to see a thing through to the end with courage

brav·er·y (bréivəri:, bréivri:) *n.* courage

brá·vo (brávou, brɑvóu) **1.** *interj.* Well done! **2.** *n.* *(pl.)* enthusiastic cries of approval

bra·vu·ra (brəvúərə, brəvjúərə) *n.* swagger ‖ *(mus.)* technical daring and display ‖ *(painting)* spirited brushwork

brawl (brɔl) **1.** *n.* a noisy, undignified fight **2.** *v.i.* to quarrel or fight noisily

brawn (brɔn) *n.* muscular strength ‖ the pickled and potted flesh of a pig **bráwn·y** *comp.* **brawn·i·er** superl. **brawn·i·est** adj. muscular

bray (brei) **1.** *n.* the cry of an ass ‖ a similar loud, rasping noise **2.** *v.i.* to make the cry or noise of an ass ‖ *v.t.* (with 'out') to utter harshly and loudly ‖ to sound harshly and loudly

bra·zen (bréiz'n) **1.** *adj. (rhet.)* made of brass ‖ of a harsh yellow color like brass ‖ harsh and loud ‖ bold and shameless **2.** *v.t.* **to brazen it out, to brazen one's way out** to extricate oneself from a difficult situation by putting on a bold act

bra·zier (bréizər) *n.* a metal holder for burning coal or coke in the open

breach (bri:tʃ) **1.** *n.* the breaking of a legal or moral obligation ‖ an estrangement ‖ a gap made by guns in a wall or fortifications ‖ a gap in a hedge, wall etc. **to stand in the breach** to be ready to beat off an attack ‖ to be ready to take responsibility in a crisis **to throw oneself into the breach** to hurl oneself wholeheartedly into some emergency task **2.** *v.t.* to break through ‖ to make a gap in

bread (bred) **1.** *n.* a food made by moistening and kneading flour (usually leavened by yeast) or meal and baking it **to know which side one's bread is buttered on** to know what is to one's advantage or when one should count oneself lucky **2.** *v.t. (cookery)* to coat with breadcrumbs

bread and butter a buttered slice or slices of bread ‖ a livelihood **bread-and-butter** (bréd'nbʌ́tər) *adj.* concerned with earning a livelihood

breadth (bredθ, bretθ) *n.* the linear dimension measured from side to side of a surface or volume and at right angles to its length ‖ a piece of cloth etc. considered in respect to its width ‖ spaciousness ‖ largeness, generosity (of mind, sympathies etc.)

break (breik) **1.** *v. pres. part.* **break·ing** past **broke** (brouk) *past part.* **bro·ken** (bróukən) *v.t.* to cause to fall into pieces, by force or by accident ‖ to cause to snap in two ‖ to interrupt the continuity of ‖ to reduce the damaging power ‖ to shatter, destroy ‖ to suppress, bring to an end ‖ to demote ‖ to disobey ‖ to disregard, violate ‖ to announce (startling or bad news) ‖ to discover or work out the secret of (a code) ‖ to split into smaller units ‖ *v.i.* to fall suddenly to pieces ‖ (of waves) to curl over and crash down in foam ‖ to burst ‖ to happen explosively or suddenly ‖ to disintegrate under pressure ‖ (of the voice) to change from one register to another ‖ to show a dramatic fall in prices or values ‖ to come to an end ‖ to come out of a clinch, huddle etc. ‖ to come into general knowledge ‖ *(phon.,* of vowels) to change into a diphthong ‖ (of a pitched baseball) to curve near the plate **to break a record** to do better than the best competitive performance officially recorded **to break away** to leave suddenly ‖ (in a race) to start too soon **to break down** to destroy ‖ to go out of working condition ‖ to have an emotional, physical or nervous collapse **to break in** to force an entry ‖ to make (a young horse) tractable ‖ to train (a person) to a new job **to break in on** to interrupt (e.g. a conversation) **to break into** to enter forcibly ‖ to enter in order to rob **to break loose** (or **free**) to escape (from clutches, handcuffs etc.) **to break off** to separate (a part) from the whole ‖ to put an abrupt end to **to break open** to force open **to break out** to start suddenly ‖ to become covered with pimples ‖ (with 'of' or 'from') to escape from **to break the bank** (gambling) to win all the dealer's money **to break up** to come to an end ‖ to put a stop to **to break with** to sever relations with ‖ to stop conforming to **2.** n. a gap, the result of breaking, a rupture ‖ (rhet., of day) the beginning ‖ an interruption ‖ a short pause, e.g. between periods of work ‖ (good or bad) fortune ‖ (mus.) the point where one register of the voice, or of certain wind instruments, changes to the next ‖ a sudden drop in prices on the exchange ‖ (pool) the shot that scatters the balls ‖ (bowling) the playing of a frame without a strike or a spare ‖ an attempt to run away, *to make a break for it* **bréak·a·ble** adj. **bréak·a·bles** pl. n. articles easily broken **bréak·age** n. a breaking ‖ a thing broken ‖ a fee or allowance for what has been broken

break·er (bréikər) n. a wave breaking into foam on the shore ‖ a huge wave with a foaming white crest

break·fast (brékfəst) **1.** n. the first meal of the day **2.** v.t. to eat breakfast

break·wa·ter (bréikwɒtər, bréikwɒtər) n. a protective seawall built to break the force of the waves

breast (brest) **1.** n. the upper front part of the human body between the neck and the abdomen ‖ the corresponding part of an animal ‖ a mammary gland ‖ that part of a coat or dress covering the breast ‖ anything analogous to a human or animal breast **to make a clean breast of** to confess **2.** v.t. to struggle up and over

breast·bone (bréstb'oun) n. the sternum

breath (breθ) n. air drawn into or expelled from the lungs ‖ a slight movement of air ‖ air carrying fragrance ‖ respiration ‖ (rhet.) the capacity to breathe ‖ a whisper, suggestion ‖ a slight pause ‖ (phon.) a hiss or puff, produced e.g. in pronouncing 's' or 'p' **a breath of fresh air** an invigorating influence **in the same breath** at the same moment **out of breath** unable to draw breath quickly enough after violent exercise **to catch one's breath** to gasp in a little air as the result of an emotional reflex ‖ to stop to rest so as to breathe normally again **to draw breath** (rhet.) to breathe, live **to save one's breath** to keep quiet, stop talking, because argument is useless **to take one's breath away** to shock or astonish one **to waste one's breath** to talk to no avail **under** (or **below**) **one's breath** in a whisper

breath·er (bri:ðər) n. (pop.) a short rest

breath·ing (brí:ðiŋ) n. respiration

breathe (bri:ð) pres. part. **breath·ing** past and past part. **breathed** v.i. to draw in air and send it out from the lungs ‖ (rhet.) to live ‖ (of wind) to blow gently ‖ v.t. to take in (air etc.) into the lungs ‖ to exhale (esp. fragrance) ‖ to make naturally evident **not to breathe a word of** to say nothing of, not tell anyone about **to breathe again** (or **freely**) to recover from fear or anxiety **to breathe new life into** to revive, encourage or invigorate **to breathe one's last** (or **last breath**) (rhet.) to die

breech (bri:tʃ) n. (mil.) the part of a cannon behind the barrel, where the shell is inserted ‖ the back part of a rifle

breed (bri:d) **1.** n. a particular group of domestic animals related by descent from common ancestors, visibly similar in most characteristics and usually incapable of maintaining its distinctive qualities in nature ‖ a similar group of plants **2.** v. pres. part. **breed·ing** past and past part. **bred** (bred) v.t. to produce (young) ‖ to give rise to ‖ to mate (animals) ‖ v.i. to reproduce

breed·ing (brí:diŋ) n. the propagation of plants or animals, esp. so as to improve their useful properties ‖ distinction of manners

breeze (bri:z) **1.** n. a gentle wind ‖ (pop.) something easy **2.** v.i. pres. part. **breez·ing** past and past part. **breezed** (pop., with 'in') to pay a casual call ‖ to move at a pleasantly easy speed

breez·y (brí:zi) comp. **breez·i·er** superl. **breez·i·est** adj. played over by pleasant light winds ‖ pleasantly windy ‖ cheerful and casual

brev·i·ty (bréviti:) n. shortness, esp. of time ‖ conciseness of speech or writing

brew (bru:) **1.** n. a drink made by brewing ‖ the process of brewing ‖ the amount or quality of something brewed **2.** v.t. to make (beer or ale) ‖ to make (tea) by infusion ‖ to foment ‖ v.i. to brew ale or beer ‖ (of beer, tea etc.) to be being prepared ‖ to gather force

brew·er·y (brú:əri:, brú:ri:) pl. **brew·er·ies** n. a building housing machinery for brewing beer or ale

bribe (braib) **1.** n. a secret gift (usually of money) offered to a person in a position of trust to persuade him to turn his power to the advantage of the person offering the gift ‖ any enticement meant to condition behavior **2.** v.t. pres. part. **brib·ing** past and past part. **bribed** to give a bribe to ‖ to secure by bribes, *to bribe one's way* **brib·er·y** n.

brick (brik) **1.** n. a block of fired clay and sand used in building ‖ a child's building block of wood, plastic etc. ‖ anything brick-shaped ‖ the red color of brick ‖ (pop.) someone brave or good-hearted **2.** v.t. (with 'up', 'in') to fill in (a space) with bricks

brid·al (bráid'l) adj. relating to a bride or a wedding

bride (braid) n. a woman on her wedding day ‖ a newly married woman

bride·groom (bráidgru:m, bráidgrum) n. a man on his wedding day

brides·maid (bráidzmeid) n. a girl or a young woman, usually unmarried, who attends the bride on her wedding day

bridge (bridʒ) **1.** n. a structure carrying a road, railroad or path over a road, railroad, river or ravine ‖ the movable wooden part of a violin or related instrument, over which the strings are stretched ‖ the part of a pair of glasses fitting over the nose ‖ (naut.) a platform amidships for the officers on watch, from which the vessel is commanded ‖ (dentistry) a device for anchoring artificial to natural teeth ‖ (engin.) a gantry ‖ the upper bony part of the nose **2.** v.t. pres. part. **bridg·ing** past and past part. **bridged** to make a bridge over ‖ to cross over, *to bridge a gap in conversation*

bridge n. a skilled card game of E. European origin, derived from whist, for four people

bri·dle (bráid'l) **1.** n. the headgear, made up of headstall, bit and reins, by which a horse is guided and controlled ‖ a check, a restraining influence ‖ (naut.) a mooring cable **2.** v. pres. part. **bri·dling** past and past part. **bri·dled** v.t. to put a bridle on (a horse) ‖ to restrain (emotions, ambitions etc.)

brief (bri:f) **1.** adj. lasting a short time ‖ concise ‖ short in length ‖ curt **2.** n. (law) a concise presentation of the facts of a client's case for counsel ‖ any concise summary prepared for someone else to act on ‖ *(pl.)* shorts, underpants **in brief** in short **to hold no brief for** not to advocate 3. *v.t.* to instruct by brief ‖ to employ as counsel ‖ to summarize (facts) in a brief

brig (brig) *n. (Am. Navy)* a ship's prison

bri·gade (brigéid) **1.** *n. (mil.)* one of the subdivisions of an army ‖ (outside an army) a disciplined group, *fire brigade* **2.** *v.t. pres. part.* **bri·gad·ing** *past and past part.* **bri·gad·ed** to form into a brigade

brig·and (brígənd) *n.* a member of a band of men who rob and plunder, a bandit **brig·and·age** *n.*

bright (brait) **1.** *adj.* reflecting or giving out light ‖ cheerful ‖ (of color) brilliant, vivid ‖ hopeful, promising success **2.** *adv.* brightly

bright·en (bráit'n) *v.t.* to make light or cheerful ‖ *v.i.* to light up ‖ to become cheerful, lively etc.

bright·ness (bráitnis) *n.* the quality of a source by which the light emitted varies from dim to bright

bril·liance (bríljəns) *n.* the quality of being brilliant ‖ extreme clarity in musical performance or richness in overtones etc. of a sound recording **bríl·lian·cy** *n.*

bril·liant (bríljənt) **1.** *adj.* sparkling, very bright ‖ outstanding in intelligence or imagination ‖ very distinguished **2.** *n.* a cut diamond with very many facets

brim (brim) **1.** *n.* the edge or lip of a cup, bowl or other hollow dish ‖ the projecting rim or edge of a hat **2.** *v.i. pres. part.* **brim·ming** *past and past part.* **brimmed** (with 'over') to be so full as to overflow **brim·ful** *adj.* full to the brim

brim·stone (brímstoun) *n.* sulfur ‖ hellfire

brin·dle (bríndʹl) **1.** *adj.* gray or tawny with darker streaks **2.** *n.* an animal marked in this way **brín·dled** *adj.*

brine pan (brain pæn) a shallow iron vessel, or pit, for extracting salt from salt water by evaporation

bring (briŋ) *pres. part.* **bring·ing** *past and past part.* **brought** (brɔt) *v.t.* to carry, lead, convey, or otherwise cause to come along with oneself ‖ to persuade ‖ to cause to come ‖ *(law)* to institute (proceedings) ‖ *(law)* to prefer ‖ to adduce, advance (an argument) ‖ to fetch (a price) **to bring about** to cause to happen ‖ to turn (a ship) around **to bring around** to win over to a new point of view ‖ to restore to consciousness **to bring back** to recall **to bring down** to cause to fall wounded or dead ‖ to lower (a price) ‖ to cause to fall **to bring forth** *(rhet.)* to give birth to ‖ to produce **to bring forward** to introduce (a topic or proposal) for discussion **to bring in** to cause to appear ‖ to yield (income etc.) ‖ to pronounce (a verdict in court) ‖ to introduce (e.g. a topic, a quotation) **to bring into play** to cause to be effective, begin using **to bring off** to achieve (something difficult or risky) **to bring on** to cause to publish or have published on one's behalf ‖ to clarify and stress ‖ to call forth, cause to be seen or realized **to bring (someone) to** to restore (someone) to consciousness **to bring to bear** to concentrate ‖ to cause to have effect **to bring to one's senses** to restore to reasonableness or sanity **to bring up** to rear, train (a child) ‖ to vomit

brink (briŋk) *n.* the top or edge of a steep place ‖ the verge ‖ the bank of a river or other stretch of water

bri·quette, bri·quet (brikét) *n.* a brick-shaped block, esp. of compressed coal dust

brisk (brisk) *adj.* lively and quick ‖ sharply refreshing and keen ‖ (of a person or manner) lively, alert ‖ (of a drink) sparkling

bris·ket (brískit) *n.* the breast or lower part of the chest of an animal, as meat for the table

bris·tle (brísʹl) **1.** *n.* a short, stiff hair on the back of an animal, esp. on swine ‖ anything resembling this **2.** *v.i. pres. part.* **bris·tling** *past and past part.* **bris·tled** (of an animal's hair) to stand on end, usually through fear, anger etc. ‖ (of people) to take offense ‖ to abound in **brís·tly** *comp.* **bris·tli·er** *superl.* **bris·tli·est** *adj.*

brit·tle (brítʹl) *adj.* of a solid in which the cohesion bewteen the molecules is fairly easily destroyed by a sudden stress, causing either fragmentation or cleavage along one or more planes

broach (broutʃ) **1.** *n.* a roasting spit ‖ any of various other pointed tools, e.g. a boring bit **2.** *v.t.* to tap, pierce (a cask) so as to let out the liquor ‖ to open and start using ‖ to introduce (a subject) into conversation

broad (brɔd) **1.** *adj.* of great width ‖ clear and explicit, easily understandable ‖ full and clear ‖ (of ideas or the mind) liberal, free from prejudice ‖ free in treatment (e.g. of brushwork in painting) ‖ general, not detailed ‖ strongly marked ‖ (of a vowel) pronounced with a wide gap between tongue and palate, open **as broad as it is long** amounting to the same thing, with no advantage one way or the other **2.** *n.* the broad part of something

broad·cast (brɔ́dkæst, brɔ́dkɑst) **1.** *adj.* transmitted by radio or television **2.** *n.* a speech or other item sent out by radio or television **3.** *v. pres. part.* **broad·cast·ing** *past and past part.* **broad·cast** *v.t.* to transmit by radio or television ‖ to spread (news, rumors etc.) about ‖ *v.i.* to speak or perform on the radio

broad-mind·ed (brɔ́dmáindid) *adj.* tolerant in thought and views, not bigoted or petty

broad·side (brɔ́dsaid) *n. (naut.)* the side of a ship from bow to quarter above the waterline ‖ all the guns on one side of a ship ‖ their simultaneous firing ‖ a spate of vigorous abuse ‖ a broadsheet

bro·cade (broukéid) **1.** *n.* a rich fabric with raised patterns woven in gold or silver thread **2.** *v.t. pres. part.* **bro·cad·ing** *past and past part.* **bro·cad·ed** to work (a cloth) with a raised design

broc·co·li, bro·co·li (brɔ́kəli:) *n.* a hardy variety of cauliflower ‖ sprouting broccoli

bro·chure (brouʃúər) *n.* a pamphlet, esp. a small stitched booklet

broil (brɔil) *v.t.* to cook by direct exposure to a fire or other radiant heat ‖ to expose to great heat ‖ *v.i.* to be cooked in this way ‖ to be exposed to great heat **bróil·er** *n.* a grill or part of a stove used for broiling ‖ a young chicken suitable for broiling ‖ a very hot day

bro·ken (bróukən) *past part.* of BREAK ‖ *adj.* fractured ‖ interrupted ‖ uneven ‖ emotionally crushed ‖ ruined and despairing ‖ violated, betrayed ‖ imperfectly spoken, esp. by a foreigner ‖ consisting of remains or siftings ‖ (of weather) uncertain ‖ (of cloud) covering much of the sky but not all of it

bro·ken-down (bróukəndáun) *adj.* reduced physically or morally to very poor condition

bro·ken·heart·ed (bróukənhártid) *adj.* grieving inconsolably

bro·ker (bróukər) *n.* a stockbroker ‖ a professional middleman in some special market **bró·ker·age** *n.* the commission earned by a broker ‖ his business **brók·ing** *n.* the profession of being a broker

bronchi *pl.* of BRONCHUS

bron·chi·a (brɔ́ŋki:ə) *pl. n.* the branches of the bronchi within the lungs **brón·chi·al** *adj.* pertaining to the bronchia or the bronchi

bron·chi·tis (brɔŋkáitis) *n.* an inflammation of the mucous membrane in the bronchial tubes

bron·chus (brɔ́ŋkəs) *pl.* **bron·chi** (brɔ́ŋkai:, brɔ́ŋki:) *n.* either of the two main divisions of the trachea leading directly into the lungs, where they ramify

bronze (brɔnz) **1.** *n.* an alloy of copper and tin, special types also containing other elements ‖ an object made of bronze ‖ the color of bronze, golden or reddish-brown **2.** *v.t. pres. part.* **bronz·ing** *past and past part.* **bronzed** to make the color of bronze

brooch (broutʃ, bru:tʃ) *n.* an ornamental, sometimes jeweled clasp

brood (bru:d) **1.** *n.* the young birds from one clutch of eggs ‖ *(rhet.)* a large family of children **2.** *v.i.* (of a bird) to sit on eggs and hatch them ‖ v.t. (of a bird) to sit on (eggs) so as to hatch them **to brood on** (or **over**) to think about and weigh in one's mind ‖ to think about sullenly, esp. after an injury or insult **brood·er** n. a heated device for rearing chicks artificially ‖ someone who broods

brook (bruk) n. a small stream

broom (bru:m, brum) n. a longhandled brush for sweeping floors etc.

broth (brɔθ, brɒθ) n. a thin soup made from meat stock and vegetables ‖ meat stock

broth·el (brɒθəl) n. a house of prostitutes

broth·er (brʌðər) pl. **broth·ers**, alt. pl. **breth·ren** (bréðrin) n. a son in his relationship to another child of the same parents ‖ a man sharing with others the same citizenship, profession, religion etc. ‖ a title in certain religious orders, sects, guilds, corporations etc.

broth·er·hood (brʌðərhud) n. the condition of being a brother ‖ a group of men living a communal life ‖ men of the same profession, business or other occupational tie, a fraternity

broth·er-in-law (brʌðərinlɔ) pl. **broth·ers-in-law** n. the brother of one's husband or wife ‖ the husband of one's sister

brow (brau) n. the forehead ‖ (usually pl.) the eyebrow ‖ the rounded top of a hill or projecting edge of a cliff

brow·beat (bráubi:t) pres. part. **brow·beat·ing** past **brow·beat** past part. **brow·beat·en** (bráubi:t'n) v.t. to bully mentally and spiritually

brown (braun) 1. n. any color of an orange-black mixture ‖ such a pigment, fabric etc. 2. adj. of the color brown 3. v.t. to make brown, esp. by exposure to sun or heat ‖ v.i. to become brown

browse (brauz) 1. n. the act of browsing 2. v. pres. part. **brows·ing** past and past part. **browsed** v.t. to nibble or feed on (leaves, bushes etc.) ‖ v.i. to nibble, feed, on leaves, bushes etc. ‖ to graze ‖ to dip into a book, read without concentration ‖ to explore a library or bookshop unsystematically, or in a leisurely, desultory fashion

bruise (bru:z) 1. n. a surface injury to the body, caused by a fall or a blow ‖ a similar injury to fruit or plants 2. v. pres. part. **bruis·ing** past and past part. **bruised** v.t. to inflict a bruise on ‖ to pound and crush into small particles, as in a mortar ‖ to make a dent in ‖ v.i. to be susceptible to, show the effect of, bruises

bru·net, **bru·nette** (bru:nét) 1. adj. having dark hair and complexion 2. n. someone with such hair and complexion

brunt (brʌnt) n. the main force or shock of a blow, attack, etc.

brush (brʌʃ) n. an implement made of bristles, wire, hair, or nylon etc. set in wood, etc. ‖ the act of brushing ‖ a bushy tail, esp. of a fox or squirrel ‖ a short, quick fight, a skirmish ‖ a controversy ‖ small trees and shrubs, land covered with thicket ‖ brushwood (undergrowth)

brush v.t. to apply a brush to ‖ to apply with a brush ‖ to force (one's way) ‖ to touch lightly in passing ‖ v.i. to use a brush ‖ to make a brushing action ‖ to force one's way, esp. through a crowd **to brush aside** to dismiss summarily **to brush away** to remove with a brush or with a brushing action of one's fingers **to brush off** to dismiss curtly **to brush over** to paint lightly ‖ to touch lightly in passing, esp. to treat lightly or superficially **to brush up** to refresh by starting to study again

brusque (brʌsk) adj. abrupt, short ‖ curt, slightly hostile in manner or speech

bru·tal (brú:t'l) adj. harsh to the point of cruelty ‖ savagely violent, a brutal attack ‖ plain and direct with no regard for feeling **bru·tal·i·ty** (bru:tǽliti:) pl. **bru·tal·i·ties** n.

bru·tal·ize (brú:t'laiz) pres. part. **bru·tal·iz·ing** past and past part. **bru·tal·ized** v.t. to render brutal, inhuman, savage ‖ to treat brutally

brute (bru:t) 1. n. an animal ‖ a brutal person 2. adj. not endowed with reason ‖ (of actions, motives, ideas etc.) like a beast's in strength or savagery **brút·ish** adj.

bub·ble (bʌb'l) 1. n. a small volume of air or gas surrounded by a liquid, a solid or an elastic membrane such as a soap solution film ‖ dome or semicylindrically shaped structure, e.g., of rubber or plastic ‖ something transient without substance and liable to burst 2. v.i. pres. part. **bub·bling** past and past part. **bub·bled** to form bubbles ‖ to make gurgling sounds **to bubble over** to be exuberant

buck (bʌk) 1. n. the male of hares, goats, rabbits, deer, antelope, rats ‖ (pop.) a dollar **to pass the buck** to dodge responsibility by passing it on to someone else 2. v.t. to throw (a rider) by bucking ‖ to resist, oppose ‖ v.i. of a horse or mule) to spring up vertically clear off the ground with the back arched ‖ (with 'up') to become more cheerful or energetic **buck up!** pull yourself together! ‖ cheer up!

buck·et (bʌkit) 1. n. a container for holding water, milk etc., a pail ‖ the amount contained in this ‖ a similar container 2. v.t. to lift in buckets ‖ v.i. to drive fast, rush along

buck·le (bʌk'l) 1. n. a stiff fastening attached to one end of a belt, ribbon, strap etc. ‖ a similar device in the form of an ornament, e.g. on some shoes 2. v. pres. part. **buck·ling** past and past part. **buck·led** v.t. (often with 'on', 'up') to fasten with a buckle ‖ to bend sharply, kink, crumple ‖ v.i. to give way ‖ to bend out of shape, twist, crumple **to buckle down to** to force oneself to concentrate and work hard at

buck·shot (bʌkʃɒt) n. coarse lead shot for big-game hunting

bu·col·ic (bju:kɒlik) 1. adj. rustic ‖ pastoral 2. n. (esp. pl.) a pastoral poem

bud (bʌd) 1. n. (bot.) a much condensed, undeveloped shoot end of the axis, composed of closely crowded young leaves, with very short internodes ‖ a gemma ‖ a half-opened flower **in bud** putting forth buds 2. v. pres. part. **bud·ding** past and past part. **bud·ded** v.t. (hort.) to engraft by inserting a bud of one variety of tree or shrub under the bark of another stock ‖ to develop ‖ v.i. to put forth buds **búd·ding** adj. promising

bud·dy (bʌdi:) pl. **bud·dies** n. a pal, friend ‖ a fellow soldier

budge (bʌdʒ) pres. part. **budg·ing** past and past part. **budged** v.t. to cause (something heavy or resisting) to move slightly ‖ to cause (a person) to modify his opinion ‖ v.i. to move ‖ to yield ‖ to modify an opinion

budg·et (bʌdʒit) 1. n. the annual estimate of revenue and expenditure for governing a country, fixing the level of taxation until the next budget ‖ (pop.) personal or household expenses 2. v.t. to allow for in a budget ‖ v.i. to plan expenditure with a given amount of money **búdg·et·ar·y** adj.

buff (bʌf) 1. adj. like buff in color, yellowish ‖ made of buff 2. n. a thick, good-quality soft leather made from buffalo or oxhide ‖ the pale brownish-yellow color of this ‖ (pop.) an enthusiast 3. v.t. to polish with a buff ‖ to dye or stain buff ‖ to give (leather) a velvety surface

buf·fa·lo (bʌfəlou) 1. n. pl. **buf·fa·lo**, **buf·fa·loes**, **buf·fa·los** any of several wild oxen, e.g. the water buffalo, the cape buffalo or bison ‖ buffalo fish **2.** *v.t.* *(pop.)* to trick, bamboozle ‖ *(pop.)* to overawe

buf·fet (bʌfit) **1.** *n.* a blow given by a storm, or strong waves ‖ **2.** *v.t.* *(old-fash.)* to strike, hit ‖ to knock about ‖ to force by striking out about one

buf·fet (buféi) *n.* a sideboard ‖ a recessed cupboard or set of shelves for displaying china etc. ‖ in informal entertaining, a table laid with food and drink to which guests help themselves ‖ (búfei) a refreshment bar, as in a railroad station

buf·foon (bʌfúːn) **1.** *n.* someone noted for playing the fool ‖ a clownish fellow **2.** *v.i.* to act like a clown **buf·foon·er·y** (bʌfúːnəri:) *pl.* **buf·foon·er·ies** *n.*

bug (bʌg) **1.** *n.* any small insect ‖ a bedbug or other hemipteran ‖ *(pop.)* a disease-producing organism, bacterium ‖ *(pop.)* a fault in an apparatus or in its working ‖ *(pop.)* a concealed microphone **2.** *v.t. pres. part.* **bug·ging** *past* and *past part.* **bugged** *(pop.)* to conceal a microphone in ‖ *(pop.)* to listen to by means of a concealed microphone ‖ *(pop.)* to pester, annoy

bug·gy (bʌgi:) *pl.* **bug·gies** *n.* a light, usually one-horse carriage for one or two persons ‖ a baby carriage

bu·gle (bjúːgˈl) **1.** *n.* a brass wind instrument like a trumpet, but with a shorter, more conical tube and no valves **2.** *v. pres. part.* **bu·gling** *past* and *past part.* **bu·gled** *v.i.* to sound a bugle ‖ *v.t.* to sound (a call) on a bugle

build (bild) **1.** *n.* shape, proportions of body **2.** *v. pres. part.* **build·ing** *past* and *past part.* **built** (bilt) *v.t.* to construct ‖ *v.i.* to construct a house etc. ‖ to cause a house etc. to be constructed **to build into** to incorporate into **to build on** to rely hopefully upon **to build up** to establish by means of hard work ‖ to endow with imaginary qualities **build·er** *n.* someone who builds ‖ a building contractor

build·ing (bíldiŋ) *n.* a permanent construction (house, factory etc.) ‖ the work of constructing houses etc.

bulb (bʌlb) *n.* the erect underground stem of a plant, reduced to a mere plate, surrounded by fleshy overlapping leaf bases, which are covered with brown scale leaves ‖ *(anat.)* a rounded part or end of a cylindrical organ, as of a hair root, urethra etc. ‖ the medulla oblongata ‖ any bulb-shaped part, esp. of a glass tube ‖ that part of an electric lamp which encloses the filament

bulge (bʌldʒ) **1.** *n.* a curving outwards, esp. when this is ugly or involves asymmetry ‖ a rounded part ‖ an abnormal increase in numbers **2.** *v. pres. part.* **bulg·ing** *past* and *past part.* **bulged** *v.t.* to cause to curve or swell outwards ‖ *v.i.* to curve or swell out **búlg·i·ness** *n.* **búlg·y** *comp.* **bulg·i·er** *superl.* **bulg·i·est** *adj.*

bulk (bʌlk) **1.** *n.* mass ‖ thickness ‖ a very large or fat human body ‖ the largest part ‖ food taken in to help digestion rather than for nutritional value **in bulk** as one mass, not packaged or bottled ‖ in large amounts **to break bulk** to begin unloading a ship **2.** *v.t.* (with out') to increase the size of (usually by adding something of little intrinsic worth) ‖ *v.i.* to occupy space **to bulk large** to be or seem very important

bulk·y (bʌlki:) *comp.* **bulk·i·er** *superl.* **bulk·i·est** *adj.* having bulk ‖ taking up a lot of room, and often of a shape difficult to handle

bull (bul) **1.** *adj.* male, esp. of large animals ‖ very strong-looking or massive ‖ *(stock exchange)* marked by rising prices, marked by the activity of bulls **2.** *n.* an uncastrated male of the bovine or ox family ‖ the male of certain other large animals, e.g. whale, elephant, elk, or moose ‖ *(stock exchange)* a person buying as a speculation in the hope that prices will rise **a bull in a china shop** a person who is destructively clumsy in a situation requiring delicacy or tact **to take the bull by the horns** to deal boldly and directly with a difficult situation

bul·let (búlit) *n.* a small, round or conical piece of lead, fired from a rifle or pistol

bul·le·tin (búlitin) *n.* a short official statement of news ‖ a periodical publication, e.g. of a club or society

bul·lion (búljən) *n.* gold or silver in bars or ingots, i.e. before coining or manufacturing processes

bull's-eye (búlzai) *pl.* **bull's-eyes** *n.* the center ring of a target ‖ a shot which hits it ‖ a guess, remark etc. which exactly hits on the truth ‖ a thick disk of glass, e.g. in a ship's side, to let in light or air ‖ a hemispherical lens of short focal distance, or a lantern with such a lens

bul·ly (búli:) **1.** *pl.* **bul·lies** *n.* someone who enjoys oppressing others weaker than himself **2.** *v. pres. part.* **bul·ly·ing** *past* and *past part.* **bul·lied** *v.t.* to persecute physically or spiritually ‖ to oppress (a weaker person or subordinate) ‖ to intimidate or force ‖ *v.i.* to be a bully or act like one

bul·rush (búlrʌʃ) *n.* a sedge of genus *Scirpus*

bul·wark (búlwərk) *n.* a defensive wall, ramparts ‖ (usually *pl.*) a ship's side above the upper deck ‖ any defensive or safeguarding structure, e.g. a breakwater ‖ a person, institution, moral principle etc. thought of as being a defense or protection

bum (bʌm) **1.** *adj. (pop.)* of poor quality **2.** *n. (pop.)* a loafer ‖ *(pop.)* a vagrant **on the bum** *(pop., of* people and machines) not working **3.** *v. pres. part.* **bum·ming** *past* and *past part.* **bummed** *v.t. (pop.)* to get (something) by sponging ‖ *v.i. (pop.)* to sponge ‖ *(pop.)* to idle

bum·ble·bee (bʌmb'lbiː) *n.* a member of *Bombus*, a genus of big, hairy, social bees which make a loud humming noise in flight

bump (bʌmp) **1.** *n.* a heavy jolt, blow or collision ‖ the swelling caused by a bump ‖ *(aviation)* a jolt felt by an aircraft in flight ‖ the variation in wind or air pressure which causes this **2.** *v.t.* to knock or strike ‖ to preempt a place, particularly on a public carrier or for an event ‖ to shape (metal) into curves ‖ *v.i.* (often with into' or against') to knock or collide suddenly **to bump into** to meet accidentally **to bump off** *(pop.)* to kill [imit.]

bump·er (bʌmpər) *n.* a device for reducing (by absorbing) the shock of a collision, esp. the metal guards at the front and back of a car

bump·tious (bʌmpʃəs) *adj.* self-assertive, full of noisy conceit

bump·y (bʌmpi:) *comp.* **bump·i·er** *superl.* **bump·i·est** *adj.* having or causing jolts or bumps

bun (bʌn) *n.* a small, soft, slightly sweetened roll, often with raisins ‖ a soft bread roll ‖ a woman's long hair done in a tight coil at the back of the head

bunch (bʌntʃ) **1.** *n.* a cluster of things growing or tied together ‖ a number of things of the same kind ‖ *(pop.)* a group of people **2.** *v.t.* to tie or gather together in bunches ‖ to work (material) in fold or gathers ‖ *v.i.* to gather into a close group

bun·dle (bʌnd'l) **1.** *n.* a number of things wrapped, rolled or tied together ‖ a set of parallel fibers, e.g. of nerves or muscles **2.** *v.t. pres. part.* **bun·dling** *past* and *past part.* **bun·dled** to tie up in a bundle ‖ to stow (things) untidily ‖ (with off') to hustle

bun·ga·low (bʌŋgəlou) *n.* a one-storied house

bun·gle (bʌŋg'l) **1.** *n.* a clumsy, unsuccessful piece of work **2.** *v. pres. part.* **bun·gling** *past* and *past part.* **bun·gled** *v.i.* to work clumsily and unsuccessfuly ‖ *v.t.* to botch, spoil

bun·ion (bʌnjən) *n.* an enlargement from chronic inflammation of the small sac on the first joint of the big toe

bunk (bʌŋk) **1.** *n.* a narrow sleeping berth, e.g. in a ship **2.** *v.i.* (often with 'down') to occupy a bed

bunk *n. (pop.)* humbug, nonsense

bun·ny (bʌni:) *pl.* **bun·nies** *n.* (child's name for) a rabbit

bunt·ing (bʌntiŋ) *n.* thin wool or cotten stuff used for flags and similar decorations ‖ flags

buoy (búːiː, bɔi) **1.** *n.* an anchored float marking a navigable channel, dangerous shallows etc. **2.** *v.t.* (usually with up') to keep afloat ‖ (usually with up') to raise to the surface ‖ (usually with up') to en-

buoy·an·cy (bɔ́iənsi:, bú:jənsi:) *n.* the ability to float or (of a fluid) to keep something afloat || *(hydrostatics)* loss of weight by immersion in a fluid || resilience of spirits, prices etc.

buoy·ant (bɔ́iənt, bú:jənt) *adj.* able to float or rise to the surface || able to keep things floating || resilient in spirit, lighthearted

bur·den (bɔ́:rd'n) **1.** *n.* a heavy load || a heavy moral obligation || the capacity or tonnage of a ship's cargo **2.** *v.t.* to put a weight on || to take on (oneself) or put on (others) a mental or moral burden

bur·den·some (bʌ́rd'nsəm) *adj.* heavy || troublesome

bu·reau (bjúərou) *pl.* **bu·reaus, bu·reaux** (bjúərouz) *n.* a chest of drawers (esp. with a mirror) for a bedroom || a government department or its subdivision || an organization or agency

bu·reauc·ra·cy (bjuərɔ́krəsi:) *pl.* **bu·reauc·ra·cies** *n.* government by officials || officialdom, the routine world of regulations || government officials **bu·reau·crat** (bjúərəkræt) *n.* **bu·reau·crát·ic** *adj.* **bu·reau·crát·i·cal·ly** *adv.*

bur·geon, bour·geon (bɔ́:rdʒən) **1.** *n.* a bud || a shoot **2.** *v.i.* to send forth shoots or other new growth || to begin to grow

bur·glar (bɔ́:rglər) *n.* someone who commits burglary

bur·gla·ry (bɔ́:rgləri:) *pl.* **bur·gla·ries** *n.* the act of breaking into houses, shops etc. to steal

bur·gle (bɔ́:rg'l) *pres. part.* **bur·gling** *past* and *past part.* **bur·gled** *v.t.* to rob by burglary || *v.i.* to be a burglar

bur·i·al (béri:əl) *n.* a burying or being buried

burl (bə:rl) **1.** *n.* a knot or lump in wool, thread or cloth || a growth, often round and flat, on tree trunks || a veneer made from such growths **2.** *v.t.* to free (cloth) from burls

bur·lap (bɔ́:rlæp) *n.* a coarse fabric of hemp, jute or flax

bur·lesque (bə:lésk) **1.** *adj.* intentionally comic through lighthearted, exaggerated imitation || unintentionally ludicrous, through inadequacy **2.** *n.* a literary or dramatic imitation mocking its model by going to comic extremes, for fun || a parody || an unintentionally ludicrous entertainment || a theatrical entertainment of low comedy, esp. incorporating striptease **3.** *v.t. pres. part.* **bur·les·quing** *past* and *past part.* **bur·lesqued** to represent grotesquely, in fun

bur·ly (bɔ́:rli:) *comp.* **bur·li·er** *superl.* **bur·li·est** *adj.* big and strong, heavily built

burn (bə:rn) **1.** *n.* damage or injury caused by fire, heat or acid **2.** *v. pres. part.* **burn·ing** *past* and *past part.* **burned, burnt** (bə:rnt) *v.t.* to consume or destroy by flames or heat || to injure by fire or heat or acid || to make by fire or heat or acid || *(cooking)* to scorch, to cause to stick to the pan || *(med.)* to cauterize (a wound etc.) || *(chem.)* to cause to undergo combustion || to cause (candles, electricity, gas, oil etc.) to give light or heat || to cause a sensation of heat in || (of sun, radiation etc.) to cause injury or discomfort to || *v.i.* to flame, blaze || to be destroyed by fire or heat || (of fires, electric lamps, gas stoves etc.) to give out light or heat || *(cooking)* to stick to a pan and char || to suffer injury or discomfort by exposure to the sun, radiation etc. || to be passionately excited or heated with anger etc. || to feel hot || *(chem.)* to undergo combustion **to burn a hole in one's pocket** (of money) to give one an urge to spend **to burn away** to diminish by burning, to burn to nothing || to continue to burn **to burn down** to destroy or be destroyed by fire **to burn into** (esp. of acid) to eat into || to make an indelible impression on, *to burn into one's memory* **to burn one's bridges** (*Am.* = *Br.* **to burn one's boats**) to take some irrevocable step **to burn oneself out** to use up one's energy by overwork or dissipation **to burn one's fingers** to suffer the result of rash behavior **to burn out** to stop burning because of lack of fuel || to come to nothing, *her burst of energy soon burned out* || to force to emerge by setting fire to a dwelling etc. **to burn up** to consume or be consumed by fire

burn·ing (bɔ́:rniŋ) *adj.* on fire || intense || exciting passion, *a burning question*

bur·nish (bɔ́:rniʃ) **1.** *n.* a gloss, luster produced by burnishing **2.** *v.t.* to polish by rubbing with a hard and smooth instrument || *v.i.* to take a polish in this way

burr (bə:r) **1.** *n.* *(bot.)* a bur || a trilling pronunciation of *r* || a rough, country pronunciation || a whirring, humming sound || *(dentistry)* a bur || a roughness left on cut or punched metal or paper || any rough edge or ridge || a disk seen around the moon or a star || a small washer placed on the end of a rivet before it is made fast || a coarse rock with quartz crystals used in millstones || any of various limestones || a whetstone **2.** *v.i.* to speak with a burr || to make a burring sound (e.g. of a drill) || *v.t.* to pronounce with a burr

bur·ro (bɔ́:rou, búərou, bʌ́rou) *n.* a small donkey used as a pack animal

bur·row (bɔ́:rou, bʌ́rou) **1.** *n.* a hole dug underground by some animals (e.g. foxes, rabbits) as a shelter and home **2.** *v.t.* (of animals) to dig (such a hole) || *v.t.* (of animals) to dig a burrow or move forward by doing this || (of people) to make a way underground or as though underground || to delve, *to burrow into a mystery*

burst (bə:rst) *n.* an explosion, a sudden disintegration || a sudden outbreak || a spouting forth, a spurt || a sudden short intensive period, *a burst of energy*

burst *pres. part.* **burst·ing** *past* and *past part.* **burst** *v.i.* to explode, disintegrate suddenly and forcefully from inner pressure || to come open suddenly, *to burst into flower* || to collapse, *to burst into tears* || to be full to overflowing, *to burst with pride* || to rush suddenly and violently, *to burst into a room* || *v.t.* to cause to burst, *to burst a balloon* || to make by bursting, *to burst a hole in a canoe* || to break, *the river will burst its banks* || (with 'open') to open forcibly **to burst into view** to appear with startling suddenness **to burst out** (with *pres. part.*) suddenly to begin, *to burst out laughing* || (with 'into') to launch oneself, *to burst out into a tirade*

bur·y (béri:) *pres. part.* **bur·y·ing** *past* and *past part.* **bur·ied** (béri:d) *v.t.* to put in the ground so as to be hidden from view || to place in a grave or tomb || to perform funeral rites over, *to be buried at sea* || to dismiss from the mind || to cover over || to hide, *to bury one's face in one's hands* || to preoccupy (oneself), *to bury oneself in one's books* || to isolate (oneself), *to bury oneself in the country* **to bury one's head in the sand** to refuse to face a difficulty

bus (bʌs) **1.** *pl.* **bus·es, bus·ses** *n.* a large public passenger vehicle serving fixed routes || a similar vehicle used privately, e.g. by firms for transporting employees **2.** *v.i. pres. part.* **bus·sing** *past* and *past part.* **bussed** to go by bus

bush (buʃ) **1.** *n.* a clump of shrubs || rough, shrubby, uncultivated country || *(pop.,* with 'the') undeveloped, remote, thinly populated country occupying a large area || *(hist.)* a bunch of ivy hung at a vintner's door **2.** *v.i.* to branch out or cluster thickly

---

bush·el (búʃəl) *n.* any of various measures of capacity, esp. *(Am.)* a dry unit equal to 2150.42 cu. ins. and *(Br.)* a dry and liquid unit equal to 2219.36 cu. ins. or 8 gallons **to hide one's light under a bushel** to keep some ability etc. secret

busi·ness (bíznis) *n.* one's regular employment, profession, occupation ‖ one's personal affair, concern, duty ‖ something requiring attention ‖ a situation, matter, happening ‖ the activity of buying and selling, trade ‖ active selling, transactions ‖ a commercial firm or enterprise **to go about one's business** to do what concerns oneself **to have no business to** to have no right to **to make it one's business** to choose to be personally responsible for **to mean business** to be in earnest **to mind one's own business** to refrain from interfering

bus·ing (bʌ́siŋ) *n.* transporting students from one school area to another to promote racial integration

bust (bʌst) *n.* a piece of sculpture showing head, neck and something of shoulders and chest ‖ the upper front part of a woman's body ‖ the measurement around a woman's body at the breasts

bust **1.** *n.* (*pop.*) a burst ‖ (*Am., pop.,* of a person) a complete failure ‖ a spree **2.** *v.t. pres. part.* **bust·ing** *past* **bust** *past part.* **bust, bust·ed** (*pop.*) to burst, break ‖ to make bankrupt ‖ (*pop.*) to demote (a soldier) ‖ (*slang*) to arrest ‖ to raid

bus·tle (bʌ́s'l) **1.** *n.* a stir ‖ brisk movement **2.** *v. pres. part.* **bus·tling** *past and past part.* **bus·tled** *v.i.* to move with busy or fussy purpose ‖ *v.t.* to cause to bustle

bus·y (bízi:) *comp.* **bus·i·er** *superl.* **bus·i·est** *adj.* engaged in work or other occupation ‖ having plenty to do ‖ full of activity ‖ always moving or working ‖ (of a telephone line) in use

busy *pres. part.* **bus·y·ing** *past and past part.* **bus·ied** *v.t.* to occupy (someone, one's hands etc.)

but (bʌt) **1.** *adv.* (*rhet.*) only, merely ‖ just **2.** *conj.* yet, and on the other hand ‖ except (that) ‖ (after a negative) without the result that **3.** *prep.* except **all but** almost **but for** except for, without **4.** *n.* (*pl.*) objections, *ifs and buts*

butch·er (bútʃər) **1.** *n.* someone who sells meat that he has prepared for sale ‖ someone who slaughters animals for market ‖ (of bad surgeons, generals etc.) a man who causes needless killing or suffering through brutality or incompetence **2.** *v.t.* to slaughter (animals) for food ‖ to kill cruelly or in great numbers ‖ to ruin the impact of (a work) by bad reading, performing or editing **bútch·er·ly** *adj.*

but·ler (bʌ́tlər) *n.* the chief manservant of a house

butt (bʌt) *n.* the thicker or handle end, esp. of a tool or weapon ‖ the base of a petiole or end of a plant nearest the roots ‖ the unburned end of a smoked cigarette etc. or used candle ‖ any of various flatfish, e.g. sole, turbot, plaice ‖ the thickest leather, from an animal's back or sides, trimmed rectangularly

butt *v.t.* to strike with the head or horns ‖ to join by making a butt joint, without overlapping ‖ to place (a plank etc.) end to end with another ‖ *v.i.* to bump ‖ to project **to butt in** to interrupt suddenly **to butt in on** to intrude on

butte (bju:t) *n.* an isolated hill, with steep, even sides, and a flat top

but·ter (bʌ́tər) **1.** *n.* the fatty substance made by churning cream, used at the table and in cooking **2.** *v.t.* to spread with butter **to butter up** to flatter

but·ter·cup (bʌ́tərkʌp) *n.* a member of *Ranunculus,* fam. *Ranunculaceae,* a genus of plants of Europe, Asia and North America

but·ter·fly (bʌ́tərflai) *pl.* **but·ter·flies** *n.* an insect of the division *Rhopalocera* of the order *Lepidoptera* ‖ a frivolous person, *a social butterfly* ‖ a fast swimming stroke **to have butterflies in one's stomach** to be in a state of acute nervous anticipation

but·ter·scotch (bʌ́tərskɒtʃ) *n.* a candy made chiefly of butter and brown sugar

but·ter·y (bʌ́təri:) *adj.* having the appearance or consistency of butter ‖ containing or covered with butter

but·tock (bʌ́tək) *n.* one of the two rounded, muscled parts of the body on which a person sits

but·ton (bʌ́t'n) *1. n.* a small disk or knob sewn on material and passed through a hole or loop to provide a loose fastening, or this used ornamentally ‖ a disk worn during political campaigns to identify one's party, candidate etc. ‖ a flower bud ‖ an unopened mushroom ‖ a knob, a small device to be pressed, e.g. to start machinery working, or on an electric bell **2.** *v.t.* (often with 'up') to fasten the buttons of or enclose within a buttoned garment ‖ *v.i.* to have buttons for fastening

but·tress (bʌ́tris) **1.** *n.* a support built against a wall ‖ a prop, a supporting factor **2.** *v.t.* to prop or support with buttresses ‖ (often with 'up') to support

buy (bai) **1.** *v.t. pres. part.* **buy·ing** *past and past part.* **bought** (bɔt) to acquire by paying money, purchase ‖ to obtain at some cost or sacrifice ‖ to win over by bribery or promises **to buy in** to buy a stock of **to buy into** to buy stocks or shares in (esp. a company) **to buy off** to get rid of (a blackmailer, claimant etc.) by payment **to buy out** to pay (a person) to give up certain privileges or rights **to buy up** to purchase (a firm etc., or a big part of it **2.** *n.* something bought, esp. a bargain **búy·er** *n.* someone who selects and buys stock for a big store

buzz (bʌz) **1.** *n.* a humming noise, esp. of bees ‖ a muted sound of many people talking ‖ a general stir **2.** *v.t.* to fly an airplane low and fast over (something) ‖ to cause to buzz ‖ *v.i.* to make a humming sound ‖ to murmur ‖ to circulate, *the rumor buzzed around the village* ‖ to use a buzzer

buz·zard (bʌ́zərd) *n.* the turkey buzzard

by (bai) **1.** *adv.* past (in space) ‖ past (in time) ‖ near ‖ aside **2.** *prep.* beside ‖ close to ‖ in the direction of ‖ along, over ‖ through, via ‖ past ‖ during ‖ not later than ‖ to the extent of ‖ concerning, with respect to ‖ through the means of ‖ with, born of ‖ (indicating progression or quantity), *little by little, to go forward by degrees, to emigrate by the thousand*

by·gone (báigɒn, báigɒn) **1.** *adj.* (*rhet.*) past, of the past **2.** *n.* (*pl.*) past offenses etc. (esp. in phrase) **to let bygones be bygones** to forgive and forget

by·law, bye·law (báilɔ) *n.* a regulation or law made by a corporation, company, club ‖ a secondary law or regulation

by·pass (báipæs, báipɒs) **1.** *n.* an alternative road around a town or through its outskirts designed to make through traffic avoid the town ‖ (*engin.*) a device to direct flow around a fixture or pipe, etc., instead of through it ‖ (*elec.*) a shunt **2.** *v.t.* to make a detour around

by·prod·uct (báiprɒdəkt) *n.* something produced during the manufacture of something else

by·stand·er (báistændər) *n.* a person present when some action takes place but not involved in it, a casual spectator

by·word (báiwə:rd) *n.* proverbial status accorded to some person, place etc., usually held in contempt ‖ a word or phrase often used

C

C, c (si:) the third letter in the English alphabet

cab (kæb) *n.* a taxi, car for hire ‖ the closed part of a truck or locomotive where the driver sits

ca·bal (kəbǽl) **1.** *n.* a plot, intrigue ‖ an association of persons secretly united to further their interests by plotting **2.** *v.i. pres. part.* **ca·bal·ling** *past* and *past part.* **ca·balled** to plot, form a cabal

cab·a·ret (kæbəréi) *n.* a place serving alcoholic drinks and providing entertainment

cab·bage (kǽbidʒ) *n.* a plant whose tightly packed, unopened leaves are eaten as a vegetable

cab·in (kǽbin) *n.* a small wooden house ‖ a room on board ship where passengers sleep ‖ a room below-decks for crew or passengers ‖ an aircraft's closed compartment for passengers

cab·i·net (kǽbinit) *n.* a piece of furniture with display shelves ‖ a metal or wood container with drawers or shelves for storing things ‖ the committee of chief ministers under a president or prime minister

ca·ble (kéib'l) **1.** *n.* a strong length of rope, wire or chain ‖ a rope of wire used to transmit electricity or messages, a telegraph line ‖ a message sent by this means ‖ a rope or chain holding a ship at anchor **2.** *v. pres. part.* **ca·bling** *past* and *past part.* **ca·bled** *v.t.*

ca·boose (kəbú:s) *n.* a ship's galley ‖ the rear car of a freight train used by trainmen

cache (kæʃ) **1.** *n.* a hiding place for treasure or stores ‖ the goods in such a hiding place, a hoard or store **2.** *v.t. pres. part.* **cach·ing** *past* and *past part.* **cached** to hide away (valuables or stores)

cack·le (kæk'l) **1.** *n.* the harsh, clucking noise of a hen ‖ a raucous laugh ‖ *(pop.)* idle talk **2.** *v. pres. part.* **cack·ling** *past* and *past part.* **cack·led** *v.i.* to make such a noise ‖ to chatter or laugh shrilly ‖ *v.t.* to utter in a harsh, shrill tone

ca·coph·o·ny (kəkɔ́fəni:) *pl.* **ca·coph·o·nies** *n.* a harsh discord ‖ dissonance

cac·tus (kǽktəs) *pl.* **cac·ti** (kǽktai), **cac·tus·es** *n.* a member of *Cactus,* a genus of spiny plants of fam. *Cactaceae*

ca·dav·er (kədǽvər, kədéivər) *n.* a human corpse **ca·dav·er·ous** (kədǽvərəs) *adj.* corpse-like ‖ gaunt ‖ deathly pale

cad·die, cad·dy (kǽdi:) **1.** *n.* an attendant paid to carry a golfer's clubs around the course **2.** *v.i. pres. part.* **cad·dy·ing** *past* and *past part.* **cad·died** to serve as a caddie

ca·dence (kéid'ns) *n.* the fall or modulation of the voice ‖ the rhythmic flow of sound, esp. of words in verse or prose ‖ a beat, measure ‖ the closing of a musical phrase

ca·det (kədét) *n.* a student at a military or naval college ‖ a member of the army being trained to be an officer

ca·dre (kǽdri:, kɑ́drə) *n.* the permanent nucleus of an organization (esp. *mil.*)

ca·fé, ca·fe (kæféi) *n.* a place providing light meals or snacks ‖ a place where coffee, other drinks and occasionally food are served

caf·e·te·ri·a (kæfitíəri:ə) *n.* a self-service restaurant

caf·feine (kǽfi:n, kæfi:n) *n.* an organic compound (alkaloid) of the purine group, occurring in esp. the coffee bean and tea leaf

cage (keidʒ) **1.** *n.* an airy container made with bars for keeping birds etc. in ‖ an open protective framework enclosing a platform, esp., used as a hoist or lift **2.**

v.t. pres. part. **cag·ing** *past* and *past part.* **caged** to place or keep in a cage

cage·y, cag·y (kéidʒi:) *comp.* **cag·i·er** *superl.* **cag·i·est** *adj. (pop.)* secretive, reluctant to give oneself away ‖ wary **cá·gi·ly** *adv.* **cá·gi·ness** *n.*

ca·hoots (kəhú:ts) *pl. n. (pop., only in the phrase)* **in cahoots** in partnership, esp. one which involves shady dealings

ca·jole (kədʒóul) *pres. part.* **ca·jol·ing** *past* and *past part.* **ca·joled** *v.t.* to persuade or coax by flattery, try to win over by playing on the sympathies of **ca·jóle·ment, ca·jól·er·y** *ns*

cake (keik) **1.** *n.* a baked mixture of flour, leaven, eggs, fats, sugar and other sweet or fruity ingredients ‖ an edible, round, flattened mixture, fried or baked, *fish cake* ‖ a small quantity of a substance molded into a bar, *a cake of soap* **2.** *v. pres. part.* **cak·ing** *past* and *past part.* **caked** *v.t.* to cover (a surface) or fill (a space) with a hardened mass ‖ *v.i.* to become a hardened mass

cal·a·boose (kǽləbu:s, kæləbú:s) *n. (pop.)* jail

ca·lam·i·ty (kəlǽmiti:) *pl.* **ca·lam·i·ties** *n.* a disastrous event causing great misery

cal·ci·fi·ca·tion (kælsifikéiʃən) *n.* conversion to calcium carbonate ‖ the deposition of insoluble calcium salts in a tissue

cal·ci·fy (kǽlsifai) *pres. part.* **cal·ci·fy·ing** *past* and *past part.* **cal·ci·fied** *v.t.* to change into calcium carbonate or into a calciferous state by the reaction of calcium salts

cal·ci·um (kǽlsi:əm) *n.* a white divalent element of the alkaline earth group found chiefly as a carbonate (chalk, limestone, marble, coral)

cal·cu·late (kǽlkjuleit) *pres. part.* **cal·cu·lat·ing** *past* and *past part.* **cal·cu·lat·ed** *v.t.* to find out or ascertain by using mathematics ‖ to figure out in one's head ‖ (usually *pass.*) to intend, plan, arrange for a particular purpose ‖ *v.i.* to make a calculation ‖ (with 'on') to rely **cál·cu·lat·ing** *adj.* working out mathematical processes ‖ planning and scheming for one's own ends

cal·cu·la·tion (kælkjuléiʃən) *n.* the act, process or result of using mathematical processes ‖ careful thinking ‖ self-seeking deliberation

cal·cu·la·tor (kǽlkjuleitər) *n.* someone who calculates ‖ a set of tables used in mathematics ‖ a calculating machine

cal·cu·lus (kǽlkjuləs) *pl.* **cal·cu·li** (kǽlkjulai), **cal·cu·lus·es** *n.* a hard concretion formed in parts of the body such as the gall bladder or kidneys ‖ *(math.)* any branch of mathematics that employs symbolic computations

cal·dron, caul·dron (kɔ́ldrən) *n.* a large deep cooking pot of iron used over an open fire

cal·en·dar (kǽləndər) **1.** *n.* a table of the days, weeks and months of the year noting public holidays etc. ‖ a register or schedule **2.** *v.t.* to enter or write in a register ‖ to arrange and index (documents)

cal·en·der (kǽləndər) **1.** *v.t.* to press (cloth, paper etc.) so as to produce a smooth, glossy or other special finish, or to adjust thickness **2.** *n.* a machine containing rollers to carry out this process

calf (kæf, kɑf) *pl.* **calves** (kævz, kɑvz) *n.* the fleshy part of the back of the leg below the knee

calf *pl.* **calves** *n.* the young of a cow, elephant, whale etc. ‖ leather made from the skin of a young cow **in**

(a) æ, cat; ɑ, car; ɔ fawn; ei, snake. **(e)** e, hen; i:, sheep; iə, deer; ɛə, bear. **(i)** i, fish; ai, tiger; ə:, bird. **(o)** o, ox; au, cow; ou, goat; u, poor; ɔi, royal. **(u)** ʌ, duck; u, bull; u:, goose; ə, bacillus; ju:, cube. x, loch; θ, think; ð, bother; z, Zen; ʒ, corsage; dʒ, savage; ŋ, orangutang; j, yak; ʃ, fish; tʃ, fetch; 'l, rabble; 'n, redden. Complete pronunciation key appears inside front cover.

calf (of a cow) pregnant

cal·i·ber, cal·i·bre (kǽlibər) n. the diameter of the bore of a gun or rifle or of a bullet or a shell ‖ the quality of a person's mind or character

cal·i·brate (kǽlibreit) pres. part. **cal·i·brat·ing** past and past part. **cal·i·brat·ed** v.t. to indicate a scale on (a measuring instrument) ‖ to measure the internal diameter of (a tube) ‖ to test the accuracy of (a measuring instrument)

cal·i·co (kǽlikou) pl. **cal·i·coes, cal·i·cos** n. inexpensive printed cotton cloth

ca·liph, ca·lif (kéilif, kǽlif) n. a successor to Mohammed as head of Islam, originally having full political as well as religious power **cal·i·phate, cal·i·fate** (kǽlifeit) n.

cal·is·then·ic (kælisθénik) adj. producing health and beauty in the body **cal·is·then·ics**

call (kɔl) **1.** v.t. to say loudly in order to get attention ‖ to summon ‖ to speak to by telephone or send a message to by radio etc ‖ to consider, regard as ‖ to attract (animals, birds) by an imitative cry or signal ‖ (finance) to demand payment of, or give notice of payment on (a loan or a bond) ‖ v.i. to shout or exclaim in order to gain attention ‖ to telephone ‖ (of a bird) to make its characteristic sound ‖ to pay a visit ‖ to stop (at a port) **to be called to the bar** to qualify as a lawyer **to call back** to summon back, recall ‖ to retract **to call for** to request, to call for help **to call into question** to challenge the truth of **to call (someone) names** to use insulting epithets to or about (someone) **to call off** to order to desist ‖ to postpone or cancel **to call on** to pay a visit to (someone) **to call to order** to request (someone) to be quiet or orderly **to call the roll** to check a list of names so as to find absentees **to call up** to telephone or contact by radio etc. ‖ to summon for military service **to call upon** (or **on**) to appeal to **2.** n. a cry or shout to attract attention ‖ a message, esp. by telephone ‖ a short visit ‖ a doctor's consultation at the patient's home ‖ the notes of a bird ‖ a vocation, a call to the presthood ‖ an inner urging ‖ a summons or invitation, the call of the sea ‖ a claim on time, money etc. ‖ (finance) a demand for payment of money **on call** (of a doctor, ambulance etc.) available for duty

call·ing (kɔ́liŋ) n. a profession or occupation ‖ a spiritual summons, a deep impulse to carry out some mission

cal·li·o·pe (kəláiəpi:) n. a musical instrument

cal·lous (kǽləs) **1.** adj. indifferent to the pain or distress of others ‖ (of the skin) hardened **2.** n. a callus

cal·low (kǽlou) adj. lacking experience of life, immature

cal·lus, cal·lous (kǽləs) pl. **cal·lus·es, cal·lous·es** n. a thickened area of skin or plant tissue ‖ a bony substance formed around a fractured bone

calm (kɑm) **1.** adj. (of the sea) still, without rough motion ‖ (of a person) placid ‖ (pop.) impudent, brazen **2.** n. a period of serenity ‖ a windless period ‖ a motionless, undisturbed state **3.** v.t. to soothe, pacify ‖ v.i. to become calm **to calm down** to regain emotional self-control after anger etc.

cal·o·rie, cal·o·ry (kǽləri:) n. (phys., abbr. cal.) a unit of heat energy ‖ (physiol.) a unit of heat energy derived by the body from food

ca·lum·ni·ate (kəlΛmni:eit) pres. part. **ca·lum·ni·at·ing** past and past part. **ca·lum·ni·at·ed** v.t. to slander ‖ to accuse falsely and maliciously by making untrue statements **ca·lum·ni·á·tion** n. **ca·lúm·ni·a·tor** n. someone who slanders **ca·lúm·ni·a·to·ry** adj. marked by, or given to, calumny ‖ slanderous **ca·lúm·ni·ous** adj.

cal·um·ny (kǽləmni:) pl. **cal·um·nies** n. a slanderous accusation, made with the intention of harming another

ca·lyp·so (kəlípsou) **1.** n. a W. Indian lilting song, usually improvised and topical like a ballad with a refrain **2.** adj. of this style

ca·lyx (kéiliks, kǽliks) pl. **ca·lyx·es, cal·y·ces** (kéilisi:z, kǽlisi:z) n. an outer whorl of floral leaves forming the protective covering of a flower bud

cam (kæm) n. an eccentric projection of a shaft which communicates the revolution of the shaft into the linear movement of another part of a machine

cam·el (kǽməl) n. either of two members of Camelus, fam. Camelidae, quadruped ruminants used in desert countries for riding or as beasts of burden: C. dromedarius of Arabia, having a single hump, and C. bactrianus of Turkestan, having two humps **cam·el·eer** (kæməlíər) n. a camel driver

cam·e·o (kǽmi:ou) n. an engraved design or portrait cut in relief on hard stone or a gem so engraves **2.** adj. miniature-scale

cam·er·a (kǽmərə, kǽmrə) n. an apparatus for taking photographs ‖ an apparatus, as used in television, for changing images into electrical impulses **in camera** in a judge's private chamber ‖ with the public excluded

cam·ou·flage (kǽməflɑʒ) n. the hiding from observation of ships or buildings ‖ the disguise used ‖ any concealment by disguise

camp (kæmp) **1.** n. (mil.) a place where forces are temporarily lodged, in tents, barracks or huts ‖ a temporary resting place for gypsies etc. ‖ tents collectively, an encampment ‖ a holiday recreational center, esp. for children **to break camp** to pack up equipment and leave a campsite **to pitch camp** to set up a camp **2.** v.i. to make a camp, pitch tents, etc. ‖ to live in a camp ‖ v.t. to station (soldiers) in a camp **to camp out** to live outdoors in a camp **3.** adj. to live elsewhere than one's home, temporarily, and in conditions involving discomfort or inconvenience

cam·paign (kæmpéin) **1.** n. a series of military actions in one area, usually with limited objectives, or a part of some larger warfare ‖ any organized attempt to gain public support **2.** v.i. to direct, or take part in, a campaign

camp·er (kǽmpər) n. a person at a camp or living in a tent etc. on holiday ‖ a pickup truck or any vehicle fitted out with temporary living arrangements

cam·pus (kǽmpəs) pl. **cam·pus·es** n. the grounds and main buildings of a school or college

can (kæn) infin. and parts lacking, neg. **can·not** (kǽnɒt) **can not, can't** (kænt, kɑnt) 3rd pers. sing. **can** past **could** (kud)

can 1. n. a receptacle, often of metal, for liquids, etc. ‖ a tinplated container in which foodstuffs are preserved **2.** v.t. pres. part. **can·ning** past and past part. **canned** to preserve by packing in an airtight can

ca·nal (kənǽl) n. an artificial waterway for irrigation or navigation ‖ (zool.) a tube through which lymph and other fluids are conveyed

ca·nard (kənɑ́rd) n. a piece of false information put out as a hoax

ca·nar·y (kənéəri:) pl. **ca·nar·ies** n. any of several varieties of singing cage birds of the finch family ‖ a bright yellow

ca·nas·ta (kənǽstə) n. a card game, somewhat similar to rummy

can·cel (kǽnsəl) **1.** v.t. pres. part. **can·cel·ing** past and past part. **can·celed** to abolish, nullify ‖ to countermand ‖ to cross out, delete ‖ to mark (postage stamps) so that they cannot be used again ‖ to neutralize **2.** n. the act of canceling

can·cel·la·tion, can·cel·a·tion (kænsəléiʃən) n. the act of canceling, nullifying or invalidating ‖ something canceled

Can·cer (kǽnsər) n. a northern constellation ‖ the fourth sign of the zodiac, represented as a crab **can·cer** a malignant tumor ‖ the disease caused by such a tumor **cán·cer·ous** adj.

can·de·la·brum (kænd'lábrəm) pl. **can·de·la·bra** (kænd'lábrə) (pl., often used as sing., with pl. **can·de·la·bras**) n. a large, branching support for a number of candles

can·did (kǽndid) adj. frankly truthful even if the truth is unpleasant ‖ honest, open

can·di·da·cy (kǽndidəsi:) pl. **can·di·da·cies** n. the position or status of being a candidate

can·di·date (kǽndideit, kǽndidit) *n.* a person who offers himself, or is nominated, for some post or office (esp. in elections) ‖ a person taking an examination

can·dle (kǽnd'l) *n.* a cylinder of tallow or wax around a core of wick, burned to give light **to burn the candle at both ends** to live too hectic a life

can·dor, *Br.* **can·dour** (kǽndər) *n.* frankness, even to the point of telling unwelcome truths ‖ openness of speech or expression

can·dy (kǽndi:) 1. *n. pl.* **can·dies** crystallized sugar ‖ a piece of sugared confectionery 2. *v. pres. part.* **can·dy·ing** *past* and *past part.* **can·died** *v.t.* to preserve by coating with sugar ‖ to turn into candy ‖ *v.i.* to become candied

cane (kein) 1. *n.* the long, hollow stem of plants such as bamboo, osier or sugarcane ‖ a stem, usually osier, used for furniture, chair seats, baskets, etc. ‖ a thin walking stick 2. *v.t. pres. part.* **can·ing** *past* and *past part.* **caned** to make (a chair seat or back etc.) with cane

ca·nine (kéinain) 1. *adj.* of or pertaining to the family *Canidae* (dogs, wolves, foxes and jackals) 2. *n.* a canine tooth

can·is·ter, can·nis·ter (kǽnistər) *n.* a small metal box for tea, coffee etc. or tobacco ‖ *(mil.)* a case containing shot

can·ker (kǽŋkər) *n.* an ulceration on the inside of the mouth or lips ‖ a disease of horses' hooves ‖ a disease of fruit trees **cán·ker·ous** *adj.*

can·na·bis (kǽnəbis) *n.* hemp

can·ni·bal (kǽnəb'l) 1. *n.* a human who eats human flesh ‖ any animal which feeds on its own kind 2. *adj.* having the habits of a cannibal **can·ni·bal·ism** *n.* **can·ni·bal·is·tic** *adj.*

can·ni·bal·ize (kǽnəbəlaiz) *pres. part.* **can·ni·bal·iz·ing** *past* and *past part.* **can·ni·bal·ized** *v.t.* to repair (vehicles or aircraft) by using parts from other vehicles, instead of using spare parts ‖ *v.i.* to repair vehicles or aircraft in this way

can·non (kǽnən) *n.* (*pl.* **can·non**) a piece of artillery fired from a mounting ‖ (*pl.* **cannon**) an automatic gun in an aircraft

can·non·ade (kænənéid) 1. *n.* continuous fire from cannon ‖ a bombardment 2. *v. pres. part.* **can·non·ad·ing** *past* and *past part.* **can·non·ad·ed** *v.t.* to bombard (a target)

can·ny (kǽni:) *comp.* **can·ni·er** *superl.* **can·ni·est** *adj.* cautious ‖ shrewd ‖ careful

ca·noe (kənú:) 1. *n.* a light, long, narrow boat, propelled by paddles 2. *v.i.* to in a canoe **ca·nóe·ist** *n.*

can·on (kǽnən) *n.* a church law ‖ any general principle or body of principles ‖ a member of the chapter, or administrative body, of a cathedral ‖ books of the Bible regarded by Christians as holy writ ‖ part of the Mass ‖ *(mus.)* a contrapuntal work in which various instruments or voices take up the same melody successively, before the previous one has finished

can·on·i·za·tion (kænənizéiʃən) *n.* a canonizing or being canonized

can·on·ize (kǽnənaiz) *pres. part.* **can·on·iz·ing** *past* and *past part.* **can·on·ized** *v.t.* to declare by authority in the Roman and Orthodox churches that a person is to be venerated as a saint

can·o·py (kǽnəpi:) 1. *pl.* **can·o·pies** *n.* an ornate covering of cloth, wood etc. suspended or held over a bed, throne, shrine or person 2. *v.t. pres. part.* **can·o·py·ing** *past* and *past part.* **can·o·pied** to cover with a canopy ‖ to serve as a canopy to

cant (kænt) 1. *n.* an external angle of slope ‖ an inclination ‖ the bevel of a sloping surface, e.g. of a buttress 2. *v.t.* to tilt ‖ to deflect ‖ to set at an angle ‖ *v.i.* to assume a tilted position

cant 1. *n.* insincere or trite statements, esp. those expressing hypocritical piety ‖ jargon used by members of a particular class or profession 2. *adj.* trite ‖ insincere

can·ta·loupe, can·ta·loup (kǽnt'loup) *n.* a variety of chiefly European muskmelon having a warty rind and orange flesh

can·tan·ker·ous (kæntǽŋkərəs) *adj.* bad-tempered ‖ quarrelsome

can·teen (kæntí:n) *n.* the restaurant of a large institution, e.g. a factory or college ‖ a shop in a military camp or barracks, selling food, liquor, etc. ‖ a box of cooking utensils for army use ‖ a water bottle

can·ter (kǽntər) 1. *n.* the gait of a horse between a trot and a gallop 2. *v.i.* to move at a canter

can·tor (kǽntər) *n.* the leader of a church choir, a precentor ‖ the singer of the liturgy and leader of chanting in a synagogue **can·to·ri·al** (kæntɔ́ri:əl, kæntóuri:əl) *adj.*

can·vas, can·vass (kǽnvəs) *n.* a strong, coarse cloth of unbleached hemp or flax, used for sails, tents, and as a surface for painting on in oils ‖ an oil painting on canvas ‖ tents or sails collectively **under canvas** in tents

can·vass, can·vas (kǽnvəs) 1. *v.t.* to seek votes, business orders, subscriptions, etc., from (potential supporters, clients, etc.) ‖ to ascertain (public opinion) by interrogating people in a certain area, etc. 2. *n.* a seeking of support, votes etc. ‖ a survey of public opinion **cán·vass·er** *n.* someone who canvasses

can·yon, ca·ñon (kǽnjən) *n.* a deep gorge or natural cleft, with very steep sides

cap (kæp 1. *n.* a usually brimless head covering ‖ any caplike cover, e.g. on a bottle or fountain pen ‖ a charge (for igniting explosive in a cartridge) 2. *v.t. pres. part.* **cap·ping** *past* and *past part.* **capped** to put a cap on (something) ‖ to cover the top or end of (an object) with metal etc. ‖ to cover as if with a cap, *mountains capped with snow* ‖ to put the finishing touch to or come as a climax to

ca·pa·bil·i·ty (keipəbíliti:) *pl.* **ca·pa·bil·i·ties** *n.* the quality of being capable, ability ‖ ability to be developed, exploited etc. ‖ (*pl.*) potentially excellent performance

ca·pa·ble (kéipəb'l) *adj.* able, having many capacities **capable of** with the ability for

ca·pac·i·ty (kəpǽsiti:) *pl.* **ca·pac·i·ties** *n.* the ability to contain or accommodate ‖ the amount which can be contained or accommodated ‖ mental ability ‖ faculty ‖ an office or position with respect to a particular function, competence etc., *in his capacity as chairman* **to be filled to capacity** to be completely full

cape (keip) *n.* a sleeveless outer garment hanging from the shoulders, worn fastened at the neck

cape *n.* a piece of land jutting out into the sea

ca·per (kéipər) 1. *v.i.* to leap or jump about playfully 2. *n.* a frisky leap or jump ‖ a fantastic antic

caper *n.* a low trailing shrub with small dark-green leaves, and three-petaled white flowers with mauve stamens, growing in the Mediterranean region ‖ (*pl.*) its unopened flower buds pickled for use in sauces, relishes etc.

cap·il·lar·y (kǽpiləri:) 1. *adj.* hairlike ‖ having a small bore or diameter 2. *pl.* **cap·il·lar·ies** *n.* one of a system of minute thin-walled blood vessels separating arterial from venous circulation

cap·i·tal (kǽpit'l) *n.* the top or head of a pillar, pier or column

capital 1. *adj.* involving forfeiture of life ‖ chief ‖ very great ‖ very good ‖ having to do with capital (wealth)

(**a**) æ, c*a*t; ɑ, c*a*r; ɔ f*aw*n; ei, sn*a*ke. (**e**) e, h*e*n; i:, sh*ee*p; iə, d*ee*r; ɛə, b*ea*r. (**i**) i, f*i*sh; ai, t*i*ger; ə:, b*i*rd. (**o**) o, *o*x; au, c*ow*; ou, g*oa*t; u, p*oo*r; ɔi, r*oy*al. (**u**) ʌ, d*u*ck; u, b*u*ll; u:, g*oo*se; ə, b*a*cillus; ju:, c*u*be. x, lo*ch*; θ, *th*ink; ð, bo*th*er; z, *Z*en; ʒ, corsa*g*e; dʒ, sava*g*e; ŋ, oranguta*ng*; j, *y*ak; ʃ, fi*sh*; tʃ, fe*tch*; 'l, rabb*le*; 'n, red*den*. Complete pronunciation key appears inside front cover.

|| (of a letter of the alphabet) in its relatively large form **2.** *n.* principal || the value of this in a given instance || the chief city of a country, state etc. || the owners of wealth (only vis-à-vis 'labor') || *(econ.)* the stock of goods and commodities in a country at any one time || a capital letter

cap·i·tal·ism (kǽpitəlizəm, *Br. also* kəpítəlizəm) *n.* an economic system in which the means of production, distribution and exchange are privately owned and operated for private profit

cap·i·tal·ist (kǽpitəlist, *Br. also* kəpítəlist) **1.** *n.* someone who owns capital stock used in business, or who has accumulated wealth from business **2.** *n.* possessing capital || defending or engaging in capitalism || characterized by capitalism **cap·i·tal·is·tic** *adj.*

cap·i·tal·ize (kǽpitəlaiz, *Br. also* kəpítəlaiz) *pres. part.* **cap·i·tal·iz·ing** *past and past part.* **cap·i·tal·ized** *v.t.* to use as capital || to convert into capital || to provide (a business) with capital || to turn (something) to account || to write with an initial capital letter

cap·i·tol (kǽpit'l) *n.* the building in which a state legislature meets || the Congressional building in Washington, D.C.

ca·pit·u·late (kəpítʃuleit) *pres. part.* **ca·pit·u·lat·ing** *past and past part.* **ca·pit·u·lat·ed** *v.i.* to surrender, often on terms agreed by both sides

ca·pit·u·la·tion (kəpítʃuléiʃən) *n.* a surrender upon terms

ca·price (kəprí:s) *n.* a sudden and illogical fancy, a whim || an arbitrary action || *(mus.)* a light, gay piece

ca·pri·cious (kəpríʃəs) *adj.* unreliable, ruled by whims || changeable, *capricious winds*

cap·size (kǽpsaiz, kæpsáiz) *pres. part.* **cap·siz·ing** *past and past part.* **cap·sized** *v.t.* to upset or cause to founder (esp. a boat or ship) || *v.i.* to turn over or become overturned on water

cap·su·lar (kǽpsələr) *adj.* of or like a capsule

cap·sule (kǽpsəl, *Br.* kǽpsju:l) *n.* *(anat.)* a saclike membrane enclosing an organ || *(bot.)* any closed boxlike vessel containing seeds, spores or fruits || *(med.)* a small case of gelatin etc., enclosing a medicinal dose || a sealed, pressurized cabin for extremely high-altitude or space flight that provides an acceptable environment for humans, animals, or equipment

cap·tain (kǽptən) **1.** *n.* *(navy)* an officer above a commander and below a rear admiral in rank || (by courtesy) the commander or master of a vessel || *(army)* an officer above a lieutenant and below a major in rank || an officer of the same rank in the U.S. air force or marine corps || a leader, chief || the leader of a team in sports **2.** *v.t.* to be captain of **cáp·tain·cy** *n.*

cap·tion (kǽpʃən) *n.* the heading of a chapter || the headline of a newspaper article || a legend to an illustration, or, in silent films, to an image

cap·ti·vate (kǽptiveit) *pres. part.* **cap·ti·vat·ing** *past and past part.* **cap·ti·vat·ed** *v.t.* to charm, enchant **cap·ti·va·tion** *n.*

cap·tive (kǽptiv) **1.** *n.* a prisoner, esp. a prisoner of war **2.** *adj.* imprisoned, kept in confinement (used both of people and animals)

cap·tiv·i·ty (kæptíviti) *pl.* **cap·tiv·i·ties** *n.* the period of being a captive || confinement

cap·ture (kǽptʃər) **1.** *v.t.* to get (someone) into one's power as a prisoner || to subdue, dominate or overcome and get possession of, *it captured our imagination* **2.** *n.* a capturing or being captured || a thing or person captured

car (kɑr) *n.* a wheeled vehicle, esp. an automobile || a passenger conveyance in an elevator || any railroad carriage or wagon

ca·rafe (kərǽf, kərɑ́f) *n.* a glass bottle for table water or wine

car·a·mel (kǽrəməl, kǽrəmel) *n.* *(cooking)* sugar melted and slightly burned over a low flame || a semi-hard candy that needs chewing || a shade of light brown

car·at, kar·at (kǽrət) *n.* an international measure of weight used for gems

car·a·van (kǽrəvæn) *n.* a company of people, e.g. merchants or pilgrims, traveling together for safety, esp. in desert areas of Asia and Africa

car·a·vel (kǽrəvel) *n.* a small, fast sailing ship of the 15th and 16th cc.

car·bo·hy·drate (kɑ́rbouháidreit) *n.* one of a biologically important group of neutral organic chemicals composed of carbon, hydrogen and oxygen and including sugars, starches and celluloses

car·bon (kɑ́rbən) *n.* a tetravalent element. It occurs in crystalline forms as diamonds and graphite

car·bon·ate (kɑ́rbəneit, kɑ́rbənit) **1.** *n.* a salt of carbonic acid **2.** (kɑ́rbəneit) *v.t. pres. part.* **car·bon·at·ing** *past and past part.* **car·bon·at·ed** to impregnate (a liquid) with carbon dioxide under pressure (e.g. aerated water) or with carbonic acid || *(chem.)* to form into a carbonate

car·bon·a·tion (kɑ́rbənéiʃən) *n.* a saturation or reaction with carbon dioxide

carbon dioxide a colorless, heavy gas that does not support combustion, that dissolved in water to form carbonic acid and that is formed by the oxidation of carbon-containing compounds (e.g. in animal respiration) and by the action of acid on carbonates

carbon monoxide a colorless, odorless, highly toxic gas that may be produced by the incomplete combustion of carbon

car·bun·cle (kɑ́rbʌŋk'l) *n.* a garnet cut in a boss, or cabochon || a painful infection of the skin **car·bún·cu·lar** *adj.* like a carbuncle

car·bu·re·tor, car·bu·re·ter (kɑ́rbəreitər, kɑ́rbjəretər) *n.* an apparatus which vaporizes a liquid fuel and controls its mixing with air for combustion in an engine

car·cass (kɑ́rkəs) *n.* a dead animal body || the human body, alive or dead

car·ci·no·ma (kɑrsinóumə) *pl.* **car·ci·no·mas, car·ci·no·ma·ta** (kɑrsinóumətə) *n.* *(med.)* an epithelial cancer

card (kɑrd) *n.* a usually rectangular piece of paper or pasteboard suitable for writing or printing on || a playing card || *(pl.)* the activity of playing with cards

card·board (kɑ́rdbɔrd, kɑ́rdbourd) *n.* stiff pasteboard, used for shoe boxes etc.

car·di·ac (kɑ́rdi:æk) **1.** *adj.* *(anat.)* pertaining to the heart **2.** *n.* a medicine or cordial which stimulates the heart || a cardiac patient

car·di·gan (kɑ́rdigən) *n.* a knitted jacket which buttons down the front

car·di·nal (kɑ́rd'n'l) **1.** *adj.* of fundamental importance || deep red **2.** *n.* one of the princes of the Catholic Church who are members of the papal council or Sacred College, and electors of the pope || a family of small red birds in the U.S.A. || a deep red color

care (keər) *n.* serious attention, watchfulness, caution || protection || charge || anxiety, concern, worry || an object of anxiety, worry **to take care** to exercise caution or prudence **to take care of** to look after

care *pres. part.* **car·ing** *past and past part.* **cared** *v.t.* to feel interest in, bother about || to be concerned as much as || *v.i.* to be willing, have the wish **to care for** to take care of || to like, enjoy

ca·reen (kərí:n) *n.* *(naut.)* a tilted position of a ship, *on the careen* **2.** *v.t.* to turn (a ship) on her side for scraping etc. || to make (a ship) heel or tip over || *v.i.* (of a ship or car) to go forward tilting to one side

ca·reer (kəríər) **1.** *n.* a swift movement, impetus || progress through life with respect to one's work || a means of earning a living, a profession **2.** *v.i.* to move swiftly and erratically

care·free (kéərfri:) *adj.* free from care

care·ful (kéərfəl) *adj.* cautious || painstaking || done with accuracy or with caution || (with 'of' or 'for') having thoughtful concern

care·less (kéərlis) *adj.* lighthearted, carefree || relaxed, casual || indifferent, thoughtless || negligent || showing negligence

ca·ress (kərés) *n.* a gentle, affectionate touch or embrace

caress *v.t.* to touch gently and lovingly, fondle

care·tak·er (kéərteikər) *n.* a person employed to take charge of property etc., and see to routine matters, esp. in the owner's absence

car·go (kárgou) *pl.* **car·goes, car·gos** *n.* the freight of goods or luggage carried by a ship, aircraft etc.

car·i·bou (kæribu:) *n.* a deer indigenous to Canada, Alaska and Greenland and related to the reindeer

car·i·ca·ture (kærikətʃuər) **1.** *n.* ridicule (by exaggeration and distortion) of a thing or person, e.g. in mime, a picture, or a literary portrait ‖ such a picture, literary portrait etc. ‖ a ludicrously poor copy or imitation **2.** *v.t. pres. part.* **car·i·ca·tur·ing** *past* and *past part.* **car·i·ca·tured** to make a caricature of **cár·i·ca·tur·ist** *n.* someone who makes caricatures, esp. pictorial ones

car·ies (kéəri:z, kéəri:i:z) *n.* the decay of animal tissues, esp. of teeth

car·il·lon (kærələn, *Br.* kəríljən) **1.** *n.* a set of bells sounded either directly by hand or from a keyboard, and playing either a tune or a series of notes repeated without any change **2.** *v.i.* to play a carillon

car·nage (kárnidʒ) *n.* slaughter, esp. in battle

car·nal (kárn'l) *adj.* pertaining to the flesh, as opposed to the spirit ‖ sexual, *carnal appetite*

car·na·tion (kɑːnéiʃən) *n.* a species of pink, having many usually double-flowering varieties

car·ni·val (kárnivəl) *n.* the festivities in Catholic countries just before Lent (Mardi Gras) and at mid-Lent ‖ any public festivity, usually with processions, dancing and sideshows ‖ a traveling amusement show

car·niv·o·rous (karnívərəs) *adj.* flesh-eating

car·ol (kærəl) **1.** *n.* a Christmas hymn ‖ (*rhet.*) a joyful song **2.** *v. pres. part.* **car·ol·ing** *past* and *past part.* **car·oled** *v.i.* (*rhet.*) to sing joyfully ‖ to sing Christmas hymns

ca·rouse (kəráuz) **1.** *v.i. pres. part.* **ca·rous·ing** *past* and *past part.* **ca·roused** to take part in a drinking bout **2.** *n.* a drinking bout

carp (karp) *n.* a long-lived bony, edible, freshwater fish

carp *v.i.* to complain **to carp at** to nag, find fault with

car·pen·ter (kárpəntər) **1.** *n.* a workman in wood ‖ a person who makes the wooden frames of a house, ship etc. **2.** *v.i.* to work as a carpenter ‖ *v.t.* to make by carpentry

car·pen·try (kárpəntri:) *n.* woodwork ‖ the carpenter's trade

car·pet (kárpit) **1.** *n.* a heavy fabric, often patterned, used esp. as a covering for floors and stairs ‖ a smooth expanse (of turf, flowers etc.) **2.** *v.t.* to cover with or as if with a carpet

car·pet·ing (kárpitiŋ) *n.* material used for laying as a carpet

car·riage (kæridʒ) *n.* a horse-drawn vehicle for people to ride in ‖ the manner of holding oneself in walking and standing ‖ the passing of a bill, proposal before a committee etc. ‖ a framework on which a gun is mounted

car·ri·er (kæri:ər) *n.* a person, company or corporation undertaking transport ‖ a luggage rack on a bicycle ‖ a person or animal carrying the germs of a disease without contracting it himself but able to infect others ‖ an aircraft carrier

car·ri·on (kæri:ən) *n.* dead, putrefying flesh of man or beast

car·rot (kærət) *n.* a biennial plant whose yellowish-red root is widely used as a vegetable ‖ the root of this plant **cár·rot·y** *adj.* yellowish red

car·rou·sel, car·ou·sel (kærəsél, *Br.* kæru:zél) *n.* a cavalry tournament ‖ a merry-go-round

car·ry (kæri:) **1.** *v. pres. part.* **car·ry·ing** *past* and *past part.* **car·ried** *v.t.* to convey from one place to another by hand or in a vehicle ‖ to convey or transmit in any manner ‖ to conduct ‖ to prolong, extend ‖ to be necessarily accompanied by ‖ to support, bear (the weight of a stationary object) ‖ to win, capture (a position held by an enemy) ‖ to secure or hold the sympathy of (an audience) ‖ to sing (a tune) in tune ‖ to play (an instrument) or sing (a part) ‖ to hold or bear (the body or head or oneself) in a certain way ‖ *v.i.* to have range, *this rifle carries half a mile* ‖ (of sound) to be so strong as to be heard at a distance **to carry away** to cause (someone) to be so absorbed or thrilled as to cease to be aware of himself and his immediate concerns **to carry forward** (*accounting*) to transfer (a total) from one column of figures to the next ‖ to progress with **to carry on** to continue ‖ to flirt **to carry out** to fulfil, put (orders etc.) into effect **to carry over** (*accounting*) to carry forward **2.** *n.* portage between rivers ‖ the range of a gun

cart (kart) **1.** *n.* a two-wheeled or four-wheeled horse-drawn or tractor-drawn vehicle, used for carrying loads ‖ a small, shafted vehicle for moving loads by hand **2.** *v.t.* to transport in a cart etc. ‖ to drag, cause to go under compulsion ‖ *v.i.* to move loads by cart **cárt·age** *n.* the act of conveying goods in a cart ‖ the charge for doing this

car·tel (kartél, kárt'l) *n.* an industrial combination in which several different firms agree on some form of joint action

car·ter (kártər) *n.* a person who drives a cart ‖ a person who transports goods for others

car·ti·lage (kárt'lidʒ) *n.* (*anat.*) a very tough, translucent, bluish-white elastic tissue, found in connection with bones in vertebrates **car·ti·lag·i·noid** (kɑrt'lædʒinɔid) *adj.* resembling cartilage

car·tog·ra·pher (kartógrəfər) *n.* a person who prepares and makes maps

car·tog·ra·phy (kartógrəfi:) *n.* mapmaking

car·ton (kárt'n) *n.* a light box made of cardboard or fiber

car·toon (kartú:n) *n.* a drawing which puts a comic construction on current events or on people ‖ a drawing for a tapestry or a painting ‖ an animated cartoon ‖ comic strip **car·tóon·ist** *n.* a person who draws cartoons

car·tridge (kártridʒ) *n.* a cased explosive charge, also containing the missile when made for rifles or shotguns ‖ a holder for a roll of film

carve (karv) *pres. part.* **carv·ing,** *past* and *past part.* **carved** *v.t.* to cut (stone, wood etc.) ‖ to form (an image, inscription etc.) by such cutting ‖ to cut (a roast, chicken etc.) into slices or pieces ‖ *v.i.* to make a statue, inscription etc. by cutting ‖ to cut up a roast, chicken etc. **to carve out** to cause to emerge by a proces of cutting away surroundings

carv·ing (kárviŋ) *n.* the act of carving ‖ a carved work or design

cas·cade (kæskéid) **1.** *n.* a waterfall ‖ anything thought of as like a rush of water, *cascades of laughter* **2.** *v.i. pres. part.* **cas·cad·ing** *past* and *past part.* **cas·cad·ed** to fall as or like a waterfall

case (keis) **1.** *n.* a box or crate ‖ any protective outer covering ‖ a glass-sided box for exhibiting specimens, e.g. in a museum ‖ (*bookbinding*) a completed book cover ready to be fitted to the sheets **2.** *v.t. pres. part.* **cas·ing** *past* and *past part.* **cased** to enclose in a case or box, encase

case *n.* a set of circumstances or conditions, a state of

---

affairs ‖ an instance ‖ the patient suffering from an illness ‖ *(law)* a matter for trial ‖ the arguments for either side in a lawsuit ‖ *(gram.)* in inflected languages the form of a noun, pronoun or adjective which indicates its relationship to other words in a sentence **in case of** in the event of

case harden *v.t.* to harden the surface of **case·hard·ened** (kéishərd'nd) *adj.* of a person grown callous through seeing too much misery

ca·sein (kéisi:n, kéisi:in) *n.* the colloidal protein in milk, caseinogen ‖ the insoluble protein which is the basis and chief protein in cheese and is used in making certain plastics

cash (kæʃ) **1.** *n.* money in the form of coins or paper, ready money **2.** *v.t.* to give or obtain cash in exchange for (a check, money order etc.) **to cash in on** *(pop.)* to turn to account, take advantage of

cash·ew (kæʃu:, kəʃú:) *n.* a tropical tree native to Brazil and grown in the West and East Indies

cash·ier (kæʃíər) *n.* an employee in a bank, who receives and pays out money ‖ an employee in a shop, restaurant etc. who takes and records customers' payments

cashier (kəʃíər) *v.t. (armed forces)* to dismiss (an officer) from the service in disgrace

cash·mere (kæ̃ʒmiər, kæ̃ʃmiər) *n.* a very soft, fine wool, or woolen material, made from the fleece of the Kashmir goat

cas·ing (kéisiŋ) *n.* a thing which encases ‖ a material for encasing something else ‖ an enclosing framework

ca·si·no (kəsí:nou) *n.* a public room for gambling and dancing ‖ a building containing gambling rooms

cask (kæsk, kɑsk) *n.* a wooden barrel for liquids ‖ a barrel and its contents ‖ the amount a cask holds

cas·ket (kǽskit, kɑ́skit) *n.* a small box, usually of some valuable material ‖ a receptacle for the ashes of a cremated person ‖ a coffin

cas·se·role (kǽsəroul) *n.* a covered dish of earthenware or toughened glass etc. in which food needing long, slow cooking is prepared ‖ food cooked in such a dish

cas·sette (kəsét) *n.* a holder for a photographic film or plate, esp. in X-ray work or for a tape-recorder tape ‖ cartridge containing magnetic tape that can be inserted into a player for listening or viewing

cas·sock (kǽsək) *n.* a long, close-fitting tunic, usually black, worn by priests and choristers

cast (kæst, kɑst) **1.** *v. pres. part.* **cast·ing,** past and past part. **cast** *v.t.* to throw ‖ to let drop, throw off ‖ to discard (a card) ‖ to add up ‖ to shape by pouring into a mold ‖ to make (an object) by this process ‖ *(angling)* to throw (a line) into the water ‖ *(theater)* to distribute (the parts) in a play to the actors ‖ to register (a vote) ‖ to drop out (an anchor) attached to a rope ‖ to direct, usually quickly, *to cast a glance* ‖ *v.i.* to turn, tack ‖ *(angling)* to throw the line into the water **to cast aside** to put away from one **to cast down** to turn (the eyes) downwards **to cast on** *(knitting)* to begin or widen a piece by making loops on a knitting needle **2.** *n.* the act of casting ‖ a throw of a fishing net or line, a sounding lead, or dice ‖ the actors in a play ‖ a model made by running molten metal, plaster etc., into a mold ‖ the mold into which metal is poured ‖ *(med.)* a rigid surgical dressing often of gauze and plaster of paris

cas·ta·net (kæstənét) *n. (mus.)* one of a pair of wooden or ivory attached, shell-like pieces which the player loops over his fingers and holds in the palm and which produce a sharp, clicking sound when struck together

caste (kæst, kɑst) *n.* an inherited socioreligious rank

cast·er, cas·tor (kǽstər, kɑ́stər) *n.* a small container for sugar, salt or pepper, with holes in the top, used at the table ‖ a small metal wheel fixed to the leg of a piece of furniture to allow it to be moved easily

cas·ti·gate (kǽstigeit) *pres. part.* **cas·ti·gat·ing** past and past part. **cas·ti·gat·ed** *v.t.* to rebuke or criticize vehemently **cas·ti·gá·tion** *n.* very severe criticism

cás·ti·ga·tor *n.* **cas·ti·ga·to·ry** (kæstigətɔ̃ri:, kæstigətɔ̃uri:) *adj.*

cast iron an iron-carbon alloy produced in a blast furnace **cást-iron** *adj.* made of cast iron ‖ *(fig.)* unbreakable, *a cast-iron will*

cas·tle (kǽs'l, kɑ́s'l) *n.* a fortified building or group of buildings within a defensive wall, a fortress ‖ *(chess)* a rook

cast-off (kǽstɔf, kɑ́stɔf, kǽstɒf, kɑ́stɒf) *adj.* (of clothes, lovers etc.) not wanted any more **cást-off** *n.* a person who has been rejected ‖ *(printing)* an estimate of the number of lines or pages, in type of a given style, required for a given quantity of copy

cas·tor (kǽstər, kɑ́stər) *n.* a substance obtained from glands of the beaver, used in medicine and perfumery

castor oil a pale yellow, thick oil, with an unpleasant taste, obtained from the seeds of the castor-oil plant

cas·trate (kǽstreit) *pres. part.* **cas·trat·ing** past and past part. **cas·trat·ed** *v.t.* to remove the testicles of (a man or male animal) **cas·trá·tion** *n.*

cas·u·al (kǽʒu:əl) *adj.* irregular, happening by chance ‖ without formality ‖ free and easy ‖ unimportant, not significant

cas·u·al·ty (kǽʒu:əlti:) *pl.* **cas·u·al·ties** *n.* an accident, esp. one involving injury or loss of life ‖ an injured person ‖ a soldier who is missing or has been captured, wounded or killed in action

cat (kæt) *n.* a carnivorous furry mammal, long domesticated and useful for keeping down mice ‖ the fur or pelt of the domestic cat ‖ any other member of fam. *Felidae*, e.g. a lion, tiger, leopard, wildcat etc. ‖ a malicious or spiteful woman **to let the cat out of the bag** to reveal a secret, esp. by a slip of the tongue

cat·a·clysm (kǽtəklizəm) *n.* any violent physical upheaval such as a flood or an earthquake ‖ a political upheaval or catastrophe **cat·a·clýs·mal, cat·a·clýs·mic** *adjs*

cat·a·comb (kǽtəkoum) *n.* a series of underground galleries and chambers with recesses for burying the dead

cat·a·log, cat·a·logue (kǽt'lɔg, kǽt'lɒg) **1.** *n.* a complete list of articles, usually in alphabetical order, or under special headings, and often with descriptions of the articles **2.** *v.t. pres. part.* **cat·a·log·ing, cat·a·logu·ing** past and past part. **cat·a·loged, cat·a·logued** to list ‖ to include in a catalog **cát·a·log·er, cát·a·logu·er** *n.*

ca·tal·y·sis (kətǽlisis) *pl.* **ca·tal·y·ses** (kətǽlisi:z) *n.* the change in the rate of chemical reaction brought about by a catalyst **cat·a·lyst** (kǽt'list) *n.* a substance that alters the rate of a chemical reaction and is itself unchanged by the process **cat·a·lýt·ic** (kæt'lítik) *adj.* causing or relating to catalysis **cat·a·lýt·i·cal·ly** *adv.*

cat·a·ma·ran (kætəmərǽn) *n.* a boat with twin hulls connected by a frame ‖ a raft of two boats lashed together

cat·a·pult (kǽtəpult, kǽtəpʌlt) **1.** *n. (hist.)* a machine for hurling stones etc., worked by a lever ‖ a machine for launching aircraft **2.** *v.t.* to launch (aircraft) with a catapult ‖ *v.i.* to rise into the air as though shot from a catapult

cat·a·ract (kǽtərækt) *n.* a waterfall ‖ any rush of water ‖ *(med.)* a disease of the eye in which the normally transparent lens becomes opaque

ca·tas·tro·phe (kətǽstrɑfi:) *n.* a sudden and terrible event, e.g. an earthquake, flood or tornado, any disaster affecting one or more persons **cat·a·stroph·ic** (kætəstrɔ́fik) *adj.*

catch (kætʃ) **1.** *v. pres. part.* **catch·ing** past and past part. **caught** (kɔt) *v.t.* to capture, ensnare ‖ to seize in flight ‖ to be in time for ‖ to hit or strike ‖ to surprise or detect (esp. in a crime or misdemeanor) ‖ to burst into ‖ to contract (an illness) ‖ to obtain briefly ‖ to attract (attention) or the attention of ‖ *v.i.* to become entangled ‖ (of the voice) to break with emotion ‖ (of breath) to stop momentarily as a result of surprise etc. ‖ *(baseball)* to play as catcher ‖ to take fire **to catch it** *(pop.)* to be punished **to catch on** *(pop.)* to understand, grasp an idea ‖ to make up arrears **to catch up with** to come level with **2.** *n.* the act of catching ‖ the number of fish caught in a fishing expedition ‖ something worth securing *(pop.,* esp. a husband or wife) ‖ a fastening on a door, window or gate ‖ a game consisting of throwing and catching a ball

catch·er (kǽtʃər) *n. (baseball)* the player who stands behind the batter to catch the pitched ball

catch·ing (kǽtʃiŋ) *adj.* (of disease, enthusiasm etc.) contagious

catch·y (kǽtʃi:) *comp.* **catch·i·er** *superl.* **catch·i·est** *adj.* attractive and easy to remember ‖ tricky, full of snags

cat·e·chism (kǽtəkizəm) *n.* a set of questions and answers on religious doctrine

cat·e·gor·i·cal (kætəgɔ́rik'l, kætəgórik'l) *adj.* unqualified, absolute ‖ explicit *(logic)* analyzable into a subject and an attribute ‖ of, pertaining to, or in a category

cat·e·go·ry (kǽtəgɔri:, kǽtəgouri:) *pl.* **cat·e·go·ries** *n.* one of the divisions in a system of classification ‖ any general division serving to classify

ca·ter (kéitər) *v.i.* to provide meals, refreshments etc. ‖ to provide something other than food, e.g. amusement **cá·ter·er** *n.* a person or company supplying food for public or private entertainment

cat·er·pil·lar (kǽtərpilər, kǽtəpilər) *n.* the larva of a moth or butterfly **Cat·er·pil·lar** (trademark) a tractor fitted with flexible steel bands around the wheels to enable it to travel over very rough or soft ground

ca·thar·sis, ka·thar·sis (kəθársis) *pl.* **ca·thar·ses, ka·thar·ses** (kəθársi:z) *n. (med.)* purgation

ca·thar·tic (kəθártik) **1.** *n.* a purgative medicine **2.** *adj.* pertaining to catharsis

ca·the·dral (kəθí:drəl) **1.** *n.* the principal church of a diocese ‖ any of various large non-episcopalian churches **2.** *adj.* pertaining to or ranking as a cathedral

cath·e·ter (kǽθitər) *n.* a tube of metal, glass or rubber passed along a mucous canal to permit the passage of fluid (esp. from the bladder) or to facilitate breathing

Cath·o·lic (kǽθəlik, kǽθlik) **1.** *adj.* any of the original Christian Church before the schism between East and West ‖ of the Roman or Western Church after this schism and before the Reformation ‖ pertaining to the whole Christian Church ‖ pertaining or adhering to Catholicism **cath·o·lic** universal, all embracing **2.** *n.* someone who subscribes to the beliefs of the universal Christian Church ‖ a member of the Roman Catholic Church

Ca·thol·i·cism (kəθɔ́lisizəm) *n.* the faith, practice or system of the Catholic Church ‖ the faith, practice or system of the Roman Catholic Church ‖ catholicity

cat·nap (kǽtnæp) *n.* a short doze by a human being who is not in bed

cat·nip (kǽtnip) *n.* an aromatic plant with blue flowers and grayish foliage

cat-o'-nine-tails (kætənáinteilz) *pl.* **cat-o'-nine-tails** *n.* a whip of nine knotted lashes used *(hist.)* for punishment esp. in the British navy

Cat·tail (kǽtteil) *n.* a reedlike plant growing in marshes, with a dense cylindrical spike of flowers

cat·ti·ness (kǽti:nis) *n.* the quality of being catty

cat·tle (kǽt'l) *n.* bovine animals collectively

cat·tle·man (kǽt'lmən, kǽt'lmæn) *pl.* **cat·tle·men** (kǽt'lmən, kǽt'lmen) *n.* the owner of a cattle ranch ‖ a man who tends cattle

cat·ty (kǽti:) *comp.* **cat·ti·er** *superl.* **cat·ti·est** *adj.* spiteful in a catty way

cau·cus (kɔ́kəs) **1.** *n.* a preliminary meeting of the leaders of a political party to make policy and decide on

candidates **2.** *v.i.* to hold a meeting of party leaders ‖ to make use of the caucus system to organize a political party

cau·li·flow·er (kɔ́ləflauər) *n.* a variety of cabbage with a fleshy hypertrophied inflorescence

caulk, calk (kɔk) *v.t.* to stop up and make watertight the seams of (a wooden ship) with pitch and oakum ‖ to stop up the crevices of (windows etc.)

cau·sal·i·ty (kozǽliti:) *pl.* **cau·sal·i·ties** *n.* the state of being a cause ‖ the relation of cause and effect ‖ the doctrine that all things have a cause

cause (kɔz) *n.* that which brings about a result ‖ basis, grounds ‖ a person whose actions or words lead to some result ‖ a matter of widespread interest and concern ‖ the side taken in a contest between individuals or between political or religious movements

cause·way (kɔ́zwei) *n.* a raised roadway across wet or low-lying ground

caus·tic (kɔ́stik) *adj.* burning, corrosive, e.g. of some chemicals, esp. strong alkalis ‖ *(fig.)* sharply biting, esp. with a sarcastic intention **cáus·ti·cal·ly** *adv.*

cau·ter·ize (kɔ́təraiz) *pres. part.* **cau·ter·iz·ing** *past* and *past part.* **cau·ter·ized** *v.t.* to destroy (living tissue) by means of heat or a caustic agent, esp. in the treatment of wounds

cau·tion (kɔ́ʃən) **1.** *n.* carefulness, concern for safety ‖ a warning, esp. one that carries a reprimand **2.** *v.t.* to warn ‖ to warn with a reprimand

cau·tious (kɔ́ʃəs) *adj.* prudent, attentive to safety

cav·al·cade (kævəlkéid, kǽvəlkeid) *n.* horsemen in a procession ‖ a procession or parade not necessarily of horsemen, *circus cavalcade*

cav·a·lier (kævəlíər, kǽvəliər) **1.** *n. (hist.)* a horseman, esp. a mounted soldier ‖ *(hist.)* a knight **Ca·va·lier 2.** *adj.* high-handed

cav·al·ry (kǽvəlri:) *pl.* **cav·al·ries** *n. (hist.)* mounted soldiers ‖ *(mil.)* a motorized unit formerly mounted

cav·al·ry·man (kǽvəlri:mən) *pl.* **cav·al·ry·men** (kǽvəlri:mən) *n.* a member of the cavalry

cave (keiv) **1.** *n.* a natural hollow in rock, or an underground chamber, with an opening at surface level **2.** *v.t. pres. part.* **cav·ing** *past* and *past part.* **caved** to make a hollow in ‖ to scoop or excavate (earth) **to cave in** to cause to collapse ‖ (of a wall etc.) to bulge inwards ‖ (of a roof) to sink in ‖ *(pop.)* to collapse, cease resisting

cave·man (kéivmæn) *pl.* **cave·men** (kéivmen) *n.* a Stone Age cave dweller ‖ a man fatuously pleased with his own strength and behaving with ostentatious aggressiveness

cav·ern (kǽvərn) *n.* a cave, esp. a large one ‖ an underground chamber

cav·ern·ous (kǽvərnəs) *adj.* full of caverns ‖ suggestive of caverns, *cavernous eye sockets*

cav·i·ar, cav·i·are (kǽvi:ɑr, kævi:ɑ́r) *n.* the roes of the sturgeon and sterlet caught in lakes and rivers of the U.S.S.R., salted and eaten as an appetizer

cav·il (kǽvəl) **1.** *v.i. pres. part.* **cav·il·ing** *past* and *past part.* **cav·iled** (with at' or about') to raise petty objections ‖ to find fault without reason **2.** *n.* a trivial, frivolous objection, a quibble ‖ the raising of such objections

cav·i·ty (kǽviti:) *pl.* **cav·i·ties** *n.* an empty space inside a solid object, e.g. in a decayed tooth

ca·vort (kəvɔ́rt) *v.i.* to prance about

cay·enne pepper (kaién, keién) a very hot powder obtained form the dried pulverized fruit of several pepper varieties used as a condiment

cease (si:s) *pres. part.* **ceas·ing** *past* and *past part.* **ceased** *v.t.* to stop, bring to an end ‖ *v.i.* to come to an end, stop

---

cease-fire (síːsfáiər) *n.* *(mil.)* an order to stop shooting ‖ an order for the cessation of hostilities as a preliminary to making peace terms ‖ the period during which the order holds

cease·less (síːslis) *adj.* without pause or interruption

ce·dar (síːdər) *n.* a genus of evergreen trees, producing durable wood used for building

cede (siːd) *pres. part.* **ced·ing** *past* and *past part.* **ced·ed** *v.t.* to grant ‖ to surrender (esp. territory or legal rights)

ceil·ing (síːliŋ) *n.* the upper, inner surface of a room ‖ the maximum height which can be reached ‖ an imposed upper limit ‖ an upper limit of capacity or ability ‖ the cloud cover above clear air, esp. with respect to altitude

cel·e·brate (séləbreit) *pres. part.* **cel·e·brat·ing** *past* and *past part.* **cel·e·brat·ed** *v.t.* to perform (a religious ceremony) publicly ‖ to honor or observe (some special occasion or event) ‖ *v.i.* to seize an occasion for being festive **cél·e·brat·ed** *adj.* famous

cel·e·bra·tion (seləbréiʃən) *n.* the act or process of celebrating

ce·leb·ri·ty (səlébriti) *pl.* **ce·leb·ri·ties** *n.* fame ‖ a famous person

ce·ler·i·ty (səlériti) *n.* rapidity, swiftness

cel·er·y (séləri) *n.* a culinary plant cultivated in fertile, moist, temperate areas. The leafstalks are blanched and eaten raw or cooked

ce·les·tial (səléstʃəl) *adj.* pertaining to the sky or heavens ‖ pertaining to a spiritual heaven, heavenly, divine

cel·i·ba·cy (sélibəsi) *n.* the unmarried state

cel·i·bate (sélibit, sélibeit) **1.** *n.* a person who has vowed to remain unmarried, or who is bound to do so **2.** *adj.* unmarried

cell (sel) *n.* a small enclosed space, small chamber ‖ a small group of militant political members within a community ‖ *(computer)* unit of computer memory with one-word capacity ‖ *(biol.)* the smallest structural unit of living tissue capable of functioning as an independent entity ‖ *(chem.)* a device for producing an electric current chemically or photoelectrically or for use in electrolysis ‖ *(chem.)* a fuel cell

cel·lar (sélər) *n.* a room, usually under a building, used as a cool storage place for wine and food **cél·lar·age** *n.* **cél·lar·er** *n.* the keeper of wine and food in a monastery

cel·list (tʃélist) *n.* a person who plays the cello

cel·lo, 'cel·lo (tʃélou) *n.* a four-stringed, bowed musical instrument

cel·lo·phane (séləfein) **1.** *n.* a thin, transparent material made from viscose **2.** *adj.* made from cellophane

cel·lu·lar (séljulər) *adj.* formed of cells ‖ having cells or compartments

cel·lu·lose (séljulous) *n.* a fibrous carbohydrate. It is the principal structural material of the cell walls of plants and is chiefly obtained from wood pulp and cotton

ce·ment (simént) **1.** *n.* a grayish powder made by heating together limestone or chalk and clay or shale, and then grinding ‖ any substance used to make materials cohere **2.** *v.t.* to join together with, or as if with, cement ‖ *v.i.* to become cemented **ce·men·ta·tion** (siːmentéiʃən, sementéiʃən) *n.* the act of cementing

cem·e·ter·y (sémiteri:, *Br.* sémitri) *pl.* **cem·e·ter·ies** *n.* a place where the dead are buried

cen·sor (sénsər) **1.** *n.* a person empowered to suppress publications or excise any matter in them thought to be immoral, seditious or otherwise undesirable ‖ any person who supervises the morals and conduct of others **2.** *v.t.* to examine (letters, literature etc.) in the capacity of a censor **cen·so·ri·al** (sensóːriəl, sensóuri:əl) *adj.*

cen·sor·ship (sénsərʃip) *n.* the institution or practice of censoring

cen·sur·a·ble (sénʃərəb'l) *adj.* deserving or subject to censure, blamable **cén·sur·a·bly** *adv.*

cen·sure (sénʃər) *n.* adverse criticism, blame, *vote of censure*

censure *pres. part.* **cen·sur·ing** *past* and *past part.* **cen·sured** *v.t.* to reprove, criticize severely

cen·sus (sénsəs) *n.* an official counting of a country's population, usually with vital statistics etc. ‖ a similar count of items in some other field (e.g. production, distribution)

cent (sent) *n.* *(symbol* [¢]*)* one hundredth of a dollar ‖ a small coin of this value in the U.S.A., Canada etc.

cen·ten·ni·al (senténi:əl **1.** *n.* a hundredth anniversary **2.** *adj.* lasting one hundred years

cen·ter (séntər) **1.** *n.* a point equidistant from the extremities of a straight line, circle, sphere or any other object ‖ an axis, pivot or point around which an object moves ‖ a place where activity is concentrated ‖ *(politics)* the group of those who hold moderate opinions ‖ the part of a target, e.g. for archery, which encircles the bull's-eye **2.** *v.* *pres. part.* **cen·ter·ing** *past* and *past part.* **cen·tered** *v.t.* to concentrate at one point ‖ to place in or bring into the middle ‖ to find the center of (an object) ‖ *v.i.* (with 'in', 'at', 'on', 'upon') to have a center ‖ to have a chief element

cen·ti·grade scale (séntigreid) *(abbr.* C.) a temperature scale for which 0° is taken as the freezing point of pure water and 100° is taken as the boiling point of pure water under standard atmospheric pressure

cen·ti·me·ter (séntimiːtər) *n.* a hundredth part of a meter

cen·tral (séntrəl) *adj.* situated at or near the center or middle point ‖ principal, chief ‖ between extremes

cen·tral·ize (séntrəlaiz) *pres. part.* **cen·tral·iz·ing** *past* and *past part.* **cen·tral·ized** *v.i.* to concentrate at one central point ‖ *v.t.* to bring under central control

cen·trif·u·gal (sentrífjug'l) *adj.* acting, moving or tending to move away from a center

cen·tri·fuge (séntrifjuːdʒ) *n.* a machine that, by rotating a liquid containing a finely divided or a dispersed liquid at high speeds, increases the rate of sedimentation of the suspended material

cen·tu·ry (séntʃuri) *pl.* **cen·tu·ries** *n.* a period of a hundred years ‖ a period of a hundred years counting from a particular point of time

ce·ram·ic (səræmik) *adj.* of or having to do with pottery **ce·rám·ics** *pl. n.* the art of pottery **cer·a·mist** (séramist) *n.* a potter

ce·re·al (síəri:əl) **1.** *n.* any of several plants (wheat, barley, oats, corn, millet, rice etc.), whose seed (grain) is cultivated for human food and for feeding livestock ‖ breakfast food made from grain **2.** *adj.* pertaining to grain used for food

cer·e·bral (sérəbrəl, səríːbrəl) *adj.* pertaining to the brain ‖ relating to the cerebrum ‖ marked by intellectual rather than passionate qualities

cer·e·mo·ni·al (serəmóuni:əl) **1.** *n.* ritual ‖ formalities observed on certain occasions ‖ *(eccles.)* a book of ritual **2.** *adj.* pertaining to ceremonies

cer·e·mo·ni·ous (serəmóuni:əs) *adj.* observing ceremony ‖ fussily polite

cer·e·mo·ny (sérəmouni) *pl.* **cer·e·mo·nies** *n.* rites or ritual ‖ an occasion observed with ritual ‖ any formalities observed on a special occasion ‖ punctilious, formal behavior **without ceremony** casually ‖ brusquely

ce·rise (səríːs, səríːz) **1.** *n.* cherry red, a bright red color **2.** *adj.* of this color

cer·tain (sə́ːrt'n) *adj.* sure ‖ convinced ‖ predictably reliable ‖ of a thing or person not specified although the identity is known ‖ some, though not very much **cér·tain·ly** *adv.* definitely ‖ admittedly ‖ (as an answer) yes ‖ yes, willingly

cer·tif·i·cate 1. (sərtífikit) *n.* a written statement attesting some fact, esp. the status and qualifications of the person holding it **2.** (sərtífikeit) *v.t. pres. part.* **cer·tif·i·cat·ing** *past* and *past part.* **cer·tif·i·cat·ed** to grant a certificate to ‖ to license **cer·ti·fi·cá·tion** *n.*

cer·ti·fy (sə́ːrtifai) *pres. part.* **cer·ti·fy·ing** *past* and *past part.* **cer·ti·fied** *v.t.* to attest formally ‖ to state in a certificate

ces·sa·tion (səséiʃən) *n.* a ceasing

ces·sion (séʃən) n. the act of ceding or giving up

chafe (tʃeif) **1.** v. pres. part. **chaf·ing** past and past part. **chafed** v.t. to irritate or make sore by rubbing ‖ to wear by rubbing ‖ to rub so as to warm ‖ to irritate, annoy ‖ v.i. to rub ‖ to become worn by rubbing **2.** n. a sore or irritation ‖ wear caused by rubbing

chaff (tʃæf, tʃɑf) **1.** n. banter, good-humored teasing **2.** v.t. to tease good-humoredly

chaff 1. n. the outer husk of grain separated by threshing or winnowing ‖ straw or hay chopped for animal fodder ‖ the bracts of the flower of grasses, esp. the inner pair ‖ useless or worthless writing, talk etc. **2.** v.t. to chop

cha·grin (ʃəgrín, Br. ʃǽgrin) **1.** n. disappointment, mortification **2.** v.t. to vex acutely because of disappointment

chain (tʃein) **1.** n. a series of rings or links of metal joined one to another ‖ an ornamental set of links worn as a necklace, as insignia etc. ‖ a series or sequence ‖ (pl.) a prisoner's fetters ‖ (pl., fig.) bonds, bondage ‖ a number of business concerns all of one kind and owned by one person or group **2.** v.t. to combine with or as if with chains or a chain

chair (tʃeər) **1.** n. a seat with four legs and a backrest, for one person ‖ the position of a professor in a university ‖ the seat and the office of a person appointed to preside over a meeting ‖ the chairman, to appeal to the chair ‖ the electric chair ‖ a rail chair **to take the chair** to act as chairman **2.** v.t. to preside over (a meeting) as chairman ‖ to install in office

chair·man (tʃéərmən) pl. **chair·men** (tʃéərmən) n. a person appointed to preside over a meeting ‖ the president of a committee **cháir·man·ship** n.

cha·let (ʃæléi, ʃǽlei) n. a small wooden house in the Alps ‖ a house built in this style

chal·ice (tʃǽlis) n. the cup used at the celebration of the Mass (Eucharist) **chál·iced** adj. (of flowers) cup-shaped

chalk (tʃɔk) **1.** n. (geol.) a soft, friable, earthy, whitish variety of limestone ‖ a short rod, formerly of chalk but now of calcium sulfate, used for writing and drawing on dark and slightly rough surfaces (esp. a blackboard) **2.** v.t. to write or mark with chalk **chálk·i·ness** n.

chalk·y (tʃɔ́ki:) comp. **chalk·i·er** superl. **chalk·i·est** adj. of or like chalk

chal·lenge (tʃǽlindʒ) n. a calling in question (of the truth of statements, rights, authority etc.) ‖ something which tests a person's qualities ‖ an invitation to play a game or accept a match ‖ an objection made against someone in respect of his qualification to vote, serve on a jury etc.

challenge pres. part. **chal·leng·ing** past and past part. **chal·lenged** v.t. (of a sentry) to demand a statement of identity of (a person) ‖ to invite or summon to a match or game or to a duel or (fig.) to comparison ‖ to dispute the truth of (a statement) ‖ to take objection to the authority or opinions of ‖ (law) to object to (a person) as voter, juryman etc. **chál·leng·er** n. someone or something that challenges

cham·ber (tʃéimbər) n. a legislative or judicial body ‖ a large room or hall used for the meetings of a legislative or judicial body ‖ (hist.) a private room, esp. a bedroom ‖ (pl.) a room where a judge deals with matters not requiring action in court ‖ a compartment or cavity ‖ the part of a gun which holds the charge

cha·me·le·on (kəmí:liːən, kəmí:ljən) n. an insectivorous lizard distinguished by its prehensile tail, long extensible tongue, independently moving eyeballs and esp. by its ability to change its skin color to match its surroundings ‖ an inconstant person **cha·me·le·on·ic** (kəmiːliːónik) adj.

cham·ois (ʃǽmiː, ʃǽmwɑ) n. a horned, goatlike antelope of the high Alps and European mountains. Its skin makes a very soft, warm leather

cham·pagne (ʃæmpéin) n. a sparkling white wine made in Champagne

cham·pi·on (tʃǽmpiːən) **1.** n. a winner of a competition in a particular field ‖ a flower or vegetable or animal which has won first prize in competition ‖ someone who defends another person or a cause **2.** v.t. to fight or argue on behalf of **3.** adj. first among all competitors ‖ (pop.) first-rate **chám·pi·on·ship** n. the state or honor of being a champion ‖ a competition in which the title of champion is contested ‖ advocacy

chance (tʃæns, tʃɑns) **1.** n. an occurrence that cannot be accounted for by any pattern of cause and effect, nor by the working of providence ‖ an opportunity **by chance** fortuitously **to leave it to chance** to trust to luck **to take a chance** to run a risk and trust to luck **2.** adj. unintentional, fortuitous **3.** v.i. pres. part. **chanc·ing** past and past part. **chanced** to happen fatefully ‖ to happen by accident ‖ v.t. to leave to luck ‖ to risk

chan·cel·lor (tʃǽnsələr, tʃɑ́nsələr) n. the chief administrative officer of some U.S. universities ‖ the presiding judge in a court of equity **chán·cel·lor·ship** n.

chan·de·lier (ʃændəlíər) n. a branched holder for several candles or electric lights, suspended from a ceiling

change (tʃeindʒ) n. alteration ‖ the exchange of one thing for another ‖ a new occupation or fresh outlook ‖ the passing from one form, phase, place or state to another ‖ a balance of money remaining out of what is tendered in payment of a smaller sum ‖ coins of small denomination

change pres. part. **chang·ing** past and past part. **changed** v.i. to become altered ‖ to put on different clothes ‖ to get out of a bus, train etc. and into another so as to continue a journey ‖ to make a change or exchange ‖ v.t. to alter ‖ to take off (clothes) and put on different ones ‖ to exchange (money) for the same amount in another denomination ‖ to abandon (one thing or person) for another ‖ to exchange ‖ to put a clean diaper on (a baby) ‖ to put fresh sheets on (a bed) **to change hands** to pass from one owner to another

chan·nel (tʃǽnˈl) **1.** n. a natural or artificial course for running water ‖ a part of a river or harbor where the water is deeper than the water on either side of it ‖ (radio) a narrow band of frequencies ‖ the course or agency through which something passes **2.** v.t. pres. part. **chan·nel·ing** past and past part. **chan·neled** to make a channel or groove in ‖ to canalize, to channel one's energies

chant (tʃænt, tʃɑnt) n. a simple melody to which a psalm may be sung ‖ a singing, esp. in choir ‖ a repetitive singsong utterance

chant v.t. to sing (a chant) ‖ to utter in a singsong voice ‖ v.i. to sing a chant **chánt·er** n. a person who chants

cha·os (kéiɒs) n. complete confusion ‖ the formless void before the creation of the universe **cha·ót·ic** adj. **cha·ót·i·cal·ly** adv.

chap (tʃæp) n. (pop.) a man or boy

chap 1. v. pres. part. **chap·ping** past and past part. **chapped** v.i. (usually of skin) to crack or split ‖ to become rough and sore ‖ v.t. to make rough and sore **2.** n. a crack or split in the skin

chap·el (tʃǽpˈl) n. a place of Christian worship other than a parish or cathedral church ‖ a part of a cathedral or large church, divided off from the rest, and having a separate altar and dedication

chap·er·on, chap·er·one (ʃǽpəroun) **1.** n. (esp. hist.)

(a) æ, cat; ɑ, car; ɔ fawn; ei, snake. (e) e, hen; i:, sheep; iə, deer; ɛə, bear. (i) i, fish; ai, tiger; ə:, bird. (o) o, ox; au, cow; ou, goat; u, poor; ɔi, royal. (u) ʌ, duck; u, bull; u:, goose; ə, bacillus; ju:, cube. x, loch; θ, think; ð, bother; z, Zen; ʒ, corsage; dʒ, savage; ŋ, orangutang; j, yak; ʃ, fish; tʃ, fetch; 'l, rabble; 'n, redden. Complete pronunciation key appears inside front cover.

someone responsible for the moral protection of a girl or the good behavior of young people at social gatherings **2.** *v.t. pres. part.* **chap·er·on·ing** *past* and *past part.* **chap·er·oned** to act as chaperon to

chap·lain (tʃǽplin) *n.* a priest or minister who officiates in a private chapel ‖ a priest, minister or rabbi who serves a school, college, prison or hospital or attached to the armed forces **cháp·lain·cy** *n.* the office of being chaplain

chap·ter (tʃǽptər) *n.* a division of a book ‖ a phase of existence ‖ the administrative body of canons of a cathedral or abbey ‖ a meeting of such a body ‖ a meeting of members of a religious community or order ‖ a local section of a national club, lodge etc.

char (tʃɑr) *pres. part.* **char·ring** *past* and *past part.* **charred** *v.t.* to reduce to carbon by slow, intense heating, or by burning ‖ to scorch ‖ *v.i.* to be burned to charcoal

char·ac·ter (kǽriktər) **1.** *n.* the total quality of a person's behavior ‖ *(genetics)* a detectable quality of an organism that is the result of the presence of a gene or group of genes, a unit of character ‖ a set of qualities or attributes distinguishing one place or country from another ‖ an imaginary person in a book or play etc. ‖ any symbol representing information ‖ a person of a bizarre or eccentric nature ‖ reputation ‖ a figure or sign used in writing **2.** *adj.* of or relating to character ‖ (of actors and parts in plays) portraying types, not individuals

char·ac·ter·is·tic (kæriktərístik) **1.** *n.* a quality typical of a person, place or object ‖ *(genetics)* a unit character ‖ *(math.)* the whole-number part of a logarithm **2.** *adj.* typical **char·ac·ter·is·ti·cal·ly** *adv.*

char·ac·ter·i·za·tion (kæriktərizéiʃən) *n.* the act, process or result of characterizing

char·ac·ter·ize (kǽriktəraiz) *pres. part.* **char·ac·ter·iz·ing** *past* and *past part.* **char·ac·ter·ized** *v.t.* to be the distinguishing feature of ‖ to describe the character of

cha·rade (ʃəréid) *n. (esp. pl.)* a party game in which each syllable of a word to be guessed is acted out or mimed

char·coal (tʃɑ́rkoul) *n.* the amorphous form of carbon

charge (tʃɑrdʒ) *n.* the price to be paid for goods or services ‖ an entry in an account of something due ‖ a duty, responsibility ‖ safekeeping ‖ a legal accusation ‖ a record of accusation kept at a police station ‖ *(mil.)* a swift concerted attack on a limited objective ‖ an explosive for a gun, or for blasting ‖ an electric charge ‖ the electricity stored in a battery ‖ a financial responsibility **to take charge** to assume control or responsibility

charge *pres. part.* **charg·ing** *past* and *past part.* **charged** *v.t.* to accuse ‖ to ask as a price ‖ to record (a debt) ‖ to give electrical energy or charge to (a battery) ‖ to saturate ‖ to load ‖ *v.i.* to rush forward in assault ‖ to ask payment ‖ to accumulate electrical energy or charge **chárge·a·ble** *adj.* liable to be accused ‖ liable or proper to be charged as debts

char·i·ot (tʃǽri:ət) *n. (hist.)* a two-wheeled, horse-drawn vehicle used in warfare and for racing, esp. in classical times **char·i·ot·eer** (tʃæri:ətíər) *n.* the driver of a chariot

cha·ris·ma (kərízmə) *pl.* **cha·ris·ma·ta** (kərízmətə) *n.* an extraordinary power in a person, group, cause etc. which takes hold of popular imagination, wins popular support ‖ **cha·ris·mat·ic** (kærizmǽtik) *adj.*

char·i·ta·ble (tʃǽritəb'l) *adj.* using Christian charity in human dealings ‖ generous in giving to the needy ‖ tolerant in judging other people ‖ of or relating to charity **chár·i·ta·bly** *adv.*

char·i·ty (tʃǽriti:) *pl.* **char·i·ties** *n.* spiritual love for others ‖ tolerance in judging other people ‖ generosity to the needy ‖ alms given to the poor ‖ an organization dispensing relief to the poor

char·la·tan (ʃɑ́rlətən) *n.* a person who pretends to have knowledge or skill that he does not possess, esp.

medical knowledge **chár·la·tan·ism** *n.*

charm (tʃɑrm) *n.* a softly or gently pleasing quality ‖ a formula or action supposed to have a supernatural power against evil ‖ an object worn to avert danger by magic ‖ a small trinket worn esp. on a bracelet **like a charm** perfectly, without the least hitch

charm *v.t.* to please and attract, esp.in a relaxed or gentle way ‖ to allay as if by magic **chármed** *adj.* pleased, *he will be charmed to see you home* **chárm·ing** *adj.* delightful

chart (tʃɑrt) **1.** *n.* a map used by navigators, showing coastlines, deeps, rocks, currents etc. ‖ an outline map giving information on a particular subject, e.g. climatic conditions ‖ a graph showing fluctuations, e.g. in temperature or prices **2.** *v.t.* to make a map of ‖ to record on a chart or graph

char·ter (tʃɑ́rtər) **1.** *n.* an official document granting rights, esp. to a new borough, company, university etc. ‖ the articles of incorporation of an organization or company ‖ the lease of an airplane, yacht, ship or bus etc. to a hirer for his exclusive use **2.** *v.t.* to grant a charter to ‖ to hire (an airplane, yacht etc.)

char·treuse (ʃɑrtrú:z) *n.* a Carthusian monastery ‖ a liqueur first made by Carthusian monks ‖ a yellow-green color

chase (tʃeis) *n.* a running after, a pursuit **to give chase** to set off in pursuit

chase *pres. part.* **chas·ing** *past* and *past part.* **chased** *v.t.* to follow at speed in order to catch ‖ to drive (someone, something) away ‖ to pursue amorously ‖ *v.i.* to rush, hurry

chas·er (tʃéisər) *n.* a short drink usually of beer or water taken after drinking neat liquor

chasm (kǽzəm) *n.* a deep cleft in the earth ‖ a deep division of opinion or interests

chas·sis (ʃǽsi:, tʃǽsi:) *n.* the frame, wheels and engine of an automobile, without the bodywork

chaste (tʃeist) *adj.* innocent of immoral sexual intercourse ‖ deliberately abstaining from sexual intercourse

chas·tise (tʃæstáiz) *pres. part.* **chas·tis·ing** *past* and *past part.* **chas·tised** *v.t.* to punish by whipping or beating ‖ to denounce or criticize vehemently **chas·tise·ment** (tʃǽstizmənt, tʃæstáizmənt) *n.*

chas·ti·ty (tʃǽstiti:) *n.* the state or virtue of being chaste ‖ total sexual abstention, continence

chat (tʃæt) **1.** *n.* light, gossipy conversation **2.** *v.i. pres. part.* **chat·ting** *past* and *past part.* **chat·ted** to talk light gossip

chat·tel (tʃǽt'l) *n. (law)* a piece of property other than real estate or a freehold

chat·ter (tʃǽtər) **1.** *n.* light, inconsequential talk ‖ (of birds) quick, short notes suggesting human speech ‖ the rattling together of teeth from cold, fear etc. **2.** *v.i.* to talk lightly and inconsequentially, chat ‖ (of teeth) to rattle together ‖ (of a machine or tool) to skid or vibrate on a surface instead of cutting it cleanly, leaving a line of irregular notches or a spiral pattern

chauf·feur (ʃóufər, ʃoufə́:r) **1.** *n.* a person employed to drive a car **2.** *v.t.* to be or act as chauffeur to ‖ *v.i.* to be or act as chauffeur

chau·vin·ism (ʃóuvinizəm) *n.* exaggerated and aggressive patriotism **cháu·vin·ist** *n.* **chau·vin·is·tic** *adj.* **chau·vin·is·ti·cal·ly** *adv.*

cheap (tʃi:p) **1.** *adj.* inexpensive ‖ easily obtained ‖ (of goods) worth more than the price paid ‖ poor in quality, tawdry ‖ facile ‖ low-down, mean **2.** *adv.* inexpensively

cheap·en (tʃí:pən) *v.t.* to lower in price ‖ to lower in cost ‖ to lower or degrade ‖ *v.i.* to become cheap or cheaper

cheat (tʃi:t) **1.** *v.t.* to trick or deceive ‖ *v.i.* to play a game not according to the rules ‖ to use unfair methods ‖ to practice fraud **2.** *n.* a person who cheats ‖ a fraud

check (tʃek) **1.** *n.* a sudden interruption of movement ‖ a restraint ‖ a control to verify information etc. ‖ a controlled test ‖ a means of preventing error, fraud ‖

a small crack ‖ a mark to show that something has been verified or checked ‖ a bill for a meal in a restaurant ‖ a receipt for deposit (of luggage etc.) ‖ (chess) the position of the king when exposed to attack 2. adj. serving to control, verify

check n. a pattern of crossing lines or alternating squares of colors ‖ a fabric woven or printed with such a pattern

check v.t. to arrest or restrain the progress or motion of ‖ to restrain ‖ to curb (a horse) ‖ to verify the correctness of (e.g. accounts) ‖ to verify the state or condition of (something) to see if it is all right ‖ to deposit or accept for safekeeping, receiving a check as a receipt ‖ to send or accept for conveyance, using a passage ticket ‖ v.i. to crack or split (e.g. of paint)

check n. an order (on a specially printed form) to a bank to pay a stated sum to a named person

check·mate (tʃékmẹit) 1. n. (chess) a move or position which places the opponent's king inescapably in check 2. v.t. pres. part. **check·mat·ing** past and past part. **check·mat·ed** to defeat or frustrate (a plan) 3. interj. the announcement of such a move in chess

cheek (tʃi:k) 1. n. the soft fleshy part of the face between the eye, mouth and edge of the jaw ‖ the side wall of the mouth ‖ impudence **to turn the other cheek** to react with submissiveness rather than retaliate in the face of injury or provocation 2. v.t. to speak or behave impudently to

cheek·i·ly (tʃí:kili:) adv. in a cheeky manner

cheek·y (tʃí:ki:) comp. **cheek·i·er** superl. **cheek·i·est** adj. impudent

cheer (tʃiər) 1. n. a shout of joy ‖ (pl.) applause ‖ (rhet.) heart-warming comfort 2. v.i. to shout for joy ‖ v.t. to applaud by shouts

cheer·ful (tʃiərfəl) adj. happy, good-humored ‖ bright and attractive

cheese (tʃi:z) n. a solid food of high protein content made from the pressed curds of milk ‖ a mass of this food set into characteristic shape

cheese·burg·er (tʃí:zbərgər) n. a hamburger with cooked cheese on top

chee·tah (tʃí:tə) n. a small leopard formerly used for hunting deer and antelope in India

chef (ʃef) n. the head cook, esp. in a hotel or restaurant

chem·i·cal (kémik'l) 1. adj. relating to the science of chemistry ‖ relating to the applications of chemistry 2. n. a substance used in or obtained by a chemical process

chem·ist (kémist) n. a person trained or engaged in chemistry

chem·is·try (kémistri:) n. the study of the composition, properties and structure of substances, and of the changes they undergo

cher·ish (tʃériʃ) v.t. to treasure ‖ to take loving care of ‖ to keep alive (an emotion, illusion, etc.)

cher·ry (tʃéri:) 1. pl. **cher·ries** n. a genus of flowering trees bearing small fruit on long stems and a skin varying in color from pink to dark red ‖ the fruit (drupe) ‖ a bright red color 2. adj. bright red

cher·ub (tʃérəb) pl. **cher·ubs**, (Bible) **cher·u·bim** (tʃérəbim) n. an order of angels ‖ a representation of such a creature, e.g. in art as a winged child's head, or a rosy baby boy **che·ru·bic** (tʃərú:bik) adj. (esp. of a child) having a round rosy face

chess (tʃes) n. an ancient, conventional, elaborate game of skill for two players, played on a chessboard

chess·man (tʃésmæn, tʃésmən) pl. **chess·men** (tʃésmẹn, tʃésmən) n. one of the 16 pieces which each player of a game has on the board at the start

chest (tʃest) n. the thorax, that part of the body between the neck and abdomen which contains the lungs and heart, parts of the esophagus, windpipe, greater blood vessels and some nerves ‖ a large, strong box with a hinged lid ‖ the funds of an institution ‖ a chest of drawers **to get something off one's chest** to unburden oneself by speaking about what is weighing on one's mind or conscience

chew (tʃu:) 1. v.t. to reduce (food) to a pulp in the mouth by grinding it between the teeth with the help of the tongue etc. ‖ (with 'on' or 'over') to think carefully and at length about the various aspects of (a matter) ‖ v.i. to chew something 2. n. the act of chewing

chic (ʃi:k) 1. n. stylishness 2. adj. elegant, stylish

chi·can·er·y (ʃikéinəri) pl. **chi·can·er·ies** n. trickery, esp. legal trickery

Chi·ca·no (masc.) (tʃikánou) **Chi·ca·na** (fem.) n. U.S. resident of Mexican descent

chick (tʃik) n. a newly hatched chicken ‖ any very young bird

chick·en (tʃíkən) 1. n. the domestic fowl, or its flesh as food 2. adj. (pop.) cowardly

chic·o·ry (tʃíkəri) n. a perennial plant whose root is roasted, pulverized and used as a coffee adulterant or substitute

chide (tʃaid) pres. part. **chid·ing** past **chid** (tʃid), **chid·ed** past part. **chid**, **chid·den** (tʃíd'n), **chid·ed** v.t. to reprove, rebuke ‖ to compel by chiding

chief (tʃi:f) 1. n. a leader or ruler, esp. of a tribe or clan ‖ the head of a department in an institution 2. adj. most important ‖ highest in rank

chief·ly (tʃí:fli:) adv. mainly, but not altogether ‖ pertaining to a chief

chief·tain (tʃí:ftən) n. the leader of a group, esp. a clan or tribe **chief·tain·cy** n.

chif·fon (ʃifón, ʃifən) 1. n. a very soft, fine transparent material, usually of silk, used in dressmaking etc. 2. adj. made of chiffon ‖ (cooking) light and fluffy in consistency

child (tʃaild) pl. **chil·dren** (tʃíldrən) n. a boy or girl at any age between infancy and adolescence ‖ a person of any age in relation to his parents **with child** pregnant

child·hood (tʃáildhud) n. the state of being a child ‖ the years between infancy and adolescence

child·ish (tʃáildiʃ) adj. like or proper to a child ‖ pertaining to childhood ‖ immature ‖ (of remarks or behavior) puerile, not befitting an adult

child·like (tʃáildlaik) adj. possessing what are commonly thought of as the good qualities of a child's character

chil·i (tʃíli:) pl. **chil·ies** n. a garden pepper grown from Chile to the middle of North America

chill (tʃil) 1. adj. cold to the touch ‖ unpleasantly cold ‖ unemotional, undemonstrative ‖ unfriendly 2. n. an unpleasant sensation of coldness ‖ a depressing influence 3. v.t. to make cold ‖ to refrigerate but not freeze (food) ‖ to bring down to the right temperature for drinking ‖ to depress or dishearten ‖ v.i. to become cold

chime (tʃaim) 1. n. a set of bells ‖ the sound made by a bell or bells, esp. (pl.) the bells in a striking clock ‖ a musical instrument consisting of a set of vertical metal tubes, struck with a hammer 2. v. pres. part. **chim·ing** past and past part. **chimed** v.i. (of a chime of bells) to ring ‖ v.t. to ring (a bell or bells)

chim·ney (tʃímni:) pl. **chim·neys** n. an enclosed vertical channel or flue in the wall of a house for carrying away the smoke from a fire ‖ the part of a flue projecting above the roof of a house ‖ anything resembling a chimney in purpose, e.g., the opening of a volcano etc. ‖ (mountaineering) a narrow, climbable crack in a cliff face

---

(a) æ, cat; ɑ, car; ɔ fawn; ei, snake. (e) e, hen; i:, sheep; iə, deer; ɛə, bear. (i) i, fish; ai, tiger; ə:, bird. (o) o, ox; au, cow; ou, goat; u, poor; ɔi, royal. (u) ʌ, duck; u, bull; u:, goose; ə, bacillus; ju:, cube. x, loch; θ, think; ð, bother; z, Zen; ʒ, corsage; dʒ, savage; ŋ, orangutang; j, yak; ʃ, fish; tʃ, fetch; 'l, rabble; 'n, redden. Complete pronunciation key appears inside front cover.

chim·pan·zee (tʃimpænzíː, tʃimpǽnzi:) *n.* an African ape allied to the gorilla and resembling man more closely than do most apes

chin (tʃin) **1.** *n.* the part of the face below the lower lip, esp. the front part of the lower jaw **2.** *pres. part.* **chin·ning** *past* and *past part.* **chinned** *v.t. (gymnastics)* to bring one's chin up to the level of (the horizontal bar etc.)

chi·na (tʃáinə) **1.** *n.* a twice-fired, finegrained ceramic ware used esp. for eating and drinking utensils and ornaments ‖ porcelain ‖ any crockery **2.** *adj.* made of china

chin·chil·la (tʃíntʃílə) *n.* South American rodent, closely allied to the rabbit, with long hind legs and a bushy tail. The soft, pearl-gray fur, used for coats, is very valuable ‖ a breed of rabbit with a fur resembling that of the chinchilla ‖ a woolen fabric with a long soft nap

chink (tʃiŋk) **1.** *n.* a narrow crack or opening, e.g. in a wall or door **a chink in someone's armor** a factor in a person's character which makes them susceptible to persuasion, or vulnerable in some way **2.** *v.t.* to fill up the chinks in

chip (tʃip) **1.** *n.* a small fragment broken or cut from wood, china, glass, stone etc. ‖ *(electr.)* miniaturized wafer disc of silicon on which an integrated circuit is printed ‖ a mark made by chipping ‖ a counter in a gambling game **2.** *v. pres. part.* **chip·ping** *past* and *past part.* **chipped** *v.t.* to cut or break a frament off (wood, stone etc.) ‖ *v.i.* to become chipped ‖ to be liable to become chipped ‖ *(golf)* to play a chip shot

chip·munk (tʃípmʌŋk) *n.* any of several species of small, squirrel-like animals found in North America

chi·rop·o·dist (kairɔ́pədist, kirɔ́pədist) *n.* a person professionally qualified to treat minor disorders of the feet **chi·rop·o·dy** (kairɔ́pədi:, kirɔ́pədi:) *n.* the care of the feet and treatment of ailments of the feet

chi·ro·prac·tic (kairəprǽktik) *n.* the manipulation of the spinal vertebrae in an attempt to cure various ailments **chi·ro·prac·tor** *n.*

chirp (tʃəːrp) **1.** *n.* a short, sharp sound made by a small bird, a cricket or grasshopper ‖ sound or other wave variation due to a variation of frequency **2.** *v.i.* to make such a sound ‖ to talk brightly ‖ *v.t.* to say with a chirping sound

chis·el (tʃíz'l) **1.** *n.* any of various steel hand tools with a beveled cutting edge for cutting or shaping wood, stone or metal **2.** *v.t. pres. part.* **chis·el·ing** *past* and *past part.* **chis·eled** *v.t.* to cut or shape (wood, stone or metal) with a chisel ‖ to cheat or defraud **chis·eled** *adj.* worked with a chisel ‖ fine, clear-cut, *chiseled features*

chit·chat (tʃíttʃæt) *n.* gossip

chiv·al·ric (ʃívəlrik, ʃivǽlrik) *adj.* chivalrous ‖ of chivalry

chiv·al·rous (ʃívəlrəs) *adj.* (of men) respectful of women ‖ having the characteristics of the ideal medieval knight: courteous, honorable, ready to help those in need ‖ pertaining to the age of chivalry

chiv·al·ry (ʃívəlri:) *n.* honorable behavior, esp. to women

chive (tʃaiv) *n.* an Old World hardy perennial plant allied to the onion. The leaf is used for seasoning

chlo·rine (klɔ́riːn, klóuriːn, klɔ́rin, klóurin) *n.* a gaseous greenish-yellow element. It occurs widely in nature in combination with metals, e.g. as sodium chloride in seawater. It is extremely reactive, and is used as a bleaching, disinfecting and oxidizing agent

chlo·ro·phyll, chlo·ro·phyl (klɔ́rəfil, klóurəfil) *n.* a green pigment in plant cells, that is essential to photosynthesis and is formed only in the presence of light

choc·o·late (tʃɔ́kəlit, tʃókəlit, tʃɔ́klit, tʃóklit) **1.** *n.* a food product made form the seeds of cacao, roasted and ground, often sweetened ‖ a small candy coated with chocolate ‖ a hot drink made from chocolate and milk **2.** *adj.* flavored with chocolate ‖ of a brown color resembling that of chocolate

choice (tʃɔis) *adj.* (esp. commercial contexts) of high quality, carefully selected

choice *n.* the act of choosing or selecting ‖ the right or possibility of choosing ‖ something chosen ‖ an alternative

choir (kwáiər) **1.** *n.* a group of singers giving public performances, a choral society ‖ the part of a cathedral, abbey or church between the nave and the sanctuary **2.** *v.t. (rhet.)* to sing (a hymn etc.) in chorus ‖ *v.i. (rhet.)* to sing in chorus

choke (tʃouk) **1.** *v. pres. part.* **chok·ing** *past* and *past part.* **choked** *v.t.* to stop or almost stop from breathing, by applying pressure on the windpipe or by blocking it ‖ to asphyxiate ‖ to restrict the air intake of (an internal-combustion engine) ‖ (with 'back', 'down') to repress (emotion) with difficulty ‖ *v.i.* to be unable to breathe ‖ to be inarticulate (with emotion) ‖ to suffer strangling or suffocation **2.** *n.* the act of choking ‖ the valve controlling the air intake in an internal-combustion engine

chol·er·a (kɔ́lərə) *n.* a highly dangerous and infectious disease

chol·er·ic (kɔ́lərik, kəlérik) *adj.* inclined to be irritable

cho·les·ter·ol (kələstəroul, kəléstərol, kəléstərol) *n.* *(biochem.)* a fat-soluble crystalline steroid alcohol, found in all animal tissues and fluids, esp. in nervous tissue

choose (tʃuːz) *pres. part.* **choos·ing** *past* **chose** (tʃouz) *past part.* **cho·sen** (tʃóuz'n) *v.t.* to select from a number, or between alternatives ‖ *v.i.* to make a choice ‖ to decide **choos·y, choos·ey** *comp.* **choos·i·er** *superl.* **choos·i·est** *adj. (pop.)* fastidious, hard to please

chop (tʃɒp) **1.** *v. pres. part.* **chop·ping** *past* and *past part.* **chopped** *v.t.* to cut by striking or dividing with a sharp instrument ‖ to hit (a ball) with a short cutting stroke ‖ *v.i.* to use a chopper **2.** *n.* a cutting stroke with a sharp instrument ‖ a cut of pork, mutton or veal including a rib or part of a rib ‖ *(boxing)* a short, downward blow ‖ the short, irregular, broken motion of waves

chop·py (tʃɒ́pi:) *comp.* **chop·pi·er** *superl.* **chop·pi·est** *adj.* (of the sea) agitated, with small tossing waves ‖ (of the wind) changing suddenly or irregularly

cho·ral (kɔ́rəl, kóurəl) *adj.* sung or intended for singing by a choir ‖ pertaining to a choir

cho·rale, cho·ral (kərǽl, kɔ́rəl, kóurəl) *n.* a hymn tune of simple rhythm, adapted from plainsong

chord (kɔrd) *n.* an emotional response ‖ *(physiol.)* a part of the body resembling a string ‖ *(math.)* a straight line joining two points on a curve ‖ *(engin.)* a principal member of a truss framework

chord *n. (mus.)* a simultaneous combination of notes, either concord or discord **chórd·al** *adj.*

cho·re·og·ra·pher (kɔri:ɔ́grəfər, kouri:ɔ́grəfər) *n.* someone who composes choreography

cho·re·og·ra·phy (kɔri:ɔ́grəfi:, kouri:ɔ́grəfi:) *n.* the art of arranging a dance performance and the notation of the steps of the dance in detail

chor·tle (tʃɔ́rt'l) **1.** *n.* a gleeful chuckle **2.** *v.t. pres. part.* **chor·tling** *past* and *past part.* **chor·tled** to utter such a chuckle

cho·rus (kɔ́rəs, kóurəs) **1.** *n.* a group of singers or dancers in musical comedy etc. ‖ a secular choir ‖ the refrain of a song in which a number of singers join the solo voice ‖ any remark made by several people simultaneously **2.** *v.t.* to sing (music) or utter (greetings etc.) in chorus ‖ *v.i.* to sing or speak in chorus

chow·der (tʃáudər) *n.* a dish of fish or clams or other foods stewed in milk with bacon, onion etc.

Christ (kraist) the anointed king or Messiah of Jewish prophecy ‖ the title given to Jesus by his followers, who believed that his coming fulfilled the Messianic prophecies

chris·ten (krís'n) *v.t.* to receive (a person usually an infant) into the Christian Church by baptism ‖ to name (a child) formally, at baptism ‖ to name (a ship) at its launching

Chris·ten·dom (krís'ndəm) *n.* the whole body of members of the Christian Church || all countries professing Christianity as opposed to those professing other religions

chris·ten·ing (krís'niŋ, krísniŋ) *n.* the religious ceremony of baptizing and naming a child

Chris·ti·an·i·ty (krĩstʃi:ǽniti:) *n.* the religion of those who accept Jesus Christ as God incarnate, are guided by the Holy Spirit, and participate in the fellowship of the Christian Church || the state of being a Christian

Christ·mas (krísmǝs) *n.* the annual festival observed by Christians on Dec. 25, commemorating the birth of Christ || the Christmas season

chro·mat·ic (kroumǽtik, krǝmǽtik) *adj.* colored or relating to color, esp. with respect to hue or saturation || *(mus.)* having notes other than those in the diatonic scale

chrome (kroum) *n.* chromium || chrome yellow

chro·mite (króumait) *n.* an ore containing chromium, from which chromium is obtained

chro·mi·um (króumi:ǝm) *n.* a metallic element, not occurring freely in nature, but produced from chromite

chro·mo·some (króumǝsoum) *n.* a microscopic, threadlike bundle of deoxyribonucleic acid molecules which collectively carry the hereditary material in subunits called genes

chron·ic (krónik) *adj.* (of disease) longlasting, deep-seated || constant, inveterate **chrón·i·cal·ly** *adv.* **chro·nic·i·ty** (krɒnísiti:) *n.* (of disease) the state or quality of being chronic

chron·i·cle (krónik'l) **1.** *n.* a list of events in the order in which they happened || a narrative of events **2.** *v.t. pres. part.* **chron·i·cling** *past* and *past part.* **chron·i·cled** to record (events) in a chronicle **chrón·i·cler** *n.* a writer of chronicles

chron·o·log·i·cal (krɒn'lɒdʒi·k'l) *adj.* of or relating to chronology

chro·nol·o·gy (krǝnólǝdʒi:) *pl.* **chro·nol·o·gies** *n.* the science of measuring time and fixing dates || order of occurrence || an arrangement (list, table, treatise etc.) in order of occurrence

chro·nom·e·ter (krǝnómitǝr) *n.* an instrument measuring the passage of time with great accuracy

chrys·a·lis (krísǝlis) *pl.* **chry·sal·i·des** (krisǽlidi:z) **chrys·a·lis·es** *n.* the pupa of certain insects, esp. butterflies and moths

chry·san·the·mum (krisǽnθǝmǝm) *n.* widely cultivated, autumn-flowering, perennial plants from China and Japan

chub·bi·ness (tʃʌbi:nis) *n.* the state or quality of being chubby

chub·by (tʃʌbi:) *comp.* **chub·bi·er** *superl.* **chub·bi·est** *adj.* (of people, esp. children) nicely plump

chuck (tʃʌk) *n.* the cut of beef or lamb between the neck and shoulder blade || a block used as a chock || a mechanical screw device for holding a tool in a machine (e.g. a bit in a drill)

chuck 1. *v.t. (pop.)* to throw lightly, toss || to tap playfully (under the chin) **2.** *n.* a playful tap under the chin || *(pop.)* a short throw

chuck·le (tʃʌk'l) **1.** *v. pres. part.* **chuck·ling** *past* and *past part.* **chuck·led** *v.i.* to laugh quietly with amusement, satisfaction, glee or triumph || to make a sound suggesting quiet laughter, e.g. of water flowing over stones **2.** *n.* such a laugh or sound suggesting laughter

chum (tʃʌm) *n.* (esp. of young people) a close friend **chúm·my** *comp.* **chum·mi·er** *superl.* **chum·mi·est** *adj.* intimately friendly

chump (tʃʌmp) *n. (pop.)* a person who has said or done something silly || a thick lump of wood

chunk (tʃʌŋk) *n.* a short, thick piece (of wood, bread etc.) || a large amount **chúnk·y** *comp.* **chunk·i·er** su-

perl. **chunk·i·est** *adj.* (of people) short and thickset || (of objects) rather thick or heavy

church (tʃǝ:rtʃ) *n.* a building for Christian worship || a service held in it || baptized Christian men and women

churl·ish (tʃǝ:rliʃ) *adj.* ill-mannered || surly

churn (tʃǝ:rn) **1.** *n.* a vessel in which milk or cream is shaken or stirred to produce butter **2.** *v.t.* to make butter by beating (milk or cream) in a churn || to make (butter) by working a churn || to agitate violently, *the propeller churned the water* || *v.i.* to work a churn **chúrn·ing** *n.* the amount of butter made at one time

chute (ʃu:t) *n.* a steep slide or trough down which things are made to pass to a lower level || a quick descent of water over a slope

chutz·pah or **chutz·pa** (xútspǝ) *n. (Yiddish)* brass, boldness, impertinence, insolence, effrontery

ci·der (sáidǝr) *n.* a nonalcoholic drink made from apple juice, sweet cider

ci·gar (sigár) *n.* a roll of tobacco leaves for smoking

cig·a·rette, cig·a·ret (sigǝrét, sígǝrẹt) *n.* a short cylinder of finely cut tobacco rolled in very thin paper, for smoking

cil·i·a (síli:ǝ) *sing.* **cil·i·um** (síli:ǝm) *pl. n.* short, hairlike cytoplasmic processes projecting from the free surface of certain cells **cíl·i·ar·y** *adj.*

cinch (sintʃ) **1.** *n.* a strong girth for a saddle || *(pop.)* something done very easily || *(pop.)* someone or something sure to be successful || *(pop.)* a tight grip **2.** *v.t.* to put a cinch on || *(pop.)* to make sure of

cinc·ture (síŋktʃǝr) *n.* (old-fash.) a girdle || (archit.) a ring at the top and bottom of a column shaft, marking off capital and base

cin·der (síndǝr) *n.* a piece of partly burned coal or other combustible material no longer flaming || slag from a furnace || *(pl.)* the residue of burned coal || *(pl.)* lava from a volcano

cin·e·ma (sínǝmǝ) *n.* the art or technique of making movies

cin·na·mon (sínǝmǝn) *n.* a spice made from the bark of certain trees of the genus *Cinnamomum* || a tree yielding this || the yellowish-brown color of this spice || its flavor

ci·pher (sáifǝr) **1.** *n.* a 0, zero, naught (*NUMBER TABLE) || a person or thing of no importance || interwoven letters, e.g. in a monogram **2.** *v.i.* (of an organ) to sound one note continually || *v.t.* to put (a message) into cipher

cir·ca (sǝ́:rkǝ) *prep. (abbr.* **c., ca.,** used with numerals) about

cir·cle (sǝ́:rk'l) **1.** *n.* (geom.) a plane figure with a bounding edge (circumference), all points on which are equidistant from a fixed point || *(pop.)* the circumference || the area of intersection of a sphere by a plane || a group of objects on the circumference of a circle || a group of persons with a common interest or an exclusive group within society, *court circles* **to argue in a circle** to base a conclusion upon a premise which is itself derived from the conclusion **to come full circle** (esp. of ideas) to return to the point of departure by a circuitous path **to run around in circles** to achieve nothing because one is in a dither **2.** *v. pres. part.* **cir·cling** *past* and *past part.* **cir·cled** *v.t.* to put a circle around || *v.i.* to move around, or around in, the circumference of a circle

cir·cuit (sǝ́:rkit) **1.** *n.* a movement around an object || a roughly circular boundary or route || *(law)* a geographical group of towns having courts of law, visited in turn by a judge || a chain of movie houses or theaters under the same ownership || the complete path traversed by an electric current || the diagram of the connections of an electrical apparatus **2.** *v.t.* to make the

---

circuit of ‖ *v.i.* to go or move in a circuit

cir·cu·lar (sə́:rkjulər) **1.** *adj.* having the shape of a circle ‖ moving in a circle **2.** *n.* a printed advertising leaflet, notice etc., sent out in large numbers **cir·cu·lar·i·ty** (sə:rkjulǽriti) *n.* **cir·cu·lar·i·za·tion** *n.* the act of circularizing **cir·cu·lar·ize** (sə́:rkjuləraiz) *v.t. pres. part.* **cir·cu·lar·iz·ing** *past* and *past part.* **cir·cu·lar·ized** to send circulars to ‖ to make into a circular letter

cir·cu·late (sə́:rkjuleit) *pres. part.* **cir·cu·lat·ing** *past* and *past part.* **cir·cu·lat·ed** *v.i.* to move around and return to a starting point ‖ to pass from place to place or from person to person ‖ *v.t.* to send or pass around

cir·cu·la·tion (sə:rkjuléiʃən) *n.* movement in a circuit, e.g. of water or air, usually with a return to the starting point ‖ the movement of blood in the blood vessels of the body ‖ distribution ‖ *(fig.)* flow ‖ the number of copies of a newspaper or magazine regularly sold

cir·cum·cise (sə́:rkəmsaiz) *pres. part.* **cir·cum·cis·ing** *past* and *past part.* **cir·cum·cised** *v.t.* to cut off the foreskin of (males) or the clitoris of (females) as a religious rite or on medical grounds

cir·cum·ci·sion (sə:rkəmsíʒen) *n.* the act of circumcising ‖ the religious rite of purification and initiation by circumcising

cir·cum·fer·ence (sərkʌ́mfərəns) *n.* the line bounding a circle, or its length

cir·cum·lo·cu·tion (sə:rkəmloukjú:ʃən) *n.* the use of many words when a few would do ‖ an indirect or roundabout expression **cir·cum·loc·u·to·ry** (sə:rkəmlɒ́kjutɔri:, sə:rkəmlɒ́kjutɔuri:) *adj.*

cir·cum·scribe (sə:rkəmskráib, sə́:rkəmskraib) *pres. part.* **cir·cum·scrib·ing** *past* and *past part.* **cir·cum·scribed** *v.t.* to draw a line around ‖ to mark the boundary of ‖ to set limits to, restrict ‖ *(geom.)* to draw (a plane figure) so as to enclose another

cir·cum·spect (sə́:rkəmspekt) *adj.* attentive to the consequences of one's behavior, cautious, discreet, prudent **cir·cum·spec·tion** *n.*

cir·cum·stance (sə́:rkəmstæns) *n.* an essential fact or detail ‖ *(of storytelling)* detail ‖ stiff ceremonial ‖ chance, fate ‖ *(pl.)* the elements of a total situation ‖ *(pl.)* the particular elements directly affecting a matter ‖ *(pl.)* the financial state of a person **cir·cum·stanced** *adj.* placed in a set of conditions, esp. with regard to financial state

cir·cum·stan·tial (sə:rkəmstǽnʃəl) *adj.* giving full and precise details ‖ incidental, related but not essential **cir·cum·stan·ti·al·i·ty** (sə:rkəmstænʃi:ǽliti:) *n.*

circumstantial evidence evidence made up of details tending to prove a fact by inference, but giving no direct proof

cir·cum·vent (sə:rkəmvént, sə́:rkəmvent) *v.t.* to prevent by counterstrategy, outwit, get around **cir·cum·ven·tion** *n.*

cir·cus (sə́:rkəs) *n.* the entertainment made up of acts including performing animals, horseback riders, acrobats, clowns etc. ‖ the arena with seats around it in which the show is performed ‖ the persons and animals making up the show

cir·rho·sis (siróusis) *n.* a chronic, noninfectious disease of the liver characterized by excessive formation of scar tissue, hardening and contraction

cir·rus (sírəs) *pl.* **cir·ri** (sírai) *n.* *(meteor.)* a lofty, white, fleecy cloud formation usually made up of ice crystals

cis·tern (sístərn) *n.* a tank for storing water ‖ a reservoir for storing rainwater

cit·a·del (sítəd'l, sítədel) *n.* a fortress protecting or dominating a town ‖ *(hist.)* a place of refuge ‖ something thought of as a defensive stronghold

ci·ta·tion (saitéiʃən) *n.* the act of citing ‖ a quotation ‖ *(mil.)* a mention in dispatches in praise of an act of courage or other soldierly virtue ‖ a summons to appear in court

cite (sait) *pres. part.* **cit·ing** *past* and *past part.* **cit·ed** *v.t.* to give (an example), or quote (an authority) e.g. in support of an argument ‖ *(mil.)* to mention in of-

ficial dispatches ‖ to summon to court to answer an accusation

cit·i·zen (sítiz'n, sítis'n) *n.* an inhabitant of a city or town ‖ a member of a country, native or naturalized, having rights and owing allegiance **cit·i·zen·ry** *n.* *(old-fash.)* citizens as a body **cit·i·zen·ship** *n.* the state of being a citizen

cit·rus (sítrəs) *n.* trees and shrubs yielding fruits which include the orange, lemon, lime, grapefruit, shaddock, tangerine and citron

cit·y (síti:) *pl.* **cit·ies** *n.* an important town ‖ a municipal corporation whose powers are confined to a fixed area and subject to the authority of the state ‖ *(Canada)* a municipality of highest rank

civ·et (sívit) *n.* any of several fierce carnivorous mammals of N. Africa and Asia ‖ a fatty substance produced in the perineal glands of these animals, and used in perfume

civ·ic (sívik) *adj.* relating to a city, its citizens or citizenship

civ·il (sív'l) *adj.* relating to a community or to citizens ‖ relating to civilian as opposed to military matters ‖ conforming to normal standards of politeness ‖ *(law)* relating to the private rights of individuals and disputes between them

ci·vil·ian (sivíljən) **1.** *adj.* not belonging to the armed forces **2.** *n.* a person not a member of the armed forces

ci·vil·i·ty (sivíliti:) *pl.* **ci·vil·i·ties** *n.* conformity with normal conventions of politeness ‖ an act or expression conforming to these conventions

civ·i·li·za·tion, civ·i·li·sa·tion (sivilizéiʃən) *n.* a making or becoming civilized ‖ the state of being civilized ‖ the sum of qualities of a particular civilized society

civ·i·lize (sívəlaiz) *pres. part.* **civ·i·liz·ing** *past* and *past part.* **civ·i·lized** *v.t.* to endow with law, order and the conditions favorable to the arts and sciences ‖ to refine the manners and tastes of

civil war war between the citizens of one country

claim (kleim) *v.t.* to demand as a right ‖ to assert as true ‖ to profess ‖ (of things) to need, require

claim *n.* the demanding of something as a right ‖ *(insurance)* a request for payment of compensation ‖ a right to demand assistance ‖ an assertion of right to possession of a thing ‖ an assertion (esp. of superiority) ‖ the thing claimed, esp. land claimed by a settler or prospector **cláim·ant** *n.* a person making a claim

clair·voy·ance (klɛərvɔ́iəns) *n.* second sight **clair·vóy·ant 1.** *adj.* having second sight **2.** *n.* someone who is clairvoyant

clam (klæm) **1.** *n.* one of various bivalve marine or freshwater mollusks, esp. those that are edible and equivalved and that live partly or completely buried in sand or mud **to shut up like a clam** to become suddenly uncommunicative **2.** *v.i. pres. part.* **clam·ming** *past* and *past part.* **clammed** to gather clams **to clam up** to shut up like a clam

clam·mi·ness (klǽmi:nis) *n.* the state or quality of being clammy

clam·my (klǽmi:) *comp.* **clam·mi·er** *superl.* **clam·mi·est** *adj.* damp, cold and sticky to the touch

clam·or (klǽmər) **1.** *n.* a loud confused noise, a hubbub ‖ a noisy outcry, a loud demanding **2.** *v.i.* to make demands or complain loudly ‖ to make a loud noise **clám·or·ous** *adj.*

clamp (klæmp) **1.** *n.* a device for holding things together tightly ‖ any of various appliances with parts brought together by screws for holding or compressing **2.** *v.t.* to fasten with, or place in, a clamp ‖ *v.i.* to close with a clamp

clan (klæn) *n.* a social group, esp. Scots, with a common ancestor, usually under patriarchal control ‖ a tribe ‖ *(pop.)* a large united family ‖ *(pop.)* a clique, a coterie

clan·des·tine (klændéstin) *adj.* existing or done in forced secrecy ‖ surreptitious

clang (klæŋ) **1.** *n.* a loud ringing sound, esp. of metal striking metal **2.** *v.i.* to make such a sound ‖ *v.t.* to cause to make such a sound

clap (klæp) *n.* a sharp, loud noise ‖ the sound of hands struck together

clap *pres. part.* **clap·ping** *past* and *past part.* **clapped** *v.i.* to strike the palms of the hands together ‖ *v.t.* to strike (the palms of the hands) together ‖ to slap lightly in friendly gestures ‖ *(pop.)* to put, impose etc. with force

clar·et (klǽrit) **1.** *n.* red Bordeaux wine **2.** *adj.* the reddish-purple color of this wine

clar·i·fi·ca·tion (klærifikéiʃən) *n.* the act or process of clarifying

clar·i·fy (klǽrifai) *pres. part.* **clar·i·fy·ing** *past* and *past part.* **clar·i·fied** *v.t.* to make understandable, explain ‖ to make (a liquid) pure and transparent ‖ *v.i.* to become easier to understand

clar·i·net (klærinét) *n.* a woodwind instrument with a single reed and keys **clar·i·nét·ist, clar·i·nét·tist** *n.* someone who plays the clarinet

clar·i·ty (klǽriti:) *n.* clearness (of liquids, sounds, meaning etc.)

clash (klæʃ) **1.** *v.i.* to make the loud, resonant noise of metal striking metal ‖ to skirmish ‖ to conflict by disagreeing ‖ to conflict by occurring at the same time ‖ (of colors) not to harmonize ‖ *v.t.* to strike together violently, usually noisily **2.** *n.* a loud strident noise as of metal being struck ‖ a skirmish ‖ a conflict

clasp (klæsp, klɑsp) **1.** *v.t.* to hold tightly in one's arms, embrace ‖ to seize in a firm hold, or with the hand ‖ to fasten together with a clasp ‖ to interlace the fingers of (one's hands) ‖ *v.i.* (of hands) to close tensely **2.** *n.* a fastening device ‖ a clip on a brooch etc. ‖ a firm hold, a grasp ‖ *(mil.)* a bar on a medal ribbon inscribed with the name of the action or campaign at which the wearer was present

class (klæs, klɑs) **1.** *n.* a group of people of the same rank or status in a community ‖ the concept or system of social divisions ‖ a division by cost ‖ a division by quality ‖ a group of students taught together ‖ the period when they meet ‖ a course of instruction ‖ *(biol.)* a comprehensive group of animals or plants ranking above an order and below a phylum **in a class apart, in a class by itself** different from, esp. better than, all others **2.** *v.t.* to place in a class ‖ to classify ‖ *v.i.* to be classed

clas·sic (klǽsik) **1.** *adj.* received into the accepted canons of excellence ‖ conforming to Greco-Roman canons of taste ‖ having familiar historical or literary association ‖ (of dress) having simple tailored lines which never go out of fashion **2.** *n.* a great work of ancient Greek or Roman literature ‖ a later work commonly received as having permanent greatness ‖ a writer or artists of recognized excellence, other than a contemporary

clas·si·cal (klǽsik'l) *adj.* of the ancient civilization of Greece and Rome ‖ (of literature and art) having the formal beauty and emotional control typical of the works of that civilization ‖ (of education) humane as distinct from scientific ‖ traditional, as distinct from modern or experimental ‖ *(mus.)* compact in form and emotionally controlled ‖ *(pop.)* of all music other than jazz or popular music ‖ *(loosely)* orthodox, within a received tradition, academic

clas·si·fi·ca·tion (klæsifikéiʃən) *n.* the act or result of classifying ‖ a system of classifying

clas·si·fied (klǽsifaid) *adj.* (of information) forbidden to be disclosed for reasons of national or military security ‖ put into a certain category or categories

clas·si·fy (klǽsifai) *pres. part.* **clas·si·fy·ing** *past* and *past part.* **clas·si·fied** *v.t.* to arrange in classes ‖ to put into groups systematically

clat·ter (klǽtər) **1.** *v.i.* to make, or move with, the noises of impact of many hard objects ‖ *v.t.* to cause to make such a confused sound **2.** *n.* a confused sharp banging, rattling or clashing ‖ noisy, confused chatter

clause (klɔz) *n.* a distinct article or proviso in a legal document, agreement or treaty ‖ a part of a sentence having a subject and predicate of its own

claus·tro·pho·bi·a (klɔstrəfóubi:ə) *n.* a morbid dread of being in confined spaces **claus·tro·pho·bic** (klɔstrəfóubik, klɔstrəfóbik) *adj.*

clav·i·cle (klǽvik'l) *n.* the vertebrate bone forming part of the pectoral arch, joined to the breastbone and the shoulder blade **cla·vic·u·lar** (kləvíkjulər) *adj.*

claw (klɔ) **1.** *n.* the sharp, hooked nail on an animal's foot ‖ the whole foot or leg so armed ‖ a pincer of a crustacean ‖ anything shaped like an animal's claw **2.** *v.t.* to scratch or tear with claws or fingernails ‖ *v.i.* to make scratching or tearing attacks with or as if with claws ‖ to make febrile grasping motions **clawed** *adj.* having claws ‖ scratched and torn by claws

clay (klei) *n.* a firm earthy substance essentially composed of aluminum silicate **clay·ey** *adj.*

clean (kli:n) **1.** *adj.* not dirty ‖ free from imperfections ‖ fresh, not soiled ‖ pure, without moral defilement ‖ free from ceremonial defilement ‖ (of animals and food) considered on hygienic or religious grounds fit to be eaten ‖ trim and definite ‖ even, without obstructions or rough edges ‖ dexterous and free from imprecision ‖ *(colloq.)* not possessing drugs ‖ not addicted to drugs ‖ not possessing any stolen merchandise **2.** *adv.* completely **3.** *v.t.* to make clean ‖ *v.i.* to remove dirt **4.** *n.* the act or process of cleaning

clean·li·ness (klénli:nis) *n.* the habit or condition of being clean

clean·ly (klí:nli:) *adv.* in a clean manner

clean·ly (klénli:) *comp.* **clean·li·er** *superl.* **clean·li·est** *adj.* (of a person or animal) habitually clean ‖ habitually kept clean

cleanse (klenz) *pres. part.* **cleans·ing** *past* and *past part.* **cleansed** *v.t.* to make thoroughly clean ‖ to purify (from sin) ‖ *(Bible)* to cure, esp. of leprosy **cléans·er** *n.* an agent which cleanses

clear (kliər) **1.** *adj.* transparent, unclouded ‖ bright, luminous ‖ distinct to the vision ‖ free from blemishes or defects ‖ untroubled ‖ (of sounds) easily audible, distinct, pure ‖ perceiving distinctly ‖ easy to understand, plain ‖ free from difficulty, obstruction or danger ‖ at a safe distance ‖ complete, entire **2.** *n.* **in the clear** innocent, having an alibi **3.** *adv.* completely **4.** *v.t.* to free from obstructions ‖ to remove (an obstruction) ‖ to free from suspicion ‖ to get over or past ‖ to make as a net profit ‖ to settle (a debt) ‖ to free (a ship, cargo or luggage) from port restrictions by payment of customs dues etc. ‖ to get rid of by selling ‖ to get (a check) approved for payment ‖ to rid (land) of bushes, weeds etc. ‖ to remove (dirty dishes etc.) from a table ‖ to rid (the throat) of phlegm by coughing slightly ‖ *v.i.* to become clear

clear·ance (klíərəns) *n.* the act or process of clearing ‖ an unobstructed space allowing passage ‖ the amount of space between two objects ‖ the act of clearing a ship, goods etc. at a customhouse ‖ the certificate showing that this has been done ‖ the passing of a check through a clearinghouse

clear·ing (klíəriŋ) *n.* a making or becoming clear ‖ a piece of land in a wood free from trees ‖ the bank process of honoring checks ‖ *(pl.)* the total of claims settled at a clearinghouse

clear·ly (klíərli:) *adv.* in a clear manner, distinctly ‖ lucidly ‖ undoubtedly, manifestly

clear·ness (klíərnis) *n.* the quality of being clear or distinct ‖ transparency ‖ freedom from ambiguity or confusion ‖ freedom from obstruction

cleat (kli:t) **1.** *n.* a device used to secure a rope by belaying it around two projecting arms ‖ a wedge-shaped piece bolted on to a spar etc. to prevent a rope from slipping ‖ one of the studs on the sole of a shoe to prevent sliding (e.g. on golf shoes) **2.** *v.t.* to fasten to, or by, a cleat

cleav·age (klí:vidʒ) *n.* a cleaving or being cleft ‖ *(biol.)* cell division ‖ *(chem.)* the splitting of a crystal along certain directions parallel to certain actual or possible crystal faces, when subjected to tension ‖ *(chem.)* the breaking down of complex molecules into simpler molecules ‖ any sharp division (e.g. of ideas)

cleave (kli:v) *pres. part.* **cleav·ing** *past* **clove** (klouv), **cleaved, cleft** (kleft) *past part.* **clo·ven** (klóuv'n), **cleaved, cleft** *v.t.* to split with an ax or chopper ‖ to make a way through as if by cutting ‖ *v.i.* to become split in two

cleav·er (klí:vər) *n.* a splitting instrument esp. a wide heavy knife with a short handle used by butchers to split up carcasses

clef (klef) *n.* *(mus.)* a sign at the beginning of the staff to show pitch by locating a particular note on the staff

cleft (kleft) *n.* an opening made by splitting, a crack, a fissure ‖ a hollow in the chin

clem·en·cy (klémənsi:) *pl.* **clem·en·cies** *n.* the disposition to be merciful ‖ mercy

clem·ent (klémənt) *adj.* inclined to be merciful

clench (klentʃ) **1.** *v.t.* to press closely together, *to clench one's teeth* ‖ to grasp firmly **2.** *n.* the act of clenching ‖ a grip

cler·gy (klɔ́:rdʒi:) *n.* ordained Christian ministers collectively **cler·gy·man** (klɔ́:rdʒi:mən) *pl.* **cler·gy·men** (klɔ́:rdʒi:mən) *n.* a member of the clergy

cler·ic (klérik) *n.* *(old-fash.)* a clergyman

cler·i·cal (klérik'l) *adj.* relating to the work of a clerk in an office ‖ connected with the clergy

clerk (klɔ:rk, *Br.* klɑ:k) **1.** *n.* an officeworker in a position of minor responsibility ‖ an official who acts as secretary to a council ‖ a shop assistant, salesman or saleswoman **2.** *v.i.* to work as a clerk **clérk·ly** *adj.*

clev·er (klévər) *adj.* quick to learn and understand ‖ skillful, good at a job ‖ artful ‖ revealing skill

click (klik) **1.** *n.* a slight, sharp momentary sound, as when a switch is put on or off ‖ a catch or detent in machinery acting with this sound **2.** *v.t.* to make a clicking sound ‖ to fit, *the clues clicked into place* ‖ *(pop.)* to succeed or be lucky ‖ *(pop., of two persons)* to get along well, be attracted to one another ‖ *v.t.* to cause to click

cli·ent (kláiənt) *n.* a person who hires the services of a professional man ‖ a customer

cliff (klif) *n.* a high steep face of rock

cli·mate (kláimit) *n.* the sum of the prevailing weather conditions of a place over a period of time ‖ an area or region with certain weather conditions ‖ the trend of opinions and attitudes pervading a community, nation or period **cli·mat·ic** (klaimǽtik) *adj.* **cli·mát·i·cal·ly** *adv.*

cli·max (kláimæks) **1.** *n.* the last of a series of ideas, events, points of interest or situations to which what has gone before seems in retrospect to have been building up ‖ the movement towards such a culmination **2.** *v.i.* to come to a climax ‖ *v.t.* to bring to a climax

climb (klaim) **1.** *v.t.* to go up, ascend, esp. using hands and footholds ‖ *v.i.* to rise to a higher point ‖ to slope upward ‖ (of plants) to grow upward by turning around a support or by tendrils ‖ to gain height in the air ‖ to rise in social rank or in reputation, by effort **2.** *n.* a climbing ‖ a place to be climbed **climb·er** *n.* a

person who climbs mountains for sport ‖ a plant which grows vigorously up a support

clinch (klintʃ) **1.** *v.t.* to settle, make conclusive ‖ to bend back the point of (a nail) after it has gone through the wood, and drive it into the wood to secure it ‖ to clench (teeth) ‖ to fasten (a rope) by a clinch ‖ *v.i.* *(boxing)* to grapple as a method of making strong punches impossible ‖ *(wrestling)* to struggle at close quarters **2.** *n.* the position or practice of clinching by boxers or wrestlers **clinch·er** *n.* a thing that clinches ‖ the remark or argument which settles a dispute

cling (kliŋ) *pres. part.* **cling·ing** *past* and *past part.* **clung** (klʌŋ) *v.i.* to hold fast ‖ to keep close ‖ to keep a sentimental feeling for something

clin·ic (klínik) *n.* a place where hospital outpatients receive medical examination, treatment or advice ‖ a similar institution where people get medical help (often free) ‖ practical instruction of medical students by letting them watch treatment of patients ‖ a class so taught **clín·i·cal** *adj.* of or concerning a clinic ‖ concerning medical teaching by demonstration ‖ concerning the study of disease by observation

clip (klip) **1.** *v. pres. part.* **clip·ping** *past* and *past part.* **clipped** *v.t.* to fasten together with a clip **2.** *n.* a device for fastening things together ‖ a brooch ‖ a device for holding cartridges for a magazine rifle

clip 1. *v. pres. part.* **clip·ping** *past* and *past part.* **clipped** *v.t.* to cut, trim, shear ‖ to cut the edge of (a coin) ‖ to omit final sounds or syllables of in pronouncing ‖ *(pop.)* to cuff with the hand ‖ *v.i.* *(pop.)* to move swiftly **2.** *n.* the act of clipping, esp. of sheepshearing ‖ the quantity of wool clipped from a sheep ‖ the season's yield of wool ‖ a cutting, esp. a sample piece of cloth ‖ a cuff with the hand ‖ *(pop.)* a rapid pace

clip·ping (klípiŋ) *n.* the act of clipping ‖ something clipped off, *nail clippings* ‖ a paragraph, article etc. cut from a newspaper or magazine

clique (kli:k, klik) **1.** *n.* *(pejorative)* a small, exclusive set of people **2.** *v.i.* to form a clique **cli·quey** (klí:ki:, klíki:), **cli·quish** (klí:kiʃ, klíkiʃ), **clí·quy** *adjs*

cloak (klouk) **1.** *n.* a loose, sleeveless outer garment sometimes worn instead of a coat, or as part of uniform or habit ‖ something which hides **2.** *v.t.* to conceal, disguise ‖ to cover as if with a cloak

clock) *n.* a device, other than a watch, for measuring and indicating time ‖ a mechanism with a dial for indicating or recording the working state or output of the machine to which it is attached ‖ a time clock ‖ a speedometer **2.** *v.t.* to time (a race, competitors) with a stopwatch ‖ *v.i.* (of employees, with 'in', 'out', 'on') to record one's entry or exit on a control mechanism

clod (klɒd) *n.* a lump of earth or mud ‖ a part of the shoulder of beef ‖ a stupid person **clód·dish** *adj.* oafish

clog (klɒg) **1.** *n.* a wooden shoe, or one with a wooden sole ‖ a movable weight to which an animal is tied to prevent its straying **2.** *v. pres. part.* **clog·ging** *past* and *past part.* **clogged** *v.t.* to choke up ‖ to encumber, make heavy ‖ to hamper the movement of (an animal) with a clog ‖ *v.i.* to become choked up

clois·ter (klɔ́istər) **1.** *n.* a place of religious seclusion ‖ a covered walk, usually walled on one side and open on to a court or quadrangle on the other, esp. of a religious building **2.** *v.t.* to shut up in, or confine to, a convent or monastery ‖ to isolate **clóis·tered** *adj.* monastic ‖ isolated from the outside world **clóis·tral** *adj.*

clone (kloun) *n.* *(biol.)* the descendants produced asexually from a single animal or plant

close (klous) **1.** *adj.* near ‖ intimate ‖ nearly alike ‖ nearly equal ‖ dense, tightly packed, compact ‖ careful, thorough ‖ secretive ‖ strictly kept or guarded ‖ mean, tightfisted ‖ stifling ‖ *(phon.,* of vowels) articulated with the tongue near the palate ‖ *(finance)* scarce, hard to obtain **2.** *adv.* in a close manner ‖ nearby, near ‖ tightly ‖ nearly ‖ compactly ‖ secretly

close (klouz) **1.** *v. pres. part.* **clos·ing** *past* and *past* *part.* **closed** *v.t.* to shut ‖ to bring together ‖ to end, finish ‖ to settle (an account) finally ‖ to come to an agreement about (a bargain) ‖ *v.i.* to become shut ‖ to come together ‖ to come to an end **2.** *n.* an end, conclusion ‖ *(mus.)* a cadence **to come** (or **draw**) **to a close** to finish gradually

clos·et (klɔ́zit) **1.** *n.* a recess built into a room and shut off with a door, or a small room for storing things ‖ a toilet (room) ‖ a water closet **2.** *v.t.* (usually *refl.*) to shut in a room, esp. for private conference **3.** *adj.* secret, undisclosed

clot (klɒt) **1.** *n.* a lump of coagulated or thickened liquid ‖ *(pop.)* a stupid person **2.** *v. pres. part.* **clot·ting** *past* and *past part.* **clot·ted** *v.i.* to undergo a series of chemical and physical reactions such that a fluid is converted into a coagulum (e.g. blood) ‖ *v.t.* to cause to form into a clot or clots

cloth (klɔθ, klɒθ) **1.** *pl.* **cloths** (klɔθs, klɒθs, klɔðz, klɒðz) *n.* woven material or fabric ‖ a piece of this material ‖ *(rhet.)* the clerical profession **2.** *adj.* made of cloth

clothe (klouð) *pres. part.* **cloth·ing** *past* and *past part.* **clothed** esp. *archaic* and *rhet.* **clad** (klæd) *v.t.* and *refl.* to provide with clothes ‖ to cover

clothes (klouðz, klouz) *pl. n.* garments, wearing apparel ‖ bedclothes ‖ laundry

cloth·ing (klóuðiŋ) *n.* clothes in general

cloud (klaud) **1.** *n.* a visible expanse of suspended droplets of water or ice particles in the air ‖ any suspension of particles in the air or any gas ‖ *(astron.)* a suspension in outer space of dispersed matter ‖ a multitude forming a cloudlike mass **2.** *v.t.* to overspread with clouds ‖ to darken ‖ to make opaque, misty or patchy ‖ to be suffused with ‖ *v.i.* to become cloudy or overcast

cloud·i·ly (kláudili:) *adv.* in a cloudy way

cloud·i·ness (kláudi:nis) *n.* the state or quality of being cloudy

cloud·y (kláudi:) *comp.* **cloud·i·er** *superl.* **cloud·i·est** *adj.* of or resembling clouds ‖ overcast with clouds ‖ difficult to understand ‖ vague, inexact ‖ lacking brightness

clove (klouv) a tropical tree ‖ the spice yielded by its dried flower buds

clo·ver (klóuvər) perennial plants, having trifoliate leaves, cultivated widely in temperate and subtropical regions as forage crops and for soil improvement **in clover** enjoying good fortune or success

clown (klaun) *n.* a buffoon in a circus ‖ someone who is clumsy, or who behaves stupidly **2.** *v.i.* to be a clown ‖ to make people laugh by one's antics **clówn·er·y** *n.* **clówn·ish** *adj.*

cloy (klɔi) *v.t.* to glut, satiate, esp. with sweetness

club (klʌb) **1.** *n.* a stout stick with a thickened end, a cudgel ‖ a golf stick ‖ a playing card of the suit marked with black trefoils (♣) ‖ an association of people with some common interest who meet periodically, *a boat club* **2.** *v.t. pres. part.* **club·bing** *past* and *past part.* **clubbed** to beat with a club or similar weapon

clue (klu:) *n.* anything serving as a guide in the solution of a mystery

clum·sy (klʌ́mzi:) *comp.* **clum·si·er** *superl.* **clum·si·est** *adj.* awkward, ungainly ‖ poorly made, without refinement or elegance

clus·ter (klʌ́stər) **1.** *n.* a number of similar things growing or gathered together **2.** *v.i.* to gather close together **3.** *adj.* of houses built close together

clutch (klʌtʃ) *n.* a tight grip ‖ the act of clutching ‖ (esp. *pl.*) power, control ‖ *(mech.)* a device for con-

necting and disconnecting driving and driven parts smoothly ‖ the lever or pedal controlling this device ‖ the grab of a crane

clutch *v.t.* to seize, catch hold of ‖ to hold firmly ‖ *v.i.* (with 'at') to make a snatching movement

clut·ter (klʌ́tər) **1.** *n.* an untidy mess, state of disorder ‖ litter, things left around untidily **2.** *v.t.* to disorder, make untidy

coach (koutʃ) **1.** *n.* a state carriage ‖ *(hist.)* a large four-wheeled carriage usually drawn by four horses, carrying passengers, parcels and mail ‖ a bus for long-distance journeys ‖ a railroad car for passengers ‖ a class of air travel less luxurious than first class ‖ a private tutor ‖ a trainer in athletics **2.** *v.t.* to teach (someone) privately ‖ to train (someone, e.g. in athletics) ‖ *v.i.* to give private tuition

co·ag·u·late (kouǽgjuleit) *pres. part.* **co·ag·u·lat·ing** *past* and *past part.* **co·ag·u·lat·ed** *v.i.* to turn from a liquid to a curdlike or jellylike consistency, congeal ‖ *v.t.* to precipitate (a suspension) ‖ to cause to congeal **co·ag·u·lá·tion, co·ág·u·la·tor** *ns*

coal (koul) **1.** *n. (geol.)* a combustible deposit of vegetable matter (mosses, ferns etc.) which grew in the Carboniferous era, rendered compact and hard by pressure and heat ‖ a burning ember **2.** *v.t.* to load (a ship) with coal ‖ *v.i.* to take in a supply of coal

co·a·lesce (kouəlés) *pres. part.* **co·a·lesc·ing** *past* and *past part.* **co·a·lesced** *v.i.* to grow or come together, fuse ‖ to combine in a political coalition **co·a·lés·cence** *n.* **co·a·lés·cent** *adj.*

co·a·li·tion (kouəlíʃən) *n.* a coalescing, union ‖ a temporary union of political parties for some common aim **co·a·li·tion·ist** *n.*

coarse (kɔrs, kours) *comp.* **coars·er** *superl.* **coars·est** *adj.* rough, large-grained, not fine ‖ inferior, of poor quality ‖ unrefined, rude ‖ vulgar, indecent

coars·en (kɔ́rs'n, kóurs'n) *v.t.* to make coarse ‖ *v.i.* to become coarse

coast (koust) **1.** *n.* the seashore, the land bordering the sea ‖ a slope for tobogganing ‖ a ride downhill on a sled etc. ‖ a ride downhill on a bicycle without pedaling or in a motor vehicle with the engine switched off **2.** *v.i.* to sail along the coast ‖ to trade between ports along the same coast ‖ to toboggan downhill ‖ to cycle downhill without pedaling or drive a car downhill with the engine switched off ‖ *v.t.* to sail near **cóast·al** *adj.*

coat (kout) **1.** *n.* an overcoat ‖ a person's jacket ‖ an animal's protective covering ‖ any outer covering, *a coat of paint* **2.** *v.t.* to cover with a coat

coat·ing (kóutiŋ) *n.* a covering (e.g. of paint etc.) ‖ cloth used for coats

coax (kouks) *v.t.* to persuade by soft words or gentle handling ‖ to cause a desired effect in (something) by persistent little efforts ‖ to get (something) out of someone by cajoling, encouragement etc. ‖ *v.i.* to wheedle, cajole

co·balt (kóubɔlt) *n.* a bivalent, hard, magnetic, silver-white, metallic element

cobalt blue a permanent greenish-blue pigment composed of cobalt oxide and alumina ‖ a strong greenish-blue color

cob·ble (kɔ́b'l) **1.** *n.* a cobblestone **2.** *v.t. pres. part.* **cob·bling** *past* and *past part.* **cob·bled** to pave with cobbles

cobble *pres. part.* **cob·bling** *past* and *past part.* **cob·bled** *v.t.* to mend (shoes) **cób·bler** *n.* a shoe repairer ‖ a fruit pie made in a deep dish and covered with a thick crust ‖ an iced drink typically of wine, sugar and citrus fruit

---

co·bra (kóubrə) *n.* a very poisonous African and Asian snake that, when on the defensive, flatten the skin behind the neck by distending and elevating the ribs to form a hood

co·caine (koukéin, kóukein) *n.* an alkaloid derived from coca leaves or which can be synthesized

cock 1. *n.* the male bird of the common domestic fowl ‖ (often in combination) the male of other birds, *cock pheasant* ‖ a weathercock ‖ a tap ‖ the hammer in a gun ‖ the raised position of this hammer ‖ an upward tilt, of a nose, hat etc. **2.** *v.t.* to erect or cause to stand on end ‖ to set aslant, tilt upwards ‖ to raise the cock of (a gun) ready to fire ‖ *v.i.* to stick up, stand on end

cock·a·too (kókətu:, kókətú:) *n.* a crested parrot found in Australia and the East Indies

cock·le (kók'l) **1.** *v. pres. part.* **cock·ling** *past and past part.* **cock·led** *v.i.* (of paper etc.) to pucker, curl up because of varying tensions ‖ *v.t.* to cause to pucker or curl up **2.** *n.* a pucker, wrinkle ‖ a bivalve mollusk, the common edible European species ‖ a cockleshell ‖ (*rhet.*) a small, frail boat

cock·roach (kókrout ʃ) *n.* an order of usually vegetarian insects

cock·tail (kókteil) *n.* a drink of liquor mixed with others or with various flavorings ‖ an appetizer served as a first course ‖ a horse with a docked tail

cock·y (kóki:) *comp.* **cock·i·er** *superl.* **cock·i·est** *adj.* cocksure ‖ pert

co·coa (kóukou) *n.* a brown powder obtained after extracting the fats from the cacao bean ‖ a drink prepared from this powder ‖ dull reddish brown

co·co·nut, co·coa·nut (kóukənʌt, kóukənət) *n.* the coconut palm, which grows on the shores of tropical islands ‖ the edible fruit (a drupe) of this palm

co·coon (kəkú:n) *n.* the silky covering which the larvae of many insects, e.g. the silkworm, spin about themselves for protection during the pupa stage ‖ the similar protective coverings produced by some animals, e.g. some annelids

cod (kɒd) *n.* a genus of bony fishes inhabiting cold and temperate seas of the northern hemisphere, particularly abundant off Newfoundland. They yield food and oil

cod·dle (kód'l) *pres. part.* **cod·dling** *past and past part.* **cod·dled** *v.t.* to treat carefully and tenderly, to pamper ‖ to cook slowly in water just below boiling point

code (koud) **1.** *n.* a collection of statutes, rules etc. methodically arranged ‖ an accepted way of behavior, esp. the mores of a society ‖ a system of signals ‖ a system in which arbitrary values are given to letters, words, numbers or symbols to ensure secrecy or brevity **2.** *v.t. pres. part.* **cod·ing** *past and past part.* **cod·ed** to put (a message) into code ‖ (*genetics*) to particularize the genetic code used in synthesizing

cod·i·cil (kódis'l) *n.* a supplementary clause added to a will, revoking or modifying it ‖ an additional provision **cod·i·cil·la·ry** *adj.*

cod·i·fy (kódifai, kóudifai) *pres. part.* **cod·i·fy·ing** *past and past part.* **cod·i·fied** *v.t.* to draw up a code of (laws etc.)

co·ed (kóuéd, kóued) *n.* (*pop.*) a female student at a coeducational college

co·ed·u·ca·tion (kóuedʒukéiʃən) *n.* the education together in a single institution of children or students of both sexes **co·ed·u·ca·tion·al** *adj.*

co·erce (kouə́:rs) *pres. part.* **co·erc·ing** *past and past part.* **co·erced** *v.t.* to compel ‖ to enforce, *to coerce obedience* **co·er·ci·ble** *adj.*

co·er·cion (kouə́:rʃən) *n.* compulsion (moral or physical) ‖ government by force

co·er·cive (kouə́:rsiv) *adj.* compelling, intended to coerce

cof·fee (kófi:, kófi:) *n.* a genus of plants of which two or three species are cultivated commercially ‖ its seeds, raw, roasted or ground ‖ a drink, made (by infusion or decoction) from the roasted and ground seeds ‖ dark brown

cof·fer (kófər, kófər) *n.* a large strongbox for storing money or valuables ‖ a place for storing money ‖ (often *pl.*) a store of funds **2.** *v.t.* (*archit.*) to adorn with coffers

cof·fin (kófin, kófin) *n.* a box in which a corpse is placed for burial

cog (kɒg, kɔg) *n.* a projection or tooth on the rim of a wheel which, by fitting between the cogs of another wheel or between the links of a chain, transmits motion and power ‖ a cogwheel ‖ (*carpentry*) a tenon ‖ a person whose efforts must combine with those of others to be effective

co·gen·cy (kóudʒənsi:) *n.* the state or quality of being cogent

co·gent (kóudʒənt) *adj.* compelling, convincing, *cogent arguments*

cog·i·tate (kódʒiteit) *pres. part.* **cog·i·tat·ing** *past and past part.* **cog·i·tat·ed** *v.i.* to think ‖ *v.t.* to plan, devise **cog·i·ta·tion** *n.* **cog·i·ta·tive** (kódʒiteitiv) *adj.*

co·gnac (kónjæk) *n.* brandy distilled in Cognac and the surrounding region

cog·ni·zance (kógnizəns, kɒ́nizəns) *n.* the range of mental observation or awareness ‖ the fact of being aware, knowledge ‖ (*law*) the power given to a court to deal with a given matter, jurisdiction **cog·nize** (kógnaiz) *pres. part.* **cog·niz·ing** *past and past part.*

co·here (kouhíər) *pres. part.* **co·her·ing** *past and past part.* **co·hered** *v.i.* to stick together, e.g. of the particles of a mass ‖ to stay united ‖ (of style, design, planning etc.) to be consistent throughout

co·her·ence (kouhíərəns) *n.* the state or quality of being coherent

co·her·ent (kouhíərənt) *adj.* cohering ‖ forming a unity ‖ consistent in sequence of thought or design

co·he·sion (kouhí:ʒən) *n.* a cohering ‖ (*phys.*) intermolecular attraction holding together particles in the mass ‖ a remaining or becoming united **co·he·sive** (kouhí:siv) *adj.*

co·hort (kóuhɔrt) *n.* a companion

coif·fure (kwɑfjúər) **1.** *n.* a way of wearing the hair **2.** *v.t. pres. part.* **coif·fur·ing** *past and past part.* **coif·fured** to provide (someone) with a coiffure ‖ to arrange (someone's hair) in a coiffure

coil (kɔil) **1.** *v.t.* to arrange in rings which lie side by side ‖ *v.i.* to wind itself **2.** *n.* something coiled ‖ a single turn of something coiled ‖ (*elec.*) a spiral or helix of wire used as a resistance for electromagnetic purposes

coin (kɔin) **1.** *n.* a piece of metal money **2.** *v.t.* to turn (metal) into coins ‖ to mint (coins of a specified sort) ‖ to invent (a new word or expression) ‖ to amass (a fortune, money) quickly

coin·age (kɔ́inidʒ) *n.* the making of coins ‖ money ‖ the inventing of a word, phrase or idea ‖ a word, phrase or idea so invented

co·in·cide (kouinsáid) *pres. part.* **co·in·cid·ing** *past and past part.* **co·in·cid·ed** *v.i.* to occur at the same time, *their holidays coincide this year, his holiday coincides with hers* ‖ to occupy the same space, esp. in geometry ‖ to be equal, or the same, in some other (non-spatial) respect, *your statement does not coincide with his*

co·in·ci·dence (kouínsidəns) *n.* the state of coinciding ‖ an event or circumstance fortuitously relating in some way to other events or circumstances

co·in·ci·dent (kouínsidənt) *adj.* coinciding ‖ (*geom.*) occupying the same space ‖ happening at the same time **co·in·ci·den·tal** (kouinsidént'l) *adj.* coincident ‖ happening by chance, not by contrivance

co·i·tion (kouíʃən) *n.* sexual intercourse

co·i·tus (kóuitəs) *n.* coition

coke (kouk) **1.** *n.* the hard, gray, porous residue, mostly carbon, obtained by destructive distillation of coal which is heated in a retort or oven, driving off coal gas and other volatile matter **2.** *v.t. pres. part.* **cok·ing** *past and past part.* **coked** to transform into coke

col·an·der (kʌ́ləndər, kɑ́ləndər) *n.* a bowl perforated with holes, used as a strainer in cooking

cold (kould) *n.* absence of heat ‖ low temperature, in comparison with that of the body ‖ *(med.)* coryza, acute infectious catarrh of the nasal mucous membrane ‖ cold weather

cold *adj.* without heat, unheated, *cold water* ‖ without warmth as felt by the human body, *a cold day* ‖ feeling the cold ‖ having cooled, grown cold ‖ without warm human feelings, unfriendly ‖ lacking enthusiasm ‖ (of scent in hunting) faint ‖ unconscious ‖ chilling in effect ‖ *(pop.* of a searcher) far from the object sought

cole·slaw (kóulslɔ) *n.* cabbage salad

co·lic (kólik) *n.* severe pains in the bowels or abdomen **col·ick·y** (kóliki:) *adj.*

col·i·se·um (kɒlisí:əm) *n.* a large building, theater, stadium etc. for sports or public entertainment

col·lab·o·rate (kəlǽbəreit) *pres. part.* **col·lab·o·rat·ing** *past* and *past part.* **col·lab·o·rat·ed** *v.i.* to work together, esp. on work of an intellectual nature ‖ to help an enemy country or an occupying power **col·lab·o·ra·tion, col·lab·o·rá·tion·ist** (only of quislings), **col·láb·o·ra·tor** *ns*

col·lapse (kəlǽps) **1.** *v. pres. part.* **col·laps·ing** *past* and *past part.* **col·lapsed** *v.i.* to fall down or apart when the component parts cease to support one another ‖ to fail ‖ to suffer a breakdown of body, mind or nerves ‖ (of a table etc. designed to do so) to fold ‖ (of a lung) to come into an airless state ‖ *v.t.* to cause to collapse **2.** *n.* a falling down ‖ a breaking to pieces ‖ a failure (of plans etc.) ‖ a mental or physical breakdown **col·láps·i·ble** *adj.* made so as to fold up when not in use

col·lar (kólər) **1.** *n.* the usually folded part of a coat, shirt, dress etc. around the neck ‖ *(zool.)* any of various markings or structures suggesting such a collar ‖ *(engin.)* a ring used to limit motion or hold something in place ‖ any structure comparable to a collar ‖ a leather band or chain put around an animal's neck ‖ part of the harness around a draft horse's neck ‖ an ornamental necklace with insignia of an order **2.** *v.t.* to snatch possession of ‖ to seize ‖ *(pop.)* to appropriate ‖ to put a collar on

col·late (kɒléit, kəléit, kóleit) *pres. part.* **col·lat·ing** *past* and *past part.* **col·lat·ed** *v.t.* to examine (a text) closely against another in order to discover variations ‖ to put (pages, illustrations) in correct order

col·lat·er·al (kəlǽtərəl) **1.** *adj.* parallel ‖ *(law)* subordinate ‖ *(commerce,* of money) lent or secured to guarantee another loan as supplement to some more important security **2.** *n.* a secondary security for a loan

col·la·tion (kɒléiʃən, kəléiʃən, kouléiʃən) *n.* the act or result of collating texts ‖ a description of the technical features of a book

col·league (kóli:g) *n.* a fellow worker, e.g. in a professional organization

col·lect (kəlékt) **1.** *v.t.* to gather in or together ‖ to accumulate (things of a similar kind) for pleasure, self-education or profit ‖ to gain or recover control of (oneself or one's mental faculties) ‖ *v.i.* to come together ‖ to take up a collection **2.** *adj.* and *adv.* to be paid for by the recipient

col·lec·tion (kəlékʃən) *n.* the act of collecting ‖ things brought together by choice ‖ money taken up from members of an audience or congregation for some intention ‖ the season's models designed by a dress designer ‖ an assembly of people

col·lege (kólidʒ) *n.* an organized body of people united for the sake of their functions, purposes or rights ‖

an educational institution within a university and part of it for some purposes but organizing its own affairs ‖ an institution for higher education ‖ the building occupied by an institution for higher education ‖ a school offering specialized professional instruction

col·le·giate (kəlí:dʒit, kəlí:dʒi:it) *adj.* having the nature of a college ‖ of or pertaining to a college or to college members ‖ characteristic of colleges

col·lide (kəláid) *pres. part.* **col·lid·ing** *past* and *past part.* **col·lid·ed** *v.i.* to come into collision ‖ to come into conflict, *your ideas collide with his*

col·li·sion (kəlíʒən) *n.* the violent coming together of a moving body with another, either moving or stationary ‖ a conflict, esp. of ideas or interests

col·lo·qui·al (kəlóukwi:əl) *adj.* (of words, idioms, etc.) thoroughly part of living language ‖ not part of conventional formal modes of expression (esp. written), though usable in speech without being classified as slang **col·ló·qui·al·ism** *n.*

col·lu·sion (kəlú:ʒən) *n.* a dishonest, secret agreement ‖ *(law)* a fraudulent secret agreement between litigating parties **col·lu·sive** (kəlú:siv) *adj.*

co·logne (kəlóun) *n.* a scented toilet water composed of alcohol and citrus or other oils

co·lon (kóulən) *n.* a punctuation mark (:) used chiefly to introduce examples, a list, a statement which illustrates or explains the previous one, or one which expresses a contrast to the previous one

colon (kóulən, kóulɒn) *n.* the major portion of the large intestine of vertebrates between the cecum and the rectum ‖ the second portion of the intestine of insects

colo·nel (kɔ́:rn'l) *n.* an officer in the U.S. army, air force or marine corps ranking below a brigadier general and above a lieutenant colonel **colo·nel·cy** (kɔ́:rn'lsi:) *n.*

co·lo·ni·al (kəlóuni:əl) **1.** *n.* an inhabitant of a colony **2.** *adj.* of or belonging to a colony ‖ of or pertaining to the 13 colonies which originated the United States of America

col·o·nist (kólənist) *n.* someone who helps to establish a colony ‖ an inhabitant of a colony

col·o·ni·za·tion (kólənizéiʃən) *n.* the act or policy of colonizing

col·on·nade (kólənéid) *n.* *(archit.)* an evenly spaced line of columns supporting an entablature ‖ a line of trees making a similar effect

col·o·ny (kóləni:) *pl.* **col·o·nies** *n.* a land or place settled by people from another country, to whose government it is in some degree subject ‖ people of the same foreign nationality, or of a special occupation, living in an unorganized community, *an artists' colony* ‖ a number of animals of the same kind living in one place, *a colony of rats* ‖ *(bot.)* a group of individuals of a species migrant in a new habitat ‖ *(bacteriol.)* a mass of organisms growing in or on a substance

col·or (kálər) **1.** *n.* a sensation experienced usually as a result of light of varying wavelengths reaching the eye ‖ a pigment ‖ the complexion of the face ‖ *(pl.)* a ribbon used as a symbol of a party, the flag of a ship or a regiment ‖ tone of conversation or behavior ‖ *(art)* the general effect of color in a painting ‖ *(printing)* the quality of the inking ‖ *(pl., navy)* the morning ceremony of hoisting the flag and the evening one of lowering it **2.** *v.t.* to impart color to ‖ *(fig.)* to make (something) seem better or worse, by selection of facts and studied emphasis, than is really the case, *to color a report* ‖ *v.i.* to assume a color, or a deeper color, to blush

col·ored (kálərd) *adj.* having color ‖ belonging to some race other than white ‖ given deliberate bias

col·or·ful (kʌ́lərfəl) *adj.* full of color || vivid, lively

col·or·ing (kʌ́ləriŋ) *n.* color scheme || the color of the face and hair || appearance, show (esp. false) || *(art)* the way in which an artist uses color || a children's pastime of putting color on outline pictures || a substance used to give color to something (esp. food)

co·los·sal (kəlɒ́səl) *adj.* huge

col·umn (kɒ́ləm) *n.* a pillar, usually with capital and base, used to support an entablature or an arch, or used decoratively in a building, or alone monumentally || something analogous to such a column, *a column of mercury* || a journalist's regular feature in a newspaper, or other regular feature || *(mil.)* a formation extending in depth behind a narrow front || a similar formation of ships **co·lum·nar** (kəlʌ́mnər) *adj.* **co·lúm·ni·form** *adj.* **cól·umn·ist** *n.* a journalist who writes a regular newspaper feature

co·ma (kóumə) *n.* the state of deep unconsciousness caused by disease, injury or poison

co·ma·tose (kóumətous, kóumətous) *adj.* relating to, resembling or affected by coma

comb (koum **1.** *n.* a toothed instrument for arranging the hair || the fleshy crest on a cock's head or a similar crest on other birds || the crest of a wave || a honeycomb **2.** *v.t.* to arrange or clean with a comb || to search through with great care || to card (wool) || *v.i.* (of a wave) to break, curl over

com·bat 1. (kɒ́mbæt, kʌ́mbæt) *n.* a fight, struggle **2,** *v.* (kəmbǽt, kɒ́mbæt, kʌ́mbæt) *pres. part.* **com·bat·ing, com·bat·ting** *past* and *past part.* **com·bat·ed, com·bat·ted** *v.t.* to fight or struggle against || to oppose || *v.i.* to fight, struggle

com·bat·ant (kəmbǽt'nt, kɒ́mbət'nt, kʌ́mbət'nt) **1.** *adj.* fighting || disposed to fight **2.** *n.* a fighter

com·bi·na·tion (kɒmbinéiʃən) *n.* a combining or being combined || the single thing formed by two or more other things joining together, e.g. business concerns acting as one unit || *(chem.)* the act or process of two or more substances joining to form a different substance || the compound so formed || *(math.)* any of the different sets into which a number of objects may be grouped, irrespective of the order within each set || a set of numbers or other symbols which controls the action of a combination lock || the mechanism operated by this

com·bine 1. (kəmbáin) *v. pres. part.* **com·bin·ing** *past* and *past part.* **com·bined** *v.i.* (of two or more things) to join to form a single unit || *(chem., of substances)* to join to form a different substance || to join with other people in order to achieve a joint purpose || *v.t.* to cause to join together || to contain in a fused state **2.** (kɒ́mbain) *n.* a combination of people or organizations, usually for keeping trade prices high or for political ends || art form utilizing various elements, e.g., collage, painting, etc. || a machine which reaps and threshes as a single process

com·bus·ti·ble (kəmbʌ́stib'l) **1.** *adj.* able to undergo combustion **2.** *n.* a substance having this property

com·bus·tion (kəmbʌ́stʃən) *n.* any chemical process accompanied by the emission of heat and light, typically by combination with oxygen

come (kʌm **1.** *v. pres. part.* **com·ing** *past* **came** (keim) *past part.* **come** *v.i.* to approach || to arrive, appear || to happen, *take life as it comes* || to occur || to reach || to occur in sequence || to occur to the mind || to fall as inheritance || to issue, be born || to result || to be available **2.** *interj.* used to call attention or express remonstrance, *come! that's enough*

co·me·di·an (kəmí:di:ən) *n.* a person who tells jokes in variety shows, nightclubs etc. || an actor in comedy parts

co·me·di·enne (kəmi:di:én, kəmeidi:én) *n.* a woman who tells jokes in variety shows, nightclubs etc. || a comedy actress

com·e·dy (kɒ́midi:) *pl.* **com·e·dies** *n.* drama which seeks to please by amusing and deals with 'some defect . . . that is not painful or destructive' || an ex-

ample of such drama || a real-life situation that suggests such drama || the laughter provoking element in a situation, real or imagined

come·ly (kʌ́mli:) *comp.* **come·li·er** *superl.* **come·li·est** *adj. (old-fash.)* of handsome appearance

com·et (kɒ́mit) *n.* a heavenly body subject to the sun's force of attraction, moving in an elliptical or parabolic orbit, which sometimes degenerates into a hyperbola leading to the escape of the comet from the solar system **com·et·ar·y** (kɒ́miteri:) *adj.*

com·fort (kʌ́mfərt) *n.* consolation (for loss etc.) || someone or something that brings consolation || well-being, contentment || someone or something that contributes to one's well-being

comfort *v.t.* to console

com·fort·a·ble (kʌ́mftəb'l, kʌ́mfərtəb'l) *adj.* providing comfort || enjoying comfort || serene, restful || quite large

com·ic (kɒ́mik) **1.** *adj.* funny, amusing || relating to comedy **2.** *n.* a comedian || an amusing person || *(pl.)* comic strips **the comic** the humorous element in life or art **cóm·i·cal** *adj.* **com·i·cal·i·ty** (kɒmikǽliti:) *n.*

com·ma (kɒ́mə) *n.* a punctuation mark (,) separating words, phrases or clauses in a sentence, items in a list etc.

com·mand (kəmǽnd, kəmɑ́nd) **1.** *v.t.* to control, be in authority over || to dominate, restrain || to order || to deserve and win || to have at one's disposal || to have a view of, overlook || to be in a position to demand || *v.i.* to be in authority **2.** *n.* an order || *(mil.)* a drilling order || authority, control || *(computer)* a signal that sets a process in motion || mastery || troops or ships under one's authority || view or effective range **in command of** in charge of **under the command of** commanded by

com·man·deer (kɒməndíər) *v.t.* to take possession of for military purposes || *(loosely)* to take arbitrary possession of

com·man·der (kəmǽndər, kəmɑ́ndər) *n.* a leader, someone in command || *(navy)* an officer ranking below a captain and above a lieutenant commander

com·mand·ment (kəmǽndmənt, kəmɑ́ndmənt) *n.* an order, esp. a divine command

com·mem·o·rate (kəméməreit) *pres. part.* **com·mem·o·rat·ing** *past* and *past part.* **com·mem·o·rat·ed** *v.t.* to recall to memory || to serve as a memorial to

com·mem·o·ra·tion (kəmeməréiʃən) *n.* a solemn act of remembrance || a religious service of remembrance

com·mence (kəméns) *pres. part.* **com·menc·ing** *past* and *past part.* **com·menced** *v.t.* to begin || *v.i.* to have a beginning

com·mence·ment (kəménsmənt) *n.* the act of beginning || the time of beginning || the fact of beginning || a ceremony in some universities etc. at which diplomas and degrees are conferred

com·mend (kəménd) *v.t.* to recommend, *to commend a book to someone* || to praise || to entrust

com·men·da·tion (kɒmendéiʃən) *n.* praise || the act of commending || something which commends

com·ment (kɒ́ment) **1.** *n.* a remark || a criticism || an explanatory note, esp. to a test **2.** *v.i.* to make comments or remarks || to write explanatory notes

com·men·tar·y (kɒ́mənteri:) *pl.* **com·men·tar·ies** *n.* an explanatory book || a set of notes or critical remarks || a continuous flow of remarks on an event or performance

com·men·ta·tor (kɒ́menteitər) *n.* the writer of a commentary || *(radio)* someone who is present at an event and broadcasts a description of it as it takes place || in a religious ceremony, a layman who explains the rituals

com·merce (kɒ́mərs) *n.* the exchange of goods, esp. on a large scale

com·mer·cial (kəmə́:rʃəl) **1.** *adj.* concerned with commerce || (of a radio program) paid for by an advertiser || (of certain films etc.) made with an eye to emphasis on sales appeal rather than artistic worth **2.** *n. (radio* and *television)* a broadcast advertisement or a program put on by an advertiser

com·mis·er·ate (kəmízəreit) *pres. part.* **com·mis·er·at·ing** *past* and *past part.* **com·mis·er·at·ed** *v.i.* (with 'with') to feel or express pity **com·mis·er·a·tion** *n.* **com·mis·er·a·tive** (kəmízəreitiv) *adj.*

com·mis·sar·y (kómiseri:) *pl.* **com·mis·sar·ies** *n.* an officer in charge of military supplies ‖ a government store supplying food and equipment to army or other governmental personnel

com·mis·sion (kəmíʃən) **1.** *n.* a paper or warrant conferring authority ‖ the entrusting of authority to a person ‖ the business entrusted to a person ‖ a committing or being committed ‖ a percentage paid to an agent or employee on the business which he transacts ‖ a group of people appointed to investigate a matter **in commission** ready for active service ‖ in active service **out of commission** not in a state for use **2.** *v.t.* to give a commission to ‖ to order as a commission, *to commission a portrait* ‖ to put (a ship) in commission

com·mit (kəmít) *pres. part.* **com·mit·ting** *past* and *past part.* **com·mit·ted** *v.t.* to give in keeping, entrust ‖ to be guilty of ‖ to consign officially to custody ‖ to consign for preservation ‖ to put in its last place **com·mit·ment** *n.* something which engages one to do something ‖ a continuing obligation, esp. financial ‖ the act of committing ‖ the state of being committed ‖ a promise, pledge ‖ *(stock exchange)* the purchase or sale of a security **com·mit·tal** (kəmít'l) *n.* the point in the burial service at which the body is placed in the grave ‖ the sending to prison of a person ‖ a commitment of oneself

com·mit·tee (kəmíti:) *n.* a body of people appointed or elected to examine or deal with particular matters ‖ *(law)* someone to whom a trust or charge is committed

com·mo·di·ous (kəmóudi:əs) *adj.* roomy

com·mod·i·ty (kəmóditi:) *pl.* **com·mod·i·ties** *n.* an article of trade ‖ *(econ.)* any concrete thing desired by purchasers, possessing utility, and available in limited supply

com·mon (kómən) *adj.* belonging or relating to more than one ‖ belonging or relating to the public ‖ ordinary, usual, of frequent occurrence ‖ vulgar ‖ second-rate, inferior ‖ *(math.)* belonging to two or more quantities

common *n.* (often *pl.)* an area of grassland, usually in or near a village, used mainly for recreation **in common** owned or shared by all the members of a group, or by two people **out of the common** specially remarkable

common law the unwritten law of custom

com·mon·place (kómənpleis) **1.** *adj.* ordinary ‖ undistinguished ‖ trite **2.** *n.* a trite saying

com·mon·wealth (kómənwelθ) *n.* a free association of self-governing units in a federation, with certain common tasks performed by the federal government

com·mo·tion (kəmóuʃən) *n.* a noisy disturbance caused by a number of people ‖ mental turmoil, confused excitement

com·mune (kómju:n) *n.* the smallest administrative division of the country in France, Belgium, Italy, Spain and some other countries ‖ the government or citizens of a commune ‖ a group protesting modern technological civilization and seeking a simpler way of living through a communal effort, usually based on craft or agriculture ‖ a collective organization for living or working in which products and property are shared

com·mune (kəmjú:n) *pres. part.* **com·mun·ing** *past* and *past part.* **com·muned** *v.i.* to be in communion (in

respect of ideas, feelings) ‖ to communicate, receive Communion

com·mu·ni·ca·ble (kəmjú:nikəb'l) *adj.* capable of being communicated

com·mu·ni·cate (kəmjú:nikeit) *pres. part.* **com·mu·ni·cat·ing** *past* and *past part.* **com·mu·ni·cat·ed** *v.t.* to give or pass on (information, feelings, disease etc.) ‖ to make others understand one's ideas ‖ to be in touch by words or signals ‖ to be joined by a common door, gate etc.

com·mu·ni·ca·tion (kəmju:nikéiʃən) *n.* a sending, giving or exchanging (of information, ideas, etc.) ‖ a method of such exchange ‖ the state of such exchange ‖ an item of such exchange ‖ a scientific paper read to a learned group ‖ (often *pl.)* travel and transport links between places

com·mun·ion (kəmjú:njən) *n.* an intimate or sublime exchange or communication of thoughts and feelings ‖ a body of people with common faith ‖ fellowship bridging divisions of the Church **Com·mun·ion** *(eccles.)* the partaking of the consecrated bread or wine ‖ the sacrament of Holy Communion

com·mun·ism (kómjunizəm) *n.* the ownership of property, or means of production, distribution and supply, by the whole of a classless society, with wealth shared on the principle of 'to each according to his need', each yielding fully 'according to his ability' **cóm·mun·ist 1.** *n.* a person who advocates communism **2.** *adj.* of, pertaining to, favoring communism

com·mu·ni·ty (kəmjú:niti:) *pl.* **com·mu·ni·ties** *n.* a body of people living near one another and in social relationship ‖ a body of people with a faith, profession or way of life in common, *the Jewish community* ‖ a collection of animals and or plants sharing the same environment ‖ common ownership ‖ a sharing

com·mute (kəmjú:t) *pres. part.* **com·mut·ing** *past* and *past part.* **com·mut·ed** *v.t.* to change (a mode of payment) to another ‖ to change (a punishment) into another less severe ‖ *(elec.)* to commutate ‖ *v.i.* to travel regularly to and from a city, usually for work

com·pact (kómpækt) *n.* an agreement between individuals or groups

com·pact 1. (kəmpækt) *adj.* densely packed ‖ closely arranged or put together so as to use space economically ‖ (of an automobile) smaller than average ‖ without waste of words **2.** (kómpækt) *n.* a small container for face powder, and sometimes rouge, with a mirror

com·pan·ion (kəmpænjən) **1.** *n.* a person who goes with or accompanies another ‖ someone who shares another's experiences ‖ a person or animal whose company one enjoys ‖ a thing made to match or harmonize with another ‖ a woman paid to live with and help another **2.** *v.t. (rhet.)* to accompany, go with

com·pa·ny (kámpəni:) *pl.* **com·pa·nies** *n.* the state of being with another or others ‖ people with whom one associates ‖ *(pop.)* a guest or guests ‖ a number of people united in an industrial or commercial enterprise, e.g. a firm of partners ‖ the officers and men of a ship ‖ an infantry unit between a platoon and a battalion in size ‖ companionship ‖ someone or something providing companionship

com·pa·ra·ble (kómpərəb'l) *adj.* capable or worthy of being compared ‖ similar **cóm·pa·ra·bly** *adv.*

com·par·a·tive (kəmpærətiv) **1.** *adj.* using or introducing comparison ‖ not absolute but existing in some degree **2.** *n. (gram.)* the comparative degree

com·pare (kəmpéər) **1.** *v. pres. part.* **com·par·ing** *past* and *past part.* **com·pared** *v.t.* to examine (two or more things) in order to discover their likenesses or differences ‖ to state a likeness of (one thing to another) ‖ to affirm the excellence of (one thing) by setting it beside another of known excellence ‖ *(gram.)* to form the comparative and superlative degrees of (adjectives and adverbs) ‖ *v.i. (usually neg.)* to sustain comparison **2.** *n.* (in phrases) **beyond compare, past compare** of such excellence that nothing comparable can be found

com·par·i·son (kəmpǽris'n) *n.* a comparing, an attempt to discover what is like and unlike ‖ a resemblance shown for the sake of explanation ‖ *(gram.)* the change in form of adjectives and adverbs to show difference of degree, e.g. 'great, greater, greatest'

com·part·ment (kəmpártmənt) *n.* one part of a space which has been divided, e.g., in an egg carton, or watertight division of a ship **com·part·men·tal** (kəmpɑrtmént'l, kəmpɑrtmént'l) *adj.*

com·pass (kʌ́mpəs) *n.* an instrument for determining direction on the earth's surface ‖ (also *pl.*) an instrument consisting of two legs connected by a metal joint, used for making circles

com·pas·sion (kəmpǽʃən) *n.* pity aroused by the distress of others, with the desire to help them

com·pas·sion·ate (kəmpǽʃənit) *adj.* feeling compassion

com·pat·i·ble (kəmpǽtəb'l) *adj.* able to exist together without mutual contradiction ‖ capable of living together harmoniously

com·pa·tri·ot (kəmpéitri:ət) *n.* someone having the same native country as another

com·pel (kəmpél) *pres. part.* **com·pel·ling** *past* and *past part.* **com·pelled** *v.t.* to oblige (someone to do something) ‖ to call forth and secure (something) in others **com·pél·la·ble** *adj.*

com·pen·sate (kʌ́mpənseit) *pres. part.* **com·pen·sat·ing** *past* and *past part.* **com·pen·sat·ed** *v.t.* to repay (someone) for a loss ‖ *(phys.)* to provide with a means of counteracting or neutralizing variation ‖ to make up for (something)

com·pen·sa·tion (kɒmpənséiʃən) *n.* an act of compensating or thing which compensates ‖ *(psychol.)* a behavior mechanism which seeks a substitute for something lacking or unacceptable

com·pete (kəmpí:t) *pres. part.* **com·pet·ing** *past* and *past part.* **com·pet·ed** *v.i.* to try to win a contest ‖ to try to get what others also seek and which all cannot have

com·pe·tence (kʌ́mpitəns) *n.* sufficient ability ‖ a modest income, enough to live on ‖ legal capacity or qualification

com·pe·tent (kʌ́mpitənt) *adj.* having the necessary qualities or skills ‖ showing adequate skill ‖ *(law)* having legal capacity or qualification

com·pe·ti·tion (kɒmpitíʃən) *n.* a contest in which people compete, *an athletic competition* ‖ a competing, *trade competition*

com·pet·i·tive (kəmpétitiv) *adj.* based on competition

com·pet·i·tor (kəmpétitər) *n.* someone who takes part in a competition ‖ a rival

com·pi·la·tion (kɒmpiléiʃən) *n.* the act of compiling ‖ something compiled

com·pile (kəmpéil) *pres. part.* **com·pil·ing** *past* and *past part.* **com·piled** *v.t.* to collect (materials, facts) for a book etc. ‖ to put together (a history, an account etc.) from facts

com·pla·cence (kəmpléisəns) *n.* complacency

com·pla·cen·cy (kəmpléisənsi:) *n.* self-satisfaction, lack of self-criticism ‖ mild contentment

com·pla·cent (kəmpléisənt) *adj.* self-satisfied, smug

com·plain (kəmpléin) *v.i.* to express dissatisfaction ‖ to express pain or distress ‖ to make a formal complaint **com·pláin·ant** *n. (law)* someone accusing another of an injury

com·plaint (kəmpléint) *n.* an expression of dissatisfaction ‖ an accusation ‖ a cause of dissatisfaction ‖ a minor or recalcitrant illness ‖ *(Am., law)* a formal allegation in a civil action

com·ple·ment (kʌ́mpləmənt) *n.* that which serves to complete ‖ the full number required, esp. of men to

man a ship, soldiers in an army unit etc. **com·ple·men·tal** (kɒmpləmént'l) *adj.* of or relating to a complement **com·ple·mén·ta·ry** *adj.* serving to complete

com·plete (kəmplí:t) *adj.* with nothing missing or lacking ‖ finished ‖ absolute, entire

complete *pres. part.* **com·plet·ing** *past* and *past part.* **com·plet·ed** *v.t.* to finish ‖ to perfect, round off ‖ to make up a desired amount **com·plé·tion** *n.*

com·plex (kɒ́mpleks) *n.* a whole made up of dissimilar parts or parts in intricate relationship ‖ *(pop.)* a fixed idea or obsession ‖ *(psychol.)* a persistent set of attitudes, having a decisive influence on the personality, and partly determined by unconscious motives ‖ *(chem.)* a complex substance, a substance formed by the union of simpler substances as distinguished from mixtures or compounds

complex (kəmpléks, kɒ́mpleks) *adj.* not simple ‖ consisting of many parts ‖ of a distinct chemical species consisting of some combination of ions, radicals, elements or compounds in which the chemical bonds are weaker than those found in compounds

com·plex·ion, com·plec·tion (kəmplékʃən) *n.* the natural color and appearance of the skin, esp. of the face **com·pléx·ioned** *adj.* (chiefly in combinations) having a (specified) complexion

com·plex·i·ty (kəmpléksiti:) *pl.* **com·plex·i·ties** *n.* the state or quality of being complex ‖ something complex

com·pli·ance (kəmpláiəns) *n.* willingness to follow or consent to another's wishes ‖ an instance of this quality

com·pli·ant (kəmpláiənt) *adj.* yielding or willing to comply

com·pli·cate (kɒ́mplikeit) **1.** *v.t. pres. part.* **com·pli·cat·ing** *past* and *past part.* **com·pli·cat·ed** to make difficult or confused ‖ to make complex ‖ *(med.)* to cause to be more severe or more difficult to treat **2.** *adj. (zool.)* folded lengthwise **cóm·pli·cat·ed** *adj.* complex, with many components ‖ difficult to understand because of its many aspects, *a complicated relationship* ‖ *(med.,* of a fracture) in which nerves or blood vessels are damaged

com·pli·ca·tion (kɒmplikéiʃən) *n.* the state of being complicated ‖ an additional difficulty or accumulation of difficulties which makes something hard to understand or which makes a situation hard to act in ‖ *(med.)* the condition resulting from the coincidence of two diseases or conditions arising in sequence, where the second disease may or may not be attributable to the first

com·plic·i·ty (kəmplísiti:) *pl.* **com·plic·i·ties** *n.* participation in wrongdoing

com·pli·ment (kɒ́mplimənt) *n.* a verbal expression of courteous praise ‖ an action showing praise and respect ‖ *(pl.)* a formula of greeting

com·pli·ment (kɒ́mpliment) *v.t.* to praise courteously ‖ to congratulate **com·pli·mén·ta·ry** *adj.* of or relating to a compliment

com·ply (kəmplái) *pres. part.* **com·ply·ing** *past* and *past part.* **com·plied** *v.i.* to act in accordance with another's wishes, or with rules and regulations

com·po·nent (kəmpóunənt) **1.** *adj.* forming part of a whole **2.** *n.* an essential part of something ‖ *(mech.)* one of the parts into which a vector or tensor quality (force, velocity etc.) may be resolved ‖ a substance of fixed composition in a chemical system

com·port (kəmpɔ́rt, kəmpóurt) *v. refl. (rhet.)* to behave (oneself) ‖ *v.i. (rhet.,* with 'with') to be in agreement, harmony **com·pórt·ment** *n. (rhet.)* one's way of behaving

com·pose (kəmpóuz) *pres. part.* **com·pos·ing** *past* and *past part.* **com·posed** *v.t.* to create in music or literature ‖ to arrange shapes and colors into (a painting etc.) ‖ to arrange (words or objects) into good order ‖ to make calm, quiet, bring under control ‖ *(printing)* to set up (copy) in printing types ‖ (of elements, parts etc.) to constitute when put together ‖ *v.i.* to compose music **com·pósed** *adj.* calm, in full self-possession

com·pós·er *n.* a person who composes music

com·po·site (kəmpózit) *adj.* made up of parts, each of which is itself a whole or taken from another whole ‖ *(math.)* of a number divisible by some number other than 1 without a remainder

com·po·si·tion (kɒmpəzíʃən) *n.* the act of creating in music or literature ‖ a work so created ‖ the act of arranging or putting into order ‖ *(printing)* the setting up of type ‖ the building up of a compound from two single words ‖ the arrangement of shapes, color and line in a picture ‖ an essay ‖ content with respect to constituent elements

com·po·sure (kəmpóuʒər) *n.* a settled state of mind, calm self-possession

com·pote (kómpout) *n.* fruit stewed with sugar

com·pound 1. (kómpaund, kəmpáund) *adj.* made up of separate substances or parts ‖ *(bot.)* composed of a number of similar parts forming a common whole **2.** (kómpaund) *n.* something made up from things combined together ‖ *(chem.)* a substance formed of two or more ingredients of constant proportion by weight ‖ *(gram.)* a word composed of two or more other words or elements **3.** (kəmpáund) *v.t.* to make (a new whole) by combining elements ‖ to combine (elements) to make a new whole ‖ to compute (interest) on the total of the principal and the interest which has accrued regularly at intervals ‖ *v.i.* to settle a debt by compromise

com·pre·hend (kɒmprihénd) *v.t.* to understand, grasp the meaning or significance of, esp. by an effort of sympathy ‖ to include

com·pre·hen·sion (kɒmprihénʃən) *n.* the act of understanding ‖ the faculty of understanding ‖ the capacity to include ‖ sympathetic understanding of differing opinions

com·pre·hen·sive (kɒmprihénsiv) *adj.* including much ‖ all-inclusive ‖ able to understand much

com·press (kómpres) *n.* a soft pad of cloth, pressing on to some part of the body to relieve pain etc. ‖ a wet cloth held by a waterproof bandage to relieve inflammation

com·press (kəmprés) *v.t.* to reduce the volume, duration etc. of, by or as if by pressure ‖ to condense, express concisely **com·préssed** *adj.* pressed together ‖ condensed ‖ flattened

com·pres·sion (kəmpréʃən) *n.* a compressing or being compressed **com·prés·sive** *adj.* having the tendency to compress

com·prise, com·prize (kəmpráiz) *pres. part.* **com·pris·ing, com·priz·ing** *past* and *past part.* **com·prised, com·prized** *v.t.* to be made up of, consist of ‖ to include, contain

com·pro·mise (kómprəmaiz) **1.** *n.* a method of reaching agreement in a dispute, by which each side surrenders something that it wants ‖ an agreement so reached ‖ a course of action intermediate between extremes ‖ a placing in jeopardy **2.** *v. pres. part.* **com·pro·mis·ing** *past* and *past part.* **com·pro·mised** *v.i.* to settle a dispute by a compromise ‖ *v.t.* to bring into danger or under suspicion, or expose to loss of reputation

comp·trol·ler (kəntróulər) *n.* (only in official titles) a controller

com·pul·sive (kəmpálsiv) **1.** *adj.* compelling ‖ *(psychol.)* irrationally compelling **2.** *n.* *(psychol.)* a person subject to compulsive drives

com·pul·so·ry (kəmpálsəri:) *adj.* that must be done or suffered, having the force of compulsion

com·punc·tion (kəmpáŋkʃən) *n.* the pricking of conscience

com·pu·ta·tion (kɒmpjutéiʃən) *n.* the act of computing

com·pute (kəmpjú:t) *pres. part.* **com·put·ing** *past* and *past part.* **com·put·ed** *v.t.* to calculate **com·pút·er, com·pú·tor** *n.* someone who computes ‖ a computing machine

com·rade (kómræd) *n.* an intimate companion who shares one's work or pleasures **cóm·rade·ship** *n.*

con- *prefix* (used before sounds other than b, p, m, l, r) with

con·cave (kɒnkéiv, kónkeiv) **1.** *adj.* curving inwards like the inside of a sphere **2.** *n.* a concave surface, line etc. **con·cav·i·ty** (kɒnkǽviti:) *n.*

con·ceal (kənsí:l) *v.t.* to hide ‖ to keep secret **con·céal·ment** *n.*

con·cede (kənsí:d) *pres. part.* **con·céd·ing** *past* and *past part.* **con·céd·ed** *v.t.* to grant to be true in an agrument ‖ to grant (a right or privilege) ‖ to admit having lost (a game, election etc.) at some stage before the end

con·ceit (kənsí:t) *n.* excessive satisfaction with one's character or achievements ‖ a complex witty figure of speech **con·céit·ed** *adj.* having too high an opinion of oneself

con·ceiv·a·ble (kənsí:vəb'l) *adj.* capable of being thought, imagined or understood **con·céiv·a·bly** *adv.*

con·ceive (kənsí:v) *pres. part.* **con·céiv·ing** *past* and *past part.* **con·ceived** *v.t.* to become pregnant with (a child) ‖ to form (an idea) ‖ *v.t.* to become pregnant ‖ (with *of*) to form a conception

con·cen·trate (kónsəntreit) **1.** *v. pres. part.* **con·cen·trat·ing** *past* and *past part.* **con·cen·trat·ed** *v.t.* to bring together into a mass ‖ to render less dilute ‖ to focus, cause to converge on an objective ‖ *v.i.* to direct or focus one's powers or actions on some limited object ‖ to come together in a mass **2.** *n.* a concentrated form of something **con·cen·trá·tion** *n.* a concentrating or being concentrated ‖ *(mil.)* a body of troops massed in an area ‖ *(chem.)* an amount present in a given volume

con·cept (kónsept) *n.* a thought or opinion, general notion or idea, esp. one formed by generalization from particular examples

con·cep·tion (kənsépʃən) *n.* the act of becoming pregnant ‖ teh state of being conceived in the womb ‖ the faculty of conceiving in the mind ‖ a thing conceived, designed, or thought out **con·cép·tion·al** *adj.*

con·cep·tu·al (kənséptʃu:əl) *adj.* pertaining to mental conception or concepts

con·cern (kənsə́:rn) **1.** *v.t.* to have as subject ‖ *(refl.)* to interest (oneself) in, take part in ‖ to implicate or involve **2.** *n.* a matter of direct interest or importance to one ‖ a business, firm or organization ‖ anxiety worry **con·cérn·ing** *prep.* about, regarding, pertaining to **con·cérn·ment** *n.* concern, anxiety ‖ relation or bearing

con·cert 1. (kənsə́:rt) *v.t.* to devise, plan, or frame together **2.** (kónsə:rt) *n.* agreement or union in an undertaking ‖ a musical performance, usually by several singers or instrumentalists **con·cért·ed** *adj.* arranged by mutual agreement

con·ces·sion (kənséʃən) *n.* a conceding or yielding ‖ the thing yielded or conceded ‖ a grant, esp. of land or property, by a government for a specified purpose ‖ a lease of a part of premises for some specific use **con·ces·sion·aire, con·ces·sion·naire** (kənséʃənɛ́ər) *n.* a person or company benefiting from a concession, esp. the beneficiary of a monopoly granted by a government to a foreign company ‖ a person or firm benefiting from the grant of a lease, e.g. to sell retail goods in a special place **con·ces·sion·ar·y** (kənséʃənɛri:) **1.** *adj.* relating to a concession **2.** *pl.* **con·ces·sion·ar·ies** *n.* a concessionaire

conch (kɒŋk, kɒntʃ) *pl.* **conchs** (kɒŋks), **con·ches** (kóntʃiz) *n.* any of a group of large spiral-shelled

---

marine mollusks, or the shell or animal individually ‖ (archit.) the domed roof of a church apse ‖ (anat.) the largest concavity of the external ear, or the whole external ear

con·cil·i·ate (kənsíli:eit) pres. part. **con·cil·i·at·ing** past and past part. **con·cil·i·at·ed** v.t. to win over from hostility ‖ to win (goodwill) by genial or soothing approaches ‖ to make compatible, reconcile (conflicting views etc.)

con·cil·i·a·tion (kənsili:éiʃən) n. a bringing of opponents into harmony ‖ reconcilement ‖ a voluntary (and not legally binding) attempt by parties to an industrial dispute to reach agreement without strike action

con·cise (kənsáis) adj. brief, condensed, expressing much in few words

con·clave (kónkleiv, kóŋkleiv) n. the room in which cardinals meet to elect a pope ‖ the body of cardinals ‖ a private or secret meeting **cón·clav·ist** n. a priest attending cardinals in a conclave

con·clude (kənklú:d) pres. part. **con·clud·ing** past and past part. **con·clud·ed** v.t. to bring to an end ‖ to effect or bring about ‖ to decide (something) on the basis of reasoning ‖ v.i. to come to an end

con·clu·sion (kənklú:ʒən) n. the end or last part ‖ a reasoned judgment or inference ‖ a settlement or arrangement of an agreement etc. ‖ the summary or upshot of an agreement etc. ‖ the summary or upshot of an argument, essay etc. **in conclusion** lastly

con·clu·sive (kənklú:siv) adj. final, decisive, a conclusive argument ‖ putting an end to further discussion, conclusive evidence ‖ belonging to an end or termination, concluding

con·coct (kɒnkókt, kənkókt) v.t. to prepare by mixing ingredients ‖ to make up, invent, devise

con·coc·tion (kɒnkókʃən, kənkókʃən) n. a concocting ‖ something concocted ‖ a lie

con·cord (kónkɔrd, kóŋkɔrd) n. a state of agreement or harmony ‖ a treaty or agreement

con·course (kónkɔrs, kónkours, kóŋkɔrs, kóŋkours) n. a flocking together of people ‖ a coming together (of things, e.g. streams) ‖ an open space where crowds may gather

con·crete (kónkri:t, kɒnkrí:t) **1.** n. a hard strong substance made by mixing sand and gravel or crushed stone with cement and water, used as a building and construction material while still moist, and allowed to set in position **2.** adj. (of a noun) naming an object as opposed to a quality or attribute ‖ real, specific, not abstract or ideal ‖ united, compounded, in a condensed or solid state ‖ made of concrete **3.** v. pres. part. **con·cret·ing** past and past part. **con·cret·ed** v.i. (kɒnkrí:t) to solidify, harden ‖ v.t. (kónkri:t) to make from, set in or cover with concrete

con·cu·bine (kóŋkjubain, kónkjubain) n. a woman who lives with a man not her husband

con·cur (kənkɔ́:r) pres. part. **con·cur·ring** past and past part. **con·curred** v.i. to agree or accord in opinion ‖ to happen together, coincide ‖ (esp. of three or more lines) to meet in one point **con·cur·rence** (kənkɔ́:rəns, kənkʌ́rəns), **con·cúr·ren·cy** ns. **con·cúr·rent** adj. running alongside, existing or happening together ‖ acting together, cooperating ‖ directed to, or intersecting in, the same point ‖ (law) having joint, equal authority

con·cus·sion (kənkʌ́ʃən) n. violent shaking, e.g. from an impact ‖ (med.) a condition of impaired activity of the brain, through a blow or violent shaking

con·cus·sive (kənkʌ́siv) adj. of an agitating or shaking nature

con·demn (kəndém) v.t. to censure, blame ‖ to prescribe punishment for ‖ to pronounce (esp. a tenement) unfit for use ‖ to pronounce (e.g. smuggled goods) taken over for public use ‖ (pop.) to declare incurable **con·dem·na·ble** (kəndémnəb'l) adj.

con·dem·na·tion (kóndemnéiʃən) n. a condemning or being condemned ‖ grounds for condemning

con·den·sa·tion (kóndenséiʃən) n. a condensing or being

condensed ‖ a making more concise and brief of written material etc. ‖ the product of such treatment ‖ (chem.) the transition of a substance from the vapor to the liquid state

con·dense (kəndéns) pres. part. **con·dens·ing** past and past part. **con·densed** v.t. to make more dense or compact ‖ to express in fewer words ‖ to concentrate, increase the strength of ‖ to reduce (gas or vapor) to a liquid form ‖ to reduce by evaporation ‖ v.i. to become more dense or compact ‖ (of gas or vapor) to become liquid or solid

con·de·scend (kɒndisénd) v.i. to behave patronizingly ‖ to agree to do something which one considers beneath one's dignity ‖ to be gracious to people of lower rank **con·de·scénd·ing** adj.

con·de·scen·sion (kɒndisénʃən) n. a condescending

con·di·ment (kóndimənt) n. a seasoning, e.g. pepper, used to flavor food

con·di·tion (kəndíʃən) v.t. (pass.) to be a condition of ‖ to subject to conditions ‖ to stipulate ‖ to put into the required state, make fit ‖ to subject (a substance) to a technological treatment in order to sterilize or preserve it etc. ‖ to impose a condition on (a student) ‖ (psychol.) to affect the reflexes or behavior of (a person or animal) by conditioning

condition n. mode or state of existence ‖ state of health ‖ state of training ‖ a stipulation, provision ‖ a prerequisite ‖ (pl.) circumstances ‖ (pl.) terms ‖ social rank ‖ (gram.) a conditional clause, protasis ‖ (logic) an antecedent ‖ a stipulation that a student who has failed to reach the required standard in a subject should pass a further examination in it before he may proceed ‖ (law) a clause in a contract etc. that modifies, revokes or suspends a stipulation or a given contingency

con·di·tion·al (kəndíʃən'l) **1.** adj. dependent, made or granted on certain conditions, not absolute ‖ (gram.) expressing or containing a condition **2.** n. (gram.) a conditional word, clause, mood etc. **con·di·tion·al·i·ty** n.

con·dole (kəndóul) pres. part. **con·dol·ing** past and past part. **con·doled** v.i. to express sympathetic grief, commiserate **con·dó·lence** n.

con·dom (kóndəm) n. a contraceptive sheath worn over the penis

con·do·min·i·um (kɒndəmíni:əm) n. a region administered jointly by two or more powers ‖ joint sovereignty ‖ part of a building owned usually for use by the purchaser, e.g. a single apartment in a multiple housing structure or office in a commercial structure

con·do·na·tion (kɒndounéiʃən) n. the act of condoning

con·done (kəndóun) pres. part. **con·don·ing** past and past part. **con·doned** v.t. to overlook (an offense or shortcoming) ‖ to allow to continue (what ought to be stopped)

con·dor (kóndər) n. a very large vulture of the High Andes

con·duce (kəndú:s, kəndjú:s) pres. part. **con·duc·ing** past and past part. **con·duced** v.i. (with 'to' or 'toward') to lead or tend towards (a generally desirable result) **con·dú·cive** adj. having power to promote

con·duct **1.** (kəndʌ́kt) v.t. to lead, guide, escort ‖ to direct, command or manage ‖ to direct (an orchestra) ‖ to behave (oneself) ‖ to transmit or be capable of transmitting (heat, light, sound or electricity) ‖ v.i. to act as a musical conductor **2.** (kóndʌkt) n. moral behavior ‖ management, mode of conducting

con·duc·tor (kəndʌ́ktər) n. the guide or leader of a party ‖ someone who conducts musical performers ‖ the official in charge of passengers on a bus or streetcar ‖ a railroad official who examines passengers' tickets during the journey ‖ a material which can conduct heat, electricity etc.

con·duit (kóndwit, kóndu:it, kóndju:it, kóndit) n. a channel or pipe for carrying fluid ‖ a tube or trough for protecting electric wires

cone (koun) n. (bot.) a mass of spirally arranged, woody carpels, bearing pollen or ovules ‖ (geom.) a solid figure with circular (or elliptical) base, tapering to a point ‖ something conical in shape ‖ a cone-shaped wafer for ice cream **2.** *v. pres. part.* **con·ing** *past and past part.* **coned** *v.t.* to shape like a cone ‖ *v.i.* to bear cones

con·fec·tion (kənfékʃən) **1.** *n.* a prepared dish, esp. jam, preserves or dessert ‖ a mixture or compounding **2.** *v.t.* to prepare or make (confections) **con·féc·tion·er** *n.* a manufacturer of, or shopkeeper selling, candies, cakes etc.

con·fec·tion·er·y (kənfékʃəneri:) *n.* candy ‖ the work of a confectioner ‖ a confectioner's shop

con·fed·er·a·cy (kənfédərəsi:, kənfédrəsi:) *pl.* **con·fed·er·a·cies** *n.* a league or alliance ‖ a union of states or peoples for a particular purpose

con·fed·er·ate (kənfédərit, kənfédrit) **1.** *adj.* allied, leagued together **2.** *n.* an ally (esp. in a pejorative sense), an accomplice **3.** (kənfédəreit) *v. pres. part.* **con·fed·er·at·ing** *past and past part.* **con·fed·er·at·ed** *v.i.* to unite in a league or conspiracy ‖ *v.t.* to bring (a person or state) into an alliance

con·fed·er·a·tion (kənfédəréiʃən) *n.* a confederating or being confederated ‖ an alliance of powers for some mutual benefit

con·fer (kənfɔ́:r) *pres. part.* **con·fer·ring** *past and past part.* **con·ferred** *v.i.* to seek advice ‖ to discuss views, hold a conference ‖ *v.t.* to give or grant **con·fer·ee** (kɒnfərí:) *n.* someone on whom something is conferred ‖ someone who takes part in a conference

con·fer·ence (kɒ́nfərəns, kɒ́nfrəns) *n.* consultation ‖ a formal meeting at which people confer **con·fer·en·tial** (kɒnfərénʃəl) *adj.*

con·fess (kənfés) *v.t.* to own up to, admit ‖ to acknowledge (one's sins) in penitence ‖ *v.i.* to acknowledge one's sins **con·féssed** *adj.* admitted, avowed

con·fes·sion (kənféʃən) *n.* an acknowledgment of a crime or fault ‖ a statement of something confessed ‖ the acknowledging of one's sins, esp. the act of disclosing them to a priest to obtain absolution **con·fés·sion·al** *adj.* pertaining to a confession or creed

con·fes·sion·al (kənféʃənəl) *n.* the enclosure in which a priest hears confession ‖ the practice of confessing sin to a priest

con·fes·sor (kənfésər) *n.* a person confessing ‖ a priest who hears confession and grants absolution

con·fet·ti (kənféti:) *pl. n.* small pieces of colored paper thrown for fun on festive occasions

con·fide (kənfáid) *pres. part.* **con·fid·ing** *past and past part.* **con·fid·ed** *v.t.* to entrust a secret ‖ to trust, have entire faith ‖ *v.i.* to tell (something) confidentially

con·fi·dence (kɒ́nfidəns) *n.* a state of trust ‖ reliance, a feeling of hope on which one relies ‖ self-reliance ‖ something told in confidence, a secret **in confidence** as a secret **to take someone into one's confidence** to tell someone something private

con·fi·dent (kɒ́nfidənt) *adj.* self-assured ‖ convinced ‖ bold, sometimes presumptuously

con·fi·den·tial (kɒ́nfidénʃəl) *adj.* spoken or written in confidence ‖ entrusted with secrets ‖ indicating close intimacy or confidence

con·fine (kənfáin) *pres. part.* **con·fin·ing** *past and past part.* **con·fined** *v.t.* to limit, keep (something, oneself) within limits ‖ to shut in, imprison ‖ (with 'to') to prevent from going out **con·fíned** *adj.* (old-fash.) about to have a child

con·fine·ment (kənfáinmənt) *n.* the state of being confined ‖ imprisonment ‖ inability to go out because of illness ‖ a lying-in, time of giving birth to a child

con·firm (kənfɔ́:rm) *v.t.* to make stronger or more persistent ‖ to corroborate, establish the truth of ‖ to ratify, endorse by writing ‖ to make (something pro-

visional) definite ‖ to administer the rite of confirmation to **con·fir·mand** (kɒnfərmǽnd, kɒ́nfərmænd) *n.* candidate for confirmation

con·fir·ma·tion (kɒnfərméiʃən) *n.* a confirming or being confirmed ‖ corroboration ‖ something that confirms, a proof ‖ the Christian rite by which baptized persons, at the age of discretion, are admitted to full communion ‖ the solemn initiation of boys and girls into the Jewish faith

con·fis·cate (kɒ́nfiskeit, kənfískeit) *pres. part.* **con·fis·cat·ing** *past and past part.* **con·fis·cat·ed** *v.t.* to seize for the public treasury as a penalty ‖ to take away (something) from somebody under discipline

con·fis·ca·tion (kɒnfiskéiʃən) *n.* a confiscating or being confiscated

con·fla·gra·tion (kɒnfləgréiʃən) *n.* a calamitous fire

con·flict 1. (kɒ́nflikt) *n.* armed fighting, a war ‖ a struggle between opposing principles or aims ‖ a clash of feelings or interests ‖ such a clash as a source of dramatic action **2.** (kənflíkt) *v.i.* to be at variance, clash ‖ to struggle, contend **con·flíc·tion** *n.*

con·flu·ence (kɒ́nflu:əns) *n.* a flowing together of streams, roads etc. ‖ a stream or body formed by such a junction

con·form (kənfɔ́rm) *v.i.* to comply ‖ to do as others do ‖ *v.t.* to adapt, cause to comply

con·form·ist (kənfɔ́rmist) **1.** *adj.* tending to conform **2.** *n.* someone who conforms

con·form·i·ty (kənfɔ́rmiti:) *pl.* **con·form·i·ties** *n.* a conforming to authority or to an accepted or implied standard ‖ compliance ‖ likeness in form, shape or manner

con·found (kɒnfáund, kənfáund) *v.t.* to fail to distinguish between, mix up, confuse ‖ (rhet.) to defeat ‖ to perplex deeply, utterly astonish ‖ (kɒnfáund, as a mild oath) to damn, *confound it!* **con·fóund·ed** *adj.* utterly confused, astonished ‖ (pop.) damned, damnable

con·front (kənfrʌ́nt) *v.t.* to face, esp. boldly or in a hostile way ‖ (with 'with') to bring face to face, force to consider something ‖ to stand in front of, lie before ‖ to put together for comparison **con·fron·ta·tion** (kɒnfrəntéiʃən) *n.*

con·fuse (kənfjú:z) *pres. part.*, **con·fus·ing** *past and past part.* **con·fused** *v.t.* to throw into disorder, jumble together ‖ to fail to distinguish between ‖ to perplex or muddle ‖ to abash, disconcert **con·fus·ed·ly** (kənfjú:zidli:, kənfjú:zdli:) *adv.* in a confused manner

con·fu·sion (kənfjú:ʒən) *n.* the state of being confused ‖ the act of confusing, mistaking one thing for another ‖ lack of clarity ‖ bewilderment, perplexity ‖ embarrassment

con·fute (kənfjú:t) *pres. part.*, **con·fut·ing** *past and past part.* **con·fut·ed** *v.t.* to refute (an argument) ‖ to prove (a person) mistaken

con·geal (kəndʒí:l) *v.i.* to change from fluid to solid through coldness, freeze ‖ to coagulate, become thick as if frozen ‖ *v.t.* to cause to freeze ‖ to cause to coagulate **con·géal·ment** *n.* a congealing ‖ a congealed mass

con·gen·ial (kəndʒí:njəl) *adj.* of the same nature, tastes ‖ suited to one's nature or tastes, agreeable ‖ suitable **con·ge·ni·al·i·ty** (kəndʒi:ni:ǽliti:) *n.*

con·gen·i·tal (kəndʒénit'l) *adj.* present at birth ‖ acquired during fetal development and not hereditary

con·gest (kəndʒést) *v.t.* to pack closely, cause clogging in by overcrowding ‖ to cause excessive accumulation of blood in the vessels of (an organ or part) ‖ *v.i.* to become crowded together **con·gést·ed** *adj.* closely packed, crowded ‖ overpopulated ‖ overcharged with blood

---

con·ges·tion (kəndʒéstʃən) *n.* the state of being congested

con·glom·er·ate (kənglómərit) **1.** *adj.* gathered or clustered into a ball or mass **2.** *n.* sedimentary rock consisting of rounded rock fragments ‖ an accumulated mass of different materials ‖ corporate entity composed of several companies in a variety of industries **3.** *v.* (kənglóməreit) *pres. part.* **con·glom·er·at·ing** *past* and *past part.* **con·glom·er·at·ed** *v.t.* to gather into a compact mass ‖ *v.i.* to form a compact mass **con·glom·er·á·tion** *n.* the state of being conglomerated

con·grat·u·late (kəngrǽtʃuleit) *pres. part.* **con·grat·u·lat·ing** *past* and *past part.* **con·grat·u·lat·ed** *v.t.* to express pleasure in the success or happiness of (another) ‖ *(refl.)* to deem (oneself) fortunate or clever in some matter

con·grat·u·la·tion (kəngrǽtʃuléiʃən) *n.* a congratulating ‖ *(pl.)* expressions of congratulation

con·gre·gate **1.** (kóŋgrəgeit) *v. pres. part.* **con·gre·gat·ing** *past* and *past part.* **con·gre·gat·ed** *v.i.* to collect into a crowd or mass ‖ *v.t.* to cause to collect into a crowd **2.** (kóŋgrəgit, kóŋgrəgeit) *adj.* collected, assembled

con·gre·ga·tion (kóŋgrəgéiʃən) *n.* an assemblage of persons or things ‖ the body of regular attenders at a particular place of worship **con·gre·gá·tion·al** *adj.* pertaining to a congregation

con·gress (kóŋgris) *n.* a formal meeting, e.g. of delegates, *a biochemical congress* **Con·gress** the federal legislature of the U.S.A. (Senate and House of Representatives) and of some other American republics

con·gres·sion·al (kəngréʃən'l) *adj.* of or pertaining to a congress **Con·gres·sion·al** pertaining to the U.S. Congress

con·gress·man (kóŋgrismən) *pl.* **con·gress·men** (kóŋgrismən) *n.* a member of the House of Representatives

con·gru·ent (kóŋgru:ənt) *adj.* possessing congruity ‖ *(geom.)* equal in all respects, able to be superimposed so as to coincide throughout

con·gru·i·ty (kəngrú:iti:, kɒngrú:iti:) *pl.* **con·gru·i·ties** *n.* a state of agreement, harmony, correspondence ‖ *(geom.)* exact coincidence of figures

co·ni·fer (kóunifər, kónifər) *n.* a large order of gymnospermous trees and shrubs. They are generally evergreen, with slender, prickly leaves or leaves with rounded points, and reproduce by means of cones **co·nif·er·ous** (kounífərəs) *adj.*

con·jec·tur·al (kəndʒéktʃərəl) *adj.* doubtful, of the nature of conjecture ‖ given to, prone to conjecture

con·jec·ture (kəndʒéktʃər) *n.* guesswork, opinion or theory based on presumption or insufficient evidence **conjecture** *pres. part.* **con·jec·tur·ing** *past* and *past part.* **con·jec·tured** *v.t.* to guess, infer on slight evidence ‖ *v.i.* to make conjectures

con·ju·gal (kóndʒug'l) *adj.* pertaining to marriage or to married persons **con·ju·gal·i·ty** (kɒndʒugǽliti:) *n.*

con·ju·gate **1.** (kóndʒugeit) *v. pres. part.* **con·ju·gat·ing** *past* and *past part.* **con·ju·gat·ed** *v.t.* to state or set out (a verb) with its various inflectional endings in order ‖ *v.i.* to join together ‖ to become fused or united **2.** (kóndʒugit, kóndʒugeit) *adj.* yoked or united, joined, connected, esp. in pairs ‖ *(gram.)* derived from the same root **3.** (kóndʒugit, kóndʒugeit) *n.* a conjugate word or conjugate axis, diameter etc.

con·ju·ga·tion (kɒndʒugéiʃən) *n.* a conjugating or being conjugated ‖ *(gram.)* a statement of the various forms of a verb ‖ a class of verbs having similar inflections **con·ju·ga·tion·al, con·ju·ga·tive** (kɒndʒugéitiv) *adjs*

con·junc·tion (kəndʒʌ́ŋkʃən) *n.* a conjoining or being conjoined ‖ the apparent meeting of two or more heavenly bodies in the same part of the sky ‖ *(gram.)* a word used to connect sentences, clauses, phrases or words, e.g. a coordinating word ('and', 'but', 'or') or a subordinating word ('if', 'as', 'though') ‖ a combination of events or circumstances **in conjunction with** together with

con·jure (kóndʒər) *pres. part.* **con·jur·ing** *past* and

past part. **con·jured** *v.t.* to summon up (a spirit) by invocation ‖ to produce by sleight of hand ‖ *(rhet.)* (kəndʒúər) to urge with pleading ‖ *v.i.* to practice sleight of hand **to conjure up** to bring vividly before the imagination as though by magic **cón·jur·er, cón·ju·ror** *n.* a magician who practices legerdemain

con·nect (kənékt) *v.t.* to join ‖ to establish a connection between in the mind ‖ *v.i.* to join on, make a connection **con·néct·ed** *adj.* joined together ‖ linked ‖ related by birth or marriage ‖ coherent

con·nec·tion (kənékʃən) *n.* a connecting or being connected ‖ a linking mechanism ‖ a link or joint ‖ relationship of thought, plot etc. ‖ something, esp. a train, timed so as to be convenient for something else, esp. another train ‖ blood relationship or personal relationship ‖ economic and business relations

con·nive (kənáiv) *pres. part.* **con·niv·ing** *past* and *past part.* **con·nived** *v.i.* to pretend ignorance of something one should condemn ‖ (with 'at') to wink, be sympathetically tolerant ‖ (with 'at') to be culpably cooperative

con·nois·seur (kɒnəsə́:r, kɒnəsúər) *n.* an expert critic (of the arts) ‖ a judge in matters of taste

con·no·ta·tion (kɒnətéiʃən) *n.* the implication of a word, apart from its primary meaning ‖ *(logic)* implication by a general name

con·note (kənóut) *pres. part.* **con·not·ing** *past* and *past part.* **con·not·ed** *v.t.* (of a word) to suggest, imply apart from its primary meaning ‖ to involve by implication ‖ *(logic)* to imply by a general name (the sum of its attributes)

con·quer (kóŋkər) *v.t.* to defeat in war ‖ to take possession of by force ‖ to overcome by moral power ‖ *v.i.* to be victorious

con·quer·or (kóŋkərər) *n.* a victor, a person who conquers

con·quest (kónkwest, kóŋkwest) *n.* the act of conquering ‖ something won or acquired by physical or moral victory ‖ someone amorously won

con·science (kónʃəns) *n.* knowledge of one's own acts as right or wrong

con·sci·en·tious (kɒnʃi:énʃəs) *adj.* governed by conscience, scrupulous ‖ characterized by or done with careful attention

con·scious (kónʃəs) *adj.* recognizing the existence, truth or fact of something ‖ in the state of knowing what goes on around one ‖ registered subjectively ‖ marked by the use of one's rational powers ‖ self-conscious ‖ intended

con·scious·ness (kónʃəsnis) *n.* the state of being conscious ‖ mental activity, including emotion and thought ‖ the upper level of mental life, as opposed to subconscious mental processes

con·se·crate (kónsikreit) *pres. part.* **con·se·crat·ing** *past* and *past part.* **con·se·crat·ed** *v.t.* to make (someone) a king or a bishop by religious rite ‖ to make or declare holy ‖ to devote to a purpose, dedicate

con·se·cra·tion (kɒnsikréiʃən) *n.* the act of consecrating

con·sec·u·tive (kənsékjutiv) *adj.* following in regular or unbroken order ‖ marked by logical sequence ‖ *(gram.)* expressing result

con·sen·sus (kənsénsəs) *pl.* **con·sen·sus·es** *n.* concord (of opinion, evidence, authority, testimony etc.)

con·sent (kənsént) *n.* permission, acquiescence, approval ‖ agreement **consent** *v.i.* to give assent

con·se·quence (kónsikwens, kónsikwəns) *n.* that which follows something and arises from it ‖ a logical inference ‖ importance

con·se·quent (kónsikwent, kónsikwənt) **1.** *n.* a thing that follows another in time or order ‖ *(math.)* the second term in a ratio **2.** *adj.* following as an effect or outcome ‖ following as a deduction, logically consistent

con·se·quent·ly (kónsikwentli:, kónsikwəntli:) **1.** *adv.* accordingly, therefore **2.** *conj.* therefore, and so

con·ser·va·tion (kɒnsərvéiʃən) *n.* the act of keeping

free from depletion, decay or injury, esp. works of art ‖ wise management and maintaining ‖ official supervision of rivers and forests ‖ a district under such supervision **con·ser·vá·tion·al** *adj.* **con·ser·vá·tion·ist** *n.* someone who is active in the conserving of natural resources

con·serv·a·tive (kənsə́:rvətiv) **1.** *adj.* desiring to preserve existing institutions ‖ tending or desiring to conserve ‖ *(loosely)* moderate, cautious ‖ *(pop.,* of ideas, views etc.) old-fashioned ‖ considered to involve little risk ‖ tending to preserve, keep from deteriorating **2.** *n.* a person of conservative disposition ‖ something that tends to preserve

con·serv·a·to·ry (kənsə́:rvətɔri:, kənsə́:rvətouri:) *pl.* **con·serv·a·to·ries** *n.* a greenhouse ‖ a school of music or art

con·serve (kɔ́nsə:rv, kənsɔ́:rv) *n.* fruit etc. preserved in sugar

con·serve (kənsə́:rv) *pres. part.* **con·serv·ing** *past and past part.* **con·served** *v.t.* to preserve in a sound state ‖ to make a preserve of (fruit etc.) by cooking with sugar

con·sid·er (kənsídər) *v.t.* to ponder, think out, weigh the advantages and disadvantages of ‖ to assess before reaching a decision ‖ to take into one's reckoning ‖ to make allowances for ‖ to be sensitively thoughtful ‖ to believe ‖ *v.i.* to reflect or deliberate

con·sid·er·a·ble (kənsídərəb'l) *adj.* quite large in amount, extent or degree ‖ important **con·sid·er·a·bly** *adv.*

con·sid·er·ate (kənsídərit) *adj.* careful not to hurt the feelings of others or cause inconvenience to them

con·sid·er·a·tion (kənsidəréifən) *n.* a considering, deliberation ‖ a point of importance, a thing worth considering as a reason ‖ a financial reward, payment ‖ considerateness, thoughtfulness for others ‖ importance, *of no consideration*

con·sid·er·ing (kənsídəriŋ) **1.** *prep.* in view of **2.** *adv.* *(pop.)* taking all circumstances into account **3.** *conj.* seeing that

con·sign (kənsáin) *v.t.* to send ‖ to entrust, give over to another's charge ‖ to make over formally **con·sign·ee** (kɒnsainí:, kɒnsiní:, kənsainí:) *n.* a person to whom goods etc. are consigned or sent **con·sign·er** *n.*

con·sist (kənsíst) *v.i.* (with 'of') to be made up or composed ‖ (with 'in') to reside or lie essentially

con·sist·ence (kənsístəns) *n.* consistency **con·sist·en·cy** (kənsístənsi:) *pl.* **con·sist·en·cies** *n.* degree of solidity, or (of liquids) of density ‖ firm coherence in applying principles or a policy ‖ agreement, correspondence

con·sist·ent (kənsístənt) *adj.* in accordance ‖ true to principles or a policy **con·sist·ent·ly** *adv.* in a consistent way ‖ regularly

con·sol·a·ble (kənsóuləb'l) *adj.* able to be consoled

con·so·la·tion (kɒnsəléifən) *n.* the alleviation of suffering, grief, disappointment etc. by comforting ‖ an instance of this, or some circumstance which consoles

con·sole (kənsóul) *pres. part.* **con·sol·ing** *past and past part.* **con·soled** *v.t.* to bring consolation to, comfort in distress ‖ *v.i.* to be a consolation

con·sole (kɔ́nsoul) *n.* a bracket supporting a shelf or cornice ‖ a table supported by brackets against a wall ‖ the part of an organ containing the keyboard or keyboards and stops ‖ a cabinet for a radio or television set standing on the floor

con·sol·i·date (kənsɔ́lideit) *pres. part.* **con·sol·i·dat·ing** *past and past part.* **con·sol·i·dat·ed** *v.t.* to strengthen, make firm ‖ *(mil.)* to strengthen (a recently captured position) ‖ to make or compress into a compact mass ‖ *v.i.* to become solid or firm ‖ to combine, merge **con·sol·i·dá·tion** *n.*

con·sol·i·da·tion *(securities)* process of firming the market price following a substantial change in prices

con·som·mé (kɒnsəméi) *n.* a clear soup made from poultry or meat

con·so·nant (kɔ́nsənənt) *adj.* having consonance, consistent ‖ harmonious ‖ corresponding in sound ‖ resonant

consonant *n.* a unit of speech sound (p, t etc.) which differs from a vowel in that there is some obstruction of the breath in its production ‖ the letter representing such a unit **con·so·nan·tal** (kɒnsənǽnt'l) *adj.*

con·sort 1. (kɔ́nsɔrt) *n.* the non-reigning wife or husband of a reigning king or queen ‖ a ship accompanying another, esp. for protection in wartime ‖ a combination of musical instruments or singers **in consort** in harmony ‖ in company (with) **2.** (kənsɔ́rt) *v.i.* to associate or keep company ‖ to harmonize, be in accord

con·spic·u·ous (kənspíkju:əs) *adj.* very readily perceived ‖ attracting attention

con·spir·a·cy (kənspírəsi:) *pl.* **con·spir·a·cies** *n.* a conspiring, esp. a joining secretly with others for an evil purpose *adj.* of or relating to conspiracy ‖ a plot

con·spir·a·tor (kənspírətər) *n.* a person taking part in a conspiracy **con·spir·a·to·ri·al** (kənspirətɔ́ri:əl, kənspirətóuri:əl) *adj.* of or relating to conspiracy

con·spire (kənspáiər) *pres. part.* **con·spir·ing** *past and past part.* **con·spired** *v.i.* to combine secretly esp. for unlawful purposes ‖ *(rhet.)* to cooperate towards an end ‖ *v.t.* *(rhet.)* to devise

con·stan·cy (kɔ́nstənsi:) *n.* steadfastness, fidelity, esp. in love, friendship etc. ‖ firm adherence to principles ‖ fortitude, endurance ‖ stability

con·stant (kɔ́nstənt) **1.** *adj.* continual, unceasing ‖ unremitting ‖ faithful, unwavering ‖ not subject to variation, uniform. **2.** *n.* *(math., phys.)* a quantity or factor that does not change, that may be universal

con·stant·ly (kɔ́nstəntli:) *adv.* without stopping, continuously ‖ frequently

con·stel·la·tion (kɒnstəléifən) *n.* a group of fixed stars, arbitrarily considered together ‖ a group of brilliant people ‖ *(psychoanal.)* a group conditions affecting behavior

con·ster·na·tion (kɒnstərnéifən) *n.* surprise and alarm, astonishment, dismay

con·sti·pate (kɔ́nstəpeit) *pres. part.* **con·sti·pat·ing** *past and past part.* **con·sti·pat·ed** *v.i.* to cause constipation ‖ *v.t.* to cause constipation in (someone)

con·sti·pa·tion (kɒnstəpéifən) *n.* infrequent passage of dry hardened feces due to poor functioning of the bowels

con·stit·u·en·cy (kənstítfu:ənsi:) *pl.* **con·stit·u·en·cies** *n.* a body of voters represented by an officeholder ‖ an area or community represented thus

con·stit·u·ent (kənstítfu:ənt) **1.** *adj.* forming a basic part of a whole ‖ having power to elect ‖ charged with making or modifying a political constitution **2.** *n.* an essential part, component ‖ a member of a constituency

con·sti·tute (kɔ́nstitu:t, kɔ́nstitju:t) *pres. part.* **con·sti·tut·ing** *past and past part.* **con·sti·tut·ed** *v.t.* to appoint to an office or function ‖ to set up, establish ‖ to give legal form to (a court, tribunal etc.) ‖ to be the constituent element of, make up ‖ *(pass.)* to have certain qualities

con·sti·tu·tion (kɒnstitú:fən, kɒnstitjú:fən) *n.* the act of constituting, a setting up ‖ the total physical condition of the body ‖ total moral or mental makeup ‖ molecular structure, physical and chemical ‖ the set of principles adopted by a state or society for its government ‖ a decree or ordinance **con·sti·tú·tion·al 1.** *adj.* of, due to, or inherent in one's constitution ‖

(a) æ, cat; ɑ, car; ɔ fawn; ei, snake. **(e)** e, hen; i:, sheep; iə, deer; ɛə, bear. **(i)** i, fish; ai, tiger; ə:, bird. **(o)** o, ox; au, cow; ou, goat; u, poor; ɔi, royal. **(u)** ʌ, duck; u, bull; u:, goose; ə, bacillus; ju:, cube. x, loch; θ, think; ð, bother; z, Zen; ʒ, corsage; dʒ, savage; ŋ, orangutang; j, yak; ʃ, fish; tʃ, fetch; 'l, rabble; 'n, redden. Complete pronunciation key appears inside front cover.

of or pertaining to a political constitution || loyal to the constitution || limited by the constitution **2.** *n.* a regular walk taken for one's health

con·strain (kənstréin) *v.t.* to persuade by strong pressure or force, compel **con·stráined** *adj.* ill at ease and embarrassed through repression of natural feelings **con·strain·ed·ly** (kənstréinidli:) *adv.*

con·straint (kənstréint) *n.* use of force to influence or prevent an acton || the state or quality of being compelled to do or not do something || restricted liberty || the sense of being ill at ease

con·struct 1. (kənstrʌ́kt) *v.t.* to put together, build || to arrange mentally || to combine (words) meaningfully **2.** (kónstrʌkt) *n.* (*psychol.*) a mental construction **con·strúct·er, con·strúc·tor** *n.*

con·struc·tion (kənstrʌ́kʃən) *n.* a thing constructed || the process of constructing || the manner of building with regard to materials || the arrangement and interrelation of words in a sentence

con·struc·tive (kənstrʌ́ktiv) *adj.* tending to or helping to construct || of construction, esp. the construction of a building, or comparable activity || (*law*) not direct or expressed, inferred

con·strue (kənstrú:) *pres. part.* **con·stru·ing** *past* and *past part.* **con·strued** *v.t.* to analyze (a sentence or clause) grammatically || to interpret the meaning of (a statement) || to combine (words) grammatically, 'aware' is construed with 'of' or 'that' || *v.i.* to admit of grammatical analysis

con·sul (kónsəl) *n.* an agent appointed by a country to look after the interests of its citizens and its commerce in a foreign town

con·su·late (kónsəlit) *n.* the premises or establishment of a consul

con·sult (kənsʌ́lt) *v.t.* to seek advice from || to seek information from || to test, finds out || *v.i.* to reflect (with others), sit in council

con·sult·ant (kənsʌ́ltənt) *n.* a person (engineer, doctor etc.) giving expert or professional advice

con·sul·ta·tion (kɒnsəltéiʃən) *n.* the act of consulting || a conference to discuss a problem, esp. among lawyers or doctors

con·sume (kənsú:m) *pres. part.* **con·sum·ing** *past* and *past part.* **con·sumed** *v.t.* to eat or drink up || to destroy by burning || to waste or absorb **con·súmed** *adj.* eaten up or as if eaten up

con·sum·er (kənsú:mər) *n.* someone who uses articles made by another

con·sum·mate 1. (kənsʌ́mit, kónsəmit) *adj.* complete, perfect, supreme **2.** (kónsəmeit) *v.t. pres. part.* **con·sum·mat·ing** *past* and *past part.* **con·sum·mat·ed** to bring to completion or perfection, esp. to complete (a marriage) by sexual intercourse

con·sum·ma·tion (kɒnsəméiʃən) *n.* the act of completing || perfection || fulfillment

con·sump·tion (kənsʌ́mpʃən) *n.* a consuming || an amount consumed || (*econ.*) the use and enjoyment of goods and services by consumers or producers || (*pop.*) tuberculosis of the lungs

con·tact (kóntækt) **1.** *n.* the state of touching or meeting || a coming into association or establishing of communication || a person who may be helpful to one || junction of two conductors enabling an electric current to flow from one to the other || a device for effecting such a junction **2.** *v.t.* to get in touch with

con·ta·gion (kəntéidʒən) *n.* the direct or indirect transmission of disease from one person to another || a contagious disease || the spreading of an influence (e.g. enthusiasm, panic) from person to person

con·ta·gious (kətéidʒəs) *adj.* (of diseases) catching, communicable by direct or indirect contact || (of persons) liable to pass on such a disease || easily spreading

con·tain (kəntéin) *v.t.* to have capacity for, hold || to enclose || to comprise || (*math.*) to be a multiple of without remainder || to control (oneself or one's feelings) **con·táin·er** *n.* a carton, crate, jar, bottle, etc. for receiving and holding something

con·tam·i·nate (kəntǽmineit) *pres. part.* **con·tam·i·nat·ing** *past* and *past part.* **con·tam·i·nat·ed** *v.t.* to infect with a contagious disease || to pollute || to harm morally **con·tam·i·ná·tion** *n.*

con·tem·plate (kóntəmpleit, kəntémpleit) *pres. part.* **con·tem·plat·ing** *past* and *past part.* **con·tem·plat·ed** *v.t.* to look steadily at || to consider attentively || to intend, but not as part of an immediate plan || *v.i.* to meditate or ponder **con·tem·plá·tion** *n.* meditation, concentration of the mind on an intellectual or religious subject || the act of looking attentively at something || the process of considering with a view to a decision

con·tem·pla·tive (kəntémplətiv, kóntəmplɛitiv) *adj.* concerned with or given to contemplation, thoughtful

con·tem·po·rar·y (kəntémpərɛri) **1.** *adj.* belonging to the same time, contemporaneous || (*pop.*) modern **2.** *n. pl.* **con·tem·po·rar·ies** a person living at the same time as another || a person of the same or nearly the same age as another

con·tempt (kəntémpt) *n.* an attitude to something which one despises as worthless, insignificant or vile || total disregard || (*law*) disobedience of lawful orders

con·tempt·i·ble (kəntémptəb'l) *adj.* worthy of contempt or scorn **con·témpt·i·bly** *adv.*

con·temp·tu·ous (kəntémptʃu:əs) *adj.* feeling or showing contempt

con·tend (kənténd) *v.i.* to struggle in rivalry || to conflict || to argue || (with 'with') to struggle (e.g. with hardship or difficulty) || *v.t.* to assert, esp. against opposition

con·tent (kəntént) *v.t.* to make content or satisfied **to content oneself with** to make do with, resign oneself to having only

con·tent (kəntént) **1.** *adj.* satisfied, not displeased **2.** *n.* the state of being contented or satisfied

con·tent (kóntent) *n.* (usually *pl.*) that which is contained || (usually *pl.*) a summary of subjects treated in a book || the amount of a certain substance contained || the volume of a solid || the gist of a speech or argument || the substance, matter (of a book)

con·tent·ed (kənténtid) *adj.* enjoying or showing contentment

con·test 1. (kəntést) *v.t.* to call in question, dispute || to refuse to recognize as lawful || to strive to win or hold || *v.i.* to strive, struggle **2.** (kóntest) *n.* a trial of skill || a competition || a struggle for domination

con·test·ant (kəntéstənt) *n.* someone who contests, in a fight, match

con·text (kóntekst) *n.* the parts of a book, speech etc. which precede or follow a word or passage and affect its significance || the conditions or circumstances which affect something **con·tex·tu·al** (kəntékstʃu:əl) *adj.*

con·ti·nent (kóntinənt) *n.* one of the seven great land masses of the world **the Continent** the mainland of Europe **con·ti·nen·tal** (kɒntinént'l) **1.** *adj.* belonging to or characteristic of a continent || belonging to or characteristic of the mainland of Europe

con·tin·gen·cy (kəntíndʒənsi:) *pl.* **con·tin·gen·cies** *n.* the quality or state of being contingent || something likely but not certain to happen || something dependent on a probable but not certain event || an unforeseeable event or circumstance || an incidental quality

con·tin·gent (kəntíndʒənt) **1.** *adj.* liable but not certain to happen || dependent on something that may not occur || incidental || conditional, dependent || (*logic*) established by sensory observation, not true || a priori **2.** *n.* a quota, esp. of troops || a representative group of people, e.g. a delegation || a contingent thing

con·tin·u·al (kəntínju:əl) *adj.* occurring frequently, often repeated || continuous, unbroken

con·tin·u·a·tion (kəntínju:éiʃən) *n.* a prolonging || the action of resuming after an interruption || the next additional part to be published in serial publication

con·tin·ue (kəntínju:) *pres. part.* **con·tin·u·ing** *past* and *past part.* **con·tin·ued** *v.t.* to go on with (an action) || to prolong || to resume, take up again || *v.i.* to extend || to remain in a given place or condition || to be retained in an official position ‖ (of a story, speech, speaker etc.) to go on

con·tin·u·ous (kəntínjuːəs) *adj.* connected throughout, uninterrupted in space, time or sequence

con·tort (kəntɔ́rt) *v.t.* to twist, force out of normal shape, distort

con·tor·tion (kəntɔ́rʃən) *n.* a twisting or contorting **con·tór·tion·ist** *n.* an acrobat who can contort his body or limbs

con·tour (kɔ́ntuər) **1.** *n.* the outline of a figure or shape ‖ a contour line **2.** *adj.* following contour lines **3.** *v.t.* to mark with contour lines ‖ to construct (a road etc.) in relation to contour lines

con·tra·band (kɔ́ntrəbænd) **1.** *n.* illegal traffic in goods, smuggling ‖ smuggled goods ‖ goods which may not be imported or exported **2.** *adj.* forbidden by law, prohibited ‖ concerned with illegal goods or smuggling

con·tra·cep·tion (kɒntrəsépʃən) *n.* birth control **con·tra·cép·tive 1.** *adj.* preventing conception **2.** *n.* a contraceptive device

con·tract (kəntrǽkt) *v.t.* to catch (cold, a disease etc.) ‖ to enter into (a marriage) ‖ to acquire (debts, habits etc.) ‖ to draw together (brows, muscles etc.) ‖ to shorten ‖ *v.i.* to shrink, become narrower or shorter ‖ (sometimes kɔ́ntrækt) to enter into a contract

con·tract (kɔ́ntrækt) *n.* an agreement, a covenant ‖ a document formulating such agreement ‖ an agreement to undertake work or supply goods at a certain price ‖ an order to assault or kill a predetermined victim for a price ‖ the work done or goods supplied under such a contract ‖ an agreement endorsed by law ‖ a promise made and accepted but only morally binding ‖ a marriage agreement ‖ contract bridge ‖ *(bridge)* the number and suit of tricks called by the highest bidder

con·trac·tion (kəntrǽkʃən) *n.* a contracting (of disease, bad habits, debts etc.) ‖ a shrinking ‖ a shortened form of a word made by omitting or combining some elements or by reducing vowels or syllables

con·trac·tor (kɔ́ntræktər, kəntrǽktər) *n.* a person or firm undertaking to do work or to supply goods, esp. on a large scale, by signing a contract ‖ a muscle which contracts

con·tra·dict (kɒntrədíkt) *v.t.* to deny the truth of (a statement) ‖ to assert the contrary to ‖ to be inconsistent with ‖ *v.i.* to deny the truth or assert the contrary of something

con·tra·dic·tion (kɒntrədíkʃən) *n.* a contradicting ‖ a contradicting statement ‖ opposition, inconsistency

con·tra·dic·to·ry (kɒntrədíktəriː) **1.** *adj.* affirming the contrary ‖ inconsistent **2.** *n. (logic)* a contradictory principle or proposition

con·tral·to (kəntrǽltou) *pl.* **con·tral·tos** *n.* the lowest female singing voice ‖ a singer with such a voice ‖ the part sung by such a singer

con·trap·tion (kəntrǽpʃən) *n.* an odd gadget, device or contrivance

con·tra·ry (kɔ́ntreriː) **1.** *adj.* opposed ‖ opposite in nature, direction etc. ‖ (of wind etc.) unfavorable ‖ (esp. kəntréəri:) vexatious, perverse, doing the opposite of what is expected or wanted **2.** *n. pl.* **con·tra·ries** the opposite, something which is the opposite of something else **3.** *adv.* counter, contrarily

con·trast (kəntrǽst) *v.t.* to display the differences between ‖ *v.i.* to show marked differences when compared

con·trast (kɔ́ntræst) *n.* a divergence between related things, ideas etc. ‖ a relationship of difference demonstrated by juxtaposition ‖ a person or thing showing this difference relationship when compared with someone or something else ‖ *(optics)* the degree to which a photographic or optical image displays sharp differences in brightness between adjacent areas **con·trast·y** (kəntrǽsti:, kɔ́ntræsti:) *comp.* **con·trast·i·er** *superl.* **con·trast·i·est** *adj. (optics)* displaying marked contrast

con·tri·bute (kəntríbjuːt) *pres. part.* **con·tri·but·ing** *past and past part.* **con·tri·but·ed** *v.t.* to give, together with others, for a common purpose ‖ to supply (an article etc.) to a newspaper or periodical ‖ *v.i.* to help to bring something about ‖ to have writings accepted by a publication

con·tri·bu·tion (kɒntrəbjúːʃən) *n.* the act of contributing ‖ something contributed

con·trite (kəntráit, kɔ́ntrait) *adj.* penitent, thoroughly sorry, esp. for sin

con·tri·tion (kəntríʃən) *n.* remorse, penitence

con·triv·ance (kəntráivəns) *n.* the act of contriving ‖ a mechanical appliance ‖ resource ‖ a dishonest device

con·trive (kəntráiv) *pres. part.* **con·triv·ing** *past and past part.* **con·trived** *v.t.* to devise ‖ to invent ‖ to manage by resourcefulness

con·trol (kəntróul) **1.** *v.t. pres. part.* **con·trol·ling** *past and past part.* **con·trolled** to govern, exercise control over ‖ to restrain ‖ to regulate ‖ to test or verify (an experiment) **2.** *n.* power, authority ‖ restraint ‖ self-restraint ‖ the right of administering or supervising ‖ dominance over the difficulties of a technique ‖ *(pl.)* the mechanisms operated by the driver's hands and feet in driving a vehicle, or those by which a pilot flies an aircraft ‖ a person who acts as a check ‖ a standard of comparison or check in an experiment ‖ *(spiritualism)* a spirit said to actuate the utterances of the medium

con·trol·ler (kəntróulər) *n.* a person who or device which governs or controls, esp. an officer controlling expenditure or a device for controlling power, pressure, speed etc. **con·tról·ler·ship** *n.*

con·tro·ver·sial (kɒntrəvə́:rʃəl) *adj.* disputable ‖ prone to controversy ‖ relating to controversy **con·tro·vér·sial·ist** *n.*

con·tro·ver·sy (kɔ́ntrəvə̀:rsi:) *pl.* **con·tro·ver·sies** *n.* a disputing ‖ an argument, esp. a prolonged one, e.g. in newspaper correspondence ‖ a quarrel or wrangle

con·tuse (kəntúːz, kəntjúːz) *pres. part.* **con·tus·ing** *past and past part.* **con·tused** *v.t.* to bruise, damage the subcutaneous tissue of, without breaking the skin

con·tu·sion (kəntúːʒən, kəntjúːʒən) *n.* a bruise, damage to subcutaneous tissue

con·va·lesce (kɒnvəlés) *pres. part.* **con·va·lesc·ing** *past and past part.* **con·va·lesced** *v.i.* to recover health, esp. gradually, after prolonged illness **con·va·lés·cence** *n.* **con·va·lés·cent 1.** *adj.* gradually recovering from illness ‖ of or suitable for convalescence **2.** *n.* a person recovering from illness

con·vene (kənvíːn) *pres. part.* **con·ven·ing** *past and past part.* **con·vened** *v.t.* to call together (a committee, assembly etc.) ‖ to summon to appear before a tribunal etc. ‖ *v.i.* to assemble

con·ven·ience (kənvíːnjəns) *n.* advantage ‖ a convenient time or arrangement ‖ something which makes for one's comfort or for saving work, or any useful appliance

con·ven·ient (kənvíːnjənt) *adj.* favorable to one's comfort, occasioning little trouble or extra work ‖ suitable as an arrangement ‖ easy of access ‖ fitting in with one's requirements

con·vent (kɔ́nvənt) *n.* a community of religious, esp. of nuns ‖ the establishment in which they live

con·ven·tion (kənvénʃən) *n.* the act of convening ‖ a conference, a body of delegates assembled for a common purpose ‖ an arbitrary but consistently observed

---

usage ‖ a polite practice observed by the majority

con·ven·tion·al (kɘnvénʃɘn'l) *adj.* depending on or deriving from convention ‖ customary, sanctioned by usage ‖ not original or spontaneous ‖ conformist ‖ *(arts)* lacking originality, merely traditional ‖ (of signs, symbols etc., e.g. in mathematics and the sciences) habitually used with a single arbitrary, well understood significance ‖ of or relating to a convention or meeting **con·ven·tion·al·ism**, **con·ven·tion·al·ist**, **con·ven·tion·al·i·ty** (kɘnvenʃɘnǽliti:) *ns* **con·ven·tion·al·ize** (kɘnvénʃɘn'laiz) *pres. part.* **con·ven·tion·al·iz·ing** *past* and *past part.* **con·ven·tion·al·ized** *v.t.* to make conventional ‖ *(arts)* to treat or represent conventionally

con·verge (kɘnvɘ́:rdʒ) *pres. part.* **con·verg·ing** *past* and *past part.* **con·verged** *v.i.* (of two or more directions) to be towards the same point in space ‖ (of two or more things having direction) to be directed towards the same point in space

con·ver·gence (kɘnvɘ́:rdʒɘns) *n.* the act or state of converging

con·ver·gent (kɘnvɘ́:rdʒɘnt) *adj.* of things in motion or of directions or actions which converge, or of that which causes things to converge

con·ver·sant (kɘnvɘ́:rsɘnt, kɔ́nvɘ:rsɘnt) *adj.* well acquainted, familiar ‖ informed about

con·ver·sa·tion (kɔnvɘrséiʃɘn) *n.* talk, esp. informal and friendly ‖ good talk practiced as an art **con·ver·sá·tion·al** *adj.* pertaining to or characteristic of conversation ‖ fond of conversation **con·ver·sá·tion·al·ist** *n.* a practiced or gifted talker

con·verse 1. (kɔ́nvɘ:rs) *n.* a statement which transposes the terms of another statement ‖ *(logic)* a proposition obtained by conversion ‖ something which is the opposite of something else **2.** (kɘnvɘ́:rs, kɔ́nvɘ:rs) *adj.* of one statement which is the converse of another

con·verse 1. (kɘnvɘ́:rs) *v.i. pres. part.* **con·vers·ing** *past* and *past part.* **con·versed** to have a conversation **2.** (kɔ́nvɘ:rs) *n.* spiritual communion

con·ver·sion (kɘnvɘ́:rʒɘn, kɘnvɘ́:rʃɘn) *n.* a converting or being converted, esp. to new beliefs ‖ a change of role, purpose etc. ‖ *(economics)* a change in a rate of interest to a lower rate ‖ *(real estate)* changeover of a rental apartment building to condominium or cooperative ownership ‖ *(chem.)* the change of one substance into another ‖ *(football)* a score made on a try for point after touchdown

con·vert 1. (kɘnvɘ́:rt) *v.t.* to change ‖ to change the chemical or physical character of ‖ to bring over to a new position, faith etc. ‖ to make a spiritual change in ‖ to turn to another use ‖ *(logic)* to change (a statement etc.) by conversion ‖ *v.i.* to undergo a conversion ‖ to be able to be converted **2.** (kɔ́nvɘ:rt) *n.* a person whose religious, philosophical or political beliefs etc. have been changed **con·vért·er** *n.* a device for transforming electrical voltage

con·vert·i·ble (kɘnvɘ́:rtɘb'l) **1.** *adj.* liable to conversion ‖ able to be converted ‖ interchangeable **2.** *n.* a car with a folding top

con·vex 1. (kɔnvéks, kɘnvéks) *adj.* curving outwards like the outside of a sphere **2.** (kɔ́nveks) *n.* a convex surface, line etc. **con·véx·i·ty** *n.*

con·vey (kɘnvéi) *v.t.* to carry, transport ‖ to act as a medium transmitting sound etc. ‖ to impart (information etc.) ‖ to suggest, present as meaning ‖ to transfer by legal process **con·véy·a·ble** *adj.*

con·vey·ance (kɘnvéiɘns) *n.* the act of conveying ‖ a means of conveying, esp. a hired vehicle ‖ *(law)* the transfer of property from one person to another ‖ *(law)* the deed conveying this transfer **con·véy·anc·ing** *n.* the work of drawing up deeds etc.

con·vey·or (kɘnvéiɘr) *n.* a conveyor belt or other device for moving articles or raw materials in a factory

con·vict (kɘnvíkt) *v.t.* to prove or find guilty after trial ‖ to show to be in error or to have done wrong ‖ *(theol.)* to impress with a sense of guilt

con·vict (kɔ́nvikt) *n.* a person convicted of crime, esp.

one serving a long sentence

con·vic·tion (kɘnvíkʃɘn) *n.* a convicting or being convicted ‖ firm belief ‖ a convincing or being convinced

con·vince (kɘnvíns) *pres. part.* **con·vinc·ing** *past* and *past part.* **con·vinced** *v.t.* to persuade by argument or proof

con·viv·i·al (kɘnvívi:ɘl) *adj.* festive, gay, sociable ‖ appropriate to feasting and drinking **con·viv·i·ál·i·ty** *n.*

con·vo·ca·tion (kɔnvɘkéiʃɘn) *n.* a calling together or convoking ‖ an assembly of representatives ‖ an ecclesiastical or academic assembly **con·vo·cá·tion·al** *adj.*

con·voy (kɔ́nvɔi) *n.* a convoying or being convoyed or escorted ‖ a group of merchant ships under aerial or naval protection ‖ a column of military supplies or motorized troops etc.

con·voy (kɔ́nvɔi, kɘnvɔ́i) *v.t.* to provide military or naval escort for

con·vulse (kɘnvʌ́ls) *pres. part.* **con·vuls·ing** *past* and *past part.* **con·vulsed** *v.t.* to throw into spasms or convulsions ‖ to affect with strong emotion

con·vul·sion (kɘnvʌ́lʃɘn) *n.* (usually *pl.*) a violent involuntary spasm of muscles, or irregular movement of limbs etc., resulting from this ‖ any violent disturbance, e.g. an earthquake, tidal wave ‖ (esp. *pl.*) violent political or social upheaval ‖ (esp. *pl.*) uncontrollable laughter

con·vul·sive (kɘnvʌ́lsiv) *adj.* of the nature of a convulsion ‖ attended with or producing convulsions ‖ emotionally violent

cook (kuk) **1.** *n.* a person who cooks food, esp. professionally **2.** *v.t.* to prepare (food) by the action of heat ‖ (with up') to invent ‖ *v.i.* to do the work of a cook ‖ to undergo the process of cooking

cook·ie, cook·y (kúki:) *pl.* **cook·ies** *n.* a small, sweet cake, usually thin

cool (ku:l) **1.** *adj.* rather colder than one would wish ‖ pleasantly cold ‖ not retaining heat, *a cool dress* ‖ self-possessed, calm ‖ unenthusiastic, verging on hostility ‖ calmly impudent ‖ untemperamental ‖ (of money) impressive in amount ‖ (of colors) near green or blue (removed from orange or red) ‖ *(jazz)* showing technical control and virtuosity ‖ *(pop.)* excellent **2.** *n.* cool air ‖ a cool time ‖ a cool place ‖ coolness

cool *v.i.* to become cool ‖ (of temper or enthusiasm) to calm down, moderate ‖ *v.t.* to make cool

cool·ant (kú:lɘnt) *n.* a liquid used to lessen friction in cutting tools, or (in industrial processes) to cool down metals, liquids etc., or (in engines) to cool them

cool·er (kú:lɘr) *n.* a vessel for cooling liquids

coop (ku:p) **1.** *n.* a box, cage, pen or enclosure for poultry, small animals etc. ‖ a place of confinement **2.** *v.t.* to put in a coop

co-op, co·op (kóup, kouɒ́p) *n.* (short for) a cooperative

co·op·er·ate (kouɒ́pɘreit) *pres. part.* **co·op·er·at·ing** *past* and *past part.* **co·op·er·at·ed** *v.i.* to work jointly with others to some end ‖ to be helpful as distinct from hostile ‖ to contribute to a joint effect

co·op·er·a·tion (kouɒpɘréiʃɘn) *n.* a cooperating, working together to a common end ‖ *(econ.)* a group of producers, distributors etc. cooperating and sharing profits

co·op·er·a·tive (kouɒ́pɘɾeitiv, kouɒ́pɘɾɘtiv) **1.** *adj.* of or pertaining to cooperation ‖ describing an association for producing goods, marketing etc. in which members share profits, and middlemen are eliminated **2.** *n.* a cooperative business or association ‖ an apartment house in which the apartments are each individually owned ‖ an apartment in such a building

co·or·di·nate (kouɔ́rd'nit, kouɔ́rd'neit) **1.** *adj.* equal in rank or order, not subordinate ‖ pertaining to or made up of coordinate things **2.** *n.* something that is coordinate

co·or·di·nate (kouɔ́rd'neit) *pres. part.* **co·or·di·nat·ing** *past* and *past part.* **co·or·di·nat·ed** *v.t.* to make coordinate ‖ to bring the parts or agents of a plan, process etc. into a common whole, to harmonize

co·or·di·na·tion (kouərd´néiʃən) *n.* a making or being coordinate

cop (kɒp) *pres. part.* **cop·ping** *past* and *past part.* **copped** *v.t. (pop.)* to catch (something that causes death, suffering, imprisonment etc.)

cop *n. (pop.)* a policeman

cope (koup) *pres. part.* **cop·ing** *past* and *past part.* **coped** *v.i.* (with 'with') to contend (with a situation, problem), esp. successfully

co·pi·ous (kóupi:əs) *adj.* plentiful, overflowing ‖ not concise

cop·per (kɒ́pər) **1.** *n.* a metallic element easily smelted from its ores ‖ a penny ‖ a large boiler **2.** *v.t.* to sheathe (e.g. a saucepan) with copper **3.** *adj.* made of copper ‖ coppercolored

cop·per·y (kɒ́pəri:) *adj.* mixed with or containing copper ‖ like copper

cop·u·late (kɒ́pjuleit) *pres. part.* **cop·u·lat·ing** *past* and *past part.* **cop·u·lat·ed** *v.i.* to unite in sexual intercourse

cop·u·la·tion (kɒpjuléiʃən) *n.* coition, sexual intercourse ‖ *(logic)* the act of joining by a copula

cop·y (kɒ́pi:) *pl.* **cop·ies** *n.* a reproduction, not an original ‖ a duplicate ‖ a work written out from a model or pattern ‖ one of the printed works which as a set comprise an edition ‖ material intended for printing ‖ material for newspaper publication

copy *pres. part.* **cop·y·ing** *past* and *past part.* **cop·ied** *v.t.* to make a copy of ‖ to imitate ‖ *v.i.* to cheat, e.g. in examination, by passing off a copy of someone else's work as one's own

cop·y·right (kɒ́pi:rait) **1.** *n.* the exclusive right to reproduce literary, dramatic, artistic or musical work, given by law for a certain period to an author etc. or his agent **2.** *v.t.* to secure a copyright on (a book, film etc.) **3.** *adj.* protected by copyright

co·quet, co·quette (koukét) *pres. part.* **co·quet·ting** *past* and *past part.* **co·quet·ted** *v.i.* to flirt ‖ to show interest but be indecisive

cor·al (kɒ́rəl, kɒ́rəl) **1.** *n.* a coelenterate of class *Anthozoa* or a colony of them. They occur as polyps only and usually are colonial, living in shallow ocean waters ‖ the hard red or white substance secreted by thse animals to protect and support the polyps **2.** *adj.* of coral, or the color of red coral **cor·al·lif·er·ous** (kɒrəlífərəs, kɒrəlífərəs) *adj.*

cord (kɒrd) **1.** *n.* a rope of small diameter or a fairly thick string ‖ a piece of such rope or string ‖ *(anat.)* a structure of the body resembling a cord ‖ a cordlike rib on textiles ‖ a ribbed fabric ‖ a cubic measure, esp. for cut wood (128 cu. ft) ‖ a quantity of wood so measured ‖ *(elec.)* insulated wire for conveying current **2.** *v.t.* to bind with cord ‖ to supply with cord ‖ to pile (wood) into cords **cord·age** (kɒ́rdidʒ) *n.* (collective term for) ropes ‖ (of wood) quantity in cords

cor·date (kɒ́rdeit) *adj.* heart-shaped

cord·ed (kɒ́rdid) *adj.* bound or supplied with cords ‖ ribbed

cor·dial (kɒ́rdʒəl) **1.** *adj.* hearty, sincere, friendly ‖ deeply felt **2.** *n.* a fortifying drink of flavored spirits or a comforting non-alcoholic drink **cor·dial·i·ty** (kɒrdʒǽliti:, kɒrdʒi:ǽliti:) *n.* friendliness, sincerity, cheerfulness

cor·du·roy (kɒ́rdərɔi, kɒrdərɔ́i) **1.** *n.* a thick cotton material with a velvetlike pile on raised ribs ‖ *(pl.)* trousers made of this **2.** *adj.* made of corduroy

core (kɔr, kour) **1.** *n.* the inner part of certain fruits containing the seeds ‖ the innermost part of anything ‖ the essence or gist ‖ *(phys.)* the uranium-containing heater of a nuclear reactor where energy is released ‖ the insulated conducting wire of a cable **2.** *v.t. pres.*

part. **cor·ing** *past* and *past part.* **cored** to take out the core of (an apple etc.)

cork (kɔrk) **1.** *n.* the bark of the cork oak ‖ a bottle stopper made of cork (or a substitute) **2.** *v.t.* to furnish with cork ‖ to stop with a cork ‖ to blacken with burned cork

cork·screw (kɔ́rkskru:) **1.** *n.* an implement, usually with a pointed spiral, for removing corks from bottles **2.** *adj.* spiral, twisted **3.** *v.i.* to move spirally or windingly ‖ *v.t.* to cause to move spirally or windingly

corn (kɔrn) **1.** *n.* maize, a tall annual American cereal grass having a terminal staminate tassel and lateral pistillate inflorescences covered with protecting leaves ‖ small hard seeds of cereals, grain in general ‖ a small hard seed of pepper and a few other plants ‖ a plant producing such seeds ‖ *(pop.)* corny music, dialogue, jokes etc. ‖ *(pop.)* corn whiskey **2.** *v.t.* to preserve with salt, *corned beef*

corn *n.* a horny hardening or thickening of the skin, esp. on the toes or feet

cor·ne·a (kɔ́rni:ə) *n.* the transparent portion of the external covering of the eyeball **cór·ne·al** *adj.*

cor·ner (kɔ́rnər) **1.** *n.* the point or place of meeting of e.g. two converging sides ‖ the area thus contained ‖ the angle formed by the meeting of two streets ‖ an angular projection ‖ a photographic print mount ‖ a protective piece to fit over a corner ‖ a position from which escape is difficult or dangerous ‖ a remote place ‖ a secret place ‖ *(loosely)* any monopolistic combination to raise prices ‖ *(soccer, hockey)* a free hit or kick from the corner **2.** *adj.* situated at or placed across a corner ‖ *(football)* of a defensive player on right or left of line **3.** *v.t.* to supply with corners ‖ to set in a corner ‖ to drive into a corner ‖ to put in a difficult position ‖ to obtain a corner or monopoly in (a stock or product) ‖ *v.i.* to make a financial corner ‖ to form, come to or drive around a corner

cor·net (kɔrnét) *n.* a brass wind instrument of the trumpet class ‖ a cornet player ‖ (kɔ́rnit, kɔrnét) something shaped like a horn ‖ *(naut.,* kɔ́rnit, kɑrnét) a signal pennant

cor·nice (kɔ́rnis) *n. (archit.)* a horizontal strip of stone, wood or plaster crowning a building, usually molded and projecting, esp. part of the entablature above a frieze ‖ a molding of the wall of a room just below the ceiling ‖ an overhanging mass of snow above a precipice

cor·nu·co·pi·a (kɔrnəkóupi:ə) *n. (mythol.)* the horn of the goat Amalthea that suckled Jupiter, shown in art as overflowing with corn, flowers and fruit, an emblem of plenty **cor·nu·có·pi·an** *adj.*

corn·y (kɔ́rni:) *comp.* **corn·i·er** *superl.* **corn·i·est** *adj.* trite, lacking in imagination ‖ mawkish ‖ out-of-date ‖ poor in quality

cor·ol·lar·y (kɔ́rəleri:, kɒ́rəleri:) **1.** *pl.* **cor·ol·lar·ies** *n.* *(math.)* a proposition which can be inferred from one already proved as self-evidently true ‖ a natural consequence or result **2.** *adj.* following as a result, consequential

co·ro·na (kəróunə) *pl.* **co·ro·nas, co·ro·nae** (kəróuni:) *n. (astron.)* the upper region of the solar atmosphere, consisting of highly ionized gases ‖ a luminous ring formed by reflection on a fogbank or cloud on the opposite side of an observer to the sun ‖ *(archit.)* the projecting part of a cornice ‖ *(bot.)* a cup-shaped body formed by the union of scales on perianth leaves ‖ *(anat.)* any of various bones etc. shaped like a crown, e.g. in the skull or a tooth ‖ *(elec.)* a visible discharge on the surface of a high-voltage conductor ‖ a circular church chandelier

cor·o·nar·y (kɔ́rəneri:, kɒ́rəneri:) *adj.* of or pertaining

(a) æ, c*a*t; ɑ, c*a*r; ɔ f*a*wn; ei, sn*a*ke. (e) e, h*e*n; i:, sh*ee*p; iə, d*ee*r; ɛə, b*ea*r. (i) i, f*i*sh; ai, t*i*ger; ə:, b*i*rd. (o) o, *o*x; au, c*o*w; ou, g*oa*t; u, p*oo*r; ɔi, r*oy*al. (u) ʌ, d*u*ck; u, b*u*ll; u:, g*oo*se; ə, b*a*cillus; ju:, c*u*be. x, lo*ch*; θ, *th*ink; ð, *b*other; z, *Z*en; ʒ, corsa*g*e; dʒ, sava*g*e; ŋ, oranguta*n*g; j, *y*ak; ʃ, *f*ish; tʃ, fe*tch*; 'l, rabb*le*; 'n, redd*en*. Complete pronunciation key appears inside front cover.

to a crown, crownlike || *(anat.)* pertaining to either of two arteries arising from the aorta and supplying blood to the heart muscles

cor·o·na·tion (kɔrənéiʃən, kɔrənéiʃən) *n.* the act or ceremony of crowning a sovereign

cor·o·ner (kɔ́rənər, kɔ́rənər) *n.* a public officer whose most usual task is to hold an inquiry into the causes of accidental or suspicious deaths **cór·o·ner·ship** *n.*

cor·po·ral (kɔ́rpərəl, kɔ́rprəl) *adj.* belonging or relating to the body

corporal *n.* a noncommissioned officer in the army ranking below sergeant

cor·po·rate (kɔ́rpərit, kɔ́rprit) *adj.* united, combined into one || incorporated || belonging to an incorporated body, or corporation

cor·po·ra·tion (kɔrpəréiʃən) *n.* a body or society entitled to act as a single person, esp. a body of municipal authorities || *(law)* an artificial person created by charter etc., made up of many persons (corporation aggregate) or one (corporation sole)

cor·po·ra·tive (kɔ́rpərᶒitiv, kɔ́rpərᶒtiv, kɔ́rprᶒtiv) *adj.* relating to or consisting of a corporation || of a political system giving supreme authority to representatives from key corporations meeting in one corporate body

corps (kɔr, kour) *pl.* **corps** (kɔrz, kourz) *n.* part of an army forming a tactical unit and consisting of two or more divisions || a body of specialist troops || a body of trained people working together, e.g. of nurses in a hospital

corpse (kɔrps) *n.* the dead body of a human being || anything defunct

cor·pu·lence (kɔ́rpjuləns) *n.* the state or quality of being corpulent **cór·pu·len·cy** *n.*

cor·pu·lent (kɔ́rpjulənt) *adj.* having a fat body

cor·pus·cle (kɔ́rpəs'l, kɔ́rpᴧs'l) *n.* any minute body, esp. one of the free-floating cells found in blood

cor·pus·cu·lar (kɔrpᴧ́skjulər) *adj.* of or pertaining to corpuscles

cor·ral (kərǽl, *Br.* kərá́l) **1.** *n.* an enclosure for cattle, horses etc. || an enclosure for the capture of wild animals **2.** *v.t. pres. part.* **cor·ral·ling** *past* and *past part.* **cor·ralled** to put or drive (animals) into a corral || *(pop.)* to capture and keep hold of

cor·rect (kərékt) **1.** *v.t.* to put right || to remove faults from || to admonish, reprove, chastise || to adjust, bring to standard || to adjust for some known or estimated deviation, *correct the reading for individual error* **2.** *adj.* true, *a correct account* || accurate || conforming to recognized standards || conventional || complying with etiquette

cor·rec·tion (kərékʃən) *n.* an emending or an emendation || a rebuking or punishing or an instance of either || an allowance made for something to ensure accuracy

cor·re·late (kɔ́rəleit, kɔ́rəleit) **1.** *n.* either of two things or words implying the other, e.g. 'father' and 'son' **2.** *v. pres. part.* **cor·re·lat·ing** *past* and *past part.* **cor·re·lat·ed** *v.t.* to bring into mutual or reciprocal relation || to connect systematically || *v.i.* to have a mutual relation **cor·re·la·tion** (kɔrəléiʃən, kɔrəléiʃən) *n.* the act of state of being correlated || *(biol.)* mutual relationship || *(statistics)* degree of relationship

cor·re·spond (kɔrispɔ́nd, kɔrispɔ́nd) *v.i.* to communicate, esp. by letter || to be similar in function, position etc. || to be equivalent or representative || to be in agreement or harmony **cor·re·spónd·ing** *adj.* agreeing in any way, e.g. in kind, degree or position || similar || related, *privileges with corresponding obligations* || communicating by or dealing with letters

cor·re·spond·ence (kɔrispɔ́ndəns, kɔrispɔ́ndəns) *n.* harmony, agreement, the state of having qualities in common || an exchange of letters

cor·re·spond·ent (kɔrispɔ́ndənt, kɔrispɔ́ndənt) **1.** *n.* a person with whom one exchanges letters || a journalist employed to send regular reports or news items to a newspaper || a person having regular commercial con-

tact with a firm, esp. one distant or overseas **2.** *adj.* corresponding

cor·ri·dor (kɔ́ridər, kɔ́ridər, kɔ́ridɔr, kɔ́ridɔr) *n.* a long passageway, e.g. in a hotel with doors leading off it into separate rooms || an outdoor passage connecting parts of a building

cor·rob·o·rate (kərɔ́bəreit) *pres. part.* **cor·rob·o·rat·ing** *past* and *past part.* **cor·rob·o·rat·ed** *v.t.* to confirm by law || to give confirmation of or evidence to support

cor·rob·o·ra·tion (kərɔbəréiʃən) *n.* confirmation, support by further evidence

cor·rode (kəróud) *pres. part.* **cor·rod·ing** *past* and *past part.* **cor·rod·ed** *v.t.* to eat away by degrees, eat into the surface of || to consume || *v.i.* to become eaten away

cor·ro·sion (kəróuʒən) *n.* the process of wearing away the surface of a solid, esp. of metals and building stone, by converting the compact, cohesive substance into a friable one as the result of chemical action or the surface action of moisture

cor·ro·sive (kəróusiv) **1.** *adj.* producing corrosion || corroding the mind **2.** *n.* a substance which corrodes

cor·ru·gate (kɔ́rəgeit, kɔ́rəgeit) *pres. part.* **cor·ru·gat·ing** *past* and *past part.* **cor·ru·gat·ed** *v.t.* to form into wrinkles, folds, alternate ridges and grooves || *v.i.* to become corrugated **cor·ru·gá·tion** *n.* the act of corrugating || a single ridge or groove of a corrugated surface

cor·rupt (kərᴧ́pt) **1.** *adj.* depraved || changed from a sound to a putrid state || dishonest, open to bribery || not genuine, full of errors **2.** *v.t.* to pervert, make wicked || to defile, taint || to falsify || to bribe, *to corrupt a judge* || *v.i.* to become corrupt

cor·rupt·i·bil·i·ty (kərᴧptəbíliti:) *n.* the state or quality of being corruptible

cor·rupt·i·ble (kərᴧ́ptəb'l) *adj.* open to corruption, esp. to bribes **cor·rúpt·i·bly** *adv.*

cor·rup·tion (kərᴧ́pʃən) *n.* a corrupting || the state of being or becoming decayed || a spoiling || corrupt practices || perversion || moral decay || a corrupting influence || a debased form of a word

cor·sage (kɔrsáʒ) *n.* the bodice of a woman's dress || a spray of flowers to be worn on a dress

cor·set (kɔ́rsit) *n.* a close-fitting, usually stiffened, woman's undergarment extending from the bust to below the hips, worn to support the body and sustain or impose shape

cos·met·ic (kɒzmétik) **1.** *adj.* designed to beautify the complexion, eyes, hair, lips, nails etc. **2.** *n.* a preparation to enhance beauty, cleanse and improve the skin etc. **cos·me·ti·cian** (kɒzmitíʃən) *n.* a person skilled in the use of cosmetics

cos·mic (kɔ́zmik) *adj.* of or pertaining to the cosmos **cós·mi·cal·ly** *adv.*

cos·mo·pol·i·tan (kɔzməpɔ́litən) **1.** *adj.* free from local, provincial or national prejudices || composed of many nationalities, languages etc., *a cosmopolitan city* || *(biol.)* common to all or most of the world **2.** *n.* someone who is cosmopolitan **cos·mo·pól·i·tan·ism** *n.*

cos·mos (kɔ́zməs, kɔ́zmous) *n.* the universe viewed as an orderly whole || an ordered system of ideas, self-inclusive and harmonious

cost (kɔst, kɒst) *n.* the price paid or to be paid for something || an item in the outlay of time, labor, trouble etc. on a job

cost *pres. part.* **cost·ing** *past* and *past part.* **cost** *v.t.* to require an outlay or expenditure of || to result in (a specified loss) || to calculate the outlay on, *to cost a job*

cost·ly (kɔ́stli:, kɒ́stli:) *comp.* **cost·li·er** *superl.* **cost·li·est** *adj.* expensive || involving great loss || sumptuous, luxurious

cos·tume 1. (kɔ́stu:m, kɔ́stju:m) *n.* style of clothing in general, including ornaments, hairstyles etc. || a suit or dress representing a particular period, nationality, personage etc., worn at fancy-dress balls || a woman's tailored suit **2.** (kɒstú:m, kɒstjú:m) *v.t. pres. part.* **cos·tum·ing** *past* and *past part.* **cos·tumed** to supply with a costume

cot (kɒt) *n.* a camp bed or other small, narrow bed

co·til·lion (koutíljən, kətíljən) *n.* a ballroom or country dance for couples ‖ music for such dances ‖ a formal ball

cot·tage (kɒ́tidʒ) *n.* a small house, esp. in the country, for a farm laborer, miner etc. ‖ any small house, esp. in the country, esp. one used as a secondary residence

cot·ton (kɒ́t'n) **1.** *n.* a plant of genus *Gossypium*, fam. *Malvaceae* ‖ the soft, white, wool-like fiber enclosing the seeds of the cotton plant ‖ a threat or textile of this fiber ‖ guncotton **2.** *adj.* made of cotton

cot·ton·y (kɒ́t'ni:) *adj.* of or like cotton ‖ covered with down like cotton

couch (kautʃ) *n.* a piece of upholstered furniture for sitting or lying on, a sofa

cough (kɔf, kɒf) **1.** *v.i.* to make a cough ‖ (of an engine) to fire irregularly **2.** *n.* a sudden forced expulsion of air from the lungs, through the partially closed vocal cords, and the noise made by this ‖ a tendency to cough

could *past, past conditional* and *pres. conditional* of CAN

coun·cil (káunsəl) *n.* a consultative or advisory assembly ‖ a body elected or appointed to advise or legislate for a term of office ‖ a meeting of such people ‖ discussion, deliberation in a council ‖ a federation of delegates from labor unions composing a legislative body ‖ (*eccles.*) an assembly of churchmen to consider doctrinal, moral, legal problems etc.

coun·cil·lor, coun·ci·lor (káunsələr, káunslər) *n.* a member of a council **cóun·cil·lor·ship, cóun·ci·lor·ship** *n.*

coun·cil·man (káunsilmən) *pl.* **coun·cil·men** (káunsilmən) *n.* a member of a council, esp. of a city council

coun·sel (káunsəl) *n.* advise resulting from consultation ‖ a legal adviser ‖ (*collect.*) lawyers involved in a case

counsel (káunsəl) *pres. part.* **coun·sel·ing** *past* and *past part.* **coun·seled** *v.t.* to advise, recommend **cóun·sel·ing** *n.* a professional guidance service for individuals, applying the techniques of psychological testing

coun·se·lor, coun·sel·lor (káunsələr) *n.* a person who counsels or advises ‖ an adviser, esp. a legal adviser, at an embassy or legation ‖ a legal adviser who may conduct a case in court for his client ‖ an academic adviser ‖ a person in charge of a group of children at camp

count (kaunt) *n.* a European title of nobility ‖ a nobleman holding it

count *v.t.* to add up (units in a collection) ‖ to check by this process ‖ to repeat (numbers in order, up to and including a specified number) ‖ to include in one's reckoning ‖ to consider (a thing or person) as belonging to a specified class ‖ *v.i.* to name or add up numbers in order ‖ to be important, have significance ‖ to come properly into a reckoning

coun·te·nance (káuntənəns) *n.* the face ‖ the expression on a face

countenance *pres. part.* **coun·te·nanc·ing** *past* and *past part.* **coun·te·nanced** *v.t.* to show open approval of, support

coun·ter (káuntər) **1.** *adj.* opposite, contrary **2.** *adv.* in the opposite direction **3.** *v.i.* to answer an attack ‖ *v.t.* to parry

count·er *n.* a flat-topped piece of shop furniture dividing sales attendants from customers, and over which

business is transacted ‖ a similar fitting in a bank ‖ a small disk of bone, plastic etc. used e.g. for scoring in games or in playing a board game

coun·ter *n.* a computer, device for counting ‖ a Geiger counter

coun·ter·act (kauntərǽkt) *v.t.* to neutralize ‖ to defeat by contrary action ‖ to act in opposition to **coun·ter·ác·tion** *adj.*

coun·ter·feit (káuntərfit) **1.** *adj.* spurious, copied or made in imitation and pretending to be genuine ‖ feigned **2.** *n.* a counterfeit object **3.** *v.t.* to imitate, esp. with fraudulent intent, to forge ‖ to feign **cóun·ter·feit·er** *n.* a person who makes false money

coun·ter·part (káuntərpɑrt) *n.* a person fulfilling a role similar to another's ‖ a person or thing almost exactly resembling another ‖ a thing complementary to, or completing, another

coun·ter·sign (káuntərsain, kauntərsáin) *v.t.* to add a ratifying signature to (a signed document)

coun·tess (káuntis) *n.* the wife or widow of an earl or a count ‖ a lady having equivalent rank in her own right

count·less (káuntlis) *adj.* too many to be counted, innumerable

coun·tri·fied (kʌ́ntrifaid) *adj.* characteristic of rural life, unsophisticated

coun·try (kʌ́ntri:) *pl.* **coun·tries 1.** *n.* a region, district, tract of land, esp. with reference to geographical or esthetic features ‖ the land in which one was born or to which one owes allegiance ‖ a political state ‖ regions of woods and fields, esp. as opposed to towns ‖ the people of a country, nation **2.** *adj.* of or relating to the country as opposed to the town

coun·try·man (kʌ́ntri:mən) *pl.* **coun·try·men** (kʌ́ntri:mən) *n.* a compatriot ‖ a person of a specified district

coun·ty (káunti:) *pl.* **coun·ties** *n.* the largest local government division within a state

coup (ku:) *pl.* **coups** (ku:z) *n.* a sudden successful stroke, blow or stratagem

coupe (ku:p) *n.* a closed automobile, esp. a two-seater, with a body shorter than the corresponding sedan

cou·ple (kʌ́p'l) *n.* a pair ‖ (*pop.*) roughly two ‖ an engaged or married pair ‖ partners in a dance

couple *pres. part.* **cou·pling** *past* and *past part.* **cou·pled** *v.t.* to join, fasten, esp. in pairs ‖ to connect (railroad cars) by coupling ‖ to bring together, pair off ‖ to associate ‖ *v.i.* to unite sexually ‖ to associate in pairs **cóu·pler** *n.* a device for joining two things ‖ (*radio*) a device for connecting electric circuits ‖ (*rail.*) a coupling

cou·pon (kú:pɒn, kjú:pɒn) *n.* a detachable slip of paper giving entitlement to a payment of interest or to some service ‖ a ration voucher for food, clothing etc. in time of war or national austerity ‖ a sales promotion voucher ‖ part of a printed advertisement to be cut out as an order form, entry for a competition etc.

cour·age (kə́:ridʒ, kʌ́ridʒ) *n.* the capacity to meet danger without giving way to fear

cou·ra·geous (kəréidʒəs) *adj.* possessing or marked by courage

cour·i·er (kʌ́:ri:ər, kúəri:ər) *n.* a person employed by a firm of travel agents etc. to make arrangements abroad for travelers ‖ a special messenger

course (kɔrs, kours) **1.** *n.* a moving from one point to another ‖ the direction of travel or path taken ‖ ordinary sequence ‖ a line of conduct ‖ a racecourse ‖ a golf links ‖ a channel in which water flows ‖ a series of lectures, seminars etc. ‖ a scheme of study leading to a degree, diploma etc. ‖ a series of remedial treatments ‖ any of the successive parts of a meal **2.** *v.*

pres. part. **cours·ing** *past* and *past part.* **coursed** *v.t.* to hunt by sight and not by scent, *to course hares* ‖ *v.i.* to move or flow quickly, *the blood coursed through his veins*

court (kɔrt, kourt) **1.** *n.* an uncovered area surrounded by walls or buildings and planned as a unit, e.g. an entrance space or area in front of stables, a courtyard ‖ a college quadrangle ‖ a subdivision of a large, multiple-unit building (e.g. a museum) ‖ an enclosed space, open or covered, marked off for certain games, *a tennis court* ‖ a division of this ‖ the residence of a sovereign, a palace ‖ a sovereign's family and his retinue of courtiers ‖ a place or hall where justice is administered ‖ the judges, magistrates, coroners and other officials acting as a tribunal to administer justice ‖ a meeting of such officials **2.** *v.t.* to try to gain the favor or affection of, by flattery or attention ‖ to seek in marriage ‖ to allure, attract, entice ‖ to behave as though seeking (harm, a disaster etc.) ‖ *v.i.* to be sweethearts

cour·te·ous (kɔ́:rtiːəs) *adj.* polite, civil, considerate in manner

cour·te·sy (kɔ:rtisiː) *pl.* **cour·te·sies** *n.* polite, kind, considerate behavior or an instance of it

court·li·ness (kɔ́rtliːnis, kóurtliːnis) *n.* the quality of being courtly

court·ly (kɔ́rtliː, kóurtliː) *comp.* **court·li·er** *superl.* **court·li·est** *adj.* having or showing very polished, formal manners

court-mar·tial (kɔ́rtmɑrʃəl, kóurtmɑrʃəl, kɔrtmɑ́rʃəl, kourtmɑ́rʃəl) **1.** *pl.* **courts-mar·tial, court-mar·tials** *n.* a judicial court of military or naval officers to try soldiers' or sailors' offenses **2.** *v.t. pres. part.* **court-mar·tial·ing, court-mar·tial·ling** *past* and *past part.* **court-mar·tialed, court-mar·tialled** to try by court-martial

court·ship (kɔ́rtʃip, kóurtʃip) *n.* the wooing of a person one wishes to marry ‖ (of birds etc.) the sequence of song, display etc. preparatory to mating

cous·in (kʌ́z'n) *n.* a first cousin ‖ a first cousin once removed, second cousin, second cousin once removed etc., or any distant relative ‖ (*pl.*) people of a group with whom one acknowledges special ties (though blood relationship is not involved)

cou·tu·ri·er (kuːtúːriːei, kuːtúːriːər, kuːtúːrjei) *n.* a dress designer of a highclass fashion house

cove (kouv) **1.** *n.* a small sheltered bay, creek or inlet of the sea ‖ a cavern or recess ‖ (*archit.*) a concave molding or arch, esp. connecting a wall and ceiling **2.** *v.i. pres. part.* **cov·ing** *past* and *past part.* **coved** to arch, esp. at a junction of ceiling and wall ‖ (e.g. of the sides of a fireplace) to slope inwards

cov·e·nant (kʌ́vənənt) **1.** *n.* an agreement, bargain ‖ a sealed contract or clause of such a contract ‖ (*Bible*) the agreement between God and his chosen people, the Israelites **2.** *v.t.* to agree to by covenent ‖ *v.i.* to enter into formal agreement

cov·er (kʌ́vər) **1.** *v.t.* to place a cover on or over ‖ to hide ‖ to keep under aim ‖ to stand or march immediately behind (another man) ‖ to bring upon (oneself) to extend over, occupy ‖ to stake a bet equal to (one's opponent's bet) ‖ to protect financially ‖ to be enough to defray the costs of ‖ to have as one's territory or area of work ‖ to deal with, embrace ‖ to pass over ‖ (*journalism*) to report (proceedings, events etc.) **2.** *n.* something which extends over a thing, e.g. a top or lid ‖ the binding of a book ‖ a loose or fitted covering on a seat to protect it against dust, dirt or wear ‖ (*philately*) a stamped envelope that has passed through the mail ‖ a screen, veil ‖ money to meet liabilities ‖ insurance to protect against loss

cov·ert (kʌ́vərt, kóuvərt) *adj.* hidden, secret, disguised

cov·et (kʌ́vit) *v.t.* to long to possess (something belonging to another person) **cóv·et·ous** *adj.* strongly desiring another person's property

cow (kau) *pl.* **cows,** *archaic pl.* **kine** (kain) *n.* a fully grown female animal of the ox family, usually kept in herds by farmers for milk ‖ the female of any animal whose male is known as a bull, e.g. the elephant, rhinoceros, whale, seal, moose

cow *v.t.* to intimidate, browbeat

cow·ard (káuərd) *n.* a person without courage

cow·ard·ice (káuərdis) *n.* a lack or failure of courage

cow·er (káuər) *v.i.* to crouch or shrink back, esp. from fear

cowl (kaul) *n.* the hood of a monk's habit ‖ a covering (often hood-shaped) fitted to a chimney or ventilating shaft to prevent wind from blowing down ‖ part of an automobile to which are fitted the windshield and dashboard

coy (kɔi) *adj.* coquettishly bashful

coy·o·te (kaióutiː, káiout) *n.* a small wolf of North America

co·zi·ness, co·si·ness (kóuziːnis) *n.* the state or quality of being cozy

co·zy, co·sy (kóuziː) **1.** *comp.* **co·zi·er, co·si·er** *superl.* **co·zi·est, co·si·est** *adj.* nicely relaxing, comfortable ‖ (of people) lovable and easy to get on with **2.** *n.* a cover placed over a teapot etc. to keep it warm

crab (kræb) **1.** *n.* the popular name for the 10-legged, short-tailed crustaceans ‖ the flesh of the larger edible species ‖ an ill-tempered person ‖ a crab louse **2.** *v.t. pres. part.* **crab·bing** *past* and *past part.* **crabbed** to hunt crabs, fish for crabs

crab *pres. part.* **crab·bing** *past* and *past part.* **crabbed** *v.t.* (of hawks) to scratch or pull to pieces ‖ *v.i.* (*pop.*) to find fault

crab apple a wild apple with bitter fruit, or its fruit

crab·by (kræbiː) *comp.* **crab·bi·er** *superl.* **crab·bi·est** *adj.* crabbed (ill-tempered, morose, peevish)

crack (kræk) **1.** *v.t.* to cause to make a sudden, sharp sound ‖ to hit with a sudden, sharp blow ‖ to break open (a nut) ‖ (*pop.*) to break into (a safe) ‖ to break down (chemical compounds) into simpler ones ‖ *v.i.* to fracture without complete separation ‖ to make a sudden, sharp sound ‖ (of the voice) to break abruptly ‖ (*pop.*) to fail, give way ‖ (*pop.*) to hurry **2.** *n.* a sudden, sharp sound ‖ a sharp but not violent blow ‖ a partial breakage without complete separation ‖ a fissure in the ground or in ice ‖ a narrow opening, a chink ‖ a break in the voice ‖ a highly potent and addictive cocaine distillate in rock form ‖ (*pop.*) a joke **3.** *adj.* first-class, of the highest quality

crack·er (krǽkər) *n.* a flat, dry, crisp cake or a piece of unleavened bread ‖ a firework that explodes with a sharp crack

crack·le (kræk'l) **1.** *n.* a slight, sharp, cracking sound, as made by burning twigs ‖ a network of surface cracks in some glazes and in some glassware **2.** *v.i. pres. part.* **crack·ling** *past* and *past part.* **crack·led** to make little cracking sounds ‖ to form a crackle (in glaze)

cra·dle (kréid'l) **1.** *n.* a small bed or cot for a baby, sometimes mounted on rockers ‖ a place where something begins or is nurtured ‖ a framework of wood or metal to support a ship during construction or repair ‖ (*mining*) a rocking device used for washing goldbearing earth **2.** *v.t. pres. part.* **cra·dling** *past* and *past part.* **cra·dled** to place (a baby) in a cradle ‖ to hold (esp. a baby) in one's arms as if in a cradle ‖ to wash in a miner's cradle

craft (kræft, krɑft) *n.* a trade or occupation that requires skill in the use of the mind and hands ‖ an art viewed as a making that requires developed skills ‖ the members of a trade collectively, a guild ‖ cunning, deceit, guile ‖ (*pl.,* **craft**) a boat or vessel or aircraft

crafts·man (kræftsmən, krɑ́ftsmən) *pl.* **crafts·men** (krǽftsmən, krɑ́ftsmən) *n.* a skilled worker practicing a particular craft ‖ an artist with respect to the technical side of his art **crɑ́fts·man·ship** *n.*

craft·y (krǽftiː, krɑ́ftiː) *comp.* **craft·i·er** *superl.* **craft·i·est** *adj.* cunning, wily, deceitful

crag (kræg) *n.* a steep, rugged rock or cliff ‖ a piece of rock projecting from a surface

crag·ged (krǽgid) *adj.* craggy

crag·gy (krǽgi:) *comp.* **crag·gi·er** *superl.* **crag·gi·est** *adj.* having many crags

cram (kræm) *pres. part.* **cram·ming** *past* and *past part.* **crammed** *v.t.* to fill very full ‖ to force ‖ to stuff with food ‖ to stuff (food) into ‖ to eat (something) greedily ‖ to teach intensively for examination purposes ‖ *v.i.* to eat greedily ‖ to learn hurriedly without prolonged study

cramp (kræmp) **1.** *n.* a sudden painful contraction of the muscles often caused by cold or strain ‖ a temporary paralysis in the muscles caused by excessive use ‖ (*pl.*) severe pains in the stomach **2.** *v.t.* to hinder, restrict, *poverty cramped his early development* ‖ to cause to have a cramp ‖ to fasten or secure with a cramp **cramped** *adj.* restricted, without room to move ‖ not properly spaced out ‖ narrow-minded

cran·ber·ry (krǽnberi:, krǽnbəri:) *pl.* **cran·ber·ries** *n.* the tart, red, edible berry produced by some members of the genus *Vaccinium,* fam. *Ericaceae,* esp. *V. macrocarpon* and *V. oxycoccus* ‖ any of these plants

crane (krein) **1.** *n.* a family of tall, wading birds related to herons and storks, of considerable size and remarkable for their long stiltlike legs ‖ a machine for raising and lowering heavy weights ‖ a water siphon with a long, flexible tube for supplying water to railroad engines ‖ an axle fixed to a fireplace for hanging a pot or kettle on **2.** *v. pres. part.* **cran·ing** *past* and *past part.* **craned** *v.t.* to raise by a crane ‖ to stretch (one's neck) ‖ *v.i.* to stretch one's neck

cra·ni·um (kréini:əm) *pl.* **cra·ni·ums, cra·ni·a** (kréini:ə) *n.* the skull of any vertebrate, esp. that part enclosing the brain

crank (kræŋk) **1.** *n.* an arm set at right angles to a shaft or axle, used for converting reciprocal (to-and-fro) motion into circular motion ‖ an odd or eccentric person **2.** *v.t.* to set going with a crank (esp. an automobile engine ‖ to provide with a crank **3.** *adj.* (of machinery) weak, loose, shaky, unreliable

crank·i·ness (krǽŋki:nis) *n.* the state or quality of being cranky

crank·y (krǽŋki:) *comp.* **crank·i·er** *superl.* **crank·i·est** *adj.* irritable, crotchety ‖ capricious ‖ crazy ‖ (of machinery) loose or liable to break down

crash (kræʃ) **1.** *n.* a sudden, violent noise ‖ a collision of vehicles or of a vehicle with an obstacle, or a falling to earth of aircraft ‖ the collapse of a business or speculative enterprise **2.** *v.i.* to make a violent noise ‖ to come into collision ‖ (of an aircraft) to fall to earth ‖ to fail in business ‖ *v.t.* to attend (a party) without being invited

crass (kræs) *adj.* gross ‖ extremely stupid

crate (kreit) **1.** *n.* a framework of wooden boards for protecting something during transport **2.** *v.t. pres. part.* **crat·ing** *past* and *past part.* **crat·ed** to pack in a crate

cra·ter (kréitər) *n.* the mouth of a volcano ‖ a hole in the ground made by the explosion of a shell or bomb ‖ any bowl-shaped depression or cavity

cra·vat (krəvǽt) *n.* an elaborate silk necktie worn with formal morning dress ‖ a trade term for any necktie

crave (kreiv) *pres. part.* **crav·ing** *past* and *past part.* **craved** *v.t.* to desire strongly, urgently and persistently ‖ *v.i.* (with 'for') to long

cra·ven (kréivən) **1.** *adj.* (*rhet.*) cowardly, abject, fearful **2.** *n.* (*rhet.*) a coward

crav·ing (kréiviŋ) *n.* a strong, urgent and persistent desire

crawl (krɔl) **1.** *v.i.* to move forward on hands and knees ‖ to make one's way slowly and painfully ‖ to abase or humiliate oneself ‖ (of plants) to creep along the ground or up a wall ‖ to be as though alive (with crawling insects) ‖ (of flesh) to register unpleasant, creepy sensations ‖ to swim the crawl **2.** *n.* the act of crawling ‖ a powerful overarm stroke in swimming, with a thrashing movement of the legs

cray·fish (kréifiʃ) *pl.* **cray·fish, cray·fish·es** *n.* any of various long-tailed, freshwater edible crustaceans

cray·on (kréiɒn, kréiən) **1.** *n.* a stick of colored chalk or chalk and wax for drawing with **2.** *v.t.* to draw with crayons

craze (kreiz) **1.** *n.* a great or fashionable enthusiasm for something **2.** *v. pres. part.* **craz·ing** *past* and *past part.* **crazed** *v.t.* (*rhet.*) to make made ‖ *v.i* (*pottery*) to show crackle in the glaze

cra·zy (kréizi:) *comp.* **cra·zi·er** *superl.* **cra·zi·est** *adj.* foolish ‖ insane ‖ unsound, full of defects and imperfections ‖ (*pop.*) very enthusiastic ‖ in love with

creak (kri:k) **1.** *n.* a harsh grating or squeaking sound, made e.g. by a loose floorboard or layers of dry leather rubbing together **2.** *v.i.* to make such a sound **créak·i·ly** *adv.* **créak·y** *comp.* **creak·i·er** *superl.* **creak·i·est** *adj.*

cream (kri:m) **1.** *n.* the rich, fatty part of milk which gathers on the top ‖ a food or confection containing cream or resembling it, *ice cream* ‖ a creamlike cosmetic ointment, *face cream* ‖ the best part of anything, *the cream of society* ‖ the color of cream, a pale yellow **2.** *v.t.* to beat to a light, smooth consistency ‖ to skim the cream from (milk) ‖ to rub a cosmetic cream into (the skin) ‖ *v.i.* (of milk) to form a cream

cream·y (krí:mi:) *comp.* **cream·i·er** *superl.* **cream·i·est** *adj.* having the consistency or color of cream

crease (kri:s) **1.** *n.* a wrinkle or fold mark, whether intended (e.g. along the length of the trouser leg) or not **2.** *v. pres. part.* **creas·ing** *past* and *past part.* **creased** *v.i.* to wrinkle ‖ to become creased ‖ *v.t.* to make creases in

cre·ate (kri:éit) *pres. part.* **cre·at·ing** *past* and *past part.* **cre·at·ed** *v.t.* to bring into being ‖ to make by applying the imagination in some artistic technique ‖ to produce ‖ to invest with rank ‖ (of an actor) to incarnate (a character), esp. playing it for the first time, or in a particularly effective manner

cre·a·tion (kri:éiʃən) *n.* the act of creating ‖ everything that has been created, the universe ‖ something that has been created with imagination, e.g. by an author, actor or fashion designer ‖ a bringing into being ‖ an investing with rank or title etc. **the Creation** (*Bible*) the creation of the world by God described in Genesis

cre·a·tive (kri:éitiv) **1.** *adj.* having the quality or power of creating ‖ imaginative **2.** *n.* (*slang*) one who is creative, esp. a writer in the advertising field

cre·a·tiv·i·ty (krị:eitíviti:) *n.* creativeness

cre·a·tor (kri:éitər) *n.* someone who creates **the Cre·a·tor** God as maker of the universe and of all life

crea·ture (krí:tʃər) *n.* a living human or animal ‖ something created ‖ a servile tool of someone else

cre·den·tials (kridénʃəls) *pl. n.* a letter establishing the authority of the bearer

cred·i·bil·i·ty (kreḍəbíliti:) *n.* the state or quality of being credible

cred·i·ble (kréḍəb'l) *adj.* believable **créd·i·bly** *adv.*

cred·it (krédit) **1.** *n.* the system of buying and selling without immediate payment or security ‖ the power to obtain goods without immediate payment ‖ time allowed for payment ‖ a favorable balance of an account ‖ belief ‖ good reputation ‖ an acknowledgment of merit ‖ a credit line **2.** *v.t.* to believe ‖ to trust ‖ to enter (a sum of money) upon the credit side of an account ‖ to enter a sum of money in (an account

---

etc.) ‖ to attribute to (a student or his record) the units of time spent in following a course of instruction **créd·it·a·ble** adj. quite good, more than just satisfactory **créd·it·a·bly** adv.

cred·i·tor (kréditər) n. someone to whom a debt is owing

cre·do (krí:dou, kréidou) pl. **cre·dos** n. a creed **Cré·do** a Christian liturgical Creed

cred·u·lous (krédʒuləs) adj. gullible, ready to believe without proof

creed (kri:d) n. a set of beliefs or opinions **Creed** one of the formal summaries of Christian beliefs used liturgically

creek (kri:k, krik) n. a short arm of a river ‖ a small tributary river or stream

creep (kri:p) 1. v.i. pres. part. **creep·ing** past and past part. **crept** (krept) to move along with the body prone and close to the ground ‖ (of babies) to crawl on all fours ‖ to move quietly and stealthily ‖ to move or act in a servile manner ‖ (of time etc.) to go slowly ‖ (of plants) to grow along the ground or up walls, trees. etc. ‖ (of the skin) to prickle in fear or disgust 2. n. the act or pace of creeping ‖ (phys.) the slow movement of a solid under stress **the creeps** a sensation of fear or horror

creep·y (krí:pi:) comp. **creep·i·er** superl. **creep·i·est** adj. having a physical sensation of fear or disgust ‖ producing such a sensation, creepy stories

cre·mate (krí:meit) pres. part. **cre·mat·ing** past and past part. **cre·mat·ed** v.t. to burn, incinerate (a dead body) **cre·ma·tion** (kriméiʃən) n.

crepe, crêpe, crape (kreip) n. a thin fabric, usually of silk, with a wrinkled surface

cres·cent (krés·nt) 1. n. the waxing moon ‖ the moon in its first or last quarter ‖ any crescentshaped object 2. adj. crescentshaped

crest (krest) 1. n. the comb or tuft on the head of a bird or animal ‖ a plume of feathers or other ornament on top of a helmet ‖ the ridge of a helmet ‖ the top of a hill or wave ‖ a mane ‖ (anat.) a ridge along a bone surface 2. v.t. to furnish with a crest ‖ to serve as a crest to ‖ to reach and pass the top of (a hill, wave etc.) ‖ v.i. to rise or form into a crest

cre·vasse (krəvǽs) n. a deep crevice, esp. in a glacier ‖ a breach in a river bank

crev·ice (krévis) n. a narrow crack or split

crew (kru:) n. (a collective term for) a ship's company, or ship's company with the officers ‖ the men manning an aircraft ‖ a body of men working together at a task ‖ a band, mob ‖ a rowing team ‖ the sport of rowing in races

crib (krib) 1. n. a barred wooden manger for animal fodder ‖ (Am. = Br. cot) a bed, usually with high sides, for a small child ‖ a crèche (model of the Nativity) ‖ a literal prose translation of a literary work in another language, used esp. by young students ‖ plagiarism, a theft of other people's ideas etc. ‖ the framework lining a mine shaft ‖ a bin for corn, salt etc. 2. v. pres. part. **crib·bing** past and past part. **cribbed** v.i. to use a crib in one's work ‖ v.t. to copy unfairly ‖ to plagiarize ‖ to line with timbers or planks

crick·et (kríkit) n. insect allied to the cicada, distinguished by long cerci and filamentous antennae

cricket n. an outdoor team game

crime (kraim) n. a violation of the law, esp. a serious one ‖ such acts in general ‖ (loosely) a foolish or ill-considered action

crim·i·nal (krímin'l) 1. adj. relating to crime ‖ guilty of crime 2. n. someone who has committed a crime **crim·i·nal·i·ty** (krìminǽliti:) n. the quality or state of being criminal

crimp (krimp) 1. v.t. to pinch into waves or ridges ‖ to form into shape, esp. (shoemaking) to mold (leather) into shape ‖ to put a crimp in 2. n. wave or undulation (e.g. in the hair) ‖ a corrugation ‖ the act or result of crimping, e.g. the warping of wood from drying too fast **crimp·y** comp. **crimp·i·er** superl. **crimp·i·est** adj. crimped in appearance

crim·son (krímzən, krímzn) 1. n. a deep red color 2. adj. of this color 3. v.t. to cause to become crimson ‖ v.i. to become crimson

cringe (krindʒ) pres. part. **cring·ing** past and past part. **cringed** v.i. to cower, shrink in fear ‖ to behave servilely

crin·kle (kríŋk'l) 1. v. pres. part. **crin·kling** past and past part. **crin·kled** v.i. to wrinkle ‖ v.t. to cause to wrinkle 2. n. a crease, wrinkle **crin·kly** comp. **crin·kli·er** superl. **crin·kli·est** adj.

crip·ple (kríp'l) 1. n. a badly lamed or disabled person 2. v.t. pres. part. **crip·pling** past and past part. **crip·pled** to disable, lame ‖ to frustrate, hinder

cri·sis (kráisis) pl. **cri·ses** (kráisi:z) n. the turning point in a disease ‖ the decisive moment, esp. in a tragedy ‖ a time of danger or suspense in politics etc.

crisp (krisp) 1. adj. firm and fresh ‖ fresh and bracing ‖ concise, clear and direct ‖ (of hair etc.) curly, crinkled 2. n. (Br.) potato chip 3. v.t. to make crisp ‖ v.i. to become crisp

crisp·y (kríspi:) comp. **crisp·i·er** superl. **crisp·i·est** adj. crisp

cri·te·ri·on (kraitíəri:ən) pl. **cri·te·ri·a** (kraitíəri:ə), **cri·te·ri·ons** n. a standard or principle by which a thing is judged

crit·ic (krítik) n. a person skilled in forming opinions and giving a judgment, esp. on literature, art, music etc. ‖ a professional reviewer ‖ a fault finder

crit·i·cal (krítik'l) adj. given to expressing severe judgments or passing unfavorable comment ‖ fond of pointing out shortcomings or error, censorious ‖ of a crisis ‖ of critics or criticism ‖ involving danger or suspense ‖ discerning, based on thorough knowledge ‖ (phys., math.) denoting a point or state at which a change in properties, characteristics etc. takes place

crit·i·cism (krítisizəm) n. the art of judging merit ‖ a spoken or written judgment concerning some matter resting on opinion ‖ censure, unfavorable comment

crit·i·cize (krítisaiz) pres. part. **crit·i·ciz·ing** past and past part. **crit·i·cized** v.t. to assess the merits and demerits of ‖ to censure ‖ v.i. to find fault

croak (krouk) 1. v.i. (e.g. of a frog or raven) to utter a deep hoarse sound ‖ to talk dismally ‖ v.t. to speak or say in a low, hoarse voice 2. n. a hoarse, harsh sound **cróak·i·ly** adv. **cróak·y** adj.

cro·chet (krouʃéi) n. a kind of needlework done with a hook

crock·er·y (krókəri:) n. earthenware vessels

croc·o·dile (krókədail) n. amphibious reptile found in the waters of all warm regions of the world

crook (kruk) 1. n. a hooked staff used by a shepherd ‖ a crosier ‖ anything hooked or bent ‖ a hook ‖ (pop.) a thief, criminal ‖ (mus.) a device on some wind instruments for changing pitch 2. v.t. to bend into a crook ‖ to grasp with a crook ‖ v.i. to bend or curve **crook·ed** (krúkid) adj. not straight, twisted ‖ bent or stooping with age or illness ‖ dishonest

croon (kru:n) 1. v.i. to sing or hum in an undertone ‖ (of entertainers) to hum or sing with the technique of a crooner ‖ (of babies) to hum or sing softly, abstractedly and contentedly ‖ v.t. to hum or sing (a song) in an undertone or with the technique of a crooner 2. n. the sound made by crooning **cróon·er** n. a singer of sentimental songs sung in a low, intimate, breathy style

crop (krɒp) 1. n. harvested grain, fruit etc. ‖ cultivated produce while growing ‖ a group of things coming together ‖ the pouchlike dilation of a bird's gullet where food is broken up for digestion ‖ a hunting whip with a loop instead of a lash ‖ the handle of a whip ‖ hair cut short ‖ the style of wearing hair so cut 2. v. pres. part. **crop·ping** past and past part. **cropped** v.t. (of animals) to eat off short ‖ to cut (hair) short and often unevenly ‖ to cut off (ends, parts of a photograph unwanted for printing etc.) ‖ to clip (ears) ‖ to reap, harvest ‖ to cultivate in ‖ v.i. to bear a crop

cro·quet (kroukéi) **1.** *n.* a game in which wooden balls are knocked with long-handled wooden mallets through a series of wickets ‖ the act of croqueting a ball **2.** *v.t.* *pres. part.* **cro·quet·ing** (kroukéiiŋ) *past* and *past part.* **cro·queted** (kroukéid)

cro·quette (koukét) *n.* a ball of minced meat, fish etc. coated with crumbs and fried

cross (krɔs, krɒs) **1.** *n.* a figure or mark made by placing one line across another (×, +, †) ‖ *(hist.)* an upright wooden stake with a horizontal crossbar to which criminals were tied or nailed, esp. the one on which Jesus Christ was crucified ‖ a model or image of this, the chief emblem of Christianity ‖ a movement of the right hand making the sign of a cross as a sacramental act ‖ suffering, tribulation one has to bear ‖ interbreeding ‖ the product of mixed breeding ‖ *(astron.)* a constellation, *the Southern Cross* ‖ *(plumbing)* a four-way joint in the form of a cross **2.** *v.t.* to go across ‖ to place crosswise ‖ to put the bar on (the letter 't') ‖ (with *off* or *out*') to draw a line through or across (written matter) to cancel it ‖ to thwart, frustrate ‖ to meet and pass ‖ to mark with a cross ‖ to make the sign of the cross over as a sacramental act ‖ *v.i.* to go across something ‖ to lie across something ‖ to interbreed ‖ to cross-fertilize **3.** *adj.* transverse, *crossbeams* ‖ contrary, opposite, *at cross-purposes* ‖ conflicting, *crosscurrents* ‖ peevish, annoyed

cross-ex·am·ine (krɔ́sigzǽmin, krɒ́sigzǽmin) *pres. part.* **cross-ex·am·in·ing** *past* and *past part.* **cross-ex·am·ined** *v.t.* to question closely (esp. a witness in a law court)

cross·ing (krɔ́siŋ, krɒ́siŋ) *n.* the act of crossing, esp. by a sea voyage ‖ an intersection ‖ a place with special arrangements for the traversing of a road, river etc.

crotch (krɒtʃ) *n.* a fork, e.g. of a tree ‖ the bifurcation of the human body

crouch (krautʃ) **1.** *v.i.* to have the tense posture of an animal preparing to spring ‖ to stand with knees slightly bent, muscles tensed, and shoulders thrust forward, ready to give or receive a blow ‖ to stoop or bend for lack or head room **2.** *n.* a crouching position

crou·ton (krú:tɒn, kru:tɔ́n) *n.* a small piece of toasted or fried bread served with soup, or used as a garnishing

crow (krou) *n.* a passerine, mainly vegetarian bird **as the crow flies** (of distances) in a straight line, i.e. not following the road etc. **to eat crow** to eat humble pie, to admit humbly that one was wrong

crow 1. *v.i.* *pres. part.* **crow·ing** *past* and *past part.* **crowed** to utter the loud shrill cry of a cock ‖ (esp. of a baby) to utter a cry of delight ‖ to boast **2.** *n.* the cry of a cock ‖ a happy sound made by babies

crow-bar (króubɑr) *n.* an iron bar with a wedge at the working end used as a lever

crowd (kraud) **1.** *n.* a large number of people collected together ‖ *(pop.)* a clique, set ‖ *(pop.)* a large number **2.** *v.t.* to throng together ‖ to press forward ‖ *v.t.* to press upon, deprive of space ‖ to fill, cram (a space etc.)

crown (kraun) **1.** *n.* a royal headdress of precious metal or jewels ‖ an emblem resembling this, used as a badge of rank ‖ the monarch himself ‖ *(rhet.)* a wreath or garland ‖ *(rhet.)* a reward ‖ the top part of the head ‖ the top of a hat ‖ the highest part of an arch ‖ the crest of a road ‖ the crest of a bird ‖ a British coin ‖ *(anat.)* the exposed part of a tooth ‖ *(bot.)* the junction of root and stem ‖ the leafy upper part of a tree ‖ a perfecting touch, completion ‖ *(naut.)* the junction of the arms and stem of an anchor ‖ the top part of a bell **the Crown** the supreme power in a monarchy **2.** *v.t.* to place a crown on (someone's head) ‖ to

complete, perfect, put the finishing touch to ‖ to be at the top of, surmount ‖ to put a top on (a broken tooth) ‖ *(pop.)* to deal (someone) a blow on the top of the head

cru·cial (krú:ʃəl) *adj.* decisive, critical ‖ fundamental ‖ *(anat.)* cross-shaped

cru·ci·ble (krú:səb'l) *n.* a vessel for melting substances requiring extreme heat ‖ *(rhet.)* a severe test

cru·ci·fix (krú:sifiks) *n.* a cross with a figure of Christ on it

cru·ci·fy (krú:sifai) *pres. part.* **cru·ci·fy·ing** *past* and *past part.* **cru·ci·fied** *v.t.* to put to death by fastening or nailing to a cross ‖ to torment ‖ to mortify (the passions etc.)

crude (kru:d) *comp.* **crud·er** *superl.* **crud·est** *adj.* raw, in a natural state, untreated ‖ unpolished, graceless ‖ unfinished, rough ‖ undisguised, blunt ‖ vulgar

cru·el (krú:əl) *adj.* liking to inflict pain and suffering ‖ showing pleasure at the suffering of others ‖ causing suffering, *a cruel blow of fate* **cru·el·ty** *pl.* **cru·el·ties** *n.* the quality of being cruel ‖ something cruel done, said, written etc.

cruise (kru:z) **1.** *v.i.* *pres. part.* **cruis·ing** *past* and *past part.* **cruised** to make a sea voyage for pleasure ‖ to sail about with no special destination ‖ *(navy)* to be on the search for enemy ships ‖ *(slang* or *colloq.)* to search for a sexual partner at bars or by driving or walking along the streets ‖ to drive slowly about (e.g. of a taxi looking for fares) **2.** *n.* a sea voyage for pleasure

cruis·er (krú:zər) *n.* a warship designed for speed, less heavily armed than a battleship ‖ a motorboat with living accommodation ‖ a squad car

crumb (krʌm) **1.** *n.* a small fragment, esp. of bread ‖ a small amount ‖ the soft inside of a loaf of bread **2.** *v.t.* to coat with crumbs ‖ to break into crumbs

crum·ble (krʌ́mb'l) *pres. part.* **crum·bling** *past* and *past part.* **crum·bled** *v.t.* to break into small pieces ‖ *v.i.* to fall to pieces (esp. through age and decay) ‖ to fail **crum·bly** *comp.* **crum·bli·er** *superl.* **crum·bli·est** *adj.*

crum·ple (krʌ́mp'l) **1.** *v.* *pres. part.* **crum·pling** *past* and *past part.* **crum·pled** *v.t.* to crush into a mass of creases ‖ *v.i.* to become creased ‖ (sometimes with *up*') to collapse **2.** *n.* an untidy crease

crunch (krʌntʃ) **1.** *v.t.* to crush noisily with the teeth ‖ to crush underfoot with a similar noise ‖ to make with a crushing noise ‖ *v.i.* to make a crushing noise by chewing, grinding etc. **2.** *n.* the act of crunching ‖ high-pressure situation ‖ the point in a situation where decision or action is necessary ‖ the noise produced

cru·sade (kru:séid) **1.** *n.* any war undertaken in the name of religion ‖ any energetic movement to remove an evil or improve a situation **2.** *v.i.* *pres. part.* **cru·sad·ing** *past* and *past part.* **cru·sad·ed** to take part in a crusade

crush (krʌʃ) **1.** *v.t.* to maim, damage or spoil by pressure ‖ to crease ‖ to reduce to a powder or to small pieces under pressure ‖ to squash ‖ to subdue ‖ to silence (a critic or opponent) in a humiliating way ‖ to hug violently ‖ *v.i.* to squeeze ‖ to become crumpled **2.** *n.* a crushing or being crushed ‖ a large crowd of people ‖ an infatuation ‖ the object of such an infatuation

crust (krʌst) **1.** *n.* the crisp outer part of bread ‖ a hard dry piece of bread ‖ the pastry cover of a pie ‖ a hard outer surface or covering, e.g. of snow, ice etc. ‖ *(geol.)* the light, thin mantle of the earth ‖ *(med.)* a scab ‖ a deposit of tartar on the inside of a wine bottle or barrel ‖ outer appearance masking true character

---

or feelings ‖ (*pop.*) impertinence, nerve **2.** *v.t.* to cover with a crust ‖ *v.i.* to form into, or become covered with a crust

crus·ta·cean (krʌstéiʃən) *n.* mostly aquatic and gill-breathing arthropod, including crabs, lobsters and shrimps

crus·ti·ness (krʌ́sti:nis) *n.* the state or quality of being crusty

crust·y (krʌ́sti:) *comp.* **crust·i·er** *superl.* **crust·i·est** *adj.* hard, crustlike ‖ (of bread) having a crisp crust ‖ (of persons, esp. men) gruff, hard to approach

crutch (krʌtʃ) *n.* a wood or metal support to help a lame person to walk ‖ (*rhet.*) a support, something one relies upon ‖ the crotch, fork of the human body ‖ the forked leg rest of a sidesaddle

cry (crai) *pres. part.* **cry·ing** *past* and *past part.* **cried** *v.i.* to call out (in pain, anger, fear, delight etc.) ‖ to weep ‖ (of an animal) to utter its call ‖ *v.t.* to shout ‖ to announce for sale by shouting

cry *pl.* **cries** *n.* a shout or wail ‖ a vendor's street call ‖ a watchword or battle cry ‖ a fit of weeping

cry·ing (kráiiŋ) *adj.* (esp. of a need, shame or evil) calling urgently for attention, flagrant

crypt (kript) *n.* an underground room or cell, esp. one underneath a church ‖ (*anat.*) a simple gland or gland cavity ‖ a follicle

cryp·tic (kríptik) *adj.* enigmatic **crýp·ti·cal·ly** *adv.*

crys·tal (krístəl) **1.** *n.* the solid state of a pure substance or mixture, characterized by a regular ordered arrangement of the constituent atoms, usually having external plane faces meeting at angles characteristic of the substance ‖ a substance having some of the properties of a crystal, usually as a result of the ordered arrangement of its molecules ‖ transparent quartz, often cut for ornamental use ‖ a very clear and transparent kind of glass ‖ (*Am.* = *Br.* watch glass) a concavo-convex cover of glass or plastic over the face of a watch **2.** *adj.* of or using a crystal ‖ perfectly clear

crys·tal·li·za·tion (krịstəlizéiʃən) *n.* the process of crystallizing ‖ a crystallized form

crys·tal·lize (krístəlaiz) *pres. part.* **crys·tal·liz·ing** *past* and *past part.* **crys·tal·lized** *v.i.* to assume the form of a crystal ‖ (of ideas) to become clear and definite ‖ *v.t.* to assume the form of a crystal or crystals ‖ to cause to become clear

cub (kʌb) *n.* a young bear, fox, lion, tiger, wolf etc. ‖ a novice, *a cub reporter* ‖ a junior boy scout

cube (kju:b) *n.* a geometrical solid bounded by six plane faces of equal area and making right angles with one another

cube (kju:b) *pres. part.* **cub·ing** *past* and *past part.* **cubed** *v.t.* to cut into cubes

cu·bic (kjú:bik) *adj.* having the properties of a cube ‖ being the volume of a cube whose edge is a specified unit **cú·bi·cal** *adj.* cube-shaped

cuck·oo (kú:ku:, kúku:) *pl.* **cuck·oos 1.** *n.* a European bird which deposits its eggs in the nests of other birds, for them to hatch **2.** *adj.* (*pop.*) foolish, crazy

cu·cum·ber (kjú:kʌmbər) *n.* a genus of annual trailing vines ‖ the long green fleshy fruit

cud·dle (kʌ́d'l) **1.** *v. pres. part.* **cud·dling** *past* and *past part.* **cud·dled** *v.t.* to hold closely and fondly ‖ *v.i.* to curl up comfortably, nestle **2.** *n.* an embrace **cud·dle·some** *adj.* **cúd·dly** *adj.*

cudg·el (kʌ́dʒəl) **1.** *n.* a short, stout stick used as a weapon **to take up the cudgels for** to defend strongly (in argument) **2.** *v.t. pres. part.* **cudg·el·ing** *past* and *past part.* **cudg·eled** to beat with a cudgel

cue (kju:) **1.** *n.* (*theater*) an agreed signal, usually a line or word of dialogue, for some action or speech on or off stage ‖ a similar guide to a musical performer ‖ a hint meant to guide behavior etc. **2.** *pres. part.* **cu·ing** *past* and *past part.* **cued** *v.t.* to give a cue to

cue *n.* a long leather-tipped rod for striking the ball in billiards and related games ‖ a queue of hair ‖ a queue of people **2.** *pres part.* **cu·ing** *past* and *past part.*

cued to strike with a cue ‖ to form (hair) into a cue

cuff (kʌf) *n.* the part of a sleeve which is turned back at the wrist, or which touches the wrist ‖ the turned-up end of a trouser leg ‖ a handcuff

cuff 1. *v.t.* to strike with the open palm or back of the hand **2.** *n.* the blow given in this way

cui·sine (kwizí:n) *n.* cooking with reference to quality or style

cu·li·nar·y (kiú:lineri:, kʌ́lineri:) *adj.* relating to cooking or the kitchen ‖ suitable for or used in cooking

cull (kʌl) **1.** *v.t.* (*rhet.*) to pick, gather (flowers, facts etc.) **2.** *n.* something picked out as substandard, e.g. an old or weak animal taken from a flock

cul·mi·nate (kʌ́lməneit) *pres. part.* **cul·mi·nat·ing** *past* and *past part.* **cul·mi·nat·ed** *v.i.* to reach a climax ‖ (*astron.*) to be on the meridian **cul·mi·ná·tion** *n.* a climax ‖ (*astron.*) the highest or lowest altitude of a heavenly body in meridian transit

cul·prit (kʌ́lprit) *n.* a guilty person ‖ (*law*) a person accused of an offense, prisoner at the bar

cult (kʌlt) *n.* a system of religious worship ‖ admiration of, or devotion to, a person or thing, esp. as a form of intellectual snobbery ‖ a passing craze or fashion ‖ a creed or sect

cul·ti·vate (kʌ́ltiveit) *pres. part.* **cul·ti·vat·ing** *past* and *past part.* **cul·ti·vat·ed** *v.t.* to prepare (land) for crops, till ‖ to raise (crops) by farming, gardening etc. ‖ to improve, refine ‖ to foster, cause to develop **cúl·ti·vat·ed** *adj.* (of land) prepared for, or planted with, crops, not left to grow wild ‖ (of people) cultured

cul·ti·va·tion (kʌltivéiʃən) *n.* a cultivating or being cultivated ‖ refinement, development (of the mind, taste etc.)

cul·tur·al (kʌ́ltʃərəl) *adj.* of, or relating to, culture or a culture ‖ produced by breeding

cul·ture (kʌ́ltʃər) **1.** *n.* the training and development of the mind ‖ the refinement of taste and manners acquired by such training ‖ the social and religious structures and intellectual and artistic manifestations etc. that characterize a society ‖ the rearing of bees, fish, oysters, silkworms etc. ‖ the cultivation of tissues or microorganisms in prepared media, or a product of this **2.** *v.t. pres. part.* **cul·tur·ing** *past* and *past part.* **cul·tured** to make a culture of ‖ to grow in a prepared medium

cul·vert (kʌ́lvərt) *n.* a drain carrying water under a road, railroad etc. ‖ an underground channel for electric wires or cables

cum·ber (kʌ́mbər) *v.t.* to hinder or burden, encumber

cum·ber·some (kʌ́mbərsəm) *adj.* burdensome ‖ (of objects) unwieldy, apt to get in the way

cu·mu·late (kjú:mjuleit) *pres. part.* **cu·mu·lat·ing** *past* and *past part.* **cu·mu·lat·ed** *v.t.* to accumulate, heap up, amass ‖ *v.i.* to become massed **cu·mu·lá·tion** *n.*

cu·mu·la·tive (kjú:mjuleitiv, kjú:mjulətiv) *adj.* gradually increasing by successive additions ‖ tending to accumulate

cun·ning (kʌ́niŋ) **1.** *adj.* crafty, full of deceit ‖ skillful, ingenious ‖ sweet, charming **2.** *n.* guile, deceit ‖ artfulness ‖ skill, dexterity

cup (kʌp) **1.** *n.* a small bowl-shaped vessel, usually with a handle, for drinking tea, coffee etc. from, and usually matched with a saucer ‖ an ornamental vessel, often with a stem of gold or silver, offered as a sports trophy etc. ‖ a cupful, *a cup of tea* ‖ a measure in cookery ‖ the wine of the Eucharist, or the chalice containing it ‖ (*rhet.*) one's portion or fate ‖ a rounded hollow, e.g. the socket of certain bones or the calyx of some flowers ‖ (*med.*) a glass vessel used in cupping **2.** *v.t. pres. part.* **cup·ping** *past* and *past part.* **cupped** to form into a cup ‖ (*med.*) to bleed by cupping

cup·cake (kʌ́pkeik) *n.* a small cake baked in a cup-shaped tin

cup·ful (kʌ́pful) *pl.* **cup·fuls** *n.* (*cookery*) as much as a cup will hold

cu·pid·i·ty (kju:píditi:) *n.* avarice, greed, esp. for wealth

cu·po·la (kjú:pələ) *n.* a rounded roof or ceiling ‖ a small dome-shaped superstructure on a roof ‖ a furnace for melting metals ‖ a revolving dome protecting guns on battleships ‖ *(anat.)* a domed organ or process, esp. the extremity of the canal of the cochlea

cup·ping (kʌ́piŋ) *n. (med.)* the application of a cup-shaped instrument to the skin to draw the blood to the surface for bloodletting

cur (kəːr) *n.* a mongrel dog, esp. a snappish, bad-tempered one ‖ *(old-fash.)* a bad-tempered, despicable fellow

cu·rate (kjúərit) *n.* an assistant to a vicar or a rector

cu·ra·tor (kjuréitər, kjúəreitər) *n.* a person in charge of a museum, art gallery or department of such an institution **cu·ra·to·ri·al** (kjuərətɔ́riːəl, kjuərətóuriːəl) *adj.* **cu·rá·tor·ship** *n.*

curb (kəːrb) **1.** *n.* a chain or strap passing under a horse's lower jaw and used to restrain ‖ a restraint, control ‖ a protective barrier ‖ *(stock exchange)* a market in stocks not listed on the exchange (orig. on the street after the closing of the exchange) ‖ a hard swelling on a horse's leg **2.** *v.t.* to put a cub on (a horse) ‖ to restrain

curd (kəːrd) *n.* (esp. *pl.*) the smooth, thickened part of sour milk

cur·dle (kə́ːrd'l) *pres. part.* **cur·dling** *past* and *past part.* **cur·dled** *v.t.* to cause to clot, congeal ‖ *v.i.* to form into curds ‖ to thicken, congeal

cure (kjuər) *n.* a remedy ‖ a course of treatment ‖ a successful treatment ‖ *(eccles.)* the pastorate ‖ an agent for curing hides

cure *v.t. pres. part.* **cur·ing** *past* and *past part.* **cured** to restore to health ‖ to remedy ‖ to preserve by smoking, salting, pickling etc. ‖ to treat (hides) with salt or chemicals so as to stop decomposition ‖ *v.i.* (of hides) to become cured

cur·few (kə́ːrfjuː) *n.* in places under martial law, a fixed time after which (or period during which) no citizen may remain outdoors ‖ *(hist.)* a medieval rule that all lights and fires should be covered at a certain time in the evening, when a bell was rung ‖ the time for this

cu·ri·o (kjúəriːou) *pl.* **cu·ri·os** *n.* an interesting object valued for its appearance or associations

cu·ri·os·i·ty (kjuəriːɔ́siti) *pl.* **cu·ri·os·i·ties** *n.* eagerness to know ‖ inquisitiveness ‖ strangeness ‖ a rare or curious object

cu·ri·ous (kjúəriːəs) *adj.* odd, unusual ‖ inquisitive, prying ‖ anxious to learn

curl (kəːrl) **1.** *v.t.* to cause to form into curls ‖ to cause to bend around ‖ *v.i.* to form into curls ‖ to assume the shape of a curl ‖ to move in spirals ‖ to play at curling **2.** *n.* a lock of hair growing in a curved or coiled shape, a ringlet ‖ anything shaped like a curl, twist or spiral **cúrl·er** *n.* a pin etc. for curling the hair ‖ a player at curling

curl·y (kə́ːrliː) *comp.* **curl·i·er** *superl.* **curl·i·est** *adj.* curling ‖ having curls ‖ (of wood) having a wavy grain

cur·rant (kə́ːrənt, kʌ́rənt) *n.* a genus of cold-climate bush fruits, with red, black or white berries, according to species ‖ a small dried grape, or from Greece, once called 'raisin of Corauntz' (Corinth)

cur·ren·cy (kə́ːrənsiː, kʌ́rənsiː) *pl.* **cur·ren·cies** *n.* the coins, notes or other tokens in circulation as a means of exchange ‖ the state of being in general use ‖ general acceptance, prevalence ‖ the time during whch something is current

cur·rent (kə́ːrənt, kʌ́rənt) *adj.* in general use ‖ prevalent ‖ of the present time

current *n.* a mass of air, water or other fluid moving in a certain direction ‖ the stream thus formed ‖ the most rapidly moving part of a river etc. ‖ electric current ‖ a general trend or direction or course of events

cur·ric·u·lum (kəríkjuləm) *pl.* **cur·ric·u·lums, cur·ric·u·la** (kəríkjulə) *n.* a course of study, esp. at a school or college ‖ a list of the courses offered at a school, college or university

cur·ry (kə́ːriː, kʌ́riː) **1.** *pl.* **cur·ries** *n.* a hot-tasting powder made from turmeric and other spices and used in meat dishes etc., esp. in India ‖ a dish flavored with this powder **2.** *v.t. pres. part.* **cur·ry·ing** *past* and *past part.* **cur·ried** to cook with curry

curry *pres. part.* **cur·ry·ing** *past* and *past part.* **cur·ried** *v.t.* to rub down and comb (a horse) ‖ to dress (tanned leather) **to curry favor** to seek favor by flattery

curse *pres. part.* **curs·ing** *past* and *past part.* **cursed, curst** *v.t.* to call for divine punishment of or utter a curse or curses on (someone) ‖ to bring harm upon ‖ to swear at ‖ *v.i.* to swear or blaspheme **curs·ed** (kə́ːrsid, kəːrst), **curst** *adj.* under a curse ‖ evil, hateful ‖ (pop., kə́ːrsid) damned

cur·so·ry (kə́ːrsəriː) *adj.* hurried, superficial

curt (kəːrt) *adj.* short in speech ‖ abrupt, impolitely brief

cur·tail (kərtéil) *v.t.* to cut short ‖ to cut off (a part) **cur·táil·ment** *n.*

cur·tain (kə́ːrt'n, kə́ːrtin) **1.** *n.* a hanging cloth used esp. to screen or adorn windows ‖ something like this ‖ the hanging drape dividing a theater stage from the auditorium ‖ the raising of this at the beginning of a play or its lowering at the end, or at the end of an act ‖ something that conceals **2.** *v.t.* to supply with curtains

curve (kəːrv) **1.** *n.* a line or direction subject to continuous deviation from the straight ‖ a thing or part shaped thus ‖ a curving ‖ an amount of curving ‖ *(baseball)* a ball pitched with spin so that it curves before passing the plate ‖ an unfair act or statement ‖ *(math.)* any line defined precisely in terms of a series of coordinates which are functions of a given equation **2.** *v. pres. part.* **curv·ing** *past* and *past parv.*
curved *v.i.* to take on the shape of a curve ‖ to move in a curved path ‖ *v.t.* to make (something) assume the shape of a curve or move in a curved path

cush·ion (kúʃən) **1.** *n.* a cloth case stuffed with down or feathers, kapok, foam rubber etc. ‖ something that resembles or serves as this ‖ something that serves as a shock absorber, e.g. the resilient lining of the sides of a billiard table ‖ the steam left in a cylinder to act as a buffer to the piston ‖ (of a pig etc.) the buttocks ‖ the soft part of a horse's foot protected by the horny hoof **2.** *v.t.* to supply with cushions ‖ to protect with cushions so as to diminish or absorb shock ‖ to shield (a person) e.g. from the full force of hostile criticism ‖ to suppress (criticism) discreetly ‖ to lean as if against a cushion ‖ *(billiards)* to leave (a ball) placed up against a cushion

cus·tard (kʌ́stərd) *n.* a sweetened mixture of eggs and milk baked or steamed ‖ a liquid form of this served as a sauce ‖ a sweetened mixture of milk and a thickening powder as a substitute for the above

cus·to·di·an (kʌstóudiːən) *n.* a guardian or keeper, esp. of some public building **cus·tó·di·an·ship** *n.*

cus·to·dy (kʌ́stədiː) *n.* guardianship, care ‖ imprisonment

cus·tom (kʌ́stəm) **1.** *n.* a generally accepted practice or habit, convention ‖ the support given to a shop or firm by dealing with it regularly ‖ *(pl.)* duties levied on imported goods ‖ *(law)* a long-established practice having the force of law **2.** *adj.* made-to-order ‖ dealing in made-to-order goods

cus·tom·ar·y (kʌ́stəmɛriː) **1.** *adj.* usual, according to custom **2.** *pl.* **cus·tom·ar·ies** *n.* a written collection of a society's customs

cus·tom·er (kÁstəmər) *n.* a person wishing to make a purchase from a store or firm ‖ someone who buys regularly from a particular store or firm ‖ *(pop.)* a person with respect to the dealings one has or may have with him

cut (kʌt) **1.** *v. pres. part.* **cut·ting** *past* and *past part.* **cut** *v.t.* to make an incision in ‖ to wound with or on something sharp ‖ to sever ‖ to separate into slices or pieces ‖ to reap ‖ to make smaller or shorter by trimming with a sharp instrument ‖ to cross, intersect ‖ to reduce ‖ to shorten ‖ to excavate ‖ to hurt (someone) in his feelings ‖ to strike (a ball) so as to put a spin on it ‖ to make, appear as ‖ to refuse to recognize (an acquaintance) ‖ to stay away from (what should be attended) ‖ to divide (a pack of playing cards) ‖ to castrate ‖ *v.i.* to make a cut ‖ to be capable of being cut ‖ to make thrashing strokes ‖ *(movies)* to cut back **2.** *n.* a gash, incision or wound ‖ a reduction ‖ an excision ‖ *(pop.)* a share ‖ a piece of meat for cooking ‖ a thrashing stroke (e.g. with a whip) ‖ a sharp glancing stroke at a ball ‖ a railroad cutting ‖ a style of fashioning clothes, hair etc. ‖ *(pop.)* a social degree ‖ a verbal attack ‖ *(printing)* a process block set in the text ‖ a woodcut **3.** *adj.* having been cut ‖ castrated ‖ reduced

cute (kju:t) *comp.* **cut·er** *superl.* **cut·est** *adj.* *(pop.)* attractive, charming ‖ *(pop.)* sharp-witted ‖ deceptively straightforward

cu·ti·cle (kjú:tik'l) *n.* the skin, esp. the outer layer or epidermis ‖ the hardened skin around the edges of fingernails and toenails ‖ *(bot.)* the superficial covering of the outer layer of epidermal cells **cu·tic·u·lar** (kju:tíkjulər) *adj.* **cu·tic·u·lar·i·zá·tion** *n.* the state of being cuticularized or the process of becoming so **cu·tic·u·lar·ized** *adj.* covered with cuticle or changed to cuticle

cut·ler·y (kÁtleri:) *n.* knives, forks and spoons used at table ‖ knives and other edged instruments (shears, razors etc.) ‖ the trade or business of a cutler

cut·let (kÁtlit) *n.* a small chop cut from the best end of mutton, lamb, veal or pork, for grilling or frying ‖ a croquette of flaked fish etc. made up into this shape

cut-rate (kÁtreit) *adj.* offered for sale at a price below the general market price, or dealing in goods offered at such prices

cut·ting (kÁtiŋ) **1.** *n.* a passage or tunnel cut through high ground for a road or railroad etc. ‖ a small shoot bearing leaf buds and used for propagation **2.** *adj.* sharp ‖ piercing, *a cutting wind* ‖ sarcastic, unkind, *cutting remarks*

cy·a·nide (sáiənaid, sáiənid) *n.* a compound of cyanogen and a metal

cy·cle (sáik'l) **1.** *n.* a series of recurring events or phenomena ‖ a period of time occupied by a set of events which will go on recurring in similar periods of time ‖ a series of poems or songs with a central theme ‖ an orbit in the heavens ‖ *(biol.)* an ordered series of phenomena in which some process is completed ‖ *(econ.)* a fluctuation showing a regular pattern ‖ the circulation of a fluid through a series of vessels ‖ *(chem.)* a ring ‖ *(phys.)* any series of changes which restores a system to its original state ‖ the period of an alternating electric current ‖ a bicycle or tricycle **2.** *v.i. pres. part.* **cy·cling** *past* and *past part.* **cy·cled** to move in cycles ‖ to ride a bicycle

cy·clic (sáiklik, síklik) *adj.* recurring in cycles ‖ of or related to a cycle ‖ *(bot.,* of a flower) with its parts arranged in a whorl ‖ *(chem.)* having some or all of the constituent atoms in ring formation ‖ *(math.)* of a figure all of whose vertices lie on a circle (è.g. a cyclic quadrilateral)

cy·clist (sáiklist) *n.* someone who rides a bicycle

cy·clone (sáikloun) *n.* a region of low atmospheric pressure characterized by rotating winds, in middle and high latitudes called a depression or low

cy·clo·tron (sáiklətrɒn, síklətrɒn) *n.* a device used to produce and focus a beam of high-energy positive ions by subjecting them to successive accelerations in a region of constant-frequency alternating electric field

cyl·in·der (sílindər) *n.* a solid figure traced out when a rectangle rotates using one of its sides as the axis of rotation ‖ a solid or hollow body having this form (esp. the chamber in which a piston is propelled by the expansion of steam or a gas mixture) ‖ the revolving part of a revolver, containing the cartridge chambers

cy·lin·dri·cal (silíndrik'l) *adj.* cylinder-shaped

cym·bal (símb'l) *n.* *(mus.)* one of a pair of shallow brass plates clashed together to make a ringing clang **cým·bal·ist** *n.*

cyn·ic (sínik) **1.** *n.* someone who believes that self-interest is the motive of all human conduct ‖ *(loosely)* a habitual scoffer **2.** *adj.* cynical thinking like a cynic or revealing such thoughts **cyn·i·cism** (sínisizəm) *n.* the quality of being cynical ‖ an expression of this quality

cy·press (sáipris) *n.* a genus of coniferous trees. The general habit is xerophytic, the leaves being much reduced and closely pressed to the stem ‖ the hard wood of these trees

cyst (sist) *n.* *(med.)* a sac containing fluid or semifluid morbid matter or parasitic larvae etc. ‖ a nonliving membrane enclosing a cell or cells ‖ *(biol.)* a hollow organ or cavity containing a liquid secretion

cyst·ic (sístik) *adj.* of or like a cyst ‖ relating to the gallbladder or urinary bladder

czar, tsar, tzar (zɑr, tsɑr) *n.* *(hist.)* the emperor of Russia

czar·e·vitch, tsar·e·vitch (zárəvitʃ, tsárəvitʃ) *n.* *(hist.)* the son of a czar

cza·ri·na, tsa·ri·na (zɑrínə, tsɑrínə) *n.* *(hist.)* the wife of a czar

D

D, d (di:) the fourth letter of the English alphabet
dab (dæb) **1.** *v. pres. part.* **dab·bing** *past and past part.* **dabbed** *v.t.* to touch lightly and quickly ‖ to apply (a substance) by light strokes ‖ *v.i.* to make a weak, ineffective striking movement **2.** *n.* a light, quick blow ‖ an applying of light, gentle pressure, esp. with a damp cloth, sponge, brush etc., the material dabbed on a surface
dab·ble (dæb'l) *pres. part.* **dab·bling** *past* and *past part.* **dab·bled** *v.t.* to splash about ‖ *v.i.* to take up a pursuit without serious and consistent effort **dáb·bler** *n.* a person who takes only superficial interest in some subject, a dillettante
daft (dæft, dɑft) *adj. (pop.)* foolish, crazy
dag·ger (dægǝr) *n.* a short, knifelike weapon for stabbing, with a sharp-edged, pointed blade
dai·ly (déili:) **1.** *adj.* happening or recurring every day **2.** *adv.* every day **3.** *pl.* **dai·lies** *n.* a newspaper appearing every weekday
dain·ty (déinti:) **1.** *pl.* **dain·ties** *n. a delicacy* **2.** *comp.* **dain·ti·er** *superl.* **dain·ti·est** *adj.* small and pretty, delicate ‖ *(rhet.)* choice
dair·y (déǝri:) *pl.* **dair·ies** *n.* the part of a farm given over to milk, cream, butter, cheese etc. ‖ a shop where milk, butter and cream etc. are sold
da·is (déiis, dáiis) *pl.* **da·is·es** *n.* a raised platform in a hall or large room
dai·sy (déizi:) *pl.* **dai·sies** *n.* any of several composite plants having flower heads that consist of a whorl or several whorls of ray florets
dale (deil) *n. (rhet.)* a valley
dal·li·ance (dæli:ǝns, dæljǝns) *n. (rhet.)* amorous by-play ‖ *(rhet.)* frivolous spending of time
dal·ly (dæli:) *pres. part.* **dal·ly·ing** *past* and *past part.* **dal·lied** *v.i.* to waste time ‖ to loiter ‖ to toy, play
dam (dæm) **1.** *n.* a barrier constructed to hold back a flow of water in order to raise its level ‖ a reservoir of water held back by such a barrier **2.** *v.t. pres. part.* **dam·ming** *past* and *past part.* **dammed** to hold back (water) by constructing a dam
dam·age (dæmidʒ) **1.** *v. pres. part.* **dam·ag·ing** *past* and *past part.* **dam·aged** *v.t.* to injure physically (usually objects) ‖ *v.i.* to incur damage **2.** *n.* injury or harm ‖ *(pl., law)* a money compensation for harm sustained **dám·age·a·ble** *adj.*
damn (dæm) **1.** *v.t.* to condemn ‖ to bring ruin upon ‖ to condemn to eternal punishment ‖ to curse **2.** *n.* 'damn' said as a curse **3.** *adv.* damned
dam·na·ble (dæmnǝb'l) *adj.* deserving condemnation ‖ detestable ‖ annoying
dam·na·tion (dæmnéiʃǝn) **1.** *n. (theol.)* a condemning or being condemned to eternal punishment ‖ a complete critical condemnation (of a play etc.) **2.** *interj.* an expression of annoyance
damp (dæmp) **1.** *n.* moisture in a permeable object, esp. a fabric ‖ moisture on the surface of a solid object ‖ moisture in the air **2.** *adj.* slightly wet ‖ impregnated with moisture **3.** *v.t.* to make slightly wet, moisten ‖ *(mus.)* to stop the vibration of (a string) ‖ to discourage **dámp·en** *v.t.* (esp. *Am.*) to make slightly wet, moisten ‖ to depress, discourage ‖ *v.i.* (esp. *Am.*) to become damp **dámp·er** *n.*
dance (dæns, dɑns) *n.* the act of dancing ‖ a series of set movements to music ‖ a party or social gathering at which the guests dance
dance *pres. part.* **danc·ing** *past* and *past part.* **danced**

v.i. to move rhythmically, alone or with a partner or other dancers ‖ to move in a lively or excited way ‖ to move quickly up and down, bounce ‖ *v.t.* to dandle
danc·er (dænsǝr, dánsǝr) *n.* a person dancing ‖ a person who makes his/her living by dancing in public, in ballet, musical comedy etc.
dan·de·li·on (dænd'laiǝn) *n.* a perennial, almost cosmopolitan plant with a thick primary root and a very short sympodial stem
dan·druff (dændrǝf) *n.* small scales of dead skin on the scalp, scurf
dan·ger (déindʒǝr) *n.* peril, exposure to harm, injury, loss, esp. loss of life ‖ a thing or circumstance that constitutes a peril
dan·gle (dæng'l) *pres. part.* **dan·gling** *past* and *past part.* **dan·gled** *v.i.* to be hanging loosely ‖ *v.t.* to cause to swing lightly to and fro
dank (dæŋk) *adj.* cold and damp ‖ smelling unpleasantly of damp
dap·per (dæpǝr) *adj.* (esp. of short, middle-aged men) neat and spruce in appearance
dap·ple (dæp'l) **1.** *adj.* dappled **2.** *pres. part.* **dap·pling** *past* and *past part.* **dap·pled** *v.t.* to mark with irregular spots or patches of color
dap·pled (dæp'ld) *adj.* marked with irregular spots or patches of color
dare (deǝr) **1.** *v.i. pres. part.* **dar·ing** *past* and *past part.* **dared** to have enough courage ‖ to have enough impudence ‖ *v.t.* to challenge (someone) to do something as test of courage ‖ *(rhet.)* to brave (e.g. someone's wrath) ‖ (as a verbal auxiliary) to have the courage to **2.** *n.* a challenge to do something as a test of courage
dar·ing (déǝriŋ) **1.** *n.* bravery **2.** *adj.* adventurous ‖ boldly unconventional
dark (dɑrk) **1.** *adj.* partly or totally devoid of light ‖ dispiriting, gloomy ‖ (of color) of a deep shade ‖ (of people) having dark hair, eyes and (often) skin ‖ very unpromising ‖ *(rhet.)* obscure ‖ mysterious ‖ *(pop.)* secretive **2.** *n.* a total absence of light ‖ bad light ‖ night ‖ dark color, esp. in painting **3.** *v.t.* to make dark
dar·ling (dárliŋ) **1.** *n.* a beloved person **2.** *adj.* loved dearly ‖ lovable
darn (dɑrn) **1.** *v.t.* to damn **2.** *interj.* damn! **3.** *n.* a damn **4.** *adj.* confounded, damnable **darned 1.** *adj.* confounded, damnable **2.** *adv.* extremely
dart (dɑrt) **1.** *n. (hist.)* a sharply-pointed light missile, a javelin, arrow etc. ‖ a feathered and pointed object thrown in the game of darts ‖ a sudden swift movement ‖ *(archit.)* an element of the ancient egg and dart pattern ‖ *(sewing)* a short, tapering tuck made to fit a garment to the figure **2.** *v.i.* to move swiftly and suddenly ‖ *v.t.* to aim (a glance, look) swiftly and suddenly
dash (dæʃ) **1.** *v.t.* to smash, shatter ‖ to throw violently ‖ to splash ‖ *v.i.* (of people and vehicles) to go in a great hurry ‖ to discourage, disappoint **2.** *(Br., pop.)* damn! **3.** *n.* a rush, sudden movement ‖ a sprint ‖ a punctuation mark (—) used to denote a break or an omission or (in pairs) parentheses ‖ a small amount ‖ the sound of water striking a solid object violently, e.g. waves on a cliff ‖ verve, spirited attack or stylish vigor in behavior or public performance ‖ a quick stroke (of the pen)
dash·board (dæʃbɔrd, dæʃbourd) *n.* the instrument panel

---

of a car, boat etc. ‖ a panel at the front or sides of a boat, carriage etc. to protect against splashing

das·tard (dǽstərd) **1.** *n.* a coward ‖ a cad **2.** *adj.* cowardly and mean **dás·tard·ly** *adj.*

date (deit) **1.** *n.* the day of the month and year, or sometimes the year only ‖ this as written or printed information on a letter, newspaper etc. ‖ *(pl.)* the years of birth and death of a person, or the length of rule of a king etc. ‖ an appointment, esp. with a person of the opposite sex ‖ *(pop.)* a person of the opposite sex with whom an appointment is made **2.** *v. pres. part.* **dat·ing** *past* and *past part.* **dat·ed** *v.t.* to write a date on ‖ to assign a date to ‖ to make an appointment with (someone of the opposite sex) ‖ to reveal the full age of ‖ *v.i.* to make a reckoning from some point in time ‖ to extend back in time ‖ to become old-fashioned **dáte·a·ble** *adj.* **dát·ed** *adj.* bearing a date ‖ outmoded **dáte·less** *adj.* undated ‖ so ancient as to be undatable

daub (dɔb) **1.** *v.t.* to apply a coating of (soft, sticky material) ‖ to coat thickly and unevenly ‖ to apply (color or coloring matter) carelessly or insensitively, esp. too thickly ‖ *v.i.* to paint a picture unskillfully **2.** *n.* any soft sticky material for coating an object ‖ a smear

daugh·ter (dɔ́tər) *n.* a female human being in relation to her parents ‖ *(rhet.)* the females of a race or country ‖ *(rhet.)* a woman whose character has been molded by a particular event or set of circumstances

daugh·ter-in-law (dɔ́tərinlɔ) *pl.* **daugh·ters-in-law** *n.* a son's wife

daugh·ter·ly (dɔ́tərli:) *adj.* of, like or proper in a daughter

daunt (dɔnt, dɑnt) *v.t.* to intimidate, fill with dismay **dáunt·less** *adj.* fearless, intrepid ‖ (of courage) unshaken

daw·dle (dɔ́d'l) *pres. part.* **daw·dling** *past* and *past part.* **daw·dled** *v.i.* to walk, or do a job, very slowly and lazily ‖ *v.t.* (with 'away') to waste (time) in idling

dawn (dɔn) **1.** *n.* the first light of day, daybreak ‖ the first sign of something **2.** *v.i.* (of day) to begin to grow light

day (dei) *n.* the time during which the sun is above the horizon ‖ a day as a point of time or date ‖ a day as marking some event ‖ (esp. *pl.*) a period of time ‖ *(pl.)* one's whole lifetime ‖ (with possessive adj.) a time when things go well ‖ without seeking to plan ahead

day·break (déibreik) *n.* dawn

day·dream (déidri:m) **1.** *n.* a reverie ‖ a wish or plan not likely to be realized **2.** *v.i.* to indulge in such fancies

daze (deiz) **1.** *v.t. pres. part.* **daz·ing** *past* and *past part.* **dazed** to bewilder, confuse or stun, by a blow, fear, surprise or grief **2.** *n.* a dazed state

daz·zle (dǽz'l) **1.** *v.t. pres. part.* **daz·zling** *past* and *past part.* **daz·zled** to confuse the vision of (a person) with bright light ‖ to blind mentally ‖ to impress by brilliant display **2.** *n.* light that dazzles **dáz·zle·ment** *n.*

dea·con (díːkən) *n.* *(eccles.)* a member of the clergy next in order below a priest, whom he assists

dead (ded) **1.** *adj.* (of animals and plants) in a state of complete and permanent cessation of vital functions ‖ inanimate, having no life ‖ having no feeling, movement or activity ‖ insensitive, hardened, *dead to feelings of remorse* ‖ no longer used ‖ inert ‖ lacking resonance ‖ *(pop.)* very tired ‖ *(elec.)* uncharged ‖ not in play or in operation **2.** *n.* **the dead** all dead persons or a dead person **3.** *adv.* completely, thoroughly

dead end a road closed at one end, a cul-de-sac ‖ a job or any situation without hope of betterment **déad-énd** *adj.* of such a road or job ‖ characteristic of, or living in, the slums

dead·ly (dédli:) **1.** *comp.* **dead·li·er** *superl.* **dead·li·est** *adj.* causing or capable of causing death or serious injury ‖ implacable ‖ deathlike ‖ *(pop.)* boring ‖ caus-ing spiritual death **2.** *adv.* intensely, *deadly dull*

deaf (def) **1.** *adj.* wholly or partly deprived of the sense of hearing ‖ unwilling to listen, obstinate **2.** *n.* **the deaf** deaf people

deaf-mute (défmjúːt) *n.* a person who is deaf and dumb

deal (diːl) **1.** *v. pres. part.* **deal·ing** *past* and *past part.* **dealt** (delt) *v.t.* to apportion, distribute among a number, esp. to distribute (cards) among cardplayers ‖ (with 'in') to engage in buying and selling some commodity ‖ (with 'with') to make a business transaction, have business relations ‖ (with 'with') to do what is necessary to meet a situation ‖ (with 'with') to treat a topic, have as subject ‖ (with 'with') to treat a person, esp. to punish him **2.** *n.* the distribution of cards, before a game ‖ treatment measured out to a person, by someone else or by fate ‖ a business transaction ‖ an illegal transaction advantageous to all transacting parties **déal·er** *n.* someone who buys and sells some commodity ‖ a cardplayer dealing the cards

dean (diːn) *n.* *(eccles.)* the head of the chapter of a cathedral or collegiate church ‖ the senior member (in length of service) of a body, the doyen

dear (diər) **1.** *n.* a loved or lovable person **2.** *adj.* a polite form of address for beginning letters, *Dear Sir* ‖ precious, cherished ‖ won at great cost **3.** *adv.* *(rhet.)* at a high price ‖ *(rhet.)* very affectionately **4.** *interj.* an exclamation of surprise, dismay or mild sympathy **déar·ly** *adv.* very affectionately ‖ expensively or at a great cost ‖ keenly, earnestly

death (deθ) *n.* a dying, the end of life ‖ the state of being dead ‖ an end, destruction ‖ a cause of death

de·ba·cle (deibάk'l, deibǽk'l, dəbάk'l, dəbǽk'l) *n.* a disastrous confusion, e.g. a complete military defeat, collapse

de·bar (dibάr) *pres. part.* **de·bar·ring** *past* and *past part.* **de·barred** *v.t.* to exclude from entry, esp. to some privilege, position or right

de·bat·a·ble (dibéitəb'l) *adj.* not decided, questionable ‖ subject to dispute

de·bate (dibéit) **1.** *v. pres. part.* **de·bat·ing** *past* and *past part.* **de·bat·ed** *v.t.* to discuss (a question) thoroughly, esp. at a public meeting or in government ‖ to consider (something requiring a decision) in one's mind ‖ *v.i.* to hold a formal discussion under rules of procedure **2.** *n.* discussion or a discussion, esp. a public one ‖ controversy

de·bauch (dibɔ́tʃ) **1.** *v.t.* to corrupt (a person) **2.** *n.* a bout of excessive self-indulgence in sensual pleasures

de·bauch·er·y (dibɔ́tʃəri:) *pl.* **de·bauch·er·ies** *n.* excessive indulgence in sensual pleasures

de·bil·i·tate (dibíliteit) *pres. part.* **de·bil·i·tat·ing** *past* and *past part.* **de·bil·i·tat·ed** *v.t.* to weaken (the body)

de·bil·i·ty (dibíliti:) *pl.* **de·bil·i·ties** *n.* physical weakness, feebleness, or an instance of this

deb·it (débit) **1.** *n.* the account book entry of a sum owed ‖ the left-hand page of an account book where debts are recorded **2.** *v.t.* to charge up (goods or an account)

deb·o·nair, deb·o·naire (dèbənɛ́ər) *adj.* (esp. of young men) having attractive manners and vitality

de·bouch (dibúːʃ, dibáutʃ) *v.i.* (of people) to emerge ‖ (of a stream) to flow from a narrow course into a lake, the sea etc. **de·bóuch·ment** *n.*

de·bris (dəbríː, déibri) *n.* the remnants of something broken to pieces ‖ broken pieces of rock detached, transported and then deposited by a rush of water, or detached from a cliff and accumulating where they fall

debt (det) *n.* something, esp. money, owed to another ‖ the state of owing

debt·or (détər) *n.* a person who owes money or service

de·but, dé·but (deibjúː, deibjúː) *n.* the first public appearance of someone (esp. an actor) ‖ the first formal presentation of a debutante in society

deb·u·tante, déb·u·tante (débjutɑnt, débjutænt) *n.* a girl making her first appearances at formal social functions

dec·ade (dékeid) *n.* a period of 10 years ‖ a series or group of 10

dec·a·dence (dékədəns, dikéid'ns) *n.* a falling away, decline **déc·a·dent 1.** *adj.* deteriorating ‖ falling to lower standards **2.** *n.* a person of low moral standards ‖ a person excessively civilized, at the cost of moral energy

de·cal·co·ma·ni·a (dikælkəméini:ə, dikælkəméinjə) *n.* the process of transferring specially prepared colored images from paper to porcelain, paper, glass, metal etc. ‖ such an image

de·cay (dikéi) **1.** *v.i.* (of a substance) to lose gradually its original form, quality or value ‖ to decrease in activity, force or quality, as in the spontaneous breakdown of radioactive material ‖ to fall into disrepair or great shabbiness ‖ to lose strength of quality **2.** *n.* the state or process of decaying

de·cease (disí:s) **1.** *n.* (in legal or formal contexts) death **2.** *v.i. pres. part.* **de·ceas·ing** *past* and *past part.* **de·ceased** to die **the de·céased** *n.* the dead person or persons

de·ceit (disí:t) *n.* a deceiving ‖ deception, guile ‖ a trick, fraud **de·céit·ful** *adj.*

de·ceive (disí:v) *pres. part.* **de·ceiv·ing** *past* and *past part.* **de·ceived** *v.t.* to make (someone) believe what is false ‖ to mislead ‖ to break faith with

De·cem·ber (disémbər) *(abbr.* **Dec.)** *n.* the 12th and last month of the year, having 31 days

de·cen·cy (dí:sənsi:) *pl.* **de·cen·cies** *n.* the quality or state of being decent ‖ accepted standards as regards propriety in language, behavior or modesty

de·cep·tion (disépʃən) *n.* a tricking, deceiving ‖ the state of being deceived ‖ something that deceives or tricks, a hoax, imposture

de·cep·tive (diséptiv) *adj.* misleading

de·cide (disáid) *pres. part.* **de·cid·ing** *past* and *past part.* **de·cid·ed** *v.i.* to choose ‖ to determine ‖ *v.t.* to bring to a decision ‖ to settle (a question or dispute) **de·cíd·ed** *adj.* clearly marked, distinct ‖ (of personality or opinions) vigorous and determined **de·cíd·ed·ly** *adv.*

dec·i·mal (désəməl) *adj.* relating to 10 ‖ of a number scale based on 10, and using multiples and submultiples of 10, *the decimal system*

de·ci·pher (disáifər) *v.t.* to put (a text transmitted in cipher) into plain writing ‖ to find out the meaning of, interpret (bad writing, hieroglyphics etc.) **de·cí·pher·a·ble** *adj.* **de·cí·pher·ment** *n.*

de·ci·sion (disíʒən) *n.* a making up of one's mind ‖ the result of making up one's mind ‖ resoluteness, *a man of decision*

de·ci·sive (disáisiv) *adj.* conclusive ‖ showing resoluteness

deck (dek) *n.* a floor in a ship ‖ *(computer)* means of storing information for future use, e.g., magnetic tape ‖ strip of material on which data can be recorded ‖ *(Am.)* a pack of playing cards **on deck** above the lower decks, in the open air

deck *v.t.* to array ‖ (often with 'out') to dress (oneself) in a fine or fancy way

dec·la·ra·tion (dɛklǝréiʃǝn) *n.* an act of declaring ‖ a manifesto ‖ a document formalizing matters to be made known publicly ‖ an announcement or affirmation ‖ a solemn statement made by the plaintiff or witnesses instead of the oath, but equally binding

de·clare (diklέǝr) *pres. part.* **de·clar·ing** *past* and *past part.* **de·clared** *v.t.* to make known explicitly or formally, announce ‖ to cause to be paid out ‖ to pronounce (a person) to be (something) ‖ to affirm or protest strongly ‖ to state (dutiable goods) in one's possession ‖ to give particulars of (income liable to tax etc.) ‖ *(bridge)* to name (the trump suit) ‖ *v.i.*

(with 'against' or 'for') to take sides, vote **de·cláred** *adj.* stated ‖ professed **de·clár·er** *n.* (esp. at cards)

de·cline (dikláin) **1.** *v. pres. part.* **de·clin·ing** *past* and *past part.* **de·clined** *v.t.* to refuse ‖ *(gram.)* to inflect (a noun, adjective, pronoun) ‖ *v.i.* to lose vigor, deteriorate ‖ to refuse ‖ to fall off, diminish (e.g. of prices or numbers) ‖ to slope downwards ‖ *(rhet.,* of the sun or of the day) to begin to go down or draw toward the close **2.** *n.* a falling off, loss of vigor, sinking or deterioration ‖ a fall in price or number ‖ a downward slope ‖ a refusal ‖ *(rhet.,* of the sun or the day) a progress downward or toward a close

de·com·pose (di:kǝmpóuz) *pres. part.* **de·com·pos·ing** *past* and *past part.* **de·com·posed** *v.i.* to break up into component parts or elements ‖ to disintegrate, rot ‖ *v.t.* to cause to break up into component parts or elements ‖ to cause to rot **de·com·po·si·tion** (di:kɒmpǝzíʃǝn) *n.*

de·con·trol (di:kǝntróul) **1.** *v.t. pres. part.* **de·con·trol·ling** *past* and *past part.* **de·con·trolled** to release from control **2.** *n.* a release from control

dec·o·rate (dékǝreit) *pres. part.* **dec·o·rat·ing** *past* and *past part.* **dec·o·rat·ed** *v.t.* to add something ornamental to, adorn ‖ to honor (someone) with a medal, ribbon etc.

dec·o·ra·tion (dekǝréiʃǝn) *n.* a decorating ‖ something decorative ‖ a ribbon or medal etc. awarded for bravery, service etc.

dec·o·ra·tive (dékǝrǝtiv, dékrǝtiv) *adj.* serving to decorate

dec·o·ra·tor (dékǝreitǝr) *n.* someone who professionally plans interior decoration schemes

de·coy (dikɔ́i, dí:kɔi) **1.** *n.* a real or imitation bird or animal used to lure other birds or animals to a place where they may be trapped or shot ‖ the place into which animals are lured ‖ a person or thing used as a trap **2.** *v.t.* to lure successfully

de·crease (dí:kri:s, dikrí:s) *n.* a diminishing ‖ the amount by which something is diminished **on the decrease** lessening

de·crease (dikrí:s) *pres. part.* **de·creas·ing** *past* and *past part.* **de·creased** *v.i.* to grow less, diminish, dwindle ‖ *v.t.* to make less or smaller

de·cree (dikrí:) **1.** *n.* an order made by a ruling body or other authority **2.** *pres. part.* **de·cree·ing** *past* and *past part.* **de·creed** *v.t.* to appoint or order by decree ‖ (of fate) to ordain ‖ *v.i.* to issue a decree

de·crep·it (dikrépit) *adj.* made dilapidated or extremely weak by age or illness

de·cry (dikrái) *pres. part.* **de·cry·ing** *past* and *past part.* **de·cried** *v.t.* to disparage, attack in speech

ded·i·cate (dédikeit) *pres. part.* **ded·i·cat·ing** *past* and *past part.* **ded·i·cat·ed** *v.t.* to devote to any serious purpose **ded·i·ca·tee** (dedikǝtí:) *n.* the person to whom a thing is dedicated

ded·i·ca·tion (dedikéiʃǝn) *n.* the act or rite of dedicating ‖ an inscription in a book or on a building etc. as a tribute to a person or persons

de·duce (didú:s, didjú:s) *pres. part.* **de·duc·ing** *past* and *past part.* **de·duced** *v.t.* to infer by reasoning from known facts ‖ to trace the descent or derivation of

de·duct (didʌ́kt) *v.t.* to subtract, take (an amount) away **de·dúct·i·ble** *adj.* able to be deducted, esp. as a tax allowance

de·duc·tion (didʌ́kʃǝn) *n.* a subtracting or taking away ‖ the amount deducted ‖ reasoning in which the conclusion follows necessarily from given premises ‖ the conclusion reached in this way

deed (di:d) **1.** *n.* something done, an act ‖ a brave or otherwise outstanding feat ‖ actual performance as opposed to mere words ‖ *(law)* a sealed written or printed agreement containing some transfer or other

---

(**a**) æ, c*a*t; ɑ, c*a*r; ɔ f*a*wn; ei, sn*a*ke. (**e**) e, h*e*n; i:, sh*ee*p; iǝ, d*ee*r; εǝ, b*ea*r. (**i**) i, f*i*sh; ai, t*i*ger; ǝ:, b*i*rd. (**o**) o, *o*x; au, c*ow*; ou, g*oa*t; u, p*oo*r; ɔi, r*oy*al. (**u**) ʌ, d*u*ck; u, b*u*ll; u:, g*oo*se; ǝ, b*a*cillus; ju:, c*u*be. x, lo*ch*; θ, *th*ink; ð, bo*th*er; z, *Z*en; ʒ, corsa*g*e; dʒ, sava*g*e; ŋ, oranguta*ng*; j, *y*ak; ʃ, fi*sh*; tʃ, fe*tch*; 'l, rabb*le*; 'n, redd*en*. Complete pronunciation key appears inside front cover.

contract **2.** *v.t.* *(law)* to convey or transfer by deed

deem (di:m) *v.t.* to consider as true in the impossibility of proving ‖ to come to believe

deep (di:p) **1.** *adj.* extending far down below the surface ‖ extending to a specified extent downwards ‖ plunged in ‖ wide, extending back ‖ completely absorbed ‖ heartfelt ‖ well concealed ‖ thorough ‖ profound ‖ (of colors) dark and intense ‖ low-pitched ‖ (of a person) hard to make out, inscrutably clever and perhaps cunning ‖ (of a remark etc.) suggesting aspects of truth not at once apparent **2.** *adv.* profoundly, deeply ‖ far down, *to dig deep* **3.** *n.* a deep part of a body of water, esp. an ocean channel **deep·en** *v.t.* to make deep or deeper ‖ *v.i.* to become deep or deeper

deer (diər) *pl.*, **deer, deers** *n.* ruminant mammal found almost universally except in much of Africa and in Australia

de·face (diféis) *pres. part.* **de·fac·ing** *past* and *past part.* **de·faced** *v.t.* to disfigure, spoil the appearance of ‖ to make illegible **de·face·ment** *n.*

de·fame (diféim) *pres. part.* **de·fam·ing** *past* and *past part.* **de·famed** *v.t.* to attack the good reputation of (someone)

de·fault (difɔ́lt) **1.** *n.* a failure to carry out an obligation ‖ failure to pay a debt ‖ (sports) failure to take part in or finish a contest **2.** *v.t.* to declare (someone) in default and enter judgment against him ‖ (sports) to fail to take part in or finish (a contest) ‖ to forfeit (a contest) by such a failure ‖ *v.i.* to be guilty of default **de·fault·er** *n.* someone who defaults

de·feat (difí:t) **1.** *n.* an overcoming or being overcome in war, sport or argument ‖ frustration, prevention from success **2.** *v.t.* to conquer in war, sport or argument ‖ to frustrate

de·fect (dífekt, difékt) **1.** *n.* a shortcoming, inadequacy ‖ a fault, blemish **2.** *v.i.* (difékt) to desert ‖ to fall away from a cause or party

de·fec·tion (difékʃən) *n.* a falling or breaking away, e.g. from a party, allegiance or religion

de·fec·tive (diféktiv) **1.** *adj.* having faults ‖ incomplete **2.** *n.* a person noticeably subnormal either physically or mentally

de·fec·tor (diféktər) *n.* someone who defects

de·fend (difénd) *v.t.* to protect from danger, slander, criticism etc. ‖ to justify ‖ (law) to plead in court on behalf of (someone) ‖ *v.i.* to plead for the defense

de·fend·ant (diféndənt) **1.** *n.* (law) the accused person in a case **2.** *adj.* (law) being the accused

de·fend·er (diféndər) *n.* someone who protects from attack ‖ (sport) the holder of a championship or other title, defending it against the challenger

de·fense (diféns) *n.* the act of resisting attack ‖ preparation to meet attack ‖ something which defends ‖ (pl., mil.) fortifications ‖ an answer ‖ (law) the defendant's denial or plea and proceedings in court **de·fense·less** *adj.*

de·fer (difɔ́:r) *pres. part.* **de·fer·ring** *past* and *past part.* **de·ferred** *v.t.* to postpone ‖ *v.i.* to put off taking action **de·fer·a·ble** *adj.*

defer *pres. part.* **de·fer·ring** *past* and *past part.* **de·ferred** *v.i.* (followed by 'to') to allow someone else's opinion, judgment etc. to have more weight than one's own, willing or politely

def·er·ence (défərəns) *n.* polite regard for someone else's wishes, ideas etc. ‖ respectful submission **in deference to** out of submissive respect for

de·fer·ment (difɔ́:rmənt) *n.* postponement

de·fi·ance (difáiəns) *n.* a deliberate challenge (to authority) by disobedience ‖ a fierce, contemptuous opposition ‖ a deliberate disregarding

de·fi·ant (difáiənt) *adj.* showing defiance

de·fi·cien·cy (difíʃənsi:) *pl.* **de·fi·cien·cies** *n.* a lack ‖ a shortage ‖ the quality or state of being deficient

de·fi·cient (difíʃənt) *adj.* lacking something which should be present ‖ below essential requirements ‖ below normal standards

def·i·cit (défisit) *n.* a financial accounting loss

de·file (difáil) *pres. part.* **de·fil·ing** *past* and *past part.* **de·filed** *v.t.* to desecrate or make ritually unclean, to profane ‖ to corrupt morally **de·file·ment** *n.*

de·fine (difáin) *pres. part.* **de·fin·ing** *past* and *past part.* **de·fined** *v.t.* to state the precise meaning of ‖ to formulate or describe precisely ‖ to mark the limits of ‖ to outline clearly

def·i·nite (définit) *adj.* clear, not vague ‖ limiting ‖ limited **def·i·nite·ly 1.** *adv.* exactly **2.** *interj.* (pop.) yes, certainly

def·i·ni·tion (definíʃən) *n.* an act of defining ‖ a set of words explaining the meaning e.g. of a word, scientific principle or property ‖ clearness of detail, esp. of the image given by a lens in a photograph, or on a television screen

de·fin·i·tive (difínitiv) *adj.* serving to define ‖ decisive, final ‖ most authoritative

de·flate (difléit) *pres. part.* **de·flat·ing** *past* and *past part.* **de·flat·ed** *v.t.* to let air or gas out of ‖ (fig.) to cause to shrink suddenly ‖ to reduce from an inflated condition ‖ *v.i.* to lose shape or rigidity through the escape of air or gas **de·flá·tion** *n.* **de·fla·tion·a·ry** (difléiʃəneri:) *adj.*

de·flect (diflékt) *v.t.* to bend or turn aside ‖ *v.i.* to deviate from a course

de·form (difɔ́rm) *v.t.* to disfigure ‖ to spoil the form or essential quality of ‖ (phys.) to subject to deformation ‖ *v.i.* to become deformed, changed in shape

de·for·ma·tion (di:fɔrméiʃən, defərméiʃən) *n.* a deforming or being deformed ‖ (phys.) an alteration of size or shape ‖ the process by which this occurs

de·form·i·ty (difɔ́rmiti:) *pl.* **de·form·i·ties** *n.* the state or quality of being deformed ‖ a misshapen part of the body

de·fraud (difrɔ́d) *v.t.* to cheat (someone) of some right or property

de·fray (difréi) *v.t.* to pay or settle (costs or expenses) **de·fráy·al, de·fráy·ment** *ns*

de·frost (difrɔ́st, difrɔ́st) *v.t.* to rid of ice or frost ‖ *v.i.* to become free of ice or frost **de·fróst·er** *n.* a device for freeing from frost or ice

deft (deft) *adj.* quick and neat ‖ clever, quick-witted

de·funct (difʌ́ŋkt) **1.** *adj.* (of people) dead ‖ (of things) extinct

de·fuse (di:fjú:z) *v.* to alleviate a tense or dangerous situation —**defusor** *n.*

de·fy (difái) *pres. part.* **de·fy·ing** *past* and *past part.* **de·fied** *v.t.* to challenge (someone) to do or prove something ‖ to disobey openly ‖ to resist successfully

de·gen·er·ate 1. (didʒénəreit) *v.i.* *pres. part.* **de·gen·er·at·ing** *past* and *past part.* **de·gen·er·at·ed** to lose former or characteristic qualities to one's detriment, to decline mentally or morally ‖ to grow much worse **2.** (biol.) to change to a less specialized or functionally less active form ‖ (med., of a tissue or organ) to become enfeebled or impaired **2.** (didʒénərit) *adj.* having lost former or characteristic qualities, degraded ‖ (biol., pathol.) showing degeneration **3.** (didʒénərit) *n.* a degenerate person, animal, tissue etc.

deg·ra·da·tion (degrədéiʃən) *n.* a degrading or being degraded

de·grade (digréid, di:gréid) *pres. part.* **de·grad·ing** *past* and *past part.* **de·grad·ed** *v.t.* to lower esp. in rank or degree ‖ to debase morally ‖ *v.i.* (chem.) to change in this way ‖ to become lower in grade **de·grád·ing** *adj.*

de·gree (digrí:) *n.* a step or stage in an ascending or descending series or process ‖ a step in line of descent ‖ a relative amount ‖ a measure of intensity or gravity ‖ (rhet.) social rank ‖ (law) a gradation of criminality ‖ a grade or title conferred to mark academic achievement ‖ (gram.) one of three grades in the comparison of adjectives and adverbs ‖ (phys., symbol °) a division of a scale of measurement ‖ (algebra) the power to which a term is raised

de·hy·drate (di:háidreit) *pres. part.* **de·hy·drat·ing** *past* and *past part.* **de·hy·drat·ed** *v.t.* to remove water from (esp. foodstuffs)

de·i·fy (díːifai) *pres. part.* **de·i·fy·ing** *past* and *past part.* **de·i·fied** *v.t.* to make a god of, treat as a god

deign (dein) *v.i.* (with 'to') to condescend ‖ *v.t. (rhet.)* to condescend to give

de·i·ty (díːiti:) *pl.* **de·i·ties** *n.* a god or goddess ‖ the state of being divine **the Deity** God

de·ject·ed (didʒéktid) *adj.* cast down in spirits

de·jec·tion (didʒékʃən) *n.* depression, lowness of spirits

de·lay (diléi) *n.* an unexpected lapse of time

delay *v.t.* to cause to be late ‖ to hinder the progress of ‖ to postpone ‖ *v.i.* to fail to make haste

de·lec·ta·ble (diléktəbˈl) *adj. (rhet.)* delightful to the mind or the senses

del·e·gate (déligeit) *pres. part.* **del·e·gat·ing** *past* and *past part.* **del·e·gat·ed** *v.t.* to appoint as a representative ‖ to give up (some degree of one's powers) to another

del·e·gate (déligit, déligeit) *n.* an official representative of some larger body ‖ someone given power to act for another

del·e·ga·tion (dẹligéiʃən) *n.* the entrusting of authority ‖ a delegacy, body of delegates

de·lete (dilíːt) *pres. part.* **de·let·ing** *past* and *past part.* **de·let·ed** *v.t.* to cross out, erase

de·le·tion (dilíːʃən) *n.* the act of deleting ‖ the thing deleted

de·lib·er·ate (dilíbərit) *adj.* made or done intentionally ‖ slow and careful

de·lib·er·ate (dilíbəreit) *pres. part.* **de·lib·er·at·ing** *past* and *past part.* **de·lib·er·at·ed** *v.i.* to think out a matter with proper care ‖ *v.t.* to think (something) out in this way

de·lib·er·a·tion (dilibəréiʃən) *n.* careful consideration, a weighing of reasons for and against ‖ formal discussion or consultation

del·i·ca·cy (délikəsi:) *pl.* **del·i·ca·cies** *n.* fineness of quality ‖ sensitivity ‖ mechanical sensitivity, fineness of adjustment etc. ‖ fine fragility ‖ susceptibility to disease, constitutional weakness ‖ something to eat of rare ōr fine quality

del·i·cate (délikit) *adj.* finely made ‖ very fragile ‖ needing careful handling ‖ requiring great tact and reflection ‖ requiring fine technique ‖ (of colors) soft or subdued ‖ subtle ‖ exquisitely considerate ‖ (of distinctions) finely graduated ‖ (of mechanisms or instruments) of great precision ‖ sheltered ‖ tending to become tired or ill easily ‖ (of health) weak, precarious ‖ (of food) choice

del·i·ca·tes·sen (dẹlikətésˈn) *n.* a shop selling prepared foods ‖ the foods sold there

de·li·cious (dilíʃəs) *adj.* delightful, giving pleasure esp. to the taste, smell, or sense of humor

de·light (diláit) *v.t.* to please very much ‖ *v.i.* (with 'in') to take great pleasure

delight *n.* great pleasure ‖ something which gives such pleasure

de·lin·e·ate (dilíni:eit) *pres. part.* **de·lin·e·at·ing** *past* and *past part.* **de·lin·e·at·ed** *v.t.* to show by drawing, or by outlining in words **de·lin·e·á·tion, de·lín·e·a·tor** ns

de·lin·quen·cy (dilíŋkwənsi:) *pl.* **de·lin·quen·cies** *n.* wrongdoing ‖ an action going against the law ‖ guilt ‖ a fault, e.g. with respect to duty

de·lin·quent (dilíŋkwənt) **1.** *adj.* guilty of wrongdoing ‖ guilty of a fault, e.g in respect of duty **2.** *n.* a delinquent person

de·lir·i·ous (dilíri:əs) *adj.* in a state of delirium, raving ‖ *(loosely)* wildly excited, in an ecstasy of joy

de·lir·i·um (dilíri:əm) *pl.* **de·lir·i·ums, de·lir·i·a**

(dilíri:ə) *n.* a temporary disorder of the mind marked by incoherent speech, ravings, hallucinations ‖ wild excitement or ecstasy

de·liv·er (dilívər) *v.t.* to distribute (mail) ‖ to transport ‖ to convey (something) to the person to whom it is destined ‖ to assist (a woman) to give birth ‖ to rescue ‖ to utter, pronounce (a speech, etc.) to an audience ‖ to declaim in a specified manner ‖ to aim, strike (a blow, attack, etc.) ‖ (with 'up', 'over') to yield

de·liv·er·ance (dilívərəns) *n.* a rescuing or setting free ‖ the state of being rescued or set free ‖ a pompous and emphatically expressed opinion

de·liv·er·y (dilívəri:) *pl.* **de·liv·er·ies** *n.* the act of giving birth ‖ a distribution, esp. of mail ‖ the transporting of merchandise on purchasers' instructions ‖ the declaiming of a speech, lecture, etc. ‖ the manner of doing this ‖ a rescuing or setting free ‖ something delivered

del·ta (déltə) *n.* the fourth letter (Δ, δ) of the Greek alphabet ‖ a low tract of alluvial land formed by the precipitation of river mud when the river water meets the tidal seawater **del·ta·ic** (deltéiik) *adj.*

de·lude (dilúːd) *pres. part.* **de·lud·ing** *past* and *past part.* **de·lud·ed** *v.t.* to cause (someone, oneself) to believe wrongly

del·uge (déljuːdʒ) **1.** *n.* a flood ‖ an overwhelming rush of water ‖ a heavy fall of rain ‖ a rush of anything (e.g. words, mail) **2.** *v.t. pres. part.* **del·ug·ing** *past* and *past part.* **del·uged** to flood ‖ to overwhelm as if with a flood

de·lu·sion (dilúːʒen) *n.* a deluding or being deluded ‖ a false opinion or idea ‖ a false, unshakable belief indicating a severe mental disorder **de·lú·sion·al** *adj.*

de·lu·sive (dilúːsiv) *adj.* deceptive, false **de·lu·so·ry** ((dilúːsəri:, dilúːzəri:) *adj.*

de luxe (dəlúks, dəlʌks) *adj.* especially lavish or elegant

delve (delv) *pres. part.* **delv·ing** *past* and *past part.* **delved** *v.i.* to search as if burrowing ‖ (of a road etc.) to dip suddenly

dem·a·gog·ic (dẹməgódʒik, dẹməgógik) *adj.* of or like a demagogue **dem·a·góg·i·cal** *adj.*

dem·a·gogue, dem·a·gog (déməgɒg) *n.* a political speaker or leader who plays upon the passions etc. of the people to win their support for himself or his party ‖ a factious orator **dém·a·gogu·er·y** *pl.* **dem·a·gogu·er·ies** *n.* demagogism **dém·a·gog·ism, dém·a·gogu·ism** *n.* the principles or practices of demagogues

de·mand (dimǽnd, dimánd) *n.* a peremptory request ‖ the thing requested ‖ an urgent claim ‖ an economic need or call

demand *v.t.* to ask for peremptorily, claim as one's due ‖ to require, call for ‖ to inquire with authority ‖ *v.i.* (with 'of') to make a demand

de·mar·cate (díːmɑrkeit, dimárkeit) *pres. part.* **de·mar·cat·ing** *past* and *past part.* **de·mar·cat·ed** *v.t.* to mark the boundaries of

de·mean (dimíːn) *v.t.* to behave (oneself) in a specified way

de·mean·or (dimíːnər) *n.* outward bearing, behavior, manner

de·ment·ed (diméntid) *adj.* mad, insane ‖ indicating madness

de·mer·it (dimérit) *n.* a quality deserving blame ‖ a fault or defect

de·mise (dimáiz) **1.** *n.* death ‖ *(law)* the conveyance of an estate by will or lease **2.** *v. pres. part.* **de·mis·ing** *past* and *past part.* **de·mised** *v.t. (law)* to convey by will or lease ‖ *v.i. (law)* to pass by bequest or inheritance

dem·i·tasse (démitæs, démitɑs) *n.* a small coffee cup

(a) æ, c*a*t; ɑ, c*a*r; ɔ f*aw*n; ei, sn*a*ke. **(e)** e, h*e*n; iː, sh*ee*p; iə, d*ee*r; ɛə, b*ea*r. **(i)** i, f*i*sh; ai, t*i*ger; əː, b*i*rd. **(o)** o, *o*x; au, c*ow*; ou, g*oa*t; u, p*oo*r; ɔi, r*oy*al. **(u)** ʌ, d*u*ck; u, b*u*ll; uː, g*oo*se; ə, b*a*cillus; juː, c*u*be. x, lo*ch*; θ, *th*ink; ð, bo*th*er; z, *Z*en; ʒ, corsa*g*e; dʒ, sava*g*e; ŋ, oranguta*n*g; j, *y*ak; ʃ, *fi*sh; tʃ, fe*tch*; 'l, rabb*le*; 'n, redd*en*. Complete pronunciation key appears inside front cover.

for serving coffee after dinner ‖ a cup of this coffee

de·moc·ra·cy (dəmókrəsi:) *pl.* **de·moc·ra·cies** *n.* government by the people, usually through elected representatives ‖ a state so governed ‖ *(pop.)* social equality

de·mol·ish (dimóliʃ) *v.t.* to destroy the structure of (a building etc.) ‖ to reduce to nothing, overthrow ‖ to refute conclusively (a theory, opponent etc.) ‖ *(pop.)* to eat up quickly

dem·o·li·tion (dḭ:məlíʃən) *n.* a demolishing or being demolished

de·mon (dí:mən) *n.* an evil spirit or devil ‖ a wicked, destructive creature ‖ an indwelling compulsive force

de·mon·ic (dimónik) *adj.* possessed or inspired by a demon or as if by a demon

dem·on·strate (démənstreit) *pres. part.* **dem·on·strat·ing** *past* and *past part.* **dem·on·strat·ed** *v.t.* to show clearly and openly by action the existence of ‖ to prove the truth of, by logical or scientific processes ‖ *v.i.* to explain and teach by performing experiments and showing examples ‖ to make a public display of sympathies, grievances or opinions ‖ to make a display of military force

dem·on·stra·tion (demənstréiʃən) *n.* an expression of public feeling for or against something through meetings, marches etc. ‖ the use of practical experiments for purposes of teaching ‖ a display of the way of working or merits of something ‖ a show of military force to intimidate, confuse or deter a potential enemy **dem·on·strá·tion·al** *adj.*

de·mon·stra·tive (dəmónstrətiv) **1.** *adj.* serving to point out, prove or show clearly ‖ (of persons) given to open display of feelings, esp. of affection ‖ *(gram.)* pointing out, *demonstrative adjectives and pronouns* **2.** *n.* a demonstrative adjective or pronoun

dem·on·stra·tor (démənstreitər) *n.* someone who demonstrates ‖ a participant in a public protest meeting ‖ someone who teaches by practical demonstration, esp. in a laboratory ‖ someone employed to show how (or how well) an article or appliance works

de·mor·i·za·tion (dimͻrəlaizéiʃən, dimͻrəlaizéiʃən) *n.* a demoralizing or being demoralized

de·mor·al·ize (dimórəlaiz, dimͻrəlaiz) *pres. part.* **de·mor·al·iz·ing** *past* and *past part.* **de·mor·al·ized** *v.t.* to destroy or weaken the morale of, undermine the confidence of ‖ to corrupt the morals of, deprave

de·mote (dimóut) *pres. part.* **de·mot·ing** *past* and *past part.* **de·mot·ed** *v.t.* to reduce to a lower rank or class **de·mó·tion** *n.*

de·mur (dimͻ:r) **1.** *v.i. pres part.* **de·mur·ring** *past* and *past part.* **de·murred** to raise objections or scruples, hesitate, show reluctance **2.** *n.* an objecting, a protesting

den (den) *n.* a wild beast's lair ‖ a cramped, dirty little room ‖ a snug, secluded room where a person may retire to study or doze in peace

de·ni·a·ble (dináiəb'l) *adj.* capable of being denied

de·ni·al (dináiəl) *n.* an assertion that something is not true ‖ a refusal to acknowledge, disavowal ‖ a refusal of a request ‖ self-denial

den·im (dénəm) *n.* a strong, coarse, twilled cotton fabric used for overalls, jeans etc.

de·nom·i·na·tion (dinͻminéiʃən) *n.* the act of denominating ‖ a name, esp. one given to a class or category ‖ one of a series of units in numbers, weights or money ‖ a religious sect **de·nom·i·ná·tion·al** *adj.* pertaining to a religious sect **de·nom·i·ná·tion·al·ism**, **de·nom·i·ná·tion·al·ist** *ns*

de·nom·i·na·tor (dinóminẹitər) *n.* the part of a fraction written below the numerator and separated from it by a usually horizontal line. It denotes the number of equal parts into which the whole is divided

de·note (dinóut) *pres. part.* **de·not·ing** *past* and *past part.* **de·not·ed** *v.t.* to be the distinguishing sign of ‖ to indicate ‖ to signify, stand for ‖ *(logic)* to be a name of, designate

de·nounce (dináuns) *pres. part.* **de·nounc·ing** *past* and *past part.* **de·nounced** *v.t.* to inform against ‖ to

censure, esp. publicly, inveigh against ‖ to announce formally the end of (a treaty, agreement etc.) **de·nóunce·ment** *n.*

dense (dens) *comp.* **dens·er** *superl.* **dens·est** *adj.* massed closely together ‖ thick ‖ rich in texture, requiring mental effort to appreciate ‖ stupid, slow-witted

dent (dent) *n.* a slight hollow made in a surface by pressure or a blow **2.** *v.t.* to make a dent in ‖ *v.i.* to become dented

den·tal (dént'l) *adj.* of or relating to the teeth or dentistry

den·tist (déntist) *n.* someone professionally qualified to treat ailments of the teeth **den·tist·ry** (déntistri:) *n.* the science of the care of the teeth ‖ the work of a dentist

den·ture (déntʃər) *n.* a set of artificial teeth

de·nude (dinú:d, dinjú:d) *pres. part.* **de·nud·ing** *past* and *past part.* **de·nud·ed** *v.t.* to strip, make bare ‖ to lay bare (rock etc.)

de·nun·ci·a·tion (dinʌnsi:éiʃən) *n.* the act of denouncing ‖ an instance of censuring, esp. publicly

de·nun·ci·a·tor (dinʌnsi:eitər) *n.* someone who denounces **de·nun·ci·a·to·ry** (dinʌnsi:ətͻri:, dinʌnsi:ətouri:) *adj.*

de·ny (dinái) *pres. part.* **de·ny·ing** *past* and *past part.* **de·nied** *v.t.* to declare to be untrue ‖ to repudiate ‖ to refuse (someone something or something to someone)

de·o·dor·ant (di:óudərənt) *n.* an agent for neutralizing unpleasant odors, esp. of perspiration

de·o·dor·ize (di:óudəraiz) *pres. part.* **de·o·dor·iz·ing** *past* and *past part.* **de·o·dor·ized** *v.t.* to neutralize a bad odor in (a room, clothes etc.)

de·part (dipárt) *v.i.* to go away ‖ to set off or out ‖ to deviate

de·part·ment (dipártmənt) *n.* a distinct branch of a whole **de·part·men·tal** (dipartmént'l, dḭ:partmént'l) *adj.* **de·part·mén·tal·ize** *pres. part.* **de·part·men·tal·iz·ing** *past* and *past part.* **de·part·men·tal·ized** *v.t.*

de·pend (dipénd) *v.i.* (with 'on' or 'upon' in all senses) to rely for livelihood, support etc. ‖ to rely trustfully ‖ to be contingent

de·pend·a·bil·i·ty (dipͻndəbíliti:) *n.* the quality of being dependable

de·pend·a·ble (dipéndəb'l) *adj.* reliable, trustworthy **de·pénd·a·bly** *adv.*

de·pend·ant, de·pend·ent (dipéndənt) *n.* someone who relies upon another for financial support

de·pend·ence, de·pend·ance (dipéndəns) *n.* a depending on another for material or emotional support ‖ trust, reliance ‖ the state of being contingent

de·pend·en·cy (dipéndənsi:) *pl.* **de·pend·en·cies** *n.* the state of being dependent ‖ something depending on or subordinate to another

de·pend·ent (dipéndənt) **1.** *adj.* (of a person) being a financial charge ‖ (of lands or peoples) subject ‖ *(gram.,* of a clause) subordinate ‖ forced to rely ‖ *(bot.)* hanging down ‖ contingent **2.** *n.* DEPENDANT

de·pict (dipíkt) *v.t.* to represent by drawing or painting ‖ to describe verbally **de·píc·tion** *n.*

de·plete (diplí:t) *pres. part.* **de·plet·ing** *past* and *past part.* **de·plet·ed** *v.t.* to reduce or empty by destroying or using up **de·plé·tion** *n.*

de·plor·a·ble (diplͻ́rəb'l, diplóurəb'l) *adj.* much to be regretted ‖ wretched **de·plór·a·bly** *adv.*

de·plore (diplͻr, diplóur) *pres. part.* **de·plor·ing** *past* and *past part.* **de·plored** *v.t.* to regret very much or express conventional regret for ‖ to be grieved and appalled by

de·port (dipͻrt, dipóurt) *v.t.* to send away from a country, exile **to deport oneself** to conduct oneself, behave in a specified way **de·por·tá·tion** (dḭ:pͻrtéiʃən, dḭ:pourtéiʃən) *n.* banishment

de·port·ment (dipͻrtmənt, dipóurtmənt) *n.* bearing, way of walking or holding oneself ‖ behavior, manners

de·pose (dipóuz) *pres. part.* **de·pos·ing** *past* and *past part.* **de·posed** *v.t.* to dethrone ‖ to remove from

office ‖ to say on oath ‖ *v.i.* to give evidence
de·pos·it (dipózit) **1.** *v.t.* to store for safety ‖ to put (something) down ‖ to leave a layer or coating of ‖ to pay (a sum) as a security **2.** *n.* something entrusted for safekeeping ‖ a sum paid as a security or as a first installment ‖ anything put down or left to settle ‖ a sediment ‖ a natural accumulation
de·pot (dí:pou, dépou) *n.* a storage place (civil or military) ‖ a place where things are deposited before distribution ‖ *(mil.)* a station for recruiting, training or holding soldiers not sent to a unit ‖ a railroad station ‖ the place from which a bus service is run
dep·ra·va·tion (dẹprəvéiʃən) *n.* a depraving or being depraved
de·prave (dipréiv) *pres. part.* **de·prav·ing** *past* and *past part.* **de·praved** *v.t.* to corrupt, pervert, esp. morally
de·prav·i·ty (diprǽviti:) *pl.* **de·prav·i·ties** *n.* moral corruption, perversion, wickedness ‖ a particular manifestation of this
de·pre·ci·ate (diprí:ʃi:eit) *pres. part.* **de·pre·ci·at·ing** *past* and *past part.* **de·pre·ci·at·ed** *v.t.* to diminish the value of ‖ to belittle ‖ *v.i.* to diminish in value **de·pre·ci·á·tion** *n.* a depreciating or being depreciated **de·pre·ci·a·to·ry** (diprí:ʃi:ətɔri:, diprí:ʃi:ətɔuri:) *adj.*
dep·re·da·tion (dẹprìdéiʃən) *n.* a laying waste ‖ *(pl.)* ravages **dép·re·da·tor** *n.*
de·press (diprés) *v.t.* to make gloomy, dispirit ‖ to press down, lower **de·prés·sant 1.** *adj.* *(med.)* lowering activity **2.** *n.* a medicine which lowers activity, a sedative **de·préssed** *adj.* dispirited, miserable ‖ *(bot.)* flattened ‖ *(bot.)* sunken so that the central part is lower than the margin ‖ substandard in economic activity ‖ having a very low standard of living
de·pres·sion (dipréʃən) *n.* a depressing or being depressed ‖ a natural hollow or low-lying place ‖ a state of low mental vitality, dejection ‖ the condition of being less active than usual
dep·ri·va·tion (dẹprivéiʃən) *n.* deprival ‖ an instance of this
de·prive (dipráiv) *pres. part.* **de·priv·ing** *past* and *past part.* **de·prived** *v.t.* (with 'of') to withhold or take away something desirable or necessary from (someone)
depth (depθ) *n.* deepness ‖ an extent of deepness downwards or inwards ‖ the representation of deepness in perspective ‖ the innermost part ‖ the most intense point ‖ the quality of being profound ‖ (of color) intensity ‖ *(pl., rhet.)* a low moral condition
dep·u·ty (dépjuti:) *pl.* **dep·u·ties** *n.* someone appointed to act on behalf of another ‖ a second-in-command who takes control in his superior's absence
de·rail (diréil) *v.t.* to cause (a train etc.) to run off the rails ‖ *v.i.* to run off the rails **de·ráil·ment** *n.*
de·range (diréindʒ) *pres. part.* **de·rang·ing** *past* and *past part.* **de·ranged** *v.t.* to make insane ‖ to throw into confusion ‖ to cause to go out of order **de·ránge·ment** *n.*
der·e·lict (dérəlikt) **1.** *adj.* abandoned, neglected, left to fall to ruin **2.** *n.* abandoned property ‖ a human wreck
der·e·lic·tion (dẹrəlíkʃən) *n.* an abandoning or being abandoned ‖ neglect (of duty)
de·ride (diráid) *pres. part.* **de·rid·ing** *past* and *past part.* **de·rid·ed** *v.t.* to laugh at in scorn, mock
de·ri·sion (dirízən) *n.* mockery, ridicule
de·ri·sive (diráisiv) *adj.* scornful, mocking ‖ contemptible
der·i·va·tion (dẹrivéiʃən) *n.* a deriving or being derived ‖ an origin, source ‖ a statement of the source of a word, or the act of tracing it ‖ the formation of a word from a root
de·riv·a·tive (dirívətiv) **1.** *adj.* derived from something else **2.** *n.* something derived ‖ a word formed from

another ‖ *(chem.)* a substance structurally related to another
de·rive (diráiv) *pres. part.* **de·riv·ing** *past* and *past part.* **de·rived** *v.t.* to receive, obtain ‖ to deduce ‖ *(chem.)* to obtain (a compound) from another ‖ *v.i.* to stem, take its origin
der·ma·tol·o·gy (dẹ:rmətólədʒi:) *n.* the branch of medicine dealing with the skin and its diseases
de·rog·a·to·ry (diróɡətɔri:, diróɡətɔuri:) *adj.* disparaging
der·rick (dérik) *n.* a hoisting apparatus consisting of a boom carrying a tackle at its outer end and pivoted at the other, often to the foot of a central mast, used (esp. aboard ship) for unloading, etc. and in construction work ‖ a tower or framework over an oil drilling etc. for supporting and manipulating drilling tackle
de·scend (disénd) *v.i.* to go downwards ‖ to debase oneself ‖ (with 'on') to make a sudden attack ‖ to be transmitted by inheritance ‖ to proceed (in a narration) from earlier to later time ‖ *v.t.* to go down
de·scend·ant, de·scend·ent (diséndənt) *n.* someone or something descended
de·scent (disént) *n.* a descending ‖ a downward slope ‖ a way down ‖ a moral stooping ‖ lineage, ancestry ‖ *(law)* the transmission of property or title by inheritance
de·scribe (diskráib) *pres. part.* **de·scrib·ing** *past* and *past part.* **de·scribed** *v.t.* to give a description of ‖ (with 'as') to qualify ‖ to draw, trace (esp. a geometrical figure) ‖ to move in the outline of
de·scrip·tion (diskrípʃən) *n.* a verbal account or portrayal of a person, scene, event etc. ‖ a technical account, definition ‖ sort, kind
de·scrip·tive (diskríptiv) *adj.* serving to describe
des·e·crate (désikreit) *pres. part.* **des·e·crat·ing** *past* and *past part.* **des·e·crat·ed** *v.t.* to outrage the sanctity of, profane **des·e·crá·tion, dés·e·cra·tor** *ns*
de·seg·re·gate (di:séɡrigeit) *pres. part.* **de·seg·re·gat·ing** *past* and *past part.* **de·seg·re·gat·ed** *v.t.* to free from the practice of segregation (esp. racial) ‖ *v.i.* to abandon the practice of segregation **de·seg·re·gá·tion** *n.*
de·sert (dizɔ́:rt) *v.t.* to abandon, forsake, and so break faith with (someone) ‖ to leave entirely unoccupied ‖ *v.i.* to run away from service in the armed forces
des·ert (dézərt) *n.* a large area of land where there is not enough vegetation to support human life
de·sert·er (dizɔ́:rtər) *n.* someone who deserts, esp. from the armed forces
de·ser·tion (dizɔ́:rʃən) *n.* a deserting or being deserted ‖ the act or crime of running away from service in the armed forces
de·serve (dizɔ́rv) *pres. part.* **de·serv·ing** *past* and *past part.* **de·served** *v.t.* to be worthy of, merit ‖ to have a claim on ‖ *v.i.* to show worthiness **de·sérved** *adj.* **de·serv·ed·ly** (dizɔ́rvidli:) *adv.* **de·sérv·ing** *adj.*
de·sign (dizáin) *n.* a decorative pattern ‖ instructions for making something which leave the details to be worked out ‖ the formal structure of a picture ‖ the combination of parts in a whole ‖ a plan conceived in the mind ‖ a purpose, intention ‖ *(pl.)* an intention to get possession of
design *v.t.* to invent and bring into being ‖ to prepare plans or a sketch or model etc. of (something to be made) ‖ to intend for a particular purpose ‖ *v.i.* to make designs
des·ig·nate (dézignit, dézigneit) **1.** *adj.* (always placed after its noun) appointed to an office but not yet in possession of it **2.** *v.t.* (dézigneit) *pres. part.* **des·ig·nat·ing** *past* and *past part.* **des·ig·nat·ed** to show, identify ‖ (often with 'as') to name, describe ‖ to appoint to office

de·sir·a·ble (dizáiərəb'l) *adj.* inspiring the wish to possess ‖ that one hopes to find in oneself, in others, or in things **de·sír·a·bly** *adv.*

de·sire (dizáiər) *n.* yearning, longing ‖ strong sexual attraction ‖ wish, request

de·sist (dizíst, disíst) *v.i.* to cease (from doing something)

desk (desk) *n.* a piece of furniture with a flat or sloping surface for writing or reading at ‖ a lectern

des·o·late (désəleit) **1.** *v.t. pres. part.* **des·o·lat·ing** *past and past part.* **des·o·lat·ed** to make desolate ‖ to depopulate ‖ to lay waste, ravage ‖ to make wretched **2.** (désəlit) *adj.* lonely ‖ forlorn ‖ wasted, barren ‖ uninhabited

des·o·la·tion (desəléiʃən) *n.* a desolating ‖ a laying waste ‖ a barren, neglected state or area ‖ extreme loneliness, misery, unhappiness

de·spair (dispéər) **1.** *v.i.* to lose hope **2.** *n.* hopelessness **de·spáir·ing** *adj.*

des·per·ate (déspərit, désprit) *adj.* beyond, or almost beyond, hope ‖ frantic ‖ reckless and violent ‖ extremely bad

des·per·a·tion (despəréiʃən) *n.* a despairing ‖ a state of recklessness caused by despair

des·pi·ca·ble (dispíkəb'l, déspikəb'l) *adj.* fit to· be despised, contemptible, mean **des·pí·ca·bly** *adv.*

de·spise (dispáiz) *pres. part.* **de·spis·ing** *past and past part.* **de·spised** *v.t.* to look down upon, feel contempt for

de·spite (dispáit) **1.** *prep.* notwithstanding **2.** *n.* (only in) **in despite of** *(rhet.)* in spite of

de·spoil (dispɔ́il) *v.t.* to plunder, pillage ‖ to strip (a person, institution etc.) of possessions ‖ to ruin (land etc.) by stripping away its valuable products **de·spóil·ment** *n.*

de·spond (dispɔ́nd) *v.i.* to become very disheartened, be dejected **de·spónd·ence, de·spónd·en·cy** *ns* **de·spónd·ent** *adj.*

des·pot (déspɒt, déspɒt) *n.* an absolute ruler, a tyrant **des·pót·ic** *adj.* **des·pót·i·cal·ly** *adv.* **dés·pot·ism** *n.*

des·sert (dizɔ́:rt) *n.* a sweet course served at the end of a meal

des·ti·na·tion (destinéiʃən) *n.* the place to which a person or thing is going

des·tine (déstin) *pres. part.* **des·tin·ing** *past and past part.* **des·tined** *v.t.* (usually *pass.*) to set apart (for a specified purpose) ‖ (of fate) to foreordain

des·ti·ny (déstini:) *pl.* **des·ti·nies** *n.* the power of fate ‖ one's predetermined lot

des·ti·tute (déstitju:t, déstitu:t) *adj.* so poverty-stricken as to be without the necessities of life **destitute of** entirely lacking **des·ti·tú·tion** *n.*

de·stroy (distrɔ́i) *v.t.* to smash the structure of, break past mending, demolish ‖ to put an end to (hopes etc.)

de·stroy·er (distrɔ́iər) *n.* a small, fast warship ‖ someone who destroys ‖ something which destroys

de·struct·i·ble (distrʌ́ktəb'l) *adj.* capable of being destroyed

de·struc·tion (distrʌ́kʃən) *n.* a destroying or being destroyed ‖ the cause of ruin, something which destroys

de·tach (ditætʃ) *v.t.* to separate, remove ‖ to send (a regiment, ships etc.) on a special mission away from the main body **de·tách·a·ble, de·táched** *adjs* (of the mind, opinions etc.) independent, uninfluenced by other people or by prejudice etc. ‖ separate ‖ standing apart

de·tach·ment (ditætʃmənt) *n.* a detaching, separation ‖ cool independence of judgment ‖ freedom from involvement ‖ indifference to worldly ambitions

de·tail (dí:teil, ditéil) *n.* a small part, an item ‖ *(fine arts)* a part of a composition or construction considered in isolation ‖ *(mil.)* a detachment for a special job, or the job itself

de·tail (ditéil) *v.t.* to itemize, list ‖ *(mil.)* to assign to a special duty

de·tain (ditéin) *v.t.* to keep from leaving ‖ to keep in custody

de·tect (ditékt) *v.t.* to find out, discover betraying signs of ‖ to discover the presence of **de·téct·a·ble** *adj.* **de·téc·tion** *n.* **de·téc·tive 1.** *adj.* serving to detect or concerned with detection **2.** *n.* a policeman whose work is to investigate crime ‖ a private crime investigator

dé·tente (deitánt) *n.* an easing of tension, esp. between nations

de·ter (ditɔ́:r) *pres. part.* **de·ter·ring** *past and past part.* **de·terred** *v.t.* to discourage from some action by making the consequences seem frightening etc.

de·ter·gent (ditɔ́:rdʒənt) **1.** *adj.* cleansing **2.** *n.* soap ‖ one of a large number of cleansing agents

de·te·ri·o·rate (ditíəri:əreit) *pres. part.* **de·te·ri·o·rat·ing** *past and past part.* **de·te·ri·o·rat·ed** *v.t.* to make worse ‖ *v.i.* to become worse **de·te·ri·o·rá·tion** *n.* **de·té·ri·o·ra·tive** *adj.*

de·ter·mi·na·tion (ditə:rminéiʃən) *n.* firmness of purpose or character, resolution ‖ the act of determining, fixing, deciding ‖ the act of finding out exactly ‖ *(law)* the settling of a controversy by a judicial decision ‖ a coming to a decision

de·ter·mine (ditɔ́:rmin) *pres. part.* **de·ter·min·ing** *past and past part.* **de·ter·mined** *v.t.* to settle, fix ‖ to cause (someone) to resolve ‖ to regulate ‖ to find out precisely ‖ *(law)* to limit, define ‖ to settle by judicial decision ‖ *v.i.* (with 'on') to make up one's mind, resolve ‖ (esp. *law*) to come to an end, terminate ‖ to come to a judicial decision **de·tér·mined** *adj.* resolved, decided ‖ resolute

de·ter·rent (ditɔ́:rənt, ditʌ́rənt, ditérənt) **1.** *adj.* meant to deter **2.** *n.* something which deters or is meant to deter

de·test (ditést) *v.t.* to hate, abhor **de·tést·a·ble** *adj.* **de·tést·a·bly** *adv.*

de·tour (dí:tuər, ditúər) **1.** *n.* a deviation from the usual route or course ‖ a circuitous path taken to avoid some obstacle, danger etc. **2.** *v.i.* to make a detour ‖ *v.t.* to make a detour around ‖ to cause to make a detour

de·tract (ditrǽkt) *v.i.* (with 'from') to lessen in value or estimation **de·trác·tion** *n.* **de·trác·tive** *adj.* **de·trác·tor** *n.*

det·ri·ment (détrəmənt) *n.* harm, damage **det·ri·mén·tal** *adj.* harmful, injurious

de·val·u·ate (di:vǽlju:eit) *pres. part.* **de·val·u·at·ing** *past and past part.* **de·val·u·at·ed** *v.t.* to lower the legal value of (a depreciated currency) in a crisis ‖ to lessen the value of **de·val·u·á·tion** *n.*

dev·as·tate (dévəsteit) *pres. part.* **dev·as·tat·ing** *past and past part.* **dev·as·tat·ed** *v.t.* to lay waste, ravage **dev·as·tá·tion, dév·as·ta·tor** *ns*

de·vel·op (divéləp) *v.t.* to cause to grow or expand ‖ to elaborate on ‖ to begin to have ‖ to realize (what was potential) ‖ to expand by putting money into ‖ *(photog.)* to treat (an exposed plate or film) chemically so that the image appears ‖ *v.i.* (of mind, body or species) to evolve ‖ to come into being ‖ to expand **de·vél·op·er** *n.* *(photog.)* a chemical reagent used to develop an exposed film **de·vél·op·ment** *n.* the act of developing ‖ evolution (of an organism) ‖ a new factor or situation ‖ a tract of land developed as a unit **de·vel·op·mén·tal** *adj.'* relating or incidental to growth

de·vi·ate (dí:vi:eit) **1.** *v. pres. part.* **de·vi·at·ing** *past and past part.* **de·vi·at·ed** *v.i.* to turn aside (from a course, custom, topic etc.) ‖ *v.t.* to cause to turn aside or diverge **2.** (dí:vi:it) *n.* someone sexually perverted

de·vi·a·tion (di:vi:éiʃən) *n.* a turning aside ‖ *(statistics)* the algebraic difference between one of a set of observed values and their mean or average value

de·vice (diváis) *n.* a scheme, trick, stratagem ‖ something designed or adapted for a special purpose ‖ a heraldic design ‖ a motto

dev·il (dévəl) **1.** *n.* an evil spirit, a demon ‖ a cruel or vicious person ‖ *(pop.)* someone full of spirit and daring ‖ (*pop.*) a fellow, person, *you lucky devil!* **the Devil** (in Jewish and Christian theologies) the spirit of evil, Satan **2.** *v. pres. part.* **dev·il·ing** past and *past part.* **dev·iled** *v.t.* to prepare (food) with hot seasoning ‖ to tease, torment ‖ *v.i.* to serve as a devil, e.g. to a lawyer

de·vi·ous (díːviːəs) *adj.* roundabout, very winding ‖ underhanded, shifty

de·vise (diváiz) **1.** *v.t. pres. part.* **de·vis·ing** past and *past part.* **de·vised** to contrive, think up (e.g. a method, plot) ‖ (*law*) to bequeath (realty) by will **2.** *n.* (*law*) a giving or leaving (of realty) by will **de·vi·see** (diˌvaizíː, dɛvizíː), **de·ví·sor** ns

de·void (divɔ́id) *adj.* (with 'of') lacking in, completely without

de·vote (divóut) *pres. part.* **de·vot·ing** past and *past part.* **de·vot·ed** *v.t.* to give wholly, dedicate ‖ to earmark or make a gift of (money) for a particular use **de·vót·ed** *adj.* bound by strong affection ‖ loyal, zealous ‖ expressing devotion **de·vót·ed·ly** *adv.*

de·vo·tion (divóuʃən) *n.* love given with the whole heart and will ‖ ardent addiction ‖ devoutness ‖ (*pl.*) prayers, worship **de·vó·tion·al** *adj.*

de·vour (diváuər) *v.t.* (of or like an animal) to eat up hungrily ‖ to take in eagerly with the senses ‖ to consume, destroy

de·vout (diváut) *adj.* worshiping ‖ attending to religious duties ‖ sincere, earnest

dew (duː, djuː) **1.** *n.* small drops of moisture condensed from the atmosphere ‖ droplets resembling this **2.** *v.t.* to wet with or as if with dew

dex·ter·i·ty (dekstériti) *n.* manual skill, deftness ‖ mental adroitness

dex·ter·ous (dékstərəs, dékstrəs) *adj.* dextrous **dex·tral** (dékstrəl) *adj.* on the right-hand side ‖ turned or moving towards the right

di·a·be·tes mel·li·tus (daiəbíːtiːzməlaitəs) *n.* a disease, characterized by the presence of excessive amounts of sugar in the urine and manifested by various metabolic disorders

di·a·bet·ic (daiəbétik) **1.** *adj.* of diabetes ‖ suffering from diabetes **2.** *n.* a person suffering from diabetes

di·a·bol·ic (daiəbɔ́lik) *adj.* wicked, evil ‖ of or like the devil ‖ having to do with sorcery ‖ fiendish in cunning or astuteness **di·a·ból·i·cal** *adj.*

di·ag·nose (dáiəgnous, dáiəgnouz) *pres. part.* **di·ag·nos·ing** past and *past part.* **di·ag·nosed** *v.t.* to determine the nature of (a disease) from its symptoms

di·ag·no·sis (daiəgnóusis) *pl.* **di·ag·no·ses** (daiəgnóusiːz) *n.* the recognition of a disease from its symptoms ‖ a formal statement of the decision reached in identifying a disease

di·ag·nos·tic (daiəgnɔ́stik) **1.** *adj.* of diagnosis **2.** *n.* a diagnosis **di·ag·nós·ti·cal·ly** *adv.* **di·ag·nos·ti·cian** (daiəgnɔstíʃən) *n.* **di·ag·nós·tics** *n.* the art of making a diagnosis

di·ag·o·nal (daiǽgən'l) **1.** *adj.* running from corner to corner in a slanting direction ‖ having oblique markings or weave **2.** *n.* a diagonal straight line or direction

di·a·gram (dáiəgræm) *n.* a figure or sketch designed to give a broad explanation ‖ a graph or chart ‖ a geometrical figure used to illustrate a theorem **di·a·gram·mát·ic** *adj.* **di·a·gram·mát·i·cal·ly** *adv.* **di·a·gram·ma·tize** (daiəgrǽmətaiz) *pres. part.* **di·a·gram·ma·tiz·ing** past and *past part.* **di·a·gram·ma·tized** *v.t.*

di·al (dáiəl, dáil) **1.** *n.* a circle around or on which a scale is marked, so that the position of one or more pointers, rotating about the center of the circle, can be stated ‖ the numbered disk of an automatic telephone instrument **2.** *v.t. pres. part.* **di·al·ing** past and *past part.* **di·aled** to compose (a desired number) with the finger on a telephone

di·a·lect (dáiəlekt) *n.* a form of a language distinguished from other forms of the same language by pronunciation, grammar or vocabulary ‖ a language in relation to the family to which it belongs **di·a·léc·tal** *adj.*

di·a·logue, di·a·log (dáiəlɔg, dáiəlɒg) *n.* a literary work in conversational form ‖ conversation in a novel, play, movie etc.

di·am·e·ter (daiǽmitər) *n.* a straight line passing through the center of a circle or other curvilinear figure and ending at the boundary of the figure ‖ this measure through or across **di·am·e·tral** (daiǽmitrəl) *adj.*

di·a·met·ric (daiəmétrik) *adj.* diametrical **di·a·mét·ri·cal** *adj.* of or pertaining to a diameter ‖ (of opposition) complete **di·a·mét·ri·cal·ly** *adv.*

di·a·mond (dáiəmənd, dáimənd) **1.** *n.* a very valuable precious stone ‖ a rhombus ‖ a playing card marked with one or more red lozenges ‖ (*pl.*) the suit so marked ‖ a tool fitted with a diamond for cutting glass ‖ (*baseball*) the infield ‖ (*baseball*) the playing field **2.** *adj.* made of or set with diamonds ‖ sparkling ‖ lozenge-shaped ‖ (of a jubilee or wedding or other anniversary) sixtieth or seventy-fifth **3.** *v.t.* to adorn with diamonds or diamondlike objects

di·a·per (dáiəpər, dáipər) **1.** *n.* a piece of absorbent cloth or other material for catching a baby's urine and feces **2.** *v.t.* to put a diaper on (a baby)

di·a·phragm (dáiəfræm) *n.* a septum or partition ‖ the midriff ‖ (*optics*) the physical element of an optical system that regulates the quantity of light (brightness) traversing the system ‖ (*photog.*) an iris diaphragm ‖ thin rubber cap fitted over the uterine cervix **di·a·phrag·mat·ic** (daiəfrægmǽtik) *adj.*

di·ar·rhe·a, esp. *Br.* **di·ar·rhoe·a** (daiəríːə) *n.* unusually frequent passage of loose, watery stools

di·a·ry (dáiəriː) *pl.* **di·a·ries** *n.* a daily written account of events, experiences or observations ‖ a book for keeping such an account

di·a·tribe (dáiətraib) *n.* a fulminating piece of invective

dice (dais) **1.** *n. pl.* of DIE ‖ a gambling game played with these **2.** *v. pres. part.* **dic·ing** past and *past part.* **diced** *v.i.* to play dice ‖ *v.t.* to cut up (vegetables, meat etc.) into small cubes ‖ to mark into squares

dic·tate **1.** (dikteit, díkteit) *v. pres. part.* **dic·tat·ing** past and *past part.* **dic·tat·ed** *v.t.* to read or say (something) aloud that is to be written down ‖ to prescribe ‖ *v.i.* to behave like an autocrat **2.** (díkteit) *n.* (usually *pl.*) an order, a compelling impulse

dic·ta·tion (diktéiʃən) *n.* a dictating ‖ something dictated ‖ something written from dictation ‖ a command

dic·ta·tor (díkteitər, diktéitər) *n.* an autocrat, an absolute ruler ‖ someone who acts like a petty tyrant

dic·ta·to·ri·al (diktətɔ́riːəl, diktətóuriːəl) *adj.* imperious, autocratic ‖ of a dictator

dic·ta·tor·ship (diktéitərʃip) *n.* the office or period of power of a dictator ‖ a form of government in which power is held by a dictator without effective constitutional checks

dic·tion (díkʃən) *n.* a way of speaking, enunciation or delivery in public speaking ‖ the selection and control of words to express ideas

dic·tion·ar·y (díkʃəneriː) *pl.* **dic·tion·ar·ies** *n.* a book containing the words or a choice of the words of a language arranged in alphabetical order, with their definitions, and often indicating their pronunciation, part of speech, common usage, provenance etc. ‖ a compilation of such words limited to a particular subject ‖ a work of informative character arranged alphabetically

did *past of* DO

die (dai) *n.* (*pl.* **dice,** dais) a small cube marked on its faces with 1–6 spots and used in playing dice ‖ (*archit.*), *pl.* **dies**) the cubic part of a pedestal ‖ (*pl.* **dies**) any of various tools for cutting, shaping or embossing

die *pres. part.* **dy·ing** *past and past part.* **died** *v.i.* to cease to live ‖ to fade away, be forgotten ‖ to fade to nothing ‖ to become feeble or cease to be ‖ to wither

di·et (dáiit) *n.* the food and drink normally taken by an individual or a group ‖ a prescribed course of what is to be eaten and what is not

diet *v.t.* to put on a diet ‖ *v.i.* to eat special food (for health reasons, athletic training etc.) ‖ to eat less so as to become thinner

di·e·tar·y (dáiiteri:) **1.** *pl.* **di·e·tar·ies** *n.* a course of diet ‖ an allowance or ration of food **2.** *adj.* relating to diet

di·e·tet·ic (daiitétik) *adj.* of or relating to diet **di·e·tét·i·cal·ly** *adv.* **di·e·tét·ics** *n.* the study of the principles of nutrition

dif·fer (dífər) *v.i.* to be different ‖ to disagree in opinion

dif·fer·ence (dífərəns, dífrəns) *n.* a differing ‖ an instance of differing ‖ a distinction ‖ the result obtained by subtracting one quantity, function or number from another of the same kind ‖ a disagreement in opinion, quarrel

dif·fer·ent (dífərənt, dífrənt) *adj.* (with 'from') dissimilar ‖ not the same ‖ (*pop.*) out of the ordinary, unusual

dif·fi·cult (dífikəlt, dífikʌlt) *adj.* hard to do ‖ hard to understand or solve ‖ hard to deal with or to please, obstinate ‖ troublesome, worrying **dif·fi·cul·ty** (dífikəlti:, dífikʌlti:) *pl.* **dif·fi·cul·ties** *n.* the quality of being difficult ‖ something which cannot easily be done, understood or believed ‖ an obstacle or hindrance ‖ an objection, demurral, *please don't raise difficulties* ‖ a disagreement or cause of hostility or estrangement ‖ (*often pl.*) trouble, esp. financial trouble

dif·fuse **1.** (difjú:z) *v. pres. part.* **dif·fus·ing** *past and past part.* **dif·fused** *v.t.* to spread widely ‖ *v.i.* (*phys.*) to undergo diffusion **2.** (difjú:s) *adj.* widely spread, dispersed ‖ not concise, wordy ‖ (*phys.*, of reflection, or the thing reflected) not coherent **dif·fus·i·ble** (difjú:zəb'l) *adj.*

dif·fu·sion (difjú:ʒən) *n.* a diffusing or being diffused ‖ the reflection of light by a mat surface or transmission of light through frosted glass etc. or the scattering caused by particles in the atmosphere ‖ the spread of cultural elements from one people or district to others

dig (dig) **1.** *v. pres. part.* **dig·ging** *past and past part.* **dug** (dʌg) *v.t.* to break up or turn (soil) with a spade, fork, paws etc. ‖ to excavate, make (a hole etc.) by digging ‖ to remove from the ground by digging ‖ to thrust, poke ‖ *v.i.* to perform the action of digging **2.** *n.* a poke or thrust ‖ a sarcastic remark ‖ a piece of digging, esp. an archaeological excavation

di·gest (dáidʒest) *n.* a synopsis of information, usually set out under headings ‖ a body of laws ‖ a form of popular anthology, superficially serious

di·gest (didʒést) *v.t.* to convert (food) into a form that can be assimilated ‖ to study and master the significance of in one's mind and store in the memory ‖ to make a digest of ‖ *v.i.* (of food) to admit of or undergo digestion **di·gest·i·bíl·i·ty** *n.* **di·gést·i·ble** *adj.*

di·ges·tion (didʒéstʃən, daidʒéstʃən) *n.* the conversion of food into chyme in the stomach and the separation from the chyme of the chyle which is absorbed into the bloodstream ‖ the assimilation of ideas

dig·it (dídʒit) *n.* a finger or a toe ‖ any of the numbers from 0 to 9

dig·it·al (dídʒit'l) *adj.* pertaining to a finger or the fingers ‖ having digits ‖ like a digit ‖ (*computer*) of an instrument that accepts data and produces output in the form of characters or digits

dig·ni·fy (dígnifai) *pres. part.* **dig·ni·fy·ing** *past and*

past part. **dig·ni·fied** *v.t.* to confer dignity upon ‖ to add an air of distinction to ‖ to give a pretentious name to

dig·ni·ty (dígniti:) *pl.* **dig·ni·ties** *n.* worth, excellence ‖ nobility of manner or bearing ‖ the quality of commanding esteem ‖ high office or rank

di·gress (daigrés, digrés) *v.i.* to wander from the main subject in speaking or writing

di·gres·sion (daigréʃən, digréʃən) *n.* a wandering from the subject in speaking or writing ‖ a deliberate turning aside from the main track

di·gres·sive (daigrésiv, digrésiv) *adj.* tending to digress, digressing

dike, dyke (daik) **1.** *n.* a raised bank constructed to prevent flooding ‖ a low wall, esp. of turf or unmortared stones ‖ a causeway ‖ a crack in a rock stratum filled with igneous matter **2.** *v. pres. part.* **dik·ing, dyk·ing** *past and past part.* **diked, dyked** *v.i.* to construct dikes ‖ *v.t.* to provide or protect with dikes

di·lap·i·date (dilǽpideit) *pres. part.* **di·lap·i·dat·ing** *past and past part.* **di·lap·i·dat·ed** *v.i.* to fall into disrepair ‖ *v.t.* to cause to fall into ruin or disrepair **di·láp·i·dat·ed** *adj.*

di·la·ta·tion (dailətéiʃən, dilətéiʃən) *n.* the quality of being dilatant ‖ a dilating, esp. an enlargement of the pupil of the eye, heart chamber, or other organ

di·late (dailéit, diléit) *v. pres. part.* **di·lat·ing** *past and past part.* **di·lat·ed** *v.i.* to expand, become wide ‖ to enlarge upon a subject by relating the details of it ‖ *v.t.* to cause to expand ‖ to stretch (something contracted) **di·lá·tion** *n.*

di·lem·ma (dilémə) *n.* a situation in which one is faced with a choice between equally unsatisfactory alternatives

dil·et·tan·te (dilitǽnti:, dílitant) **1.** *pl.* **dil·et·tant·ti** (dilitánti:), **dil·et·tan·tes** *n.* someone who genuinely loves the fine arts without being a professional ‖ someone who dabbles in art, literature, music etc., without any deep knowledge or application **2.** *adj.* superficial ‖ amateur **dil·et·tánt·ism** *n.*

dil·i·gence (dílidʒəns) *n.* the quality of being diligent

dil·i·gent (dílidʒənt) *adj.* hard-working, industrious ‖ conscientious, not negligent

dill (dil) *n.* an annual whose seeds are used as a carminative, and also as a flavoring in pickles etc.

di·lute (dailú:t, dilú:t) **1.** *v. pres. part.* **di·lut·ing** *past and past part.* **di·lut·ed** *v.t.* to lessen the concentration of (a mixture) by adding more water or a thinner etc. ‖ to reduce the strength or brilliance of (a color etc.) ‖ to weaken, water down (a story, doctrine etc.) ‖ *v.i.* to become diluted **2.** *adj.* diluted, weakened **di·lú·tion** *n.*

dim (dim) **1.** *comp.* **dim·mer** *superl.* **dim·mest** *adj.* not bright or clear ‖ indistinct, not clearly visible ‖ vague ‖ (of sound) muffled, faint ‖ (of vision) blurred ‖ (*pop.*) stupid **2.** *v. pres. part.* **dim·ming** *past and past part.* **dimmed** *v.t.* to make dim ‖ to lower the beam of (headlights) ‖ *v.i.* to become dim

dime (daim) *n.* (U.S.A. and Canada) a coin worth 10 cents, one-tenth of a dollar

di·men·sion (diménʃən) *n.* a measurement in a single direction (e.g. length, breadth, thickness or circumference) ‖ (*pl.*) size ‖ (*pl.*) extent or scope ‖ (*phys.*) the powers to which the fundamental units of mass, length and time are raised **di·mén·sion·al** *adj.*

di·min·ish (dimíniʃ) *v.t.* to make less ‖ (*mus.*) to reduce (a perfect or minor interval) by a chromatic semitone ‖ *v.i.* to become less

dim·i·nu·tion (dimini:ʃən, diminjú:ʃən) *n.* the act of diminishing ‖ a decrease ‖ (*mus.*, e.g. in some fugues) a passage repeated but in notes with smaller time values

di·min·u·tive (dimínjutiv) **1.** *adj.* very small ‖ (*gram.*) expressing diminution **2.** *n.* a word expressing diminution

dim·mer (dímər) *n.* a device for controlling the intensity of illumination (esp. of stage lighting) or for lowering the beam of car headlights

dim·ple (dímp'l) 1. *n.* a small hollow, esp. in the cheek or chin 2. *v. pres. part.* **dim·pling** *past* and *past part.* **dim·pled** *v.t.* to cause or produce dimples in ‖ *v.i.* to show dimples ‖ (of a stream) to break into little ripples

din (din) 1. *n.* a clamor of discordant, deafening noises 2. *v. pres. part.* **din·ning** *past* and *past part.* **dinned** *v.t.* (with 'into') to drive home by constant repetition ‖ (of noise) to assail (the ears) ‖ *v.i.* to make a din

dine (dain) *pres. part.* **din·ing** *past* and *past part.* **dined** *v.i.* to have dinner ‖ *v.t.* to entertain to dinner ‖ to provide dining accommodation for **dín·er** *n.* someone who dines ‖ a dining car on a train ‖ a restaurant built to resemble a dining car on a train

di·nette (dainét) *n.* a small informal dining room, usually just off the kitchen ‖ a small table and chairs styled for use in this room

din·ghy (díngi:, díŋi:) *pl.* **din·ghies** *n.* a ship's small boat ‖ a small rowboat often fitted for sailing ‖ a small inflatable rubber boat carried on an aircraft

din·gy (díndʒi:) *comp.* **din·gi·er** *superl.* **din·gi·est** *adj.* drab, dull-colored, dirtylooking

din·ner (dínər) *n.* the main meal of the day whether taken at midday or in the evening ‖ a festive but formal evening meal with guests

di·no·saur (dáinəsɔr) *n.* a group of fossil lizards of the Triassic to the Mesozoic

di·o·cese (dáiəsis, dáiəsi:s) *n.* the district under a bishop's authority

dip (dip) 1. *v. pres. part.* **dip·ping** *past* and *past part.* **dipped** *v.t.* to immerse momentarily in a liquid ‖ to dye by immersing in a liquid ‖ to take up with a ladle, hand, scoop etc. ‖ to lower momentarily (a flag, sail etc.) ‖ *v.i.* to reach into something ‖ to sink, drop down ‖ (of a bird or airplane) to drop suddenly before climbing ‖ to slope downwards ‖ (with 'into') to make a cursory appraisal of a book or subject etc. 2. *n.* a dipping ‖ a quick swim ‖ a downward slope ‖ a liquid into which something may be dipped ‖ (*geol.*) the downward slope of a stratum ‖ a sudden drop in flight before climbing

diph·the·ri·a (difθíəri:ə, dipθíəri:ə) *n.* an acute infectious disease, chiefly of children

diph·thong (dífθɒŋ, dífθɒŋ, dípθɒŋ, dípθɒŋ) *n.* a speech sound consisting of two vowels pronounced glidingly in one syllable (as in 'house') **diph·thón·gal** *adj.* **diph·thong·ize** *pres. part.* **diph·thong·iz·ing** *past* and *past part.* **diph·thong·ized** *v.t.* and *i.*

di·plo·ma (diplóumə) *n.* a document conferring some honor or privilege, esp. one recording successful completion of a course of academic study ‖ a state document or charter

di·plo·ma·cy (diplóuməsi:) *pl.* **di·plo·ma·cies** *n.* the science of international relations ‖ the conduct of negotiations between nations ‖ a tactful dealing with people

dip·lo·mat (dípləmæt) *n.* someone officially employed in international diplomacy ‖ a tactful person skilled in handling people

dip·lo·mat·ic (dipləmǽtik) *adj.* relating to diplomacy ‖ tactful **dip·lo·mát·i·cal·ly** *adv.*

dire (dáiər) *comp.* **dir·er** *superl.* **dir·est** *adj.* dreadful, terrible ‖ most pressing ‖ extreme

di·rect (dirékt, dairékt) 1. *v.t.* to explain or point out the way to (someone) ‖ to address, aim (e.g. a criticism or remark) ‖ to address (a parcel etc.) ‖ to turn (something) in a certain direction ‖ to supervise ‖ to control the making of (a film), guiding the actors, cameramen etc. ‖ to direct the actors in and supervise

the presentation of (a play) ‖ to order, instruct ‖ *v.i.* to give orders 2. *adj.* straight, without detours ‖ straightforward, candid, blunt ‖ immediate ‖ not turned aside, *direct rays* ‖ (of descent) in unbroken line from parent to child ‖ (of a descendant) lineal 3. *adv.* by the direct way or in a direct manner

di·rec·tion (dirékʃən, dairékʃən) *n.* the act of directing, aiming or managing ‖ a command ‖ instruction, esp. moral or spiritual ‖ (*pl.*) instructions, esp. about how to use or make something or how to go somewhere ‖ the course which something is taking or is pointed towards ‖ a channel of activity **di·réc·tion·al** *adj.* (*radio*) depending upon direction for a good performance

dirt (dəːrt) *n.* any unclean substance, anything that soils ‖ soil ‖ mud ‖ excrement

dirt·y (dɔ́ːrti:) 1. *comp.* **dirt·i·er** *superl.* **dirt·i·est** *adj.* soiled, not clean ‖ indecent ‖ mean, despicable ‖ (of color) murky, tending to black or brown ‖ (*pop.*) resentful, or likely to be resented ‖ (of nuclear explosions) generating excessive fallout 2. *v. pres. part.* **dirt·y·ing** *past* and *past part.* **dirt·ied** *v.t.* to soil ‖ *v.i.* to become dirty

dis·a·bil·i·ty (disəbíliti:) *pl.* **dis·a·bil·i·ties** *n.* a being physically or mentally disabled ‖ a cause of this ‖ a legal disqualification or incapacity

dis·a·ble (diséib'l) *pres. part.* **dis·a·bling** *past* and *past part.* **dis·a·bled** *v.t.* to incapacitate physically or mentally ‖ to incapacitate legally **dis·á·ble·ment** *n.*

dis·ad·van·tage (disədvǽntidʒ, disədvántidʒ) 1. *n.* an unfavorable circumstance, drawback, handicap ‖ loss, detriment 2. *pres. part.* **dis·ad·van·tag·ing** *past* and *past part.* **dis·ad·van·taged** *v.t.* to place at a disadvantage

disadvantaged *adj.* of economically deprived or handicapped people or groups of people **disadvantaged** *n.*

dis·a·gree (disəgrí:) *v.i. pres. part.* **dis·a·gree·ing** *past* and *past part.* **dis·a·greed** to differ in opinion or total ‖ to quarrel, squabble ‖ (with 'with') to be harmful or unsuitable ‖ to upset the digestion

dis·a·gree·a·ble (disəgrí:əb'l) *adj.* unpleasant ‖ ill-natured

dis·a·gree·ment (disəgrí:mənt) *n.* a disagreeing ‖ a being opposed or at variance

dis·ap·pear (disəpíər) *v.i.* to vanish, cease to be visible ‖ to be lost **dis·ap·péar·ance** *n.*

dis·ap·point (disəpɔ́int) *v.t.* to fail to come up to the expectations of ‖ to thwart, frustrate ‖ to break a promise to (someone) **dis·ap·póint·ed** *adj.* unhappy because of frustrated hopes etc. **dis·ap·póint·ing** *adj.* **dis·ap·póint·ment** *n.* someone who or something which disappoints ‖ the state of distress resulting from being disappointed

dis·ap·prov·al (disəprú:vəl) *n.* moral condemnation ‖ administrative rejection

dis·ap·prove (disəprú:v) *pres. part.* **dis·ap·prov·ing** *past* and *past part.* **dis·ap·proved** *v.t.* to have or express an unfavorable opinion of ‖ to refuse to sanction ‖ *v.i.* to withhold approval **dis·ap·próv·ing·ly** *adv.*

dis·arm (disárm) *v.t.* to deprive of weapons ‖ to deprive of the power to harm ‖ to allay the wrath or suspicion of, or turn aside the criticism of ‖ *v.i.* to cut down armaments, or renounce them

dis·ar·ray (disəréi) 1. *n.* a lack of order ‖ a state of confusion ‖ disorderly dress 2. *v.t.* to throw into disorder

dis·as·ter (dizǽstər, dizástər) *n.* an event causing great loss, hardship or suffering to many people ‖ a great or sudden misfortune ‖ a fiasco **dis·ás·trous** *adj.*

dis·a·vow (disəváu) *v.t.* to refuse to acknowledge or accept responsibility for, disclaim **dis·a·vów·al** *n.*

dis·band (disbǽnd) *v.t.* to end the existence of (an organization, e.g. a theatrical company) || *v.i.* to disperse, break up **dis·bánd·ment** *n.*

dis·bar (disbár) *pres. part.* **dis·bar·ring** *past* and *past part.* **dis·barred** *v.t. (law)* to expel from the bar, to deprive of the status of attorney **dis·bár·ment** *n.*

dis·be·lieve (dịsbilí:v) *pres. part.* **dis·be·liev·ing** *past* and *past part.* **dis·be·lieved** *v.i.* (with 'in') to refuse to believe || (with 'in') to lack faith || *v.t.* to refuse to accept as true **dis·be·liev·er** *n.*

dis·burse (disbə́:rs) *pres. part.* **dis·burs·ing** *past* and *past part.* **dis·bursed** *v.t.* to pay out (money) || *(rhet.)* to defray (expenses) **dis·búrse·ment** *n.* a disbursing || the money paid out

dis·card 1. (diskárd) *v.t.* to get rid of as being of no further use || *v.i. (card games)* to throw out a card or cards from a hand **2.** (dískərd) *n. (card games)* the act of discarding || the card or cards thrown out || something gotten rid of or rejected

dis·cern (disə́:rn, dizə́:rn) *v.t.* to see, or make out through any of the senses || to perceive with the mind **dis·cérn·i·ble** *adj.* **dis·cérn·i·bly** *adv.* **dis·cérn·ing** *adj.* discriminating, perceptive **dis·cérn·ment** *n.* a discerning || discrimination, insight, perception

dis·charge 1. (distʃárdʒ) *v.t. pres. part.* **dis·charg·ing** *past* and *past part.* **dis·charged** to unload || to send forth, give out || to absolve, free oneself from (an obligation or debt) by an act or payment || to release (an arrow or bullet etc.), fire (a gun) || to rid of an electric charge || to dismiss (a servant, employee) || to release (e.g. a prisoner or patient) || to remove the dye from (a fabric) || *(med.)* to emit (e.g. pus) || (of a gun) to go off, fire || to lose a charge of electricity || to shed a load **2.** (dístʃardʒ) *n.* an unloading of a ship or cargo || a sending forth or thing sent forth || the fulfilment of an obligation, esp. the payment of a debt || the firing of a gun etc. || a release || a dismissal || *(law)* an acquittal || *(law)* a dismissal of a court order || a certificate of release or payment etc. || *(med.)* the emission of matter || the process of removing dye **dis·chárg·er** *n.* someone who discharges || an apparatus for discharging electricity

dis·ci·ple (disáip'l) *n.* someone who accepts the doctrine or teachings of another, esp. an early follower of Christ || one of the 12 Apostles **dis·ci·ple·ship** *n.*

dis·ci·pli·nar·y (dísəplineri:) *adj.* of or relating to discipline || concerned with mental training

dis·ci·pline (dísəplin) **1.** *n.* the training of the mind and character || a branch of learning || a mode of life in accordance with rules || self-control || control, order, obedience to rules || *(eccles.)* a system of practical rules for the members of a Church or an order || a scourge for religious penance **2.** *v.t. pres. part.* **dis·ci·plin·ing** *past* and *past part.* **dis·ci·plined** to bring under control || to train || to punish

dis·claim (diskléim) *v.t.* to refuse to acknowledge (e.g. responsibility) || *(law)* to renounce a legal claim to || *v.i. (law)* to make a disclaimer

dis·claim·er (diskléimər) *n.* a renunciation, e.g. of a legal claim || a disavowal, e.g. of statements made in one's praise || a repudiation, e.g. of someone's self-criticism

dis·close (disklóuz) *pres. part.* **dis·clos·ing** *past* and *past part.* **dis·closed** *v.t.* to reveal (e.g. a secret) || to expose to view **dis·clo·sure** (disklóuʒər) *n.* the act of disclosing || the thing disclosed

dis·col·or (diskʌ́lər) *v.t.* to spoil the color of, stain || *v.i.* to become changed or spoiled in color **dis·col·or·á·tion** *n.* **dis·cól·or·ment** *n.*

dis·com·fort (diskʌ́mfərt) *n.* physical or mental uneasiness

dis·con·cert (dịskənsə́:rt) *v.t.* to give a mental jolt to, confuse || to upset, spoil (e.g. plans) **dis·con·cért·ment** *n.*

dis·con·nect (dịskənékt) *v.t.* to cause to be no longer connected **dis·con·néct·ed** *adj.* disjoined, not connected || (of speech, writing) disjointed, incoherent **dis·con·nec·tion** (dịskənékʃən) *n.* a disconnecting or

being disconnected

dis·con·so·late (diskɔ́nsəlit) *adj.* cast down in spirits, utterly dejected

dis·con·tent (dịskəntént) **1.** *n.* dissatisfaction **2.** *v.t.* to make dissatisfied **dis·con·tént·ed** *adj.* **dis·con·tént·ment** *n.*

dis·con·tin·u·ance (dịskəntínju:əns) *n.* a discontinuing || *(law)* the discontinuing of an action because the plaintiff has not observed the formalities needed to keep it pending

dis·con·tin·u·a·tion (dịskəntinju:éiʃən) *n.* a discontinuing

dis·con·tin·ue (dịskəntínju:) *pres. part.* **dis·con·tin·u·ing** *past* and *past part.* **dis·con·tin·ued** *v.t.* to stop, give up || *v.i.* to cease

dis·con·tin·u·ous (dịskəntínju:əs) *adj.* not continuous, interrupted, intermittent

dis·cord (dískɔrd) *n.* disagreement, quarreling || a jarring combination of sounds **dis·córd·ance** *n.* **dis·córd·ant** *adj.*

dis·count (dískaunt) *n.* a sum deducted (by courtesy, not by right) from an account, e.g. if it is paid immediately or in advance || a sum deducted from the value of a bill of exchange etc. || a discounting || a reduction in price offered to the public for sales promotion

dis·count (diskáunt) *v.t.* to refuse to accept as being wholly true || to lend money on (e.g. negotiable paper) and deduct a discount or allowance for interest || to sell at a reduced price || to leave out of account deliberately as being of small importance, dismiss as negligible || to take (some future event of probability) into account in advance and so lessen its effect

dis·cour·age (diskə́:ridʒ, diskʌ́ridʒ) *pres. part.* **dis·cour·ag·ing** *past* and *past part.* **dis·cour·aged** *v.t* to sap or take away the courage of || to deter || to lessen enthusiasm for and so restrict or hinder || to tend no encouragement to || to seek to prevent (by homily etc., not by law) **dis·cóur·age·ment** *n.* a discouraging or being discouraged || something which discourages

dis·cour·te·ous (diskə́:rti:əs) *adj.* unmannerly, impolite

dis·cov·er (diskʌ́vər) *v.t.* to find out || to find by exploration || to come across || *v.i.* to make a discovery **dis·cóv·er·y** *pl.* **dis·cóv·er·ies** *n.* a discovering || the thing discovered

dis·cred·it (diskrédit) **1.** *v.t.* to destroy the trustworthiness of (someone or something) || to refuse to believe or have confidence in **2.** *n.* disesteem || a cause of loss of repute || doubt, disbelief

dis·creet (diskrí:t) *adj.* circumspect in word or deed || able to keep silent about matters where prudence requires it || tactful || quietly tasteful, not showy

dis·crep·an·cy (diskrépənsi:) *pl.* **dis·crep·an·cies** *n.* the state of being discrepant || an instance of this

dis·crim·i·nate (diskrímineit) *pres. part.* **dis·crim·i·nat·ing** *past* and *past part.* **dis·crim·i·nat·ed** *v.i.* to use good judgment in making a choice || to observe or make distinctions || *v.t.* to distinguish (one thing) from another, *to discriminate good from bad* || to serve to distinguish **to discriminate against** to single out for unfavorable treatment **dis·crím·i·nat·ing** *adj.* having fine judgment or taste || treating differently, making distinctions, *a discriminating tariff*

dis·crim·i·na·tion (diskriminéiʃən) *n.* a choosing with care || good taste, discernment || the making of distinctions (often unfair) in meting out treatment, service etc.

dis·cus (dískəs) *pl.* **dis·cus·es, dis·ci** (díski) *n. (athletics)* a heavy disk (4 lbs 6.4 ozs), thrown as far as possible as a trial of strength and skill from a circle 8 ft 2½ ins in diameter

dis·cuss (diskʌ́s) *v.t.* to exchange ideas about (e.g. a problem, plan) || to debate (a set theme) || to gossip about || to allow one's opinions on (a matter) to be questioned **dis·cúss·i·ble** *adj.*

dis·dain (disdéin) **1.** *v.t.* to scorn || to have contempt for (e.g. subterfuge) || to dismiss as not to be taken into consideration **2.** *n.* contempt, scorn **dis·dáin·ful**

adj.

dis·ease (disíːz) *n.* an unhealthy condition ‖ a particular malady **dis·eased** *adj.*

dis·en·chant (dǝsintʃǽnt, dǝsintʃánt) *v.t.* to disillusion, free from enchantment **dis·en·chánt·ment** *n.*

dis·fig·ure (disfígjǝr) *pres. part.* **dis·fig·ur·ing** *past* and *past part.* **dis·fig·ured** *v.t.* to spoil the appearance of **dis·fig·ure·ment** *n.* a disfiguring or being disfigured ‖ something which disfigures

dis·grace (disgréis) **1.** *n.* loss of honor or esteem ‖ shame, ignominy ‖ someone or something causing shame or discredit **2.** *v.t. pres. part.* **dis·grac·ing** *past* and *past part.* **dis·graced** to bring shame or discredit upon ‖ to remove from favor or position **dis·gráce·ful** *adj.*

dis·guise (disgáiz) **1.** *v.t. pres. part.* **dis·guis·ing** *past* and *past part.* **dis·guised** to change the normal appearance, sound etc. of, so as to conceal identity ‖ to hide, conceal **2.** *n.* an altering of appearance to conceal identity ‖ the clothing etc. used to work this change **dis·gúise·ment** *n.*

dis·gust (disgást) *n.* strong aversion, loathing

dis·gust *v.t.* to fill with loathing ‖ to make indignant ‖ to offend the modesty of (someone) **dis·gúst·ing** *adj.*

dis·gust·ed (disgástid) *adj.* (with 'at', 'with' or 'by') feeling or showing disgust **dis·gúst·ed·ly** *adv.*

dish (diʃ) **1.** *n.* a shallow vessel, typically of glass or earthenware, esp. for serving or holding food at meals ‖ the food served in such a dish ‖ the quantity a dish will hold **2.** *v.t.* to put (food) into a dish ‖ *(pop.)* to frustrate (hopes), put an end to (chances)

dis·heart·en (dishárt'n) *v.t.* to discourage, dispirit **dis·héart·en·ing** *adj.* **dis·héart·en·ment** *n.*

dis·hon·est (disónist) *adj.* not honest, lacking integrity ‖ insincere

dis·hon·es·ty (disónistiː) *pl.* **dis·hon·es·ties** *n.* lack of honesty ‖ a dishonest act, fraud

dis·hon·or (disónǝr) *n.* disgrace ‖ something which brings disgrace ‖ someone who causes disgrace

dishonor *v.t.* to treat disrespectfully ‖ to bring shame or disgrace on ‖ (of a bank) to refuse to pay or accept (a check etc.)

dis·hon·or·a·ble (disónǝrǝb'l) *adj.* not honorable, disgraceful **dis·hón·or·a·bly** *adv.*

dis·il·lu·sion (disilúːʒǝn) **1.** *v.t.* to free from illusion, disenchant **2.** *n.* the state of being disillusioned **dis·il·lú·sion·ment** *n.*

dis·in·fect (dǝsinfékt) *v.t.* to free from infection by destroying harmful microorganisms

dis·in·fect·ant (dǝsinféktǝnt) **1.** *n.* an agent used to kill harmful microorganisms, esp. a chemical used for such a purpose **2.** *adj.* suitable for use in disinfecting

dis·in·her·it (dǝsinhérit) *v.t.* to deprive of an inheritance **dis·in·hér·i·tance** *n.*

dis·in·te·grate (disíntigreit) *pres. part.* **dis·in·te·grat·ing** *past* and *past part.* **dis·in·te·grat·ed** *v.t.* to separate or break up into fragments ‖ *v.i.* to break up, lose unity, go to pieces **dis·in·te·grá·tion, dis·in·te·gra·tor** *ns*

disk, disc (disk) *n.* a flat circular plate ‖ *(computer)* magnetic disc round, magnetic coated plastic record for storing data ‖ (esp. **disc**) a phonograph record ‖ anything which is, or appears, round and flat ‖ any such structure in a plant or in the body, esp. the gristly pads cushioned between the vertebrae

dis·like (disláik) **1.** *v.t. pres. part.* **dis·lik·ing** *past* and *past part.* **dis·liked** to feel an antipathy for **2.** *n.* an aversion, antipathy

dis·lo·cate (dísloukeit) *pres. part.* **dis·lo·cat·ing** *past* and *past part.* **dis·lo·cat·ed** *v.t.* to put out of joint, displace ‖ to upset (e.g. plans) **dis·lo·cá·tion** *n.*

dis·mal (dízmǝl) *adj.* gloomy, dreary, depressed ‖ depressing

dis·man·tle (dismǽnt'l) *pres. part.* **dis·man·tling** *past* and *past part.* **dis·man·tled** *v.t.* to take to pieces ‖ to strip of furniture and equipment ‖ to deprive (a fortification etc.) of defenses, guns etc.

dis·may (disméi) **1.** *v.t.* to fill with consternation or alarm **2.** *n.* consternation, alarm

dis·mem·ber (dismémbǝr) *v.t.* to divide limb from limb ‖ to divide, partition (esp. a country) **dis·mém·ber·ment** *n.*

dis·miss (dismís) *v.t.* to send away, tell to go ‖ to discharge from employment, office etc. ‖ to discard mentally, put out of one's thoughts ‖ to treat briefly ‖ *(law)* to refuse further hearing to (a case) **dis·míss·al** *n.* a dismissing or being dismissed

dis·o·be·di·ence (dǝsǝbíːdiːǝns) *n.* failure or refusal to obey **dis·o·bé·di·ent** *adj.* failing or refusing to obey

dis·o·bey (dǝsǝbéi) *v.t.* to refuse or fail to obey (a person, orders etc.) ‖ *v.i.* to be disobedient

dis·or·der (disɔ́rdǝr) **1.** *n.* a state of confusion ‖ disarray, untidiness ‖ riot, lawlessness ‖ a disease, ailment **2.** *v.t.* to confuse, disarrange ‖ to upset the health of **dis·ór·der·ly** *adj.* unruly, wild ‖ untidy ‖ *(law)* violating public order

dis·or·gan·i·za·tion (disɔrgǝnizéiʃǝn) *n.* a disorganizing or being disorganized

dis·or·gan·ize (disɔ́rgǝnaiz) *pres. part.* **dis·or·gan·iz·ing** *past* and *past part.* **dis·or·gan·ized** *v.t.* to upset the planned scheme of (things) ‖ to bring about a state of disorder in

dis·o·ri·ent (disɔ́riːent, disóuriːent) *v.t.* to confuse (a person) about his bearings ‖ to make (a person) unsure of where he belongs, make (him) ill-adjusted

dis·o·ri·en·tate (disɔ́riːenteit, disóuriːenteit) *pres. part.* **dis·o·ri·en·tat·ing** *past* and *past part.* **dis·o·ri·en·tat·ed** *v.t.* to construct (a church) with the chancel not to the east **dis·o·ri·en·tá·tion** *n.*

dis·own (disóun) *v.t.* to deny authorship of ‖ to repudiate ‖ to disclaim, deny

dis·par·age (dispǽridʒ) *pres. part.* **dis·par·ag·ing** *past* and *past part.* **dis·par·aged** *v.t.* to talk to the detriment of (a person etc.) ‖ to belittle, deprecate **dis·pár·age·ment** *n.* **dis·pár·ag·ing** *adj.*

dis·par·i·ty (dispǽritiː) *pl.* **dis·par·i·ties** *n.* inequality, great difference

dis·patch, des·patch (dispǽtʃ) **1.** *v.t.* to send off (a letter etc.) ‖ to put to death, kill ‖ to put a quick end to, finish off promptly (a piece of work, business etc.) **2.** *n.* a sending off (e.g. of a letter or messenger) ‖ a putting to death ‖ a discharging (of business or a duty) ‖ promptitude ‖ a message, esp. one sent in to a newspaper ‖ an official report, esp. military or diplomatic

dis·pel (dispél) *pres. part.* **dis·pel·ling** *past* and *past part.* **dis·pelled** *v.t.* to drive away, disperse

dis·pen·sa·ble (dispénsǝb'l) *adj.* capable of being done without, not necessary ‖ capable of being given out or distributed

dis·pen·sa·tion (dispenséiʃǝn, dispǝnséiʃǝn) *n.* the act of meting out ‖ a particular fate ordained by providence ‖ an exemption from a rule, penalty or law

dis·pense (dispéns) *pres. part.* **dis·pens·ing** *past* and *past part.* **dis·pensed** *v.t.* to distribute, give out ‖ to prepare and give out (medicine) ‖ to administer (justice) ‖ to grant a dispensation to ‖ to exempt (from a rule) ‖ *v.i.* (with 'with') to do without **dis·péns·er** *n.* someone who dispenses or something which dispenses ‖ a person who makes up medical prescriptions

dis·perse (dispɔ́ːrs) *pres. part.* **dis·pers·ing** *past* and *past part.* **dis·persed** *v.t.* to scatter, disseminate ‖ to

---

(a) æ, c**a**t; ɑ, c**a**r; ɔ f**a**wn; ei, sn**a**ke. **(e)** e, h**e**n; iː, sh**ee**p; iǝ, d**ee**r; ɛǝ, b**ea**r. **(i)** i, f**i**sh; ai, t**i**ger; ǝː, b**i**rd. **(o)** o, **o**x; au, c**o**w; ou, g**o**at; u, p**oo**r; ɔi, r**o**yal. **(u)** ʌ, d**u**ck; u, b**u**ll; uː, g**oo**se; ǝ, b**a**cillus; juː, c**u**be. x, lo**ch**; θ, **th**ink; ð, bo**th**er; z, **Z**en; ʒ, corsa**g**e; dʒ, sava**g**e; ŋ, oranguta**n**g; j, **y**ak; ʃ, **fish**; tʃ, fe**tch**; 'l, rabb**l**e; 'n, redd**en**. Complete pronunciation key appears inside front cover.

cause to break up and go away ‖ to put in position at separate points ‖ *(optics)* to separate (wavelengths) usually by their different velocities in a refracting medium, but also by diffraction ‖ *v.i.* to break up, go away in different directions ‖ to become dispersed **dis·pér·sive** *adj.*

dis·place (displéis) *pres. part.* **dis·plac·ing** *past and past part.* **dis·placed** *v.t.* to take the place of, oust ‖ to remove from office ‖ to remove from its usual place

dis·play (displéi) 1. *v.t.* to exhibit ‖ (of birds) to exhibit (plumage) in courtship, or aggressively ‖ to reveal, show (qualities etc.) ‖ to set out in large or distinctive printing type ‖ to show ostentatiously ‖ *v.i.* (of birds) the characteristic behavior (e.g. the exhibition of plumage etc.) of a male bird before the female while courting or to protect his own territory ‖ a showing ‖ an ostentatious showing ‖ an arragnement of printing type (usually large) to set out titles etc. or command attention

dis·please (displí:z) *pres. part.* **dis·pleas·ing** *past and past part.* **dis·pleased** *v.t.* to annoy, offend

dis·pleas·ure (displéʒər) *n.* annoyance, disapproval

dis·pos·a·ble (dispóuzəb'l) 1. *adj.* that can be disposed of, got rid of ‖ available for use 2. *n.* something that is to be thrown away after use, e.g., beer cans

dis·pose (dispóuz) *pres. part.* **dis·pos·ing** *past and past part.* **dis·posed** *v.t.* to place in position, arrange ‖ to incline ‖ *v.i.* to determine the outcome **to dispose of** to get rid of ‖ to deal as one wishes with ‖ to make final arrangements about ‖ to demolish (arguments etc.) ‖ to stow ‖ to eat (food, a meal) ‖ to sell

dis·po·si·tion (dịspəzíʃən) *n.* a being disposed ‖ temperament ‖ a placing, arrangement ‖ the power to dispose of something ‖ a making over of property, bestowal ‖ a dispensation ‖ a plan or preparatory countermeasure

dis·pos·sess (dịspəzés) *v.t.* to deprive of property ‖ to oust **dis·pos·sés·sion, dis·pos·sés·sor** *ns*

dis·prove (disprú:v) *pres. part.* **dis·prov·ing** *past and past part.* **dis·proved** *v.t.* to prove to be false

dis·put·a·ble (dispjú:təb'l, díspjutəb'l) *adj.* questionable, open to dispute **dis·pút·a·bly** *adv.*

dis·pute (dispjú:t) 1. *v. pres. part.* **dis·put·ing** *past and past part.* **dis·put·ed** *v.i.* to quarrel, argue ‖ *v.t.* to question the truth of ‖ *(rhet.)* to fight hard for 2. *n.* a quarrel

dis·qual·i·fi·ca·tion (diskwɒlifikéiʃən) *n.* a disqualifying or being disqualified ‖ something which disqualifies

dis·qual·i·fy (diskwólifai) *pres. part.* **dis·qual·i·fy·ing** *past and past part.* **dis·qual·i·fied** *v.t.* to render unfit ‖ *(sport)* to judge ineligible to continue a game, or receive a prize, etc. ‖ to take a legal right or privilege from

dis·re·gard (dịsrigárd) 1. *v.t.* to pay no heed to, ignore ‖ to treat as not mattering 2. *n.* a lack of proper regard ‖ indifference ‖ neglect

dis·re·pair (dịsripéər) *n.* the state of needing repair

dis·re·spect (dịsrispékt) *n.* lack of respect, incivility **dis·re·spéct·ful** *adj.*

dis·rupt (disrápt) *v.t.* to tear apart, shatter ‖ to interrupt or cause to cease entirely

dis·rup·tion (disrápʃən) *n.* a disrupting or being disrupted

dis·sat·is·fac·tion (dịssætisfǽkʃən, dịssætisfǽkʃən) *n.* a being dissatisfied

dis·sat·is·fied (dissǽtisfaid) *adj.* not satisfied ‖ discontented

dis·sat·is·fy (dissǽtisfai) *pres. part.* **dis·sat·is·fy·ing** *past and past part.* **dis·sat·is·fied** *v.t.* to fail to satisfy ‖ to make discontented

dis·sect (disékt, daisékt) *v.t.* to cut up ‖ to cut open in order to display and examine the parts of (a plant, animal, etc.) ‖ to examine in detail **dis·séc·ted** *adj.* cut in pieces, cut open

dis·sen·sion (disénʃən) *n.* a difference of opinions, discord, strife

dis·sent (disént) 1. *v.i.* to withhold assent ‖ to be in positive opposition, hold a declared contrary opinion ‖ to refuse to conform to the doctrines or practices of orthodoxy or the established Church **dis·sént·er** *n.* someone who dissents 2. *n.* disagreement, difference of opinion ‖ nonconformity in religion

dis·serv·ice (dissɔ́:rvis) *n.* a well-meant but in fact harmful attempt to be of service

dis·si·pate (dísəpeit) *pres. part.* **dis·si·pat·ing** *past and past part.* **dis·si·pat·ed** *v.t.* to break up and drive away, dispel ‖ to waste, squander ‖ *v.i.* to disperse, vanish **dís·si·pat·ed** *adj.* dissolute ‖ squandered, wasted ‖ dispersed

dis·solve (dizólv) 1. *v. pres. part.* **dis·solv·ing** *past and past part.* **dis·solved** *v.t.* to cause to pass into a solution ‖ to put an end to ‖ to disperse ‖ *v.i.* to pass into solution ‖ (*fig.*, with 'into') to break, melt ‖ *(movies,* of a sequence) to fade gradually (into another shot) 2. *n.* *(movies)* the fading of one shot into another **dis·sól·vent** 1. *adj.* capable of dissolving something 2. *n.* a dissolving agent, a solvent

dis·so·nance (dísənəns) *n.* *(mus.)* discord ‖ disagreement ‖ inconsistency between words and actions, or words and beliefs, or between beliefs

dis·suade (diswéid) *pres. part.* **dis·suad·ing** *past and past part.* **dis·suad·ed** *v.t.* to change the intention of (a person) by persuasion **dis·sua·sion** (diswéiʒən) *n.* **dis·sua·sive** (diswéisiv) *adj.*

dis·taff (dístæf, dístaf) 1. *n.* a cleft staff or stick on which wool or flax is wound for spinning by hand ‖ the corresponding part of a spinning wheel 2. *adj.* *(rhet.)* relating to a woman or women, female

dis·tance (dístəns) 1. *n.* an interval in space ‖ the remoter part of a view ‖ an interval of time ‖ reserve, aloofness ‖ *(sports)* the specified length of a race 2. *v.t. pres. part.* **dis·tanc·ing** *past and past part.* **dis·tanced** to put or maintain at a distance ‖ to outstrip

dis·tant (dístənt) *adj.* far away ‖ remote in time ‖ far removed in relationship, likeness etc. ‖ standoffish, reserved, aloof

dis·taste (distéist) *n.* dislike ‖ aversion **dis·táste·ful** *adj.* disagreeable to the taste ‖ causing aversion

dis·till, dis·til (distíl) *pres. part.* **dis·till·ing, dis·til·ling** *past and past part.* **dis·tilled** *v.i.* (of a liquid or solid) to undergo a process of evaporation and condensation for puritification or fractionation ‖ *v.t.* to cause to undergo this process ‖ to extract the pure essence of (something) **dis·til·late** (dístəlit, dístəleit, distílit) *n.* the product of distillation

dis·til·la·tion (dịstəléiʃən) *n.* a distilling or being distilled

dis·till·er·y (distíləri) *pl.* **dis·till·er·ies** *n.* a building where spirits are manufactured by distilling

dis·tinct (distíŋkt) *adj.* clear, plain ‖ marked, definite ‖ separate, individual, serving to distinguish

dis·tinc·tion (distíŋkʃən) *n.* the making of a difference, discrimination ‖ a difference so made ‖ a being different ‖ modest fame ‖ breeding or eminence ‖ a mark of honor, a decoration or award

dis·tin·guish (distíŋgwiʃ) *v.t.* to recognize (something) as distinct from other things ‖ to tell the difference between ‖ to make distinct, characterize ‖ to make out, perceive ‖ to win honor for (oneself etc.) ‖ *v.i.* to draw distinctions, discriminate ‖ to point out a difference (esp. in syllogistic disputation) **dis·tín·guish·a·ble** *adj.* **dis·tín·guished** *adj.* famous, eminent ‖ showing distinction

dis·tort (distɔ́rt) *v.t.* to twist out of shape ‖ to give a false significance to, misrepresent **dis·tór·tion** *n.* a distorting or being distorted ‖ *(radio)* the alteration of wave form during transmission or reception ‖ *(optics)* the lens aberration due to the variation of magnification with distance from the lens axis **dis·tór·tion·al** *adj.*

dis·tract (distrǽkt) *v.t.* to divert (attention) ‖ to divert the attention of ‖ to disturb, confuse ‖ to bewilder ‖ to drive nearly mad

dis·trac·tion (distrǽkʃən) *n.* a distracting or being distracted ‖ an interest that provides relaxation ‖ a diversion, interruption ‖ something which prevents concentration ‖ perplexity, bewilderment ‖ frenzy, near madness

dis·traught (distrɔ́t) *adj.* almost crazy with anxiety etc., frantic

dis·tress (distrés) *n.* considerable mental or physical discomfort or pain ‖ acute financial hardship ‖ a being in great difficulty or danger ‖ *(law)* the act of distraining ‖ *(law)* that which is seized in distraining **distress** *v.t.* to cause considerable mental or physical discomfort or pain

dis·trib·ute (distríbju:t) *pres. part.* **dis·trib·ut·ing** *past and past part.* **dis·trib·ut·ed** *v.t.* to deal out, divide out ‖ to spread, scatter, put at different places

dis·tri·bu·tion (distrəbjú:ʃən) *n.* a distributing or being distributed ‖ the marketing of industrial products ‖ concentration or diffusion **dis·tri·bú·tion·al** *adj.*

dis·trib·u·tor (distríbjutər) *n.* someone who distributes ‖ an agent who markets goods ‖ a device which distributes electric power to the plugs of an internal-combustion engine

dis·trict (dístrikt) **1.** *n.* a region ‖ a political or geographical division of a city, county, state etc. marked off for administrative or other purposes **2.** *v.t.* to divide into districts

dis·trust (distrʌ́st) **1.** *n.* a lack of trsut **2.** *v.t.* to have no trust in ‖ to regard with suspicion **dis·trúst·ful**

dis·turb (distɔ́:rb) *v.t.* to upset the peace of, bother ‖ to worry ‖ to move out of place

dis·turb·ance (distɔ́:rbəns) *n.* a disturbing or being disturbed ‖ public disorder, tumult ‖ *(law)* an interfering with rights or property

dis·u·nite (disju:náit) *pres. part.* **dis·u·nit·ing** *past and past part.* **dis·u·nit·ed** *v.t.* to destroy the harmony or solidarity of (a number of people) ‖ *v.i.* to fall apart, separate **dis·u·ni·ty** (disjú:niti:) *pl.* **dis·u·ni·ties** *n.*

ditch (ditʃ) **1.** *n.* a narrow, shallow trench, esp. for drainage or irrigation **2.** *v.i.* to make or repair ditches ‖ *v.t.* to provide with a ditch or ditches ‖ to drive (a vehicle) into a ditch ‖ *(pop.)* to abandon, get rid of

di·ur·nal (daiɔ́:rn'l) *adj.* *(astron.)* completed once in one day ‖ daily ‖ *(zool.)* active mainly in the daytime

di·van (divǽn, divɑ́n, dáivæn) *n.* a long low couch without back or ends, generally usable as a bed ‖ an Oriental council of state ‖ an Oriental court of justice

dive (daiv) **1.** *pres. part.* **div·ing** *past* **dived, dove** (douv) *past part.* **dived** *v.i.* to plunge headfirst into water, esp. with controlled grace ‖ (of a submarine, water bird etc.) to go underwater ‖ (of an airplane, bird of prey etc.) to plunge down steeply through the air ‖ to dart quickly, esp. so as to hide or flee ‖ (with 'into') to plunge one's hand ‖ to immerse oneself (e.g. in a subject) **2.** *n.* a diving into water ‖ any of the graceful classical figures of the art of diving ‖ a sudden swift plunge of the body ‖ (of a submarine or aircraft) a plunging ‖ *(pop.)* a low-class establishment for drinking, gambling etc.

div·er (dáivər) *n.* someone who dives ‖ someone who works below water in a diving bell or diving suit

di·verge (daivɔ́:rdʒ, divɔ́:rdʒ) *pres. part.* **di·verg·ing** *past and past part.* **di·verged** *v.i.* to go in branching directions ‖ (with 'from') to turn aside ‖ to deviate from the normal, differ **di·vér·gence** *n.* **di·vér·gen·cy** *pl.* **di·vér·gen·cies** *n.* **di·vér·gent** *adj.* diverging ‖ (of a lens) causing a change in the direction of rays away from a common direction or point

di·verse (divɔ́:rs, daivɔ́:rs, dáivɔ:rs) *adj.* different, unlike in character or qualities ‖ various

di·ver·si·fi·ca·tion (divə:rsifikéiʃən, daivə:rsifikéiʃən) *n.* a diversifying or being diversified

di·ver·si·fy (divɔ́:rsifai, daivɔ́:rsifai) *pres. part.*

di·ver·si·fy·ing *past and past part.* **di·ver·si·fied** *v.t.* to make varied

di·ver·sion (divɔ́:rʒən, divɔ́:rʃən, daivɔ́:rʒən, daivɔ́:rʃən) *n.* a turning aside, deviating ‖ something which brings pleasant mental distraction ‖ *(mil.)* a ruse to divert the attention of an enemy **di·ver·sion·ar·y** (divɔ́:rʒəneri:, divɔ́:rʃəneri:, daivɔ́:rʒəneri:, daivɔ́:rʃəneri:) *adj.* *(mil.)* intended to create a diversion

di·ver·si·ty (divɔ́:rsiti:, daivɔ́:rsiti:) *pl.* **di·ver·si·ties** *n.* the state or quality of being diverse ‖ an instance of this ‖ variety

di·vert (daivɔ́:rt, divɔ́:rt) *v.t.* to turn aside ‖ to distract ‖ to amuse, entertain **di·vért·ing** *adj.*

di·vide (diváid) **1.** *v. pres. part.* **di·vid·ing** *past and past part.* **di·vid·ed** *v.t.* to separate ‖ to deal out, share ‖ to put into separate groups ‖ to cause a disagreement between ‖ to mark out, graduate ‖ *(math.)* to find out how many times one number is contained in (another) ‖ *v.i.* to do mathematical division ‖ *(math.,* of one number) to be contained a specified number of times in another number ‖ to separate, branch **2.** *n.* a watershed ‖ a line of division **di·víd·ed** *adj.*

div·i·dend (dívidend) *n.* the interest or share of profits payable to shareholders on stock or bonds ‖ the share due to creditors of an insolvent estate ‖ the individual's share of a sum divided ‖ *(math.)* the number to be divided by another ‖ a bonus or share of surplus given to a policyholder by an insurance company

di·vine (diváin) **1.** *adj.* of God or a god ‖ addressed to God ‖ coming from God ‖ having the nature of a god ‖ *(pop.)* superlatively good or beautiful **2.** *n.* a theologian ‖ a priest or clergyman **3.** *v. pres. part.* **di·vin·ing** *past and past part.* **di·vined** *v.t.* to guess ‖ to foretell ‖ *v.i.* to detect the presence of water or metals underground by means of a forked, esp. hazel, twig or rods ‖ to practice divination **di·vín·er** *n.*

di·vin·i·ty (divíniti:) *pl.* **di·vin·i·ties** *n.* the quality of being divine ‖ a god ‖ theology ‖ the study in schools etc. of the Bible and of Church doctrine **the Di·vin·i·ty** God

di·vis·i·ble (divízʌb'l) *adj.* capable of being divided ‖ *(math.)* capable of being divided without a remainder **di·vís·i·bly** *adv.*

di·vi·sion (divíʒən) *n.* a dividing or being divided ‖ a distribution ‖ a sharing ‖ something which divides ‖ a section of a larger group ‖ *(math.)* the process of finding out how many times one number is contained in another ‖ lack of harmony, disagreement ‖ the separation of the members of a debating chamber for voting ‖ *(mil.)* a section of a corps, grouping a number of regiments ‖ a special-purpose formation **di·ví·sion·al** *adj.*

di·vorce (divɔ́rs, divóurs) *n.* a legal dissolution of marriage ‖ any marked or total separation

di·vulge (daivʌ́ldʒ, divʌ́ldʒ) *pres. part.* **di·vulg·ing** *past and past part.* **di·vulged** *v.t.* to make known, reveal **di·vúlge·ment, di·vúl·gence** *ns*

diz·zi·ness (dízi:nis) *n.* the state of being dizzy

diz·zy (dízi:) **1.** *adj. comp.* **diz·zi·er** *superl.* **diz·zi·est** experiencing a sensation of vertigo ‖ mentally confused ‖ such as to cause vertigo or mental turmoil **2.** *v.t. pres. part.* **diz·zy·ing** *past and past part.* **diz·zied** to make dizzy

do (du:) *v. 1st and 2nd pers. sing. pres.* **do** *3rd pers. sing. pres.* **does** (dʌz) *1st, 2nd and 3rd pers. pl. pres.* **do** *pres. part.* **do·ing** *past* **did** *past part.* **done** (dʌn) *v.t.* to perform (an action or activity) ‖ to work at, have as occupation ‖ to deal with in required fashion ‖ to accomplish, finish ‖ to have a mechanical performance of ‖ to cook ‖ to render ‖ to play the part of ‖ to present (a play) ‖ *(pop.)* to swindle

---

(**a**) æ, c*a*t; ɑ, c*a*r; ɔ f*aw*n; ei, sn*a*ke. (**e**) e, h*e*n; i:, sh*ee*p; iə, d*ee*r; ɛə, b*ea*r. (**i**) i, f*i*sh; ai, t*i*ger; ə:, b*i*rd. (**o**) o, *o*x; au, c*ow*; ou, g*oa*t; u, p*oo*r; ɔi, r*oy*al. (**u**) ʌ, d*u*ck; u, b*u*ll; u:, g*oo*se; ə, b*a*cillus; ju:, c*u*be. x, lo*ch*; θ, *th*ink; ð, bo*th*er; z, *Z*en; ʒ, corsa*g*e; dʒ, sava*g*e; ŋ, oranguta*ng*; j, *y*ak; ʃ, *fi*sh; tʃ, fe*tch*; 'l, rabb*le*; 'n, redd*en*. Complete pronunciation key appears inside front cover.

|| to make a tour of || (*pop.*) to upset, ruin || to translate || *v.i.* to act, behave || to progress || to be suitable || to suffice || used as a substitute verb to avoid repetition || used as an auxiliary verb in negation

doc·ile (dɒ́s'l) *adj.* tractable, amenable, easy to manage **do·cil·i·ty** (dɒsíliti:) *n.*

dock (dɒk) **1.** *n.* an enclosure or artificial basin in which ships may be loaded, unloaded, repaired etc. || a pier **2.** *v.t.* to bring or receive (a ship) into dock || *v.i.* to come into dock

doc·tor (dɒ́ktər) **1.** *n.* a person qualified to practice medicine || (*abbr.* Dr.) the title of a medical practitioner || (*abbr.* Dr.) the title of the holder of the highest university degree **2.** *v.t.* to give first aid to || to adulterate || to alter so as to improve || to alter so as to falsify || to patch up (machinery etc.) || *v.i.* to practice medicine **dóc·tor·al** *adj.* **doc·tor·ate** (dɒ́ktərit) *n.* the degree or rank of doctor **doc·to·ri·al** (dɒktɔ́ri:əl, dɒktóuri:əl) *adj.*

doc·tri·nal (dɒ́ktrin'l, dɒktráin'l) *adj.* of or relating to doctrine

doc·trine (dɒ́ktrin) *n.* the tenets of a literary or philosophical school or of a political or economic system, or the dogma of a religion

doc·u·ment 1. (dɒ́kjumənt) *n.* an official paper, a certificate || anything written that gives information or supplies evidence **2.** (dɒ́kjument) *v.t.* to support or supply with documents **doc·u·men·ta·rist** (dɒkjuméntərist) *n.* **doc·u·men·ta·ry** (dɒjuméntəri:) **1.** *adj.* set down in writing || fully supported by documents || having the validity of a document **2.** *pl.* **doc·u·men·ta·ries** *n.* a documentary film

dodge (dɒdʒ) **1.** *v. pres. part.* **dodg·ing** *past* and *past part.* **dodged** *v.i.* to move suddenly in order to avoid a blow, being seen etc. || to be constantly on the move from place to place with no clear line of progress || to be evasive || *v.t.* to avoid by trickery || to get quickly out of the way of || to evade (a difficulty or choice) **2.** *n.* a quick evasive movement || a trick, **dódg·er** *n.* someone who dodges || a person full of subterfuge || a handbill

doe (dou) *pl.* **does, doe** *n.* a female deer, hare or rabbit

doff (dɔf, dɒf) *v.t.* to take off (one's hat) in salutation

dog (dɒg, dɔg) **1.** *n.* a common quadruped of many breeds || a male of the species || (*pop.*) a fellow || a term of contempt or abuse || a mechanical gripping device || an iron bar spiked at each end for joining timbers together || (*pl.*) a pair of metal supports for logs burning on an open hearth **2.** *v.t. pres. part.* **dog·ging** *past* and *past part.* **dogged** to track like a hound || (*mech.*) to grip with a dog

dog·ged (dɒ́gid, dɔ́gid) *adj.* obstinate, pertinacious, persistent

dog·ma (dɔ́gmə, dɒ́gmə) *pl.* **dog·mas, dog·ma·ta** (dɔ́gmətə, dɒ́gmətə) *n.* a basic doctrinal point in religion or philosophy || such basic points collectively

dog·mat·ic (dɔgmǽtik, dɒgmǽtik) *adj.* of or relating to dogma, doctrinal || asserting views as if they were facts, esp. in an arrogant way **dog·mát·i·cal** *adj.* **dog·mát·ics** *n.*

doi·ly, doy·ley (dɔ́ili:) *pl.* **doi·lies** *n.* a small, usually round, ornamental mat of lace, paper or plastic placed on a cake plate or under a vase, ornament etc. or on the arms and backs of chairs to protect the material

dole (doul) **1.** *n.* a weekly relief payment made by a government to the unemployed || a share || a charitable distribution (esp. a stingy one) **2.** *v.t. pres. part.* **dol·ing** *past* and *past part.* **doled** (with 'out') to give out in small portions, often grudgingly

doll (dɒl) **1.** *n.* a miniature human figure, usually of a child, made as a toy || a pretty, empty-headed woman **2.** *v.t.* and *i.* (*pop.*, with 'up') to dress or make up too conspicuously

dol·lar (dɒ́lər) *n.* the basic monetary unit of the U.S.A., containing 100 cents || a monetary units containing 100 cents used also in Canada and some other countries || the symbol ($) of the dollar || a note of the value of one dollar || a U.S. silver coin

doll·y (dɒ́li:) *pl.* **doll·ies** *n.* a child's word for doll || a small wheeled trolley for carrying beams etc. || (*movies*) such a trolley for moving the camera about the set

dol·or·ous (dɒ́lərəs, dóulərəs) *adj.* (*rhet.*) sad, mournful || (*rhet.*) distressing

dolt (doult) *n.* a dull, stupid person, an oaf **dólt·ish** *adj.*

do·main (douméin) *n.* an estate or territory over which authority is exerted || a sphere of action or thought **do·mái·nal, do·má·ni·al** *adjs*

dome (doum) **1.** *n.* a large, hemispherical structure surmounting the highest part of a roof || anything thought of as resembling the dome of a building **2.** *v. pres. part.* **dom·ing** *past* and *past part.* **domed** *v.t.* to cover with, or shape like, a dome || *v.i.* to rise in a dome

do·mes·tic (dəméstik) **1.** *adj.* belonging to the home or house || relating to family affairs || home-loving and capable in household matters || tame || of one's own country, not foreign **2.** *n.* a household servant **do·més·ti·cal·ly** *adv.* in a domestic way || as regards a country's home affairs

do·mes·ti·cate (dəméstikeit) *v.t. pres. part.* **do·mes·ti·cat·ing** *past* and *past part.* **do·mes·ti·cat·ed** to tame (animals) and teach them to live with man and under his control || to make fond of home and skilled in household affairs **do·mes·ti·cá·tion** *n.*

dom·i·cile (dɒ́misail, dɒ́mis'l, dóumisail, dóumis'l) **1.** *n.* a home, dwelling place || a principal place of residence as fixed for legal purposes (taxation, etc.) **2.** *v.t. pres. part.* **dom·i·cil·ing** *past* and *past part.* **dom·i·ciled** to establish in a domicile **dom·i·cil·i·ar·y** (dɒmisíli:ɛri) *adj.*

dom·i·nance (dɒ́minəns) *n.* the quality of being dominant || a dominating influence

dom·i·nant (dɒ́minənt) **1.** *adj.* controlling, ruling || most noticeable || commanding by position || (*biol.*) of a character possessed by one parent which in a hybrid masks the corresponding alternative character derived from the other parent || of a species of plant or animal prevalent in a particular ecological community or at a given period of time || (*mus.*) of or related to the dominant **2.** *n.* (*mus.*) the fifth note of the scale relative to the tonic || (*biol.*) a dominant character or species

dom·i·nate (dɒ́mineit) *pres. part.* **dom·i·nat·ing** *past* and *past part.* **dom·i·nat·ed** *v.t.* to exert authority over, control || to tower above || to have a position which commands (e.g. a valley, view) || *v.i.* to exercise domination || to be predominant

dom·i·na·tion (dɒminéiʃən) *n.* authority, control || tyranny || predominance

dom·i·neer (dɒminíər) *v.i.* to force one's wishes, opinions or commands overbearingly on others || to tyrannize **dom·i·néer·ing** *adj.*

do·min·ion (dəmínjən) *n.* sovereignty, supreme authority || (*pl.*) an order of angels **Do·min·ion** the title of some self-governing, independent countries within the Commonwealth

don (dɒn) *pres. part.* **don·ning** *past* and *past part.* **donned** *v.t.* (*rhet.*) to put on (robes, armor etc.)

do·nate (douneit, dóuneit) *pres. part.* **do·nat·ing** *past* and *past part.* **do·nat·ed** *v.t.* to give or present (esp. money) to a society, institution etc.

do·na·tion (dounéiʃən) *n.* a gift, esp. of money, to a society or institution || the act of making such a gift

done (dʌn) *past. part.* of DO || *adj.* finished, completed || cooked as long as thought desirable

don·key (dɒ́ŋki:, dɑ́ŋki:) *pl.* **don·keys** *n.* the ass || (*pop.*) a stupid person

do·nor (dóunər) *n.* someone who makes a gift || a person giving some of his blood for transfusion or skin for grafting etc.

doom (du:m) **1.** *n.* a calamitous fate || ruin, complete destruction || the Last Judgment **2.** *v.t.* to destine to a fate involving death, suffering or unhappiness ‖ to destine to be destroyed

door (dor, dour) *n.* a solid barrier, swinging on hinges or sliding, to close the entrance of a building, a room, a cupboard etc. ‖ a means of obtaining something

dope (doup) **1.** *n.* *(pop.)* a narcotic ‖ a lubricant ‖ an additive used to produce a desired quality ‖ a coating used to give a fabric certain qualities ‖ *(pop.)* information that lets one into a secret ‖ *(pop.)* a very stupid person **2.** *v.t. pres. part.* **dop·ing** *past* and *past part.* **doped** to drug

dor·mant (dórmənt) *adj.* quiescent ‖ sleeping, or as if sleeping ‖ *(bot.)* inactive, resting ‖ *(zool.)* hibernating ‖ *(heraldry)* in a sleeping position

dor·mer (dórmər) *n.* a projecting window built out from the slope of a roof

dor·mi·to·ry (dórmitɔri:, dórmitɔuri:) *pl.* **dor·mi·to·ries** a communal sleeping room with a number of beds

dor·sal (dórsəl) **1.** *adj.* *(anat.)* on or lying near the back, in human anatomy sometimes posterior ‖ *(bot.)* away from the axis **2.** *n.* a dossal

dos·age (dóusidʒ) *n.* the amount and frequency in which a medicine is administered ‖ the administration of medicine in doses ‖ the adding of an ingredient to a mixture so as to secure some quality in it, e.g. sugar added to wine to increase the alcoholic content

dose (dous) **1.** *n.* the amount of medicine to be taken at one time ‖ *(pop.)* an amount of punishment or anything else one can stand in limited quantities **2.** *v.t. pres. part.* **dos·ing** *past* and *past part.* **dosed** to administer medicine to ‖ to treat (wine) with another ingredient, e.g. sugar

dos·si·er (dósi:ei, dósjei) *pl.* **dos·si·ers** (dósi:eiz, dósjeiz) *n.* a set of papers giving information about one particular subject, esp. one person's personal record

dot (dɒt) **1.** *n.* a small spot or point, usually round ‖ a point in printing or writing, e.g. a period, or over an *i* or *j* ‖ *(mus.)* a point placed after a note denoting the lengthening of the note by half its value ‖ *(mus.)* a point placed over a note, denoting staccato ‖ a short sound as part of a letter on a Morse transmitter **2.** *v.t. pres. part.* **dot·ting** *past* and *past part.* **dot·ted** to mark with a dot or dots ‖ to mark as though with dots **dót·ted** *adj.* *(mus.)* increased by half its time value

dot·age (dóutidʒ) *n.* a feeblemindedness as a result of old age **in one's dotage** senile

dou·ble (dʌ́b'l) *pres. part.* **dou·bling** *past* and *past part.* **dou·bled** *v.t.* to make double, multiply by two ‖ *(mus.)* to duplicate (a melody) ‖ to sail around, *to double the Cape*

double 1. *adj.* having two parts, layers, decks, etc. ‖ forming a pair ‖ of twice the usual speed, number or quantity ‖ (of a bed or room) for two people ‖ *(bot.,* of a flower) having more than the normal number or floral leaves ‖ *(bot.,* of a plant) bearing such flowers **2.** *adv.* twice over, two together, *to see double* **3.** *n.* something twice as much ‖ a person or thing that resembles another extremely closely ‖ *(mil.)* a running pace ‖ one bet placed on two contests, with very high odds ‖ a sharp backward turn ‖ *(baseball)* a hit which enables a batter to reach second base ‖ *(horse racing)* a wager on horses to win two races in the day, also daily double ‖ *(movies)* an actor who substitutes for the star, esp. in dangerous scenes ‖ *(pl., tennis)* a game between two pairs

doubt (daut) *n.* feeling of uncertainty ‖ *(esp. pl.)* misgivings

doubt *v.t.* to disbelieve ‖ to distrust ‖ to be in doubt about ‖ *v.i.* to be in a state of doubt

doubt·ful (dáutfəl) *adj.* full of doubt ‖ of an uncertain

but probably bad character ‖ open to doubt

doubt·less (dáutlis) **1.** *adv.* without doubt, certainly **2.** *adj.* *(rhet.,* with 'of') entertaining no doubt

dough (dou) *n.* a mass of slightly moistened flour or meal, sometimes with yeast or fat added, esp. for making bread or pastry ‖ *(pop.)* money

dough·nut (dóunʌt, dóunət) *n.* a ring or ball of sweetened dough fried in deep fat and often coated with sugar

dour (duər, dáuər) *adj.* sullen, sour ‖ stern, harsh

douse, dowse (daus) *pres. part.* **dous·ing, dows·ing** *past* and *past part.* **doused, dowsed** *v.t.* to drench with water ‖ to immerse in water ‖ *(naut.)* to lower (sail) ‖ *(pop.)* to extinguish (a light)

dow·a·ger (dáuədʒər) *n.* a widow whose title derives from her dead husband ‖ *(loosely)* a formidably dignified elderly lady

dow·dy (dáudi:) **1.** *comp.* **dow·di·er** *superl.* **dow·di·est** *adj.* (of a woman or her clothes) shabby, drab and unfashionable **2.** *pl.* **dow·dies** *n.* a dowdy woman

down (daun) *n.* the soft fluff on very young birds before they are fledged ‖ the fluff under the feathers of fully-fledged birds ‖ the breast feathers of certain birds, used for stuffing cushions etc. ‖ any fluffy growth resembling down, e.g. soft, very fine hair on the cheeks, or the fuzz on a peach or on some leaves

down 1. *adv.* from a higher to a lower position ‖ in a direction or place thought of as lower ‖ in a lower position, on the ground ‖ below the horizon ‖ from generation to generation, or from ancestor to descendant ‖ into a low mental or emotional state ‖ into a low physical condition ‖ to a smaller amount ‖ in writing ‖ in check ‖ to a less active condition ‖ less in value ‖ as an initial cash payment **2.** *prep.* in a lower position on ‖ further along ‖ descending toward, through, into ‖ towards the mouth or outlet of **3.** *adj.* descending ‖ in a low or lower place or at a low or lower level ‖ brought, gone, fallen, pulled, paid ‖ ill ‖ depressed ‖ *(games)* behind an opponent in points ‖ *(football,* of the ball) out of play ‖ *(baseball)* put out ‖ (of a boxer) with a part of the body other than the feet touching the floor **4.** *n.* *(football)* one of four plays in which the team having the ball must score or advance the ball at least 10 yds in order to keep it **5.** *v.t.* to knock, throw, put, bring or drink down

down·cast (dáunkæst, dáunkást) *adj.* depressed, dispirited ‖ directed downward

down·fall (dáunfɔl) *n.* a heavy fall of rain or snow ‖ a fall from greatness or prosperity ‖ a cause of ruin ‖ a deadfall

down·grade (dáungreid) **1.** *n.* a downward slope **2.** *adj.* and *adv.* downhill **3.** *v.t. pres. part.* **down·grad·ing** *past* and *past part.* **down·grad·ed** to reduce to a status carrying less salary, or put in a lower category

down·heart·ed (dáunhártid) *adj.* depressed, dejected

down·ward (dáunwərd) **1.** *adj.* from a higher to a lower level ‖ towards an inferior state **2.** *adv.* in a downward direction

down·wards (dáunwərdz) *adv.* downward

doze (douz) **1.** *v.i. pres. part.* **doz·ing** *past* and *past part.* **dozed** to sleep lightly ‖ to be half asleep **to doze off** to fall lightly asleep **2.** *n.* a short sleep, catnap

doz·en (dʌ́z'n) *pl.* **doz·ens, doz·en** *n.* a group of 12 ‖ a small but unspecified number **dóz·ens** *pl. n.* a large but unspecified number

drab (dræb) *comp.* **drab·ber** *superl.* **drab·best** *adj.* dull brown in color ‖ dull, monotonous

draft, draught (dræft, drɑft) **1.** *n.* a rough plan of a work to be executed ‖ a writing, drawing, plan etc. as first put on paper and intended to be revised later

---

‖ the payment of money from an account held for this purpose, esp. by a bank ‖ the written order for this payment ‖ a number of men selected for service with the armed forces or for performing a particular task ‖ conscription ‖ a current of air in a room, chimney etc. ‖ a device for controlling the flow of air in a chimney, fireplace etc. ‖ the act of dragging with a net ‖ the act of drinking ‖ a quantity of liquid drunk **2.** *adj.* used for pulling loads ‖ drawn from a barrel **3.** *v.t.* to call up for military service ‖ to detail (esp. troops) for a particular purpose ‖ *(baseball, football)* to select new professional players ‖ to make a rough, preliminary version of (a document, letter etc.) ‖ to draw up (a statute etc.) **draftee** (dræftí:, drɑftí:) *n.* a conscript **dráft·i·ly** *adv.* **dráft·i·ness** *n.*

draft·y (dræfti:, drɑfti:) *comp.* **draft·i·er** *superl.* **draft·i·est** *adj.* exposed to currents of air

drag (dræg) **1.** *v. pres. part.* **drag·ging** *past* and *past part.* **dragged** *v.t.* to pull or haul along, esp. with an effort ‖ to move (one's feet) in walking without completely lifting them from the ground ‖ to search the bottom of (a river, lake etc.) with a grapnel or net in order to recover a body, lost object etc. ‖ to break (land) with a drag or harrow ‖ *v.i.* to be dragged, pulled or trailed ‖ to use a drag ‖ (of time) to pass slowly **2.** *n.* *(agric.)* a heavy harrow ‖ a device, such as a grapnel, for searching the bottom of a river or lake etc. ‖ something or someone that hinders ‖ *(aeron.)* the total air resistance to the flight of an aircraft ‖ *(colloq.)* a boring activity ‖ *(pop.)* women's clothes worn by a man

drag·on (drægən) *n.* a mythical, winged animal with a huge scaly body, enormous claws and sharp teeth ‖ a formidably fierce person, esp. a woman

drain (drein) **1.** *v.t.* to conduct water away from (land) by means of drains, conduits, canals etc. ‖ (of a river or stream) to carry away the water from (a district) ‖ to remove surplus water from by sieving, standing in racks etc. ‖ to empty (a vessel) of liquid, esp. by drinking ‖ to exhaust of energy, wealth etc. ‖ *v.i.* (of liquid) to flow or trickle away ‖ (often with 'away') to disappear slowly **2.** *n.* a pipe or channel carrying away water or sewage from a street or a building ‖ a channel for draining off water from flat land ‖ the metal grating and stone or concrete edging surrounding the inlet of a house drain ‖ *(med.)* a tube or catheter for drawing off the discharge from an abscess or open wound ‖ a constant or protracted demand on wealth, energy or other resources **dráin·age** *n.* the draining of land etc. ‖ a system of drains or water courses

dra·ma (drɑmə, dræmə) *n.* a play written for actors to perform ‖ a play which in general is serious, not comic, but which does not rise to tragedy ‖ plays for acting as a literary genre ‖ a slice of real life with the intensity of a play

dra·mat·ic (drəmætik) *adj.* pertaining to drama or the theater ‖ as striking as a play ‖ (of people) inclined to give falsely heightened emphasis to ordinary events, conversation etc. **dra·mát·i·cal·ly** *adv.*

dra·mat·ics (drəmætiks) *pl. n.* the performance of plays by amateurs ‖ the technique of acting as a branch of study ‖ dramatic behavior

dram·a·tist (dræmətist, drɑmətist) *n.* a playwright

dram·a·ti·za·tion (dræmətizéiʃən, drɑmətizéiʃən) *n.* a turning into a play ‖ a rendering vivid by acting

dram·a·tize (dræmətaiz, drɑmətaiz) *pres. part.* **dram·a·tiz·ing** *past* and *past part.* **dram·a·tized** *v.t.* to put (a novel etc.) into the form of a play ‖ to behave dramatically over (an ordinary situation) ‖ to exaggerate histrionically

drape (dreip) **1.** *v.t. pres. part.* **drap·ing** *past* and *past part.* **draped** to cover or ornament with material, hangings, flags etc. ‖ to arrange (materials) in decorative folds **2.** *n.* a draped tapestry or curtain ‖ the manner of hanging

dras·tic (dræstik) *adj.* acting violently, having extreme effects ‖ rigorous, thoroughgoing **drás·ti·cal·ly** *adv.*

draw (drɔ) **1.** *v. pres. part.* **draw·ing** *past* **drew** (dru:) *past part.* **drawn** (drɔn) *v.t.* to pull ‖ to attract ‖ to pull out, extract ‖ to remove the entrails from (a chicken etc.) ‖ to make a picture or plan of with pencil, pen and ink, charcoal, crayon etc. ‖ to delineate in words ‖ to deduce and formulate ‖ to try to get information out of (someone) ‖ to stretch out to greater length ‖ to cause to discharge ‖ to obtain from a source of supply ‖ to write out (a check) ‖ to get in a lottery ‖ *v.i.* to infuse ‖ to end a match or game without either side winning ‖ to make the same score as, or arrive level with, another competitor ‖ (with 'on') to obtain something from a reserve, store etc. ‖ to draw lots ‖ (of smoking, with 'on') to inhale (through a pipe etc.) ‖ to have a draft **2.** *n.* a stunt, personality etc. that attracts customers or an audience ‖ a game or match that ends without either side winning ‖ the drawing of lots ‖ a raffle ‖ the pulling of a revolver out of its holster to shoot ‖ the movable part of a drawbridge ‖ *(card games)* the choosing of a card from the pack ‖ a deal of cards to improve the hands of players after discarding in draw poker

draw·back (drɔbæk) *n.* a disadvantage, esp. in something otherwise satisfactory ‖ a withdrawal ‖ money refunded, esp. secretly as a bribe or favor ‖ compensation payment

draw·er (drɔər) *n.* someone who draws ‖ (drɔr) a boxlike receptacle for clothes, papers etc. which slides in and out of a table, cabinet etc. or on a special frame ‖ *(pl., old-fash., drɔrz)* underpants

draw·ing (drɔiŋ) *n.* a sketch, picture or plan in pencil, charcoal, crayon, etc. ‖ the art of producing these ‖ a gathering at which lots are drawn in order to reach some decision

drawl (drɔl) **1.** *v.i.* to speak indistinctly, lengthening the vowels, and slurring one word into the next in a slow, lazy way ‖ *v.t.* to utter in this way **2.** *n.* this manner of speech

dread (dred) **1.** *v.t.* to be very much afraid of, esp. to anticipate with great apprehension **2.** *n.* apprehension ‖ great fear ‖ something that is greatly feared **3.** *adj.* *(rhet.)* feared, dreaded

dread·ful (drédfəl) *adj.* inspiring dread ‖ very bad **dréad·ful·ly** *adv.*

dream (dri:m) **1.** *n.* an idea or image present in the sleeping mind ‖ a reverie, daydream ‖ something greatly desired ‖ *(pop.)* something excellent or very beautiful ‖ an extravagant fancy **2.** *v. pres. part.* **dream·ing** *past* and *past part.* **dreamt** (dremt), **dreamed** (dremt, dri:md) *v.t.* to experience mentally while asleep ‖ *v.i.* to have experience of ideas and images during sleep ‖ to indulge in reverie or imagination, usually of a pleasant kind, esp. to daydream **dréam·er** *n.* an impractical person who tends to live in a world of fantasy

drear·y (dríəri) *comp.* **drear·i·er** *superl.* **drear·i·est** *adj.* dull and gloomy ‖ depressing ‖ uninteresting

dredge (dredʒ) **1.** *v. pres. part.* **dredg·ing** *past* and *past part.* **dredged** *v.t.* to clear mud etc. from (a harbor or riverbed) with a dredge ‖ *v.i.* to use a dredge **2.** *n.* an apparatus, such as a crane and grab, for clearing mud etc. from a riverbed or harbor, to increase the depth

dredge *pres. part.* **dredg·ing** *past* and *past part.* **dredged** *v.t.* to sprinkle (food) with flour, sugar etc. **drédg·er** *n.* a container with a perforated lid, used for sprinkling flour, sugar etc. over food

drench (drentʃ) *v.t.* to wet thoroughly, soak ‖ to force (an animal) to take a medicinal dose ‖ to steep (leather) for tanning ‖ a device for administering a medicinal dose to an animal

dress (dres) **1.** *v.t.* to put clothes on ‖ to provide with clothes ‖ to arrange decoratively for display ‖ to decorate (streets or a ship) with flags ‖ to draw up (soldiers or companies of soldiers) into alignment ‖ to clean and bandage (a wound) ‖ to treat the surface of (stone, leather, textiles etc.) ‖ to groom (a horse)

|| to clean and truss (poultry, game) || to garnish (a dish) || to treat (soil) with manure or other fertilizer || to style, arrange (hair) || to prepare (ore) for smelting by removing impurities || *v.i.* to put on or change one's clothes, esp. to put on formal or evening clothes || *(mil.)* to get one's dressing or alignment **2.** *n.* attire || a woman's frock or gown

dress·er (drésər) *n.* a chest of drawers, often with a mirror || a long, low cupboard or sideboard with extra shelves fitted to a high back above the cupboard, for holding china and kitchen utensils

drib·ble (dríb'l) **1.** *v. pres. part.* **drib·bling** *past* and *past part.* **drib·bled** *v.i.* (esp. of babies) to drool || to flow, in a small trickle || *v.t.* to cause to flow in a trickle || to squeeze (paint) directly on to a canvas without using a brush || *(sports)* to control (a ball or puck) while running or riding, in such a way that it advances by a series of short kicks (or pats, hits etc.) **2.** *n.* slaver || a small trickle || an instance of dribbling a ball, puck etc.

drift (drift) **1.** *n.* the process of being driven, usually slowly, in a certain direction by wind, water etc. in motion || a phenomenon compared with this || the thing driven (snow, sand etc.) || the general meaning of a statement, speech etc. as distinct from the details || *(naut.)* deviation due to current || *(geol.)* a loose mass of debris accumulated by ice, water or wind || *(naut.)* the rate of flow (in knots) of an ocean current **2.** *v.i.* to be carried along by a current of water or by wind or as if by these || to be piled up by wind || to live without any apparent aim || to move aimlessly || *(pop.)* to walk slowly || to fish with a drift net || *v.t.* (of a current of water or wind) to carry along or pile up **drift·age** *n.* the action of drifting || the distance drifted || material washed up on the shore **drift·er** *n.* a fishing boat, used in fishing with a drift net || someone who drifts, esp. a rather unstable, aimless person who changes jobs constantly etc.

drift·wood (dríftwʊd) *n.* pieces of wood floating in the sea or cast up on the shore

drill (dril) *n.* a series of exercises in physical training, in the use of weapons or equipment, or in procedure || training in such exercises || a mental exercise, regularly repeated || a tool or machine for making holes in wood, metal, stone etc.

drill *v.t.* to train in physical or military exercises || to teach by making (a pupil) repeat a set of facts etc. frequently || to bore (holes) through or in something with a drill or as if with a drill || to break up or remove with a drill || *v.i.* to use a drill || to perform exercises in physical or military training

drink (driŋk) *n.* a liquid to be swallowed or (by plants) absorbed || alcoholic liquor || excessive drinking of alcohol

drink (driŋk) *pres. part.* **drink·ing** *past* **drank** (dræŋk) *past part.* **drunk** (drʌŋk) *v.t.* to swallow (a liquid) or the contents of (a cup) || (of plants) to absorb (moisture) || to join in (a toast) by drinking || *v.i.* to swallow liquid or absorb moisture || to be in the habit of taking alcoholic liquors, esp. to excess **drink·er** *n.*

drip (drip) **1.** *v. pres. part.* **drip·ping** *past* and *past part.* **dripped** *v.i.* (of liquid) to fall in drops || (of a solid object) to allow liquid to fall off in drops || to be so saturated that liquid exudes || *v.t.* to cause to fall in drops **2.** *n.* the falling of liquid in drops || the sound of dripping || a drop of liquid falling or about to fall from something **drip·ping** *n.* the act of falling in drops, or of allowing something to fall in drops || (also *pl.*) the fat drained off roasting meat

drive (draiv) **1.** *v. pres. part.* **driv·ing** *past* **drove** (drouv)

past part. **driv·en** (drívən) *v.t.* to control the course of (a car, bus, truck etc., or an animal drawing a vehicle) || to convey in a vehicle || to impel by force, violence, threats, shouts etc. || to hit or push in some direction || to cause to tend to be in a specified state || (of power) to activate (a piece of machinery) || to cause to work very hard || to conclude (a bargain) || to frighten (game) on to the guns || to force into a course of action, compel || (of wind) to impel || *(golf)* to strike (a ball) from the tee || *(mining* and *engin.)* to cut (a tunnel, road or mine gallery) || *v.i.* to travel by car or in a carriage || to know how to drive a car or be in the habit of driving a car || to advance with great force || to hit a golf ball from the tee **2.** *n.* an excursion in a car or bus || the driving of animals or game || a concerted effort by a numebr of people, e.g. to raise money for a charity etc. || a major military offensive || energy and willpower || *(psychol.)* a source of motivation || *(sport)* the act or manner of hitting a ball || *(mech.)* the part driving a piece of machinery || a private road through the grounds of a house

driv·el (drívəl) **1.** *v. pres. part.* **driv·el·ing**, esp. *Br.* **driv·el·ling** *past* and *past part.* **driv·eled**, esp. *Br.* **driv·elled** *v.i.* to allow saliva to run from the mouth || *(pop.)* to talk foolishly || *v.t.* *(pop.)* to utter (inanities) **2.** *n.* foolish talk, nonsense

driv·er (dráivər) *n.* someone who drives a car, bus etc. || a person who drives animals, a drover || *(mech.)* a driving wheel, or other part of a machine that receives the power directly || *(golf)* a wood for driving the ball a long distance from the tee

driz·zle (dríz'l) **1.** *v.i. pres. part.* **driz·zling** *past* and *past part.* **driz·zled** (of rain) to fall in very small drops || to rain slightly **2.** *n.* a slight, very fine rain **driz·zly** *adj.*

droll (droul) *adj.* amusing || odd, surprising, but humorous

drom·e·dar·y (drómidęri:, drʌmədęri:) *pl.* **drom·e·dar·ies** *n.* a swift variety of one-humped camel used in the Arabian and African deserts for riding or for carrying burdens

drone (droun) **1.** *n.* the male of the honeybee, which does no work in the hive || a very lazy man, esp. one who lives like a parasite || a pilotless aircraft or boat guided by remote control || a monotonous speaker || low, monotonous speech, humming or singing **2.** *v. pres. part.* **dron·ing** *past* and *past part.* **droned** *v.t.* to hum or utter monotonously at a low pitch || *v.i.* to make a monotonous, low-pitched humming noise

droop (dru:p) **1.** *v.i.* to hang down || to be lowered || to slouch || to go limp || to flag, weary or begin to give up hope || *v.t.* to allow to hang down, slouch etc. **2.** *n.* the act or state of drooping

drop (drɒp) *n.* a very small amount of liquid in a round or pear-shaped mass, either falling or clinging to a surface || *(pl.)* medicine measured in a number of such drops || *(pop.)* a small amount of liquid, esp. to drink || a small pendant ornament || a dropping or falling or the amount by which something falls || a very steep slope || a sheer fall || a thing that drops or falls, esp. *(theater)* a piece of cloth scenery not on a frame || a parachute descent || men or materials or supplies dropped by parachute

drop *pres. part.* **drop·ping** *past* and *past part.* **dropped** *v.t.* to allow to fall, accidentally or on purpose || to make (a remark, hint) casually or with studied unconcern || *(knitting)* to fail to prevent (a stitch) from sliding off the needle || *(shooting)* to cause to fall by hitting || to give up || *(slang)* to take orally, esp. drugs || to cease to discuss (a subject) || to cease to be friendly with || to write (a short note, postcard etc.) and mail

---

(a) æ, c*a*t; ɑ, c*a*r; ɔ f*aw*n; ei, sn*a*ke. **(e)** e, h*e*n; i:, sh*ee*p; iə, d*ee*r; ɛə, b*ea*r. **(i)** i, f*i*sh; ai, t*i*ger; ə:, b*i*rd. **(o)** o, *o*x; au, c*ow*; ou, g*oa*t; u, p*oo*r; ɔi, r*oy*al. **(u)** ʌ, d*u*ck; u, b*u*ll; u:, g*oo*se; ə, b*a*cillus; ju:, c*u*be. x, lo*ch*; θ, *th*ink; ð, bo*th*er; z, *Z*en; ʒ, corsa*g*e; dʒ, sava*g*e; ŋ, oranguta*ng*; j, *y*ak; ʃ, *fi*sh; tʃ, fe*tch*; 'l, rabb*le*; 'n, redd*en*. Complete pronunciation key appears inside front cover.

it ‖ to land (men, supplies or material) by parachute ‖ to lower (the voice) ‖ to set down from a car, ship etc. ‖ (of an animal) to give birth to ‖ (*math.*) to draw (a line) from a point to a line, plane etc. 3. *v.i.* to fall ‖ to let oneself fall ‖ to fall from exhaustion ‖ to become less or lower ‖ to assume a lower position ‖ to go to a position thought of as lower ‖ (*mus.*) to become lower or flat

drought (draut) *n.* a prolonged period of dry weather, a lack of rain **dróught·y** *adj.*

drown (draun) *v.i.* to die of suffocation by immersion in a liquid ‖ *v.t.* to kill by suffocation in a liquid ‖ to submerge or flood ‖ to make inaudible because of greater sound

drowse (drauz) 1. *v.i. pres. part.* **drows·ing** past and *past part.* **drowsed** to be half-asleep, doze ‖ *v.t.* (with 'away') to pass (time) sleepily 2. *n.* the condition of being half asleep

drow·si·ly (dráuzili:) *adv.* in a drowsy way

drow·si·ness (dráuzi:nis) *n.* the state of being drowsy

drow·sy (dráuzi:) *comp.* **drow·si·er** *superl.* **drow·si·est** *adj.* half-asleep, sleepy ‖ inducing sleep, lulling

drudge (drʌdʒ) 1. *n.* someone who has to work hard at uninteresting tasks, esp. domestic work 2. *v.i. pres. part.* **drudg·ing** past and *past part.* **drudged** to work very hard at uninteresting tasks **drudg·er·y** (drʌdʒəri:) *n.* uninteresting work or any time-consuming work one has no wish to do

drug (drʌg) 1. *n.* a substance used as or in a medicine ‖ a chemical substance used to alter the state of the body or the mind ‖ a narcotic substance, esp. one which induces addiction, such as opium 2. *v. pres. part.* **drug·ging** past and *past part.* **drugged** *v.t.* to administer drugs to ‖ to act on as though a drug ‖ *v.i.* to be a drug addict

drug·gist (drʌgist) *n.* a dealer in medicinal drugs ‖ someone who dispenses or sells medical drugs, toiletries etc.

drum (drʌm) 1. *n.* any of various types of percussive musical instrument consisting of a hollow cylinder or hemisphere of wood, metal etc. ‖ the sound made by such an instrument, or a similar sound ‖ something resembling a drum in shape, e.g. a cylindrical container, or a cylinder or barrel on which cable is wound 2. *v.i. pres. part.* **drum·ming** past and *past part.* **drummed** to play a drum ‖ to make a rhythmic beating sound

drum·stick (drʌmstik) *n.* a stick for beating a drum ‖ the leg bone of a chicken or other fowl

drunk (drʌŋk) 1. *adj.* intoxicated by alcoholic drink ‖ elated, *drunk with success* **to get drunk** to become intoxicated 2. *n.* a person who is drunk ‖ a drinking bout **drunk·ard** (drʌŋkərd) *n.* a person habitually drunk

drunk·en (drʌŋkən) *adj.* (rarely predicative) in the habit of becoming intoxicated, frequently drunk, *a drunken sot* ‖ caused by or showing the effects of drunkenness

dry (drai) 1. *adj. comp.* **dri·er** *superl.* **dri·est** free from moisture ‖ needing rain ‖ dried up ‖ not underwater ‖ (of a poet etc.) temporarily not creative ‖ not yielding milk ‖ (of bread) served without butter ‖ (of masonry) built without mortar ‖ (of wines) not sweet ‖ thirsty ‖ having laws prohibiting the manufacture and sale of alcoholic liquors ‖ written without an effort to win the reader's attention ‖ given to making humorous remarks in a matter-of-fact way ‖ quietly ironic ‖ bare, plain ‖ (of a cough) unaccompanied by mucus in the throat 2. *v. pres. part.* **dry·ing** past and *past part.* **dried** *v.t.* to make dry ‖ *v.i.* to become dry

du·al (dú:əl, djú:əl) *adj.* double

dub (dʌb) *pres. part.* **dub·bing** past and *past part.* **dubbed** *v.t.* to make (a man) ceremonially a knight by lightly touching his shoulder with a sword ‖ to give (someone) a nickname ‖ to fit a new sound track to (a film) ‖ (often with 'in') to add (sound effects) to a television program etc. ‖ to rerecord ‖ to treat (leather) by smearing with grease

du·bi·ous (dú:bi:əs, djú:bi:əs) *adj.* doubtful, having doubts ‖ of questionable value or truth ‖ of questionable character, shady ‖ of uncertain outcome

duch·ess (dʌtʃis) *n.* a duke's wife or widow ‖ a woman holding a duchy in her own right

duck (dʌk) *n.* any of the smallest webfooted swimming birds of fam. *Anatidae*. They are widely distributed, and in the wild state are often migratory ‖ the female of the species ‖ the flesh of the bird as food

duck 1. *v.i.* to bob or bend down quickly ‖ to dart off quickly in a new direction so as to avoid someone or something ‖ to make a brief curtsy ‖ to plunge the head under the water and come up quickly ‖ to miss a turn or not score in certain games deliberately ‖ *v.t.* to lower abruptly ‖ to dodge, avoid ‖ to push and hold (someone) under the water for a moment 2. *n.* a quick forcing of someone else's head underwater ‖ a quick plunge ‖ a sudden lowering of the head

duct (dʌkt) *n.* a tube which conveys fluid or some other substance ‖ (*biol.*) a tube formed by a series of cells which have lost their walls at the point of contact ‖ a pipe or conduit for electric cables etc.

duc·tile (dʌktil) *adj.* (of metals) capable of being drawn out into wire ‖ (of clay) plastic, easily molded ‖ (of persons) easily led or influenced **duc·til·i·ty** *n.*

dud (dʌd) 1. *n.* a shell, bomb etc. that fails to explode, or a bullet that fails to fire ‖ a person or plan turning out a failure or an object that turns out to be no good ‖ (*pl., pop.*) personal belongings, esp. clothes 2. *adj.* counterfeit ‖ not sound, useless

dude (du:d, dju:d) *n.* a dandy, a man of affected speech, dress and manners

due (du:, dju:) 1. *adj.* payable ‖ morally owing ‖ proper, fitting, adequate ‖ expected to arrive (at a given time) ‖ (with 'on') scheduled to speak, sing, perform etc. ‖ justified in expecting ‖ (*pop.*) about (to) ‖ owing, attributable 2. *adv.* directly, exactly 3. *n.* that which is morally owed to someone ‖ (*pl.*) fees, charges

du·el (dú:əl, djú:əl) 1. *n.* (*hist.*) a fight, arranged and conducted according to a code of honor between two gentlemen ‖ any contest between two antagonists, esp. where they are very evenly matched 2. *v.i. pres. part.* **du·el·ing** past and *past part.* **du·eled** to fight a duel or duels **dú·el·ist** *n.* someone who fights a duel

du·et (du:ét, dju:ét) *n.* a piece of music for two singers or performers **du·ét·tist** *n.*

duke (du:k, dju:k) *n.* (in some parts of Europe and in former times) a sovereign price ruling a duchy ‖ (in Great Britain and some other European countries) a nobleman holding the highest hereditary title outside the royal family **dúke·dom** *n.* a territory (duchy) ruled by a duke ‖ the office or rank of a duke

dul·cet (dʌlsit) 1. *adj.* (of sounds) sweet, soothing 2. *n.* (*mus.*) an organ stop like the dulciana, but an octave higher

dull (dʌl) 1. *adj.* stupid, slow in understanding ‖ lacking sensitivity ‖ tedious ‖ uninteresting, colorless in personality ‖ blunt ‖ (of pain) not sharp ‖ (of colors and lights) dim, not bright or vivid ‖ (of sounds) muffled, not clear and ringing ‖ (of trade) sluggish ‖ (of weather) cloudy, overcast ‖ without vitality, depressed 2. *v.t.* to make dull ‖ *v.i.* to become dull **dull·ard** (dʌlərd) *n.* a slow, stupid person

dull·ness, dul·ness (dʌlnis) *n.* the quality or state of being dull

du·ly (djú:li:, dú:li:) *adv.* in a due and proper manner or degree ‖ at the right time

dumb (dʌm) *adj.* permanently unable to speak, mute ‖ temporarily unable to speak ‖ unwilling to speak ‖ without the use of words, soundless ‖ inarticulate ‖ (*pop.*) stupid

dumb·found, dum·found (dʌmfáund) *v.t.* to shock with amazement, utterly astonish

dum·my (dʌmi:) 1. *n. pl.* **dum·mies** an imitation of, or substitute for, something, esp. a dressmaker's or tailor's figure for fitting clothes or mannequin for displaying clothes ‖ someone pretending to act for himself but really acting for another ‖ a person put up as a figurehead who plays no real part, a puppet ‖ *(pop.)* a stupid person ‖ *(cards)* an exposed hand played by one of the players in addition to his own ‖ *(cards)* the player who lays his hand down to be so played ‖ *(publishing)* a pattern volume, usually of blank pages, made in advance of an edition for designing or publicity purposes **2.** *adj.* sham ‖ simulating real conditions **3.** *v.i. pres. part.* **dum·my·ing** *past* and *past part.* **dum·mied**

dump (dʌmp) **1.** *v.t.* to unload, tip ‖ to let fall with a bump ‖ to set down temporarily ‖ to get rid of, dispose of ‖ *(commerce)* to sell in quantity at a very low price, esp. to sell (surplus goods) abroad at much less than the market price at home, so as to capture a new market and keep home prices up ‖ to land (surplus immigrants) in a foreign country **2.** *n.* a scrap heap ‖ a shabby, untidy house, room or place ‖ an unexciting place where there is nothing going on ‖ a place where military supplies are temporarily stored ‖ a cache of supplies for an expedition

dump·ling (dʌmpliŋ) *n.* a lump of dough boiled esp. with stew ‖ a baked pudding of fruit (esp. a whole apple) wrapped in pastry ‖ a short, fat, dumpy person (esp. a child)

dunce (dʌns) *n.* a very slow child at school ‖ a stupid person

dune (du:n, dju:n) *n.* a mound or ridge of loose sand piled up by the wind on coasts or in deserts

dun·ga·ree (dʌŋgəri:) *n.* a coarse Indian calico ‖ *(pl.)* overalls or trousers of dungaree or strong cotton cloth, jeans

dun·geon (dʌndʒən) *n. (hist.)* an underground prisoners' cell, esp. in a castle

dupe (du:p, dju:p) **1.** *n.* someone easily deceived or tricked **2.** *v.t. pres. part.* **dup·ing** *past* and *past part.* **duped** to deceive, cheat, make a fool of **dúp·er·y** *n.* a duping or being duped

du·pli·cate 1. *v.t.* (dú:plikeit, djú:plikeit) *pres. part.* **du·pli·cat·ing** *past* and *past part.* **du·pli·cat·ed** to do or cause to be done twice over ‖ to make in duplicate ‖ to be a copy of ‖ to make several copies of **2.** (dú:plikit, djú:plikit) *adj.* double, twofold ‖ exactly like another or several others **3.** (dú:plikit, djú:plikit) *n.* a thing that is exactly like another or others ‖ a second copy of a form or document ‖ *(cards)* duplicate bridge, whist etc. **in duplicate** in two copies **du·pli·cá·tion** *n.* a duplicating or being duplicated ‖ a duplicate **dú·pli·ca·tive** *adj.* **dú·pli·ca·tor** *n.* a machine which quickly makes many copies of a document

du·pli·ca·tion (du:plikéiʃən) *n. (genetics)* deviation from normal chromosome formation resulting in repetition of material

du·plic·i·ty (du:plísiti:, dju:plísiti:) *pl.* **du·plic·i·ties** *n.* double-dealing, deceitfulness, deceiving by thinking one thing and saying another ‖ by willfully saying different things at different times ‖ an instance of this

du·ra·bil·i·ty (duərəbíliti:, djuərəbíliti:) *n.* the quality of being durable

du·ra·ble (dúərəb'l, djúərəb'l) *adj.* lasting, enduring ‖ not likely to wear out or decay for a long time **dúr·a·bly** *adv.*

du·ra·tion (duəréiʃən, djuəréiʃən) *n.* continuance in time ‖ the time that something lasts

du·ress (duərés, djuərés) *n.* compulsion, threats, esp. as used illegally to force someone to do something

dur·ing (dúəriŋ, djúəriŋ) *prep.* throughout (time) ‖ in the course of

dusk (dʌsk) *n.* the time of day just before it gets quite dark ‖ shade, gloom **dúsk·i·ly** *adv.* **dúsk·i·ness** *n.* **dúsk·y** *comp.* **dusk·i·er** *superl.* **dusk·i·est** *adj.* shadowy, rather dark ‖ dark-skinned

dust (dʌst) **1.** *n.* minute particles of mineral or plant material, lying on the ground or on the surfaces of things, or suspended in the atmosphere ‖ other matter in the form of powder ‖ turmoil, commotion, row ‖ pollen ‖ gold dust ‖ *(rhet.)* a dead person's remains **2.** *v.t.* to remove dust from ‖ to sprinkle with powder ‖ *v.i.* to remove the dust from furniture etc.

dust·y (dʌsti:) *comp.* **dust·i·er** *superl.* **dust·i·est** *adj.* covered with, full of, or like dust

du·ti·ful (dú:tifəl, djú:tifəl) *adj.* mindful of one's duties, properly respectful and obedient ‖ showing a sense of duty

du·ty (dú:ti:, djú:ti:) *pl.* **du·ties** *n.* obligations of behavior or conduct in relation to others or to God which have a stronger claim on a person than his self-interest ‖ the work someone is expected to do because of his vocation ‖ *(pl.)* the detailed content of this work ‖ payment due to the government for import, export, manufacture or sale of goods

dwarf (dwɔrf) **1.** *n.* a freakishly small person ‖ someone made by comparison to seem of relatively little capacity or achievement ‖ a plant or animal far below the usual size of its species ‖ a dwarf star ‖ *(Teutonic and Norse mythol.)* a small being with supernatural powers and esp. skill in working metal **2.** *adj.* undersized, deliberately stunted, esp. of plant varieties **3.** *v.t.* to stunt or inhibit in growth ‖ to make small by comparison ‖ *v.i.* to become dwarf ‖ to seem small by comparison **dwárf·ish** *adj.* dwarflike

dwell (dwel) *pres. part.* **dwell·ing** *past* and *past part.* **dwelt** (dwelt), **dwelled** *v.i. (rhet.)* to reside **to dwell on** to linger over or concentrate upon (a subject) ‖ to prolong (e.g. a note in music, or a syllable in versespeaking) **dwéll·er** *n.* (usually in compounds) an inhabitant, *a cave-dweller* **dwéll·ing** *n.* the place where one lives, a house, esp. a primitive one

dwin·dle (dwínd'l) *pres. part.* **dwin·dling** *past* and *past part.* **dwin·dled** *v.i.* to grow gradually less in size, extent, quality or importance

dye (dai) *n.* a substance capable of coloring materials (e.g. textiles, paper, plastics) and generally applied in solution or dispersion, sometimes with the aid of a mordant ‖ a color produced by dyeing

dy·nam·ic (dainæmik) **1.** *adj. (phys.)* pertaining to dynamics ‖ active, forceful, energetic, capable of giving a sense of power and transmitting energy ‖ *(med.)* to do with the function of an organ rather than its structure **2.** *n.* a moving or driving force **dy·nám·i·cal** *adj.* dynamic ‖ *(theol.)* endowing with divine power

dy·na·mite (dáinəmait) **1.** *n.* a powerful explosive. It consists essentially of nitroglycerine made stable by mixing with some absorbent ‖ a personality, or an element in a situation, likely to produce violent reactions **2.** *v.t. pres. part.* **dy·na·mit·ing** *past* and *past part.* **dy·na·mit·ed** to blow up or destroy with dynamite

dy·nas·ty (dáinəsti:, *Br.* also dínəsti:) *pl.* **dy·nas·ties** *n.* a line of rulers of the same family ‖ its period of rule

dys·en·ter·y (dísənteri:) *n.* a usually endemic disease of the colon characterized by diarrhea and the passage of blood, pus and mucus in the stools, which are highly infectious

---

(a) æ, cat; ɑ, car; ɔ fawn; ei, snake. **(e)** e, hen; i:, sheep; iə, deer; ɛə, bear. **(i)** i, fish; ai, tiger; ə:, bird. **(o)** o, ox; au, cow; ou, goat; u, poor; ɔi, royal. **(u)** ʌ, duck; u, bull; u:, goose; ə, bacillus; ju:, cube. x, loch; θ, think; ð, bother; z, Zen; ʒ, corsage; dʒ, savage; ŋ, orangutang; j, yak; ʃ, fish; tʃ, fetch; 'l, rabble; 'n, redden. Complete pronunciation key appears inside front cover.

E

E, e (i:) the fifth letter in the English alphabet

each (i:tʃ) **1.** adj. every one of two or more **2.** pron. every one of two or more **3.** adv. for or to every one ‖ apiece

ea·ger (í:gər) adj. keen ‖ having a strong desire (to attain some end)

ea·gle (í:g'l) n. a large diurnal bird of prey of cosmopolitan distribution ‖ a representation of this bird, as an emblem ‖ (golf) a hole played in two below par

ea·glet (í:glit) n. a young eagle

ear (iər) **1.** n. the compound spike or inflorescence of most cereals, esp. of the mature fruit **2.** v.i. to form ears, come into ear

ear n. the organ of hearing in men and animals, esp. the external part ‖ the power of hearing correctly or of distinguishing and appreciating sounds ‖ something resembling the external ear

ear·drum (íərdrʌm) n. the membrane in the ear which receives sound impulses

earl (ə:rl) n. (in the peerages of Great Britain and Northern Ireland) a nobleman ranking between a viscount and a marquess **éarl·dom** n.

ear·ly (ə́:rli:) comp. **ear·li·er** superl. **ear·li·est 1.** adj. at or near the beginning of a period of time, piece of work, series etc. ‖ belonging to a distant or comparatively distant time in the past ‖ in the near future ‖ coming or happening before the usual or expected time **2.** adv. at or near the beginning of a period of time, piece of work, series, etc. ‖ long ago ‖ unusually or unexpectedly soon, or soon by comparison with others of a comparable kind

earn (ə:rn) v.t. to get as a payment, reward or yield in return for work or services ‖ to deserve or obtain by merit or wrongdoing ‖ (of money, shares etc.) to bring in ‖ v.i. to be doing paid work **earned** adj. (of income) worked for, not derived from investments ‖ deserved

ear·nest (ə́:rnist) n. a token or pledge ‖ money paid as a deposit to confirm a sale or agreement

earnest adj. heartfelt ‖ serious and diligent ‖ emotionally intense and solemn

earn·ing (ə́:rniŋ) n. the act of earning or the thing earned ‖ (pl.) money earned by work or commerce

ear·ring (íəriŋ) n. a small ring, often of gold and set with a stone, or a hook supporting an ornament, worn on the earlobe, which is pierced to receive it ‖ a small ornament screwed or clipped to the lobe

ear·shot (íərʃɒt) n. the distance within which a shout or call can be heard

earth (ə:rθ) **1.** n. the fifth largest planet of the solar system ‖ the planet on which we live ‖ land and sea as opposed to the sky ‖ the topsoil of the earth's crust ‖ a natural pigment (e.g. ocher) found in the earth **2.** v.t. (with 'up') to heap earth around

earth·en·ware (ə́:rθənwɛ̯ər) n. glazed or unglazed pots, plates, crockery, etc., made of clay fired at a lower temperature than that at which its particles would fuse

earth·i·ness (ə́:rθi:nis) n. the quality of being earthy

earth·quake (ə́:rθkwe̯ik) n. a pressure wave in the earth's crust caused by a deep-seated disturbance

earth·y (ə́:rθi:) comp. **earth·i·er** superl. **earth·i·est** adj. of or like earth ‖ unspiritual, robust and pleasure-loving ‖ gross or bawdy

ease (i:z) **1.** n. physical comfort and relaxation ‖ mental calm ‖ freedom from awkwardness or shyness ‖ freedom from difficulty **2.** v. pres. part. **eas·ing** past and past part. **eased** v.t. to lessen the discomfort or anxiety of, relieve ‖ to loosen (e.g. a bolt) ‖ to make less difficult, trying, or tense ‖ to handle (something) carefully and move it gradually ‖ v.i. to become less difficult, trying or tense ‖ (of stocks or the stock market) to fall in price **éase·ful** adj.

ea·sel (í:z'l) n. an adjustable frame of wood or metal to support esp. an artist's canvas

eas·i·ly (í:zili:) adv. in an easy way ‖ without strain or exertion ‖ comfortably ‖ smoothly ‖ by far ‖ very possibly

eas·i·ness (í:zi:nis) n. freedom from difficulty ‖ the state of being comfortable or free from care ‖ (econ.) a state of economic weakness involving falling prices and diminished trade

east (i:st) **1.** adj. towards the east **2.** n. (usually with 'the') one of the four cardinal points of the compass ‖ the states of the U.S.A. east of the Mississippi, esp. the northern states on the Atlantic seaboard **3.** adj. of, belonging to or situated towards the east ‖ facing east ‖ (of winds) blowing from the east ‖ (eccles.) of the end of a church where the chancel is

East·er (í:stər) **1.** n. the chief Christian feast, which celebrates the Ressurrection of Christ **2.** adj. coming at or near Easter

east·ern (í:stərn) adj. situated, facing or moving towards the east

east·ward (í:stwərd) **1.** adv. and adj. towards the east **2.** n. the eastward direction or part **éast·wards** adv.

eas·y (í:zi) comp. **eas·i·er** superl. **eas·i·est 1.** adj. not difficult ‖ obtained without difficulty ‖ free from hardship, anxiety or worry ‖ gentle and comfortable, smooth ‖ not demanding or oppressive, not strict ‖ not stiff or awkward, easy prose ‖ not at all tight ‖ not difficult to get the better of **easy on the eyes** (old-fash.) good-looking **on easy terms** (commerce) by installments **2.** adv. **easy does it!** go gently, be very careful ‖ to treat carefully **to take it easy**, not to work too hard or go too fast ‖ not to get excited

eas·y·go·ing (í:zi:gou̯iŋ) adj. not strict, very tolerant ‖ lazy, not diligent or methodical

eat (i:t) pres. part. **eat·ing** past **ate** (eit) past part. **eat·en** (í:t'n) v.t. to take as food ‖ to corrode ‖ v.i. to have a meal ‖ to be of a specified quality when eaten ‖ (with 'into') to reduce something gradually as if by eating it, e.g., by corrosion ‖ to begin to use something up **éat·a·ble 1.** adj. fit, but hardly pleasant, to eat **2.** n. (pl.) things to eat **éat·er** n. someone who or something which eats as specified

eaves (í:vz) pl. n. the part of a roof which projects over the top of a wall and allows rain to fall clear of the wall or into a gutter

eaves·drop (í:vzdrɒp) pres. part. **eaves·drop·ping** past and past part. **eaves·dropped** v.i. to listen to what is not meant for one's own ears, without letting oneself be seen **éaves·drop·per, éaves·drop·ing** ns

ebb (eb) **1.** n. the drawing back of tidal water from the shore ‖ decline **2.** v.i. (of the tide) to draw back from the shore ‖ to decline, worsen, diminish

eb·on·y (ébəni:) **1.** n. the wood of many trees, blackened by a deposition of gum resin in the heartwood ‖ any of these trees **2.** adj. black as ebony ‖ made of ebony

ec·cen·tric (ikséntrik) **1.** adj. (of circles, etc.) not having a common center ‖ with its axle not at the center ‖ not conforming to conventions, odd, eccentric behavior **2.** n. someone who behaves unconventionally ‖ (engin.) a device for converting circular motion into to-and-fro rectilinear motion **ec·cén·tri·cal·ly** adv. **ec·cen·tric·i·ty** (ẹksentrísiti:) pl. **ec·cen·tric·i·ties** n. the state of being eccentric ‖ oddness of behavior ‖ an example of such behavior ‖ the distance of an axis or point of rotation from the center of the orbit, e.g., from the sun to the center of a planet's orbit

ec·cle·si·as·tic (iklị:zi:ǽstik) n. a priest, clergyman **ec·cle·si·ás·ti·cal** adj. of or relating to the Christian Church or clergy ‖ of or used in churches **ec·cle·si·as·ti·cism** (iklị:zi:ǽstisịzəm) n. the principles that govern the organization of the Church and its well-being ‖ interest in, and support of, such principles

ech·o (ékou) **1.** *pl.* **cdh·oes** *n.* a second reception of sound waves, etc., when these return after reflection from a surface at some distance ‖ a repetition or close imitation ‖ an answering sympathetic effect ‖ *(mus.)* the soft repetition of a phrase **2.** *v.i.* to produce an echo ‖ *v.t.* to reflect back and so cause an echo ‖ to imitate, esp. weakly ‖ to agree completely with (another's opinions)

é·clat (eiklá, F. eiklǽ) *n.* (of performance or display) manifest brilliance

ec·lec·tic (iklέktik) **1.** *adj.* taking from different sources what seems most suitable for one's purpose ‖ not confined to one source or to one point of view ‖ *n.* an eclectic philosopher, thinker, writer, scientist, etc. **ec·léc·ti·cal·ly** *adj.* **ec·lec·ti·cism** (iklέktisįzəm) *n.*

e·clipse (iklíps) **1.** *n.* the total or partial cutting off of light received from a celestial body, due to another celestial body's moving into an intercepting position ‖ a loss of brightness, reputation, etc. **2.** *v. pres. part.* **e·clips·ing** *past and past part.* **e·clipsed** *v.t.* to cause an eclipse of ‖ to diminish the brightness, glory, etc., of, esp. by excelling ‖ *v.i. (astron.)* to be eclipsed

e·clip·tic (iklíptik) **1.** *n.* the apparent circular path relative to the fixed stars followed by the sun in one year, as seen from the earth **2.** *adj.* of or relating to the eclipse of a heavenly body ‖ relating to the ecliptic

ec·o·log·i·cal (ękəlódʒik'l) *adj.* of or relating to ecology **e·col·o·gist** (ikólədʒist) *n.* a specialist in ecology

e·col·o·gy, oe·col·o·gy (ikólədʒi:) *n.* the branch of biology concerned with the relation between organisms and their environment ‖ the set of relationships between an organism and its environment ‖ a balanced environment used for a natural or artificial environment

e·co·nom·ic (į:kənómik, ękənómik) *adj.* relating to or concerned with economics ‖ financially sound, reasonably profitable ‖ useful in the production of wealth or promotion of commercial prosperity **e·co·nóm·i·cal** *adj.* thrifty, not wasteful ‖ cheap, costing little ‖ (esp. in titles of learned societies, journals, etc.) of or relating to economics **e·co·nóm·i·cal·ly** *adv.* **e·co·nóm·ics** *n.* the study of the way in which natural resources are used and how the wealth they produce is divided, and of the application of the underlying principles of the needs and prosperity of society ‖ this science as applied to the financial structure of an organization, industry, etc.

e·con·o·mist (ikónəmist) *n.* an expert in economics **e·con·o·mize** (ikónəmaiz) *pres. part.* **e·con·o·miz·ing** *past and past part.* **e·con·o·mized** *v.t.* to refrain from wasting ‖ to reduce the amount normally used of ‖ *v.i.* to reduce expenses

e·con·o·my (ikónəmi:) *pl.* **e·con·o·mies** *n.* thrift, avoidance of waste ‖ a means of saving money or avoiding waste ‖ part of a system that deals with man's material needs ‖ a system of producing and distributing the material needs of society

ec·sta·sy (ékstəsi:) *pl.* **ec·sta·sies** *n.* a state in which reason yields to intense (generally delighted) feeling and one is beside oneself ‖ a state in which an overpowering spiritual influence takes charge of one

ec·stat·ic (ikstǽtik) **1.** *adj.* feeling, expressing, or causing ecstasy **2.** *n.* someone experiencing mystical joy **ec·stát·i·cal·ly** *adv.*

ec·u·men·ic, oec·u·men·ic (ękjuménik) *adj.* ecumenical **ec·u·mén·i·cal, oec·u·mén·i·cal** *adj.* of or encouraging universal Christian unity ‖ of, pertaining to or being a movement toward universal Christian unity ‖ worldwide **ec·u·mén·i·cal·ism, oec·u·mén·i·cal·ism** *n.* the principles of the ecumenical movement **ec·u·men·i·cism, oec·u·men·i·cism** (ękjuménisįzəm) *n.* ecumenicalism **ec·u·men·i·cist, oec·u·men·i·cist** (ękjuménisist) *n.*

ec·ze·ma (éksəmə, igzí:mə) *n.* a skin disease, characterized in the acute stage by red, 'weeping' areas, which may later become dry, rough, scaly and irritable **ec·zem·a·tous** (eksémətəs, igzémətəs) *adj.*

ed·dy (édi:) **1.** *pl.* **ed·dies** *n.* a whirling movement, such as that seen when water runs out of a bath or is checked by the bank of a river ‖ a similar movement of air or of some things that float **2.** *v. pres. part.* **ed·dy·ing** *past and past part.* **ed·died** *v.t.* to cause to move with a circular or eddying motion ‖ *v.i.* to move in eddies

edge (edʒ) **1.** *n.* the extreme (generally horizontal) limit, e.g., of a table, cliff, wood, sheet of paper, pond, coin ‖ the fringe, region of the outer limit ‖ the line formed by the meeting of two surfaces ‖ the sharp side or end of a cutting tool **2.** *v. pres. part.* **edg·ing** *past and past part.* **edged** *v.t.* to make, or serve as, an edge or border for ‖ to sharpen ‖ to move gradually in a confined or awkward place ‖ to make (one's way) sideways, cautiously or stealthily ‖ *v.i.* to advance sideways cautiously, e.g. along a cliff ledge ‖ (with 'away', 'towards', etc.) to move in such a way as not to be noticed ‖ (with 'out of') to take avoiding action by stealth

edg·ing (édʒiŋ) **1.** *n.* a border **2.** *adj.* serving to make edges

edg·y (édʒi:) *comp.* **edg·i·er** *superl.* **edg·i·est** *adj.* nervous, jumpy, easily annoyed or upset

ed·i·bil·i·ty (edəbíliti:) *n.* the quality of being edible **ed·i·ble** (édəb'l) **1.** *adj.* wholesome to eat, eatable **2.** *n. (pl.)* things to eat, eatables

e·dict (í:dikt) *n.* an official order published by a ruler or by authority **e·dic·tal** *adj.*

ed·i·fi·ca·tion (ędifikéiʃən) *n.* enlightening of ignorance, or moral or spiritual instruction

ed·i·fice (édifis) *n.* a building, esp. an imposing one ‖ an organized system

ed·i·fy (édifai) *pres. part.* **ed·i·fy·ing** *past and past part.* **ed·i·fied** *v.t.* to improve spiritually or morally by instruction or example

ed·it (édit) *v.t.* to prepare (literary or musical work) for publication, esp. to establish or prepare a commentary on (a text) ‖ to prepare (a film, radio or television material) in the form in which it is to be seen or heard ‖ to alter (matter for publication) so as to make it more suitable for one's purpose ‖ to be in charge of (a newspaper or periodical) and decide its policy and contents

e·di·tion (idíʃən) *n.* a published literary or musical text ‖ a particular form (selected on commercial or aesthetic grounds) in which a book is produced for sale ‖ the copies of a version of a text printed at one time ‖ one of the several issues of a daily newspaper ‖ a thing or person closely resembling another of the same type

ed·i·tor (éditər) *n.* someone who edits a manuscript, book or series of books, newspaper, periodical, film, radio or television material, etc. ‖ someone who is in charge of a particular section of a newspaper or periodical **ed·i·to·ri·al** (ędit̄óri:əl, ędit̄óuri:əl) **1.** *adj.* of or relating to an editor **2.** *n.* an article in a newspaper or periodical which gives the views of those who decide its policy **ed·i·tor·ship** (éditərʃip) *n.*

ed·u·cate (édʒukeit, édjukeit) *pres. part.* **ed·u·cat·ing** *past and past part.* **ed·u·cat·ed** *v.t.* to instruct and train, esp. in such a way as to develop the mental,

---

moral and physical powers of ‖ to provide or obtain such training or instruction for ‖ to train or develop (a particular power or skill, etc.) ‖ to train for a particular end **ed·u·cat·ed** *adj.* properly taught or trained ‖ showing signs of a good education

ed·u·ca·tion (ẹdȝukéiʃən, ẹdjukéiʃən) *n.* instruction or training by which people (generally young) learn to develop and use their mental, moral and physical powers ‖ the art of giving such training ‖ a gaining of experience, either improving or harmful ‖ a branch, system, or stage of instruction ‖ the fruit of training or instruction **ed·u·cá·tion·al** *adj.* concerned with training and teaching ‖ instructive **ed·u·cá·tion·al·ist**, **ed·u·cá·tion·ist** *ns* (often used disparagingly) a theorist in educational matters

eel (i:l) *n.* any of several genera of teleostean fish of the order *Apodes*. They are characterized by a smooth, serpent-like body, devoid of ventral fins and with a continuous dorsal fin

ee·rie, ee·ry (íəri:) *comp.* **ee·ri·er** *superl.* **ee·ri·est** *adj.* mysteriously frightening, uncanny **ée·ri·ly** *adv.* **ée·ri·ness** *n.*

ef·face (iféis) *pres. part.* **ef·fac·ing** *past* and *past part.* **ef·faced** *v.t.* to rub or wipe out, obliterate ‖ to cause to be as though canceled or forgotten ‖ to outshine **ef·fáce·a·ble** *adj.* **ef·fáce·ment** *n.*

ef·fect (ifékt) **1.** *n.* the result produced by a cause ‖ influence, power to change ‖ general meaning or purport ‖ a specific scientific phenomenon, usually named after its discoverer ‖ a general appearance or impression ‖ an impression (often false) deliberately produced ‖ (*pl.*) artistic contrivances ‖ (*pl.*) possessions, assets **2.** *v.t.* to cause to happen, to bring about ‖ to accomplish

ef·fec·tive (iféktiv) **1.** *adj.* causing or capable of causing a desired or decisive result ‖ in use, in force or in operation ‖ causing a telling or striking effect ‖ (*mil.*) actually available for service **2.** *n.* (*pl., mil.*) men ready and fit to fight

ef·fec·tu·al (iféktʃu:əl) *adj.* capable of, or successful in, bringing about a desired effect

ef·fem·i·nate (iféminit) **1.** *adj.* (of men or boys) womanish or girlish, not virile **2.** *n.* a womanish man or girlish boy

ef·fer·vesce (efərvés) *pres. part.* **ef·fer·vesc·ing** *past* and *past part.* **ef·fer·vesced** *v.i.* to produce a great number of bubbles (esp. of carbon dioxide), which rise to the surface and burst with a fizzing sound ‖ to manifest high spirits or great excitement **ef·fer·vés·cence**, **ef·fer·vés·cen·cy** *ns* **ef·fer·vés·cent** *adj.*

ef·fi·ca·cious (ẹfikéiʃəs) *adj.* useful or successful in bringing about a desired result

ef·fi·cien·cy (ifíʃənsi:) *n.* the degree of effectiveness with which something is done, or of the person who does it ‖ (of a machine) the ratio of the work done to the work needed to operate the machine ‖ (of an engine) the ratio of the work done by the engine to the work equivalent of the energy supplied to it

ef·fi·cient (ifíʃənt) *adj.* competent, working properly ‖ (of a machine) producing nearly as much work as it uses (in the form of fuel, etc.)

ef·fi·gy (éfidȝi:) *pl.* **ef·fi·gies** *n.* a statue, image or dummy of a person

ef·fort (éfərt) *n.* an expense of bodily or mental energy to achieve a desired end ‖ the thing achieved by such an expense of energy ‖ a force as distinct from the movement caused by its application

ef·fort·less (éfərtlis) *adj.* making or appearing to make no effort, easy and graceful

ef·fuse (ifjú:z) *pres. part.* **ef·fus·ing** *past* and *past part.* **ef·fused** *v.t.* to pour out or forth

ef·fu·sion (ifjú:ȝən) *n.* a pouring out, a shedding ‖ an extravagant or uncontrolled expression of thought or emotion

ef·fu·sive (ifjú:siv) *adj.* unduly demonstrative, gushing

e·gal·i·tar·i·an (igæliṭéəri:ən) **1.** *adj.* holding the view that all men have equal social and political rights **2.**

n. someone who holds this view **e·gal·i·tár·i·an·ism** *n.*

egg (eg) *n.* the female gamete, ovum ‖ an animal reproductive body consisting of an ovum with its protective coverings or membranes ‖ (*pop.*) the pupa of ants and some other insects

egg *v.t.* (with 'on') to urge or encourage (someone) persistently

e·go (í:gou, égou) *n.* the individual self, looked on as an organized being distinct from others ‖ (*pop.*) one's image of oneself, *to bolster up one's ego* ‖ (*psychoanal.*) the conscious personality as opposed to the unconscious

e·go·tism (í:gəṭizəm, égəṭizəm) *n.* the frame of mind which causes a person to pay too much attention to himself, to be conceited and selfish or refer to himself frequently in writing **é·go·tist** *n.* **e·go·tís·tic**, **e·go·tís·ti·cal** *adjs*

e·gre·gious (igrí:dȝəs) *adj.* flagrant ‖ outstanding for some bad quality

e·gress (í:grəs) *n.* a way out, exit ‖ the act of going out ‖ the right to go out ‖ (*astron.*) the reappearance of a heavenly body (except the moon) at the end of an eclipse or transit

e·gret (í:gret) *n.* a genus of tall, elegant, snowy white birds related to herons

eight (eit) **1.** *adj.* being one more than seven (*NUMBER TABLE) **2.** *n.* twice four ‖ the cardinal number representing this (8, VIII) ‖ eight o'clock ‖ a playing card marked with eight symbols ‖ a team of eight members, esp. in rowing ‖ (*pl.*) races for eight-oared boats

eight·een (éiti:n) **1.** *adj.* being one more than 17 (*NUMBER TABLE) **2.** *n.* ten plus eight ‖ the cardinal number representing this (18, XVIII)

eight·eenth (éiti:nθ) **1.** *adj.* being number 18 in a series (*NUMBER TABLE) ‖ being one of the 18 equal parts of anything **2.** *n.* the person or thing next after the 17th ‖ one of 18 equal parts of anything (1/18) ‖ the 18th day of a month

eighth (eitθ) **1.** *adj.* being number eight in a series (*NUMBER TABLE) ‖ being one of the eight equal parts of anything **2.** *n.* the person or thing next after the seventh ‖ one of eight equal parts of anything (1/8) ‖ the eighth day of a month ‖ (*mus.*) an octave **3.** *adv.* in the eighth place ‖ (followed by a superlative) except seven, *the eighth biggest*

eight·i·eth (éiti:iθ) **1.** *adj.* being number 80 in a series (*NUMBER TABLE) ‖ being one of the 80 equal parts of anything **2.** *n.* the person or thing next after the 79th ‖ one of 80 equal parts of anything (1/80)

eight·y (éiti:) **1.** *adj.* being ten more than 70 (*NUMBER TABLE) **2.** *pl.* **eight·ies** *n.* eight times ten ‖ the cardinal number representing this (80, LXXX) **the eighties** (of temperature, a person's age, a century, etc.) the span 80–9

ei·ther (í:ðər, áiðər) **1.** *adj.* each one of two ‖ one or other of two **2.** *pron.* each one of two ‖ one or other of two **3.** *conj.* used with 'or' to connect two or more alternatives

e·ject (idȝékt) *v.t.* to throw out ‖ to turn out, force to leave ‖ (*law*) to evict from property

e·jec·tion (idȝékʃən) *n.* an ejecting or being ejected

e·jec·tor (idȝéktər) *n.* something which ejects, esp. the mechanism in a firearm which ejects the spent cartridge

e·lab·o·rate 1. (ilǽbərit) *adj.* made with care and much fine detail ‖ complicated **2.** (ilǽbəreit) *v. pres. part.* **e·lab·o·rat·ing** *past* and *past part.* **e·lab·o·rat·ed** *v.t.* to make or develop (a complicated thing) with care, to work out in detail ‖ *v.i.* to add extra complication or ornament, esp. to go into details about a matter **e·lab·o·rá·tion** *n.* **e·láb·o·ra·tive** (ilǽbəreiṭiv, ilǽbərətiv) *adj.* **e·láb·o·ra·tor** *n.*

e·lapse (ilǽps) *pres. part.* **e·laps·ing** *past* and *past part.* **e·lapsed** *v.i.* (of time, or an equivalent) to pass by

e·las·tic (ilǽstik) **1.** *adj.* having the ability to recover its original size or shape after deformation ‖ springy, with the power to give or bend without snapping or breaking ‖ adaptable to circumstances ‖ (of persons) recovering quickly after a setback ‖ made of (or partly of) elastic, *an elastic band* **2.** *n.* vulcanized rubber thread, often covered with or woven into fabric, which can be stretched and which returns to its original size when released ‖ *(pop.)* a rubber band **e·lás·ti·cal·ly** *adv.* **e·las·tic·i·ty** (ilæstísiti:, ɪ:læstísiti:) *n.* the ability to resume the original size or shape after deformation ‖ the capacity to recover after emotional or other stress

e·late (iléit) *pres. part.* **e·lat·ing** *past* and *past part.* **e·lat·ed** *v.t.* to fill with joy, cause to be jubilant **e·lát·ed** *adj.*

e·la·tion (iléiʃən) *n.* the quality or state of being filled with joy or jubilation

el·bow (élbou) **1.** *n.* the joint connecting the forearm and upper arm ‖ the point formed at this joint when the arm is bent ‖ a bend or corner resembling a bent arm, e.g. in a pipe **out at elbows** shabby ‖ poor, without money **2.** *v.t.* to jostle with the elbow ‖ to make (one's way) in this manner ‖ *v.i.* to make one's way in this manner

eld·er (éldər) **1.** *adj.* (of one of two persons) born at an earlier date ‖ of higher rank, dignity, validity or other seniority, by virtue of an earlier origin **2.** *n.* a person who is respected, and whose authority is recognized, because of his age or worthiness ‖ (in Presbyterian Churches) a lay official who shares with the minister the responsibility for running a church ‖ (in the Mormon Church) a grade of the high, or Melchizedek, order of priesthood

eld·er·ly (éldərli:) *adj.* approaching old age, past middle age

eld·est (éldist) *adj.* (of three or more persons, generally of the same family) oldest

e·lect (ilékt) **1.** *adj.* chosen, esp. *(theol.)* chosen by God, predestined to salvation ‖ (following the noun to which it applies) chosen or elected for, but not yet filling, an office or position **2.** *pl. n.* **the elect** those chosen by God, those predestined to salvation ‖ a group of people specially privileged in some way **3.** *v.t.* to choose by voting ‖ *(rhet.)* to decide on (a certain course of action) or choose (to do something) ‖ to choose (an optional course of study) in high school or college

e·lec·tion (ilékʃən) *n.* the act or process of electing, esp. of choosing by vote **e·lec·tion·éer** *v.i.* to try to obtain votes for a political candidate

e·lec·tive (iléktiv) **1.** *adj.* chosen by election or voting ‖ with the power to choose by vote ‖ relating to election by vote ‖ (of a course of studies) optional **2.** *n.* an optional course of studies

e·lec·tor (iléktər) *n.* someone who has the right to vote, esp. in the election of representatives in a national assembly ‖ a member of the electoral college

e·lec·tor·ate (iléktərit) *n.* the whole body of those who have the right to vote in a political election

e·lec·tric (iléktrik) *adj.* of or pertaining to electricity, containing, produced by, producing or worked by electricity ‖ extremely tense, nervously excited **e·léc·tri·cal** *adj.*

e·lec·tri·cian (ilektríʃən) *n.* someone whose trade is making, installing, maintaining or repairing electrical equipment

e·lec·tric·i·ty (ilektrísiti:) *n.* a basic form of energy that is a property of certain fundamental particles of matter and consists of mutually attractive positively and negatively charged particles (protons and electrons, respectively, or positrons and electrons). It is characterized by magnetic, chemical and radiant prop-

erties ‖ an electric current, or stream of electrons ‖ static electricity ‖ the science or study of electricity

e·lec·tri·fy (iléktrifai) *pres. part.* **e·lec·tri·fy·ing** *past* and *past part.* **e·lec·tri·fied** *v.t.* to produce an electric charge or current in ‖ to cause to function by electric power ‖ to thrill or startle as though by an electric shock

e·lec·tro·cute (iléktrəkju:t) *v.t. pres. part.* **e·lec·tro·cut·ing** *past* and *past part.* **e·lec·tro·cut·ed** to administer a fatal electric shock to ‖ to put (a criminal) to death in this way **e·lec·tro·cú·tion** *n.*

e·lec·trode (iléktroud) *n.* one of the two conductors (anode or cathode) by which an electric current is passed through a device such as an electrolytic cell or a discharge tube by an electrical circuit (electrons being emitted by the cathode)

e·lec·trol·y·sis (ilektrólisis) *n.* the passing of an electric current through an electrolyte to produce chemical changes in it ‖ depilation by means of an electric current applied to the body with a needle-shaped electrode

e·lec·tro·lyte (iléktrəlait) *n.* a liquid solution or fused salt that conducts electricity **e·lec·tro·lyt·ic** (ilektrəlítik) *adj.*

e·lec·tron (iléktrɒn) *n.* a constituent of the atom

e·lec·tron·ic (ilektrónik) *adj.* of or relating to electronics ‖ working or produced by the action of electrons **e·lec·trón·i·cal·ly** *adv.* **e·lec·trón·ics** *n.* the branch of physics dealing with the behavior of electrons

el·e·gance (éligəns) *n.* the state or quality of being elegant

el·e·gant (éligənt) *adj.* gracefully refined ‖ neatly and beautifully made or constructed, e.g., of a mathematical proof ‖ showing good taste, refined, polite ‖ fashionable, smart ‖ *(pop.)* very good of its kind

el·e·gize (élidʒaiz) *pres. part.* **el·e·giz·ing** *past* and *past part.* **el·e·gized** *v.t.* to lament the death of (someone) in an elegy ‖ *v.i.* to write an elegy

el·e·gy (élidʒi:) *pl.* **el·e·gies** *n.* a poem which laments the death of someone ‖ a poem written in a nostalgic or melancholy mood

el·e·ment (éləmənt) *n.* one of the simplest parts into which something can be divided, or a component of a composite whole ‖ something which is present in small quantity in a larger whole ‖ *(pl.)* the simplest and most basic parts of a branch of knowledge ‖ *(pl., rhet.)* atmospheric forces (to force oneself to go out into the storm) ‖ *(pl.)* earth, air, fire and water, formerly regarded as the basic constituents of the material universe ‖ *(biol.)* the natural habitat of an organism (water, dry land etc.) ‖ *(chem.)* any of more than 100 substances that never have been separated into simpler substances by ordinary chemical means ‖ *(elec.)* the resistance coil, wire, of an electric heater, kiln, etc. **el·e·men·tal** (ələmént'l) **1.** *adj.* pertaining to the primitive forces of nature ‖ elementary **2.** *n.* a spirit identified with one of the primitive forces of nature

el·e·men·ta·ry (ələméntəri:, ələméntri:) *adj.* very simple, basic ‖ consisting of the simplest parts of a branch of knowledge ‖ consisting of a single chemical element

el·e·phant (élifənt) *n.* the Indian or the African, the largest living land animals, standing 9–12 ft high and weighing 5–6 tons

el·e·phan·tine (elifánti:n, elifæntain) *adj.* of or like an elephant ‖ huge and clumsy ‖ pompous and heavy-handed

el·e·vate (éliveit) *pres. part.* **el·e·vat·ing** *past* and *past part.* **el·e·vat·ed** *v.t.* to raise to a higher level ‖ to raise in rank or dignity ‖ to raise in price, value, importance, etc. ‖ to raise to a higher moral or intellectual level ‖ to encourage (hopes) or raise (spirits)

el·e·va·tion (elivéiʃən) *n.* an elevating or being elevated ‖ height above sea level ‖ loftiness, grandeur ‖ *(archit.)* a side or end view of a building, etc. or a drawing of this view ‖ a hill or piece of rising ground ‖ *(ballet)* a leap, the dancer appearing to hang for a moment in the air ‖ *(astron.)* the angular distance of a heavenly body above the horizon

el·e·va·tor (éliveitər) *n.* a machine that can raise or carry a weight from one level to another ‖ a mechanical apparatus for raising or lowering people or things from floor to floor in a building ‖ a tall building or tower into which grain is mechanically hoisted for storage ‖ a muscle which controls the lifting of a part of the body

e·lev·en (ilévən) **1.** *adj.* being one more than 10 (*NUMBER TABLE) **2.** *n.* 10 plus one ‖ the cardinal number representing this (11, XI) ‖ 11 o'clock ‖ a team of 11 members, e.g., in field hockey

e·lev·enth (ilévənθ) **1.** *adj.* being number 11 in a series (*NUMBER TABLE) ‖ being one of the 11 equal parts of anything **at the eleventh hour** at the last possible moment ‖ in the nick of time **2.** *n.* the person or thing next after the tenth ‖ one of 11 equal parts of anything (1/11) ‖ the 11th day of a month

elf (elf) *pl.* **elves** (elvz) *n.* a little creature of folklore with magic power, often mischievous or malicious, but sometimes kind and helpful ‖ an elflike child or person

elf·in (élfin) **1.** *adj.* of or relating to elves, elflike ‖ fey **2.** *n.* an elf

elf·ish (élfiʃ) *adj.* of or relating to elves ‖ mischievous

e·lic·it (ilísit) *v.t.* to draw forth in response ‖ to arrive at (the truth, etc.) by questioning or other logical process

el·i·gi·bil·i·ty (elidʒəbíliti) *n.* the state or quality of being eligible

el·i·gi·ble (élidʒəb'l) *adj.* qualified to be chosen ‖ entitled to receive ‖ desirable, suitable, esp. having the advantages looked for by prospective mothers-in-law

e·lim·i·nate (ilímineit) *pres. part.* **e·lim·i·nat·ing** *past and past part.* **e·lim·i·nat·ed** *v.t.* to get rid of ‖ to cause to be no longer included ‖ *(physiol.)* to get rid of by expelling, excrete ‖ *(math.)* to remove (a quantity) from an equation **e·lim·i·ná·tion, e·lím·i·na·tor** *ns* **e·lim·i·na·to·ry** (ilíminətɔri:, ilíminətouri:) *adj.*

e·lite (ilí:t, eilí:t) *n.* the few who are considered socially, intellectually or professionally superior to the rest in a group or society

e·lix·ir (ilíksər) *n.* a substance sought by alchemists for converting base metals into gold ‖ *(pharm.)* an aromatic preparation, often sweetened and containing alcohol, used for flavoring drugs

elk (elk) *n.* the largest of the deer family inhabiting N. Europe and Asia ‖ a member of the Elks, a prominent fraternal society

el·lipse (ilíps) *n.* *(geom.)* a plane figure obtained when a plane intersects a cone obliquely

el·lip·tic (ilíptik) *adj.* having the form of an ellipse ‖ characterized by ellipsis **el·líp·ti·cal** *adj.*

el·o·cu·tion (eləkjú:ʃən) *n.* the art of speaking or reading correctly, clearly, pleasantly and forcefully, esp. in public **el·o·cú·tion·ar·y** *adj.* **el·o·cú·tion·ist** *n.* someone skilled in, or who teaches, the art

e·lon·gate (iló ŋgeit, ilóŋgeit, í:lɔŋgeit) **1.** *v. pres. part.* **e·lon·gat·ing** *past and past part.* **e·lon·gat·ed** *v.t.* to make longer ‖ *v.i.* to increase in length **2.** *adj.* *(biol.)* long and slender

e·lope (ilóup) *pres. part.* **e·lop·ing** *past and past part.* **e·loped** *v.i.* (of a lover or pair of lovers) to run away with the intention of getting married

el·o·quence (éləkwəns) *n.* the fluent, skillful use of words to persuade or move hearers or readers

el·o·quent (éləkwənt) *adj.* speaking or writing with eloquence ‖ spoken or written with eloquence

else (els) **1.** *adv.* in a different way ‖ at a different time

‖ in a different place ‖ otherwise, if not (usually preceded by 'or') **2.** *adj.* (after an indefinite or interrogative pronoun) other, different

else·where (élshwɛər, élswɛər) *adv.* in, to or at another or a different place

e·lu·ci·date (ilú:sideit) *pres. part.* **e·lu·ci·dat·ing** *past and past part.* **e·lu·ci·dat·ed** *v.t.* to make easier to understand, give an explanation of **e·lu·ci·dá·tion, e·lú·ci·da·tor** *ns*

e·lude (ilú:d) *pres. part.* **e·lud·ing** *past and past part.* **e·lud·ed** *v.t.* to slip away from, avoid capture by, dodge away from ‖ to escape the notice, understanding or memory of

e·lu·sive (ilú:siv) *adj.* hard to catch, find, pin down or keep hold of ‖ hard to grasp with the mind, remember exactly or define precisely

E·ly·sian (ilíʒən, ilí:ʒən) *adj.* of or pertaining to Elysium ‖ (of joy, happiness) perfect

E·lys·i·um (ilízi:əm) *pl.* **E·lys·iums, E·lys·i·a** (ilízi:ə) *n. (Gk. mythol.)* the Elysian Fields, the abode after death of the brave and good ‖ a place or state of ideal happiness

e·ma·ci·ate (iméiʃi:eit) *pres. part.* **e·ma·ci·at·ing** *past and past part.* **e·ma·ci·at·ed** *v.t.* to make thin and worn, to waste by, or as if by, hunger and want **e·má·ci·at·ed** *adj.* **e·ma·ci·á·tion** *n.*

em·a·nate (émaneit) *pres. part.* **em·a·nat·ing** *past and past part.* **em·a·nat·ed** *v.i.* to come, arise (from a source or origin)

e·man·ci·pate (imǽnsəpeit) *pres. part.* **e·man·ci·pat·ing** *past and past part.* **e·man·ci·pat·ed** *v.t.* to set free from oppression or slavery ‖ to free from restrictive rules or conventions **e·mán·ci·pa·tor** *n.* **e·man·ci·pa·to·ry** (imǽnsəpətɔri:, imǽnsəpətouri:) *adj.*

e·man·ci·pa·tion (imænsipéiʃən) *n.* a setting free or being set free, esp. from slavery ‖ freedom from political, moral, intellectual or social restraints offensive to reason or justice

em·balm (imbɑ́m) *v.t.* to preserve (a corpse) from decay by the application of ointments, resins etc. or by injections **em·bálm·ment** *n.*

em·bar·go (imbɑ́rgou) **1.** *pl.* **em·bar·goes** *n.* a government order forbidding foreign ships to enter or leave its ports (esp. before an outbreak of war) ‖ an order forbidding the import, export or carriage of certain commodities ‖ a prohibition (generally in an industrial or commercial context) **2.** *v.t.* to lay under an embargo

em·bark (imbɑ́rk) *v.t.* to put or take on board ship ‖ *v.i.* to go on board ship ‖ *(rhet.)* to make a start (on something long, difficult or dangerous)

em·bar·rass (imbǽrəs) *v..t* to cause to feel self-conscious, awkward, shy or ashamed ‖ to make things difficult or complicated for ‖ to hinder ‖ (esp. *pass.*) to involve in debt **em·bár·rass·ing** *adj.* **em·bár·rass·ment** *n.* an embarrassing or being embarrassed ‖ something which embarrasses

em·bas·sy (émbəsi:) *pl.* **em·bas·sies** *n.* an official mission or delegation, esp. one which represents one country in another at the highest diplomatic level ‖ the residence or offices of the head of such a body ‖ the office or function of an ambassador ‖ *(rhet.)* the mission of a private person who acts as an intermediary

em·bel·lish (imbéliʃ) *v.t.* to make more decorative, to add flourishes or ornament to ‖ to add made-up details to (a story) so as to increase the pleasure of telling it or listening to it **em·bél·lish·ment** *n.*

em·ber (émbər) *n.* a hot or red-hot fragment of burning coal or wood ‖ *(pl.)* the hot remains of a fire

em·bez·zle (imbéz'l) *pres. part.* **em·bez·zling** *past and past part* **em·bez·zled** *v.t.* to steal or use for one's own purposes (money or other property which has been entrusted to one as an employee, servant or agent) **em·béz·zle·ment** *n.*

em·blem (émbləm) *n.* an object, or the representation of an object, which serves as a recognized symbol ‖

a design (which may represent an object), e.g. a publisher's device, used to show who owns or has produced the thing in or on which it appears ‖ a heraldic device in a coat of arms or crest **em·blem·át·i·cal** *adj.* **em·blem·a·tist** (imblémətist) *n.* **em·blém·a·tize** *pres. part.* **em·blem·a·tiz·ing** *past* and *past part.* **em·blem·a·tized** *v.t.* to symbolize, represent by an emblem or serve as an emblem of

em·boss (imbós, imbós) *v.t.* to produce a raised design, pattern or lettering on (a plain surface, e.g. metal, leather, cloth, paper), esp. by stamping or impressing on it an engraved die ‖ to produce (a raised design etc.) on such a surface

em·brace (imbréis) **1.** *v. pres. part.* **em·brac·ing** *past* and *past part.* **em·braced** *v.t.* to put one's arms lovingly around ‖ to accept gladly, seize ‖ to adopt (a faith, opinion etc.) ‖ to include, incorporate ‖ to encompass, take in with the eye or understanding ‖ *v.i.* to join in an embrace, hug one another **2.** *n.* a clasping or folding in the arms, a hug ‖ a tight grip ‖ an adoption (of a faith, opinion etc.)

em·broi·der (imbrɔ́idər) *v.t.* to ornament (cloth, silk, leather etc.) with needlework ‖ to carry out (a design) in needlework ‖ to add to (a story etc.) details that are interesting or entertaining but not true

em·broi·der·y (imbrɔ́idəri:) *pl.* **em·broi·der·ies** *n.* the art or process of embroidering cloth etc. ‖ the work so produced ‖ the embroidering of a story, or the details so added

em·bry·o (émbri:ou) *pl.* **em·bry·os** *n.* an animal organism during the early stages of growth and development merging in higher animals into fetal stages or ending (as in primitive species) with the larva ‖ a human individual from the time of implantation to the eighth week after conception ‖ a young sporophyte in seed plants, usually consisting of a rudimentary plant embedded in endosperm **em·bry·on·ic** (ęmbri:ɔ́nik) *adj.*

em·er·ald (émərəld) **1.** *n.* a bright green precious stone, the green beryl (a silicate of beryllium and aluminum) ‖ the color of an emerald **2.** *adj.* of or like an emerald ‖ of the color of an emerald

e·merge (imɔ́:rdʒ) *pres. part.* **e·mer·ging** *past* and *past part.* **e·merged** *v.i.* to come out (from), to appear (from) ‖ to come out from a less desirable or less developed state to one more desirable or more advanced ‖ to be brought out in discussion or investigation as a fact or logical conclusion ‖ to come to light, be discovered **e·mér·gence** *n.* the act of emerging

e·mer·gen·cy (imɔ́:rdʒənsi:) *pl.* **e·mer·gen·cies** *n.* a situation, often dangerous, which arises suddenly and calls for prompt action ‖ an immediate need

em·er·y (éməri:) *pl.* **em·er·ies** *n.* a very hard, granular corundum, intimately mixed with hematite and magnetite, used as an abrasive

em·i·grant (émigrənt) **1.** *n.* a person emigrating or who has emigrated **2.** *adj.* emigrating ‖ of or relating to emigration or emigrants

em·i·grate (émigreit) *pres. part.* **em·i·grat·ing** *past* and *past part.* **em·i·grat·ed** *v.i.* to leave one's own country or home and settle in another ‖ *v.t.* to cause or help (a person) to emigrate **em·i·grá·tion** *n.* **em·i·gra·to·ry** (émigrətɔ:ri:, émigrətouri:) *adj.*

em·i·nent (éminənt) *adj.* distinguished, widely thought of as superior in some way ‖ outstanding, conspicuous

em·is·sar·y (émiseri:) **1.** *pl.* **em·is·sar·ies** *n.* an agent sent on a mission, sometimes in secret, sometimes with great pomp **2.** *adj.* of, or serving as, an emissary

e·mis·sion (imíʃən) *n.* a sending out or giving out, e.g. of light, heat, gas, smoke ‖ that which is given out

‖ an involuntary discharge of semen ‖ an issuing and putting into circulation of paper money ‖ *(elec.)* the throwing off or sending out of electrons, esp. from a heated cathode ‖ the electronic current so produced

e·mit (imít) *pres. part.* **e·mit·ting** *past* and *past part.* **e·mit·ted** *v.t.* to give out, give off ‖ to put (currency etc.) in circulation

e·mote (imóut) *pres. part.* **e·mot·ing** *past* and *past part.* **e·mot·ed** *v.i.* *(pop.)* to display or affect emotion, esp. in a film or play ‖ *(pop.)* to behave histrionically

e·mo·tion (imóuʃən) *n.* a strong feeling (such as fear, wonder, love, sorrow, shame) often accompanied by a physical reaction (e.g. blushing or trembling) **e·mó·tion·al** *adj.* of or relating to the emotions ‖ showing deep feeling or emotion ‖ aimed at the arousing of emotion ‖ ruled by emotion rather than by reason **e·mó·tion·al·ism** *n.* a tendency to delight in **e·mó·tion·al·ist** *n.* **e·mo·tion·ál·i·ty** *n.* the quality or state of being too emotional **e·mo·tion·al·ize** (imóuʃən'laiz) *pres part.* **e·mo·tion·al·iz·ing** *past* and *past part.* **e·mo·tion·al·ized** *v.t.* to adopt an emotional attitude toward

em·pa·thy (émpəθi:) *n.* the power to enter into emotional harmony with a work of art and so derive aesthetic satisfaction ‖ *(psychol.)* the power to enter into the feeling or spirit of others **em·pa·thet·ic** (ęmpəθétik), **em·path·ic** (impǽθik) *adjs*

em·per·or (émpərər) *n.* the ruler of an empire **ém·per·or·ship** *n.*

em·pha·sis (émfəsis) *pl.* **em·pha·ses** (émfəsi:z) *n.* a special stress or deliberate accent laid on a word or syllable in order to make a meaning or intention unmistakable ‖ a special vigor or deliberation given to an action so as to convey an attitude of mind ‖ a special importance given to a thing ‖ sharpness, esp. of contrast **em·pha·size** (émfəsaiz) *pres. part.* **em·pha·siz·ing** *past* and *past part.* **em·pha·sized** *v.t.* to lay emphasis on, stress

em·phat·ic (imfǽtik) *adj.* expressed in words or action with emphasis ‖ (of words) adding emphasis or intensifying meaning ‖ strongly marked, strikingly noticeable ‖ having a firm opinion and expressing it **em·phát·i·cal·ly** *adv.*

em·phy·se·ma (ęmfisí:mə) *n.* *(med.)* a condition, often a complication in bronchitis, in which the lungs and their constituent air cells are distended with air to the point of inefficiency **em·phy·sem·a·tous** (ęmfisémətəs) *adj.*

em·pire (émpaiər) **1.** *n.* a sovereign state whose possessions have been extended by military or economic conquest, colonization, or federation, to include countries or territories originally independent of it ‖ supreme power or sovereignty ‖ an organization (commercial, industrial, financial) having great wealth and power **2.** *adj.*

em·pir·ic (empírik) **1.** *n.* someone who believes that in science and philosophy there is no truth other than that obtained by sense, observation and experiment ‖ someone who acquires knowledge or practices a science by methods of trial and error without constructing an ordered or scientific system **2.** *adj.* **em·pír·i·cal** making use of, or based on, experience, trial and error, or experiment, rather than theory or systematized knowledge ‖ derived from the senses and not by logical deduction **em·pir·i·cism** (empíriṣiẓəm) *n.* **em·pír·i·cist** *n.*

em·ploy (implɔ́i) **1.** *v.t.* to pay (a person) to work for one ‖ to require the work of, keep busy ‖ to use, make use of **2.** *n.* (in the phrase **in** (someone's) **employ** working for (someone) **em·plóy·a·ble** *adj.*

---

em·ploy·ee (implɔ́ii:, ɛmplɔií:) *n.* someone paid to work esp. on a regular rather than a casual basis

em·ploy·er (implɔ́iər) *n.* someone who pays another or others to work for him ‖ a user

em·ploy·ment (implɔ́imənt) *n.* the state of being employed ‖ work done, or to be done, by someone employed, work as livelihood

em·pow·er (impáuər) *v.t.* to delegate legal power to, authorize ‖ to enable

em·press (émpris) *n.* the wife of an emperor ‖ a woman ruler of an empire in her own right

emp·ti·ly (émptili:) *adv.* in an empty way

emp·ti·ness (émpti:nis) *n.* the state of being empty

emp·ty (émpti:) **1.** *comp.* **emp·ti·er** *superl.* **emp·ti·est** *adj.* with nothing in it ‖ unoccupied, *an empty chair* ‖ (with 'of') totally without ‖ silly, without substance ‖ (with 'of') totally without ‖ silly, without seriousness ‖ (*pop.*) hungry **2.** *pl.* **emp·ties** *n.* an empty packing case, bottle, or other container **3.** *v. pres. part.* **emp·ty·ing** *past* and *past part.* **emp·tied** *v.t.* to cause to become empty, take the contents out of ‖ to transfer (something) from one container to another ‖ *v.i.* to flow or discharge ‖ to become empty

em·py·re·al (ɛmpairí:əl, ɛmpíri:əl) *adj.* of the empyrean

em·py·re·an (ɛmpairí:ən, ɛmpíri:ən) *n.* the vault of the sky

em·u·late (émjuleit) *pres. part.* **em·u·lat·ing** *past* and *past part.* **em·u·lat·ed** *v.t.* to try to do as well as **em·u·la·tion** *n.* **em·u·la·tive** (émjuleitiv, émjulətiv) *adj.*

e·mul·sion (imʌ́lʃən) *n.* a colloidal dispersion of two incompletely miscible liquids, one of which is in the form of fine droplets, or of a finely divided insoluble solid in a liquid ‖ (*photog.*) the coating, sensitive to light, of a photographic plate or film, consisting of finely divided silver halide crystals in a viscous liquid (e.g. gelatin)

e·mul·sive (imʌ́lsiv) *adj.* having the nature of an emulsion

en·a·ble (inéib'l) *pres. part.* **en·a·bling** *past* and *past part.* **en·a·bled** *v.t.* to make it possible for or to allow (a person or thing to do something)

en·act (inǽkt) *v.t.* to make (a bill) into a law ‖ to play out, perform as though on the stage **en·ác·tive** *adj.* **en·áct·ment** *n.* an enacting or being enacted ‖ an order, decree, regulation

e·nam·el (inǽməl) **1.** *n.* a glass rendered opaque or translucent by an admixture of tin oxide or other infusible substance and often strongly colored ‖ something worked with this ‖ enamel paint ‖ the hard, white, calcareous substance which coats the crown of a tooth ‖ a cosmetic applied to the nails to give a hard shiny coating **2.** *v.t. pres. part.* **e·nam·el·ing** *past* and *past part.* **e·nam·eled** to coat with enamel

e·nam·ored (inǽmərd) *adj.* (*rhet.*, with 'of') in love

en·camp (inkǽmp) *v.i.* (of troops) to set up a camp ‖ *v.t.* to quarter (troops) in a camp **en·cámp·ment** *n.* a camp ‖ the act of setting up a camp or of quartering troops in a camp

en·case, in·case (inkéis) *pres. part.* **en·cas·ing, in·cas·ing** *past* and *past part.* **en·cased, in·cased** *v.t.* to enclose in an outer cover or case

en·chant (intʃǽnt, intʃɑ́nt) *v.t.* to cast a spell on ‖ to fill with delight **en·chánt·ed** *adj.* under a spell **en·chánt·er** *n.* a magician ‖ someone who fascinates **en·chánt·ing** *adj.* delightful ‖ fascinating **en·chánt·ment** *n.* a magic spell or charm ‖ the state of being under a spell ‖ delight ‖ delightfulness **en·chánt·ress** *n.*

en·cir·cle (insɔ́:rk'l) *pres. part.* **en·cir·cling** *past* and *past part.* **en·cir·cled** *v.t.* to surround ‖ to move in a circular path around **en·cir·cle·ment** *n.* a surrounding or being surrounded

en·close, in·close (inklóuz) *pres. part.* **en·clos·ing, in·clos·ing** *past* and *past part.* **en·closed, in·closed** *v.t.* to shut in with a wall or other protection ‖ to put (something) into an envelope or parcel with something else ‖ to surround on all sides, hem in

en·clo·sure, in·clo·sure (inklóuʒər) *n.* something enclosed in a letter or parcel ‖ a place shut in, fenced in or otherwise marked off for a special purpose ‖ a fence or other boundary that encloses an area

en·com·pass (inkʌ́mpəs) *v.t.* to surround or enclose, hem in on every side ‖ to embrace within its scope etc.

en·core (ɑ́ŋkɔr, ɑ́ŋkour) **1.** *interj.* the cry of an audience when it is pleased and wants a performer to play (or sing etc.) again **2.** *n.* the additional performance called for in this way **3.** *v.t. pres. part.* **en·cor·ing** *past* and *past part.* **en·cored** to call on (a performer) to play (or sing etc.) again ‖ to call on the performer of (a song etc.) to perform it again

en·coun·ter (inkáuntər) **1.** *v.t.* to come upon, meet ‖ to come up against, meet in conflict or battle, or as rivals in sport **2.** *n.* a meeting by chance, not by design ‖ a conflict, battle, or match or game between rival teams ‖ in health care, any contact between a patient and health professional in which care is given, sometimes excluding telephone contacts

en·cour·age (inkɔ́:ridʒ, inkʌ́ridʒ) *pres. part.* **en·cour·ag·ing** *past* and *past part.* **en·cour·aged** *v.t.* to give courage or confidence to ‖ to raise the hopes of ‖ to help on by sympathetic advice and interest ‖ to advise and make it easy for (someone to do something) ‖ to promote, stimulate ‖ to strengthen (a belief or idea) **en·cóur·ag·ing** *adj.* **en·cóur·age·ment** *n.* a heartening or being heartened ‖ something that cheers and helps on ‖ an inducement

en·croach (inkróutʃ) *v.i.* (with 'on' or 'upon') to overstep the limits of what belongs or is due to one ‖ (with 'on' or 'upon') to make gradual inroads **en·cróach·ment** *n.*

en·cum·ber (inkʌ́mbər) *v.t.* to hamper, impede ‖ to burden ‖ to litter, block up

en·cy·clo·pe·di·a, en·cy·clo·pae·di·a (insaiklɔpí:di:ə) *n.* a book or series of books giving information (generally arranged alphabetically) on all subjects or on all aspects of one subject **en·cy·clo·pé·dic, en·cy·clo·pǽ·dic** *adj.* in or like an encyclopedia ‖ covering a wide range of knowledge or all aspects of a subject **en·cy·clo·pé·di·cal, en·cy·clo·pǽ·di·cal** *adj.* **en·cy·clo·pé·dism, en·cy·clo·pǽ·dism** *n.* the possession of wide and exact knowledge **en·cy·clo·pé·dist, en·cy·clo·pǽ·dist** *n.* someone who writes, edits or contributes to an encyclopedia

end (end) *n.* the last part of a thing, i.e. the furthest in distance, latest in time, or last in sequence or series ‖ the limit beyond which a thing cannot be extended ‖ the tip or extremity of a thing ‖ a piece that is left over, a remnant ‖ the conclusion of what has gone before ‖ a final result or ultimate state ‖ death ‖ aim or purpose ‖ the reason for which someone or something exists

end *v.t.* to stop ‖ to conclude ‖ *v.i.* to come to an end ‖ to result in **to end off** to conclude **to end up**

en·dan·ger (indéindʒər) *v.t.* to cause danger to or constitute a cause of danger to

en·dear (indíər) *v.t.* to cause to be held in affection **en·déar·ment** *n.* a word, phrase, act, gesture etc. which expresses affection

en·deav·or (indévər) **1.** *v.i.* to make a determined effort **2.** *n.* a determined effort

end·ing (éndiŋ) *n.* the action of coming or bringing to an end ‖ conclusion, finish ‖ (*gram.*) a morpheme added to a word to make inflectional forms, e.g. in English '-s' for the plural of most nouns, or '-ed' for the past of most verbs

en·dorse, in·dorse (indɔ́rs) *pres. part.* **en·dors·ing, in·dors·ing** *past* and *past part.* **en·dorsed, in·dorsed** *v.t.* to sign one's name on the back of (a check etc.) in order to obtain the cash it represents ‖ to make (a check etc.) payable to another by writing his name on the back and signing ‖ to sign or initial, or add a comment or qualification to (a document) ‖ to confirm, sanction, show approval of or agreement with (an option, action, proposal etc.) **en·dórse·ment, in·dórse·ment** *n.*

en·dow (indáu) *v.t.* to give money or other property for the permanent upkeep or benefit of (an institution, organization etc.) ‖ (with 'with') to provide with a natural gift, attribute etc. **en·dów·ment** *n.* the act of endowing (with money or other property) ‖ the money or property so given ‖ a natural gift or ability

en·dur·a·ble (indúərəb'l, indjúərəb'l) *adj.* that can be endured

en·dur·ance (indúərəns, indjúərəns) *n.* the capacity to keep going or put up with pain, hardship etc. for a long time ‖ the act of doing this ‖ the length of time that an aircraft can remain in the air under specified conditions without refueling

en·dure (indúər, indjúər) *pres. part.* **en·dur·ing** *past* and *past part.* **en·dured** *v.t.* to bear, stand ‖ to suffer patiently ‖ to put up with, tolerate ‖ *v.i.* to remain set in purpose, hold out, under suffering, trial etc. ‖ to last for a long time

en·e·my (énəmi) **1.** *pl.* **en·e·mies** *n.* a hostile nation, or a member of it ‖ *(collect.)* a hostile nation's armed forces or part of them ‖ a person who bears another ill will and actively works or fights against him ‖ someone who opposes, disapproves, or works against (ideas, beliefs etc.) ‖ something harmful or troublesome **2.** *adj.* being or pertaining to an enemy

en·er·get·ic (ɛnərdʒétik) *adj.* active, showing great physical or mental energy ‖ requiring great physical effort ‖ forceful, vigorous **en·er·gét·i·cal·ly** *adv.* **en·er·gét·ics** *n.* the study of the production of energy and its transformations

en·er·gize (énərdʒaiz) *pres. part.* **en·er·giz·ing** *past* and *past part.* **en·er·gized** *v.t.* to give energy to ‖ to cause electricity to flow in

en·er·gy (énərdʒi:) *pl.* **en·er·gies** *n.* forcefulness and vigor in actions or words ‖ (often *pl.*) busy activity ‖ *(phys.)* the unifying concept of all physical science that associates with any system a capacity for work either as a result of the motion of mass in the system (kinetic energy), the configuration of masses or charges in the system (potential energy) or the presence of photons in the system (radiant energy)

en·er·vate (énərveit) *pres. part.* **en·er·vat·ing** *past* and *past part.* **en·er·vat·ed** *v.t.* to lower the vitality of ‖ to sap the willpower of or weaken the mental vigor of **en·er·vá·tion** *n.*

en·force (infórs, infúrs) *pres. part.* **en·forc·ing** *past* and *past part.* **en·forced** *v.t.* to impose by force, compel ‖ to give strength to ‖ to press home ‖ to put into force **en·fórce·a·ble** *adj.* **en·fórce·ment** *n.*

en·gage (ingéidʒ) *pres. part.* **en·gag·ing** *past* and *past part.* **en·gaged** *v.t.* to take into one's employment ‖ to make a promise binding on (oneself), esp. a promise of marriage ‖ to occupy the time of or compel the attention of ‖ (in warfare or other dispute) to come to grips with, to attack ‖ *v.i.* to join battle ‖ *(mech.,* with 'with') to interlock, mesh ‖ (with 'in') to busy oneself **en·gáged** *adj.* pledged to marry ‖ busy, already occupied, and so not free ‖ (of a gear) meshed **en·gáge·ment** *n.* an undertaking or obligation, esp. a promise to marry ‖ an agreement to employ or be employed ‖ an appointment for a fixed time ‖ a battle ‖ *(mech.)* the state of being meshed **en·gág·ing** *adj.* attractive, charming

en·gen·der (indʒéndər) *v.t.* to give rise to

en·gine (éndʒin) *n.* a device used to transform one form of energy into another, esp. into kinetic energy ‖ a locomotive

en·gi·neer (ɛndʒiníər) **1.** *n.* an expert in the design and construction of engines, *mechanical engineer* or of electrical equipment, *electrical engineer* or expert in the organization of civil works (roads, bridges etc.), *civil engineer* ‖ a person qualified in any branch of engineering ‖ the driver of a locomotive ‖ *(mil.)* one of a corps trained for roadmaking, bridge-building etc. ‖ someone active behind the scenes in achieving something **2.** *v.t.* to carry out (a piece of engineering work) ‖ to manage, by using tact, craft or ingenuity, to achieve (a result) **en·gi·néer·ing** *n.* the science of applying knowledge of the properties of matter and the natural sources of energy to the practical problems of industry

Eng·lish (íŋgliʃ) **1.** *adj.* of, relating to or characteristic of the country, state or people of England ‖ of the official language spoken in Great Britain, Northern Ireland, the U.S.A., Canada, Australia and in other Commonwealth countries **2.** *n.* the English language **the English** *(pl.)* the people of England or its representatives (e.g. armed forces, or a team in international sport

en·grain, in·grain (ingréin) *v.t.* to instil (habits, tastes etc.) so that they become deep-rooted

en·grave (ingréiv) *pres. part.* **en·grav·ing** *past* and *past part.* **en·graved** *v.t.* to cut a design or lettering on (a hard surface, e.g. copper, glass, etc.) by hand with a burin or other sharp tool, either for decoration or to produce a plate from which the image can be printed ‖ to fix deeply in the mind, memory etc. **en·gráv·er** *n.* **en·gráv·ing** *n.* the hand engraver's art or the allied mechanical process ‖ an impression or print taken from an engraved surface

en·gross (ingróus) *v.t.* to occupy (a person or his attention) to the exclusion of everything else ‖ to make a fair copy of (a legal document) in careful, formal handwriting ‖ to draw up in proper legal form **en·gróss·ing** *adj.* holding one absorbed in interest **en·gróss·ment** *n.*

en·gulf (ingʌ́lf) *v.t.* (of a flood, the sea etc.) to swallow up ‖ overwhelm, bury

en·hance (inhǽns, inhǻns) *pres. part.* **en·hanc·ing** *past* and *past part.* **en·hanced** *v.t.* to increase, add to (a quality, price or value) **en·hánced** *adj.* heightened, intensified **en·hánce·ment** *n.*

e·nig·ma (inígmə) *n.* something hard to define or understand fully ‖ an unfathomable person ‖ an obscure saying, riddle

en·ig·mat·ic (ɛnigmǽtik) *adj.* puzzling, deliberately veiled in meaning **en·ig·mát·i·cal** *adj.*

en·join (indʒɔ́in) *v.t.* to impose as a rule, order or duty ‖ to command, urge authoritatively ‖ *(law)* to forbid or restrain (an action) by an injunction

en·joy (indʒɔ́i) *v.t.* to take pleasure or delight in, be pleased by ‖ to have the use, benefit or advantage of **to enjoy oneself** to have a pleasant time **en·jóy·a·ble** *adj.* pleasant, giving pleasure **en·jóy·ment** *n.* the pleasure or satisfaction given by what is enjoyed ‖ something enjoyed ‖ the right to possess and use

en·large (inlάrdʒ) *pres. part.* **en·larg·ing** *past* and *past part.* **en·larged** *v.t.* to make bigger ‖ to expand ‖ *v.i.* to become bigger ‖ to widen in scope ‖ (with 'on' or 'upon') to speak or write more fully about **en·lárge·ment** *n.* the act of enlarging ‖ the state produced by enlarging ‖ *(photog.)* a print larger than the original negative **en·lárg·er** *n. (photog.)* an apparatus for enlarging photographs

en·light·en (inláit'n) *v.t.* to give (someone) information about, or help him to understand, what is obscure or difficult ‖ to shed light on (a problem) ‖ to civilize by freeing from ignorance, superstition etc. ‖ to give spiritual light to **en·líght·en·ment** *n.* an enlightening or being enlightened ‖ something which enlightens

en·list (inlíst) *v.i.* to join the armed forces (in the ranks, not as a commissioned officer) ‖ *v.t.* to take into the armed forces ‖ to recruit (persons to help), *to enlist helpers for a mission* ‖ to call in (help or support)

en·list·ment (inlístmənt) *n.* an enlisting, or being enlisted ‖ the period for which someone enlists

en·liv·en (inláivən) *v.t.* to make more lively, give animation to ‖ to make gayer or brighter

en·mi·ty (énmiti:) *n.* a state or feeling of hatred or hostility (either shared by two parties or confined to one)

en·no·ble (inóub'l) *pres. part.* **en·no·bling** *past and past part.* **en·no·bled** *v.t.* to make spiritually, intellectually or morally elevated ‖ to raise to the ranks of the nobility **en·nó·ble·ment** *n.*

en·nui (ɑ̃nwi:) *n.* boredom, weariness and discontent

e·nor·mi·ty (inɔ́rmiti:) *pl.* **e·nor·mi·ties** *n.* shocking wickedness ‖ a shocking crime or offense ‖ a terrible blunder ‖ huge size

e·nor·mous (inɔ́rməs) *adj.* huge, very great **e·nór·mous·ly** *adv.* to a very great degree ‖ an intensive form of 'very'

e·nough (inʌ́f) **1.** *adj.* as much (in number, quantity or degree) as is needed **2.** *adv.* (invariably placed after the word it modifies) sufficiently, in the degree or quantity that is needed **3.** *n.* a sufficient quantity ‖ as much as one can put up with or manage **4.** *interj.* stop!, no more!

en·rage (inréidʒ) *pres. part.* **en·rag·ing** *past and past part.* **en·raged** *v.t.* to make furiously angry ‖ to torment to madness

en·rich (inrítʃ) *v.t.* to make rich or richer in money or goods ‖ to improve the quality of ‖ to add fullness of flavor or richness to ‖ to add a precious or costly ornament to ‖ to make a valuable addition to (a collection, museum etc.) **en·rích·ment** *n.*

en·roll, en·rol (inróul) *pres. part.* **en·roll·ing, en·rol·ling** *past and past part.* **en·rolled** *v.t.* to include (a person's name) in a list ‖ to enter (a document) in an official or legal register ‖ *v.i.* to enlist (in the armed forces) ‖ to join a particular body of persons **en·róll·ment, en·ról·ment** *n.*

en·sconce (inskɔ́ns) *pres. part.* **en·sconc·ing** *past and past part.* **en·sconced** *v.t.* (often *refl.*) to tuck (oneself) away in, install (oneself) in some snug or desirable place

en·sem·ble (ɑnsɑ́mb'l, ɑ̃sɑ́mb'l) *n.* a thing looked at or judged as a whole or from the point of view of the general effect ‖ (*mus.*) a performance or passage in which all the players or singers take part together ‖ a chamber orchestra ‖ (*theater*) the whole company or cast ‖ a complete matching outfit of clothes

en·shrine (inʃráin) *pres. part.* **en·shrin·ing** *past and past part.* **en·shrined** *v.t.* to place in a shrine or honored place of safety ‖ to keep dear or sacred (in one's heart, mind, memory etc.) **en·shrine·ment** *n.*

en·sign (énsain, énsən) *n.* (esp. *naut.*) a flag, standard ‖ an emblem, badge, etc., esp. a symbol of office ‖ (énsən) a U.S. naval officer ranking immediately below a lieutenant junior grade **én·sign·ship** *n.*

en·slave (insléiv) *pres. part.* **en·slav·ing** *past and past part.* **en·slaved** *v.t.* to make a slave of **en·sláve·ment** *n.*

en·sue (insú:) *pres. part.* **en·su·ing** *past and past part.* **en·sued** *v.i.* to happen or come afterwards or as a result

en·tail (intéil) **1.** *v.t.* to bring as a necessary consequence ‖ (*law*) to settle (landed property) in such a way that it cannot be sold and must be inherited and bequeathed in a certain way **2.** *n.* such a legal settlement ‖ an entailed estate **en·táil·ment** *n.*

en·tan·gle (intǽŋg'l) *pres. part.* **en·tan·gling** *past and past part.* **en·tan·gled** *v.t.* to catch up in, seemingly inextricably ‖ to make into a tangle or complicated muddle ‖ to involve in difficulties, complications or undesirable circumstances **en·tán·gle·ment** *n.*

en·ter (éntər) *v.t.* to go or come in or into ‖ to penetrate into ‖ to take up, adopt (an occupation, profession etc.) ‖ to join (a body or organization) ‖ to admit or cause to be admitted to a body or organization ‖ to put (oneself, someone else, something) down for a competition ‖ to make a note or record of (in the appropriate book, list, or other record) ‖ (*law*) to bring (a writ etc.) before a court in proper form ‖ *v.i.* to go in ‖ to come in ‖ (*theater*) to come on stage **to enter into** to start upon, begin to take part in ‖ to form part of, have a bearing or influence upon, be a factor in

en·ter·prise (éntərpraiz) *n.* a venture, esp. one calling for determination, energy and initiative ‖ the character needed for such a venture ‖ a commercial or industrial undertaking **én·ter·pris·ing** *adj.* with plenty of initiative, ready to undertake new ventures or try new methods or ideas

en·ter·tain (entərtéin) *v.t.* to receive as a visitor or guest ‖ to give interest and pleasure to, amuse ‖ to have in one's mind ‖ to give thought or consideration to, *not even to entertain the possibility of failure* ‖ *v.i.* to show hospitality **en·ter·táin·er** *n.* a person who entertains professionally, esp. by telling funny stories **en·ter·táin·ing** *adj.* **en·ter·táin·ment** *n.* an entertaining or being entertained ‖ any interesting or diverting performance or spectacle, usually public ‖ hospitality meant to amuse and divert a guest

en·thrall, en·thral (inθrɔ́l) *pres. part.* **en·thrall·ing, en·thral·ling** *past and past part.* **en·thralled** *v.t.* to capture the interest or attention of, hold as if spellbound, delight **en·thráll·ing, en·thrál·ling** *adj.* **en·thráll·ment, en·thrál·ment** *n.*

en·thu·si·asm (inθú:zi:æzəm) *n.* passionate admiration or interest ‖ an object of such feelings

en·thu·si·ast (inθú:zi:æst) *n.* an ardent fan, supporter or admirer, someone passionately interested in something **en·thu·si·ás·tic** *adj.* **en·thu·si·ás·ti·cal·ly** *adv.*

en·tice (intáis) *pres. part.* **en·tic·ing** *past and past part.* **en·ticed** *v.t.* to cause (a person or animal) to cease resisting and to do as one wishes, by offering some inducement **en·tíce·ment** *n.*

en·tire (intáiər) *adj.* whole and complete, absolute and unqualified ‖ not broken or damaged, intact ‖ (*bot.*, of leaves) with an unbroken outer edge ‖ (of male animals) not castrated **en·tíre·ly** *adv.* wholly and completely ‖ solely

en·tire·ty (intáiərti:, intáirəti:) *pl.* **en·tire·ties** *n.* completeness ‖ (*law*) sole and undivided possession **in its entirety** as an undiminished whole

en·ti·tle (intáit'l) *pres. part.* **en·ti·tling** *past and past part.* **en·ti·tled** *v.t.* to give (someone) a right ‖ to give a title to

en·ti·tle·ments (intáit'lmənts) *pl. n.* benefits that one may receive upon request, esp. from a government agency

en·ti·ty (éntiti:) *pl.* **en·ti·ties** *n.* something existing complete in itself, by its own right

en·tou·rage (ɑnturɑ́ʒ) *n.* the companions or servants who attend or surround a person ‖ surroundings

en·trance (éntrəns) *n.* a door or other opening by which one can enter a building or other place ‖ the act of coming or going in ‖ the act of starting, being admitted etc. ‖ the right to come or go in or to be admitted ‖ a fee paid for the right to be admitted ‖ the coming on stage of a player

en·trance (intrǽns, intrɑ́ns) *pres. part.* **en·tranc·ing** *past* nad *past part.* **en·tranced** *v.t.* to overcome with joy, delight or wonder ‖ to put into a trance **en·tránc·ing** *adj.* delightful **en·tránce·ment** *n.*

en·treat (intrí:t) *v.t.* to plead with ‖ (*rhet.*) to plead for, implore **en·tréat·y** *pl.* **en·tréat·ies** *n.* an entreating, pleading, beseeching

en·trée, en·tree (ɑ́ntrei) *n.* freedom of entry ‖ a dish served between the fish and the meat ‖ the main course of a dinner

en·trench (intréntʃ) *v.t.* to surround or protect with a trench ‖ to settle (oneself) securely e.g. in a job or some other position thought of as safe ‖ *v.i.* to dig protective trenches ‖ (with 'on') to encroach **en·trénch·ment** *n.*

en·trust (intrʌ́st) *v.t.* to give for safekeeping or to be looked after ‖ to give a task or duty to

en·try (éntri:) *pl.* **en·tries** *n.* entrance ‖ the part of a building, around the door, which leads to the interior ‖ someone or something entered for a competition, race etc. ‖ *(law)* the actual taking possession of a property by setting foot in it ‖ the noting, recording or registering of something in a book, list, or other record, or the thing so recorded

e·nu·mer·ate (inú:məreit, injú:məreit) *pres. part.* **e·nu·mer·at·ing** *past and past part.* **e·nu·mer·at·ed** *v.t.* to state or name one by one **e·nu·mer·á·tion** *n.* **e·nú·mer·a·tive** *adj.*

e·nun·ci·ate (inʌ́nsi:eit) *pres. part.* **e·nun·ci·at·ing** *past and past part.* **e·nun·ci·at·ed** *v.t.* to pronounce (sounds, syllables etc.) ‖ to state, give expression to ‖ *v.i.* to articulate **e·nun·ci·á·tion** *n.* the act or way of pronouncing ‖ the stating (of a proposition, theory, doctrine etc.) **e·nún·ci·a·tive** *adj.* **e·nún·ci·a·tor** *n.*

en·vel·op (invéləp) *v.t.* to wrap up, esp. in a garment ‖ to cover completely, shroud ‖ *(mil.)* to surround **en·vél·op·ment** *n.*

en·ve·lope (énvəloup, ɑ́nvəloup) *n.* a paper cover with a gummed or tuck-in flap, to hold a letter etc. ‖ the outer skin of an airship or balloon ‖ *(biol.)* a membrane, shell or other covering

en·vi·ous (énvi:əs) *adj.* feeling, showing or prompted by envy

en·vi·ron·ment (inváirənmənt, inváiərnmənt) *n.* surroundings, esp. the material and spiritual influences which affect the growth, development and existence of a living being **en·vi·ron·mén·tal** *adj.*

en·voy (énvɔi) *n.* someone sent on a mission or with a message, usually official ‖ an envoy extraordinary

en·vy (énvi:) *pres. part.* **en·vy·ing** *past and past part.* **en·vied** *v.t.* to feel malicious envy of or for ‖ to affirm the goodness of (something) by wishing to share it

envy *pl.* **en·vies** *n.* a feeling of antagonism towards someone because of some good which he is enjoying but which one does not have oneself ‖ a coveting for oneself of the good which someone else is enjoying (traditionally one of the seven deadly sins) ‖ an innocent desire to share another's good ‖ something which arouses this desire

en·zyme (énzaim) *n.* one of a large class of complex proteinaceous substances of high molecular weight formed in and produced by living matter which are responsible for promoting the chemical reactions upon which life depends

e·phem·er·a (ifémərə) *pl.* **e·phem·er·as, e·phem·er·ae** (iféməri:) *n.* a mayfly ‖ something short-lived **e·phém·er·al 1.** *adj.* short-lived, of only passing interest or value ‖ (of plants and insects) with a mature or adult life of a few days or less **2.** *n.* something ephemeral

ep·ic (épik) **1.** *n.* a long narrative poem conceived on a grand scale, telling a story of great or heroic deeds **2.** *adj.* of or having the nature of an epic

ep·i·cure (épikjuər) *n.* a discriminating person, esp. one who cultivates and enjoys his taste for the best in food and drink

ep·i·dem·ic (epidémik) **1.** *n.* a disease which becomes widespread in a particular place at a particular time ‖ an occurrence, generally unpleasant, which is widespread or intense **2.** *adj.* widespread, esp. of disease **ep·i·dém·i·cal** *adj.*

ep·i·der·mis (epidə́:rmis) *pl.* **ep·i·der·mis·es, ep·i·der·mes** (epidə́:rmi:z) *n.* the outer protective monocellular layer of plants ‖ the protective external skin of vertebrates, consisting of thin layers of horny cells which are sometimes modified to hair and nails etc. **ep·i·dér·moid, ep·i·der·mói·dal** *adjs* resembling epidermis

ep·i·lep·sy (épələpsi:) *n.* a chronic nervous disorder of the brain of man and other animals affecting consciousness and muscular control with various degrees of severity **ep·i·lép·tic** *n. and adj.*

ep·i·logue, ep·i·log (épələɡ, épələɡ) *n.* the concluding part of, or a final note added to, a literary work ‖ a short final speech or scene after the end of a play

ep·i·sode (épisoud) *n.* a part of a story subordinate to the main theme and generally self-contained ‖ a similar passage in a musical work ‖ a self-contained part of a serial story ‖ an isolated event or instance, separate from the run of events **ep·i·sód·i·cal** *adj.* consisting of linked episodes ‖ spasmodic

e·pis·tle (ipís'l) *n. (rhet.)* a letter ‖ a literary work (prose or poetry) cast in the form of a letter

ep·i·taph (épitæf, épitɑf) *n.* words inscribed on a gravestone or other monument in memory or in praise of a dead person or persons ‖ a short, pithy tribute to a dead person, sometimes in verse **ep·i·táph·ic** *adj.*

e·pit·o·me (ipítəmi:) *n.* a summary of the contents of a book or other writing or piece of exposition ‖ a person or thing typical of, or serving as a model of, something larger or wider **e·pít·o·mist** *n.* **e·pít·o·mize** *pres. part.* **e·pit·o·miz·ing** *past and past part.* **e·pit·o·mized** *v.t.* to make or serve as an epitome of

ep·och (épək) *n.* a period of time characterized by momentous events or changes ‖ the beginning of such a period ‖ *(geol.)* a division of geological time shorter than a period **ép·och·al** *adj.*

ep·os (épɒs) *n.* early folk-epic poetry, either recited or written ‖ an epic of this kind

eq·ua·bil·i·ty (ękwəbíliti:) *n.* the state or quality of being equable

eq·ua·ble (ékwəb'l) *adj.* not changing much, steadily even, without extremes ‖ calm, not easily upset or excited **éq·ua·bly** *adv.*

e·qual (í:kwəl) **1.** *adj.* the same in number, degree, value, rank or other standard of comparison ‖ with no advantage on either side, even ‖ impartial ‖ without subservience or domination ‖ (with 'to') the same in number, degree, value, rank etc. as ‖ (with 'to') able to face up to ‖ (with 'to') equivalent to **2.** *n.* someone or something equal in some point of comparison to another **3.** *v.t. pres. part.* **e·qual·ing** *past and past part.* **e·qualed** to be or become equal to ‖ to come up (or sink) to the standard of

e·qual·i·ty (ikwóliti:) *pl.* **e·qual·i·ties** *n.* the state or an instance of being equal in number, amount, rank, meaning etc.

e·qual·ize (í:kwəlaiz) *pres. part.* **e·qual·iz·ing** *past and past part.* **e·qual·ized** *v.t.* to make equal ‖ to make regular or even ‖ *v.i. (sports)* to score a goal which makes the scores equal **é·qual·iz·er** *n. (sports)* a goal which makes the score equal ‖ *(elec.)* a conductor connecting two points, normally of the same potential, on the armature of an electrical machine

e·qual·ly (í:kwəli:) *adv.* to the same degree ‖ in equal shares or parts

e·qua·nim·i·ty (į:kwənímiti:, ękwənímiti:) *n.* steady calmness, the state of being unperturbed

e·quate (ikwéit) *pres. part.* **e·quat·ing** *past and past part.* **e·quat·ed** *v.t. (math.)* to state the equality of ‖ to regard as equal in value or as mutually

---

equation 122 **escape**

interdependent

e·qua·tion (ikwéiʒən, ikwéiʃən) *n.* the act of making equal ‖ *(math.)* a statement of the equality between mathematical expressions ‖ *(chem.)* a quantitative statement of chemical change, using the symbol → to represent the process **e·quá·tion·al** *adj.*

e·qua·tor (ikwéitər) *n.* the great circle of the earth, in a plane perpendicular to the axis of the earth and equidistant from the poles, dividing the northern and southern hemispheres **e·qua·to·ri·al** (į:kwətóri:əl, į:kwətóuri:əl, ękwətóri:əl, ękwətóuri:əl) *adj.* on or near or pertaining to the equator

e·ques·tri·an (ikwéstri:ən) **1.** *adj.* concerned with or representing horseback riding **2.** *n.* (esp. of acrobats) a horseback rider **e·ques·tri·enne** (ikwęstri:én) *n.* a female horseback rider

e·qui·lib·ri·um (į:kwəlíbri:əm) *n.* a state of balance between opposing forces or effects, the system involved undergoing no total change

e·qui·nox (í:kwinɒks, ékwinɒks) *pl.* **e·qui·nox·es** *n.* the moment or point at which the sun crosses the equator during its apparent annual motion from north to south or from south to north. At the equinoxes day and night are of equal length

e·quip (ikwíp) *pres. part.* **e·quip·ping** *past* and *past part.* **e·quipped** *v.t.* to provide with what is needed to carry out a particular purpose or function

e·quip·ment (ikwípmənt) *n.* what is needed or is provided to carry out a particular purpose or function ‖ the personal gear, arms, kit etc. carried by troops ‖ a person's knowledge, training, skill, experience etc. ‖ *(rail.)* rolling stock ‖ the act or process of equipping

eq·ui·ta·ble (ékwitəb'l) *adj.* fair and just ‖ *(law)* relating to, or valid in, equity as distinct from statute law **éq·ui·ta·bly** *adv.*

eq·ui·ty (ékwiti) *pl.* **eq·ui·ties** *n.* fairness and justice, esp. the common fairness that follows the spirit rather than the letter of justice ‖ *(law)* an equitable claim or right ‖ *(law)* an equity of redemption ‖ the value of a property after deducting any charges to which it is liable

e·quiv·a·lence (ikwívələns) *n.* the state of being equivalent **e·quív·a·len·cy** *n.*

e·quiv·a·lent (ikwívələnt) **1.** *adj.* (with 'to') equal, having the same effect or value. **2.** *n.* that which is equivalent to something else

e·quiv·o·cal (ikwívək'l) *adj.* capable of being understood in more than one way ‖ suspect, of doubtful validity, honesty or sincerity **e·quiv·o·cál·i·ty** *n.*

e·quiv·o·cate (ikwívəkeit) *pres. part.* **e·quiv·o·cat·ing** *past* and *past part.* **e·quiv·o·cat·ed** *v.i.* to avoid a plain statement or answer and so evade the truth **e·quiv·o·cá·tion, e·quív·o·ca·tor** *ns*

e·ra (íərə) *n.* a system of dating events from one particular event or moment ‖ a period of time in history or any relatively prolonged stage of development ‖ a date or event which is taken as the beginning of an era ‖ *(geol.)* one of the major divisions of geological time

e·rad·i·cate (irǽdikeit) *pres. part.* **e·rad·i·cat·ing** *past* and *past part.* **e·rad·i·cat·ed** *v.t.* to stamp out or destroy utterly **e·rad·i·cá·tion** *n.* **e·rádi·i·ca·tor** *n.* a chemical substance for removing ink or stain

e·rase (iréis) *pres. part.* **e·ras·ing** *past* and *past part.* **e·rased** *v.t.* to rub out, efface **e·rás·er** *n.* something used for erasing marks

e·rect (irékt) **1.** *adj.* upright, without stooping or bowing ‖ (of a dog's hair etc.) on end, bristling ‖ (of the penis or clitoris) stiff and swollen from being distended with blood ‖ *(bot.)* growing vertically, growing at right angles to the stem or branch **2.** *v.t.* to cause to have built or put up ‖ to put in place, *to erect a fence* ‖ to set upright ‖ to cause to become erect ‖ *(geom.)* to draw, construct ‖ *v.i.* (of the penis or clitoris) to become erect

e·rec·tion (irékʃən) *n.* an erecting or being erected ‖ a building or other similar structure ‖ a hardening and

swelling of the penis or clitoris when distended with blood

e·rode (iróud) *pres. part.* **e·rod·ing** *past* and *past part.* **e·rod·ed** *v.t.* to eat away ‖ to wear away (land) ‖ *v.i.* to become eroded

e·ro·sion (iróuʒən) *n.* an eroding or being eroded, esp. *(geol.)* the wearing away of land by water, wind or ice

e·rot·ic (irɒ́tik) *adj.* of or relating to sexual love ‖ licentious

e·rot·i·cism (irɒ́tisiʒəm) *n.* sexual excitement or desire ‖ the character of being erotic

err (ə:r, er) *v.i.* to make a mistake, to be wrong ‖ to contain a relative amount of error

er·rand (érənd) *n.* a short journey to carry out some particular task or to take a message ‖ the task itself

er·rant (érənt) *adj.* erring, tending to do wrong ‖ straying ‖ *(rhet.)* roving

er·rat·ic (irǽtik) **1.** *adj.* not fitting into any regular pattern of events or behavior ‖ uneven in quality ‖ unstable, unbalanced ‖ *(geol.,* of boulders) transported from their place of origin ‖ *(med.)* moving from one place in the body to another **2.** *n. (geol.)* a boulder transported from its place of origin **er·rát·i·cal·ly** *adv.*

er·ro·ne·ous (iróuni:əs) *adj.* (of a statement, opinion, doctrine etc.) mistaken, wrong

er·ror (érər) *n.* departure from the truth in a statement or in a belief ‖ a mistake ‖ departure from right conduct ‖ *(math.)* the difference between the correct result and the computed one ‖ *(law)* a legal or factual mistake in court proceedings, giving grounds for review upon a writ of error

er·satz (érzɑts, éərsɑts) **1.** *adj.* (of a product) synthetic **2.** *n.* a synthetic product replacing a natural one

erst·while (ə́:rsthwail, ə́:rstwail) *adj. (rhet.)* former, esp. operative or existing until then or until now

er·u·dite (érjudait, érudait) *adj.* (of a man or a work) learned **er·u·di·tion** (ęrjudíʃən, ęrudíʃən) *n.* scholarly learning

e·rupt (irʌ́pt) *v.i.* (of a volcano) to pour forth rocks, lava etc. ‖ (of a geyser) to shoot forth steam ‖ to break or burst out violently from restraint, or as if from restraint ‖ (of teeth) to cut through the gums ‖ (of a rash) to break out on the skin ‖ *v.t.* (of a volcano or geyser, or of someone or something compared to these) to throw out violently, eject

e·rup·tion (irʌ́pʃən) *n.* an outbreak, explosion (of a natural force) ‖ an outbreak (of violence, passion, disease etc.) ‖ a breaking out in a skin rash ‖ the rash itself

es·ca·late (éskəleit) *pres. part.* **es·ca·lat·ing** *past* and *past part.* **es·ca·lat·ed** *v.t.* and *i.* to increase gradually but steadily **es·ca·lá·tion** *n.*

es·ca·la·tor (éskəleitər) *n.* a moving staircase working on the principle of an endless chain

es·ca·pade (éskəpeid, ęskəpéid) *n.* a wild, often innocent, adventure involving a throwing over of restraints

es·cape (iskéip) **1.** *v. pres. part.* **es·cap·ing** *past* and *past part.* **es·caped** *v.i.* to get free by flight, regain one's liberty ‖ to leak, flow or otherwise issue from a container ‖ to find release or relief from worries, troubles or responsibilities ‖ *v.t.* (of words or sounds) to be uttered or released involuntarily by ‖ to get away from (pursuit or restraint) ‖ to avoid, keep or be kept safe from, get away from (death, danger, disaster, punishment etc.) ‖ to elude the memory, understanding or notice of **2.** *n.* the act of getting free from prison or other confinement, from pursuit or from a pursuer etc. ‖ a way out, a means of getting free from confinement or danger ‖ a leak, flowing out or overflow ‖ avoidance of, preservation from, or getting away from death, danger, punishment etc. ‖ a release or relief from misery, worries or responsibilities **es·cap·ée** *n.* someone who has escaped **es·cápe·ment** *n.* a device for checking and regulating the movements of the wheels in a clock or watch

es·chew (istʃú:) *v.t.* *(rhet.)* to do without, refrain from using, avoid **es·chéw·al** *n.*

es·cort 1. (éskɔrt) *n.* a person or group accompanying another person or group out of politeness, for company, to give protection, by way of ceremonial etc. ‖ warships or aircraft acting in a protective or ceremonial role ‖ an accompanying by a person, group or formation ‖ a man accompanying a woman on some social occasion ‖ a guard responsible for a prisoner in transit **under escort** accompanied by guards **2.** (iskɔ́rt) *v.t.* to accompany as an escort ‖ to accompany as a courtesy or protection

es·crow (éskrou) *n.* *(law)* a formal contract or deed which does not come into effect until some specified condition has been fulfilled. (Until that time it is held by a third person.) **in escrow** on trust as an escrow

e·soph·a·gus, oe·soph·a·gus (isɔ́fəgəs) *pl.* **e·soph·a·gi, oe·soph·a·gi** (isɔ́fədʒai) *n.* *(anat.)* the tube through which food passes from the mouth to the stomach

es·o·ter·ic (esətérik) *adj.* (of religious, mystical or philosophical teaching or practice) with a meaning that is understood only by those who have received the necessary instruction or training ‖ trained to understand such teaching or practices ‖ difficult to understand ‖ with a private or secret meaning or purpose **es·o·tér·i·cal·ly** *adv.*

es·pe·cial (ispéʃəl) *adj.* particular ‖ outstanding, exceptional **in especial** in particular ‖ especially **es·pé·cial·ly** *adv.* particularly ‖ exceptionally

es·pi·o·nage (éspi:ɑnɑʒ, espi:ənɑʒ) *n.* spying or the use of spies to obtain military, political, scientific, industrial etc. secrets

es·pous·al (ispáuz'l) *n.* *(rhet.)* an adoption or taking up (of a cause, doctrine or line of action etc.)

es·pouse (ispáuz) *pres. part.* **es·pous·ing** *past* and *past part.* **es·poused** *v.t.* to adopt, take up, support (a cause, doctrine, line of action etc.)

es·prit (esprí:) *n.* wit

es·py (ispái) *pres. part.* **es·py·ing** *past* and *past part,* **es·pied** *v.t.* *(rhet.)* to catch sight of, notice

es·say (eséi) *v.t.* to test, try out, esp. to assay (metals) ‖ *v.i.* to attempt

essay (ései) *n.* a writing (often quite short) dealing with a particular subject ‖ *(rhet.,* also eséi) a trial or experiment ‖ a proof of a rejected design for a stamp or for paper money **és·say·ist** *n.* a writer of essays

es·sence (és·ns) *n.* the most significant part of a thing's nature ‖ *(philos.)* the sum of the intrinsic properties without which a thing would cease to be what it is, and which are not affected by accidental modifications ‖ *(philos.)* the subject in which attributes adhere ‖ a concentrated extract, e.g. of vanilla **in essence** in fundamental respects

es·sen·tial (isénʃəl) **1.** *adj.* necessary, such that one cannot do without it ‖ of the utmost importance ‖ relating to, or arising from, the real nature of a thing or person, basic, fundamental ‖ ideal, as perfect as the mind can conceive ‖ containing all that is best or most important in a thing **2.** *n.* something that one cannot do without ‖ (esp. *pl.)* the basic or fundamental part or element in a thing **es·sen·ti·al·i·ty** (isenʃi:æliti:) *n.*

es·tab·lish (istǽbliʃ) *v.t.* to set up, found ‖ to place on a firm basis ‖ to bring into being ‖ to set up (oneself or another) in a profession or trade or cause to settle in a locality etc. ‖ to achieve, secure ‖ to make clear, prove, win general recognition for ‖ (of a post in the civil service, a large corporation etc.) permanent and carrying full benefits ‖ beyond question **es·táb·lish·ment** *n.* an establishing or being estab-

lished ‖ a place of business or a residence ‖ the servants of a household ‖ a body of people employed in one organization ‖ an organization as a whole

es·tate (istéit) *n.* a landed property ‖ the whole of a person's property, incl. real estate and personal estate ‖ a class in society sharing in the government of a country

es·teem (istí:m) **1.** *n.* good opinion, regard **2.** *v.t.* to have a high opinion of, value ‖ *(rhet.)* to value (something) as being (something) ‖ to consider (oneself) as being (something)

es·thet·ic (esθétik) *adj.* aesthetic

es·ti·ma·ble (éstəməb'l) *adj.* worthy of esteem ‖ capable of being estimated **és·ti·ma·bly** *adv.*

es·ti·mate 1. (éstəmit) *n.* a judgment of size, number, quantity, value, distance, quality etc., esp. of something which needs calculation or assessment ‖ a statement of the cost or charge which would be involved in a given piece of work, or a tender to carry it out for a certain sum **2.** (éstəmeit) *v. pres. part.* **es·ti·mat·ing** *v. pres. part.* **es·ti·mat·ing** *past* and *past part.* **es·ti·mat·ed** *v.t.* to make an estimate of ‖ *v.i.* to submit an estimate

es·ti·ma·tion (estəméiʃən) *n.* an opinion ‖ an assessing of value or importance ‖ an estimate ‖ esteem

es·ti·ma·tor (éstəmeitər) *n.* someone who works out cost estimates in a firm ‖ *(statistics)* one who makes a conclusion from a sampling

es·trange (istréindʒ) *pres. part.* **es·trang·ing** *past* and *past part.* **es·tranged** *v.t.* to cause (a person or persons) to become unloving or unfriendly **es·tránge·ment** *n.*

es·tro·gen, oes·tro·gen (éstrədʒən) *n.* one of a group of female sex hormones that is produced by the ovaries and is responsible for initiating estrus and for the development of secondary sexual charcteristics in the female **es·tro·gén·ic, oes·tro·gén·ic** *adj.*

es·tu·ar·y (éstʃuːɛri:) *pl.* **es·tu·ar·ies** *n.* the tidal mouth of a river

et cet·er·a (etsétərə, etsétrə) *(abbr.* etc., used to indicate the incompleteness of a list) and others, and so on **et·cet·er·as** *pl. n.* sundry items, extras

etch (etʃ) *v.t.* to engrave (a design etc.) on glass or a metal plate, esp. copper, from which a picture or design can be printed ‖ to engrave (a plate) ‖ *v.i.* to practice this art **étch·ing** *n.* the art of producing such plates ‖ a print from an etched plate

e·ter·nal (itɔ́:rn'l) *adj.* never ending, lasting for ever ‖ without beginning or end in time ‖ ceaseless, or constantly repeated ‖ annoyingly incessant ‖ seemingly limitless **e·tér·nal·ize** *pres. part.* **e·ter·nal·iz·ing** *past* and *past part.* **e·ter·nal·ized** *v.t.* to eternalize

e·ter·ni·ty (itɔ́:rniti:) *pl.* **e·ter·ni·ties** *n.* time or existence without beginning or end ‖ the endless state after death ‖ a seemingly endless time or distance

e·ther, ae·ther (í:θər) *n.* a hypothetical substance proposed in the wave theory of light as being the medium of propagation of electromagnetic waves ‖ *(chem.)* a volatile, inflammable colorless liquid, diethyl ether, with a sweet, pungent smell, used as an anesthetic and as a solvent ‖ *(rhet.)* the upper regions of the sky

e·the·re·al (iθíəri:əl) *adj.* light, airy and intangible ‖ heavenly ‖ *(chem.)* pertaining to ether **e·the·re·ál·i·ty** *n.* **e·thé·re·al·ize** *pres. part.* **e·the·re·al·iz·ing** *past* and *past part.* **e·the·re·al·ized** *v.t.*

eth·ic (éθik) **1.** *n.* a system of ethics **2.** *adj.* ethical **éth·i·cal** *adj.* dealing with ethics ‖ relating to morality of behavior ‖ conforming with an accepted standard of good behavior, e.g. in a profession or trade **éth·i·cal·ly** *adv.* in an ethical way ‖ so far as ethics is concerned **eth·ics** n. moral philosophy or moral science ‖ a treatise on this science ‖ the moral principles which determine the rightness or wrongness of particular acts or activities

eth·nic (éθnik) adj. of or relating to a people whose unity rests on racial, linguistic, religious or cultural ties ‖ deriving from or belonging to such racial etc. ties of a people or country **eth·ni·cal** adj. **eth·ni·cal·ly** adv. according to ethnic grouping

et·i·quette (étikit, étiket) n. the rules of behavior standard in polite society ‖ the rules governing professional conduct ‖ court ceremonial or conventions of official life

é·tude (éitu:d, éitju:d) n. (mus.) a short composition, written either as an exercise or to demonstrate technique, or to develop a particular limited theme or mood

et·y·mol·o·gist (ętəmɔ́lədʒist) n. a specialist in etymology

et·y·mol·o·gy (ętəmɔ́lədʒi:) pl. **et·y·mol·o·gies** n. the branch of the study of language dealing with the origin, derivation and development of words ‖ the derivation of a word

eu·lo·gize (jú:lədʒaiz) pres. part. **eu·lo·giz·ing** past and past part. **eu·lo·gized** v.t. to praise highly in speech or writing

eu·lo·gy (jú:lədʒi:) pl. **eu·lo·gies** n. a written or spoken expression of high praise

eu·nuch (jú:nək) n. castrated man or boy

eu·phe·mism (jú:fəmɪzəm) n. the use of a pleasant, polite or harmless-sounding word or expression to mask harsh, rude or infamous truths ‖ the word or phrase so used **eu·phe·mis·tic** adj. **eu·phe·mis·ti·cal·ly** adv.

eu·phon·ic (ju:fɔ́nik) adj. euphonious **eu·phon·i·cal·ly** adv.

eu·pho·ny (jú:fəni:) pl. **eu·pho·nies** n. a pleasant concordance of sound ‖ (phon.) a tendency towards ease of pronunciation, e.g. the use of 'an' instead of 'a' before words beginning with a vowel

eu·pho·ri·a (ju:fɔ́ri:ə, ju:fóuri:ə) n. a feeling of well-being or elation (often, as in drunkenness, deceptive) **eu·phor·ic** (ju:fɔ́rik, ju:fóurik) adj.

eu·tha·na·sia (ju:θənéiʒə, ju:θənéizi:ə) n. the deliberate, painless killing of persons who suffer from a painful and incurable disease or condition, or who are aged and helpless

e·vac·u·ate (ivǽkju:eit) pres. part. **e·vac·u·at·ing** past and past part. **e·vac·u·at·ed** v.t. (mil.) to abandon (a town or position) ‖ to empty (a dangerous place) of troops, civilians, material etc. ‖ to remove (troops, civilians, material etc.) from a dangerous place ‖ to empty ‖ to discharge the contents of (a bodily organ, the bowels) **e·vac·u·a·tion** n. **e·vac·u·ee** (ivækju:í:) n. an evacuated person

e·vade (ivéid) pres. part. **e·vad·ing** past and past part. **e·vad·ed** v.t. to escape from by skill, cunning, deception, dexterity etc. ‖ to find a way of getting out of (something demanded, asked or expected of one), dodge ‖ to be too difficult, puzzling or baffling for ‖ v.i. to be evasive

e·val·u·ate (ivǽlju:eit) pres. part. **e·val·u·at·ing** past and past part. **e·val·u·at·ed** v.t. to determine or assess the value of ‖ (math.) to express the value of (a quantity) numerically **e·val·u·a·tion** n.

e·van·gel·i·cal (i:vænʤélik'l) adj. concerned with, or relating to, the preaching of the Christian gospel ‖ contained in, or in accordance with, the teaching of the Gospels ‖ of, like, or relating to the Gospels ‖ of or relating to the school of theology within the Protestant Church

e·van·ge·lism (ivǽnʤelizəm) n. the preaching of the Christian gospel, missionary activity

e·van·ge·list (ivǽnʤəlist) n. an author of one of the four Gospels ‖ a preacher of the Christian gospel, an evangelizer or missionary **e·van·ge·lis·tic** adj. of, or relating to, or like the Christian gospel or one of the four Gospels ‖ of or relating to preaching the Christian gospel

e·vap·o·rate (ivǽpəreit) pres. part. **e·vap·o·rat·ing** past and past part. **e·vap·o·rat·ed** v.i. (of a liquid or solid) to assume the vapor state by a gradual physical change to which all solids and liquids are subject, at all temperatures, though the rate of change may be very slow ‖ to disappear, leaving no trace ‖ v.t. to cause to evaporate, by raising the temperature or reducing the pressure of

e·vap·o·ra·tion (ivæpəréiʃən) n. an evaporating or being evaporated ‖ disappearance without trace

e·va·sion (ivéiʒən) n. the act or a means of evading (a danger, a duty, the law etc.) ‖ a dodging or avoiding e.g. of a question, the truth, a point under discussion etc.

e·va·sive (ivéisiv) adj. not candid, evading or dodging the material point ‖ serving to avoid trouble or danger ‖ not easily caught

eve (i:v) n. the day before some named day, esp. a Church festival, *Christmas Eve* or before a day important for some event ‖ the brief period before some momentous or culminating event ‖ (rhet.) evening, dusk

e·ven (í:vən) adj. (of a surface) smooth, without irregularities ‖ steady, constant, uniform, not jerky or irregular ‖ (of temper, disposition, mental state) equable, not easily ruffled ‖ of equal height ‖ equal, *an even balance between opposing forces* ‖ exact, exactly whole, without a fraction ‖ giving a whole number when divided by two, *2, 4, 6, 8, 10 are even numbers*

even adv. exactly, precisely, just (emphasizing the exact time or manner of an event or action)

even v.t. (often with 'out', 'up', 'off') to make even, equal or level ‖ v.i. (often with 'out', 'up', or 'off') to become even

eve·ning (í:vniŋ) n. the later part of the day as darkness approaches ‖ the interval between sunset and bedtime ‖ (rhet.) the later or closing years (of a man's life, a nation's history, a civilization etc.) ‖ an entertainment or other function or occupation taking place in the evening

e·vent (ivént) n. an occurrence, esp. one regarded as having importance ‖ an occurrence notable as being an exception to routine ‖ a separate item in a program of games, athletic contests, racing etc. ‖ (math.) one of several independent probabilities **e·vént·less** adj. without any notable happenings

e·vent·ful (ivéntfəl) adj. full of important, exciting or interesting events ‖ important because associated with an important event

e·ven·tu·al (ivéntʃu:əl) adj. final, occurring as a final result or end **e·ven·tu·ál·i·ty** pl. **e·ven·tu·al·i·ties** n. something that may possibly occur **e·vén·tu·al·ly** adv. in the end

ev·er (évər) adv. (with a negative, a partial negative, a doubt, a question or a condition) at any time ‖ (with a comparison) *it is hotter than ever* ‖ (to intensify a comparison or emphasize a question) *why ever didn't you write to me?* ‖ (with 'before', to add emphasis) *before airplanes were ever thought of* ‖ always, *he came late—as ever* **ever after, ever since** for all subsequent time

eve·ry (évri:) adj. each and all (followed by a singular noun and verb), or used with a possessive pronoun) *he anticipates my every wish* ‖ each possible or conceivable, *he has had every advantage* ‖ strong or well founded

e·vict (ivíkt) v.t. to turn (a person) out, esp. to turn (a tenant) out of a house or land ‖ (law) to recover (property, a right or title) by legal proof and judgment, of or from the person who holds it **e·vic·tion, e·víc·tor** ns

ev·i·dence (évidəns) **1.** n. anything that provides material or information on which a conclusion or proof may be based, an indication ‖ (law) information, given by a witness in court (oral), contained in documents (documentary), or provided by things (real), used to prove or disprove the point at issue or to arrive at the truth || (*theol.*) the certainty of an undeniable truth **2.** *v.t. pres. part.* **ev·i·denc·ing** *past* and *past part.* **ev·i·denced** to be evidence for, show

ev·i·dent (évidənt) *adj.* clear, obvious to the eye or the mind **ev·i·dent·ly** *adv.* clearly, obviously

e·vil (í:vəl) **1.** *adj.* wicked || arising from or caused by real or supposed wickedness || indicating wickedness || foul, disgusting, *an evil stench* || (*rhet.*) disastrous, ill-omened **2.** *n.* what is morally wrong, what hinders the realization of the good || what is materially, esp. socially, very harmful

e·vil·do·er (í:vəldu̟:ər, i̟:vəldú:ər) *n.* (*rhet.*) someone whose actions are evil

e·voke (ivóuk) *pres. part.* **e·vok·ing** *past* and *past part.* **e·voked** *v.t.* to cause to be expressed or made manifest in response || to bring to mind, cause to be felt || to summon (a spirit) by the use of magic

ev·o·lu·tion (evəlú:ʃən) *n.* a continuous change from a simple to a more complex form || the gradual development e.g. of an idea, argument, plot, institution or social group || (*pl.*) changes in military or naval or airplane formations || (*math.*) the extraction of roots from an expression || (*phys.*) continuous emission || the theory that all living things have changed in response to environmental conditions by the natural selection of randomly occurring mutations **ev·o·lú·tion·al, ev·o·lú·tion·ar·y** *adjs* **ev·o·lú·tion·ist** *n.* someone who accepts the theory of evolution

e·volve (ivólv) *pres. part.* **e·volv·ing** *past* and *past part.* **e·volved** *v.i.* to change continuously from the simple to the more complex || *v.t.* to cause to unfold or develop || (*phys.*) to emit **e·vólve·ment** *n.*

ewe (ju:) *n.* a female sheep

ew·er (jú:ər) *n.* a widemouthed pitcher

ex·ac·er·bate (iksǽsərbeit, igzǽsərbeit) *pres. part.* **ex·ac·er·bat·ing** *past* and *past part.* **ex·ac·er·bat·ed** *v.t.* to make (a quarrel) more violent || to irritate or provoke (someone) to anger || to make (a disease) more serious **ex·ac·er·bá·tion** *n.*

ex·act (igzǽkt) **1.** *adj.* completely correct or accurate || precise || (used to intensify) very || precisely determined || meticulous || calling for precision and accuracy || (of numbers, measures etc.) neither more nor less **2.** *v.t.* to insist upon having, demand || to enforce payment of (a penalty, debt, tax etc.) **ex·áct·a·ble** *adj.* **ex·áct·ing** *adj.* making great, trying or continual demands || difficult to satisfy or please

ex·ag·ger·ate (igzǽdʒəreit) *pres. part.* **ex·ag·ger·at·ing** *past* and *past part.* **ex·ag·ger·at·ed** *v.t.* to go beyond the truth in describing, estimating or representing || to lay increased emphasis upon || to make larger than normal **ex·ag·ger·á·tion** *n.* **ex·ag·ger·a·tive** (igzǽdʒərei̟tiv, igzǽdʒərətiv) *adj.* **ex·ag·ger·a·tor** (igzǽdʒərei̟tər) *n.*

ex·alt (igzólt) *v.t.* (*rhet.*) to raise up (in position or dignity) || to praise highly, give glory to || to fill with elation

ex·al·ta·tion (egzɔltéiʃən) *n.* a state of mental or spiritual elation or excitement || a raising or being raised to a high position or dignity

ex·am·i·na·tion (igzǽminéiʃən) *n.* an inspection || a considering || a questioning || (often shortened to 'exam') a testing of knowledge or capabilities **ex·am·i·ná·tion·al** *adj.*

ex·am·ine (igzǽmin) *pres. part.* **ex·am·in·ing** *past* and *past part.* **ex·am·ined** *v.t.* to look carefully and closely at, inspect (in order to discover the facts, carry out a test, detect a mistake or fraud etc.) || to inquire into,

give careful thought to || to question || to test the knowledge or capabilities of || *v.i.* to act as examiner **ex·am·i·nee** (igzæminí:) *n.* a student who is examined **ex·ám·in·er** *n.*

ex·am·ple (igzǽmp'l, igzámp'l) *n.* a specimen or instance || a mode of behavior to imitate || a punishment meant also as a warning, or a victim of this || something which illustrates the working of a general rule or principle, or which helps to make a meaning clearer **for example** (*abbr.* e.g.) as an instance

ex·as·per·ate (igzǽspəreit) *pres. part.* **ex·as·per·at·ing** *past* and *past part.* **ex·as·per·at·ed** *v.t.* to annoy or irritate beyond measure (*rhet.*) to make more violent or bitter **ex·as·per·á·tion** *n.*

ex·ca·vate (ékskəveit) *pres. part.* **ex·ca·vat·ing** *past* and *past part.* **ex·ca·vat·ed** *v.t.* (*archaeol.*) to expose by digging away the covering earth etc. from || to hollow out by digging, *to excavate a trench*

ex·ca·va·tion (ekskəvéiʃən) *n.* a digging out or being dug out || a hole made by excavating || (esp. *pl.*) a site where excavating has been done

ex·ca·va·tor (ékskəvei̟tər) *n.* someone who excavates || a mechanical digger

ex·ceed (iksí:d) *v.t.* to go beyond (a given or proper limit) || to be greater in number or degree **ex·céed·ing** *adj.* (*rhet.*) very great in quality **ex·céed·ing·ly** *adv.* very

ex·cel (iksél) *pres. part.* **ex·cel·ling** *past* and *past part.* **ex·celled** *v.t.* to be superior to in quality, degree, performance etc. || *v.i.* to be outstandingly skilled or gifted **to excel oneself** to do outstandingly well

ex·cel·lence (éksələns) *n.* very great merit, quality or ability

ex·cel·lent (éksələnt) *adj.* extremely good

ex·cel·si·or (iksélsi:ər) *n.* very fine wood shavings used for packing, stuffing upholstery etc.

ex·cept (iksépt) *v.t.* to exclude from a list, rule, statement, classification etc. || *v.i.* (with 'to' or 'against') to take exception

except 1. *prep.* apart from, excluding **2.** *conj.* (often with 'that') only, but

ex·cep·tion (iksépʃən) *n.* an excluding or being excluded || someone or something excepted from a general rule, class etc. || (*law*) an objection against a decision made by the judge during the course of an action **ex·cép·tion·a·ble** *adj.* open to objection **ex·cép·tion·al** *adj.* unusual, outstanding

ex·cerpt 1. (éksə:rpt) *n.* a selected passage from a written work or musical composition **2.** (iksó:rpt) *v.t.* to pick out (pieces or passages) from literary or other compositions **ex·cérp·tion** *n.*

ex·cess 1. (iksés) *n.* the state of being greater than something else || the amount by which something is greater than what is usual or permitted etc. || (*pl.*) acts which are more violent than accepted standards of conduct allow || (*pl.*) inordinate indulgence in sensual pleasure || (*chem.*) an amount of one substance greater than is necessary to complete reaction with another **in excess of** over **to excess** beyond normal limits, immoderately **2.** (ékses, iksés) *adj.* of something greater than what is usual or permitted

ex·ces·sive (iksésiv) *adj.* going beyond the limit of what is needed, tolerable, desirable etc. || very great

ex·change (ikstʃéindʒ) *pres. part.* **ex·chang·ing** *past* and *past part.* **ex·changed** *v.t.* to give or receive (one thing in return for something else) || to interchange, take or receive from another (the same thing as that which one gives, or its equivalent) || to change over from (one thing to another), to substitute (one for another) || to change (money) from one currency to another ‖ *v.i.* (of money, with 'at' or 'for') to have a specified value in another currency ‖ to change places, holidays, jobs etc. with someone

ex·change *n.* the giving or receiving of one thing in return for something else ‖ a reciprocal giving and receiving of things of the same kind ‖ an interchange of visits, jobs etc. ‖ a changeover from one thing to another ‖ a thing given in return for something else ‖ the conversion of the money of one country into that of another ‖ the price of one country's money in the currency of another ‖ a central place of business for merchants, brokers or financiers ‖ *(telephone)* the local center to which subscribers are connected and through which they make and receive calls ‖ *(pl., banking)* checks etc. sent to a central clearinghouse **ex·change·a·bil·i·ty** *n.* the state of being exchangeable **ex·chánge·a·ble** *adj.* capable of being exchanged

ex·cise **1.** (éksaiz) *n.* a tax duty levied on the manufacture, sale or consumption within a country of certain commodities, or the charge for a license to manufacture or sell them **2.** (iksáiz) *v.t. pres. part.* **ex·cis·ing** *past* and *past part.* **ex·cised** to lay excise duty on

ex·cise (iksáiz) *pres. part.* **ex·cis·ing** *past* and *past part.* **ex·cised** *v.t.* to cut away by surgery ‖ to remove, strike out **ex·ci·sion** (iksíʒən) *n.* a cutting out ‖ the thing cut out

ex·cite (iksáit) *pres. part.* **ex·cit·ing** *past* and *past part.* **ex·cit·ed** *v.t.* to cause the emotions of (a person) to be intense ‖ to arouse (admiration, jealousy etc.) ‖ to stir up (the imagination etc.) ‖ to incite (a mob) to collective action or hysteria ‖ *(biol.)* to stimulate, cause to respond ‖ *(elec.)* to cause to be electrically active or magnetic **ex·cit·a·bil·i·ty** *n.* **ex·cít·a·ble** *adj.* able to be excited ‖ emotionally unbalanced, quickly enraged or worked up **ex·cit·ant** (iksáit·nt, éksitənt) *n.* something which excites ‖ *(med.)* a stimulant **ex·ci·ta·tion** (ęksaitéiʃən) *n.* **ex·ci·ta·to·ry** (iksáitətɔri:, iksáitətɔuri:) *adj. (med.)* stimulating **ex·cite·ment** *n.* an exciting or being excited ‖ a thing or event that causes excitement **ex·cít·ing** *adj.*

ex·claim (ikskléim) *v.i.* to cry out in emotion or excitement‖ *v.t.* to utter under the stress of sudden thought or emotion

ex·cla·ma·tion (ękskləméiʃən) *n.* the act of exclaiming ‖ the words exclaimed ‖ an interjection

ex·clude (iksklú:d) *pres. part.* **ex·clud·ing** *past* and *past part.* **ex·clud·ed** *v.t.* to keep out, prevent or forbid the entry of ‖ to leave out ‖ to make impossible, prevent ‖ to leave out of account **ex·clúd·ing** *prep.* except, excepting

ex·clu·sion (iksklú:ʒən) *n.* an excluding or being excluded **to the exclusion of** in such a way as to exclude **with the exclusion of** except for

ex·clu·sive (iksklú:siv) **1.** *adj.* sole, not shared with any others ‖ confined to a selected few (esp. the rich or snobbish) ‖ fastidiously selective ‖ having the effect of excluding **2.** *adj.* (of dates, numbers etc.) not counting the first and last mentioned

ex·com·mu·ni·cate 1. (ękskəmjú:nikeit) *v.t. pres. part.* **ex·com·mu·ni·cat·ing** *past* and *past part.* **ex·com·mu·ni·cat·ed** *(eccles.)* to exclude partially or totally from communion with the Church **2.** (ękskəmjú:nikit) *adj.* excommunicated **3.** (ękskəmjú:nikit) *n.* an excommunicated person **ex·com·mu·ni·cá·tion** *n.* an excommunicating or being excommunicated

ex·co·ri·ate (iksk5ri:eit, ikskóuri:eit) *pres. part.* **ex·co·ri·at·ing** *past* and *past part.* **ex·co·ri·at·ed** *v.t.* to remove the skin from by tearing, rubbing, grazing, scalding etc. ‖ *(rhet.)* to criticize savagely **ex·co·ri·á·tion** *n.*

ex·cre·ment (ékskrəmənt) *n.* waste matter expelled from the bowels **ex·cre·men·tal** (ękskrəmént'l) *adj.*

ex·crete (ikskrí:t) *pres. part.* **ex·cret·ing** *past* and *past part.* **ex·cret·ed** *v.t.* to eliminate (waste matter) from the plant or animal system **ex·cré·tive** *adj.* **ex·cre·to·ry**

(ékskrətɔri:, ékskrətɔuri:) **1.** *adj.* of or for excretion **2.** *n. pl.* **ex·cre·to·ries** an excretory organ

ex·cre·tion (ikskrí:ʃən) *n.* the act of excreting ‖ the matter excreted

ex·cur·sion (ikskɔ́:rʒən, ikskɔ́:rʃən) *n.* a short pleasure trip to and from a place, esp. one at reduced rates on public transport ‖ a wandering from the subject, a digression ‖ the attempting of an activity other than one's usual one **ex·cúr·sion·ist** *n.*

ex·cuse (ikskjú:z) *pres. part.* **ex·cus·ing** *past* and *past part.* **ex·cused** *v.t.* to free (oneself or someone else guilty of a fault) from blame ‖ to be a reason for not blaming ‖ to forgive, overlook ‖ to release (someone) from an obligation, undertaking or duty ‖ to give exemption from ‖ to permit (someone) to leave a classroom etc.

ex·cuse (ikskjú:s) *n.* the act of excusing ‖ something which serves to excuse ‖ a pretext ‖ *(pl.)* apologies

ex·e·cute (éksikju:t) *pres. part.* **ex·e·cut·ing** *past* and *past part.* **ex·e·cut·ed** *v.t.* to carry out, put into effect ‖ to perform ‖ to make, esp. as a craftsman ‖ *(law)* to draw up and complete in correct legal form ‖ to fulfill ‖ to meet (a trade order) ‖ to put (a condemned person) to death

ex·e·cu·tion (ęksikjú:ʃən) *n.* a carrying out, putting into effect or fulfilling ‖ a performance, esp. of a musical work ‖ the inflicting or suffering of the death penalty ‖ the act of completion in a legally valid form **ex·e·cú·tion·er** *n.* someone who carries out the death sentence

ex·ec·u·tive (igzékjutiv) **1.** *adj.* concerned with, or relating to, the putting into effect of orders, plans or policies **2.** *n.* the executive branch of a government ‖ a person holding an executive position in a business firm etc.

ex·ec·u·tor (igzékjutər) *n.* a person appointed by a testator to carry out the provisions of his will ‖ someone who puts something into execution, esp. a craftsman or artist **ex·ec·u·to·ry** (igzékjutɔri:, igzékjutɔuri:) *adj.* administrative ‖ designed to have effect at some future time or in a certain contingency **ex·ec·u·trix** (igzékjutriks) *pl.* **ex·ec·u·tri·ces**

ex·em·pla·ry (igzémpləri:) *adj.* without fault, worthy to be copied ‖ serving as a warning example ‖ typical, serving as an example or illustration

ex·empt (igzémpt) **1.** *adj.* (with 'from') not liable to, free from, a duty, law, tax etc. **2.** *v.t.* to cause to be exempt **ex·émpt·i·ble** *adj.*

ex·emp·tion (igzémpʃən) *n.* an exempting ‖ immunity from some obligation, e.g. military service

ex·er·cise (éksərsaiz) **1.** *n.* the use of practice of a quality, power, right ‖ the use of a bodily power ‖ physical exertion for the sake of bodily health ‖ training or practice to develop skill, aptitude, mental or spiritual powers, or something designed to do this ‖ a task set for students, to give practice or to test knowledge ‖ a training operation for troops ‖ *(pl.)* a program of songs, speeches etc. given at a school or college ‖ a work of art that is in the nature of a trial or practice attempt **2.** *v. pres. part.* **ex·er·cis·ing** *past* and *past part.* **ex·er·cised** *v.t.* to use, practice (a quality, power etc.) ‖ to give exercise to ‖ to train, give practice to ‖ to carry out (duties, a function) ‖ to make demands on ‖ to be a difficulty to ‖ *v.i.* to take bodily exercise ‖ *(mil.)* to take part in practice operations

ex·ert (igzɔ́:rt) *v.t.* to make effective use of, bring into operation **ex·ér·tive** *adj.*

ex·hale (ekshéil, igzéil) *pres. part.* **ex·hal·ing** *past* and *past part.* **ex·haled** *v.i.* to breathe out ‖ to be given off ‖ *v.t.* to give off (a scent) ‖ to breathe out (air, tobacco smoke etc.)

ex·haust (igzɔ́st) **1.** *v.t.* to use up completely, come to the end of (one's patience, ammunition etc.) ‖ to tire out, drain of strength ‖ to empty (a container) ‖ to draw out (contents) ‖ to destroy the fertility of (soil) ‖ to treat or discuss (a subject) so thoroughly that no more is left to be said **2.** *n.* the expulsion of steam exhibit 127 expend

or spent gases from the cylinder of a heat engine after their expansion ‖ the steam or spent gases expelled ‖ the pipe through which the spent gases are expelled **ex·haust·i·bil·i·ty** *n.* **ex·háus·tion** (igzɔ́stʃən) *n.* **ex·háus·tive** *adj.* thorough, painstaking, searching, *exhaustive inquiries*

ex·hib·it (igzíbit) **1.** *v.t.* to show, display ‖ to show (paintings etc.) to the public in a specially assembled collection ‖ to display (goods) for sale **2.** *n.* a thing or collection put on show ‖ something produced as evidence in a court of law **on exhibit** out on view ‖ away on view

ex·hi·bi·tion (eksəbíʃən) *n.* an exhibiting or being exhibited ‖ a display of something beautiful, valuable, salable, or of historic or other interest ‖ a performance meant to show off skill for the pleasure of an audience ‖ a person who makes himself look ridiculous in public **ex·hi·bi·tion·ism** *n.* a form of sexual gratification in which a man displays his genitals or a woman her naked body ‖ the tendency to show off or make oneself the center of interest **ex·hi·bi·tion·ist** *n. and adj.*

ex·hib·i·tor (igzíbitər) *n.* someone who exhibits at an exhibition ‖ a movie house owner or manager

ex·hil·a·rate (igzíləreit) *pres. part.* **ex·hil·a·rat·ing** *past and past part.* **ex·hil·a·rat·ed** *v.t.* to fill with strong feelings of delight or of well-being **ex·hil·a·rant** *adj.* exhilarating **ex·hil·a·rá·tion** *n.* **ex·hil·a·ra·tive** (igzíləreitiv, igzílərətiv) *adj.* tending to exhilarate

ex·hort (igzɔ́rt) *v.t.* to urge or advise strongly, seek earnestly to persuade

ex·hor·ta·tion (egzɔrtéiʃən, eksɔrtéiʃən) *n.* an earnest persuading ‖ a persuasive sermon or speech addressed to the minds and hearts of its hearers

ex·hume (ekshjú:m, igzú:m) *pres. part.* **ex·hum·ing** *past and past part.* **ex·humed** *v.t.* to disinter (a body) after burial ‖ to bring to notice again (what was long forgotten)

ex·i·gent (éksidʒənt) *adj.* demanding a great deal, exacting ‖ urgent, pressing

ex·ile (égzail, éksail) *pres. part.* **ex·il·ing** *past and past part.* **ex·iled** *v.t.* to send into exile or as if into exile

exile *n.* banishment or expulsion from one's home or country ‖ long absence from one's home or country or from some place or activity dear to one ‖ a person banished from, or suffering long absence from, his home or country **ex·il·ic, Ex·il·ic** (egzílik, eksílik) *adjs*

ex·ist (igzíst) *v.i.* to have real being ‖ to live ‖ to be able to maintain life ‖ to have life but no more than life

ex·ist·ence (igzístəns) *n.* real being ‖ the state of being in the world of actuality ‖ a way of life ‖ a life ‖ *(philos.)* a thing that has immediate and concrete reality **ex·íst·ent** *adj. and n.* **ex·is·ten·tial** (egzisténʃəl, eksisténʃəl) *adj.* relating to existence

ex·it (égzit, éksit) a stage direction for an actor to go off

exit *n.* a way out (from a public building or enclosure) ‖ an actor's leaving of the stage

ex·o·dus (éksədəs) *n.* a departure in great numbers **Ex·o·dus** the departure of the people of Israel led by Moses from Egypt

ex·on·er·ate (igzɔ́nəreit) *pres. part.* **ex·on·er·at·ing** *past and past part.* **ex·on·er·at·ed** *v.t.* to free from blame ‖ to release from a duty or obligation **ex·on·er·á·tion** *n.*

ex·or·bi·tant (igzɔ́rbitənt) *adj.* much greater than is justified, greatly excessive

ex·or·cise, ex·or·cize (éksɔrsaiz) *pres. part.* **ex·or·cis·ing, ex·or·ciz·ing** *past and past part.* **ex·or·cised,**

ex·or·cized *v.t.* to drive out or ward off (an evil spirit) by commanding it, in the name of God, to depart, or by using incantations, charms etc. ‖ to free (a person or place) from the possession of evil spirits

ex·or·cism (éksɔrsizəm) *n.* the act or process of exorcising ‖ the words etc. used

ex·or·cist (éksɔrsist) *n.* someone who exorcises evil spirits

ex·ot·ic (igzɔ́tik) **1.** *adj.* brought in from a foreign country (e.g. of non-native plants) or from a foreign language ‖ like or imitating the foreign ‖ *(pop.)* very unusual, attractively strange **2.** *n.* a plant, word etc. introduced into a country from outside ‖ an exotic-looking person **ex·ót·i·cal·ly** *adv.* **ex·ot·i·cism** (igzɔ́tisizəm) *n.*

ex·pand (ikspǽnd) *v.t.* to make larger, swell ‖ to cause to increase ‖ to express in detail (a formula, an algebraic expression etc.) ‖ to enlarge on, treat (a topic) more fully ‖ *v.i.* to become larger, swell ‖ to increase in scope ‖ to spread out, open out ‖ to grow genial, unbend

ex·panse (ikspǽns) *n.* a wide, open stretch of earth, sky or water

ex·pan·sion (ikspǽnʃən) *n.* an expanding or being expanded ‖ the extent to which something expands or has expanded **ex·pán·sion·ism** *n.* a belief in, or policy of, expansion (e.g. of territory, influence, economic production, currency) **ex·pán·sion·ist** *n.*

ex·pan·sive (ikspǽnsiv) *adj.* happy to communicate thoughts and feelings ‖ broad, wide ‖ tending to expand or relating to expansion ‖ working by expansion **ex·pan·siv·i·ty** (ekspænsíviti:) *n.* capacity to expand ‖ coefficient of expansion

ex·pect (ikspékt) *v.t.* to think likely ‖ to anticipate the coming of, either with pleasure or with none ‖ to hope for ‖ to require (something) of somebody ‖ to require (someone) to do something ‖ to suppose

ex·pect·an·cy (ikspéktənsi:) *pl.* **ex·pect·an·cies** *n.* a state of expectation ‖ the quality of hopefulness ‖ an amount that is actuarially probable

ex·pect·ant (ikspéktənt) *adj.* expressing pleasurable hope or anticipation ‖ having prospects ‖ pregnant

ex·pec·ta·tion (ekspektéiʃən) *n.* an expecting ‖ something anticipated ‖ a looking forward with hope or pleasure ‖ a reasonable chance ‖ something regarded as almost certain or fit and proper ‖ *(pl.)* prospects of inheriting ‖ an amount that is actuarially probable, expectancy

ex·pe·di·en·cy (ikspí:di:ənsi:) *pl.* **ex·pe·di·en·cies** *n.* expedience ‖ an expedient

ex·pe·di·ent (ikspí:di:ənt) **1.** *adj.* suitable for the end in view, advisable ‖ bringing a particular limited (often selfish or material) advantage, but one which is not right or just **2.** *n.* a way or means of achieving an end in view, a device **ex·pe·di·en·tial** (ikspi:di:énʃəl) *adj.*

ex·pe·dite (ékspidait) *pres. part.* **ex·pe·dit·ing** *past and past part.* **ex·pe·dit·ed** *v.t.* to haste, *to expedite an order* ‖ to send, dispatch

ex·pe·di·tion (ekspidíʃən) *n.* a journey or voyage to a particular place or for a particular purpose ‖ the people taking part in this, with their equipment ‖ a pleasure trip ‖ promptness, quickness **ex·pe·dí·tion·ar·y** *adj.* *(mil.)* of or being an expedition **ex·pe·dí·tious** *adj.* prompt, quick and effective

ex·pel (ikspél) *pres. part.* **ex·pel·ling** *past and past part.* **ex·pelled** *v.t.* to deprive of membership (of a school, political party etc.) ‖ to eject by force, force out **ex·pél·la·ble** *adj.* **ex·pél·lent, ex·pél·lant** *n. and adj.*

ex·pend (ikspénd) *v.t.* to spend (time, money, mental or physical effort etc.) ‖ to use up (ammunition etc.)

(a) æ, cat; ɑ, car; ɔ fawn; ei, snake. (e) e, hen; i:, sheep; iə, deer; ɛə, bear. (i) i, fish; ai, tiger; ə:, bird. (o) o, ox; au, cow; ou, goat; u, poor; ɔi, royal. (u) ʌ, duck; u, bull; u:, goose; ə, bacillus; ju:, cube. x, loch; θ, think; ð, bother; z, Zen; ʒ, corsage; dʒ, savage; ŋ, orangutang; j, yak; ʃ, fish; tʃ, fetch; 'l, rabble; 'n, redden. Complete pronunciation key appears inside front cover.

ex·pénd·a·ble *adj.* (of equipment etc.) meant to be used up in the normal course of work ‖ (of a person) that can be sacrificed as of no further usefulness

ex·pend·i·ture (ikspénditʃər) *n.* an expending ‖ the amount or amounts expended

ex·pense (ikspéns) *n.* cost in terms of money ‖ cost in terms of anything else paid or sacrificed to achieve an end, e.g. in casualties ‖ a source of expense ‖ (*pl.*) money paid out in running a business or household, doing a job etc.

ex·pen·sive (ikspénsiv) *adj.* costly in money or damage, or in whatever is sacrificed to achieve an end ‖ high-priced or making a high charge

ex·pe·ri·ence (ikspíəri:əns) **1.** *n.* the knowledge or feeling obtained through direct impressions ‖ an instance of direct knowledge ‖ the skill or judgment gained by practice ‖ an interesting or remarkable event in a person's life, or something suffered by a person ‖ all that has happened to a person, in his life or in a particular sphere of activity **2.** *v.t. pres. part.* **ex·pe·ri·enc·ing** *past* and *past part.* **ex·pé·ri·enced** to have experience of, undergo, feel **ex·pé·ri·enced** *adj.* endowed with experience, with the knowledge and skill derived from experience

ex·per·i·ment (ikspérimənt) **1.** *n.* an operation carried out under determined conditions to discover, verify or illustrate a theory, hypothesis or fact ‖ a method or procedure adopted without knowing just how it will work ‖ experimentation **2.** *v.i.* to make experiments **ex·per·i·men·tal** (ikspɛrəmént'l) *adj.* based on or derived from experiences or experiment ‖ making use of experiment ‖ made or designed as a trial or for use in experiment **ex·per·i·mén·tal·ism**, **ex·per·i·mén·tal·ist** *ns* **ex·per·i·men·ta·tion** (iksperəmentéiʃən) *n.* the use of experiment as a method of obtaining or confirming knowledge

ex·pert 1. (ékspəːrt) *n.* someone whose knowledge or skill is specialized and profound, esp. as the result of much practical experience ‖ (*U.S. Army*) the highest proficiency rating for marksmanship ‖ a soldier with this rating **2.** (ékspəːrt, ikspə́ːrt) *adj.* pertaining to such knowledge or skill ‖ provided by an expert

ex·per·tise (ɛkspərti:z) *n.* expert knowledge

ex·pi·ra·tion (ɛkspəréiʃən) *n.* a coming to an end (of what is limited in time) ‖ breathing out

ex·pire (ikspáiər) *pres. part.* **ex·pir·ing** *past* and *past part.* **ex·pired** *v.i.* (of a period of time, or of what is limited to a period of time) to come to an end ‖ to die ‖ (of a patent etc.) to become void at the end of a term of years ‖ (of a title) to become extinct ‖ to breathe out ‖ *v.t.* to breathe out (carbon dioxide etc.) **ex·pi·ry** (ikspáiəri:, ékspəri:) *n.* a coming to an end, expiration

ex·plain (ikspléin) *v.t.* to make clear ‖ to give a detailed exposition of ‖ to give a reason that accounts for or justifies (an event or action) ‖ (with 'away') to account for completely, show that no problem or difficulty exists ‖ *v.i.* to give an explanation **to explain oneself** to justify one's conduct ‖ to clarify one's meaning **ex·pláin·a·ble** *adj.*

ex·pla·na·tion (ɛksplənéiʃən) *n.* a making clear ‖ something which makes clear ‖ an accounting for or justifying of an event or action ‖ the facts put forward in justification ‖ an attempt on the part of the persons involved to settle a dispute or clear up a misunderstanding by defining terms, stating motives etc.

ex·ple·tive (éksplitiv) **1.** *adj.* expressing strong emotion, using expletives ‖ used to pad out a sentence or a line of verse **2.** *n.* an exclamation, often an oath, expressing strong emotion ‖ a word or phrase used to pad out a sentence, line of verse etc. **ex·ple·to·ry** (éksplitɔri:, éksplitɔuri:) *adj.*

ex·plic·it (iksplísit) *adj.* clearly and openly stated or defined, not left to be understood ‖ direct and unambiguous in speech or writing

ex·plode (iksplóud) *pres. part.* **ex·plod·ing** *past* and *past part.* **ex·plod·ed** *v.i.* to undergo a large sudden increase of volume (usually accompanied by the production of heat, light and sound) resulting in destructive pressures on the surrounding materials ‖ (of a container) to fly to pieces as the result of the sudden large increase in volume of its contents ‖ to release emotional tension suddenly ‖ *v.t.* to cause to explode ‖ (*pop.*) to destroy (a myth, theory etc.)

ex·ploit (iksplɔ́it) *v.t.* to derive unjust profit from (the work of another) ‖ to use for one's own selfish ends or profit ‖ to develop the use of, make the best use of **ex·plóit·a·ble** *adj.* **ex·ploi·ta·tion** (ɛksplɔitéiʃən) *n.* **exploít·a·tive** *adj.*

ex·ploit (éksplɔit) *n.* a heroic or remarkable deed

ex·plo·ra·tion (ɛkspləréiʃən) *n.* the act of exploring ‖ a journey of exploration ‖ (*med.*) an examination of a wound or part of the body

ex·plore (iksplɔ́r, iksplóur) *pres. part.* **ex·plor·ing** *past* and *past part.* **ex·plored** *v.t.* to travel in or voyage through (an unknown or little known region) in order to add to man's knowledge ‖ to conduct a search into, investigate ‖ to consider carefully (a possible course of action) ‖ (*med.*) to probe or examine (a wound etc.) ‖ *v.i.* to make a voyage of exploration **ex·plór·er** *n.* someone who explores ‖ (*med.*) an instrument for exploring

ex·plo·sion (iksplóuʒən) *n.* a violent expansion, usually accompanied by noise, caused by a sudden release of energy from a very rapid chemical or nuclear reaction or by the release of highly compressed fluids ‖ an outburst of violent emotion or energy ‖ (*phon.*) the sharp puff of breath sometimes accompanying a stop (e.g. p, t)

ex·plo·sive (iksplóusiv) **1.** *adj.* used or designed to explode or to cause an explosion ‖ liable to explode ‖ very dangerous ‖ suddenly violent ‖ (*phon.*) pronounced with a sudden output of breath **2.** *n.* a substance which is capable of undergoing very rapid decomposition to more stable products (releasing energy in the form of heat, light and sound), accompanied by a rapid expansion of these products ‖ (*phon.*) an explosive consonant

ex·po·nent (ikspóunənt) *n.* someone who expounds ‖ (*math.*) an index, a symbol indicating to what power a quantity is to be raised **ex·po·nen·tial** (ɛkspounénʃəl) *adj.* serving to expound, explain or interpret ‖ (*math.*) of an expression involving exponents which are variable quantities

ex·port 1. (ikspɔ́rt, ikspóurt, éksature, ékspourt) *v.t.* to send from one country to another in return for goods, money or services **2.** (ékspɔrt, ékspourt) *n.* the act or trade of exporting ‖ an article or commodity exported **3.** (ékspɔrt, ékspourt) *adj.* pertaining to what is exported or to exportation, *an export license* **ex·pórt·a·ble** *adj.*

ex·por·ta·tion (ɛkspɔrtéiʃən, ɛkspourtéiʃən) *n.* the act or business of exporting ‖ an export

ex·pose (ikspóuz) *pres. part.* **ex·pos·ing** *past* and *past part.* **ex·posed** *v.t.* to leave uncovered, bare, without clothing or other protection or shelter ‖ to leave open to attack, danger etc. ‖ to subject to, allow to be affected by ‖ to allow light to fall upon (a photographic plate or film) ‖ (*eccles.*) to display for veneration or adoration ‖ to bring to light, uncover ‖ to reveal (something secret) ‖ to show up (a crime, fault, mistake etc.) **to be exposed** (of a house) to face (a given direction)

ex·po·si·tion (ɛkspəzíʃən) *n.* an explaining and interpreting of a theme, writing etc. ‖ the words which do this ‖ (*mus.*) the statement of a theme in a sonata, symphony or fugue ‖ an exposing, displaying in public ‖ (*eccles.*) the displaying of the consecrated Host for adoration, or of relics for veneration ‖ an exhibition of works of art, industry, commerce etc.

ex·po·sure (ikspóuʒər) *n.* an exposing or being exposed (to light, heat, cold, sickness etc.) ‖ the period during which something or someone is exposed ‖ (*photog.*) any piece of a roll of film or of cut film that is exposed for a single photograph or (as a measure of amount of film) that is intended to be so exposed ‖ the act of making something shameful publicly known ‖ the aspect (of a house)

ex·pound (ikspáund) v.t. to explain and interpret (e.g. the Scriptures) ‖ to state with great detail

ex·press (iksprés) **1.** adj. explicitly stated or laid down ‖ particular, special ‖ specially fast ‖ concerned with the specially fast transport of goods or delivery of money **2.** n. an express train ‖ an express rifle ‖ a fast service for transporting goods or delivering money ‖ a firm which undertakes such work ‖ a firm which undertakes such work ‖ goods or money sent by express **3.** adv. by express train ‖ by an express delivery service

express v.t. to state explicitly in words ‖ to indicate by gesture or behavior ‖ to convey implicitly ‖ (math.) to represent by using symbols ‖ to send by express delivery ‖ to press out, squeeze out ‖ to put under pressure so as to yield an extract **to express oneself** to communicate one's meaning or feelings **ex·press·age** (iksprésidʒ) n. the sending of goods by express delivery ‖ the charge made for this **ex·préss·i·ble** adj.

ex·pres·sion (ikspréʃən) n. the act of expressing something thought or felt ‖ something expressed ‖ a squeezing out ‖ an idiom ‖ (math.) a representation by symbols ‖ (mus.) subjective interpreting of a passage ‖ a look, or tone of voice, revealing what a person thinks or feels

ex·pres·sion·ism (ikspréʃənizəm) n. a mode of artistic expression in which direct communication of feeling or emotion is the main intention

ex·pres·sive (iksprésiv) adj. of or relating to expression ‖ showing what a person thinks or feels

ex·pul·sion (ikspʌ́lʃən) n. an expelling or being expelled **ex·púl·sive** adj. serving to expel

ex·qui·site (ékskwizit, ikskwízit) **1.** adj. showing perfection in taste or workmanship of a delicate though often elaborate kind ‖ highly sensitive to quality **2.** n. a mannered young man displaying overrefined taste in his dress

ex·tant (ikstǽnt, ékstənt) adj. still in existence, esp. of books or documents not lost or destroyed in the course of time

ex·tem·po·ra·ne·ous (ikstempəréiniːəs) adj. extempore

ex·tem·po·re (ikstémpəriː) **1.** adv. without advance preparation, on the spur of the moment **2.** adj. made or done on the spur of the moment **ex·tem·po·ri·za·tion** (ikstempəraizéiʃən) n. an extemporizing or something extemporized **ex·tém·po·rize** pres. part. **ex·tem·po·riz·ing** past and past part. **ex·tem·po·rized** v.i. to speak or act without advance preparation ‖ v.t. to compose, speak, act etc. (something) extempore

ex·tend (iksténd) v.t. to lengthen in space or time ‖ to make wider, greater or more inclusive ‖ to stretch (one's body) at or to full length ‖ to hold out ‖ (mil.) to spread out with a regular distance between (men) ‖ to tax the powers of, stretch ‖ to write out (notes etc.) in a full or fuller form ‖ (with 'to') to offer ‖ (with 'to') to make available ‖ (bookkeeping) to carry forward (figures, an entry) ‖ v.i. to stretch out in space or time ‖ to reach **ex·ténd·ed** adj. lengthened ‖ relatively long ‖ stretched out ‖ compelled to put forth a great effort ‖ enlarged in scope, meaning etc. ‖ widespread ‖ (printing, of type) having a wider face than is normal for the height **ex·ténd·er** n. a substance used to adulterate, dilute or otherwise modify a product **ex·ténd·i·ble, ex·ténd·a·ble** adj. capable of being extended **ex·ten·si·ble** (iksténsəbˈl) adj. extendible ‖ (of the tongue) capable of being protruded

ex·ten·sion (iksténʃən) n. an extending or being ex-

tended ‖ something added so as to make longer or bigger ‖ an extra allowance of time, e.g. for paying a debt, finishing a game, or deferring army service ‖ (logic) the class of things which a general term can designate, denotation ‖ (phys.) the state of having magnitude in three-dimensional space ‖ (med.) the stretching of a limb to enable the ends of a broken bone to fit accurately together ‖ a telephone subconnection to a particular room in a building ‖ the making available of resources or services (e.g. of a central library) to people to whom they are not immediately available, or the system which achieves this

ex·ten·sive (iksténsiv) adj. covering a wide area ‖ great in scope ‖ (farming) based on the use of a big area of land with minimum upkeep and expenses (e.g. cattle ranching or sheep farming)

ex·tent (ikstént) n. the length to which a thing stretches or reaches or the area it covers ‖ a very large area ‖ compass ‖ limit

ex·te·ri·or (ikstíəriːər) **1.** adj. outer ‖ visible from or on the outside **2.** n. the outside, e.g. of a building ‖ outward appearance or manner ‖ (movies) a background or scene filmed outdoors

ex·ter·mi·nate (ikstə́ːrmineit) pres. part. **ex·ter·mi·nat·ing** past and past part. **ex·ter·mi·nat·ed** v.t. to destroy, wipe out, get rid of completely **ex·ter·mi·ná·tion** n. **ex·ter·mi·na·tive** (ikstə́ːrmineitiv, ikstə́ːrminətiv) adj. **ex·tér·mi·na·tor** n. **ex·ter·mi·na·to·ry** (ikstə́ːrminətɔːriː, ikstə́ːrminətɔuriː) adj.

ex·ter·nal (ikstə́ːrnˈl) **1.** adj. situated on, pertaining to, or derived from the outside ‖ merely superficial, not backed by feeling or conviction ‖ on the outside of the body ‖ (of state affairs) foreign ‖ of what lies outside the mind **2.** n. (pl.) outward appearances **ex·tér·nal·i·ty** (ekstəːrnǽlitiː) n.

ex·tinct (ikstíŋkt) adj. (of a fire, flame etc.) put out, burnt out ‖ (of a volcano) no longer active ‖ (of passions, hopes) no longer entertained ‖ (of species) died out, no longer found ‖ (of a title or office) no longer existing, either because abolished or because there is no one to carry it on

ex·tinc·tion (ikstíŋkʃən) n. (of fire etc.) an extinguishing or being extinguished ‖ a making or becoming extinct ‖ an annihilating or being annihilated **ex·tínc·tive** adj. serving or tending to extinguish

ex·tin·guish (ikstíŋgwiʃ) v.t. to put out (a fire, light etc.) ‖ to put an end to, destroy (hope etc.) ‖ to outshine completely (another person or thing) ‖ to silence (an opponent) ‖ to wipe out (a debt) ‖ (law) to make null **ex·tín·guish·er** n. a fire extinguisher ‖ someone who extinguishes

ex·tol, ex·toll (ikstóul, ikstɔ́l) pres. part. **ex·tol·ling, ex·toll·ing** past and past part. **ex·tolled** v.t. to praise enthusiastically

ex·tort (ikstɔ́rt) v.t. to obtain by force, threats, deception etc. ‖ to force (a meaning, conclusion etc.) from words which cannot reasonably yield it

ex·tor·tion (ikstɔ́rʃən) n. an extorting, esp. of money, overcharging **ex·tór·tion·ate** adj. using extortion ‖ (of prices or charges) much greater than is fair or reasonable **ex·tór·tion·er, ex·tór·tion·ist** ns

ex·tra (ékstrə) **1.** adj. over and above what is usual or normal ‖ (commerce) of superior quality **2.** n. an extra charge ‖ something for which an extra charge is made ‖ (movies) a person hired to take part in crowd scenes etc. ‖ a special (esp. a late) edition of a newspaper **3.** adv. more than usually, specially

extra- (ékstrə) prefix outside or beyond a thing, not coming within its scope

ex·tract 1. (ékstrækt) *n.* a passage taken from a book, speech, letter etc. || a concentrated essence, used esp. for flavoring || the solid or semisolid matter which remains of a substance after evaporation of moisture or the use of solvents **2.** (ikstrǽkt) *v.t.* to draw, pull or otherwise take out || to obtain (an essence, juice etc.) by pressure, distillation, evaporation, treatment with a solvent etc. || to obtain esp. by force or with difficulty || to obtain (a substance) from the raw materials in which it is contained || to pick out (a passage from a book, speech, document etc.) || *(math.)* to find (the root of a number) **ex·tráct·a·ble** *adj.* **ex·trác·tor** *n.* a device for extracting, esp. one which extracts the spent round from a gun

ex·trac·tion (ikstrǽkʃən) *n.* the act or process of extracting, esp. the pulling out of a tooth || something extracted || descent, lineage

ex·traor·di·nar·y (ikstrɔ́rd'nɛri:) *adj.* beyond what is normal or ordinary || bizarre || astonishing || (of an official) specially appointed, serving in addition to the officials regularly appointed and usually for some particular mission

ex·trav·a·gance (ikstrǽvəgəns) *n.* a being extravagant or an instance of this

ex·trav·a·gant (ikstrǽvəgənt) *adj.* spending more money than one can afford, or spending foolishly, carelessly or wastefully || using too much of anything involving expense || going beyond what is reasonable, justified or normal || exaggerated, overemphatic

ex·trav·a·gan·za (ikstrævgəgǽnzə) *n.* a freely imaginative or fanciful musical stage entertainment, esp. farce or burlesque

ex·treme (ikstrí:m) **1.** *adj.* furthest out, furthest from the center || utmost, maximum || very great, with as great a degree as possible of whatever is referred to || (of views, opinions etc. and those who hold them) not moderate, esp. far to the left or right || as severe and forcible as possible **2.** *n.* (esp. *pl.*) the highest or extreme degree (generally of two opposites) || either end of a whole range || *(pl.)* extreme measures, actions, views etc. || *(math.)* the first or last term of a series or ratio || *(logic)* the subject or predicate of a proposition || the major or minor term of a syllogism

ex·trem·i·ty (ikstrémiti:) *pl.* **ex·trem·i·ties** *n.* the very end, the tip || *(pl.)* the most distant parts || *(pl.)* the hands and feet, esp. the fingers and toes, sometimes the tip of the nose, ears and chin || a situation involving great trouble, difficulty or danger || extreme-

ness (of views or actions) || *(rhet.)* the utmost degree of emotion || the limit || (esp. *pl.*) an extreme measure

ex·tri·cate (ékstrikeit) *pres. part.* **ex·tri·cat·ing** *past* and *past part.* **ex·tri·cat·ed** *v.t.* to disentangle or free (a person or thing) from some tangle, difficulty, danger or muddle **ex·tri·cá·tion** *n.*

ex·tro·ver·sion (ɛkstrəvə́:rʒən, ɛkstrəvə́:rʃən) *n.* the psychological state of an extrovert || a manifestation of this

ex·tro·vert (ékstrəvə:rt) *n.* a person interested and taking pleasure more in what happens outside him than in his own emotions or states of mind

ex·u·ber·ance (igzú:bərəns) *n.* the state or quality of being exuberant, or an instance of it

ex·u·ber·ant (igzú:bərənt) *adj.* bubbling over with joy, high spirits, enthusiasm, health etc || abundant in growth || unrestrainedly inventive

ex·ude (igzjú:d, iksú:d) *pres. part.* **ex·ud·ing** *past* and *past part.* **ex·ud·ed** *v.t.* to ooze with, to cause to ooze out || to give off, emit || *v.i.* to ooze out in small drops

ex·ult (igzʌ́lt) *v.i.* to feel and express tremendous joy || (with 'over') to rejoice in the defeat of a rival **ex·últ·an·cy** *n.* **ex·últ·ant** *adj.* **ex·ul·ta·tion** (ɛgzʌltéiʃən, ɛksʌltéiʃən) *n.*

eye (ai) **1.** *n.* an organ of sight that converts light impinging on it into nervous impulses. In vertebrates the impulses travel from the eye via the optic nerve to the brain, where they produce the sensation of seeing || the iris or colored part of the eyeball || the part around the eyes || the power of seeing || the power of judging and appreciating what one sees || a thing like an eye in shape, e.g. the hole for the thread in a needle, the marking on a peacock's tail, the leaf bud of a potato || (often *pl.*) judgment || *(meteor.)* the low-pressure center of e.g. a hurricane || an aperture allowing the entry of light, esp. the lens of a camera **2.** *v.t. pres. part.* **eye·ing, ey·ing** *past* and *past part.* **eyed** to look attentively at || to make an eye in (a rope) || to remove the leaf buds of (a potato)

eye·sight (áisait) *n.* the power of vision || range of vision

eye·sore (áisɔr, áisɔur) *n.* something that offends by its ugliness

eye·tooth (áitu:θ) *pl.* **eye·teeth** (áiti:θ) *n.* one of the two upper canine teeth

eye·wit·ness (áiwítnis) **1.** *n.* a person who actually saw a crime, accident etc. take place **2.** *adj.* emanating from such a person

F

F, f (ef) the sixth letter of the English alphabet

F. Fahrenheit

fa·ble (féib'l) *n.* a fanciful, epigrammatic story, usually illustrating a moral precept or ethical observation. The characters are often animals, gifted with speech, and possessing the human traits commonly attributed to them, or they may be gods, persons, or things

fa·bled (féib'ld) *adj.* celebrated in legend || fictitious, falsely boasted

fab·ric (fǽbrik) *n.* woven stuff || a framework, structure || the texture of a textile || structural material

fab·ri·cate (fǽbrikeit) *pres. part.* **fab·ri·cat·ing** *past* and *past part.* **fab·ri·cat·ed** *v.t.* to construct, esp. to put together standard parts of || to make up, invent (nonexistent facts)

fab·ri·ca·tion (fæbrikéiʃən) *n.* a fabricating or being

fabricated || something fabricated || a structure of falsehoods

fab·u·lous (fǽbjuləs) *adj.* belonging to the realm of fable || extraordinary

fa·cade, fa·çade (fəsád, fæsád) *n.* the main front of a building || an appearance or manner intended as a pretense or mask

face (feis) **1.** *n.* the front part of the head from forehead to chin, including the features (eyes, nose, mouth etc.) || the expression of a person's countenance || a grimace || *(pop.)* impudence || an outward show of self-possession || a mask || the front or main side of a building, monument etc. || a surface || the working surface of a tool || any of the planes of a many-sided object or of a crystal || *(printing)* the part of a type, or other raised printing surface, which takes the ink

|| *(printing)* the collective types of a single design (e.g. of an alphabet), which may be available in many sizes || a dial of a clock etc. || the area of immediate operations in mining, quarrying or climbing **2.** *v. pres. part.* **fac·ing** *past* and *past part.* **faced** *v.t.* to be the opposite to || to turn or have one's face towards || to put a visible covering on (a surface) || to confront || (often with 'up to') to meet resolutely || *(mil.)* to cause (troops) to turn in a certain direction || *v.i.* to be situated so as to have the front in a specified direction

fac·et (fǽsit) *n.* any of the small planes which constitute the surface of a crystal or cut gem || any of the single surface segments of the many simple ocelli of a compound eye || any of the separate aspects of an involved problem, situation etc.

fa·ce·tious (fəsí:ʃəs) *adj.* (of a person) given to sly or pointless joking || (of a remark) characterized by such joking

fa·cial (féiʃəl) **1.** *adj.* of or pertaining to the face **2.** *n.* a face massage

fac·ile (fǽsil, *esp. Br.* fǽsail) *adj.* performing or performed easily, without great effort || easily won || fluent, even if lacking qualities of greater worth || merely superficial

fa·cil·i·tate (fəsíliteit) *pres. part.* **fa·cil·i·tat·ing** *past* and *past part.* **fa·cil·i·tat·ed** *v.t.* to make easy or easier **fa·cil·i·ta·tion** (fəsilitéiʃən) *n.*

fa·cil·i·ty (fəsíliti:) *pl.* **fa·cil·i·ties** *n.* an aptitude for doing some specified thing easily || the quality of being easy to do || dexterity or apparent lack of effort in performing something relatively difficult || *(pl.)* things that make some specified activity, task etc. easier

fac·sim·i·le (fæksímili:) *n.* an exact reproduction of a picture, document, coin, print etc. || the process of long-distance reproduction of print or pictures by telegraph or radio

fact (fækt) *n.* a thing known to be true || a statement about something which has occurred || *(law,* in certain phrases only) a crime

fac·tion (fǽkʃən) *n.* a small opposition group within a larger group, or one tending to split off from the larger group, generally with a suggestion of unscrupulous self-interest || excessive liking for political strife or troublemaking **fác·tion·al** *adj.* of, relating to or characteristic of a faction || tending to create a faction **fác·tion·al·ism** *n.*

fac·ti·tious (fæktíʃəs) *adj.* artificial, fabricated || deliberately worked up, not natural

fac·tor (fǽktər) **1.** *n. (math.)* a number or term which, divided into a larger number or expression, has an integral remainder || any of the facts or circumstances which, taken together, constitute a result or situation || *(biol.)* a causative agent in heredity || *(biol.)* any agent (biotic, climatic, nutritional etc.) contributing to a result || someone who acts as agent for, or is appointed to conduct the affairs of, another **2.** *v.t.* to factorize

fac·to·ry (fǽktəri:) *pl.* **fac·to·ries** *n.* a building or group of buildings where goods are manufactured by collective production

fac·tu·al (fǽktʃuəl) *adj.* concerned with facts || full of facts

fac·ul·ty (fǽkəlti:) *pl.* **fac·ul·ties** *n.* a mental or physical power || a gift for some special activity || a branch of studies (law, medicine etc.) in a university || the teachers of a school, college or university || the members of a particular profession, esp. medicine

fad (fæd) *n.* a short-lived fashion or craze **fád·dish** *adj.* inclined to take up fads **fád·dist** *n.* **fád·dy** *comp.*

fad·di·er *superl.* **fad·di·est** *adj.* **faddish**

fade (feid) *pres. part.* **fad·ing** *past* and *past part.* **fad·ed** *v.i.* to lose color || to lose freshness or vigor || (of a sound) to lose intensity gradually || (of an image, memory or dream) to become gradually less and less distinct || *v.t.* to cause to lose color, freshness, intensity or distinctness gradually **fáde·less** *adj.* not liable to fade

Fah·ren·heit scale (fǽrənhaitskeil) *(abbr.* **F.)** a temperature scale on which the freezing point of water is 32° and its boiling point 212°

fail (feil) *n.* (only in) **without fail** for certain

fail *v.i.* to omit or forget to do something required || (of supplies etc.) to become exhausted, give out || (of someone old or seriously ill, or of the mental faculties) to grow feeble || to die out, cease to function || to crash financially, go bankrupt || to be unsuccessful, *the attack failed* || to be inadequate or deficient || *v.t.* to be unsuccessful in (an exam etc.) || to declare (a candidate) to be unsuccessful || to let (someone) down completely, to disappoint utterly || to be lacking to || to abandon suddenly **fáil·ing 1.** *n.* a weakness in character **2.** *prep.* in the absence of, in default of

fail·ure (féiljər) *n.* lack of success || lack or sudden end of performance || the fact of failing || an unsuccessful person, thing or project || neglect or omission, *failure to comply* || a financial crash || a running short

faint (feint) **1.** *adj.* likely to faint, weak, feeble || pale, dim, indistinct || slight **2.** *n.* a sudden loss of consciousness from shock, exhaustion, loss of blood etc. **3.** *v.i.* to lose consciousness in a faint

fair (fɛər) *adj.* (of the hair or complexion) light-colored, blond || just, equitable || according to the rules || (of a wind) favorable || (of weather) cloudless || (of a chance or probability) quite good || of medium quality || *(rhet.)* beautiful || *(pop.)* complete, thorough

fair *adv.* according to the rules || squarely

fair *n.* a traveling collection of sideshows and amusements || a large-scale exhibition to promote trade || a traditional market held on a specific date, with amusements and sideshows || a specialized market

fair·ly (fɛərli:) *adv.* in a just and equitable manner || moderately || positively

fair·y (fɛəri:) **1.** *n. pl.* **fair·ies** *(folklore)* a small supernatural being, capable of intervening in human affairs, usually in order to help **2.** *adj.* of or relating to fairies

faith (feiθ) *n.* trust, confidence || complete acceptance of a truth which cannot be demonstrated or proved by the process of logical thought || a religion based upon this || the virtue by which a Christian believes in the revealed truths of God **faith·ful 1.** *adj.* steadfast in faith || loyal || accurate, true to the original **2.** *n.* **the faithful** conscientious adherents to a system of religious belief

faith·less (féiθlis) *adj.* disloyal, breaking pledges || having no religious faith

fake (feik) **1.** *v. pres. part.* **fak·ing** *past* and *past part.* **faked** *v.t.* to make a false imitation of, counterfeit || to contrive (something) so as to deceive || (with 'up') to contrive (something) as a working substitute || *v.i.* to pretend, sham **2.** *n.* something faked **3.** *adj.* artificial, false

fal·con (fɔ́lkən, fǽlkən) *n.* a diurnal bird of prey that has a very strong, compact body with powerful, long, pointed wings, a large head and a sharp, hooked beak. It is carnivorous, and cosmopolitan in distribution

fall (fɔl) **1.** *pres. part.* **fall·ing** *past* **fell** *past part.* **fall·en** (fɔ́lən) *v.i.* to drop by gravity || to lose balance and drop to the ground || to allow oneself to drop to the ground or to one's knees ‖ to decrease ‖ to lose position ‖ (of temperature) to become lower in degree ‖ to decline in value or in price level ‖ (of clothes, curtains etc.) to hang ‖ to be killed ‖ to be captured ‖ (of a government) to be voted out of office ‖ to slope downwards ‖ (of wind, floodwater, sound etc.) to subside, diminish ‖ (of the face) to take on an expression of disappointment or dismay ‖ (of the eyes) to be suddenly lowered ‖ to seem to descend ‖ to happen by way of obligation ‖ to pass by right ‖ to pass into some state ‖ to occur ‖ to cease to resist a temptation ‖ to have its position ‖ to divide analytically ‖ (of the young of some animals, esp. sheep and hares) to be born **2.** *n.* the act or an instance of falling ‖ a distance fallen ‖ falling matter ‖ the way a thing falls ‖ autumn ‖ a descent to a level below ‖ a decrease, decline ‖ an amount by which something drops ‖ a downfall, collapse ‖ the taking or surrendering of a stronghold after a siege or attack ‖ (*wrestling*) a scoring throw ‖ the rope of a hoisting tackle ‖ a quantity of timber cut down ‖ (*pl.*) a cascade, waterfall ‖ (of animals) a birth or the number of young born

fal·la·cious (fəléiʃəs) *adj.* based on error ‖ misleading
fal·la·cy (fǽləsi:) *pl.* **fal·la·cies** *n.* a false notion ‖ a piece of false reasoning ‖ the quality in reasoning of being false or unsound
fal·li·bil·i·ty (fæləbíliti:) *n.* the quality of being fallible
fal·li·ble (fǽləb'l) *adj.* subject to the possibility of erring or being mistaken
fall·out (fɔ́lạut) *n.* the radioactive material produced by a nuclear explosion, which is distributed through the atmosphere and settles on the earth ‖ the settling of this material ‖ an unexpected byproduct of a process
fal·low (fǽlou) **1.** *adj.* (of land) plowed and harrowed but left without crops for a season **2.** *n.* land so treated **3.** *v.t.* to break up (land) with plow and harrow, but without seeding
false (fɔls) **1.** *adj.* untrue ‖ logically wrong ‖ incorrect, mistaken ‖ not genuine, artificial ‖ deceitful, lying ‖ meant to deceive ‖ fake ‖ (*archit.*) not structurally necessary or not permanent ‖ (*mus.*) off pitch ‖ not natural, straining for effect ‖ misconceived, mistaken ‖ (*bot.*) incorrectly so-named **2.** *adv.* not honestly ‖ not on the note
false·hood (fɔ́lshud) *n.* falsity ‖ a lie ‖ lying
fal·si·fi·ca·tion (fɔlsifikéiʃən) *n.* a falsifying or being falsified ‖ something falsified
fal·si·fy (fɔ́lsifai) *pres. part.* **fal·si·fy·ing** *past* and *past part.* **fal·si·fied** *v.t.* to alter with intent to defraud ‖ to misrepresent ‖ to pervert
fal·si·ty (fɔ́lsiti:) *pl.* **fal·si·ties** *n.* the quality of being false, deceitfulness ‖ an untrue assertion
fal·ter (fɔ́ltər) **1.** *v.i.* to stumble in movement, action or speech ‖ to begin to lose one's determination ‖ *v.t.* (often with 'out') to say in a hesitant or feeble way **2.** *n.* a faltering ‖ a faltering sound
fame (feim) *n.* the state of being widely known and esteemed or acclaimed, renown ‖ (*rhet.*) reputation
famed (feimd) *adj.* renowned, celebrated ‖ (*rhet.*) generally reported
fa·mil·iar (fəmíljər) **1.** *adj.* knowing intimately ‖ accustomed, well known by frequently repeated experience ‖ much seen ‖ (of personal relations) close and pleasantly free from formality ‖ presumptuous, impudent **2.** *n.* a familiar spirit
fa·mil·i·ar·i·ty (fəmili:ǽriti:) *pl.* **fa·mil·i·ar·i·ties** *n.* close knowledge or acquaintance ‖ the state of being well known ‖ an unjustified presumption of intimacy in speech or behavior ‖ (*pl.*) unwelcome gestures of affection
fa·mil·iar·ize (fəmíljəraiz) *pres. part.* **fa·mil·iar·iz·ing** *past* and *past part.* **fa·mil·iar·ized** *v.t.* to cause (someone, oneself) to get to know something well
fam·i·ly (fǽmili:) *pl.* **fam·i·lies** *n.* a group consisting of parents and their children ‖ the children of two parents ‖ a group of people closely related by blood, e.g

children and their parents, their cousins, their aunts and uncles ‖ a group consisting of individuals descended from a common ancestry ‖ a household ‖ unit of a crime syndicate usu. in a specific geographic area ‖ a group of related genera of animals, plants, languages etc. ‖ (*rhet.*) a harmonious group bound together by common interest
fam·ine (fǽmin) *n.* extreme scarcity of food ‖ starvation ‖ a scarcity of something
fam·ished (fǽmiʃt) *adj.* hungry to the point of starvation ‖ (*pop.*) feeling very hungry
fa·mous (féiməs) *adj.* celebrated ‖ (*pop.*) excellent
fá·mous·ly *adv.* excellently
fan (fæn) *n.* a devotee of a particular sport, pursuit, entertainer, entertainment etc.
fan **1.** *n.* a manually operated device for agitating the air before one's face so as to make one feel cooler ‖ a mechanically operated propeller setting up currents of air for cooling rooms or attached to water-cooled engines for the same purpose ‖ a small sail on a windmill to keep it in the wind ‖ the blade of a propeller ‖ (*hist.*) a device for winnowing **2.** *v. pres. part.* **fan·ning** *past* and *past part.* **fanned** *v.t.* to agitate the air in front of (a person, with cooling effect, or a fire, with heating effect) with or as if with a fan ‖ to agitate (the air) in this way ‖ (of a breeze) to blow gently upon ‖ (*hist.*) to winnow (grain) or winnow away (chaff) with a fan ‖ to knock back the hammer of (a revolver) rapidly and repeatedly with the edge of one hand while keeping the trigger depressed with the first finger of the other, for more rapid firing ‖ to cause (cards etc.) to spread out like a fan ‖ (*baseball*) to strike (a batter) out ‖ *v.i.* (with 'out') to open like a fan or (*mil.*) in fan-shaped formation
fa·nat·ic (fənǽtik) **1.** *adj.* overenthusiastic, zealous beyond the bounds of reason **2.** *n.* an inordinately zealous adherent or supporter, esp. in politics or religion
fa·nát·i·cal *adj.* **fa·nat·i·cism** (fənǽtisizəm) *n.* wild and often dangerous enthusiasm, esp. in politics or religion
fan·cied (fǽnsi:d) *adj.* favorite ‖ imagined
fan·ci·er (fǽnsi:ər) *n.* a person specially interested in the breeding of a certain kind of animal or plant in order to establish particular characteristics in the breed
fan·ci·ful (fǽnsifəl) *adj.* produced by fancy, unreal ‖ arranged in an unusual or odd way
fan·ci·ly (fǽnsili:) *adv.* in a fancy way
fan·cy (fǽnsi:) **1.** *pl.* **fan·cies** *n.* the faculty of forming mental images, esp. the light, superficial play of this faculty (contrasted with imagination) ‖ a product of this faculty ‖ a whim, caprice ‖ a delusion ‖ a vague intuition ‖ a liking **2.** *adj. comp.* **fan·ci·er** *superl.* **fan·ci·est** (of artifacts) ornamental, not plain ‖ (of prices) unreasonably high ‖ (of birds and animals) bred for particular characteristics ‖ (of canned goods) of superior quality **the fancy** enthusiastic followers of some pastime, or narrow interest, or of boxing as a sport **3.** *v.t. pres. part.* **fan·cy·ing** *past* and *past part.* **fan·cied** to call up a mental picture of ‖ (used imperatively as an exclamation of surprise) imagine ‖ to suppose, suspect ‖ to be attracted to ‖ to wish to have ‖ to have a high opinion of
fan·fare (fǽnfɛər) *n.* a flourish of trumpets, bugles or other brass instruments
fang (fæŋ) *n.* a long, pointed tooth, esp. in dogs or wolves, or one of the long, hollow or grooved teeth of poisonous snakes through which venom is passed ‖ one of the prongs in the root of a tooth ‖ the spike of a tool driven into the handle or stock **fanged** (fæŋd) *adj.* having fangs
fan·tail (fǽnteil) *n.* a tail in the shape of a fan ‖ a variety of domestic pigeon having such a tail ‖ a genus of flycatchers of Asia and Australia
fan·tas·tic (fæntǽstik) *adj.* belonging to the realm of fancy ‖ very peculiar ‖ wilfully elaborated ‖ (*pop.*) incredible **fan·tás·ti·cal·ly** *adv.*

fan·ta·sy, phan·ta·sy (fǽntəsi:) *pl.* **fan·ta·sies, phan·ta·sies** *n.* playful imagination, fancy ‖ a grotesque mental image ‖ *(psychol.)* a daydream satisfying some desire ‖ *(pop.)* thinking, planning etc. not based on sound reason or prudence

far (fɑr) *comp.* **far·ther** (fɑ́rðər), **fur·ther** (fɔ́:rðər) *superl.* **far·thest** (fɑ́rðist), **fur·thest** (fɔ́:rðist) **1.** *adv.* at a considerable distance or to a great extent (in space or time) ‖ very much **as far as** to but not beyond ‖ to the extent that **by far** by a large degree **far from it** not at all **how far** to what extent **so far** up to now ‖ to a certain extent **so far so good** up to this point all is well **thus far** up to this point or moment **to go far** to be eminently successful **to go too far** to overstep the bounds of truth or politeness **2.** *adj.* very distant, remote ‖ the more distant of two

far·a·way (fɑ́rəwẹi) *adj.* remote ‖ (of a facial expression) dreamy

farce (fɑrs) *n.* a dramatic representation intended only to amuse ‖ the class of such dramas ‖ any event with a futile or absurd outcome **far·ci·cal** *adj.* **far·ci·cál·i·ty** *n.* the quality of being farcical

fare (fɛər) *n.* the cost of a journey (by train, bus, airplane, ship etc.) ‖ *(commerce)* a passenger in a hired vehicle ‖ food, diet

fare *pres. part.* **far·ing** *past* and *past part.* **fared** *v.i.* to manage, get along ‖ (with 'well' or 'ill') to experience luck of the kind indicated ‖ (with 'well' or 'ill') to be fed with the amount and quality of food indicated

fare·well (fɛ́ərwẹl) **1.** *interj. (rhet.)* goodbye **2.** *n.* a leavetaking, *to make one's farewells* **3.** (fɛ́ərwẹl) *adj.* last, parting

far·fetched (fɑ́rfétʃt) *adj.* (of jokes, comparisons, excuses etc.) laboriously contrived, not plausible

far·flung (fɑ́rflʌ́ŋ) *adj. (rhet.)* of huge extent ‖ *(rhet.)* remote

farm (fɑrm) **1.** *n.* an area of land used for cultivation or animal breeding under individual or collective management ‖ a tract of water for cultivating fish, oysters etc. ‖ *(baseball)* a minor-league team attached to a major-league team and providing it with recruits for training **2.** *v.t.* to raise (crops, stock, poultry etc.) on a farm for the market ‖ to use (land) for this purpose ‖ *(hist.,* often with 'out') to lease for a fixed sum or fixed percentage the right to collect taxes etc.) to someone ‖ *(hist.)* to pay a certain sum for (the right to collect taxes etc.) ‖ (often with 'out') to delegate (work) to outside workers ‖ *v.i.* to be a farmer, cultivate the land **fárm·er** *n.* a person who owns or rents a farm

far·off (fɑ́rɔf, fɑ́rɔf) *adj.* remote in space or time

far·sight·ed (fɑ́rsáitid) *adj.* hypermetropic (opp. NEAR-SIGHTED) ‖ prudent

fas·ci·cle (fǽsik'l) *n. (bot.)* a bunch, bundle, cluster ‖ *(anat.)* a bundle of nerve fibers ‖ a single part of a book published in sections **fás·ci·cled, fas·cíc·u·lar** (fəsíkjulər), **fas·cíc·u·late** (fesíkjuleit, fəsíkjulit), **fas·cíc·u·lat·ed** *adjs (bot.)* arranged in clusters **fas·cic·u·lá·tion** *n.*

fas·ci·nate (fǽsineit) *pres. part.* **fas·ci·nat·ing** *past* and *past part.* **fas·ci·nat·ed** *v.t.* to compel delighted interest in ‖ *(pop.,* of snakes, stoats etc.) to paralyze by ocular hypnosis ‖ to hold (someone) as if under a spell **fás·ci·nat·ing** *adj.* **fas·ci·ná·tion, fás·ci·na·tor** *ns*

Fas·cism (fǽʃizəm) *n. (hist.)* the ideological outlook and its extremist manifestations in Mussolini's Italian counterrevolutionary movement (1919–22) and in his dictatorship (1922–43)

Fas·cist (fǽʃist) **1.** *n.* an adherent or supporter of Fascism ‖ a member of the Fascist political party **fas·cist** a someone who holds fascist views **2.** *adj.* of or pertaining to Fascist ideas or to the Fascist régime **fas·cist** characterized by or advocating fascism

fash·ion (fǽʃən) **1.** *n.* way, manner ‖ the style of clothes worn at a particular period ‖ modishness, *a slave to fashion* ‖ social prominence ‖ a prevailing mode in speech, personal adornment, social behavior etc. ‖ dress in its aspect of changing style **2.** *v.t.* to mold, shape **fásh·ion·a·ble** *adj.* currently in style, modish ‖ being the object of a modish interest **fásh·ion·a·bly** *adv.*

fast (fæst, fɑst) **1.** *v.i.* to abstain from food, either entirely or partly **2.** *n.* an act of abstinence from food ‖ a period of time during which adherents of a faith are required to abstain from food

fast *adj.* swift ‖ speedy ‖ lasting a short time ‖ allowing rapid progress ‖ (of a clock or watch) in advance of the real time ‖ loyal ‖ firmly fixed ‖ (of dyes) that will not wash out or fade ‖ *(photog.)* having a high shutter speed ‖ gay and dissipated ‖ *(bacteriol.)* resistant to destruction or staining

fast *adv.* quickly, hurriedly ‖ fixedly ‖ soundly ‖ wildly, in a dissipated way

fas·ten (fǽs'n, fɑ́s'n) *v.t.* to make secure ‖ to fix firmly, tie, attach ‖ (with 'on') to fix (thoughts, attention) ‖ to get firm hold with (the teeth) ‖ *v.i.* (with 'on') to get firm hold ‖ (with 'on') to fix one's attention ‖ to close securely

fas·tid·i·ous (fæstídi:əs) *adj.* having highly developed taste ‖ fussily particular ‖ meticulous

fast·ness (fǽstnis, fɑ́stnis) *n.* fixedness, irremovability, e.g. of dyes

fat (fæt) **1.** *n.* the greasy material constituting the largest portion of the cells of adipose tissue and occurring in other parts of animals and in plants ‖ one of a class of neutral compounds which may be solid or liquid, and insoluble in water, and which are glycerides of one or more fatty acids ‖ a solid or semisolid fat as distinguished from a fatty oil ‖ the best part of something **2.** *adj.* (of the body) bulky due to fat rather than to bone or muscle ‖ thick ‖ financially rewarding ‖ (of animals) made fat for slaughtering ‖ (esp. of meat) containing a high proportion of fat ‖ (of clay) sticky ‖ (of coal) bituminous ‖ *(printing,* of type) broadfaced ‖ (of a printed page) with large spaces

fa·tal (féit'l) *adj.* resulting in death ‖ calamitous ‖ fateful **fá·tal·ism** *n.* the belief that all events are naturally or supernaturally predetermined ‖ a fatal accident ‖ the mental attitude of submission to the inevitability of the power of fate **fá·tal·ist** *n.* someone who adopts a fatalistic attitude, or believes in fatalism **fa·tal·ís·tic** *adj.* accepting one's fate with stoicism or lethargy

fa·tal·i·ty (fətǽliti:, feitǽliti:) *pl.* **fa·tal·i·ties** *n.* subjection to the power of fate ‖ the quality of being predestined to disaster ‖ the quality of causing death or calamity ‖ fate ‖ a disaster, esp. one causing death ‖ a person killed in an accident or disaster

fate (feit) *n.* a power that supposedly predetermines events ‖ the history of an individual or of a social group (family, tribe, country etc.) considered as predetermined ‖ the future of a person or persons ‖ doom, destruction ‖ one's ultimate end **fát·ed** *adj.* predetermined, destined **fáte·ful** *adj.* controlled by fate ‖ critical, decisive in effect

fa·ther (fɑ́ðər) **1.** *n.* the male parent ‖ *(rhet.)* an ancestor ‖ an originator ‖ a venerable person ‖ the oldest member of an institution or community **Father** a title of reverence for a priest **the Father** *(theol.)* the first

---

person of the Trinity **2.** *v.t.* to be the father of ‖ to originate and guide through the early stages ‖ (with 'on') to fix the original responsibility for (an idea etc.)

fa·ther·hood (fáðərhud) *n.* the state of being a father

fa·ther-in-law (fáðərinlɔ̜) *pl.* **fa·thers-in-law** *n.* a husband's or wife's father

fath·om (fǽðəm) **1.** *n.* a measure of depth of water equal to 6 ft ‖ **fáth·om·less** *adj.* (*rhet.*) too deep to measure ‖ too profound to understand **2.** *v.t.* to measure the depth of, to sound ‖ to get to the bottom of, to comprehend

fa·tigue (fətí:g) **1.** *n.* weariness after exertion or hard work ‖ (*zool.*) a condition of cells, tissues or organs which, as a result of excessive activity, temporarily lose the power to respond to further stimulation ‖ a condition of a material, esp. a metal, causing loss of elasticity and tendency to fracture after long or repeated stress ‖ (*mil.*) a noncombatant task for soldiers ‖ (*pl., mil.*) clothing worn while doing fatigue duty **2.** *v.t. pres. part* **fa·ti·guing** *past* and *past· part.* **fa·tigued** to make weary

fat·ten (fǽt'n) *v.t.* to make fat ‖ to make (animals) fat for slaughtering ‖ to make (soil) fertile or rich ‖ *v.i.* to grow fat

fat·ty (fǽti:) *comp.* **fat·ti·er** *superl.* **fat·ti·est** *adj.* containing fat, adipose ‖ caused by an accumulation of fat

fat·u·ous (fǽtʃu:əs) *adj.* foolish, esp. empty-headed or vacuously self-satisfied

fau·cet (fɔ́sit) *n.* a device for controlling the flow of a fluid from a pipe or container

fault (fɔlt) **1.** *n.* something for which one is rightly open to blame ‖ a mistake ‖ a blemish ‖ a moral failing ‖ (*geol.*) a fracture within the earth's crust caused by vertical slipping or folding, distinguished from a simple crack by the break in continuity of the rock strata ‖ an imperfect insulation or leakage in a telecommunications line ‖ (*tennis* etc.) a failure to serve the ball correctly **fáult·i·ly** *adv.* **fáult·less** *adj.* not to blame ‖ without blemish **fáult·y** *comp.* **fault·i·er** *superl.* **fault·i·est** *adj.* imperfect, defective **2.** *v.t.* to criticize (someone) with justice ‖ (*geol.*) to cause a fault in

fau·na (fɔ́nə) *pl.* **fau·nas, fau·nae** (fɔ́ni:) *n.* animal life in general, as distinguished from flora, esp. the indigenous animals of a certain region, environment or period ‖ a classification of the animals of a region, environment or period **fáu·nal** *adj.*

faux pas (foupá) *pl.* **faux pas** (foupáz) *n.* a social blunder

fa·vor (féivər) *v.t.* to be to the advantage of ‖ to suit ‖ (*commerce*) to oblige ‖ to show partiality towards ‖ to resemble in looks ‖ to be in favor of

favor *n.* approbation ‖ an act of kindness going beyond what could normally be expected ‖ advantage ‖ the condition of being approved or liked ‖ unfair partiality ‖ an emblem or mark of support for some cause or individual, e.g. a rosette or ribbon ‖ a decorative trinket or knick-knack such as party guests may be given ‖ (*commerce*) a letter

fa·vor·a·ble (féivərəb'l) *adj.* giving or expressing approval ‖ auspicious ‖ (of a wind) following ‖ (of business or bargaining terms) attractive **fá·vor·a·bly** *adv.*

fa·vored (féivərd) *adj.* granted special concessions

fa·vor·ite (féivərit) **1.** *n.* an object or person regarded with esteem or affection above others ‖ (*racing*) the animal generally backed to win **2.** *adj.* most or very much liked, regarded with special affection **fá·vor·it·ism** *n.* the showing of a special liking for one person or a few individuals in a group by acts of partiality where impartiality is called for

fawn (fɔn) **1.** *n.* a deer less than one year old **2.** *adj.* light yellowish-brown **3.** *v.i.* (of a doe) to give birth to a fawn

fawn *v.i.* (of animals, esp. dogs) to show affection or seek attention by hand-licking, rubbing up against one etc. ‖ (of persons) to seek favor by servile and flattering behavior **fáwn·ing** *adj.*

faze (feiz) *pres. part.* **faz·ing** *past* and *past part.* **fazed** *v.t.* to disconcert, daunt

fear (fiər) **1.** *n.* the instinctive emotion aroused by impending or seeming danger, pain or evil ‖ likelihood ‖ danger ‖ (*pl.*) anxiety ‖ awe, reverence **2.** *v.t.* to be afraid of ‖ to imagine or assume in fear ‖ to regret politely or conventionally ‖ to revere with awe ‖ *v.i.* to be afraid, feel fear **féar·ful** *adj.* causing fear ‖ reluctant through misgiving ‖ (*pop.*) appalling, extreme ‖ (*rhet.*) frightened or showing fear **féar·ful·ly** *adv.* (*pop.*) extremely **féar·less** *adj.* having no fear **féar·some** *adj.* causing fear ‖ daunting ‖ (*pop.*) very great

fea·si·bil·i·ty (fi:zəbíliti:) *n.* the quality of being feasible

fea·si·ble (fí:zəb'l) *adj.* possible to do or achieve ‖ possible to believe **féa·si·bly** *adv.*

feast (fi:st) **1.** *n.* a fine, elaborate meal designed for celebration ‖ a date in the calendar appointed for the celebration of some religious anniversary ‖ an abundance of anything giving enjoyment **2.** *v.t.* to provide with a feast ‖ *v.i.* to enjoy a feast

feat (fi:t) *n.* a deed (physical, intellectual or moral) out of the ordinary

feath·er (féðər) *v.t.* to furnish with feathers ‖ to shave down the edge of (something) so that it is very fine ‖ (*rowing*) to turn (the oar) so that its blade is horizontal and skims the water's surface lightly ‖ (*aeron.*) to turn (the propeller) so that its blades move with minimum resistance through the air ‖ (*shooting*) to knock feathers out of (a bird) but not kill it ‖ *v.i.* to grow or sprout feathers ‖ to move like feathers ‖ to feather an oar or propeller ‖ (of a hound) to make quivering movements of the stern and tail when searching for the scent

feather *n.* one of the epidermal outgrowths that cover the body of a bird ‖ (usually *pl.*) plumage ‖ the vane of an arrow ‖ a plume worn in a hat ‖ a flaw marked like a feather, e.g. in an eye or a gem ‖ (*rowing*) the action of feathering

feath·er·weight (féðərweit) *n.* a professional boxer whose weight does not exceed 126 lbs. ‖ an amateur boxer whose weight does not exceed (*Am.*) 125 lbs. ‖ somebody who does not matter much ‖ something very light

fea·ture (fí:tʃər) **1.** *n.* a part of the face, esp. as regards appearance ‖ (*pl.*) the face in general ‖ the distinctive part, trait or characteristic of a thing ‖ a distinctive article, picture etc. in a newspaper or periodical ‖ the main item in a movie program **2.** *v.t. pres. part.* **fea·tur·ing** *past* and *past part.* **fea·tured** to give prominence to ‖ (of a film) to present as the star actor or actress **féa·tured** *adj.* displayed, advertised as a special feature **féa·ture·less** *adj.* lacking distinctive features

Feb. February

Feb·ru·ar·y (fébru:ɛri:, fébju:ɛri:) *n.* (*abbr.* **Feb.**) the 2nd month of the year, having 28 days except in leap year, when it has 29

fe·ces, fæ·ces (fí:si:z) *pl. n.* bodily waste discharged through the anus

fe·cund (fí:kənd, fékʌnd) *adj.* prolific, fertile ‖ rich in inventive power

fed·er·a·cy (fédərəsi:) *pl.* **fed·er·a·cies** *n.* an alliance, federation of states

fed·er·al (fédərəl) *adj.* characterizing an agreement between states to unite, forgoing some sovereignty but remaining independent in internal affairs ‖ pertaining to this consolidated state ‖ relating to the central government of the U.S.A.

fed·er·al·ism (fédərəlizəm) *n.* the federal principle of government ‖ the support of this principle

fed·er·al·ist (fédərəlist) *n.* a supporter of federalism

fed·er·ate (fédəreit) **1.** *v. pres. part.* **fed·er·at·ing** *past* and *past part.* **fed·er·at·ed** *v.i.* to come together in federation ‖ *v.t.* to organize (states) into a federation **2.** *adj.* federated

fed·er·a·tion (fẹdəréiʃən) *n.* the act of uniting with a league for common purposes, esp. in forming a sovereign power with control of foreign affairs, defense etc., while each member state retains control of internal matters ‖ a group of states so united ‖ a sovereign state so produced ‖ a federated society, e.g. a league of clubs, societies, trade unions

fee (fi:) **1.** *n.* a payment for the services of a professional man (e.g. a doctor or lawyer) or a public body (e.g. a library or professional body) ‖ the entrance charge for an examination etc. ‖ (*usually pl.*) money paid terminally to a private school ‖ (*law*) inheritable land or estate ‖ (*hist.*) land held in feud **2.** *v.t. pres. part.* **fee·ing** *past* and *past part.* **feed**

fee·ble (fí:b'l) *adj.* lacking in energy or strength, weak ‖ lacking in character or intelligence ‖ lacking in effectiveness ‖ dim, unclear, indistinct

fee·ble·mind·ed (fí:b'lmáindid) *adj.* mentally deficient ‖ silly, foolish

feed (fi:d) **1.** *v. pres. part.* **feed·ing** *past* and *past part.* **fed** (fed) *v.t.* to give food to ‖ to suckle (a baby) ‖ to put food into the mouth of ‖ to fortify ‖ to supply food for ‖ to supply (material) to ‖ to feed material to ‖ to supply as fuel to ‖ to supply fuel to ‖ to supply (electrical energy) to ‖ to supply electrical energy to ‖ to be a source of supply of ‖ to supply as food ‖ (*theater*) to supply (esp. a comedian) with cue lines, improvising material on which he makes jokes ‖ (*games,* e.g. field hockey) to give a pass to ‖ *v.i.* (esp. of animals) to eat **2.** *n.* food, esp. for livestock, fodder etc. ‖ a meal ‖ the process of feeding a machine with raw material etc. ‖ the material thus supplied ‖ the mechanism for such feeding ‖ the part of the action of a firearm which moves up the cartridge from the clip or magazine to the chamber

feed·back (fí:dbæk) *n.* the return to a system, process or device of part of its output ‖ (*elec.*) the return to the input of an amplification system of part of the output in order to control amplification ‖ response following an action, e.g., comments after a speech, esp. when designed to correct a situation ‖ (*med.*) return to input that stimulates the proper adjustment, e.g., biofeedback

feel (fi:l) **1.** *pres. part.* **feel·ing** *past* and *past part.* **felt** (felt) *v.t.* to perceive, learn, explore by touching ‖ to become aware of through the senses ‖ to experience (an emotion) ‖ to sense ‖ to experience the effects of ‖ *v.i.* to be, or become aware of being ‖ to affect one's senses as being ‖ to have sympathy or compassion **2.** *n.* the sense of touch ‖ the effect on the sense of touch ‖ an instinctive understanding of, esp. as manifesting an aptitude **féel·er** *n.* someone who or something that feels, esp. an organ for testing by touch, e.g. the tentacle of an octopus or antenna of an insect ‖ a remark, hint, proposal etc. put out to sound the opinions of others **feel·ing** (fí:liŋ) **1.** *n.* the act or state of someone who feels ‖ the effect conveyed by the sense of touch ‖ sensation in general ‖ bodily power to feel ‖ an emotion ‖ resentment, antagonism ‖ (*pl.*) susceptibilities, emotions ‖ emotional solidarity ‖ sympathy ‖ an intuitive belief, conviction based on other grounds than reason ‖ opinion ‖ (with 'for') sensitive understanding or response ‖ the ability to use sensitively **2.** *adj.* that feels ‖ sensitive **feel·ing·ly** *adv.* in a way that shows the speaker's sympathy, self-pity, prejudice etc.

feign (fein) *v.t.* to represent by false appearance, simulate ‖ to pretend **feigned** (feind) *adj.* sham, fictitious ‖ fraudulent

feint (feint) **1.** *n.* a false appearance, pretense ‖ a mock attack meant to deceive an opponent about the attack proper, e.g. in military strategy or in boxing ‖ a deceptive movement, e.g. in fencing **2.** *v.i.* to make a feint

fe·lic·i·tate (filísiteit) *pres. part.* **fe·lic·i·tat·ing** *past* and *past part.* **fe·lic·i·tat·ed** *v.t.* to congratulate **fe·lic·i·tá·tion** *n.* congratulation

fe·lic·i·tous (filísitəs) *adj.* notably apt, happily expressed, well chosen

fe·lic·i·ty (filísiti:) *pl.* **fe·lic·i·ties** *n.* marked aptness or grace of language ‖ a well-chosen expression ‖ a state of great happiness

fe·line (fí:lain) **1.** *adj.* of cats ‖ catlike ‖ cunningly spiteful **2.** *n.* an animal of the cat family **fe·lin·i·ty** (filíniti:) *n.*

fell (fel) **1.** *v.t.* to cut down ‖ to cause to fall, to knock down ‖ (*sewing*) to stitch down the folded back projection of (a seam) **2.** *n.* an amount of timber cut ‖ a seam formed by felling **féll·er** *n.* someone who fells timber

fel·low (félou) *n.* a man, esp. a man of whom one speaks with familiarity or condescension ‖ a person, one ‖ (*often pl.*) a companion, associate ‖ a counterpart, one of a pair ‖ (in combination with nouns) one of the same class ‖ an elected graduate holding endowment for a period of research etc., or a member of the governing body of a college **Fel·low** a member of a learned society

fel·low·man (féloumæn) *pl.* **fel·low·men** (féloumén) *n.* another human being thought of as being like oneself by virtue of his humanity

fel·low·ship (félouʃip) *n.* the companionship and comradeship characteristic of group solidarity or the friendly exchange between individuals that springs from shared work, shared religious practices etc. ‖ (in titles) a guild, association, fraternity etc. ‖ communion between church members etc. ‖ the position, status or salary of a college fellow

fel·on (félən) *n.* (*law*) someone guilty of a felony

fe·lo·ni·ous (filóuni:əs) *adj.* wicked, criminal ‖ (*law*) of the nature of a felony

fel·o·ny (féləni:) *pl.* **fel·o·nies** *n.* (*law*) a grave crime (e.g. murder, arson) more serious than a misdemeanor

felt (felt) **1.** *n.* a fabric made by pressing and rolling (wool, hair, fur etc.) with size or lees ‖ an undercarpet or stair tread etc. made of this ‖ material like felt **2.** *v.t.* to make into felt ‖ to cover with felt ‖ to put felt under ‖ *v.i.* to mat together, e.g. after repeated washings

fe·male (fí:mail) **1.** *adj.* of the sex in animals or plants that produces or is capable of producing eggs or bearing young (symbol ♀) ‖ (*bot.*) pertaining to any reproductive structure that contains elements to be fertilized by male elements ‖ pertaining to women ‖ (*engin.*) describing a hollow part, tool etc. fitted to take a corresponding male part **2.** *n.* a female person, animal or plant

fem·i·nine (fén inin) **1.** *adj.* of the female sex ‖ of women ‖ characteristic of women ‖ having qualities thought of as proper to women ‖ (*gram.*) having female gender **2.** *n.* the feminine gender ‖ a word in this gender

fem·i·nin·i·ty (femininíti:) *n.* the quality of being feminine

fem·i·nism (féminizəm) *n.* the policy, practice or advocacy of political, economic and social equality for women **fém·i·nist** *n.* an advocate of feminism

fe·mur (fí:mər) *pl.* **fe·murs, fem·o·ra** (fémərə) *n.* the thighbone ‖ the corresponding part of an insect's leg

fen (fen) *n.* low marshy land, partially covered with water if not drained, or often flooded

fence (fens) **1.** *n.* a railing (of wood, wire etc.) en-

(**a**) æ, c*a*t; ɑ, c*a*r; ɔ f*aw*n; ei, sn*a*ke. (**e**) e, h*e*n; i:, sh*ee*p; iə, d*ee*r; ɛə, b*ea*r. (**i**) i, f*i*sh; ai, t*i*ger; ə:, b*i*rd. (**o**) o, *o*x; au, c*ow*; ou, g*oa*t; u, p*oo*r; ɔi, r*oy*al. (**u**) ʌ, d*u*ck; u, b*u*ll; u:, g*oo*se; ə, b*a*cillus; ju:, c*u*be. x, lo*ch*; θ, *th*ink; ð, bo*th*er; z, *Z*en; ʒ, cor*s*age; dʒ, sava*g*e; ŋ, oranguta*ng*; j, *y*ak; ʃ, *fi*sh; tʃ, fe*tch*; 'l, rabb*le*; 'n, redd*en*. Complete pronunciation key appears inside front cover.

closing a field, garden etc. to keep beasts in or intruders out or simply to mark a boundary ‖ an artificial obstacle for a horse to jump over in show jumping or steeplechasing ‖ fencing with saber, épée etc. as an art ‖ a person receiving stolen goods ‖ a place where stolen goods are received ‖ a guard or guide in various machines 2. *v. pres. part.* **fenc·ing** *past* and *past part.* **fenced** *v.i.* to fight in contest with a saber, épée etc. ‖ to practice fencing as a sport ‖ to avoid answering questions in debate by shifting ground or parrying ‖ to deal in stolen goods ‖ *v.t.* to enclose, provide or surround with a fence **fénc·er** *n.* someone skilled in fencing ‖ someone who builds, erects or repairs fences **fénc·ing** *n.* the art of attack, defense etc. with sword or foil ‖ the art of parrying etc. in debate ‖ fences collectively ‖ material for making fences

fend (fend) *v.t.* (with 'off') to repel, parry ‖ *v.i.* (with 'for') to struggle to look after **fénd·er** *n.* a device to defend or protect ‖ a bundle of rope or a log of wood etc. to protect the side of a ship against the quayside or another ship ‖ shock absorber on a locomotive ‖ a metal cover or guard over the wheel of a vehicle to deflect or catch splashes of mud from the wheels

fer·ment (fərmént) *v.i.* to undergo fermentation ‖ *v.t.* to cause fermentation in ‖ to inflame, excite, stir with anger etc.

fer·ment (fə́:rmənt) *n.* any agent able to produce fermentation by enzyme action ‖ fermentation ‖ commotion, unrest, tumult

fer·men·ta·tion (fə:rmentéiʃən) *n.* a chemical change produced by enzymes, particularly an energy-producing transformation of carbohydrate material yielding esp. alcohols, acids and carbon dioxide ‖ restless excitement **fer·men·ta·tive** (fə:rméntətiv) *adj.* able to ferment or to cause to ferment

fern (fə:rn) *n.* vascular, nonflowering plant characterized by alternation of generations

fe·ro·cious (fəróuʃəs) *adj.* savage, fierce ‖ cruel, violent

fe·roc·i·ty (fərósiti:) *pl.* **fe·roc·i·ties** *n.* the quality of being ferocious ‖ an act of intense cruelty

fer·ret (férit) **1.** *n.* variety of the European polecat, often kept half-tamed for use in netting rabbits **2.** *v.i.* to hunt with ferrets ‖ *v.t.* to clear (an area, burrow etc.) by using ferrets **to ferret out** to search out, esp. by close questioning or guile **fér·ret·y** *adj.* (of people) shifty, ferretlike

fer·ric (férik) *adj.* pertaining to, or containing iron

fer·ry (féri:) **1.** *pres. part.* **fer·ry·ing** *past* and *past part.* **fer·ried** *v.t.* to transport in a boat ‖ to deliver (an automobile, aircraft, naval craft, etc.) under its own power, esp. from the factory to the purchaser ‖ to transport (troops etc.) by aircraft which shuttle back and forward between two points **2.** *pl.* **fer·ries** *n.* a ferryboat ‖ a place where passengers or goods are ferried, or the service which ferries them ‖ *(law)* the right to ferry for a fee ‖ the regular service route of aircraft

fer·ry·boat (féri:bout) *n.* a boat working a ferry service

fer·tile (fə́:rt'l, *Br.* fə́:rtail) *adj.* highly productive ‖ (of seeds, eggs etc.) capable of developing ‖ capable of breeding or reproducing ‖ productive, creative

fer·til·i·ty (fərtíliti:) *pl.* **fer·til·i·ties** *n.* the state or quality of being fertile ‖ *(demography)* birthrate

fer·ti·lize (fə́:rt'laiz) *v.t. pres. part.* **fer·ti·liz·ing** *past* and *past part.* **fer·ti·lized** to make (an egg, ovum) capable of developing by the union of sperm with it ‖ to make fertile or productive ‖ to make (soil) productive by enriching it with nitrogen compounds, phosphorus, potassium etc.

fer·ven·cy (fə́:rvənsi:) *n.* the quality of being fervent

fer·vent (fə́:rvənt) *adj.* ardent, emotionally intense

fer·vid (fə́:rvid) *adj.* fervent

fer·vor (fə́:rvər) *n.* intensity of feeling, passion, devotion

fes·tal (féstəl) *adj.* of or pertaining to a feast ‖ gay, festive

fes·ter (féstər) **1.** *v.i.* (of a wound etc.) to produce pus ‖ to produce bitter feelings, rankle ‖ to rot, putrefy **2.** *n.* a festering sore, pustule

fes·ti·val (féstivəl) **1.** *n.* a joyful celebration or occasion ‖ a local season of entertainment, often annual, when cultural works are produced or performed **2.** *adj.* of a feast day ‖ of a festival

fes·tive (féstiv) *adj.* of feasts or festivals ‖ gay, *a festive party*

fes·tiv·i·ty (festíviti:) *pl.* **fes·tiv·i·ties** *n.* merrymaking, gaiety ‖ *(pl.)* festive activities

fetch (fetʃ) **1.** *v.t.* to go and get, bring ‖ to obtain as its price, to sell for ‖ to deal (a blow) **2.** *n. (naut.)* a continuous line or course from point to point (e.g. of a bay) **fétch·ing** *adj.* attractive

fete, fête (feit) **1.** *n.* a festival, entertainment, esp. an outdoor sale for charity ‖ the day dedicated to the saint after whom a child is named commemorated by Roman Catholics as a second birthday **2.** *v.t.* to entertain (a person, in celebration of some event or exploit) ‖ to celebrate (a success etc.)

fet·id, foet·id (fétid) *adj.* having a strong offensive smell

fet·ish (fétiʃ, fí:tiʃ) *n.* an object believed by certain primitive peoples to embody a spirit and exert magical powers, e.g. to protect its owner, cure diseases etc. ‖ an idea, practice etc. regarded with excessive or irrational reverence **fáet·ish·ism** *n.* the worship of fetishes ‖ excessive or irrational reverence for some idea, practice etc. ‖ *(psychol.)* the centering of strong sexual emotion in objects (e.g. shoes or furs) or parts of the body not normally associated with such emotion **fét·ish·ist** *n.* **fet·ish·is·tic** *adj.*

fet·ter (fétər) **1.** *n.* a chain or shackle for the feet of a prisoner ‖ a tether for an animal ‖ *(pl., rhet.)* captivity **2.** *v.t.* to put fetters on ‖ to restrain, hamper

fe·tus, foe·tus (fí:təs) *n.* a vertebrate that has passed the early stages of development and attained the basic final form prior to parturition

feud (fju:d) *n. (hist.)* an estate held by a tenant on condition of services being rendered to an overlord **in feud** held in this way

feud 1. *n.* a long-standing quarrel, esp. deadly enmity between families, clans, tribes etc. **2.** *v.i.* to wage a feud

feu·dal (fjú:d'l) *adj.* pertaining to feuds, fiefs or fees ‖ pertaining to the feudal system, *feudal law* ‖ of ideas of social relations characteristic of the feudal system **féu·dal·ism** *n.* the feudal system **féu·dal·ist** *n.* **feu·dal·is·tic** *adj.*

feudal system *(hist.)* the system of economic, political and social organization which flourished in Europe (9th—14th cc.)

fe·ver (fí:vər) **1.** *n.* human body temperature above the normal 98.6° F. or 37.0 C., usually accompanied by rapid pulse and general malaise ‖ a disease causing such high temperature ‖ a high state of excitement, agitation ‖ a wave of irrational enthusiasm **2.** *v.t.* to put in a state of great excitement and agitation

fe·ver·ish (fí:vəriʃ) *adj.* having a fever ‖ marked by fever ‖ caused by fever ‖ causing fever ‖ restlessly excited

few (fju:) **1.** *adj.* consisting of a small, indefinite number ‖ (with 'a') a small number of **2.** *n.* a small number of people, things etc. **the few** the minority of people **the happy few** the priviliged minority ‖ *(mil.)* in air intercept usage, seven or less aircraft **3.** *pron.* a small, indefinite number of people or things

fi·an·cé (fi:ɑːséi, fi:ɑ́nsei) *n.* a man in relation to the woman to whom he is engaged to be married **fi·an·cée** (fi:ɑːséi) *n.* a woman in relation to the man to whom she is engaged

fi·as·co (fi:ǽskou) *pl.* **fi·as·cos, fi·as·coes** *n.* an absurd or complete failure

fib (fib) **1.** *n.* a trivial lie **2.** *v.i. pres. part.* **fib·bing** *past* and *past part.* **fibbed** to tell such a lie

fi·ber, fi·bre (fáibər) *n.* a fine thread ‖ a threadlike structure of animal or vegetable tissue ‖ *(bot.)* an elongate cell typical of some sclerenchymas that is found in wood, leaves, phloem, cortex and dry fruits ‖ a substance made of threads ‖ a fibrous structure ‖ a substance, natural or man-made, that can be spun, woven, felted etc. ‖ a threadlike root or twig ‖ moral strength

fiber glass, *Br.* **fibre glass** the trade name for fine glass fibers used for textile manufacture, and for material made from these which is used for the bodies of light cars, boats etc. and in felted form for insulation

fi·brous (fáibrəs) *adj.* containing fibers

fic·tion (fíkʃən) *n.* literature consisting of invented narrative, esp. the novel and short story ‖ a false story or statement ‖ a pretense, invention ‖ a falsehood conventionally accepted as true because it is useful to make the assumption **fíc·tion·al** *adj.* pertaining to fiction ‖ not restricted to fact

fic·ti·tious (fiktíʃəs) *adj.* imagined, not factual ‖ (of a name or character) assumed ‖ imaginary, feigned ‖ pertaining to action or like fiction ‖ existing by virtue of a legal or polite fiction

fid·dle (fíd'l) **1.** *n.* a violin ‖ (in an orchestra) a violin player ‖ *(naut.)* a rack or railing, often of cord, to prevent dishes etc. from sliding off the table in rough weather **2.** *v. pres. part.* **fíd·dling** *past* and *past part.* **fíd·dled** *v.i.* (often familiar or contemptuous) to play the violin ‖ to make aimless, interfering, indecisive or annoyingly distracting movements ‖ *v.t.* to play (a tune) on a violin

fid·dler (fídlər) *n.* someone who plays the fiddle, esp. someone hired to do so ‖ a fiddler crab

fiddler crab a small crab, the males of which have one of the claws greatly enlarged

fi·del·i·ty (fidéliti:) *pl.* **fi·del·i·ties** *n.* the faithful performance of duty ‖ loyalty ‖ adherence to the contract of marriage ‖ exactness ‖ *(elec.,* in radio, television etc.) the degree of accuracy in the reproduction of the sound or picture

fidg·et (fídʒit) **1.** *v.i.* to be constantly making restless little movements ‖ to be uneasy, worry ‖ *v.t.* to make (someone) disturbed or worried **2.** *n.* (also *pl.*) restlessness, accompanied by frequent nervous movements ‖ someone who fidgets or disturbs others **fídg·et·i·ness** *n.* **fídg·et·y** *adj.*

fi·du·ci·ar·y (fidú:ʃi:eri:, fidjú:ʃi:eri:) **1.** *adj.* of the nature of a trust or trusteeship ‖ held or given in trust ‖ (of paper money etc.) having a valuale depending on public confidence **2.** *pl.* **fi·du·ci·ar·ies** *n.* someone acting in a fiduciary capacity, a trustee

field (fi:ld) **1.** *n.* an area of land, usually enclosed, devoted to pasture or the cultivation of crops ‖ *(pl.)* meadows or arable land ‖ *(rhet.)* a battleground ‖ (in compounds) an area of land yielding minerals ‖ an area of land set aside and made suitable for a particular use ‖ the area on which something is drawn, painted etc., e.g. the ground color of a flag, the background of a picture or coin, or *(heraldry)* the surface of a shield ‖ *(phys.)* a space within which electric, gravitational or magnetic etc. effects exist and can be, in principle, specified at each point ‖ a particular body of interest, study, knowledge or thought ‖ *(racing)* the competing horses ‖ all runners except the favorite ‖ all those taking part in a sport or contest out-of-doors **2.** *v.t. (baseball, cricket)* to stop or catch (the ball) ‖ to answer without previous preparation, e.g., to field questions **3.** *adj.* of or relating to a field ‖ growing in fields

fiend (fi:nd) *n.* the Devil, Satan ‖ any demon or evil spirit ‖ a person actuated by intense wickedness, esp.

by cruelty ‖ (with an attributive noun etc.) an addict, *a dope fiend* or devotee, *a fresh-air fiend* **fíend·ish** *adj.* devilish

fierce (fiərs) *comp.* **fierc·er** *superl.* **fierc·est** *adj.* savage, violently hostile ‖ raging, violent ‖ intense, passionate

fi·er·y (fáiəri:) *comp.* **fi·er·i·er** *superl.* **fi·er·i·est** *adj.* flaming with fire ‖ looking like fire, blazing red ‖ (of eyes) glowing, flashing ‖ seeming to burn ‖ vehement ‖ passionate ‖ *(rhet.,* of horses) mettlesome

fif·teen (fiftí:n) **1.** *adj.* being one more than 14 (*NUMBER TABLE) **2.** *n.* 10 plus five ‖ the cardinal number representing this (15, XV) ‖ a team of 15 members, esp. in Rugby Union

fif·teenth (fiftí:nθ) **1.** *adj.* being number 15 in a series (*NUMBER TABLE) ‖ being one of the 15 equal parts of anything **2.** *n.* the person or thing next after the 14th ‖ one of 15 equal parts of anything (1/15) ‖ the 15th day of a month

fifth (fifθ) **1.** *adj.* being number five in a series (*NUMBER TABLE) being one of the five equal parts of anything **2.** *n.* the person or thing next after the fourth ‖ one of five equal parts of anything (1/5) ‖ the fifth day of a month ‖ *(mus.)* the note five steps above or below a given note in a diatonic scale, inclusive of both notes ‖ *(mus.)* the interval between these notes ‖ *(mus.)* a combination of these notes **3.** *adv.* in the fifth place ‖ (followed by a superlative) except four, *the fifth biggest*

fif·ti·eth (fífti:iθ) **1.** *adj.* being number 50 in a series (*NUMBER TABLE) ‖ being one of the 50 equal parts of anything **2.** *n.* the person or thing next after the 49th ‖ one of 50 equal parts of anything (1/50)

fif·ty (fífti:) **1.** *adj.* being 10 more than 40 (*NUMBER TABLE) **2.** *pl.* **fif·ties** *n.* five times 10 ‖ the cardinal number representing this (50, L) **the fifties** (of temperature, a person's age, a century etc.) the span 50–9

fif·ty-fif·ty (fífti:fífti:) **1.** *adv. (pop.)* equally **2.** *adj.* *(pop.)* shared equally ‖ *(pop.,* of a division) equal, half-and-half

fig (fig) *n.* a genus of tropical trees and shrubs of most varied habit, commonly having adventitious and aerial roots ‖ the fruit of the fig tree ‖ the least little bit

fight (fait) *pres. part.* **fíght·ing** *past* and *past part.* **fought** (fɔt) *v.i.* to give mutual blows ‖ to take part in a war ‖ to be one of two or more combatants in physical combat ‖ to strive, struggle ‖ to engage in a legal contest ‖ *v.t.* to win (one's way) by fighting ‖ to try to stop, prevent or overcome ‖ to make war upon ‖ to oppose by legal action ‖ to defend one's interests in (a legal case) ‖ to engage in (a war or battle) ‖ to box against ‖ to engage in (a boxing contest) ‖ to cause to fight

fight *n.* a physical struggle for victory ‖ a battle ‖ single combat ‖ an effort to overcome something ‖ fighting spirit, a will to fight **fíght·er** *n.* someone who fights, esp. someone full of determination to win ‖ an aircraft designed mainly for aerial combat

fig·ment (fígmənt) *n.* something made up with no basis of truth

fig·ur·a·tive (fígjurətiv) *adj.* expressed by means of metaphor or other figure of speech ‖ addicted to or abounding in figures of speech ‖ representing by means of a figure

fig·ure (fígjər) **1.** *n.* the written or printed symbol for a number ‖ *(pl., pop.)* addition, accounting etc. ‖ price ‖ a diagram, esp. a plane geometrical form enclosed by lines, e.g. a triangle ‖ a three-dimensional form enclosed by surfaces e.g. a cylinder ‖

any such plane or solid form ‖ a drawing of a form ‖ a diagram in a printed text ‖ the human form ‖ a piece of sculpture, esp. a representation of the human form ‖ a personage ‖ a decorative pattern or design ‖ a movement in a dance (esp. a folk dance or country dance) ‖ a set pattern cut by the skates in display skating ‖ *(gram.)* a permitted deviation from the rules, e.g. ellipsis **2.** *v. pres. part.* **fig·ur·ing** *past* and *past part.* **fig·ured** *v.t.* to represent by means of a figure, diagram, picture etc. ‖ to decorate with patterns or designs ‖ to employ figures of speech in ‖ *(pop.)* to consider ‖ *v.i.* to work out figures, do arithmetic ‖ to be a personage of some note **fig·ured** *adj.* represented by a painted or sculpted figure ‖ ornamented, patterned ‖ shaped, fashioned

fig·ur·ine (fígjuri:n) *n.* a small statue, carved or molded

fil·a·ment (fíləmənt) *n.* a fine threadlike body or fiber ‖ *(elec.)* a thin thread of metal, carbon etc. heated or made incandescent in some electric lamps etc. ‖ a thin metallic fiber that serves as the cathode in electron tubes ‖ *(bot.)* the stalk of a stamen, bearing the anther ‖ a hypha, a threadlike string of cells or a long single cell in certain fungi, bacteria etc. **fil·a·men·ta·ry** (fìləméntəri:), **fil·a·men·tous** (fìləméntəs) *adjs*

filch (filtʃ) *v.t.* to steal, pilfer

file (fail) **1.** *n.* a steel instrument with a surface of cutting ridges or teeth used for smoothing, cutting through or abrading surfaces of metal etc. **2.** *v.t. pres. part.* **fil·ing** *past* and *past part.* **filed** to cut or smooth with or as if with a file

file 1. *n.* a device of various kinds for keeping papers, or for organizing them for ease of reference etc. ‖ a set of papers so kept ‖ a series of issues, e.g. of a newspaper or periodical, kept in order ‖ a row of persons or things arranged one behind the other ‖ a soldier in the front rank of a formation and the man (or men) behind him **in file** (esp. *mil.*) one behind the other **2.** *v. pres. part.* **fil·ing** *past* and *past part.* **filed** *v.t.* to place (a paper) in or on a file ‖ to place (a document) with others so as to be available for reference ‖ (with 'off' or 'out') to cause (soldiers) to move in file ‖ *(law)* to submit (a petition), e.g. for divorce ‖ *v.i.* to march or move in file ‖ to apply

fi·let (filéi) *n.* a lace or net with a geometrical pattern worked on a square mesh

fil·i·al (fíli:əl) *adj.*) of, relating to or appropriate to a son or daughter

fil·i·bus·ter (fíləbəstər) **1.** *n. (hist.)* a freebooter ‖ the obstruction of legislative action by delaying tactics, e.g. by making long speeches to consume time (esp. in the U.S. Senate) **2.** *v.i.* to act as a filibusterer **fil·i·bus·ter·er** *n.* someone who filibusters

fil·i·gree (fíligri:) *n.* lacy ornamental work, formerly of metal beads, now of fine wire (gold, silver, copper etc.) ‖ any delicate or fragile openwork **fíl·i·greed** *adj.*

fill (fil) *v.t.* to make full ‖ to distend to the full extent ‖ to occupy the whole space of ‖ to stock lavishly ‖ to plug up a cavity in (a tooth) with metal etc. in order to arrest decay ‖ a plug (a crack or hole) ‖ to occupy (an office) ‖ to appoint someone to (a vacant post) ‖ to treat (fabrics, leather etc.) so as to block the crevices, pores etc. ‖ to occupy (time) ‖ to satisfy, glut ‖ to dispense (a prescription etc.) ‖ to fulfill (an order) ‖ *v.i.* to become full

fill *n.* a full supply, enough to satisfy one's needs ‖ enough to satiate ‖ *(securities)* a trading order that demands immediate execution or cancellation

fil·let 1. *n.* (filéi) a boneless piece of meat, fish or esp. of beef from the loin ‖ (filit) a narrow band to bind the hair ‖ a thin narrow strip of material, e.g. cotton, leather ‖ *(archit.)* a flat band separating two moldings or between flutings of a column ‖ *(heraldry)* a horizontal division of a shield, quarter of the chief in depth ‖ *(bookbinding)* a plain or ornamental line stamped on a book cover ‖ the tool used for this **2.** (filéi) *v.t.* to remove the bone from (fish or meat)

and divide it into long, thin slices

fil·ling (fíliŋ) *n.* the act of filling ‖ a substance used in filling, esp. cement used to fill a decayed tooth ‖ the woof or weft in woven fabrics ‖ yarn as prepared for the shuttle

fil·ly (fíli:) *pl.* **fil·lies** *n.* a young mare

film (film) **1.** *n.* a thin layer ‖ a growth on the eye ‖ a haze dimming the sight ‖ a sheet or strip of celluloid or other material that has been coated with a light-sensitive emulsion **2.** *v.t.* to make a movie of ‖ to cover with or as if with a film ‖ *v.i.* to be in the process of making a movie ‖ to be suitable for making into a movie

fil·ter (fíltər) **1.** *n.* a device for separating solids from liquids, or suspended particles from gases, consisting of a porous substance through which only the liquid or gas can pass ‖ *(phys.)* a device for removing or reducing waves or oscillations of certain frequencies without affecting other vibrations passing through it ‖ *(photog.)* a lens screen which has different absorptive powers for different wavelengths of light **2.** *v.t.* to pass (something) through or as if through a filter ‖ *v.i.* to go through or as if through a filter

filth (filθ) *n.* foul matter, esp. of a nauseating character ‖ obscene language or thoughts ‖ anything that corrupts or defiles, physically or morally **filth·y** *comp.* **filth·i·er** *superl.* **filth·i·est** *adj.* extremely dirty ‖ obscene

fin (fin) *n.* one of the paired membranous limbs or unpaired dermal outgrowths used by a fish to propel and steer itself ‖ anything resembling this, e.g. the limb of a seal or whale, or the ridge left on a metal casting ‖ *(aeron.)* an external rib, parallel to the axis of symmetry, preserving balance and direction by dividing the airflow ‖ a rib to provide a cooling surface, e.g. on a car radiator

fi·na·gle (finéig'l) *pres. part.* **fi·na·gling** *past* and *past part.* **fi·na·gled** *v.i. (pop.)* to practice guile, wangle ‖ *v.t. (pop.)* to get (something) by guile

fi·nal (fáin'l) **1.** *adj.* the last of a series ‖ coming at the end ‖ ultimate ‖ decisive, conclusive, *a final judgment* ‖ concerned with the end product or purpose ‖ *(gram.)* describing a clause of purpose (stating 'in order that', 'lest' etc.) **2.** *n.* a deciding race, game, contest etc. ‖ (often *pl.*) the last of a series of examinations or an examination at the end of a course ‖ the latest edition of a newspaper in any one day ‖ *(mus.)* the note on which an ecclesiastical mode ends **fi·nal·ist** *n.* a competitor in a deciding game, competition etc. **fi·nal·ly** *adv.* lastly, in conclusion ‖ completely, once for all

fi·na·le (finéili:, fináli:) *n.* the last movement of a musical composition ‖ the last aria, chorus etc. of an act of an opera ‖ the last piece performed at a concert ‖ the last scene of a play ‖ the last event in a dramatic series of events

fi·nal·i·ty (fainǽliti:) *pl.* **fi·nal·i·ties** *n.* the state or quality of being final

fi·nal·ize (fáin'laiz) *pres. part.* **fi·nal·iz·ing** *past* and *past part.* **fi·nal·ized** *v.t.* to put into final form

fi·nance (fainǽns, fáinæns, finǽns) **1.** *n.* monetary affairs ‖ the management of public or company revenue ‖ *(pl.)* monetary resources **2.** *v.t. pres. part.* **fi·nanc·ing** *past* and *past part.* **fi·nanced** to provide with money or provide money for ‖ to raise the money for **fi·nan·cial** (fainǽnʃəl, finǽnʃəl) *adj.* pertaining to financiers or financial operations

fin·an·cier (fainənsí:r, finənsí:r) *n.* a large-scale investor, capitalist ‖ someone skilled in financial matters, esp. those of a public concern

finch (fintʃ) *n.* a small, seed-eating bird of fam. *Fringillidae*

find (faind) **1.** *v. pres. part.* **find·ing** *past* and *past part.* **found** (faund) *v.t.* to discover (what was lost) ‖ to discover by seeking ‖ to discover by experiment or study ‖ to discover by trial or experience ‖ to discover by the feelings ‖ to discover by chance ‖ to arrive at ‖ to make (a way) somehow ‖ to obtain ‖ to succeed in getting or raising ‖ to summon up ‖ to perceive (oneself) to be as specified ‖ to declare (a verdict) ‖ to declare (a person) as specified (guilty, insane etc.) ‖ to provide ‖ to discover (the scent) or start (game) in hunting ‖ *v.i.* to discover the scent or start game in hunting ‖ to reach and deliver a verdict **2.** *n.* a finding ‖ something valuable that is found ‖ a starting of game or picking up of the scent in hunting ‖ someone discovered to be of great quality, esp. when this is not expected **find·er** (fáindər) *n.* someone who or something which finds ‖ a small telescope attached to a large one, to simplify directing it on to a particular object ‖ a lens in a microscope for a similar purpose ‖ *(photog.)* a viewfinder

fine (fain) **1.** *adj.* highly satisfactory, excellent ‖ very skilled and delicate ‖ made or worked with delicacy ‖ consisting of small particles, *fine sand* ‖ made of slender threads ‖ highly refined ‖ (of gold and silver) containing a specified proportion of pure metal ‖ thin, sharp ‖ highly accomplished ‖ dressy ‖ subtle ‖ able to see and appreciate subtleties ‖ refined ‖ mannered, ornate ‖ (used as an intensive) tremendous ‖ (of the weather) bright and clear **2.** *adv.* very well **3.** *v. pres. part.* **fin·ing** *past* and *past part.* **fined** *v.t.* (often with 'down') to make finer, thinner or less coarse ‖ (often with 'away') to remove gradually until fineness is achieved ‖ (often with 'down') to taper

fine 1. *n.* a sum of money paid as an imposed penalty for an offense **2.** *v.t. pres. part.* **fin·ing** *past* and *past part.* **fined** to punish by imposing a fine on **fine·a·ble** *adj.*

fin·e·ry (fáinəri:) *n.* showy, elaborate clothing, ornaments etc.

fi·nesse (finés) **1.** *n.* subtlety of contrivance, judgment etc. ‖ a skillful strategic maneuver ‖ *(cards)* an attempt at taking a trick by choosing to play a card lower than some as yet unplayed card, taking the chance that this unplayed card is in a hand whose turn has passed **2.** *v. pres. part.* **fi·ness·ing** *past* and *past part.* **fi·nessed** *v.i. (cards)* to make a finesse ‖ *v.t.* to make or achieve by subtlety

fin·ger (fíŋgər) **1.** *n.* a terminal digit of the hand, esp. other than the thumb ‖ something shaped like, or as thin as, a finger ‖ the breadth of a finger ‖ the part of a glove into which a finger is inserted ‖ a pointer on a dial ‖ *(taboo slang)* an obscene gesture of contemptuous rejection **2.** *v.t.* to touch with the fingers, handle ‖ to perform (a piece of music) with a certain fingering ‖ to mark (notes of printed or written music) so as to indicate which fingers are to be used

fin·ger·print (fíŋgərprint) **1.** *n.* an impression of a fingertip left on a surface ‖ such an impression taken in ink to record or check identification **2.** *v.t.* to take an impression of the fingerprints of (a person)

fin·ger·tip (fíŋgərtip) *n.* the tip of a finger ‖ a protective covering for the end of a finger

fin·ish (fíniʃ) **1.** *v.t.* to casue to come to an end ‖ to arrive at the end of ‖ to complete (esp. the remainder of something) ‖ to consume entirely ‖ to put the final touches to ‖ *v.i.* to come to an end **2.** *n.* conclusion, end ‖ a manner or style of finishing ‖ the material used for a decorative surface ‖ *(fine arts)* surface refinement (often excessive) ‖ social polish, cultivated manners, speech etc. **fin·ished** *adj.* concluded ‖ perfected ‖ thorough ‖ incapable of further achievement **fin·ish·er** *n.* someone who or something which finishes, esp. a craftsman, machine or substance involved in some final process of manufacture ‖ *(pop.)*

a crushing blow **finishing school** a private school putting emphasis on social and cultural accomplishments for girls

fi·nite (fáinait) *adj.* having definable bounds ‖ (of numbers) able to be counted, not infinite or infinitesimal ‖ *(gram.)* of a verb which is limited by tense, number and person

fink (fiŋk) *n. (slang)* one who tells tales; a betrayer

fiord, fjord (fjɔrd, fjourd) *n.* a narrow inlet of the sea enclosed by high cliffs

fir (fə:r) *n.* an evergreen tree of genus *Abies,* fam. *Pinaceae*

fire (fáiər) **1.** *n.* a chemical change accompanied by the emission of heat and light, and often flame, usually a change consisting in the combination of carbon compounds with the oxygen of the air ‖ a mass of material undergoing this change or gotten ready for this ‖ the act of undergoing this chemical change ‖ the discharge of a gun or guns ‖ passion **2.** *v. pres. part.* **fir·ing** *past* and *past part.* **fired** *v.t.* to discharge (a gun etc.) ‖ to cause (bullets, rounds etc.) to be propelled from a gun ‖ to make by gunfire ‖ to ask (questions) or make (remarks etc.) in rapid succession ‖ to set fire to, esp. so as to destroy ‖ *(pop.)* to dismiss, discharge (an employee) ‖ to stimulate ‖ to bake (bricks, pottery etc.) in a kiln ‖ to cure (tobacco, tea etc.) by heat ‖ to cauterize (horses' hooves etc.) ‖ to supply with fuel ‖ to light the fuse of (an explosive) ‖ *v.i.* to shoot a gun or guns etc. ‖ (of a gun etc.) to go off ‖ to be detonated ‖ to be affected by fire ‖ (of an internal-combustion engine) to have the compressed mixture in the cylinders ignited ‖ (of wheat etc.) to turn yellow prematurely, as in a drought

fire·arm (fáiərárm) *n.* any portable weapon firing shot or bullets by gunpowder

fire·crack·er (fáiərkrækər) *n.* a small, cylindrical firework which goes off with a sharp, cracking noise when its fuse is lit

fire·fly (fáiərflai) *pl.* **fire·flies** *n.* any of several winged, nocturnal insects emitting light by the oxidation of luciferin

fire·man (fáiərmən) *pl.* **fire·men** (fáiərmən) *n.* a member of a fire department ‖ the man responsible for feeding the fire, e.g. of a steam engine, furnace etc.

fire·work (fáiərwə:rk) *n.* a device used in quantity for entertainment by effects of colored light, smoke, noise etc. caused by combustion or explosion ‖ *(pl.)* a display of fireworks ‖ *(pl.)* a verbal display of wit or anger

firm (fə:rm) **1.** *adj.* compact, solid ‖ stable ‖ steady ‖ steadfast, resolute ‖ exercising authority with discipline ‖ not liable to cancellation or modification (of prices, stock market etc.) steady, not fluctuating much **2.** *adv.* firmly, *to stand firm* **3.** *v.t.* to make firm ‖ *v.i.* to become firm

firm *n.* a partnership or business house ‖ the name under which such a partnership (not having the legal status of a company) conducts business

fir·ma·ment (fə́:rməmənt) *n.* the whole vault of the sky with its myriad stars etc.

first (fə:rst) **1.** *adj.* being number one in a series (*NUMBER TABLE) ‖ earliest in time ‖ nearest the front ‖ foremost in importance, rank etc. ‖ earliest available ‖ earliest with relation to an unspecified time ‖ fundamental ‖ rudimentary ‖ *(mus.,* of an instrument or voice) having a part generally higher in pitch than that of the second instrument or voice of the same kind ‖ of low gear in a vehicle **2.** *n.* the first person or thing mentioned or the first of a series ‖ a first prize or a victory in a race or other contest ‖ the first

---

day of a month ‖ low gear in a vehicle ‖ *(pl.)* certain products (lumber, flour, butter etc.) of the highest quality **3.** *adv.* before any other person or thing ‖ for the first time ‖ before anything else

first aid the emergency treatment of someone wounded or taken ill

first·hand (fə́:rsthænd) *adv.* and *adj.* from the original sources or by personal experience

First Lady the wife of the president of the U.S.A. or of the governor of a state of the U.S.A., or whoever presides for him at social functions if the man has no wife

fis·cal (fískəl) *adj.* of or pertaining to the public treasury or revenue ‖ financial

fish (fiʃ) *pl.* **fish, fish·es** *n.* a class of backboned aquatic animals ‖ the flesh, whether raw or cooked

fish *v.i.* to try to catch fish, e.g. with a net or line ‖ to search for something underwater by dredging, hooking etc. ‖ to try to get something, usually by indirect methods ‖ *v.t.* to fish in, *to fish a river* ‖ to draw up or out from water or as if from water

fish·er·man (fíʃərmən) *pl.* **fish·er·men** (fíʃərmən) *n.* someone who lives by fishing ‖ someone who fishes for pleasure

fish·er·y (fíʃəri:) *pl.* **fish·er·ies** *n.* the fishing industry ‖ an area where fishing is carried on ‖ a place where fish are bred ‖ *(law)* the right to fish in particular waters

fis·sion (fíʃən) *n.* the act of process of splitting into parts, esp. *(biol.)* asexual reproduction by means of division into two equal parts (binary fission) or more than two (multiple fission), e.g. in bacteria, corals etc. ‖ *(phys.)* the splitting of an atomic nucleus into approximately equal parts, e.g. by bombardment with neutrons **fis·sion·a·ble** *adj.*

fis·sure (fíʃər) **1.** *n.* a narrow opening or cleft made by splitting, esp. in rock ‖ a cleaving or cleavage ‖ *(anat.)* a narrow opening in an organ, a groove separating certain skull bones or a cleft in the lobes of the brain **2.** *v.t.* and *i. pres. part.* **fis·sur·ing** *past* and *past part.* **fis·sured** to split into fissures

fist (fist) *n.* the hand when clenched, with the fingers folded tightly into the palm

fist·i·cuffs (fístikʌfs) *pl. n. (old-fash.)* fighting with bare fists

fit (fit) **1.** *adj.* suited to a particular end ‖ (with 'for') good enough ‖ proper, right ‖ competent or suitably endowed by nature ‖ brought into a specified condition, ready ‖ in good physical condition, healthy **2.** *v. pres. part.* **fit·ting** *past* and *past part.* **fit·ted, fit** *v.t.* to suit ‖ to qualify, make competent ‖ to answer to, correspond with ‖ to be the right size or shape for ‖ to adjust the size or shape of so as to be right ‖ (with 'for') to measure (someone or something) ‖ to insert into a position where there is just enough room ‖ to install, put in as equipment etc. ‖ *v.i.* to be correct in size or shape ‖ to be in harmony or agreement ‖ (of statistical data) to correspond with a standard **3.** *n.* the manner or degree of fitting ‖ the degree of correspondence of statistical data with a standard ‖ something which fits

fit *n.* a seizure, convulsion ‖ a short sudden attack or outburst, e.g. of depression or coughing ‖ a short spell **by fits and starts** in irregular bursts of activity **to have** (or **throw) a fit** to become suddenly and violently angry or upset

fit·ful (fítfəl) *adj.* spasmodic

fit·ness (fítnis) *n.* the state of being fit, suitable, appropriate ‖ good health

fit·ting (fítiŋ) *n.* (esp. *pl.*) a piece of fixed equipment or furnishing ‖ a small part for a piece of apparatus or an installation ‖ a trying-on of tailor-made clothes

five (faiv) **1.** *adj.* being one more than four (*NUMBER TABLE) **2.** *n.* four plus one ‖ the cardinal number representing this (5, V) ‖ five o'clock ‖ a playing card (domino etc.) marked with five symbols ‖ a team of five members, esp. in basketball

fix (fiks) **1.** *v.t.* to fasten firmly, make fast ‖ to make as if rigid ‖ to look or stare steadily at (something or someone) ‖ (of an object) to seize and hold (one's attention) ‖ to commit (details) to one's mind or memory ‖ to determine, establish ‖ to place (oneself), establish (one's residence etc.) with a degree of permanency ‖ to arrange ‖ to prepare ‖ to repair ‖ *(chem.)* to convert (a gas) into a solid compound ‖ *(dyeing)* to make (a color) fast ‖ *(microscopy)* to preserve for examination ‖ *(photog.)* to make (a negative or print) permanent by dissolving and washing away unreduced bromide etc. ‖ *(pop.)* to influence the result of (a race, fight, election etc.) by bribery etc. ‖ *(pop.)* to deal with (someone) so as to punish, reduce to silence, counter etc. ‖ *(mil.)* to attach (bayonets) to rifles as a parade drill ‖ *v.i.* to become fixed **2.** *n.* a difficult situation, dilemma ‖ the position of a ship or aircraft, as determined by bearings, radio etc. ‖ the process of finding such a position

fix·a·tion (fikséiʃən) *n.* the act of fixing ‖ *(chem.)* the conversion of a gas, esp. atmospheric nitrogen, into a solid compound ‖ the preparation of specimens for study by treating them with formaldehyde ‖ *(psychol.)* the partial arrest of psychosexual development at an infantile stage with consequent immaturity of sexual or other relationships ‖ the accurate direction and focusing of the eyes, for optimum vision

fix·a·tive (fíksətiv) **1.** *adj.* able to fix or make permanent **2.** *n.* any of various substances used to make something more permanent, e.g. to keep the hair tidy, preserve a specimen for display, prevent a photographic print or film from fading

fix·ture (fíkstʃər) *n.* a thing fixed permanently in position ‖ any of the fixed items bought or sold with a building (e.g. gas pipes, electric fittings) of with land (e.g. a greenhouse, fencing) ‖ the date fixed in advance for a game or athletics meeting, or the meeting itself ‖ *(pop.)* someone or something thought of as invariably present

fiz·zle (fíz'l) **1.** *v.i. pres. part.* **fiz·zling** *past* and *past part.* **fiz·zled** to hiss or splutter feebly **to fizzle out** to come to nothing, esp. after a good start **2.** *n. (pop.)* a complete failure, fiasco

flab·bi·ness (flǽbi:nis) *n.* the state or quality of being flabby

flab·by (flǽbi:) *comp.* **flab·bi·er** *superl.* **flab·bi·est** *adj.* lacking firmness ‖ having soft, slack flesh ‖ hanging loosely

flac·cid (flǽksid) *adj.* limp, flabby ‖ feeble **flac·cíd·i·ty** *n.*

flag (flæg) **1.** *n.* a piece of cloth or bunting, usually with a pattern or a device, generally oblong or square in shape, attached to a pole or staff, and used to denote nationality, party or ownership, to mark a position, or to exchange information ‖ the admiral's flag hoisted on his flagship when he is in command at sea ‖ the tail of a setter or Newfoundland dog ‖ the 'for hire' signal of a taxi **2.** *v.t. pres. part.* **flag·ging** *past* and *past part.* **flagged** to signal (orders etc.) by means of flags (with 'down') to bring to a stop by means of flags ‖ to put flags on or over (something) ‖ to mark out with flags ‖ to draw attention to, e.g. attach markers to (selected documents in a file etc.) ‖ to convey a message to with flag signals or with motions of the hand

flag *pres. part.* **flag·ging** *past* and *past part.* **flagged** *v.i.* (e.g. of a plant) to hang down limply, droop ‖ (of a person) to show signs of exhaustion ‖ (of attentive interest) to begin to fail

flag·on (flǽgən) *n.* a vessel for holding liquor, esp. one with a handle, spout and lid, for serving wine etc. at table ‖ a large globular glass bottle

fla·grant (fléigrənt) *adj.* conspicuously evil ‖ glaringly wrong

flair (flɛər) *n.* an intuitive gift of discrimination ‖ a natural ability, aptitude

flak (*colloq.*) complaints ‖ criticism difficult to handle ‖ from the exploded bullets of antiaircraft fire

flake (fleik) **1.** *n.* a small, thin, loose-textured fragment ‖ a thin but broad piece that scales off ‖ (*pl.*) pieces into which the flesh of certain fish separates ‖ a flake tool ‖ (*slang*) an eccentric person **2.** *v. pres. part.* **flak·ing** *past* and *past part.* **flaked** *v.i.* to fall as or like snow ‖ to come away in flakes ‖ to separate into flakes ‖ *v.t.* to cover with flakes ‖ to make flaky ‖ to work (flint) into flake tools or to chip (flake tools) from flint

flak·y (fléiki:) *comp.* **flak·i·er** *superl.* **flak·i·est** *adj.* consisting of flakes or tending to break up into flakes

flam·boy·ance (flæmbɔ́iəns) *n.* the state or quality of being flamboyant

flam·boy·ant (flæmbɔ́iənt) **1.** *adj.* florid, ornate, vivid in color ‖ ostentatious, overelaborate, showy **2.** *n.* a tropical tree widely cultivated for its flaming red racemes of flowers

flame (fleim) *n.* a body of glowing, burning gas ‖ the state of burning with a blaze ‖ a blaze of red ‖ (*rhet.*) intense feeling, passion ‖ (*old-fash., pop.*) a sweetheart ‖ a strong reddish-orange color like a flame

flame (fleim) *pres. part.* **flam·ing** *past* and *past part.* **flamed** *v.i.* to burst into flame or burn with flames ‖ to look as though in a blaze ‖ *v.t.* to treat with a flame, pass through a flame e.g. so as to sterilize

flam·ma·ble (flæməb'l) *adj.* (in technical contexts) liable to ignite

flank (flæŋk) **1.** *n.* the side of an animal between the ribs and thigh ‖ the side of a hill, mountain, building etc. ‖ the right or left side of an army, fleet etc. **2.** *v.t.* to be situated on the flanks of ‖ (*mil.*) to guard on the flank ‖ (*mil.*) to attack from the flank ‖ to pass around the flank of

flap (flæp) **1.** *n.* something broad and flat that is attached on one side only and hangs down from the attachment or can be moved freely around it, e.g. the part for sealing an envelope or the cover of a coat pocket ‖ the movement made by a bird's wing or by a sail in the breeze or by something comparable, e.g. a shirt hung out to dry ‖ the sound accompanying such a movement ‖ a sudden unreasoning loss of self-confidence resulting in confused and often foolish actions or words ‖ (*aeron.*) a movable airfoil on the trailing edge of an aircraft wing ‖ (*med.*) a piece of skin or bone partly separated from the adjoining tissue ‖ a group of sightings of unidentified flying objects at a similar time and place **2.** *v. pres. part.* **flap·ping** *past* and *past part.* **flapped** *v.i.* (with 'at') to strike out weakly with something broad and flat ‖ (of a bird's wings) to move up and down, esp. while the bird remains perched or standing ‖ to lose self-confidence suddenly and say or do silly things as a result ‖ *v.t.* to move (the wings) up and down ‖ to cause to move lightly one way and another with a dry, slapping sound

flare (fleər) **1.** *n.* a sudden emission of bright flame ‖ a spurt of flame, e.g. from an acetylene burner in the open air ‖ a device used esp. by ships and aircraft to illuminate a position, target etc. ‖ a gradual spreading and widening ‖ (*photog.*) a defect caused by too great a local concentration of light ‖ (*football*) a short lateral pass **2.** *v. pres. part.* **flar·ing** *past* and *past part.* **flared** *v.i.* (of a fire) to emit flames which are bright and fierce but unsteady ‖ to become wider ‖ *v.t.* to cause to flare **to flare up** to emit bright flame suddenly ‖ to become suddenly angry

flash (flæʃ) **1.** *v.i.* to give out a momentary, intensely bright light ‖ to give out flames or sparks ‖ to emit light suddenly ‖ to reflect light brilliantly ‖ to move quickly ‖ to come into the mind as quick as lightning ‖ (*glassmaking*) to spread out in a sheet ‖ *v.t.* to send (signals etc.) by flashes of light ‖ to make known over great distances in little time ‖ to allow to be seen briefly ‖ (*building*) to protect against rain by laying sheet metal on (joints, roof valleys etc.) ‖ to fill or flood (a stream, river etc.) with water, esp. suddenly and rapidly ‖ (of water) to rush along ‖ to give out in flashes ‖ to display ostentatiously **2.** *n.* a sudden burst or gleam of light ‖ a photograph taken by flashbulb ‖ flame ‖ an instant of time ‖ a sudden, short-lived feeling ‖ a sudden manifestation ‖ a short news dispatch, esp. by radio ‖ a chute of water down a weir to carry a boat over, or the mechanism for producing this chute **3.** *adj.*

flash·back (flǽʃbæk) *n.* a short insertion in the plot sequence e.g. of a film or novel to relate events prior to the time of the narrative ‖ a sudden recurrence in the memory of an incident or emotion from the past ‖ (*drug culture*) recurrence of a hallucination and accompanying emotional disturbance

flash·light (flǽʃlait) *n.* a small, portable container fitted with an electric light bulb and dry-cell battery ‖ the light that flashes from a lighthouse ‖ (*photog.*) a sudden bright light used for taking photographs at night or indoors

flash·y (flǽʃi:) *comp.* **flash·i·er** *superl.* **flash·i·est** *adj.* showy but worthless ‖ given to empty display

flask (flæsk, flɑsk) *n.* a narrow-necked vessel, normally of blown glass, used in laboratories ‖ a flat broad bottle, often of metal, for carrying liquor in one's pocket

flat (flæt) **1.** *adj.* (of a surface) even and level ‖ unbroken by depressions or projections ‖ (*racing*) uninterrupted by jumps ‖ stretched out ‖ spread out ‖ completely in ruins ‖ broad, smooth and lacking thickness, e.g. like a coin ‖ uniform ‖ without gloss ‖ outright ‖ dull, monotonous ‖ without energy or zest ‖ lacking sparkle or effervescence, stale ‖ inactive ‖ (of feet) having the instep arch fallen ‖ (of a tire) deflated ‖ (of a sail) taut ‖ (of a curve) shallow ‖ (*mus.*) lower by half a tone ‖ (*mus.*) below the correct pitch **2.** *adv.* absolutely, precisely ‖ in a downright way **3.** *n.* the flat part of something ‖ level ground ‖ (*pl.*) low-lying ground over which the tide flows ‖ (*theater*) a section of scenery mounted on a wooden frame ‖ a punctured tire ‖ a flat-bottomed boat ‖ a flat basket ‖ a flat box for growing seedlings ‖ a flatcar ‖ (*mus.*) a note lowered a semitone below the note named ‖ (*mus.*) a sign (b) indicating this lowering **4.** *v. pres. part.* **flat·ting** *past* and *past part.* **flat·ted** *v.t.* to cause to have a nonglossy surface, or to remove the gloss from (a surface) ‖ to lower (a note) by a semitone ‖ to plant or transplant in a flat ‖ *v.i.* (*mus.*) to go flat

flat *n.* an apartment (set of rooms) on one floor

flat·ten (flǽt'n) *v.t.* to make flat ‖ to make dull, dispirit ‖ to knock down ‖ *v.i.* to become flat

flat·ter (flǽtər) *v.t.* to praise excessively, esp. in a calculating way ‖ to gratify the vanity of ‖ to cause to look more handsome (e.g. in a painting) or seem to have more quality (e.g. in a description) than is really the case **to flatter oneself** to delude oneself into a hope or belief ‖ to venture to think **flát·ter·y** *n.* insincere or excessive praise

flaunt (flɔnt) **1.** *v.t.* to display proudly or brazenly ‖ to flout ‖ *v.i.* to wave brightly ‖ to display oneself **2.** *n.* the act of flaunting, a display

fla·vor (fléivər) **1.** *n.* the quality belonging to food, drink etc. that is experienced through the combined senses of taste and smell ‖ flavoring ‖ a characteristic quality 2. *v.t.* to give flavor to **flá·vor·ing** *n.* a substance for adding flavor, esp. an essence to give a particular taste to food

flaw (flɔ) 1. *n.* a crack or gap ‖ a blemish, defect ‖ a weakness that invalidates 2. *v.t.* to cause a defect in ‖ to crack ‖ *v.i.* to become cracked **fláw·less** *adj.* perfect

flax (flæks) *n.* a plant of the genus *Linum*, fam. *Linaceae*, esp. *L. usitatissimum* ‖ its fibers, raw or dressed

flax·en (flǽksən) *adj.* like flax or of flax ‖ of the color of dressed flax, blond

flay (flei) *v.t.* to strip the skin or flesh from ‖ to peel off the skin or bark from ‖ to fleece, charge (a person) extortionately ‖ to criticize harshly

flea (fli:) *n.* a small, wingless insect

fleck (flek) 1. *n.* a small mark or speck ‖ a freckle or other colored mark on the skin ‖ a patch of light or color 2. *v.t.* to spot with flecks **fléck·er** *v.t.* to mark in patches, dapple, fleck

fledg·ling, fledge·ling (flédʒliŋ) *n.* a bird just fledged ‖ an immature or inexperienced person

flee (fli:) *pres. part.* **flee·ing** *past* and *past part.* **fled** (fled) *v.i.* (*rhet.*) to run away, esp. from danger or evil ‖ (*rhet.*) to pass swiftly away, vanish ‖ *v.t.* (*rhet.*) to run away from ‖ (*rhet.*) to shun

fleece (fli:s) 1. *n.* the coat of wool covering a sheep or similar animal ‖ the amount of wool taken from sheep etc. at one shearing ‖ a thick and woolly hair or covering ‖ something resembling wool ‖ a thin sheet of cotton or wool fiber ‖ a fabric with a silky pile 2. *v.t. pres. part.* **fleec·ing** *past* and *past part.* **fleeced** to rob (someone) by overcharging, or by cheating at cards **fléec·y** *comp.* **fleec·i·er** *superl.* **fleec·i·est** *adj.* covered with, consisting of or resembling wool

fleet (fli:t) *n.* a number of warships under one command ‖ any naval force ‖ a national navy ‖ a number of ships sailing together ‖ a group of vehicles under one control

fleet *adj.* (*rhet.*) swift and agile ‖ (*rhet.*) transient

fleet·ing (flí:tiŋ) *adj.* transient, passing swiftly away

flesh (fleʃ) 1. *n.* the muscular substance, together with the fat and connective tissues, of man and animals ‖ the human body as distinct from mind, soul or spirit ‖ the part of an animal body that is considered food ‖ the pulpy part of a fruit ‖ sensual human nature 2. *v.t.* to train (hounds) for hunting by giving them flesh from the kill to eat ‖ to remove the flesh from (skin, hides etc.)

flesh·y (fléʃi:) *comp.* **flesh·i·er** *superl.* **flesh·i·est** *adj.* (of a person) plump ‖ (of a chicken etc.) yielding more than average meat for eating ‖ succulent, pulpy

flex (fleks) *v.t.* to bend (a joint) by the flexors ‖ to move (a muscle) so as to bend a joint

flex·i·bil·i·ty (fleksəbíliti:) *n.* the quality of being flexible

flex·i·ble (fléksəb'l) *adj.* easily bent, not rigid ‖ pliable ‖ adaptable, capable of being modified ‖ responsive to changing conditions ‖ open to influence

flick·er (flíkər) 1. *v.i.* to waver, quiver ‖ to burn fitfully ‖ (with 'out') to waver and then become extinguished 2. *n.* a flickering movement, light or flame ‖ a momentary stir of feeling

fli·er, fly·er (fláiər) *n.* a bird or insect with reference to the quality of its flight ‖ an aviator ‖ an animal, vehicle etc. that is exceptionally fast ‖ a flying jump ‖ a widely distributed handbill ‖ (*pop.*) a reckless gamble, esp. in the stock market ‖ the part which twists the thread on a spinning machine as it winds on to the bobbin ‖ one of the steps in a flight of identical, rectangular steps

flight (flait) 1. *n.* the act or mode of flying ‖ the power of flying ‖ a journey by air ‖ the distance that an aircraft, rocket etc. can fly ‖ a journey on the schedule of an airline ‖ a flock of birds, insects etc. ‖ (*pl.*) a bird's flight feathers ‖ a volley ‖ (of time) a swift passing ‖ (of stairs) a unit block ‖ a soaring or sally ‖ a small unit of aircraft ‖ (*angling*) a device enabling

the bait to spin rapidly ‖ (*archery*) a light, low-feathered arrow for shooting long distances, or a contest with these 2. *v.t.* to vary the pace and trajectory of (a cricket ball) so as to deceive the batsman

flight *n.* the act of fleeing ‖ a sudden hastening away

flim·sy (flímzi:) *comp.* **flim·si·er** *superl.* **flim·si·est** *adj.* lacking substance ‖ poorly made, or made of poor material, and lacking requisite strength ‖ easily torn ‖ unsound, weak

flinch (flintʃ) 1. *v.i.* to shrink or draw back ‖ to wince 2. *n.* the act or process of flinching

fling (fliŋ) 1. *v.t. pres. part.* **fling·ing** *past* and *past part.* **flung** (flʌŋ) to throw or hurl from the hand ‖ to move violently ‖ to put summarily ‖ to throw to the ground ‖ to send (troops etc.) into attack ‖ *v.i.* to go violently or in a temper ‖ (of a horse etc., esp. with 'out') to kick and plunge 2. *n.* the act or an instance of flinging ‖ a lively, esp. Scottish, dance with quick arm and leg movements ‖ the music for this ‖ a sarcastic attack ‖ a period of going all out for sensual pleasure ‖ a sudden violent movement

flint (flint) *n.* a heavy and hard variety of silica which emits sparks when struck with steel and is easily chipped to a cutting edge ‖ a stone of this material used in building ‖ a prehistoric tool of knapped flint ‖ anything hard and unyielding ‖ (*hist.*) a piece of flint used with steel for striking fire, e.g. in a flintlock gun ‖ a small piece of metal alloy used to produce a spark in a cigarette lighter ‖ a pebble made of flint

flip (flip) 1. *v. pres. part.* **flip·ping** *past* and *past part.* **flipped** *v.t.* to toss or flick with a quick movement of the fingers, esp. so as to cause (e.g. a coin) to turn over in midair ‖ to lose control of oneself, creating either a good or bad response ‖ to cause (a pancake) to do this and land back in the pan reverse side up ‖ to strike lightly ‖ to flick (the fingers) together ‖ to move with a flick or jerk ‖ *v.i.* to make a flipping motion 2. *n.* a light blow ‖ a flick ‖ a short aircraft flight ‖ (*banking*) flexible loan insurance plan, in which a down payment is made to a savings account, drawn upon to supplement interest and amortization when the loan is due 3. *adj.* (*pop.*) flippant

flip·pan·cy (flípənsi:) *pl.* **flip·pan·cies** *n.* the state or quality of being flippant ‖ a flippant remark

flip·pant (flípənt) *adj.* treating serious matters with levity or lack of respect

flirt (fləːrt) 1. *v.t.* to move, esp. to open and close, with quick little movements ‖ *v.i.* to show amorous interest without any depth of feeling ‖ (with 'with') to take a superficial or half-serious interest 2. *n.* someone who flirts ‖ a quick little movement ‖ (esp. *horol.*) a lever or other mechanical device for controlling periodic motion **flir·tá·tion** *n.* the act of flirting or an instance of it **flir·tá·tious** *adj.* fond of amorous flirting

flit (flit) 1. *v.i. pres. part.* **flit·ting** *past* and *past part.* **flit·ted** to make sudden, brief flights from place to place ‖ to come or go swiftly 2. *n.* the act or motion of flitting ‖ an instance of flitting

float (flout) *n.* something that floats on a fluid, or itself enables something else to float ‖ a cork or quill on a fishing line ‖ a cork or hollow ball supporting a fishing net in the water ‖ an inflated part helping to support a fish or aircraft ‖ the hollow metal ball at the end of a lever controlling the water level in a tank, cistern etc., or a similar device in a carburetor controlling the gasoline level ‖ a low-wheeled movable platform for displays etc. in a procession or carnival, or the display itself and its movable platform ‖ a mass of floating ice or weeds ‖ (*theater, pl.*) footlights ‖ any of various tools for smoothing surfaces used by masons, plasterers etc. ‖ a single-cut file for filing metal ‖ a raft ‖ (*banking*) the total of outstanding checks in the process of collection at any given time ‖ money kept in a cash register for making change

float *v.i.* (of a body which displaces its own weight of a fluid and therefore becomes weightless) to rest on or near the surface of a fluid ‖ to be held up by air, gas or fluid ‖ to be suspended in a fluid ‖ to move gently, drift ‖ to wander aimlessly ‖ to hover in front of the eyes ‖ (of a boat) to get afloat ‖ *v.t.* (of liquid) to support (a buoyant object) ‖ to set afloat ‖ to start and obtain support for (a scheme or company) ‖ to negotiate (a loan) ‖ to circulate (a rumor) ‖ *(plastering* etc.) to level or smooth with a float ‖ to grind and wash (pigments) in running water **flóat·a·ble** *adj.* capable of floating ‖ (of a river etc.) able to float rafts, logs etc. ‖ (of ores) suitable for treatment by flotation

flock (flɒk) **1.** *n.* a number of birds living, feeding or moving together ‖ a number of goats or sheep herded together ‖ a crowd of people ‖ the body of Christians in relation to Christ, or a church congregation in relation to its pastor **2.** *v.i.* to come together in a flock or large crowd ‖ to move like a flock

floe (flou) *n.* an ice floe

flog (flɒg, flɔg) *pres. part.* **flog·ging** *past* and *past part.* **flogged** *v.t.* to beat or strike hard and repeatedly with a cane etc. ‖ *(fishing)* to cast time and again into (a stream) ‖ to drive too hard, obtain exhausting effort from

flood (flʌd) **1.** *n.* a large quantity of water covering what is usually dry land, as the result of a river or sea's flowing over its usual limits ‖ the state of a river that is very full of water ‖ the point of high tide ‖ an abundance of something which seems to flow **the Flood** *(Bible)* the flood in the time of Noah **2.** *v.t.* to cover with a flood ‖ to cause (a river) to be in spate ‖ to irrigate ‖ to fill (e.g. a carburetor) to overflowing ‖ *(pop.)* to add a lot of water to (whiskey etc.) ‖ to overwhelm, e.g. with work or orders ‖ *v.i.* to be in a state of flood ‖ to be subject to submersion by a flood

floor (flɔr, flour) *n.* the lower horizontal surface of a room, on which one stands ‖ the bottom of a sea, river, cave, mine, gallery or platform of a bridge etc. ‖ the space for dancing in a restaurant or nightclub ‖ a structure dividing a building horizontally into stories ‖ a story ‖ a level surface ‖ a minimum level, e.g. of prices ‖ *(shipbuilding)* a timber or metal plate across the keel between the inner and outer bottoms ‖ (in a legislative or debating chamber) the part where members speak from **to have the floor** to have the right to speak or to go on speaking in a legislative or debating assembly

flop (flɒp) **1.** *v. pres. part.* **flop·ping** *past* and *past part.* **flopped** *v.i.* to move clumsily ‖ to let oneself drop (into a chair, on to a bed, to the ground etc.) in an ungainly way ‖ (of a fish taken out of the water) to make convulsive movements ‖ (of a bird) to flap its wings clumsily ‖ to be a conspicuous failure (e.g. of a novel or play, or of a person) ‖ *v.t.* to throw with a flop ‖ (of a bird) to move (its wings) up and down with a loud flapping sound **2.** *n.* a flopping motion or sound ‖ a failure **3.** *adv.* with a flop **flóp·py** *comp.* **flop·pi·er** *superl.* **flop·pi·est** *adj.* lacking firmness and tending to bob about in a limp way

flo·ra (flɔ́rə, flóurə) *pl.* **flo·ras, flo·rae** (flɔ́ri:, flóuri:) *n.* plant life in general, esp. plants of a certain region, environment or period ‖ a classification of the plants of a region, environment or period

flo·ral (flɔ́rəl, flóurəl) *adj.* of flowers ‖ like flowers ‖ of floras

flo·ret (flɔ́rit, flóurit) *n.* one of the small individual flowers of a composite flower

flor·id (flɔ́rid, flóurid) *adj.* heavily ornate ‖ flowery in style ‖ flushed

flo·rist (flɔ́rist, flóurist, flɑ́rist) *n.* someone who sells

flowers ‖ someone who cultivates and breeds flowers

flo·til·la (floutílə) *n.* a small fleet ‖ a fleet of small vessels

flot·sam (flɒ́tsəm) *n.* the wreckage of a ship or its cargo found floating on the sea ‖ people who are drifters ‖ accumulated objects of little value

flounce (flauns) **1.** *n.* a brusque, self-conscious movement of the body, usually expressing petulance or high rage, sometimes merely to attract attention **2.** *v.i. pres. part.* **flounc·ing** *past* and *past part.* **flounced** to go with such movements ‖ (of a horse) to plunge, make struggling movements

flounce 1. *n.* a strip of cloth or lace gathered and sewn (e.g. on a woman's skirt) by the upper edge only **2.** *v.t. pres. part.* **flounc·ing** *past* and *past part.* **flounced** to trim or adorn with a flounce or flounces

floun·der (fláundər) *n.* a small, edible flatfish

flounder *v.i.* to struggle, stumble about (in mud etc.) ‖ to do things badly, blunder

flour (fláuər) **1.** *n.* finely ground and sieved wheat meal ‖ the ground meal of rye, barley or other cereals ‖ the ground meal of other food products, e.g. potato or cassava ‖ any fine, soft powder **2.** *v.t.* to make into flour ‖ to sprinkle with flour

flour·ish (flɔ́:riʃ, flʌ́riʃ) **1.** *v.i.* to grow well ‖ to succeed, do well ‖ (used to indicate a person's date or a main period of literary or artistic activity) to live, work, be in its developed stage ‖ *v.t.* to display ostentatiously ‖ to cause to move with a sweeping, wavelike motion **2.** *n.* a calculated showiness of manner ‖ an ostentatious gesture, a waving (of hands, handkerchiefs) or brandishing (of a weapon or the fist) ‖ a curving, decorative stroke of the pen around a letter or word in calligraphy ‖ *(mus.)* a showy passage, impromptu addition etc. ‖ a fanfare

flout (flaut) *v.t.* to treat with contempt, set aside brazenly ‖ *v.i.* (with 'at') to mock, jeer

flow (flou) **1.** *v.i.* (of matter, esp. fluids) to move with a continuous change in shape, as a result of the absence of forces of interaction between the constituent particles of a substance ‖ to move like a straem contained by banks ‖ (of a liquid, or something that behaves comparably, e.g. grain) to run or spread freely ‖ (of the blood) to circulate ‖ (of blood) to be spilled, esp. in violence ‖ (of the tide) to rise ‖ (of a stream etc.) to be full and running fast ‖ to run smoothly and effortlessly ‖ (of hair, draperies etc.) to hang with graceful freedom ‖ to be dispensed abundantly ‖ to gush forth in a spring ‖ to issue from **2.** *n.* the act of flowing ‖ the rate of flowing, e.g. of a current ‖ a quantity of substance passing a given point in a flowing system in unit time ‖ the rising of the tide ‖ a smooth falling in waves or folds ‖ a steady, copious, progressive movement of goods, ideas, talk etc.

flow·age (flóuidʒ) *n.* a flooding or being flooded

flow·er (fláuər) **1.** *n.* a flowering plant ‖ its blossom only ‖ *(pl., chem.)* the powdery substance left after sublimation ‖ *(pl.)* the scum on wine etc. formed by fermentation ‖ *(pl.)* rhetorical ornament ‖ a printer's ornament, fleuron ‖ *(rhet.)* the choicest part or specimen **in flower** blooming **2.** *v.i.* to blossom, produce flowers ‖ *(rhet.)* to develop and flourish ‖ *v.t.* to bring into flower ‖ to decorate with flowers or a floral design **flow·er·er** (fláuərər) *n.* a flowering plant with respect to its time or manner of flowering **flow·er·et** (fláuərit) *n.* a floret

flu, flue (flu:) *n. (pop.)* influenza

fluc·tu·ate (flʌ́ktʃueit) *pres. part.* **fluc·tu·at·ing** *past* and *past part.* **fluc·tu·at·ed** *v.i.* to change constantly, esp. between opposites ‖ to show irregular variation **fluc·tu·á·tion** *n.*

---

flue (flu:) *n.* a pipe or vent for carrying off smoke, gases, etc. to the outside air ‖ *(engin.)* a channel for conveying a current of hot or cold air for heating, air conditioning etc.

flu·en·cy (flú:ənsi) *n.* the quality of being fluent

flu·ent (flú:ənt) *adj.* having or showing ease of command of speaking in public, writing, using a foreign language etc.

fluff (flʌf) **1.** *n.* soft down worn off blankets etc. ‖ any soft downy mass of feathers, fur, hair etc. ‖ *(pop.)* a stumble in a speech or misplay in a game **2.** *v.t.* to shake so as to make plump ‖ to shake out into a fluffy mass ‖ *(pop.)* to make an error in (spoken lines in a play) or misplay (a shot) in a game ‖ to smooth and whiten (the flesh side of leather) ‖ *v.i.* to become fluffy **flúff·i·ness** *n.* **flúff·y** *comp.* **fluff·i·er** *superl.* **fluff·i·est** *adj.* of or like fluff

flu·id (flú:id) **1.** *n.* a substance (e.g. a liquid or gas) that under the influence of small forces flows and is capable of assuming the shape of its container **2.** *adj.* able to flow ‖ able or likely to change

fluke (flu:k) **1.** *n.* a stroke of luck, an accidentally successful or lucky stroke, esp. at billiards **2.** *v. pres. part.* **fluk·ing** *past* and *past part.* **fluked** *v.i.* to make a fluke, esp. at billiards ‖ *v.t.* to get by a fluke

fluk·y (flú:ki) *comp.* **fluk·i·er** *superl.* **fluk·i·est** *adj.* lucky, done or won by luck ‖ (of a breeze) light and veering often

flunk (flʌŋk) *v.t.* *(pop.)* to fail (esp. an examination) ‖ *(pop.)* to fail (someone) in an examination **to flunk out** *(pop.)* to be dismissed, esp. from college, for failure

fluo·resce (flurés, flɔrés, flourés) *pres. part.* **fluo·resc·ing** *past* and *past part.* **fluo·resced** *v.i.* to show fluorescence

fluo·res·cence (flurés'ns, flɔrés'ns, flourés'ns) *n.* *(phys.)* a luminescence which may or may not persist after removal of the excitation but whose decay does not depend on temperature ‖ the property of emitting such radiation ‖ the radiation so emitted, often in the visible region **fluo·rés·cent** *adj.*

fluorescent lamp a tubular glass electric lamp containing mercury vapor and equipped with an electron gun and anode, whose inner surface is coated with fluorescent substances

fluor·i·da·tion (fluəridéiʃən, flɔridéiʃən, flouridéiʃən) *n.* the addition of fluorides to (drinking water) so as to combat tooth decay

flur·ry (flɔ́:ri, flʌ́ri) **1.** *pl.* **flur·ries** *n.* a sharp sudden gust of wind ‖ a sudden gusty shower of rain or snow ‖ a fit of nervous excitement ‖ the struggles of a dying whale **2.** *v.i. pres. part.* **flur·ry·ing** *past* and *past part.* **flur·ried** to fluster, esp. by causing to hasten, divide attention, etc.

flush (flʌʃ) **1.** *v.i.* to blush ‖ to flow and spread suddenly and freely ‖ to glow suddenly red, e.g. with reflected sunset ‖ *v.t.* to cause (water etc.) to flow ‖ to cleanse by sending a rush of water over or through ‖ to redden, inflame ‖ to cause a rush of emotion in, *flushed with pride* ‖ to make level **2.** *n.* a sudden flow (esp. of water or blood) ‖ a rush of emotion ‖ a feverish rush of heat ‖ *(rhet.)* a state of fresh and confident vigor ‖ a fresh growth of grass or leaves etc. **3.** *adj.* (of a river) in flood ‖ *(pop.)* affluent ‖ level with adjoining surfaces ‖ immediately adjacent and in line ‖ *(printing)* level with the left edge of the printed matter of the page, not indented **4.** *adv.* so as to be level ‖ so as to be adjacent and in line

flus·ter (flʌ́stər) **1.** *v.t.* to make nervous, agitate and confuse ‖ *v.i.* to be in such a state **2.** *n.* a state of confused agitation, flurry

flute (flu:t) **1.** *n.* a woodwind instrument consisting of a hollow wooden (sometimes metal) cylinder, played by blowing through a lateral blowhole and stopping other holes with fingers or keys ‖ an organ stop of flutelike quality ‖ *(archit.)* a long vertical rounded groove in a column, esp. in classical orders ‖ a similar groove cut into the walls of a pot, glass etc. or fashioned in cloth **2.** *v. pres. part.* **flut·ing** *past* and *past part.* **flut·ed** *v.i.* to play on a flute ‖ *v.t.* to utter in a soft, clear, high-pitched voice ‖ to form rounded grooves in (a pillar, pot etc.) **flút·ing** *n.* decorative flutes on a column etc. **flút·ist** *n.* a flute player

flut·ter (flʌ́tər) **1.** *v.i.* to flap the wings in a short flight ‖ to flit ‖ to wave with flapping motions ‖ to vibrate or beat irregularly ‖ to tremble, to be thrown into confusion or uncertainty ‖ *v.t.* to flap (the wings) in a short flight or without flying ‖ to cause to wave with flapping motions ‖ to make agitated little movements with (a fan) ‖ to throw into a state of agitation or confusion **2.** *n.* a quick irregular movement ‖ an irregular pulse or vibration ‖ a state of agitated excitement ‖ an effect of surprise causing comment or stir ‖ the rapid alternate beating of the legs in swimming the crawl and backstroke ‖ rapid changes in pitch on a recording, due to variations in speed ‖ *(med.)* an abnormal cardiac vibration ‖ *(aeron.)* an abnormal oscillation or up-and-down movement in a wing or tail, occurring at a critical speed

flux (flʌks) **1.** *n.* the act of flowing ‖ the condition of continuously changing ‖ a substance added to another in order to give a lower melting point and promote fusion, or (as in soldering) to remove a film of oxide ‖ *(phys.)* the rate of transfer of energy (e.g. light) or matter (e.g. a liquid) across a given surface area **2.** *v.t.* to make more fusible by adding a flux to ‖ to cause to flow or melt ‖ *v.i.* to become fluid, melt ‖ to fuse

fly (flai) **1.** *v. pres. part.* **fly·ing** *past* **flew** (flu:) *past part.* **flown** (floun) *v.i.* to move through the air by means of wings, jets, propellers etc. ‖ to travel by air ‖ (of bullets etc.) to be impelled through the air ‖ (of kites, flags etc.) to float or wave in the air ‖ to operate an aircraft ‖ to rush ‖ *(pop.)* to hasten away ‖ (of time) to pass quickly ‖ (of money) to be quickly spent ‖ to run away, flee ‖ *(baseball, past and past part.* **flied**) to hit a fly ‖ *v.t.* to cause to float or move through the air ‖ to hoist (a flag) or keep (a flag) hoisted ‖ to operate (an aircraft) **2.** *pl.* **flies** *n.* the act of flying or the course or distance flown ‖ the flap covering the fastening up the front of trousers ‖ the flap at a tent entrance ‖ the outer canvas of a double-topped tent ‖ the flyleaf of a book ‖ *(baseball)* a flyball ‖ *(football)* forward pass tactic in which the receiver moves directly past the line of scrimmage ‖ a device for regulating speed in clockwork etc. ‖ a flywheel

fly *pl.* **flies** *n.* almost any dipteran insect, esp. the housefly ‖ *(angling)* a hook dressed with feathers, used as bait

fly·weight (fláiweit) *n.* a professional or amateur boxer whose weight does not exceed 112 lbs ‖ a professional or amateur weightlifter whose weight does not exceed 114.5 lbs

fly·wheel (fláihwi:l, fláiwi:l) *n.* a solid heavy disk mounted on a shaft, serving to offset fluctuations of the speed of the associated machinery by its inertia

foal (foul) **1.** *n.* the young of a horse, donkey or other member of fam. *Equidae*, esp. under one year of age **in** (or **with**) **foal** (of a horse etc.) pregnant **2.** *v.t.* to give birth to (a foal) ‖ *v.i.* to give birth to a foal

foam (foum) **1.** *n.* a mass of whitish bubbles formed on liquid by agitation, fermentation etc. ‖ a dispersion of a gas or vapor in a liquid ‖ froth formed in an animal's mouth by saliva or on its skin by perspiration ‖ a lightweight cellular material, e.g. of rubber **2.** *v.i.* to foam or gather foam ‖ to rage ‖ *v.t.* to produce a lightweight cellular material by forming air bubbles in (a plastic etc.)

foam·y (fóumi) *comp.* **foam·i·er** *superl.* **foam·i·est** *adj.* consisting of foam or like foam ‖ covered with foam

fo·cus (fóukəs) **1.** *pl.* **fo·cus·es, fo·ci** (fóusai) *n.* *(phys.)* a point to which waves from a distant source converge, or from which they appear to diverge, after reflection or refraction ‖ focal length ‖ adjustment for, or the condition of, distinct vision or sharpness ‖ (math.) one of the two fixed points to which any point on a curve has a definite distance relationship ‖ a center of interest, importance etc. ‖ (seismology) the point of origin of an earthquake ‖ (med.) the part of the body where a disease is centered 2. v. pres. part. fo·cus·ing, fo·cus·sing past and past part. fo·cused, fo·cussed v.t. to cause to converge to a focus ‖ to adjust (a mirror, lens etc.) so that waves from each point of an extended source converge to a point image ‖ to concentrate and direct (the attention etc.) ‖ v.i. to come to a focus

fod·der (fódər) 1. n. dried food (hay, straw etc.) for cattle, sheep, horses etc. 2. v.t. to feed with fodder

foe (fou) n. (rhet.) an enemy, adversary

fog (fog) 1. n. water vapor condensed on fine suspended particles, forming a dense opaque cloud at or just above the earth's surface ‖ the condition of the atmosphere when visibility is less than 1,100 yds. ‖ (photog.) cloudiness or opaqueness obscuring a film or print **in a fog** bewildered, mentally at a loss 2. v. pres. part. **fog·ging** past and past part. **fogged** v.t. to cover or surround with fog ‖ to confuse or perplex (the mind) ‖ to cause (a matter for thought) to be obscure for lack of clear presentation ‖ (photog.) to cause (a film or print) to become cloudy

fog·gy (fógi:) comp. **fog·gi·er** superl. **fog·gi·est** adj. misty, thick with fog ‖ (photog.) fogged ‖ muddled, indistinct

foi·ble (fóib'l) n. an odd feature or mild failing in a person's character ‖ a fad ‖ (fencing) the weaker part of a sword blade, between the middle and the point

foil (foil) 1. n. a leaf or very thin sheet of metal, such as is used to protect packaged cigarettes or food against moisture ‖ a thin metallic coat, e.g. of silver, tin or tin amalgam, used as a mirror backing ‖ a thin polished leaf of metal, sometimes colored, placed under paste or inferior stones or clear enamels to increase brilliancy ‖ something that sets off or enhances something else, esp. a character in a play or novel who serves to bring out the qualities of another 2. v.t. to back or cover with foil

foil n. (fencing) a light, thin, blunt-edged sword with a button on its point to prevent injury

foil v.t. to frustrate (efforts etc.) or wreck (schemes etc.), by countering with guile ‖ to thwart (a person) in his designs ‖ (of animals) to cross over or run back on (their scent or trail) so as to throw off pursuit

foist (foist) v.t. to get rid of (something) by fraud or deception

fold (fould) 1. n. an enclosure, often of movable hurdles, to contain and protect sheep ‖ a flock of sheep ‖ (rhet.) the community of those who subscribe to some organized religious or pseudoreligious system 2. v.t. to enclose (sheep) in a fold ‖ to put sheep enclosed in this way on (land) to crop and manure it by sections

fold 1. v.t. to cause one part of (something) to lie on another ‖ to clasp around, embrace and draw close to one ‖ to reduce into a small space, by making folds in ‖ to cross and hold (the arms) close to the body ‖ to clasp (the hands) together in a relaxed way ‖ (of birds or aircraft) to bring (the wings) in close to the body ‖ (cooking) to work in to a mixture gently without stirring ‖ v.i. to be able to be folded ‖ (pop., esp. of a contest or enterprise) to fail, collapse 2. n. the arrangement or crease caused by folding ‖ a little undulation in a fabric ‖ (geol.) a bending back of strata

fold·er (fóuldər) n. a paper or cardboard holder for loose papers ‖ a folded printed leaflet ‖ a paper-folding machine

fold·ing (fóuldiŋ) 1. n. (geol.) a bending of rock strata, caused by compression of the earth's crust 2. adj. designed to fold away or fold into a compact shape

fo·li·age (fóuli:idʒ) n. the leaves of a plant or tree ‖ sprays of leaves

folk (fouk) 1. pl. **folk, folks** n. people as belonging to a class ‖ the great mass of common people that make up a nation, produce its unsophisticated art and continue its traditions ‖ (pl., Am. **folks**) relatives 2. adj. used by or springing from the mass of common people as distinguished from the individual or the few, *folk art*

folk·lore (fóuklɔr, fóuklour) n. the stories, sayings, local customs, songs, dances etc., handed down from generation to generation among the unsophisticated members of a race or nation ‖ the science and study of these

fol·li·cle (fólik'l) n. (bot.) a dry, one-celled, monocarpellary fruit with several seeds dehiscing along a ventral suture only (e.g. peony, larkspur) ‖ (anat.) a small cavity, e.g. that in which a hair root grows **fol·lic·u·lar** (fəlíkjulər), **fol·lic·u·late** (fəlíkjulit), **fol·lic·u·lat·ed** adjs

fol·low (fólou) 1. v.t. to go or come after ‖ to go in pursuit of ‖ to succeed in order of time ‖ to succeed (someone) in a position ‖ to result from, be a necessary consequence of ‖ to proceed along ‖ to imitate ‖ to act in accordance with ‖ to accept as an authority or guide ‖ to pay attention to, watch ‖ to take an interest in and make a study of ‖ to understand ‖ (oldfash.) to practice (a profession) ‖ v.i. to come or go after a person or thing in time, sequence or place ‖ to occur as a consequence ‖ to pay attention so as to understand ‖ as is about to be said 2. n. (billiards) a stroke in which the player hits his ball above center so that it continues to roll on after hitting the opponent's ball **fól·low·er** n. an adherent, disciple **fól·low·ing** 1. n. a group of adherents or disciples 2. adj. succeeding, next ‖ about to be mentioned ‖ moving in the same direction 3. prep. immediately after

fol·ly (fóli:) pl. **fol·lies** n. behavior arising from stupidity ‖ misguided behavior liable to end disastrously ‖ a foolish act or idea ‖ a lapse from moral rectitude ‖ (pl.) a light theatrical revue

fo·ment (foumént) v.t. to excite, foster or instigate (disorder, hatred, revolt) ‖ to treat with warm water or hot moist cloths **fo·men·tá·tion** n.

fond (fond) adj. affectionate, loving ‖ foolishly tender, indulgent ‖ foolishly cherished **to be fond of** to hold in affection ‖ to take pleasure in ‖ (with pres. part.) to have the habit of

fon·dle (fónd'l) pres. part. **fon·dling** past and past part. **fon·dled** v.t. to handle lovingly, caress ‖ v.i. (with 'with') to play amorously

fond·ly (fóndli:) adv. affectionately ‖ credulously

font (font) n. (printing) a complete set of types of a particular size and face

food (fu:d) n. any substance which, by a process of metabolism, a living organism can convert into fresh tissue, energy etc. ‖ a solid substance eaten for nourishment ‖ something which can be put to constructive use

fool (fu:l) 1. n. someone lacking common sense or judgment ‖ (hist.) a jester, a professional clown ‖ someone made to appear stupid 2. adj. (pop.) foolish, silly 3. v.i. to trifle, not be serious ‖ v.t. to deceive ‖ to cheat, trick ‖ to play stupidly or irresponsibly **fóol·er·y** n. foolish behavior

fool·har·dy (fú:lhɑrdi:) comp. **fool·har·di·er** superl. **fool·har·di·est** adj. fearless but taking thoughtless, unnecessary risks

fool·ish (fúːliʃ) *adj.* silly, ridiculous ‖ lacking in good sense, prudence or judgment or showing such a lack

fool·proof (fúːlpruːf) *adj.* absolutely safe against misinterpretation or misuse ‖ guaranteed never to go wrong

foot (fut) **1.** *pl.* **feet** (fiːt) *n.* the part at the end of the leg usually below the ankle joint on which vertebrates stand or walk ‖ any of various organs of locomotion in invertebrates ‖ a step, tread ‖ the lowest part ‖ a base ‖ the low end of a leg of a piece of furniture ‖ the end of a bed etc. furthest from the head ‖ a unit of length used in English-speaking countries equal to 12 ins, one-third of the standard yard ‖ *(printing)* the lowest part of the body of a type on either side of the groove ‖ that part of a sewing machine which keeps the cloth steady ‖ *(poetry)* a group of measured syllables constituting a metrical unit **on foot** walking (as distinct from using transportation) **2.** *v.t.* to make or renew a foot for (a stocking or sock) **fóot·age** *n.* length in feet ‖ *(movies)* the total length of a film ‖ frontage

foot·ball (fútbɔl) *n.* any of various team games played with a ball (round or elliptical according to the game played) **fóot·ball·er** *n.* someone who plays football or *(Br.)* soccer

foot·hold (fúthould) *n.* a place to put one's foot where it will bear one's weight when climbing ‖ an initial position of advantage

foot·ing (fútiŋ) *n.* a firm placing of the feet ‖ a secure place to stand on ‖ a basis of organization ‖ a social relationship ‖ *(archit.)* a projecting course at the lower end of a wall, column etc. used for distributing the load

foot·note (fútnout) **1.** *n.* a note at the bottom of a printed page to elucidate a minor point raised in the text without burdening the narrative, or to give a reference **2.** *v.t. pres. part.* **foot·not·ing** *past* and *past part.* **foot·not·ed** to add a footnote to

foot·print (fútprint) *n.* a mark made by the foot

foot·step (fútstep) *n.* a footfall ‖ a footprint

fop (fɔp) *n.* a man excessively interested in his dress **fóp·per·y** *pl.* **fop·per·ies** *n.* **fóp·pish** *adj.*

for (fɔr) **1.** *prep.* as a representative of, on behalf of ‖ in honor of ‖ in support of, in favor of ‖ with the purpose of ‖ with the aim of going to ‖ for the benefit of ‖ given over to ‖ destined to (a specific person or thing) ‖ to allow of ‖ (of feelings or capacities) towards ‖ in its or their effect on ‖ as being ‖ in place of ‖ considering the usual nature of ‖ in spite of ‖ as the effect of ‖ as a result of ‖ to set against ‖ to the amount ‖ at the amount of ‖ to the extent or duration of ‖ at (a certain time) ‖ regarding ‖ in order to have, get etc. ‖ because of **for all that** nevertheless **for oneself** without help ‖ for one's own benefit **2.** *conj.* (used to introduce an explanation or proof of something previously stated) because, since, seeing that

for·age (fɔ́ridʒ, fɔ́ridʒ) **1.** *n.* food for horses and cattle ‖ the act of foraging, a hunt for provisions **2.** *v. pres. part.* **for·ag·ing** *past* and *past part.* **for·aged** *v.t.* to collect forage from ‖ to supply with forage ‖ to get by making a forage ‖ *v.i.* to go out in search of forage ‖ to search

for·ay (fɔ́rei, fɔrei) **1.** *n.* a raid to get food, capture booty, or just pillage **2.** *v.i.* to make a raid, pillage

for·bear (fɔrbéər) *pres. part.* **for·bear·ing** *past* **for·bore** (fɔrbɔ́r, fɔrbóur) *past. part.* **for·borne** (fɔrbɔ́rn, fɔrbóurn) *v.i.* to control one's patience, not give way to anger ‖ to abstain ‖ *v.t.* to refrain from (using, doing etc.) **for·béar·ance** *n.*

for·bid (fɔrbíd, fɔrbíd) *pres. part.* **for·bid·ding** *past* **for·bade** (fɔrbéid), **for·bad** (fɔrbǽd, fɔrbǽd) *past. part.* **for·bid·den** (fɔrbíd'n, fɔrbíd'n) *v.t.* to command (someone) not to do something ‖ to put an interdiction against (something) ‖ to put (a place) out of bounds ‖ to make impossible, prevent **for·bíd·dance** *n.* **for·bíd·ding** *adj.* frighteningly difficult ‖ angry, *forbidding looks* ‖ unlovely, *a forbidding country* ‖ lowering, *forbidding cliffs* **for·bíd·den** *adj.*

force (fɔrs, fours) **1.** *n.* the exertion of physical strength ‖ physical vigor ‖ mental or moral strength, esp. in the overcoming of opposition ‖ the capacity to convince, influence or affect ‖ *(law)* violence exerted on a person or thing ‖ *(phys.)* any influence or agency that produces a change in the velocity of an inelastic object, whether it be in speed or direction ‖ *(esp. pl.)* an organized body of men, troops, warships, etc. **by force** by using force or by being forced **in force** required by law or regulation ‖ in large numbers **to come into force** to become required by law or regulation **2.** *v.t. pres. part.* **forc·ing** *past* and *past part.* **forced** to compel by using physical or moral strength ‖ to produce with difficulty ‖ to cause to open by using physical strength ‖ to drive or impel against physical resistance ‖ *(cards)* to compel (a player) to use a trump card, or to play a particular card, or to reveal by his play the strength of his hand ‖ *(baseball)* to put out (a man on base) by compelling him to make room for another runner ‖ *(baseball,* of a pitcher) to allow (a run) to be scored when the bases are full by giving a base on balls which automatically brings home the player on third base ‖ *(hort.)* to hasten the growth of (plants etc.) by artificial means **forced** (fɔrst, fourst) *adj.* compelled by force ‖ opened by force ‖ insincere

force·ful (fɔ́rsfəl, fóursfəl) *adj.* forcible

for·ceps (fɔ́rseps) *pl.* **for·ceps** *n.* a two-pronged instrument, esp. surgical and obstetrical pincers ‖ *(anat.)* a limb shaped like a forceps

for·ci·ble (fɔ́rsəb'l, fóursəb'l) *adj.* made or done by using force, *a forcible entry* ‖ convincing, impressive, powerful, *a forcible argument* **fór·ci·bly** *adv.*

ford (fɔrd, fourd) **1.** *n.* a place where a river is shallow and can be crossed by wading **2.** *v.t.* to cross by wading

fore (fɔr, four) **1.** *n.* the bows of a ship **at the fore** *(naut.)* on the foremast masthead **to the fore** (of personalities) in the public eye, conspicuous ‖ *(of money)* ready and available **2.** *adj.* placed in front, forward, advanced **3.** *adv. (naut.)* in or towards the bows

fore- (fɔr, four) *prefix* in front, beforehand, in advance ‖ anticipatory

fore·arm (fɔrárm, fourárm) *n.* to arm in advance

fore·arm (fɔ́rɑrm, fóurɑrm) *n.* the part of the arm between the elbow and the wrist

fore·bode (fɔrbóud, fourbóud) *pres. part.* **fore·bod·ing** *past* and *past part.* **fore·bod·ed** *v.t.* to betoken, portend (usually evil or trouble) ‖ to have a presentiment of (disaster etc.) **fore·bód·ing** *n.* a sign of something to come ‖ a presentiment, esp. of evil

fore·cast (fɔ́rkæst, fóurkæst, fɔ́rkɑst, fóurkɑst) **1.** *v.t. pres. part.* **fore·cast·ing** *past* and *past part.* **fore·cast,** **fore·cast·ed** to predict on the basis of scientific observation and applied experience (e.g. in meteorology), or by simple estimate of probability **2.** *n.* something predicted

fore·close (fɔrklóuz, fourklóuz) *pres. part.* **fore·clos·ing** *past* and *past part.* **fore·closed** *v.t. (mortgage law)* to deprive (a person) of the equity of redemption for nonpayment of money due ‖ to bar, remove (the right of redemption) ‖ *v.i.* to take away the right to redeem a mortgage **fore·clos·ure** (fɔrklóuʒər, fourklóuʒər) *n.*

fore·fath·er (fɔ́rfɑðər, fóurfɑðər) *n.* (esp. *pl.*) an ancestor, esp. a remote ancestor

fore·fin·ger (fɔ́rfiŋgər, fóurfiŋgər) *n.* the finger next to the thumb

fore·go·ing (fɔrgóuiŋ, fourgóuiŋ) *adj.* mentioned above

foregone conclusion a result that could be foreseen ‖ a decision reached before a matter could be properly considered

fore·ground (fɔ́rgraund, fóurgraund) *n.* the part of a scene nearest the viewer ‖ the most noticeable position

fore·hand (fɔ́rhænd, fóurhænd) **1.** *adj. (racket games,* of a stroke) made with the palm of the hand turned in the direction of the stroke (opp. BACKHAND) **2.** *adv.* with a forehand stroke **3.** *n. (tennis* etc.) a forehand stroke or the capacity to play forehand strokes ‖ the part of a horse in front of a rider

fore·head (fɔ́rid, fɔ́rid, fɔ́rhẹd, fɔ́rhẹd) *n.* the front of the vertebrate head, in man above the eyebrows to where the hair begins to grow

fore·eign (fɔ́rin, fɔ́rin) *adj.* not of one's own country or race ‖ coming from or typical of some country outside one's own ‖ having to do with other countries ‖ relating to or coming from a district, province or society other than one's own ‖ introduced from outside ‖ outside one's knowledge ‖ unrelated, extraneous ‖ *(law)* outside the jurisdiction of the governmental unit in question

fore·eign·er (fɔ́rinər, fɔ́rinər) *n.* someone whose nationality is other than one's own ‖ a ship from another country

fore·man (fɔ́rmən, fóurmən) *pl.* **fore·men** (fɔ́rmən, fóurmən) *n.* someone who supervises other workmen ‖ a member of a jury who acts as leader and spokesman

fore·most (fɔ́rmoust, fóurmoust) **1.** *adj.* first of several in place or time, rank or status **2.** *adv.* first ‖ most importantly

fore·noon (fɔ́rnṵːn, fóurnṵːn) *n.* the part of the day from dawn until midday, or between breakfast and lunch

fo·ren·sic (fərénsik) **1.** *adj.* relating to law courts or to public debate **2.** *n.* an oral or written argumentative exercise, e.g. in the teaching of rhetoric **fo·ren·si·cal·ly** *adv.*

fore·run (fɔrrʌ́n, fourrʌ́n) *pres. part.* **fore·run·ning** *past* **fore·ran** (fɔrrǽn, fourrǽn) *past part.* **fore·run** *v.t.* to be the precursor of, to come before as a token of what is to follow **fóre·run·ner** *n.* a precursor ‖ a predecessor

fore·see (fɔrsíː, foursíː) *pres. part.* **fore·see·ing** *past* **fore·saw** (fɔrsɔ́, foursɔ́) *past part.* **fore·seen** (fɔrsíːn, foursíːn) *v.t.* to have a vision of (a future event), e.g. in a dream ‖ to arrive at a reasonable estimate of (what is probable), esp. with a view to taking measures in advance **fore·sée·a·ble** *adj.* of what can be anticipated ‖ of the future that lies sufficiently close to allow forecasting

fore·sight (fɔ́rsait, fóursait) *n.* prophetic capacity, prevision ‖ provident care for the future ‖ the aiming device at the front of the barrel of a rifle etc. used in conjunction with the backsight **fóre·sight·ed** *adj.*

fore·skin (fɔ́rskịn) *n.* the fold of skin covering the end of the penis

for·est (fɔ́rist, fɔ́rist) **1.** *n.* a large area of land covered with trees and brush growing thickly ‖ the trees on such land ‖ something which, in its density, is like a forest of trees **2.** *v.t.* to cause to become forest

fore·stall (fɔrstɔ́l, fourstɔ́l) *v.t.* to frustrate the intentions of (someone) by acting before him ‖ to act in anticipation of (future circumstances or possibilities)

for·est·er (fɔ́ristər, fɔ́ristər) *n.* someone in charge of a forest ‖ that who plants and cares for forest trees

for·est·ry (fɔ́ristriː, fɔ́ristriː) *n.* the science of planting and tending forests ‖ *(rare)* forest land

fore·tell (fɔrtél, fourtél) *pres. part.* **fore·tell·ing** *past* and *past part.* **fore·told** (fɔrtóuld, fourtóuld) *v.t.* to announce (an event) before it happens

for·ev·er (fərévər, forévər) *adv.* eternally ‖ without a break or so often as to seem so

fore·word (fɔ́rwəːrd, fóurwəːrd) *n.* a preface

for·feit (fɔ́rfit) **1.** *n.* a fine for breach of contract or negligence ‖ a small fine for breaking the rules of a club etc. ‖ the act of forfeiting ‖ something forfeited ‖ *(pl.)* a game in which items taken from players are

recovered by the performance of imposed and often ridiculous or embarrassing tasks **2.** *adj.* lost or taken away as a forfeit **3.** *v.t.* to be deprived of as a penalty for a crime, fault, error etc. or as a necessary result or consequence, to surrender, lose

for·fei·ture (fɔ́rfitʃər) *n.* the act of forfeiting ‖ something forfeited

forge (fɔrdʒ) *n.* the workshop of a blacksmith, with its furnace, anvil and bellows ‖ the furnace itself, or the hearth used to shape wrought iron ‖ a workshop and furnace where metals are melted and refined

forge *pres. part.* **forg·ing** *past* and *past part.* **forged** *v.t.* to heat and hammer (metal) into shape ‖ to form or shape (something) by heating and hammering metal ‖ to imitate (something) and attempt to pass it off as genuine ‖ *v.i.* to commit forgery

forge *pres part.* **forg·ing** *past* and *past part.* **forged** *v.i.* to move forward with effort, esp. so as to secure an advance ‖ (with 'ahead') to make rapid progress ‖ (with 'ahead') to increase one's lead over others in a race rapidly

for·ger·y (fɔ́rdʒəriː, fóurdʒəriː) *pl.* **for·ger·ies** *n.* the act or art of forging or falsifying (documents, signatures etc.) ‖ something counterfeit

for·get (fərgét) *pres. part.* **for·get·ting** *past* **forgot** (fərgɔ́t) *past part.* **for·got·ten, for·got** *v.t.* to fail to keep in the memory ‖ to overlook unintentionally, neglect ‖ to leave behind unintentionally ‖ to stop thinking about ‖ *v.i.* to be apt to forget things ‖ to suffer a lapse of memory **for·gét·ful** *adj.* apt to forget

for·giv·a·ble, for·give·a·ble (fərgívəb'l) *adj.* that may be forgiven or pardoned **for·gív·a·bly** *adv.*

for·give (fərgív) *pres. part.* **for·giv·ing** *past* **for·gave** (fərgéiv) *past part.* **for·giv·en** (fərgívən) *v.t.* to excuse (a wrong or a wrongdoer) ‖ to pardon ‖ to remit or cancel (a debt) ‖ *v.i.* to show or grant forgiveness or pardon **for·give·a·ble** *adj.* **for·give·ness** *n.* a forgiving or being forgiven **for·giv·ing** *adj.* willing to forgive, *a forgiving spirit*

for·go, fore·go (fɔrgóu) *pres. part.* **for·go·ing, fore·go·ing** *past* **for·went, fore·went** (fərwént) *past part.* **for·gone, fore·gone** (fɔrgɔ́n, fɔrgɔ́n) *v.t.* to go without, renounce for oneself

fork (fɔrk) **1.** *n.* an agricultural implement consisting of two or more prongs on a long handle and used for digging, carrying, picking up or pitching ‖ a pronged instrument for handling food, in cooking, serving or eating ‖ the place where something divides, e.g. a road into two roads, a tree trunk into branches, or the crotch of the human body ‖ one of the branches into which a river, road, tree etc. is divided ‖ a sharp point (e.g. of an arrow) ‖ a support with two prongs ‖ *(mus.)* a tuning fork **2.** *v.i.* to divide or develop into branches ‖ to form into the shape of a fork ‖ to pick up or pitch with a fork ‖ *(pop.,* with 'out', 'over' or 'up') to pay **forked** *adj.* Y-shaped, cleft

for·lorn (fərlɔ́rn) *adj.* hopeless ‖ deserted, forsaken ‖ wretched-looking, pitiful

form (fɔrm) *n.* shape ‖ outward appearance apart from color, esp. the essential structure of a thing ‖ a person, animal or thing considered as a shape ‖ a variety, manifestation, example ‖ pattern ‖ the relationship of parts of a work of art in the organization of the whole ‖ a document with blank spaces for information to be written in ‖ that which gaves shape, a mold ‖ *(engin.)* a frame for holding assembled parts in place ‖ *(gram.)* one of the varieties of a word in spelling, pronunciation or inflection ‖ state of performance or training (physical or mental) ‖ behavior according to rule, custom, convention or etiquette ‖ a formula, prescribed order or layout of words, or established practice or ritual ‖ *(philos.)* the formative principle, nature or essence of a thing as distinguished from the matter it is composed of ‖ *(printing)* a body of type secured in a chase ‖ a hare's nest

form *v.t.* to make, shape ‖ to put together ‖ to mold by instruction or discipline ‖ to develop, *to form a habit* ‖ to conceive, *to form an idea* ‖ to organize into or become arranged as ‖ to constitute ‖ *(gram.)* to construct (a new word or a variant) by derivation etc. ‖ to assume the form of ‖ *v.i.* to arise, to take form ‖ *(esp. mil.)* to draw up, to assume formation

for·mal (fɔ́rməl) **1.** *adj.* of or pertaining to form, rule or ceremonial ‖ having form without spirit, perfunctory ‖ explicit, not merely understood ‖ *(philos.)* of the essence of a thing rather than its matter **2.** *n.* a social event for which one has to wear formal dress

for·mal·ism (fɔ́rməlizəm) *n.* strict adherence to prescribed forms, esp. in religion, art and literature **fór·mal·ist** *n.* someone characterized by formalism or who advocates formalism **for·mal·ís·tic** *adj.*

for·mal·i·ty (formǽliti) *pl.* **for·mal·i·ties** *n.* conformity or attention to rule, custom or etiquette ‖ *(esp. pl.)* an official or customary requirement, *customs formalities* ‖ a merely formal act ‖ the quality of being formal

for·mal·ize (fɔ́rməlaiz) *pres. part.* **for·mal·iz·ing** *past and past part.* **for·mal·ized** *v.t.* to put on a legal, official or regular basis ‖ *v.i.* to act with formality

for·mat (fɔ́rmæt) **1.** *n.* the linear measurements of a publication ‖ *(loosely)* the general typographical style and physical characteristics of a publication ‖ the general characteristics of organization of something, e.g. a radio program **2.** *v.* to produce in a special plan, size, shape, or proportion

for·ma·tion (forméiʃən) *n.* a forming or being formed ‖ that which has been formed ‖ *(geol.)* rock beds sufficiently homogeneous to be regarded as a unit in geological mapping ‖ the form in which something is arranged, e.g. the arrangement of wild ducks on the wing ‖ an arrangement of troops ‖ an arrangement of aircraft flying at small fixed intervals from one another

for·mer (fɔ́rmər) **1.** *adj.* earlier ‖ of the first or first mentioned of two ‖ having once held a certain post or office **2.** *pron.* the first or first-mentioned of two **fór·mer·ly** *adv.* at a time in the past

for·mi·da·ble (fɔ́rmidəb'l, formídəb'l) *adj.* likely to prove hard ‖ to be feared ‖ impressive **fór·mi·da·bly** *adv.*

form·less (fɔ́rmlis) *adj.* without shape, amorphous ‖ needing better arrangement ‖ incorporeal

for·mu·la (fɔ́rmjulə) *pl.* **for·mu·las, for·mu·lae** (fɔ́rmjuliː) *n.* *(chem.)* a symbolic representation of the composition, constitution or configuration of a substance ‖ *(logic, math.)* a statement expressed in symbols showing the relationships of interrelated facts ‖ a form of words defining a doctrine, principle etc. ‖ a verbal phrase or any set form accepted as conventional ‖ a form of words for ritual or ceremonial usage **for·mu·lar·i·za·tion** *n.* **fór·mu·lar·ize** *pres. part.* **for·mu·lar·iz·ing** *past and past part.* **for·mu·lar·ized** *v.t.*

for·mu·late (fɔ́rmjuleit) *pres. part.* **for·mu·lat·ing** *past and past part.* **for·mu·lat·ed** *v.t.* to express (a doctrine, problem etc.) in a clear or systematic way ‖ to express in a formula **for·mu·lá·tion** *n.* a formulating or being formulated ‖ an expression resulting from formulating

for·ni·cate (fɔ́rnikeit) *pres. part.* **for·ni·cat·ing** *past and past part.* **for·ni·cat·ed** *v.t.* to commit fornication

for·ni·ca·tion (fornikéiʃən) *n.* voluntary sexual intercourse between an unmarried man and an unmarried woman

for·sake (forséik) *pres. part.* **for·sak·ing** *past* **for·sook** (forsúk) *past part.* **for·sak·en** (forséikən) *v.t.* *(rhet.)* to desert, abandon ‖ *(old-fash.)* to break off from, give up (esp. bad habits) **for·sák·en** *adj.* deserted

fort (fort, fourt) *n.* a fortified place occupied only by troops ‖ *(hist.)* a fortified trading post

forth (forθ, fourθ) *adv.* out from concealment or as if from concealment **and so forth** and so on, et cetera **back and forth** backwards and forwards **from this (or that, which) time forth** from this (or that, which) time on

forth·com·ing (forθkʌ́miŋ, fourθkʌ́miŋ) *adj.* approaching ‖ shortly to appear ‖ made available when required, *the expected aid was not forthcoming*

forth·right (fɔ́rθrait, fóurθrait) *adj.* direct, frank, decisive

forth·with (fɔ́rθwiθ, fóurθwiθ, fɔ́rθwið, fóurθwið) *adv.* at once, immediately

for·ti·eth (fɔ́rtiːiθ) **1.** *adj.* being number 40 in a series (*NUMBER TABLE) ‖ being one of the 40 equal parts of anything **2.** *n.* the person or thing next after the 39th ‖ one of 40 equal parts of anything (1/40)

for·ti·fi·ca·tion (fortifikéiʃən) *n.* a fortifying or being fortified ‖ the science of fortifying ‖ something that fortifies ‖ *(mil., esp. pl.)* works constructed so as to fortify

for·ti·fy (fɔ́rtifai) *pres. part.* **for·ti·fy·ing** *past and past part.* **for·ti·fied** *v.t.* to strengthen structurally ‖ *(mil.)* to strengthen (a defensive position etc.) against attack ‖ to give moral strength to, encourage ‖ to add nutritive value to, enrich ‖ to strengthen (wine) with alcohol ‖ *v.i. (mil.)* to build fortifications

for·ti·tude (fɔ́rtituːd, fɔ́rtitjuːd) *n.* endurance or courage in the face of pain or adversity ‖ moral strength, one of the cardinal virtues

fort·night (fɔ́rtnait) *n.* *(esp. Br.)* a continuous period of two weeks **fórt·night·ly 1.** *adj.* occurring or appearing once every two weeks **2.** *adv.* once every two weeks **3.** *pl.* **fort·night·lies** *n.* a periodical issued at intervals of two weeks

for·tress (fɔ́rtris) *n.* a fortified place, military stronghold

for·tu·i·tous (fortúːitəs, fortjúːitəs) *adj.* happening by chance or accident **for·tú·i·ty** *pl.* **for·tu·i·ties** *n.* chance, accident ‖ a chance occurrence

for·tu·nate (fɔ́rtʃunit) *adj.* owing to good luck or receiving good luck, luck ‖ favorable

for·tune (fɔ́rtʃən) *n.* the power of chance in mankind's affairs ‖ an instance of how this affects someone ‖ personal wealth ‖ a large sum of money ‖ success in general ‖ destiny

for·ty (fɔ́rtiː) **1.** *adj.* being ten more than 30 (*NUMBER TABLE) **2.** *pl.* **for·ties** *n.* four times ten ‖ the cardinal number representing this (40, XL) **the forties** (of temperature, a person's age, a century, etc.) the span 40–9

fo·rum (fɔ́rəm, fóurəm) *pl.* **fo·rums, fo·ra** (fɔ́rə, fóurə) *n.* *(Rom. hist.)* the marketplace or public square of a city, a center of judicial and public business ‖ any place or institution where questions of public concern can be discussed or decided

for·ward (fɔ́rwərd) **1.** *adj.* toward the front ‖ *(of seasons)* early ‖ *(of growth)* advanced ‖ precociously developed ‖ showing substantial progress ‖ progressive, radical ‖ onward, advancing ‖ eager, prompt ‖ overbold in a too familiar way ‖ *(naut., fɔ́rəd)* of the front (bow) section of a ship ‖ *(commerce, of goods etc.)* not immediately available) of or for the future **2.** *adv.* towards the front, in the direction one is facing, ahead ‖ towards improvement or progress ‖ in advance ‖ into prominence, into view, to the attention of someone ‖ onward in time ‖ *(naut.)* at the forepart of a ship **3.** *n.* *(football, hockey* etc.) one of the players positioned near or towards the opponents' goal, having an attacking, scoring function **4.** *v.t.* to send (a letter etc.) to a further destination ‖ to convey, dispatch (goods etc.) ‖ to advance, promote ‖ *(bookbinding)* to trim, line and put (a sewn book) into its cover, ready for finishing **fór·ward·er** *n.* someone who forwards ‖ someone who receives goods for transportation and delivers them to the carrier for transmission to the proper destination

for·wards (fɔ́rwərdz) *adv.* (of a direction or movement) forward

fos·sil (fɔ́s'l) **1.** *n.* the recognizable remains, or an impression left by them, of a plant or animal of the remote, geological past, preserved in the earth's crust ‖ *(pop.)* someone or something out of date, esp. a person holding outworn opinions **2.** *adj.* of the nature of a fossil **fos·sil·á·tion** *n.* **fos·sil·íf·er·ous** *adj.* containing fossils, rich in fossils **fos·sil·i·zá·tion** *n.* **fós·sil·ize** *pres. part.* **fos·sil·iz·ing** *past* and *past part.* **fos·sil·ized** *v.t.* to make a fossil of ‖ *v.i.* to become a fossil ‖ to become set in outworn opinions

fos·ter (fóstər, fóstər) *v.t.* to rear ‖ to encourage, promote (ideas, feelings, plants etc.) ‖ to harbor, nurse (ambitions etc.) in oneself

foul (faul) *v.t.* to make foul ‖ to pollute ‖ to bring dishonor on ‖ to block or choke with foreign matter ‖ to jam (e.g. a road crossing) ‖ to tangle ‖ to come into collision with ‖ *(baseball)* to bat (a ball) outside the foul lines ‖ *v.i.* to become foul ‖ to become entangled ‖ to collide ‖ *(sports)* to commit a foul

foul 1. *adj.* extremely offensive to the senses, dirty, disgusting, stinking ‖ polluted with noxious matter ‖ (of a gun barrel, ship's bottom etc.) clogged up or covered with foreign matter ‖ entangled ‖ in collision ‖ indecent or profane, *foul language* ‖ obnoxious, unpleasant ‖ morally repulsive, evil ‖ *(sports)* contrary to the rules of the game ‖ *(baseball)* outside the foul lines ‖ (of weather) stormy ‖ (of wind or tide) contrary ‖ defaced by alterations **2.** *n.* a collision esp. of boats ‖ an entanglement ‖ *(sports)* an act forbidden by the rules ‖ *(baseball)* a foul ball

found (faund) *v.t.* to originate ‖ to establish (an institution) by endowment ‖ to begin the building of ‖ (with 'on' or 'upon') to base

foun·da·tion (faundéiʃən) *n.* a founding or being founded ‖ the solid base, either natural or prepared from concrete etc. on which a building is raised ‖ the lowest courses of a wall, building etc., usually underground ‖ the establishment and endowment of an institution ‖ an endowed institution or endowed charity or fund ‖ a basis, esp. a basis of truthfulness ‖ an underlying principle ‖ the body or ground material on which something is overlaid, e.g. material to stiffen a dress ‖ a foundation garment ‖ a liquid or cream cosmetic used as the base for makeup

found·er (fáundər) *n.* someone who founded or helped to found an institution

founder 1. *v.i.* (of a building etc.) to fall down, collapse ‖ to go lame, stumble ‖ to sink or stick fast in soft ground ‖ to fail, esp. financially ‖ (of a ship) to become filled with water and sink ‖ (of a horse) to have founder ‖ *v.t.* to cause to founder ‖ *(vet.)* to cause (a horse) to become afflicted with founder **2.** *n.* inflammation of sensitive tissue in a horse's hoof

found·ling (fáundliŋ) *n.* an abandoned infant

found·ry (fáundri:) *pl.* **found·ries** *n.* a building where metal or glass is founded ‖ the art or process of casting metals ‖ metal castings

fount (faunt) *n.* *(rhet.)* a source, spring or fountain

foun·tain (fáuntən) *n.* a water spring ‖ the source or head of a stream etc. ‖ a contrived ornamental jet of water, e.g. in a courtyard, garden or public square ‖ a jet of drinking water, e.g. in a park or station ‖ the structure containing a jet of water ‖ a soda fountain

four (fɔr, four) **1.** *adj.* being one more than three (*NUMBER TABLE) **2.** *n.* twice two ‖ the cardinal number representing this (4, IV) ‖ four o'clock **on all fours** with hands and knees on the ground

four-di·men·sion·al (fɔrdiménʃən'l, fourdiménʃən'l) *adj.* having four dimensions

four·score (fórskór, fóurskóur) *adj.* (*old-fash.*) eighty

four·some (fórsəm, fóursəm) *n.* *(golf)* a game between two pairs of players, each pair sharing a ball ‖ *(pop.)* a group of four persons

four·teen (fɔrtíːn, fóurtíːn) **1.** *adj.* being one more than 13 (*NUMBER TABLE) **2.** *n.* 10 plus four ‖ the cardinal number representing this (14, XIV)

four·teenth (fɔrtíːnθ, fóurtíːnθ) **1.** *adj.* being number 14 in a series (*NUMBER TABLE) ‖ being one of the 14 equal parts of anything **2.** *n.* the person or thing next after the 13th ‖ one of 14 equal parts of anything (1/14) ‖ the 14th day of a month

fourth (fɔrθ, fourθ) **1.** *adj.* being number four in a series (*NUMBER TABLE) ‖ being one of the four equal parts of anything ‖ of or pertaining to the gear immediately above third in some vehicles **2.** *n.* the person or thing next after the third ‖ a quarter, a fourth part ($^1/_4$) ‖ *(mus.)* the note four steps above or below a given note in a diatonic scale, inclusive of both notes ‖ *(mus.)* the interval between these notes ‖ *(mus.)* a combination of these notes **3.** *adv.* in the fourth place ‖ (followed by a superlative) except three, *the fourth biggest*

fowl (faul) **1.** *pl.* **fowl, fowls** *n.* a domestic cock, hen, duck or turkey **2.** *v.i.* to hunt wildfowl

fox (fɒks) **1.** *pl.* **fox·es, fox** *n.* a mammal of fam. *Canidae*, esp. genus *Vulpes*. They are carnivores, closely related to dogs, but with a more elongated body ‖ the fur of this animal ‖ someone cunning or full of guile **2.** *v.t.* *(pop.)* to trick, baffle ‖ to discolor, stain (manuscripts, prints, leaves of a book) with specks of brown, esp. through dampness ‖ to renew (the upper leather of a shoe) ‖ *v.i.* (of papers, book leaves etc.) to become discolored

fox terrier a small, lively wirehaired or smooth-haired breed of dog

fox·y (fóksi:) *comp.* **fox·i·er** *superl.* **fox·i·est** *adj.* foxlike, full of guile, wily in ways or looks ‖ *(sexist slang)* sexy, as describing a woman

fra·cas (fréikəs) *pl.* **fra·cas·es** (frǽkɑz) *n.* a noisy disturbance, brawl, row

frac·tion (frǽkʃən) **1.** *n.* a very small proportion ‖ an amount less than the whole, a part ‖ *(math.)* a noninteger quantity expressed in terms of a numerator and a denominator (e.g. 3/4) or in decimal form (e.g. 0.75)) ‖ *(chem.)* a part of a component that may be separated by fractionation **2.** *v.t.* to separate into fractions **frác·tion·al** *adj.* *(math.)* pertaining to fractions, *a fractional expression* ‖ of that which is a fraction, esp. a small fraction, *a fractional risk of failure* ‖ *(chem.)* of any process of fractionation, *fractional distillation of petroleum* **frac·tion·ate** (frǽkʃəneit) *pres. part.* **frac·tion·at·ing** *past* and *past part.* **frac·tion·at·ed** *v.t.* to separate (a mixture or substance) into smaller portions having different properties by distillation, precipitation etc. **frac·tion·á·tion** *n.* **frác·tion·ize** *pres. part.* **frac·tion·iz·ing** *past* and *past part.* **frac·tion·ized** *v.t.* to divide into fractions

frac·tious (frǽkʃəs) *adj.* with frequent outbreaks of temper, peevish, unruly

frac·ture (frǽktʃər) **1.** *n.* a breaking or being broken ‖ a break in a bone or cartilage ‖ *(geol.)* the surface revealed in a stone sample broken along other than cleavage planes **2.** *v. pres. part.* **frac·tur·ing** *past* and *past part.* **frac·tured** *v.t.* to break ‖ *v.i.* to be liable to break ‖ to become broken

frag·ile (frǽdʒəl, *Br.* frǽdʒail) *adj.* easily broken or damaged ‖ (of health) delicate **fra·gil·i·ty** (frədʒíliti:) *n.*

frag·ment (frǽgmənt) *n.* a piece broken off from the whole ‖ an incomplete or isolated part ‖ the existing part of something unfinished or incomplete, esp. of a writing or work of art **frag·men·tal** (frǽgmént'l) *adj.* fragmentary ‖ *(geol.)* clastic **frag·men·tar·y** (frǽgmənteri:) *adj.* composed of broken parts ‖ dissociated, broken up **frag·men·tá·tion** *n.* a breaking into fragments

fra·grance (fréigrəns) *n.* sweetness of scent ‖ a sweet scent

fra·grant (fréigrənt) *adj.* having a delicious smell ‖ (*rhet.*, of the past) delectable

frail (freil) *adj.* easily broken, fragile ‖ feeble, *frail arguments* ‖ morally weak

frail·ty (fréilti:) *pl.* **frail·ties** *n.* moral weakness ‖ an example of this, a shortcoming

frame (freim) **1.** *n.* an arrangement of parts fitted together, holding something in place or keeping the form of something unchanged ‖ an ideal or established order ‖ the build of a person ‖ a cold frame ‖ a single exposure in the run of exposures of a film or filmstrip ‖ (*television*) one isolated image in the succession of images transmitted ‖ a border of wood or other material put around a picture or mirror ‖ the basic unit of programmed instruction for a student ‖ a punch position or recording on a tape, etc. ‖ (*embroidery*) an adjustable structure for keeping work taut ‖ (*pool, snooker*) a triangular form used in setting up the balls ‖ (*bowling*) the period of play from when the pins have been set up to when they are set up again ‖ (*beekeeping*) a structure put in the hive for the bees to build their honeycombs in **2.** *v.t. pres. part.* **fram·ing** *past* and *past part.* **framed** to surround with a frame, or as if with one ‖ to assemble (ideas etc.) in an orderly way ‖ to devise ‖ to make a structure for ‖ (*pop.*) to place (someone) in an incriminating position by falsifying the evidence ‖ (*movies*) to bring (an image) into register with the projector aperture

frame·work (fréimwə:rk) *n.* a basic structure which supports and gives shape, or a broad outline plan etc. thought of as having a similar function

fran·chise (frǽntʃaiz) *n.* (with 'the') full rights of citizenship, esp. the right to vote in public elections ‖ a privilege or right usually granted by a government charter to a person or company, to exercise an exclusive service or office, or to form a company to do this ‖ the jurisdiction over which a franchise extends

frank (fræŋk) *adj.* without guile, open ‖ stating unwelcome facts or giving critical opinions without trying to soften their impact ‖ undisguised

frank 1. *v.t.* to send (mail) free of charge ‖ to mark (mail) for free delivery **2.** *n.* a mark or sign indicating that mail is to be sent free ‖ the right to send mail free ‖ a letter etc. sent free

frank·furt·er, frank·fort·er (frǽŋkfərtər) *n.* a smoked beef, or beef and pork, sausage

fran·tic (frǽntik) *adj.* nearly mad with anger, pain, grief, fear etc. or suggesting such near-madness **frán·ti·cal·ly** *adv.*

fra·ter·nal (frətə́:rn'l) *adj.* of a brother or brothers ‖ brotherly ‖ (*biol.*) designating twins from two ova ‖ (*Am.*) of or relating to a fraternity **fra·tér·nal·ism** *n.*

fra·ter·ni·ty (frətə́:rniti:) *pl.* **fra·ter·ni·ties** *n.* the state of being brothers ‖ brotherliness ‖ men with common professional interests ‖ a religious brotherhood ‖ (in U.S. colleges) a private, usually residential, social club of male students

frat·er·ni·za·tion (frætərnizéiʃən) *n.* a fraternizing

frat·er·nize (frǽtərnaiz) *pres. part.* **frat·er·niz·ing** *past* and *past part.* **frat·er·nized** *v.i.* to be friendly ‖ to behave as friends ‖ (of occupying troops) to be intimate with civilians in the country occupied

fraud (frɔd) *n.* the use of deception for unlawful gain or unjust advantage ‖ something that constitutes a criminal deception ‖ someone who is not what he pretends he is

fraud·u·lence (frɔ́dʒuləns) *n.* the quality or state of being fraudulent

fraud·u·lent (frɔ́dʒulənt) *adj.* characterized by fraud, *a fraudulent claim* ‖ obtained by fraud

fraught (frɔt) *adj.* (with 'with') filled with ‖ (with 'with') involving or potentially filled with

fray (frei) *n.* (*rhet.*) a fight, brawl

fray *v.t.* to break threads in (part of a garment, esp. sleeves, collar or elbows) by hard wear ‖ to cause the threads in (a rope or the edge of material) to separate instead of remaining close ‖ to strain (the nerves, temper etc.) almost to breaking point ‖ *v.i.* to become frayed ‖ (of deer) to rub the velvet off new horns against trees

freak (fri:k) *n.* a person or animal malformed in a way which makes him or it an object of curiosity ‖ (*pop.*) an eccentric person ‖ an inexplicable act or happening ‖ combining suffix meaning 'addicted to,'' e.g., drug freak, old-book freak ‖ a sudden, capricious notion, whim **2.** *adj.* occurring as a freak **fréak·ish** *adj.*

freck·le (frék'l) **1.** *n.* a small brownish fleck in the skin caused by exposure to sunlight or ultraviolet light **2.** *v.t. pres. part.* **freck·ling** *past* and *past part.* **freck·led** to cover or mark with freckles ‖ *v.i.* to become covered or marked with freckles **fréck·ly** *adj.* covered with freckles

free (fri:) **1.** *adj.* not subject to external constraints or domination ‖ not captive, at liberty ‖ able to moove, loose ‖ not having to be paid for ‖ (with 'from') clear of (a specified condition) ‖ not busy, without prior engagements ‖ not reserved or occupied ‖ not being used ‖ without trade or tariff restrictions ‖ unhampered ‖ able to act and choose for oneself, *a free agent* ‖ spontaneous, voluntary ‖ generous, profuse ‖ unrestrained from the point of view of manners and morality ‖ unconstrained by convention ‖ not literal, not wholly faithful to the original ‖ open to all without restrictions ‖ unimpeded ‖ not fastened ‖ (*chem.*) not combined ‖ (of power, energy) available ‖ (*naut.*, of a wind) blowing from a direction more than six points from straight ahead **2.** *adv.* without expense ‖ without penalty ‖ (*naut.*) with the wind blowing more than six points from straight ahead **3.** *v.t.* to release from constraint, set free ‖ to disengage, *to free one's hands* ‖ to relieve

free·dom (frí:dəm) *n.* enjoyment of personal liberty, of not being a slave nor a prisoner ‖ the enjoyment of civil rights (freedom of speech, freedom of assembly etc.) generally associated with constitutional government ‖ the state of not being subject to determining forces ‖ liberty in acting and choosing ‖ immunity to or release from obligations, undesirable states of being etc. ‖ ability to move with ease ‖ excessive familiarity ‖ unrestricted use or enjoyment ‖ (with 'from') an absence of ‖ (in the arts) spontaneity unfettered by rules and conventions

free-for-all (frí:fərɔl) *n.* a fight without rules in which any number of people join or become involved

freeze (fri:z) **1.** *v. pres. part.* **freez·ing** *past* **froze** (frouz) *past part.* **fro·zen** (fróuz'n) *v.i.* to change from a liquid to a solid by heat loss, esp. to turn into ice ‖ to be cold enough to turn water into ice ‖ to have the contents turned to ice ‖ to suffer intense cold ‖ to die by frost ‖ to become rigid as a result of shock or fright ‖ to try to avoid being seen, heard etc. by becoming rigid and silent ‖ (with 'to') to become fixed to by freezing or become as though fixed in this way ‖ *v.t.* to form ice in or on ‖ to preserve (meat, fruit, vegetables, fish etc.) by refrigeration below freezing point ‖ to anesthetize (a part of the body) by artificial freezing ‖ to fix (a price, wage etc.) unchangeably until further authorized adjustment ‖ (*finance*) to immobilize (assets) by governmental authority, prohibiting exchange, wighdrawal or expenditure within the country where the assets are **2.** *n.* a freezing or being frozen ‖ a cessation of changes, usu. in economic factors, e.g., a job freeze, a wage freeze ‖ a period of freezing ‖ financial, legislative or administrative action intended to have an immobilizing effect **fréez·er** *n.* a machine for freezing ice cream ‖ the part of a refrigerator in which the temperature is below freezing point ‖ a refrigerated room or compartment for quick-freezing perishable food

freight (freit) **1.** *n.* the hire of a ship for transporting goods || the transporting of goods by ship, or by other means of transport, esp. ordinary transport service by common carrier, charged at a lower rate than express, and taking longer || a charge for transporting goods, **freightage** || a shipload, cargo or a load transported by other means || a train carrying goods **2.** *adj.* carrying goods rather than passengers, *a freight plane* **3.** *v.t.* to load (a ship) with cargo || to load (other transport) with goods for transporting || to transport by freight **freight·age** *n.* the charge for the transportation of goods || transportation of goods || cargo

freight·er (fréitər) *n.* a ship which carries cargo || anyone concerned in the transportation of goods by freight || someone who loads a ship || someone who receives and forwards goods || a freight-carrying aircraft

fre·net·ic, phre·net·ic (frinétik) *adj.* frenzied, frantic

fren·zy (frénzi) *pl.* **fren·zies** *n.* a state of tense emotional excitement or mental disturbance close to madness || *(pop.)* intense activity || a hectic rush

fre·quen·cy (frí:kwənsi:) *pl.* **fre·quen·cies** *n.* the quality or condition of occurring repeatedly || the number of times a periodic phenomenon or process occurs in a unit of time, e.g. the number of alternations (cycles) per second of an alternating electric current or the number of vibrations of a pendulum per minute || the number of objects falling into a single class in a statistical survey of the variation of specified characteristics

fre·quent (frí:kwənt) *adj.* occurring often || in close proximity || habitual

fre·quent (fri:kwént, frí:kwənt) *v.t.* to resort habitually to, go often to **fre·quen·ta·tion** *n.*

fre·quen·ta·tive (frikwéntətiv) **1.** *adj.* (gram.) expressing by its form frequent repetition or intensification of an action **2.** *n.* (gram.) a frequentative verb || (gram.) a frequentative verb || (gram.) frequentative aspect

fres·co (fréskou) **1.** *pl.* **fres·coes, fres·cos** *n.* a method of painting pictures on plaster, usually on a wall or ceiling, by laying on the color before the plaster is dry || a picture painted by this method **2.** *v.t.* to paint (a wall etc. or a subject) in this medium

fresh (freʃ) **1.** *adj.* just picked, gathered, made etc. || not salted || not salted, cured or preserved in any way || (of water) not salt || brisk and cold, refreshing || (of the wind) fairly strong, of more than breeze force || not tired, in full vigor || not soiled || further || new, different || opening up a new field of experience || having full youthful bloom || healthy-looking || (with 'from') just come || too familiar, impertinent **2.** *adv.* freshly, quite recently **3.** *n.* a stream of fresh water, a freshet || the part of a tidal river just above the flow of salt water **fresh·en** *v.t.* to make fresh || *(naut.)* to relieve (a rope) of strain by changing its position || (with 'up') to make (oneself) clean and neat and get rid of strain and fatigue by washing, changing one's clothes etc. || to remove saltiness from (salted meat, fish etc.) the soaking or parboiling || *v.i.* to become fresh || (with 'up') to freshen oneself up

fresh·man (fréʃmən) *pl.* **fresh·men** (fréʃmən) *n.* a student in his first year at a university or college || a student in the first year of a four-year high school

fret (fret) **1.** *v. pres. part.* **fret·ting** *past* and *past part.* **fret·ted** *v.i.* to be in a state of anxiety, vexation or discontent || to become chafed or rubbed || *v.t.* to cause to be in a state of anxiety, vexation or discontent || to wear away, chafe, rub || to make uneven, ruffle || to make (a hole, channel etc.) by wearing away **2.** *n.* a state of anxiety, vexation or discontent || erosion or an instance of it **fret·ful** *adj.* inclined to

fret, e.g. from vexation or illness

fri·a·bil·i·ty (fraiəbíliti:) *n.* the state or quality of being friable

fri·a·ble (fráiəb'l) *adj.* (of soil etc.) easily crumbled, apt to crumble

fric·as·see (frikəsí:) **1.** *n.* a dish of meat, poultry or game cut up and cooked in a sauce **2.** *v.t.* to cook (meat etc.) in this way

fric·tion (fríkʃən) *n.* (mech.) the force which opposes the movement of one surface sliding or rolling over another with which it is in contact || the act of rubbing the surface of the body, e.g. with a lotion to stimulate the skin after shaving || emotional opposition to the acts or behavior of another person, discord between individuals or within a group **fric·tion·al** *adj.*

Fri·day (fráidi:, fráidei) *n.* the sixth day of the week

friend (frend) *n.* someone on terms of affection and regard for another who is neither relative nor lover || someone who freely supports and helps out of good will || an acquaintance || an ally

friend·li·ness (fréndli:nis) *n.* the quality or state of being friendly

friend·ly (fréndli:) **1.** *adj. comp.* **friend·li·er** *superl.* **friend·li·est** showing interest and good will, amiable || manifesting kindness || sympathetic || not hostile || (rhet.) causing feelings of well-being and good will, welcoming || (of a game) played for the sport and not as part of a competition or for a prize || (of a legal action) brought merely to get a legal decision **2.** *adv.* amicably

friend·ship (fréndʃip) *n.* a relationship of mutual affection and good will || the state of being a friend or of being friends || harmonious cooperation

frieze (fri:z) *n.* an ornamental band, e.g. along the top of a wall || (archit.) that part of the entablature of a building between the architrave and the cornice, usually decorated with sculpture, or the band of sculpture itself || the decorative border of a wallpaper below the ceiling or cornice

fright (frait) *n.* a sudden shock of fear or alarm, a feeling of sudden terror || a grotesque-looking object or person **fright·en** *v.t.* to cause to feel fear || to make loath to run the risk of **fright·ful** *adj.* causing horror || causing anxiety || (pop.) provoking ridicule || (pop.) very bad || (pop.) extreme, intense **fright·ful·ly** *adv.* in a frightful way || (pop.) very, extremely

frig·id (frídʒid) *adj.* extremely cold || forbidding, *a frigid silence* || marked by a chilling formality || of a person not being able to achieve orgasm in sexual intercourse

fri·gid·i·ty (fridʒíditi:) *n.* the quality or state of being frigid, esp. a person's lack of sexual desire or inability to achieve orgasm

frill (fril) **1.** *n.* an ornamental edging used to trim clothes, curtains etc., formed by gathering the inner edge and leaving the outer edge loose || a similar decoration made with paper to ornament e.g. the knucklebone of a ham || (pl.) superficial embellishments || (biol.) a natural ruff of feathers, fur or membrane **2.** *v.t.* to ornament with a frill **fril·ly** *comp.* **fril·li·er** *superl.* **fril·li·est** *adj.* adorned with frills || like a frill

fringe (frindʒ) **1.** *n.* an ornamental border of loose or twisted threads made at an edge or made separately for attachment || a border or edge of hair on an animal or plant || an outer margin || (optics) any of the light or dark bands produced by the diffraction or interference of light || a marginal or extremist group of any society **2.** *v.t. pres. part.* **fring·ing** *past* and *past part.* **fringed** to form a border for || to border on || to put a fringe on **3.** *adj.* at the limit or border

frisk (frisk) **1.** *v.i.* to scamper and jump about playfully || *v.t.* (pop.) to search (a person or his clothes) for weapons or stolen goods, by quickly feeling over his clothing ‖ *(pop.)* to steal from (someone) in this manner **2.** *n.* a frolic, gambol ‖ *(pop.)* a quick search of a person for concealed weapons or stolen goods

frisk·y (fríski:) *comp.* **frisk·i·er** *superl.* **frisk·i·est** *adj.* lively and playful

frit·ter (frítǝr) *n.* a small lump of batter, containing sliced fruit, vegetables or meat, fried in deep fat

fritter *v.t.* (with 'away') to waste (time, money etc.) on too many or frivolous interests ‖ to cause to break into fragments or as if into fragments

friv·ol (frívǝl) *v. pres. part.* **friv·ol·ing** *past* and *past part.* **friv·oled** *v.i.* to behave frivolously ‖ *v.t.* (with 'away') to waste in trifling, spend frivolously

fri·vol·i·ty (frivóliti:) *pl.* **fri·vol·i·ties** *n.* the quality of being frivolous ‖ a frivolous piece of behavior

friv·o·lous (frívǝlǝs) *adj.* gay and lighthearted in pursuit of trivial or futile pleasures ‖ lacking in proper seriousness ‖ empty, without importance

frog (frɔg, frɒg) *n.* a small, coldblooded, tailless, leaping animal living both on land and in water

frog *n.* an attachment to a belt for a bayonet or a sword ‖ a coat-fastening consisting of a loop (often of braid) and a spindle-shaped button (sometimes tasselled), used e.g. on duffel coats and in a highly ornamental form on some military full-dress uniforms ‖ a perforated flower holder used to assist with arrangements

frol·ic (frólik) **1.** *v.i. pres. part.* **frol·ick·ing** *past* and *past part.* **frol·icked** to frisk, gambol **2.** *n.* an outburst of high spirits ‖ a bit of gay, harmless fun **fról·ic·some** *adj.*

from (frǝm, frɒm) *prep.* indicating outward movement or distance in relation to a point in space or time ‖ indicating a point of departure, or starting point in place or time or abstract calculation ‖ indicating a place of origin ‖ indicating cause ‖ indicating separation ‖ indicating a relationship of distinction ‖ describing a change of amount, state or quality ‖ indicating source or derivation ‖ indicating selection ‖ (with 'to') indicating limits ‖ (with 'to' and extreme cases or examples) indicating wide scope ‖ sent or given by

frond (frɒnd) *n. (bot.)* the leaf of a palm ‖ the leaf of a fern, often bearing spores ‖ *(bot.)* the thallus of some seaweeds and lichens ‖ *(rhet.)* any leaf or leaflike appendage **frónd·ed** *adj.* having fronds

front (frʌnt) **1.** *n.* the most forward part or surface of anything‖ the most advanced position ‖ (in static warfare) the most advanced battle line, where the fighting takes place ‖ the scene of a particular activity ‖ a grouping of separate bodies of people, esp. political parties, for some common objective ‖ *(archit.)* a face of a building, esp. the one having the main entrance ‖ (of land) frontage ‖ a dicky, shirtfront ‖ outward demeanor ‖ the part of the human body opposite the back ‖ a person appointed to a post as a figurehead to bring prestige, or a person or group used to cover up some illegal activity ‖ *(meteor.)* the surface of separation between cold and warm masses of air, usually lying along a trough of low pressure ‖ the auditorium of a theater and all that is in front of the curtain, including the personnel who work there **2.** *adj.* of the, or in the, more or most forward position, *front legs* ‖ *(phon.)* articulated with the front of the tongue, *a front vowel* **3.** *adv.* at or to the front, esp. in **out front** *(theater)* in the audience **up front** *(mil.)* in the front line

front *v.t.* to face toward ‖ to be in front of ‖ *(archit.)* to supply a front or face to ‖ to confront ‖ *(phon.)* to pronounce with the tongue in the forward position ‖ *v.i.* to serve as a front ‖ to be facing

front·age (frʌ́ntidʒ) *n.* the front of a plot of land, esp. with respect to its length and the direction it faces ‖ the land between the front of a building and the street, road or river which it faces ‖ the front of a building

fron·tal (frʌ́nt'l) *adj.* in or at or relating to the forward part ‖ directly towards the front ‖ *(anat.)* pertaining

to the forehead ‖ relating to a meteorological front

fron·tier (frʌntíǝr) **1.** *n.* the border separating one country from another ‖ (esp. *pl.*) an area of mental activity where much remains to be done ‖ a marginal region between settled and unsettled lands **2.** *adj.* at or relating to a frontier

fron·tiers·man (frʌntíǝrzmǝn) *pl.* **fron·tiers·men** (frʌntíǝrzmǝn) *n. (Am. hist.)* someone living in a frontier territory

frost (frɔst, frɒst) **1.** *n.* the crystallization of the water in the atmosphere upon exposed surfaces occurring when their temperature falls below freezing point ‖ the ice thus formed ‖ temperature below freezing point ‖ coldness of manner **2.** *v.t.* to damage by frost ‖ to cover with ice crystals ‖ to roughen the surface of (glass) and thus destroy its transparency, though not its translucency ‖ to coat with frosting

frost·bite (frɔ́stbɒit, frɒ́stbɒit) **1.** *n.* an injury to the tissues of part of the body caused by exposure to freezing cold **2.** *v.t. pres. part.* **frost·bit·ing** *past* **frost·bit** (frɔ́stbit, frɒ́stbit) *past* and *past part.* **frost·bit·ten** (frɔ́stbit'n, frɒ́stbit'n), **frost·bit** to injure (a part of the body) by exposure to freezing cold

frost·ing (frɔ́stiŋ, frɒ́stiŋ) *n.* a mixture of fine sugar, white of egg etc. used to coat a cake ‖ an unglossed finish on metal or glass ‖ a decorative substance made from powdered glass flakes, varnish and glue ‖ *(cosmetology)* creation of two-tone style by bleaching small sections of hair

froth (frɔθ, frɒθ) **1.** *n.* the mass of small bubbles produced by the agitation or fermentation of a liquid ‖ foam ‖ spume ‖ frivolous or trivial talk or writing **2.** *v.t.* to cause to form froth ‖ to cause to be covered with froth ‖ *v.i.* to foam ‖ to cover with something insubstantial **fróth·i·ly** *adv.* **fróth·i·ness** *n.* **fróth·y** *comp.* **froth·i·er** *superl.* **froth·i·est** *adj.* light as froth ‖ covered in froth ‖ frivolous, superficial

fro·ward (fróuǝrd) *adj. (old-fash.)* stubbornly self-willed

frown (fraun) **1.** *v.i.* to wrinkle the brow, e.g. in displeasure, puzzlement or deep thought ‖ (with 'on', 'upon', 'at') to be disapproving in attitude ‖ *(rhet.,* of inanimate things) to look foreboding ‖ *v.t.* to subdue (someone) with a frown **2.** *n.* a wrinkling or drawing together of the brows indicating e.g. displeasure, puzzlement or concentration

frowz·y (fráuzi:) *comp.* **frowz·i·er** *superl.* **frowz·i·est** *adj.* (of people or things) unkempt, slovenly ‖ (of the atmosphere) stale, musty

fru·gal (frú:g'l) *adj.* scanty ‖ economical **fru·gal·i·ty** (fru:gǽliti:) *n.*

fruit (fru:t) **1.** *n.* the enlarged or developed reproductive body of a seed plant, consisting of one or more seeds and usually various protective and supporting structures ‖ such a fruit with an edible pulp commonly eaten as dessert, e.g. an orange ‖ dessert fruits collectively ‖ the result of effort, esp. success **2.** *v.i.* to bear fruit ‖ *v.t.* to cause to bear fruit

fruit·ful (frú:tfǝl) *adj.* fertile, productive in abundance ‖ producing beneficial results

fru·i·tion (fru:íʃǝn) *n.* the state of bearing fruit ‖ (of plans etc.) a being realized, a coming to fulfillment

fruit·less (frú:tlis) *adj.* yielding no fruit ‖ unprofitable, useless

fruit·y (frú:ti:) *comp.* **fruit·i·er** *superl.* **fruit·i·est** *adj.* like fruit in taste, appearance or smell ‖ (of wine) having a rich taste of grapes ‖ (of the voice) thickly sweet

frus·trate (frʌ́streit) *pres. part.* **frus·trat·ing** *past* and *past part.* **frus·trat·ed** *v.t.* to prevent (someone) from achieving an object or prevent (an attempt etc.) from being made successfully, often by foiling ‖ to cause feelings in (someone) of being thwarted or baffled, deprived of what was due, or having some fundamental need unsatisfied

frus·tra·tion (frʌstréiʃǝn) *n.* a frustrating or being frustrated ‖ something which frustrates

fry (frai) **1.** *n. pl.* **fries** (*pop.*) a dish of fried food ‖ (*pop.*) an outdoor social gathering at which the main dish is fried ‖ the heart, liver etc. of an animal, usually eaten fried, *pig's fry* **2.** *v. pres. part.* **fry·ing** *past* and *past part.* **fried** (fraid) *v.t.* to cook in hot fat or oil in a shallow open pan ‖ *v.i.* to be cooked in this way

fuch·sia (fjúːʃə) *n.* perennial shrubs found mainly in tropical America

fudge (fʌdʒ) **1.** *n.* a soft candy made of sugar, chocolate or other flavoring, milk and butter etc. ‖ nonsense **2.** *v. pres. part.* **fudg·ing** *past* and *past part.* **fudged** *v.i.* to talk nonsense ‖ *v.t.* to fake ‖ to make or do (something) in a makeshift or blurry way

fu·el (fjúːəl) **1.** *n.* combustible material used as a source of heat or energy ‖ food as a source of energy ‖ fissionable material used as a source of atomic energy ‖ anything that makes strong feelings or passions (anger etc.) stronger **2.** *v. pres. part.* **fu·el·ing** *past* and *past part.* **fu·eled** *v.t.* to provide with fuel ‖ *v.i.* to take in fuel

fu·ga·cious (fjuːgéiʃəs) *adj.* (*rhet.*) evanescent, fleeting ‖ (*bot.,* of sepals, petals etc.) falling off soon after the flower opens **fu·gac·i·ty** (fjuːgǽsiti:) *n.*

fu·gi·tive (fjúːdʒitiv) **1.** *n.* someone fleeing from punishment, danger, pursuit, authority etc. **2.** *adj.* in flight, running away ‖ liable to change, not durable ‖ of literary compositions) scattered, occasional ‖ ephemeral

ful·crum (fʌ́lkrəm, fúlkrəm) *pl.* **ful·crums, ful·cra** (fʌ́lkrə, fúlkrə) *n.* the point about which a lever turns or on which it is supported ‖ (*bot.*) a supporting organ, e.g. a tendril or stipule ‖ (*zool.*) a chitinous structure in the base of the rostrum of insects ‖ (*zool.*) a spinelike scale on the anterior fin rays of many ganoid fish

ful·fill, ful·fil (fulfíl) *pres. part.* **ful·fill·ing, ful·fil·ling** *past* and *past part.* **ful·filled** *v.t.* to carry out (a promise) ‖ to obey (a law, command) ‖ to satisfy (a prayer, desire) ‖ to complete, accomplish (a task) ‖ to answer (a purpose) ‖ to comply with (conditions) ‖ to prove true (a prophecy) ‖ to realize (a destiny) **to fulfill oneself** to realize all one's potentialities as a person **ful·fill·ment, ful·fil·ment** *n.*

full (ful) **1.** *adj.* completely filled ‖ filled with emotion ‖ crowded ‖ characterized by a pronounced trait ‖ well filled with food ‖ ample, thoroughly adequate ‖ well supplied ‖ at maximum development, size etc. ‖ (of sounds) having depth or volume ‖ (of light, color) strong ‖ (of materials) arranged in gathers or folds ‖ expanded ‖ well filled out, plump ‖ unqualified ‖ (with 'of') having much or many ‖ (with 'of') having an abundance ‖ having the same parents ‖ (*binding*) on spine and boards **2.** *n.* (with 'the') the highest point **3.** *adv.* exactly ‖ directly, squarely ‖ (*rhet.*) perfectly, entirely, very **4.** *v.t.* to gather or pleat (cloth) for greater fullness ‖ *v.i.* (of the moon) to become full

full-fledged (fúlfléd3d) *adj.* (of birds) having all their feathers ‖ completely qualified

full·ness, ful·ness (fúlnis) *n.* the quality or state of being full

ful·ly (fúli:) *adv.* entirely, completely ‖ at least

ful·mi·nate (fʌ́lmineit) **1.** *v. pres. part.* **ful·mi·nat·ing** *past* and *past part.* **ful·mi·nat·ed** *v.i.* to flash like lightning or to explode like thunder ‖ *v.t.* to thunder forth (threats, denunciations or commands) **2.** *n.* a (usually explosive) salt of fulminic acid, esp. mercury fulminate

ful·some (fúlsəm) *adj.* (esp. of flattery or praise) excessively or offensively exaggerated

fum·ble (fʌ́mbˈl) **1.** *v. pres. part.* **fum·bling** *past* and *past part.* **fum·bled** *v.t.* to deal with clumsily or

awkwardly, bungle ‖ (*sports*) to fail to catch or control (a ball), bungle (a pass etc.) ‖ *v.i.* to grope awkwardly ‖ to speak as though finding it hard to express oneself **2.** *n.* a clumsy or groping use of the hands ‖ a bungling of an action

fume (fjuːm) **1.** *n.* (esp. *pl.*) pungent, often noxious, vapor or smoke ‖ a suspension of particles in gas or air **2.** *v. pres. part.* **fum·ing** *past* and *past part.* **fumed** *v.i.* to give off fumes ‖ to be angry in a pent-up way ‖ *v.t.* to subject (wood) to the action of fumes of ammonia so as to darken it

fu·mi·gate (fjúːmigeit) *pres. part.* **fu·mi·gat·ing** *past* and *past part.* **fu·mi·gat·ed** *v.t.* to subject to smoke or fumes, esp. in order to disinfect, kill insects, etc. **fu·mi·gá·tion, fú·mi·ga·tor** *ns* a device for fumigating ‖ someone who fumigates

fum·y (fjúːmi:) *comp.* **fum·i·er** *superl.* **fum·i·est** *adj.* full of fumes ‖ giving off fumes

fun (fʌn) **1.** *n.* pleasure and amusement ‖ gaiety, playfulness **2.** *v.i. pres. part.* **fun·ning** *past* and *past part.* **funned** (*pop.*) to joke **3.** *adj.* characterized by or providing fun

func·tion (fʌ́ŋkʃən) **1.** *n.* a characteristic activity or the activity for which something exists ‖ end or purpose ‖ an official duty ‖ a ceremony or social gathering of some formality ‖ chemical behavior due to the presence of a functional group ‖ a functional group ‖ (*math.*) a relation that associates with every ordered set of numbers $(x, y, z ...)$ a number $f (x, y, z ...)$ for all the permitted values of $x, y, z ...$ ‖ any quantity, trait or fact that depends upon and varies in accordance with another **2.** *v.i.* to act, perform a function ‖ to be in working order, *to stop functioning* **func·tion·al** (fʌ́ŋkʃənˈl) *adj.* pertaining to function ‖ designed primarily in accordance with criteria determined by use, rather than according to canons of taste ‖ (*med.*) affecting the functions but not the substance of an organ ‖ (*math.*) pertaining to a function or functions

fund (fʌnd) **1.** *n.* an available store of immaterial resources ‖ an accumulation of money, esp. one set aside for a certain purpose ‖ (*pl.*) financial resources **2.** *v.t.* to convert (a floating debt) into a long-term debt at fixed interest ‖ to put in a fund

fun·da·ment (fʌ́ndəmənt) *n.* the anus ‖ the buttocks

fun·da·men·tal (fʌndəmént'l) **1.** *adj.* basic, essential ‖ affecting the foundations of something ‖ deep-rooted in a person or being part of the elementary nature of a thing ‖ (*mus.,* of a tone) being the lowest primary note, determining pitch, in a harmonic series **2.** *n.* something fundamental

fu·ner·al (fjúːnərəl) **1.** *n.* the ceremony of burial or cremation of a dead person ‖ the procession attending a burial or cremation ‖ the burial service ‖ (*pop.*) problem (concern) **2.** *adj.* of or pertaining to a funeral or funerals

fu·ne·re·al (fjuːníːəri:əl) *adj.* mournful, gloomy

fungi *pl.* of FUNGUS

fun·gus (fʌ́ŋgəs) *pl.* **fun·gi** (fʌ́ndʒai, fʌ́ŋgai) *n.* parasitic or saprophytic plants, devoid of chlorophyll

fun·nel (fʌ́nˈl) **1.** *n.* a cone-shaped vessel ending in a tube at the base, used for pouring liquids or powders through a small opening ‖ the metal flue of a ship or steam engine, a smokestack ‖ a lighting or ventilating shaft **2.** *v. pres. part.* **fun·nel·ing** *past* and *past part.* **fun·neled** *v.t.* to cause to pass through a funnel or as if through one ‖ *v.i.* to take the shape of a funnel ‖ to pass through a funnel or as if through one

fun·nies (fʌ́ni:z) *pl. n.* (*pop.*) comic strips

fun·ny (fʌ́ni:) *comp.* **fun·ni·er** *superl.* **fun·ni·est** *adj.* that makes one laugh ‖ (*pop.*) puzzling ‖ (*pop.*) ill

fur (fə:r) **1.** *n.* the dressed pelt of certain animals (mink, beaver, fox, rabbit, seal etc.) ‖ this as an item of apparel, worn loose around the neck and over the shoulders ‖ a coat, wrap, stole etc. made of several such pelts ‖ the soft, fine, thick hair that covers many animals, e.g. a cat ‖ *(pl.)* the skins of animals with the fur attached **2.** *adj.* made of, or pertaining to, fur, *a fur coat* **3.** *v. pres. part.* **fur·ring** *past* and *past part.* **furred** *v.t.* to provide, cover, trim or clothe (something or someone) with fur ‖ to coat with a deposit ‖ to make (a floor or ceiling) level by inserting strips of wood ‖ *v.i.* to become coated with a deposit

fur·bish (fə́:rbiʃ) *v.t.* to polish, cause to shine ‖ (with 'up') to give a new look to, renovate ‖ to refresh one's knowledge of

fu·ri·ous (fjúəri:əs) *adj.* passionately angry ‖ violent, frantic

furl (fə:rl) **1.** *v.t.* to roll up (a sail) and tie it to a yard or boom ‖ to fold up, close (a flag, umbrella, fan etc.) ‖ *v.i.* to become furled ‖ (with 'off') to roll off ‖ (with 'away') to roll away **2.** *n.* a furling or being furled ‖ a roll of something furled

fur·long (fə́:rlɒŋ, fə́:rlɒŋ) *n.* a unit of distance equaling one eighth of a statute mile or 220 yds (201.17 meters), used esp. in horse racing and surveying

fur·lough (fə́:rlou) **1.** *n.* leave of absence, *on furlough* ‖ a leave of absence, esp. one given to a soldier ‖ the document granting this **2.** *v.t.* to grant a furlough to ‖ *v.i.* to spend a furlough

fur·nace (fə́:rnis) *n.* an apparatus in chamber form for the production of intense heat to melt metals, reduce ores etc. ‖ the firebox of a hot-water or hot-air heating system in a building

fur·nish (fə́:rniʃ) *v.t.* to provide (a house etc.) with furnishings ‖ to supply, equip ‖ to yield, provide **fúr·nish·ings** *pl. n.* furniture and fittings for a house etc. ‖ haberdashery

fur·ni·ture (fə́:rnitʃər) *n.* movable articles (bed, table etc.) put in a room to make it habitable and decorative ‖ accessories or equipment, e.g. the tackle of a ship or the stilts, shelves etc. used in packing a kiln ‖ *(printing)* pieces of metal or wood used to make margins, blank spaces etc. and secure the type in its form or chase

fu·ror (fjúərər) *n.* a furore

fu·rore (fjúərɔr) *n.* intense mass enthusiasm ‖ mass rage, uproar

fur·ri·er (fə́:ri:ər, fʌ́ri:ər) *n.* a dealer in furs or fur garments ‖ someone who dresses furs ‖ someone who makes fur garments **fur·ri·er·y** (fə́:ri:əri:, fʌ́ri:əri:) *n.* the craft or trade of a furrier

fur·row (fə́:rou, fʌ́rou) **1.** *n.* a trench in the earth made by a plow ‖ the track of a ship ‖ any track, channel or groove ‖ *(rhet.)* a deep wrinkle, *furrows of care* **2.** *v.t.* to make a furrow, channel or groove in ‖ to wrinkle deeply ‖ *v.i.* to make a furrow, channel or groove ‖ to become deeply wrinkled

fur·ry (fə́:ri:) *comp.* **fur·ri·er** *superl.* **fur·ri·est** *adj.* covered with or clothed in fur ‖ resembling fur ‖ (esp. of the tongue) coated with fur

fur·ther (fə́r:ðər) alt. *comp.* of FAR ‖ *adj.* additional, *a further topic of conversation* ‖ more remote in time ‖ more distant

further *v.t.* to advance, promote **fúr·ther·ance** *n.*

fur·ther·more (fə́:rðərmɔr, fə́:rðərmọur) *adv.* moreover, besides

fur·thest (fə́:rðist) alt. *superl.* of FAR ‖ **1.** *adj.* most distant ‖ extreme **2.** *adv.* at or to the greatest distance or degree

fur·tive (fə́:rtiv) *adj.* stealthy ‖ shifty ‖ done so as not to be noticed

fu·ry (fjúəri:) *pl.* **fu·ries** *n.* violent rage ‖ a fit of rage ‖ violence (of weather, mental disease etc.) ‖ a violently angry woman **like fury** in an intense degree, furiously

fuse (fju:z) **1.** *v. pres. part.* **fus·ing** *past* and *past part.* **fused** *v.t.* to melt (a solid) ‖ to join by melting together or as if by melting together ‖ *v.i.* to melt ‖ to become joined by being melted together or as if melted together ‖ (of lights etc. in an electric circuit) to fail because the circuit is broken by a melted fuse wire **2.** *n.* a short length of wire or metal or low melting point inserted in an electric circuit and melting (thus breaking the circuit) if the current flow heats it above its melting point

fuse, fuze (fju:z) **1.** *n.* a combustible or detonating tube, piece of cord, metal etc. which ignites or detonates an explosive ‖ a detonating device inserted into an explosive weapon (e.g. a torpedo or shell) designed to set off the charge on impact **2.** *v.t. pres. part.* **fus·ing, fuz·ing** *past* and *past part.* **fused, fuzed** to furnish with a fuse

fu·se·lage (fjú:sələʒ, fjú:zələʒ, fjú:səliʒ, fjú:zəliʒ) *n.* the body structure of an airplane, to which the wings and tail are attached

fu·sion (fjú:ʒən) *n.* a melting together into a fused mass, e.g. of metals ‖ *(phys.)* the union of light atomic nuclei to form heavier ones under extreme conditions of temperature and pressure, taking place with overall loss in mass and resulting in great energy release ‖ a blending together such that the component parts are not distinguishable ‖ a coalition **fú·sion·ist** *n.* someone joining in a coalition

fuss (fʌs) **1.** *n.* unnecessary excitement ‖ worry about trifles ‖ complaint, objection **2.** *v.i.* to be in a state of restless commotion ‖ to worry unduly or about trifles ‖ to raise objections, complain ‖ *v.t.* to bother (someone), esp. with unwanted attentions

fuss·y (fʌ́si:) *comp.* **fuss·i·er** *superl.* **fuss·i·est** *adj.* given to fussing ‖ hard to plase, fastidious, exacting ‖ bustling ‖ (of clothes, ornament etc.) having too many small or unnecessary details

fus·ty (fʌ́sti:) *comp.* **fus·ti·er** *superl.* **fus·ti·est** *adj.* musty, moldy, rank ‖ out-of-date, old-fashioned

fu·tile (fjú:t'l) *adj.* unavailing ‖ pointless, trifling and wearisome **fu·til·i·ty** (fju:tíliti:) *pl.* **fu·til·i·ties** *n.* the quality of being futile ‖ something futile

fu·ture (fjú:tʃər) **1.** *adj.* of or in time to come ‖ destined to be ‖ *(gram.,* of a tense) relating to time yet to come **2.** *n.* time yet to come ‖ prospects ‖ future events ‖ *(gram.)* the future tense or a verb in this tense ‖ *(pl., commerce)* goods or securities bought or sold on a contract for future delivery

fuzz (fʌz) **1.** *n.* a fluffy mass or coating of fine particles or fibers etc. e.g. on cloth or a peach ‖ a blurred effect **2.** *v.t.* t cover with fuzz ‖ to blur ‖ *v.i.* to become covered with fuzz ‖ to become blurred

fuzz·y (fʌ́zi:) *comp.* **fuzz·i·er** *superl.* **fuzz·i·est** *adj.* like fuzz, covered with fuzz, downy, frayed etc. ‖ (of hair) consisting of tightly interlaced curls ‖ indistinct, blurred, not clear

G

G, g (dʒi:) the seventh letter of the English alphabet

ga·ble (géib'l) *n.* the triangular upper part of a wall closing the end of a ridged roof ‖ the gable-topped end wall of a building ‖ a triangular architectural decoration, e.g. over a doorway or window **gá·bled** *adj.*

gad (gæd) *v.i. pres. part.* **gad·ding** *past* and *past part.* **gad·ded** (in the phrase) **to gad about** to be constantly going out in search of pleasure

gad·a·bout (gǽdəbaut) *n.* someone constantly moving around, esp. for frivolous reasons

gad·fly (gǽdflai) *pl.* **gad·flies** *n.* any of various flies (e.g. the botflies, warble flies, tabanids) that bite cattle ‖ an irritating person, esp. one who goads others into action by persistent criticism

gadg·et (gǽdʒit) *n.* a small, ingenious and useful fitting, e.g. in machinery ‖ a useful device, *kitchen gadgets* ‖ a clever but trivial device that is hardly more than a knickknack

gaff (gæf) **1.** *n.* a barbed fishing spear ‖ an iron hook for lifting heavy fish into a boat ‖ (*naut.*) a spar on which the upper edge of a fore-and-aft sail is extended **2.** *v.t.* to strike or catch hold of with a gaff

gag (gæg) **1.** *v. pres. part.* **gag·ging** *past* and *past part.* **gagged** *v.t.* to stop up the mouth of (someone) with a gag ‖ to fasten open the jaws of, e.g. for surgery ‖ to restrict the freedom of speech of ‖ *v.i.* to retch or choke ‖ (*theater*) to interpolate jokes into a script **2.** *n.* something crammed into the mouth to prevent sound ‖ a device used to hold the mouth open, e.g. in dentistry ‖ any suppression of freedom of speech ‖ a joke, esp. one interpolated in a play etc. ‖ a hoax, trick

gai·e·ty, gay·e·ty (géiiti:) *pl.* **gai·e·ties, gay·e·ties** *n.* the quality of being or looking gay ‖ merrymaking, entertainment

gai·ly, gay·ly (géili:) *adv.* in a gay fashion

gain (gein) *n.* financial profit ‖ (*pl.*) winnings or profits ‖ an improvement or increase ‖ the acquiring of wealth ‖ advantage

gain *v.t.* to acquire, obtain ‖ to obtain as a profit ‖ to earn ‖ to win ‖ to reach ‖ to obtain by steady increase ‖ *v.i.* to improve, advance ‖ (of clocks and watches) to become increasingly fast **gáin·er** *n.* a back-somersault dive made from a front-dive takeoff position **gáin·ful** *adj.* profitable, money-earning, *a gainful occupation* **gáin·ings** *pl. n.* profits, earnings

gain·say (geinséi, géinsei) *pres. part.* **gain·say·ing** *past* and *past part.* **gain·said** (geinséid, geinséd, géinseid, géinsed) *v.t.* (*old-fash.*) to contradict, deny

gait (geit) **1.** *n.* a manner of walking, running etc. ‖ (of horses) a manner of moving the feet, e.g. a trot, canter **2.** *v.t.* to train (a horse) to a particular gait

ga·la (géilə, gúlə) **1.** *n.* a festival, a grand social occasion **2.** *adj.* highly festive

gal·ax·y (gǽləksi:) *pl.* **gal·ax·ies** *n.* one of the vast number of systems containing stars, nebulae, star clusters and interstellar matter that make up the universe ‖ a brilliant company

gale (geil) *n.* (*meteor.*) a wind having a speed from 32 to 63 m.p.h. ‖ a strong wind ‖ a gust, noisy outburst

gall (gɔl) **1.** *n.* an injury to a horse's skin caused by chronic chafing ‖ a cause of intense irritation ‖ impertinence ‖ bile ‖ the gallbladder **2.** *v.t.* to chafe so as to cause a sore ‖ to irritate or mortify ‖ *v.i.* to become sore through chafing

gall *n.* a growth, which may take many varied forms, on the tissues of plants, caused by plant or animal parasites

gal·lant (gǽlənt) *adj.* showing noble courage ‖ (gəlánt) showily attentive to women

gal·lant·ry (gǽləntri:) *pl.* **gal·lant·ries** *n.* dashing bravery ‖ showily attentive behavior to women ‖ a compliment made to a woman by a man flirting with her

gal·ler·y (gǽləri:) *pl.* **gal·ler·ies** *n.* an indoor balcony projecting from the wall of a church or hall, providing extra accommodation ‖ (*theater*) the highest balcony, with the cheapest seats ‖ the people who sit there ‖ a long narrow room, e.g. one for exhibiting pictures in stately homes ‖ a room or series of rooms used for exhibiting works of art ‖ an art dealer's premises ‖ a covered passage, partly open at one side, and usually above ground level ‖ an underground passage made by animals, e.g. by moles or ants ‖ (*mining*) a working drift or level ‖ an underground passage

gal·ley (gǽli:) *n.* (*hist.*) a long, low, narrow, single-decked ship propelled by sails and oars ‖ an ancient Greek or Roman warship with one or several banks of oars ‖ a large open rowing boat, such as is used by the captain of a warship ‖ the kitchen of a ship ‖ (*printing*) an oblong tray with upright sides, to hold type which has been set ‖ a galley proof

galley proof a printer's proof taken from type locked in a galley to permit correction before the type is made up in pages

gal·li·vant (gǽlivænt) *v.i.* to gad about

gal·lon (gǽlən) *n.* (*abbr.* gal.) a liquid measure

gal·lop (gǽləp) **1.** *n.* the fastest pace of horses and similar animals, in which all four feet are off the ground in each stride ‖ a ride at this pace **at a gallop, at full gallop** at full speed **2.** *v.t.* to make (a horse) gallop ‖ *v.i.* to go at a gallop ‖ to progress quickly, hurry

gal·lows (gǽlouz) *pl. n.* (often treated as *sing.*) a wooden structure for the execution of the death sentence by hanging ‖ the punishment of hanging

ga·losh (gəlɔʃ) *n.* a waterproof boot worn over the shoe to keep out snow or water

gal·va·ni·za·tion (gælvənizéiʃən) *n.* a galvanizing or being galvanized

gal·va·nize (gǽlvənaiz) *pres. part.* **gal·va·niz·ing** *past* and *past part.* **gal·va·nized** *v.t.* to stimulate by electric currents ‖ to coat with metal by electrolysis ‖ to coat (iron or steel) with zinc ‖ to rouse to sudden action through shock or excitement

gam·bit (gǽmbit) *n.* an opening move or series of moves in chess, in which the player risks losing a pawn or a piece, to secure an advantageous position ‖ any purposeful or provocative opening to a conversation, contest etc.

gam·ble (gǽmb'l) **1.** *v. pres. part.* **gam·bling** *past* and *past part.* **gam·bled** *v.i.* to play a game for money ‖ to take risks in the hope of getting better results than by some safer means ‖ to stake one's money or hopes ‖ *v.t.* to risk by staking **2.** *n.* the act of gambling ‖ a risky undertaking **gam·bler** *n.*

gam·bol (gǽmb'l) **1.** *n.* a frisking, playful leaping **2.** *v.i. pres. part.* **gam·bol·ing** *past* and *past part.* **gam·boled** to frisk, leap about

game (geim) **1.** *n.* a contest played for sport or amusement according to rules ‖ the method employed in such a contest ‖ any playful activity for amusement

---

or diversion ‖ (pl.) organized outdoor sporting activities, esp. at school ‖ a single round or part of a contest (tennis, bridge etc.) ‖ the number of points that must be scored to win such a round ‖ a scheme, plan or intrigue against others ‖ (collect.) wild animals or birds hunted for sport or food ‖ the flesh of these used for food **2.** adj. pertaining to game (animals), game laws **3.** v.i. pres. part. **gam·ing** past and past part. **gamed** to gamble, play for money

game adj. (of a limb) chronically stiff and painful

game adj. plucky ‖ ready and willing to perform any challenging action

ga·mut (gǽmət) n. the entire range or scope of something ‖ the compass of a voice or musical instrument ‖ the whole series of recognized musical notes

gan·der (gǽndər) n. the male goose ‖ (pop.) a look, glance

gang (gæŋ) **1.** n. a team of workmen working together ‖ a number of men or boys banding together, esp. lawlessly. Occasionally girls are members ‖ a set of tools etc. arranged to work together **2.** v.i. (often with 'up') to band together, join **gang·er** (gǽŋər) n. a man in charge of a gang of workmen

gan·gling (gǽŋgliŋ) adj. lanky and awkward

gang·plank (gǽŋplæŋk) n. a long, narrow movable bridge or plank for passing between quay and boat

gan·grene (gǽŋgri:n) **1.** n. (med.) the necrosis of part of a living body, e.g. a toe or a single muscle **2.** v. pres. part. **gan·gren·ing** past and past part. **gan·grened** v.t. to affect with gangrene ‖ v.i. to become affected with gangrene **gan·gre·nous** (gǽŋgrənəs) adj.

gang·ster (gǽŋstər) n. a member of a gang of criminals or gunmen

gap (gæp) n. an opening or breach in a wall, fence, hedge etc. ‖ a breach in defenses ‖ a pass through hills, a defile ‖ a break in continuity, a pause ‖ a wide difference in views or ideas

gape (geip) **1.** v.i. pres. part. **gap·ing** past and past part. **gaped** to open the mouth wide ‖ to be wide open ‖ to show a gap, be split ‖ to stare in wonder or surprise **2.** n. the act of gaping ‖ an open-mouthed stare ‖ (zool.) the distance between the wide-open jaws of birds, fishes etc. ‖ the part of a bird's beak where it opens ‖ the opening between the shells of a bivalve ‖ a gap or rent ‖ a fit of yawning

ga·rage (gəráʒ, gərádʒ) **1.** n. a building in which cars etc. are kept ‖ a commercial enterprise for the repair, and often the sale, of motor vehicles ‖ a place where gasoline and oil are sold **2.** v.t. pres. part. **ga·rag·ing** past and past part. **ga·raged** to put (a vehicle) in a garage

garb (gɑrb) **1.** n. manner of dress, esp. when distinctive or odd, or the clothes themselves **2.** v.t. (esp. pass. and refl.) to dress, esp. in some distinctive or odd way

gar·bage (gárbidʒ) n. animal or vegetable refuse, kitchen waste, rubbish ‖ (computer) inaccurate or unsuitable data

gar·ble (gárb'l) pres. part. **gar·bling** past and past part. **gar·bled** v.t. to give a confused version of (a message, facts) ‖ to tell (a story) with the facts mixed up or wrong ‖ to select parts of (a story) and recount them in an incompetent, unfair or malicious way

gar·den (gárd'n) **1.** n. a piece of ground where flowers, fruit and vegetables are grown, usually near a house ‖ (often pl.) a big area of laid-out garden open to the public ‖ (rhet.) a region of great fertility or beauty **2.** v.i. to work in a garden

gar·gan·tu·an (gɑrgǽntʃu:ən) adj. huge, enormous

gar·gle (gárg'l) **1.** v. pres. part. **gar·gling** past and past part. **gar·gled** v.i. to wash the throat with esp. antiseptic liquid kept in motion in the mouth or throat by breath expelled from the lungs ‖ to make gargling noises ‖ v.t. to wash (the throat) by gargling **2.** n. the liquid used in gargling ‖ the act of gargling

gar·ish (gέəriʃ, gέriʃ) adj. harsh, glaring and gaudy

in color ‖ vulgarly bright and showy

gar·land (gárlənd) **1.** n. a circlet of flowers ‖ a circlet of gold, jewels etc. ‖ (hist.) a laurel or other wreath as a festive sign of victory ‖ (naut.) a ring of rope lashed to a spar to prevent chafing ‖ (skiing) a sideslip on a slope **2.** v.t. to deck or crown with a garland

gar·lic (gárlik) n. any of several plants of the genus Allium, fam. Liliaceae, esp. A. sativum. The bulb is a compound of several small cloves, stronger and more pungent in smell and flavor than an onion, and much used for flavoring **gár·lick·y** adj.

gar·ment (gármənt) n. any article of clothing ‖ (pl., esp. commerce) clothes

gar·ner (gárnər) **1.** n. (rhet.) a granary, storehouse **2.** v.t. (rhet.) to collect or gather in or as if in a granary

gar·net (gárnit) n. a hard, brittle, crystalline mineral found in gneiss and mica schist. The precious garnet is a deep red gem. The common garnet is used as an abrasive

gar·nish (gárniʃ) **1.** v.t. to decorate (esp. a dish) with something savory or pretty ‖ (law) to garnishee ‖ (law) to summon (a person) to take part in a litigation pending between others **2.** n. a savory or decorative addition, esp. to a dish at table **gar·nish·ee** (gárniʃí:) **1.** n. (law) a person who has in his possession a defendant's money or property and is ordered not to dispose of it pending settlement of the lawsuit **2.** v.t. (law) to order (someone) not to dispose of a defendant's money or property pending settlement of a lawsuit ‖ (law) to attach (wages, property etc.) by court authority in order to pay a debt **gár·nish·ment** n. (law) a summons to a third person to appear in court in connection with a lawsuit between two other parties ‖ (law) a warning to a third person to keep possession of property belonging to a defendant in a lawsuit in case it is needed to pay off a debt ‖ a garnish

gar·ri·son (gǽris'n) **1.** n. the troops stationed in a fort or town **2.** v.t. to place a garrison in ‖ to occupy as a garrison ‖ to put on garrison duty

gar·ru·lous (gǽrələs) adj. given to constant idle, trivial, tedious talking

gar·ter (gártər) **1.** n. a band of elastic used to keep up one's stocking ‖ a strap of elastic hanging from a girdle etc., with a fastener to keep a woman's stocking up ‖ an elastic device with a fastener for keeping a sock or stocking up **2.** v.t. to put a garter around

gas (gæs) **1.** n. pl. **gas·es, gas·ses** a fluid substance that fills and thus takes the shape of its container ‖ (chem. and phys.) a fluid substance at a temperature above its critical temperature ‖ a substance or mixture of substances in a gaseous state used to produce light and heat (e.g. natural gas), anesthesia (e.g. laughing gas), or a poisonous or irritant atmosphere (e.g. tear gas) ‖ (pop.) fluent trivial talk or empty boasting or rhetoric ‖ gasoline **2.** v. pres. part. **gas·sing** past and past part. **gassed** v.i. to give off gas (esp. of a battery during charging) ‖ (pop.) to talk trivially and too much ‖ v.t. to submit (something) to the action of gas, esp. to singe (fabric) so as to remove unnecessary fibers ‖ to harm or kill (someone) by poison gas

gas·e·ous (gǽsi:əs, gǽʃəs) adj. in the form of a gas ‖ of or pertaining to gas

gash (gæʃ) **1.** n. a deep long cut or slash ‖ the act of gashing **2.** v.t. to make a gash in

gas·ket (gǽskit) n. a thin sheet of rubber, leather or metal placed between two flat surfaces to seal the joint, e.g. between the cylinder block and cylinder head in a car engine ‖ a packing of hemp or tow used to seal a joint ‖ (naut.) a rope used to secure a furled sail to a yard

gas·o·line, gas·o·lene (gǽsəli:n, gǽsəlí:n) n. a refined mixture of lower members of the hydrocarbon series, esp. hexane, heptane and octane. It is used, mixed with air and in a fine spray, as the fuel in an internal-combustion engine

gasp (gæsp, gɑsp) **1.** v.i. to catch the breath suddenly in astonishment ‖ to pant, heave through breathlessness ‖ *v.t.* to utter breathlessly 2. *n.* the act of gasping ‖ a convulsive struggle to draw breath

gas·tric (gǽstrik) *adj.* of or relating to the stomach

gas·tron·o·my (gæstrónəmi:) *n.* good eating as an art or science

gate (geit) 1. *n.* a wooden or metal barrier on hinges or pivots, capable of being opened and shut, and filling the opening in a wall or fence ‖ an opening or passageway through any wall or barrier ‖ the structure built about an entrance ‖ any means of entrance or exit ‖ a mountain pass or defile ‖ a device regulating the passage of water ‖ the slotted guide for the gearshift of an internal-combustion engine ‖ the number of people paying to see an athletic contest etc., or the amount of money collected from them ‖ *(computer)* a logic element with outputs under set conditions 2. *v.t. pres. part.* **gat·ing** *past* and *past part* **gat·ed**

gath·er (gǽðər) 1. *v.t.* to collect as harvest ‖ to pluck ‖ to amass ‖ to gain ‖ to cause to collect or come together ‖ to summon up (one's thoughts, strength) for an effort ‖ to draw parts together ‖ to wrinkle, pucker ‖ to deduce, learn indirectly ‖ to infer ‖ *v.i.* to come together, assemble ‖ to mass, accumulate ‖ (of a sore) to generate pus 2. *n.* (usually *pl.*) part of a dress, cloth etc. that has been gathered in **gáth·er·ing** *n.* an assembly of people ‖ *(printing)* a signature, a number of leaves of a book folded for stitching

gauche (gouʃ) *adj.* awkward ‖ lacking in social graces

gaud·y (gɔ́di:) *comp.* **gaud·i·er** *superl.* **gaud·i·est** *adj.* showy and cheap, tastelessly ornate

gauge, gage (geidʒ) 1. *n.* a standard measure, esp. of the thickness of wire or sheet metal and of the diameter of bullets ‖ the diameter of the bore of a gun ‖ an instrument for measuring quantity of rainfall, force of wind etc. ‖ the width between the insides of the rails of a railroad track ‖ measure, means of estimating, criterion ‖ a device attached to a container to show the height of its contents ‖ *(plastering)* the amount of plaster of paris used with common plaster to make it set more quickly 2. *v.t. pres. part.* **gaug·ing, gag·ing** *past* and *past part.* **gauged, gaged** to measure with a gauge ‖ to measure the capacity of (a cask etc.) ‖ to estimate, appraise ‖ to make conformable to a standard: to make (bricks, stones etc.) uniform ‖ to mix (plasters) in certain proportions for quick drying **gáuge·a·ble** *adj.* **gáug·er, gág·er** *n.* someone who measures the capacity of casks etc.

gaunt (gɔnt) *adj.* (of persons) haggard, emaciated, esp. from illness or suffering

gaunt·let (gɔ́ntlit, gántlit) *n.* a strong glove with a covering for the wrist ‖ *(hist.)* a steel glove of mail or plate worn with armor from the 14th c.

gaunt·let, gant·let (gɔ́ntlit, gántlit) *n.* *(hist.,* in phrase) **to run the gauntlet** to be forced as punishment to run between rows of men and be struck by them

gauze (gɔz) *n.* a thin, open-woven fabric of silk, cotton or linen ‖ any such semitransparent material, e.g. wire gauze ‖ a thin haze **gáuz·i·ness** *n.* **gáuz·y** *comp.* **gauz·i·er** *superl.* **gauz·i·est** *adj.*

gav·el (gǽvəl) *n.* the hammer with which e.g. the chairman of a meeting calls for attention or silence, or with which an auctioneer marks a sale

gawk (gɔk) 1. *n.* *(pop.)* a stupid and awkward person 2. *v.i.* *(pop.)* to stare stupidly **gáwk·i·ly** *adv.* in a gawky way **gáwk·i·ness** *n.* the state or quality of being gawky **gáwk·y** *comp.* **gawk·i·er** *superl.* **gawk·i·est** *adj.* clumsy and stiffly awkward, ungainly

gay (gei) *adj.* merry, cheerful, lighthearted ‖ bright in

color, brilliant ‖ pleasure-loving ‖ a homosexual, usu. male

gaze (geiz) 1. *n.* a long, intent look 2. *v.t. pres. part.* **gaz·ing** *past* and *past part.* **gazed** to look intently

ga·zelle (gəzél) *n.* a genus of small, swift, graceful antelopes of N. Africa and Arabia

ga·zette (gəzét) 1. *n.* *(hist.)* a periodical news sheet 2. *v.t. pres. part.* **ga·zet·ting** *past* and *past part.* **ga·zet·ted**

gaz·et·teer (gæzitíər) *n.* a geographical dictionary

gear (giər) 1. *n.* *(collect.)* the tools, materials etc. needed, and assembled, for a piece of work or particular activity ‖ personal belongings ‖ a combination of moving parts with a specified mechanical function ‖ a device for connecting the moving parts of a machine, usually by the engagement of toothed wheels or their equivalent, so that the speed of rotation of one part causes a different speed of rotation of the other part 2. *v.t.* to furnish with a gear or apply a gear to ‖ to put into gear ‖ to adjust according to need ‖ *v.i.* (with 'with') to be in gear ‖ (with 'into') to fit exactly

gel·a·tin, gel·a·tine (dʒélətin, dʒélət'n) *n.* a brittle, transparent, tasteless colloidal protein, soluble in water, extracted with glue and size from animal hides, skins and bones, and used in foods, photography and the making of sizing, plastic compounds etc. ‖ a substance having physical properties similar to those of gelatin, e.g. agar-agar ‖ blasting gelatin **ge·lat·i·nate** (dʒəlǽtineit) *pres. part.* **ge·lat·i·nat·ing** *past* and *past part.* **ge·lat·i·nat·ed** *v.t.* and *i.* to gelatinize **ge·lát·i·nize** *pres. part.* **ge·lat·i·niz·ing** *past* and *past part.* **ge·lat·i·nized** *v.t.* to make gelatinous ‖ *(photog.)* to treat or coat with gelatin ‖ *v.i.* to become gelatinous

ge·lat·i·nous (dʒəlǽt'nəs) *adj.* jellylike ‖ of or containing gelatin

geld (geld) *pres. part.* **geld·ing** *past* and *past part.* **geld·ed, gelt** (gelt) *v.t.* to castrate (an animal) ‖ to spay

geld·ing (géldiŋ) *n.* a gelded animal, esp. a gelded horse

gem (dʒem) 1. *n.* a precious stone, esp. when cut and polished for ornament ‖ an engraved precious or semiprecious stone ‖ something treasured particularly ‖ someone who ought to be treasured ‖ a work of art that is small and exquisite 2. *v.t. pres. part.* **gem·ming** *past* and *past part.* **gemmed** to adorn with gems

gen·der (dʒéndər) *n.* *(gram.)* the classification of words, or the class to which a word belongs by virtue of such classification, according to the sex of the referent (natural gender) or according to arbitrary distinctions of form and syntax (grammatical gender) ‖ *(pop.)* sex (male or female)

gene (dʒi:n) *n.* a portion of a chromosome which, if further subdivided into parts, would lose the character of a hereditary unit, i.e. the ability to copy itself during the reproductive process of the cell, and the ability to copy itself even after undergoing a mutation

ge·ne·al·o·gy (dʒi:ni:ólədʒi:, dʒi:ni:ǽlədʒi:) *pl.* **ge·ne·al·o·gies** *n.* the study of family pedigrees ‖ the descent of a person or family from an ancestor, generation by generation ‖ the record of this descent, a pedigree ‖ the line of development of a plant or animal from earlier forms

gen·er·al (dʒénərəl) 1. *adj.* pertaining to a whole or to most of its parts, not particular, not local ‖ prevalent, widespread ‖ customary, usual ‖ concerned with main features and not with details ‖ not restricted ‖ indefinite, vague ‖ not specialized ‖ above the rank of colonel ‖ of top rank 2. *n.* an army officer ranking below a general of the army ‖ any army commander as military strategist ‖ *(eccles.)* the head of a religious order **in general** for the most part

---

(a) æ, cat; ɑ, car; ɔ fawn; ei, snake. **(e)** e, hen; i:, sheep; iə, deer; ɛə, bear. **(i)** i, fish; ai, tiger; ə:, bird. **(o)** o, ox; au, cow; ou, goat; u, poor; ɔi, royal. **(u)** ʌ, duck; u, bull; u:, goose; ə, bacillus; ju:, cube. x, loch; θ, think; ð, bother; z, Zen; ʒ, corsage; dʒ, savage; ŋ, orangutang; j, yak; ʃ, fish; tʃ, fetch; 'l, rabble; 'n, redden. Complete pronunciation key appears inside front cover.

gen·er·al·i·ty (dʒenərǽliti:) pl. **gen·er·al·i·ties** n. a general point ‖ a vague statement ‖ the state of being general

gen·er·al·i·za·tion (dʒenərəlizéiʃən) n. a general notion or statement (whether true or false) derived from particular instances ‖ the forming of such notions or statements

gen·er·al·ize (dʒénərəlaiz) pres. part. **gen·er·al·iz·ing** past and past part. **gen·er·al·ized** v.i. to draw a general rule or statement from particular instances ‖ to use generalities ‖ v.t. to draw (a general rule or statement) from particular instances ‖ to base a generalization upon (particular instances) ‖ to bring into general use, popularize

gen·er·al·ly (dʒénərəli:) adv. usually, for the most part ‖ widely ‖ in a general sense, without particulars

gen·er·ate (dʒénəreit) pres. part. **gen·er·at·ing** past and past part. **gen·er·at·ed** v.t. to cause to be, produce ‖ (biol.) to procreate ‖ (math.) to trace out or produce (a line or figure) by motion (of a point, line or other element)

gen·er·a·tion (dʒenəréiʃən) n. a producing or being produced ‖ procreation ‖ a whole body of persons, animals or plants removed in the same degree from an ancestor ‖ the whole body of persons thought of as being born about the same time ‖ a period of time, about 25 or 30 years, roughly corresponding to the age of parents when their children are born

gen·er·a·tive (dʒénəreitiv, dʒénərətiv) adj. of the production of offspring ‖ able to produce

gen·er·a·tor (dʒénəreitər) n. an apparatus for converting mechanical energy into electricity, a dynamo ‖ an apparatus for producing gas or steam

ge·ner·ic (dʒənérik) adj. (biol.) of or pertaining to a genus ‖ of or pertaining to a group or class ‖ having a wide or general application, not specific **ge·nér·i·cal·ly** adv.

gen·er·os·i·ty (dʒenərɔ́siti:) pl. **gen·er·os·i·ties** n. the quality of being generous ‖ an instance of this

gen·er·ous (dʒénərəs) adj. giving freely, liberal, not stingy ‖ noble-minded, magnanimous ‖ plentiful, copious ‖ (of wine) full and rich ‖ (rhet., of soil) very fertile

Gen·e·sis (dʒénisis) the first book of the Old Testament and of the Pentateuch

gen·e·sis (dʒénisis) pl. **gen·e·ses** (dʒénisi:z) n. origin ‖ mode of generation

ge·net·ic (dʒənétik) adj. or of relating to the origin or development of something ‖ of or relating to genetics **ge·nét·i·cal·ly** adv. **ge·net·i·cist** (dʒənétisist). **ge·nét·ics** n. the branch of biology concerned with the heredity and variation of organisms ‖ the genetic constitution of an organism, group or kind

gen·ial (dʒí:njəl) adj. pleasant, cheerful, kindly ‖ (of climate, air etc.) mild, warm

gen·i·tal (dʒénit'l) adj. pertaining to the reproductive organs

gen·i·tals (dʒénit'lz) pl. n. the organs of reproduction, eps. the external organs

gen·ius (dʒí:njəs) pl. **gen·ius·es**, **gen·i·i** (dʒí:ni:ai) n. extraordinary power of intellect, imagination or invention ‖ a person gifted with this ‖ extraordinary aptitude (for some pursuit) ‖ the special characteristics or spirit of an age, culture, people or institution ‖ (rhet., pl. **genii**) a guardian spirit of a person, place or institution

gen·o·cide (dʒénəsaid) n. the deliberate extermination of a race of people, such as the Nazis attempted against the Jews

gen·teel (dʒentí:l) adj. (of manners or people) excessively refined through social pretension ‖ (old-fash.) of or relating to the upper class

gen·tile (dʒéntail) **1.** adj. not Jewish, esp. Christian ‖ (among Mormons) not Mormon **2.** n. a non-Jew, esp. a Christian ‖ (among Mormons) a non-Mormon

gen·til·i·ty (dʒentíliti:) n. refinement in conduct and manners ‖ excessive and affected refinement or delicacy

gen·tle (dʒént'l) **1.** adj. mild, sensitively light ‖ moderate, not strong or violent ‖ docile **2.** n. a maggot used as bait in fishing

gen·tle·man (dʒént'lmən) pl. **gen·tle·men** (dʒént'lmən) n. a man of the wealthy, leisured class ‖ a man of high principles, honorable and courteous (regardless of social position) ‖ (in polite and conventional usage) a man

gen·tly (dʒéntli:) adv. in a gentle manner

gen·try (dʒéntri:) n. people of good family, esp. those next in rank to the nobility

gen·u·ine (dʒénju:in) adj. real, not pretended ‖ authentic ‖ frank, honest, sincere

ge·nus (dʒí:nəs) pl. **gen·e·ra** (dʒénərə), **ge·nus·es** n. (biol.) a group of animals or plants within a family, closely connected by common characteristics ‖ a class of things

ge·og·ra·pher (dʒi:ɔ́grəfər) n. a specialist in geography

ge·o·graph·ic (dʒi:əgrǽfik) adj. of or relating to geography **ge·o·gráph·i·cal** adj.

ge·og·ra·phy (dʒi:ɔ́grəfi:) pl. **ge·og·ra·phies** n. the science of the earth, broadly divided into physical geography, which deals with the composition of the earth's surface and the distribution of its features, and human geography, which includes econmic, political and social geography and is concerned essentially with the changes wrought by man on his environment ‖ the data with which this science deals ‖ a treatise or textbook of geography

ge·o·log·ic (dʒi:əlɔ́dʒik) adj. of or pertaining to geology **ge·o·lóg·i·cal** adj.

ge·ol·o·gist (dʒi:ɔ́lədʒist) n. a specialist in geology

ge·ol·o·gy (dʒi:ɔ́lədʒi:) pl. **ge·ol·o·gies** n. the scientific study of the nature, formation, origin and development of the earth's crust and of its layers ‖ these data ‖ a treatise on this subject

ge·o·met·ric (dʒi:əmétrik) adj. of or pertaining to geometry ‖ formed of regular lines, curves and angles **ge·o·mét·ri·cal** adj.

ge·om·e·try (dʒi:ɔ́mitri:) pl. **ge·om·e·tries** n. the mathematical study of the properties of, and relations between, points, lines, angles, surfaces and solids in space ‖ a treatise on this subject ‖ the dimensional relations within a composite

ge·o·phys·i·cal (dʒi:oufízik'l) adj. of or pertaining to geophysics

ge·o·phys·ics (dʒi:oufíziks) n. the application of the methods of physics to the study of the earth and its atmosphere. It includes meteorology, terrestrial magnetism, seismology, hydrology etc.

ge·ra·ni·um (dʒiréini:əm) n. a plant having brightly colored flowers and pungent-smelling leaves. Geraniums are widely distributed, esp. in temperate areas. Perfume oil is extracted from the foliage of many species

ger·i·at·ric (dʒeri:ǽtrik) adj. (med.) pertaining to geriatrics ‖ (med.) of or relating to aging or the aged **ger·i·át·rics** n. the branch of medicine dealing with old age and its diseases

germ (dʒə:rm) n. a microorganism, often pathogenic ‖ the earliest stage in the development of an organism, e.g. the formative protoplasm of an egg ‖ a seed or embryo ‖ a thing from which something may develop as if from a seed

ger·mane (dʒərméin) adj. relevant

ger·mi·nate (dʒə́:rmineit) pres. part. **ger·mi·nat·ing** past and past part. **ger·mi·nat·ed** v.i. to begin to grow, sprout, develop ‖ v.t. to cause to sprout ‖ to produce (ideas, forces etc.)

ger·mi·na·tion (dʒə́:rminəeiʃən) n. the beginning of growth

ger·und (dʒérənd) n. (Latin gram.) a verbal noun used in all but the nominative case ‖ (English gram.) a verbal noun ending in '-ing' **ge·run·di·al** (dʒərʌ́ndi:əl) adj.

ges·ta·tion (dʒestéiʃən) n. the inter-uterine period in the development of the mammalian embryo, which from fertilization to birth is supplied with food and oxygen through the blood system of the parent carrying it

ges·tic·u·late (dʒestíkjuleit) *pres. part.* **ges·tic·u·lat·ing** *past and past part.* **ges·tic·u·lat·ed** *v.i.* to wave the arms about, make expressive gestures while speaking or instead of speech ‖ *v.t.* to express by gestures **ges·tic·u·la·tion** *n.* **ges·tic·u·la·tive** (dʒestíkjuleitiv, dʒestíkjulətiv) *adj.* **ges·tic·u·la·tor** *n.* **ges·tic·u·la·tor·ry** (dʒestíkjulətɔri:, dʒestíkjulətouri:) *adj.*

ges·ture (dʒéstʃər, dʒéʃtʃər) 1. *n.* a movement of the hand or body to express an emotion or intention ‖ some word or deed either intended to convey an attitude or intention or dictated by diplomacy or respect for form 2. *v.i. pres. part.* **ges·tur·ing** *past and past part.* **ges·tured** to make gestures, gesticulate

get (get) *pres. part.* **get·ting** *past* **got** (gɒt) *past part.* **got, got·ten** (gɒt'n) *v.t.* to acquire ‖ to procure ‖ to fetch ‖ to buy ‖ to receive ‖ to earn ‖ to arrive at by calculation ‖ to hit ‖ to catch (an illness) ‖ to prepare ‖ *(pop.)* to grasp the meaning of, understand ‖ to establish communication with by radio, telephone etc. ‖ to induce, persuade ‖ *(pop.)* to baffle, puzzle ‖ *(pop.)* to irritate ‖ *(pop.)* to charm, enchant ‖ *v.i.* (with 'across', 'over', 'here', 'there' etc.) to succeed in moving, arriving etc. ‖ to become ‖ (with *infin.*) to grow, come gradually ‖ to go, take oneself off ‖ (with *pres. part.*) to begin ‖ *(pop., imper.)* clear out!, go away!

gey·ser (gáizər) *n.* a spring which throws up jets of hot water and steam from time to time, found in regions that are, or recently have been, volcanic

ghast·ly (gǽstli:, gáːstli:) 1. *adj. comp.* **ghast·li·er** *superl.* **ghast·li·est** horrifying, gruesome ‖ deathlike, ghostlike ‖ *(pop.)* very unpleasant 2. *adv.* in a ghastly manner

gher·kin (gɔ́ːrkin) *n.* a plant yielding a knobbly fruit, like a small cucumber, used mainly for pickles ‖ the fruit of this plant ‖ an immature cucumber selected for pickling

ghet·to (gétou) *pl.* **ghet·tos, ghet·toes** *n.* *(hist.)* the quarter of a city in which Jews were required to reside ‖ a quarter of a city largely inhabited by Jews ‖ a quarter where members of a minority reside as a result of social or economic pressure

ghost (goust) 1. *n.* the specter of a person appearing after their death, an apparition ‖ a slight trace, a glimmer ‖ a ghost-writer ‖ *(phys.)* a false line in a line spectrum due to the defective ruling of the diffraction grating ‖ *(optics)* a secondary image or bright spot caused by a defect in the lens of an instrument 2. *v.t.* to be the ghost-writer of (a book) ‖ *v.i.* to act as ghost-writer

ghost·ly (góustli:) *comp.* **ghost·li·er** *superl.* **ghost·li·est** *adj.* like a ghost ‖ eerie, preternatural ‖ *(archaic)* concerned with spiritual matters

ghoul (guːl) *n.* (in Oriental stories) a spirit which robs graves and devours corpses ‖ *(pop.)* a person of weird or macabre appearance or habits **ghóul·ish** *adj.*

G.I. (dʒiːái) 1. *n.* an American serviceman, esp. an enlisted man 2. *adj.* of, characteristic of or belonging to the U.S. Army [GOVERNMENT ISSUE]

gi·ant (dʒáiənt) 1. *n.* a mythical person of superhuman size, often appearing in children's stories or in folklore ‖ an abnormally tall person ‖ anything large of its kind ‖ someone of exceptional ability 2. *adj.* exceptionally big **gí·ant·ess** *n.*

gib·ber·ish (dʒíbəriʃ, gíbəriʃ) *n.* rapid inarticulate chatter ‖ speech that is not understood and therefore sounds like a confused gabble

gib·bon (gíbən) *n.* an anthropoid ape native to S.E. Asia. Gibbons are tailless, have exceptionally long

arms, and give a loud, piercing cry

gib·bous (gíbəs, dʒíbəs) *adj.* rounded out, convex ‖ (of the moon or a planet) above half and less than full ‖ humpbacked, having a hump

gibe, jibe (dʒaib) 1. *v. pres. part.* **gib·ing, jib·ing** *past and past part.* **gibed, jibed** *v.t.* to jeer, scoff ‖ *v.t.* to mock 2. *n.* an expression of mockery, a taunt, sneer

gib·lets (dʒíblits) *pl. n.* the gizzard and edible innards of a fowl, commonly removed before it is cooked and used for making gravy or soup

gid·di·ness (gídi:nis) *n.* the quality or state of being giddy

gid·dy (gídi:) *comp.* **gid·di·er** *superl.* **gid·di·est** *adj.* dizzy ‖ making one feel dizzy ‖ *(old-fash.)* frivolous

gift (gift) 1. *n.* a thing given ‖ a natural talent 2. *v.t.* to endow with a natural talent ‖ to give as a gift ‖ to bestow gifts upon

gi·gan·tic (dʒaigǽntik) *adj.* giantlike, very large **gi·gán·ti·cal·ly** *adv.*

gig·gle (gíg'l) 1. *v. pres. part.* **gig·gling** *past and past part.* **gig·gled** to laugh foolishly or nervously or in an attempt to repress outright laughter 2. *n.* foolish, nervous or half-suppressed laughter **the giggles** a fit of such laughter **gig·gly** *adj.*

gig·o·lo (dʒígəlou, ʒígəlou) *pl.* **gig·o·los** *n.* a man kept by a woman ‖ a professional male dancing partner or paid escort

gild (gild) *pres. part.* **gild·ing** *past and past part.* **gild·ed, gilt** (gilt) *v.t.* to cover with a fine layer of gold or gold leaf ‖ *(rhet.)* to make golden ‖ to give a speciously attractive appearance to

gill (gil) 1. *n.* the vascular respiratory organ in fish and other water-breathing animals ‖ the dewlap of a fowl ‖ one of the vertical radiating plates on the underside of mushrooms or toadstools 2. *v.t.* to gut (fish) ‖ to catch (fish) by the gill covers in a gill net

gilt (gilt) 1. *n.* gilding ‖ superficial glitter 2. *adj.* gilded

gim·mick (gímik) *n.* a gadget ‖ any clever scheme ‖ a hidden device for controlling a gambling wheel ‖ any deceptive trick or device

gin (dʒin) *n.* a strong liquor distilled from grain and flavored with juniper berries or a substitute for them ‖ gin rummy

gin (dʒin) 1. *n.* a spring trap with steel teeth, a snare ‖ a hoisting device, usually a tripod with one hinged leg ‖ a machine for removing seeds etc. from fiber, esp. cotton 2. *v.t. pres. part.* **gin·ning** *past and past part.* **ginned** to trap, snare with a gin ‖ to remove seeds from (cotton) with a gin

gin·ger (dʒíndʒər) 1. *n.* a perennial native to Asia but widely cultivated for its aromatic rhizome, which is used as a spice, in sweetmeats and in medicine ‖ a sandy reddish color 2. *adj.* of a sandy, reddish color 3. *v.t.* *(pop., with 'up')* to liven, animate ‖ to add ginger to

gin·ger·bread (dʒíndʒərbrɛd) *n.* cake made with molasses and ginger ‖ cheap, gaudy ornamentation

gin·ger·ly (dʒíndʒərli:) 1. *adv.* very cautiously or warily, so as not to damage or disturb, or so as to avoid close contact 2. *adj.* very cautious or wary

ging·ham (gíŋəm) *n.* an inexpensive cotton fabric, usually checked or striped

gi·raffe (dʒirǽf, *Br.* dʒiráf) *n.* an African ruminant quadruped, the tallest living animal (18–20 ft) with an extraordinarily long neck and long forelegs

gir·an·dole (dʒírəndoul) *n.* an elaborate, branched candle holder ‖ an earring or pendant, with a large jewel set in a circle of smaller ones ‖ a rotating firework ‖ a rotating water jet

gird (gɔːrd) *v.i.* (with 'at') to jeer, gibe, scoff

gird *pres. part.* **gird·ing** *past* and *past part.* **gird·ed, girt** (gə:rt) *v.t.* *(rhet.)* to encircle (the waist) with a belt ‖ *(archaic)* to fasten with a belt ‖ *(rhet.)* to surround, encircle ‖ *(refl., rhet.)* to clothe oneself, equip oneself **gird·er** *n.* an iron or steel (rarely wooden) beam used in building and bridge construction ‖ (in floors) one of the main joist-supporting, horizontal members

gir·dle (gə:rd'l) **1.** *n.* a belt or sash encircling the waist ‖ anything which encircles like a girdle ‖ a usually elastic undergarment worn by women to hold in the waist, hips and buttocks ‖ the ring made around a tree by cutting away the bark ‖ *(anat.)* a bony arch to support a limb ‖ the outer rim of a cut gem clasped by the setting **2.** *v.t.* *pres. part.* **gir·dling** *past* and *past part.* **gir·dled** to bind with a girdle ‖ to encircle, enclose ‖ to cut a ring around the bark of

girl (gə:rl) *n.* a female child ‖ a young unmarried woman ‖ *(pop.)* a single or married woman at any age ‖ a female servant, maid ‖ a girlfriend, sweetheart

girl·ish (gə:rliʃ) *adj.* of, like or suitable to a girl

girth (gə:rθ) **1.** *n.* the band which fastens around the body of a horse or other animal to secure the saddle, pack etc. ‖ the circumference of a thing **2.** *v.t.* to fit or secure with a girth

gist (dʒist) *n.* the main point, the heart of the matter ‖ *(law)* the real ground or point of an action

give (giv) **1.** *v. pres. part.* **giv·ing** *past* **gave** (geiv) *past part.* **giv·en** (gívən) *v.t.* to offer as a present ‖ to hand over ‖ to put into someone's hands ‖ to pay as price ‖ to make involuntarily ‖ to provide with, supply ‖ to furnish as product ‖ to offer as host or sponsor ‖ to produce, yield ‖ to show ‖ to grant, confer ‖ to confer ownership of ‖ to inflict ‖ to pronounce ‖ to administer ‖ to pledge ‖ to allow, permit ‖ to concede, admit ‖ to deliver (a message) ‖ to bestow in charity, by legacy, as alms etc. ‖ to bestow (friendship, trust etc.) ‖ to perform before an audience ‖ to name for a toast ‖ to sacrifice ‖ to bestow in marriage ‖ *v.i.* to make a gift ‖ to yield to pressure ‖ to open or look out **2.** *n.* elasticity, springiness

giv·en (gívən) *past part.* of GIVE ‖ *adj.* agreed, fixed ‖ executed, esp. in official documents ‖ *(math., logic)* granted, admitted as the basis of a calculation, or as data or premises

gla·cial (gléiʃəl) *adj.* icy, frozen ‖ *(geol.)* of or pertaining to glaciers ‖ *(chem.)* having icelike crystals

gla·cier (gléiʃər) *n.* a river of ice in a high mountain valley formed by the consolidation under pressure of snow falling on higher ground

glad (glæd) *comp.* **glad·der** *superl.* **glad·dest** *adj.* joyful ‖ (used only predicatively) happy about some specific circumstance, pleased **glad·den** (glǽd'n) *v.t.* to make glad

glade (gleid) *n.* a clear, open space in a forst ‖ an everglade

glad·i·a·tor (glǽdi·ẹitər) *n.* *(hist.)* a fighter with a sword or other weapon at a Roman circus **glad·i·a·tor·i·al** (glædi:ətóri:əl, glædi:ətóuri:əl) *adj.*

glad·i·o·lus (glædi:óuləs) *pl.* **glad·i·o·li** (glædi:óulai), **glad·i·o·lus**, **glad·i·o·lus·es** *n.* a plant of genus *Gladiolus*, fam. *Iridaceae*, having long, sword-shaped leaves and bright, variously colored flowers

glad·ly (glǽdli:) *adv.* with gladness ‖ willingly

glam·or·ous (glǽmərəs) *adj.* having glamour

glam·our, glam·or (glǽmər) *n.* dazzling charm, allure and mysterious fascination

glance 1. *v. pres. part.* **glanc·ing** *past* and *past part.* **glanced** *v.i.* to look briefly ‖ to be deflected obliquely at the point of impact ‖ (usually with 'over') to allude with deliberate brevity ‖ to flash, gleam **2.** *n.* a brief look ‖ a sudden gleam of light

gland (glænd) *n.* a single structure of cells, which takes certain substances from the blood and secretes them in a form which the body can use or eliminate ‖ a similar structure in a plant

glan·du·lar (glǽndʒulər) *adj.* of, like, consisting of, or

containing a gland or gland cells

glare (gleər) **1.** *v. pres. part.* **glar·ing** *past* and *past part.* **glared** *v.i.* to shine brightly and fiercely ‖ to stare fiercely ‖ to be too conspicuous ‖ *v.t.* to express (anger etc.) with a look **2.** *n.* a strong, fierce light ‖ a fierce, intense look ‖ (of colors) the quality of being uncomfortably bright **glar·ing** *adj.* bright and dazzling ‖ staring fiercely ‖ flagrant ‖ garish, too vivid

glass (glæs, glɑs) **1.** *pl.* **glass·es** *n.* a hard, brittle, transparent or translucent, greenish solid solution made by melting a mixture of silica (esp. sand) and various silicates, with metallic oxides added to give the product special qualities ‖ a drinking vessel made of glass ‖ its contents ‖ a mirror made of glass backed by a bright film or reflecting metal ‖ a protective cover made of glass ‖ a glass lens ‖ an optical device having a glass lens or lenses, e.g. a telescope or microscope ‖ *(pl.)* spectacles ‖ *(pl.)* binoculars ‖ an hourglass ‖ a pane of glass ‖ glassware **2.** *v.t.* to fit with, cover with, or encase in glass **3.** *adj.* made of glass, pertaining to glass

glass·y (glǽsi:, glɑsi:) *comp.* **glass·i·er** *superl.* **glass·i·est** *adj.* like glass ‖ dull, lifeless ‖ smooth, calm

glau·co·ma (glɔkóumə, glaukóumə) *n.* a disease of the eye, characterized by an increase of pressure of the fluids within the eyeball, leading to gradual loss of vision and blindness **glau·có·ma·tous** *adj.*

glaze (gleiz) **1.** *v. pres. part.* **glaz·ing** *past* and *past part.* **glazed** *v.t.* to fit (a window or picture frame) with glass ‖ to apply a vitreous coating to (pottery etc.) ‖ to give a smooth, glossy coating to (leather, cloth, certain foods etc.) ‖ to cover (a painted surface) with a thin transparent layer so as to modify the underlying color ‖ to polish ‖ *v.i.* to become glassy **to glaze in** to enclose with glass panels **2.** *n.* the glassy compound fired on pottery etc. to make it watertight or to please the eye ‖ a brightness, sheen ‖ a smooth coating (given to cloth, leather, food etc.) ‖ a glassy film ‖ a transparent coat applied to a painted surface ‖ ice formed by rain falling on objects below freezing temperature ‖ a stretch of ice

gla·zier (gléiʒər) *n.* someone who cuts and sets glass in windows professionally **glá·zier·y** *n.*

gleam (gli:m) **1.** *n.* a glint ‖ a faint light, or something compared to this **2.** *v.i.* to glint ‖ to glow, to shine dimly

glean (gli:n) *v.i.* to gather leavings of grain after the reaping ‖ *v.t.* to gather leavings of grain in (a field) after reaping ‖ to collect little by little **gléan·ing** *n.* (usually *pl.*) something gathered by gleaning

glee (gli:) *n.* effervescent, demonstrative mirth ‖ laughing satisfaction at the misfortunes of others ‖ *(mus.)* an unaccompanied part-song mainly of the 18th c. for three or more voices (usually male)

glee·ful (glí:fəl) *adj.* filled with glee

glen (glen) *n.* a narrow valley

glib (glib) *comp.* **glib·ber** *superl.* **glib·best** *adj.* too pat ‖ shallow and facile

glide (glaid) **1.** *v. pres. part.* **glid·ing** *past* and *past part.* **glid·ed** *v.i.* to move smoothly forward without apparent effort ‖ *(aeron.)* to fly without engine power ‖ to move silently ‖ to pass imperceptibly ‖ *(mus.)* to pass from one note to another with a glide ‖ *v.t.* to cause to glide **2.** *n.* the act of gliding ‖ a sliding step used in dancing ‖ *(mus.)* a slur ‖ *(phon.)* the transitional sound made when changing from one speech position to another **glíd·er** *n.* an engineless aircraft used for sport and, as a towed transport, esp. for military purposes

glim·mer (glímər) **1.** *v.i.* to shine feebly or intermittently **2.** *n.* a feeble or intermittent light ‖ a faint gleam (of hope etc.) ‖ a glimpse **glím·mer·ing** *n.*

glimpse (glimps) **1.** *v.t. pres. part.* **glimps·ing** *past* and *past part.* **glimpsed** to catch sight of briefly or fleetingly **2.** *n.* a brief view

glint (glint) **1.** *v.i.* to flash, sparkle ‖ *v.t.* (of the eyes) to express (an emotion) by flashing **2.** *n.* a flash, gleam

glis·ten (glís'n) 1. *v.i.* to sparkle, glitter ‖ to appear bright, usually by reflecting light 2. *n.* a glitter

glitch (glitʃ) *n. (slang)* a misfunction in machinery, esp. in electricity input resulting in a surge in power

glit·ter (glítər) 1. *v.i.* to sparkle very brightly ‖ to be resplendent 2. *n.* sparkle, brilliance ‖ bits of tinsel, glass etc. used for ornamentation **glit·ter·y** *adj.*

gloat (glout) *v.i.* to look at or think about something with malicious, greedy or lustful pleasure

glo·bal (glóub'l) *adj.* spherical ‖ involving the whole world ‖ comprehensive, total

globe (gloub) *n.* a sphere ‖ a spherical model of the earth or the heavens ‖ *(rhet.)* the earth

glob·ule (glóbju:l) *n.* a small round particle or drop

gloom (glu:m) 1. *v.i. (rhet.)* to look morose, be sullen ‖ *(rhet., of the sky, etc.)* to look menacing, lower 2. *n.* semidarkness ‖ heavy shadow ‖ melancholy, dejectedness

gloom·y (glú:mi:) *comp.* **gloom·i·er** *superl.* **gloom·i·est** *adj.* dark, obscure ‖ melancholy ‖ dismal, depressing

glo·ri·fi·ca·tion (glɔrifikéiʃən, glɔurifikéiʃən) *n.* a glorifying or being glorified

glo·ri·fy (glɔ́rifai, glɔ́urifai) *pres. part.* **glo·ri·fy·ing** *past* and *past part.* **glo·ri·fied** *v.t.* to ascribe glory to, praise ‖ to make radiantly beautiful ‖ to swell pompously the importance of, esp. by naming pretentiously

glo·ri·ous (glɔ́ri:əs, glɔ́uri:əs) *adj.* full of glory or worthy of glory, illustrious ‖ splendid, thrilling ‖ *(pop.)* immensely enjoyable

glo·ry (glɔ́ri:, glɔ́uri:) 1. *pl.* **glo·ries** *n.* praise, adoration ‖ great renown ‖ particular distinction ‖ magnificence, splendor ‖ sublime beauty ‖ *(art)* the luminous aureole surrounding the whole body of Christ ‖ the splendor of heaven, beatitude 2. *v.i. pres. part.* **glo·ry·ing** *past* and *past part.* **glo·ried** to exult, rejoice ‖ to take pride (in)

gloss (glɔs, glɔs) 1. *n.* an interlinear translation ‖ an explanatory interlinear or marginal insertion in the text of a book ‖ a glossary ‖ a verbal interpretation or paraphrase ‖ a sophistical, misleading interpretation 2. *v.t.* to insert glosses in or provide a glossary for (a text) ‖ to comment on or interpret in a misleading or prejudiced way ‖ *v.i.* to make glosses

gloss 1. *n.* sheen ‖ deceitful appearance 2. *v.t.* to give a gloss to ‖ (with 'over') to cause to seem less serious, difficult, unfavorable etc. than is really the case by specious argument etc.

glos·sa·ry (glɔ́səri:, glɔ́səri:) *pl.* **glos·sa·ries** *n.* a list of difficult, old, technical or foreign words with explanations, usually at the end of a text

gloss·y (glɔ́si:, glɔ́si:) 1. *adj. comp.* **gloss·i·er** *superl.* **gloss·i·est** shiny, smooth, highly polished ‖ superficially attractive, specious 2. *pl.* **gloss·ies** *n.* a magazine printed on glossy paper

glot·tis (glɔ́tis) *n.* the opening between the vocal cords in the throat which controls the modulation of speech sounds

glove (glʌv) 1. *n.* one of a pair of coverings for the hands, usually with separate divisions for the fingers and for the thumb, worn for warmth, protection or adornment 2. *v.t. pres. part.* **glov·ing** *past* and *past part.* **gloved** to cover with or as if with a glove ‖ to furnish with gloves **glov·er** *n.* someone who makes or sells gloves

glow (glou) 1. *v.i.* to emit light, esp. red light, without the smoke or flame of rapid combustion ‖ to be radiant ‖ to have a bright, warm color 2. *n.* the emission of light without smoke or flame ‖ warmth produced by physical exertion ‖ warmth of emotion or passion

glow·er (gláuər) 1. *v.i.* to stare with sullen anger 2. *n.* a look of sullen anger

glue (glu:) 1. *n.* a hard, brown, brittle substance obtained from crude gelatin and used as an adhesive when softened by heating or solution ‖ any similar adhesive 2. *v. pres. part.* **glu·ing** *past* and *past part.* **glued** *v.t.* to attach with glue or as if with glue ‖ *v.i.* to become glued

glum (glʌm) *comp.* **glum·mer** *superl.* **glum·mest** *adj.* gloomy, morose

glut (glʌt) 1. *v.t. pres. part.* **glut·ting** *past* and *past part.* **glut·ted** to fill to excess, oversupply ‖ to satisfy utterly ‖ to overfeed, gorge 2. *n.* oversupply

glut·ton (glʌ́t'n) *n.* someone who eats excessively ‖ someone with a remarkable willingness to endure or perform something of a specified nature **glút·ton·ous** *adj.*

glut·ton·y (glʌ́t'ni:) *n.* excessive eating and drinking

gnash (næʃ) *v.t.* to grind (the teeth) together, in anger etc. ‖ *v.i.* to grind the teeth together, in anger etc.

gnat (næt) *n.* any of various very small, two-winged flies ‖ any very small fly that bites or stings, e.g. the sand fly

gnaw (nɔ) *pres. part.* **gnaw·ing** *past* **gnawed** (nɔd) *past part.* **gnawed, gnawn** (nɔn) *v.t.* to scrape and wear away with the teeth ‖ (of hunger, worry etc.) to be a continuous inner torment to ‖ *v.i.* to bite on something continuously **gnáw·ing** *n.* a persistent fretting discomfort, pain or anxiety

gnome (noum) *n.* a member of a race of small, misshapen imaginary beings, originally guardians of the earth's subterranean treasures ‖ a goblin or dwarf

gnu (nu:, nju:) *pl.* **gnu, gnus** *n.* one of several southern African antelopes, having a heavy neck, an oxlike head, and a tail like that of a horse

go (gou) 1. *v.i. pres. part.* **go·ing** *past* **went** (went) *past part.* **gone** (gɒn) *v.i.* to be in motion ‖ to move with a specified purpose ‖ to leave ‖ to disappear ‖ to extend, reach ‖ to be working, perform its proper function ‖ (of time) to pass ‖ to be on the average ‖ to take a certain course ‖ to remain ‖ to share ‖ to die ‖ to become worn ‖ to be a regular or frequent attender ‖ to commit oneself to action or expense ‖ to have recourse ‖ to fit, be contained ‖ to belong ‖ (of colors) to harmonize, be compatible ‖ to be sold ‖ to be applied ‖ to be allotted ‖ to be valid ‖ (used in the pres. or past continuous tense with an infin.) to be about or intending ‖ *v.t.* to travel on, *to go on a journey* ‖ to travel a distance of ‖ to follow (a way, road etc.) 2. *pl.* **goes** *n.* energy, drive ‖ an attempt

goad (goud) 1. *n.* a pointed stick for driving beasts ‖ something that torments or spurs to action 2. *v.t.* to use a goad on ‖ to urge on by continually irritating

goal (goul) *n. (football, ice hockey* etc.) the pair of posts etc. between or into which the ball or puck has to be sent to score points ‖ the act of sending the ball or puck between the two posts or into the hoop etc. ‖ the point thus scored ‖ an aim or objective

goat (gout) *n.* a wild or domesticated horned ruminant closely allied to the sheep ‖ *(pop.)* a lecher ‖ a scapegoat

goat·ee (goutí:) *n.* a small, pointed or tufted beard on the chin

gob·ble (gɔ́b'l) 1. *v.i. pres. part.* **gob·bling** *past* and *past part.* **gob·bled** (of a turkeycock) to make its characteristic guttural sound 2. *n.* this sound

gob·let (gɔ́blit) *n. (hist.)* a drinking vessel of glass or metal without handles but with a stem, a stand and sometimes a cover ‖ a wineglass with a foot and a stem

gob·lin (gɔ́blin) *n.* a mischievous, ugly spirit

god (gɒd) *n.* (in polytheistic religions) a being to whom worship is ascribed ‖ an image of such a deity ‖ an

---

idolized person or thing **God** (in monotheistic religions) the supreme being, seen as the omnipotent creator and ruler of the universe **the gods** pl. n. the theater audience up in the gallery ‖ the gallery itself
god·dess (gɔ́dis) n. a female deity
god·fa·ther (gɔ́dfɑðər) n. a man who sponsors a child at baptism, assuming responsibility for the child's religious guidance up to confirmation ‖ chief-of-chiefs in the Mafia and, by extension, other organizations
god·ly (gɔ́dli:) comp. **god·li·er** superl. **god·li·est** adj. pious, devout
god·moth·er (gɔ́dmʌðər) n. a woman who sponsors a child at baptism and assumes responsibility for the child's religious guidance up to confirmation
god·par·ent (gɔ́dpɛərənt) n. a godfather or a godmother
god·send (gɔ́dsend) n. something received unexpectedly just when needed
gog·gle (gɔ́g'l) 1. v. pres. part. **gog·gling** past and past part. **gog·gled** v.i. to stare with eyes protruding or rolling ‖ (of eyes) to protrude ‖ v.t. to roll (the eyes) 2. n. a rolling of the eyes
go·ing (gɔ́uiŋ) 1. n. departure ‖ the state of a path, racecourse or road ‖ rate of progress 2. adj. working, in operation ‖ (pop.) available ‖ viable ‖ prevailing, current [pres. part. of GO]
goi·ter, goi·tre (gɔ́itər) n. an enlargement of the thyroid gland that often results from deficient iodine in the diet and may be associated with hypothyroidism or, sometimes, with hyperthyroidism **goi·trous** adj.
gold (gould) 1. n. a yellow, malleable, ductile metallic element that occurs naturally in the uncombined state. It is monovalent and trivalent, and resists most chemical attack (save e.g. by chlorine or aqua regia). It is used in coinage, dentistry and jewelry, hardened by being alloyed esp. with copper or silver ‖ (collect.) coins minted from this metal ‖ the color of gold, a deep yellow 2. adj. made of gold, or having the color of gold
gold·en (gɔ́uldən) adj. having the color of gold ‖ made of gold ‖ eminently favorable ‖ having the qualities associated with gold, e.g. purity, splendor, excellence ‖ (of a jubilee, wedding or other anniversary) fiftieth
golf (gɔlf, gɔlf) 1. n. an outdoor game, originating in Scotland, in which a small, white, resilient ball is hit with one of a set of long-shafted clubs into a series of 9 or 18 holes up to about 550 yards apart from one another and distributed over a course having natural or artificial hazards (trees, sand-filled bunkers etc.) 2. v.i. to play golf
go·nad (gɔ́unæd, gɔ́næd) n. (biol.) a primary sexual gland, the testicle or ovary
gon·do·la (gɔ́nd'lə) n. a graceful narrow flat-bottomed boat about 30 ft long used on the canals of Venice, propelled by a single oar at the stern, and with upward-curving prow and stern ‖ a car suspended from a dirigible or balloon ‖ a flat-bottomed barge ‖ an open railroad car
gon·do·lier (gɔnd'líər) n. the rower of a gondola
gong (gɔŋ, gɔŋ) n. a metal disk with its rim turned back. It hangs freely, and when struck gives a muffled, resonant note ‖ a mechanism consisting of a saucer-shaped bell sounded by a hammer
gon·or·rhe·a, gon·or·rhoe·a (gɔnərí:ə) n. a venereal disease caused by gonococci and characterized by the discharge of pus from the genital organs
good (gud) 1. comp. **bet·ter** (bétər) superl. **best** (best) adj. serving its purpose well, having desired qualities ‖ morally excellent, virtuous ‖ well behaved, dutiful ‖ kind ‖ agreeable, pleasant ‖ beneficial ‖ sound, wholesome ‖ worthwhile, serious ‖ thorough ‖ considerable ‖ full, rather more than ‖ efficient, competent ‖ sound, reliable ‖ orthodox and devout ‖ valid 2. n. that which is morally right ‖ profit, benefit, advantage ‖ use, value, worth **for good** forever **to the good** beneficial ‖ in profit 3. adv. very 4. interj. an exclamation of satisfaction or pleasure

good-bye, good-by (gudbái) 1. interj. farewell 2. n. a farewell
good-heart·ed (gúdhɑ́rtid) adj. kind, quick to offer friendship or help
good·ly (gúdli:) comp. **good·li·er** superl. **good·li·est** adj. (old-fash.) sizable
good·ness (gúdnis) 1. n. the quality or state of being good ‖ the good element of something 2. interj. used as a euphemism for 'God' in mild expletives
goose (gu:s) pl. **geese** (gi:s) n. a waterfowl of fam. Anatidae, between a duck and swan in size, esp. a member of one of the domesticated varieties living chiefly on land, feeding on herbage and valued for their meat and feathers ‖ the female goose ‖ the flesh of the goose as food ‖ a silly person ‖ (pl. **goos·es**) a tailor's iron **to cook someone's goose** to destroy someone's chances
gore (gɔr, gour) pres. part. **gor·ing** past and past part. **gored** v.t. to pierce or wound with horns or tusks
gore n. (rhet.) blood, esp. blood that has been shed
gore 1. n. a triangular piece of material used to give a flare to a skirt etc. ‖ a triangular panel in an umbrella, sail, balloon etc. 2. v.t. pres. part. **gor·ing** past and past part. **gored** to vary width with a gore ‖ to cut into a triangular shape
gorge (gɔrdʒ) n. a narrow ravine between hills ‖ (hist.) the rear entrance to a fortification or outwork ‖ a choking mass, e.g. of ice ‖ the line made where the collar and lapels of a jacket or coat turn over **to make one's gorge rise** to give one a feeling of revulsion
gorge 1. v. pres. part. **gorg·ing** past and past part. **gorged** v.i. to eat greedily ‖ v.t. to fill (oneself) with food ‖ to fill up, choke, stuff 2. n. a gluttonous feed
gor·geous (gɔ́rdʒəs) adj. splendid, sumptuous, magnificent ‖ (pop.) excellent, fine, nice, good
gosh (gɔʃ) interj. used to express mild surprise or sudden pleasure
gos·ling (gɔ́zliŋ) n. a young goose
Gos·pel (gɔ́spəl) n. one of the first four books (Matthew, Mark, Luke and John) of the New Testament ‖ part of one of these books read at Mass or the Communion Service **gos·pel** the record of Christ's life contained in Matthew, Mark, Luke and John ‖ the message about redemption preached by Christ ‖ the content of Christian preaching ‖ (pop.) anything that is to be firmly believed ‖ a principle that one acts upon **gós·pel·er** n. the reader of the gospel at High Mass
gos·sa·mer (gɔ́səmər) 1. n. a light film of spiders' threads, such as is seen spread over grass and traced out in sparkling drops of dew ‖ one single such thread ‖ exceedingly light, gauzy material 2. adj. as light and delicate as gossamer ‖ of gossamer
gos·sip (gɔ́sip) 1. n. easy, fluent, trivial talk ‖ an instance of this ‖ talk about people behind their backs ‖ a person who indulges in gossip 2. v.i. to talk idly, chatter, esp. about people **gós·sip·y** adj.
gouge (gaudʒ) 1. n. a chisel with a concavo-convex cross section for cutting grooves 2. v.t. pres. part. **goug·ing** past and past part. **gouged** to cut out with a gouge ‖ to scoop or force out, as if with a gouge
gou·lash (gú:lɑʃ, gú:læʃ) n. a stew of beef or veal and vegetables flavored with paprika
gourd (guərd) n. any of several large, hard-rinded, inedible fruits of genus Lagenaria, used for making vessels etc. ‖ a small, ornamental, hard-rinded, inedible variety of pumpkin ‖ a gourd-bearing plant ‖ the hollowed out hard rind of any of these fruits, used for holding liquids etc.
gour·mand (guərmənd) n. someone who appreciates good food but without the refinement of taste of a gourmet, and usually with gluttonous excess
gour·met (guərmei, guərméi) n. someone who is an expert judge of good food and wine
gout (gaut) n. an intensely painful form of arthritis affecting the joints, esp. the big toe, and most often found in men **góut·y** comp. **gout·i·er** superl. **gout·i·est**

adj. having or tending to have gout || resulting from or causing gout || resembling gout

gov·ern (gʌ́vərn) *v.t.* to control and direct, rule || to be dominant in, determine || to restrain, control || to serve as or constitute a law or rule || to control the speed or power of (a machine) esp. by an automatic control || *v.i.* to rule **gov·ern·a·ble** *adj.*

gov·ern·ess (gʌ́vərnis) *n.* a woman employed to teach children in their own homes

gov·ern·ment (gʌ́vərnmənt, gʌ́vərmənt) *n.* a governing, nationwide rule, authoritative control || a system of governing (the ministers who govern a country || *(gram.)* a governing (of the number or case etc. of one word by another) **gov·ern·men·tal** (gʌvərnméntəl, gʌvərmént'l) *adj.*

gov·er·nor (gʌ́vərnər) *n.* someone who governs || the chief executive of each state of the U.S.A. || a member of the governing board of an institution, e.g. of a school or hospital || *(mech.)* a device for keeping the speed of rotation of a driven shaft constant as the load on it varies

gown (gaun) 1. *n.* a woman's dress, esp. a particularly elegant one || a loose robe, esp. worn as official dress by judges, lawyers, aldermen etc. or as academic dress 2. *v.t.* to clothe in a gown

grab (græb) 1. *v. pres. part.* **grab·bing** past and past part. **grabbed** *v.t.* to seize suddenly, snatch || *(pop.)* to capture || to seize illegally, forcibly or greedily || *(colloq.)* to hold excited attention || *v.i.* to make a snatching gesture 2. *n.* the act of grabbing || a sudden snatch or grasp || a forcible or unscrupulous seizure || a mechanical device for grabbing and lifting

grace (greis) 1. *n.* charm, elegance, attractiveness, esp. of a delicate, slender, refined, light or unlabored kind || a sense of what is fitting || courtesy || delay conceded as a favor || an attractive feature || a social accomplishment || favor || *(theol.)* unconstrained and undeserved divine favor or goodwill, God's loving mercy displayed to man for the salvation of his soul || a short prayer of thanksgiving offered before or after a meal || a title used in referring to or addressing a duke, duchess or archbishop **with good (bad, ill) grace** gladly, willingly (reluctantly, grudgingly) **to be in someone's good graces** to enjoy someone's favor 2. *v.t. pres. part.* **grac·ing** past and past part. **graced** to add grace to, adorn || to honor, do credit to

grace·ful (gréisfəl) *adj.* elegant in proportions or movement, slender or lithe || courteous, charmingly expressed || pleasing, attractive

gra·cious (gréiʃəs) 1. *adj.* showing grace in character, manners or appearance || courteous, *a gracious host* || condescendingly kind (often used ironically) || having qualities associated with good breeding and refinement of taste || *(theol.)* bestowing divine grace, merciful 2. *interj.* an exclamation of surprise etc.

gra·da·tion (greidéiʃən) *n.* a grading or being graded || a stage in the transition from one grade or type to another || the gradual passing of one color into another

grade (greid) 1. *n.* a degree or step in rank, quality or value || a class of persons or things of the same rank, quality etc. || a yearly stage in a child's school career || the pupils in such a stage || a mark or rating awarded to a pupil || a crossbred variety (of cattle etc.) having one purebred parent || a gradient **on the upgrade (downgrade)** rising, improving (falling, worsening) **to make the grade** to achieve the required standard 2. *v. pres. part.* **grad·ing** past and past part. **grad·ed** *v.t.* to arrange in grades, sort || to gradate, blend || to award a grade or mark to || to level out the gradients of (a road etc.) || *v.i.* to pass from one grade to another

to grade up to improve (bloodstock) by crossing with superior stock

grad·u·al (grǽdʒuːəl) *adj.* proceeding or taking place slowly, step by step, not steep or abrupt

grad·u·ate (grǽdʒuːit) 1. *n.* someone who has taken a bachelor's degree || someone who has completed a set course of study at school or college and received a diploma || *(chem.)* a graduated flask or tube 2. *v.* (grǽdʒuːeit) *pres. part.* **grad·u·at·ing** past and past part. **grad·u·at·ed** *v.i.* to become a graduate || to pass by gradations, gradate || *v.t.* to grant a degree or diploma to || to attach a scale of numbers to (a measuring instrument), or to mark (it) at fixed places of measurement || to graduate according to a certain scale

grad·u·a·tion (grædʒuːéiʃən) *n.* a graduating or being graduated || the ceremony of conferring academic degrees etc. || a mark on a vessel, gauge etc. to indicate measurement

graf·fi·to (græfíːtou) *pl.* **graf·fi·ti** (græfíːtiː) *n.* an inscription or design scratched into an ancient wall || a rude scribbling on a wall, e.g. in a public toilet || an incised decoration to reveal a second color, e.g. on a pot

graft (græft, grɑft) 1. *n.* *(hort.)* a shoot or bud from one plant inserted in a slit or groove cut in another plant (the stock) || *(med.)* a piece of transplanted living tissue || the process of grafting || the dishonest use of public office for private gain || the gains thus secured 2. *v.t. (hort.)* to insert as a graft || *(med.)* to transplant (living tissue) || to insert (something) into an alien position so that it is accepted as belonging || *v.i.* to become joined in a graft || to make a graft

Grail (greil) *n.* the cup used by Christ at the Last Supper

grain (grein) 1. *n.* the seed of a cereal grass || such seeds collectively || harvested cereals in general || a minute, hard particle || the smallest unit of weight || a very small amount || the hairy surface of leather || a stamped pattern imitating the grain of leather || the direction and pattern in which wood fibers grow, or the natural arrangement of strata in stone, coal etc. **against the grain** against one's natural tendency or inclination 2. *v.t.* to paint (something) so that it appears to have the natural grain of wood or marble || to give a granular surface to || *v.i.* to become granulated

gram (græm) *n.* *(abbr.* gm) the unit of mass in the metric system, defined as the thousandth part of the standard kilogram mass

gram·mar (grǽmər) *n.* the science dealing with the systematic rules of a language, its forms, inflections and syntax, and the art of using them correctly || the system of forms and syntactical usages characteristic of any language || a book of grammar

gram·mat·i·cal (grəmǽtik'l) *adj.* of or pertaining to grammar || in accordance with the rules of grammar **gram·mát·i·cal·ly** *adv.*

gran·a·ry (grǽnəriː, gréinəriː) *pl.* **gran·a·ries** *n.* a storehouse for threshed grain || a region producing or exporting much grain

grand (grænd) 1. *adj.* accompanied by pomp and display, splendid || imposing, distinguished, *grand company* || self-important || highest, or very high in rank || main, principal || summing up all the others, final || noble, dignified, lofty || *(pop.)* very enjoyable, excellent || (used only in compounds) indicating the second degree of ancestry or descent, as in 'grandparent' 2. *n.* a grand piano

grand·child (grǽntʃaild) *pl.* **grand·chil·dren** (grǽntʃildrin) *n.* a child of one's son or daughter

grand·daugh·ter (grǽndɔtər) *n.* the daughter of one's child

grand·fa·ther (grǽndfɑðər) *n.* the father of either of one's parents

gran·dil·o·quence (grændíləkwəns) *n.* the quality of being grandiloquent

gran·dil·o·quent (grændíləkwənt) *adj.* pompous and overeloquent in style or delivery

gran·di·ose (grǽndi:ous) *adj.* grand in an impressive way, imposing ‖ of inflated importance or magnificence

grand jury a jury of 12 to 23 persons which investigates certain indictments in private session and decides whether or not there is sufficient evidence to warrant a trial

grand·moth·er (grǽnmʌðər) *n.* the mother of either of one's parents

grand·par·ent (grǽnpɛərənt) *n.* a grandfather or grandmother

grand·stand (grǽnstænd) *n.* a roofed-over stand with tiered seats, commanding the best view at football games etc.

grange (gréindʒ) *n.* a country house, esp. with associated farm buildings

gra·nite (grǽnit) *n.* a very hard crystalline igneous rock normally composed of quartz, feldspar and mica', valuable for building **gra·nit·ic** *adj.*

grant (grænt, grɑnt) **1.** *v.t.* to agree to fulfill ‖ to allow to have, give ‖ to admit, concede ‖ to concede (a proposition) without proof for the sake of argument ‖ *(law)* to bestow ownership, transfer **to take for granted** to assume ‖ to accept (someone or something) thoughtlessly, without proper appreciation, esp. through familiarity **2.** *n.* the act of granting ‖ something granted, esp. money ‖ *(law)* the formal bestowal of property ‖ *(law)* the property bestowed **gran·tée** *n.* *(law)* someone who receives a grant

gran·u·lar (grǽnjulər) *adj.* consisting of grains ‖ as if composed of grains in surface or structure

gran·u·late (grǽnjuleit) *pres. part.* **gran·u·lat·ing** *past* and *past part.* **gran·u·lat·ed** *v.t.* to form into grains ‖ to roughen the surface of ‖ *v.i.* to become granular ‖ (of a wound when forming a scab) to form tiny prominences of fresh tissue **gran·u·lá·tion** *n.*

gran·ule (grǽnju:l) *n.* a small grain

grape (greip) *n.* a green or purple berry growing in bunches on a vine which can be eaten fresh or dried, or pressed and fermented to make wine

grape·fruit (gréipfru:t) *n.* a small tree native to the West Indies ‖ the large yellow citrus fruit which it yields

graph (græf, grɑf) **1.** *n.* a diagram showing the relation of one variable quantity to another, by expressing their values as distances from usually two, sometimes three, axes at right angles to one another **2.** *v.t.* to denote by a graph

graph·ic (grǽfik) *adj.* concerned with decoration and representation on a flat surface ‖ (of descriptive writing, drawing etc.) conjuring up a clear picture in the mind, vivid ‖ having to do with graphs or diagrams ‖ *(mineral.)* showing marks like written characters on the surface or in section **gráph·i·cal** *adj.* **graph·i·cal·ly** *adv.*

graph·ite (grǽfait) *n.* a naturally occurring form of carbon. It is a softish black material, used in the manufacture of pencils, dry lubricants, paints, in electrical apparatus, and as a moderator in nuclear reactors

grap·nel (grǽpnəl) *n.* a small, clawed anchor or other hooked instrument, used e.g. in dragging ‖ *(mil.)* in naval mine warfare, a device fitted to a mine mooring designed to grapple the sweep wire when the mooring is cut

grap·ple (grǽp'l) **1.** *n.* a grip, grasp ‖ a grapnel **2.** *v. pres. part.* **grap·pling** *past* and *past part.* **grap·pled** *v.i.* to fight at close quarters or hand to hand ‖ to try hard to find a solution ‖ *v.t.* to seize or hold with or as if with a grapnel

grasp (græsp, grɑsp) **1.** *v.t.* to seize hold of firmly with the hand ‖ to hold firmly ‖ to understand, comprehend ‖ *v.i.* to reach out eagerly ‖ to try to seize advantage **2.** *n.* a tight hold, grip ‖ control ‖ intellectual control,

understanding **within (beyond) one's grasp** within (out of) reach **grásp·ing** *adj.* aggressively out for one's own advantage

grass (græs, grɑs) **1.** *n.* the low green herbage of pastureland and lawns ‖ a member of *Gramineae*, one of the largest and most cosmopolitan of the monocotyledonous families (including cereals, reeds, bamboos, as well as pasture grasses), with fibrous roots, hollow jointed stems, alternate, linear, bladed, sheathing leaves, and fruit in the form of a caryopsis ‖ pasture, grazing ‖ pastureland ‖ grass-covered ground ‖ *(pop.)* marijuana **to let the grass grow under one's feet** to waste time when there is an opportunity to be grasped **2.** *v.t.* to plant with grass ‖ to feed on grass ‖ pasture ‖ to lay on the grass for bleaching

grass·hop·per (grǽshɒpər, grɑ́shɒpər) *n.* any of several leaping, orthopterous, plant-eating insects, predominantly nocturnal and allied to locusts

grass·y (grǽsi:, grɑ́si:) *comp.* **grass·i·er** *superl.* **grass·i·est** *adj.* planted with grass ‖ of or pertaining to grass, grasslike

grate (greit) *n.* a frame of metal bars to contain fuel in a fireplace or furnace ‖ the fireplace itself ‖ a grating, grill (of a window or over an opening)

grate *pres. part.* **grat·ing** *past* and *past part.* **grat·ed** *v.t.* to reduce to small pieces by rubbing against a sharp or rough surface ‖ to rub or grind (something) against something else, making a harsh noise ‖ *v.i.* to make a harsh sound ‖ to have an irritating effect

grate·ful (graǽitfəl) *adj.* feeling or showing gratitude ‖ *(rhet.)* comforting, pleasant

grat·i·fi·ca·tion (grætifikéiʃən) *n.* a gratifying or being gratified ‖ a source of satisfaction

grat·i·fy (grǽtifai) *pres. part.* **grat·i·fy·ing** *past* and *past part.* **grat·i·fied** *v.t.* to do a favor to, please ‖ to indulge, satisfy

grat·ing (gréitiŋ) *n.* a partition, frame or cover of bars, parallel or crossed ‖ *(phys.)* a diffraction grating

grating *pres. part.* of GRATE ‖ *adj.* harsh, discordant ‖ irritating

gra·tis (gréitis, grǽtis, grɑ́tis) **1.** *adv.* without charge **2.** *adj.* free, given away

grat·i·tude (grǽtitju:d) *n.* a feeling of appreciation for a kindness or favor received

gra·tu·i·tous (grətú:itəs, grətjú:itəs) *adj.* given or received free ‖ unwarranted, uncalled for, *a gratuitous insult* ‖ *(law)* given without compensation

gra·tu·i·ty (grətú:iti:, grətjú:iti:) *pl.* **gra·tu·i·ties** *n.* a tip for services rendered

grave 1. (greiv) *adj.* warranting anxiety ‖ solemn, thoughtful ‖ important, weighty ‖ (grɑv) of, or marked with, an accent (`) used to indicate vowel quality (e.g. in French) or various kinds of stress **2.** (grɑv) *n.* a grave accent

grave (greiv) *n.* a trench dug for the burial of a corpse ‖ a burial place, tomb ‖ *(rhet.)* any place that receives the dead **to turn in one's grave** to have one's eternal peace destroyed (by words or acts that one would have vehemently disapproved in one's lifetime)

grav·el (grǽvəl) **1.** *n.* a loose mixture of small pebbles and rock fragments, and sometimes sand ‖ *(geol.)* a stratum of this ‖ *(med.)* a collection of granular crystals in the kidneys and bladder ‖ the condition characterized by this **2.** *v.t. pres. part.* **grav·el·ing** *past* and *past part.* **grav·eled** to cover with gravel **gráv·el·ly** *adj.*

grave·yard (gréivjɑrd) *n.* a burial ground, cemetery

grav·i·tate (grǽviteit) *pres. part.* **grav·i·tat·ing** *past* and *past part.* **grav·i·tat·ed** *v.i.* to move under the force of gravity ‖ to move or be attracted compulsively towards some center of influence

grav·i·ta·tion (grævitéiʃən) *n.* the act or process of gravitating ‖ *(phys.)* a force of attraction acting between two bodies that is independent of the chemical nature of the bodies or the presence of intervening matter **grav·i·tá·tion·al** *adj.*

grav·i·ty (grǽviti:) *pl.* **grav·i·ties** *n.* solemn importance

‖ seriousness ‖ seriousness of demeanor ‖ weight, heaviness ‖ *(phys.)* the gravitational attraction between the earth and bodies at or near its surface ‖ *(phys.)* gravitation in general

gra·vy (gréivi:) *n.* the juice that comes out of meat while it is cooking ‖ a sauce made from this juice

gray, grey (grei) **1.** *adj.* of a color between white and black ‖ overcast or gloomy ‖ depressing, cheerless ‖ gray-haired ‖ of the members of a religious order wearing a gray habit ‖ (of fabric) just as it leaves the loom or spinning machine, unbleached and undyed, but not necessarily gray in color **2.** *n.* a gray color, pigment, fabric etc. ‖ a dull gray light ‖ a white horse ‖ (of cloth) the state of being unbleached and undyed **3.** *v.t.* to make gray ‖ *v.i.* to become gray

graze (greiz) **1.** *v. pres. part.* **graz·ing** *past* and *past part.* **grazed** *v.t.* to touch or rub lightly in passing ‖ to rub the skin from, abrade ‖ to suffer a slight abrasion of ‖ *v.i.* to come into light scraping contact **2.** *n.* a superficial abrasion or rub caused by grazing

graze *pres. part.* **graz·ing** *past* and *past part.* **grazed** *v.i.* to feed on growing grass ‖ *v.t.* to put out to pasture ‖ to put cattle etc. to feed on (a field) ‖ to feed on (growing grass) ‖ to look after (grazing cattle etc.)

grease 1. (gri:s) *n.* soft, melted or rendered animal fat ‖ any oily or fatty matter, esp. when used as a lubricant or protective film on cars, machinery etc. ‖ the oily matter in wool ‖ the raw state of wool just after shearing and before being cleaned, *wool in the grease* **2.** (gri:s, gri:z) *v.t. pres. part.* **greas·ing** *past* and *past part.* **greased** *v.t.* to put or rub grease on, lubricate **to grease the hand** (or **palm**) **of** to bribe **to grease the wheels** to make affairs run smoothly (esp. with the aid of money)

greas·y (grí:si:, grí:zi:) *comp.* **greas·i·er** *superl.* **greas·i·est** *adj.* covered with grease ‖ containing, made of or like grease ‖ damp and slippery, *greasy roads* ‖ dirty-looking, unwashed ‖ insinuating, using a veneer of politeness to ingratiate oneself

great (greit) *adj.* large in size, big ‖ as an intensive, emphasizing a following adjective ‖ large in number or extent ‖ a high degree of ‖ beyond the ordinary ‖ specially important, memorable ‖ powerful, important ‖ significant in history ‖ chief, preeminent ‖ favorite ‖ eminent, distinguished, having remarkable ability etc. ‖ noble ‖ of high rank or position ‖ fully deserving the name of (intensifying the sense of the following noun) ‖ enthusiastic in the pursuing of some interest or activity ‖ excellent, satisfactory, very pleasing (amusing, exciting etc.) ‖ (used only in compounds) one degree further removed in ancestry or descent, e.g. in 'great-grandfather' **great at** very good at, proficient at **great in** *(pop.)* excelling in **great on** *(pop.)* keen on, knowledgeable about

great·ly (gréitli:) *adv.* much, to a great degree (esp. with comparatives, participles and certain verbs

greed (gri:d) *n.* excessive desire, esp. for food or wealth

greed·y (grí:di:) *comp.* **greed·i·er** *superl.* **greed·i·est** *adj.* inordinately fond of food, gluttonous ‖ inordinately desirous, avaricious

green (gri:n) **1.** *adj.* of the color sensation stimulated by the wavelengths of light in that portion of the spectrum between blue and yellow, being the color e.g. of emeralds ‖ covered with herbage or foliage, in leaf ‖ having a pale, sickly complexion, e.g. from fear ‖ vegetable ‖ not yet ripe or mature ‖ young and flourishing ‖ immature, unskilled, inexperienced ‖ gullible, easily fooled **to be green around the gills** to look as though about to be sick **2.** *n.* a green color, pigment, fabric etc. ‖ the green part of something ‖ green vegetation or foliage, verdure ‖ *(pl.)* leafy veg-

etables, e.g. spinach, beet tops etc. ‖ *(pl.)* leaves or branches of trees used for wreaths, decorations etc. ‖ a stretch of grass for public use, *the village green* ‖ *(golf)* the area of short-cut turf surrounding the hole

green *v.i.* to become green ‖ *v.t.* to make green

green·er·y (grí:nəri:) *n.* green foliage, esp. used for decoration

greet (gri:t) *v.t.* to address with courteous words or gestures on meeting ‖ to salute the arrival of in a specified manner ‖ to make an impression on the senses of (someone arriving)

greet·ing (grí:tiŋ) *n.* an expression or gesture used when meeting someone ‖ a form of address at the beginning of a letter, e.g. 'Dear Sir' ‖ an expression of goodwill

gre·gar·i·ous (grigéəri:əs) *adj.* living in or pertaining to flocks or communities ‖ fond of being among other people

gre·nade (grinéid) *n.* a small, fused, explosive shell, with a round or oval segmented iron casing, thrown by hand or fired from a rifle ‖ a round glass bottle thrown to put out fires, spread tear gas etc. by dispersing its chemical contents

grid (grid) **1.** *n.* a frame of spaced parallel bars, a grating ‖ *(elec.)* a lattice or spiral electrode positioned between two others in an electron tube ‖ a frame of numbered squares superimposed on a map so that exact reference may be made to any point on the map ‖ a gridiron for cooking ‖ *(typography)* on a phototypesetting machine, the glass screen on which the typeset text is exposed ‖ *(auto racing)* the starting point **2.** *v.t. pres. part.* **grid·ding** *past* and *past part.* **grid·ded** to furnish with a grid

grid·dle (gríd'l) *n.* a circular plate, usually of iron, for cooking pancakes etc. on

grid·i·ron (grídaiərn) *n.* a framework of metal bars with legs or a handle, used for broiling ‖ *(naut.)* a frame of parallel beams used to support a ship in dock ‖ *(theater)* a framework of planks and beams over a stage, supporting the mechanism for curtains and scenery ‖ *(football)* the playing field, so called from its network of marked lines

grief (gri:f) *n.* deep sorrow ‖ a cause of sorrow or anxiety **to come to grief** to meet with disaster ‖ to fail

griev·ance (grí:vəns) *n.* a real or fancied wrong, hardship, or cause of complaint

grieve (gri:v) *pres. part.* **griev·ing** *past* and *past part.* **grieved** *v.t.* to cause deep sorrow to ‖ *v.i.* to feel grief, mourn

griev·ous (grí:vəs) *adj.* bringing great suffering and trouble ‖ (of disease, injury etc.) very painful, severe ‖ exciting grief, pitiful ‖ serious, heinous

grif·fin, grif·fon, gryph·on (grífin) *n.* a fabulous creature with the head and wings of an eagle and the body of a lion

grill 1. *n.* a form of postal cancellation consisting of a rectangular pattern of small dots made by a metal roll with points **2.** *v.t.* to emboss with a grill

grill 1. *v.t.* to broil on a gridiron or under the broiling apparatus of a gas or electric stove ‖ to torture with great heat ‖ to interrogate closely, torment by severe questioning ‖ to be broiled on a gridiron **2.** *n.* a gridiron ‖ a device on gas and electric stoves for radiating an intense direct red heat for cooking meat, making toast, browning the tops of savory dishes etc ‖ a dish of grilled food ‖ a grillroom ‖ the act or process of grilling

grim (grim) *comp.* **grim·mer** *superl.* **grim·mest** *adj.* stern, severe ‖ unrelenting ‖ forbidding, threatening ‖ unalleviated by humor or cheerfulness ‖ sinister ‖ mirthless

---

(a) æ, c*a*t; ɑ, c*a*r; ɔ f*aw*n; ei, sn*a*ke. **(e)** e, h*e*n; i:, sh*ee*p; iə, d*ee*r; εə, b*ea*r. **(i)** i, f*i*sh; ai, t*i*ger; ə:, b*i*rd. **(o)** o, *o*x; au, c*ow*; ou, g*oa*t; u, p*oo*r; ɔi, r*oy*al. **(u)** ʌ, d*u*ck; u, b*u*ll; u:, g*oo*se; ə, b*a*cillus; ju:, c*u*be. x, lo*ch*; θ, *th*ink; ð, bo*th*er; z, *Z*en; ʒ, cor*s*age; dʒ, *s*avage; ŋ, oranguta*ng*; j, *y*ak; ʃ, *fi*sh; tʃ, fe*tch*; 'l, rabb*le*; 'n, redd*en*. Complete pronunciation key appears inside front cover.

gri·mace (griméis, gríməs) **1.** *n.* a twisted expression of the face caused by slight pain or shyness, or to convey disgust, distaste, annoyance etc., or to frighten, irritate or amuse, or as an affectation **2.** *v.i. pres. part.* **gri·mac·ing** *past* and *past part.* **gri·maced** to make a grimace

grime (graim) **1.** *n.* ingrained dirt or soot **2.** *v.t. pres. part.* **grim·ing** *past* and *past part.* **grimed** to cover with dirt, soil

grim·y (gráimi:) *comp.* **grim·i·er** *superl.* **grim·i·est** *adj.* covered with grime, dirty

grin (grin) **1.** *v. pres. part.* **grin·ning** *past* and *past part.* **grinned** *v.i.* to smile broadly, showing the teeth, in amusement, pleasure, pain, contempt etc. ‖ (of dogs) to bare the teeth, e.g. when snarling ‖ *v.t.* to express by grinning **to grin and bear it** to suffer without complaining **2.** *n.* the act of grinning ‖ a broad or distorted smile

grind (graind) **1.** *v. pres. part.* **grind·ing** *past* and *past part.* **ground** (graund) *v.t.* to crush to powder or tiny pieces by friction, e.g. between millstones, or between one's teeth, or in a coffee or pepper mill ‖ to produce by grinding ‖ (with 'down') to crush with harsh rule or misery, treat cruelly ‖ to sharpen, smooth, file down or shape by friction ‖ (with 'down') to suppress by wearing down ‖ to cause to grate ‖ to thrust with a twisting motion ‖ to work by turning a handle ‖ to produce (music) by being worked in this way ‖ (with 'out') to produce with toil and (unwilling) effort, force out ‖ to compel by repeated effort to absorb (learning, sense etc.) ‖ *v.i.* to perform the activity of reducing something to fine particles by friction ‖ to admit of being ground ‖ (of a vehicle) to move laboriously ‖ to work or study hard (esp. for an examination) ‖ to grate **2.** *n.* a period of unbroken hard work or study to which one forces oneself ‖ (*pop.*) an unremitting student ‖ a long, steady gradient or the effort needed to climb it ‖ the act of grinding

grind·stone (gráindstoun) *n.* a thick stone disk revolving on an axle and used for grinding, sharpening and smoothing ‖ a stone from which grindstones are made **to keep one's nose to the grindstone** to keep steadily at a task by an effort of the will

grip (grip) **1.** *n.* a tight hold, strong grasp ‖ the power to grasp ‖ a way of holding ‖ (*fig.*) hold, power ‖ mental grasp, intellectual mastery ‖ the power to hold attention ‖ any device that grips ‖ the part of a racket etc. that one holds ‖ a traveling bag **to come to grips** to fight in close struggle ‖ to make a serious struggle or attempt at mastery **to lose one's grip** to lose control or mastery, e.g. of affairs or of an art or skill **2.** *v. pres. part.* **grip·ping** *past* and *past part.* **gripped** *v.t.* to take a firm hold of, grasp, seize ‖ to seize the attention of ‖ *v.i.* to take hold by friction

gripe (graip) **1.** *v. pres. part.* **grip·ing** *past* and *past part.* **griped** *v.i.* (*pop.*) to complain continually ‖ (*naut.*) to tend to veer into the wind ‖ *v.t.* (*naut.*, *past part.* only) to tie up with gripes **2.** *n.* (*pop.*) a bout of complaining ‖ (*pl.*) pain in the bowels, colic

gris·ly (grízli:) *comp.* **gris·li·er** *superl.* **gris·li·est** *adj.* horrifying, terrifying ‖ ghastly, esp. relating to physical mutilation, wounds etc.

grist (grist) *n.* grain for grinding ‖ malt crushed for brewing ‖ the quantity of grain ground at one time **to bring grist to one's mill** to bring in (a little) revenue **it's all grist to his mill** he turns anything to his profit or advantage

gris·tle (grís'l) *n.* cartilage, esp. the tough, flexible, whitish tissue in meat **gris·tli·ness** (gríslinis) *n.* **grís·tly** *adj.*

grit (grit) **1.** *n.* tiny particles of stone or sand ‖ a kind of coarse sandstone ‖ the grain or structure of stone ‖ pluck and tenacity **2.** *v. pres. part.* **grit·ting** *past* and *past part.* **grit·ted** *v.t.* to grate or grind ‖ *v.i.* to emit a grating sound

grits (grits) *pl. n.* oats with the husk removed, but not ground ‖ coarse oatmeal ‖ coarse hominy ‖ loose gravel for road-surfacing

grit·ty (gríti:) *comp.* **grit·ti·er** *superl.* **grit·ti·est** *adj.* like or containing grit ‖ plucky, brave

griz·zle (gríz'l) *pres. part.* **griz·zling** *past* and *past part.* **griz·zled** *v.t.* to make gray or gray-haired ‖ *v.i.* to become gray or gray-haired **griz·zled** *adj.* grayish ‖ gray-haired

griz·zly (grízli:) **1.** *comp.* **griz·zli·er** *superl.* **griz·zli·est** *adj.* gray-haired or turning gray **2.** *pl.* **griz·zlies** *n.* a grizzly bear

groan (groun) **1.** *v.i.* to make a deep moaning sound through pain, grief or distress ‖ (*rhet.*) to suffer, be oppressed ‖ (*rhet.*) to be heavily loaded down ‖ *v.t.* to utter with a groan **2.** *n.* a deep moaning sound

gro·cer·y (gróusəri:) *pl.* **gro·cer·ies** *n.* the grocer's trade ‖ (*pl.*) goods bought at the grocer's ‖ a grocer's store

groin (grɔin) **1.** *n.* the fold or depression between belly and thighs ‖ (*archit.*) the sharp curved edge formed by the intersection of two vaults **2.** *v.t.* to build with groins

groom (gru:m, grum) **1.** *n.* a bridegroom ‖ a man or boy who looks after horses **2.** *v.t.* to look after, esp. clean and brush (horses) ‖ to smarten (oneself) up ‖ to prepare, train (someone for a certain job)

groove (gru:v) **1.** *n.* a channel or rut ‖ a routine which makes for dullness ‖ (*colloq.*) a good time **2.** *v.t. pres. part.* **groov·ing** *past* and *past part.* **grooved** to make a groove or grooves in ‖ to enjoy, esp. with excitement along with others

grope (group) *pres. part.* **grop·ing** *past* and *past part.* **groped** *v.i.* to feel about, search blindly ‖ to feel or search mentally, with uncertainty and difficulty

gross (grous) **1.** *adj.* repulsively fat ‖ outrageous, flagrant, glaring ‖ not refined, vulgar ‖ indecent, obscene ‖ total, all-inclusive ‖ (of the senses) dull, insensitive, crude **2.** *n.* a totality, sum total **in gross, in the gross** in bulk, wholesale **3.** *v.t.* to gain as gross profit

gro·tesque (groutésk) *adj.* (*art*) combining human, animal and plant forms in a fantastic way ‖ (*literary criticism*) combining elements of tragedy and comedy inextricably ‖ (*loosely*) strangely fanciful, bizarre ‖ ludicrously incongruous, absurd ‖ unnaturally distorted ‖ ridiculously bad

grot·to (grótou) *pl.* **grot·toes, grot·tos** *n.* a picturesque cave ‖ an artificial cave once fashionable in gardens

grouch (grautʃ) **1.** *n.* a bad-tempered, grumbling person ‖ a fit of sulkiness ‖ a fit of grumbling ‖ a cause for grumbling **2.** *v.i.* to complain ‖ to be bad-tempered **grouch·i·ly** *adv.* **grouch·i·ness** *n.* **gróuch·y** *comp.* **grouch·i·er** *superl.* **grouch·i·est** *adj.*

ground (graund) **1.** *n.* the surface of the earth ‖ the upper soil ‖ a place or area on the earth's surface ‖ (*pl.*) land, often with lawns, flower gardens etc., attached to a house for ornament and recreation ‖ an area of land devoted to and equipped for some special purpose ‖ (often *pl.*) a basis for action or belief, motive, sound reason ‖ a basic surface or foundation color in painting, embroidery etc. ‖ (*elec.*) an electrical conductor enabling electricity to pass into the earth **from the ground up** thoroughly **on grounds of** because of ‖ on the pretext of **to break ground** to begin work on a building site ‖ to break fresh ground **to cover the ground** to deal with everything required to be dealt with **to cut the ground from under someone's feet** to anticipate someone's arguments or ideas and dispose of them before they are put forward **to keep one's** (or **both**) **feet on the ground** to be realistic and not idealistic, not forget practical realities **to lose ground** to fall behind or fail to maintain the full extent of a lead in a race ‖ to weaken in any competitive situation, e.g. to lose sales appeal **2.** *adj.* of, at or near the ground, pertaining to the ground **3.** *v.t.* to run (a ship) aground ‖ to confine (an aircraft, a pilot) to the ground, prevent from flying ‖ to base or establish ‖ (*elec.*) to connect with a ground ‖ to prepare the ground of (embroidery etc.) ‖ *v.i.* *(baseball)* to hit a grounder ‖ to touch bottom

ground·hog (gráundhɔg, gráundhɒg) *n.* a woodchuck

ground·work (gráundwəːrk) *n.* a foundation, basis ‖ essential basic labor or study ‖ the background to an embroidered or other pattern etc.

group (gruːp) **1.** *n.* a number of people or things gathered closely together and considered as a whole ‖ an organized body of people with a common purpose ‖ a number of persons or things classed together ‖ *(chem.)* a radical ‖ *(math.)* a set of elements and an operation (e.g. addition, multiplication or a symmetry operation) that obey the axioms of a group ‖ (in scientific classification) a cross-division falling outside the regular system ‖ a blood group **2.** *v.t.* to put into groups ‖ to arrange artistically ‖ to classify ‖ *v.i.* to form a group

grouse (graus) **1.** *v.i. pres. part.* **grous·ing** *past* and *past part.* **groused** to grumble **2.** *n.* a fit of grumbling

grouse *pl.* **grouse** *n.* any of several game birds having plump bodies and feathered legs

grove (grouv) *n.* a group of trees without undergrowth growing naturally as if arranged by man ‖ (of certain trees) an orchard

grov·el (gróvəl, grávəl) *pres. part.* **grov·el·ing** *past* and *past part.* **grov·eled** *v.i.* to lie face down or crouch or crawl at someone's feet as if begging for mercy or favor ‖ to abase oneself abjectly ‖ to take pleasure in what is base, wallow **gróv·el·ing** *adj.* abject ‖ obsequious

grow (grou) *pres. part.* **grow·ing** *past* **grew** (gruː) *past part.* **grown** (groun) *v.i.* to exist or develop as a living plant ‖ to be cultivated ‖ to increase in size as a living organism ‖ to increase in any way, become larger ‖ (with the infin.) to come to ‖ *v.t.* to cause to grow, cultivate ‖ to allow to grow ‖ to develop **to grow into** to become ‖ to grow to fit (clothes) **to grow out of** to become too big for ‖ to abandon in the process of maturing **to grow together** to become united by growth **to grow up** to reach adulthood ‖ to become prevalent **grów·er** *n.* a plant that grows in a specified way ‖ a person who grows vegetables etc., as distinguished from a distributor

growl (graul) **1.** *v.i.* to make the characteristic threatening guttural sound of a dog ‖ *v.t.* to utter in a gruff, rumbling voice, esp. angrily **2.** *n.* the sound made in growling

grown-up 1. (gróunʌp) *adj.* adult, past adolescence **2.** (gróunʌp) *n.* an adult (always in contradistinction to children)

growth (grouθ) *n.* the process of growing or developing ‖ increase in size ‖ origin, development, cultivation ‖ something growing or grown ‖ a morbid formation such as a cancer or tumor ‖ *adj.* *(securities)* of investments expected to increase in value due to expansion of the industry or the company

grub *pres. part.* **grub·bing** *past* and *past part.* **grubbed** *v.i.* to dig or poke in the ground ‖ to search or work laboriously ‖ *v.t.* (with 'up' or 'out') to dig up or out ‖ (with 'up' or 'out') to discover by laborious search

grub·by (grʌ́bi) *comp.* **grub·bi·er** *superl.* **grub·bi·est** *adj.* dirty, unwashed ‖ grub-infested

grudge (grʌdʒ) **1.** *v.t. pres. part.* **grudg·ing** *past* and *past part.* **grudged** to be reluctant to give, grant or allow (something) through envy, spite or meanness ‖ to resent (doing something) **2.** *n.* a feeling of resentment, envy or spite **grúdg·ing** *adj.* reluctant, forced

gru·el·ing (grúːəliŋ) **1.** *adj.* severely testing, exhausting **2.** *n.* a harsh testing, questioning or punishing

grue·some (grúːsəm) *adj.* ghastly, sickening, revolting, esp. associated with blood and mutilation

gruff (grʌf) *adj.* (of the voice) hoarse, rough and harsh ‖ (of speech or manner) blunt, almost surly

grum·ble (grʌ́mbˈl) **1.** *v. pres. part.* **grum·bling** *past* and *past part.* **grum·bled** *v.i.* to complain in a persistent, bad-tempered way, show discontent ‖ to make a low growling sound, rumble ‖ *v.t.* to utter in a sullen complaining way, mutter surlily **2.** *n.* a complaint ‖ something said in a nagging, complaining way ‖ a low growling sound **grúm·bler** *n.*

grump·y (grʌ́mpi) *comp.* **grump·i·er** *superl.* **grump·i·est** *adj.* bad-tempered, disagreeable

grunt (grʌnt) **1.** *v.i.* (esp. of hogs) to make a low, gruff, snorting sound ‖ (of persons) to make a similar sound, expressing discontent, tiredness, effort, irritation, boredom, self-satisfaction etc. ‖ *v.t.* to utter as if with grunts **2.** *n.* a low gruff sound made by hogs or like that made by hogs

guar·an·tee (gærəntíː) **1.** *n.* a pledge given by the makers of an article that they will repair or replace it free if it is unsatisfactory or develops defects within a stated time from the date of purchase ‖ *(law)* a written undertaking made by one person to a second person to be responsible if a third person fails to perform a certain duty, e.g. pay a debt ‖ the person who gives such a guarantee, a guarantor ‖ the person to whom such a guarantee is given ‖ *(law)* a thing given as a security for payment of a loan or fulfillment of a duty ‖ a firm promise, assurance, something that makes another thing seem sure **2.** *v.t. pres. part.* **guar·an·tee·ing** *past* and *past part.* **guar·an·teed** to accept responsibility for the genuineness, proper working or quality of (an article) ‖ to act as guarantor for ‖ to give a security for, secure ‖ to undertake to answer for (the debt or default of another person) ‖ to engage (that something has happened or will happen) ‖ to promise, assure someone of (something)

guar·an·ty (gærənti) *pl.* **guar·an·ties** *n.* *(law)* a guarantee

guard (gɑrd) *v.t.* to keep watch over so as to check or control ‖ to keep watch over so as to protect from danger, defend ‖ to keep in check, control ‖ to provide with a guard, protective device etc. ‖ *(lawn bowling, curling)* to protect (a bowl, stone) by screening it with a second one from a later player ‖ *(chess)* to protect (one piece) with another ‖ *v.i.* to be cautious or watchful, take precautions

gun·ny (gʌ́ni) *n.* coarse cloth, usually made from jute, used for sacks

gun·pow·der (gʌ́npaudər) *n.* an explosive made from saltpeter, sulfur and charcoal now largely superseded by more powerful explosives, but still used in fireworks

gun·smith (gʌ́nsmiθ) *n.* someone who makes and repairs small firearms

gun·wale, gun·nel (gʌ́nˈl) *n.* the upper edge of the side of a ship or boat

gup·py (gʌ́pi) *pl.* **gup·pies** *n.* a small ornamental freshwater fish popular in home aquariums

gur·gle (gə́ːrgˈl) **1.** *v. pres. part.* **gur·gling** *past* and *past part.* **gur·gled** *v.i.* to make a bubbling sound like water being poured from a bottle or sucked over stones ‖ *v.t.* to utter with such a bubbling sound **2.** *n.* the sound made in gurgling

gush (gʌʃ) **1.** *v.i.* to flow or pour out in torrents ‖ to behave or speak with sloppy or affected excess of feeling ‖ to produce a copious flow of something ‖ *v.t.* to emit suddenly or copiously **2.** *n.* an outpour ‖ the fluid etc. emitted in such an outpour ‖ exaggerated display of feeling, esp. insincere **gúsh·er** *n.* an oil well in which the oil spurts from the ground without pumping **gúsh·i·ly** *adv.* in a gushy manner **gúsh·i·ness** *n.* the quality or state of being gushy **gúsh·y** *comp.* **gush·i·er** *superl.* **gush·i·est** *adj.* ful-

---

(a) æ, cat; ɑ, car; ɔ fawn; ei, snake. **(e)** e, hen; iː, sheep; iə, deer; ɛə, bear. **(i)** i, fish; ai, tiger; əː, bird. **(o)** o, ox; au, cow; ou, goat; u, poor; ɔi, royal. **(u)** ʌ, duck; u, bull; uː, goose; ə, bacillus; juː, cube. x, loch; θ, think; ð, bother; z, Zen; ʒ, corsage; dʒ, savage; ŋ, orangutang; j, yak; ʃ, fish; tʃ, fetch; ˈl, rabble; ˈn, redden. Complete pronunciation key appears inside front cover.

somely effusive

gust (gʌst) *n.* a strong burst of wind ‖ a sudden brief rush, emission, puff etc. ‖ an outburst of emotion

gus·ta·to·ry (gʌ́stətɔri:, gʌ́stətɔuri:) *adj.* pertaining to the act of tasting or sense of taste

gut (gʌt) **1.** *n.* (*pl.*, *pop.*) entrails ‖ (*pl.*, *pop.*) pluck and determination ‖ (*pl.*, *pop.*) forceful content ‖ (*physiol.*) the alimentary canal or its lower part ‖ a piece of animal intestine used for the strings of musical instruments, fishing lines, tennis rackets and surgical stitching ‖ (*angling*) the silken substance taken from silkworms ready to spin their cocoons, used for snoods ‖ a narrow passage of water **2.** *v.t. pres. part.* **gut·ting** *past* and *past part.* **gut·ted** to remove the entrails of ‖ to destroy all but the framework of ‖ to extract what is essential from **3.** *adj.* (*colloq.*) intuitive, *gut reaction* ‖ basic

gut·ter (gʌ́tər) **1.** *n.* a metal trough along the edge of a roof to catch and carry away rainwater ‖ a channel in a road for draining off rainwater, specifically the channel formed along the sides of town streets by the angle between curb and road surface ‖ slum environment ‖ the space formed by the adjoining inside margins at the center opening of a book ‖ a channel, conduit or groove **2.** *v.t.* to make channels in ‖ *v.i.* (of water) to flow in channels ‖ (of candles) to melt away as the wax runs down at the side and burn fitfully or feebly

gut·tur·al (gʌ́tərəl) **1.** *adj.* of the throat ‖ (of speech sounds) produced in the throat, e.g. 'k' and 'g' ‖ throaty, harsh, grating **2.** *n.* a guttural sound in speech **gút·tur·al·ize** *pres. part.* **gut·tur·al·iz·ing** *past* and *past part.* **gur·tur·al·ized** *v.t.* (*phon.*) to make guttural

guy (gai) **1.** *n.* a rope or chain to keep something steady or in place **2.** *v.t.* to fasten with a guy

guy 1. *n.* a man, fellow **2.** *v.t.* to ridicule, esp. by burlesque parody

guz·zle (gʌ́z'l) *pres. part.* **guz·zling** *past* and *past part.* **guz·zled** *v.t.* and *i.* to drink or eat greedily and rapidly

gym (dʒim) *n.* a gymnasium ‖ gymnastics

gym·na·si·um (dʒimnéizi:əm) *pl.* **gym·na·si·a** (dʒimnéizi:ə), **gym·na·si·ums** *n.* a room or building for physical exercise, with ropes, vaulting horses, wall bars etc. and changing rooms, shower baths etc., and sometimes also equipped for indoor sports ‖ a type of secondary school in Europe, esp. in Germany, for students preparing for the university

gym·nast (dʒímnæst) *n.* a person skilled in gymnastics

gym·nas·tic (dʒimnǽstik) *adj.* having to do with gymnastics **gym·nás·tics** *n.* exercises to teach body control and agility and strengthen the muscles

gy·ne·col·o·gist, gy·nae·col·o·gist (gainikólədʒist) *n.* a specialist in gynecology

gy·ne·col·o·gy, gy·nae·col·o·gy (gainikólədʒi:) *n.* the study of women's diseases, esp. diseases of the female genital organs and urinary disturbances, excluding problems occurring in late pregnancy

gyp (dʒip) **1.** *n.* (*pop.*) a cheat, swindle ‖ (*pop.*) a swindler **2.** *v.i.* and *t. pres. part.* **gyp·ping** *past* and *past part.* **gypped** (*pop.*) to swindle, cheat

gyp·sum (dʒípsəm) **1.** *n.* a mineral, hydrated calcium sulfate, used as a fertilizer, and to make plaster of paris **2.** *v.t.* to treat with gypsum as manure

gyp·sy, gip·sy (dʒípsi:) *pl.* **gyp·sies, gip·sies 1.** *n.* a member of a swarthy Caucasoid people believed to have originated in India and to have entered Europe in the 14th or 15th c. **2.** *adj.* of or relating to a gypsy or gypsies

gy·rate 1. (dʒairéit, dʒáireit) *v.i. pres. part.* **gy·rat·ing** *past* and *past part.* **gy·rat·ed** to go around in a circle or spiral, whirl, revolve **2.** (dʒáireit) *adj.* (*biol.*) having convolutions **gy·rá·tion** *n.* **gy·ra·to·ry** (dʒáirətɔri:, dʒáirətɔuri:) *adj.*

gy·ro·scope (dʒáirəskoup) *n.* a rapidly spinning wheel mounted in such a way that its plane of rotation can vary. Its moment of inertia, however, keeps this plane constant in space unless a very large couple is ap-

plied. Gyroscopes are used in navigation (e.g. in the gyrocompass), as stabilizers and in scientific instruments **gy·ro·scop·ic** (dʒairəskópik) *adj.*

guard·i·an (gúrdi:ən) *n.* someone who undertakes legal custody of the person and property of someone unable to look after themselves, esp. a person who assumes parental responsibilities for an orphaned child ‖ a protector, keeper, custodian

gu·ber·na·to·ri·al (gu:bərnətɔ́ri:əl, gu:bərnətóuri:əl) *adj.* pertaining to a governor or a governor's office

gudg·eon (gʌ́dʒən) *n.* a pivot at the end of a beam or axle ‖ a ring on a gate which drops over a hook on the gatepost ‖ the socket in which a rudder turns ‖ a pin holding together two blocks (e.g. of stone)

guer·ril·la, guer·ril·la (gərílə) *n.* someone engaged in harassing, raiding or sabotage operations carried out by small bands of irregulars acting independently

guess (ges) **1.** *v.t* to hazard an opinion about without full knowledge or detailed reasoning ‖ to conjecture correctly ‖ to think likely, suppose ‖ *v.i.* to conjecture **to guess at** to attempt to arrive at (an answer) by conjecture **to keep someone guessing** to keep someone in a state of uncertainty **2.** *n.* a rough estimate ‖ a conjecture

guest (gest) *n.* someone who receives hospitality ‖ a person staying at a hotel ‖ (*biol.*) a parasitic insect or other organism

guf·faw (gʌfɔ́:) **1.** *n.* a loud, coarse laugh **2.** *v.i.* to make such a laugh ‖ *v.t.* to utter with such a laugh

guid·ance (gáid'ns) *n.* the act of guiding ‖ direction, advice ‖ leadership

guide (gaid) *pres. part.* **guid·ing** *past* and *past part.* **guid·ed** *v.t.* to go before or with in order to show the way ‖ to direct the course of, steer ‖ to control, direct, influence ‖ *v.i.* to act as a guide

guide *n.* a person who shows the way to strangers, esp. to tourists or to mountaineers ‖ a book of information esp. for visitors to a place ‖ a book of rudiments for beginners ‖ an adviser ‖ the principle governing behavior or choice ‖ (*mech.*) any device which steadies or directs motion

guild, gild (gild) *n.* (*hist.*) a medieval association of merchants or craftsmen ‖ a society of people with common interests and aims

guile (gail) *n.* deceiving trickery, low cunning ‖ wiliness **guíle·ful, guíle·less** *adjs*

guil·lo·tine (gíləti:n, gílətí:n, gí:ləti:n) **1.** *n.* a machine adopted in the French Revolution (and still used in France) for beheading people, by means of a blade sliding down between grooved posts ‖ a surgical instrument for cutting out the tonsils and uvula ‖ a machine for cutting paper **2.** *v.t. pres. part.* **guil·lo·tin·ing** *past* and *past part.* **guil·lo·tined** to use the guillotine on

guilt (gilt) *n.* the fact of having committed a legal offense ‖ the fact of having transgressed the moral law ‖ a feeling of culpability

guilt·y (gílti:) *comp.* **guilt·i·er** *superl.* **guilt·i·est** *adj.* having committed an offense ‖ showing guilt ‖ feeling guilt

guin·ea pig (gíni:pi:g) a small, tailless, short-eared South American rodent, nocturnal, fast-maturing and prolific. Guinea pigs are kept as pets, and are also widely used in medical and biological research ‖ any person or animal used for experiment

guise (gaiz) *n.* (*rhet.*) outward appearance, esp. assumed to conceal the truth

gui·tar (gitár) *n.* a musical instrument, normally with six strings. These are plucked, the tone intervals being controlled by a fret **gui·tár·ist** *n.*

gulch (gʌltʃ) *n.* a short, steepsided ravine

gulf (gʌlf) *n.* an area of sea partly surrounded by coast, larger and with a relatively narrower opening than a bay ‖ (*rhet.*) a great abyss ‖ a huge gap

gull (gʌl) *n.* a cosmopolitan genus of web-footed, long-winged seabirds usually found near coasts, where they feed largely on fish and mollusks and scavenge refuse

gul·let (gˈʌlit) *n.* the esophagus ‖ the throat ‖ *(biol.)* something like the esophagus in appearance or purpose ‖ a channel for water ‖ a gully

gul·li·ble (gˈʌləb'l) *adj.* easily deceived or cheated

gul·ly (gˈʌli:) **1.** *pl.* **gul·lies** *n.* a small steep valley made by water **2.** *v.t.* *pres. part.* **gul·ly·ing** *past* and *past part.* **gul·lied** to make channels in

gulp (gʌlp) **1.** *v.t.* (often with 'down') to swallow (usually a drink) quickly or greedily ‖ (with 'down') to suppress by the action of swallowing convulsively ‖ *v.i.* to swallow food or drink quickly or greedily ‖ to gasp, pant **2.** *n.* the act of gulping ‖ an action like a swallow, e.g. a suppressed sob ‖ a large mouthful

gum (gʌm) **1.** *n.* a sticky liquid that exudes from some trees and shrubs and is also obtained from some seaweeds, dissolving in water, hardening in air, and used as an adhesive or thickening agent in making emulsions, cosmetics and food preparations, and in calico printing ‖ a substance resembling this ‖ a candy made from gelatin or from some other gumlike substance ‖ chewing gum ‖ a gum tree ‖ the secretion which collects in the corner of the eyes ‖ a disease of fruit trees marked by morbid secretion of gum **2.** *v. pres.*

part. **gum·ming** *past* and *past part.* **gummed** *v.t.* to stick with gum ‖ to clog with gum ‖ to smear with gum ‖ *v.i.* to exude gum ‖ to become gummy **to gum up the works** to cause great delay or bring things to a halt in confusion

gum *n.* the flesh by which the teeth are partly surrounded ‖ (often *pl.*) the alveolar part of the jaw

gum·bo (gˈʌmbou) *n.* the okra plant or its pods ‖ a soup thickened with gummy okra pods and containing vegetables and meat or seafood ‖ fine silty soil, chiefly in the western U.S.A., which becomes waxy when it is saturated with water

gun (gʌn) **1.** *n.* any weapon, e.g. a revolver, rifle, machine gun, cannon or piece of artillery, having a metal tube along which a bullet or shell is propelled by explosive force ‖ an air gun ‖ a toy imitation of any such weapon ‖ a tool etc. like a gun in that it ejects some object, substance etc. **to stick to one's guns** to defend doggedly one's position in argument or refuse to give up in any situation **2.** *v. pres. part.* **gun·ning** *past* and *past part.* **gunned** *v.t.* (esp. with 'down') to shoot ‖ *(pop.)* to accelerate (a motor, engine etc.) ‖ *v.i.* *(pop.)* to go at high speed **to gun for** to hunt for with a gun ‖ to look for in order to harm or reprimand ‖ *(pop.)* to try to get

H

H, h (eitʃ) the eighth letter of the English alphabet

hab·it (hˈæbit) *n.* a tendency to repeat an act again and again ‖ a behavior pattern that has a degree of automatism ‖ a monk's or nun's robe ‖ *(biol.)* a characteristic mode of growth and appearance or occurrence

hab·it·a·ble (hˈæbitəb'l) *adj.* able to be lived in

hab·i·tat (hˈæbitæt) *n.* a place or region inhabited by an animal or plant in the natural state ‖ underwater housing for researchers

hab·i·ta·tion (hæbitéiʃən) *n.* the act of living in a place ‖ *(rhet.)* a place or building lived in

ha·bit·u·al (həbítʃu:əl) *adj.* (of an act) performed as the result of a habit ‖ (of a person) having a fixed habit, confirmed ‖ (of a thing) usual, accustomed

ha·bit·u·ate (həbítʃu:eit) *pres. part.* **ha·bit·u·at·ing** *past* and *past part.* **ha·bit·u·at·ed** *v.t.* to make familiar by repetition **ha·bit·u·a·tion** *n.* a habituating or being habituated

ha·bit·u·é (həbítʃu:ei, həbítʃu:éi) *n.* someone who assiduously frequents a place, e.g. a particular restaurant

hack (hæk) **1.** *n.* a horse for riding (as distinguished from a hunter etc.) ‖ a horse let out for hire ‖ a writer employed to write matter of no originality or no great literary merit ‖ *(pop.)* a taxi **2.** *v.i.* to ride on a hired horse ‖ to ride out for pleasure ‖ to do the work of a hack writer ‖ *(pop.)* to drive a taxi **3.** *adj.* (of a writer) employed to write matter of no originality or no great literary merit ‖ (of writing) of no originality nor great literary merit

hack 1. *v.t.* to cut by using a sharp blow or succession of blows ‖ to cut unskillfully, carve badly ‖ *v.i.* to cough repeatedly and raspingly ‖ (with 'at') to make cutting blows ‖ (with 'at') to make wild kicks or hits **2.** *n.* *(sports)* a bruise or wound caused by a kick ‖ a rough cut made by a sharp blow ‖ a tool used for

hacking ‖ a harsh, dry cough

hack·ney (hˈækni:) **1.** *pl.* **hack·neys** *n.* a horse of compact, strong build kept for riding or for driving **2.** *adj.* (of a cab) let out for hire

hack·neyed (hˈækni:d) *adj.* made tedious or commonplace by frequent repetition

had *past* and *past part.* of HAVE ‖ used with adjectives and adverbs of comparison to indicate necessity

hag (hæg) *n.* an ugly old woman ‖ a hagfish

hag·gard (hˈægərd) *adj.* looking worn out by suffering, worry or overexertion

hag·gle (hˈæg'l) **1.** *v.i.* *pres. part.* **hag·gling** *past* and *past part.* **hag·gled** to argue about the price of an article as a process of buying and selling or about the conditions attached to an agreement etc. **2.** *n.* an argument about price, terms of agreement etc.

hail (heil) **1.** *n.* pieces of ice varying in size from a pea to a small ball formed by repeated convectional vertical movements within clouds at low temperature ‖ a thick shower of anything **2.** *v.i.* (impers., of hail) to fall ‖ to fall like hail

hail 1. *v.t.* to call out to (a person) ‖ *(rhet.)* to welcome, *he hailed the news with joy* ‖ *v.i.* (with 'from') to be a native or inhabitant of a named place **2.** *n.* a call made to attract attention ‖ a salute **within hail** near enough to hear a shout

hail·stone (héilstoun) *n.* a single piece of hail

hail·storm (héilstɔrm) *n.* a violent storm during which hail falls

hair (heir) *n.* a threadlike tube of horny, fibrous substance with a core containing pigment cells, rooted in the skin and growing freely outwards, kept pliable by oil from glands in the skin, tending to lose its pigmentation with age or (where protective coloring of animals is concerned) in regions of ice or snow, or because of disease ‖ the covering of these on the human head or an animal body ‖ a threadlike growth on plants **to get in someone's hair** to get on someone's nerves **to let one's hair down** (*pop.*) to discard formality and restraint and give free expression to one's feelings ‖ (*pop.*) to impart confidences without reserve **to make one's hair stand on end** to horrify or terrify one **to split hairs** to draw unimportant distinctions in an argument

hair·breadth (héərbredθ, héərbretθ) **1.** *n.* a very small margin or distance **2.** *adj.* extremely narrow

hair·y (héəri) *comp.* **hair·i·er** *superl.* **hair·i·est** *adj.* covered with hair ‖ having more than the usual quantity of hair ‖ like hair

hale (heil) *adj.* (esp. of an elderly person) physically sound and well

hale *pres. part* **hal·ing** *past* and *past part.* **haled** *v.t.* to force to go

half (hæf, hɑf) **1.** *pl.* **halves** (hævz, hɑvz) *n.* one of the two equal parts into which something is or may be divided ‖ one of two equal periods in a game divided by a break **to go halves** to share equally **2.** *adj.* being one half of something **3.** *adv.* to the extent of a half ‖ almost ‖ partly

half-heart·ed (hæfhártid, hɑfhártid) *adj.* lacking the enthusiasm that comes of full conviction

half·way (hæfwéi, hɑfwéi) **1.** *adj.* equally distant between two points ‖ (*fig.*) not taken far enough **2.** *adj.* half the distance ‖ at the point of compromise

halfway house sheltered workshop or residence designed to help adjustment of institutionalized persons in the process of release, e.g., mental patients, prisoners

half-wit (hæfwit, hɑfwit) *n.* someone of subnormal intelligence **hálf-wit·ted** *adj.*

hal·i·but (hælibət, hɔlibət) *pl.* **hal·i·but**, **hal·i·buts** *n.* a food fish, one of the largest flatfish

hal·i·to·sis (hælitóusis) *n.* bad-smelling breath

hall (hɔl) *n.* a large or small entrance space into which the main door of a house opens and from which there is access to other rooms ‖ a connecting passage or corridor between rooms ‖ a communally owned building where public business is transacted or where people meet for social or recreative purposes ‖ a large room used for meetings or social occasions

hal·le·lu·jah (hælilú:jə) *n.* alleluia [Heb. *halleluyah*, praise Jehovah]

hal·low (hælou) *v.t.* to make holy or sacred ‖ to revere as holy

hal·lu·ci·nant (həlú:sinənt) *n.* cause of hallucinations —**hallucinate** *v.* to see what does not exist **hallu·cinogenic** *n.* a causative drug

hal·lu·ci·nate (həlú:sineit) *pres. part.* **hal·lu·ci·nat·ing** *past* and *past part.* **hal·lu·ci·nat·ed** *v.t.* to cause (a person) to suffer from hallucinations ‖ *v.i.* to experience hallucinations **hal·lu·ci·na·tion** *n.* perception unaccompanied by reality, e.g. hearing voices when no one is present ‖ an object of such perception **hal·lu·ci·na·to·ry** (həlú:sinətɔri:, həlú:sinətouri:) *adj.*

hal·lu·cin·o·gen (həlú:sinədʒən) *n.* a drug (e.g. mescaline) which induces hallucinations **hal·lu·cin·o·gén·ic** *adj.*

hall·way (hɔ́lwei) *n.* an entrance hall ‖ a passage connecting two or more rooms

ha·lo (héilou) *pl.* **ha·loes**, **ha·los** *n.* a disk of diffused light surrounding the sun or moon or a lamp etc. ‖ (*painting*) a bright disk or ring painted above, or surrounding, the head of a holy person as a symbol of glory ‖ glory investing a person in the eyes of others

halt (hɔlt) **1.** *n.* a cessation of movement or action **2.** *v.i.* to stop suddenly ‖ (*mil.*) to stop marching or marking time ‖ *v.t.* to cause (someone or something) to come to a halt ‖ (*mil.*) to cause (troops) to stop marching or marking time

halt·er (hɔ́ltər) **1.** *n.* a rope or strap fastened at one end around the head of a horse or riding camel and used

to lead the animal or to tie it to a firm support ‖ the rope used to hang a criminal ‖ a woman's garment encircling the waist and held in place by straps around the neck, so as to leave the arms and back bare **2.** *v.t.* to put a halter on (an animal)

halt·ing (hɔ́ltiŋ) *adj.* (of steps) dragging, slow ‖ (of rhythm) ragged, uneven ‖ (of utterance, translation etc.) marked by hesitance or awkwardness ‖ (of grammar, argument etc.) betraying imperfect command

halve (hæv, hɑv) *pres. part.* **halv·ing** *past* and *past part.* **halved** *v.t.* to divide into two equal portions ‖ to share equally ‖ to lessen by half ‖ to fit (wooden beams) together at the ends by cutting away half the thickness of each

ham (hæm) **1.** *n.* a whole thigh of a hog, salted and smoke-dried, eaten roasted, boiled or fried ‖ the back of an animal's thigh ‖ a ham actor or performer ‖ a licensed amateur operator of a radio station **2.** *adj.* of an actor or performer who plays his part without intelligence and with overemphasis of gesticulation or voice ‖ of or relating to amateur radio **3.** *v. pres. part.* **ham·ming** *past* and *past part.* **hammed** *v.t.* to play (a part) like a ham actor ‖ *v.i.* to behave like a ham actor

ham·burg·er (hæmbə:rgər) *n.* chopped beef ‖ a hamburg steak ‖ a bun or bread roll containing fried or grilled chopped steak

ham·let (hæmlit) *n.* a small group of dwellings in a rural district, not large enough to warrant a church or school

ham·mer (hæmər) **1.** *n.* a tool consisting of a short, heavy crosspiece made of a hard substance (often steel) fitted at one end of a handle ‖ a hinged lever with a knob at its free end, used as a striker e.g. in a carriage clock or a piano ‖ a gavel ‖ the part of the mechanism of a firearm which strikes the cap of the cartridge ‖ (*anat.*) the malleus ‖ (*athletics*) a spherical weight at one end of a flexible handle, thrown in the 'throwing the hammer' contest ‖ a steam hammer ‖ a drop hammer **to come under the hammer** to be put up for sale by auction **2.** *v.t.* to hit with a hammer blow or series of hammer blows ‖ to shape (metal) by striking it with a series of hammer blows ‖ *v.i.* to deliver a series of blows **to hammer at** to make a prolonged attack on **to hammer home** to drive well in

ham·mock (hæmək) *n.* a rectangle of canvas or strong net suspended from firm supports by several thin ropes at each end

ham·per (hæmpər) **1.** *v.t.* to make (action or progress) difficult **2.** *n.* (*naut.*) rigging, equipment or other gear disposed on or below deck and making it difficult for men to move around a ship

hamper *n.* a large rectangular basket usually of coarse wickerwork, with a lid ‖ a large basket divided into compartments for packing and transporting bottles of wine etc. or food delicacies

ham·ster (hæmstər) *n.* a genus of thick-bodied, short-tailed rodents

hand (hænd) **1.** *n.* the part of the human body from the wrist to the fingertips ‖ a pointer on a dial ‖ a style of penmanship ‖ (*card games*) the cards held by a player ‖ a pledge of fidelity ‖ (*pop.*) applause by an audience ‖ four inches (the breadth of a hand) as a unit of measurement for the height of a horse ‖ a member of a ship's crew ‖ an employee on a farm or in a factory **a free hand** unrestricted powers of decision and action **at first** (**second** etc.) **hand** directly (indirectly as specified) from the person concerned **at hand** near and available ‖ (*rhet.*) very close in future time **by hand** with the hands as distinct from by machinery **from hand to hand** from person to person **from hand to mouth** without provision beyond the immediate present **hands down** (of winning) by an easy victory **hands off!** don't touch! **on hand** available **on the one hand . . . on the other (hand)** from this point of view . . . from that (point of view) **out of hand** beyond control ‖ summarily **out of one's hands** not in one's control or sphere of influence **the upper hand** (in a contest, argument, struggle etc.) domination **to force someone's hand** to compel someone by oblique methods to do what one wishes him to do **to have one's hands full** to be fully occupied ‖ **to lay hands on** to get within one's power, capture ‖ to use violence on (someone) ‖ to find (something temporarily mislaid or concealed) **to lend** (or **give**) **a hand** to assist **to lift a hand** (in negative and interrogative expressions) to make an effort to help **2.** v.t. to give with the hand ‖ to assist or guide with the hand **to hand down** to leave to a successor **to hand out** to distribute **3.** adj. of or pertaining to the hand ‖ worked, used, carried etc. by hand ‖ created by hand

hand·bag (hǽndbæg) n. a woman's bag held in the hand, chiefly used to carry small necessities

hand·ball (hǽndbɔl) n. a game for two or four players, something like squash, but in which the hard rubber ball is struck with the hand. It is played on either one-wall or four-wall courts ‖ the ball used

hand·book (hǽndbuk) n. a book containing summarized information on a particular subject ‖ a guidebook ‖ a book in which a bookmaker records bets

hand·cuff (hǽndkʌf) **1.** n. a steel band which can be clamped around the wrist and locked **2.** v.t. to fasten handcuffs on (a person)

hand·ful (hǽndful) pl. **hand·fuls** n. as much as the hand will hold ‖ a small number ‖ (pop.) a person or thing that is hard to manage

hand·i·cap (hǽndikæp) **1.** n. a disadvantage possessed by one person as compared with others, esp. a physical disability which limits the capacity to earn ‖ a contest in which an allowance of distance, weight or time is made to the weaker competitors, or an artificial disadvantage imposed on the stronger ones ‖ the allowance given or disadvantage imposed ‖ (golf) the number of strokes by which a player is expected to exceed the standard for the course **2.** v.t. pres. part. **han·di·cap·ping** past and past part. **hand·i·capped** to allot a handicap to (a competitor) ‖ to put at a disadvantage, esp. a physical disadvantage **hand·i·cap·per** n. an official who decides what handicap to allot

hand·i·craft (hǽndikræft, hǽndikrɑft) n. a craft (trade or occupation)

hand·i·ly (hǽndʼli:) adv. in a handy way ‖ conveniently ‖ easily

hand·i·work (hǽndiwəːrk) n. the product of handwork

hand·ker·chief (hǽŋkərtʃif, hǽŋkərtʃiːf) n. a usually square piece of fabric carried in a pocket or handbag, used esp. for blowing the nose, weeping into, and waving goodbye with

han·dle (hǽndʼl) n. the part of a tool, utensil, weapon etc. designed for the hand or fingers to grasp ‖ something that can be used as a pretext **to fly off the handle** to become suddenly very angry indeed **handle** pres. part. **han·dling** past and past part. **han·dled** v.t. to touch or take in the hands ‖ to deal with (a person, problem) ‖ to be concerned with, treat ‖ v.i. to respond to control

hand·ler (hǽndlər) n. someone who handles ‖ someone who professionally exhibits dogs etc. in shows ‖ someone who helps in the training of a boxer, or who acts as his second in a fight

hand·out (hǽndaut) n. a leaflet or folder of information or publicity supplied by official departments or an agency ‖ an item of clothing or food given to a beggar or tramp, or anything given for nothing

hand·some (hǽnsəm) adj. (of men) good-looking ‖ (of women) beautiful in a way which commands admiration ‖ (of animals) well-shaped and good to look at ‖ ample, generously large ‖ gracious, highly praising ‖ impressive and pleasing

hand·y (hǽndi:) comp. **hand·i·er** superl. **han·di·est** adj. conveniently near ‖ able to do useful small manual jobs, esp. about the house ‖ dexterous ‖ convenient and practical

hand·y·man (hǽndi:mæn) pl. **hand·y·men** (hǽndi:men) n. a man able to do many useful kinds of work with his hands reasonably well, esp. a man employed to do a variety of jobs

hang (hæŋ) **1.** v. pres. part. **hang·ing** past and past part. **hung** (hʌŋ) v.i. to be suspended ‖ to be so that the weight supported ‖ to await a decision ‖ (of drapery) to fall in folds or (of a jacket etc.) in an elegant loose fit ‖ (of flowers) to droop for lack of moisture ‖ (pres. part. **hang·ing** past and past part. **hanged**) to suffer death by being suspended by the neck ‖ v.t. to suspend (something) ‖ to attach (wallpaper, a poster etc.) to a wall ‖ to display (a picture) on a wall ‖ (pres. part. **hang·ing** past and past part. **hanged**) to kill by suspending by the neck **to go hang** to become a matter of indifference or neglect **to hang about** (or **around**) to linger or loiter in a place or near a person **to hang back** to hesitate to commit oneself **to hang on** (or **upon**) to depend on ‖ to pay rapt attention to ‖ (pop.) to persevere, continue ‖ (pop.) to wait **to hang on to** to hold firmly to **to hang out** to put (laundry) out to dry ‖ to display (a flag or signal) ‖ (pop.) to reside ‖ (pop.) to be (at a specified place) more often than not **2.** n. the manner in which something hangs ‖ (pop.) a very small bit **to get the hang of** to grasp the meaning or way of working of

han·gar (hǽŋər) n. a very large shed used to house aircraft

hang·er (hǽŋər) n. a coat hanger

hang·er-on (hǽŋərɔn, hǽŋərɔ́n) pl. **hang·ers-on** n. someone attaching himself to an influential person or group in the hope of personal advantage

hang·ing (hǽŋiŋ) **1.** n. the act of suspending (e.g. pictures in an exhibition) ‖ execution or killing by suspending by the neck ‖ (pl.) curtains or draperies **2.** adj. suspended from a support above ‖ situated on a steep slope

han·ker (hǽŋkər) v.i. (with 'after' or 'for', or the infinitive) to have a continual nagging desire (for something or to possess or do something) **hán·ker·ing** n.

hap·haz·ard (hæphǽzərd) **1.** adj. of events occurring by chance or illogically rather than by design **2.** adv. according to no set plan or system

hap·less (hǽplis) adj. (rhet.) unlucky

hap·pen (hǽpən) v.i. to occur, take place ‖ to occur quite by accident or spontaneously ‖ to chance **to happen on** (or **upon**) (something or someone) to find or meet by chance **to happen to** (someone) to befall **háp·pen·ing** n.

hap·pen·ing (hǽpəniŋ) n. a special or unusual staged event involving many spectators, esp. in the arts

hap·pen·stance (hǽpənstæns) n. a chance circumstance

hap·pi·ness (hǽpi:nis) n. feelings of joy and pleasure mingled in varying degree ‖ the satisfaction of the deepest desire

hap·py (hǽpi:) comp. **hap·pi·er** superl. **hap·pi·est** adj. experiencing joy and pleasure ‖ expressing such feelings ‖ lucky, fortunate ‖ apt

ha·rangue (hərǽŋ) **1.** n. a long and forceful speech made to a gathering of people **2.** v.t. pres. part. **ha·rangu·ing** past and past part. **ha·rangued**

har·ass (hǽrəs, hərǽs) *v.t.* to subject (someone) to continuous vexatious attacks, questions, demands or other unpleasantness || *(mil.)* to make repeated raids or attacks on **hár·ass·ment** *n.*

har·bor (hárbər) *n.* a bay or inlet of quiet water protected from stormy waves by man-made or natural walls permitting ships to enter and leave through a narrow entrance (the harbor mouth) for anchorage or shelter || a place of refuge

harbor *v.t.* to shelter || to cherish secretly || *v.i.* to take refuge or anchor in a harbor

hard (hard) **1.** *adj.* (of solid things) difficult to cut, crack or crush || not easy || not easy to do || not easy to comprehend or accept || not easy to bear || oppressive || unkind || unfeeling || tough || energetic and persistent || of nonbiodegradable pesticides || of news of events with immediate importance || ungenerous || unfavorable || (of prices) high and tending to stay high || (of water) having in solution esp. salts of calcium or magnesium which react with soap and so prevent the soap from lathering || (of liquor) having a high percentage of alcohol || *(pop., of 'c' and 'g')* pronounced as in 'come' and 'go' **2.** *adv.* strongly **hard up** acutely short of money **hard up for (something)** lacking

hard-core *adj.* **1.** of persons whose status is not easily changed, e.g., *hard-core unemployed* **2.** of pornography, explicit

hard·en (hárd'n) *v.i.* to become hard || (of prices) to rise, or cease to fall, on the market || to become tougher in mind and character || to become callous or intolerant || *v.t.* to make (something) hard or harder || to make hardy || to make hardhearted, callous or cynical **hárd·en·er** *n.* a substance added to give a paint or varnish a harder finish

hard·head·ed (hárdhédid) *adj.* realistic and practical, unswayed by sentiment

hard·heart·ed (hárdhártid) *adj.* callous, unfeeling

hard·ly (hárdli:) *adv.* not to any great degree, scarcely || only just, barely || not quite, not at all || *(rhet.)* with effort or difficulty || severely, harshly

hard·ness (hárdnis) *n.* the quality of being hard || difficulty || unfeelingness || harshness || physical toughness || resistnace of a metal to deformation and indentation || resistance of a mineral to abrasion

hard·ship (hárdʃip) *n.* suffering or privation difficult to bear, or an instance of either

hard·ware (hárdwɛ̯ər) *n.* metal goods || *(electronics)* equipment used in computing

har·dy (hárdi:) *comp.* **har·di·er** *superl.* **har·di·est** *adj.* strong, robust || (of plants) able to flourish outdoors all year without special protection

hare (hɛər) **1.** *pl.* **hares, hare** *n.* a herbivorous lagomorph. Hares are up to 2 ft in length and have long ears, large eyes, short tail, long hind legs and a divided upper lip **2.** *v.t. pres. part.* **har·ing** *past* and *past part.* **hared** to run very fast

har·em (hɛ́ərəm, hǽrəm) *n.* the women's apartments in a Moslem household || the wives and servants of the master of the house who live in these apartments

hark (hark) *v.i.(archaic)* to listen closely || *v.t. (archaic)* to listen to **to hark back** (with 'to') to refer to (a time in the past) || (of hounds) to go back in their tracks to try to recover lost scent

Har·le·quin (hárlikwin, hárlikin) *n.* a character (partner to Columbine, a dancer) in commedia dell'arte. He survives as a buffoon in European and American pantomime. He plays wearing a mask and dressed in particolored tights, and carrying a wooden wand or sword **har·le·quin** *adj.* of variegated, bright colors

har·lot (hárlət) *n.* *(old-fash.)* a prostitute **hár·lot·ry** *n.* *(old-fash.)* prostitution

harm (harm) **1.** *n.* injury, hurt || moral wrong **2.** *v.t.* to injure, hurt

harm·ful (hármfəl) *adj.* injurious, hurtful

harm·less (hármlis) *adj.* not injurious, not hurtful || not likely to cause trouble

har·mon·i·ca (harmónikə) *n.* a small rectangular wind instrument in which free reeds are agitated by the exhalation or inhalation of the breath

har·mo·ni·ous (harmóuni:əs) *adj.* pleasing to the ear, tuneful || interrelated in a pleasing way || free from jarring differences of feeling or opinion

har·mo·nize (hármənaiz) *pres. part.* **har·mo·niz·ing** *past* and *past part.* **har·mo·nized** *v.i.* to be, sing or play in harmony || to be in agreement || to blend tastefully || *v.t.* to provide (a melody) with harmonies || to bring into agreement || to cause to blend tastefully

har·mo·ny (hárməni:) *pl.* **har·mo·nies** *n.* a pleasing combination of musical sounds || the relationship between two or more notes sung or played simultaneously || the science of combinations of musical sounds and of their use in composition || agreement || peace || pleasing relationship

har·ness (hárnis) **1.** *n.* the complete set of leather belts and straps with their metal fittings worn by a draft animal || the working contrivance in some mechanical operations, e.g. in raising or lowering the warp threads in a loom || reins for children learning to walk || *(hist.)* the armor and accessories of a knight or man-at-arms **in double harness** working with a partner, or as partners **in harness** at work **to die in harness** to die before retiring from work **2.** *v.t.* to put a harness on (an animal) || to fasten by means of a harness || to control and utilize (a source of power) || to tie together as though in harness

harp (harp) *n.* a musical instrument consisting of taut wires within a large, roughly triangular, wooden frame, the wires being plucked with the fingertips

harp *v.i.* to play on a harp || (with 'on') to make frequent, boring or annoying reference

harp·ist (hárpist) *n.* someone who plays the harp

har·poon (harpú:n) **1.** *n.* a barbed spear with an attached line, hurled from a boat or fired from a gun to bury itself in the flesh of a whale or large fish **2.** *v.t.* to spear with a harpoon

har·row (hǽrou) **1.** *n.* an iron frame with spikes or disks in echelon, drawn by a tractor or horse and used after plowing to break up clods of soil into a fine tilth, to cover seed with tilth, or to tear up weeds **2.** *v.t.* to work over (a field) with a harrow || to lacerate (the feelings) **hár·row·ing** *adj.*

har·ry (hǽri:) *pres. part.* **har·ry·ing** *past* and *past part.* **har·ried** *v.t.* to harass || to make repeated attacks on || to lay waste, ravage

harsh (harʃ) *adj.* without mercy || finding fault with acerbity || oppressive || displeasing to one of the senses || stark

har·vest (hárvist) **1.** *n.* the gathering in of ripe crops or fodder || the time of year when crops are gathered in || crops with respect to their yield || the result of action or behavior **2.** *v.t.* to gather in (a crop) to obtain (the result of action or behavior)

har·ves·ter (hárvistər) *n.* a machine used in harvesting || a harvest worker

has *3rd pers. sing. pres. tense* of HAVE

hash (hæʃ) **1.** *n.* meat, esp. meat previously cooked, chopped with potatoes and baked or fried **to make a hash of** to make a lamentable failure of **2.** *v.t.* to cut (esp. meat) into small pieces || *(pop.)* to make a muddle or failure of **to hash over** to talk about in detail, consider minutely the various aspects of

hasp (hæsp, hɑsp) **1.** *n.* a bar, usually of metal hinged at one end and pierced near the other end, used with a staple and toggle or padlock as a fastening for a door, window, lid etc. **2.** *v.t.* to fasten by means of a hasp

has·sle (hǽs'l) **1.** *n.* *(pop.)* a wrangle, dispute || *(pop.)* an annoying struggle **2.** *v. pres. part.* **has·sling** *past* and *past part.* **has·sled** *v.i.* *(pop.)* to bicker || *v.t.* to bother, annoy

has·sock (hǽsək) *n.* a small, firm, stuffed cushion, often covered with carpet material, used for kneeling on or as a footrest || a matted tuft of coarse grass

haste (heist) *n.* deliberate speediness ‖ an attempt to be more speedy than is reasonable **in haste** hastily **to make haste** to hurry **has·ten** (héis'n) *v.i.* to move with hurry ‖ *v.t.* to bring on sooner than if events were left to run their course ‖ to treat as urgent, execute with added speed ‖ to cause (someone) to make haste or be precipitate

hast·i·ly (héistili:) *adv.* in a hurry ‖ in too great a hurry

hast·i·ness (héisti:nis) *n.* the state or quality of being hasty

hast·y (héisti:) *comp.* **hast·i·er** *superl.* **hast·i·est** *adj.* impetuous, precipitate ‖ made or done with haste ‖ (of the temper) quickly flaring into anger

hat (hæt) **1.** *n.* an article designed to protect or adorn the head, and distinguished from a cap esp. by having a brim or by being voluminous in the crown **to keep something under one's hat** to keep something a secret **to take one's hat off** to affirm one's admiration for **to talk through one's hat** to talk nonsense **2.** *pres. part.* **hat·ting** *past* and *past part.* **hat·ted** *v.t.* to put a hat on, supply with a hat

hatch (hætʃ) **1.** *v.i.* to emerge from an egg as a result of incubation ‖ (of eggs) to open when incubation is completed ‖ to emerge from a chrysalis ‖ *v.t.* to produce (young) from eggs by incubation ‖ (often with 'up') to produce as a result of scheming **2.** *n.* the act or process of hatching ‖ the brood hatched

hatch *n.* an aperture, fitted with a door or lid, in a wall, in the deck of a ship (e.g. giving access to a hold), in a ceiling (e.g. giving access to a loft), or in a roof ‖ a covering for a ship's hold or stairway ‖ a hatchway ‖ a sliding door in a lock gate or weir controlling the flow of water

hatched (hætʃt) *v.* dismissed from federally funded employment on the grounds of violating the Hatch Act, which prohibits political activity by federal employees

hatch·er·y (hætʃəri:) *pl.* **hatch·er·ies** *n.* a device where eggs (e.g. of trout) are hatched under care

hatch·way (hætʃwẹi) *n.* a large opening in the deck of a ship giving access to the hold ‖ any opening that may be shut by a hatch

hate (heit) **1.** *n.* intensely hostile aversion, compounded of anger and fear, and centered on a real or supposed cause of injury **2.** *v.t. pres. part.* **hat·ing** *past* and *past part.* **hat·ed** to experience the sensation of hate in relation to (persons or things) ‖ (*pop.*) to dislike strongly **hate·ful** *adj.* arousing the sensation of hate ‖ unkind, mean

ha·tred (héitrid) *n.* the passion of hate

haugh·ti·ly (hɔ́t'li:) *adv.* in a haughty manner

haugh·ti·ness (hɔ́ti:nis) *n.* the quality or state of being haughty

haugh·ty (hɔ́ti:) *comp.* **haugh·ti·er** *superl.* **haugh·ti·est** *adj.* displaying overbearing pride, with disdain for others

haul (hɔl) **1.** *v.t.* to pull with an effort ‖ to transport by road, railroad etc. ‖ (*naut.*) to alter the course of (a ship), esp. by sailing closehauled ‖ *v.i.* to give a long, steady pull ‖ (*naut.*) to alter course by sailing close-hauled **to haul down the flag** to surrender **to haul up** (*pop.*) to bring to trial **2.** *n.* a strong steady pull ‖ a transporting or the distance over which a load is transported ‖ the quantity of fish taken in a net or in a catch ‖ the valuables stolen by a thief on one job **haul·age** *n.* the act of hauling goods ‖ the charge made for this **haul·er** *n.* someone who transports goods by road **haul·ier** (hɔ́ljər) *n.*

haunch (hɔntʃ, hɑntʃ) *n.* the lateral part of the body between the ribs and the thigh ‖ a leg and loin of meat cut in one piece ‖ (*archit.*) the shoulder of an arch, between the crown and the piers **to squat** (or sit) **on one's haunches** to sit resting one's hind-quarters on one's upturned heels

haunt (hɔnt, hɑnt) **1.** *v.t.* (of ghosts, spirits etc.) to pay frequent visits to, or be continually present in ‖ to visit very frequently ‖ to follow (someone) about in an unwelcome way ‖ to be always present as a nagging anxiety in the mind of **to be haunted** to be frequented by ghosts, spirits etc. **2.** *n.* a place which one frequents ‖ a den or feeding place of an animal

haut·bois, haut·boy (óubɔi, hóubɔi) *pl.* **haut·bois, haut·boys** *n.* (*mus.*) the former name for an oboe ‖ an organ stop giving an oboelike quality

haute cou·ture (outku:tyr) *n.* the art and industry of the leading women's fashion houses

hau·teur (outɔ́:r, houtɔ́:r) *n.* haughtiness

have (hæv) **1.** *v. 1st* and *2nd pers. sing. pres.* **have** *3rd pers. sing. pres.* **has** (hæz) *1st, 2nd* and *3rd pers. pl. pres.* **have** *pres. part.* **hav·ing** *past* and *past part.* **had** (hæd) *v.t.* ('have' is often replaced by 'have got') to hold in the hand, *what have you there?* ‖ to own, possess ‖ to be in a specified personal relationship to, *I have four brothers* ‖ to contain ‖ to take ‖ to receive, *I have my reward* ‖ to experience mentally ‖ to experience, undergo, *to have an operation* ‖ to be afflicted with, *to have gout* ‖ to cause to do (with infin.) or suffer (with past part.) ‖ to be under an obligation or necessity as regards ‖ to hold at a disadvantage ‖ used as an auxiliary with past participles of most verbs to form their perfect tenses, *I have seen my tailor* ‖ (often haef) used with infinitives to express obligation or necessity, *I have to go now* **to have at** (*rhet.*) to attack **to have done with** to have finished with, finished using (or doing etc.) **to have it coming** to observe what one gets, esp. punishment or bad luck **to have it in one** to have the courage or ability **to have it out** to discuss or fight in order to settle a problem, quarrel etc. **to have it over** to be in a better position than (someone) **to have nothing on** to have no information to the discredit of ‖ to have no advantage over **to have something on** to possess information to the discredit of **to let someone have it** to hurt someone physically or with words etc. **2.** *n.* (*pop.*) a person or nation with wealth, *the haves and the have-nots*

ha·ven (héivən) *n.* a small natural bay or inlet providing shelter and anchorage for ships ‖ a refuge

hav·er·sack (hǽvərsæk) *n.* a bag slung over the shoulder by a strap and used to carry food etc.

hav·oc (hǽvək) *n.* destruction on a wide and intense scale **to play** (or **make, raise**) **havoc with** to cause intense disturbance in or disruption to, *the weather played havoc with our plans*

hawk (hɔk) **1.** *n.* a diurnal bird of prey ‖ a person who advocates a military or bellicose solution to a disagreement **2.** *v.i.* to hunt with hawks trained for this sport

hawk *v.t.* to carry about for sale ‖ to peddle (goods) in the street by shouting ‖ *v.t.* to be a hawker

haw·ker (hɔ́kər) *n.* someone who peddles goods esp. from a cart etc., moving from place to place and shouting out his wares

haw·ser (hɔ́zər) *n.* (*naut.*) a cable, often of steel, used in mooring or warping a ship

hay (hei) **1.** *n.* stems and leaves of grasses etc. as a crop that is cut and dried for fodder **2.** *v.t.* to make hay ‖ *v.t.* to cut and dry (grasses) for hay ‖ to feed with hay **to make hay while the sun shines** to profit from favorable circumstances, grasp an opportunity

hay·ride (héiraid) *n.* a ride in an open truck or wagon with some hay in it, esp. at night, by a group, for fun

---

hay·stack (héistæk) *n.* a quantity of hay built up outdoors into a compressed mass, with a thatched, ridged or conical top to drain off the rain

hay·wire (héiwaiər) **1.** *n.* a wire used to bind bales of hay, straw etc. **2.** *adj.* (*pop.*) mixed up, out of order ‖ (*pop.*) crazy **to go haywire** (*pop.*) to behave as if crazy or to become crazy

haz·ard (hǽzərd) *v.t.* to place (something) in a dangerous or risky situation wittingly or unwittingly ‖ to attempt (an answer, guess etc.)

hazard *n.* a risk or chance associated with danger ‖ (*golf*) a ground obstacle in the direct path of the ball **ház·ard·ous** *adj.* risky

haze (heiz) *n.* a cloudy, misty appearance of the air, caused by intense heat producing irregular and changing densities of its layers or by a fine suspension of dust or vapor particles, affecting the transmission of light and lessening visibility ‖ a cloudy appearance in a liquid or on a solid surface ‖ obscurity of mental vision

haze *pres. part.* **haz·ing** *past* and *past part.* **hazed** *v.t.* (*pop.*) to place (someone, esp. an initiate into a fraternity) in an embarrassing or humiliating situation by forcing him to do menial or foolish tasks

ha·zel (héiz'l) **1.** *n.* a genus of hairy-leaved shrubs or small trees found in temperate climates. Its fruit is the hazelnut ‖ the wood of such a tree **2.** *adj.* (esp. of eyes) having the reddish-brown color of hazelnuts

ha·zel·nut (héiz'lnʌt) *n.* the fruit of the hazel, an edible hard-shelled nut

ha·zy (héizi) *comp.* **ha·zi·er** *superl.* **ha·zi·est** *adj.* (of the air) characterized by haze ‖ indistinct, as if seen through a haze ‖ (of mental processes) not clear

he (hi:) **1.** *pron., 3rd person sing., nominative case* a male person, animal or personified thing already mentioned **2.** *adj.* (*prefixed*) male, *a he-goat* **3.** *n.* a male

head (hed) **1.** *n.* the top part of the human body or foremost part of an animal's body ‖ the leading person in a community, institution etc., or the position he holds ‖ the foremost, most effective part of a tool ‖ (*engin.*) the part of a machine containing the cutting tool ‖ (*slang*) a drug user ‖ the foremost or front part ‖ the uppermost part, *the head of a river* ‖ the froth on beer etc. ‖ (*bot.*) a compact or rounded mass of flowers, leaves or leafstalks at the top of the stem ‖ the pillow end of a bed ‖ one individual out of a number of persons or animals ‖ a critical stage, *things have come to a head* ‖ a headland ‖ the height or length of a head ‖ (also *pl.*) the obverse side of a coin ‖ (*mus.*) the skin of a drum ‖ (*naut.*) the bow and adjacent parts of a ship ‖ the part of a bell between the crown and the sound bow **head and shoulders** by far **head over heels** deeply, overwhelmingly (in debt, love etc.) **to act** (or **go) over someone's head** to act without someone's knowledge or consent, esp. by ignoring the proper chain of command **to be weak in the head** (*pop.*) to be of subnormal intelligence **to go out of one's head** to be forgotten **to go to one's head** (of alcohol) to make one a little drunk ‖ (of praise, success, power etc.) to make someone vain conceited **to keep one's head** to remain calm with the reason under control **to keep one's head above water** to remain solvent or otherwise manage to cope with pressing obligations **to lose one's head** to lose one's self-control, to become irrational **to make head or tail of** to understand, make sense of **to put it into someone's head** to suggest something to someone **to put our** (etc.) **heads together** to consult one another (each other) **to talk someone's head off** (*pop.*) to talk at great length to someone **to turn someone's head** (of flattery, success etc.) to make someone vain **2.** *adj.* chief in authority, *head waiter* **3.** *v.i.* to move in a certain direction ‖ to grow to a head ‖ *v.t.* to lead ‖ to be at the top of ‖ to remove the head or top from (grain, a tree etc.) ‖ to cause (something) to move in a certain direction ‖ to proceed around the upper part

of (a stream) ‖ to propel (a soccer ball) with the head

head·ache (hédeik) *n.* a usually persistent pain in the head ‖ (*pop.*) a vexing problem

head·ing (hédiŋ) *n.* the title of a piece of writing or of a section of one ‖ (*mining*) a drift ‖ (*mining*) a passageway connecting two larger tunnels

head lamp a headlight

head·land (hédlənd) *n.* a point of land projecting into the sea, a lake etc. ‖ a strip of unplowed land left at either end of a plowed field

head·less (hédlis) *adj.* having no head ‖ lacking a leader ‖ lacking prudence or proper thought

head·light (hédlait) *n.* a powerful light, with reflector and lens, fitted on the front of a motor vehicle, locomotive or aircraft ‖ a light at a ship's masthead

head·line (hédlain) **1.** *n.* the title of a news item in a newspaper, printed in large, bold type ‖ (*printing*) a line at the head of a page giving the title of the book and page number ‖ a news summary given at the beginning of a news broadcast ‖ the rope along the top of a fishing net **to make the headlines** to be important enough to warrant a newspaper account with headlines **2.** *v.t. pres. part.* **head·lin·ing** *past* and *past part.* **head·lined** to be performing as the headliner in **héad·lin·er** *n.* a starring performer

head·long (hédlɔŋ, hédlɒŋ) **1.** *adv.* headfirst ‖ full tilt ‖ impetuously **2.** *adj.* done or proceeding with the head foremost ‖ done with utmost haste ‖ impetuous

head·most (hédmoust) *adj.* leading, foremost

head-on (hédɔn, hédɒn) *adj.* with the head, or foremost part (e.g. of a ship, vehicle etc.) moving toward or facing another person or thing **head on** *adv.* in a head-on way

head·phone (hédfoun) *n.* (*radio, telephone* etc.) a set of receivers for both ears attached to a headband

head·quar·ters (hédkwɔrtərz) *n.* (*mil., abbr.* H.Q.) the command post of a commanding officer and his staff ‖ a center from which operations are directed

head·room (hédru:m, hédrum) *n.* the clear space above a person's head e.g. in a doorway or an automobile, or above a truck, train etc., e.g. when passing under a bridge

head·stone (hédstoun) *n.* a stone erected at the head of a grave ‖ a cornerstone

head·strong (hédstrɔŋ, hédstrɒŋ) *adj.* willful and obstinate ‖ resulting from a determination to have one's own way

head·way (hédwei) *n.* progress ‖ the rate of progression ‖ the time span between movement of successive transportation vehicles, e.g., trains ‖ headroom

head·y (hédi:) *comp.* **head·i·er** *superl.* **head·i·est** *adj.* (of alcoholic drinks) likely to intoxicate ‖ (of speech, writing etc.) intended to incite or inflame

heal (hi:l) *v.i.* to become well or whole again ‖ *v.t.* to restore (someone) to health ‖ to restore (a diseased or damaged bone or tissue or a wound) to its normal condition ‖ to cause (painful emotions) to be no longer grievous **to heal a breach** to bring about a reconciliation

health (helθ) *n.* the state of fitness of the body or of the mind ‖ this state when it is good **to drink to the health of, to drink to (someone's) health** to toast (someone)

health·ful (hélθfəl) *adj.* promoting good health

health·i·ness (hélθi:nis) *n.* the state or quality of being healthy

health·y (hélθi:) *comp.* **health·i·er** *superl.* **health·i·est** *adj.* normally having good physical and mental health ‖ conducive to good health ‖ appearing to have, or indicate, good health ‖ likely to be for one's good ‖ (*pop.*, of appetite etc.) good and large

heap (hi:p) **1.** *n.* any material gathered or thrown together into a pile ‖ (*pop.*) a large number or quantity **heaps of** (*pop.*) many, a lot of ‖ plenty of **2.** *v.t.* to gather or throw into a heap ‖ to load **to heap coals of fire** to return good for evil **to heap up** to gather together, collect

hear (hiər) *pres. part.* **hear·ing** *past* and *past part.* **heard** (hɔːrd) *v.t.* to experience or be aware of (sounds), usually as a result of stimulation of the auditory system by sound waves ‖ to listen to so as to check ‖ to listen to so as to consider ‖ to attend, *to hear Mass* ‖ *(law)* to take evidence from ‖ *(law)* to conduct the trial of (a case) ‖ *v.i.* to experience or be aware of sounds usually as a result of stimulation of the auditory system by sound waves ‖ (with 'of' or 'from') to receive information or news ‖ to be informed **hear! hear!** an interjection by a member of an audience expressing approval **not to hear of** not to permit **to hear out** to listen to to the end

hear·er (híərər) *n.* someone who hears, esp. one of several

hear·ing (híəriŋ) *n.* the act of apprehending or the ability to apprehend sounds aurally ‖ an act or instance of listening ‖ *(law)* the listening to evidence and pleas in a law court ‖ *(law)* a trial, esp. one heard only by a judge or judges ‖ the distance over which a sound can be heard, *out of hearing* **hard of hearing** a little deaf **to give fair hearing to** to offer an opportunity to be heard without prejudice

heark·en, hark·en (hárkən) *v.i. (rhet.)* to listen, pay attention (to what is said)

hear·say (híərsei) *n.* that which one has been told but has not directly experienced ‖ the process of acquiring such information

hearse (hɔːrs) *n.* a vehicle used for conveying a corpse in its coffin to the place of burial etc.

heart (hart) *n.* the hollow muscular organ which, by rhythmical contraction and expansion, forces the blood through the circulatory system of vertebrates ‖ the central part of something ‖ the most important part of something ‖ the fount of man's emotions and deepest feelings ‖ kindness, affection ‖ courage and zeal, *to have no heart for a task* ‖ a state of mind or feeling, *with a heavy heart* ‖ *(pl., cards)* a suit marked with a representation of one or more red hearts (♡) ‖ a card of this suit **have a heart!** *(pop.)* be merciful! **not to have the heart to** to be unwilling to (do something distressing) **to break one's heart** to be acutely distressed in one's affections or sensitivity **to cry one's heart out** to grieve so much, and for so long, that emotion is exhausted **to give** (or **lose**) **one's heart to** to give all one's affection to **to have a change of heart** to change from being unkind or unsympathetic to being kind or sympathetic **to have one's heart in the right place** to be kind and affectionate **to have something at heart** to have great interest in or sympathy for **to learn** (or **know**) **something by heart** to memorize (or have memorized) something **to lose heart** to be discouraged and ready to give up **to take to heart** to heed with seriousness ‖ to mind so much as to be upset by **to take to one's heart** to take into one's affections **with all one's heart** *(rhet.)* most willingly

heart·ache (hárteik) *n.* persistent mental suffering through loss of a loved person or disappointment in love

heart·beat (hártbiːt) *n.* one of the rhythmical muscular movements of the heart

heart·break (hártbreik) *n.* overwhelming sorrow **héart·break·ing** *adj.* causing overwhelming sorrow ‖ tending to crush the spirits **heart·bro·ken** (hártbroukən) *adj.* suffering overwhelming sorrow

heart·burn (hártbəːrn) *n.* a burning sensation felt in the stomach (near the heart) caused by indigestion

heart·en (hárt'n) *v.t.* to inspire with fresh determination

heart·felt (hártfelt) *adj. (rhet.)* deeply and sincerely felt

hearth (harθ) *n.* the floor of a fireplace or the area immediately in front of a fireplace

heart·i·ly (hártili:) *adv.* very warmly ‖ with a good appetite ‖ enthusiastically ‖ thoroughly

heart·i·ness (hárti:nis) *n.* the quality of being hearty

heart·less (hártlis) *adj.* devoid of all feelings of affection ‖ cruel, pitiless ‖ showing cruelty or lack of affection

heart·rend·ing (hártrendiŋ) *adj.* causing grief and pity, *heartrending cries*

heart·sick (hártsik) *adj. (rhet.)* depressed and weak with yearning, or marked by such depression

heart·y (hárti:) *comp.* **heart·i·er** *superl.* **heart·i·est** *adj.* very warm ‖ vigorous ‖ abundant ‖ exuberant, genial and energetic to the point of excess

heat (hiːt) *n.* high temperature ‖ the condition of being hot ‖ hot weather ‖ intensity of emotional feeling ‖ intensity of action ‖ excessive bodily temperature associated e.g. with sunburn, a boil etc. ‖ (with 'in') a period of intense sexual excitement in a female animal ‖ pungency of flavor ‖ a preliminary race or other contest **heat** *v.t.* (often with 'up') to supply heat to, make hot or hotter ‖ *v.i.* (often with 'up') to become hot or hotter

heat·ed (híːtid) *adj.* subjected to heat ‖ emotionally violent

heat·er (híːtər) *n.* a device that gives off heat, e.g. an electric stove ‖ a device that heats its contents, e.g. a water heater

heath (hiːθ) *n.* a plant, usually found growing in open, barren, poorly drained soil

hea·then (híːðən) **1.** *pl.* **hea·thens, hea·then** *n.* a person who does not worship the God of the Christians, Jews or Moslems **2.** *adj.* of or relating to heathens, their beliefs and practices

heave (hiːv) **1.** *v. pres. part.* **heav·ing** *past* and *past part.* **heaved,** *(naut.)* **hove** (houv) *v.t.* to raise with much effort ‖ *(pop.)* to throw (a heavy object) ‖ to emit (a long-drawn-out sigh) ‖ *(naut.)* to move (a ship) or haul, or pull (something on a ship) ‖ *(geol.)* to displace (a stratum) ‖ *v.i.* to rise and fall rhythmically under powerful compulsion ‖ *(naut.,* of a ship) to move **to heave around** *(naut.)* to come closer **to heave down** *(naut.)* to careen **to heave to** *(naut.)* to bring a ship to a standstill heading into the wind **2.** *n.* the act of heaving ‖ *(geol.)* the horizontal component of the slip along a fault

heav·en (hévən) *n.* the upper regions, regarded in many religions as the abode of the deity or deities, and of the blessed ‖ *(pop.)* perfect happiness ‖ *(rhet.)* the upper air ‖ *(pl.)* the space above us seeming to form a vault **Heav·en** (in exclamations) God, *Heaven protect you!* **to move heaven and earth** to do one's utmost

heav·en·ly (hévənli:) *adj.* pertaining to heaven or the heavens ‖ *(pop.)* very delightful

heav·i·ly (hévəli:) *adv.* in a heavy manner

heav·i·ness (hévi:nis) *n.* the state or quality of being heavy

heav·y (hévi:) **1.** *comp.* **heav·i·er** *superl.* **heav·i·est** *adj.* of considerable weight ‖ of more than the usual amount ‖ weighing down on one or threatening to do so, oppressive ‖ joyless, *a heavy heart* ‖ clumsy in conception or execution, *a heavy speech* ‖ (of people) uninteresting ‖ (of soil) clayey ‖ lacking in grace ‖ difficult to accomplish ‖ tiresomely grave ‖ steep **to make heavy weather of** (a job) to make a labor of (a light task) **2.** *pl.* **heav·ies** *n. (theater)* the actor who plays the part of the villain, or the part or character itself

heavy *adv.* heavily **to hang heavy** to be oppressive to

(a) æ, c*a*t; ɑ, c*a*r; ɔ f*aw*n; ei, sn*a*ke. **(e)** e, h*e*n; iː, sh*ee*p; iə, d*ee*r; ɛə, b*ea*r. **(i)** i, f*i*sh; ai, t*i*ger; əː, b*i*rd. **(o)** o, *o*x; au, c*ow*; ou, g*oa*t; u, p*oor*; ɔi, r*oy*al. **(u)** ʌ, d*u*ck; u, b*u*ll; uː, g*oo*se; ə, b*a*cillus; juː, c*u*be. x, lo*ch*; θ, *th*ink; ð, bo*th*er; z, *Z*en; ʒ, corsa*g*e; dʒ, sava*g*e; ŋ, oranguta*ng*; j, *y*ak; ʃ, *fi*sh; tʃ, fe*tch*; 'l, rabb*le*; 'n, redd*en*. Complete pronunciation key appears inside front cover.

lie heavy to be a burden

heav·y-hand·ed (hévi:hǽndid) *adj.* domineering, oppressive ‖ clumsy

heav·y-heart·ed (hévi:hártid) *adj.* worried and sad

heck·le (hék'l) *pres. part.* **heck·ling** *past* and *past part.* **heck·led** *v.t.* to harass (a public speaker) by interrupting, asking awkward questions etc. ‖ to hackle (flax)

hec·tare (héktɛər, héktɑr) *n.* a metric unit of area equal to 10,000 sq. meters, or 2.471 acres

hec·tic (héktik) *adj.* exciting, wildly agitated

hedge (hedʒ) **1.** *n.* a continuous line of thick shrubs or low trees, planted around the edge of a field, garden etc. ‖ a protective line, e.g. of police keeping back a crowd ‖ an act or instance of hedging on speculations **2.** *v. pres. part.* **hedg·ing** *past* and *past part.* **hedged** *v.t.* to enclose, protect or obstruct with a hedge or as if with a hedge ‖ to reduce (a risk) by making opposing speculations ‖ *v.i.* to make or tend a hedge ‖ to avoid giving a direct answer or statement ‖ to make a speculation that reduces the risk on one previously made

he·don·ism (hí:d'nɪzəm) *n.* the doctrine that pleasure is the highest good and that moral duty is fulfilled through the pursuit of pleasure **hé·don·ist** *n.* someone who subscribes to the doctrine of hedonism **he·do·nís·tic** *adj.* **he·do·nís·ti·cal·ly** *adv.*

heed (hi:d) **1.** *n.* (*rhet.*) careful attention and consideration **2.** *v.t.* to take into consideration so as to profit by (advice, a warning etc.) **héed·ful** *adj.* attentive **héed·ful·ly** *adv.* **héed·ful·ness** *n.* **héed·less** *adj.* negligent **héed·less·ly** *adv.* **héed·less·ness** *n.*

heel (hi:l) **1.** *n.* the rounded hind part of the human foot ‖ the corresponding part of an animal's hind limb (often above the foot) ‖ (*pl.*) the hind feet of an animal ‖ the back part of a boot or shoe into which the heel of the foot fits ‖ the back part of the base of a boot or shoe ‖ the part of a sock or stocking which covers the heel of the foot ‖ something shaped or positioned like a heel ‖ (*pop.*) either end crust of a loaf of bread ‖ (*pop.*) a cad **to be at one's heels** to be close behind one **to be down at the heel, down at heel** to be shabby, poverty-stricken **to turn on one's heel** to turn away sharply **2.** *v.t.* to add a heel to, renew the heel of ‖ (*golf*) to hit (the ball) with the heel of the club ‖ *v.i.* (in a dance step) to touch the ground with the heel ‖ (of a dog) to follow along at the heels of an owner or trainer

heel 1. *v.i.* (of a ship) to list under the wind or because of unbalanced loading ‖ *v.t.* to make (a ship) list **2.** *n.* the list (of a ship)

heft (heft) **1.** *n.* heaviness **2.** *v.t.* to hoist ‖ to test the weight of by lifting and holding

heft·y (héfti:) *comp.* **heft·i·er** *superl.* **heft·i·est** *adj.* heavily built and strong

heif·er (héfər) *n.* a young cow that has not borne any young

heigh (hei, hai) *interj.* used to hail someone or to remonstrate with him

height (hait) *n.* (of an object, person etc.) the distance or measurement from the base or foot to the top ‖ distance above a plane of reference nearer to the center of the earth ‖ distance above the earth, altitude ‖ considerable altitude ‖ a natural elevation (hill or mountain) ‖ the highest degree or position

height·en (háit'n) *v.t.* to increase the height of (something) ‖ to increase the intensity of (something) ‖ *v.i.* to increase in amount or degree ‖ to become more intense

hei·nous (héinəs) *adj.* (of a crime or conduct) very wicked ‖ (of an offender) very hateful

heir (ɛər) *n.* a person who will become or who has become the owner of all or part of another's property or titles on that other's death ‖ a person, group etc. inheriting a trait, responsibility etc.

heir·ess (ɛ́əris) *n.* a female who is or will become an heir

heir·loom (ɛ́ərlu:m) *n.* a piece of valuable personal property (e.g. a picture, a jewel) that has been handed down within a family for a considerable period of time

hel·i·cop·ter (hélikɒptər, hí:likɒptər) *n.* a lightweight, relatively small aircraft supported in the air solely by the reaction to a vertical airstream produced by propellers rotating in a horizontal plane

he·li·um (hí:li:əm) *n.* a light, colorless, odorless, chemically inert gaseous element

he·lix (hí:liks) *pl.* **he·li·ces** (hélisi:z), **he·lix·es** *n.* a curved path taken by a point which has both a constant rate of change of direction and a constant rate of change of plane ‖ a wire, groove etc. having this form ‖ (*archit.*) a spiral ornament ‖ (*anat.*) the outer rim of the external ear

hell (hel) *n.* traditionally the abode of Satan and his fallen angels and a place of physical anguish for impenitent souls after death ‖ (in some modern theology) the condition of being aware of separation from God ‖ (*pop.*) something intensely good, *a hell of a good time* or intensely bad, *a hell of a raw deal*

hell·ish (hélif) *adj.* relating to hell ‖ like or worthy of hell

hel·lo (helóu, həlóu) **1.** *interj.* an informal greeting expressing pleasure or surprise or both ‖ a call to attract or ensure attention, e.g. to someone at some distance or on the telephone **2.** *pl.* **hel·los** *n.* the greeting 'hello'

helm (helm) *n.* (*naut.*) a device (e.g. a tiller or wheel) attached to the rudder for steering a vessel **to put down (up) the helm** (*naut.*) to bring the rudder to windward (leeward)

hel·met (hélmit) *n.* a protective covering for the head, e.g. the steel headpiece of medieval armor, the rounded steel hat worn by a soldier, the part of a deep-sea diver's suit enclosing the head ‖ a round, stiff hat of pith or other light substance giving protection from the sun ‖ (*football*) a head protector

helms·man (hélmzmən) *pl.* **helms·men** (hélmzmən) *n.* the person at the helm who steers the ship

help (help) *n.* the act of helping or an instance of this ‖ someone who or something which helps ‖ a way of avoiding or rectifying a situation, *there's no help for it* ‖ a domestic servant, farmhand ‖ (*collect.*) employees, *factory help*

help *v.t.* to join (someone) and contribute to the performance or completion of a task, *to help a friend dig his garden* ‖ used as a cry of distress indicating that one urgently needs intervention from outside to rescue one ‖ to contribute to the relief, remedy or cure of, benefit, *good light helps eyestrain* ‖ to be useful and effective to (someone) in the attainment of a desired end, *to help someone get well* ‖ to make easier, likelier or more probable, *mnemonics help remembering* ‖ to prevent oneself from, *he cannot help saying these things* ‖ to prevent, *we cannot help his resigning if he wants to* ‖ to serve (food) at a meal ‖ to serve (someone) with food at a meal **to help someone off with** to pull gently at (e.g. a coat) that someone is trying to take off so as to make it easier for him to do this **to help someone on with** to make it easier for someone to put on (a garment) by e.g. holding it for him **to help oneself** (*pop.*) to steal, misappropriate ‖ to serve oneself without putting others to the trouble of serving one ‖ *v.i.* to supply help **hélp·er** *n.*

help·ful (hélpfəl) *adj.* giving or offering help

help·ing (hélpiŋ) *n.* a serving of food, *a second helping of potatoes*

help·less (hélplis) *adj.* unable to tend one's own needs ‖ unable to act at will ‖ lacking all help

hem (hem) **1.** *n.* the edge of a garment, handkerchief etc. folded back and stitched in place **2.** *v. pres. part.* **hem·ming** *past* and *past part.* **hemmed** *v.t.* to make a hem around ‖ *v.i.* to make a hem **to hem in** to surround and keep tight in

hem·i·sphere (hémisfiər) *n.* the half of a sphere on either side of a plane passing through its center ‖ one half of the roughly spherical surface of the earth as bisected either by the equator or a line of longitude chosen so that the Americas are in one half and the remainder of the land masses in the other half ‖ one half of the celestial sphere as bisected by the horizon, the celestial equator or the ecliptic ‖ *(anat.)* either of the two chief parts of the brain **hem·i·spher·ic** (hemisférik), **hem·i·spher·i·cal** *adjs*

hem·lock (hémlɒk) *n.* any of several poisonous flower-bearing plants whose leaves and fruit produce the alkaloid coniine ‖ hemlock spruce

hem·or·rhage (hémridʒ, héməridʒ) **1.** *n.* a heavy bleeding from the blood vessels. It may occur internally in body cavities, e.g. the abdominal cavity, or within organs, e.g. the brain **2.** *pres. part.* **hem·or·rhag·ing** *past* and *past part.* **hem·or·rhaged** *v.i.* to suffer this heavy bleeding

hem·or·rhoids (hémrɔidz, hémərɔidz) *pl. n.* groups of distended veins at the anus, giving rise to pain and bleeding

hemp (hemp) *n.* a genus of widely cultivated annuals, esp. the common hemp ‖ this plant's fiber used for twines, ropes and coarse fabrics ‖ a narcotic made from hemp, e.g. hashish, marijuana, bhang ‖ the hemplike fibers of other plants, e.g. Manila hemp, agave

hen (hen) *n.* a female bird, esp. of the domestic chicken

hence (hens) *adv.* at a time in the future measured from now ‖ therefore

hence·forth (hénsfɔrθ, hénsfóurθ) *adv.* from now on

hence·for·ward (hénsfɔ́·rwərd, hénsfóurwərd) *adv.* henceforth

hench·man (héntʃmən) *pl.* **hench·men** (héntʃmən) *n.* a reliable underling ‖ a worker for a political candidate, usually rewarded for his services

hep·a·ti·tis (hepətáitis) *n.* inflammation of the liver, occasionally of infective origin

her (hər) *possessive adj.* of, pertaining to or belonging to a female person or animal or something personified as female ‖ experienced, made or done by a female person or animal or something personified as female

her *pron., objective case* of SHE

her·ald (hérəld) *v.t. (rhet.)* to announce as imminent

herald *n. (hist.)* the official messenger of a royal person, or his representative ‖ a state officer who superintends state ceremonies **he·ral·dic** (herǽldik) *adj.* pertaining to the office or duties of a herald ‖ pertaining to heraldry **her·ald·ry** (hérəldri:) *n.* the art or science of a herald ‖ the office of a herald ‖ *(collect.)* coats of arms ‖ heraldic pomp and show

herb (ərb, hər:b) *n.* a plant (e.g. mint, thyme) valued for flavoring food, for medicinal purposes, or for its fragrance ‖ *(biol.)* an annual, biennial or perennial plant (e.g. clover, grass) with no persistent, woody parts

her·ba·ceous (hə:rbéiʃəs, ə:rbéiʃəs) *adj.* of, or like, herbs, esp. (of stems) not becoming woody ‖ (of flowers, sepals) like a leaf in color, shape etc.

herb·age (ɔ́:rbidʒ, hɔ́:rbidʒ) *n. (collect.)* herbaceous plants in growth, esp. as pasturage ‖ the edible parts of herbaceous plants

her·biv·ore (hə́:rbivɔr, hə́:rbivour) *n. (zool.)* an animal feeding chiefly on plant food **her·biv·o·rous** (hə:rbívərəs) *adj.*

Her·cu·le·an (hə:rkjulí:ən, hə:rkjú:li:ən) *adj.* exceptionally strong ‖ demanding exceptional effort

herd (hə:rd) **1.** *n. (collect.)* a number of animals of one kind, esp. cattle, feeding or gathered together ‖ *(collect.)* a large number of people ‖ *(collect.)* the common run of people, the masses **2.** *v.t.* to watch and tend (a herd) ‖ to drive (a herd or something compared with a herd) ‖ *v.i.* to form a herd or crowd

herds·man (hɔ́:rdzmən) *pl.* **herds·men** (hɔ́:rdzmən) *n.* a man who tends herds

here (hiər) **1.** *adv.* in this place ‖ at this or at that moment in time, action, thought etc. ‖ who or which is present, *Mary, here, thinks we should go* **here!** (used in answering a roll call) present! ‖ used as an interjection to remonstrate or to console **here's to you!** a drinking toast **neither here nor there** irrelevant ‖ of no importance **2.** *n.* this place, *he lives near here*

here·af·ter (hiərǽftər, hiəráftər) **1.** *adv.* from now on ‖ in the future **2.** *n.* a life after death

he·red·i·tar·y (hərédiṭeri:) *adj.* of physical or psychological qualities transmitted or able to be transmitted by heredity ‖ of something that is or may be transmitted by legacy or recognized rules of descent

he·red·i·ty (həréditi:) *n.* the transmission of qualities from parent to offspring

here·in (hiərín) *adv.* (esp. *legal contexts*) in this, *. . . and all the conditions herein*

her·e·sy (hérisi:) *pl.* **her·e·sies** *n.* religious or ideological belief opposed to orthodoxy ‖ an instance of this

her·e·tic (héritik) *n.* someone who believes in or advocates a heresy

he·ret·i·cal (hərétik'l) *adj.* of or relating to a heresy or heretic

here·to·fore (hiərtufɔ́r, hiərtufóur) *adv. (legal contexts)* until now ‖ formerly

her·it·age (héritidʒ) *n.* what has been, or can be, inherited

her·met·ic (hə:rmétik) *adj.* impervious to air or airtight, *a hermetic seal*

her·mit (hɔ́:rmit) *n.* someone who withdraws from the society of his fellowmen and lives in solitude, esp. devoting himself to prayer and meditation

her·mit·age (hɔ́:rmitidʒ) *n.* the abode of a hermit ‖ a very isolated dwelling

her·ni·a (hɔ́:rni:ə) *pl.* **her·ni·as, her·ni·ae** (hɔ́:rni:i:) *n.* the protrusion of a bodily organ, esp.one located in the area of the abdomen, from the cavity in which it is normally contained

he·ro (híərou) *pl.* **heroes** *n.* a man of exceptional quality who wins admiration by noble deeds, esp. deeds of courage ‖ the male character of a play, novel etc. about whom the action turns and in whose fate the readers or audience are sympathetically involved

he·ro·ic (hiróuik) *adj.* of or relating to a hero or heroine ‖ of or relating to the acts of a hero or heroine or acts which might be expected of a hero or heroine ‖ larger than life-size ‖ of or relating to the meter of heroic verse **he·ró·i·cal·ly** *adv.*

her·o·in (hérouin) *n.* a white, crystalline narcotic derived from morphine, that can cause addiction

her·o·ine (hérouin) *n.* a female hero

her·o·ism (hérouizəm) *n.* extreme courage ‖ an instance of this

her·on (hérən) *n.* migratory wadings bird having long, slender legs, a long neck and a tapering, pointed bill **her·on·ry** (hérənri:) *pl.* **her·on·ries** *n.* a breeding place of herons

hers (hɔ:rz) *possessive pron.* that or those things belonging to a female person or animal or something personified as female

her·self (hə:rsélf) *pron. refl.* form of SHE, *she washed herself* ‖ emphatic form of SHE, *she saw it herself*

hes·i·tance (hézitəns) *n.* hesitancy

hes·i·tan·cy (hézitənsi:) *pl.* **hes·i·tan·cies** *n.* the quality of being hesitant or an instance of this

hes·i·tant (hézitənt) *adj.* (of speech) marked by pauses

(a) æ, cat; ɑ, car; ɔ fawn; ei, snake. **(e)** e, hen; i:, sheep; iə, deer; ɛə, bear. **(i)** i, fish; ai, tiger; ə:, bird. **(o)** o, ox; au, cow; ou, goat; u, poor; ɔi, royal. **(u)** ʌ, duck; u, bull; u:, goose; ə, bacillus; ju:, cube. x, loch; θ, think; ð, bother; z, Zen; ʒ, corsage; dʒ, savage; ŋ, orangutang; j, yak; ʃ, fish; tʃ, fetch; 'l, rabble; 'n, redden. Complete pronunciation key appears inside front cover.

‖ having doubts about taking an action or a decision

hes·i·tate (héziteit) *pres. part.* **hes·i·tat·ing** *past* and *past part.* **hes·i·tat·ed** *v.i.* to pause before acting, e.g. because of doubt as to the wisdom or ethics of the action ‖ to be loath (to do something) ‖ to be indecisive ‖ to pause repeatedly when speaking

hes·i·ta·tion (hezitéiʃən) *n.* the act of hesitating or an instance of this

het·er·o·ge·ne·ous (hetərədʒí:ni:əs, hetərədzí:njəs) *adj.* dissimilar in character ‖ composed of different or disparate ingredients or elements ‖ *(phys.* and *chem.)* of or being a system composed of one or more phases

hew (hju:) *pres. part.* **hew·ing** *past* **hewed** *past part.* **hewn** (hju:n), **hewed** *v.t.* (often with 'down', 'off', 'away' etc.) to cut by blows with an ax or other sharp-edged instrument ‖ to shape with such an instrument ‖ *v.i.* to make blows with an ax or other sharp-edged instrument **héw·er** *n.* a person who hews

hex·a·gon (héksəgən, héksəgɒn) *n. (geom.)* a two-dimensional figure with six sides and six angles **hex·ag·on·al** (heksǽgən'l) *adj.* having six sides ‖ *(crystall.)* having six faces

hey (hei) *interj.* used to hail someone or to remonstrate with him

hey·day (héidei) *n.* a time of greatest prosperity and vigor

hi·a·tus (haiéitəs) *pl.* **hi·a·tus·es, hi·a·tus** *n.* a break or pause in the continuity of action, speech, writing etc., esp. a pause between adjacent vowels in order that both may be pronounced

hi·ber·nate (háibə:rneit) *pres. part.* **hi·ber·nat·ing** *past* and *past part.* **hi·ber·nat·ed** *v.i.* to spend the winter in a torpid state, with all the body functions greatly slowed down and the body temperature reduced to just above 32°F. **hi·ber·ná·tion** *n.*

hic·cup, hic·cough (híkʌp) **1.** *n.* a sudden, spasmodic contraction of the diaphragm and audible closing of the glottis when breathing in ‖ an attack of this ‖ *(securities)* a stock market decline of short duration **2.** *v.i. pres. part.* **hic·cup·ing, hic·cup·ping, hic·cough·ing** *past* and *past part.* **hic·cuped, hic·cupped, hic·coughed** to make the sound of a hiccup

hide (haid) *v. pres. part.* **hid·ing** *past* **hid** (hid) *past part.* **hid·den** (híd'n), **hid** *v.t.* to put or keep (something) out of sight ‖ to keep (something) from the knowledge of others ‖ to block the view of ‖ *v.i.* to keep out of sight

hide *n.* the raw or dressed skin of an animal, esp. a large animal ‖ *(pop.)* the skin of a human being

hid·e·ous (hídi:əs) *adj.* so ugly as to be repulsive ‖ fearful, dreadful ‖ *(pop.)* very unattractive

hie (hai) *v.i.* to go off with haste ‖ *v.t.* to cause (oneself) to go off with haste

hi·er·ar·chy (háiərɑrki:, háiərɑrki:) *pl.* **hi·er·ar·chies** *n.* a group of priests holding high office within an organized religion and having graded authority to govern the organization ‖ the group of persons in any organization vested with power and authority ‖ any arrangement of principles, things etc. in an ascending or descending order (e.g. in logic or science) ‖ *(theol.)* the angels as classified in nine orders

hi·er·o·glyph (háiərəglif, háirəglif) *n.* a character used in hieroglyphics

hi·er·o·glyph·ic (haiərəglífik, hairəglífik) **1.** *adj.* of or written in hieroglyphs **2.** *n (pl.)* a method of writing in which a symbol, usually pictorial, represents a word, syllable or sound, used by the Mayas, the Aztecs and others ‖ such a symbol ‖ a drawing or mark used to convey a secret meaning

high (hai) **1.** *adj.* being at, or reaching to, a position at a relatively large distance above some plane of reference (e.g. the ground or sea level) ‖ (of action) reaching to or done from a height ‖ great in degree, *high stakes, high prices* ‖ (of sounds) produced by a relatively large number of vibrations ‖ (of latitude) far from the equator ‖ occupying an important posi-

tion, *high up in one's profession* ‖ noble, *high ideals* ‖ intense, *high hopes* ‖ elated, *high spirits* ‖ at the zenith ‖ *(pop.)* intoxicated ‖ *(colloq.)* a state of exhilaration ‖ sophisticated **high and dry** *(pop.)* stranded **high and low** everywhere **high living** living luxuriously **it is high time** *(pop., intensive)* it is quite certainly time without more delay **2.** *adv.* at or to a great distance above or up ‖ in or to an elevated degree, price, station etc. **3.** *n.* an area having a high barometric pressure ‖ top gear

high *(colloq.)* **1.** a state of exhilaration; to be high on **2.** sophisticated, e.g., ''high camp''

high·fa·lu·tin (haifəlú:t'n) *adj. (pop.,* esp. of ideas and manner of talking) pretentious, high-flown

high·fa·lu·ting (haifəlú:tiŋ) *adj.* highfalutin

high-hat (háihæt) **1.** *adj. (pop.)* affecting superiority, supercilious **2.** *v.i. (pop.) pres. part.* **high-hat·ting** *past* and *past part.* **high-hat·ted** to snub

high·light (háilait) **1.** *n.* the part of a surface that catches most light ‖ such a part so treated in a painting or etching ‖ the outstanding part of a performance, book etc. ‖ an event of special importance **2.** *v.t.* to draw special attention to (something) ‖ to render the light-catching surfaces of (in painting or etching)

high-ten·sion (háiténʃən) *adj.* having a high voltage or operating at a high voltage

high·way (háiwei) *n.* a public road, esp. one that is wide, well-paved and direct

hi·jack, high-jack (háidʒæk) *v.t. (pop.)* to steal (something) while it is in transit

hike (haik) **1.** *v.i. pres. part.* **hik·ing** *past* and *past part.* **hiked** to walk a long way for pleasure in the open country ‖ to raise (prices) with a jerk **2.** *n.* a long walk for pleasure ‖ a raising ‖ a price increase

hi·lar·i·ous (hilɛ́əri:əs, hilǽri:əs, hailɛ́əri:əs, hailǽri:əs) *adj.* (of a person) shaking with laughter ‖ farcical or highly comic

hi·lar·i·ty (hilǽriti:, hilɛ́əriti:, hailǽriti:, hailɛ́əriti:) *n.* the state or condition of being hilarious

hill (hil) **1.** *n.* an elevation of the earth's surface that typically has a rounded top and is not as high as a mountain ‖ a small quantity of material formed into such a shape, e.g. by ants ‖ a cluster of plants, roots etc. with earth piled about it **2.** *v.t.* to surround with piled earth

hill·ock (hílək) *n.* a small hill or mound

hilt (hilt) *n.* the handle of a sword or dagger **up to the hilt** deeply, *up to the hilt in debt*

him (him) *pron., objective case of* HE

him·self (himsélf) *pron.,* refl. form of HE ‖ emphatic form of HE, *he did it himself*

hind (haind) *adj.* at the back, *the hind legs of a horse*

hind *pl.* **hinds, hind** *n.* a female deer

hin·der (híndər) *v.t.* to impede, slow down, or hold up ‖ *v.i.* to be a hindrance

hind·er (háindər) *adj.* located at the back or rear

hind·most (háindmoust) *adj.* furthest back

hin·drance (híndrəns) *n.* a hindering or being hindered ‖ that which hinders

hind·sight (háindsait) *n.* the understanding that is brought to bear on an event thanks to the passage of time

hinge (hindʒ) **1.** *n.* an attachment connecting two solid objects which, by the relative motion of its own two parts, enables one object to rotate in relation to the other, e.g. a gate on a gatepost ‖ a natural joint which serves the same purpose, e.g. that connecting the two parts of a bivalve shell ‖ *(philately)* a small strip of gummed paper used in mounting a stamp **2.** *v. pres. part.* **hing·ing** *past* and *past part.* **hinged** *v.i.* (with 'on' or 'upon') to depend upon ‖ *v.t.* to connect by a hinge

hint (hint) **1.** *n.* an aid in guessing or in drawing a conclusion ‖ an oblique piece of advice ‖ an indirect mention ‖ a slight suggestion **to take a hint** to perceive an oblique piece of advice and act on it in the way that was intended **2.** *v.t.* to suggest ‖ *v.i.* (with 'at') to make an oblique reference to or suggestion of

hip (hip) *n.* the flesh-covered, lateral extension of the pelvis and the upper thighbone on either side of the body below the waist ‖ *(archit.)* the external angle at the junction of two sides of a roof whose supporting walls adjoin

hip·po·pot·a·mus (hipəpótəməs) *pl.* **hip·po·pot·a·mus·es, hip·po·pot·a·mi** (hipəpótəmai) *n.* a genus of four-toed, ungulate Old World mammals, many of which exist only as fossils

hire (haiər) *n.* a payment for temporary use of something ‖ the act of hiring or an instance of this

hire *pres. part.* **hir·ing** *past* and *past part.* **hired** *v.t.* to obtain the use of (something) temporarily for an agreed payment ‖ to obtain the services of (someone) for an agreed wage ‖ (with 'out') to provide (something) or the services of (someone) temporarily for an agreed payment

hire·ling (háiərliŋ) *n.* someone with a merely mercenary interest in the job for which he has been hired

hir·sute (hə́:rsu:t) *adj.* hairy, esp. having shaggy hair

his (hiz) **1.** *possessive pron.* that or those things belonging to him, *the house is his* **2.** *possessive adj.* of, pertaining to or belonging to him, *his house* ‖ experienced, done or made by him

hiss (his) **1.** *v.i.* to make the sound of a prolonged 's' ‖ to make a similar sound (e.g. of a snake, or of drops of water landing on a very hot surface) ‖ *v.t.* to show disapproval of by making this sound **2.** *n.* the sound itself

his·to·ri·an (históri:ən, históuri:ən) *n.* someone who specializes in history

his·tor·ic (histórik, histórik) *adj.* of or relating to the past ‖ having important associations with famous events or developments in the past, *a historic monument* ‖ (of an event) likely to be remembered or recorded in the future

his·tor·i·cal (histórik, histórik) *adj.* of or relating to history ‖ authenticated in history, not legendary ‖ based on or about events in history, *a historical novel* **his·tór·i·cal·ly** *adv.*

his·to·ry (hístəri:, hístri:) *pl.* **his·to·ries** *n.* a record of past events, usually with an interpretation of their cause and an assessment of their importance ‖ the study and writing of such records ‖ past events ‖ a narrative of real or fictitious events connected with a particular person, country, object etc.

his·tri·on·ic (histri:ónik) *adj.* relating to actors, acting or the theater ‖ excessively theatrical **his·tri·on·i·cal·ly** *adv.* **his·tri·on·ics** *pl. n.* theatrical behavior off the stage

hit (hit) **1.** *v. pres. part.* **hit·ting** *past* and *past part.* **hit** *v.t.* to succeed in landing a missile or thrown object on (a desired spot) ‖ (of a missile or thrown object) to reach, meet or make contact with (something aimed at) ‖ to strike with a blow ‖ to strike by throwing an object or sending a missile ‖ to strike against with a sudden impact ‖ to cause something to strike or knock against another, *he hit his head on the lamp* ‖ to deliver (a blow) ‖ to hurt emotionally or financially ‖ to criticize adversely ‖ *(baseball)* to make (a hit having a particular value) ‖ *v.i.* to make a blow, strike etc. **to be hard hit** to be the victim of very adverse circumstances **to hit a man when he is down** to injure someone already suffering under misfortune **to hit below the belt** to take an unfair advantage **to hit it off** to get on well together **to hit the mark** to hit an object aimed at ‖ to reach a standard **to hit the road** to start or resume traveling **to hit the spot** (of food or drink) to be exactly what is

wanted at the moment **2.** *n.* the act of hitting or an instance of this ‖ a criticism, esp. on oblique one ‖ a popular success ‖ *(underworld slang)* a murder committed under a ''contract'' from the underworld

hitch (hitʃ) **1.** *v.t.* to move (something) by little jerks ‖ to fasten temporarily or loosely ‖ to attach (something to be towed) firmly by a hook etc. ‖ *v.i.* to move slowly and jerkily ‖ to become caught by or fastened to something **to hitch up** to pull up with a little tug ‖ to harness (a draft animal) **2.** *n.* an obstacle, impediment ‖ an accident or breakdown ‖ a jerky pull

hitch·hike (hítʃhaik) *pres. part.* **hitch·hik·ing** *past* and *past part.* **hitch·hiked** *v.i.* to travel by begging free rides in motor vehicles

hith·er (híðər) **1.** *adv.* *(rhet.)* to, or towards, this place **2.** *adv.* *(rhet.)* on this side ‖ *(rhet.)* toward this side, nearer

hith·er·to (hiðərtú:, híðərtu:) *adv.* up till this time

hive (haiv) **1.** *n.* a man-made shelter for honeybees to live in ‖ a swarm of bees in such a shelter ‖ a building etc. thronged with busy people **2.** *v. pres. part.* **hiv·ing** *past* and *past part.* **hived** *v.t.* to cause (a swarm of bees) to enter an empty hive ‖ to store (e.g. honey) in a hive ‖ *v.i.* to live in or go to a hive

hives (haivz) *pl. n.* (construed as *sing.* or *pl.*) a temporary skin condition of allergic origin characterized by raised itchy patches of skin and caused by reaction to various agents, e.g. certain foods, inhalants or drugs

hoard (hɔrd, hourd) *v.t.* to collect, keep and store away as a hoard

hoard *n.* a number of things, or quantity of material, esp. money or valuables, put together in a safe, usually secret place ‖ a body of ideas, knowledge etc. stored up for future use

hoard·ing (hɔ́rdiŋ, hóurdiŋ) *n.* a temporary board wall placed around construction work

hoarse (hɔrs, hours) *adj.* (of a voice) rough, scratchy or husky ‖ (of a person) having such a voice **hóars·en** *v.t.* to make hoarse ‖ *v.i.* to become hoarse

hoax (houks) **1.** *v.t.* to deceive (someone), esp. in fun **2.** *n.* a deception, esp. one meant as a joke

hob·ble (hób'l) **1.** *v. pres. part.* **hob·bling** *past* and *past part.* **hob·bled** *v.i.* (esp. of an old or lame person) to walk with short, unsteady steps ‖ *v.t.* to join the legs of (a horse, camel etc.) by a short rope so that it can take only short steps and will not stray far **2.** *n.* a hobbling gait ‖ the rope used in hobbling an animal

hob·by (hóbi:) *pl.* **hob·bies** *n.* a spare time interest or occupation, esp. one taken up just for pleasure

hob·nob (hóbnɒb) *pres. part.* **hob·nob·bing** *past* and *past part.* **hob·nobbed** *v.i.* (with 'with') to be on familiar terms (esp. with those richer or socially more distinguished than oneself)

ho·bo (hóubou) *pl.* **ho·boes, ho·bos** *n.* a tramp, a seasonal migratory worker

hock (hɒk) *n.* a joint of the hind leg in some quadrupeds which bends backward. It corresponds to the human ankle

hock **1.** *n.* *(pop.)* (in the phrase) **in hock** at the pawnshop ‖ in debt **2.** *v.t.* *(pop.)* to pawn

hock·ey (hóki:) *n.* ice hockey ‖ field hockey

hod (hɒd) *n.* a V-shaped trough mounted on a long staff, used for carrying bricks, mortar etc. up and down scaffolding ‖ a coal scuttle

hodge·podge (hódʒpɒdʒ) *n.* an ill-assorted mixture, medley

hoe (hou) **1.** *n.* a hand tool used in cultivation, consisting of a narrow, thin, flat piece of steel with a

---

sharp edge, fixed almost at right angles to the end of a long pole and used for breaking up clods of earth, loosening the topsoil, dragging out or cutting weeds, drawing earth into a ridge etc. **2.** *v. pres. part.* **hoe·ing** *past* and *past part.* **hoed** *v.t.* to take a hoe to (weeds, earth etc.) ‖ *v.i.* to use a hoe **to have a long row to hoe** to have a long grueling task to perform

hog (hɔg, hɒg) **1.** *pl.* **hogs, hog** *n.* omnivorous mammals having stout bodies with thick, usually bristled skin, long broad snouts and cleft hoofs ‖ *(pop.)* a greedy or filthy person **to go the whole hog** to carry an action to its absolute limit **2.** *v.t. pres. part.* **hog·ging** *past* and *past part.* **hogged** to take more than one's share of

hoi pol·loi (hɔipəlɔ́i) *n.* the common people, the masses viewed with condescension

hoist (hɔist) *adj.* carried off ‖ (only in) **hoist with one's own petard** made the victim of one's own scheming

hold (hould) **1.** *v. pres. part.* **hold·ing** *past* and *past part.* **held** (held) *v.t.* to have and continue to have in one's hand or hands ‖ to support or keep in place with some part of one's body ‖ to detain ‖ to contain, *this box holds all my clothes* ‖ to retain, *does this pan hold water?* ‖ to consider, regard as having a specified value, quality or nature ‖ to keep in a certain position or condition ‖ to keep, *to hold someone's attention* ‖ to force (someone) to abide by a promise etc. ‖ *(mil.)* to keep control of ‖ to preside over, *to hold court* ‖ *(mus.)* to sustain (a note) ‖ *v.i.* to continue ‖ to remain whole under pressure ‖ to remain valid **hold on!** wait! ‖ keep firm hold! **to hold back** to suppress (truth) ‖ to keep in reserve ‖ to be reticent ‖ to be slow to attack **to hold down** to keep under restraint ‖ to keep (a job) **to hold forth** to speak at length to an audience or as if to an audience **to hold in one's hands** to have power over **to hold off** to keep at a distance ‖ to keep (someone) from advancing or attacking **to hold one's breath** to be in a state of sympathetic anxiety **to hold one's ground** (or **one's own**) to keep one's position in fighting or argument **to hold one's head high** to face the world confidently with one's honor unquestioned **to hold one's tongue** to stop talking ‖ to refrain from speaking out when one should or when one longs to do so **to hold out** to continue to be sufficient to the end or for a specified time ‖ to continue to resist **to hold out on someone** to keep back something (money, information etc.) from someone **to put on hold** to ask a telephone caller to wait **to hold water** to be valid **to hold with** to agree with, approve of **2.** *n.* the act of holding ‖ something providing a grip for the fingers ‖ in a missile-launching countdown, an order to stop; by extension, any order to delay ‖ *(wrestling)* a seizing or holding of an opponent in a particular manner **to take hold** (of ideas etc.) to begin to become established

hold·er (hóuldər) *n.* someone who holds ‖ something which holds

hold·ing (hóuldiŋ) *n.* a having or keeping hold ‖ land, shares etc. owned

hole (houl) *n.* a small space or cavity partly or wholly surrounded by matter ‖ an empty space made in the earth or other material by an animal, to serve as a home or hiding place ‖ a small, dark, often dirty place ‖ a situation that is embarrassing or from which there is apparently no escape ‖ *(golf)* a small cuplike pit into which the ball must be played ‖ *(golf)* the distance between two such successive pits ‖ *(golf)* the contest between players to play a ball over such a distance in the fewest strokes ‖ *(golf)* a win in such a contest, *two holes up* **to make a hole in** to use up a considerable amount of a large supply of **to pick holes in** to find or draw attention to defects in (an argument etc.)

hol·i·day (hólidei) *n.* a day on which one does not go to work, school etc.

ho·li·ness (hóuli:nis) *n.* the quality of being holy **Hol-**

iness *(Roman Catholicism,* with possessive) a title for the pope

hol·ler (hólər) **1.** *v.i.* and *t.* to shout or cry out **2.** *n.* a yell, shout

hol·low (hólou) *n.* a little hole ‖ a saucer-shaped piece of ground

hol·ly (hóli:) *pl.* **hol·lies** *n.* evergreen shrubs and trees usually having prickly leaves with a shiny surface

hol·o·caust (hóləkɔst, hóuləkɔst) *n.* a large-scale sacrifice or destruction esp. of life, esp. by fire

hol·ster (hóulstər) *n.* a pistol case attached to the belt or the saddle or slung from the shoulder and carried under the arm

ho·ly (hóuli:) *comp.* **ho·li·er** *superl.* **ho·li·est** *adj.* of God or a god, his works, dwelling place, attributes etc. ‖ (of a person) living a life of spiritual purity ‖ (of things) dedicated, set apart, for sacred usage

hom·age (hómidʒ, ómidʒ) *n.* a mark or testimony of esteem, respect or veneration **to do** (or **pay**) **homage** to express homage by word or gesture

home (houm) **1.** *n.* the private living quarters of a person or family ‖ the place, city etc. where a person lives ‖ the place, city etc. where one was born or reared ‖ a building where orphans, old people etc. are housed and cared for ‖ the native environment of an animal or plant ‖ the place where something originated, developed etc. ‖ *(baseball* etc.) the point to which a player seeks to move or return **at home** in one's own home **to be at home with** to be familiar with, or used to **2.** *adj.* of or associated with a home, one's home or native country ‖ *(sports)* played on one's usual field, court etc., not on one's opponent's, *a home game* **3.** *adv.* to or into one's home ‖ all the way, *he drove the nail home* ‖ exactly where intended, *the remark hit home* **nothing to write home about** *(pop.)* not very good **4.** *v. pres. part.* **hom·ing** *past* and *past part.* **homed** *v.i.* (esp. of some pigeons) to locate and make for home ‖ (of aircraft, guided missiles etc., with 'in') to move directly to a specified target, place etc. ‖ *v.t.* to guide (an aircraft, missile etc.) to a specific place by radio etc.

home·li·ness (hóumli:nis) *n.* the quality of being homely

home·ly (hóumli:) *comp.* **home·li·er** *superl.* **home·li·est** *adj.* simple, plain ‖ plain-featured, not attractive

home·made (hóummeid) *adj.* made at home, not in a factory ‖ crudely made by an amateur, not professional

home plate *(baseball)* a piece of rubber set into the ground beside which the batter stands and which a player must touch after completing the round of bases in order to score a run

home run *(baseball)* a hit which enables the batter to run all the bases and score a run

home·sick (hóumsik) *adj.* longing for home

home·spun (hóumspʌn) **1.** *n.* cloth woven from yarn spun at home or cloth imitating this **2.** *adj.* of such cloth ‖ plain, unsophisticated

home·ward (hóumwərd) **1.** *adv.* towards home **2.** *adj.* going in the direction of home

hom·e·y, hom·y (hóumi:) *comp.* **hom·i·er** *superl.* **hom·i·est** *adj.* appropriately cozy and unpretentious ‖ *(pejorative)* inappropriately lacking a sense of style

hom·i·ci·dal (hɒmisáid'l) *adj.* pertaining to homicide ‖ tending towards homicide

hom·i·cide (hómisaid) *n.* the killing of a human being by another, whether murder or manslaughter ‖ someone who kills another

hom·i·ly (hómili:) *pl.* **hom·i·lies** *n.* a sermon in which spiritual values are discussed in relation to some practical subject ‖ a wearisome moralizing lecture

hom·i·ny (hómini:) *n.* hulled corn kernels with the germ removed, often ground, and eaten boiled or fried

ho·mo·ge·ne·ous (houməd ʒí:njəs, houməd ʒí:ni:əs, hɒməd ʒí:njəs, hɒməd ʒíni:əs) *adj.* similar in character ‖ having at all points the same composition and properties

ho·mog·e·nize (houmódʒenaiz, həmódʒənaiz) *pres. part.* **ho·mog·e·niz·ing** *past* and *past part.* **ho·mog·e·nized**

v.t. to make homogeneous (e.g. milk, by breaking down the fat globules and casein)

hom·o·nym (hómənim) *n.* a word having the same sound, or the same spelling and sound, as another which has a different meaning, e.g. 'bare' and 'bear' ‖ a namesake

ho·mo·sex·u·al (hóumousékʃuːəl) 1. *adj.* of, characterized by or involving sexual attraction felt by a person for another person of the same sex 2. *n.* a person (esp. male) so attracted **ho·mo·sex·u·al·i·ty** (houmousekʃuːǽliti:) *n.*

hone (houn) 1. *n.* a piece of stone with a very fine abrasive surface, used to grind a cutting tool (e.g. razor, scythe) to a sharp edge 2. *v.t. pres. part.* **hon·ing** *past* and *past part.* **honed** to sharpen by using a hone

ho·nest (ónist) *adj.* never deceiving, stealing, or taking advantage of the trust of others ‖ sincere, truthful ‖ obtained by fair means **hó·nest·ly** *adv.* with honesty ‖ (used as an intensive) really

hon·es·ty (ónisti:) *n.* the act or condition of being honest

hon·ey (háni:) 1. *pl.* **hon·eys** *n.* a sweet viscous fluid made by bees, esp. honeybees, from nectar and stored to serve as food during the winter ‖ *(pop.)* a term of endearment 2. *pres. part.* **hon·ey·ing** *past* and *past part.* **hon·eyed, hon·ied** *v.t. (pop.,* often with 'up') to blandish (someone) ‖ to sweeten with honey, or as if with honey

hon·ey·comb (háni:koum) 1. *n.* an aggregate of hexagonal wax cells, made by bees for their eggs, larvae and store of honey ‖ anything having a comparable complex structure ‖ a small cavity in cast metal 2. *v.t.* to make a honeycomb pattern on

hon·ey·moon (háni:muːn) 1. *n.* a holiday taken by a newly married couple 2. *v.i.* to spend a honeymoon

hon·ey·suck·le (háni:sʌkˈl) *n.* a member of *Lonicera,* fam. *Caprifoliaceae,* esp. the woodbine

honk (hɔŋk, hɑŋk) 1. *n.* the call of the wild goose ‖ a similar sound, e.g. of a car horn 2. *v.i.* to make such a sound

hon·or (ónər) *n.* moral integrity ‖ *(rhet.)* the esteem accorded to virtue or talent ‖ conventional respect for a person of high rank or public distinction or for a worthy symbol ‖ an award or distinction ‖ *(pl.)* awards or special ceremonies to express public respect ‖ a person who reflects credit on someone or something, *an honor to his country* ‖ *(pl.)* academic distinction ‖ *(pl.)* the honors program ‖ *(pl., bridge)* ace to ten in a trump suit ‖ *(pl., bridge, whist)* the scoring value of such cards **Honor** (with possessive) a title of respect used esp. for judges **honor bound** compelled by considerations of upright behavior **to do honor to** to make a public show of respect for **to do the honors** to do what is expected of the host

honor *v.t.* to feel or show honor for ‖ to confer honor on ‖ *(commerce)* to treat as valid, *to honor a check*

hon·or·a·ble (ónərəbˈl) *adj.* showing great respect or self-respect ‖ worthy of respect ‖ (of the details of an agreement) consistent with the honor of all parties, *an honorable peace* **Honorable** a U.S. courtesy title of certain government officials, e.g. members of Congress

hon·or·ar·y (ónərəri:) *adj.* of an unpaid office or the person holding it ‖ of duties which are merely nominal ‖ of something intended to do honor, *an honorary degree*

hood (hud) 1. *n.* a loose bonnetlike covering for the head and neck, often attached to a coat or cloak ‖ the cover over the engine of a car etc. ‖ a loose cape worn over the upper part of an academic gown ‖ *(falconry)* a loose cover for the falcon's head 2. *v.t.* to cover, or furnish, with a hood

hood·lum (húːdləm, húdləm) *n. (pop.)* a hooligan ‖ *(pop.)* a gangster

hood·wink (húdwiŋk) *v.t.* to deceive by concealing the truth or by trickery

hoof (huf, huːf) 1. *pl.* **hooves** (huvz, huːvz), **hoofs** *n.* the sheath of horn covering the forepart of the foot in a horse, cow, sheep, pig etc. ‖ the foot of such an animal **on the hoof** (of hoofed animals for slaughtering) alive 2. *v.t. (pop.,* often with 'it') to walk ‖ *v.t. (pop.)* to dance

hook (huk) 1. *n.* a piece of a durable material, esp. metal, curved or bent sharply and able to support a considerable strain, used for taking hold of or suspending things ‖ a fishhook ‖ *(boxing)* a short swinging blow given with the elbow held bent and rigid ‖ *(golf)* a drive which sends the ball far to the left (or to the right if the player is left-handed) **by hook or by crook** by fair means or foul **hook, line and sinker** *(pop.)* completely 2. *v.t.* to use a hook to catch, fasten or suspend (something) ‖ to form (e.g. one's arm) into a hook ‖ to catch (a fish) on a hook ‖ to make (a rug) by drawing thread or lengths of wool through a canvas using a hook ‖ *(golf, cricket)* to hit (the ball) with a hook ‖ *(boxing)* to hit with a hook ‖ *(baseball)* to pitch (the ball) so that it curves ‖ *(pop.)* to steal ‖ *(pop.)* to trap (someone) into doing something ‖ *v.i.* to curve like a hook ‖ to be fastened by means of hooks

hoop (huːp, hup) 1. *n.* a strip of metal, wood etc. bent to form the circumference of a circle, used in binding the staves of a cask ‖ a child's toy consisting of a large circle made of wood, metal or plastic, played with by rolling it 2. *v.t.* to fasten with a hoop or hoops ‖ to encircle

hoot (huːt) 1. *n.* an aspirated, loud sound of derision or laughter ‖ a similar sound, e.g. of an automobile horn ‖ the call of an owl **not to care** (or **give**) **a hoot** *(pop.)* not to care at all **not worth a hoot** utterly worthless or useless 2. *v.i.* to make a hoot ‖ *v.t.* to make derisive hoots at (someone) **hóot·er** *n.* something that makes a hooting sound

hop (hɔp) 1. *v. pres. part.* **hop·ping** *past* and *past part.* **hopped** *v.i.* (of persons) to make a little jump from the ground using only one foot or both feet or to progress by a series of such little jumps ‖ (with 'over') to jump quickly over ‖ to make a short flight or a quick short journey ‖ *v.t.* to jump over ‖ to jump into ‖ to obtain (a ride) by hitchhiking **to hop from one thing to another** to change the subject of one's conversation, attention etc. quickly and repeatedly 2. *n.* an instance of hopping ‖ a short trip, esp. by airplane ‖ *(pop.)* a dance

hope (houp) *pres. part.* **hop·ing** *past* and *past part.* **hoped** *v.i.* to have hope ‖ *v.t.* to wish and expect **to hope against hope** to cling to one's hopes despite the unlikelihood of their being fulfilled

hope *n.* a confident expectation that a desire will be fulfilled ‖ wishful trust ‖ something which one longs to see realized ‖ a person in whom confidence is placed or who could provide what is wanted, *he is her last hope*

hope·ful (hóupfəl) *adj.* being full of hope ‖ likely to fulfill hopes

hope·less (hóuplis) *adj.* without hope ‖ affording no reason for hope

hop·per (hópər) *n.* (esp. in compounds) something that hops ‖ the larva of various insects, e.g. the grasshopper, locust ‖ a container, usually narrow at the bottom and wide at the top, which delivers its contents to something below it

horde (hɔrd, hourd) *n.* a vast number of people, as-

---

sembled or loosely associated

hor·i·zon (həráiz'n) *n.* the apparent line of junction of earth or sea with sky (the apparent or visible horizon)

hor·i·zon·tal (hɔrizónt'l, hɔrizónt'l) **1.** *adj.* at right angles to a radius of the earth ‖ (of machinery) having its parts arranged or moving in a plane at right angles to a radius of the earth ‖ of or located at the horizon **2.** *n.* a line, plane etc. that is horizontal

hor·mone (hɔ́rmoun) *n.* one of a group of substances of variable composition which are produced in most living systems and are transported by the circulation of the body fluids or sap

horn (hɔrn) **1.** *n.* a hard, pointed, permanent outgrowth of epidermis, usually curved and paired, on the head of some animals, e.g. cattle, antelope ‖ *(mus.)* any of various wind instruments (originally made from an animal's horn) ‖ a French horn ‖ an instrument for making loud warning noises, e.g. a foghorn, a car horn ‖ something shaped like a horn **to draw in one's horns** to be less aggressive in manner ‖ to economize ‖ to be less active **2.** *v.t.* to furnish with horns ‖ (of an animal with horns) to pierce with a horn ‖ *v.i.* **to horn in** (with 'on') to intrude

hor·net (hɔ́rnit) *n.* any of various large, strong members of *Vespidae,* a family of wasps **to stir up a hornets' nest** to arouse the fierce anger of a number of people

ho·rol·o·gy (hɔrólədʒi:, hourólədʒi:) *n.* the science of measuring time by mechanical devices ‖ the art of making timepieces

hor·o·scope (hɔ́rəskoup, hórəskoup) *n.* the configuration of the planets, esp. at the time of a person's birth, from which astrologers predict his future ‖ a diagram representing the configuration of the stars and planets at any given time **ho·ros·co·py** (hɔróskəpi:, houróskəpi:) *n.* this practice

hor·ren·dous (hɔréndəs, hɔréndəs) *adj.* of a kind to inspire horror, dreadful

hor·ri·ble (hɔ́rəb'l, hórəb'l) *adj.* giving rise to horror ‖ extremely unpleasant or unpleasing **hor·ri·bly** *adv.*

hor·rid (hɔ́rid, hórid) *adj.* very unkind ‖ horrible

hor·ri·fy (hɔ́rifai, hórifai) *pres. part.* **hor·ri·fy·ing** *past* and *past part.* **hor·ri·fied** *v.t.* to cause horror to ‖ to shock

hor·ror (hɔ́rər, hórər) *n.* intense fear joined with repulsion ‖ something which causes horror ‖ *(pop.)* someone, esp. a child, who behaves in a horrid way

hors d'oeu·vre (ɔrdə:vr) *pl.* **hors d'oeu·vres, hors d'oeu·vre** (ɔrdə:vr) *n.* various dishes served as appetizers before the principal luncheon or dinner courses

horse (hɔrs) **1.** *n.* a large, herbivorous animal with a flowing mane and a tail or coarse hair, and with the hoof undivided ‖ a stallion or gelding as distinguished from a mare, filly, colt or pony ‖ a clotheshorse ‖ a vaulting horse **a horse of a different color** quite a different matter **from the horse's mouth** from the source, not from some third person **hold your horses!** don't be impatient, wait a moment! **2.** *v. pres. part.* **hors·ing** *past* and *past part.* **horsed** *v.t.* to provide a horse for (someone) ‖ *v.i.* **to horse around** *(pop.)* to fool around

horse·rad·ish (hɔ́rsrædiʃ) *n.* a perennial plant cultivated for its fleshy white root ‖ this root ‖ a pungent condiment made from this root

horse-shoe (hɔ́rsʃu:) *n.* a curved bar of iron with a flat face, shaped to fit the rim of a horse's hoof, to which it is nailed for protection ‖ *(pl.)* a game played by trying to throw horseshoes over a stake fixed 40 ft away

hor·ti·cul·ture (hɔ́rtikʌltʃər) *n.* the art of growing flowers, fruit and vegetables **hor·ti·cúl·tur·ist** *n.*

ho·san·na (houzǽnə) *n.* a cry of praise and worship

hose (houz) **1.** *n.* a flexible tube used for conveying water ‖ *(collect., hist.* and *commerce)* stockings **2.** *v.t. pres. part.* **hos·ing** *past* and *past part.* **hosed** to spray with a hose

ho·sier (hóuʒər) *n.* someone who deals in stockings, socks **hó·sier·y** *n. (collect.)* the goods dealt in by a

hosier ‖ his business

hos·pice (hóspis) *n.* a building, usually kept by a religious order, where travelers can obtain rest and food

hos·pi·ta·ble (hóspitəb'l, hospítəb'l) *adj.* gladly and generously receiving guests and attending to their needs and comfort ‖ receptive **hós·pi·ta·bly, hos·pít·a·bly** *adv.*

hos·pi·tal (hóspit'l) *n.* an institution equipped and staffed to provide medical and surgical and sometimes psychiatric care for the sick and injured

hos·pi·tal·i·ty (hospitǽliti:) *pl.* **hos·pi·tal·i·ties** *n.* the receiving of a guest ‖ the treatment given to or received by a guest ‖ a tendency to, and liking for, the frequent receiving of guests

hos·pi·tal·i·za·tion (hospit'lizéiʃən) *n.* a hospitalizing or being hospitalized ‖ the period of being in a hospital as a patient

hos·pi·tal·ize (hóspit'laiz) *pres. part.* **hos·pi·tal·iz·ing** *past* and *past part.* **hos·pi·tal·ized** *v.t.* to place as a patient in a hospital

host (houst) *n.* someone who provides hospitality ‖ *(hist.)* the landlord of an inn ‖ *(biol.)* any organism in which a parasite spends part or the whole of its existence and from which it derives nourishment or protection or both

host *n.* a great number, *a host of enemies*

hos·tage (hóstidʒ) *n.* a person held as a pledge that certain conditions will be fulfilled, failing which his life or well-being will be forfeited ‖ the condition of being a hostage

hos·tile (hóstəl) *adj.* antagonistic ‖ warlike ‖ of or relating to an enemy

hot (hɒt) *adj.* at a high temperature, esp. at a considerably higher temperature than one's body temperature ‖ (of body temperature) above normal ‖ producing a sensation similar to heat, *a hot mustard* ‖ (of an emotion) causing a sensation of body heat ‖ controversial, *a hot issue* ‖ following or pressing closely, *hot on his heels* ‖ *(hunting,* of the scent) clear and strong ‖ (in guessing games) close to the solution ‖ of a communications medium offering much information but requiring minimal attention ‖ electrically charged ‖ radioactive ‖ *(pop.)* stolen ‖ *(jazz)* characterized by exciting rhythm and tonality and by improvisation

hot-blood·ed (hótblʌdid) *adj.* (of people) passionate ‖ (of people) rash, impetuous

hot dog *n.* a hot, freshly cooked sausage (esp. a frankfurter) sandwiched in a split roll of bread

ho·tel (houtél) *n.* a large building with a resident staff, providing accommodation and often meals

hot·house (hóthaus) *pl.* **hot·hous·es** (hóthauziz) *n.* a greenhouse whose temperature is maintained at an artificially high level

hound (haund) **1.** *n.* a dog used in hunting or tracking, that follows the prey by scent **2.** *v.t.* to pursue relentlessly ‖ (with 'on') to urge

hour (áuər) *n.* a 24th part of the mean solar day, subdivided into 60 minutes, i.e. 60 minutes of sidereal time ‖ a fixed period of time, *the lunch hour* ‖ time of day ‖ *(pl.)* times for habitual activities, esp. getting up and going to bed ‖ a measure of distance expressed as the amount of time necessary to travel it, *our home is an hour from here*

hour-glass (áuərglæs, áuərglɒs) *n.* a device for measuring the period of one hour, this being the time taken by a measured quantity of fine, dry sand to pass through a narrow tube from an upper glass bulb into a lower one

hour hand (the shorter hand of a watch or clock, indicating the hour)

hour·ly (áuərli:) **1.** *adj.* done, or occurring, every hour **2.** *adv.* every hour ‖ very soon

house (hauz) *pres. part.* **hous·ing** *past* and *past part.* **housed** *v.t.* to provide or be a home or shelter for (someone or something)

house (haus) *pl.* **hous·es** (háuziz) *n.* a building for a person or family to live in ‖ a household ‖ the audience in a theater or the theater itself, *a full house* ‖ the place where a legislature meets or the legislative body itself ‖ a residence in a university, college, school etc. or the persons residing there ‖ a religious community or its residence ‖ a sign of the zodiac regarded as the seat of a planet's greatest influence ‖ *(astrology)* one of the 12 equal parts into which the celestial sphere is divided **like a house afire** with great success **on the house** paid for by the owners or management, not by the customer **to clean house** to put a house in order **to keep house** to manage the domestic arrangements of another person

hov·el (hávəl, hóvəl) *n.* a small, squalid dwelling

hov·er (hávər, hóvər) *v.i.* (often with 'over', 'above', 'aloft' etc.) to remain in the same place in the air for a short time as though suspended ‖ (with 'about', 'around', 'near' etc.) to move about, but keep near to

how (hau) *adv.* in what way or manner, *to know how to cook, how did it happen?* ‖ in or to what degree, amount, number, *he didn't know how fast he could run, how much does it cost?* **how about** used to introduce a suggestion, *how about a little walk?* **how do you do?** (as a greeting) how are you?

how·ev·er (hauévər) **1.** *adv.* in whatever way or manner ‖ in or to whatever degree, amount, number **2.** *conj.* nevertheless, but

howl (haul) **1.** *v.i.* (of wolves, dogs etc.) to make a prolonged, hollow, wailing call ‖ (of high winds etc.) to make a similar sound ‖ (of a person) to make a similar sound e.g. from grief, fear etc. ‖ to laugh very loudly and unrestrainedly ‖ *v.t.* to utter with a howl **2.** *n.* any of these sounds or cries

how·so·ev·er (hausouévər) *adv.* *(archaic)* in whatever way ‖ to whatever extent

hub (hʌb) *n.* the central part of a wheel from which the spokes radiate ‖ the point of greatest interest and importance

hub·bub (hábʌb) *n.* a noisy confused mingling of sounds ‖ a tumult or uproar

hu·bris (hjú:bris) *n.* a scornful, overweening pride

huck·ster (hákstər) *n.* a peddler or market vendor dealing in small articles ‖ *(pop.)* an advertising man

hud·dle (hád'l) **1.** *v. pres. part.* **hud·dling** past and *past part.* **hud·dled** *v.t.* (with 'up') to draw (oneself) in, esp. defensively ‖ *v.t.* (of a number of people or animals) to gather together very close to one another **2.** *n.* a group of people or animals gathered very close together ‖ *(football)* the grouping of a team behind the line of scrimmage where the quarterback (offensive team) or the captain (defensive team) tells his team the secret play for the next play or plays **to go into a huddle** to get together in order to discuss something privately

hue (hju:) *n.* that quality of a color which allows it to be classed as red, yellow, green, blue or an intermediate

huff (hʌf) *v.t.* to cause (someone) to be offended **húff·i·ly** *adv.* **húff·i·ness** *n.* **húff·y** *comp.* **huff·i·er** *superl.* **huff·i·est** *adj.*

hug (hʌg) **1.** *n.* a tight clasp or squeeze with the arms, esp. as an affectionate embrace ‖ a wrestling grip **2.** *v. pres. part.* **hug·ging** past and *past part.* **hugged** *v.t.* to clasp tightly between one's arms ‖ to dwell on (a feeling, memory etc.), esp. keeping it a secret, *to hug a grievance* ‖ to keep close to (something)

huge (hju:dʒ) *adj.* extremely large

hulk (hʌlk) *n.* the body, or hull, of a ship no longer seaworthy, sometimes used for storage ‖ a big clumsy man **húlk·ing** *adj.* big and clumsy

hull (hʌl) **1.** *n.* the body framework of a ship ‖ the framework of an airship **2.** *v.t.* to hit or pierce the hull of (a ship), e.g. with a torpedo

hull 1. *n.* the pod, shell etc. of a seed or fruit ‖ the calyx of some fruits, e.g. the strawberry **2.** *v.t.* to remove the hull or hulls from

hum (hʌm) **1.** *v. pres. part.* **hum·ming** past and *past part.* **hummed** *v.i.* to make a continuous sound in the throat, with the mouth closed ‖ (of bees, moving machine parts etc.) to make a similar sound ‖ *v.t.* to sing (a song, tune etc.) by humming **to make things hum** to be very active and make others work too **2.** *n.* the sound or act of humming

hu·man (hjú:mən) **1.** *adj.* of or characteristic of man ‖ being a person ‖ resembling man **2.** *n.* (pop.) a person

hu·mane (hju:méin) *adj.* showing kindness, consideration etc. to persons or animals ‖ of or relating to the humanities

hu·man·ism (hjú:mənizəm) *n.* any of several movements purporting to advocate the universally human as against utilitarian science, religious dogma, uncontrolled passion (e.g. Romanticism), political strivings etc.

hu·man·i·tar·i·an (hju:mænitéəri:ən) **1.** *n.* someone who actively promotes the welfare of the human race **2.** *adj.* being or characteristic of a humanitarian **hu·man·i·tár·i·an·ism** *n.*

hu·man·i·ty (hju:mæniti:) *pl.* **hu·man·i·ties** *n.* *(collect.)* mankind ‖ kindness to other people, or to animals ‖ *(pl.,* usually with 'the') studies (history, art, literature, classics etc.) emphasizing the cultural aspects of civilization

hum·ble (hámb'l) **1.** *comp.* **hum·bler** *superl.* **hum·blest** *adj.* possessing or marked by the virtue of humility ‖ of little worth, of lowly condition or rank **2.** *v.t. pres. part.* **hum·bling** past and *past part.* **hum·bled** to cause to feel humble **to humble oneself** to perform an act of submission by way of apology or penitence

hum·bug (hámbʌg) **1.** *n.* the hiding of falsehood under an appearance of sincerity ‖ insincere talk or writing ‖ a person behaving insincerely **2.** *v. pres. part.* **hum·bug·ging** past and *past part.* **hum·bugged** *v.t.* to mislead (someone) by a sham ‖ *v.i.* to be a humbug

hum·drum (hámdrʌm) *adj.* uninspired, flat, *a humdrum speech*

hu·mid (hjú:mid) *adj.* (of atmosphere) containing a high percentage of water vapor ‖ damp, moist **hu·mid·i·fy** (hju:mídifai) *pres. part.* **hu·mid·i·fy·ing** past and *past part.* **hu·mid·i·fied** *v.t.* to make humid

hu·mid·i·fi·er (hju:mídifaiər) *n.* a device for humidifying a room or building

hu·mid·i·ty (hju:míditi:) *n.* the state of being humid

hu·mil·i·ate (hju:míli:eit) *pres. part.* **hu·mil·i·at·ing** past and *past part.* **hu·mil·i·at·ed** *v.t.* to make (a person) suffer by lessening his dignity or self-esteem

hu·mil·i·a·tion (hju:mili:éiʃən) *n.* a humiliating or being humiliated ‖ an instance of this

hu·mil·i·ty (hju:míliti:) *n.* the quality of being without pride ‖ voluntary self-abasement

hum·ming (hámiŋ) *adj.* making the sound of a hum ‖ very active, *business is humming*

hu·mor (hjú:mər) **1.** *n.* something which arouses amusement, laughter etc. ‖ the capacity for recognizing, reacting to, or expressing something which is amusing, funny etc. ‖ a mood, frame of mind **out of humor** cross **2.** *v.t.* to let (someone) have his own way for the sake of peace and quiet ‖ to keep (someone) in a good temper

hu·mor·ist (hjú:mərist) *n.* someone who expresses humor in his writing, conversation etc. **hu·mor·ís·tic** *adj.*

(**a**) æ, cat; ɑ, car; ɔ fawn; ei, snake. (**e**) e, hen; i:, sheep; iə, deer; ɛə, bear. (**i**) i, fish; ai, tiger; ə:, bird. (**o**) o, ox; au, cow; ou, goat; u, poor; ɔi, royal. (**u**) ʌ, duck; u, bull; u:, goose; ə, bacillus; ju:, cube. x, loch; θ, think; ð, bother; z, Zen; ʒ, corsage; dʒ, savage; ŋ, orangutang; j, yak; ʃ, fish; tʃ, fetch; 'l, rabble; 'n, redden. Complete pronunciation key appears inside front cover.

hu·mor·ous (hjú:mərəs) *adj.* having, or giving rise to, humor

hump (hʌmp) **1.** *n.* a rounded, raised protrusion **2.** *v.t.* to make (something) hump-shaped

hu·mus (hjú:məs) *n.* the organic part of soil, formed by the partial decomposition of vegetable or animal matter

hunch (hʌntʃ) **1.** *n.* a hump on a person's back or a rounding of the shoulders ‖ a large hunk or piece ‖ *(pop.)* an intuitive feeling about a situation or a coming event **2.** *v.t.* to bend into a hump ‖ (with 'up' or 'out') to cause to form a hump

hunch·back (hʌntʃbæk) *n.* a humpback **húnch·backed** *adj.* humpbacked

hun·dred (hʌndrid) **1.** *pl.* **hun·dred, hun·dreds** *n.* ten times ten (*NUMBER TABLE) ‖ the cardinal number representing this (100, C) ‖ *(pl.)* in mathematical calculations, the column of figures three places to the left of the decimal point **2.** *adj.* being ten more than 90

hun·ger (hʌŋgər) **1.** *n.* a desire or craving for food ‖ a strong desire for anything ‖ a condition of physical weakness and distress suffered as the result of a long period of undernourishment **2.** *v.i.* to feel hunger for food or other objects of desire

hun·gry (hʌŋgri) *comp.* **hun·gri·er** *superl.* **hun·gri·est** *adj.* feeling hunger ‖ characterized by or showing hunger ‖ having a strong desire for ‖ (of land or soil) poor, lacking humus or other essentials for plant growth

hunk (hʌŋk) *n.* a large, thick piece of something

hunt (hʌnt) **1.** *v.t.* to pursue (game, a person) with the intention of capturing or killing ‖ to cover (an area) in search of game ‖ to attempt to find by careful and thorough searching ‖ *v.i.* to participate in a hunt ‖ to search **to hunt after** (or **for**) to try to discover **2.** *n.* the act of hunting or an instance of this ‖ the persons engaged in hunting ‖ the district hunted over **húnt·er** *n.* someone who hunts, esp. for game ‖ a horse bred and trained to be ridden for hunting ‖ a dog trained for use in hunting

hur·dle (hɔ́:rd'l) **1.** *n.* movable, short section of a fence of light construction used as part of an enclosure, as a gate etc., or as an obstacle to be jumped over by horses ‖ an open frame to be cleared by athletes in a race ‖ *(pl.)* such a race ‖ an obstacle to a course of action **2.** *v. pres. part.* **hur·dling** *past* and *past part.* **hur·dled** *v.i.* to compete in a hurdles race ‖ *v.t.* to surround with hurdles ‖ to jump (a hurdle) **húr·dler** *n.* someone who competes in a hurdles race

hurl (hɔ:rl) **1.** *v.t.* to throw violently ‖ to utter (threats, abuse etc.) with vehemence **2.** *n.* the act of hurling or an instance of this

hur·rah, hoo·rah (hərá) **1.** *interj.* used to express triumph, appreciation etc. **2.** *n.* this cry

hur·ray, hoo·ray (həréi) *interj.* and *n.* hurray

hur·ri·cane (hɔ́:rikein, hʌ́rikein) *n.* a cyclone with wind velocities exceeding 73 and often reaching over 100 miles per hour, usually covering a large area and accompanied by thunder, lightning and heavy rain, occurring esp. in the West Indies and Gulf of Mexico

hur·ry (hɔ́:ri:, hʌ́ri:) **1.** *n.* the performing of an action quickly and without delay ‖ the need to act in this way **in a hurry** quickly ‖ soon, *they won't invite us again in a hurry* ‖ wishing to act without delay **2.** *v. pres. part.* **hur·ry·ing** *past* and *past part.* **hur·ried** *v.i.* (often with 'up') to be quick, waste no time ‖ *v.t.* (often with 'up' or 'along') to make (someone or something) act, move etc. more quickly ‖ to do quickly or too quickly

hurt (hɔ:rt) *v. pres. part.* **hurt·ing** *past* and *past part.* **hurt** *v.t.* to cause bodily or mental pain to ‖ to damage ‖ to lessen the well-being or status of ‖ *v.i.* to cause or feel pain

hurt *n.* something which causes pain

hur·tle (hɔ́:rt'l) *v. pres. part.* **hur·tling** *past* and *past part.* **hur·tled** *v.i.* to move with great force and noise ‖ *v.t.* to make (something) move with great force and

noise

hus·band (hʌ́zbənd) *n.* the male partner in a marriage

hus·band·ry (hʌ́zbəndri:) *n.* farming ‖ *(rhet.)* management, esp. thrifty management

hush (hʌʃ) **1.** *v.i.* to stop making noise ‖ *v.t.* to cause (someone or something) to cease to make a noise **to hush up** to keep from being generally known **2.** *n.* a cessation of noise ‖ silence

husk (hʌsk) **1.** *n.* a dry, outer covering of some seeds and fruits, e.g corn ‖ *(fig.)* the worthless part of something after the useful or valuable part has been removed **2.** *v.t.* to remove the husk from

husk·y (hʌ́ski:) *pl.* **hus·kies** *n.* an Eskimo dog

husk·y *comp.* **husk·i·er** *superl.* **husk·i·est** *adj.* full of husks ‖ husklike ‖ (of speech, or a voice) having a dry, rough sound of lower pitch than normal ‖ tough, strong and heavily built

hus·sy (hʌ́si:, hʌ́zi:) *pl.* **hus·sies** *n.* *(old-fash.)* a saucy girl ‖ *(old-fash.)* a shamelessly immoral woman

hus·tle (hʌ́s'l) **1.** *v. pres. part.* **hus·tling** *past* and *past part.* **hus·tled** *v.t.* to shove, jostle rudely ‖ to push quickly forward, off, out etc. ‖ to force (someone) to act quickly ‖ *v.i.* to push one's way quickly ‖ to act, or appear to act, quickly and forcefully, esp. in getting things done **2.** *n. (pop.)* a hurry **hús·tler** *n.* *(pop.)* an energetic, bustling person

hut (hʌt) *n.* a small, roughly-built single-story and usually one-room building used as a dwelling, office or shelter

hutch (hʌtʃ) *n.* a box, usually with one side made of slats or wire netting, used to house small animals, e.g. rabbits ‖ *(mining)* a truck for hoisting coal out of a pit ‖ *(mining)* a trough for washing ore ‖ a low cupboard topped by rocks for china

hy·brid (háibrid) **1.** *n. (biol.)* an offspring resulting from crossbreeding ‖ *(gram.)* a word composed of elements from two or more languages **2.** *adj.* of or being a hybrid

hy·brid·ism (háibridi̩zəm) *n.* hybridity ‖ the production of hybrids

hy·drant (háidrənt) *n.* a pipe, fitted with tap and nozzle, by which water may be drawn from a supply main, e.g. for fire fighting, street cleaning etc.

hy·drau·lic (haidrɔ́lik, haidrɔ́lik) *adj.* of fluids, esp. water, in motion ‖ of the pressure exerted by water when conveyed through pipes ‖ of substances, machinery etc. affected by or operated by fluids in motion, *hydraulic brakes* **hy·dráu·li·cal·ly** *adv.*

hy·dro·e·lec·tric (haidrouiléktrik) *adj.* of the production of electricity by water power

hy·dro·gen (háidrədʒən) *n.* a nonmetallic, monovalent element that is the lightest of all the elements and has the simplest structure (one proton and one electron)

hydrogen bomb *(abbr.* H-bomb) a bomb releasing enormous energy by the fusion at extremely high temperature and pressure of nuclei of isotopes of hydrogen to form helium

hy·dro·pho·bi·a (haidrəfóubi̩ə) *n.* aversion to water, esp. as a symptom of rabies ‖ rabies, esp. in man **hy·dro·phó·bic** *adj.* of or affected by hydrophobia ‖ *(chem.)* denoting a lack of affinity for water

hy·dro·phone (háidrəfoun) *n.* an instrument for detecting sound transmitted through water

hy·dro·plane (háidrəplei̩n) *n.* a light motorboat which, by means of hydrofoils, can rise partially or completely out of the water at high speed ‖ a seaplane

hy·drous (háidrəs) *adj.* containing water

hy·e·na, hy·ae·na (háii̩:nə) *n.* a carnivorous Old World quadruped having powerful jaws, strong teeth and well-developed forelimbs

hy·giene (háidʒi:n) *n.* the science of health, its preservation and the prevention of disease ‖ the practice of measures designed to attain and preserve health **hy·gi·en·ic** (haidʒi:énik, haidʒí:nik), **hy·gi·én·i·cal** *adjs* **hy·gien·ics** *n.* the science of hygiene **hy·gien·ist** (haidʒí:nist, haidʒénist) *n.*

hy·men (háimən) *n.* the thin fold of mucous membrane

at the entrance to the vagina

hymn (him) **1.** *n.* a song or ode in praise, adoration or supplication of God, esp. one sung at a religious service **2.** *v.t. (rhet.)* to praise or supplicate in a hymn ‖ *v.i. (rhet.)* to sing a hymn

hym·nal (hímnəl) *n.* a book containing a collection of hymns

hymn·book (hímbu̯k) *n.* a hymnal

hyper- *prefix* excessive, overmuch, above

hy·per·crit·i·cal (haipərkrítik'l) *adj.* too critical, esp. of trivial faults

hy·per·sen·si·tive (haipərsénsitiv) *adj.* acutely, excessively or abnormally sensitive **hy·per·sen·si·tiv·i·ty** *n.*

hy·per·son·ic (haipərsónik) *adj.* of speed more than five times that of sound in air

hy·per·ten·sion (haipərténʃən) *n.* abnormally high blood pressure in the arteries that may or may not be associated with observable organic disorders (e.g. kidney diseases, obesity, diabetes) ‖ a condition resulting from such abnormally high blood pressure and often accompanied by nervousness, dizziness and headaches

hy·phen (háifən) **1.** *n.* a punctuation mark (-) used to join two words or two elements of a word, e.g. in 'counselor-at-law', and to divide a word syllabically, e.g. at the end of a line **2.** *v.t.* to hyphenate

hy·phen·ate (háifəneit) *pres. part.* **hy·phen·at·ing** *past* and *past part.* **hy·phen·at·ed** *v.t.* to join or divide by a hyphen ‖ to write with a hyphen **hy·phen·a·tion** *n.*

hyp·no·sis (hipnóusis) *pl.* **hyp·no·ses** (hipnóusi:z) *n.* an artificially induced state, resembling sleep, but characterized by exaggerated suggestibility and continued responsiveness to the voice of the hypnotist

hy·po·chon·dri·a (haipəkóndri:ə) *n.* hypochondriasis ‖ a state of mental depression often accompanying hypochondriasis

hy·po·chon·dri·a·sis (haipoukɒndráiəsis) *n. (med.)* excessive (often pathological) preoccupation with real or fancied ailments

hy·poc·ri·sy (hipókrəsi) *pl.* **hy·poc·ri·sies** *n.* pretense of virtue, benevolence or religious devotion ‖ an instance of such pretense

hy·po·crite (hípəkrit) *n.* someone guilty of hypocrisy

hy·po·der·ma (haipədɔ́:rmə) *n. (zool.)* the hypodermis ‖ *(bot.)* a layer of supporting tissue just under the epidermis **hy·po·dér·mal** *adj.* being beneath the epidermis ‖ of the hypoderma or the hypodermis **hy·po·dér·mic 1.** *adj.* of the area just beneath the skin ‖ administered just beneath the skin, *a hypodermic injection* ‖ pertaining to an injection just beneath the skin **2.** *n.* a hypodermic syringe ‖ a hypodermic injection **hy·po·dér·mi·cal·ly** *adv.*

hy·po·der·mis (haipədɔ́:rmis) *n. (bot.)* the hypoderma ‖ *(zool.)* a cellular layer which secretes the horny integument or cuticle of annulates, arthropods etc.

hy·pos·ta·sis (haipóstəsis) *pl.* **hy·pos·ta·ses** (haipóstəsi:z) *n. (philos.)* the substantial essence of things as distinguished from their attributes

hy·pos·ta·tize (haipóstətaiz) *pres. part.* **hy·pos·ta·tiz·ing** *past* and *past part.* **hy·pos·ta·tized** *v.t.* to attribute personality or substantial essence to

hy·pot·e·nuse (haipót'nu:s, haipót'nju:s) *n. (geom.)* the side opposite the right angle of a right-angled triangle

hy·poth·e·sis (haipóθisis) *pl.* **hy·poth·e·ses** (haipóθisi:z) *n.* an idea or proposition not derived from experience but formed and used to explain certain facts (e.g. in science) or to provide the foundation or primary assumption of an argument **hy·poth·e·size** (haipóθisaiz) *pres. part.* **hy·poth·e·siz·ing** *past* and *past part.* **hy·poth·e·sized** *v.i.* to make a hypothesis ‖ *v.t.* to assume

hy·po·thet·ic (haipəθétik) *adj.* involving a hypothesis ‖ of or based on a hypothesis **hy·po·thét·i·cal** *adj.*

hys·ter·ec·to·my (histəréktəmi:) *pl.* **hys·ter·ec·to·mies** *n.* surgical removal of the womb

hys·ter·i·a (histíəri:ə, histéri:ə) *n.* a condition, due to a psychological disturbance, characterized by excessive excitability and anxiety ‖ behavior in an individual or group characterized by uncontrolled, excessive anxiety, emotionalism etc.

hys·ter·ic (histérik) **1.** *adj.* of or characterized by hysteria **2.** *n.* a hysterical person ‖ *(pl.)* a fit of uncontrolled laughing, crying etc. **hys·tér·i·cal** *adj.*

I

I, i (ai) the ninth letter of the English alphabet

I 1. *pron., 1st person sing., nominative case* oneself, as named by oneself **2.** *n.* the self or ego

i·bex (áibeks) *pl.* **i·bex·es, i·bex** *n.* any of several wild mountain goats of Europe and Asia

i·bi·dem (ibídəm, ibáidəm) in the same already specified book, chapter etc.

i·bis (áibis) *pl.* **i·bis·es, i·bis** *n.* any of several wading birds allied to the storks, found esp. in tropical regions

ice (ais) **1.** *n.* water solidified by freezing ‖ the frozen surface of water ‖ a dessert of frozen, sweetened water flavored with fruit juice etc. **to break the ice** to break down the formality or reserve in human intercourse ‖ *(slang)* an illegal bonus paid for a ticket to a public event **to skate (or be or tread) on thin ice** to be dealing with a matter where there is great danger of making a mistake or causing personal offense unless great care is taken **2.** *v. pres. part.* **ic·ing** *past* and *past part.* **iced** *v.t.* to convert into ice ‖ to cover with ice ‖ to cool by adding or applying ice to or by refrigerating ‖ to cover with icing, *to ice a cake* ‖ *v.i.* to become coated with ice **3.** *adj.* of or pertaining to ice ‖ used on or for ice

ice·berg (áisbə:rg) *n.* a large, floating mass of ice, only one-ninth projecting above water

ice cream a frozen dessert made of cream, eggs and sugar, and flavored with syrups, fresh fruit etc.

i·ci·cle (áisik'l) *n.* a hanging, tapering piece of ice formed by the successive freezing of drops of water as they prepare to fall from the point of attachment

ic·ing (áisiŋ) *n.* any sweet coating for cakes etc., esp. frosting

i·con, i·kon (áikɒn) *n.* a painting, mosaic or enamel of Christ, the Virgin Mary or a saint, revered as a sacred object in the Eastern Church

i·con·o·clasm (aikónəklæzəm) *n.* the practice or beliefs of an iconoclast

i·con·o·clast (aikónəklæst) *n.* a person who destroys

(a) æ, cat; ɑ, car; ɔ fawn; ei, snake. **(e)** e, hen; i:, sheep; iə, deer; ɛə, bear. **(i)** i, fish; ai, tiger; ə:, bird. **(o)** o, ox; au, cow; ou, goat; u, poor; ɔi, royal. **(u)** ʌ, duck; u, bull; u:, goose; ə, bacillus; ju:, cube. x, loch; θ, think; ð, bother; z, Zen; ʒ, corsage; dʒ, savage; ŋ, orangutang; j, yak; ʃ, fish; tʃ, fetch; 'l, rabble; 'n, redden. Complete pronunciation key appears inside front cover.

religious images, or who opposes their use in worship ‖ a person who seeks to destroy the established order or accepted beliefs, customs, reputations etc. **i·con·o·clás·tic** *adj.* **i·con·o·clás·ti·cal·ly** *adv.*

i·cy (áisi:) *comp.* **i·ci·er** *superl.* **i·ci·est** *adj.* covered with ice ‖ so cold that ice forms ‖ very cold in manner

i·de·a (aidíə) *n.* a mental image, conception ‖ an opinion ‖ *(loosely)* knowledge, *have you any idea of the time?* ‖ a vague sense of probability, hunch ‖ appraisal, estimate **to get ideas into one's head** to hope for more than will be fulfilled **what's the big idea?** *(pop.)* what is all this nonsense about?

i·de·al (aidíəl) **1.** *n.* a model of perfection or beauty **2.** *adj.* pertaining to an ideal ‖ supremely good or desirable ‖ existing only in thought

i·de·al·ism (aidíəlizəm, aidí:əlizəm) *n.* the attitude which consists in conceiving ideals and trying to realize them

i·de·al·ist (aidíəlist, aidí:əlist) *n.* a person who accepts and adheres to the concepts of idealism ‖ a person who attaches more importance to ideals than to practical considerations **i·de·al·is·tic** *adj.* **i·de·al·is·ti·cal·ly** *adv.*

i·de·al·i·za·tion (aidi̱:əlizéiʃən) *n.* an idealizing or being idealized ‖ something idealized

i·de·al·ize (aidí:əlaiz) *pres. part.* **i·de·al·iz·ing** *past and past part.* **i·de·al·ized** *v.t.* to attribute ideal perfection to ‖ to show something in its ideal form

i·de·al·ly (aidí:əli:) *adv.* in an ideal way, perfectly ‖ theoretically

i·den·tic (aidéntik) *adj.* of a communication made in precisely the same terms by each of several governments to another

i·den·ti·cal (aidéntik'l) *adj.* (of two or more things) the same in all respects ‖ *(biol.)* designating twins produced from one zygote ‖ *(pop.)* the very same

i·den·ti·fi·ca·tion (aide̱ntifikéiʃən) *n.* an identifying or being identified

i·den·ti·fy (aidéntifai) *pres. part.* **i·den·ti·fy·ing** *past and past part.* **i·den·ti·fied** *v.t.* to recognize the identity of (someone or something) ‖ to establish or demonstrate the identity of ‖ to consider as being the same or as being necessarily associated ‖ *v.i.* to think of oneself as being one with another person or thing

i·den·ti·ty (aidéntiti) *pl.* **i·den·ti·ties** *n.* the fact of being the same in all respects ‖ who a person is, or what a thing is

i·de·ol·o·gy (aidi:ólədʒi:, idi:ólədʒi:) *pl.* **i·de·ol·o·gies** *n.* a body of ideas used in support of an economic, political or social theory ‖ the way of thinking of a class, culture or individual ‖ *(philos.)* the science of ideas, esp. those springing from sensory stimulation

ides (aidz) *pl. n.* (in the ancient Roman calendar) the 15th day of March, May, July and October and the 13th day of all other months

id·i·om (ídi:əm) *n.* the language peculiar to a people, country, class, community or, more rarely, an individual ‖ the structure of the usual patterns of expression of a language ‖ a construction, expression etc. having a meaning different from the literal one or not according to the usual patterns of the language ‖ a writer's characteristic use of words ‖ a characteristic style in music, art. etc.

id·i·o·mat·ic (i̱di:əmǽtik) *adj.* peculiar to the patterns of expression of a particular language ‖ of or pertaining to idioms ‖ (of a language) having many idioms **id·i·o·mát·i·cal·ly** *adv.*

id·i·o·syn·cra·sy (idi:əsíŋkrəsi:) *pl.* **id·i·o·syn·cra·sies** *n.* a distinguishing habit of thought, feeling or behavior characteristic of an individual, esp. a personal peculiarity **id·i·o·syn·crat·ic** (i̱di:ousinkrǽtik) *adj.* **id·i·o·syn·crát·i·cal·ly** *adv.*

id·i·ot (ídi:ət) *n.* a person afflicted by idiocy, having a mental age of two years or less, and requiring constant care ‖ *(pop.)* a dolt **id·i·ot·ic** (idi:ótik) *adj.* **id·i·ot·i·cal·ly** (idi:ótikli:) *adv.* in an idiotic manner

i·dle (áid'l) **1.** *adj.* unwilling to work ‖ not working ‖

casual, not serious, *an idle jest* **2.** *v. pres. part.* **i·dling** *past and past part.* **i·dled** *v.i.* to let time pass without working ‖ to waste time ‖ (of an engine) to consume fuel without being connected with moving parts ‖ *v.t.* (with 'away') to let (a period of time) pass without working **íd·ler** *n.* someone who is idle ‖ an idler wheel

idler wheel a cogged wheel which transmits motion from another wheel to a third wheel without altering the velocity ratio or direction of the revolution

i·dly (áidli:) *adv.* in an idle manner

i·dol (áid'l) *n.* an image of a god constructed of wood, stone etc. and worshipped as if it were the god it represents ‖ a person or object of intense admiration or love

i·dol·a·ter (aidólətər) *n.* someone who worships idols **i·dól·a·tress** *n.* a female idolater

i·dol·a·trous (aidólətrəs) *adj.* of, pertaining to or having the nature of idolatry ‖ practicing idolatry

i·dol·a·try (aidólətri:) *n.* the worship of an idol or of idols

i·dol·ize (áid'laiz) *pres. part.* **i·dol·iz·ing** *past and past part.* **i·dol·ized** *v.t.* to treat as an idol, esp. to love with inordinate affection

if (if) **1.** *conj.* in case, in the event that, *if it rains we will stay at home* ‖ on the assumption that, *if x = y and y = z then x = z* ‖ granting that, *if you are right we are really in trouble* ‖ on condition that ‖ although, *he is kindly, if a bit too impulsive* ‖ whether, *ask if he can come* **2.** *n.* a condition

ig·loo, ig·lu (íglu:) *n.* an Eskimo dwelling, esp. one in the shape of a dome built of blocks of snow ‖ dome-shaped portable plastic structure designed for protective covering

ig·nite (ignáit) *pres. part.* **ig·nit·ing** *past and past part.* **ig·nit·ed** *v.t.* to heat (something) so strongly that it begins to burn ‖ to set on fire ‖ *v.i.* to begin to burn

ig·ni·tion (igníʃən) *n.* the act of making something begin to burn ‖ the method or process of igniting a fuel mixture, e.g. in an internal-combustion engine

ig·no·ble (ignóub'l) *adj.* unworthy or degraded in character or quality

ig·no·min·i·ous (i̱gnəmíni:əs) *adj.* disgraceful, characterized by or deserving ignominy ‖ degrading, humiliating

ig·no·min·y (ígnəmini:) *n.* public disgrace ‖ base conduct leading to disgrace

ig·no·ra·mus (ignəréiməs, ignərǽməs) *n.* someone who has little or no knowledge or education

ig·no·rance (ígnərəns) *n.* the state of not knowing, *to act in ignorance* ‖ a lack of education

ig·no·rant (ígnərənt) *adj.* not knowing ‖ lacking education ‖ showing or resulting from ignorance

ig·nore (ignɔ́r, ignóur) *pres. part.* **ig·nor·ing** *past and past part.* **ig·nored** *v.t.* to refuse to take notice of, refuse to consider

i·gua·na (igwánə) *n.* a family of edible, herbivorous, usually arboreal, tropical American lizards reaching 5 ft or more in length, having a long tail, a large, wide mouth, denticulate teeth and sharp claws

ilk (ilk) *n.* (esp. in the phrase) **of that ilk** of that sort

ill (il) **1.** *adj. comp.* **worse** (wə:rs) *superl.* **worst** (wə:rst) in bad health, not well, sick *(comp.* also **ill·er** *superl.* also **ill·est)** ‖ causing or tending to cause evil or harm, *ill will* ‖ far below standard, faulty, *ill breeding* **ill at ease** uneasy **to be taken ill** to become ill suddenly **2.** *n.* anything causing evil, harm, pain, trouble etc. **3.** *adv. comp.* **worse** *superl.* **worst** adversely, badly ‖ scarcely or not at all

ill-ad·vised (íləðváizd) *adj.* done without proper consideration, not judicious

il·le·gal (ilí:g'l) *adj.* violating the law **il·le·gál·i·ty** *pl.* **il·le·gal·i·ties** *n.* the quality or state of being illegal ‖ an illegal act

il·leg·i·bil·i·ty (ile̱dʒəbíliti:) *n.* the state or quality of being illegible

il·leg·i·ble (ilédʒəb'l) *adj.* not legible **il·lég·i·bly** *adv.*

il·le·git·i·ma·cy (ilidʒítəməsi:) *n.* the state or quality of being illegitimate

il·le·git·i·mate (ˌilidʒítəmit) *adj.* born out of wedlock ‖ contrary to law ‖ not authorized by the law ‖ not in accordance with the rules of logic

il·lic·it (ilísit) *adj.* not permitted by law

il·lit·er·a·cy (ilítərəsi:) *n.* the quality or state of being illiterate

il·lit·er·ate (ilítərit) **1.** *adj.* unable to read or write ‖ unfamiliar with books ‖ having little knowledge of the correct use of language ‖ (of writing or speech) showing little knowledge of the correct use of language ‖ having little or no knowledge of a specified subject **2.** *n.* a person who is illiterate

ill·ness (ílnis) *n.* the state of being ill (in health) ‖ a particular disease

il·log·i·cal (ilódʒik'l) *adj.* contrary to the laws of logic ‖ (of persons) thinking or acting in a way incompatible with logic

il·lu·mi·nate (ilú:mineit) *pres. part.* **il·lu·mi·nat·ing** *past* and *past part.* **il·lu·mi·nat·ed** *v.t.* to give light to (a region or space) ‖ to decorate with bright or colored lamps ‖ to light up by floodlighting ‖ to decorate (a manuscript) by means of colored initials, borders, pictures etc. ‖ to make clear to the mind ‖ to enlighten (someone)

il·lu·mi·na·tion (ilu:minéiʃən) *n.* the act of illuminating ‖ the decoration of streets or buildings by bright or colored lights ‖ the lights themselves ‖ the lighting up of buildings etc. with floodlights ‖ the decoration of a manuscript ‖ the act of making or becoming clear to the mind

il·lu·sion (ilú:ʒən) *n.* a delusion ‖ a false interpretation by the mind of a sense perception ‖ a belief or hope that has no real substance **il·lu·sion·ar·y** *adj.* **il·lú·sion·ist** *n.* a conjurer

il·lu·so·ry (ilú:səri:, ilú:zəri:) *adj.* illusive

il·lus·trate (íləstreit) *pres. part.* **il·lus·trat·ing** *past* and *past part.* **il·lus·trat·ed** *v.t.* to supplement (a written or verbal account) by pictures or designs ‖ to ornament (a book, periodical etc.) with pictures or designs ‖ to make clear by means of examples ‖ *v.i.* to make something clear with pictures, designs or examples **il·lus·tra·tive** (ilʌ́strətiv, íləstreitiv) *adj.* (esp. of an example or story) serving to illustrate **il·lus·tra·tor** (íləstreitər) *n.* someone who illustrates books etc., esp. for a living

il·lus·tra·tion (iləstréiʃən) *n.* the act of illustrating ‖ an example used to explain or demonstrate ‖ a picture, ornament etc. used to illustrate a book or paper

il·lus·tri·ous (ilʌ́stri:əs) *adj.* held in or conferring the highest public esteem

im·age (ímidʒ) **1.** *n.* a carved, painted or drawn effigy of a person or thing ‖ a mental picture or concept ‖ a person or thing resembling another person or thing, a likeness ‖ *(television)* reproduction of a view on a receiver ‖ *(psych.)* presentation of a sensory experience **2.** *v.t. pres. part.* **im·ag·ing** *past* and *past part.* **im·aged** to form an image of

im·ag·i·na·ble (imǽdʒinəb'l) *adj.* capable of being conceived by the imagination

im·ag·i·nar·y (imǽdʒineri:) *adj.* existing only in the imagination

im·ag·i·na·tion (imædʒinéiʃən) *n.* the power to form mental images of objects not perceived or not wholly perceived by the senses ‖ the power to form new ideas by a synthesis of separate elements of experience, and the ability to define new ideas ‖ the gift of employing images in writing or painting ‖ the tendency to attribute reality to unreal things, situations and states ‖ intuitive understanding

im·ag·i·na·tive (imǽdʒinətiv, imǽdʒineitiv) *adj.* having, using or showing imagination ‖ having intuitive understanding

im·ag·ine (imǽdʒin) *pres. part.* **im·ag·in·ing** *past* and *past part.* **im·ag·ined** *v.i.* to use the imagination viably ‖ *v.t.* to picture in the imagination ‖ to conceive of ‖ to form delusory ideas about, invent (something without any basis of truth)

im·bal·ance (imbǽləns) *n.* lack of balance

im·be·cile (ímbisəl, ímbisil) **1.** *n.* a mentally deficient person having a mental age of about 3–7 years, who requires supervision and help in dressing and feeding himself etc. ‖ *(pop.)* a dolt **2.** *adj.* of or relating to an imbecile ‖ stupid

im·be·cil·i·ty (imbisíliti:) *n.* mental deficiency somewhat less severe than idiocy

im·bibe (imbáib) *pres. part.* **im·bib·ing** *past* and *past part.* **im·bibed** *v.t.* to take in (liquid, moisture etc.) ‖ to take into the mind by a gradual process, *to imbibe knowledge*

im·bro·glio (imbróuljou) *n.* a very involved, confused situation

im·bue (imbjú:) *pres. part.* **im·bu·ing** *past* and *past part.* **im·bued** *v.t.* to fill, esp. with moisture or color ‖ to fill, e.g. with an emotion

im·i·tate (ímiteit) *pres. part.* **im·i·tat·ing** *past* and *past part.* **im·i·tat·ed** *v.t.* to use as a model for one's own actions ‖ to mimic, ape ‖ to resemble externally

im·i·ta·tion (imitéiʃən) **1.** *n.* the act of imitating ‖ a copy produced by imitating ‖ *(mus.)* repetition of a phrase or subject in another key or voice **2.** *adj.* made so as to be mistakable for what is genuine

im·mac·u·late (imǽkjulit) *adj.* impeccably clean ‖ having no fault ‖ *(biol.)* without spots or marks of different color

im·ma·nent (ímənənt) *adj.* inherent, intrinsic ‖ *(theol.,* of God) actually present throughout the material universe

im·ma·te·ri·al (imətíəri:əl) *adj.* having no physical substance ‖ having no importance or relevance **im·ma·te·ri·ál·i·ty** *n.* the quality or state of being immaterial

im·ma·ture (imətúər, imətjúər, imətʃúər) *adj.* not mature **im·ma·tú·ri·ty** *n.* the quality or state of being immature

im·meas·ur·a·ble (iméʒərəb'l) *adj.* incapable of being measured, esp. because too large **im·méas·ur·a·bly** *adv.*

im·me·di·a·cy (imí:di:əsi:) *n.* the state or quality of being immediate

im·me·di·ate (imí:di:it) *adj.* without an intervening lapse or interval, instant ‖ *(philos.)* intuitive ‖ direct ‖ *(loosely)* closest, *in the immediate neighborhood*

im·me·di·ate·ly (imí:di:itli:) **1.** *adv.* at once, with no intervening lapse of time ‖ directly, with no intervening agent ‖ with no intervening space or object ‖ closely **2.** *conj.* as soon as, directly

in·me·mo·ri·al (iməmɔ́ri:əl, iməmóuri:əl) *adj.* so old as to have its origin beyond the recall of memory or historical record

im·mense (iméns) *adj.* tremendously large

im·men·si·ty (iménsiti:) *pl.* **im·men·si·ties** *n.* the state or quality of being immense ‖ something immense

im·merse (imɔ́:rs) *pres. part.* **im·mers·ing** *past* and *past part.* **im·mersed** *v.t.* to put in below the surface level of a liquid or gas ‖ (esp. *refl.* and *pass.*) to absorb (oneself) in one thing to the exclusion of all others

im·mer·sion (imɔ́:rʒən, imɔ́:rʃən) *n.* an immersing or being immersed ‖ baptism by immersing the whole body in water

im·mi·grant (ímigrənt) **1.** *n.* someone who immigrates into a country 2. *adj.* of or pertaining to immigrants or immigration

im·mi·grate (ímigreit) *pres. part.* **im·mi·grat·ing** *past and past part.* **im·mi·grat·ed** *v.i.* to enter a country of which one is not a native, in order to live in it permanently ‖ *v.t.* to bring (a foreigner) into a country for this purpose **im·mi·grá·tion** *n.* the act of immigrating

im·mi·nent (íminənt) *adj.* about to happen, *his arrival is imminent* ‖ threateningly impending, *imminent danger*

im·mo·bile (imóub'l, imóubi:l) *adj.* not in motion ‖ inactive ‖ immovable

im·mo·bil·i·ty (imoubíliti:) *n.* the quality or state of being immobile

im·mod·er·ate (imódərit) *adj.* unreasonably large ‖ going beyond the proper limits

im·mo·dest (imódist) *adj.* violating conventional standards of decency ‖ lacking humility

im·mor·al (imórəl, imóurəl) *adj.* violating accepted standards of moral (esp. sexual) behavior

im·mo·ral·i·ty (imərǽliti:) *pl.* **im·mo·ral·i·ties** *n.* the quality or state of being immoral ‖ an immoral act

im·mor·tal (imórt'l) *adj.* not subject to death ‖ everlasting ‖ never to be forgotten

im·mor·tal·i·ty (imortǽliti:) *n.* the quality or state of being immortal

im·mov·a·ble (imú:vəb'l) 1. *adj.* not subject to being moved ‖ unyielding in attitude, purpose etc. 2. *n.* (*law,* usually *pl.*) property which cannot be moved, e.g. land, buildings etc.

im·mune (imjú:n) *adj.* having immunity (against illness) ‖ protected or safe from a danger etc. ‖ exempt, *immune from taxation*

im·mu·ni·ty (imjú:niti:) *pl.* **im·mu·ni·ties** *n.* (*med.*) the state of being temporarily or permanently able to resist an infection ‖ (*law*) exemption from a tax, duty or jurisdiction ‖ freedom from danger of penalty

im·mu·nize (ímjunaiz) *pres. part.* **im·mu·niz·ing** *past and past part.* **im·mu·nized** *v.t.* to render immune, esp. against a particular disease

im·mu·ta·bil·i·ty (imju:təbíliti:) *n.* the quality or state of being immutable

im·mu·ta·ble (imjú:təb'l) *adj.* incapable of being changed **im·mú·ta·bly** *adv.*

imp (imp) *n.* a little or young devil ‖ a mischievous sprite

im·pact 1. (ímpækt) *n.* a clash or collision imparting force ‖ the impression made by a person, thing or idea 2. (impǽkt) *v.t.* to press together, or into a limited space **im·páct·ed** *adj.* (of a fracture) wedged together at the broken ends ‖ (of a tooth) wedged in between the jawbone and another tooth

im·pair (impéər) *v.t.* to lessen in quality or strength, damage **im·páir·ment** *n.*

im·part (impárt) *v.t.* to give a share of (something) ‖ to make known, communicate

im·par·tial (impárʃəl) *adj.* without prejudgment ‖ not favoring one side more than the other **im·par·ti·al·i·ty** (impɑrʃi:ǽliti:) *n.*

im·pas·sioned (impǽʃənd) *adj.* full of passionate emotion, *an impassioned speech*

im·pas·sive (impǽsiv) *adj.* not giving any outward sign of emotion ‖ not feeling pain, sensation or emotion **im·pas·sív·i·ty** *n.*

im·pa·tience (impéiʃəns) *n.* the state or quality of being impatient

im·pa·tient (impéiʃənt) *adj.* lacking or showing a lack of patience, restless and fretful under delay, opposition or difficulty ‖ eagerly desiring and restive at delay ‖ (with 'of') unwilling to put up with

im·peach (impí:tʃ) *v.t.* to charge with a crime, esp. to accuse (a state official) of treason or corruption before a special tribunal ‖ to question the honesty or sincerity of (something) **im·péach·a·ble** *adj.* **im·péach·ment** *n.*

im·pec·ca·ble (impékəb'l) *adj.* without fault or flaw

im·péc·ca·bly *adv.*

im·pede (impí:d) *pres. part.* **im·ped·ing** *past and past part.* **im·ped·ed** *v.t.* to hamper, obstruct or hold back, *to impede progress*

im·ped·i·ment (impédəmənt) *n.* something which impedes ‖ a speech defect, e.g. a lisp

im·pel (impél) *pres. part.* **im·pel·ling** *past and past part.* **im·pelled** *v.t.* to drive forward ‖ to urge, *impelled by conscience to confess*

im·pend (impénd) *v.i.* (esp. of something feared) to be on the verge of happening

im·per·a·tive (impérətiv) 1. *adj.* which must at all costs be obeyed or which cannot in any way be ignored ‖ (*emphatic*) necessary ‖ (*gram.*) of the mood that expresses command 2. *n.* that which is imperative, an order ‖ (*gram.*) the imperative mood ‖ (*gram.*) a verb in this mood

im·per·fect (impɔ́:rfikt) 1. *adj.* not perfect ‖ not complete ‖ (*gram.,* of a tense) expressing continuous but unfinished action or state, e.g. 'he was walking' (past imperfect), 'he will be walking' (future imperfect) 2. *n.* the imperfect tense ‖ a verb form in this tense

im·per·fec·tion (impərfékʃən) *n.* the quality or state of being imperfect or defective ‖ a defect

im·pe·ri·al (impíəri:əl) *adj.* pertaining to an emperor or an empire ‖ (*loosely*) majestic

im·per·il (impérəl) *pres. part.* **im·per·il·ing** *past and past part.* **im·per·iled** *v.t.* to expose to danger, esp. the danger of loss

im·pe·ri·ous (impíəri:əs) *adj.* overbearing in manner ‖ imperative, *imperious necessity*

im·per·ish·a·bil·i·ty (imperiʃəbíliti:) *n.* the quality or state of being imperishable

im·per·ish·a·ble (impériʃəb'l) *adj.* of that which will not perish, decay or be destroyed, *imperishable fame* **im·pér·ish·a·bly** *adv.*

im·per·ma·nence (impɔ́:rmənəns) *n.* the quality or state of being impermanent **im·pér·ma·nen·cy** *n.*

im·per·ma·nent (impɔ́:rmənənt) *adj.* not permanent

im·per·me·a·ble (impɔ́:rmi:əb'l) *adj.* not permeable **im·pér·me·a·bly** *adv.*

im·per·son·al (impɔ́:rsən'l) *adj.* without personal content, reference or quality ‖ (*gram.,* of verbs) without a specified subject or having a subject which does not indicate an actual agent, e.g. 'it rains' ‖ (*gram.,* of pronouns) having indefinite reference, e.g. 'one', 'people', 'they' etc. **im·per·son·ál·i·ty** *n.*

im·per·son·ate (impɔ́:rsəneit) *pres. part.* **im·per·son·at·ing** *past and past part.* **im·per·son·at·ed** *v.t.* to pretend to be (someone else) ‖ to imitate or mimic in order to entertain **im·per·son·á·tion** *n.* an impersonating or being impersonated **im·pér·son·a·tor** *n.* an entertainer who mimics well-known people

im·per·ti·nence (impɔ́:rt'nəns) *n.* the quality or state of being impertinent ‖ something impertinent **im·pér·ti·nen·cy** *n.* **im·pér·ti·nen·cies** *n.*

im·per·ti·nent (impɔ́:rt'nənt) *adj.* acting or speaking disrespectfully or showing an offensive lack of respect ‖ not pertinent

im·per·vi·ous (impɔ́:rvi:əs) *adj.* impenetrable ‖ not open (to reason, persuasion etc.)

im·pe·ti·go (impitáigou) *n.* a contagious pustular skin disease caused by streptococci or staphylococci

im·pet·u·ous (impétʃu:əs) *adj.* showing or acting with impulsiveness ‖ (*rhet.*) rushing violently

im·pe·tus (ímpitəs) *n.* the force which causes a given motion or activity ‖ a stimulus resulting in increased activity ‖ the property a body possesses due to its mass and speed, esp. when moving with violence and suddennness (not used technically) ‖ incentive, driving force

im·pinge (impíndʒ) *pres. part.* **im·ping·ing** *past and past part.* **im·pinged** *v.i.* (with 'on', 'against') to come into sharp contact ‖ (with 'on') to make an impression (on the mind, senses etc.) ‖ (with 'on') to encroach

im·pi·ous (ímpi:əs) *adj.* lacking piety ‖ wicked

imp·ish (ímpiʃ) *adj.* mischievous

im·plac·a·ble (implǽkəb'l) *adj.* not to be placated, deaf to all appeals ‖ inexorable **im·plác·a·bly** *adv.*

im·plant 1. (implǽnt, implánt) *v.t.* to plant deeply or firmly ‖ *(med.)* to insert (e.g. a living tissue, as in grafting, or drugs for gradual absorption) beneath the skin ‖ *(med.)* to introduce (a living embryo) into the uterus of a host mother ‖ to instill firmly in the mind **2.** (ímplænt, ímplɑnt) *n. (med.)* the tissue, drug etc. used in implanting

im·plan·ta·tion (implæntéiʃən, implɑntéiʃən) *n.* an implanting or being implanted ‖ the passage of cells (esp. of tumors) from one part of the body to another part where they grow again

im·plau·si·ble (implɔ́zəb'l) *adj.* lacking the appearance of truth **im·pláu·si·bly** *adv.*

im·ple·ment (ímpləmənt) **1.** *n.* a tool ‖ a thing or person serving as an instrument **2.** *v.t.* to carry into effect **im·ple·men·tal** (impləmént'l) *adj.* serving as an implement, helpful **im·ple·men·tá·tion** *n.*

im·pli·cate (ímplikeit) *pres. part.* **im·pli·cat·ing** *past and past part.* **im·pli·cat·ed** *v.t.* to involve, often in an unpleasant, incriminating manner

im·pli·ca·tion (implikéiʃən) *n.* an implying or being implied ‖ something implied ‖ an implicating or being implicated

im·plic·it (implísit) *adj.* understood though not stated ‖ unquestioning, absolute

im·plied (impláid) *adj.* suggested without being stated, involved without being specified

im·plode (implóud) *pres. part.* **im·plod·ing** *past and past part.* **im·plod·ed** *v.t. (phon.)* to pronounce by implosion ‖ *v.i.* to burst inward

im·plore (implɔ́r, implóur) *pres. part.* **im·plor·ing** *past and past part.* **im·plored** *v.t.* to beseech with great intensity of feeling ‖ to beg for

im·plo·sion (implóuʒən) *n.* a bursting inwards ‖ *(phon.)* an internal compression of air, e.g. before sounding 'k', 'p' and 't' **im·plo·sive** (implóusiv) *adj.*

im·ply (impláí) *pres. part.* **im·ply·ing** *past and past part.* **im·plied** *v.t.* to suggest without actually stating ‖ to involve logically

im·po·lite (impəláit) *adj.* having or showing bad manners

im·pol·i·tic (impólitik) *adj.* lacking in tact or prudence ‖ inexpedient

im·pon·der·a·bil·i·ty (imppndərəbíliti:) *n.* the state or quality of being imponderable

im·pon·der·a·ble (impóndərəb'l) **1.** *adj.* having no measurable weight ‖ having an importance impossible to estimate **2.** *n.* (usually *pl.*) a factor in a situation whose importance is unknowable

im·port 1. (impɔ́rt) *v.t.* to bring in (goods) from abroad ‖ to introduce (ideas etc.) taken from some outside source ‖ *(rhet.)* to mean, imply ‖ *v.i. (rhet.)* to be of importance **2.** (ímpɔrt, ímpour) *n.* something imported ‖ *(rhet.)* meaning ‖ *(rhet.)* importance

im·por·tance (impɔ́rt'ns) *n.* the quality of being important

im·por·tant (impɔ́rt'nt) *adj.* producing a great effect, having great influence or significance ‖ mattering greatly ‖ having a high social position ‖ self-important, pompous

im·por·tune (impɔrtú:n, impɔrtjú:n, impɔ́rtʃən) *pres. part.* **im·por·tun·ing** *past and past part.* **im·por·tuned** *v.t.* to vex (someone) by demanding too often or too vehemently or unreasonably ‖ *v.i.* to be importunate

im·pose (impóuz) *pres. part.* **im·pos·ing** *past and past part.* **im·posed** *v.t.* to place (a tax, fine etc.) as a burden ‖ to use superior strength or authority to secure submission to (one's will etc.) ‖ to force others to receive (esp. oneself) as guest, companion etc. ‖ to

fob off, cause to be accepted as genuine, flawless etc. (what is not) ‖ *(printing)* to arrange (pages) in a form ‖ *v.i.* (with 'on') to take unfair advantage ‖ (with 'on') to use deception **im·pós·ing** *adj.* impressive

im·po·si·tion (impəzíʃən) *n.* an imposing or being imposed ‖ a tax or duty ‖ the taking of an unfair advantage ‖ *(printing)* the arranging of pages in a form

im·pos·si·ble (impósəb'l) *adj.* incapable of occurring or being done ‖ unacceptable ‖ hard to tolerate **im·pós·si·bly** *adv.*

im·pos·tor, im·pos·ter (impóstər) *n.* a person pretending to be someone he is not, or pretending to possess a quality he does not have

im·po·tence (ímpətəns) *n.* the quality or state of being impotent **ím·po·ten·cy** *n.*

im·po·tent (ímpətənt) *adj.* having no power or force, *impotent gestures* ‖ (of a male) unable to perform the sexual act

im·pound (impáund) *v.t.* to take into temporary protective legal custody ‖ to confine (stray animals) in a pound

im·pov·er·ish (impóvəriʃ) *v.t.* to make poor ‖ to exhaust the strength or productivity of (esp. soil) **im·póv·er·ish·ment** *n.*

im·prac·ti·ca·ble (imprǽktikəb'l) *adj.* (of an idea or plan) not feasible ‖ not usable **im·prác·ti·ca·bly** *adv.*

im·prac·ti·cal (imprǽktik'l) *adj.* not practical ‖ impracticable

im·pre·cate (ímprikeit) *pres. part.* **im·pre·cat·ing** *past and past part.* **im·pre·cat·ed** *v.t.* to invoke (evil) ‖ to curse ‖ *v.i.* to utter imprecations

im·pre·ca·tion (imprikéiʃən) *n.* cursing ‖ a curse

im·pre·cise (imprisáis) *adj.* not precise, vague

im·preg·na·ble (imprégnəb'l) *adj.* (of an egg etc.) capable of being impregnated

im·preg·nate 1. (imprégnit, imprégneit) *adj.* impregnated **2.** (imprégneit) *v.t. pres. part.* **im·preg·nat·ing** *past and past part.* **im·preg·nat·ed** to make pregnant ‖ to interpenetrate or saturate ‖ to cause to be interpenetrated or saturated ‖ to imbue (with an idea) **im·preg·ná·tion** *n.* an impregnating or being impregnated

im·pre·sa·ri·o (imprisári:ou, i:mpresárjo) *n.* someone who promotes, manages or organizes concerts, variety shows, plays, boxing tournaments etc.

im·pre·scrip·ti·ble (impriskríptəb'l) *adj.* of that which cannot be taken away by any external authority **im·pre·scrip·ti·bly** *adv.*

im·press 1. (imprés) *v.t.* to make a mark on (something), using pressure ‖ to make (a mark) on something, using pressure ‖ to have an effect on (the mind, emotions etc.) ‖ to cause (an idea) to have an effect ‖ *v.i.* to arouse admiration **2.** (ímpres) *n.* an imprint ‖ *(rhet.)* an effect on the mind, mode of development, character etc.

im·pres·sion (impréʃən) *n.* an impressing or being impressed ‖ a mark made by impressing ‖ *(printing)* a copy made from type or a plate ‖ *(printing)* the mark made by inked type on paper under pressure ‖ *(printing)* the group of copies made at one time without removing the form from the printing press ‖ an effect produced on the feelings or senses ‖ a vague notion or belief ‖ *(dentistry)* an imprint in plastic etc. of the teeth and parts of the jaw

im·pri·ma·tur (imprimátər, impriméitər) *n.* official license to print or publish ‖ any sanction, approval

im·print (ímprint) *n.* a mark or design produced by pressure ‖ a characteristic effect ‖ a publisher's imprint ‖ a printer's imprint

im·pris·on (impríz'n) *v.t.* to confine in a prison ‖ to confine, restrict, *imprisoned by dogmatic beliefs*

(a) æ, c*a*t; ɑ, c*a*r; ɔ f*a*wn; ei, sn*a*ke. **(e)** e, h*e*n; i:, sh*ee*p; iə, d*ee*r; ɛə, b*ea*r. **(i)** i, f*i*sh; ai, t*i*ger; ə:, b*i*rd. **(o)** o, *o*x; au, c*ow*; ou, g*oa*t; u, p*oo*r; ɔi, r*o*yal. **(u)** ʌ, d*u*ck; u, b*u*ll; u:, g*oo*se; ə, b*a*cillus; ju:, c*u*be. x, lo*ch*; θ, *th*ink; ð, bo*th*er; z, *Z*en; ʒ, cor*s*age; dʒ, sa*v*age; ŋ, oranguta*ng*; j, *y*ak; ʃ, *fi*sh; tʃ, fe*tch*; 'l, rabb*le*; 'n, redd*en*. Complete pronunciation key appears inside front cover.

im·prob·a·ble (imprób∂b'l) *adj.* not probable ‖ hard to believe **im·prób·a·bly** *adv.*

im·promp·tu (imprómptu:, imprómptju:) **1.** *adj.* without preparation, extemporaneous **2.** *adv.* done without preparation, extemporaneously

im·prop·er (imprópǝr) *adj.* offending against accepted standards of decency ‖ not conforming to what is conventionally thought suitable ‖ not right, unlawful

im·pro·pri·e·ty (ịmprǝpráiiti:) *pl.* **im·pro·pri·e·ties** *n.* the quality of being improper ‖ an improper action ‖ an improper or incorrect use of language

im·prove (imprú:v) *pres. part.* **im·prov·ing** *past* and *past part.* **im·proved** *v.t.* to make better in quality ‖ to make more productive ‖ *v.i.* to become better ‖ (with 'on' or 'upon') to do better (than), *you can improve on your last effort*

im·prove·ment (imprú:vmǝnt) *n.* an improving or being improved ‖ an instance of this ‖ an addition to a house etc. which increases its economic value

im·prov·i·dent (impróvidǝnt) *adj.* not provident

im·prov·i·sa·tion (improvizéiʃǝn, ịmprǝvizéiʃǝn) *n.* an improvising or being improvised ‖ something improvised

im·prov·i·sa·tor (impróvizẹitǝr, ímprǝvizẹitǝr) *n.* someone who improvises poems or songs

im·pro·vise (ímprǝvaiz) *pres. part.* **im·pro·vis·ing** *past* and *past part.* **im·pro·vised** *v.t.* to compose, perform or say extemporaneously ‖ to select, make or provide (a substitute for something not available) ‖ *v.i.* to compose, perform or speak extemporaneously ‖ to select, make or provide a substitute for something not available ‖ (*mus.*, with 'on') to use (a composition) as the basis of free invention

im·pru·dent (imprú:d'nt) *adj.* lacking or showing a lack of prudence

im·pu·dence (ímpjudǝns) *n.* the quality of being impudent ‖ impudent behavior

im·pu·dent (ímpjudǝnt) *adj.* bold and shameless ‖ disrespectful in a way that avoids plain rudeness

im·pugn (impjú:n) *v.t.* to challenge the integrity, veracity etc. of

im·pulse (ímpʌls) *n.* a force applied suddenly ‖ motion produced by a suddenly applied force ‖ a sudden desire to do something, not arising from reason or passion

im·pu·ni·ty (impjú:niti:) *n.* immunity to or exemption from punishment

im·pure (impjúǝr) *adj.* not pure ‖ not hygienic ‖ not chaste ‖ lewd, *impure thoughts* ‖ ritually unclean ‖ (*art*) of mixed style ‖ (of language) ungrammatical or containing foreign elements

im·pu·ri·ty (impjúǝriti:) *pl.* **im·pu·ri·ties** *n.* the quality or state of being impure ‖ something impure ‖ something which renders a thing impure

im·pute (impjú:t) *pres. part.* **im·put·ing** *past* and *past part.* **im·put·ed** *v.t.* to attribute (esp. blame, misfortune etc.)

in- (in) *prefix* in, into, on, upon, towards, against

in- *prefix* not, non-, un-

in (in) **1.** *prep.* contained by, placed physically so as to be surrounded by, *the car is in the garage* ‖ into, *put the car in the garage* ‖ within ‖ affecting, *a cold in the head* ‖ having as a condition or state, *in poor health* ‖ with regard to, *they differ in height* ‖ under the influence of, *in a trance* ‖ within the sphere or realm of, *in my experience* ‖ working for or as part of, *he is in a law firm* ‖ at, *in school* ‖ at the end of (a period of time), *he'll do it in an hour from now* ‖ while performing the act of, *in crossing the street* ‖ using, *speaking in French* ‖ within the capacity of, *she didn't have it in her* **in that** because, in the respect that, with regard to the fact that **2.** *adv.* from the outside to the inside, *please come in* ‖ so as to agree, *his plans fell in with hers* **in for it** committed to some action ‖ sure to be punished **in with** on good terms with **3.** *adj.* reserved for people or things arriving, *the in door, the in tray* ‖ at home ‖ (*colloq.*) currently

popular among important people, e.g., the in place ‖ doing or knowing what is currently popular **4.** *n.* (*pop.*) influence, *he has an in with the boss* **the ins and outs** all the involved facts (of a situation etc.)

-in *suffix* compounded with an infinitive to indicate a group activity, esp. one involving protest, passive resistance etc., or mutual encouragement, *a sit-in, a love-in*

in. inch

in·a·bil·i·ty (inǝbíliti:) *n.* the state or quality of being unable

in ab·sen·tia (inæbsénʃǝ) (esp. of an accused person being tried or sentenced, or of someone being given an award) in his or her absence

in·ac·ces·si·ble (ịnæksésǝb'l) *adj.* which cannot be reached ‖ (of a person) difficult to approach and make contact with **in·ac·cés·si·bly** *adv.*

in·ac·cu·ra·cy (inǽkjurǝsi:) *pl.* **in·ac·cu·ra·cies** *n.* the quality of being inaccurate ‖ an instance of this

in·ac·cu·rate (inǽkjurit) *adj.* not accurate, making or containing errors

in·ac·tive (inǽktiv) *adj.* not active ‖ making no effort ‖ (*mil.*) not on actual duty

in·ad·e·quate (inǽdikwit) *adj.* not enough ‖ not capable (of fulfilling a requirement)

in·ad·mis·si·ble (ịnǝdmísǝb'l) *adj.* not admissible **in·ad·mís·si·bly** *adv.*

in·ad·vert·ent (ịnǝdvɔ́:rt'nt) *adj.* not intended, accidental

in·ad·vis·a·ble (ịnǝdváizǝb'l) *adj.* not advisable, not prudent

in·al·ien·a·ble (inéiljǝnǝb'l) *adj.* of that which cannot be given or taken away, *inalienable rights* **in·ál·ien·a·bly** *adv.*

in·ane (inéin) *adj.* having no meaning or sense

in·an·i·mate (inǽnǝmit) *adj.* having no organic life ‖ not having animal life ‖ showing no sign of having life ‖ lacking liveliness

in·an·i·ty (inǽniti:) *pl.* **in·an·i·ties** *n.* the quality or state of being inane ‖ something inane

in·ap·pre·ci·a·ble (ịnǝpri:ʃí:ǝb'l, ịnǝpri:ʃǝb'l) *adj.* too small or unimportant to be taken into account **in·ap·pré·ci·a·bly** *adv.*

in·ap·pro·pri·ate (ịnǝpróupri:it) *adj.* not appropriate

in·ar·tic·u·late (ịnɑrtíkjulit) *adj.* unable to speak intelligibly ‖ (of speech sounds) indistinct ‖ not good at putting one's thoughts into words

in·as·much (ịnǝzmʌ́tʃ) *adv.* (with 'as') insofar as ‖ (with 'as') since, because

in·au·gu·rate (inɔ́ɡjǝreit) *pres. part.* **in·au·gu·rat·ing** *past* and *past part.* **in·au·gu·rat·ed** *v.t.* to initiate formally into public use with ceremony ‖ to install in office with ceremony

in·au·gu·ra·tion (inɔ̣ɡjǝréiʃǝn) *n.* an inaugurating or being inaugurated ‖ a formal beginning

in·aus·pi·cious (ịnɔspíʃǝs) *adj.* not auspicious, unfavorable

in·born (ínbɔ́rn) *adj.* inherent

in·cal·cu·la·ble (inkǽlkjulǝb'l) *adj.* not able to be reckoned ‖ unpredictable ‖ (*loosely*) very great, *incalculable risks* **in·cál·cu·la·bly** *adv.*

in·can·desce (ịnkǝndés) *pres. part.* **in·can·desc·ing** *past* and *past part.* **in·can·desced** *v.i.* to be or become incandescent ‖ *v.t.* to make incandescent

in·can·des·cence (ịnkǝndés'ns) *n.* the quality or state of being incandescent

in·can·des·cent (ịnkǝndés'nt) *adj.* (of bodies heated to a high temperature) emitting a white or bright red light

in·ca·pa·bil·i·ty (inkeipǝbíliti:) *n.* the quality or state of being incapable

in·ca·pa·ble (inkéipǝb'l) *adj.* not capable ‖ incompetent **in·cá·pa·bly** *adv.*

in·ca·pac·i·tate (ịnkǝpǽsiteit) *pres. part.* **in·ca·pac·i·tat·ing** *past* and *past part.* **in·ca·pac·i·tat·ed** *v.t.* to make incapable ‖ to disqualify **in·ca·pac·i·tá·tion** *n.*

in·car·cer·ate (inkɑ́rsǝreit) *pres. part.* **in·car·cer·at·ing**

past and past part. **in·car·cer·at·ed** v.t. to imprison **in·car·cer·á·tion** n.

in·car·nate 1. (inkárnit) adj. embodied, esp. in human flesh **2.** (inkárneit) pres. part. **in·car·nat·ing** past and past part. **in·car·nat·ed** v.t. to embody, esp. in human form ‖ to give material form to ‖ to be the embodiment of

in·car·na·tion (inkɑrnéiʃən) n. an incarnating or being incarnated ‖ an embodiment

in·cen·di·ar·y (inséndi:ɛri:) **1.** adj. pertaining to the malicious burning of property ‖ (of certain chemicals, bombs etc.) causing fires to start ‖ arousing or tending to arouse rebellion, conflict etc. **2.** pl. **in·cen·di·ar·ies** n. someone who is incendiary ‖ an incendiary substance, bomb etc.

in·cense (ínsens) **1.** n. a mixture of gums, spices etc. which when burned emit perfumed vapor, used in religious ceremonies etc. **2.** v. pres. part. **in·cens·ing** past and past part. **in·censed** v.t. to make fragrant with incense ‖ to burn incense for (a god, a dead spirit etc.)

in·cense (inséns) pres. part. **in·cens·ing** past and past part. **in·censed** v.t. to make angry

in·cen·tive (inséntiv) n. something that serves as a stimulus to action by appealing to self-interest

in·cep·tion (insépʃən) n. a beginning, originating

in·ces·sant (insés'nt) adj. never ceasing ‖ continuous

in·cest (ínsest) n. sexual intercourse between persons so closely related that marriage between them is forbidden by law

in·ces·tu·ous (inséstʃu:əs) adj. of or having the nature of incest ‖ guilty of incest

inch (intʃ) **1.** n. a unit of length equal to the twelfth part of a foot (2.54 cm.) ‖ a small amount, not an inch of room ‖ a unit of pressure equal to that of a vertical column of mercury one inch in height every inch thoroughly, in every respect **2.** v.t. and i. to move very gradually (as though an inch at a time)

in·cho·ate (inkóuit, ínkoueit) adj. in its first stage of development, just begun **in·cho·a·tive** (ínkoueitiv) **1.** adj. (gram.) inceptive **2.** n. (gram.) an inceptive verb

in·ci·dence (ínsidəns) n. the rate or extent to which something occurs

in·ci·dent (ínsidənt) **1.** n. an event seen as part of a whole situation, occurring by chance, not by design ‖ an episode ‖ a limited occurrence of trouble ‖ (law) a privilege etc. dependent upon something else **2.** adj. of that which falls upon a surface etc. ‖ (law) dependent upon something else ‖ (with 'to') arising or liable to arise in the course of, risks incident to a profession

in·ci·den·tal (insidént'l) **1.** adj. occurring by chance ‖ of secondary importance ‖ arising out of something else ‖ (with 'to') likely to arise from, the worries incidental to motherhood **2.** n. something incidental ‖ (pl.) casual expenses **in·ci·dén·tal·ly** adv. used to introduce a remark made parenthetically ‖ in a way not primarily intended

in·cin·er·ate (insínəreit) pres. part. **in·cin·er·at·ing** past and past part. **in·cin·er·at·ed** v.t. and i. to burn to ashes **in·cin·er·á·tion** n. **in·cín·er·a·tor** n. a device constructed for burning refuse etc. in

in·cip·i·ent (insípi:ənt) adj. beginning, at an early stage

in·ci·sion (insíʒən) n. an incising ‖ a cut made by incising ‖ the quality of being incisive

in·ci·sive (insáisiv) adj. keen and penetrating

in·ci·sor (insáizər) n. a tooth adapted for cutting ‖ one of the front teeth between the canines in either jaw **in·ci·so·ry** adj. (of teeth) adapted for cutting

in·cite (insáit) pres. part. **in·cit·ing** past and past part. **in·cit·ed** v.t. to stir (someone) to action ‖ to cause by

encouraging **in·cite·ment** n. an inciting ‖ something that incites

in·cle·ment (inklémənt) adj. (of weather or climate) severe, rough, stormy ‖ (rhet.) harsh, merciless

in·cli·na·tion (inklinéiʃən) n. a mental propensity ‖ liking ‖ a physical tendency ‖ an inclining or being inclined from the vertical or horizontal ‖ an incline ‖ the angle of approach of one line or plane to another ‖ dip (angle between the direction of the earth's magnetic field and the horizontal)

in·cline 1. (inkláin) v. pres. part. **in·clin·ing** past and past part. **in·clined** v.i. to deviate from the vertical or horizontal, to slant or slope ‖ to tend ‖ v.t. to cause to deviate from the vertical or horizontal ‖ to bow or bend, to incline one's head ‖ to dispose, to be inclined to agree with someone **2.** (inkláin) n. an inclined plane, a slope **in·clined** adj. mentally disposed ‖ at an angle, sloping, slanting

inclined plane a plane surface at an oblique angle to the plane of the horizon

in·clude (inklú:d) pres. part. **in·clud·ing** past and past part. **in·clud·ed** v.t. to contain as part of a whole **in·clúd·ed** adj. comprised or contained

in·clu·sion (inklú:ʒʌn) n. an including or being included ‖ (geol.) a gaseous, liquid or solid foreign body enclosed by a mineral

in·clu·sive (inklú:siv) adj. including everything, comprehensive ‖ including the specified limits, pages 10–15 inclusive ‖ (with 'of') taking account of

in·cog·ni·to (inkɒgnítou, inkɒgní:tou) **1.** adj. being under an assumed name or character **2.** adv. with an assumed name or character **3.** pl. **in·cog·ni·tos** n. a person who is incognito ‖ the assumed identity of a person who is incognito

in·co·her·ent (inkouhíərənt) adj. (of ideas, language, speech etc.) not arranged in any logical order, disjointed and unintelligible ‖ unable to speak clearly and with continuity

in·come (ínkʌm) n. whatever is received as gain, e.g. wages or salary, receipts from business, dividends from investments etc.

in·com·pa·ra·ble (inkɒmpərəb'l) adj. of things that cannot be compared ‖ of a thing or quality so superior that no other can be compared with it **in·cóm·pa·ra·bly** adv.

in·com·pat·i·bil·i·ty (inkəmpætəbíliti:) n. the state or quality of being incompatible

in·com·pat·i·ble (inkəmpǽtəb'l) **1.** adj. not compatible ‖ (of benefices) not able to be filled by the same person at the same time ‖ (med., of drugs etc.) not able to be mixed together without undesirable results **2.** n. (pl.) things that are not compatible **in·com·pát·i·bly** adv.

in·com·pe·tence (inkɒmpitəns) n. the state or quality of being incompetent

in·com·pe·tent (inkɒmpitənt) **1.** adj. not competent **2.** n. a person who is incompetent

in·com·plete (inkəmplí:t) adj. not complete

in·com·pre·hen·si·ble (inkɒmprihénsəb'l) adj. that cannot be understood **in·com·pre·hén·si·bly** adv.

in·con·ceiv·a·ble (inkənsí:vəb'l) adj. not mentally conceivable, not imaginable ‖ not believable **in·con·céiv·a·bly** adv.

in·con·clu·sive (inkənklú:siv) adj. failing to lead to or result in a conclusion

in·con·gru·ous (inkɒ́ngru:əs) adj. not in harmony or agreement ‖ incompatible with the context or surroundings

in·con·se·quence (inkɒ́nsikwəns) n. lack of logical sequence or of relevance ‖ an instance of this

in·con·se·quent (inkɒ́nsikwənt) adj. not derived logically from a premise, illogical ‖ irrelevant ‖ unimportant

in·con·se·quen·tial (ınkɒnsikwénʃəl) *adj.* of no importance or significance ‖ irrelevant ‖ not worthy of being taken seriously

in·con·sid·er·ate (ınkənsídərit) *adj.* lacking, or showing a lack of, regard for the feelings or well-being of someone else

in·con·sist·ent (ınkənsístənt) *adj.* self-contradictory ‖ (with 'with') in contradiction, not in harmony ‖ (of behavior) changing for no apparent reason ‖ (of a person) showing such behavior

in·con·spic·u·ous (ınkənspíkju:əs) *adj.* not attracting attention, hardly noticeable

in·con·ti·nent (ınkɒntinənt) *adj.* lacking self-restraint, esp. sexually ‖ unable to control the evacuation of the bladder or bowels

in·con·ven·ience (ınkənví:njəns) **1.** *n.* something which causes difficulty or annoyance esp. by interfering with one's plans or routine ‖ the difficulty or annoyance thus caused **2.** *v.t. pres. part.* **in·con·ven·ienc·ing** *past and past part.* **in·con·ven·ienced** to cause to suffer inconvenience

in·con·ven·ient (ınkənví:njənt) *adj.* not convenient

in·cor·po·rate 1. (ınkɔ́rpəreit) *v. pres. part.* **in·cor·po·rat·ing** *past and past part.* **in·cor·po·rat·ed** *v.t.* to unite into a whole ‖ to form into a legal corporation ‖ to receive into a legal corporation ‖ *v.i.* to form a legal corporation ‖ to become combined or united **2.** (ınkɔ́rpərit) *adj.* formed or united in a whole ‖ formed into a corporation

in·cor·po·ra·tion (ınkɔrpəréiʃən) *n.* an incorporating or being incorporated

in·cor·rect (ınkərékt) *adj.* not true, in error ‖ containing inaccuracies ‖ not conforming to accepted standards, improper

in·cor·ri·gi·ble (ınkɔ́ridʒəb'l, ınkɒ́ridʒəb'l) *adj.* (of a person, bad habit etc.) not capable of being corrected, esp. bad beyond hope of reform **in·cór·ri·gi·bly** *adv.*

in·crease 1. (ınkrí:s) *v. pres. part.* **in·creas·ing** *past and past part.* **in·creased** *v.i.* to become greater in size, amount, number, value, degree etc. ‖ *v.t.* to make greater in size, amount, number, value, degree etc. **2.** (ínkri:s) *n.* a growth in size, amount, number, value, degree etc. ‖ the amount by which something grows ‖ something produced by growth **on the increase** growing, increasing **in·créas·ing·ly** *adv.* to a continually increasing degree

in·cred·i·bil·i·ty (ınkrɛdəbíliti:) *n.* the quality or state of being incredible

in·cred·i·ble (ınkrédəb'l) *adj.* impossible to believe ‖ so remarkable as to be hard to believe or to believe possible **in·créd·i·bly** *adv.*

in·cre·du·li·ty (ınkrədú:liti:, ınkrədjú:liti) *n.* the quality or state of being incredulous

in·cred·u·lous (ınkrédʒuləs) *adj.* not believing, skeptical ‖ showing disbelief

in·cre·ment (ínkrəmənt) *n.* an increase or growth, esp. in profits, salary etc. ‖ the amount by which something increases **in·cre·men·tal** (ınkrəmént'l) *adj.*

in·crim·i·nate (ınkrímineit) *pres. part.* **in·crim·i·nat·ing** *past and past part.* **in·crim·i·nat·ed** *v.t.* to involve in a charge of crime **in·crim·i·na·to·ry** (ınkrímınətɔri:, ınkrímınətouri:) *adj.*

in·cu·ba·tor (ínkjubeitər, íŋkjubeitər) *n.* an apparatus for keeping eggs warm until they hatch ‖ an apparatus for surrounding premature babies with a controlled environment

in·cul·cate (ınkʌ́lkeit, ínkʌlkeit) *pres. part.* **in·cul·cat·ing** *past and past part.* **in·cul·cat·ed** *v.t.* to teach (something), impress upon the mind, by constant repetition and emphasis **in·cul·ca·tion** *n.* **in·cúl·ca·tor** *n.*

in·cum·bent (ınkʌ́mbənt) *adj.* (with 'on', 'upon') resting as an obligation or duty ‖ (*biol.*) lying or pressing (upon something)

incumbent *n.* the holder of an ecclesiastical benefice ‖ the holder of any office

in·cur (ınkə́:r) *pres. part.* **in·cur·ring** *past and past*

part. **in·curred** *v.t.* to lay oneself open to, bring upon oneself ‖ to meet with (esp. something undesirable)

in·cur·a·ble (ınkjúərəb'l) *adj.* incapable of being cured ‖ incapable of being corrected **in·cúr·a·bly** *adv.*

in·debt·ed (ındétid) *adj.* owing money ‖ owing gratitude

in·de·cen·cy (ındí:s'nsi:) *pl.* **in·de·cen·cies** *n.* the quality or state of being indecent ‖ an instance of this

in·de·cent (ındí:s'nt) *adj.* morally offensive ‖ lacking modesty ‖ indecorous

in·de·ci·sion (ındisíʒən) *n.* the state or quality of being indecisive

in·deed (ındí:d) **1.** *adv.* admittedly, in fact, certainly **2.** *interj.* an expression denoting surprise, disbelief etc.

in·de·fat·i·ga·ble (ındifǽtigəb'l) *adj.* impossible to tire out **in·de·fát·i·ga·bly** *adv.*

in·de·fen·si·ble (ındifénsəb'l) *adj.* not possible to justify or condone ‖ not possible to defend against armed attack **in·de·fén·si·bly** *adv.*

in·def·i·nite (ındéfinit) *adj.* not clearly stated, vague ‖ not limited ‖ (*gram.*, of adjectives, pronouns etc.) not specifying or limiting

in·del·i·ble (ındéləb'l) *adj.* not possible to rub out or delete ‖ that cannot be eradicated from the mind ‖ making a mark that cannot be erased **in·dél·i·bly** *adv.*

in·del·i·cate (ındélikit) *adj.* coarse, mildly indecent ‖ showing tactlessness or insensitivity

in·dem·ni·fy (ındémnifai) *pres. part.* **in·dem·ni·fy·ing** *past and past part.* **in·dem·ni·fied** *v.t.* to secure against harm or loss ‖ to compensate for loss or injury

in·dem·ni·ty (ındémniti:) *pl.* **in·dem·ni·ties** *n.* insurance or protection against loss or injury ‖ legal exemption from a penalty incurred ‖ compensation for a loss or injury sustained ‖ the money paid to a victorious enemy by a defeated country

in·dent 1. (ındént) *v.t.* to notch, made jagged ‖ to set in (written matter or type) from a margin ‖ *v.i.* to set written or printed matter in from a margin ‖ to form a notch or jagged edge **2.** (índent) *n.* an indentation ‖ an indenture

in·dent 1. (ındént) *v.t.* to impress (a mark, pattern etc.) in something ‖ to make a dent in **2.** (índent) *n.* an indentation (notch)

in·den·ta·tion (ındentéiʃən) *n.* a notch, jagged cut ‖ a deep recess in a coastline ‖ a line of type or written matter set in from the margin ‖ the space left by this setting in

in·de·pend·ence (ındipéndəns) *n.* the quality or state of being independent

in·de·pend·ent (ındipéndənt) *adj.* free from the authority, control or influence of others, self-governing ‖ self-supporting, not dependent on others for one's living ‖ not having to work for one's living ‖ not committed to an organized political party ‖ (*gram.*, of a clause) not subordinate ‖ (*math.*, of a variable) not depending on another for its value *n.* an independent person or thing, esp. a person who acts and votes without being committed to a party

in·de·scrib·a·ble (ındiskráibəb'l) *adj.* not possible to describe ‖ surpassing description **in·de·scrib·a·bly** *adv.*

in·de·struct·i·ble (ındistrʌ́ktəb'l) *adj.* impossible to destroy **in·de·strúct·i·bly** *adv.*

in·dex (índeks) **1.** *pl.* **in·dex·es, in·di·ces** (índisi:z) *n.* the forefinger ‖ a pointer on a dial or measuring instrument ‖ something that indicates, a sign ‖ an alphabetical list of names, subjects, titles etc., giving page numbers where reference is made, and generally placed at the back of a book ‖ (*math.*, *pl.* indices) a symbol showing the power or root of a given quantity **2.** *v.t.* to make an index for (a book etc.) ‖ to include in an index

in·di·cate (índikeit) *pres. part.* **in·di·cat·ing** *past and past part.* **in·di·cat·ed** *v.t.* to direct attention to ‖ to point out, show ‖ to denote the probability of

in·di·ca·tion (ındikéiʃən) *n.* something that indicates ‖ an indicating or being indicated

in·dic·a·tive (ındíkətiv) **1.** *adj.* showing, giving an indication ‖ *(gram.)* of the mood that expresses an action definitely, as distinct from stating a possible action, thought or desire **2.** *n. (gram.)* the indicative mood ‖ *(gram.)* a verb in this mood

in·di·ca·tor (índikeitər) *n.* something which points out or gives information, e.g. an instrument giving readings on a machine, or a board in a station showing train arrivals and departures ‖ *(chem.)* a substance (e.g. litmus) which shows by its color or change in color that a particular concentration of hydrogen or hydroxyl ions is present

in·dict (indáit) *v.t.* (esp. of a grand jury) to accuse formally of an offense **in·dict·a·ble** *adj.* liable to be indicted ‖ (of an action) making the doer liable for indictment

in·dict·ment (indáitmənt) *n.* an indicting or being indicted ‖ *(law)* a formal written statement accusing a person or persons of a crime

in·dif·fer·ence (indífərəns, indífrəns) *n.* lack of interest or feeling ‖ unimportance

in·dif·fer·ent (indífərənt, indífrənt) *adj.* not interested ‖ having no preference, impartial ‖ affording no grounds for preference ‖ rather poor, mediocre

in·di·gence (índidʒəns) *n.* the quality or state of being indigent

in·dig·e·nous (indídʒənəs) *adj.* born, growing or originating in the locality, not imported ‖ of or relating to natives ‖ (with 'to') innate, inborn

in·di·gent (índidʒənt) *adj.* needy, poor

in·di·ges·tion (indidʒéstʃən) *n.* difficulty in digesting food ‖ pain caused by difficulty in digesting food

in·dig·nant (indígnənt) *adj.* angered by unwarranted accusation, injustice, meanness etc. ‖ showing such anger, *indignant looks*

in·dig·na·tion (indignéiʃən) *n.* anger aroused by injustice, unkindness, unwarranted accusation, meanness etc. ‖ (with 'to') innate, inborn

in·dig·ni·ty (indígniti) *pl.* **in·dig·ni·ties** *n.* treatment that makes one feel humiliated ‖ an insult or outrage ‖ the quality of being humiliating

in·di·rect (indirékt) *adj.* not following the shortest route from one point to another, roundabout ‖ not going straight to the point, oblique ‖ dishonest, not straightforward ‖ not immediate

in·dis·creet (indiskrí:t) *adj.* lacking or showing a lack of prudence, good judgment or tact

in·dis·cre·tion (indiskréʃən) *n.* lack of prudence, tact etc. ‖ an indiscreet speech or action

in·dis·crim·i·nate (indiskríminit) *adj.* having or showing a lack of discernment, failing to make proper distinctions ‖ making no distinctions, random

in·dis·pen·sa·ble (indispénsəb'l) *adj.* absolutely necessary, impossible to do without **in·dis·pén·sa·bly** *adv.*

in·dis·pose (indispóuz) *pres. part.* **in·dis·pos·ing** *past* and *past part.* **in·dis·posed** *v.t.* to upset somewhat the state of mind or health of **in·dis·pósed** *adj.* slightly unwell ‖ unwilling, averse

in·dis·po·si·tion (indispəzíʃən) *n.* a slight illness, esp. one that does not last long ‖ a disinclination

in·dis·tinct (indistíŋkt) *adj.* difficult to see or hear for want of clarity ‖ confused, vague

in·dis·tinc·tive (indistíŋktiv) *adj.* not distinctive, having nothing to distinguish it from others

in·di·vid·u·al (indivídʒu:əl) **1.** *adj.* existing as a complete and separate entity ‖ of, relating to, used by or intended for only one person or thing ‖ distinctive, strikingly different from others **2.** *n.* one person, animal, organism etc. as distinguished from a class, group etc.

in·di·vid·u·al·i·ty (individʒu:æliti) *n.* the quality or characteristics that make one person or thing different

from others ‖ the quality or state of being individual

in·di·vis·i·ble (indivízəb'l) *adj.* impossible to divide into parts ‖ *(math.)* impossible to divide without leaving a remainder **in·di·vís·i·bly** *adv.*

in·doc·tri·nate (indóktrineit) *pres. part.* **in·doc·tri·nat·ing** *past* and *past part.* **in·doc·tri·nat·ed** *v.t.* to instill certain ideas or beliefs into, esp. so as to cause to embrace an ideology **in·doc·tri·ná·tion** *n.*

in·do·lence (índ'ləns) *n.* the state or quality of being indolent

in·do·lent (índ'lənt) *adj.* disliking exertion, lazy

in·dom·i·ta·ble (indómitəb'l) *adj.* unconquerable, not to be subdued **in·dóm·i·ta·bly** *adv.*

in·du·bi·ta·ble (indú:bitəb'l, indjú:bitəb'l) *adj.* that cannot be doubted, unquestionable **in·dú·bi·ta·bly** *adv.*

in·duce (indú:s, indjú:s) *pres. part.* **in·duc·ing** *past* and *past part.* **in·duced** *v.t.* to persuade ‖ to give rise to, cause ‖ to infer, draw (a conclusion) by induction **in·dúce·ment** *n.* an inducing or being induced ‖ something that persuades or motivates **in·dúc·i·ble** *adj.*

in·duct (indʌkt) *v.t.* to install formally in office ‖ to bring in as a member, initiate ‖ to bring into the armed forces under a draft law **in·duc·tée** *n.* someone inducted into the armed forces

in·duc·tile (indʌktəl, *Br.* indʌktail) *adj.* not ductile **in·duc·til·i·ty** (indəktíliti) *n.*

in·duc·tion (indʌkʃən) *n.* the formalities by which someone is made a member of the armed forces under a draft law

in·duc·tive (indʌktiv) *adj. (logic)* based on, or pertaining to, induction

in·dulge (indʌldʒ) *pres. part.* **in·dulg·ing** *past* and *past part.* **in·dulged** *v.t.* to treat with excessive kindness and affection, pamper ‖ to comply with, humor (a caprice etc.) ‖ to give way to ‖ *v.i.* to allow oneself a gratification ‖ (with 'in') to treat oneself to

in·dul·gence (indʌldʒəns) *n.* an indulging or being indulged ‖ self-indulgence ‖ a gratification, habit etc. that is indulged in ‖ an extension of time for payment of a bill or note, granted as a favor

in·dul·gent (indʌldʒənt) *adj.* having or showing indulgence

in·du·rate (índureit, índjureit) *pres. part.* **in·du·rat·ing** *past* and *past part.* **in·du·rat·ed** *v.t.* and *i.* to harden physically or morally

in·dus·tri·al (indʌstri:əl) **1.** *adj.* of, connected with or characterized by industry **2.** *n.* (*pl.* stocks, bonds or other securities of industrial companies

in·dus·tri·ous (indʌstri:əs) *adj.* hardworking

in·dus·try (índəstri:) *pl.* **in·dus·tries** *n.* the section of an economy concerned with manufacturing ‖ a specific type of manufacturing, business etc. ‖ any of various large-scale money-making activities ‖ diligence, application

in·e·bri·ate 1. (iní:bri:eit) *v.t. pres. part.* **in·e·bri·at·ing** *past* and *past part.* **in·e·bri·at·ed** to intoxicate ‖ to exhilarate emotionally **2.** (iní:bri:it) *adj. (rhet.)* drunk **3.** (iní:bri:it) *n.* a habitual drunkard **in·é·bri·at·ed** *adj.* **in·é·bri·á·tion** *n.*

in·ef·fa·ble (inéfəb'l) *adj.* incapable of being expressed or adequately described **in·éf·fa·bly** *adv.*

in·ef·fec·tive (iniféktiv) *adj.* not producing the desired effect ‖ (of a person) incompetent, ineffectual

in·ef·fec·tu·al (inéféktʃu:əl) *adj.* not effectual

in·el·i·gi·bil·i·ty (inelidʒəbíliti:) *n.* the quality or state of being ineligible

in·el·i·gi·ble (inélidʒəb'l) **1.** *adj.* not eligible **2.** *n.* someone not eligible

in·ept (inépt) *adj.* out of place, not apt ‖ incompetent ‖ silly, foolish

in·ept·i·tude (inéptitu:d, inéptitju:d) *n.* the quality or state of being inept ‖ something inept

in·ert (inɔ́:rt) *adj.* incapable of moving, acting, or resisting an opposing force ‖ devoid of mental energy, making no imaginative effort, hard to get to move or act ‖ *(chem.)* unreactive with other substances

in·er·tia (inɔ́:rʃə) *n.* the property of matter that causes its velocity to be constant in the absence of external forces ‖ the quality or state of being inert **in·ér·tial** *adj.*

in·es·ca·ble (ịniskéipəb'l) *adj.* impossible to escape or avoid, *inescapable conclusions*

in·es·ti·ma·ble (inéstəməb'l) *adj.* too great to be assessed **in·és·ti·ma·bly** *adv.*

in·ev·i·ta·ble (inévitəb'l) *adj.* unavoidable ‖ certain to happen **in·év·i·ta·bly** *adv.*

in·ex·o·ra·ble (inéksərəb'l) *adj.* impossible to move or influence by entreating **in·éx·o·ra·bly** *adv.*

in·ex·pe·di·en·cy (ịnikspí:di:ənsi:) *n.* the quality or state of being inexpedient

in·ex·pe·di·ent (ịnikspí:di:ənt) *adj.* not expedient

in·ex·pen·sive (ịnikspénsiv) *adj.* not expensive

in·ex·pe·ri·ence (ịnikspíəri:əns) *n.* lack of experience of a practical nature ‖ lack of the skill resulting from experience

in·ex·pert (inékspə:rt, ịnikspɔ́:rt) *adj.* lacking or showing a lack of skill

in·ex·pli·ca·ble (inéksplikəb'l, ịnikspĺíkəb'l) *adj.* not capable of being explained **in·éx·pli·ca·bly** *adv.*

in·ex·tri·ca·ble (inékstrikəb'l, ịnikstríkəb'l) *adj.* from which one cannot extricate oneself ‖ not capable of being solved ‖ that cannot be untied or unraveled **in·éx·tri·ca·bly** *adv.*

in·fal·li·bil·i·ty (infæləbíliti:) *n.* the quality or state of being infallible

in·fal·li·ble (infǽləb'l) *adj.* incapable of error ‖ never failing ‖ (of the pope) incapable of error when speaking ex cathedra on questions of faith and morals **in·fál·li·bly** *adv.*

in·fa·mous (ínfəməs) *adj.* of foul reputation ‖ arousing horror, deserving to be detested

in·fa·my (ínfəmi:) *pl.* **in·fa·mies** *n.* the quality of being infamous ‖ an infamous action ‖ public disgrace of a criminal convicted of an infamous crime

in·fan·cy (ínfənsi:) *pl.* **in·fan·cies** *n.* the state or period of being an infant

in·fant (ínfənt) **1.** *n.* a very young child, esp. one not yet able to walk or talk ‖ *(law)* a person not yet legally independent, a minor **2.** *adj.* of or pertaining to infants or being in infancy

in·fan·tile (ínfəntail, ínfəntəl) *adj.* of or pertaining to infants ‖ not appropriate in an adult, childish

in·fan·try (ínfəntri:) *pl.* **in·fan·tries** *n.* a branch of an army consisting of soldiers trained to fight on foot

in·fat·u·ate (infǽtʃu:eit) *pres. part.* **in·fat·u·at·ing** *past* and *past part.* **in·fat·u·at·ed** *v.t.* to inspire with a foolish and excessive passion **in·fat·u·á·tion** *n.*

in·fect (infékt) *v.t.* to transfer a disease or a disease-causing agent to (an individual or an organ) ‖ to contaminate with pathogens, *to infect a water supply* ‖ to affect (another) with one's own emotion, belief etc.

in·fec·tion (infékʃən) *n.* an infecting or being infected ‖ a disease etc. produced by infecting ‖ something which infects

in·fec·tious (infékʃəs) *adj.* able to cause infection ‖ caused by infection ‖ easily communicated, *infectious laughter*

in·fer (infɔ́:r) *pres. part.* **in·fer·ring** *past* and *past part.* **in·ferred** *v.t.* to arrive at by reasoning, deduce ‖ *(loosely)* to guess ‖ to hint, imply **in·fér·a·ble, in·fér·i·ble** *adj.*

in·fer·ence (ínfərəns) *n.* an inferring ‖ something inferred **in·fer·en·tial** (ịnfərénʃəl) *adj.*

in·fe·ri·or (infíəri:ər) **1.** *adj.* of poor quality ‖ of low or lower rank, status etc. ‖ *(anat.)* situated below a like part or organ or below the normal position **2.** *n.* a person of lower rank or capacity or thing that is inferior **in·fe·ri·or·i·ty** (infị̄əri:ɔ́riti:, infị̄əri:ɔ́riti:) *pl.*

in·fe·ri·or·i·ties *n.*

inferiority complex a neurotic condition resulting from subconscious belief in one's inferiority to others, leading to timidity or else overcompensated by aggressive behavior

in·fer·nal (infɔ́:rn'l) *adj.* of hell or the underworld ‖ *(pop.)* as unbearable as hell, fiendish ‖ *(pop.)* tiresome, irritating

in·fer·tile (infɔ́:rt'l) *adj.* not fertile, barren **in·fer·til·i·ty** (ịnfə:rtíliti:) *n.*

in·fest (infést) *v.t.* to overrun or swarm about in, in large numbers, so as to be dangerous or unpleasant, *infested with mice*

in·fes·ta·tion (ịnfestéiʃən) *n.* an infesting or being infested

in·fi·del (ínfid'l) **1.** *n.* *(hist.)* a person professing a religious faith other than that of the speaker ‖ *(loosely)* someone having no religious faith, an atheist **2.** *adj.* pertaining to an infidel

in·fi·del·i·ty (ịnfidéliti:) *pl.* **in·fi·del·i·ties** *n.* failure in loyalty ‖ an instance of this ‖ adultery ‖ lack of religious belief

in·fil·trate (ínfiltreit, infíltreit) **1.** *v. pres. part.* **in·fil·trat·ing** *past* and *past part.* **in·fil·trat·ed** *(mil.)* to penetrate in small numbers at various points into enemy territory ‖ to work unobtrusively and in small numbers into an organization etc. ‖ so as to form a threat to its integrity ‖ to permeate or pass through a substance, by or as if by filtering ‖ *v.t.* to permeate by or as if by filtration, *to infiltrate enemy lines* **2.** *n.* something that infiltrates, esp. a substance that passes into body tissues and forms an unhealthy accumulation **in·fil·trá·tion** *n.*

in·fi·nite (ínfinit) **1.** *adj.* absolutely without limits, endless ‖ too great to be measured on any imaginable scale ‖ *(loosely)* very great ‖ *(math.)* of a value or series the limit of which cannot be defined or expressed **2.** *n.* something infinite

in·fin·i·tes·i·mal (ịnfinitésəməl) *adj.* too small to be measured

in·fin·i·tive (infínitiv) **1.** *adj.* of an uninflected verb form conveying simply the idea of the action of the verb without limitation of person, number or mood, and used with 'to' or with an auxiliary verb: e.g. 'come' in the sentences 'try to come' and 'you may come' **2.** *n.* such a verb form

in·fin·i·ty (infíniti:) *pl.* **in·fin·i·ties** *n.* the quality of being infinite ‖ that which is infinite ‖ *(loosely)* an indefinitely large amount or number ‖ *(math., symbol ∞)* an infinite quantity that may be positive or negative

in·firm (infɔ́:rm) *adj.* physically weak (esp. through age) ‖ morally weak, *infirm of purpose*

in·fir·ma·ry (infɔ́:rməri:) *pl.* **in·fir·ma·ries** *n.* a place where the sick are cared for in a school or other institution ‖ (in names of institutions) a hospital

in·fir·mi·ty (infɔ́:rmiti:) *pl.* **in·fir·mi·ties** *n.* the quality or state of being infirm ‖ an instance of this ‖ a defect in character, flaw

in·flame (infléim) *pres. part.* **in·flam·ing** *past* and *past part.* **in·flamed** *v.t.* to excite passion in, arouse, esp. to anger ‖ to redden with or as if with flames ‖ *(med.)* to cause inflammation in

in·flam·ma·bil·i·ty (inflæməbíliti:) *n.* the state or quality of being inflammable

in·flam·ma·ble (inflǽməb'l) *adj.* easily set on fire ‖ easily excited or angered ‖ liable to degenerate into violence **in·flám·ma·bly** *adv.*

in·flam·ma·tion (ịnfləméiʃən) *n.* the response of body tissue to infection or to many kinds of injury, characterized by an increase of blood flow to the injured part, with heat, redness, pain, swelling and, occasionally, loss of function ‖ the state of being inflamed ‖ the stirring up of passion, esp. anger

in·flate (infléit) *pres. part.* **in·flat·ing** *past* and *past part.* **in·flat·ed** *v.t.* to cause to swell out with air or gas ‖ to cause to swell with pride, vanity etc. ‖ *(econ.)* to raise (prices) artificially ‖ *(econ.)* to increase the volume of (currency) so that a rise in prices follows

in·flat·ed *adj.* puffed out with air or gas ‖ (of language) bombastic ‖ elated with excessive pride, vanity etc. ‖ (of currency) increased abnormally in volume ‖ (of prices) raised artificially

in·fla·tion (infléiʃən) *n.* an inflating or being inflated ‖ a general rise in prices brought about by an increase in the ratio of currency and credit to the goods available ‖ *(econ.)* a sharp increase in the amount of paper money put into circulation **in·flá·tion·ar·y** *adj.*

in·flect (inflékt) *v.t. (gram.)* to treat (word forms) with inflection ‖ to modulate (the voice) ‖ *(bot.)* to bend (part of a plant) inward or toward the main axis ‖ *v.i. (gram.)* to be characterized by inflection

in·flec·tion (inflékʃən) *n.* a turning or bending, *inflection of light* ‖ a change in tone or pitch of voice ‖ *(gram.)* a change of word forms and endings to indicate change of case, tense etc. ‖ *(gram.)* the use of inflected forms ‖ *(gram.)* an inflectional element, e.g. a suffix ‖ *(math.)* the change of a curve or arc from convex to concave or conversely **in·fléc·tion·al** *adj.*

in·flex·i·ble (infléksəb'l) *adj.* not capable of being bent ‖ unchangeable ‖ incapable of change, rigid, unadaptable **in·fléx·i·bly** *adv.*

in·flict (inflíkt) *v.t.* to cause or give (wounds, pain etc.) by or as if by striking ‖ to impose (a penalty etc.)

in·flic·tion (inflíkʃən) *n.* the act of inflicting ‖ that which is inflicted

in·flic·tive (inflíktiv) *adj.* tending to inflict

in·flu·ence (ínflu:əns) **1.** *n.* a person's indirect power over men, events or things, e.g. through wisdom, wealth, force of character etc., and not as the exercise of physical force or formal authority ‖ a comparable power in a thing ‖ a person or thing having such power ‖ such power used to sway authority **2.** *v.t. pres. part.* **in·flu·enc·ing** *past* and *past part.* **in·flu·enced** to have or exert influence on

in·flu·en·tial (ˌinfluénʃəl) *adj.* possessing or exerting influence

in·flu·en·za (influénzə) *n.* an acute, infectious respiratory disease

in·flux (ínflʌks) *n.* a flowing in (of a liquid, gas etc.) ‖ the place where a river joins another body of water ‖ the mouth of a river ‖ a flowing in of people or things, *an influx of visitors*

in·form (infórm) *v.t.* to communicate information to ‖ to be the principle that gives form or character to ‖ *v.i.* to give information ‖ (with 'against') to denounce someone, supply information leading to an accusation

in·for·mal (infórməl) *adj.* free of conventional forms or restrictions ‖ suitable for relaxed, casual, ordinary circumstances **in·for·mál·i·ty** *pl.* **in·for·mal·i·ties** *n.* the quality or state of being informal ‖ an informal action

in·form·ant (infórmənt) *n.* someone who communicates information

in·for·ma·tion (ˌinfərméiʃən) *n.* the communication of news, knowledge etc. ‖ a fact or facts told or communicated ‖ knowledge obtained by search, study etc. ‖ *(law)* a complaint or accusation communicated to a magistrate ‖ *(law)* a formal accusation by the public prosecutor, often substituted for indictment **in·for·má·tion·al** *adj.*

in·form·a·tive (infórmətiv) *adj.* giving information, instructive

in·form·er (infórmər) *n.* someone who informs, esp. someone who sells information to the police etc.

infra- *prefix* below

in·fra·red (infrəréd) **1.** *adj.* producing, relating to, or produced by infrared radiation **2.** *n.* such radiation

in·fre·quent (infrí:kwənt) *adj.* happening rarely

in·fringe (infríndʒ) *pres. part.* **in·fring·ing** *past* and *past part.* **in·fringed** *v.t.* to fail to conform with, violate ‖ *v.i.* to encroach **in·fringe·ment** *n.*

in·fu·ri·ate (infjúəri:eit) *pres. part.* **in·fu·ri·at·ing** *past* and *past part.* **in·fu·ri·at·ed** *v.t.* to fill with fury, enrage

in·fuse (infjú:z) *pres. part.* **in·fus·ing** *past* and *past part.* **in·fused** *v.t.* to inspire ‖ to instill ‖ to soak (tea leaves etc.) in liquid that has boiled, so as to extract the flavor *v.i.* to be soaked thus

in·fu·sion (infjú:ʒən) *n.* an infusing or being infused ‖ a liquid resulting from infusing, e.g. tea ‖ something blended or mixed in

in·gen·ious (indʒí:njəs) *adj.* clever in inventing or contriving ‖ cleverly invented, contrived

in·gé·nue, in·ge·nue (ɛ̃ʒənu:, ɛ̃ʒanju:, ɛ̃ʒeinu) *n.* a naïve, unsophisticated girl ‖ *(theater)* the role of such a character ‖ an actress who plays such a role

in·ge·nu·i·ty (ˌindʒənjú:iti:, indʒənú:iti:) *n.* cleverness in contriving or inventing

in·gest (indʒést) *v.t.* to take (food) into the digestive system

in·got (íŋgət) *n.* a lump of metal, esp. of gold, silver or steel, cast in convenient form (usually oblong) for transport and storage

in·grained (ingréind, ingréind) *adj.* thoroughly imbued ‖ inveterate, thorough

in·gra·ti·ate (ingréiʃi:eit) *pres. part.* **in·gra·ti·at·ing** *past* and *past part.* **in·gra·ti·at·ed** *v.t.* to get (oneself) into the good graces of another, esp. by guile

in·grat·i·tude (ingrǽtitu:d, ingrǽtitju:d) *n.* lack of gratitude ‖ an instance of this

in·gre·di·ent (ingrí:di:ənt) *n.* an element in a mixture, constituent, *the ingredients of a cake*

in·gress (íngres) *n.* the right or ability go in ‖ *(rhet.)* a going in

in·grown (íngroun) *adj.* grown inward, esp. (of a finger or toe nail) having the tip embedded in the flesh ‖ innate

in·hab·it (inhǽbit) *v.t.* to live in

in·hab·it·a·ble (inhǽbitəb:l) *adj.* capable of being inhabited or fit to be inhabited

in·hab·it·ant (inhǽbitənt) *n.* a permanent resident in a place

in·hale (inhéil) *pres. part.* **in·hal·ing** *past* and *past part.* **in·haled** *v.t.* to breathe (something) in ‖ *v.i.* to breathe in **in·hál·er** *n.* an apparatus which facilitates the inhalation of medicines ‖ someone who inhales

in·her·ent (inhíərənt, inhérənt) *adj.* existing in someone or something as a permanent characteristic or quality

in·her·it (inhérit) *v.t.* to receive by legacy ‖ to receive by heredity ‖ to receive (something) previously in another's possession) as if by legacy ‖ *v.i.* to come into an inheritance

in·her·it·ance (inhéritəns) *n.* the act of inheriting ‖ something inherited

in·hib·it (inhíbit) *v.t.* to hold in check, restrain (a natural impulse) either consciously or unconsciously ‖ to obstruct, hinder

in·hi·bi·tion (inhibíʃən) *n.* an inhibiting or being inhibited ‖ one of the conscious or unconscious mechanisms whereby unacceptable impulses (sexual, aggressive etc.) are subdued or repressed

in·hos·pi·ta·ble (inhóspitəb'l, ˌinhɑspítəb'l) *adj.* not offering hospitality ‖ (of a place or region) not affording sustenance, barren **in·hós·pi·ta·bly** *adv.*

in·hos·pi·tal·i·ty (ˌinhɒspitǽliti:) *n.* lack of hospitality

in·hu·man (inhjú:mən) *adj.* lacking, or showing a lack of, the qualities of mercy etc. considered proper to human beings ‖ machinelike, lacking or showing a lack of human warmth ‖ not belonging to or suggestive of the human race

---

(a) æ, cat; ɑ, car; ɔ fawn; ei, snake. **(e)** e, hen; i:, sheep; iə, deer; ɛə, bear. **(i)** i, fish; ai, tiger; ə:, bird. **(o)** o, ox; au, cow; ou, goat; u, poor; ɔi, royal. **(u)** ʌ, duck; u, bull; u:, goose; ə, bacillus; ju:, cube. x, loch; θ, think; ð, bother; z, Zen; ʒ, corsage; dʒ, savage; ŋ, orangutang; j, yak; ʃ, fish; tʃ, fetch; 'l, rabble; 'n, redden. Complete pronunciation key appears inside front cover.

in·im·i·ta·ble (inímitəb'l) *adj.* not capable of being imitated, esp. too good to be successfully imitated **in·ím·i·ta·bly** *adv.*

in·iq·ui·ty (iníkwiti) *pl.* **in·iq·ui·ties** *n.* great wickedness or injustice || an instance of this

in·i·tial (iníʃəl) **1.** *adj.* of or occurring at the very beginning || designating the first letter or syllable of a word **2.** *n.* (*esp. pl.*) the first letter of a personal name || a large decorative letter used esp. at the beginning of a chapter in a book **3.** *v.t. pres. part.* **in·i·tial·ing** *past* and *past part.* **in·i·tialed** to sign or mark with an initial or initials

in·i·ti·ate 1. (iníʃi:eit) *v.t. pres. part.* **in·i·ti·at·ing** *past* and *past part.* **in·i·ti·at·ed** to cause to begin || to instruct in the fundamentals of a subject || to introduce ceremonially into a society etc. **2.** (iníʃi:it) *adj.* having been initiated **3.** (iníʃi:it) *n.* someone who has been initiated

in·i·ti·a·tion (iniʃi:éiʃən) *n.* an initiating or being initiated || the rite of introduction into a society etc.

in·i·ti·a·tive (iníʃi:ətiv) *n.* personal capacity for thinking up and initiating action || an inception that shows this quality **on one's own initiative** acting on one's own idea without prompting **to take the initiative** to be the first to act

in·i·ti·a·tor (iníʃi:ętitər) *n.* a person who or thing that initiates

in·ject (indʒékt) *v.t.* to force (a fluid) into a body esp. by means of a hypodermic syringe || to force a fluid into (a cavity, tissue etc.) || to administer an injection to || to introduce (a new or different quality) into a person or a thing

in·jec·tion (indʒékʃən) *n.* the act of injecting || the introduction of a substance, esp. a drug, into the body esp. by means of a hypodermic syringe || a substance, esp. a drug in solution, that is injected

in·ju·di·cious (indʒu:díʃəs) *adj.* lacking or showing a lack of good judgment

in·junc·tion (indʒʌ́ŋkʃən) *n.* an authoritative command || (*law*) a written order from a court forbidding or requiring some action

in·jure (índʒər) *pres. part.* **in·jur·ing** *past* and *past part.* **in·jured** *v.t.* to inflict a wound, fracture or other physical hurt upon || to cause intangible detriment or hurt to

in·ju·ri·ous (indʒúəri:əs) *adj.* causing or likely to cause injury || (of language) offensive, insulting, likely to damage a reputation

in·ju·ry (índʒəri:) *pl.* **in·ju·ries** *n.* physical impairment resulting from violence or accident || unjust or offensive treatment || an instance of physical or moral hurt || (*law*) an actionable wrong

in·jus·tice (indʒʌ́stis) *n.* violation of justice, unfairness || an instance of this **to do an injustice to someone** to judge someone unfairly

ink (iŋk) **1.** *n.* a colored fluid used for writing or printing || (*zool.*) a black liquid ejected by cephalopods to screen escape **2.** *v.t.* to cover or mark with ink

ink·ling (íŋkliŋ) *n.* the slightest notion || a faint suggestion, intimation

in·land (ínlənd) **1.** *n.* the interior of a country, away from the coast **2.** *adj.* away from the coast toward the interior of a country **3.** *adv.* in or toward the interior of a country

in-law (ínlɔ) *n.* (*pop.*, usually *pl.*) a relative by marriage

in·lay (ínlei) **1.** *v.t. pres. part.* **in·lay·ing** *past* and *past part.* **in·laid** (ínleid) to set (a material or pattern) into another material or object by cutting a design out of its surface and filling the space with a different material || to decorate (a material or object) in this way **2.** *n.* the process of inlaying || a design made by inlaying || the material used in inlaying || (*dentistry*) a filling of metal etc. cemented into a cavity

in·let (ínlit) *n.* a narrow arm of the sea or of a river || a passage between islands into a lagoon || an opening, entrance

in·mate (ínmęit) *n.* a person living in an institution, esp. in a mental hospital

inn (in) *n.* (*hist.*) a hotel || (*hist.*, now used in names) a tavern

in·nards (ínərdz) *pl. n.* (*pop.*) viscera, entrails

in·nate (inéit) *adj.* belonging to a person's nature || inherent in a thing || (*philos.*) originating in the mind itself, i.e. not acquired from direct experience, *innate ideas*

in·ner (ínər) *adj.* located within, contained near the center || of the mind or spirit, *the inner life* || not obvious, hidden, *the inner meaning*

in·ner·vate (ínə:rveit) *pres. part.* **in·ner·vat·ing** *past* and *past part.* **in·ner·vat·ed** *v.t.* (*physiol.*) to provide (a part of the body) with nerves || to stimulate (a nerve or organ) to activity **in·ner·vá·tion** *n.* an innervating or being innervated

in·no·cence (ínəs'ns) *n.* the quality or state of being innocent

in·no·cent (ínəs'nt) **1.** *adj.* free from guilt || knowing nothing of evil || naive, simple-minded || harmless || (*med.*) benign **2.** *n.* an innocent person

in·noc·u·ous (inɒ́kju:əs) *adj.* not actively harmful || calculated to give no offense || lacking in force

in·no·vate (ínouveit) *pres. part.* **in·no·vat·ing** *past* and *past part.* **in·no·vat·ed** *v.i.* to make changes, introduce new practices etc.

in·no·va·tion (inouvéiʃən) *n.* the act of innovating || something newly introduced

in·no·va·tor (ínouveitər) *n.* someone who innovates **in·no·va·to·ry** (ínouvətɔ́ri:, ínouvətǫuri:) *adj.*

in·nu·en·do (inju:éndou) *pl.* **in·nu·en·does** *n.* an oblique referring or insinuating || an instance of such hinting, always critical and usually malicious || (*law*, in an action for libel or slander) that part of the complaint which interprets the expressions alleged to be libelous or slanderous

in·nu·mer·a·ble (inú:mərəb'l, injú:mərəb'l) *adj.* too many to be counted || very many **in·nú·mer·a·bly** *adv.*

in·oc·u·late (inɒ́kjuleit) *pres. part.* **in·oc·u·lat·ing** *past* and *past part.* **in·oc·u·lat·ed** *v.t.* to introduce a disease into (an organism) to protect against subsequent infection || to introduce microorganisms etc. into (soil etc.) || to introduce particular ideas into (a person's mind) so as to imbue him with them

in·oc·u·la·tion (inɒkjuléiʃən) *n.* the act of inoculating || an instance of this || mental preparation or conditioning

in·oc·u·la·tor (inɒ́kjuleitər) *n.* a person who or thing that inoculates

in·op·er·a·ble (inɒ́pərəb'l) *adj.* (*surg.*) not able to be treated by operation

in·op·por·tune (inɒpərtú:n, inɒpərtjú:n) *adj.* not opportune, esp. happening at a wrong or inconvenient time

in·or·gan·ic (inɔrgǽnik) *adj.* (*chem.*) of or relating to elements and compounds not regarded as organic || not composed of plant or animal material || not arising from natural processes, artificial **in·or·gán·i·cal·ly** *adv.*

in·pa·tient (ínpęiʃənt) *n.* a person who is lodged, fed and treated in a hospital

in·put (ínput) *n.* something put in, esp. power or energy supplied to a machine or storage system || effort put into any project || (*computer*) data fed into a computer

in·quest (ínkwęst) *n.* a judicial or official inquiry esp. before a jury, usually to inquire into the cause of death where this is not certified by a doctor or where the possibility of crime cannot be ruled out || the jury engaged in such an inquiry || the result of the inquiry || a minute and semi-accusing investigation

in·quire, en·quire (inkwáiər) *pres. part.* **in·quir·ing, en·quir·ing** *past* and *past part.* **in·quired, en·quired** *v.t.* to seek (information) by asking || *v.i.* to ask questions || (with 'after') to ask about the health or welfare of || (with 'for') to seek to get by asking, *to inquire for a book* || (with 'for') to ask to see (a person) || (with 'into') to investigate

in·quir·y, en·quir·y (inkwáiəri:, ínkwəri:, énkwəri:) *pl.* **in·quir·ies, en·quir·ies** *n.* the act of inquiring || a question || an investigation

in·qui·si·tion (ịnkwizíʃən) n. an investigation by close interrogation, esp. one which disregards the feelings of the person subjected to it || (law, in certain contexts) a judicial inquiry **in·qui·si·tion·al** adj.

in·quis·i·tive (inkwízitiv) adj. wanting to ferret out the private concerns of other people || asking a lot of questions

in·quis·i·tor (inkwízitər) n. a person officially appointed to investigate || a cruel, severe questioner

in·road (ínroud) n. (usually pl.) a heavy encroachment, inroads on one's time || a raid, inroads into enemy territory

in·sane (inséin) adj. afflicted with a mental illness severe enough to make one incapable of leading a normal life || showing such affliction, insane delusions || (loosely) highly reckless or foolish

in·san·i·ty (insǽniti:) pl. **in·san·i·ties** n. the state of being insane || (law) such a lack of mental health as to exempt a person from legal responsibility || (loosely) a foolish act

in·sa·tia·ble (inséiʃəb'l, inséiʃi:əb'l) adj. incapable of being satisfied || continually craving **in·sá·tia·bly** adv.

in·scribe (inskráib) pres. part. **in·scrib·ing** past and past part. **in·scribed** v.t. to write or engrave (words or symbols) on a surface || to impress ineffaceably (on the mind or memory) || to dedicate (a book etc.) informally

in·scrip·tion (inskrípʃən) n. an inscribed text || the art of inscribing || an informal dedication, e.g. in a book **in·scrip·tion·al** adj.

in·scru·ta·ble (inskrú:təb'l) adj. of such a kind that the meaning or intention cannot be perceived **in·scru·ta·bly** adv.

in·sect (ínsekt) n. a member of the class Insecta, phylum Arthropoda, with external skeleton and jointed legs || any creature (the spider, tick, mite etc.) resembling an insect

in·se·cure (insikjúər) adj. not safe, liable to collapse, give way etc.

in·sen·sate (insénseit) adj. inhumane, brutal || without sense perception || lacking moral or emotional perception, insensitive || foolish

in·sen·si·ble (insénsəb'l) adj. indifferent || not aware || not feeling || unconscious **in·sén·si·bly** adv.

in·sen·si·tive (insénsitiv) adj. not mentally or emotionally sensitive || not physically sensitive

in·sep·a·ra·ble (insépərəb'l) adj. incapable of being separated || (of people) utterly devoted in friendship **in·sép·a·ra·bly** adv.

in·sert 1. (insə́:rt) v.t. to put inside || to add as an integral part **2.** (ínsə:rt) n. something inserted || an extra page set within a newspaper, magazine or book **in·sért·ed** adj.

in·ser·tion (insə́:rʃən) n. an inserting or being inserted || something inserted || one inclusion of a newspaper announcement or advertisement

in·side (ínsáid) **1.** n. the inner portion or side of something || the side of a path, sidewalk etc. furthest from the road || (pl., pop.) the stomach and intestines **2.** adj. situated in the inner portion or on the inner surface || of or relating to knowledge etc. that is not generally available **3.** adv. in or into the inner part of something **4.** prep. at or toward the inner side or portion of, stay inside the gates

in·sid·er (ínsáidər) n. a member of a group, organization etc. who, because of his position, has special information, rights, privileges etc.

in·sid·i·ous (insídi:əs) adj. working or acting maliciously with subtlety and stealth || acting gradually and imperceptibly

in·sight (ínsait) n. the imaginative power to see into and understand immediately (a person, situation etc.) || an item of knowledge gained through this power

in·sig·ni·a (insígni:ə) pl. n. symbols of authority or importance || emblems used as distinguishing marks or signs

in·sig·nif·i·cance (insignífikəns) n. the quality or state of being insignificant

in·sig·nif·i·cant (insignífikənt) adj. having no importance || meaningless || small || personally unimpressive or lacking social standing

in·sin·cere (insinsíər) adj. not sincere **in·sin·cer·i·ty** (insinsériti:) pl. **in·sin·cer·i·ties** n. the quality or state of being insincere || something insincere

in·sin·u·ate (insínju:eit) pres. part. **in·sin·u·at·ing** past and past part. **in·sin·u·at·ed** v.t. to suggest or hint indirectly, imply slyly, esp. maliciously

in·sin·u·a·tion (insinju:éiʃən) n. the act of insinuating || an oblique, esp. malicious suggestion

in·sip·id (insípid) adj. (of food) tasteless || (of people or things) vapid, uninteresting **in·si·píd·i·ty** pl. **in·si·pid·i·ties** n. the quality or state of being insipid || an insipid remark etc.

in·sist (insíst) v.t. to assert emphatically || to demand peremptorily || v.i. to repeat a request, assertion etc. with persistence || (with 'on' or 'upon') to make a specified demand authoritatively **in·síst·ence** n. the state or quality of being insistent || the act of insisting **in·síst·en·cy** n.

in·sist·ent (insístənt) adj. compelling attention || persistent **in·síst·ent·ly** adv.

in·so·lence (ínsələns) n. the quality of being insolent || an instance of this

in·so·lent (ínsələnt) adj. rudely disrespectful

in·sol·u·ble (insóljub'l) adj. (chem.) not soluble, or soluble only slightly or with difficulty || unable to be solved **in·sól·u·bly** adv.

in·sol·vent (insólvənt) adj. unable to pay one's debts || (of an estate etc.) not sufficient to pay all debts || relating to insolvency or insolvents

in·som·ni·a (insómni:ə) n. persistent inability to sleep **in·som·ni·ac** (insómni:æk) n. a person suffering from this inability

in·spect (inspékt) v.t. to examine formally, e.g. for completeness or quality || to pass in review ceremonially || to look closely at, scrutinize

in·spec·tion (inspékʃən) n. the process of inspecting || an instance of this

in·spec·tor (inspéktər) n. someone officially appointed to make inspections and report to an authority || a police officer ranking below a superintendent **in·spéc·to·ral** adj. **in·spec·tor·ate** (inspéktərit) n. the office of an inspector **in·spec·to·ri·al** (inspektɔ́ri:əl, inspektóuri:əl) adj. of or pertaining to an inspector

in·spi·ra·tion (inspəréiʃən) n. the creative impulse of an artist, often seen as a supernatural prompting || a person who or thing that inspires || an inspired idea || a breathing in, inhaling **in·spi·rá·tion·al** adj.

in·spire (inspáiər) pres. part. **in·spir·ing** past and past part. **in·spired** v.t. to fill with creative power || to stimulate || to affect || to suggest, be the motivating but unnamed power behind

in·spis·sate (inspíseit, ínspiseit) pres. part. **in·spis·sat·ing** past and past part. **in·spis·sat·ed** v.t. and i. to thicken, condense

in·sta·bil·i·ty (instəbíliti:) pl. **in·sta·bil·i·ties** n. lack of physical, moral or emotional stability || an instance of this

in·stall (instɔ́l) v.t. to place (a person) ceremonially in a position of power or dignity || to set in position for use || to settle, establish in some place or state

in·stal·la·tion (ɪnstəléiʃən) n. an installing or being installed ‖ an apparatus set in position for use ‖ a military establishment, incl. the base and all its equipment

in·stall·ment, in·stal·ment (ɪnstɔ́lmənt) n. one of the parts of a serial ‖ part of the sum paid at regular intervals over an extended period

in·stance (ínstəns) 1. n. an example, illustration **for instance** as an illustration **in the first instance** initially, at the first stage 2. v.t. pres. part. **in·stanc·ing** past and past part. **in·stanced** to cite as example ‖ to illustrate by citing an example

in·stant (ínstənt) 1. adj. urgent ‖ immediate ‖ (of coffee, soup etc.) in soluble form, ready to be prepared by adding a liquid 2. n. a short space of time ‖ a particular moment, come here this instant

in·stan·ta·ne·ous (ɪnstəntéiniːəs) adj. happening in an instant ‖ done immediately

in·stead (ɪnstéd) adv. as an alternative **instead of** in place of, rather than

in·step (ínstɛp) n. the arching area of the middle of the human foot, esp. the upper surface of this area ‖ the part of a shoe or stocking covering this area

in·sti·gate (ínstigeit) pres. part. **in·sti·gat·ing** past and past part. **in·sti·gat·ed** v.t. to bring about by inciting ‖ to incite (someone)

in·sti·ga·tion (ɪnstigéiʃən) n. an instigating or being instigated ‖ something that instigates, a stimulus

in·sti·ga·tor (ínstigeitər) n. someone who instigates

in·still, in·stil (ɪnstíl) pres. part. **in·still·ing, in·stil·ling** past and past part. **in·stilled** v.t. to cause someone to absorb (ideas, feelings etc.) gradually ‖ to put in drop by drop

in·stil·la·tion (ɪnstɪléiʃən) n. the act of instilling ‖ something instilled

in·stinct 1. (ínstɪŋkt) n. a specific, complex pattern of responses by an organism, supposedly inherited, which is quite independent of any thought processes ‖ (pop.) the ability to form a judgment without using the reasoning process ‖ (pop.) any drive or impulse 2. (ɪnstíŋkt) adj. (rhet., with 'with') deeply imbued **in·stínc·tive, in·stinc·tual** adjs

in·sti·tute (ínstitju:t, ínstitju:t) n. an institution for study or research ‖ an institution devoted to some specific welfare purpose ‖ (pl.) a collection or summary of principles, esp. in law

institute pres. part. **in·sti·tut·ing** past and past part. **in·sti·tut·ed** v.t. to set up, found ‖ to take the initial steps that will cause (something) to come into being

in·sti·tu·tion (ɪnstitú:ʃən, ɪnstitjú:ʃən) n. an organization whose purpose is to further public welfare, learning etc. ‖ the building or group of buildings used by such an establishment ‖ the act of instituting something ‖ an established law or custom ‖ (pop.) a person who is a familiar sight in a locality ‖ (pl.) a collection of rules or laws **in·sti·tú·tion·al** adj. pertaining to an institution or institutions

in·struct (ɪnstrʌ́kt) v.t. to teach (a person) ‖ to command, order, esp. formally ‖ to advise, inform

in·struc·tion (ɪnstrʌ́kʃən) n. the act of instructing ‖ knowledge imparted by instructing ‖ (pl.) a direction for procedure ‖ (pl.) a set of orders or an order ‖ (computer) a code that sets in motion an operation in a program **in·strúc·tion·al** adj.

in·struc·tive (ɪnstrʌ́ktiv) adj. serving to instruct, instructive criticisms

in·struc·tor (ɪnstrʌ́ktər) n. someone who instructs, a teacher ‖ a college or university teacher ranking next below an assistant professor **in·strúc·tor·ship** n. **in·strúc·tress** n. a female instructor

in·stru·ment (ínstrəmənt) 1. n. any object used for making, doing, achieving or promoting something, an implement ‖ a means, language is an instrument for communication ‖ a person made use of by another ‖ a device for producing music 2. v.t. to equip with instruments ‖ to orchestrate (a score)

in·stru·men·tal (ɪnstrəmént'l) adj. serving as an instrument, helping to bring something about ‖ (mus.) writ-

ten for or performed on instruments or an instrument, not vocal ‖ of, relating to or involving mechanical instruments ‖ (gram.) of or designating a case denoting the means in an action **in·stru·men·tál·i·ty** n. the quality or state of being instrumental ‖ agency or means

in·suf·fer·a·ble (ɪnsʌ́fərəb'l) adj. very hard to endure, insufferable agonies ‖ not to be tolerated **in·súf·fer·a·bly** adv.

in·suf·fi·cien·cy (ɪnsəfíʃənsi:) pl. **in·suf·fi·cien·cies** n. the quality or state of being insufficient ‖ an instance of this ‖ (med.) failure of an organ or tissue (esp. a muscle or heart valve) to perform its normal function

in·suf·fi·cient (ɪnsəfíʃənt) adj. not sufficient

in·su·late (ínsuleit, ínsjuleit) pres. part. **in·su·lat·ing** past and past part. **in·su·lat·ed** v.t. to place in an isolated situation, to segregate **in·su·lá·tion** n. an insulating or being insulated ‖ material used to insulate **ín·su·la·tor** n. a material or device that serves to insulate

in·su·lin (ínsulin, ínsjulin) n. a hormone, produced by the islets of Langerhans, that maintains the level of sugar in the blood

in·sult (ínsʌlt) n. a remark or act showing contempt and calculated to offend someone in his dignity

in·sult (ɪnsʌ́lt) v.t. to abuse in speech or action in such a way as to show contempt

in·sur·ance (ɪnʃúərəns) n. the practice by which an individual secures financial compensation for a specified loss or damage resulting from risk of any sort, by contract with a company to which he pays regular premiums ‖ the profession of drawing up such contracts ‖ the contract drawn up ‖ the protection afforded by this ‖ the premium demanded for such protection ‖ the sum for which something is insured

in·sure (ɪnʃúər) pres. part. **in·sur·ing** past and past part. **in·sured** v.t. to take out insurance for ‖ to issue an insurance policy for ‖ to ensure ‖ v.i. (often with 'against') to make provision ‖ to contract for or take out insurance **in·súr·er** n. a person or company issuing an insurance policy

in·sur·gen·cy (ɪnsɔ́:rdʒənsi:) n. the state or quality of being insurgent

in·sur·gent (ɪnsɔ́:rdʒənt) 1. n. a rebel against a lawful government or civil authority 2. adj. rebelling against a lawful government or civil authority

in·sur·rec·tion (ɪnsərékʃən) n. organized opposition to authority ‖ a revolt **in·sur·réc·tion·al** adj. **in·sur·réc·tion·ar·y** 1. adj. of, involving or producing insurrection 2. pl. **in·sur·rec·tion·ar·ies** n. someone who takes part in an insurrection **in·sur·réc·tion·ist** n.

in·tact (ɪntǽkt) adj. left in its complete state, undamaged

in·tan·gi·ble (ɪntǽndʒəb'l) 1. adj. not tangible ‖ not readily defined, vague 2. n. something that is not tangible **in·tán·gi·bly** adv.

in·te·ger (íntidʒər) n. (math.) a whole number ‖ an entity

in·te·gral (íntigrəl) adj. necessary to complete an entity, essentially part of some whole ‖ forming a single unit with something else ‖ whole and complete ‖ (math.) related to an integer 2. n. the integral whole **in·te·gral·i·ty** (ɪntigrǽliti:) n.

in·te·grate (íntigreit) pres. part. **in·te·grat·ing** past and past part. **in·te·grat·ed** v.t. to make complete by adding parts ‖ to absorb into an existing whole ‖ to end the racial segregation of, give full, equal membership in a group or in society to ‖ v.i. to become racially integrated

in·te·gra·tion (ɪntigréiʃən) n. an integrating or being integrated ‖ the coordination of personality and environment ‖ (psychol.) the organizing of psychological reactions, perceptions etc. into a balanced, whole personality ‖ the unification of educational systems previously segregated by race ‖ the giving of full civil or membership rights to those deprived of them on racial grounds **in·te·grá·tion·ist** n. someone in favor of integration

in·teg·ri·ty (intégriti:) n. moral soundness, probity ‖

wholeness, completeness ‖ the quality or state of being unimpaired

in·teg·u·ment (intégjumənt) n. an outer covering, esp. (biol.) a coating structure or layer, e.g. skin, shell or rind **in·teg·u·men·ta·ry** (integjuméntəri:) adj.

in·tel·lect (íntəlekt) n. the faculty of knowing, as distinct from feeling or willing ‖ mental power, intelligence ‖ a person of superior reasoning power

in·tel·lec·tu·al (intəléktʃu:əl) 1. adj. relating to, using or performed by the intellect ‖ (of a person) concerned with the activities of the intellect **in·tel·léc·tu·al·ism** n. preoccupation with the process of thought at the expense of its aims

in·tel·li·gence (intélidʒəns) n. the ability to perceive logical relationships and use one's knowledge to solve problems and respond appropriately to novel situations ‖ news, information ‖ the obtaining of secret information, esp. for military purposes ‖ an organization for the obtaining of such information

in·tel·li·gent (intélidʒənt) adj. having or showing a high degree of intelligence ‖ endowed with intelligence, capable of reasoning

in·tel·li·gi·ble (intélidʒəb'l) adj. that can be understood ‖ (philos.) that can be perceived by the intellect **in·tél·li·gi·bly** adv.

in·tem·per·ance (intémpərəns) n. lack of moderation, esp. habitual excessive indulgence in alcohol

in·tend (inténd) v.t. to have as intention ‖ to have in mind a specified purpose, use or destination for

in·tend·ed (inténdid) 1. adj. planned ‖ deliberate 2. n. (pop.) one's fiancé or fiancée

in·tense (inténs) adj. very great, extreme ‖ (of a color) very deep or concentrated ‖ (of a person) fervently earnest

in·ten·si·fy (inténsifai) pres. part. **in·ten·si·fy·ing** past and past part. **in·ten·si·fied** v.t. to render (a quality, emotion etc.) more intense ‖ (photog.) to increase the sharpness of (the image) by chemical action ‖ v.i. (of a quality, emotion etc.) to become more intense

in·ten·si·ty (inténsiti:) pl. **in·ten·si·ties** n. the quality or state of being intense ‖ (phys.) the magnitude of force or energy per unit area, charge or mass, used as a measure of the activity or effect of physical agencies, e.g. electric-field intensity, luminous-flux intensity, sound intensity etc.

in·ten·sive (inténsiv) 1. adj. concentrated ‖ (gram.) of a word giving force or emphasis to another, e.g. 'himself' in the sentence 'he did it himself' 2. n. (gram.) an intensive word, prefix etc.

in·tent (inténtt) adj. (with 'on' or 'upon') having a firm intention ‖ (with 'on' or 'upon') having one's attention concentrated ‖ intense, searching

intent n. intention **to all intents and purposes** virtually, practically

in·ten·tion (inténʃən) n. that which one is resolved to do, purpose ‖ meaning, significance ‖ (logic) a concept

in·ten·tion·al (inténʃən'l) adj. done on purpose ‖ of or relating to a logical concept

in·ter (intə́:r) pres. part. **in·ter·ring** past and past part. **in·terred** v.t. to put (a dead body) in the ground or in a tomb

inter- (íntər) prefix between, within ‖ reciprocal ‖ occurring, played, carried on etc. between ‖ involving two or more

in·ter·act (intərǽkt) v.i. to act upon each other **in·ter·ac·tion** (intərǽkʃən) n. **in·ter·ác·tive** adj.

in·ter·breed (intərbrí:d) pres. part. **in·ter·breed·ing** past and past part. **in·ter·bred** (intərbréd) v.t. to crossbreed (plants or animals of different varieties) ‖ v.i. (of plants or animals of different varieties) to undergo crossbreeding

in·ter·cede (intərsí:d) pres. part. **in·ter·ced·ing** past and past part. **in·ter·ced·ed** v.i. to intervene on behalf of another ‖ to intervene so as to attempt reconciliation

in·ter·cept (intərsépt) 1. v.t. to seize (something) before it can reach its destination ‖ (math.) to bound (part of a line, curve etc.) between two points 2. n. (math.) a part of a line, curve etc. bounded in this way **in·ter·cep·tion** (intərsépʃən) n. **in·ter·cép·tive** adj.

in·ter·cép·tor n. someone who or something that intercepts ‖ a fighting plane with strong climbing power used in defense

in·ter·ces·sion (intərséʃən) n. the act of interceding ‖ a prayer or petition on another's behalf

in·ter·change (íntərtʃeindʒ) n. a substitution for one another of two things or two sets of things ‖ mutual exchange ‖ a junction on separate levels of two or more highways, allowing vehicles to change from one to another without lines of traffic crossing

in·ter·change (intərtʃéindʒ) pres. part. **in·ter·chang·ing** past and past part. **in·ter·changed** v.t. to substitute (two things or sets of things) for each other ‖ to exchange ‖ v.i. (of two things or sets of things) to change places

in·ter·change·a·ble (intərtʃéindʒəb'l) adj. (of two or more things) capable of being mutually substituted **in·ter·chánge·a·bly** adv.

in·ter·con·ti·nen·tal (intərkɒntinént'l) adj. between or among continents

in·ter·cos·tal (intərkɔ́stəl, intərkóstəl) adj. (anat.) between the ribs ‖ (bot.) between the veins or nerves of a leaf

in·ter·course (íntərkɔrs, íntərkours) n. reciprocal social or commercial dealings between individuals, groups or nations ‖ sexual union between two people

in·ter·est (íntərist, íntrist) 1. n. curiosity about, or intellectual or emotional involvement in something ‖ something on which these feelings are fixed ‖ concern for one's own advantage or profit ‖ advantage, profit ‖ a legal or financial stake, right or title to a thing, she holds a 60% interest in the firm ‖ a premium paid for the use of capital ‖ the money so paid ‖ a group having a common concern in industry etc. **in the interest of** for the sake of, in the interest of humanity 2. v.t. to arouse the attention or curiosity of ‖ to cause to participate, to involve the welfare of, affect **in·ter·est·ed** adj. feeling or showing attention or curiosity ‖ having a share or concern in something and esp. likely to be prejudiced for this reason ‖ motivated by a concern for one's own welfare or gain **ín·ter·est·ing** adj.

in·ter·face (íntərfeis) n. a surface forming the common boundary of two bodies or two spaces ‖ (jargon) a device that bridges different systems, people, ideas, technologies, etc. ‖ point at which two elements of a system join ‖ the method of integrating these two elements **in·ter·fa·cial** (intərféiʃəl) adj.

in·ter·fere (intərfíər) pres. part. **in·ter·fer·ing** past and past part. **in·ter·fered** v.i. (with 'with') to conflict in such a way as to hinder something ‖ to take an active but unwelcome part in someone else's activity **in·ter·fér·ence** n. the act of interfering **in·ter·fe·ren·tial** (intərfərénʃəl) adj.

in·ter·im (íntərim) 1. n. an interval between two actions **in the interim** meanwhile 2. adj. provisional, temporary, an interim decision

in·te·ri·or (intíəri:ər) 1. adj. of, relating to or placed at the inner part of something ‖ having to do with the domestic affairs of a country ‖ in or towards the part of a country away from the coast or frontier ‖ having to do with the mind or soul ‖ having to do with the essential nature of something 2. n. the inner part of

---

(**a**) æ, cat; ɑ, car; ɔ fawn; ei, snake. (**e**) e, hen; i:, sheep; iə, deer; ɛə, bear. (**i**) i, fish; ai, tiger; ə:, bird. (**o**) o, ox; au, cow; ou, goat; u, poor; ɔi, royal. (**u**) ʌ, duck; u, bull; u:, goose; ə, bacillus; ju:, cube. x, loch; θ, think; ð, bother; z, Zen; ʒ, corsage; dʒ, savage; ŋ, orangutang; j, yak; ʃ, fish; tʃ, fetch; 'l, rabble; 'n, redden. Complete pronunciation key appears inside front cover.

something ‖ the inner character or nature of someone or something

in·ter·ject (ĭntərdʒékt) *v.t.* to interpose (a remark or question) abruptly in a conversation etc.

in·ter·jec·tion (ĭntərdʒékʃən) *n.* (*gram.*) an exclamation expressing emotion, not forming part of a sentence: it may be a word or phrase or an inarticulate cry (e.g. 'ouch!') ‖ an interjected remark ‖ the act of interjecting **in·ter·jéc·tion·al, in·ter·jec·to·ry** (ĭntərdʒéktəri:) *adjs*

in·ter·lock (ĭntərlók) *v.t.* to engage locking parts of (two things) so that they are held rigidly together ‖ to arrange (the parts of a mechanical system) so that they cannot move independently of each other ‖ *v.i.* to be connected in this way

in·ter·lope (ĭntərlóup) *pres. part.* **in·ter·lop·ing** *past* and *past part.* **in·ter·loped** *v.i.* to meddle in the affairs of others ‖ (*hist.*) to interfere illegally in the trading of others **ín·ter·lop·er** *n.* someone who interlopes ‖ someone who intrudes on the property of another

in·ter·mar·riage (ĭntərmǽridʒ) *n.* marriage between members of different social, racial, religious or tribal groups ‖ marriage between close relations

in·ter·mar·ry (ĭntərmǽri:) *pres. part.* **in·ter·mar·ry·ing** *past* and *past part.* **in·ter·mar·ried** *v.i.* (of members of different social, racial, religious or tribal groups) to marry ‖ (of closely related people) to marry

in·ter·me·di·ate (ĭntərmí:di:it) **1.** *adj.* being between two things, events, extremes etc. **2.** *n.* someone through whom two other parties communicate ‖ something between others in a series

in·ter·me·di·ate (ĭntərmí:di:eit) *pres. part.* **in·ter·me·di·at·ing** *past* and *past part.* **in·ter·me·di·at·ed** *v.i.* to act as an intermediary **in·ter·me·di·á·tion, in·ter·mé·di·a·tor** *ns*

in·ter·ment (ĭntə́:rmənt) *n.* a burial

in·ter·mi·na·ble (ĭntə́:rminəb'l) *adj.* seemingly endless, tediously long **in·tér·mi·na·bly** *adv.*

in·ter·mis·sion (ĭntərmíʃən) *n.* an interval between acts of a play or parts of any performance ‖ an interval coming between periods of activity

in·ter·mit (ĭntərmít) *pres. part.* **in·ter·mit·ting** *past* and *past part.* **in·ter·mit·ted** *v.t.* to cause to cease for a while or from time to time ‖ *v.i.* to stop for a while or from time to time

in·ter·mit·tent (ĭntərmít'nt) *adj.* stopping from time to time ‖ occurring at intervals

in·tern (ĭntə:rn) **1.** *n.* (also **ín·terne**) a newly qualified doctor serving in a hospital to complete his training **2.** *v.i.* (of a newly qualified doctor) to serve in a hospital to complete one's training ‖ *v.t.* (ĭntə́:rn) to detain (someone, esp. an alien or a prisoner of war) within prescribed boundaries

in·ter·nal (ĭntə́:rn'l) *adj.* of or on the inside ‖ inside the body ‖ involving the mind, soul, conscience etc. ‖ pertaining to the domestic affairs of a country ‖ pertaining to the essential nature of a thing, intrinsic

in·ter·na·tion·al (ĭntərnǽʃən'l) *adj.* common to, involving or used by two or more nations ‖ known or operating in more than one country

in·ter·na·tion·al·ize (ĭntərnǽʃən'laiz) *pres. part.* **in·ter·na·tion·al·iz·ing** *past* and *past part.* **in·ter·na·tion·al·ized** *v.t.* to make international in character ‖ to bring (a territory) under the combined control of several nations

in·tern·ist (ĭntə:rnist, ĭntə́:rnist) *n.* a specialist in internal medicine

in·tern·ship (ĭntə́:rnʃip) *n.* the position of an intern in a hospital ‖ the period of serving as an intern

in·ter·plan·e·tar·y (ĭntərplǽnitəri:) *adj.* situated between the planets

in·ter·play **1.** (ĭntərplei) *n.* an acting upon each other with reciprocal effect **2.** (ĭntərpléi) *v.i.* to act upon each other

in·ter·po·late (ĭntə́:rpəleit) *pres. part.* **in·ter·po·lat·ing** *past* and *past part.* **in·ter·po·lat·ed** *v.t.* to put (new words, passages etc.) into a text ‖ to alter or corrupt

(a text) by such additions ‖ to enter with (a remark) into a conversation between others ‖ (*math.*) to insert (intermediate values or terms) in a given series ‖ *v.i.* to introduce new words or passages in a text or a remark into a conversation

in·ter·po·la·tion (ĭntə:rpəléiʃən) *n.* an interpolating or being interpolated ‖ something interpolated

in·ter·pose (ĭntərpóuz) *pres. part.* **in·ter·pos·ing** *past* and *past part.* **in·ter·posed** *v.t.* to introduce (a remark etc.) into a conversation ‖ to introduce (something) so that it intervenes ‖ to introduce as an insertion ‖ *v.i.* to interrupt ‖ to intervene

in·ter·po·si·tion (ĭntərpəzíʃən) *n.* an interposing or being interposed ‖ something interposed

in·ter·pret (ĭntə́:rprit) *v.t.* to explain the meaning of (a work of art, dream etc.) ‖ to attribute a specified meaning to ‖ to express one's conception of (a role, musical work etc.) by performing it ‖ *v.i.* to act as a linguistic interpreter

in·ter·pre·ta·tion (ĭntə:rpritéiʃən) *n.* an interpreting or being interpreted ‖ an explanation produced by interpreting ‖ the act of translating a speech orally from one language into another ‖ an instance of this

in·ter·pret·er (ĭntə́:rpritər) *n.* someone who interprets, esp. someone who translates a foreign language orally, e.g. in a conversation carried on in different languages

in·ter·ro·gate (ĭntérəgeit) *pres. part.* **in·ter·ro·gat·ing** *past* and *past part.* **in·ter·ro·gat·ed** *v.t.* to ask questions of, esp. formally ‖ *v.i.* to make an interrogation

in·ter·ro·ga·tion (ĭnterəgéiʃən) *n.* the act of interrogating ‖ an instance of this ‖ a question

in·ter·rupt (ĭntərʌ́pt) *v.t.* to stop abruptly but briefly (a discussion, a person who is speaking etc.) esp. by starting to speak oneself ‖ to obstruct (a view etc.) ‖ to make a break in the continuity of ‖ *v.i.* to interfere in some action ‖ to cause a discussion, person speaking etc. to cease abruptly, esp. by entering in with a remark etc. **in·ter·rúpt·er, in·ter·rúp·tor** *n.* someone who or something that interrupts, esp. (*elec.*) a device used to open and close a circuit

in·ter·rup·tion (ĭntərʌ́pʃən) *n.* an interrupting or being interrupted ‖ something that interrupts ‖ the time during which something is interrupted

in·ter·sect (ĭntərsékt) *v.t.* to divide by passing through or across ‖ *v.i.* to meet and cross each other

in·ter·sec·tion (ĭntərsékʃən) *n.* the act of intersecting ‖ the point at which lines cut across each other (or the line at which planes do so) ‖ a place where two roads cross each other **in·ter·séc·tion·al** *adj.*

in·ter·sperse (ĭntərspə́:rs) *pres. part.* **in·ter·spers·ing** *past* and *past part.* **in·ter·spersed** *v.t.* to put here and there among other things ‖ to diversify **in·ter·sper·sion** (ĭntərspə́:rʃən) *n.*

in·ter·state (ĭntərstéit) *adj.* common to, involving or taking place between two or more states

in·ter·val (ĭntərvəl) *n.* a period of time between two actions or events ‖ a space between two points ‖ (*mus.*) the difference of pitch between two tones **at intervals** here and there ‖ now and then

in·ter·vene (ĭntərví:n) *pres. part.* **in·ter·ven·ing** *past* and *past part.* **in·ter·vened** *v.i.* to happen unexpectedly esp. so as to modify or prevent some event etc. ‖ to happen between points of time, events etc. ‖ (*law*) to impose oneself as a third party to a lawsuit so as to protect one's own interests

in·ter·ven·tion (ĭntərvénʃən) *n.* the act of intervening ‖ interference in the affairs of others, e.g. by one state in the affairs of another

in·ter·view (ĭntərvju:) **1.** *n.* a meeting of persons face to face esp. for formal discussion ‖ a formal meeting between an applicant (e.g. for a job) and the person who is to examine his qualifications ‖ a meeting between a press, radio or television reporter and a person who is to be the subject of an article, program etc. ‖ the published article or program resulting from this meeting **2.** *v.t.* to meet with (someone) to examine his qualifications or to get information etc. from him

in·tes·tate (intéstit) **1.** adj. not having made any valid will ‖ not bequeathed in a will **2.** n. a person who dies without having made a valid will

in·tes·ti·nal (intéstin'l) adj. relating to or in the intestines

in·tes·tine (intéstin) n. (usually pl.) the portion of the alimentary canal in vertebrates between the stomach and the anus

in·ti·ma·cy (íntəməsi:) pl. **in·ti·ma·cies** n. the quality or state of being intimate ‖ an intimate act ‖ (a euphemism for) illicit sexual intercourse

in·ti·mate 1. (íntəmit) adj. being on familiar, esp. affectionate, personal terms ‖ relating to or showing such an acquaintance ‖ very private and personal ‖ warmly personal ‖ resulting from close study ‖ having illicit sexual relations ‖ of or pertaining to the essential nature of something **2.** (íntəmit) n. a familiar friend **3.** (íntəmeit) v.t. pres. part. **in·ti·mat·ing** past and past part. **in·ti·mat·ed** to hint, give someone to understand (something)

in·ti·ma·tion (intəméiʃən) n. something that gives an insight or inkling ‖ the act of intimating

in·tim·i·date (intímideit) pres. part. **in·tim·i·dat·ing** past and past part. **in·tim·i·dat·ed** v.t. to frighten, esp. to influence by threats **in·tim·i·da·tion, in·tím·i·da·tor** ns

in·to (íntu:) prep. from the outside to the inside of ‖ toward the middle of (a period of time) ‖ up against ‖ acquiring the substance, form or condition of, driven into a frenzy ‖ (math.) expressing division, 3 into 27 is 9

in·tol·er·a·ble (intólərəb'l) adj. that cannot be tolerated **in·tól·er·a·bly** adv.

in·tol·er·ance (intólərəns) n. the quality or state of being intolerant

in·tol·er·ant (intólərənt) adj. not tolerating beliefs etc. that differ from one's own ‖ unfriendly or hostile towards persons of another racial or religious group

in·to·nate (íntouneit) pres. part. **in·to·nat·ing** past and past part. **in·to·nat·ed** v.t. to intone **in·to·ná·tion** n. the modulation of the voice ‖ (eccles.) the act of intoning ‖ the producing of musical sounds, with regard to accuracy of pitch **in·tone** (intóun) pres. part. **in·ton·ing** past and past part. **in·toned** v.i. to utter a droning or monotonous singing sound

in to·to (intóutou) adv. as a whole, completely, altogether

in·tox·i·cate (intóksikeit) pres. part. **in·tox·i·cat·ing** past and past part. **in·tox·i·cat·ed** v.t. (of an alcoholic drink, drug etc.) to cause to lose physical or mental control ‖ to exhilarate ‖ (med.) to poison **in·tox·i·cá·tion** n.

in·trac·ta·ble (intrǽktəb'l) adj. not docile, not easily led or persuaded ‖ (of things) unmanageable, difficult to deal with **in·trác·ta·bly** adv.

in·tra·mu·ral (intrəmjúərəl) adj. occurring within the limits of specific (esp. academic) groups, intramural athletics ‖ (biol.) within the substance of the walls of an organ or cell

in·tran·si·gence (intrǽnsidʒəns) n. the quality or state of being intransigent **in·trán·si·gen·cy** n.

in·tran·si·gent (intrǽnsidʒənt) **1.** adj. refusing to compromise, immovably adhering to a position or point of view **2.** n. a person who refuses to change his opinion or point of view

in·tran·si·tive (intrǽnsitiv) **1.** adj. (gram., of verbs) not governing a direct object **2.** n. (gram.) an intransitive verb

in·tra·per·son·al (intrəpə́:rsən'l) adj. occurring within a person's mind

in·tra·state (intrəstéit) adj. within a state

in·tra·u·ter·ine device or **intrauterine contraceptive device** (intrəjú:tərən) (med.) plastic or steel coil or loop, etc., placed within the uterus to prevent conception (abbr. IUD or IUCD)

in·tra·ve·nous (intrəví:nəs) adj. in or into a vein, intravenous feeding

in·trep·id (intrépid) adj. fearlessly facing up to danger, risk or hardship **in·tre·pid·i·ty** (intrəpíditi:) n.

in·tri·ca·cy (íntrikəsi:) pl. **in·tri·ca·cies** n. the quality or state of being intricate ‖ an intricate part or detail

in·tri·cate (íntrikit) adj. having a complicated organization, with many parts or aspects difficult to follow or grasp

in·tri·gant, in·tri·guant (íntri:gənt) n. someone who engages in intrigue **in·tri·gante, in·tri·guante** (intri:gént) n. a woman who does this

in·trigue (intrí:g, íntri:g) n. secret plotting, scheming to secure an advantage or hurt an adversary ‖ a plot

in·trigue (intrí:g) pres. part. **in·tri·guing** past and past part. **in·trigued** v.i. to use intrigue, plot secretly ‖ v.t. to arouse the interest or curiosity of

in·trin·sic (intrínsik) adj. inherent, essential ‖ (anat., esp. of certain muscles) contained completely within an organ or part **in·trín·si·cal·ly** adv.

in·tro·duce (intrədú:s, intrədjú:s) pres. part. **in·tro·duc·ing** past and past part. **in·tro·duced** v.t. to make someone acquainted with (a person) formally ‖ to make (two persons) formally acquainted with each other ‖ to bring into use or practice ‖ to add as a feature ‖ to bring into conversation etc. as a topic ‖ to lead (someone) to discover a specified subject, author etc. ‖ to offer (something new) for sale ‖ to insert, to introduce a tube into a patient's windpipe ‖ to bring (a bill etc.) before a legislative body for discussion

in·tro·duc·tion (intrədʌkʃən) n. something that introduces a subject, action etc. ‖ an explanatory or commenting section of a book, preceding the text proper and often by someone other than the book's author ‖ the opening section of a muscial composition ‖ an introducing or being introduced **introduction**

in·tro·spect (intrəspékt) v.i. to examine one's own thoughts and feelings **in·tro·spéc·tion** n. **in·tro·spéc·tive** adj.

in·tro·ver·sion (intrəvə́:rʒən, intrəvə́:rʃən) n. an introverting or being introverted ‖ (psychol.) an inclination or tendency toward introspection **in·tro·vér·sive** adj.

in·tro·vert (íntrəvə:rt) **1.** v.t. to direct (one's mind, thoughts) upon oneself ‖ (zool.) to draw (an organ) into its sheath or base **2.** n. (psychol.) someone who is more interested in himself and his own mental or emotional processes than in outside events etc. ‖ (zool.) an organ that is or can be drawn into its sheath or base **in·tro·vér·tive** adj.

in·trude (intrú:d) pres. part. **in·trud·ing** past and past part. **in·trud·ed** v.t. to thrust or force (something) in an unwelcome way ‖ (geol.) to force (molten rock) between other rock strata ‖ v.i. to enter, break in an unwelcome way

in·tru·sion (intrú:ʒən) n. the act of intruding ‖ an instance of this ‖ (law) wrongful entry upon someone else's property or seizure of his goods

in·tu·i·tion (intu:íʃən, intju:íʃən) n. (philos.) a perception or view ‖ immediate apprehension of truth, or supposed truth, in the absence of conscious rational processes **in·tu·i·tion·al** adj.

in·tu·i·tive (intú:itiv, intjú:itiv) adj. having, perceived by, or relating to intuition

in·ure (inúər, injúər) pres. part. **in·ur·ing** past and past part. **in·ured** v.t. to accustom (to something unpleasant), cause by habituation to be less sensitive ‖ v.i.

(a) æ, cat; ɑ, car; ɔ fawn; ei. snake. **(e)** e, hen; i:, sheep; iə, deer; ɛə, bear. **(i)** i, fish; ai, tiger; ə:, bird. **(o)** o, ox; au, cow; ou, goat; u, poor; ɔi, royal. **(u)** ʌ, duck; u, bull; u:, goose; ə, bacillus; ju:, cube. x, loch; θ, think; ð, bother; z, Zen; ʒ, corsage; dʒ, savage; ŋ, orangutang; j, yak; ʃ, fish; tʃ, fetch; 'l, rabble; 'n, redden. Complete pronunciation key appears inside front cover.

(law) to come into operation, take effect **in·úre·ment** *n.*

in·vade (invéid) *pres. part.* **in·vad·ing** *past* and *past part.* **in·vad·ed** *v.t.* to enter (a country, region etc.) esp. by armed force ‖ to crowd into as if taking possession of ‖ to encroach on ‖ to intrude upon ‖ *v.i.* to make an invasion

in·val·id (invǽlid) *adj.* not valid, having no legal force, *an invalid contract*

in·va·lid (ínvəlid) 1. *adj.* ill, esp. chronically ill or disabled ‖ suitable for a sick person 2. *n.* an invalid person 3. *v.t.* to make ill, disable ‖ (with 'out of') to remove, release from esp. military service as an invalid

in·val·u·a·ble (invǽlju:əb'l) *adj.* having a value too great to be measured ‖ *(loosely)* very valuable **in·vál·u·a·bly** *adv.*

in·var·i·a·ble (invέəri:əb'l) 1. *adj.* never changing, constant 2. *n.* something constant **in·vár·i·a·bly** *adv.*

in·va·sion (invéiʒən) *n.* an invading or being invaded ‖ *(med.,* of a disease) the onset

in·vent (invént) *v.t.* to devise, originate (a new device, method etc.) ‖ to think up

in·ven·tion (invénʃən) *n.* the act of inventing ‖ something invented ‖ the ability to think things up, ingenuity

in·ven·to·ry (ínvəntɔri:, ínvəntɔuri:) 1. *pl.* **in·ven·to·ries** *n.* an itemized list, esp. of property ‖ the making of such a list ‖ *(commerce)* stocktaking 2. *v.t. pres. part.* **in·ven·to·ry·ing** *past* and *past part.* **in·ven·to·ried** to make an inventory of

in·verse (invə́:rs, ínvə:rs) 1. *adj.* inverted in position or relation, reversed 2. *n.* a direct opposite

in·ver·sion (invə́:rʒən, invə́:rʃən) *n.* an inverting or being inverted ‖ something inverted ‖ *(gram.)* a reversal of the usual order of the words in a sentence ‖ *(meteor.)* an unusual condition in a layer of air in which the warmest portion is closest to the earth, near the surface ‖ homosexuality

in·vert 1. (invə́:rt) *v.t.* to turn upside down ‖ to reverse the order or position of ‖ *(mus.)* to change the relative position of the notes of (a chord, interval or phrase) ‖ *v.i. (chem.)* to undergo inversion 2. (ínvə:rt) *n.* a homosexual

in·ver·te·brate (invə́:rtəbrit, invə́:rtəbreit) 1. *adj.* having no backbone 2. *n.* an animal having no internal skeleton or backbone

in·vest (invést) *v.t.* to put (money) to a use expected to yield a profit or income ‖ to confer the insignia of office or rank upon ‖ to envelop, wrap up as if in a cloak

in·ves·ti·gate (invéstigeit) *pres. part.* **in·ves·ti·gat·ing** *past* and *past part.* **in·ves·ti·gat·ed** *v.t.* to seek information about by searching into or examining ‖ *v.i.* to make an investigation

in·ves·ti·ga·tion (invèstigéiʃən) *n.* an examination for the purpose of discovering information about something ‖ the process of investigating

in·ves·ti·ga·tor (invéstigeitər) *n.* someone who investigates

in·ves·ti·ture (invéstitʃər) *n.* the act or ceremony of investing someone with an honor or office

in·vest·ment (invéstmənt) *n.* the act of investing, esp. of money ‖ something invested, esp. money ‖ something in which money is invested ‖ the outer covering of an animal ‖ *(zool.)* the outer layer of an organ

in·ves·tor (invéstər) *n.* someone who invests

in·vet·er·ate (invétərit) *adj.* deep-rooted, firmly established ‖ confirmed in some habit

in·vid·i·ous (invídi:əs) *adj.* causing envy or ill-feeling, esp. by unfair discrimination

in·vig·o·rate (invígəreit) *pres. part.* **in·vig·o·rat·ing** *past* and *past part.* **in·vig·o·rat·ed** *v.t.* to fill with vigor, enliven **in·vig·o·rá·tion** *n.*

in·vin·ci·ble (invínsəb'l) *adj.* that cannot be conquered or overcome **in·vín·ci·bly** *adv.*

in·vi·o·la·ble (inváiələb'l) *adj.* that cannot be violated ‖ that must not be violated **in·ví·o·la·bly** *adv.*

in·vis·i·ble (invízəb'l) *adj.* that cannot be seen because

of its nature ‖ that cannot be seen because it is concealed, very small etc. ‖ *(commerce,* e.g. of goodwill) not accountable in regular statements

in·vite (inváit) *pres. part.* **in·vit·ing** *past* and *past part.* **in·vit·ed** *v.t.* to ask (someone) hospitably to come somewhere or to do or participate in something ‖ to ask for ‖ to request (someone to do something) ‖ to tend to bring about unintentionally **in·vít·ing** *adj.* tempting, attractive

in·voice (ínvɔis) 1. *n.* an itemized list of goods dispatched or delivered to a buyer, with prices and charges 2. *v.t. pres. part.* **in·voic·ing** *past* and *past part.* **in·voiced** to make an invoice of (goods)

in·voke (invóuk) *pres. part.* **in·vok·ing** *past* and *past part* **in·voked** *v.t.* to appeal to (God, a deity etc.) in prayer etc. ‖ to ask for in supplication ‖ to refer to for support etc.

in·vol·un·tar·i·ly (invɔ́lənteri:, invɔləntέərili:) *adv.* in an involuntary manner

in·vol·un·tar·y (invɔ́lənteri:) *adj.* not intended ‖ *(physiol.)* of reactions which are not controlled by the will, e.g. the movements of the esophagus in swallowing

in·volve (invɔ́lv) *pres. part.* **in·volv·ing** *past* and *past part.* **in·volved** *v.t.* to include, concern ‖ to entail **in·vólved** *adj.* complicated **in·vólve·ment** *n.*

in·vul·ner·a·ble (invʌ́lnərəb'l) *adj.* not susceptible to injury, damages etc. ‖ able to resist any attack **in·vúl·ner·a·bly** *adv.*

in·ward (ínwərd) 1. *adj.* directed toward the inside ‖ relating to the mind or soul 2. *adv.* toward the inside ‖ into the mind or soul

in·ward·ly (ínwərdli:) *adv.* internally ‖ in mind or spirit ‖ so as not to be audible

in·wards (ínwərdz) *adv.* inward

i·o·dine (áiədain) *n.* a nonmetallic element

i·on (áiɒn, áiən) *n. (chem.)* an atom or group of atoms which has either an excess or a deficiency of electrons and is thus electrically charged

i·o·ta (aióutə) *n.* a very small amount

i·rate (airéit) *adj.* angry or showing anger

ire (áiər) *n. (rhet.)* anger **íre·ful** *adj.*

ir·i·des·cent (ìridés'nt) *adj.* having shifting rainbowlike colors

i·ris (áiris) *pl.* **i·ris·es, i·ri·des** (íridi:z, áiridi:z) *n.* the broad colored muscular ring surrounding the pupil of the eye ‖ *(pl.* also **i·ris**) a member of *Iris,* fam. *Iridaceae,* a genus of perennial plants with rhizomes or bulbs

irk (ə:rk) *v.t.* to irritate, annoy **irk·some** (ə́:rksəm) *adj.*

i·ron (áiərn) 1. *n.* a widely occurring and widely used metallic element that is heavy, malleable, ductile, magnetic, and silver gray in color ‖ an implement, formerly of iron but now usually of stainless steel, used hot to press garments etc. ‖ a branding iron ‖ *(golf)* a club with an iron or steel head used for lofting the ball ‖ a preparation containing iron, used to combat anemia etc. **to have other** (or **many) irons in the fire** to have other (or many) projects in hand 2. *v.t.* to press with an iron ‖ to cover or furnish with iron **to iron out** to remove (a difficulty etc.)

i·ron·clad (áiərnklæd) 1. *adj.* protected with iron plates ‖ (e.g. of contracts or agreements) hard to break, not readily changed 2. *n. (hist.)* a wooden ship armored with iron plates

i·ron·ic (airɒ́nik) *adj.* of, using, or said in irony **i·rón·i·cal** *adj.*

i·ro·ny (áiərni:) *pl.* **i·ro·nies** *n.* a manner of speaking or writing in which the meaning literally expressed is the opposite of the meaning intended and which aims at ridicule, humor or sarcasm

ir·ra·di·ate (iréidi:eit) *pres. part.* **ir·ra·di·at·ing** *past* and *past part.* **ir·ra·di·at·ed** *v.t.* to treat by exposure to infrared, ultraviolet, X rays or other rays ‖ to shine on, light up ‖ to give out, radiate ‖ to make suddenly intensely clear

ir·ra·di·a·tion (irèidi:éiʃən) *n.* treatment by exposure to radiation (e.g. heat, X rays, radioactive emanations)

‖ the emission of radiation as heat, light etc. ‖ the apparent increase in brightness of a white or light-colored object when seen against a dark background

ir·ra·tion·al (irǽʃən'l) *adj.* not rational, unreasonable ‖ without reasoning power ‖ *(math.)* not commensurable with a finite number

ir·rec·on·cil·a·ble (irékənsáiləb'l, irękənsáiləb'l) **1.** *adj.* incapable of being placated or won over ‖ incompatible, inconsistent **2.** *n.* a person who is irreconcilable, esp. one who opposes compromise as a matter of principle ‖ *(pl.)* ideas, beliefs etc. that cannot be brought into agreement **ir·réc·on·cil·a·bly** *adv.*

ir·re·deem·a·ble (iridí:məb'l) *adj.* that cannot be reclaimed or reformed ‖ (of paper money) not capable of being exchanged for coin ‖ (of a government loan or annuity) not redeemable **ir·re·déem·a·bly** *adv.*

ir·re·duc·i·ble (iridú:səb'l, iridjú:səb'l) *adj.* that cannot be reduced or made smaller ‖ unable to be expressed in simpler terms **ir·re·dúc·i·bly** *adv.*

ir·ref·u·ta·ble (iréfjutəb'l, irifjú:təb'l) *adj.* that cannot be refuted **ir·réf·u·ta·bly** *adv.*

ir·reg·u·lar (irégjulər) **1.** *adj.* not following an even pattern or sequence of occurrence, activity etc. ‖ asymmetrical ‖ not in accordance with normal practice ‖ *(gram.)* not inflected or declined in the usual manner ‖ *(mil.,* of a soldier) not belonging to the standing army of a country ‖ *(bot.,* of the parts of a plant) not uniform in shape etc. **2.** *n. (pl.)* irregular troops

ir·reg·u·lar·i·ty (iręgjulǽriti) *pl.* **ir·reg·u·lar·i·ties** *n.* the quality or state of being irregular ‖ something irregular

ir·rel·e·vance (iréləvəns) *n.* the quality or state of being irrelevant ‖ something irrelevant **ir·rél·e·van·cy** *pl.* **ir·rel·e·van·cies** *n.*

ir·rel·e·vant (iréləvənt) *adj.* not applicable, not related to whatever is being considered, discussed etc.

ir·re·me·di·a·ble (irimí:di:əb'l) *adj.* that cannot be remedied or corrected **ir·re·mé·di·a·bly** *adv.*

ir·re·mis·si·ble (irimísəb'l) *adj.* unpardonable ‖ (of an obligation etc.) inescapable **ir·re·mis·si·bly** *adv.*

ir·rep·a·ra·ble (irépərəb'l) *adj.* that cannot be repaired, remedied, retrieved etc. **ir·rép·a·ra·bly** *adv.*

ir·re·place·a·ble (iripléisəb'l) *adj.* for whom or for which there is no substitute, that cannot be replaced if broken, lost etc.

ir·re·pres·si·ble (iriprésəb'l) *adj.* that cannot be controlled or repressed **ir·re·prés·si·bly** *adv.*

ir·re·proach·a·ble (iripróutʃəb'l) *adj.* not subject to reproach, having or showing no faults or flaws **ir·re·próach·a·bly** *adv.*

ir·re·sist·i·ble (irizístəb'l) *adj.* too powerful, tempting, charming etc. to be resisted **ir·re·síst·i·bly** *adv.*

ir·res·o·lute (irézəlu:t) *adj.* hesitant, undecided ‖ habitually lacking firmness of purpose

ir·re·spec·tive (irispéktiv) *adv.* (only in the phrase) **irrespective of** without regard to

ir·re·spon·si·ble (irispónsəb'l) *adj.* having or showing no sense of responsibility ‖ not legally responsible for one's actions **ir·re·spón·si·bly** *adv.*

ir·rev·er·ence (irévərəns) *n.* the quality or state of being irreverent ‖ an irreverent action, remark etc.

ir·rev·er·ent (irévərənt) *adj.* lacking reverence ‖ lacking respect

ir·rev·o·ca·ble (irévəkəb'l) *adj.* that cannot be revoked or altered **ir·rév·o·ca·bly** *adv.*

ir·ri·gate (írigeit) *pres. part.* **ir·ri·gat·ing** *past and past part.* **ir·ri·gat·ed** *v.t.* to provide (land) with water by building artificial channels, flooding, spraying etc. ‖ *(med.)* to wash (a wound etc.) with a constant flow of liquid

ir·ri·ga·tion (įrigéiʃən) *n.* the artificial increase of water supply to assist the growing of crops ‖ *(med.)* washing with a flow of water for cleansing and disinfecting **ir·ri·gá·tion·al** *adj.*

ir·ri·ta·ble (íritəb'l) *adj.* easily annoyed, apt to become impatient or exasperated ‖ (of a part of the body) oversensitive, apt to become sore, inflamed etc. ‖ *(physiol.,* of nerves etc.) very sensitive to stimuli **ir·ri·ta·bly** *adv.*

ir·ri·tate (íriteit) *pres. part.* **ir·ri·tat·ing** *past and past part.* **ir·ri·tat·ed** *v.t.* to cause to be impatiently angry, annoy ‖ to make sore or uncomfortable

ir·ri·ta·tion (įritéiʃən) *n.* an irritating or being irritated ‖ something that irritates

is·land (áilənd) **1.** *n.* a piece of land, smaller than a continent, entirely surrounded by water **2.** *v.t.* to cause to be or to resemble an island ‖ to isolate ‖ to cause to be dotted with or as if with islands **is·land·er** *n.* someone who lives or was born on an island

is·let (áilit) *n.* a small island

i·so·late (áisəleit) *pres. part.* **i·so·lat·ing** *past and past part.* **i·so·lat·ed** *v.t.* to place apart and alone ‖ to place (a patient with a contagious disease) apart from others to prevent the spread of the disease ‖ *(chem.)* to obtain (a substance) from one of its compounds ‖ *(elec.)* to insulate

i·so·la·tion (àisəléiʃən) *n.* an isolating or being isolated **i·so·la·tion·ism** (aisəléiʃənįzəm) *n.* the policy of avoiding alliances and undertakings with other countries

i·sos·ce·les (aisósəli:z) *adj.* (of a triangle) having two sides equal

is·sue (íʃu:) **1.** *n.* a flowing, going or passing out ‖ a place or means of going or flowing out, outlet ‖ a publishing or giving out ‖ something published or given out ‖ a question, point etc. under dispute or discussion, a matter of concern ‖ *(law)* offspring **at issue** in disagreement ‖ in dispute **2.** *v. pres. part.* **is·su·ing** *past and past part.* **is·sued** *v.i.* to come or flow forth ‖ to be derived, result ‖ *(law)* to be descended ‖ to be put into circulation ‖ *v.t.* to publish or give out

isth·mus (ísməs) *n.* a narrow strip of land joining two larger tracts

it (it) **1.** *pron.*, *3rd person sing., nominative and objective cases* an inanimate object, infant, animal, group or collection, unidentified person, idea, situation etc. already mentioned or under examination, *what is it?, he saw the house the day before it burned, he saw it, they argued about it for hours* ‖ the subject of an impersonal verb, expressing a state or condition ‖ the anticipatory subject or object of a verb whose actual subject, object or complement is another word, phrase or clause, *it is my sister whom you are looking for* ‖ the indefinite object after verbs which usually have no object, *to rough it, to go it alone* **2.** *n. (children's games)* the player whose turn it is to chase or hunt for the other players

I·tal·ic (itǽlik) **1.** *adj.* of or relating to ancient Italy, usually excluding Rome ‖ designating the branch of Indo-European languages incl. Latin, ancient Italian languages, and the Romance languages descended from Latin **i·tal·ic** of, relating to or printed in a type slanting to the upper right **2.** *n.* the Italic languages collectively **i·tal·ics** *pl. n.* italic letters

i·tal·i·cize (itǽlisaiz) *pres. part.* **i·tal·i·ciz·ing** *past and past part.* **i·tal·i·cized** *v.t.* to print in italics ‖ to underline (printer's copy) to indicate that it should be set in italics ‖ *v.i.* to use italics

itch (itʃ) *n.* an irritation or tickle in the skin ‖ a restless longing

itch *v.i.* to feel an irritating or tickling sensation ‖ to

(**a**) æ, cat; ɑ, car; ɔ fawn; ei, snake. (**e**) e, hen; i:, sheep; iə, deer; ɛə, bear. (**i**) i, fish; ai, tiger; ə:, bird. (**o**) o, ox; au, cow; ou, goat; u, poor; ɔi, royal. (**u**) ʌ, duck; u, bull; u:, goose; ə, bacillus; ju:, cube. x, loch; θ, think; ð, bother; z, Zen; ʒ, corsage; dʒ, savage; ŋ, orangutang; j, yak; ʃ, fish; tʃ, fetch; 'l, rabble; 'n, redden. Complete pronunciation key appears inside front cover.

have a restless longing

itch·y (ítʃi:) *comp.* **itch·i·er** *superl.* **itch·i·est** *adj.* feeling or causing an itch

i·tem (ítəm) **1.** *adv.* likewise (used only when introducing a new article in a list etc.) **2.** *n.* a single article, unit, feature or particular in a list, account, series, collection etc. ‖ a piece of news **i·tem·ize** (áitəmaiz) *pres. part.* **i·tem·iz·ing** *past* and *past part.* **i·tem·ized** *v.t.* to set down and specify the items of, *to itemize a bill*

it·er·ate (ítəreit) *pres. part.* **it·er·at·ing** *past* and *past part.* **it·er·at·ed** *v.t.* to say again, repeat

i·tin·er·ant (aitínərənt, itínərənt) *adj.* traveling from place to place ‖ involving travel from place to place

i·tin·er·ar·y (aitínərəri:, itínərəri:) *pl.* **i·tin·er·ar·ies** *n.* a route taken or planned ‖ a record or account of a journey ‖ a guidebook

its (its) *possessive adj.* of, pertaining to or belonging to it, *he dropped the pitcher and broke its spout* ‖ experienced, made or done by it

it·self (itsélf) *pron.* refl. form of IT ‖ emphatic form of IT **by itself** unaided ‖ in isolation, alone **in itself** considered for itself alone, intrinsically

i·vo·ry (áivəri:, áivri:) *pl.* **i·vo·ries** *n.* the hard creamy-white dentine forming the tusks of the elephant, and the canine teeth of the hippopotamus, narwhal and walrus ‖ the dentine of any teeth ‖ the color of ivory ‖ *(pl.)* things made of ivory, esp. *(pop.)* piano keys, teeth, dice

i·vy (áivi:) *n.* an evergreen woody climbing or creeping plant

J

J, j (dʒei) the tenth letter of the English alphabet

jab (dʒæb) **1.** *v.t. pres. part.* **jab·bing** *past* and *past part.* **jabbed** to penetrate suddenly with a pointed object ‖ to thrust ‖ to poke sharply ‖ to give a short straight blow with the fist to ‖ *v.i.* (with 'at') to make short thrusts **2.** *n.* a quick poke or stab

jab·ber (dʒǽbər) **1.** *v.i.* to talk rapidly without making the meaning clear ‖ to make unintelligible sounds resembling speech ‖ *v.t.* to say in a confused manner **2.** *n.* this kind of speech or noise

jack (dʒæk) **1.** *n.* a device for raising an automobile or other heavy load, e.g. by a screw or lever system or by a hydraulic system ‖ *(naut.)* a small flag flown usually from the bow to show nationality, or as a signal ‖ a playing card depicting a soldier or servant, ranking in value just below a queen ‖ the male of various animals ‖ the white ball in a game of bowls ‖ a jackstone **2.** *v.t.* (with 'up') to lift with a jack ‖ (with 'up') to raise or increase

jack·ass (dʒǽkæs) *n.* the male ass ‖ a stupid person

jack·et (dʒǽkit) **1.** *n.* a short coat, worn as part of a suit or with nonmatching trousers or skirt ‖ a detachable paper cover of a book ‖ the metal casing of a projectile ‖ the skin of a cooked potato **2.** *v.t.* to surround with a jacket

jack·knife (dʒǽknaif) *pl.* **jack·knives** (dʒǽknaivz) *n.* a large pocketknife ‖ a dive in which the diver keeps his legs straight and touches his feet before straightening out to enter the water **2.** *v.i. pres. part.* **jack·knif·ing** *past* and *past part.* **jack·knifed** to perform a jackknife dive

jack·pot (dʒǽkpɒt) *n.* *(gambling,* esp. *poker)* the accumulated kitty **to hit the jackpot** *(pop.)* to win all there is to win ‖ *(pop.)* to be suddenly very successful

jade (dʒeid) *n.* a hard stone that is either jadeite or nephrite, used in jewelry, ornaments etc.

jad·ed (dʒéidid) *adj.* dulled by satiety ‖ tired

jag·uar (dʒǽgwɑr) *pl.* **jag·uars, jag·uar** *n.* a large carnivore found in the American tropics, having brownish-yellow fur with dark spots each encircled with a dark ring

jai a·lai (háilai) *pl.* **jai a·lais** *n.* a game of Basque origin involving two or four players who use wicker baskets attached to the wrist to catch and fling a small hard ball against the wall of a long court of varying dimensions

jail (dʒeil) **1.** *n.* a civil prison **2.** *v.t.* to put in prison

jail·bird (dʒéilbə:rd) *n.* someone who is, or who is often, in jail

ja·lop·y (dʒəlópi:) *pl.* **ja·lop·ies** *n.* *(pop.)* an old dilapidated model, esp. an automobile

jal·ou·sie (dʒǽləsi:) *n.* a shutter or blind consisting of horizontal, often adjustable, overlapping slats inclined at an angle to the vertical

jam (dʒæm) *n.* a sweet thick mixture made by simmering fruit with sugar at the boiling point

jam *v. pres. part.* **jam·ming** *past* and *past part.* **jammed** *v.t.* to force (a body) to enter a confined or small space ‖ to bruise by crushing between two solid objects ‖ (with 'against' or 'down') to force or push ‖ to block or impede the movement of by crowding etc. ‖ to force or wedge (a movable part of a machine) ‖ *(radio)* to interfere with (reception) by superimposing signals on the transmitting wavelength ‖ *v.i.* to become immovably fixed or wedged ‖ to crowd tightly together **to jam on the brakes** to apply the brakes of a vehicle suddenly and forcefully

jamb (dʒæm) *n.* one of the vertical sides of a doorframe, windowframe, fireplace etc.

jam·bo·ree (dʒæmbəri:) *n.* an international scouts' camp ‖ *(pop.)* a festive gathering ‖ *(pop.)* a spree

jan·gle (dʒǽg'l) **1.** *n.* an unpleasant combination of clanging or ringing sounds **2.** *v. pres. part.* **jan·gling** *past* and *past part.* **jan·gled** *v.i.* to produce this sound ‖ *v.t.* to make (something) produce this sound

jan·i·tor (dʒǽnitər) *n.* a caretaker of a building, set of offices etc. ‖ a doorkeeper **jan·i·tress** *n.* a woman janitor

Jan·u·ar·y (dʒǽnju:eri:) *n.* (*abbr.* Jan.) the 1st month of the year, having 31 days

jar (dʒɑr) *n.* a container of earthenware, glass or stone, usually without a handle, and cylindrical in shape, with a short wide neck (or none) and wide mouth ‖ the quantity contained in a jar

jar 1. *v.t. pres. part.* **jar·ring** *past* and *past part.* **jarred** to make an impact on (a body) which causes it to vibrate irregularly ‖ to make a discordant sound by impact on (the eardrum) ‖ to stimulate (someone) in such a way as to cause unpleasant nervous responses ‖ *v.i.* to vibrate in an irregular way ‖ (of colors, shapes, styles etc., or of a sound, or of opinions or interests) to be discordant ‖ (with 'on' or 'upon') to have an unpleasant effect on the sympathies **2.** *n.* a discordant sound or an irregular vibration resulting from an impact or stimulus

jar·di·niere, jar·di·nière (dʒɑrd'niér, esp. *Br.* ʒɑrdinjéər) *n.* an ornamental stand for plant pots ‖ a large ornamental receptacle for a potted plant

jar·gon (dʒɑrgən) *n.* the vocabulary of a specialized field, esp. when it is unnecessarily obscure to the uninitiated

jaun·dice (dʒɔ́ndis) **1.** *n.* a yellowish coloring of the skin, whites of the eyes and various body tissues and body fluids. It results from excessive bile in the bloodstream due to damage to or malfunction of the liver or bile ducts **2.** *pres. part.* **jaun·dic·ing** *past* and *past part.* **jaun·diced** *v.t.* to cause (someone) to become hostile or embittered **jáun·diced** *adj.* afflicted with jaundice ‖ hostile, embittered

jaunt (dʒɔnt) **1.** *n.* a short journey made purely for pleasure **2.** *v.i.* to make such a journey

jaun·ty (dʒɔ́nti:) *comp.* **jaun·ti·er** *superl.* **jaun·ti·est** *adj.* gay and perky, spirited

jave·lin (dʒǽvlin, dʒǽvəlin) *n.* a lightweight spear, thrown by hand, esp. *(hist.)* as a weapon of war or for hunting ‖ *(sports)* an adaptation of this, with a shaft not less than 260 cm. (about 8½ ft), thrown for distance as a field event

jaw (dʒɔ) **1.** *n.* either of two bony or cartilaginous structures of vertebrates forming part of the mouth ‖ *(pl.)* these structures and the attached muscles and nerves which make it possible to open and close the mouth ‖ a similar structure in invertebrates ‖ *(pl.)* the parts of a tool between which things are gripped or crushed ‖ *(pl.)* the narrow entrance into a ravine etc. **2.** *v.i.* to talk at great length, esp. in reproach ‖ to chat

jazz (dʒæz) **1.** *n.* syncopated music played over strong dance rhythm ‖ dance music derived from this ‖ a dance to this music **2.** *v.i.* to play or dance jazz ‖ *v.t.* to transform or arrange (music) into jazz ‖ (with 'up') *(pop.)* to make more lively **jázz·y** *comp.* **jazz·i·er** *superl.* **jazz·i·est** *adj.* resembling jazz ‖ *(pop.)* excessively vivid or ostentatious

jeal·ous (dʒéləs) *adj.* racked by jealousy ‖ manifesting jealousy

jeal·ous·y (dʒéləsi:) *pl.* **jeal·ous·ies** *n.* a state of fear, suspicion or envy caused by a real or imagined threat or challenge to one's possessive instincts ‖ a zealous desire to preserve an existing situation or relationship

jeans (dʒi:nz) *pl. n.* pants made from a heavy durable cotton cloth in a twill weave

jeep (dʒi:p) *n.* (esp. *mil.*) a small, strong motor vehicle with four-wheel drive

jeer (dʒiər) **1.** *v.i.* to speak in mockery or derision ‖ (with 'at') to scoff or laugh with contempt, *to jeer at an idea* ‖ *v.t.* to pour scorn on **2.** *n.* the act of jeering ‖ a jeering remark or noise

Je·ho·vah (dʒihóuvə) *n.* an Old Testament name for God used by Christians

je·june (dʒidʒú:n) *adj.* *(rhet.)* lacking substance or nourishment ‖ (of a speech or writing) lacking interest or substance ‖ juvenile, immature

jel·ly (dʒéli:) **1.** *pl.* **jel·lies** *n.* a semitransparent, soft food preparation, having an elastic consistency due to the presence of gelatin or other gelatinous substances, used e.g. as a garnish or preservative for meats, or with the addition of fruit juices as a dessert ‖ a food prepared by boiling fruit containing pectin with sugar and allowing the juice to cool ‖ any substance resembling this in consistency **2.** *v. pres. part.* **jel·ly·ing** *past* and *past part.* **jel·lied** *v.i.* to become jelly ‖ *v.t.* to make into jelly

jel·ly·fish (dʒéli:fiʃ) *n.* any of several marine coelenterates that are the sexually reproducing forms of hydrozoans and scyphozoans which exhibit alternation of generations ‖ *(pop.)* someone lacking in self-reliance and firmness of will

jeop·ard·ize (dʒépərdaiz) *pres. part.* **jeop·ard·iz·ing** *past* and *past part.* **jeop·ard·ized** *v.t.* to put in jeopardy

jeop·ard·y (dʒépərdi:) *n.* the state of being exposed to danger ‖ *(law)* the state of being liable to conviction

jerk (dʒəːrk) **1.** *n.* a sudden, abrupt movement or change of motion ‖ an involuntary muscular spasm due to reflex action **2.** *v.t.* to move (a body) by applying a short, sudden force ‖ to throw or bowl (a ball) without following through ‖ to utter in short, abrupt phrases ‖ *v.i.* to move with sudden stops and starts ‖ to make a sudden, short movement ‖ to throw or bowl a ball without following through

jerk *v.t.* to cure (meat, esp. beef) by drying long thin strips of it in the sun

jerk·y (dʒə́ːrki:) *comp.* **jerk·i·er** *superl.* **jerk·i·est** *adj.* moving in jerks ‖ characterized by jerks

jer·sey (dʒə́ːrzi:) *n.* a machine-knitted cloth of wool, cotton, silk etc. ‖ an article of clothing for the upper body, knitted of wool or cotton, with long or short sleeves

jest (dʒest) **1.** *n.* a word or deed designed to evoke laughter ‖ a taunting remark or action ‖ an object which excites both laughter and contempt **2.** *v.i.* to speak frivolously or jokingly ‖ to speak tauntingly **jést·er** *n.* a person who jests ‖ *(hist.)* a professional buffoon employed by a king or nobleman as a member of his household

Je·sus (dʒí:zəs) (c. 6 B.C.–30 A.D.) a Jewish religious leader whom Christians worship as the Son of God and Savior of Mankind, the Christ

jet (dʒet) **1.** *n.* a stream of vapor, gas or liquid coming out fast from a narrow orifice ‖ the narrow pipe or orifice which controls such a stream ‖ an airplane having a jet engine ‖ a jet engine **2.** *v. pres. part.* **jet·ting** *past* and *past part.* **jet·ted** *v.i.* to issue as a jet ‖ *v.i.* to emit a jet of

jet engine a motor deriving propulsive power from jets of fuel combustion products and heated air that are discharged rearward with great velocity, to give forward motion

jet lag fatigue, irritability, and other mental and physical symptoms resulting from travel through several times zones *also* jet fatigue, jet syndrome

jet·sam (dʒétsəm) *n.* the cargo, gear etc. thrown overboard from a ship in distress to lighten the load. It sinks or is washed ashore

jet stream a narrow current of high-velocity westerly winds, close to the tropopause

jet·ti·son (dʒétis'n) **1.** *n.* the act of throwing cargo, gear etc. overboard to lighten the load of a ship in distress **2.** *v.t.* to throw overboard as jetsam ‖ to discard (part of any load) which has become an encumbrance

jet·ty (dʒéti:) *pl.* **jet·ties** *n.* a structure built out into the water of a sea, lake or river to shelter a harbor or to break waves or currents ‖ a small landing wharf

Jew (dju:) *n.* a member of the worldwide Semitic group who claim descent from Abraham and whose religion is Judaism ‖ a descendant of Jacob, an Israelite ‖ a member of the Hebrew tribe of Judah ‖ *(hist.)* an inhabitant of the ancient kingdom of Judah

jew·el (dʒú:əl) *n.* a precious stone prized for its beauty and rarity, e.g. an emerald or ruby ‖ an ornament of gold, platinum, silver or other costly metal set with precious stones ‖ a pivot bearing made of precious stone, esp. a ruby, in a watch ‖ a person, often one socially inferior, whose qualities one is praising **jéw·eled, jéw·elled** *adj.* set with jewels

jew·el·er, jew·el·ler (dʒú:ələr) *n.* someone who trades in or makes jewelry

jew·el·ry, esp. *Br.* **jew·el·ler·y** (dʒú:əlri) *n.* *(collect.)* personal ornaments made of precious or base metals, and precious or imitation stones

jib (dʒib) *n.* *(naut.)* a triangular sail stretching from the masthead to the bowsprit or from the foretopmast head to the jibboom ‖ the long arm of a crane ‖ the boom of a derrick

jig (dʒig) **1.** *n.* a rapid, gay, springy dance ‖ the music for such a dance ‖ a gigue ‖ *(engin.)* a device which maintains the proper positional relationship between a material and the machine that is working on it **2.** *v. pres. part.* **jig·ging** *past* and *past part.* **jigged** *v.t.* to dance as a jig ‖ to move (something) up and down in rapid succession ‖ *(engin.)* to use a jig on ‖ *v.i.* to dance a jig ‖ to move with rapid up-and-down motions **jig·ger** *n.* a person or thing that jigs

jig·gle (dʒíg'l) *pres. part.* **jig·gling** *past* and *past part.* **jig·gled** *v.i.* to move in quick little successive motions ‖ *v.t.* to cause (something) to move with quick little successive motions

jig·saw (dʒígsɔ) *n.* a mechanical saw with a vertical blade used to cut along irregular or curved lines ‖ a jigsaw puzzle

jilt (dʒilt) *v.t.* to break with (a lover who does not want to end the relationship) in a callously light hearted way

jim·my (dʒími:) **1.** *pl.* **jim·mies** *n.* a thick bar of iron with one end flattened as a chisel edge, used by burglars for forcing doors or windows **2.** *v.t. pres. part.* **jim·my·ing** *past* and *past part.* **jim·mied** to pry open esp. with a jimmy

jin·gle (dʒíŋg'l) **1.** *v. pres. part.* **jin·gling** *past* and *past part.* **jin·gled** *v.t.* to cause (something) to produce a jingle ‖ *v.i.* to make a jingle **2.** *n.* a pleasing sound composed of a number of high-pitched percussion notes in continuous but unrhythmical combination ‖ something which produces a jingle ‖ a catchy succession of words that ring against one another due to alliteration, rhyme etc. **jin·gly** *adj.*

jinx (dʒinks) **1.** *n.* *(pop.)* a person or thing bringing bad luck ‖ *(pop.)* an evil spell **2.** *v.t.* *(pop.)* to cause (someone) bad luck ‖ *(pop.)* to put a jinx on (someone)

jit·ter (dʒítər) **1.** *v.i.* to tremble with anxiety **2.** *n.* (esp. *pl.*) a fit of acute anxiety **jit·ter·y** *adj.*

job (dʒɒb) **1.** *n.* a specific piece of work, esp. done for pay ‖ an occupation as a steady source of livelihood ‖ *(pop.)* a robbery or burglary etc. ‖ a public office turned to private advantage **to make a good job of something** to do something well **2.** *v.t. pres. part.* **job·bing** *past* and *past part.* **jobbed** to pass (specific pieces of work) to others for an agreed price ‖ to buy and sell (goods) as a middleman ‖ to buy and sell (stocks and shares) ‖ *v.i.* to do various pieces of work, from time to time, for pay ‖ to turn public office to private advantage **jób·ber** *n.* a stockjobber ‖ a middleman ‖ a corrupt public servant **jób·ber·y** *n.* the act of jobbing by a public servant

job lot a collection of miscellaneous articles, usually of small value, offered for sale as a single lot ‖ an inferior set (of goods, objects etc.) ‖ (of paper) an amount less than a standard saleable quantity

jock·ey (dʒɒki:) **1.** *n.* a professional rider in horse racing **2.** *v.t.* to edge (a person, thing, situation) by tact in the direction one wishes to impose ‖ to ride (a horse) as jockey ‖ *v.i.* to work one's way into a better position by deft handling of a person, thing or situation

jo·cose (dʒoukóus) *adj.* given to joking, full of jokes **jo·cos·i·ty** (dʒoukɔ́siti:) *n.*

joc·u·lar (dʒɒkjulər) *adj.* joking or given to joking **joc·u·lar·i·ty** (dʒɒkjulǽriti:) *n.*

joc·und (dʒɒkənd, dʒóukənd) *adj.* *(rhet.)* likely to inspire joyfulness ‖ cheerful **joc·ún·di·ty** *n.*

jodh·purs (dʒɒdpuərz) *pl. n.* pants for horseback riding, fitting tightly from the knee to the ankle, worn with a low boot

jog (dʒog) **1.** *v. pres. part.* **jog·ging** *past* and *past part.* **jogged** *v.t.* to give (something) a slight push ‖ to cause (something) to move or become active ‖ *v.i.* to move as if forced to do so by a series of pushes ‖ (with 'on' or 'along') to move along at a regular pace without hurrying ‖ to exercise using such a pace **2.** *n.* a slight push ‖ a slow pace or movement

jogging *(sports)* slow running

join (dʒɔin) **1.** *v.t.* to bring (things or persons) together to make a single unit ‖ to bring (two things) together so that they communicate ‖ to fasten (one thing to another) ‖ to become a member of (an organization or group) ‖ to enter into the company of (another person or persons) ‖ *v.i.* to become united ‖ to be contiguous ‖ to become a member of an organization or group **to join in** to take part in **to join up** to enlist in the armed forces **2.** *n.* the act of joining ‖ a point, line or surface of contact

joint (dʒɔint) **1.** *n.* the place where two or more things or parts of things are joined together ‖ the structure, mechanism or material effecting such a joining together ‖ *(anat.)* a place where two or more bones come together, together with cartilage, fluid etc. in the case of movable joints ‖ *(bot.)* the articulation point on a stem from which a leaf arises ‖ *(geol.)* a line of fissure in rock, not causing dislocation ‖ *(pop.)* any establishment, esp. a low-class place of entertainment **out of joint** (of a bone) no longer having its head in the socket **2.** *v.t.* to fit (something) together by means of a joint ‖ to divide (a carcass) into joints ‖ to plane and prepare (planks of wood) so that they may be fitted together ‖ to point (masonry)

joint *adj.* owned, made or done in common with one or more persons, groups, governments etc.

joist (dʒɔist) *n.* one of a number of parallel wood or steel beams which support floorboards or ceiling laths etc.

joke (dʒouk) **1.** *n.* an action, saying, event or circumstance which causes or is intended to cause amusement or laughter ‖ something to be treated lightly, as not important, and with humor ‖ a person who is laughed at because he is ridiculous **2.** *v.t. pres. part.* **jok·ing** *past* and *past part.* **joked** to make jokes **jók·er** *n.* someone who makes jokes ‖ *(cards)* a 53rd card usually depicting a jester, used only in certain games, as either wild or having the highest value **jók·ing·ly** *adv.*

jol·ly (dʒɒli:) **1.** *comp.* **jol·li·er** *superl.* **jol·li·est** *adj.* full of good humor and fun **2.** *v.t. pres. part.* **jol·ly·ing** *past* and *past part.* **jol·lied** to chaff or joke with (someone) good-humoredly

jolt (dʒoult) **1.** *v.t.* to cause (something) to move or shake by a sudden jerk ‖ *v.i.* to move with jolts **2.** *n.* a rough jerk ‖ a sudden shock to one's feelings

josh (dʒɒʃ) *v.t.* *(pop.)* to tease (someone) without malice ‖ *(pop.)* to exchange jokes with (someone) ‖ *v.i.* *(pop.)* to joke

jos·tle (dʒɒs'l) **1.** *n.* a jostling or being jostled **2.** *v. pres. part.* **jos·tling** *past* and *past part.* **jos·tled** *v.t.* to push and shove against (someone) ‖ to struggle with (someone) ‖ *v.i.* to push and shove ‖ to struggle with someone for something

jot (dʒot) **1.** *n.* (in negative or quasinegative constructions) a very small amount **2.** *v.t. pres. part.* **jot·ting** *past* and *past part.* **jot·ted** (with 'down') to make a quick written note **jót·ting** *n.* a brief note or memorandum

jour·nal (dʒɚːrn'l) *n.* a record of events, personal experiences and thoughts etc., kept day by day ‖ a daily record of business transactions ‖ a newspaper or magazine published at regular intervals ‖ the account of the proceedings of e.g. a learned society ‖ *(naut.)* a logbook

jour·nal·ism (dʒɚːrn'lizəm) *n.* the profession of collecting news for, writing for, editing or managing a newspaper or other periodical ‖ journalistic writing

jour·nal·ist (dʒɚːrn'list) *n.* a professional writer for or editor of a newspaper or other periodical **jour·nal·is·tic** *adj.* of journalists or journalism, esp. of journalese

jour·ney (dʒɚːrni:) **1.** *pl.* **jour·neys** *n.* a movement over a considerable distance from one place to another, esp. by land or air ‖ a distance as defined by the time taken to cover it, *a day's journey* **2.** *v.i.* to make a journey

jour·ney·man (dʒə́:rni:mən) *pl.* **jour·ney·men** (dʒə́:rni:mən) *n.* a craftsman who has completed his training and works for an employer ‖ someone who is competent but not exceptional in his work

jo·vi·al (dʒóuvi:əl) *adj.* good-humored and full of jokes or conviviality **jo·vi·al·i·ty** *n.*

jowl (dʒaul) *n.* the chin and neck, when heavy with sagging flesh ‖ the dewlap of a cow etc. ‖ the wattle of a turkey etc.

jowl *n.* a jawbone, esp. the lower jaw ‖ a cheek

joy (dʒɔi) *n.* intense happiness or great delight ‖ that which gives rise to this emotion, or on which the emotion centers ‖ the outward expression of the emotion

joy·ful (dʒɔ́ifəl) *adj.* filled with, causing or showing joy

joy·ous (dʒɔ́iəs) *adj.* full of joy ‖ expressing joy

ju·bi·lant (dʒú:bələnt) *adj.* rejoicing, esp. in celebration of success or victory

ju·bi·late (dʒú:bəleit) *pres. part.* **ju·bi·lat·ing** *past* and *past part.* **ju·bi·lat·ed** *v.i.* to be jubilant

ju·bi·la·tion (dʒu:bəléiʃən) *n.* a jubilating ‖ an instance of this

ju·bi·lee (dʒú:bəli:, dʒu:bəlí:) *n.* a 50th anniversary ‖ an anniversary other than the 50th, *silver jubilee* (25th), *diamond jubilee* (60th) ‖ celebration of such anniversaries

Ju·da·ism (dʒú:di:izəm, dʒú:deiizəm) *n.* the religion of the Jews ‖ the Jews at large

judge (dʒʌdʒ) *pres. part.* **judg·ing** *past* and *past part.* **judged** *v.t.* to hear (a case) and pronounce sentence upon (a person) ‖ to hear (a case) and apply the law to (a question) ‖ to examine and determine the relative merits of (exhibits, contestants etc.) ‖ to estimate, *to judge a distance* ‖ *v.i.* to arrive at an opinion ‖ to act as a judge

judge *n.* a civil law officer of the highest rank, who tries cases in a court of law ‖ a courtesy title for any of several law officers who may try cases in lower courts ‖ any person appointed to settle a dispute, or to decide the relative merits of competitors (exhibitors, athletes etc.) ‖ a person qualified by knowledge and experience to assess quality, *a good judge of horses*

judg·ment, judge·ment (dʒʌ́dʒmənt) *n.* the process of judging in law ‖ the pronouncement of a decision ‖ a legal decision or sentence ‖ an opinion ‖ the process of assessing ‖ *(pop.)* a blow of fate thought of by onlookers as a just retribution

ju·di·cial (dʒu:díʃəl) *adj.* of the administration of justice or of acts, places, persons or powers associated with it ‖ of the use of the power and process of critical judgment

ju·di·ci·ar·y (dʒu:díʃi:eri:, dʒu:díʃəri:) *pl.* **ju·di·ci·ar·ies** *n.* the apparatus of law and its administrators ‖ the judicial branch of government

ju·di·cious (dʒu:díʃəs) *adj.* (of acts etc.) governed by or arising from sound judgment ‖ (of persons) using sound judgment

ju·do (dʒú:dou) *n.* a modern form of jujitsu

jug (dʒʌg) *n.* a vessel for holding and pouring liquids, never with a lip

jug·ger·naut (dʒʌ́gərnɔt) *n.* an irresistible destructive force

jug·gle (dʒʌ́g'l) **1.** *v. pres. part.* **jug·gling** *past* and *past part.* **jug·gled** *v.i.* to perform tricks of dexterity, esp. to throw several objects into the air one after another, catching them and throwing them again, repeatedly and rhythmically without a pause ‖ (with 'with') to make complex, confusing play, *to juggle with ideas* ‖ *v.t.* to perform tricks of dexterity with (objects) by

juggling ‖ to alter (facts or figures) with the intention of deceiving **2.** *n.* an act of juggling ‖ a fraud

jug·gler (dʒʌ́glər) *n.* someone who juggles, esp. professionally

jug·u·lar (dʒʌ́gjulər) **1.** *adj. (anat.)* of or located in the neck or throat **2.** *n.* a jugular vein ‖ a vulnerable point

jugular vein, internal a vein, running through the neck, which collects blood from the internal areas of the skull and the external areas of the face

juice (dʒu:s) *n.* the fluid contained in or extracted from fruits and vegetables ‖ a fluid in or extracted from the animal body ‖ *(pop.)* gasoline, electricity etc.

juic·y (dʒú:si:) *comp.* **juic·i·er** *superl.* **juic·i·est** *adj.* rich in juice ‖ *(pop.)* profitable ‖ *(pop.)* sexy, racy, *juicy stories*

ju·ji·tsu, ju·ju·tsu (dju:dʒítsu:) *n.* a Japanese method of self-defense by which one attempts to disable an opponent with the minimum of personal risk and physical exertion, turning the opponent's strength to one's own advantage by upsetting his balance

Ju·ly (dʒu:lái, dʒəlái) *n.* the seventh month of the year, having 31 days

jum·ble (dʒʌ́mb'l) **1.** *n.* a disorderly or confused group of things, persons etc. **2.** *v.t. pres. part.* **jum·bling** *past* and *past part.* **jum·bled** (with 'up' or 'together') to mix (things) in a jumble

jum·bo (dʒʌ́mbou) **1.** *n. (pop.)* someone or something conspicuously larger than the norm **2.** *adj.* very large, *jumbo jet*

jump (dʒʌmp) **1.** *v.i.* to rise momentarily into the air, esp. by springing with the aid of leg and foot muscles ‖ to leap from one place to another ‖ to make a sudden involuntary movement, esp. when startled ‖ to shift quickly from one state, topic etc. to another ‖ (of prices, wages etc.) to rise quickly ‖ *(computer)* to depart from a normal sequence to another ‖ to deviate from an expected course, order etc. ‖ *v.t.* to pass over (something) by jumping ‖ to cause to jump ‖ to pass over, evade or ignore (something) ‖ to make (prices, wages etc.) rise quickly ‖ *(pop.)* to attack (someone) esp. with malicious intent **to jump ahead** to move rapidly in front, passing others on the way **to jump at** to accept at once, without hesitation, *to jump at a chance* **to jump down someone's throat** to reprimand someone with sudden vehemence **to jump into** to enter suddenly, rashly or enthusiastically into (a situation, undertaking etc.) **to jump ship** (of a sailor etc.) to leave the ship while legally obliged to remain **to jump the gun** *(pop.)* to start too soon **to jump to conclusions** to make an unjustified assumption **2.** *n.* the act of jumping ‖ a sudden startled movement ‖ a sudden rise, *prices went up with a jump* ‖ a distance jumped ‖ a gap in an otherwise continuous process, e.g. in an argument, or a train of thought etc. **to be one jump ahead** to be in advance of rivals by virtue of smartness or cleverness

jump·er (dʒʌ́mpər) *n.* a loose jacket worn by workmen, sailors etc. ‖ a sleeveless, one-piece dress worn over a blouse

jumper *n.* someone or something that jumps, esp. a horse trained to jump obstacles in show riding ‖ *(elec.)* a short length of wire used to mend a break in or cut off part of a circuit

jump·y (dʒʌ́mpi:) *comp.* **jump·i·er** *superl.* **jump·i·est** *adj.* marked by jumps ‖ proceeding in jumps ‖ in a nervous or apprehensive state

junc·tion (dʒʌ́kʃən) *n.* the place where two or more things join ‖ a joining or being joined

junc·ture (dʒʌ́nktʃər) *n.* a joining or being joined ‖ (esp. *anat.*) a place of joining or structure effecting a joining ‖ a point in time as determined by certain events and circumstances

June (dʒuːn) *n.* the sixth month of the year, having 30 days

jun·gle (dʒʌŋˈgl) *n.* an area of land overgrown with tangled shrubs, vines, trees, roots and tall vegetation, found in the Tropics ‖ this dense growth ‖ an intermingled number of things difficult to analyze or sort out

jun·ior (dʒúːnjər) **1.** *(abbr.* jr) *adj.* younger, used esp. to distinguish son from father when both have the same name ‖ lower in status, *junior partner* ‖ less advanced ‖ of or relating to the third year of studies in a high school or college **2.** *n.* a younger person or person of lower status ‖ a high school or college student in the third year of studies

ju·ni·per (dʒúːnəpər) *n.* a genus of evergreen shrubs and trees

junk (dʒʌŋk) *n.* (*naut.*) a sailing vessel used in the Orient, esp. China and Java. It has a flat bottom, high poop and overhanging stern, and carries lugsails

junk 1. *n.* (*collect.*) objects having neither value nor further use for their owner ‖ (*pop.*) rubbish **2.** *v.t.* to sell or give up (soemthing) as junk

jun·ket (dʒʌ́kit) **1.** *n.* a food prepared from milk set with rennet, with sugar and flavoring added ‖ an excursion, outing ‖ a pleasure trip made at public expense and ostensibly as an official duty **2.** *v.i.* to go on a junket ‖ (*old-fash.*) to feast

jun·ta (húntə, dʒʌ́ntə) *n.* (*hist.*) a legislative or administrative council in Spain, Italy or South America ‖ a junto

jun·to (dʒʌ́ntou) *pl.* **jun·tos** *n.* a political or other group of persons united by a common purpose

ju·ris·dic·tion (dʒuərisdíkʃən) *n.* the legal power to administer and enforce the law ‖ the exercising of this power ‖ the region within which this power is valid or in which a person has authority ‖ authority **ju·ris·dic·tion·al** *adj.*

ju·ris·pru·dence (dʒuərisprúːdns) *n.* the science or philosophy of law ‖ a legal system or body of laws **ju·ris·pru·dén·tial** *adj.*

ju·rist (dʒúərist) *n.* a lawyer or judge ‖ a scholar of jurisprudence, esp. one who writes on this subject **ju·ris·tic, ju·ris·ti·cal** *adjs* of or relating to a jurist ‖ legal ‖ instituted by law

ju·ror (dʒúərər) *n.* a member of a jury ‖ someone who has sworn an oath

ju·ry (dʒúəriː) *pl.* **ju·ries** *n.* a body of (usually 12) responsible, impartial citizens summoned to hear evidence in a court of law and bound under oath to give an honest answer based on this evidence to questions put before them ‖ a body of persons appointed to judge a contest etc.

just (dʒʌst) **1.** *adj.* appropriate in kind and degree in the generally accepted body of ethical law ‖ obeying the currently accepted ethical laws ‖ legally valid ‖ deserved, merited ‖ well founded ‖ accurate **2.** *adv.* exactly, precisely, *it is just as you said* ‖ very recently ‖ directly, *the house is just across the road* ‖ no more than, *he is just a private* ‖ (*pop.*) very, *your policemen are just wonderful* ‖ (*pop.*, as an intensive) won't you, *just listen to this! just help me to clear the table* **just about** very nearly ‖ a short time ago **just then** exactly at that time or moment **just the same** nevertheless

jus·tice (dʒʌ́stis) *n.* behavior to oneself or to another which is strictly in accord with currently accepted ethical law or as decreed by legal authority ‖ rectitude of the soul enlivened by grace ‖ the process of law ‖ a person appointed to administer the law as judge or magistrate **in justice to** in order to be fair to **to do oneself justice** to make one's real abilities apparent **to do justice to** to behave with justice towards ‖ (*pop.*) to act in such a way as to show full appreciation of the worth or importance of

jus·ti·fi·a·ble (dʒʌ́stifiəbl, dʒʌstifáiəbl) *adj.* able to be justified

jus·ti·fi·ca·tion (dʒʌstifikéiʃən) *n.* a justifying or being justified ‖ that which justifies ‖ (*printing*) the arranging of a line of type so that it evenly fills the measure

jus·ti·fy (dʒʌ́stifai) *pres. part.* **jus·ti·fy·ing** *past* and *past part.* **jus·ti·fied** *v.t.* to show or prove (something or someone) to be just or right ‖ (*printing*) to make (lines of type) equal in length by adjusting the spaces between the words

jut (dʒʌt) **1.** *v. pres. part.* **jut·ting** *past* and *past part.* **jut·ted** *v.i.* to protrude from, stick out ‖ *v.t.* to cause (something) to protrude **2.** *n.* a projection

jute (dʒuːt) *n.* a fiber made from the bark of plants native to tropical Asia ‖ these plants

ju·ve·nile (dʒúːvənail, dʒúːvənl) **1.** *adj.* relating to youth or young people ‖ meant for young people ‖ immature **2.** *n.* a child or young person ‖ (*publishing, librarianship*) a book meant for young people ‖ an actor who plays the role of a young man, or such a role

jux·ta·pose (dʒʌ́kstəpouz) *pres. part.* **jux·ta·pos·ing** *past* and *past part.* **jux·ta·posed** *v.t.* to place (things, facts etc.) side by side

jux·ta·po·si·tion (dʒʌ́kstəpəzíʃən) *n.* a juxtaposing or being juxtaposed

K

K, k (kei) the 11th letter of the English alphabet

ka·lei·do·scope (kəláidəskoup) *n.* a tubular viewing device containing two plane mirrors set at an angle of 60° to one another and multiple fragments of colored glass or paper etc. These produce symmetrical patterns, which shift when the instrument is rotated ‖ something which is continually changing **ka·lei·do·scop·ic** (kəlaidəskópik) *adj.*

kan·ga·roo (kæŋgərúː) *pl.* **kan·ga·roos, kan·ga·roo** *n.* a member of a family of herbivorous, marsupial mammals of Australia and the nearby islands

kar·at (kǽrət) *n.* a measure of the purity of gold. Pure gold is 24 karat, 18-karat gold has six parts of alloy

ka·ra·te (kərúti) *n.* a Japanese system of unarmed self-defense, by body blows with the hands, knees, feet etc.

kay·ak (káiæk) *n.* an Eskimo canoe made of sealskins stretched taut over a light wooden frame, completely closed in around the paddler ‖ a similar canvas-covered canoe

keel (kiːl) **1.** *n.* the curved base of the framework of a ship, extending from bow to stern ‖ a similar structure in an airship ‖ (*biol.*) a carina, e.g. in birds, flowers and grasses **to be on an even keel** (of a ship) to have no list ‖ (of a person) to be well balanced **2.** *v.t.* to turn (a ship) so that its keel is uppermost ‖ *v.i.* (of a ship) to roll over **to keel over** to capsize

keen (kiːn) *adj.* (of a cutting edge) sharp ‖ (*fig.*) cutting or piercing ‖ (of a sensual stimulus) strong ‖ (of the mind or the senses) acute ‖ (of a mental process) acute, incisive ‖ (of feelings) intense ‖ enthusiastic **to be keen on** to like (someone or something) very much

keep (ki:p) *pres. part.* **keep·ing** *past* and *past part.*
kept (kept) *v.t.* to continue to have in one's hands,
mind, a place etc. ‖ to refrain from destroying, continue to have in one's possession ‖ to be responsible
for providing with the necessities of life, *a large
family to keep* ‖ to own and manage, *to keep a shop*
‖ to fulfill (a promise etc.) ‖ to maintain (a written
record) ‖ to maintain ‖ to raise (livestock) ‖ to maintain
(someone, something) in a certain condition, position
etc. ‖ to refrain from disclosing, *to keep a secret* ‖
v.i. to continue, to stay, *if you keep on this road
you'll arrive at the village* ‖ to remain in good condition, not be spoiled, over a period of time, *this
wine doesn't keep* **to keep at** to continue to work on
‖ to nag **to keep away** to prevent (someone or something) from coming closer ‖ to remain at a distance
to keep away from to avoid **to keep back** to force
back ‖ to refrain from revealing **to keep from** to
prevent from ‖ to refrain from disclosing (something)
to (someone) **to keep going** to persevere with an
action, *although ill and exhausted, he kept going* ‖
to enable (someone) to continue, live etc. ‖ to act so
that (something) does not fail, stop etc. **to keep in**
to hide (feelings, emotions etc.) ‖ to force (someone)
to stay indoors, after school, as punishment **to keep
in mind** to remember constantly **to keep in touch
with** to maintain contact with **to keep it up** to maintain one's effort **to keep off** to stay clear of **to keep
to oneself** to avoid other people, esp. to avoid taking
others into one's confidence **to keep to the right
(left)** to stay on the right-hand (left-hand) side of the
road, path etc. **to keep track of** to continue informing
oneself about **to keep up** to sustain, *keep up your
spirits* **to keep up with the Joneses** to attempt to
have as high a standard of living as one's neighbors
to keep well to continue to have good health **kéep·er**
n. someone, esp. a gamekeeper, who keeps, manages, guards etc. ‖ a contrivance for maintaining
something in position, e.g. a latch **kéep·ing** *n.* care,
charge, *to have in one's keeping* ‖ the action of one
who keeps **in (out of) keeping (with)** in (out of)
harmony (with)

keg (keg) *n.* a small cask or barrel holding *(Am.)* less
than 30 gals

kelp (kelp) *n.* any of various large brown seaweeds esp.
of order *Laminariales* or *Fucales*

ken·nel (kén'l) **1.** *n.* (*pl.*) a place where dogs are kept,
bred, trained etc. **2.** *v.t. pres. part.* **ken·nel·ing** *past*
and *past part.* **ken·neled** to keep or put (a dog) in a
kennel

ker·chief (kə́:rtʃif) *n.* a cloth, usually folded to a triangular shape, worn by a woman over her head

ker·nel (kə́:rn'l) *n.* the soft, usually edible, innermost
part of a seed ‖ the whole grain of a cereal ‖ the
center, or essential part, of an argument etc.

ker·o·sene, ker·o·sine (kérəsi:n, kǽrəsi:n, kɛrəsí:n,
kǽrəsí:n) *n.* any of various mixtures of similar hydrocarbons which are liquid to semisolid and are used
as fuels and solvents

ket·tle (két'l) *n.* a teakettle ‖ a large metal cooking
utensil **a pretty (or fine) kettle of fish** a state of
affairs involving confusion, embarrassment etc.

ket·tle·drum (két'ldrʌm) *n.* ((*mus.*) a large drum having
a hemispherical brass or copper shell and a parchment
drumhead

key (ki:) *n.* a reef or low island, esp. a coral island off
S. Florida

key 1. *pl.* **keys** *n.* an instrument for locking and un-
locking a lock ‖ an instrument used to wind up a
spring, e.g. in a clock ‖ a pin, wedge etc. of metal

or wood driven into component parts of a machine,
joint etc. to fasten or tighten them ‖ a slotted instrument for opening e.g. a can of sardines ‖ a device
which fastens together and finshes off something,
e.g. a keystone ‖ *(fig.)* something which affords or
prohibits entrance, possession etc., *the key to the
Mediterranean* ‖ something which enables someone
to explain, solve or decipher a problem, dilemma,
code etc. ‖ *(biol.)* a table listing the chief characteristics of groups etc. to facilitate the identification of
a specimen ‖ *(mus.)* a series or system of notes, related in frequency to that of a particular note, *the key
of B minor* ‖ the disk which actuates a printing lever,
e.g. in a typewriter, Linotype machine etc. ‖ *(elec.)*
a switch or plug which opens or cuts a circuit ‖ a
tone or style of writing or expression **2.** *adj.* of critical
importance, *a key industry*

key *v.t. pres. part.* **key·ing** *past* and *past part.* **keyed**
to furnish with a key or keys ‖ to attune ‖ to roughen
or pit (a surface) to help it to hold applied plaster
etc. **to key up** to make nervously tense

key·board (kí:bɔrd, kí:bourd) **1.** *n.* the keys of a piano,
organ, typewriter etc. **2.** *v.t. (printing)* to set (copy)
by using a composing machine with a keyboard ‖
(computer) to use the keyboard to record data

key·note (kí:nout) *n.* the tone to which the other tones
of a musical key are related by their frequencies ‖
the basic idea or principle informing a speech, policy
etc.

key·stone (kí:stoun) *n.* (*archit.*) the central stone in an
arch, bearing the lateral and vertical stresses and
binding the structure of the arch together

khak·i (kǽki:, kɑ́ki:) *pl.* **khak·is** *n.* a light yellowish-
brown color ‖ the cloth of this color, esp. as used for
the uniforms of soldiers

kick (kik) **1.** *v.t.* to hit (something) with the foot voluntarily or involuntarily ‖ to move (something) by
hitting it with the foot ‖ *(football, soccer)* to score (a
goal or point) by propelling the ball thus ‖ *v.i.* to
strike out with the foot ‖ (of a firearm) to recoil when
fired ‖ *(pop.)* to protest or complain **to be alive and
kicking** *(pop.)* to be well and strong **to kick around**
to treat roughly **to kick oneself** to heap reproaches
upon oneself **to kick up** to cause (a fuss, row etc.)
2. *n.* the act of kicking or an instance of this ‖ a jolt
from a firearm recoil ‖ *(soccer* etc.) power in kicking
‖ *(pop.)* a pleasant stimulus or thrill of pleasure

kick·back (kíkbæk) *n.* a percentage of the sale price
given secretly to the middleman or the purchaser by
the seller ‖ a money exaction made by someone in a
position to give or withhold favors

kick·off (kíkɔf, kíkɒf) *n.* the act of beginning something, e.g. a football game

kid (kid) *pres. part.* **kid·ding** *past* and *past part.* **kid·ded**
v.t. (pop.) to deceive ‖ *(pop.)* to tease (someone)
good-naturedly ‖ *v.i. (pop.)* to tease someone or
something good-naturedly ‖ *(pop.)* to joke, esp. to
say something without really meaning it

kid 1. *n.* a young goat, esp. less than one year old ‖
kidskin ‖ the young of various other animals, e.g. an
antelope ‖ *(pop.)* a child **2.** *v.i. pres. part.* **kid·ding**
past and *past part.* **kid·ded** (of goats) give birth **3.**
adj. made of kidskin ‖ *(pop.)* younger, *a kid brother*

kid·nap (kídnæp) *pres. part.* **kid·nap·ping, kid·nap·ing**
past and *past part.* **kid·napped, kid·naped** *v.t.* to
take away and hold (a person) by force

kid·ney (kídni:) *pl.* **kid·neys** *n.* one of a pair of abdominal organs in all vertebrates. They filter impurities
from the blood and excrete them as urine

kill (kil) **1.** *v.t.* to cause life to cease in ‖ to deprive of
further existence or effectiveness ‖ to defeat or veto

(a) æ, c*a*t; ɑ, c*ar*; ɔ f*aw*n; ei, sn*a*ke. **(e)** e, h*e*n; i:, sh*ee*p; iə, d*ee*r; ɛə, b*ea*r. **(i)** i, f*i*sh; ai, t*i*ger; ə:, b*i*rd. **(o)** o,
*o*x; au, c*ow*; ou, g*oa*t; u, p*oo*r; ɔi, r*oy*al. **(u)** ʌ, d*u*ck; u, b*u*ll; u:, g*oo*se; ə, b*a*cillus; ju:, c*u*be. x, lo*ch*; θ, *th*ink;
ð, bo*th*er; z, *Z*en; ʒ, cor*s*age; dʒ, sa*v*age; ŋ, oranguta*ng*; j, *y*ak; ʃ, *fi*sh; tʃ, fe*tch*; 'l, rabb*le*; 'n, redd*en*. Complete
pronunciation key appears inside front cover.

(legislation) ‖ (*pop.*) to cut off power in (an engine, machine etc.) ‖ (*pop.*) to cause (someone) to be overcome with laughter, admiration etc. ‖ (*racket games*) to play (a ball) so that one's opponent can make no effective stroke ‖ *v.i.* to destroy life **dressed to kill** showily overdressed ‖ dressed to make a stunning impression **to kill time** to occupy oneself with some activity in order to pass time **2.** *n.* the act of killing

kiln (kil, kiln) *n.* a chamber of brick etc., with a fire, used to burn, bake or dry

kil·o·cy·cle (kíləsaik'l) *n.* (*abbr.* kc.) a unit of frequency equal to 1,000 cycles per second

kil·o·gram, kil·o·gramme (kíləgræm) *n.* (*abbr.* kg. or shortened to kilo) the standard metric unit of mass

kil·o·hertz (kí:ləhə:rts) *n.* (*abbr.* kHz) a radio-frequency unit equal to 1,000 cycles per second

kil·o·me·ter (kíləmí:tər, kilómitər) *n.* (*abbr.* km.) 1,000 meters

kil·o·watt (kíləwɒt) *n.* (*abbr.* kw.) a unit of power equal to 1,000 watts

kilt (kilt) *n.* a heavily pleated knee-length tartan skirt worn esp. by the Highlanders of Scotland

ki·mo·no (kimóunə, kəmóunou) *pl.* **ki·mo·nos** *n.* a long, loose Japanese robe, having a sash and wide sleeves, worn by men or women ‖ a dressing gown in imitation of this

kin (kin) *n.* (*old-fash., collect.*) ancestral family ‖ (*old-fash.* except in anthropology, *collect.*) relatives

kind (kaind) *n.* a group or division of persons or things having one or more characteristics, qualities, interests etc. in common **in kind** in goods, not money ‖ in a similar way, *to reply to insults in kind* **nothing of the kind** (*emphatic*) quite different **of a kind** belonging to the same group ‖ of a poor or bad variety within a group **something of the kind** something similar

kind *adj.* sympathetic, helpful, friendly ‖ thoughtful and gentle ‖ well-disposed ‖ showing such qualities ‖ pleasant or beneficial in action

kin·der·gar·ten (kíndərgɑrt'n, kíndərgɑrd'n) *n.* a school or class in which very young children are encouraged to develop their skills and social behavior by games, exercises, handicrafts etc.

kind·heart·ed (káindhɑ́rtid) *adj.* having a kind nature

kin·dle (kínd'l) *pres. part.* **kin·dling** *past* and *past part.* **kin·dled** *v.t.* to cause (a fire) to begin to burn ‖ (*rhet.*) to cause (an emotion) to be felt or intensified, *the speech kindled their anger* ‖ *v.i.* to begin to burn ‖ (*rhet.*, of emotions) to begin to be excited

kin·dling (kíndliŋ) *n.* the act of lighting a fire or an instance of this ‖ dry twigs, pieces of wood etc. used to start a fire

kind·ly (káindli:) *adj.* in a kind way **to take something kindly** to consider something to be meant as kind **to take kindly to** to like

kind·ness (káindnis) *n.* the quality of being kind or an instance of this

kin·dred (kíndrid) **1.** *n.* (*old-fash., collect.*) kin **2.** *adj.* having kinship ‖ having a common origin ‖ being in many ways similar

ki·net·ic (kinétik, kainétik) *adj.* of or relating to motion ‖ producing motion

king (kiŋ) *n.* a male monarch ‖ a magnate ‖ the chief person or thing of its kind or class ‖ (*cards*) a card representing a king, intermediate in value between queen and ace ‖ (*chess*) the piece in whose defense the game is played ‖ (*checkers*) a crowned piece, which can be moved diagonally in any direction

king·dom (kíŋdəm) *n.* the territory over which a king or queen has authority ‖ a state, area etc. having a monarchal form of government ‖ one of the three most comprehensive groups used to classify nature, *the animal, plant and mineral kingdoms*

kink (kiŋk) *n.* a sharp twist or loop in a wire, rope, hair etc. ‖ a sudden, slight deviation interrupting a straight line ‖ a sharp muscle pain in e.g. the back or a leg ‖ (*pop.*) an odd trait of character or mental

quirk

kink *v.i.* to form a kink ‖ *v.t.* to cause (something) to form a kink

kink·y (kíŋki:) *comp.* **kink·i·er** *superl.* **kink·i·est** *adj.* (esp. of hair) having kinks ‖ (*colloq.*) of peculiar tastes in sexual satisfaction; by extension, in other areas

kin·ship (kínʃip) *n.* the condition of being related ‖ the condition of being similar

ki·osk (kí:ɒsk, káiɒsk) *n.* a small outdoor structure, e.g. a newsstand or bandstand

kiss (kis) *n.* an instance of kissing ‖ any of several kinds of small, highly sweetened candy or meringue

kiss *v.t.* to press or touch with the lips as an expression of passion, affection or respect ‖ (*billiards*, of a ball) to hit (another ball) with a light, glancing impact ‖ *v.i.* to join lips ‖ (*billiards*) to hit another ball or (of two balls) to come together with a light impact

kit (kit) **1.** *n.* a collection of tools, accessories and supplies necessary for a particular profession, act or service and usually contained in a bag, box etc. **2.** *v.t. pres. part.* **kit·ting** *past* and *past part.* **kit·ted**

kitch·en (kítʃən) *n.* the part of a house, restaurant etc. where food is prepared

kite (kait) *n.* a family of small hawks having a forked tail, long wings and a buoyant flight ‖ a light, usually wooden, typically diamond-shaped framework covered with paper or material and flown on the wind at the end of a long string ‖ (*pl.*) the highest and topmost sails of a ship, used only in very light winds ‖ (*commerce*) a check, bill or other document having no solid backing but used to raise money or sustain credit ‖ a trial balloon ‖ airborne radar reflector dropped from a craft to deceive the enemy

kit·ten (kít'n) **1.** *n.* a young cat, esp. a domesticated cat **2.** *v.i.* to bring forth kittens **kít·ten·ish** *adj.* playful and winning

kit·ty (kíti:) *pl.* **kit·ties** *n.* (*card games*) a pool into which each player puts a stake ‖ (*card games*) the cards left over after a deal ‖ a pool or fund of money or goods

kitty *pl.* **kitties** *n.* (*pop.*) cat, kitten

klep·to·ma·ni·a (kleptəméini:ə, kleptəméinjə) *n.* a compulsive, neurotic desire to steal, esp. when not motivated by any desire or need for economic gain **klep·to·má·ni·ac** *n.*

knack (næk) *n.* a special deftness learned by practice, *a knack for remembering names*

knap·sack (næpsæk) *n.* a canvas bag, used to carry supplies, worn strapped to the back

knave (neiv) *n.* (*old-fash.*) a cheat, a rogue ‖ (*cards*) a jack **knav·er·y** (néivəri:) *pl.* **knav·er·ies** *n.* the practice of low cunning ‖ an instance of this **knáv·ish** *adj.*

knead (ni:d) *v.t.* to work (dough, clay) into a homogeneous mass with the hands ‖ to massage (a muscle or limb) as if working dough

knee (ni:) **1.** *n.* the knee joint in man ‖ the area surrounding this joint ‖ the corresponding joint in an animal ‖ something resembling a bent knee, e.g. a piece of wood or iron used to connect upright beams **to bring (someone) to his knees** to cause (someone) to submit **to go on one's knees to** to beg humbly of **2.** *v.t.* to strike (someone) with the knee

kneel (ni:l) *pres. part.* **kneel·ing** *past* and *past part.* **knelt** (nelt), **kneeled** *v.i.* to rest or fall on one or both knees

knell (nel) **1.** *n.* the sonorous, doleful sound of a single bell tolled as a token of mourning ‖ (*rhet.*) a warning of death or disaster **2.** *v.i.* to toll a bell ‖ *v.t.* to summon by a bell or as if by a bell

knick-knack (níknæk) *n.* any trivial small ornamental article

knife (naif) **1.** *pl.* **knives** (naivz) *n.* a hand tool, culinary utensil or weapon used for cutting, consisting of a blade (usually steel) fixed to a handle and having one edge sharp ‖ a cutting edge in a machine **to get** (or have) **one's knife into someone** to have taken a strong dislike to someone and use every opportunity to attack him in one way or another **2.** *v.t. pres. part.* **knif·ing** *past* and *past part.* **knifed** to cut or stab with a knife || to use sly methods on in order to defeat, harm or betray

knight (nait) **1.** *n.* a man given the rank of knighthood by the British monarch in recognition of merit, esp. in public service || *(hist.)* a man of noble birth who, having served as page and squire, was given an honorable military rank || *(chess)* a piece shaped like a horse's head **2.** *v.t.* to make a knight of

knight·hood (náithud) *n.* the rank of a knight || *(hist.)* the profession of a knight

knit (nit) *pres. part.* **knit·ting** *past* and *past part.* **knit·ted, knit** *v.t.* to fashion (a garment, fabric etc.) by working yarn of wool, silk etc. on knitting needles or specialized machines in a succession of interlocking stitches || to work (yarn) in this way || to cause to join as if grown together or interwoven || *v.i.* to practice knitting || (esp. of a broken bone) to unite **to knit one's brows** to draw the eyebrows together in a frown **knit·ting** *n.* the act of someone who knits, or the process of a machine which knits || work being knitted

knob (nɒb) *n.* a rounded, protuberant part of an object || a rounded handle, e.g. of a door || a rounded hill

knock (nɒk) **1.** *v.t.* to make a sudden impact on || (esp. with 'down', 'in', 'off', 'onto' etc.) to cause to move or fall by a sudden impact || (with 'down') to demolish (a building etc.) || to cause to come together with a sudden impact || to cause by making a sudden impact on || *(pop.)* to find fault with || *v.i.* to rap on a door with the knuckles or a knocker || to come together with a sudden impact || (of an internal-combustion engine) to make a rapping sound due to faulty combustion || *(pop.)* to find fault **to knock around** (or **about**) to subject to rough treatment || to lead a roving life **to knock off** to do (a piece of work) esp. quickly and shoddily || to cease (work) || to deduct from **to knock out** to empty by knocking || to render unconscious || to do (something) hastily || *(pop.)* to exhaust, make weary **to knock together** to construct in a rough and ready way **to knock up** *(pop.)* to make (a woman) pregnant **2.** *n.* the impact or sound made by knocking || a piece of bad luck or misfortune

knock·out (nɒkaut) *n.* (abbr. **K.O.**) a blow in boxing which makes a boxer unable to get up before he is counted out || the act of delivering such a blow or an instance of this || someone or something superlatively attractive

knoll (noul) *n.* a small rounded hill

knot (nɒt) **1.** *n.* a place in a thread, string etc. where the thread passes through a loop in its own length and is pulled tight || a place where two or more threads, strings etc. are joined by passing each of them through loops in the other and pulling tight || a lump, protrusion etc. in animal tissue or bone, esp. a constriction in a muscle || a protrusion of growing plant tissues, e.g. in a grass stem, or where a branch grows from a tree trunk (or the hard cross section of this in a plank) || a cluster of persons or things || a difficulty, a problem hard to solve || *(naut.)* a portion, marked

off by knots, of a line attached to a log, formerly used to measure a ship's speed || *(naut.)* a unit of speed, being 1 nautical mile per hour **2.** *v. pres. part.* **knot·ting** *past* and *past part.* **knot·ted** *v.t.* to tie in or with a knot || to cause to form a knot || *v.i.* to become tied in a knot

knot·ty (nɒti:) *comp.* **knot·ti·er** *superl.* **knot·ti·est** *adj.* having knots || (of a problem etc.) hard to solve

know (nou) **1.** *v. pres. part.* **know·ing** *past* **knew** (nu:, nju:) *past part.* **known** (noun) *v.t.* to apprehend with the conscious mind || to be acquainted with by experience || to recognize || to have acquired skill in, *she knows how to swim* || to be informed about, be in possession of the facts about || to have committed to memory || to realize || *v.i.* to possess knowledge, understanding or awareness of something || to be certain of or convinced about something **to be known as** to be widely reputed to be **to know better than to** to be prudent or disciplined enough not to **to know of** to be aware of **to know one's own mind** to be firm in one's opinions, wishes or decisions **to make oneself known** to introduce oneself **2.** *n.* (only in) **in the know** having inside information or sharing a secret

know·ing (nóuiŋ) *adj.* of a gesture or of behavior which suggests that a person has penetrated a secret or knows more than he admits or knows more than you do || shrewd **know·ing·ly** *adv.* in a knowing manner || deliberately

knowl·edge (nɒlidʒ) *n.* the state of knowing, cognition || understanding || that which is known **to one's knowledge** so far as one knows **knowl·edge·a·ble** (nɒlidʒəb'l) *adj.* knowing a great deal, well-informed

knuck·le (nʌk'l) **1.** *n.* a joint in the finger, esp. one at the base of each finger || a bony knob formed at each finger joint when the hand is clenched || the middle joint of the tarsus of an animal || a piece of meat comprising this joint and the surrounding flesh || a joint in a structure which has the shape of a knuckle or functions like one, e.g. the parts of a hinge containing the rotating pin **2.** *v. pres. part.* **knuck·ling** *past* and *past part.* **knuck·led** *v.t.* to hit or rub with the knuckles || *v.i.* **to knuckle down** to discipline oneself into beginning work **to knuckle under** to submit

ko·a·la (kouálə) *n.* a sturdy marsupial of E. Australia, about 2 ft long, with thick gray fur, sometimes called a bear

kook (ku:k) *n. (colloq.)* an eccentric —**kookily** *adv.* —**kookiness** *n.* —**kooky** *adj.*

kook·a·bur·ra (kʊkəbə́:rə) *n.* a large Australian kingfisher having a raucous laughlike call

Ko·ran (kɔrán, kourán, kɔrǽn, kourǽn) *n.* the holy scripture of Islam, claimed to be a direct transmission of the word of God revealed to Mohammed **Ko·ran·ic** (kɔrǽnik, kourǽnik) *adj.*

ko·sher (kóuʃər) *adj.* (of food) conforming to the requirements of the Jewish dietary laws || (of shops, restaurants etc.) selling, preparing or serving such food || *(pop.)* genuine, legitimate

kum·quat, cum·quat (kʌ́mkwɔt) *n.* a genus of Asiatic citrus trees || a fruit of any of these trees

---

L

L, l (el) the 12th letter of the English alphabet

la (lɑ) *n. (mus.)* the note A in the fixed-do system of solmization ‖ the sixth note in any diatonic scale in movable-do solmization

la·bel (léib'l) **1.** *n.* a piece of paper, card, metal etc. to be attached to an article with the name, ownership, destination, description etc. of the article inscribed on it ‖ short name or phrase applied to a person to indicate broadly allegiance, persuasion etc., *political labels* **2.** *v.t. pres. part.* **la·bel·ing** *past* and *past part.* **labeled** to attach a label to ‖ *(pop.)* to classify

la·bi·al (léibi:əl) **1.** *adj.* of the lips or labia ‖ serving as or resembling a lip **2.** *n. (phon.)* a labial sound **la·bi·al·i·za·tion** *n.* **lá·bi·al·ize** *pres. part.* **la·bi·al·iz·ing** *past* and *past part.* **la·bi·al·ized** *v.t.* to utter as or change to a labial sound

la·bor (léibər) *n.* prolonged hard work ‖ a task demanding great effort ‖ the muscular uterine contractions preceding childbirth ‖ the period of time that these contractions last ‖ *(econ.)* work as a production factor ‖ those who work in contrast to those who own or manage ‖ workers as an economic or political force

labor *v.i.* to work hard ‖ to make slow, painful progress ‖ (of a ship) to pitch and roll in heavy seas ‖ (with 'under') to suffer from, be impeded by ‖ *v.t.* to express in unnecessary detail and at length

lab·o·ra·to·ry (lǽbrətɔ:ri:, lǽbrətouri:) *pl.* **lab·o·ra·to·ries** *n.* (often shortened to 'lab') a place equipped and used for experimental study, research, analysis, testing or (usually small-scale) preparation, in any branch of science

la·bored (léibərd) *adj.* done, or seeming to be done, with difficulty

la·bor·er (léibərər) *n.* a wage earner who does unskilled work

la·bo·ri·ous (ləbɔ́:ri:əs, ləbóuri:əs) *adj.* involving prolonged, hard work ‖ hardworking ‖ labored

lab·y·rinth (lǽbərinθ) *n.* a confusion of winding passages through which it is extremely difficult to find one's way ‖ a maze of paths bordered by high hedges in a park etc. ‖ *(anat.)* the inner ear **lab·y·rín·thine** *adj.*

lace (leis) **1.** *n.* a patterned fabric of open texture, worked in silk, linen or cotton thread ‖ a braid of gold or silver for trimming uniforms ‖ a cord or thin strip of leather, passed through eyelets and used to draw together the opposite edges of a shoe, tent flap etc.

lace *pres. part.* **lac·ing** *past* and *past part.* **laced** *v.t.* to draw together using a lace ‖ to pass (a lace) through eyelets etc. ‖ to attach ornamental lace to ‖ to add liquor to (coffee etc.) ‖ to compress the waist of (a person) by pulling tight the laces of a corset etc. ‖ *(pop.)* to lash, beat ‖ to streak or mark as if with braid ‖ *v.i.* to be fastened by a lace

lac·er·ate (lǽsəreit) *pres. part.* **lac·er·at·ing** *past* and *past part.* **lac·er·at·ed** *v.t.* to rend (the flesh) with a tearing movement ‖ to affect with painful emotions **lác·er·at·ed** *adj.* mangled, torn ‖ *(biol.)* having edges deeply and irregularly incised **lac·er·á·tion** *n.*

lac·ing (léisiŋ) *n.* laces used for fastening ‖ ornamental trimming, esp. on a uniform ‖ a small addition of alcoholic liquor, e.g. brandy, to coffee or some other drink, or to food ‖ *(pop.)* a beating, lashing ‖ the act of someone who laces

lack (læk) **1.** *n.* want, need, the fact or state of not having something or enough of something ‖ that which is missing or needed **2.** *v.t.* to be wanting in ‖ *v.i.* to be wanting

lack·a·dai·si·cal (lækədéizik'l) *adj.* (of a person or attitude) lacking in proper carefulness, seriousness, energy etc.

lack·ey (lǽki:) *pl.* **lack·eys** *n. (hist.)* a liveried manservant ‖ a servile and obsequious person

lack·ing (lǽkiŋ) *prep.* short of, without

lack·lus·ter (lǽklʌstər) *adj.* lacking in vitality or brilliance

la·con·ic (lʌkɔ́nik) *adj.* using terse, unemotional language **la·con·i·cal·ly** *adv.* **la·con·i·cism** (ləkɔ́nisiẓəm) *n.* unemotional brusque speech or an instance of this

lac·quer (lǽkər) **1.** *n.* a hard, glossy varnish derived from shellac, colored, and applied to wood and to some metals for decoration and protection ‖ *(commerce)* any hard gloss paint ‖ coated with lacquer and often inlaid with metal, ivory etc. ‖ a liquid coating containing a cellulose derivative used as a protective finish in industrial processes ‖ a hair spray ‖ any natural varnish, esp. the sap of the Japanese varnish tree **2.** *v.t.* to coat with lacquer

la·crosse (ləkrɔ́s, ləkrɔ́:s) *n.* a field game of North American Indian origin, played with two teams of *(Am.)* 10 players

lac·tic (lǽktik) *adj.* of or pertaining to milk ‖ pertaining to the production of lactic acid

la·cy (léisi:) *comp.* **la·ci·er** *superl.* **la·ci·est** *adj.* of or resembling lace

lad (læd) *n.* a boy or youth

lad·der (lǽdər) *n.* a portable device consisting usually of two long wood or metal uprights or two ropes joined at short intervals by crosspieces (rungs) which serve as footrests, for climbing up and down ‖ any means of personal step-by-step advancement

lade (leid) *pres. part.* **lad·ing** *past* **lad·ed** *past part.* **lad·en** (léid'n) *v.t.* to put goods on board (a ship) or to take goods) on board **lád·en** *adj.* loaded ‖ *(rhet.)* heavily burdened

la·dle (léid'l) **1.** *n.* a spoon with a long handle and a large, cuplike bowl, used for transferring soup, stew etc. from one receptacle to another ‖ a similarly shaped instrument for transferring molten metal **2.** *v.t. pres. part.* **la·dling** *past* and *past part.* **la·dled** (often with 'out') to transfer with a ladle ‖ to distribute freely

la·dy (léidi:) *pl.* **la·dies** *n.* a woman of the wealthy, leisured class ‖ any woman who behaves with the dignity and social grace ascribed to women of this class ‖ (in polite and conventional usage) a woman ‖ used as a courtesy title, *lady mayoress* **La·dy** a British title of rank

lag (læg) **1.** *v.i. pres. part.* **lag·ging** *past* and *past part.* **lagged** to go slowly ‖ (with 'behind') to fail to keep up with others **2.** *n.* the act of lagging or an instance of this ‖ the distance or time between one thing, event etc. and another ‖ *(phys.)* the time lapse between a cause and its effect

lag·gard (lǽgərd) **1.** *adj.* lagging **2.** *n.* a person who is slow, lazy or slack in his duty

la·gniappe, la·gnappe (lænjǽp, lǽnjæp) *n.* a small gift presented to a customer by a storekeeper ‖ a gratuity or unexpected gift

la·goon (ləgú:n) *n.* a shallow stretch of water partly or completely separated from the sea by a strip of sand or an atoll ‖ a shallow freshwater lake incompletely or narrowly separated from a larger lake or river

la·ic (léiik) **1.** *adj.* lay **2.** *n.* a layman **lá·i·cal** *adj.*

lair (lɛər) *n.* a place in which a wild animal rests and feeds its young ‖ a hiding place of outlaws

la·i·ty (léiiti:) *n.* laymen

lake (leik) *n.* a large expanse of water surrounded by land or by land and a manmade retainer, e.g. a dam. It may be fed by rivers, springs or local precipitation

lamb (læm) **1.** *n.* a young sheep ‖ the flesh of this as food ‖ a meek, mild, innocent, or particularly lovable person ‖ lambskin **2.** *v.i.* (of a ewe) to give birth ‖ *v.t.* to give birth to (a lamb)

lam·baste (læmbéist) *pres. part.* **lam·bast·ing** *past* and *past part.* **lam·bast·ed** *v.t.* to give a hard whipping to ‖ to scold

lame (leim) **1.** *adj.* unable to walk, run etc. normally because of a defect of, or injury to, a foot or leg ‖

(of a leg or foot) having such an injury or defect ‖ stiff and sore ‖ having no force or effectiveness ‖ (of meter) faltering **2.** *v.t. pres. part.* **lam·ing** *past* and *past part.* **lamed** to make lame

la·mé (læméi) *n.* a fabric woven from metal thread, usually gold or silver, mixed with silk or other fiber

la·ment (ləmént) *v.t.* to mourn for ‖ to show or feel regret for ‖ *v.i.* to mourn ‖ to show or feel regret

lament *n.* an expression of mourning or grieving ‖ such mourning or grieving in a literary or musical form

lam·en·ta·ble (læməntəb'l, ləméntəb'l) *adj.* giving cause for adverse comment ‖ giving cause for lament **lám·en·ta·bly** *adv.*

lam·en·ta·tion (læmontéiʃən) *n.* the act of lamenting or an instance of this

lam·i·na (læminə) *pl.* **lam·i·nae** (læmini:), **lam·i·nas** *n.* any thin plate or scale (e.g. of bone or metal) ‖ *(bot.)* the blade of a leaf or petal **lám·i·nar** *adj.*

lam·i·nate (læmineit) *pres. part.* **lam·i·nat·ing** *past* and *past part.* **lam·i·nat·ed** *v.t.* to make or split into thin plates or layers ‖ to make (plywood, plastic etc.) by uniting layer upon layer ‖ *v.i.* to split into laminae

lam·i·na·tion (læminéiʃən) *n.* a laminating or being laminated ‖ *(geol.)* the occurrence of minor layers of stratified sedimentary rock

lamp (læmp) *n.* a device for giving off light without being consumed itself, e.g. an oil lamp ‖ a similar device for giving off invisible radiation, e.g. an infrared lamp

lam·poon (læmpú:n) **1.** *n.* a piece of satirical verse or other writing designed to ridicule or discredit someone **2.** *v.t.* to attack (someone) in this way

lam·prey (læmpri:) *n.* a member of *Hyperoartia,* an order of marine or freshwater vertebrates, found in North American, Eurasian and subarctic waters

lance (læns, lɑns) *n. (hist.)* a mounted soldier's weapon consisting of a long shaft with a pointed steel end ‖ a similar weapon for killing a harpooned whale, spearing fish etc. ‖ a lancet (instrument) ‖ a launce

lance *pres. part.* **lanc·ing** *past* and *past part.* **lanced** *v.t.* to pierce with a lance ‖ to pierce or cut with a lancet

lan·cet (lænsit, lɑnsit) *n.* a sharp-pointed, two-edged surgical instrument

land (lænd) **1.** *n.* the solid surface of the earth where it is not covered with water ‖ a particular area of this, distinguished from other areas by political, geographical, economic or other considerations ‖ such an area in relation to its owner, *their land goes up to that wood* **the land** the country, esp. agricultural areas, as distinct from the city **to see how the land lies** to find out the true state of affairs, esp. secretly or unobtrusively, in order to assess a situation **2.** *v.i.* to step onto land from a ship ‖ to arrive, *to land at one's destination* ‖ (of an aircraft) to come to rest on the ground or on water ‖ (of a boat) to come into port or ashore ‖ *v.t.* to put on shore from a ship ‖ to bring (an aircraft) to land ‖ to bring (someone) to his destination ‖ to deliver (a blow) ‖ to bring (a fish) to shore **to land on one's feet** to be fortunate or successful ‖ to emerge safely from an awkward situation

land·ing (lændiŋ) *n.* a disembarking or being disembarked ‖ a bringing or coming to land or to shore ‖ an alighting of an aircraft ‖ a place where goods or persons are landed or taken aboard ‖ a level place at the top of a flight of stairs or between two flights of stairs

land·la·dy (lændleidi:) *pl.* **land·la·dies** *n.* a woman who runs a boarding house or an inn, or takes in lodgers ‖ a woman who leases property to others

land·locked (lændɒkt) *adj.* (of water) almost or com-

pletely surrounded by land ‖ (of fish, e.g. some salmon) prevented from leaving fresh water for the sea, or not doing so ‖ (of a country) without a seacoast

land·lord (lændlɔrd) *n.* a man who leases property to another ‖ the owner of a boardinghouse or inn

land·mark (lændmɑrk) *n.* a prominent feature on land, esp. one which acts as a guide in following a route or marking a boundary ‖ any monument of historic etc. interest ‖ an event which is of special significance in a process or period of change

land·scape (lændskeip) **1.** *n.* a painting or photograph of a piece of inland scenery ‖ such a piece of scenery **2.** *v. pres. part.* **land·scap·ing** *past* and *past part.* **land·scaped** *v.t.* to beautify (land, property etc.) by modifying or enhancing the natural scenery ‖ *v.i.* to engage in landscape gardening or landscape architecture

land·slide (lændslaid) *n.* the slipping down from a hillside or cliff of masses of earth and rock ‖ this rock and earth ‖ an overwhelming majority of votes cast for one political party or one politician ‖ an overwhelming electoral victory

lane (lein) *n.* a narrow country road, esp. one edged with hedges or fences ‖ a narrow street or alley, esp. one edged with walls or buildings ‖ a prescribed channel for sea or air traffic ‖ one of a series of parallel marked sections of road ‖ one of a series of similar marked strips on a running track ‖ a passage left between rows of persons ‖ a channel of water in an ice field ‖ a wooden bowling alley

lan·guage (læŋgwidʒ) *n.* the organized system of speech used by human beings as a means of communication among themselves ‖ any such differentiated system as used by a section of the human race ‖ such a system adapted to a special purpose, *the language of diplomacy* ‖ a manner of expressing oneself, *strong language* ‖ any other organized system of communication, e.g. by symbols, *mathematical language,* or gestures, *deaf-and-dumb language* ‖ any apparently organized system of communication, *the language of animals* ‖ literary style, use of words

lan·guish (læŋgwiʃ) *v.i.* to become languid ‖ to live under dispiriting conditions ‖ to pine ‖ to assume a languid expression in an effort to win sympathy or affection ‖ to wane

lan·guor (læŋgər) *n.* a state of languishing or being languid **lan·guor·ous** (læŋgərəs) *adj.*

lank (læŋk) *adj.* extremely slim ‖ (of plants) inordinately long and slender ‖ (of hair) long, straight and lifeless-looking

lank·i·ness (læŋki:nis) *n.* the state or quality of being lanky

lank·y (læŋki:) *comp.* **lank·i·er** *superl.* **lank·i·est** *adj.* (of a person) tall, thin and ungainly ‖ (of limbs) longer and thinner than is graceful

lan·o·lin (læn'lin) *n.* a waxy substance obtained from wool grease, readily absorbed by the skin and used in ointments and cosmetics

lan·tern (læntərn) *n.* a portable case with transparent sides containing a source of light and protecting this from wind and rain ‖ a glass structure in a roof or in the upper part of a dome, admitting light ‖ the chamber of a lighthouse containing the light

lap (læp) *n.* the crook of the body between waist and knees of someone sitting down

lap 1. *v. pres. part.* **lap·ping** *past* and *past part.* **lapped** *v.t.* to drink (liquid) by taking it up with the tongue ‖ (of water) to come repeatedly against (something) with a soft slapping sound ‖ *v.i.* to drink liquid by taking it up with the tongue ‖ to make a soft slapping sound **to lap up** to absorb or accept eagerly and quickly **2.** *n.* an instance or the sound of lapping ‖ the amount drunk in a lap

lap 1. *v. pres. part.* **lap·ping** *past* and *past part.* **lapped** *v.i.* (with 'about', 'around', 'in') to wrap ‖ (with 'over') to fold, esp. on itself ‖ to cause to overlap ‖ to overlap ‖ to make a circuit of (a racecourse) ‖ to outdistance (a racing opponent) by one or more laps ‖ *v.i.* to cover partially ‖ to cover and extend beyond ‖ to make a circuit of a racecourse **2.** *n.* a section that overlaps ‖ an amount of overlap ‖ a circuit of a racecourse ‖ a section or phase of a whole

la·pel (ləpél) *n.* the part of the front of a coat or dress folded back along the neckline

lap·i·dar·y (lǽpidẹri:) **1.** *pl.* **lap·i·dar·ies** *n.* someone who cuts, polishes or engraves gems **2.** *adj.* pertaining to precious stones ‖ engraved on stone ‖ (of literary style) tersely elegant and pithy

lapse (læps) **1.** *n.* a passing away ‖ a slip or minor mistake ‖ a falling into disuse ‖ the invalidation of some right through failure to exercise it or lack of attention **2.** *v.t. pres. part.* **laps·ing** *past* and *past part.* **lapsed** to cease to be ‖ to become void through lack of attention ‖ to slip or fall back ‖ to slip from virtue or right conduct ‖ (of time) to pass

lar·ce·nous (lɑ́rsənəs) *adj.* of or pertaining to larceny ‖ guilty of larceny

lar·ce·ny (lɑ́rsəni:) *pl.* **lar·ce·nies** *n.* (*law*) the illegal taking and removal of another's personal property without his knowledge or consent and with the express intention of depriving the owner of such property

lard (lɑrd) *n.* the rendered fat of pigs, esp. the abdominal fat, used in cooking

lard *v.t.* to flavor and make more fatty by inserting bacon or pork strips before cooking ‖ to cover with lard ‖ to flavor or enrich (speech or writing) by using flowery phrases, foreign words etc.

lar·der (lɑ́rdər) *n.* a cool room in which meat and other foods are stored until ready for use, or the foods themselves

large (lɑrdʒ) **1.** *adj.* extensive in area or scope ‖ of greater size, capacity or number than average for its kind ‖ broad ‖ (*naut.*, of a wind) favorable **2.** *adj.* (*naut.*) with the wind aft of the beam, *sailing large* **-at-large** (used postpositively representing or selected by a whole body or area rather than any part, *a congressman-at-large*

large·ly (lɑ́rdʒli:) *adv.* in large measure, mostly

lar·gess, lar·gesse (lɑrdʒés, lɑ́rdʒis) *n.* the giving of bounty by a superior to an inferior ‖ (*rhet.*) the bounty given ‖ generosity on a big scale

lar·i·at (lǽri:ət) *n.* a lasso ‖ a long rope or leather line used with or without a noose for tethering a grazing animal

lark (lɑrk) *n.* any of several songbirds native to Europe, Asia and N. Africa, and having a long hind claw, esp. the skylark ‖ any of various unrelated ground birds, e.g. a meadowlark

lark 1. *n.* (*pop.*) something done for fun or mild adventure, often with gently mischievous intent **2.** *v.i.* (with 'around' or 'about') to play around

lar·va (lɑ́rvə) *pl.* **lar·vae** (lɑ́rvi:), **lar·vas** *n.* the free-living, immature state in many insects (e.g. butterflies) and certain animals (e.g. frogs) that is basically unlike the adult form, usually passing after a period of growth and minor changes to the pupa and thence to the imago **lár·val** *adj.*

la·ryn·ge·al (ləríndʒi:əl, lærindʒí:əl) *adj.* of or pertaining to the larynx

lar·yn·gi·tis (lærindʒáitis) *n.* inflammation of the larynx

lar·ynx (lǽriŋks) *pl.* **la·ryn·ges** (ləríndʒi:s), **lar·ynx·es** *n.* an organ of the respiratory system of air-breathing vertebrates situated above the windpipe

las·civ·i·ous (ləsívi:əs) *adj.* marked by pressing sexual lust ‖ stimulating sexual lust

la·ser (léizər) *n.* a maser operating at optimal frequencies to produce a high-energy monochromatic beam of light or infrared radiation (*Light Amplification by Stimulated Emission of Radiation*)

lash (læʃ) *v.t.* (esp. *naut.*) to fasten or bind with a rope etc. **lásh·ing** *n.* (esp. *naut.*) a rope, wire etc. so used

lass (læs) *n.* (*rhet.* or esp. *Scot.*) a girl or young woman

las·si·tude (lǽsitu:d, lǽsitju:d) *n.* weariness of spirit

las·so (lǽsou) **1.** *pl.* **las·sos, las·soes** *n.* a long leather thong or rope with a running noose, used esp. by Argentine gauchos and North American cowboys for catching cattle or horses **2.** *v.t.* to catch with a lasso

last (læst, lɑst) *n.* a wood or iron form shaped like the human foot used in shoemaking **to stick to one's last** to attend to one's own business ‖ to restrict oneself to one's proper field of activity

last *v.i.* to go on existing for a period of time ‖ to continue without being used up ‖ to exist in good condition for a period of time ‖ *v.t.* to go on meeting the need of (someone) ‖ (with 'out') to arrive at the end of (a period of time or whatever occupies it)

last 1. *adj.* most distant from an observer ‖ nearest to the present time ‖ which will not, or cannot, be followed by any other person or thing of the same kind ‖ being the least likely **last but not least** final in order of mention but not least important **the last** (or **latest**) **thing** the newest fashion **2.** *n.* someone or something which comes or is last ‖ the just-mentioned person or thing ‖ the end ‖ (*rhet.*) death ‖ (*rhet.*) the final performance of a specific action **at last** in the end, finally **at long last** finally after much delay **3.** *adv.* finally ‖ most recently, *I saw him last in Paris*

last·ing (lǽstiŋ, lɑ́stiŋ) **1.** *adj.* existing for a long period of time **2.** *n.* a durable, closely woven fabric used for the top part of shoes, for covering buttons etc.

last·ly (lǽstli:, lɑ́stli:) *adv.* in the last place ‖ in conclusion

latch (lætʃ) **1.** *n.* a fastening for a door or window, consisting of a pivoted bar which falls into, and can be lifted out of, a catch ‖ any similar door or window fastening ‖ a spring lock which fastens a door that can be opened without a key **2.** *v.t.* to fasten by means of a latch

late (leit) *adj.* coming or happening after the usual, expected or proper time ‖ at or near the expected period of time, piece of work, series etc. ‖ belonging to a recent or relatively recent time in the past ‖ recently in existence but now over ‖ recently resigned ‖ recently deceased ‖ opening or blooming after earlier varieties

late *adv.* after the usual, expected or proper time ‖ at or to a time far on in a period of time ‖ recently **of late** recently **late in the day** too late to be of any help or to be taken seriously

late·ly (léitli:) *adv.* recently, in recent years

la·ten·cy (léit'nsi:) *n.* the quality or state of being latent

la·tent (léit'nt) *adj.* hidden, dormant, but capable of being developed ‖ present but not seen until some change occurs

lat·er·al (lǽtərəl) **1.** *adj.* of, to or from a side ‖ (*anat.*) located to one side of the central axis of the body ‖ (*bot.*) located on one side of a plant, an organ or to one side of the central axis of the plant, branch etc. ‖ (of a family line) descended from a brother or sister of someone in the direct line **2.** *n.* something or a part of something located at the side, e.g. a lateral branch

la·tex (léiteks) *pl.* **lat·i·ces** (lǽtisi:z), **la·tex·es** *n.* a milky, usually whitish fluid obtained from various trees and plants, e.g. rubber plants, euphorbias etc. ‖ any of several similar synthetic products, used e.g. as binders in paint

lath (læθ, lɑθ) **1.** *pl.* **laths** (læθs, lɑθs, læðz, lɑðz) *n.* a long, thin, narrow strip of wood, used esp. nailed to joists as a foundation for plaster or for supporting slates **2.** *v.t.* to provide with laths

lathe (leið) **1.** *n.* a machine used to shape or cut wood, metal etc., which holds the material fast in rapid rotation against the cutting component **2.** *v.i. pres. part.* **lath·ing** *past* and *past part.* **lathed** to shape or cut on a lathe

lath·er (lǽðər) **1.** *n.* the foamy froth produced when soap (or other detergent) is agitated in water ‖ foamy froth from excessive sweat, esp. on a horse **2.** *v.i.* to form lather, or become covered with it ‖ *v.t.* to cover with lather **láth·er·y** *adj.*

lath·ing (lǽθiŋ, lάθiŋ) *n.* the act or process of constructing with laths ‖ laths collectively

lat·i·tude (lǽtitu:d, lǽtitju:d) *n.* the angular distance of a place on the earth's surface from the equator as measured in degrees, minutes and seconds ‖ the possibility of acting as one pleases, esp. the permitted extent of departure from some line of conduct or set of conventions ‖ *(astron.)* the angular distance of a heavenly body from the ecliptic ‖ (esp. *pl.*) a region in relation to average distance from the equator **lat·i·tú·di·nal** *adj.*

la·trine (lətrí:n) *n.* a toilet in any army camp, factory etc.

lat·ter (lǽtər) **1.** *adj.* of the second of two ‖ of the second-mentioned of two **2.** *pron.* the latter person or thing

lat·ter·ly (lǽtərli) *adv. (old-fash.)* recently, of late

lat·tice (lǽtis) **1.** *n.* a framework or structure of wooden or metal laths crossing one another at regular intervals, leaving spaces between them and used, e.g. as a screen or ornamental feature ‖ something resembling the crisscross pattern of this **2.** *v.t. pres. part.* **lat·tic·ing** *past* and *past part.* **lat·ticed** to furnish with a lattice ‖ to make a lattice of

laud·a·bil·i·ty (lɔdəbíliti) *n.* the quality of being laudable

laud·a·ble (lɔ́dəb'l) *adj.* worthy of praise **láud·a·bly** *adv.*

laud·a·to·ry (lɔ́dətɔri:, lɔ́dətouri:) *adj.* praising, complimentary, *a laudatory speech*

laugh (læf, lɑf) **1.** *v.i.* to express amusement, mirth, contempt, fear etc. by inarticulate, explosive sounds, usually accompanied by convulsive muscular movements, esp. of the face ‖ to experience these emotions, esp. silently or inwardly ‖ *v.t.* to utter with a laugh or as if with a laugh ‖ to cause (someone) to do something by playfully mocking him **to laugh in someone's face** to treat someone with mocking defiance to his face **2.** *n.* an instance of laughing ‖ *(pop.)* a joke, cause of amusement **good for a laugh** likely to produce a laugh but not much else **láugh·a·ble** *adj.* such as to cause amusement or contempt **láugh·a·bly** *adv.*

laugh·ing (lǽfiŋ, lάfiŋ) *adj.* that laughs ‖ causing amusement, esp. in the phrase **no** (or **not a**) **laughing matter** something likely to have serious consequences

laugh·ter (lǽftər, lάftər) *n.* the act of laughing ‖ the sound accompanying this

launch (lɑntʃ) **1.** *v.t.* to cause (esp. a newly built ship) to move from land into water ‖ to cause (a glider) to become airborne ‖ to plan and cause to become operative ‖ to cause (something) to be propelled up or forward **2.** *n.* the act of launching a ship, missile etc.

launch *n.* a fast, small, power-driven boat, used on rivers or for short sea trips

laun·der (lɔ́ndər) **1.** *n. (mining)* an orewashing trough **2.** *v.t.* to wash (clothes etc.) ‖ *v.i.* to wash and iron ‖ to do laundry ‖ (of clothes etc.) to bear laundering ‖ to legitimatize illegally obtained funds by processing through a third party business

laun·der·ette (lɔndərét, lɔndərət) *n.* ə laundromat

laun·dress (lɔ́ndris) *n.* a woman whose job is laundering clothes

laun·dro·mat (lɔ́ndrəmæt) *n.* premises where customers can use washing machines and usually dryers for a fee

laun·dry (lɔ́ndri:) *pl.* **laun·dries** *n.* a place in a home,

apartment house etc. equipped for laundering clothes etc. ‖ a commercial establishment equipped and staffed to launder clothes etc. ‖ a batch of clothes etc. to be laundered

lau·rel (lɔ́rəl, lɒ́rəl) *n.* a tree of S. Europe ‖ any of various evergreen trees or shrubs resembling the European laurel, e.g. the spurge laurel **to look to one's laurels** to make the effort needed to retain some threatened distinction **to rest on one's laurels** to be content with past achievement and make no more effort

la·va (lάvə) *n.* molten rock which issues from a volcano or volcanic vent in the liquid state ‖ any of the solid materials obtained when this is cooled

la·va·liere (lævəlíər) *n.* a pendant worn on a chain around the neck

lav·a·to·ry (lǽvətɔri:, lǽvətɒuri:) *pl.* **lav·a·to·ries** *n.* a room with a toilet and a washbasin ‖ a room with a washbasin

lav·en·der (lǽvəndər) *n.* a small European shrub, native to the S. Alps ‖ the color of the flowers ‖ the dried flowers and stalks of the plant used in sachets etc.

lav·ish (lǽviʃ) **1.** *adj.* given or provided with great generosity and abundance ‖ giving or providing in this way **2.** *v.t.* to bestow with large generosity

law (lɔ) *n.* a custom or practice recognized as binding by a community, esp. as a result of having been so decreed by the governing authority ‖ the whole body of such customs or practices ‖ obedience to such customs or practices ‖ such customs or practices considered as a branch of knowledge ‖ the profession of interpreting and enforcing such customs or practices ‖ an aspect of such customs or practices, *civil law,* or a body of customs or practices applicable to a specific group, community etc., *military law* ‖ a relationship between cause and effect, or a statement of what occurs in nature, as found by observation and experiment to be true, *the law of supply and demand* ‖ (in a discipline or moral code) a practice accepted as correct, a rule **to lay down the law** to be pompously authoritative and dogmatic **to take the law into one's own hands** to act, esp. to punish, outside the sanction of the law

law-a·bid·ing (lɔ́əbaidiŋ) *adj.* obedient to the law

law·ful (lɔ́fəl) *adj.* allowed by law ‖ legitimate, *a lawful ruler* ‖ valid, enforceable by law

law·less (lɔ́lis) *adj.* having no regard for laws ‖ without law, *a lawless region* ‖ illegal ‖ disorderly

lawn (lɔn) *n.* a stretch of grass-covered land kept closely cut

law·suit (lɔ́su:t) *n.* a claim brought for judgment before a lawcourt

law·yer (lɔ́jər, lɔ́iər) *n.* someone qualified to practice law, as an attorney, advocate etc.

lax (læks) *adj.* free from tension, slack ‖ not strict ‖ careless, negligent ‖ *(phon.,* of vowels) pronounced with relaxed tongue and associated muscles ‖ (of the bowels) loose

lax·a·tive (lǽksətiv) **1.** *adj.* loosening the bowels and relieving constipation **2.** *n.* a laxative medicine

lax·i·ty (lǽksiti:) *n.* the quality or condition of being lax

lay (lei) **1.** *v. pres. part.* **lay·ing** *past* and *past part.* **laid** (leid) *v.t.* to place in a more or less horizontal position on a more or less horizontal surface with a minimum of impact ‖ to do this ceremonially ‖ to apply (paint, plaster etc.) to ‖ to place in position ‖ to bring forth (an egg) ‖ to stake as a bet or wager ‖ to get (the table) ready for a meal ‖ to cover, *the floor was laid with carpet* ‖ to impute (blame, responsibility etc.) ‖ *v.i.* to bring forth eggs **to be able to lay**

one's hand (or hands) on to be able to find at once (what one is looking for) to lay bare (*rhet.*) to uncover to lay before to present to for discussion, consideration etc. to lay down to surrender (arms) || to sacrifice (one's life) || to place (a bet) || to store away (wine) to lay eyes on to see to lay hands on to seize to lay it on to flatter extravagantly || to charge excessively || to boast outrageously to lay low (*pop.*) to knock (someone) down || (of a disease) to cause (someone) to be sick or physically weakened to lay off to discharge from employment, esp. temporarily || (*pop.*) to refrain from (some activity) || (*pop.*) to stop interfering with || to stop work to lay on the line to put up (money) in full || to make (an offer, statement) without reservations or conditions to lay out to spend (money) in a planned way || to prepare (a corpse) for burial || (*pop.*) to render (someone) unconscious to lay over to stop for a usually short period during a journey 2. *n.* the manner, position or direction in which something lies || an animal's lie the lay of the land the main aspects of a situation as one discerns it

lay·er (léiər) 1. *n.* one thickness, coating etc. of one or more substances lying upon or under one or more other substances || a laying hen || a machine that twists rope || a shoot or branch of a plant which is set into the ground to take root while still attached to the parent plant (from which it is later severed) || a plant propagated in this way 2. *v.t.* to root (a plant) from a layer || *v.i.* to form in layers, strata etc. || (of a plant) to form a layer or layers

lay·ette (leiét) *n.* the outfit of clothing, furniture, linen etc. for a newborn child

lay·man (léimən) *pl.* lay·men (léimən) *n.* a person who is not a priest or cleric || a person without recognized status or expert knowledge, in contrast to a professional man

lay·out (léiaut) *n.* the act of arranging or disposing something in an orderly fashion || the way in which things are laid in relation to one another, esp. print and illustration for typographical display || a plan or mockup for such display

laz·i·ly (léizili:) *adv.* in a lazy manner

laz·i·ness (léizi:nis) *n.* the quality or state of being lazy

la·zy (léizi:) *comp.* la·zi·er *superl.* la·zi·est *adj.* with little will to work, idle || characterized by or inducing lack of exertion || slow-moving

lead (li:d) 1. *v. pres. part.* lead·ing *past* and *past part.* led (led) *v.t.* to show (someone) the way to go by accompanying him || to force (someone) to go with oneself || (of a road etc.) to take (someone) to a place || to hold and take (someone or something) to a place || to show (someone) the way to go by markings, indications etc. || to cause (water etc.) to go in a specific direction || to persuade to do or believe something || to cause to do or believe something || to conduct (an orchestra, chorus etc.) || to be moving at the head of (a procession, race etc.) || to hold first place in || to cause to follow one's example || (*cards*) to play as the first card of a hand || to go through, pass, live (life etc.) || to cause someone to go through, pass, live (a particular sort of life) || *v.i.* to be at the head of a group in motion || to show the way || (of a road etc.) to go in a certain direction || to bring about a specified result || to hold the directorial or foremost position || (*cards*) to make the first play || (*boxing*) to begin a series of blows to lead on to entice (someone of the opposite sex) || to cause (someone) to go further in some action than his prudence or moral sense would otherwise have allowed to lead up to to prepare the way for, e.g. in conversation or in a plot 2. *n.* a showing of the way || a clue as to direction || the principal or guiding part in a group action || the foremost or front position || the state of being in this position || the distance, time etc. by which one is in front of others || leadership || example, *they all followed his lead* || (*cards*) the act or opportunity of

playing first || (*cards*) the card so played || (*acting*) the most important role || (*acting*) someone who plays such a role || (*boxing*) the first blow of a series of attacking blows || (*journalism*) the most important news article in a newspaper || (*journalism*) the opening paragraph or paragraphs of a news story containing the essential facts || (*mining*) a lode || (*mining*) a stratum of gold-bearing gravel in an old riverbed

lead (led) 1. *n.* a soft, very dense, malleable and ductile, divalent or tetravalent metallic element || (*printing*) a thin strip of metal inserted between lines of type || (*pl., glazing*) thin strips of lead between which small panes of glass are held 2. *v.t.* to cover or frame with lead || (*printing*) to separate (lines of type) with leads

lead·en (léd'n) *adj.* made of lead || of a dull gray color || very heavy, hard to lift || oppressive || sluggish, lacking animation

lead·er (lí:dər) *n.* someone who acts as a guide || a directing head or chief e.g. of a political party || someone who or something that leads a body of moving troops, animals etc. || someone or something that holds first place || a conductor of a musical group, esp. of one in which he also performs || (*bot.*) a shoot growing from the apex of a stem or branch || (*pl., printing*) a series of dots to lead the eye horizontally along a line (e.g. in tabular display) || the front horse in a harnessed team || (*fishing*) a length of gut to which the hook is attached lead·er·ship *n.* the position of a leader || the quality displayed by a leader || the act of leading or an instance of this

lead·ing (lí:diŋ) 1. *adj.* coming first, e.g. in a procession || prominent, influential 2. *n.* the act of someone or something that leads

lead·ing (lédiŋ) *n.* (*printing*) lead (thin strip of metal) or the spacing between lines achieved by such leads

leaf (li:f) 1. *pl.* leaves (li:vz) *n.* a thin expanded outgrowth of a plant stem or a twig, usually green and consisting essentially of a broad blade and a stalk || a single sheet of folded paper, consisting in a book of two pages back to back || the movable section of a table top which can be added or removed, or one which can be raised on hinges to extend the surface area || a similar hinged section in a folding shutter or door etc. || leaves of tea, tobacco etc. as an item of commerce || (*pop.*) a petal, esp. of a rose to take a leaf out of someone's book to follow someone's example to turn over a new leaf to make a fresh start in an attempt to improve one's behavior 2. *v.i.* to produce leaves || (with 'through') to turn over the pages of (a book etc.) quickly and glance at the contents

leaf·let (lí:flit) *n.* a small printed sheet of paper, single or folded but not stitched, distributed free and usually containing advertising, propaganda etc. || an individual unit of a compound leaf || a small or immature leaf

leaf·y (lí:fi:) *comp.* leaf·i·er *superl.* leaf·i·est *adj.* full of leaves || like a leaf

league (li:g) 1. *n.* an association of persons, cities etc. formed to assist one another in some way || an association of football, baseball or other athletic clubs agreeing to play against one another under agreed rules in league with in alliance with (usually implying that no good will come of the alliance) 2. *v.i.* and *t. pres. part.* lea·guing *past* and *past part.* lea·gued to unite in a league

league *n.* (*hist.*) a measure of distance, usually about three miles

leak (li:k) *n.* a small hole, crack etc. in a wall, container etc. through which e.g. fluid or light escapes or penetrates || that which leaks or is leaked to spring a leak to develop a hole etc. through which a fluid or light escapes or penetrates

leak *v.i.* (e.g. of a fluid or light, with 'in' or 'out') to pass through a small hole or crack in a retaining or excluding wall, container etc. || to have a small hole or crack through which something (e.g. usually retained or excluded fluid or light) can pass || (of secret or restricted information) to become known to people not intended to have the information ‖ *v.t.* to allow (e.g. fluid or light) to leak ‖ to allow (secret or restricted information) to lead **leak·age** *n.* the act of leaking or an instance of this ‖ something which has leaked or the amount leaked

leak·y (líːki:) *comp.* **leak·i·er** *superl.* **leak·i·est** *adj.* allowing fluids etc. to leak in or out

lean (liːn) **1.** *v. pres. part.* **lean·ing** *past* and *past part.* **leaned,** *Br.* also **leant** (lent) *v.i.* to be or stand not quite upright ‖ to place the body, or part of the body, in such a position ‖ (with 'on' or 'upon') to depend for support or encouragement ‖ to incline in opinion or feeling ‖ *v.t.* to cause to lean ‖ to place for support **to lean over backward** to spare no effort in trying (to do something) **2.** *n.* the act of leaning or an instance of this

lean 1. *adj.* having little fat ‖ (of a person or animal) thin but not excessively so ‖ having or producing little of value **2.** *n.* that part of meat which has little fat

lean·ing (líːniŋ) *n.* tendency, inclination

leap (liːp) *n.* the act of leaping ‖ the distance leaped ‖ something to be leaped ‖ an abrupt change **by leaps and bounds** very fast

leap *pres. part.* **leap·ing** *past* and *past part.* **leaped, leapt** (lept) *v.i.* to project the body through the air from one place to another with a sudden movement by the muscular effort of the legs or feet, esp. with more force than is usually suggested by 'jump' ‖ to rise quickly as if with a leap ‖ *v.t.* to pass over by leaping ‖ to cause to leap

learn (ləːrn) *pres. part.* **learn·ing** *past* and *past part.* **learned, learnt** (ləːrnt) *v.t.* to acquire knowledge of or skill in by study, instruction, practice or experience ‖ to commit to memory ‖ to come to know or be aware of ‖ *v.i.* to acquire knowledge or skill ‖ (with 'of') to become aware, to be told **learn·ed** (ləːrnid) *adj.* having a great deal of knowledge ‖ characterized by or demanding profound knowledge **léarn·er** *n.* **léarn·ing** *n.* a large and well organized body of usually nonscientific ideas, acquired and retained by long and great effort ‖ the mental process itself ‖ the acquisition of skills or mental attitudes

lease (liːs) *n.* a legal contract between lessor and lessee putting land or property of the former at the disposal of the latter usually for a stated period, for a stipulated rent, and under other specified conditions ‖ the document itself ‖ the period stated **to get** (or **take, have**) **a new lease on** (or **of**) **life** to survive a dangerous or difficult period and renew one's energy, drive, optimism etc.

lease *pres. part.* **leas·ing** *past* and *past part.* **leased** *v.t.* to put (land, buildings etc.) at the disposal of a lessee under a lease ‖ to take (property, buildings etc.) into one's own use under a lease

leash (liːʃ) **1.** *n.* a strap, cord or chain fastened to the collar of an animal or jess of a hawk for control **2.** *v.t.* to put a leash on

least (liːst) **1.** *adj.* (*superl.* of LITTLE) smallest in size, amount, quality, importance etc. **the least** (usually after a negative) smallest, slightest, *not the least suspicion* **2.** *n.* the smallest amount **at least** as the bare minimum to satisfy legitimate expectations, even if any wider statement could be disputed **at the least** at a minimum estimate **not in the least** not in the slightest degree **least of all** with the smallest justification **3.** *adv.* in the smallest degree

leath·er (léðər) **1.** *n.* the skin of an animal, cleaned and made flexible and durable by tanning, and used for shoes, luggage, harness etc. ‖ something made

of this, e.g. a stirrup leather ‖ a piece of chamois leather used for polishing **2.** *adj.* pertaining to, or made of, leather

leath·er·y (léðəri:) *adj.* like leather in consistency or appearance ‖ tough

leave (liːv) *n.* permission, esp. to be absent from (esp. *mil.*) duty or from a place of duty ‖ the period of such absence, *seven days' leave* **on leave** absent from duty with permission **to take leave of** to say goodbye to **to take leave of one's senses** to behave so foolishly as to seem temporarily insane **to take one's leave** to say goodbye and go

leave *v. pres. part.* **leav·ing** *past* and *past part.* **left** (left) *v.i.* to depart, go away ‖ to cease to reside in a certain place, attend school, serve an employer etc. ‖ *v.t.* to allow to remain by oversight, *he left his hat on the train* ‖ to cause to remain as a consequence, *sign etc., the wound left a scar* ‖ to be survived by, *he leaves a wife and three children* ‖ to bequeath, *he left her all his money* ‖ to deposit for transmission or collection, *she left a message for him* **to leave alone** to stop interfering with or not interfere with **to leave behind** to go away without **to leave off** to cease, *to leave off work* ‖ to stop wearing (a garment) **to leave out** to omit ‖ to put (something) where it will be available **to leave to chance** to allow chance to settle a matter

leave *pres. part.* **leav·ing** *past* and *past part.* **leaved** *v.i.* to put out leaves

leav·en (lévən) **1.** *n.* a substance added to dough which, by fermentation, produces carbon dioxide gas and thus makes the dough rise and become porous **2.** *v.t.* to cause (dough) to ferment by adding leaven ‖ to cause a general change for the better in, esp. to make as though light and airy

lech (letʃ) *v.* to lust; to be a lecher —**lech** *n.* one who leches

lech·er (létʃər) *n.* a man given to lechery

lech·er·ous (létʃərəs) *adj.* given to, characterized by or encouraging lechery

lech·er·y (létʃəri:) *n.* gross indulgence in carnal pleasure

lec·tern (léktəːrn) *n.* a raised desk in a church on which the Bible is placed for reading the Scriptures aloud ‖ a similar desk for supporting music in the choir ‖ a stand with a sloping top for holding a reader's or lecturer's book, papers etc.

lec·ture (léktʃər) **1.** *n.* a prepared disquisition made to an audience, class, etc., designed to instruct or explain at some length ‖ a long and tedious reprimand **2.** *v. pres. part.* **lec·tur·ing** *past* and *past part.* **lec·tured** *v.i.* to deliver a lecture or series of lectures ‖ *v.t.* to instruct by giving a lecture ‖ to reprimand (someone) tediously and at length **léc·tur·er** *n.* someone who professionally instructs by giving lectures

ledge (ledʒ) *n.* a narrow horizontal projection in a vertical or steep surface ‖ a ridge of rock, esp. under water ‖ (*mining*) a stratum of rock rich in ore

ledg·er (lédʒər) *n.* (*bookkeeping*) a large book in which are recorded the credits and debits of commercial transactions ‖ a flat gravestone ‖ (*building*) a horizontal scaffold pole parallel to the wall

lee (liː) **1.** *n.* the sheltered side, opposite to that against which the wind blows **2.** *adj.* of, pertaining to or located on the sheltered side

leech (liːtʃ) *n.* a class of segmented, chiefly aquatic, suctorial annelids, which cling hard to the skin of an animal while sucking blood and relinquish their hold when fully distended ‖ a human parasite

leek (liːk) *n.* an edible vegetable, native to S. Asia, allied to the onion but having a long slender cylindrical bulb

---

leer (liər) **1.** *v.t.* to cast a knowing sidelong look that travesties a smile, and may indicate lust, malicious triumph or stupidity **2.** *n.* such a look

leer·y (líːəriː) *adj.* suspicious, wary

lee·way (líːweɪ) *n.* *(naut.)* the drift of a vessel to the leeward of her proper course ‖ *(aeron.)* the angle of drift of an aircraft due to crosswind ‖ a margin of freedom of action ‖ a margin of time, money etc.

left (left) **1.** *adj.* of or on the side of the body where the heart is situated, or on this side of a person's vertical axis of symmetry ‖ or on to this side as perceived by an observer ‖ (of a river bank) on this side of an observer facing downstream **2.** *adv.* in or to a left direction or side **3.** *n.* the left side or direction ‖ *(boxing)* the left hand or a blow with this hand ‖ *(marching, dancing* etc.) the left foot

leg (leg) **1.** *n.* one of the limbs supporting a human or animal body and used in moving it from place to place ‖ this portion of an animal (or part of it) as food ‖ a support for an object raised above the ground ‖ the part of a garment which covers a human leg ‖ one section of a V-shaped instrument, e.g. a pair of compasses ‖ *(math.)* a side of a triangle other than the base or hypotenuse ‖ one section or stage of a journey, a relay race etc. **not to have a leg to stand on** to lack any rational support **on one's last legs** at the end of one's endurance **on its last legs** hardly stable or useful any longer **to pull (someone's) leg** to make a fool of (someone) by making him believe what is not true **2.** *v.i. pres. part.* **leg·ging** *past* and *past part.* **legged** (with 'it') to walk in a hurry or run

leg·a·cy (légəsiː) *pl.* **leg·a·cies** *n.* money or property bequeathed in a will ‖ something resulting from and left behind by an action, event or person, *a legacy of hatred*

le·gal (líːgʼl) *adj.* of or pertaining to law ‖ in agreement with, or as prescribed by, the law ‖ valid in law as distinct from equity ‖ *(theol.)* of or pertaining to the Law

le·gal·i·ty (liːgǽlitiː) *pl.* **le·gal·i·ties** *n.* accordance with the law ‖ *(theol.)* legalism ‖ *(pl.)* the requirements and procedure of the law

le·gal·ize (líːgʼlaɪz) *pres. part.* **le·gal·iz·ing** *past* and *past part.* **le·gal·ized** *v.t.* to make legal

le·ga·tion (ligéɪʃən) *n.* the official residence and office of a diplomatic representative of lower status than an ambassador ‖ the representative and his staff ‖ a diplomatic mission ‖ legateship

leg·end (léʤənd) *n.* a story, handed down from the past, which lacks accurate historical evidence but has been, and may still be, popularly accepted as true ‖ a body of such stories ‖ an inscription, esp. on a coin or medal ‖ an explanation or comment beneath a photograph or cartoon, e.g. in a newspaper ‖ a key to a map etc. **leg·end·ar·y** (léʤənderiː) *adj.* told of in legends

leg·er·de·main (leʤərdəméɪn) *n.* deception of the eye by quickness of the hand, esp. in conjuring

legged (legd, légid) *adj.* (in combination) having legs of a specified numebr or type

leg·gings (légiŋz) *pl. n.* a sturdy, protective outer covering for the legs, of various materials and lengths

leg·gy (légiː) *adj.* having long legs, esp. in comparison with the size of the body

leg·i·bil·i·ty (leʤəbíliti) *n.* the quality of being legible

leg·i·ble (léʤəbʼl) *adj.* (of handwriting, inscriptions etc.) able to be read **lég·i·bly** *adv.*

le·gion (líːʤən) *n.* *(Rom. hist.)* a division of the Roman army, of 3,000–6,000 foot soldiers, often with additional cavalry, divided into 10 cohorts ‖ a great number, *legions of ants*

le·gion·naire (liːʤənέər) *n.* a member of a legion, e.g. the foreign legion

leg·is·late (léʤisleɪt) *pres. part.* **leg·is·lat·ing** *past* and *past part.* **leg·is·lat·ed** *v.i.* to make laws ‖ *v.t.* to effect or cause to become by making laws

leg·is·la·tion (leʤisléɪʃən) *n.* the process of legislating

a law or body of laws enacted ‖ a law, bill etc. under consideration by a legislative body

leg·is·la·tive (léʤisleɪtiv) **1.** *adj.* empowered to legislate ‖ of or effected by legislation ‖ of a legislature **2.** *n.* a legislature

leg·is·la·tor (léʤisleɪtər) *n.* someone who makes laws, esp. a member of a legislative body

leg·is·la·ture (léʤisleɪtʃər) *n.* the body empowered to make, amend or repeal laws for a nation or unit of a nation

le·git·i·ma·cy (liʤítəməsiː) *n.* the quality or state of being legitimate

le·git·i·mate 1. (liʤítəmit) *adj.* born of a legally recognized marriage ‖ in accord with the provisions of law ‖ in accord with accepted rules and procedures ‖ in accord with rules of hereditary right ‖ in accord with the laws of logic, admissible **2.** (liʤítəmeit) *v.t. pres. part.* **le·git·i·mat·ing** *past* and *past part.* **le·git·i·mat·ed** to make legitimate ‖ to establish as legitimately born ‖ to justify **le·git·i·ma·tize** (liʤítəmitaɪz) *pres. part.* **le·git·i·ma·tiz·ing** *past* and *past part.* **le·git·i·ma·tized** *v.t.* to legitimate

le·git·i·mize (liʤítəmaɪz) *pres. part.* **le·git·i·miz·ing** *past* and *past part.* **le·git·i·mized** *v.t.* to make legitimate

lei·sure (líːʒər, léʒər) **1.** *n.* time when one is free from the need to do any work **at leisure** not working or busy ‖ without hurrying **at one's leisure** when convenient and without any compulsion to hurry **2.** *adj.* free from work ‖ leisured **léi·sured** *adj.* having plenty of leisure

lei·sure·ly (líːʒərliː, léʒərliː) **1.** *adj.* unhurried **2.** *adv.* in an unhurried manner

lem·on (lémən) *n.* a tree, probably native to S.E. Asia, that is widely cultivated in Mediterranean countries and the southern U.S.A. ‖ its yellow oval fruit ‖ the color of the ripe fruit

lem·on·ade (leménéid) *n.* a drink made by mixing lemon juice and sugar with water ‖ a commercially made, lemon-flavored soft drink

lend (lend) *pres. part.* **lend·ing** *past* and *past part.* **lent** (lent) *v.t.* to place in the temporary possession of another (for his use, enjoyment etc.) with the expectation of resuming possession later ‖ to loan (money) at interest ‖ to let out (books) for a fee ‖ to transfer (someone) to another job or service temporarily ‖ *(fig.)* to furnish, supply, *to lend dignity to a scene* ‖ *v.i.* to make a loan or loans **to lend a hand** to assist **to lend itself to** to be serviceable or well suited for

length (leŋθ, leŋkθ) *n.* linear extent in space from end to end measured in certain arbitrary units ‖ the longer of the two linear dimensions of a surface or plane or the longest of the three linear dimensions of a solid ‖ extent in time from beginning to end ‖ the length of a horse, boat etc., used as a unit in stating the distance between competitors in a race, *to win by two lengths* ‖ the quantity of a vowel or syllable **at length** at last, after a long time **to go to any length** (or **lengths**) to set no limits to what one is prepared to do **to go to great length** (or **lengths**) to set hardly any limits on what one is prepared to do **to keep at arm's length** to avoid too intimate a contact with

length·en (léŋθən, léŋkθən) *v.i.* to become longer ‖ *v.t.* to cause (something) to become longer

length·wise (léŋθwaɪz, léŋkθwaɪz) **1.** *adv.* in the direction of the length **2.** *adj.* of, being or going in the direction of the length

length·y (léŋθiː, léŋkθiː) *comp.* **length·i·er** *superl.* **length·i·est** *adj.* unusually or excessively long, *a lengthy journey, a lengthy speech*

le·ni·ence (líːniːəns, líːnjəns) *n.* the quality of being lenient or an instance of this

le·ni·en·cy (líːniːənsiː, líːnjənsiː) *n.* lenience

le·ni·ent (líːniːənt, líːnjənt) *adj.* tolerant, disinclined to punish severely ‖ (of punishment, sentences etc.) mild, not as severe as the fault might justify

lens (lenz) *pl.* **lens·es** *n.* a piece of glass, or other transparent refracting substance, with two opposite regular surfaces, of which at least one is curved, used in optical systems (a camera, a magnifying glass etc.) to converge or diverge light rays to form an image ‖ a device used to focus or direct radiation other than light (e.g. a beam of electrons in an electron microscope) ‖ a transparent, almost spherical body behind the pupil of the eye, focusing light on to the retina ‖ a facet of a compound eye

leop·ard (lépərd) *n. Felis pardus,* fam. *Felidae,* a large, fierce, carnivorous mammal native to Africa and S. Asia, usually having a fawn to reddish-buff coat marked with irregular black spots ‖ any of various similar felines, e.g. the snow leopard, the cheetah ‖ the fur of a leopard

lep·er (lépər) *n.* a person suffering from leprosy ‖ (*rhet.*) a social outcast

lep·ro·sy (léprəsi:) *n.* a chronic infective disease due to the leprosy bacillus

Les·bi·an (lézbiːən) **1.** *adj.* pertaining to Lesbos ‖ relating to homosexuality in women **2.** *n.* a woman homosexual **Lés·bi·an·ism** *n.*

le·sion (líːʒən) *n.* a change in the structure of a tissue or an organ due to injury or disease, usually resulting in impairment of normal function ‖ an injury

less (les) alt. *comp.* of LITTLE, c.f. LESSER ‖ **1.** *adj.* smaller in size, degree, extent etc. ‖ not so much ‖ lower in rank **in less than no time** very quickly **no less than** as much as ‖ as many as **2.** *prep.* made smaller by, *ten less seven is three* **3.** *adv.* in or to a smaller degree or extent **4.** *n.* the smaller in amount, size, degree, number, importance

less·ee (lesíː) *n.* someone who is granted a lease

less·en (lés'n) *v.t.* to cause to become less ‖ *v.i.* to become less

less·er (lésər) alt. *comp.* of LITTLE ‖ *adj.* smaller in size, amount, quality, importance etc., *choose the lesser of two risks*

less·son (lés'n) *n.* that which is taught to a pupil by a teacher, esp. during a given period of time ‖ this period of time ‖ something to be learned ‖ (*pl.*) a series of sessions of instruction ‖ one unit in a series of sessions of instruction ‖ something, usually unpleasant, which serves as a warning or example

less·sor (lésɔr, lesɔ́r) *n.* someone who grants a lease

lest (lest) *conj.* (relating an act to its negative result) in order that . . . not ‖ (relating a feeling of fear, anxiety etc. to an undesired but possible event) that

let (let) *v. pres. part.* **let·ting** *past* and *past part.* **let** *v.t.* to permit to ‖ (often with 'out') to assign (a contract) ‖ used as an auxiliary in the imperative 1st and 3rd persons in commands **let alone** without mentioning **to let down** to lower ‖ to cause (someone) disappointment by failing to do what was expected **to let (someone) down gently** to soften the blow of a reproof, humiliation or disappointment by administering it mildly to (someone) **to let go** to cease to hold on to **to let in on** to make (someone) party to (a secret etc.) **to let on** to reveal a secret ‖ to pretend **to let oneself go** to throw off restraints **to let up** to relax one's efforts ‖ to become less

let *n.* (*law,* only in) **without let or hindrance** without impediment ‖ (*lawn tennis, rackets* etc.) an obstruction of the ball, esp. contact with the top of the tennis net, necessitating a replay

-let *suffix* added to nouns to express smallness or minor importance

let·down (létdaun) *n.* a disappointment, esp. of confident expectations, or total failure to do what was relied on ‖ a relaxation or lowering of standards ‖ a drop in amount or volume

le·thal (líːθəl) *adj.* causing or able to cause death

le·thar·gic (ləθɑ́rdʒik) *adj.* of, marked by or causing lethargy **le·thár·gi·cal·ly** *adv.*

leth·ar·gy (léθərdʒiː) *n.* the state of lacking energy and interest

let·ter (létər) **1.** *n.* one of the printed or written symbols of an alphabet, used in representing speech sounds ‖ a written, printed or typed personal communication ‖ (often *pl.*) a document, written statement etc. constituting the authority for a particular action, status, privilege etc. ‖ (*printing*) a font of type ‖ (*pl.*) literature ‖ (*pl.*) scholarly study or knowledge, esp. of literature **to the letter** precisely and completely **2.** *v.t.* to inscribe with letters ‖ to impress (letters) on a book cover or page

let·tered (létərd) *adj.* marked with letters ‖ (*rhet.*) cultured ‖ (*rhet.*) learned, esp. in literature

let·ter·head (létərhed) *n.* the heading (address etc.) printed at the top of writing paper ‖ (*commerce*) a piece of paper so printed

let·ter·ing (létəriŋ) *n.* the act of marking with letters ‖ such letters, esp. in regard to style or quality, as used in calligraphy

let·tuce (létəs) *n.* a crisp-leaved, annual plant, widely cultivated in temperate regions and usually eaten raw in salads

leu·ke·mi·a, leu·ce·mi·a, leu·kae·mi·a, leu·cae·mi·a (luːkíːmiːə) *n.* (*med.*) an acute or chronic disease of unknown origin which affects the leukocytes in the tissues, their number greatly increasing, sometimes without an equal increase in the leukocytes of the bloodstream

lev·ee (léviː) *n.* an embankment built to prevent a river from overflowing ‖ a landing place from a river ‖ an embankment built to enclose an area of land to be flooded

lev·el (lévəl) **1.** *n.* an instrument, esp. a spirit level, for testing whether something is horizontal ‖ a horizontal line, plane or surface ‖ a surveyor's level ‖ a piece of country which is horizontal or relatively so ‖ a horizontal condition ‖ a position in a scale of importance, *the wage increase applies at all levels in the industry* ‖ a degree of attainment, *the general level of the class is high* **on the level** (*pop.*) honest, truthful ‖ (*pop.*) honestly, truthfully **to find one's own level** to find a position (in a society) that corresponds with one's status and abilities **2.** *adj.* horizontal, having no part higher than another ‖ (of two or more persons, things etc., sometimes with 'with') being on the same level ‖ unflustered, *a level head* ‖ not betraying emotion, *level tones* ‖ steady and direct, *a level look* ‖ (*phys.*) equipotential **3.** *v. pres. part.* **lev·el·ing** *past* and *past part.* **lev·eled** *v.t.* to make level ‖ to make level with the ground ‖ to aim, direct, *to level a gun, to level an accusation* ‖ *v.i.* to become level **to level off** to make level, smooth

lev·el·er (lévələr) *n.* someone or something which brings things or people to the same level

lev·el·head·ed (lévəlhédid) *adj.* showing balanced judgment and good sense

lev·er (lévər, líːvər) **1.** *n.* a rigid bar turning about a fixed point, the fulcrum, used to modify or transmit a force or motion applied at a second point so that it acts at a third point ‖ anything which brings influence to bear **2.** *v.t.* to move with or as if with a lever ‖ *v.i.* to use a lever **lév·er·age** *n.* the action or effect of a lever ‖ the way in which influence is brought to bear

lev·i·tate (léviteit) *pres. part.* **lev·i·tat·ing** *past* and *past part.* **lev·i·tat·ed** *v.i.* to rise or float in the air as if weightless ‖ *v.t.* to cause to rise or float in the air **lev·i·tá·tion** *n.*

lev·i·ty (léviti:) *pl.* **lev·i·ties** *n.* lighthearted and frivolous behavior, esp. when not appropriate to the circumstances ‖ an instance of such behavior

lev·y (lévi:) **1.** *pl.* **lev·ies** *n.* the imposition by a state or organization of a tax, duty, fine etc. ‖ the amount demanded, esp. per head ‖ *(rhet.)* the calling up of men for military service or the men called up ‖ *(law)* the seizure of property in accordance with a legal claim or judgment **2.** *v. pres. part.* **lev·y·ing** *past* and *past part.* **lev·ied** *v.t.* to impose (a tax, fine etc.) ‖ *(rhet.)* to call up (men) for military service ‖ *(rhet.)* to begin, make or carry on (war) ‖ *(law)* to seize (property) in accordance with a legal claim or judgment ‖ *v.i. (law)* to make a levy

lewd (lu:d) *adj.* offending modesty, indecent ‖ lascivious

lex·i·cal (léksik'l) *adj.* having to do with the words of a language or their meaning as defined in a dictionary (as opposed to their structural meaning) ‖ of or pertaining to a lexicon or lexicography

lex·i·cog·ra·pher (lɛksikrógrəfər) *n.* someone who compiles or writes a dictionary **lex·i·co·graph·i·cal** (lɛksikəgrǽfik'l) *adj.* **lex·i·cóg·ra·phy** *n.* the process of compiling or writing a dictionary

lex·i·con (léksikən, léksikɒn) *n.* a dictionary ‖ the special vocabulary of a group, an individual, an occupational field etc., or the vocabulary of a language

li·a·bil·i·ty (lɑiəbíliti:) *pl.* **li·a·bil·i·ties** *n.* the quality or condition of being liable ‖ that which one is liable for ‖ *(pl.)* debts

li·a·ble (lɑiəb'l) *adj.* (with 'for') legally bound or responsible ‖ (with 'to') subject (to a tax, law, penalty etc.) ‖ (with 'to') having a tendency, apt ‖ (with 'to') likely

li·ai·son (li:éizɔ̃, li:eizɔ̃) *n. (rhet.)* a love affair outside marriage ‖ *(mil.,* li:éizən) the establishment of harmonious cooperation between separate units of an armed force

li·ar (lɑiər) *n.* someone who tells a lie or habitually tells lies

li·ba·tion (lɑibéiʃən) *n.* the act of pouring wine or oil upon the ground as a sacrifice to a god ‖ the wine or oil so sacrificed

li·bel (lɑib'l) **1.** *n. (law)* a published statement, photograph etc. which without due cause has the result, or is intended to have the result, of bringing its subject into disrepute ‖ the act of publishing such a statement etc. ‖ *(pop.)* any false and insulting statement ‖ (with 'on') something that brings undeserved discredit **2.** *v.t. pres. part.* **li·bel·ing** *past* and *past part.* **li·beled** to publish a libel about ‖ *(pop.)* to insult, make false and malicious statements about ‖ *(law)* to bring suit against by filing a libel **li·bel·ous** *adj.*

lib·er·al (líbərəl, líbrəl) **1.** *adj.* giving freely, giving more than is necessary or usual ‖ generously large, more in quantity than is necessary or usual ‖ involving a general enlarging of the mind beyond the merely professional or technical ‖ not subject to the common prejudices or conventions ‖ *(politics)* favorable to individual liberty, social reform and the removal of economic restraints ‖ admitting a free interpretation of religious doctrine and of its application to ritual and conduct **Lib·er·al** (of or belonging to the Liberal party **2.** *n. (politics)* a person who holds liberal views **Liberal** a member or supporter of the Liberal party

lib·er·al·ism (líbərəlizəm, líbrəlizəm) *n.* the quality or state of being liberal ‖ a body of social, political, religious or economic doctrines or attitudes which are liberal

lib·er·al·i·ty (lɪbərǽliti:) *pl.* **lib·er·al·i·ties** *n.* the quality or state of being liberal ‖ an instance of liberal giving

lib·er·al·ize (líbərəlaiz, líbrəlaiz) *pres. part.* **lib·er·al·iz·ing** *past* and *past part.* **lib·er·al·ized** *v.t.* to make liberal ‖ *v.i.* to become liberal

lib·er·ate (líbəreit) *pres part.* **lib·er·at·ing** *past* and *past part.* **lib·er·at·ed** *v.t.* to set free, release ‖ *(chem.)* to free (e.g. a gas) from combination ‖ to change the status or ownership of, e.g. a nation, a piece of property

lib·er·a·tion (lɪbəréiʃən) *n.* a liberating or being liberated

lib·er·a·tor (líbəreitər) *n.* someone who liberates, esp. someone who sets people free from political oppression

lib·er·ty (líbərti:) *pl.* **lib·er·ties** *n.* the condition of being free to choose, esp. as between ways of acting or living, with an implication of wisdom and voluntary restraint ‖ the right to do as one pleases ‖ the condition of being free from physical confinement or captivity ‖ *(navy)* a short period of leave ‖ *(philos.)* free will **at liberty** free ‖ *(pop.)* unemployed, not busy ‖ authorized ‖ possessing the right, *I am not at liberty to tell you* **to take the liberty** (polite usage) to presume

li·bi·do (libí:dou, libáidou) *n. (psychol.)* the vital impulse or energy motivating human behavior ‖ the sexual urge

li·brar·i·an (laibréari:ən) *n.* a person in charge of a library ‖ a member of a staff of library workers

li·brar·y (láibreri:, líbrəri:) *pl.* **li·brar·ies** *n.* a room or building housing a collection of books, usually arranged according to some plan ‖ such a collection of books

li·bret·to (librétou) *pl.* **li·bret·tos, li·bret·ti** (librétí:) *n.* the words of an opera, oratorio etc. ‖ a book in which these are printed

li·cense, li·cence (láis'ns) **1.** *n.* a right formally granted in writing by an authority (who also has the power to withhold it), e.g. to drive a vehicle, marry, conduct certain businesses, possess a firearm etc. ‖ the official certificate of this right ‖ the generally recognized right of an artist, writer etc. to depart from strict adherence to rules or truth in his work ‖ a degree of freedom ‖ behavior in which liberty is abused or used in a socially undesirable way ‖ licentious behavior **2.** *v.t. pres. part.* **li·cens·ing, li·cenc·ing** *past* and *past part.* **li·censed, li·cenced** to grant a license to (someone) or for (something) **li·cen·see** (laisənsí:) *n.* someone to whom a license is granted **li·cens·er** *n.* someone who grants a license

li·cen·tious (laisénʃəs) *adj.* (of a person, book, play etc.) disregarding the laws of morality, esp. in sexual matters

lick (lik) **1.** *v.t.* to draw the tongue over ‖ (of waves, fire, flames etc.) to play lightly over the surface of ‖ *(pop.)* to beat soundly in a competition ‖ *(pop.)* to get the better of ‖ *(pop.)* to thrash, beat **to lick someone's shoes** (or **boots**) to be servile towards someone **2.** *n.* the act of licking or an instance of this ‖ the amount taken up by the tongue in such a lick ‖ a quick light coating, e.g. of paint ‖ *(pop.)* a great speed ‖ a salt lick

lic·o·rice, liq·uo·rice (líkəriʃ) *n.* a black extract made from the dried root of *Glycyrrhiza glabia,* fam. *Papilionaceae,* used as a demulcent and expectorant, in confectionery, and for flavoring tobacco ‖ this plant or its root

lid (lid) *n.* a cover closing the top of a receptacle fitting inside or outside its walls ‖ an eyelid ‖ an operculum in mosses ‖ the upper part of a pyridium

lie (lai) **1.** *v.i. pres. part.* **ly·ing** (láiiŋ) *past* **lay** (lei) *past part.* **lain** (lein) to have the body more or less horizontal upon a surface ‖ (usually with 'down') to assume such a position ‖ to be in the grave ‖ (of ships) to float at anchor ‖ to press, weigh heavily e.g. on the consciousness or conscience **to take lying down** to accept without protest **2.** *n.* the manner, position or direction in which something lies ‖ the place where a wild animal sleeps

lie *pres. part.* **ly·ing** (láiiŋ) *past* and *past part.* **lied** *v.i.* to tell a lie ‖ to deceive by making a false impression ‖ *v.t.* to get (one's way) by lying

lie *n.* an intentionally false statement or impression ‖ something thought of as like this

lie detector a device which registers the physical changes in the body (e.g. respiration, blood pressure) of someone under questioning. The record is interpreted as a guide to the person's veracity

lien (li:n, lí:ən) *n. (law)* the right to hold another's goods or property until a claim is met

lieu (lu:) *n.* (only in the phrases) **in lieu** instead **in lieu of** as a substitute for

lieu·ten·ant (lu:ténənt) *n.* someone acting for (i.e. holding the place of) a superior in rank ‖ *(navy)* an officer ranking immediately below a lieutenant commander ‖ *(mil.)* a first or second lieutenant

life (laif) *pl.* **lives** (laivz) *n.* the state of an organism characterized by certain processes or abilities that include metabolism, growth, reproduction and response ‖ the fact of being in this state ‖ the period of time from birth to the present ‖ the period of time from the present or another specified time to death ‖ a specified period or aspect of one's existence, *his school life, his spiritual life* ‖ a way or manner of existence, *city life, the life of the natives* ‖ a human being, *to save a life* ‖ the gay, animating presence, *he was the life of the party* **a matter of life and death** something that someone's life depends on ‖ a very critical matter **for dear life** as if or because one's life depended on it **for the life of me** (used for emphasis) even if my life depended on it **from life** *(art)* from the living model **not on your life** certainly not **to bring to life** to cause to be lively **to come to life** to begin to be lively **to have the time of one's life** to enjoy oneself very much **to take life** to kill

life·guard (láifgɑrd) *n.* an expert swimmer employed to prevent or deal with swimming casualties at a swimming pool etc.

life·less (láiflis) *adj.* without life ‖ providing no stimulus, arousing no interest

life·long (láifloŋ, láifloŋ) *adj.* for the period of a lifetime

life·size (láifsaiz) *adj.* (of a portrait, sculpture etc.) of the same size as the subject **life-sized** *adj.*

life·time (láiftaim) *n.* the duration of the life of a person, thing, institution etc. ‖ *(pop.)* a very long time

lift (lift) **1.** *v.t.* to raise to a higher position, hoist ‖ *(rhet.)* to direct up to God ‖ to take from the ground ‖ *(pop.)* to steal ‖ to plagiarize (material) ‖ to remove ‖ *v.i.* to move upwards, disperse **to lift one's hand against** to strike **to lift** (or **lift up**) **one's voice against** *(rhet.)* to protest against **2.** *n.* the act of lifting or an instance of this ‖ a mechanical hoist ‖ the load that is lifted ‖ the distance through which something is lifted or rises ‖ *(pop.)* an emotional bolstering up ‖ a free ride in a vehicle offered to someone to help him on his journey ‖ *(envir.)* compacted solid waste covered over in a sanitary landfill ‖ one of the layers of leather in the heel of a shoe ‖ *(aeron.)* the upward force exerted by air pressure agaisnt the undersurface of the wings of an aircraft, counteracting the force of gravity ‖ an airlift

lift-off (liftɔf, liftɒf) *n.* the action of a rocket leaving its launch pad or of a helicopter etc. becoming airborne ‖ the moment this action occurs

lig·a·ment (lígəmənt) *n.* *(anat.)* a short fibrous band which connects one bone with another or supports an organ ‖ any similar band of connective tissue **lig·a·men·tal** (lɪgəmént'l), **lig·a·men·tar·y** (lɪgəméntəri:), **lig·a·mén·tous** *adjs*

lig·a·ture (lígətʃər, lígətʃuər) **1.** *n.* something used to bind or unite ‖ *(med.)* a piece of nylon, wire etc. used as a surgical suture ‖ the action of binding with such a suture ‖ *(mus.)* a slur or tie joining notes together **2.** *v.t. pres. part.* **lig·a·tur·ing** *past* and *past part.* **lig·a·tured** to bind with a ligature

light (lait) *n.* the wave band of electromagnetic radiation to which the retina of the eye is sensitive and which the brain interprets ‖ the portion of the electromagnetic spectrum including infrared, visible and ultraviolet radiation, e.g. ultraviolet light ‖ the presence

of this radiation ‖ a source of this radiation ‖ a brightness ‖ a vivacious or spirited look ‖ someone who is a luminary, *a light of the English court* ‖ the aspect in which something is seen, *in a favorable light* ‖ daylight ‖ daytime ‖ a flame or spark used to ignite something, or the thing providing this flame or spark ‖ *(painting)* a bright part of a picture, *light and shade* ‖ a light used as a signal ‖ *(pl., theater)* illuminated letters outside a theater **in the light of** as a result of taking into consideration **to bring** (or **come**) **to light** to make (or become) known **to see the light** to be born, come into being ‖ to come to understand ‖ to have a spiritual revelation

light *adj.* of little weight, not heavy ‖ having low specific gravity and small weight in relation to volume ‖ having less than the correct wieght ‖ having less than the usual weight or amount ‖ constructed of light parts or materials ‖ having, because of its texture, small mass in relation to volume, *light pastry* ‖ making a small impact, *a light touch* ‖ quick-moving, nimble, *light on her feet* ‖ not strenuous, easy to do ‖ easy to bear, *a light punishment* ‖ designed merely to amuse and give pleasure, *light entertainment* ‖ dizzy, having a feeling of slight loss of stablity ‖ (of food) easy to digest, not very substantial ‖ (of wine, ale etc.) having a relatively small alcoholic content ‖ (of a building) not massive ‖ (of soil) easily broken up, free of clay **to make light of** to appear to attach little importance to **to travel light** to travel with little luggage **with a light heart** cheerfully

light *adj.* having considerable light, not dark ‖ pale in color ‖ (of a color) pale

light *pres. part.* **light·ing** *past* and *past part.* **lit** (lit), **light·ed** *v.t.* to cause to emit light or burn ‖ to show the way to by carrying a light ‖ *v.i.* to become lit **to light up** to give light (or more light) to ‖ to become brighter ‖ to start smoking one's pipe or cigarette

light *pres. part.* **light·ing** *past* and *past part.* **lit**, **light·ed** *v.i.* to come to rest, as a bird does from flight **to light on** (or **upon**) to discover by chance

light·en (láit'n) *v.t.* to make lighter ‖ to reduce the load of ‖ to relieve, mitigate ‖ to make more interesting or amusing ‖ *v.i.* to become lighter

lighten *v.t.* to make (a dark place) lighter ‖ to make (a color etc.) lighter ‖ *v.t.* to become brighter ‖ (of lightning) to flash

light·er (láitər) *n.* a device for lighting a cigarette etc.

lighter 1. *n.* a large, usually flat-bottomed, boat used to transport goods to or from a ship which cannot be docked or brought to a jetty etc. **2.** *v.t.* to transport by lighter **light·er·age** *n.* this transporting or the cost of it **light·er·man** (léitərmən) *pl.* **light·er·men** (láitərmən) *n.* someone employed on a lighter

light-head·ed (láithédid) *adj.* not quite in control of one's words or behavior, from delirium, drink, exhaustion etc. ‖ frivolous, silly

light-heart·ed (láithɑ́rtid) *adj.* free from cares or worries, cheerful

light heavyweight a professional boxer whose weight does not exceed 175 lbs ‖ an amateur boxer whose weight does not exceed 178 lbs

light·ly (láitli) *adv.* in a manner devoid of heaviness

light·ness (láitnis) *n.* the quality of an object that depends on its ability to reflect or transmit light ‖ degree of illumination

lightness *n.* the quality of being by no means heavy

light·ning (láitniŋ) **1.** *n.* an electric discharge, e.g. a flash or a spark, between clouds or between a cloud and the earth **2.** *adj.* as quick as lightning ‖ of or pertaining to lightning

lightning rod an earthed metal rod attached to a build-

---

ing to divert lightning from it or to reduce the likelihood of damage by lightning

light·weight (láitweit) **1.** *n.* a professional boxer whose weight does not exceed 135 lbs ‖ an amateur boxer whose weight does not exceed 132 lbs **2.** *adj.* of a lightweight ‖ of less than usual weight

light-year (láitjiər) *n.* an astronomical unit of distance: the distance traveled by light in one terrestrial year, i.e. 5.88×10^{12} miles

lig·nite (lígnait) *n.* coal intermediate between peat and bituminous coal and containing much volatile matter

lik·a·ble, like·a·ble (láikəb'l) *adj.* amiable, of a kind that elicits liking

like (laik) **1.** *adj.* identical, equal or almost equal ‖ faithful to the original ‖ resembling each other or one another in appearance or character **of like minds** of the same opinion **something like** *(pop.)* as it should be, or almost so **2.** *prep.* characteristic of ‖ indicative of ‖ to compare with ‖ of the same nature as, to be compared with ‖ identical or almost so, *he looks like his father* **to feel like** to be in the mood for **3.** *adv.* (in the phrases) **as like as not, like as not, like enough,** probably **4.** *conj. (pop.)* as, in the same way as ‖ *(pop.)* similar to **5.** *n.* counterpart, equal **and the like** and similar things **the likes of me (you, him** etc.) people of the same rank, class etc. as me (you, him etc.)

like 1. *v.t. pres. part.* **lik·ing** *past* and *past part.* **liked** to find pleasing, agreeable or attractive ‖ to be fond of ‖ (with infinitive) to make it a practice (to do something) from prudence ‖ to choose in a spirit of self-congratulation, *he likes to think he never makes mistakes* ‖ (in conditional constructions) to want to have, *he would like a cup of tea* ‖ (in conditional constructions) to wish, *he'd like to help* ‖ (with 'how') to feel about, *how do you like his new play?* **2.** *n.* *(pl.)* preferences, *we share the same likes and dislikes*

like·li·hood (láikli:hud) *n.* probability

like·ly (láikli:) **1.** *adj. comp.* **like·li·er** *superl.* **like·li·est** probable ‖ plausible, credible ‖ suitable, promising for a certain purpose ‖ appearing capable, *a likely candidate* **likely to** probably going to **2.** *adv.* (often with 'most' or 'very') probably **as likely as not, likely as not** quite possibly

lik·en (láikən) *v.t.* (with 'to', 'with') to represent as similar

like·ness (láiknis) *n.* a similarity, resemblance ‖ a portrait, esp. with respect to its lifelike quality ‖ form

like·wise (láikwaiz) **1.** *adv.* similarly, in the same way **2.** *conj.* also, moreover

li·lac (láilək, láilæk) **1.** *n.* a small deciduous tree native to Europe widely cultivated for its highly scented pinkish-mauve flowers, or a cultivated white variety ‖ flowers of these trees ‖ pinkish-mauve color **2.** *adj.* of this color

lilt (lilt) *n.* a gentle, pleasing, rising and falling rhythm in songs, voices, etc. ‖ a gay melody with a lightly swinging rhythm ‖ a light swaying or sprightly movement **lilt·ing** *adj.* having or characterized by a lilt

lil·y (líli:) *pl.* **lil·ies** *n.* a genus of bulbous, perennial plants, native to the northern hemisphere and widely cultivated for their showy flowers ‖ such a flower ‖ any of various plants of the same family bearing flowers like those of genue *Lilium,* e.g. the day lily ‖ something compared to a lily in purity, delicacy, whiteness etc. ‖ *(heraldry)* the fleur-de-lis

limb (lim) **1.** *n.* one of the projecting paired appendages (e.g. arm, leg, wing, fin, parapodium) of an animal body ‖ a large bough of a tree ‖ an arm of a cross ‖ a spur of a mountain ‖ either half of an archery bow **out on a limb** in a vulnerable position from which there is no going back **2.** *v.t.* to tear or cut away a limb of

lim·ber (límbər) **1.** *adj.* bending easily, flexible ‖ having a supple body **2.** *v.i.* (with 'up') to flex one's muscles and make one's limbs supple before some physical exertion ‖ *v.t.* (with 'up') to make supple

lime (laim) **1.** *n. (chem.)* a caustic and highly infusible solid consisting essentially of calcium oxide, obtained when calcium carbonate is strongly heated. It is used in building, agriculture, metallurgy and for the treatment of sewage etc. ‖ birdlime **2.** *v.t. pres. part.* **lim·ing** *past* and *past part.* **limed** to spread lime over (a field etc.) ‖ to dress (hides), using lime and water ‖ to smear with birdlime

lime *n.* a citrus tree native to the East Indies and cultivated in the U.S.A. and West Indies for its yellowish-green fruits ‖ this fruit

lime·light (láimlait) *n.* an intense white light produced when lime is heated in an oxyhydrogen flame, formerly used in signaling and for stage lighting ‖ the flood of publicity accorded to a public figure

lim·er·ick (límərik) *n.* a five-lined nonsense verse

lime·stone (láimstoun) *n.* a hard rock formed by the deposition of organic remains (e.g. seashells) that consists mainly of calcium carbonate

lim·it (límit) **1.** *n.* (often *pl.*) the furthest extent, amount etc. ‖ (often *pl.*) boundary, confines ‖ a point which may not or cannot be passed, *speed limit* ‖ an established highest or lowest amount, quantity, size etc., *the limit is six players per game* ‖ someone or something that goes too far and cannot be endured **within limits** within moderation, to a moderate extent **without limit** without restriction **2.** *v.t.* to restrict ‖ to serve as a limit to

lim·i·ta·tion (limitéiʃən) *n.* a limiting or being limited ‖ something that limits ‖ a limit of capability ‖ *(law)* the period fixed by statute of limitation after which a claimant cannot bring an action

lim·ou·sine (líməzi:n, liməzí:n) *n.* a car with a closed body and a partitioned seat for the driver ‖ a luxurious car

limp (limp) **1.** *v.i.* to walk awkwardly or painfully because of some deformity or injury to one leg ‖ to move slowly or with difficulty ‖ (of verse) to have a halting rhythm **2.** *n.* a lame or crippled walk

limp *adj.* floppy, not stiff or crisp ‖ lacking in energy, weak, feeble

lim·pid (límpid) *adj. (rhet.)* clear, transparent **lim·pid·i·ty**

lim·y (láimi:) *comp.* **lim·i·er** *superl.* **lim·i·est** *adj.* like, made of, containing or covered with lime

lin·age, line·age (láinidʒ) *n.* the number of lines in printed or written matter ‖ payment to the writer according to the number of lines

line (lain) **1.** *n.* *(esp. naut.)* a length of rope ‖ a length of cord, thread etc. with a hook, used with or without a rod for catching fish ‖ a clothesline ‖ a telephone wire or cable, or this route of communication ‖ a pipe or similar retainer through which liquids, gases etc. may be transported, e.g. a gas line ‖ a long thin stroke marked on a surface ‖ the way an artist uses such lines, *purity of line* ‖ *(math.)* that which has length but not breadth ‖ an outline, contour ‖ the style or cut of a garment ‖ a wrinkle or crease in the skin ‖ a row, *a line of trees* ‖ a row of written, typed or printed words ‖ a brief letter ‖ a single row of words in a poem ‖ *(pl.)* the words of an actor's part, *to forget one's lines* ‖ *(football)* the line of scrimmage ‖ *(mil.)* a linked series of trenches and fortifications, *the front line* ‖ a number of things, persons or events which come one after another in time in a regular manner or series, *a long line of distinguished public servants, direct line of descent* ‖ *(rhet.)* lineage, family, *he comes of a good line* ‖ route, *lines of communication* ‖ a single track of rail ‖ a rail route, or part of a rail system ‖ a course of conduct, direction of thought, or mode of procedure ‖ a branch of business or activity, *he's in the building line* ‖ *(commerce)* a stock of a certain kind of goods, *a cheap line in ready-made suits* **all along the line** at every point **to bring into line** to make agree **to draw the line at** to consider to be beyond the limit of what is acceptable **to drop a line** to write a brief letter or note **to fall into line with** to adjust oneself to the wishes of **to get a line on** to obtain information on **to read between the lines** to understand what is being implied without its being made explicit **2.** *v. pres. part.* **lin·ing** *past* and *past part.* **lined** *v.t.* to mark or cover with lines ‖ to stand or be in a line along ‖ to place or arrange in a line along ‖ to set or arrange in a line ‖ (with 'up') to make arrangements about, *to line up support for a candidate* ‖ *v.i.* (with 'up') to form a line

line *pres. part.* **lin·ing** *past* and *past part.* **lined** *v.t.* to provide with an inner layer ‖ to be such an inner layer for **to line one's purse** (or **pocket**) to enrich oneself by dishonest or surreptitious methods, esp. by accepting bribes

lin·e·age (líni:idʒ) *n.* (*rhet.*) a line of descent, ancestry, *a family of ancient lineage*

lin·e·al (líni:əl) *adj.* in the direct line of descent ‖ of or in lines

lin·e·ar (líni:ər) *adj.* of or in lines ‖ (of a unit of measure) involving one dimension only ‖ able to be shown as a straight line on a graph ‖ (esp. *bot.*) long and narrow and of uniform width ‖ (*electronics*) responding in a manner directly proportional to the input or stimulus or being such a response ‖ (of a painting etc.) having well-defined lines and outlines ‖ (*psych.*) of the tendency to follow the sequence of a printed line ‖ (*math.*) of an equation where both sides are linear functions of the variables ‖ (*computer*) of a programming technique for solving a problem to maximize or minimize the ratio of various quantities in a mix for a best result

lin·en (línən) **1.** *n.* cloth made from flax fiber, varying in coarseness from cambric to canvas ‖ yarn or thread made from flax ‖ (*collect.*) articles made of this cloth or formerly usually made of it, e.g. shirts, underclothes, sheets, towels, tablecloths **to wash one's dirty linen in public** to discuss matters which reflect badly on oneself or one's close associates in front of other people or in print **2.** *adj.* made of flax or linen

line-up (láinʌp) *n.* a row of people made to assemble, esp. by the police, for identification of suspected criminals ‖ (*football, baseball*) a list of players and their respective playing positions ‖ an enumeration of people with a common purpose, *a lineup of the prospective candidates*

lin·ger (língər) *v.i.* to dawdle ‖ to loiter ‖ to stay on because one is loath to go ‖ to dwell (upon a subject) ‖ to be slow in dying or in dying out ‖ *v.t.* (with 'out') to pass (time) slowly, often in suffering

lin·ge·rie (lɑnʒəréi, lɛ̃ʒari:) *n.* (esp. *commerce*) women's underclothing

lin·go (língou) *pl.* **lin·goes, lin·gos** *n.* (*pop.*) a foreign language, considered as being peculiar ‖ jargon ‖ an unusual vocabulary or a way of using words that is peculiar to an individual

lin·gual (língwəl) *adj.* of, like or near the tongue ‖ (*phon.*) articulated esp. with the tongue, e.g. the 'l' sound ‖ linguistic

lin·guist (língwist) *n.* someone who is proficient in several foreign languages ‖ someone who exhibits a facility in learning a foreign language ‖ a specialist in linguistics **lin·guís·tic** *adj.* of or relating to languages or linguistics **lin·guís·tics** *n.* the scientific study of language or languages whether from a historical and comparative or from a descriptive, structural point of view

lin·i·ment (línəmənt) *n.* a liquid medicinal preparation for rubbing into the skin to relieve pain and muscular stiffness

lin·ing (láiniŋ) *n.* the material which lines an inner surface, e.g. of a garment ‖ (*bookbinding*) the ma-

terial used to reinforce a book's spine ‖ a providing with a lining

link (liŋk) **1.** *n.* a ring or loop of a chain ‖ a sausage forming part of a chain ‖ a cuff link ‖ someone or something that joins other people or things ‖ (*mech.*) a joining part needed to transmit force or motion ‖ (*computer*) portion of a program or equipment that directs information from one part to another, e.g., data link **2.** *v.t.* (often with 'up') to join ‖ to entwine (arms) by looping one's arm around another's ‖ *v.i.* (often with 'up') to join up, form an association

link·age (líŋkidʒ) *n.* a linking or being linked

linked (liŋkt) *n.* (of genes) exhibiting linkage

links (liŋks) *pl. n.* a golf course

link·up (líŋkʌp) *n.* a connection or contact ‖ a means of contact, communication or connection

li·no·le·um (linóuli:əm) *n.* a floor covering made by coating canvas with oxidized linseed oil mixed with resins and fillers (e.g. cork)

lin·seed (línsi:d) *n.* the seed of flax, from which linseed oil is extracted. It is also used medicinally as a demulcent and emollient

lint (lint) *n.* a material used for dressing wounds and made by rubbing linen cloth on one side until it is soft and fluffy ‖ bits of loose thread, fluff etc., esp. when these collect in dust on clothing etc.

li·on (láiən) *n.* a large carnivorous mammal, up to 12 ft in length and 600 lbs in weight, native to Africa and S. Asia **the lion's share** the largest share

li·on·ess (láiənis) *n.* the female lion

li·on·ize (láiənaiz) *pres. part.* **li·on·iz·ing** *past* and *past part.* **li·on·ized** *v.t.* to treat as a celebrity and make a great fuss over

lip (lip) **1.** *n.* one of the two fleshy, muscular, highly sensitive folds bordering the mouth, lined on the outside by skin, and on the inside by the translucent membrane of the mouth ‖ (*biol.*) a lip-shaped structure ‖ the edge of a cavity, opening, vessel, wound etc. ‖ the rim of a vessel, esp. that part which juts out to form a pouring spout ‖ (*pop.*) impudent talk, answering back etc. **to hang on someone's lips** to listen to someone with complete attention **to keep a stiff upper lip** to endure without flinching, show fortitude **to lick** (or **smack**) **one's lips** to show eager anticipation **2.** *adj.* (*phon.*) labial

lip·read (lípri:d) *pres. part.* **lip·read·ing** *past* and *past part.* **lip·read** (lípred) *v.t.* to understand by lipreading ‖ *v.i.* to do lipreading

lip·read·er (lípri:dər) *n.* someone who does lipreading

lip·read·ing (lípri:diŋ) *n.* a method of understanding speech by observing the movements of the speaker's lips. It may be learned by deaf people

lip·stick (lípstik) *n.* a stick of cosmetic, usually in a retractable holder, for coloring the lips

liq·ue·fi·er (líkwifaiər) *n.* an apparatus in which gases are liquefied

liq·ue·fy (líkwifai) *v. pres. part.* **liq·ue·fy·ing** *past* and *past part.* **liq·ue·fied** *v.t.* to make liquid ‖ *v.i.* to become liquid

li·queur (likə́:r) *n.* a strongly flavored and highly fortified alcoholic liquor, e.g. chartreuse or benedictine ‖ a mixture of sugar and aged wine for inducing second fermentation in the making of champagne

liq·uid (líkwid) **1.** *adj.* of or being a fluid substance which under the influence of small forces assumes a shape imposed by its container but does not expand indefinitely ‖ transparent, clear ‖ (of sounds) flowing, musical ‖ (*phon.*, of a consonant) pronounced with the slightest contact of the tongue and mouth, e.g. 'l' and 'r' ‖ readily changeable for cash **2.** *n.* a liquid substance ‖ a liquid consonant

---

(**a**) æ, cat; ɑ, car; ɔ fawn; ei, snake. (**e**) e, hen; i:, sheep; iə, deer; ɛə, bear. (**i**) i, fish; ai, tiger; ə:, bird. (**o**) o, ox; au, cow; ou, goat; u, poor; ɔi, royal. (**u**) ʌ, duck; u, bull; u:, goose; ə, bacillus; ju:, cube. x, loch; θ, think; ð, bother; z, Zen; ʒ, corsage; dʒ, savage; ŋ, orangutang; j, yak; ʃ, fish; tʃ, fetch; 'l, rabble; 'n, redden. Complete pronunciation key appears inside front cover.

liq·ui·date (líkwideit) *pres. part.* **liq·ui·dat·ing** *past* and *past part.* **liq·ui·dat·ed** *v.i.* to pay or settle (a debt) ‖ to wind up (a company or business) by realizing its assets, paying its debts and distributing the balance to the shareholders ‖ to clear up, put an end to ‖ to eradicate, exterminate (opponents, enemies etc.) ‖ to convert into cash ‖ *v.i.* to become liquidated **liq·ui·dá·tion** *n.* a liquidating or being liquidated ‖ the condition of being liquidated **líq·ui·da·tor** *n.* someone appointed to supervise the liquidation of a company

liq·uor (líkər) *n.* drink (gin, whiskey etc.) of high alcoholic content ‖ any liquid or juice, e.g. the water in which something has been cooked ‖ water used in brewing ‖ *(pharm.)* a solution of a specified drug in water

lisp (lisp) **1.** *v.i.* to mispronounce 's' or 'z' as 'th' ‖ to speak with a lisp or as if with a lisp ‖ *v.t.* to utter with a lisp or as if with a lisp **2.** *n.* a lisping pronunciation

lis·some, lis·som (lísəm) *adj.* lithe, slim and supple

list (list) **1.** *n.* a number of names of persons or things having something in common, written out systematically one beneath or after another ‖ a catalog **2.** *v.t.* to make a list of ‖ to put on a list ‖ to register (a security) on a stock exchange

list 1. *n.* (esp. of a ship) a lean to one side **2.** *v.i.* (esp. of a ship) to lean to one side

lis·ten (lís'n) *v.i.* to use one's ears consciously in order to hear ‖ to pay attention to speech, music etc. ‖ to be influenced by

list·less (lístlis) *adj.* lacking energy ‖ spent in languor ‖ uninterested, indifferent

li·ter, li·tre (lí:tər) *n.* a metric unit of capacity, approximately 0.22 gallon or 1.76 pints

lit·er·a·cy (lítərəsi:) *n.* the condition or quality of being literate

lit·er·al (lítərəl) **1.** *adj.* true in the usual sense of the words used, not metaphorical or exaggerated ‖ (of a translation) following the original closely or even word for word ‖ prosaic, matter-of-fact ‖ of, relating to or expressed by a letter of the alphabet **2.** *n.* a literal misprint **lít·er·al·ism** *n.* a tendency to interpret words, statements etc. in their literal sense ‖ (in painting, writing etc.) realism **lít·er·al·ist** *n.* someone practicing literalism

lit·er·ar·i·ly (lítərerili:) *adv.* in a literary way or manner **lit·er·ar·y** (lítəreri:) *adj.* of, being or about literature ‖ producing, well versed in or connected with literature ‖ characteristic of a written as distinct from a spoken style

lit·er·ate (lítərit) **1.** *adj.* able to read and write **2.** *n.* someone who can read and write

lit·er·a·ture (lítərətʃər) *n.* written compositions in prose or verse, esp. of lasting quality and artistic merit ‖ writings produced in a certain country or during a certain period ‖ *(rhet.)* the occupation or profession of writing or studying such works ‖ the realm of written composition ‖ books or treatises on a particular subject ‖ *(pop.)* any printed matter even if devoid of literary merit, e.g. travel folders

lithe (laið) *adj.* slim, sinewy and supple ‖ indicating suppleness and agility

lith·o·graph (líθəgræf, líθəgraf) **1.** *v.t.* to print by the process of lithography **2.** *n.* an impression or print so made **li·thog·ra·pher** (liθógrəfər) *n.* someone skilled in lithography

lith·o·graph·ic (liθəgræfik) *adj.* of, pertaining to or produced by lithography

li·thog·ra·phy (liθógrəfi:) *n.* the art or process of printing from a smooth surface (a prepared stone, aluminum or zinc) on which the image to be printed is ink-receptive, the rest being ink-repellent

lith·o·log·i·cal (liθəlódʒik'l) *adj.* of or relating to lithology

li·thol·o·gy (liθóládʒi:) *n.* the study of stones and rocks ‖ the nature of a rock or rock formation described in terms of its composition, color, texture and structure

lit·i·gate (lítigeit) *pres. part.* **lit·i·gat·ing** *past* and *past part.* **lit·i·gat·ed** *v.i.* to go to law, to carry on a lawsuit ‖ *v.t.* to contest at law **lit·i·gá·tion** *n.*

lit·ter (lítər) **1.** *n.* rubbish, e.g. scraps of paper, orange peel etc., lying about in disorder ‖ a state of disorder or untidiness ‖ the young brought forth at one birth by a multiparous animal, e.g. a sow or bitch ‖ straw or other bedding provided for animals or as a protection for plants ‖ the top layer of leaves, twigs and other organic matter on a forest floor ‖ a stretcher **2.** *v.t.* to be litter in (a place) ‖ to leave litter in (a place) ‖ to throw down as litter ‖ to bed down (an animal) with straw etc.) ‖ to cover (a floor) with straw etc. ‖ *v.i.* (of an animal) to bring forth young

lit·ter·bug (lítərbʌg) *n.* someone who drops litter on a street or in some other public area

lit·tle (lít'l) **1.** *adj. comp.* **less** (les), **less·er** (lésər), **lit·tler** *superl.* **least** (li:st), **lit·tlest** small in size, amount, number, degree etc. ‖ (of children) young ‖ short, not having great height ‖ (of distance or duration) short, brief ‖ trivial, *little details* ‖ petty, mean, *little minds* ‖ operating on a small scale **2.** *adv. comp.* **less** *superl.* **least** not much, very slightly ‖ (with 'to care', 'dream', 'guess', 'know', 'think' etc.) not at all **3.** *n.* a small amount, *the little I possess, what little I could do* ‖ not much, *he did little to help* **a little** a short time, *stay for a little* ‖ a short distance, *go along the road a little* **in little** on a small scale **little by little** gradually **little or nothing** hardly anything **to think little of** to have a low opinion of ‖ to have no hesitancy about

lit·ur·gy (lítərdʒi:) *pl.* **lit·ur·gies** *n.* the public rites and services of the Christian Church ‖ the Eucharist office in the Orthodox Eastern Church

liv·a·ble, live·a·ble (lívəb'l) *adj.* good for living in ‖ able to be lived, worth living

live (liv) *pres. part.* **liv·ing** *past* and *past part.* **lived** *v.i.* to have life as an animal or plant ‖ to continue in this state ‖ (with 'on', 'upon') to subsist, maintain life ‖ (with 'on', 'upon', 'by') to obtain the means of life ‖ to flourish, remain in people's memory ‖ to conduct or pass one's life in a certain manner, *to live quietly, live like a pig* ‖ to reside, dwell ‖ *v.t.* to pass, spend, *live a happy life* ‖ to carry out in one's life the principles of, *to live one's religion* **to live and let live** to live as one wishes and allow others to do the same ‖ to be tolerant of others' views, weaknesses etc. **to live** (something) **down** to live so that people forget (a past failure or mistake in one's life **to live for** to devote oneself wholly to **to live up to** to attain expected standards in ‖ to put (one's ideals) into practice

live (laiv) *adj.* living, not dead ‖ existing, not fictional ‖ energetic, lively ‖ full of interest and importance ‖ unexploded, *a live bomb* ‖ (of a broadcast) direct, not recorded ‖ carrying electric current, *a live wire* ‖ (of machinery) imparting or having motion

live·li·hood (láivli:hud) *n.* means of subsistence

live·ly (láivli:) *comp.* **live·li·er** *superl.* **live·li·est 1.** *adj.* brisk, vigorous, full of zest and spirit ‖ vivid ‖ active, intense ‖ brilliant, fresh ‖ fast and quick to respond, *a lively little car* **2.** *adv.* in a lively way

liv·en (láivən) *v.t.* (often with 'up') to enliven ‖ *v.i.* (often with 'up') to become brisker, brighter, more active

liv·er (lívər) *n.* a large, vascular, glandular organ of vertebrates that plays an important role in digestion (e.g. the production of bile), that converts carbohydrates to glycogen, which it then stores, and that elaborates many important substances (esp. of the blood) ‖ any of various large organs associated with the digestive tract of invertebrates ‖ the liver of an animal eaten as food

liver *n.* a person who lives in a specified manner, *a clean liver, a loose liver*

live·stock (láivstɒk) *n.* animals, esp. cattle, kept on a farm for breeding, dairy products, sale etc.

liv·id (lívid) *adj.* bluish-gray in color, like lead ‖ discolored as if by bruising ‖ *(pop.)* exceedingly angry **li·víd·i·ty** *n.*

liv·ing (lívin̦) **1.** *n.* the condition of having life ‖ the action of a being having life ‖ livelihood **2.** *adj.* endowed with life ‖ having continuing effect ‖ still spoken, *a living language* ‖ now existing, *the greatest living sculptor* ‖ natural, not moved or detached by man ‖ of or pertaining to life ‖ sufficient for life, *a living wage* **in living memory** capable of being remembered by people still alive

living room the room in a house where the family spends most of the day when at home, esp. as distinct from bedroom or kitchen

liz·ard (lízərd) *n.* a suborder of reptiles found chiefly in warm climates ‖ leather made from lizard skin

lla·ma (lámə) *pl.* **lla·mas, lla·ma** *n.* any of several domesticated or wild South American ruminant mammals, closely allied to the camel but smaller (about 4 ft high), humpless and woolly-coated ‖ cloth made from the wool of these animals

lo (lou) *interj. (rhet.)* esp. in the phrase **lo and behold!** by a curious chance

load (loud) **1.** *n.* something which is supported by or carried in something, *a full load of passengers* ‖ the weight of a mass on its support ‖ the forces to which a support is subjected ‖ an amount usually carried or delivered of a specified material, often in a specified mode of conveyance, *a truck load of gravel* ‖ an amount of work expected to be done ‖ *(engin.)* the resistance, apart from friction, offered to the working of an engine, *the working load* ‖ *(elec.)* the amount of electrical energy taken from a source at a given time ‖ the quantity of electrical power used by a machine, circuit etc. ‖ *(pl., pop.)* a large amount, *loads of money* **2.** *v.t.* (often with 'up') to put a load on or in ‖ to put as a load ‖ to be a load or weight on ‖ to make heavier ‖ to treat with an adulterant, filler etc. ‖ to add a weight to (dice) so that they fall as one wants them to ‖ to add weight or importance to ‖ to insert the charge, cartridge or shell in (a firearm or gun) ‖ to insert (film) in a camera ‖ (often with 'with') to burden ‖ (often with 'on') to place as a burden upon ‖ (often with 'with') to give (someone) a great deal of ‖ *v.i.* (often with 'up') to take on a load ‖ to charge a firearm or put the ammunition into a gun

load·er (lóudər) *n.* someone or something that loads ‖ (in compounds) a gun loaded in a specified way, *a muzzle-loader*

load·ing (lóudin̦) *n. (insurance)* an amount added to an insurance premium in special circumstances ‖ a filler or stuffing used by paper, rubber or cloth manufacturers etc.

loaf (louf) *pl.* **loaves** *n.* a portion of bread baked in a separate, shaped piece ‖ meat or other food done up in a similar shaped piece ‖ a sugar loaf

loaf *v.i.* to waste time, be idle ‖ *v.t.* (usually with 'away') to pass (time) in idleness **lóaf·er** *n.* a lazy person

loaf·er (lóufər) *n.* a type of leather walking shoe with a broad flat heel and uppers like moccasins

loam (loum) *n.* a loose rich soil of clay and sand, with some organic matter ‖ a clay and sand mixture used in making bricks and molds ‖ any fertile soil **lóam·y** *comp.* **loam·i·er** *superl.* **loam·i·est** *adj.*

loan (loun) **1.** *n.* something lent, usually money, on condition that it is returned, with or without interest ‖ a lending, permission to use ‖ a loanword **on loan** under conditions of lending **2.** *v.t.* to grant a loan of

loan·word (lóunwə:rd) *n.* a word adopted from a foreign language and freely used

loath, loth (louθ) *adj. (rhet.,* used predicatively) unwilling, reluctant **nothing loath** without any reluctance

loathe (louð) *pres. part.* **loath·ing** *past* and *past part.* **loathed** *v.t.* to regard with disgust or abhorrence ‖ *(pop.)* to dislike strongly **lóath·ing** *n.* detestation, abhorrence **loath·some** (lóuðsəm) *adj.* exciting disgust, repulsive ‖ nauseating

lob (lɒb) **1.** *v.t. pres. part.* **lob·bing** *past* and *past part.* **lobbed** to toss or propel (e.g. a ball) without great force in a fairly high parabola ‖ *(tennis)* to hit (the ball) in a high parabola, usually to the back of the opponent's court **2.** *n.* a ball tossed, bowled or hit in this manner

lob·by (lɒbi) **1.** *pl.* **lob·bies** *n.* a corridor or room, esp. one from which the main rooms lead off, used as an entrance hall, vestibule, waiting room, anteroom etc. ‖ the part of a legislative building to which the public has access to meet with legislators ‖ a group of people trying to bring pressure to bear on legislators to pursue policies favorable to their interests **2.** *v. pres. part.* **lob·by·ing** *past* and *past part.* **lob·bied** *v.t.* to try to influence (legislators) in favor of a certain policy by constantly seeking interviews, writing letters, bringing external pressures to bear etc. ‖ *v.i.* to influence legislators in this way **lób·by·ist** *n.* a person who lobbies

lobe (loub) *n.* the soft rounded lower end of the human ear ‖ any similarly shaped part of an organ, esp. of the brain or lungs **lobed** *adj.* having a lobe or lobes

lob·ster (lɒbstər) *pl.* **lob·sters, lob·ster** *n.* a family of marine crustaceans, esp. *Homarus americanus* found off the Atlantic seaboard of North America ‖ their flesh eaten as food

lo·cal (lóuk'l) **1.** *adj.* of, relating to or restricted to a particular place or area ‖ narrow, restricted, parochial ‖ affecting or being in one part only ‖ (of trains, buses etc.) stopping at every station **2.** *n.* someone who lives or works in a particular neighborhood or area ‖ a local train, bus etc. ‖ a postage stamp valid only in a limited area ‖ the local branch of a large organization, esp. of a trade union

lo·cale (loukǽl, loukál) *n.* a place or location, esp. as the site of certain activities, a setting

lo·cal·i·ty (loukǽliti:) *pl.* **lo·cal·i·ties** *n.* a particular district or neighborhood ‖ the fact or state of being situated in time or space ‖ place with regard to the ability to find one's way around

lo·cate (lóukeit, loukéit) *pres. part.* **lo·cat·ing** *past* and *past part.* **lo·cat·ed** *v.t.* to look for and discover ‖ to situate, set in position ‖ to define the limits of a claim to land or a mining right ‖ *v.i.* to take up residence or set up business

lo·ca·tion (loukéiʃən) *n.* a locating or being located ‖ a geographical situation ‖ a tract of land located ‖ *(movies)* a site chosen outside the studio for purposes of filming

lock (lɒk) *n.* a curl, tress or tuft of hair as it naturally grows and divides on the head ‖ *(pl., rhet.)* the hair of the head ‖ a tuft of wool, cotton or flax

lock 1. *n.* a fastening device for doors, lids, drawers etc., in which a bolt is secured and released by a mechanism operated usually by a key acting on moving components (wards), or by some other means, such as a combination ‖ a device for preventing movement in a wheel ‖ *(hist.)* a mechanism for exploding the charge of a gun ‖ any of several holds in wrestling which prevent the part held from moving ‖ a part of a canal or river enclosed between gates, in which the level of the water can be controlled, thus providing access from one level reach of navigable water to another ‖ an airlock **under lock and key** put away

---

(a) æ, c*a*t; ɑ, c*a*r; ɔ f*aw*n; ei, sn*a*ke. **(e)** e, h*e*n; i:, sh*ee*p; iə, d*ee*r; ɛə, b*ea*r. **(i)** i, f*i*sh; ai, t*i*ger; ə:, b*i*rd. **(o)** o, *o*x; au, c*ow*; ou, g*oa*t; u, p*oo*r; ɔi, r*oy*al. **(u)** ʌ, d*u*ck; u, b*u*ll; u:, g*oo*se; ə, b*a*cillus; ju:, c*u*be. x, lo*ch*; θ, *th*ink; ð, bo*th*er; z, *Z*en; ʒ, corsa*g*e; dʒ, sava*g*e; ŋ, oranguta*ng*; j, *y*ak; ʃ, *fi*sh; tʃ, fe*tch*; 'l, rabb*le*; 'n, redd*en*. Complete pronunciation key appears inside front cover.

very safely **2.** *v.t.* to fasten (a door etc.) with a lock ‖ to fasten by fitting parts together ‖ *(printing)* to fasten (type) in a chase by securing the quoins ‖ to move (a ship) by means of a lock or locks ‖ to join tightly ‖ *v.i.* to become fastened with a lock ‖ to become fastened as if locked ‖ (of a ship) to pass by means of a lock or locks ‖ (of a vehicle) to allow the front wheels to turn across the plane of the back wheels ‖ (of wheels) to move in this way ‖ to become fixed, stop revolving **to lock out** to prevent from entering ‖ to prevent (employees) from working

lock·er (lókər) *n.* a small cupboard usually with a lock, allotted to an individual for storage, coats etc., e.g. in a factory or school ‖ a storeroom or compartment in a ship ‖ a storage compartment in a deep-freezing plant available for rent

lock·et (lókit) *n.* a small, usually precious metal case worn or hung around the neck, e.g. on a chain, often containing a portrait or lock of hair kept for sentimental reasons

lock·jaw (lókdʒɔ) *n. (med.)* an early symptom of tetanus marked by muscular spasms of the jaws and inability to open them

lo·co·mo·tive (loukəmóutiv) **1.** *n.* a self-propelled vehicle running on rails, used to haul railroad trains **2.** *adj.* having power of or used in locomotion

lo·cus (lóukəs) *pl.* **lo·ci** (lóusai) *n. (math.)* a system of points, lines or surfaces representing a given condition or law ‖ *(genetics)* the relative position of a gene on a chromosome ‖ (esp. *legal contexts)* the exact place of something

lo·cust (lóukəst) *n.* a family of grasshoppers having short antennae, esp. those members which migrate in countless numbers, devouring all vegetation in their path ‖ a cicada ‖ a locust tree ‖ the wood of a locust tree

lo·cu·tion (loukjú:ʃən) *n.* a turn of speech, a word, phrase or idiom considered from a stylistic point of view

lode (loud) *n.* a deposit of ore as a vein in a rock

lode·stone, load·stone (lóudstoun) *n.* a naturally occurring magnetic iron ore ‖ a thing that exerts a very strong attraction over people or a person

lodge (lɒdʒ) *n.* a small house at the gates of the park or on the grounds of a large country house, usually occupied by an employee or leased to a tenant ‖ the meeting hall of a branch of a Masonic or similar body, or the members of the branch collectively ‖ the den of a beaver or otter ‖ an American Indian's tepee or wigwam ‖ the inhabitants of such a dwelling, thought of as a unit

lodge *pres. part.* **lodg·ing** *past* and *past part.* **lodged** *v.i.* to live in someone else's house, paying for accommodation ‖ to become fixed, come to a resting-place, *a bullet lodged in his brain* ‖ to cause to be held securely ‖ to place, deposit ‖ to put in a place for safety ‖ to vest, *power lodged in a junta* ‖ to beat down (vegetation) ‖ to make formal statement of, *to lodge an official complaint* **lódg·er** *n.* someone who occupies a rented room in another person's house **lódg·ing** *n.* temporary accommodation in a lodging house etc. ‖ a place providing this ‖ *(pl.)* a room or rooms to live in rented in someone else's house

lo·ess, löss (lóues, les) *pl.* **lo·ess, löss·es** *n. (geol.)* a deposit of fine yellowish soil transported by the wind. Mixed with silt and humus it is very fertile

loft (lɔft, lɒft) **1.** *n.* a room in the roof, an attic ‖ a room over a stable for hay ‖ the upper story of a warehouse or factory ‖ a pigeon house ‖ a gallery in a church or hall ‖ *(golf)* the backward slope in the head of a club ‖ *(golf)* a stroke which sends a ball in a high arc above the ground **2.** *v.t.* (esp. *golf*) to hit in a high arc above the ground ‖ to send into space **lóft·er** *n. (golf)* an iron club with a slanted face used to loft the ball

loft·y (lɔ́fti:, lɒ́fti:) *comp.* **loft·i·er** *superl.* **loft·i·est** *adj. (rhet.)* imposingly tall, towering ‖ proud, haughty ‖ sublime, elevated

log (lɔg, lɒg) **1.** *n.* a long and heavy piece of the trunk or a branch of a tree, usually cut and trimmed but otherwise unshaped, and with the bark still on ‖ a shorter segment of similarly unshaped timber used for fuel ‖ *(naut.)* a device for gauging the speed of a ship ‖ a logbook or the record entered in it **2.** *v. pres. part.* **log·ging** *past* and *past part.* **logged** *v.t.* to enter in a logbook ‖ to go (a specified distance) as entered in a logbook ‖ to have experience of flying or sailing for (a specified distance or amount of time) ‖ to cut (trees) into logs ‖ to cut down the trees of (an area) ‖ *v.i.* to cut down trees into logs and transport them to a place of sale

log·a·rithm (lɔ́gəriðəm, lɒ́gəriðəm) *n. (abbr.* log) the power to which a selected number b (the base) must be raised in order to be equal to the number a under consideration: if $a = b^n$, n is the logarithm of a to base b (written as $\log_b a$) **log·a·rith·mic** *adj.* **log·a·rith·mi·cal·ly** *adv.*

log·book (lɔ́gbuk, lɒ́gbuk) *n.* a book containing a record of the progress of a ship and all events of the voyage, kept daily ‖ any similar record, e.g. of a plane's flight, the flying hours of a pilot, a traveler's journey, the mechanical history of an engine or its components etc.

loge (louʒ) *n.* a box in a theater or opera house

log·ger (lɔ́gər) *n.* someone who earns his living by logging

log·ic (lɒ́dʒik) *n.* the science of pure reasoning ‖ conformity with the principles of this science, rationality ‖ a sequence of reasoning ‖ a way of reasoning or arguing ‖ compelling power, the inevitability by which certain causes have certain results ‖ inherent guiding principles, *the logic of art*

log·i·cal (lɒ́dʒik'l) *adj.* related to or employed in logic ‖ consistent with correct reasoning ‖ capable of or skilled in logical argument ‖ inevitably following from the application of reason **log·i·cal·i·ty** (lɒdʒikǽliti:) *n.*

lo·gi·cian (loudʒíʃən) *n.* a specialist in logic

lo·gis·tic (loudʒístik) *adj.* of or pertaining to logistics

lo·gis·tics (loudʒístiks) *n.* the branch of military science concerned with troop movements and supplies ‖ symbolic logic

log·o·gram (lɔ́gəgræm, lɒ́gəgræm) *n.* an arbitrary symbol (e.g. in shorthand) representing a complete word

loin (lɔin) *n.* the cut of meat taken from the hindquarters of an animal ‖ (esp. *pl.*) the area in a man or quadruped on either side of the spinal column between the hipbone and ribs

loi·ter (lɔ́itər) *v.i.* to hang around, stay or wander about near some spot apparently aimlessly ‖ to be slow in the running of an errand, making of a journey etc., with stops for idling, gossip, play etc. ‖ *v.t.* (with 'away') to waste in idleness

loll (lɒl) *v.i.* to hang in a loosely relaxed, drooping way ‖ (of the tongue) to hang out ‖ to stand or sit in a lazy, comfortable attitude ‖ *v.t.* to allow to dangle

lone (loun) *adj. (rhet.)* single, alone, not one of a pack or group ‖ *(rhet.)* isolated **lóne·li·ness** *n.* the state or quality of being lonely ‖ an instance of this **lóne·ly** *comp.* **lone·li·er** *superl.* **lone·li·est** *adj.* solitary and feeling miserable because of the lack of company ‖ isolated ‖ unfrequented ‖ *(rhet.)* completely without companions **lóne·some** *adj.* (of people) lonely and sad because of the lack of company ‖ (of places etc.) unfrequented

long (lɒŋ, lɔŋ) **1.** *comp.* **long·er** (lɔ́ŋgər, lɒ́ŋgər) *superl.* **long·est** (lɔ́ŋgəst, lɒ́ŋgəst) *adj.* measuring a considerable or more than usual distance from one end to the other in space or duration ‖ of specified length or duration ‖ of or being the longer or longest in dimension ‖ extending to relatively remote time, far back or forward, *a long memory, a long friendship* ‖ *(phon.,* of a vowel or syllable) of relatively extended duration ‖ *(prosody,* of a syllable) stressed ‖ (esp.

classical prosody, of a syllable) of relatively extended duration ‖ *(finance)* holding goods in expectation of a rise in prices ‖ (of betting odds) in which a bettor stands to win a large multiple of his stake ‖ served in a tall glass, *a long drink* **in the long run** eventually **of long standing** with a lengthy history **2.** *n.* a long interval or period of time ‖ (esp. in *classical prosody*) a long syllable ‖ *(finance)* someone who holds goods in expectation of a rising market **the long and the short of it** the result or total outcome, briefly stated

long *comp.* **long·er** (lɔ́ŋgər, lɔ́ŋgər) *superl.* **long·est** (lɔ́ŋgəst, lɔ́ŋgəst) *adv.* for a long time ‖ by a long time ‖ throughout a specified period ‖ (comp., with 'no', 'any', 'much' etc.) after a specified or implied time **as** (or **so**) **long as** provided that, *you can come home late as long as you tell me in advance* **so long** *(pop.)* goodbye

long *v.i.* to desire earnestly and intensely

lon·gev·i·ty (lɔndʒéviti:) *n.* long life or unusually long life

long·ing (lɔ́ŋiŋ, lɔ́ŋiŋ) *n.* intense desire for what is not immediately attainable, or an instance of this

lon·gi·tude (lɔ́ndʒitu:d, lɔ́ndʒitju:d) *n.* the angular distance between the meridian passing through a given point on the earth's surface and the poles, and the standard meridian at Greenwich, England

lon·gi·tu·di·nal (lɔndʒitú:d'n'l, lɔndʒitjú:d'n'l) *adj.* of longitude ‖ lengthwise

long·shore·man (lɔ́ŋʃɔrmən) *pl.* **long·shore·men** (lɔ́ŋʃɔrmən) *n.* a stevedore

long-suf·fer·ing (lɔ́ŋsʌfəriŋ, lɔ́ŋsʌfəriŋ) *adj.* patient, not easily provoked

look (luk) *v.i.* to use the faculty of sight, make an effort to see ‖ (esp. imperative) to pay attention ‖ to direct the eyes in a particular direction ‖ to direct one's mental faculties in a particular direction, *look at the facts* ‖ to appear, *he looks ill* ‖ *v.t.* to direct one's eyes at, examine, regard intensely ‖ to find out, come to know through seeing ‖ (followed by an infinitive) to expect, anticipate, *he is looking to be promoted* **look here!** an expostulating or calling for attention **to look after** to take care of **to look ahead** to consider the future **to look alive** to be quick and alert **to look around** (or **about**) to examine one's surroundings **to look as if** (or **though**) to indicate a specified possibility **to look at** (in neg. sentences) to consider as a possible option, to take an interest in **to look back** to look into the past **to look down on** (or **upon**) to consider inferior **to look for** to search for ‖ to hope for expectantly **to look forward to** to anticipate, esp. with pleasure **to look into** to inquire into **to look like** to resemble ‖ *(probability)* to promise or threaten **to look out** (often with 'for') to be on one's guard, *look out for snakes* ‖ (with 'for') to see if one can discover, *look out for George on the train* ‖ to have a view, *the house looks out on fields* **to look over** to inspect esp. briefly **to look to** to attend to ‖ *(rhet.)* to be careful of, *look to your manners* ‖ to rely on, *he looks to you for a bit of sense* **to look up** to show improvement **to look up to** to admire, respect **to look (someone) up** to call on, visit **to look (someone or something) up and down** to inspect closely, esp. contemptuously **2.** *n.* a glance, a regard ‖ appearance ‖ *(pl.)* personal, esp. facial aspect, *she has her mother's looks* **to take a look at** to look at briefly ‖ to examine with a view to verification or correction

look·out (lúkaut) *n.* the act of looking out, a keeping watch ‖ an observation post for this purpose, e.g. a crow's nest ‖ someone stationed to keep watch **on the lookout** in a state of watchfulness

loom (lu:m) **1.** *v.i.* to appear indistinctly, to come into sight, usually somewhat menacingly, e.g. through a mist ‖ to figure as a future threat or ordeal **2.** *n.* the indistinct and somewhat menacing appearance of something seen e.g. through mist or fog

loom *n.* a frame or machine operated by hand or driven by power for weaving cloth

loon (lu:n) *n.* an order of large, aquatic, diving birds native to northern climates ‖ a grebe

loon *n.* someone extremely silly, esp. someone who has just done something extremely silly

loon·y (lú:ni:) *comp.* **loon·i·er** *superl.* **loon·i·est** *adj.(pop.)* crazy ‖ *(pop.)* extremely silly or foolish

loop (lu:p **1.** *n.* a closed figure with a curved outline and central aperture, as formed when a curve, string or wire etc. crosses itself ‖ anything of this shape, e.g. the running noose of a lasso ‖ a figure curving back on itself but not closed, *a loop in the road* ‖ a rail or telegraph line that breaks away from the main line and later rejoins it ‖ *(elec.)* a closed circuit ‖ *(phys.)* an antinode ‖ the figure performed in looping the loop **to knock** (or **throw**) **for a loop** to throw into a totally unexpected state of surprise, bewilderment or inactivity ‖ to cause to suffer a sudden reversal of fortune **2.** *v.t.* to form into a loop ‖ to fasten with a loop ‖ to enclose or encircle in or with a loop ‖ *v.t.* to move in a loop or loops ‖ to become or form a loop **to loop the loop** *(aeron.)* to travel around a complete loop in a vertical plane

loop·hole (lú:phoul) *n.* a narrow vertical slit in a wall to admit light and air ‖ *(hist.)* a similar slit for firing missiles through ‖ a way of evading a situation, rule, law etc.

loose (lu:s) **1.** *adj.* not fitting tightly ‖ not bound together ‖ not fastened, not firmly fixed ‖ made or allowed to hang freely, *loose draperies* ‖ unconfined, *there are loose dogs at the farm* ‖ (of build, limbs) long or tall and rather gangly ‖ slack, *loose reins* ‖ careless, vague ‖ not exact, *a loose definition* ‖ free, not literal, *a loose translation* ‖ lacking moral restraint, *loose morals* ‖ not under strict control ‖ not in a container, *loose change* **2.** *adv.* in a loose way **to break** (or **get**) **loose** to escape from confinement or control **to cut loose** to free oneself from ties **to let** (or **set**) **loose** to release from confinement or control **3.** *n.* **on the loose** freed from control or restrictions **4.** *v. pres. part.* **loos·ing** *past* and *past part.* **loosed** *v.t.* to set free ‖ to unfasten, release ‖ to untie (a rope) or make (a boat) free of its mooring ‖ (with 'off') to fire (a gun, ammunition etc.) ‖ *v.i.* (with 'off') to fire a gun

loos·en (lú:s'n) *v.t.* to make less tight ‖ to unfasten ‖ to make less restrained ‖ to make less firm, less fixed in place ‖ to make less tightly packed or arranged ‖ to relax (the bowels) ‖ to ease (a cough) ‖ to relax (regulations, discipline) ‖ *v.i.* to become loose

loot (lu:t) **1.** *n.* booty, plunter ‖ *(pop.)* goods stolen or come by illicitly **2.** *v.t.* to pillage (a place), esp. after a battle or some other calamity ‖ to carry off as booty ‖ *v.i.* to steal by pillaging

lop (lɔp) **1.** *v.t. pres. part.* **lop·ping** *past* and *past part.* **lopped** (often with 'off') to trim (branches) from a tree ‖ to trim (a tree) by cutting off branches ‖ (with 'off') to cut off, reduce as though by one swift blow **2.** *n.* the small branches and twigs of a tree that can't be sold to a lumber dealer

lop *pres. part.* **lop·ping** *past* and *past part.* **lopped** *v.i.* to hang loosely, droop, e.g. of a spaniel's ears ‖ (of a rabbit) to go with short unhurried bounds

lop **1.** *v.i. pres. part.* **lop·ping** *past* and *past part.* **lopped** (of water) to break in small choppy waves **2.** *n.* the breaking of such waves

---

lope (loup) **1.** *v.i. pres. part.* **lop·ing** *past* and *past part.* **loped** (esp. of animals) to move at less than a run with a long effortless stride and the body well down to the ground

lope *n.* (esp. in animals) a loping stride

lop·sid·ed (lópsaidid) *adj.* drooping at one side, *a lopsided smile* ‖ unevenly balanced

lo·qua·cious (loukwéiʃəs) *adj.* talkative

lord (lɔrd) *n.* (*Br.*) a nobleman or person entitled to use 'Lord' before his name ‖ (*hist.*) a master, ruler, sovereign ‖ (*hist.*) a feudal estate owner in relation to his tenants ‖ a business magnate, *the steel lords* ‖ the House of Lords **to live like a lord** to live in great luxury

lord·ly (lɔ́rdli:) *comp.* **lord·li·er** *superl.* **lord·li·est** *adj.* (*rhet.*) magnificent, of or befitting a lord ‖ haughty, lofty

lore (lɔr, lour) *n.* the knowledge and stock of beliefs relating to a certain subject place, person etc.

lose (lu:z) *pres. part.* **los·ing** *past* and *past part.* **lost** (lɔst, lɒst) *v.t.* to become unable to find ‖ to cease to have, fail to keep ‖ to be deprived of, *to lose a leg* ‖ to be deprived of through death ‖ to get rid of, *to lose weight* ‖ to waste ‖ to fail to win, *to lose a game* ‖ to miss, *she hates to lose a day in the sun* ‖ to fail to keep in sight ‖ to shake off (someone trailing) ‖ to fail to grasp or understand ‖ to cause the loss of, cost, *her rudeness lost her the job* ‖ (of a timepiece) to become slow by, *my watch is losing three minutes a day* ‖ to decrease in ‖ *v.i.* to fail to win, be defeated ‖ to suffer loss, be at a disadvantage **to lose ground** to fall back, give way, lose a lead or advantage **to lose interest** to cease to interest ‖ to cease to be interested **to lose oneself** to become engrossed in **to lose sight of** to fail to keep in view **to lose track of** to cease to keep in touch with or be fully informed about **to lose out** (*pop.*) to be unsuccessful **los·er** (lú:zər) *n.* someone who or something that loses **to be a good (bad) loser** to accept defeat with good (bad) grace

loss (lɔs, lɒs) *n.* a losing or an instance of this ‖ a person, thing or quantity that is lost ‖ the harm, trouble, sadness etc. caused by losing someone or something ‖ defeat ‖ (*pl.*) soldiers reported as having been killed, wounded or captured ‖ excess of cost over selling price ‖ the financial detriment suffered by an insured person as a result of damage to property, theft etc. ‖ energy wasted in a machine, circuit etc. e.g. through poor insulation or ventilation ‖ decrease in quality or degree, *loss in weight*

lost (lɔst, lɒst) *past* and *past part.* of LOSE ‖ *adj.* in verbal senses, esp. unable to be found ‖ unable to find the way ‖ wasted ‖ missed ‖ that one has failed to win ‖ ruined ‖ (of persons) killed ‖ bewildered ‖ helpless ‖ no longer practiced or known ‖ (*rhet.*) damned, *a lost soul* ‖ (*rhet.*) insensible ‖ engrossed **lost to the world** so engrossed in something as to be unaware of one's surroundings

lot (lɒt) **1.** *n.* one of a number of portions into which a quantity or substance may be divided for allotment ‖ (*rhet.*) one's fate or destiny in life ‖ an article or set of articles offered as an item for sale at an auction ‖ a plot or area of land having established limits ‖ (*movies*) a studio and the surrounding land belonging to it ‖ a set of people or things **to draw lots** to decide by using some method of random choice **a bad lot** (*pop.*) a person of bad character **a lot, lots** a large number or amount **by lot** by drawing lots **to throw in one's lot with** to elect to share the fortunes of, join up with **2.** *adv.* **a lot** much, considerably, to a great extent

lo·tion (lóuʃən) *n.* a liquid medicinal or cosmetic preparation applied to the skin

lot·ter·y (lɒ́təri:) *pl.* **lot·ter·ies** *n.* a method of raising money by the sale of a large number of tickets and the subsequent chance selection of certain ones entitling the bearers of these to a prize

lot·to (lɒ́tou) *n.* a form of bingo using slightly different numbered cards

loud (laud) *adj.* producing a powerful stimulus on the ear ‖ clamoring, noisy ‖ showy, conspicuous, *loud colors* ‖ vulgar, unrefined, *loud manners* **to be loud in one's praises** to praise with emphasis and insistence

loud *adv.* in a loud manner

loud·speak·er (láudspí:kər) *n.* a device that converts electrical impulses into sounds loud enough to be heard some distance away

lounge (laundʒ) **1.** *v. pres. part.* **loung·ing** *past* and *past part.* **lounged** *v.i.* to loll, sit or stand in a lazy manner ‖ to saunter idly ‖ *v.t.* (with 'away') to pass (time) in idleness or loafing **2.** *n.* a room in a hotel, club etc. with easy chairs for relaxation ‖ a long sofa with a headrest at one end

louse (laus) *pl.* **lice** (lais) *n.* orders of small wingless parasitic insects with mouthparts adapted for sucking or biting ‖ any of various small arthropods which are parasitic on plants or animals, e.g. plant lice ‖ (*pop., pl.* **louses**) a person for whom one feels contempt

lous·y (láuzi:) *comp.* **lous·i·er** *superl.* **lous·i·est** infested with lice ‖ (*pop.*) rotten, disgusting, bad in quality ‖ (*pop.*, with 'with') as if infested with lice ‖ (*pop.*) excessively well supplied, *he's lousy with money*

lout (laut) *n.* a rough, clumsy, stupid fellow

lou·ver, lou·vre (lú:vər) *n.* an arrangement of overlapping boards or slats with gaps between them so that air is admitted but rain excluded ‖ one of these boards or slats ‖ a slit-like opening in the body of a car for ventilation or escape of engine heat **lóu·vered, lóu·vred,** *adj.*

lov·a·ble, love·a·ble (lʌ́vəb'l) *adj.* for whom people instinctively feel warm affection **lóv·a·bly, lóve·a·bly** *adv.*

love (lʌv) *n.* a powerful emotion felt for another person manifesting itself in deep affection, devotion or sexual desire ‖ the object of this emotion ‖ God's regard for his creatures ‖ charity (the virtue) ‖ a great liking, fondness ‖ (*tennis, rackets* etc.) no score, nothing **for love or** (or **nor**) **money** (after a negative) by any means, *you couldn't get a ticket for love or money* **in love** feeling love, esp. sexual love **there's no love lost between them** they heartily dislike each other **to fall in love** to experience the emotions of love, esp. suddenly and unexpectedly ‖ to be taken with a possessive liking **to give one's love** to convey one's affectionate greetings **to make love** to show by one's actions one's feelings of sexual love, esp. to have sexual intercourse **to send one's love** to ask for one's affectionate greetings to be conveyed

love *pres. part.* **lov·ing** *past* and *past part.* **loved** *v.t.* to feel the passion of love for ‖ to be fond of ‖ to delight in, enjoy ‖ *v.i.* to be in love

love·li·ness (lʌ́vli:nis) *n.* the state or quality of being lovely

love·ly (lʌ́vli:) *comp.* **love·li·er** *superl.* **love·li·est** *adj.* beautiful ‖ delightful, pleasing

lov·er (lʌ́vər) *n.* a man in relation to his mistress ‖ a man in relation to some person (other than a mistress) whom he loves ‖ (*pl.*) two people in love with one another ‖ someone who greatly enjoys something specified

lov·ing (lʌ́viŋ) *adj.* devoted, affectionate ‖ expressing or feeling love

low 1. *adj.* being at, or reaching to, a position at a relatively small distance above some plane of reference (e.g. the ground or sea level) ‖ (of latitude) close to the equator ‖ coming or reaching far downward, *a low bow* ‖ at or near the bottom of some real or imagined scale of measurement ‖ at or near the bottom of some scale of moral or social values or ranking ‖ mean, contemptible ‖ obscene, *a low remark* ‖ depressed, *low spirits* ‖ small in number or amount ‖ depleted to the point of being nearly gone or exhausted ‖ unfavorable, *a low opinion* ‖ little advanced in biological evolution || (*phon.*, of a vowel) open || quiet, soft || (*mus.*, of a note etc.) produced by relatively few vibrations || (of a gear) having the smallest ratio of wheel revolutions to engine revolutions **to lie low** to stay hidden || to avoid attracting attention while awaiting a change in events **2.** *adv.* in or to a low position || in or to a mean or abject position, *he wouldn't sink as low as that* || quietly, softly, *speak lower* || deeply, in or to a low pitch **3.** *n.* low gear || (*meteorol.*) an area of low barometric pressure

low·down *n.* (*pop.*) the real facts of a situation as known to someone with inside information

low·er (lóuər) **1.** *adj. comp.* of LOW || (*biol.*) relatively little advanced in biological evolution **2.** *v.t.* to let down || to reduce || to make less loud || (*mus.*) to depress in pitch || to reduce the height of || to bring down, degrade || *v.i.* to become lower || to decrease **3.** *n.* a lower berth

low·er·ing (láuəriŋ, láuriŋ) *adj.* (of the sky, clouds) black and threatening || (of someone's face, expression etc.) scowling, sullen

low·li·ness (lóuli:nis) *n.* the quality or state of being lowly

low·ly (lóuli:) **1.** *adj. comp.* **low·li·er** *superl.* **low·li·est** (*rhet.*) humble, modest, unpretentious || far down in a scale or hierarchy **2.** *adv.* in a lowly manner

loy·al (lɔ́iəl) *adj.* faithful to any person to whom fidelity is owed || faithful in allegiance to the government of one's country || personally devoted to a sovereign or ruler || displaying fidelity **lóy·al·ist** *n.* someone who is loyal, esp. someone who remains loyal in times of revolt

loy·al·ty (lɔ́iəlti:) *pl.* **loy·al·ties** *n.* the quality or state of being loyal or an instance of this

loz·enge (lɔ́zindʒ) *n.* a four-sided figure having all sides equal and having two oblique and two obtuse angles, e.g. a rhombus, a diamond || a small medicinal candy (originally lozenge-shaped) to be dissolved in the mouth || a diamond-shaped windowpane

lub·ber (lʌ́bər) *n.* a clumsy unskilled sailor

lu·bri·cant (lú:brikənt) **1.** *n.* a substance (e.g. grease, oil, soap) that when introduced between solid surfaces which move over one another reduces resistance to movement, heat production and wear (i.e. friction and its effects) by forming a fluid film between the surfaces **2.** *adj.* lubricating

lu·bri·cate (lú:brikeit) *pres. part.* **lu·bri·cat·ing** *past* and *past part.* **lu·bri·cat·ed** *v.t.* to make smooth or slippery || to diminish friction by applying a lubricant to **lu·bri·cá·tion, lú·bri·ca·tor** *ns*

lu·cid (lú:sid) *adj.* clear, easily understood || sane **lu·cíd·i·ty** *n.*

luck (lʌk) *n.* chance || good fortune || success due to chance || the tendency of a person to be persistently fortunate or unfortunate **as luck would have it** fortunately || unfortunately **to be down on one's luck** to be going through a time of bad luck **to be in (out of) luck** to be fortunate (unfortunate), esp. in some specified set of circumstances **to try one's luck** to take a chance, esp. in gambling

luck·i·ly (lʌ́kili:) *adv.* in a lucky manner, fortunately

luck·i·ness (lʌ́ki:nis) *n.* the state or quality of being lucky

luck·y (lʌ́ki:) *comp.* **luck·i·er** *superl.* **luck·i·est** *adj.* having good luck, esp. habitually || being more successful than one deserves or could expect || bringing or supposed to bring good luck || successful due to chance

lu·cra·tive (lú:krətiv) *adj.* bringing in plenty of money, very profitable

lu·di·crous (lú:dikrəs) *adj.* absurd, arousing mocking laughter

lug (lʌg) **1.** *v. pres. part.* **lug·ging** *past* and *past part.* **lugged** *v.t.* to haul (something heavy) clumsily, with great expenditure of effort, half pulling and half carrying || to introduce or bring in irrelevantly, *to lug anecdotes into a discussion* || to bring or take (someone) along at great effort || *v.i.* to tug **2.** *n.* an act of lugging

lug·gage (lʌ́gidʒ) *n.* suitcases, bags and trunks full of a traveler's belongings || empty suitcases, trunks etc.

lu·gu·bri·ous (lugú:bri:əs, lugjú:bri:əs) *adj.* dismal, mournful

luke·warm (lú:kwɔrm) *adj.* tepid, not very warm || unenthusiastic, halfhearted

lull (lʌl) **1.** *v.t.* to calm, soothe, e.g. by rocking or singing || to quiet, esp. by guile, *to lull suspicions with a plausible story* || *v.i.* to become less in intensity or strength **2.** *n.* a temporary period of peace and quiet || a temporary drop in activity

lull·a·by (lʌ́ləbai) *pl.* **lull·a·bies** *n.* a soothing song to put a baby to sleep

lum·ber (lʌ́mbər) **1.** *n.* wood suitable for, or prepared for, use in construction, esp. just felled and roughly sawn into logs and planks || little-used pieces of furniture or junk, stored away and taking up room **2.** *v.t.* to fell and saw timber into logs and remove it from (an area) || (often with 'up') to fill up (a room or other place) with lumber || *v.i.* to cut down trees and saw them into logs

lumber *v.i.* to move clumsily, heavily and noisily

lu·mi·nar·y (lú:mineri:) *pl.* **lu·mi·nar·ies** *n.* a body giving light, esp. the sun or moon || a person of outstanding intellectual, spiritual or moral quality

lu·mi·nes·cence (lu:minés'ns) *n.* the emission of electromagnetic radiation esp. in the visible region by a substance (e.g. a phosphor) during and/or following stimulation by any of various forms of energy except heat

lu·mi·nes·cent (lu:minés'nt) *adj.* of, relating to or exhibiting luminescence

lu·mi·nos·i·ty (lu:minɔ́siti:) *pl.* **lu·mi·nos·i·ties** *n.* the state or quality of being luminous || the amount of radiation emitted by a star or other heavenly body

lu·mi·nous (lú:minəs) *adj.* emitting a steady, diffused light || shining, bright || lucid, enlightening and inspiring

lump (lʌmp) **1.** *n.* a firm irregular mass || (of sugar) a cube || a large amount or quantity || a dull, heavy awkward person || a swelling, or other hard bump, such as is caused by a heavy blow **a lump in one's throat** a feeling of pressure in one's throat, caused by repressed emotion **in a lump** all at one time **in the lump** taking things as a whole **2.** *v.t.* to put together in a lump || to treat alike without discrimination || *v.i.* to move heavily || to form into lumps

lump·y (lʌ́mpi:) *comp.* **lump·i·er** *superl.* **lump·i·est** *adj.* full of or covered with lumps || (of water) choppy

lu·na·cy (lú:nəsi:) *n.* the state of being a lunatic || (*law*) insanity || (*loosely*) incredible foolishness

lu·nar (lú:nər) *adj.* to do with the moon || measured according to the phases of the moon || similar to that of the moon || crescent-shaped || of or pertaining to silver

lu·na·tic (lú:nətik) **1.** *adj.* mad, insane || exceptionally foolish or irresponsible || wildly frivolous **2.** *n.* (*law*) a person who is insane || a wildly foolish or eccentric person

lunch (lʌntʃ) **1.** *n.* the midday meal **2.** *v.i.* to eat lunch

lunch·eon (lʌ́ntʃən) *n.* the midday meal, lunch, esp. this meal taken with ceremony

---

(**a**) æ, c**a**t; ɑ, c**a**r; ɔ f**a**wn; ei, sn**a**ke. (**e**) e, h**e**n; i:, sh**ee**p; iə, d**ee**r; ɛə, b**ea**r. (**i**) i, f**i**sh; ai, t**i**ger; ə:, b**i**rd. (**o**) o, **o**x; au, c**ow**; ou, g**oa**t; u, p**oo**r; ɔi, r**oy**al. (**u**) ʌ, d**u**ck; u, b**u**ll; u:, g**oo**se; ə, b**a**cillus; ju:, c**u**be. x, lo**ch**; θ, **th**ink; ð, bo**th**er; z, **Z**en; ʒ, corsa**g**e; dʒ, sava**g**e; ŋ, oranguta**n**g; j, **y**ak; ʃ, **fi**sh; tʃ, fe**tch**; 'l, rabb**le**; 'n, redd**en**. Complete pronunciation key appears inside front cover.

lung (lʌŋ) *n.* one of the pair of spongy saclike organs that oxygenate the blood in air-breathing vertebrates and remove carbon dioxide from it

lunge (lʌndʒ) **1.** *n.* a sudden thrust, e.g. with a foil in fencing ‖ a sudden, forward plunging movement of the body **2.** *v. pres. part.* **lung·ing** *past* and *past part.* **lunged** *v.i.* to make a lunge ‖ to start off suddenly ‖ *v.t.* to cause to make a lunge

lure (luər) **1.** *n.* some quality or thing that entices or attracts, *the lure of adventure* ‖ a device to attract animals, esp. fish, by guile **2.** *v.t. pres. part.* **lur·ing** *past* and *past part.* **lured** to entice, tempt with the promise of pleasure or gain

lu·rid (lúərid) *adj.* gaudy, sensational ‖ fascinatingly repulsive ‖ reddish and menacing ‖ ashen, pallid

lurk (lə:rk) *v.i.* to lie hidden waiting to attack ‖ to prowl or skulk around, esp. with some mischief in mind ‖ to be latent or hardly noticed

lus·cious (lʌ́ʃəs) *adj.* rich, full and delicious in flavor or smell ‖ affording other rich sensual delights ‖ excessively rich or luxuriant ‖ *(pop.)* voluptuously attractive, *a luscious blonde*

lush (lʌʃ) *adj.* growing thickly and richly, luxuriant ‖ characterized by luxuriant vegetation ‖ luscious, *lush imagery* ‖ effusive, extravagant

lust (lʌst) **1.** *n.* strong sexual desire without idealized or spiritualized feelings ‖ any passionate desire, *a lust for power* **2.** *v.i. (rhet.,* often with 'for') to have a passionate desire

lus·ter (lʌ́stər) **1.** *n.* a surface sheen or gloss on a surface reflecting light ‖ the quality of having such a gloss ‖ radiance, brightness ‖ splendor, renown, distinction ‖ a glass pendant, or chandelier hung with them ‖ lusterware ‖ *(mineral.)* the appearance of the surface of a mineral with regard to its light-reflecting quality **2.** *v.t. pres. part.* **lus·ter·ing, lus·tring** *past* and *past part.* **lus·tered, lus·tred** to add luster to ‖ to give (pottery or cloth) a luster finish

lust·ful (lʌ́stfəl) *adj.* full of lust ‖ characterized by lust

lust·i·ness (lʌ́sti:nis) *n.* the state or quality of being lusty

lus·trous (lʌ́strəs) *adj.* shining, having a luster

lust·y (lʌ́sti:) *comp.* **lust·i·er** *superl.* **lust·i·est** *adj.* vigorous, strong, sturdy

Lu·ther·an (lú:θərən) **1.** *adj.* of or relating to Martin Luther ‖ of the Protestant denomination founded by Luther, or its teachings **2.** *n.* a member of the Lutheran Church **Lú·ther·an·ism** *n.* a Protestant faith following the doctrines of Luther

lux·u·ri·ance (lʌgʒúəri:əns, lʌkʃúəri:əns) *n.* the state or quality of being luxuriant

lux·u·ri·ant (lʌgʒúəri:ənt, lʌkʃúəri:ənt) *adj.* abundant or exuberant in growth ‖ prolific, richly varied ‖ (of style) richly figurative, florid

lux·u·ri·ous (lʌgʒúəri:əs, lʌkʃúəri:əs) *adj.* opulent, sumptuous, richly comfortable ‖ self-indulgent, extravagant, *a luxurious life* ‖ sensually delightful

lux·u·ry (lʌ́kʃəri:, lʌ́gʒəri:) *pl.* **lux·u·ries** *n.* habitual indulgence in expensive food, clothes, comforts etc. ‖ something enjoyable, relatively costly, but not indispensable ‖ something voluptuously enjoyed ‖ abundance of rich comforts

lymph (limf) *n.* a colorless, plasmalike fluid that bathes many of the tissues of vertebrates, is conducted from these tissues by a system of ducts and channels to the blood circulatory system, and serves to lubricate and cleanse them

lym·phat·ic (limfǽtik) **1.** *adj.* relating to, produced by or conveying lymph ‖ (of a person or his temperament) sluggish, flabby, languid **2.** *n.* any of the fine-walled vessels draining most tissues and conducting lymph to the thoracic duct. The vessels range in size from capillary to veinlike ducts

lynch (lintʃ) *v.t.* (of a mob) to take the law into its own hands and kill (someone) in punishment for a real or presumed crime

lynx (liŋks) *pl.* **lynx, lynx·es** *n.* a genus of wildcats native to the northern hemisphere, e.g. the bobcat ‖ the fur of a lynx

lyr·ic (lírik) **1.** *adj.* (of poetry) expressing the poet's intense personal emotions, usually in short poems divided into stanzas ‖ (of a poet) writing such poetry ‖ (of a singing voice) pure, light and free, not brilliant or deeply charged with emotion ‖ meant to be sung set to music **2.** *n.* a lyric poem ‖ *(pl.)* the words of a popular song

lyr·i·cal (lírik'l) *adj.* *(old-fash.,* of poetry) lyric ‖ written or expressed in language appropriate to lyric poetry ‖ *(pop.)* passionately enthusiastic, esp. in praising

lyr·i·cist (lírisist) *n.* someone who writes the words for popular songs

M

M, m (em) the 13th letter of the English alphabet

ma·ca·bre (məkábr, məkábər) *adj.* suggestive of the terrifying aspect of death

mac·ad·am (məkǽdəm) *n.* small broken stones which, having angular faces, fit closely together when pressed by a heavy roller and so constitute an even and durable road surface ‖ a road having such a surface **mac·ád·am·ize** *pres. part.* **mac·ad·am·iz·ing** *past* and *past part.* **mac·ad·am·ized** *v.t.* to construct (a road surface) of layers of macadam, generally using tar as a binding surface

mac·a·ro·ni (mækəróuni:) *pl.* **mac·a·ro·nies** *n.* a pasta made of semolina, usually rolled into long thin tubes which are hard and brittle when dried, softening when boiled for eating

ma·caw (məkɔ́) *n.* any of several large, bright-feathered parrots of Central and South America

mace (meis) *n.* *(hist.)* a club with a heavy, spiked metal head, used as a weapon for shattering armor, esp. helmets ‖ an ornamented staff of office, carried before certain officials

mace *n.* a spice made from the outer covering of the nutmeg kernel

Mace tradename of a temporarily incapacitating liquid nerve irritant in aerosol form that is sprayed into a person's face and causes irritation of eyes, dizziness, etc. It is often used as a personal defense weapon and by the police to disable rioters —**mace** *v.t.* to use mace

mac·er·ate (mǽsəreit) *pres. part.* **mac·er·at·ing** *past* and *past part.* **mac·er·at·ed** *v.t.* to soften or separate (e.g. food in the digestive tract) by soaking ‖ to cause to waste away, esp. by fasting ‖ *v.i.* to become softened or separated by soaking ‖ to waste away, esp. by fasting **mac·er·á·tion** *n.*

ma·chet·e (mətʃéti:, məʃéti:) *n.* a long, heavy, broad-bladed knife used esp. in Central and South America and the West Indies as a tool and a weapon

mach·i·nate (mǽkineit) *pres. part.* **mach·i·nat·ing** *past* and *past part.* **mach·i·nat·ed** *v.i.* to form a plot or intrigue, esp. in order to work harm

mach·i·na·tion (mækinéiʃən) *n.* the act of machinating

‖ a plot, scheme

ma·chine (məʃíːn) **1.** *n.* an apparatus, made of organized, interacting parts, which takes in some form of energy, modifies it, and delivers it in a more suitable form for a desired function ‖ a thing or system resembling such an apparatus in acting with regularity as a result of the interaction of its component parts ‖ a person who acts like such an apparatus, apparently without exercising his will, thought or imagination ‖ an organization whose members collaborate for some purpose, *a political machine* **2.** *v.t. pres. part.* **ma·chin·ing** *past and past part.* **ma·chined** to make or operate on by machinery

ma·chin·er·y (məʃíːnəri) *n. (collect.)* machines in general ‖ the assembled parts of a machine ‖ the organization of various processes so that a certain purpose may be fulfilled

ma·chin·ist (məʃíːnist) *n.* someone who makes, assembles, repairs or operates machines

ma·chis·mo or **ma·cho** (mɑtʃíːzmou) *n.* exaggerated masculinity; manly assurance —**macho** *adj.*

mack·i·naw (mǽkinɔ) *n. (Am. hist.)* a heavy woolen blanket originally distributed by the U.S. government to North American Indians ‖ a short, double-breasted, belted coat of thick wool napped and felted

mac·ro·bi·ot·ics (mækroubaiótiks) *n.* a Zen-influenced food cult that holds that foods are yin (feminine) and/or yang (masculine), and that a vegetarian diet is in balance and in harmony with the cosmos

mac·ro·cosm (mǽkrəkɒzəm) *n.* the universe as contrasted with a microcosm **mac·ro·cós·mic** *adj.*

mac·ro·or·gan·ism (mækrouɔ́rgənizəm) *n.* an organism visible to the naked eye *ant.* microorganism

mac·ro·scop·ic (mækrəskópik) *adj.* visible to the unaided eye

mad (mæd) *comp.* **mad·der** *superl.* **mad·dest** *adj.* insane ‖ showing insanity ‖ *(pop.)* utterly foolish, irrational ‖ *(pop.)* rash ‖ *(pop.,* often with 'at') angry ‖ *(pop.,* with 'about' or 'on') wildly enthusiastic about some specified thing, person etc. ‖ (of a dog) rabid **like mad** with great enthusiasm ‖ frantically

mad·am (mǽdəm) *n. (pl.* **mes·dames**, meidǽm) a polite title used in addressing a woman ‖ *(pl.* **mad·ams**) a woman in charge of a brothel

ma·dame (mǽdəm, mədǽm, mədám) *pl.* **mes·dames** (meidǽm, meidám) *n.* a courtesy title for a married Frenchwoman (the equivalent of 'Mrs') ‖ a courtesy title for a married woman who is neither American nor English

mad·cap (mǽdkæp) **1.** *n.* someone given to capricious behavior conspicuously lacking prudence **2.** *adj.* (of a person or action) foolishly impulsive

mad·den (mǽd'n) *v.t.* to make mad

mad·e·moi·selle (mædəməzél, mædmwəzél) *n.* a courtesy title for an unmarried French girl or woman (the equivalent of 'Miss') ‖ a courtesy title for an unmarried girl or woman who is neither American nor English

mad·house (mǽdhaus) *pl.* **mad·hous·es** (mǽdhauziz) *n. (pop.)* a mental hospital ‖ *(pop.)* a scene of uproar or confusion

mad·man (mǽdmæn, mǽdmən) *pl.* **mad·men** (mǽdmɛn, mǽdmən) *n.* a man who is insane or acts as if he were

ma·don·na (mədónə) *n.* a statue or picture of the Virgin Mary

mad·ri·gal (mǽdrig'l) *n. (mus.)* a contrapuntal secular composition for several voices, either unaccompanied or with instrumental doubling or replacing of one or more parts

mael·strom (méilstrəm) *n.* a large and dangerous whirl-

pool ‖ *(rhet.)* a turbulent situation

maes·tro (máistrou, maéstrɔ) *pl.* **maes·tros, ma·es·tri** (maéstri:) *n.* a great musical conductor, composer or teacher ‖ a master in any art

ma·ga·zine (mǽgəzíːn) *n.* a paperback periodical publication of writings by different authors, often illustrated and with advertisements ‖ a storage place for arms, ammunition and explosives ‖ a receptacle for cartridges which are to be fed into the breech of a rifle, machine gun etc., or for films or plates to be fed into some cameras

ma·gen·ta (mədʒéntə) **1.** *n.* a brilliant, bluish-red aniline dye prepared from aniline and toluidine ‖ the color of this dye **2.** *adj.* having this color

mag·got (mǽgət) *n.* an insect larva, e.g. that of the housefly, without appendages or distinct head **mág·got·y** *adj.*

mag·ic (mǽdʒik) *n.* the art which claims to control and manipulate the secret forces of nature by occult and ritualistic methods ‖ the practice of this art ‖ any mysterious power or phenomenon which defies analysis or explanation ‖ the art or practice of producing illusions etc. by sleight of hand

magic *adj.* of, relating to, used in or produced by magic ‖ having an effect like one produced by magic **mág·i·cal** *adj.*

ma·gi·cian (mədʒíʃən) *n.* a person who practices magic

mag·is·trate (mǽdʒistreit, mǽdʒistrit) *n.* an inferior judicial officer, esp. a civil justice of the peace ‖ *(broadly)* a civil legislative or executive officer

mag·nan·i·mous (mægnǽniməs) *adj.* generously and benevolently overlooking faults, not subject to resentment, envy etc.

mag·nate (mǽgneit, mǽgnit) *n.* a person of great prominence and wealth, esp. someone important in big business or industry

mag·ne·sia (mægníːʒə, mægníːʃə) *n.* a white low-melting solid oxide of magnesium that occurs naturally or is obtained by calcining the carbonates of magnesium **mag·né·sian** *adj.*

mag·ne·sium (mægníːʒəm, mægníːziːəm) *n.* a light divalent silvery metallic element that occurs in nature in combination only in sea water, plants and animals (e.g. in chlorophyll and animal bones)

mag·net (mǽgnit) *n.* a piece of steel, iron, cobalt, nickel or alloy exhibiting ferromagnetism ‖ the magnetized needle of a compass ‖ the soft-iron core and surrounding coil of an electromagnet ‖ something or someone exerting a powerful attraction

mag·net·ic (mægnétik) *adj.* of or relating to a magnet or to magnetism ‖ taking the north magnetic pole as reference ‖ (esp. of a ferromagnetic substance) magnetized or capable of being magnetized ‖ strongly attractive **mag·nét·i·cal·ly** *adv.*

mag·net·ism (mǽgnitizəm) *n.* a group of physical phenomena associated with the interaction of a magnetic field with matter ‖ the study of the behavior and effects of magnetic fields ‖ *(fig.)* the ability to attract by·personal charm

mag·net·i·za·tion (mægnitizéiʃən) *n.* a magnetizing or being magnetized ‖ intensity of magnetic force measured by magnetic moment per unit volume

mag·net·ize (mǽgnitaiz) *pres. part.* **mag·net·iz·ing** *past and past part.* **mag·net·ized** *v.t.* to make (something) magnetic ‖ to exert an irresistible influence upon

mag·ni·fi·ca·tion (mægnifikéiʃən) *n. (phys.)* the act or process of apparently changing the dimensions of an object by optical methods ‖ the ability to be apparently changed in this way ‖ *(rhet.)* a celebrating with praise

mag·nif·i·cence (mægnífis'ns) *n.* the quality of being magnificent ‖ an instance of this

---

(**a**) æ, c**a**t; ɑ, c**a**r; ɔ f**aw**n; ei, sn**a**ke. (**e**) e, h**e**n; iː, sh**ee**p; iə, d**ee**r; ɛə, b**ea**r. (**i**) i, f**i**sh; ai, t**i**ger; ə, b**i**rd. (**o**) o, **o**x; au, c**ow**; ou, g**oa**t; u, p**oo**r; ɔi, r**oy**al. (**u**) ʌ, d**u**ck; u, b**u**ll; uː, g**oo**se; ə, b**a**cillus; juː, c**u**be. x, lo**ch**; θ, **th**ink; ð, bo**th**er; z, **Z**en; ʒ, corsa**g**e; dʒ, sava**g**e; ŋ, oranguta**n**g; j, **y**ak; ʃ, **f**ish; tʃ, fe**tch**; 'l, rabb**le**; 'n, redd**en**. Complete pronunciation key appears inside front cover.

mag·nif·i·cent (mægnífis'nt) *adj.* so splendid, lavish, beautiful etc. as to arouse admiration and wonder

mag·ni·fy (mǽgnifai) *pres. part.* **mag·ni·fy·ing** *past* and *past part.* **mag·ni·fied** *v.t.* to make (something) appear larger or more important than it is ‖ *(phys.)* to make (an object) look larger by substituting for it an image which subtends a wider angle at the eye ‖ *(rhet.)* to celebrate with praise, laud ‖ *v.i.* to increase or be able to increase the size of the appearance of an object

mag·ni·tude (mǽgnitu:d, mǽgnitju:d) *n.* size ‖ largeness in size or number ‖ importance ‖ *(astron.)* a number designating the relative brightness of a star ‖ *(math.)* a number denoting the relative measure of a quantity

mag·no·lia (mægnóuljə) *n.* a genus of trees and shrubs native to Asia and North America

ma·hog·a·ny (məhɔ́gəni:) *pl.* **ma·hog·a·nies 1.** *n.* the wood of any of several trees of fam. *Meliaceae*, esp. the reddish brown wood of the West Indian *Swietonia mahogani*, which takes a high polish and is widely used in cabinetmaking ‖ the color of the wood ‖ a tree producing this wood **2.** *adj.* of, pertaining to or made of mahogany ‖ of the dark-reddish-brown color of mahogany

maid (meid) *n.* a female domestic servant ‖ *(rhet.)* a girl ‖ *(rhet.)* a virgin

maid·en (méid'n) **1.** *n.* *(rhet.)* a girl ‖ *(rhet.)* a virgin **2.** *adj.* *(rhet.)* virgin ‖ *(rhet.)* unmarried ‖ being the first of its kind ‖ of a horse that has not won a race ‖ of a race open only to such horses

mail (meil) **1.** *n.* the public organization dealing with the collection and delivery of correspondence and other postal matter ‖ the letters and parcels sent by this organization **2.** *v.t.* to send by this organization

mail·box (méilbɒks) *n.* a box, provided by the public organization dealing with the mail, into which people drop their letters for dispatch ‖ a box into which letters etc. delivered to an address are placed

mail·man (méilmæn) *pl.* **mail·men** (méilmen) *n.* a man employed to collect and deliver mail

maim (meim) *v.t.* to deprive of the full or partial use of a limb or limbs by inflicting an injury

main (mein) **1.** *n.* a principal pipe system, duct etc. for drainage, gas, water etc. ‖ *(rhet.)* the high sea **2.** *adj.* most important, chief, principal

main·land (méinlənd, méinlænd) *n.* a continuous land mass as compared with an island

main·ly (méinli:) *adv.* chiefly, principally

main·spring (méinsprin) *n.* the chief spring in a clockwork mechanism ‖ the principal activating power or motive

main·tain (meintéin) *v.t.* to cause to remain unaltered or unimpaired ‖ to declare to be true, valid etc. ‖ to defend the truth, validity etc. of ‖ to preserve against attack ‖ to provide for the needs of, *to maintain a large household*

main·te·nance (méintənəns) *n.* a maintaining or being maintained ‖ the provisions, money etc. needed for subsistence

maize (meiz) *n.* corn

ma·jes·tic (mədʒéstik) *adj.* having majesty **ma·jes·ti·cal** *adj.*

maj·es·ty (mǽdʒisti:) *pl.* **maj·es·ties** *n.* royal stateliness, splendor etc. ‖ sovereign power **Maj·es·ty** (with second or third person possessive pronoun) the title used in addressing or referring to a king, queen or emperor

ma·jor (méidʒər) *n.* an army officer ranking below a lieutenant colonel and above a captain ‖ an officer of the same rank in the U.S. air force or marine corps

ma·jor·i·ty (mədʒɔ́riti:, mədʒɔ́riti:) *pl.* **ma·jor·i·ties** *n.* the greater number or part, esp. more than half the total number ‖ the amount by which a greater part exceeds a smaller

make (meik) **1.** *v. pres. part.* **mak·ing** *past* and *past*

part. **made** (meid) *v.t.* to bring (something) into being, cause to exist ‖ to use (something already in being) in order to bring something else into being ‖ to contrive by imaginative effort, *to make a design* ‖ to arrive at (a choice, decision, conclusion) ‖ to cause to occur, *to make a noise* ‖ to cause to acquire some specified quality ‖ (with 'of') to cause (someone or something) to become or seem (something), *to make a mess of a job* ‖ to cause to acquire a specified mental or emotional state, *to make someone sad* ‖ to compel ‖ to cause to perform a specified action ‖ to utter (a remark, a statement) ‖ to deliver (a speech) ‖ to arrange, *to make the bed* ‖ to establish, frame, *to make a set of rules* ‖ *(law)* to draw up (e.g. a contract) ‖ to add up to, be the equivalent of, *2 pints make 1 quart* ‖ to turn out to be, have the qualities needed for, *he will make a good lawyer* ‖ to assure the success of, *that performance will make him* ‖ (often with 'it') to succeed in arriving at (a desired goal) ‖ to gain (money etc.), *to make a profit* ‖ to earn (money etc.) ‖ to achieve, *to make a high score* ‖ *(cards)* to shuffle ‖ *v.i.* (with 'for') to lead to a specified result, *it makes for harmony* ‖ (with an adjective) to cause oneself to become as specified, *to make sure* **to make a break with** to cease to have relations with **to make as if** to pretend **to make believe** to pretend **to make do with** to manage with (what is available) **to make much of** to cherish or be particularly attentive to **to make off** to run away **to make off with** to steal **to make or break, to make or mar** to have a decisive effect on for good or bad **to make out** to understand ‖ to decipher ‖ *(pop.)* to succeed, get along satisfactorily ‖ *(pop.)* to neck **to make over** to transfer ownership of **to make time** to advance at a specified rate of progress **to make up** to invent (a story) ‖ to put an end to (a quarrel) by being reconciled ‖ to apply cosmetics **2.** *n.* provenance of manufacture ‖ style or quality of making ‖ *(cards)* a turn at shuffling ‖ quality of personality **on the make** aggressively seeking financial or social advantage

mak·er (méikər) *n.* someone who makes, usually in compounds indicating the thing made, *brickmaker, shoemaker* **Mak·er** God

make·shift (méikʃift) **1.** *n.* something used temporarily as a substitute **2.** *adj.* serving as, or resembling, a makeshift

make·up (méikʌp) *n.* the way in which the parts of something are put together ‖ cosmetics ‖ the art of applying cosmetics ‖ *(printing)* the arrangement of various elements (text, titles, illustrations etc.) of printed matter on a page ‖ *(pop.)* a special examination taken to make up for one missed through illness etc.

mal·ad·just·ed (mælədʒʌ́stid) *adj.* (of a person) psychologically unable to adjust his behavior to the conditions of his social environment

mal·ad·just·ment (mælədʒʌ́stmənt) *n.* the quality or state of being maladjusted ‖ an instance of this

mal·a·dy (mǽlədi:) *pl.* **mal·a·dies** *n.* a physical, mental or moral disorder

ma·laise (mæléiz) *n.* a feeling of general discomfort, of being below one's normal standard of health ‖ a feeling of being emotionally ill at ease or apprehensive

mal·a·prop·ism (mǽləprɒpizəm) *n.* a ludicrous misuse of a word

mal·ap·ro·pos (mælæprəpóu) **1.** *adv.* at an unsuitable time, or in an inappropriate manner **2.** *adj.* inopportune

ma·lar·i·a (məléəri:ə) *n.* an infectious, chiefly tropical disease characterized by periodic chills and fever, splenic enlargement and anemia **ma·lár·i·ous** *adj.*

mal·con·tent (mǽlkəntent) *n.* someone who is discontented, esp. with the government, and ready to make trouble

male (meil) **1.** *adj.* of the sex in animals or plants that fertilizes in order to reproduce ‖ *(bot.)* pertaining to any reproductive structure that contains elements for fertilizing female elements ‖ of, pertaining to or characteristic of men ‖ manly ‖ *(engin.)* of or being a part designed to fit into another part ‖ (of a gem) having hardness, depth or brilliance **2.** *n.* a male person, animal or plant

mal·e·dic·tion (mælidíkʃən) *n.* a curse called down upon someone

mal·e·fac·tion (mæləfǽkʃən) *n.* an evil deed, crime

mal·e·fac·tor (mǽləfæktər) *n.* someone who does evil, esp. someone who commits a crime

ma·lev·o·lence (məlévələns) *n.* the quality of being malevolent

ma·lev·o·lent (məlévələnt) *adj.* having or showing a desire to do harm

mal·fea·sance (mælfíːzːns) *n.* *(law)* the committing of illegal acts by a public official ‖ *(law)* an instance of this **mal·féa·sant** *adj.* and *n.*

mal·for·ma·tion (mælfɔːrméiʃən) *n.* the quality of being malformed ‖ something malformed **mal·fórmed** *adj.* abnormal in structure, badly made

mal·func·tion (mælfʌ́ŋkʃən) **1.** *v.i.* (esp. used in the pres. part.) to function improperly **2.** *n.* malfunctioning ‖ an instance of this

ma·lice (mǽlis) *n.* the will to do harm to another

ma·li·cious (məlíʃəs) *adj.* having or showing malice

ma·lign (məláin) *adj.* having an evil effect, doing harm ‖ *(med.)* malignant

malign *v.t.* to make false or misleading statements about (someone) so as to injure him

ma·lig·nan·cy (məlígnənsiː) *pl.* **ma·lig·nan·cies** *n.* the quality or state of being malignant ‖ an instance of this ‖ *(med.)* a malignant tumor

ma·lig·nant (məlígnənt) *adj.* feeling, showing or acting with extreme ill will ‖ *(med.,* of a disease) tending to be fatal without treatment ‖ *(med.,* of a tumor) tending to metastasize and lead to death

ma·lin·ger (məlíŋgər) *v.i.* to pretend to be ill, or exaggerate a real illness, in order to avoid one's work or responsibility

mall (mɔl) *n.* a usually public, tree-lined walk

mal·lard (mǽlərd) *pl.* **mal·lard, mal·lards** *n.* the common wild duck. The name applies to both sexes

mal·le·a·bil·i·ty (mæliːəbíliːtiː) *n.* the quality or state of being malleable

mal·le·a·ble (mǽliːəbʼl) *adj.* (esp. of a metal) able to have its shape changed permanently through the applying of stress, e.g by hammering ‖ (of a person's character) easily affected or formed by external influences

mal·let (mǽlit) *n.* a hammer, usually of wood, used to strike a wooden object (chisel handle, tent peg etc.) without the risk of splitting it ‖ *(croquet, polo)* a long-handled hammer used to strike the ball

mal·nu·tri·tion (mælnuːtríʃən, mælnjuːtríʃən) *n.* poor nutrition caused by an inadequate or unbalanced diet, or by defective assimilation or utilization of nutrients

mal·o·dor·ous (mælóudərəs) *adj.* having a foul smell

mal·prac·tice (mælprǽktis) *n.* *(law)* the improper treatment of a patient by a doctor ‖ *(law)* illegal action taken in one's own interest by a person in a position of trust

malt (mɔlt) **1.** *n.* grain, esp. barley, allowed to germinate in water and then heated and dried, used in brewing and distilling **2.** *v.t.* to convert (grain) into malt ‖ to prepare with malt ‖ *v.i.* to become malt

mam·ma, ma·ma (múmə, məmú) *n.* (a child's word for) mother

mam·mal (mǽməl) *n.* a member of *Mammalia,* the highest class of vertebrates, including man. The many distinguishing characteristics include warm blood, hair

more or less covering the body, mammary glands to nourish the young **mam·ma·li·an** (məméiliːən) *adj.*

mam·moth (mǽməθ) **1.** *n.* any of several extinct elephants, distinguished by great size, long hair and long curved tusks ‖ something of very great size **2.** *adj.* of very great size

man (mæn) *pl.* **men** (men) *n. Homo sapiens,* a member of a race of erect, biped mammals, with a highly developed brain, having the powers of articulate speech, abstract reasoning and imagination ‖ the human race in general ‖ an adult human male ‖ a husband (only in 'man and wife') ‖ *(chess* etc.) one of the pieces used in playing **as one man** in unison, unanimously **to a man** (in apposition) every individual without exception

man *pres. part.* **man·ning** *past* and *past part.* **manned** *v.t.* to supply (a post, vessel, field gun etc.) with the man or men needed ‖ to take one's operational position at (a gun, helm etc.)

man·a·cle (mǽnəkʼl) **1.** *n.* (usually *pl.*) a steel clasp, heavy chain or handcuff used to bind a person's wrists close together *v.t. pres. part.* **man·a·cling** *past* and *past part.* **man·a·cled** to fasten manacles on (someone) ‖ to restrict the freedom of action of (someone) as if by manacles

man·age (mǽnidʒ) *v. pres. part.* **man·ag·ing** *past* and *past part.* **man·aged** *v.t.* to exercise control over ‖ to handle, manipulate ‖ to influence (someone) so that he does as one wishes ‖ to use economically and with forethought ‖ *v.i.* to be able to cope with a situation ‖ to contrive to make one's budget suffice **man·age·a·bíl·i·ty** *n.* **mán·age·a·ble** *adj.* **mán·age·a·bly** *adv.*

man·age·ment (mǽnidʒmənt) *n.* a managing or being managed ‖ (of a business or other collective enterprise) the body of those in positions of administrative authority

man·ag·er (mǽnidʒər) *n.* someone who manages a company, department, institution etc. **man·ag·er·ess** (mǽnidʒəris) *n.* a female manager **man·a·ge·ri·al** (mænidʒíəriːəl) *adj.*

man·da·tar·y (mǽndəteriː) *pl.* **man·da·tar·ies** *n.* a nation to which a mandate is given

man·date (mǽndeit) **1.** *n.* an instruction or authorization given or conferred ‖ instructions concerning policy, assumed to be given by constituents to a legislative body or its members ‖ *(law)* an order by a court or legal officer to an inferior court or officer ‖ a mandated territory **2.** *v.t. pres. part.* **man·dat·ing** *past* and *past part.* **man·dat·ed** to assign (a territory) as a mandate

man·da·to·ry (mǽndətɔːriː, mǽndətɔuriː) **1.** *adj.* of, relating to or having the force of a mandate **2.** *pl.* **man·da·to·ries** *n.* an instance of this

man·di·ble (mǽndəbʼl) *n. (anat.)* the lower jaw, formed either of a single bone or of fused bones ‖ *(zool.)* either part of the beak of a bird ‖ *(zool.)* either of the pair of outermost mouth appendages in an arthropod, often forming biting jaws **man·dib·u·lar** (mændíbjulər) *adj.*

man·drill (mǽndril) *n.* a large, ferocious baboon of W. Africa. It has red buttock callosities and, in the male, cheek protuberances striped with brilliant red and blue

mane (mein) *n.* the long hair growing on the top or sides of the neck of some animals, e.g. of the horse or lion

ma·nège, ma·nege (mænéʒ, mænéiʒ) *n.* a riding academy ‖ the training of horses ‖ the exercises used in training horses

---

(a) æ, cat; ɑ, car; ɔ fawn; ei, snake. **(e)** e, hen; iː, sheep; iə, deer; ɛə, bear. **(i)** i, fish; ai, tiger; əː, bird. **(o)** o, ox; au, cow; ou, goat; u, poor; ɔi, royal. **(u)** ʌ, duck; u, bull; uː, goose; ə, bacillus; juː, cube. x, loch; θ, think; ð, bother; z, Zen; ʒ, corsa*g*e; dʒ, sava*g*e; ŋ, oranguta*ng*; j, *y*ak; ʃ, fish; tʃ, fetch; ʼl, rabble; ʼn, redden. Complete pronunciation key appears inside front cover.

ma·neu·ver (mənú:vər) *n.* a tactical movement of military troops, naval vessels etc. || (usually *pl.*) training exercises involving such movement || a cleverly thought-out or dextrous movement, action or plan
maneuver *pres. part.* **ma·neu·ver·ing** *past* and *past part.* **ma·neu·vered** *v.t.* to cause (troops etc.) to perform maneuvers || to move, manage or guide cleverly and dextrously || to cause by clever contriving || (with 'into' or 'out of') to cause to acquire or lose a specified condition, position etc. || *v.i.* to engage in a maneuver or maneuvers **ma·neu·ver·a·bíl·i·ty** *n.* **ma·néu·ver·a·ble** *adj.*
man·ga·nese (mǽngəni:s, mǽngəni:z) *n.* a grayish-white, polyvalent metallic element that is usually hard and brittle, occurring in nature usually as an oxide, carbonate or silicate
mange (meindʒ) *n.* any of several contagious skin diseases of domestic animals and sometimes man, caused by parasitic mites, and marked esp. by hair loss
man·ger (méindʒər) *n.* a trough from which horses and cattle feed in their stalls
man·gle (mǽng'l) *pres. part.* **man·gling** *past* and *past part.* **man·gled** *v.t.* to hack or cut or crush with or as if with repeated blows || to ruin by bad interpretation, pronunciation, etc.
man·gle 1. *n.* a machine having heated rollers between which damp linen is pressed smooth **2.** *v.t. pres. part.* **man·gling** *past* and *past part.* **man·gled** to press in a mangle
man·go (mǽngou) *pl.* **man·goes, man·gos** *n.* a large Indian tree cultivated widely for its fruit || the fruit of this tree, a large, juicy drupe with aromatic pulp, eaten ripe or used green in jam, pickles etc.
man·gy (méindʒi:) *comp.* **man·gi·er** *superl.* **man·gi·est** *adj.* infected with mange || of or relating to mange || shabby, poorly kept-up
man·han·dle (mǽnhænd'l) *pres. part.* **man·han·dling** *past* and *past part.* **man·han·dled** *v.t.* to handle roughly, beat up
man·hole (mǽnhoul) *n.* a hole in a floor, street etc. allowing access to a sewer, pipe etc.
man·hood (mǽnhud) *n.* the state or period of being an adult male || manly qualities of courage and fortitude || (*rhet.*) men collectively
man-hour (mǽnauər) *n.* the amount of work done by one man in one hour, as a statistical unit of measurement of labor cost in production
ma·ni·a (méini:ə) *n.* a form of mental disorder marked by great elation and violent action || (*pop.*) an irrational and prolonged desire or enthusiasm || used as a suffix in compounds denoting specific kinds of mental disorder, e.g. kleptomania
ma·ni·ac (méini:æk) **1.** *adj.* of, relating to or typical of mania **2.** *n.* a person affected with mania **ma·ni·a·cal** (mənáiək'l) *adj.*
man·ic (mǽnik) *adj.* (*psychol.*) affected with mania || pertaining to or resembling mania
man·i·cure (mǽnikjuər) **1.** *n.* a beauty treatment for the hands, esp. the nails **2.** *v.t. pres. part.* **man·i·cur·ing** *past* and *past part.* **man·i·cured** to give a manicure to (the hands) || to give a manicure to the hands of (a person) **mán·i·cur·ist** *n.* a person who gives manicures
man·i·fest (mǽnifest) *n.* a detailed list of a ship's cargo, submitted to Customs officers
manifest *v.t.* to show plainly, make manifest || to list in a ship's manifest
manifest *adj.* immediately evident to sense perception or to the mind
man·i·fes·ta·tion (mænifestéiʃən) *n.* a manifesting or being manifested || a public demonstration, esp. by a political group || something that makes manifest the presence or existence of something else || a form or phenomenon by which a spirit makes itself manifest
man·i·fes·to (mæniféstou) *pl.* **man·i·fes·tos, man·i·fes·toes** *n.* a public statement of opinions or intentions, esp. on behalf of an organized and au-

thoritative body of persons
man·i·fold (mǽnifould) **1.** *adj.* having many different parts, applications, forms etc. || (of things, qualities etc.) numerous and varied **2.** *n.* a copy made by manifolding || (*engin.*) a pipe with several lateral outlets for connecting it with other pipes **3.** *v.t.* to make a number of carbon copies of (a letter etc.)
man·i·kin, man·ni·kin (mǽnikin) *n.* a tiny man || an anatomical model of the human body with detachable parts for revealing structures || a mannequin (dummy)
ma·nip·u·late (mənípjuleit) *pres. part.* **ma·nip·u·lat·ing** *past* and *past part.* **ma·nip·u·lat·ed** *v.t.* to handle, esp. with skill || to deal with mentally || to cause by clever maneuvering to act as one wishes || to make dishonest changes in (e.g. election results) so as to suit one's purpose || (*commerce*) to influence (a market) by cunningly calculated trading acts
ma·nip·u·la·tion (mənipjuléiʃən) *n.* a manipulating or being manipulated || an instance of this
ma·nip·u·la·tor (mənípjuleitər) *n.* someone who or something that manipulates
man·kind (mǽnkaind) *n.* the human race || men as contrasted with women
man·li·ness (mǽnli:nis) *n.* the state or quality of being manly
man·ly (mǽnli:) *comp.* **man·li·er** *superl.* **man·li·est** *adj.* having qualities regarded as proper in a man, e.g. courage || befitting a man
man·na (mǽnə) *n.* (*Bible*) food miraculously supplied to the Israelites in the wilderness (Exodus xvi, 14–36) || any food for the mind or spirit that is felt as something miraculously given
man·ne·quin (mǽnikin) *n.* a model (person who demonstrates clothes) || a dummy figure used by dressmakers, tailors or artists
man·ner (mǽnər) *n.* a way of doing something || (*pl.*) social behavior with respect to standards || (*pl.*) correct social behavior || (*pl.*) human behavior as manifested in society **mán·nered** *adj.* (usually in combination) having manners of a given kind, *well-mannered*
man·ner·ism (mǽnərizəm) *n.* an affected gesture, habit, manner of speaking etc. || adherence to a personal artistic or literary style marked by affectation
man·ner·li·ness (mǽnərli:nis) *n.* the quality of being mannerly
man·ner·ly (mǽnərli:) *adj.* having or showing good manners
man·or (mǽnər) *n.* (*hist.*) a medieval landed estate held by a lord under the feudal system and worked by serfs or tenant farmers as a largely self-sufficient economic unit, chiefly in W. Europe **ma·no·ri·al** (mənɔ́ri:əl, mənóuri:əl) *adj.*
man·pow·er (mǽnpauər) *n.* the persons available for some purpose, regarded as one of the resources of a nation, industry etc.
man·sard (mǽnsərd) *n.* a roof divided into a steep lower part and a less steep upper part on all four sides || the story under such a roof
man·sion (mǽnʃən) *n.* a very large, imposing house
man·slaugh·ter (mǽnslɔtər) *n.* (*law*) the unlawful killing of a human being without malicious intent
man·tel (mǽnt'l) *n.* an ornamental structure above and around a fireplace
man·tle (mǽnt'l) **1.** *n.* a loose outer garment or sleeveless cloak || anything that covers or conceals, *the mantle of secrecy* || (*metall.*) a blast furnace's outer wall and casing, above the hearth || a small hood of net material coated with any of certain substances which, when heated by a gas flame, emit bright light **2.** *v. pres. part.* **man·tling** *past* and *past part.* **man·tled** *v.t.* to cover with or as if with a mantle || *v.i.* (of liquids) to become coated with scum etc.
man·u·al (mǽnju:əl) **1.** *adj.* relating to, done with or operated by the hands **2.** *n.* a book containing information set out briefly
man·u·fac·ture (mænjufǽktʃər) **1.** *n.* the making of

things on a large scale, by hand or machine or both, esp. with division of labor ‖ something made in this way **2.** *v.t. pres. part.* **man·u·fac·tur·ing** *past* and *past part.* **man·u·fac·tured** to make (goods) in this way ‖ to make up, fabricate (evidence, an excuse etc.) **man·u·fac·tur·er** *n.*

ma·nure (mənúər, mənjúər) **1.** *v.t. pres. part.* **ma·nur·ing** *past* and *past part.* **ma·nured** to add dung, compost or chemicals to (soil) in order to fertilize it **2.** *n.* matter, esp. dung, added to soil for fertilizing

man·u·script (mǽnjuskrɪpt) **1.** *n. (abbr.* MS, *pl.* MSS) a document or book written by hand ‖ an author's written or typewritten copy of his work, as opposed to the printed copies made from it **2.** *adj.* written by hand

man·y (méni:) **1.** *adj. comp.* **more** (mɔr, mour) *superl.* **most** (moust) consisting of a large but indefinite number ‖ *(rhet.,* before 'a' or 'an') being one of a large but undefinite number of things, people etc. **2.** *n.* (followed by 'of') a large, indefinite number (of people, things etc.) **3.** *pron.* a large, indefinite number of people or things

map (mæp) **1.** *n.* a representation in scale, usually on a flat surface, of part or the whole of the earth's surface, showing physical, political or other features ‖ a similar representation of part of the heavens **2.** *v.t. pres. part.* **map·ping** *past* and *past part.* **mapped** to represent on a map ‖ (often with 'out') to establish the main features of (a plan, project etc.) **to put on the map** to make well known **to wipe off the map** to destroy completely (a city etc.)

ma·ple (méip'l) *n.* a large genus of hardwood trees and shrubs, largely of the north temperate zone ‖ their hard, light-colored, close-grained wood, used for furniture etc. ‖ the flavor of maple sap

maple syrup a syrup consisting of the concentrated sap of the sugar maple

mar (mɑr) *pres. part.* **mar·ring** *past* and *past part.* **marred** *v.t.* to lessen the perfection of

ma·ra·ca (mərɑ́kə) *n.* a dried gourd containing pebbles, usually one of a pair used as a musical percussion instrument

ma·ras·ca (mərǽskə) *n.* a small, black, bitter Dalmatian cherry from which maraschino is made [Ital.]

mar·a·schi·no (mæəskí:nou, mærəʃí:nou) *n.* a liqueur distilled from the marasca

mar·a·thon (mǽrəθɒn, mǽrəθən) *n.* a long-distance race, esp. one run over 26 miles 385 yards in the Olympic Games ‖ any contest testing endurance over a long period

ma·raud (mərɔ́d) *v.i.* to roam about making raids and pillaging ‖ *v.t. (esp. pass.)* to raid

mar·ble (mɑ́rb'l) **1.** *n.* naturally occurring calcium carbonate which has been crystallized from limestone under heat and pressure, forming a hard rock capable of taking a high polish and often veined or mottled by the presence of other crystallized minerals ‖ a piece of sculpture made of this material ‖ a small ball made of something resembling this material, used as a toy ‖ *(pl.)* a game played with these small balls **2.** *v.t. pres. part.* **mar·bling** *past* and *past part.* **mar·bled** to treat (something) so as to give it the mottled or veined appearance of marble **3.** *adj.* of, pertaining to, or like marble

March (mɑrtʃ) *n. (abbr.* Mar.) the 3rd month of the year, having 31 days

march (mɑrtʃ) *n.* the act of marching ‖ a steady regular gait used in marching ‖ a distance covered by marching ‖ steady progress ‖ a piece of music to accompany marching

mare (mɛər) *n.* a female horse ‖ the female of any equine animal

mar·ga·rine (mɑ́rdʒərin, mɑ́rdʒəri:n, mɑ́rgəri:n) *n.* a substitute for butter prepared from milk and certain edible purified animal or vegetable fats, with added vitamins etc.

mar·gin (mɑ́rdʒin) **1.** *n.* an outer limiting edge ‖ a narrow area adjacent to the border of something ‖ the space between written or printed matter and an edge of the paper, esp. at the left or right of the text ‖ an extra supply of something forming a reserve in case of need ‖ *(commerce)* the difference between net sales and costs, out of which expenses and profits come ‖ *(econ.)* the least profit at which a transaction is economically sound ‖ *(stock exchange)* cash or collateral paid to a broker as security ‖ *(stock exchange)* a speculation in which the broker shares ‖ *(stock exchange)* a buyer's equity if his account is closed at the market price **2.** *v.t. (stock exchange)* to deposit a margin upon (stock)

mar·gin·al (mɑ́rdʒin'l) *adj.* of or written in the margin of a page ‖ close to the limit of acceptability ‖ at or close to an edge

mar·i·gold (mǽrigould) *n.* an annual composite garden plant with yellow or orange flowers, native to Europe ‖ any of several plants bearing yellow or orange flowers

mar·i·jua·na (mærəwɑ́nə, mærəhwɑ́nə) *n.* the dried leaves and top of *Cannabis sativa,* the common hemp, often smoked as a narcotic

ma·rim·ba (mərímbə) *n.* a musical instrument of African origin, resembling a xylophone

ma·ri·na (mərí:nə) *n.* a boat basin that rents moorings and provides other services for small craft

mar·i·nade (mærinéid) **1.** *n.* a combination of wine or vinegar with oil, herbs and spices, in which meat or fish is sometimes steeped **2.** *v.t. pres. part.* **mar·i·nad·ing** *past* and *past part.* **mar·i·nad·ed** to marinate

mar·i·nate (mǽrineit) *pres. part.* **mar·i·nat·ing** *past* and *past part.* **mar·i·nat·ed** *v.t.* to season by steeping in a marinade

ma·rine (mərí:n) **1.** *adj.* of, relating to, found in or produced by the sea ‖ of or relating to shipping or navigation **2.** *n.* a member of a class of soldiers specially trained in combined operations with the navy ‖ seagoing ships collectively, *the merchant marine*

mar·i·ner (mǽrinər) *n.* a sailor ‖ *(esp. law)* someone employed on a seagoing ship

mar·i·on·ette (mæri:ənét) *n.* a puppet moved by strings

mar·i·tal (mǽrit'l) *adj.* of or relating to marriage or married life

mar·i·time (mǽritaim) *adj.* of, connected with, or bordering on the sea

mar·jo·ram (mɑ́rdʒərəm) *n.* any of several aromatic plants used in cookery

mark (mɑrk) *n.* a spot, stain, scratch etc. breaking the uniform appearance of a solid surface ‖ any distinguishing characteristic ‖ an object whose position is known, used as a fixed reference point or guide ‖ a letter, numeral etc. put on something to indicate quality, provenance, ownership etc. ‖ an impression or influence ‖ a letter or numeral used by a teacher to indicate his assessment of the quality of a piece of work ‖ something aimed at ‖ a cross or other symbol used as a substitute for a signature by a person who cannot write ‖ *(vet.)* a hollow on a horse's incisor, by which its age can be estimated **below** (or **not up to) the mark** unsatisfactory **to make one's mark** to achieve recognition of some personal quality or attainment

---

mark *v.t.* to make a mark on ‖ to disfigure ‖ to be a distinguishing trait of ‖ to indicate ‖ to assess the merit of (a piece of work) by a letter, numeral etc. ‖ to show the position of ‖ to heed, pay attention to **to mark down (up)** to lower (raise) the price of **to mark off** to indicate the extent or limit of, *he marked off six feet on the plank* **to mark out** to indicate the shape or plan of

mark *n.* a deutsche mark ‖ a coin representing this value

marked (mɑrkt) *adj.* bearing a mark or marks ‖ noticeable **a marked man** a man wanted by his enemies **mark·ed·ly** (mɑ́rkidli:) *adv.*

mark·er (mɑ́rkər) *n.* someone who marks ‖ a device for marking

mar·ket (mɑ́rkit) **1.** *n.* a place where many sellers display and sell their goods ‖ the demand for a commodity ‖ a region or outlet for successful trading ‖ the body of persons concerned with buying and selling a particular class of goods ‖ the class of persons to whom a particular commodity can readily be sold ‖ dealing in stocks or goods **in the market for** looking for a chance to buy **2.** *v.t.* to sell (goods) in a market ‖ *v.i.* to go shopping for provisions ‖ to see to the business of selling goods **mar·ket·a·bil·i·ty** *n.* **már·ket·a·ble** *adj.* able to attract a buyer if offered for sale

mark·ing (mɑ́rkiŋ) *n.* the making of a mark ‖ the awarding of a mark ‖ a mark ‖ the arrangement of marks on an object

mar·lin (mɑ́rlin) *n.* a member of *Makaira,* fam. *Istiophoridae,* a genus of big-game sea fish

mar·ma·lade (mɑ́rməleid) *n.* a preserve made by boiling shredded oranges, or other citrus fruits, with sugar

ma·roon (mərú:n) *v.t.* to land (someone) on a desolate shore and leave him to his fate

ma·roon (mərú:n) **1.** *n. a dark brownish-red color* **2.** *adj.* of the color maroon

mar·quee (mɑrkí:) *n.* a large tent set up for outdoor receptions, garden parties etc. ‖ a permanent rooflike projection over the entrance to a theater, moviehouse etc.

mar·quis (mɑ́rkwis, mɑrkí:) *n.* a European and English title of nobility ranking below duke and above earl or count ‖ the holder of this title

mar·riage (mǽridʒ) *n.* the institution under which a man and a woman become legally united on a permanent basis ‖ the act of entering into this institution ‖ the wedding ceremony ‖ the entering into the married state as a religious rite ‖ an intimate linking together **mar·riage·a·bil·i·ty** *n.* **mar·riage·a·ble** *adj.* fit for marriage

mar·row (mǽrou) *n.* a soft tissue filling up the cavities in most bones, where many cells of the blood are manufactured ‖ the pith of certain plants ‖ the essential part of something

mar·ry (mǽri:) *pres. part.* **mar·ry·ing** *past* and *past part.* **mar·ried** *v.t.* to join (two people) in marriage ‖ to take in marriage ‖ to give in marriage ‖ to join closely or match (two things, e.g. two materials, two colors) ‖ *v.i.* to enter into marriage **to marry into** to become part of (a family) by marriage **to marry (someone) off** to give (someone) in marriage so as to cease to be responsible for (her)

marsh (mɑrʃ) *n.* a tract of low-lying land, usually wet or periodically wet

mar·shal (mɑ́rʃəl) **1.** *n.* a military commander of the highest rank in certain armies ‖ someone who regulates ceremonies and directs processions ‖ a U.S. civil officer responsible in a judicial district for the processes of the law **2.** *v.t. pres. part.* **mar·shal·ing** *past* and *past part.* **mar·shaled** to arrange in correct order

marsh·mal·low (mɑ́rʃmɛlou, mɑ́rʃmælou) *n.* a perennial plant growing in marshes, the root of which yields abundant mucilage formerly used in medicine and confectionery ‖ a soft white confection made from glucose, sugar, albumen and gelatin

mar·su·pi·al (mɑrsú:pi:əl) **1.** *n.* a member of *Marsu-*

pialia, the lowest order of mammals incl. the kangaroo, opossum etc. The female usually has no placenta, and bears imperfectly developed young, nourished and carried by the mother, until fully developed, in an external abdominal pouch **2.** *adj.* of, relating to or being a marsupial

mar·tial (mɑ́rʃəl) *adj.* of, relating to, suited to or suggestive of war

martial art any of several Oriental techniques of self-defense, e.g., karate, judo, tai-chi

mar·tyr (mɑ́rtər) **1.** *n.* someone who suffers death rather than renounce his faith ‖ someone who suffers greatly for some cause or principle **2.** *v.t.* to put to death for refusing to renounce the faith ‖ to inflict great suffering upon

mar·tyr·dom (mɑ́rtərdəm) *n.* the death or putting to death of a martyr ‖ great suffering

mar·vel (mɑ́rvəl) *n.* something that causes astonishment and admiration

mas·car·a (mæskǽrə) *n.* a cosmetic for darkening esp. the eyelashes

mas·cot (mǽskət, mǽskɒt) *n.* an object, animal or person whose presence is supposed to bring good luck

mas·cu·line (mǽskjulin) **1.** *adj.* of the male sex ‖ relating to or characteristic of men ‖ mannish ‖ *(gram.)* designating or belonging to the gender of words referring to things male or originally regarded as male **2.** *n. (gram.)* the masculine gender ‖ a word having this gender

mas·cu·lin·i·ty (mæskjulíniti:) *n.* the quality or state of being masculine

mash (mæʃ) **1.** *n.* a mixture of things crushed together into a pulp, usually with liquid added ‖ a dry or moistened mixture of ground grain used as poultry and livestock feed ‖ *(brewing)* a mixture of crushed grain or malt with hot water to form wort **2.** *v.t.* to cause to become a mash, by grinding, crushing etc. ‖ *(brewing)* to mix (grain, malt etc.) with hot water to form wort

mask (mæsk, mɑsk) **1.** *n.* any of several coverings for the face, worn as a disguise, as protection, or to filter air breathed in or out ‖ *(fig.)* a disguise or method of concealment ‖ a likeness, esp. a cast of a face ‖ a respirator, esp. one through which an anesthetic is inhaled ‖ *(photog.)* a screen used to modify the size or shape of an image ‖ *(printing)* an opaque screen used to cover part of a plate **2.** *v.t.* to cover with a mask ‖ *(fig.)* to conceal with some disguise, *to mask one's feelings*

mas·o·chism (mǽsəkizəm, mǽzəkizəm) *n. (psychol.)* a condition in which the subject delights in being hurt or humiliated, esp. as a form of sexual perversion **más·o·chist** *n.* **mas·o·chís·tic** *adj.*

ma·son (méis'n) *n.* a craftsman who builds with stone, brick etc.

ma·son·ry (méis'nri:) *n.* that which is built by a mason ‖ the mason's craft

mas·quer·ade (mæskəréid) **1.** *n.* a ball at which masks are worn ‖ a false show for pretense or concealment of the truth **2.** *v.i. pres. part.* **mas·quer·ad·ing** *past* and *past part.* **mas·quer·ad·ed** to wear a disguise ‖ to put on a false outward show **mas·quer·ád·er** *n.*

mass (mæs) *n. (phys.)* a property of matter that (with length and time) constitutes one of the fundamental, undefined quantities upon which all physical measurements are based, and which is intuitively associated with the amount of matter a body contains ‖ an aggregation of a quantity of matter ‖ *(loosely)* a large amount or number ‖ massiveness ‖ an expanse, esp. of color or shade in a painting ‖ the larger part or number **the masses** the ordinary working people in a community, as opposed to the privileged

mas·sa·cre (mǽsəkər) *n.* a ruthless, indiscriminate killing of many people or animals

massacre *pres. part.* **mas·sa·cring** *past* and *past part.* **mas·sa·cred** *v.t.* to kill (many people or animals) ruthlessly and indiscriminately

mas·sage (məsáʒ) **1.** *n.* treatment of the muscles etc. by rubbing or kneading **2.** *v.t. pres. part.* **mas·sag·ing** *past* and *past part.* **mas·saged** to apply this treatment to

mas·seur (mæsə́:r) *n.* a man who professionally gives massage **mas·seuse** (mæsə́:z) *n.* a female masseur

mas·sif (mǽsi:f) *n.* an elevated mass, usually mountainous, with a number of peaks rising from it ‖ a large portion of the earth's crust which has shifted as a block without internal folding, faulting etc.

mass-pro·duce (mǽsprədú:s, mǽsprədjú:s) *pres. part.* **mass-pro·duc·ing** *past* and *past part.* **mass-pro·duced** *v.t.* to manufacture (goods) by mass production **máss-pro·dúced** *adj.*

mass production production of one article or type of goods in large numbers by a standardized mechanical process

mast (mæst, mɑst) **1.** *n.* a long pole of wood or metal set up on a ship's keel or deck to carry sails or other rigging ‖ an upright pole or other structure for carrying radio aerials etc. **2.** *v.t.* to put a mast or masts on

mas·ter (mǽstər, mɑ́stər) **1.** *n.* a man in control or authority ‖ someone who gets the better of a rival ‖ a spiritual leader or guide ‖ someone regarded as great in his field, who serves as inspiration to later generations ‖ a person of consummate skill, in an art, technique etc. ‖ an employer, as contrasted with 'man', 'servant', 'apprentice' ‖ a skilled workman qualified to work on his own ‖ the captain of a merchant ship ‖ a person with a degree between a bachelor's and a doctor's ‖ the owner of a pet animal ‖ the owner of a slave ‖ (used esp. by servants) the male head of a household ‖ the head of a college, guild, masonic lodge etc. ‖ a matrix from which duplicates (e.g. phonograph records) can be made **2.** *v.t.* to gain control over, overcome ‖ to become completely skilled in **3.** *adj.* largest, most important, *master bedroom* ‖ clearly outstanding in some profession, occupation etc. ‖ controlling the operation of a number of individually controlled devices

mas·ter·ful (mǽstərfəl, mɑ́stərfəl) *adj.* domineering, wanting to dictate to others ‖ having or showing the qualities appropriate to a master, e.g. the ability to command

mas·ter·piece (mǽstərpi:s, mɑ́stərpi:s) *n.* a work of art etc. made with consummate skill ‖ an individual's best piece of creative work

mas·ter·y (mǽstəri:, mɑ́stəri:) *n.* command, control ‖ thorough knowledge or skill in a specified field

mas·ti·cate (mǽstikeit) *pres. part.* **mas·ti·cat·ing** *past* and *past part.* **mas·ti·cat·ed** *v.t.* to chew ‖ to grind (rubber etc.) to a pulp ‖ *v.i.* to chew food etc. **mas·ti·cá·tion, más·ti·ca·tor** *ns*

mas·tiff (mǽstif) *n.* big, powerful, short-haired dog with drooping ears and hanging lips, used formerly as fighting dogs, now as watchdogs

mas·to·don (mǽstədɒn) *n.* any of several extinct mammals of fam. *Mammutidae* related to modern elephants, but differing from them esp. in the shape of their molar teeth

mas·toid (mǽstɔid) **1.** *adj.* shaped like a breast or nipple ‖ of or designating the nipplelike process of the temporal bone behind the ear **2.** *n.* this process

mas·tur·bate (mǽstərbeit) *pres. part.* **mas·tur·bat·ing** *past* and *past part.* **mas·tur·bat·ed** *v.i.* to produce orgasm in oneself by manipulation of the genitals, erotic fantasies etc., exclusive of sexual intercourse ‖ *v.t.* to produce orgasm in (someone) by manipulation of the genitals **mas·tur·bá·tion** *n.*

mat, matt, matte *pres. part.* **mat·ting, matt·ing** *past* and *past part.* **mat·ted, matt·ed** *v.t.* to render dull (gilding, metal etc.) ‖ to frost (glass)

mat, matt, matte **1.** *n.* a mount (for pictures) ‖ the dull finish of unburnished gold, e.g. in painting or gilding ‖ *(metalwork)* a dull, roughened or frosted groundwork **2.** *adj.* without luster or shine

ma·ta·dor (mǽtədɔr) *n. (bullfighting)* the man whose role is to kill the bull with his sword

match (mætʃ **1.** *n.* someone who or something that can be opposed to or compete with another on an equal footing ‖ one of two persons or things exactly alike ‖ a person or thing harmonizing well with another ‖ a person with regard to his or her suitability as a husband or wife ‖ a marriage ‖ a game or contest between two teams or persons **2.** *v.t.* to bring into competition ‖ to equal ‖ to be in harmony with ‖ to cause (two people or things) to be in harmony ‖ to toss coins with (a person) to decide something ‖ *v.i.* to have the same color, shape etc. as what is taken for comparison ‖ to harmonize with something ‖ (of two things) to be exactly the same with respect to color, shape etc.

match *n.* a small, thin piece of wood (sometimes of plastic), covered at one end with material of low ignition point which will burn when heated by the friction of striking it on a rough surface

mate (meit) **1.** *n.* checkmate **2.** *v.t. pres. part.* **mat·ing** *past* and *past part.* **mat·ed** to checkmate

mate **1.** *n.* the male or female of a couple ‖ one of a pair of objects ‖ (in compounds) a companion, *classmate* ‖ a deck officer on a merchant ship who ranks below the captain and carries out his orders ‖ *(U.S. Navy)* an assistant to a warrant officer, ranking as a petty officer ‖ any assistant, *plumber's mate* **2.** *v. pres. part.* **mat·ing** *past* and *past part.* **mat·ed** *v.t.* to pair (birds, animals) for breeding ‖ *v.i.* (of birds, animals) to copulate

ma·te·ri·al (mətíəri:əl) **1.** *adj.* of or consisting of matter ‖ (of behavior, ideas) worldly, not spiritual ‖ connected or concerned with bodily comfort, *material needs* ‖ substantially important ‖ *(law)* important for the determination of a cause or for the outcome of a case **2.** *n.* the stuff from which a thing is made ‖ cloth ‖ data constituting the basis of a more finished composition ‖ *(pl.)* necessary tools, equipment etc., *writing materials*

ma·te·ri·al·ism (mətíəri:əlizəm) *n. (philos.)* the theory that matter is the basic reality of the universe, hence that everything is material or can be shown to derive ultimately from matter

ma·te·ri·al·ist (mətíəri:əlist) *n.* someone who values material things more than spiritual ones ‖ someone who holds the philosophical beliefs of materialism **ma·te·ri·al·ís·tic** *adj.* **ma·te·ri·al·ís·ti·cal·ly** *adv.*

ma·te·ri·al·i·za·tion (mətìəri:əlizéiʃən) *n.* a materializing or being materialized ‖ an apparition of a spirit

ma·te·ri·al·ize (mətíəri:əlaiz) *pres. part.* **ma·te·ri·al·iz·ing** *past* and *past part.* **ma·te·ri·al·ized** *v.t.* to give material characteristics or form to ‖ to cause (a spirit) to appear ‖ *v.i.* to become tangible ‖ (of spirits) to appear in bodily form

ma·te·ri·al·ly (mətíəri:əli:) *adv.* to a considerable degree, substantially ‖ with regard to matter or material things ‖ of matter as distinguished from form

ma·ter·nal (mətə́:rn'l) *adj.* of or pertaining to a mother ‖ motherly ‖ related through the mother, *a maternal uncle*

ma·ter·ni·ty (mətə́:rniti:) **1.** *n.* the state of being a mother ‖ motherliness **2.** *adj.* of or pertaining to the time when a woman is pregnant or has just had a baby, or to pregnancy or childbirth

math·e·mat·i·cal (mæθəmætik'l) *adj.* of, pertaining to or using mathematics ‖ used in mathematics ‖ very precise

math·e·ma·ti·cian (mæθəmətíʃən) *n.* a specialist in mathematics

math·e·mat·ics (mæθəmætiks) *n.* the science of expressing and studying the relationships between quantities and magnitudes as represented by numbers and symbols

mat·i·nee, mat·i·née (mæt'néi) *n.* an afternoon performance at a moviehouse or theater

ma·tri·arch (méitri:ɑrk) *n.* a woman who rules a group, esp. a mother having authority over her immediate family or over a larger family group ‖ a venerable old woman **ma·tri·ár·chal** *adj.* of or like a matriarch ‖ based on or pertaining to a matriarchy **má·tri·ar·chate** *n.* a community etc. ruled by a matriarch **má·tri·ar·chy** *pl.* **ma·tri·ar·chies** *n.* a form of social organization in which descent is traced through the mothers ‖ government by women ‖ a matriarchate

ma·tric·u·late (mətríkjuleit) *pres. part.* **ma·tric·u·lat·ing** *past and past part.* **ma·tric·u·lat·ed** *v.t.* to enroll in a university or college ‖ *v.i.* to be enrolled as a member of a university or college **ma·tric·u·lá·tion** *n.*

mat·ri·mo·ni·al (mætrəmóuni:əl) *adj.* pertaining to marriage or married life

mat·ri·mo·ny (mætrəmọuni:) *pl.* **mat·ri·mo·nies** *n.* the state of being married ‖ marriage as a Christian sacrament

ma·trix (méitriks, mætriks) *pl.* **mat·ri·ces** (méitrisi:z, mætrisi:z), **ma·trix·es** *n.* a mold in which type or other matter in relief is shaped or cast ‖ the impression left in a rock when a fossil etc. has been removed ‖ *(computer)* a table of variables ‖ an arrangement of circuit elements to perform particular functions

ma·tron (méitrən) *n.* a married woman or a widow, usually having children and no longer young ‖ a person who superintends the domestic affairs of a public institution, e.g. a prison or hospital ‖ a female attendant or guard in a women's prison or in some other public institution **má·tron·li·ness** *n.* **má·tron·ly** *adj.*

mat·ter (mætər) **1.** *n.* that which any physical thing is composed of ‖ *(phys.)* that which occupies space and possesses inertia ‖ a substance serving a specified purpose ‖ content as distinct from form, subject matter ‖ importance ‖ a circumstance, issue, topic etc. ‖ trouble, difficulty, *what's the matter?* ‖ *(law)* the facts as opposed to principles ‖ pus ‖ type set up or impressions from this **for that matter** as far as that is concerned **in the matter of** as regards **2.** *v.i.* to be of importance

mat·ting (mætiŋ) *n.* woven material, esp. of hemp, grass, bast etc., used for floor covering etc.

mat·tress (mætris) *n.* a flat case of some strong fabric, e.g. canvas, stuffed with hair, feathers, sponge rubber etc., put on a bedstead or serving as a bed

ma·ture (mətúər, mətjúər, mətʃúər) *adj.* having reached a state of full natural development ‖ ripe ‖ of or relating to the time when development is complete ‖ (of decisions etc.) involving or arrived at after prolonged and careful thought ‖ (of a bond etc.) due

ma·tu·ri·ty (mətúəriti:, mətjúəriti:, mətʃúəriti:) *n.* the quality or state of being mature ‖ (of bonds etc.) a becoming due

ma·tu·ti·nal (mətú:t'n'l, mətjú:t'n'l) *adj.* of or occurring in the morning

mat·zo, mat·zoh (mátzə) *pl.* **mat·zoth** (mátsout), **mat·zos** *n.* an unleavened bread eaten by Jews at Passover

maud·lin (mɔ́dlin) *adj.* weakly and tearfully sentimental, esp. when drunk

maul (mɔl) **1.** *n.* (also **mall**) any of several kinds of heavy hammer, usually wooden, for driving in stakes, wedges etc. **2.** *v.t.* (also **mall**) to attack savagely and injure, *the lion mauled its trainer* ‖ to treat roughly ‖ to attack with violent criticism ‖ to split (wood) with a maul and wedge

maun·der (mɔ́ndər) *v.i.* to talk ramblingly, with no obvious purpose ‖ to move or act aimlessly and slowly

mau·so·le·um (mɔsəlí:əm, mɔzəlí:əm) *pl.* **mau·so·le·ums, mau·so·le·a** (mɔsəli:ə, mɔzəli:ə) *n.* a large and elaborate tomb, or a building housing tombs

mauve (mouv) **1.** *n.* a pale purple dye obtained from crude aniline, the first to be prepared synthetically ‖ the color of this dye **2.** *adj.* having this color

mav·er·ick (mævərik) *n. (pop.)* a person who refuses to conform and acts independently ‖ a member of a political party who will not toe the party line ‖ an unbranded animal on the range, esp. a motherless calf

max·il·la (mæksílə) *pl.* **max·il·lae** (mæksíli:), **max·il·las** *n.* either of the parts of the upper jaw behind the premaxilla ‖ the upper jaw ‖ an appendage of most arthropods, posterior to the mandible, modified in various ways according to function **max·il·lar·y** (mæksiləri:, mæksələri:) **1.** *adj.* of, pertaining to, or in the region of the maxilla **2.** *n. pl.* **max·il·lar·ies** *(anat.)* the maxilla

max·im (mæksim) *n.* a succinct general truth, moral reflection or rule of conduct

max·i·mal (mæksəməl) *adj.* to the greatest possible degree ‖ pertaining to or being a maximum

max·i·mum (mæksəməm) **1.** *pl.* **max·i·mums, max·i·ma** (mæksəmə) *n.* the greatest possible amount, number or degree ‖ the greatest amount, number or degree actually reached **2.** *adj.* greatest in amount, number or degree, *at maximum speed* ‖ relating to, marking or setting a maximum

May (mei) *n.* the fifth month of the year, having 31 days

may *infin.* and *parts.* lacking, *neg.* **may not, mayn't** *3rd pers. sing.* **may** *past* **might** (mait) (or, by suppletion, 'was', 'were able to') *auxiliary v.* to be permitted to ‖ expressing possibility ‖ used in clauses expressing result, purpose, concession or condition ‖ used to express a wish, hope, prayer, *may they both be happy*

may·be (méibi:) *adv.* perhaps, possibly but not certainly

may·flow·er (méiflauər) *n.* any of several plants blooming in May or in early spring, esp. the trailing arbutus, and any of several anemones **May·flow·er** the ship in which the Pilgrims sailed (1620)

may·hem (méihem) *n. (law)* the malicious, permanent maiming or mutilating of a person, rendering him partly or wholly defenseless

may·on·naise (meiənéiz) *n.* a thick creamy dressing of egg yolks beaten with oil, vinegar and seasoning, usually served as a garnish for cold fish, salads etc.

may·or (méiər, mɛər) *n.* the head of a municipal corporation of a city, town etc. **máy·or·al** *adj.*

may·or·al·ty (méiərəlti:, mɛərəlti:) *pl.* **may·or·al·ties** *n.* the office, or term of office, of a mayor

maze (meiz) *n.* a contrived ornamental, complex layout of paths, often hedged ‖ something intricately complicated or confusing

me (mi:) *pron., objective case* of **"I"**

mead·ow (médou) *n.* a piece of grassland, esp. one used for hay

mea·ger (mí:gər) *adj.* low in quantity or quality, *meager rewards, a meager supper*

meal (mi:l) *n.* the edible part of coarsely ground grain ‖ any similarly ground substance

meal *n.* food eaten alone or in company to satisfy hunger or at a set hour as part of daily routine ‖ the time or occasion of taking this food

meal·y (mí:li:) *comp.* **meal·i·er** *superl.* **meal·i·est** *adj.* powdery and dry, like meal ‖ of or containing meal ‖ (of complexion) sallow, unhealthy looking ‖ covered with meal or powder ‖ (of an animal) spotted with a second color ‖ mealymouthed

mean (mi:n) **1.** *adj.* midway between two extremes in number, quantity, degree, kind, value etc. ‖ having the value which is most frequent, *mean rainfall* **2.** *n.* something occupying a mean position with regard to number, quantity, degree, kind, value etc. ‖ *(math.)* an average

mean *adj.* stingy ‖ small-minded, petty ‖ unkind or positively spiteful ‖ bad-tempered ‖ of poor quality, esp. shabby or squalid

mean *pres. part.* **mean·ing** *past* and *past part.* **meant** (ment) *v.t.* to intend ‖ to intend to signify ‖ *v.i.* to have a specified degree of importance **to mean well** to be well intentioned

me·an·der (mi:ǽndər) **1.** *n.* a winding of a stream or river ‖ (often *pl.*) a rambling stroll ‖ an ornamental linear pattern, e.g. in ancient Greek design **2.** *v.i.* (of a stream) to follow a winding course ‖ to wander aimlessly

mean·ing (mí:niŋ) **1.** *n.* that which is intended or meant **2.** *adj.* expressive, conveying emotion etc. ‖ (in compounds) having intentions of a specified kind **mean·ing·ful, mean·ing·less** *adjs*

mean·time (mí:ntaim) **1.** *adv.* during the intervening time ‖ during the same time as something else is or was going on **2.** *n.* (only in) **the meantime** the intervening time ‖ the same time as something else is or was going on

mea·sles (mí:z'lz) *n.* a contagious disease caused by a virus and common in children. It is characterized by catarrh, fever and skin eruption ‖ German measles ‖ a disease of cattle and swine caused by the larvae of certain tapeworms

meas·ur·a·bil·i·ty (meʒərəbíliti:) *n.* the state or quality of being measurable

meas·ur·a·ble (méʒərəb'l) *adj.* that can be measured **méas·ur·a·bly** *adv.*

meas·ure (méʒər) *n.* the magnitude of something as determined by measuring ‖ an instrument used to determine magnitude ‖ a unit of length, volume etc. as a standard for measuring ‖ a system of units used in measuring, *metric measure* ‖ amount, extent or degree ‖ a criterion for determining quality, degree etc. ‖ an act designed to achieve a purpose ‖ a legislation bill or statute ‖ *(mus.)* a bar ‖ rhythm in verse or music **made to measure** (of clothes) made according to the measurements of the individual

measure *pres. part.* **meas·ur·ing** *past* and *past part.* **meas·ured** *v.t.* to determine the magnitude, extent, degree etc. of in terms of some standard ‖ to judge the quality or nature of in terms of some standard ‖ (with 'against') to bring into comparison (with) **to measure up to** to reach the standard of, *to measure up to expectations* **méas·ured** *adj.* accurately determined and serving as a standard ‖ (of speech etc.) carefully thought out, calculated **méas·ure·less** *adj.* of boundless size or extent ‖ vast **méas·ure·ment** *n.* a measuring or being measured ‖ the magnitude, length, degree etc. of something in terms of a selected unit

meat (mi:t) *n.* the flesh of animals (usually excepting fish and poultry) used for food ‖ the edible part of an animal, *the meat of a lobster* ‖ *(fig.)* the substance or essence of something

meat·y (mí:ti:) *comp.* **meat·i·er** *superl.* **meat·i·est** *adj.* of, like or consisting of meat ‖ *(fig.)* full of substance, stimulating thought

me·chan·ic (məkǽnik) *n.* a workman skilled in making, using or repairing machinery

me·chan·i·cal (məkǽnik'l) *adj.* pertaining to or involving machines ‖ operated by or produced by a machine ‖ made or done as if by machinery and therefore lacking spontaneity or interest ‖ of or pertaining to the subject matter of mechanics

me·chan·ics (məkǽniks) *n.* a branch of physics that deals with energy and force in their relation to material bodies ‖ the application of mechanics to the operation and design of machines ‖ the mechanism or way of operating of a machine or process, *the mechanics of advertising*

mech·a·nism (mékənizəm) *n.* a structure of interacting parts working mechanically ‖ any system, process etc. composed of parts which, working together, resemble the workings of a machine ‖ a machine-like device, system, process etc. by means of which some result is achieved, *a defense mechanism* ‖ *(philos.)* the theory that the workings of the universe can be explained by physics and chemistry **méch·a·nist** *n.* someone who believes in the mechanistic theory of the universe **mech·a·nis·tic** *adj.*

mech·a·ni·za·tion (mekənizéiʃən) *n.* a mechanizing or being mechanized

mech·a·nize (mékənaiz) *pres. part.* **mech·a·niz·ing** *past* and *past part.* **mech·a·nized** *v.t.* to make mechanical ‖ to operate by machinery ‖ to introduce the use of machines in (an industry etc.) ‖ to equip (an army etc.) with tanks, armored motor vehicles etc.

med·al (méd'l) *n.* a small, flat piece of metal, cast with an inscription or design, that commemorates an event or is awarded in recognition for distinguished service, for an achievement etc. ‖ such a piece of metal bearing a religious image

me·dal·lion (mədǽljən) *n.* a large medal ‖ something shaped like this, e.g. a decorative tablet, panel or carpet design ‖ a license to operate a taxicab

med·dle (méd'l) *pres. part.* **med·dling** *past* and *past part.* **med·dled** *v.i.* (with 'in' or 'with') to concern or busy oneself impudently or interferingly, *don't meddle in my affairs* **méd·dle·some** *adj.* given to meddling

me·di·an (mí:di:ən) **1.** *adj.* designating a plane dividing a body or part into symmetrical halves ‖ situated in this plane ‖ of or pertaining to a median **2.** *n.* something situated in the middle ‖ *(geom.)* a line joining a vertex of a triangle to the middle of the opposite side ‖ *(math.)* a quantity situated in a series so as to have as many quantities below it as above, *the median of 3, 6, 8, 14 and 15 is 8* ‖ a median artery, vein, nerve etc.

me·di·ate 1. (mí:di:eit) *v. pres. part.* **me·di·at·ing** *past* and *past part.* **me·di·at·ed** *v.t.* to bring about (a settlement) by reconciling conflicting parties ‖ to settle (a dispute etc.) by reconciling conflicting parties ‖ to act as agent in conveying, communicating etc. ‖ *v.i.* to intervene in order to bring about a reconciliation **2.** (mí:di:it) *adj.* acting indirectly, through some agency

me·di·a·tion (mi:di:éiʃən) *n.* a mediating or being mediated

me·di·a·tor (mí:di:eitər) *n.* someone who mediates **me·di·a·to·ri·al** (mi:di:ətɔ́ri:əl, mi:di:ətóuri:əl), **mé·di·a·to·ry** *adjs*

med·ic (médik) *n.* *(pop.)* a physician or surgeon, or a student or military corpsman doing medical work

Med·i·caid (médikeid) *n.* government-administered program in U.S. to provide medical services to the poor; financed jointly by federal and state governments

med·i·cal (médik'l) **1.** *adj.* of, concerned with or relating to the practice of medicine (often as contrasted with surgery etc.) **2.** *n.* *(pop.)* a medical examination required by authority

Med·i·care, med·i·care (médikɛər) *n.* a U.S. govern-

---

ment insurance program that provides medical care for old people

med·i·cate (médikeit) *pres. part.* **med·i·cat·ing** *past* and *past part.* **med·i·cat·ed** *v.t.* to saturate with a medical preparation **med·i·ca·tion** *n.* the act of medicating ‖ a substance used in medicating **med·i·ca·tive** (médikeitiv, médikətiv) *adj.*

me·dic·i·nal (medísin'l) *adj.* relating to medicine, esp. having healing properties **me·dic·i·nal·ly** *adv.*

med·i·cine (médisin) *n.* any preparation or substance used in the treatment of disease ‖ the science of the prevention and cure of disease and of health preservation ‖ the branch of this science dealing with curative substances rather than with surgery, obstetrics etc. ‖ the medical profession **to take one's medicine** to submit stoically to punishment etc. that one deserves

med·i·e·val, med·i·ae·val (medi:í:vəl, mi:di:í:vəl) *adj.* of, relating to or characteristic of the Middle Ages

me·di·o·cre (mi:di:óukər) *adj.* neither good nor bad, without distinction ‖ of distinctly poor quality

me·di·oc·ri·ty (mi:di:ókriti:) *pl.* **me·di·oc·ri·ties** *n.* the state or quality of being mediocre ‖ a mediocre person

med·i·tate (méditeit) *pres. part.* **med·i·tat·ing** *past* and *past part.* **med·i·tat·ed** *v.i.* (with 'on' or 'upon') to reflect deeply ‖ to spend time in the spiritual exercise of thinking about some religious theme ‖ *v.t.* to contemplate, esp. as a plan

med·i·ta·tion (meditéiʃən) *n.* deep, serious thought ‖ reflection on a religious subject as a spiritual exercise

me·di·um (mí:di:əm) **1.** *pl.* **me·di·ums, me·di·a** *n.* a means ‖ a middle quality or degree ‖ something through which a force is transmitted ‖ the material that an artist works with ‖ a liquid in which a dry pigment can be suspended ‖ the substance making up the natural habitat of an organism ‖ *(pl.,* **me·di·a**) environment ‖ *(biol., pl.* **me·di·a**) the substance in which displayed or preserved specimens are put ‖ *(biol., pl.* **me·di·a**) a substance in which a culture can be grown ‖ *(spiritualism, pl.* **me·di·ums**) a person credited with special powers for communicating between the living and the dead **2.** *adj.* of that which is a mean with regard to quality, degree, size, distance etc. ‖ average, *medium height*

med·ley (médli:) *pl.* **med·leys** *n.* a confused mixture ‖ a miscellaneous musical or literary collection

me·dul·la (mədʌlə) *pl.* **me·dul·las, me·dul·lae** (mədʌli:) *n. (anat.)* the central part of an organ, e.g. the kidney ‖ the marrow of bone ‖ the medulla oblongata ‖ the sheath of some nerve fibers

me·dul·la ob·lon·ga·ta (mədʌləɒblɔŋgátə, mədʌləɒblɔŋgátə) *pl.* **me·dul·la ob·lon·ga·tas, me·dul·lae ob·lon·ga·tae** (mədʌli:ɒblɔŋgáti:, mədʌli:ɒblɔŋgáti:) *n.* that part of the brainstem continuous posteriorly with the spinal cord. It contains centers controlling many involuntary vital functions, e.g. cardiovascular activities and respiration

meek (mi:k) *adj.* humbly submissive ‖ too mild, lacking spirit

meet (mi:t) **1.** *v. pres. part.* **meet·ing** *past* and *past part.* **met** (met) *v.t.* to come face-to-face with ‖ to be present at the arrival of, *to meet a plane* ‖ to make the acquaintance of, be introduced to ‖ to keep an appointment with ‖ to satisfy (a demand, need etc.) ‖ to face up to (criticism, trouble etc.) ‖ to come into the company of ‖ to come into contact with ‖ to deal with, *to meet a problem* ‖ *v.i.* to come face-to-face or into one another's company ‖ to be united, *the rivers meet below the city* ‖ to become acquainted ‖ to come together to contend ‖ to assemble ‖ (with 'with') to encounter ‖ (with 'with') to confer **to meet (someone) halfway** to offer (someone) a generous compromise **2.** *n.* a gathering for a sporting event **méet·ing** *n.* a coming together of people or things ‖ a gathering of people, esp. for business purposes ‖ the people so assembled

meg·a·phone (mégəfoun) *n.* a trumpet-shaped instru-

ment used to magnify or direct the voice

meg·a·ton (mégətʌn) *n.* an explosive power equal to that of a million tons of TNT

mel·an·cho·li·a (melənkóuli:ə) *n.* a form of mental disorder characterized by extreme dejection

mel·an·chol·ic (melənkólik) *adj.* having a tendency towards melancholy ‖ in a melancholy mood ‖ producing melancholy

mel·an·chol·y (mélənkɒli:) **1.** *n.* depression, low spirits ‖ sad thoughtfulness **2.** *adj.* sad, depressed ‖ expressing sadness, *a melancholy smile* ‖ causing sadness

mé·lange, me·lange (meilá:ʒ) *n.* a heterogeneous mixture

meld (meld) **1.** *v.t.* to declare (a card or cards) for scoring ‖ *v.i.* to declare a card or combination of cards for scoring **2.** *n.* a melding ‖ the cards declared ‖ the score made by melding

me·lee, mê·lée (méilei, mélei) *n.* a confused struggle involving a group or groups

mel·lif·lu·ous (məlíflu:əs) *adj.* (of a voice or words) sweet to listen to

mel·low (mélou) **1.** *adj.* (of sound, color etc.) full and rich, not harsh ‖ (of mood) warmly human, genial ‖ (of a person) having the kindly understanding and sympathy that comes from age and experience ‖ (of wine) well-matured, smooth, free of acidity ‖ (of fruit) soft, ripe and sweet ‖ very mildly, benignly drunk **2.** *v.t.* to make mellow ‖ *v.i.* to become mellow

me·lod·ic (məlódik) *adj.* of, pertaining to or containing melody **me·lód·i·cal·ly** *adv.*

me·lo·di·ous (məlóudi:əs) *adj.* (of sound) pleasing to the ear, esp. through being melodic

mel·o·dra·ma (mélədramə, mélədræmə) *n.* a play with a sensational plot and violent emotional appeal ‖ sensational events or dramatic, exaggerated behavior **mel·o·dra·mat·ic** (melədrəmætik) *adj.* **mel·o·dra·mát·i·cal·ly** *adv.*

mel·o·dy (mélədi:) *pl.* **mel·o·dies** *n. (mus.)* a succession of single notes of different pitch so arranged in relation to each other as to be a recognizable entity ‖ *(mus.)* the principal part in a piece of harmonized music ‖ sweet, pleasing music

mel·on (mélən) *n.* the edible fruit of either the muskmelon or the watermelon ‖ either of these plants

melt (melt) **1.** *v. pres. part.* **melt·ing** *past* and *past part.* **melt·ed,** *(rhet.* and *adjectival)* **mol·ten** (móultən) *v.i.* (of something solid) to become liquefied by the action of heat ‖ to dissolve ‖ *(fig.)* to become soft as if by dissolving ‖ (with 'into', of an image, sound etc.) to blend (with another) ‖ *v.t.* to cause to become liquid, by heating ‖ to dissolve ‖ *(fig.)* to soften as if by dissolving ‖ (with 'down') to cause (metal objects) to be reduced to liquefied metal, by heating **2.** *n.* something molten ‖ an amount of some substance melted in one operation

melt·down (méltdaun) *n. (nuclear phys.)* the melting of the protective cases surrounding a nuclear reactor, resulting in release of radiation

mem·ber (mémbər) *n.* a person who belongs to a group or organization ‖ a part of the body, esp. a limb ‖ a distinct part of a whole, esp. of a building, a sentence, a mathematical equation etc.

mem·ber·ship (mémbərʃip) *n.* the state of being a member ‖ the total number of members

mem·brane (mémbrein) *n.* a very thin, strong, pliable tissue which covers, lines or connects parts of an animal or vegetable body ‖ a piece of parchment forming part of a roll

me·men·to (məméntou) *pl.* **me·men·toes, me·men·tos** *n.* an object kept as a reminder of a person, event etc.

me·men·to mo·ri (məméntoumɔ́rai, məméntoumóurai) *pl.* **me·men·to mo·ri** *n.* something that serves as a reminder of death

mem·o (mémou) *pl.* **mem·os** *n.* a memorandum

mem·oir (mémwɑr) *n.* a history or record of events written by someone who has special knowledge of them, usually through personal experience ‖ an essay on a specialized subject by an expert ‖ (usually *pl.*) an autobiography, esp. about the writer's part in public life ‖ a biography, normally of a person known to the writer

mem·o·ra·bil·i·a (mẹmərəbíli:ə) *pl. n.* memorable things or events

mem·o·ra·ble (mémərəb'l) *adj.* outstanding, worthy of being remembered **mém·o·ra·bly** *adv.*

mem·o·ran·dum (mẹmərǽndəm) *pl.* **mem·o·ran·dums, mem·o·ran·da** (mẹmərǽndə) *n.* a brief record of an event or analysis of a situation, made for one's own future reference or to inform others, and sometimes embodying an instruction or recommendation ‖ an informal letter, usually unsigned, used e.g. in inter-office communication ‖ *(diplomacy)* an informal written statement or inquiry ‖ *(law)* a short document recording the terms of an agreement

me·mo·ri·al (məmɔ́ri:əl, məmóuri:əl) **1.** *adj.* commemorative, *a memorial tablet* **2.** *n.* a monument commemorating a person or event ‖ a statement of facts prepared as the basis of a petition ‖ an informal state paper, or memorandum ‖ *(pl.)* a historical account

me·mo·ri·al·ize (məmɔ́ri:əlaiz, məmóuri:əlaiz) *pres. part.* **me·mo·ri·al·iz·ing** *past and past part.* **me·mo·ri·al·ized** *v.t.* to commemorate ‖ to petition with a memorial

mem·o·rize (méməraiz) *pres. part.* **mem·o·riz·ing** *past and past part.* **mem·o·rized** *v.t.* to commit to memory

mem·o·ry (méməri:) *pl.* **mem·o·ries** *n.* the faculty by which sense impressions and information are retained consciously or unconsciously in the mind and subsequently recalled ‖ a person's capacity to remember ‖ a mental image or impression of a past event, something learned etc. ‖ the total store of mentally retained impressions and knowledge ‖ the length of time over which recollection extends ‖ the posthumous reputation of a person **in memory of** as an affectionate or respectful record of

men·ace (ménis) *n.* a threat ‖ anything that constitutes a threat

menace *pres. part.* **men·ac·ing** *past and past part.* **men·aced** *v.t. and i.* to threaten

me·nag·er·ie (mənǽdʒəri:) *n.* a collection of animals exhibited in cages ‖ the place where the animals are kept or exhibited

mend (mend) **1.** *v.t.* to repair (cloth, china etc.) ‖ to repair (a hole, tear, break etc.) ‖ to cause to become better, *to mend one's ways* ‖ *v.i.* to improve, esp. to recover from an illness **2.** *n.* a mended place, e.g. a patched hole, a glued break in china etc. **on the mend** improving, esp. in health after illness

me·ni·al (mí:ni:əl, mí:njəl) **1.** *adj.* (of work) servile, lowly **2.** *n. (rhet.)* a domestic servant ‖ *(rhet.)* a servile person

men·o·pause (ménəpɔz) *n.* the time when the menstrual cycle ceases, either abruptly or gradually, usually between the ages of 40 and 50

men·ses (ménsi:z) *pl. n.* the discharge of the mucous lining of the womb occurring in the menstrual cycle

men·stru·al (ménstru:əl) *adj.* of or pertaining to the menses

menstrual cycle the cycle of changes in the reproductive organs of women and female higher anthropoids. It culminates in uterine bleeding about every 28 days

men·stru·ate (ménstru:eit) *pres. part.* **men·stru·at·ing** *past and past part.* **men·stru·at·ed** *v.i.* to discharge the menses **men·stru·á·tion** *n.*

men·tal (mént'l) *adj.* of or pertaining to the mind ‖ done by or taking place in the mind ‖ intended for the care of the insane

men·tal·i·ty (mentǽliti) *pl.* **men·tal·i·ties** *n.* the manner of thinking, esp. the attitude toward life, society etc., of an individual or group ‖ intellectual capacity

men·thol (ménθɔl) *n.* a white crystalline substance with a strong smell of peppermint, obtained from oil of peppermint and used to relieve pain, itching and nasal congestion **men·tho·lat·ed** (ménθəleitid) *adj.* containing menthol ‖ treated iwth menthol

men·tion (ménʃən) *n.* a mentioning or being mentioned ‖ an instance of this

mention *v.t.* to refer to, esp. casually ‖ to cite the name of (a person) as official recognition of merit **don't mention it** thanks (or apologies) are unnecessary

men·tor (méntər, méntɔr) *n.* an experienced and trusted friend and adviser

men·u (ménju:) *n.* a restaurant's list of the dishes available ‖ a list of the dishes served at a formal meal ‖ the dishes served

mer·can·tile (mɔ́:rkəntail, mɔ́:rkəntil) *adj.* pertaining to or engaged in trade or commerce **mér·can·til·ism** *n.* trade and commerce

mer·ce·nar·i·ness (mɔ́:rsənɛri:nis) *n.* the state or quality of being mercenary

mer·ce·nar·y (mɔ́:rsənɛri:) **1.** *adj.* inspired merely by a desire for gain **2.** *pl.* **mer·ce·nar·ies** *n.* a hired soldier serving a country other than his own

mer·cer·ize (mɔ́:rsəraiz) *pres. part.* **mer·cer·iz·ing** *past and past part.* **mer·cer·ized** *v.t.* to treat (cotton thread or fabric) with caustic alkali to strengthen it and make it slightly glossy

mer·chan·dise 1. (mɔ́:rtʃəndaiz, mɔ́:rtʃəndais) *n. (collect.)* goods bought and sold in commerce **2.** (mɔ́:rtʃəndaiz) *v. pres. part.* **mer·chan·dis·ing** *past and past part.* **mer·chan·dised** *v.t.* to promote the sale of (goods) ‖ *v.i.* to practice the buying and selling of goods

mer·chant (mɔ́:rtʃənt) **1.** *n.* a person who directs large-scale trade, esp. with a foreign country ‖ a retailer **2.** *adj.* of or pertaining to a merchant or to trade

mer·ci·ful (mɔ́:rsifəl) *adj.* showing or feeling mercy

mer·ci·less (mɔ́:rsilis) *adj.* showing no mercy

mer·cu·ri·al (mərkjúəri:əl) **1.** *adj.* having the qualities associated with the god Mercury, esp. quick-wittedness, eloquence, changeability ‖ pertaining to or containing mercury **2.** *n.* a drug containing mercury **mer·cú·ri·al·ism** *n. (med.)* mercury poisoning

mer·cu·ry (mɔ́:rkjəri:) *n.* a silverwhite, poisonous, metallic element liquid above −35.85°C and boiling at 356.9°C under normal pressure. Mercury is used in thermometers and other scientific instruments, and in dentistry, pharmacy etc.

mer·cy (mɔ́:rsi:) *pl.* **mer·cies** *n.* compassionate rather than severe conduct towards someone in one's power ‖ a thing to be thankful for **at the mercy of** completely in the power of (something or someone potentially harmful or adverse)

mere (miər) *adj.* being no more or better than

mere·ly (míərli:) *adv.* in no way more than as specified

merge (mɔ:rdʒ) *pres. part.* **merg·ing** *past and past part.* **merged** *v.t.* to unite or blend (two or more things) ‖ *v.i.* to become united or blended **mérg·er** *n.* the combination of two companies or businesses

me·rid·i·an (mərídi:ən) **1.** *adj.* pertaining to noon, esp. to the posiition of the sun at noon ‖ *(rhet.)* at the highest point of success or greatness **2.** *n.* a great circle of the celestial sphere, passing through its poles and the zenith of a given point ‖ a great circle on the surface of the earth, passing through the poles and a given place ‖ *(rhet.)* the highest point of success or greatness

---

(a) æ, c*a*t; ɑ, c*a*r; ɔ f*aw*n; ei, sn*a*ke. **(e)** e, h*e*n; i:, sh*ee*p; iə, d*ee*r; ɛə, b*ea*r. **(i)** i, f*i*sh; ai, t*i*ger; ə:, b*i*rd. **(o)** o, *o*x; au, c*ow*; ou, g*oa*t; u, p*oo*r; ɔi, r*oy*al. **(u)** ʌ, d*u*ck; u, b*u*ll; u:, g*oo*se; ə, b*a*cillus; ju:, c*u*be. x, lo*ch*; θ, *th*ink; ð, bo*th*er; z, *Z*en; ʒ, cor*s*age; dʒ, sa*v*age; ŋ, oranguta*ng*; j, *y*ak; ʃ, *fish*; tʃ, fe*tch*; 'l, rabb*le*; 'n, redd*en*. Complete pronunciation key appears inside front cover.

me·ringue (mərǽŋ) *n*. a light, fluffy baked mixture of sugar and beaten egg whites used as topping on cakes etc. ‖ a small cake made of this

mer·it (mérit) *n*. excellence, the quality of deserving praise ‖ the intrinsic goodness or badness of something or someone ‖ spiritual credit ‖ *(pl., esp. law)* the intrinsic rights and wrongs of a case

merit *v.t.* to be worthy of

mer·i·to·ri·ous (mèritɔ́ri:əs, mèritóuri:əs) *adj.* deserving praise or reward

mer·maid (mɔ́:rmeid) *n*. a mythical sea creature with the tail of a fish and the head, arms and trunk of a woman

mer·ri·ment (méri:mənt) *n*. laughter and gaiety

mer·ry (méri:) *comp.* **mer·ri·er** *superl.* **mer·ri·est** *adj.* gay, cheerful and happy ‖ showing these qualities

mer·ry-go-round (méri:gouṛaund) *n*. a machine in a fair or amusement park, with a circular, revolving platform, colored canopy and models of horses etc. as seats on which children ride around to music ‖ a revolving device on which children ride in a playground

me·sa (méisə) *n*. a high, steep-sided rock plateau, esp. in the southwest U.S.A.

mesh (meʃ) **1.** *n*. one of the open spaces between the strands of a net ‖ *(pl.)* the strands of a net ‖ *(pl.)* something which captures and holds fast, *the meshes of the law* ‖ a network or net **in mesh** (of gears) engaged **2.** *v.t.* to cause to become interlocked ‖ *v.i.* (of cogwheels etc.) to become interlocked

mes·mer·ism (mézmərizəm) *n*. hypnotism ‖ the state of being hypnotized ‖ the theory of the uses of hypnotism **més·mer·ist** *n*. **més·mer·ize** *pres. part.* **mes·mer·iz·ing** *past* and *past part.* **mes·mer·ized** *v.t.* to induce the state of being hypnotized in (someone)

mes·quite, mes·quit (meskí:t) *n*. a S.W. North American tree which yields a gum resembling gum arabic. Its sugary pods are used as food and fodder

mess (mes) **1.** *n*. a state of untidiness or disorder ‖ an unpleasant, troubling, awkward situation or condition ‖ *(mil.)* a number of men or women, usually of the same rank, who have meals together ‖ the place where they eat ‖ the meals they eat together **2.** *v.t.* to make a mess of ‖ *v.i.* to take meals in a mess **to mess around** to amuse oneself without any clear program ‖ (with 'with') to handle something inexpertly

mes·sage (mésidʒ) *n*. a written or spoken communication from one person to another ‖ an inspired revelation ‖ ethical or spiritual teaching ‖ an official communication

mes·sage *v. (substandard)* to send a message to

mes·sen·ger (mésəndʒər) *n*. a person who carries a message ‖ a person employed by a firm to do errands ‖ a courier

mes·sy (mési:) *comp.* **mess·i·er** *superl.* **mess·i·est** *adj.* untidy or disordered ‖ (of a task, situation etc.) disagreeably confused, awkward and troublesome

met·a·bol·ic (mètəbólik) *adj.* of, involving, characterized by, or caused by metabolism

me·tab·o·lism (mətǽbəlizəm) *n*. the sum total of the chemical processes of living organisms, which result in growth, the production of energy and the maintenance of the vital functions, and in which the waste products of these processes are rendered harmless **me·táb·o·lite** *n*. a substance produced in metabolism ‖ a substance essential to a metabolic change **me·táb·o·lize** *pres. part.* **me·tab·o·liz·ing** *past* and *past part.* **me·tab·o·lized** *v.t.* and *i.* to change by metabolism

met·al (mét'l) **1.** *n*. an element, the structure of whose atoms is such that these readily lose electrons to form positively charged ions ‖ a compound or alloy of such an element ‖ *(printing)* type metal **2.** *v.t. pres. part.* **met·al·ing** *past* and *past part.* **met·aled** to supply or cover with metal

me·tal·lic (mətǽlik) *adj.* made of, like or having the properties of a metal **me·tál·li·cal·ly** *adv.*

met·al·lur·gic (mèt'lɔ́:rdʒik) *adj.* metallurgical

met·al·lúr·gi·cal *adj.* of or pertaining to metallurgy

met·al·lur·gist (mét'lə:rdʒist) *n*. a specialist in metallurgy

met·al·lur·gy (mét'lə:rdʒi:) *n*. the science of extracting metals from their ores, of freeing them from impurities, of studying their physical and chemical suitability for particular uses etc.

met·a·mor·phic (mètəmɔ́rfik) *adj.* causing or resulting from metamorphosis

met·a·mor·pho·sis (mètəmɔ́rfəsis) *pl.* **met·a·mor·pho·ses** (mètəmɔ́rfəsi:z) *n*. a marked change of form and structure undergone by an animal from embryo to adult stage, e.g. in insects, amphibians, echinoderms etc. ‖ a transformation of one structure into another, e.g. stamens into petals ‖ a striking change of appearance, character, form etc.

met·a·phor (métəfər, métəfɔr) *n*. a figure of speech in which a name or quality is attributed to something to which it is not literally applicable, e.g. 'an icy glance', 'nerves of steel' **met·a·phor·ic** (mètəfɔ́rik, mètəfórik), **met·a·phór·i·cal** *adjs*

me·ta·phys·ics (mètəfiziks) *n*. the branch of philosophy dealing with the first principles of things. It includes ontology and cosmology

me·tas·ta·sis (mətǽstəsis) *pl.* **me·tas·ta·ses** (mətǽstəsi:z) *n*. the spreading of disease from one part of the body to another, e.g. in cancer ‖ an instance of this **me·tás·ta·size** *pres. part.* **me·tas·ta·siz·ing** *past* and *past part.* **me·tas·ta·sized** *v.i.* to spread by metastasis

mete (mi:t) *pres. part.* **met·ing** *past* and *past part.* **met·ed** *v.t.* (with 'out') to distribute, apportion, deal out, *to mete out punishment*

me·te·or (mí:ti:ər) *n*. a solid body from outer space, which glows with the heat generated by friction as it enters the earth's atmosphere

me·te·or·ic (mì:ti:ɔ́rik, mì:ti:órik) *adj.* of or pertaining to meteors ‖ brilliant and rapid ‖ of, relating to or originating in the earth's atmosphere **me·te·ór·i·cal·ly** *adv.*

me·te·o·rite (mí:ti:ərait) *n*. a meteor which reaches the surface of the earth in solid form, either in one piece or in fragments

me·te·or·o·log·ic (mì:ti:ərəlódʒik) *adj. meteorological* **me·te·or·o·lóg·i·cal** of or pertaining to meteorology

me·te·or·ol·o·gist (mì:ti:ərólədʒist) *n*. a specialist in meteorology

me·te·or·ol·o·gy (mì:ti:ərólədʒi:) *n*. the study of conditions in the earth's atmosphere, esp. for making weather forecasts ‖ the general weather conditions of a region

me·ter (mí:tər) **1.** *n*. an instrument for measuring and recording the amount of flow of something (e.g. gas) or the amount of duration of use of something **2.** *v.t.* to measure with a meter ‖ to stamp (mail) with a postage meter

me·ter (mítər) *n. (abbr.* m.) the fundamental unit of length in the metric system. 1 m. = about 39.37 ins

meter *n*. the rhythmic recurrence of patterns within a line of poetry or in lines of poetry, based e.g. on stress or on number of syllables or on a combination of these or on number of feet ‖ musical rhythm

meth·a·done (méθədoun) a synthetic narcotic used to relieve pain and to detoxify drug addicts

meth·ane (méθein) *n*. an odorless, colorless, inflammable hydrocarbon which forms explosive mixtures with air. It results from the decay of organic matter and is found in natural gas and in coal mines

meth·od (méθəd) *n*. a way of doing something ‖ a procedure for doing something ‖ orderliness in doing, planning etc. ‖ an orderly arrangement or system **me·thód·i·cal** (məθódik'l) *adj.*

me·tic·u·lous (mətíkjuləs) *adj.* paying or showing scrupulous attention to detail

met·ric (métrik) *adj.* pertaining to the meter (unit of length)

met·ri·cal (métrik'l) *adj.* pertaining to or composed in meter ‖ pertaining to measurement

metric system a decimal system of measurement of

length (incl. area and volume) and mass (incl. weight). The unit of mass is the kilogram, the unit of length is the meter, and occasionally a distinction is made between volume, measured in units based upon the cubic meter, and capacity, based upon the liter

met·ro·nome (métrənoum) n. a clockwork device with a moving, audible indicator, which can be regulated to different speeds, used esp. to mark musical time **met·ro·nom·ic** (metrənómik) adj.

me·trop·o·lis (mətrópəlis) n. the chief city of a country or region ‖ any busy center of commerce etc. ‖ the see of a metropolitan bishop

met·ro·pol·i·tan (metrəpólitən) 1. adj. of, pertaining to or characteristic of a metropolis ‖ pertaining to a metropolitan 2. n. (Orthodox Eastern Church) a head of an ecclesiastical province, ranking between archbishop and patriarch ‖ (Western Church) an archbishop

met·tle (mét'l) n. (rhet.) spirit, courage or fortitude **mét·tle·some** adj. (esp. of a horse) spirited

mez·za·nine (mézəni:n, mezəni:n) n. a low-ceilinged extra story between two main ones, usually just above the ground floor ‖ the first balcony in some theaters or the first few rows of it

mez·zo for·te (métsoufɔ́rti:, médzoufɔ́rti:) adv. (mus.) moderately loud

mi·ca (máikə) n. any of several transparent silicates which can be split into very thin, pliable sheets. Mica is used as an electrical insulator and as a heat resistant substitute for glass in stove doors etc. **mi·cá·ceous** adj.

micro- (máikrou) prefix. (esp. in scientific terms) small, minute

mi·crobe (máikroub) n. a microorganism, esp. one which causes disease **mi·cró·bi·al, mi·cró·bic** adjs

mi·cro·bi·ol·o·gy (maikroubaióladʒi:) n. the branch of biology concerned with microorganisms

mi·cro·cosm (máikrəkɒzəm) n. (philos.) the universe in miniature ‖ anything regarded as being the universe in miniature **mi·cro·cós·mic** adj.

mi·cro·film (máikrəfilm) 1. n. a very small photographic film, convenient for storage and transportation, used esp. for photographing documents etc. 2. v.t. to reproduce on microfilm

mi·crom·e·ter (maikrómitər) n. an instrument fitted with scale and vernier for measuring very small objects and distances

mi·cro·phone (máikrəfoun) n. an instrument for amplifying or transmitting sound **mic·ro·phon·ic** (maikrəfónik) adj.

mi·cro·pho·to·graph (maikroufóutəgræf, maikrou- fóutəgraf) n. a very small photograph which normally is magnified to make details clear

mi·cro·scope (máikrəskoup) n. an optical instrument used to examine minute objects by giving an enlarged, well resolved image of them

mi·cro·scop·ic (maikrəskópik) adj. too small to be visible to the naked eye ‖ very small ‖ of, pertaining to or involving the use of a microscope **mi·cro·scóp·i·cal** adj. **mi·cro·scóp·i·cal·ly** adv.

mi·cro·wave (máikrouwẹiv) n. an electromagnetic wave of wavelength less than 10 m. in the radio-frequency range

microwave oven an oven that utilizes electromagnetic energy below the microwave spectrum for rapid food preparation

mid (mid) adj. (only in compounds) in the middle of, midmorning ‖ (phon., of certain vowels) pronounced with the tongue in a position between high and low

mid·air (mídẹər) n. the air thought of as a region well above the ground

mid·day (míddẹi) n. the middle of the day, when the sun appears to be directly overhead

mid·dle (míd'l) 1. adj. central ‖ intermediate ‖ medium or average in size, quality, status etc. 2. n. a place or moment or thing occupying a middle position ‖ (pop.) the waist

middle class the class of people including those in professional and commercial occupations. Other usual criteria are: relatively median income, secondary or higher education, and the holding of generally conformist views **míd·dle-cláss** adj.

mid·dle·man (míd'lmæn) pl. **mid·dle·men** (mídl'lmen) n. anyone engaged in trade who buys goods from the producer and sells them to the retailer or consumer

midg·et (mídʒit) 1. n. a very small person, esp. one normally proportioned ‖ anything much smaller than others of its kind 2. adj. very small

mid·night (mídnait) 1. n. 12 o'clock at night 2. adj. of or happening at this time **to burn the midnight oil** to work late into the night

mid·riff (mídrif) n. the part of the body including the lower ribs and the top of the abdominal cavity

mid·ship·man (mídʃipmən) pl. **mid·ship·men** (mídʃipmən) n. a student training for the rank of ensign in the U.S. Navy

midst (midst) n. (only in phrases) **in our midst** among us **in the midst of** in the middle of ‖ in the course of

mid·way 1. (mídwẹi) n. the part of an exhibition, fair etc. where sideshows and amusements are located 2. (mídwéi) adv. halfway

mid·wife (mídwaif) pl. **mid·wives** (mídwaivz) n. a woman who assists in the delivery of babies **mid·wife·ry** (mídwaifəri:, mídwaifri:) n. obstetrics

mien (mi:n) n. (rhet.) bearing, demeanor or appearance as signs an observer can interpret

miff (mif) v.t. (pop.) to offend

might (mait) n. strength, power

might past of MAY ‖ used as an auxiliary verb to express a degree of possibility less than that expressed by 'may'

might·i·ly (máitili:) adv. (rhet.) with great might ‖ (pop.) extremely

might·y (máiti:) 1. comp. **might·i·er** superl. **might·i·est** adj. (rhet.) large and strong, esp. in physique ‖ (rhet.) great and powerful 2. adv. (pop.) very, mighty fine

mi·graine (máigrein) n. a severe, periodically recurring headache, usually on one side of the head, often accompanied by nausea, vertigo etc.

mi·grant (máigrənt) 1. adj. making a periodical migration 2. n. an animal, esp. a bird, that migrates ‖ a person who migrates

mi·grate (máigreit) pres. part. **mi·grat·ing** past and past part. **mi·grat·ed** v.i. (of certain birds, fishes etc.) to change habitat, esp. at certain seasons ‖ (of people) to leave one country or region to settle or work for a period in another ‖ (of a plant) to extend its habitat into a new area

mi·gra·tion (maigréiʃən) n. the act or process of migrating ‖ an instance of this ‖ a group of migrating animals, persons etc.

mi·gra·to·ry (máigrətɔri:, máigrətouri:) adj. given to migrating ‖ relating to migration ‖ roving or wandering

mi·ka·do (mikádou) n. a title (used esp. by non-Japanese) of the emperor of Japan

mil (mil) n. a unit of measurement, used esp. for the diameter of wire, equivalent to 1/1000 in. or 0.0254 mm.

mild (maild) adj. gentle and moderate, not severe or extreme ‖ (of weather) fairly warm and windless ‖

(of food etc.) not having a strong taste || (of a disease) not acute || (of ale or beer) not strongly flavored with hops

mil·dew (míldu:, míldju:) 1. *n.* a whitish, fuzzy growth produced on the surface of various forms of organic matter and living plants by certain fungi || a fungus causing this growth 2. *v.t.* to affect with mildew || *v.i.* to become covered with mildew **míl·dew·y** *adj.*

mile (mail) *n.* a unit of linear measurement equaling 1,760 yds (1,609.35 m.) || a nautical mile **míle·age, míl·age** *n.* a number of miles traveled || the distance in miles from one place to another || an allowance for traveling expenses at a given rate per mile

mile·stone (máilstoun) *n.* a stone by the roadside showing the distance in miles from nearby important towns || an event of significance in the history of a nation, person etc.

mi·lieu (mi:ljə́:) *n.* environment

mil·i·tan·cy (mílitənsi:) *n.* the quality or state of being militant

mil·i·tant (mílitənt) 1. *adj.* engaged in fighting || aggressive in support of a cause 2. *n.* a militant person

mil·i·ta·rism (mílitərizəm) *n.* the policy of constantly building up armaments and the armed forces or of threatening armed aggression || the tendency in a society to encourage an excessively military spirit

mil·i·ta·rist (mílitərist) 1. *n.* a person who encourages militarism 2. *adj.* characterized by or imbued with militarism **mil·i·ta·rís·tic** *adj.* **mil·i·ta·rís·ti·cal·ly** *adv.*

mil·i·ta·rize (mílitəraiz) *pres. part.* **mil·i·ta·riz·ing** *past and past part.* **mil·i·ta·rized** to build up the military strength of, make military || to imbue with military spirit

mil·i·tar·y (mílitəri:) *adj.* of, pertaining to or involving the armed forces or warfare **the military** the army

mi·li·tia (milíʃə) *n.* a reserve body of citizens enrolled for military duties, called upon only in an emergency **mi·li·tia·man** (milíʃəmən) *pl.* **mi·li·tia·men** (milíʃəmən) *n.* a member of the militia

milk (milk) *n.* a white or yellowish liquid consisting of small fat globules suspended in a watery solution, secreted by the mammary glands for the nutrition of the newborn. It contains all the nutrient substances (proteins and enzymes, fats, sugars, minerals and vitamins) necessary for growth, but is deficient in iron || such a secretion drawn from a cow, goat etc. for use as human food || a liquid resembling this secretion, e.g. coconut juice or latex **to cry over spilled** (or **spilt**) **milk** to regret or fuss about something that cannot be remedied

milk *v.t.* to draw or press milk from (a cow, goat etc.) || to extract (milk) from an animal || to extract (money etc.) to one's advantage from someone or something, esp. over a period of time || to exploit (someone), esp. to extract money from || to draw the sap from (a plant) || to draw the venom from (a snake) || *v.i.* to yield milk || to draw milk

milk·er (mílkər) *n.* a person who milks || a machine for milking cows || a cow etc. that gives milk

milk·sop (mílksɒp) *n.* a man or boy who lacks proper spirit

milk·y (mílki:) *comp.* **milk·i·er** *superl.* **milk·i·est** *adj.* of, like or containing milk || (of a liquid) cloudy, whitish in color

mill (mil 1. *n.* a building containing machinery which grinds grain into flour || a machine that grinds grain || a small hand-operated machine for grinding some solid substance, e.g. coffee beans or pepper || a building containing machinery used in some kinds of manufacture, *cotton mill* || one of the machines used in such manufacture 2. *v.t.* to grind (grain, beans etc.) || to work (something) in a mill || to full (cloth) || to cut grooves across the rim edge of (a coin) || *v.i.* (with 'around') (of a crowd, herd etc.) to move about in a confused mass

mil·len·ni·um (miléni:əm) *pl.* **mil·len·ni·ums, mil·len·ni·a** (miléni:ə) *n.* a period of 1,000 years || a 1,000th anniversary

milli- (mili) *prefix* (esp. in terms of the metric system) one thousandth

mil·liard (míljərd, míljard) *n.* *NUMBER TABLE

mil·li·me·ter (míləmi:tər) *n.* (*abbr.* mm.) one thousandth of a meter

mil·li·ner (mílinər) *n.* someone who makes, trims or sells women's hats and headdresses **mil·li·ner·y** (mílineri:) *pl.* **mil·li·ner·ies** *n.* the hats and headdresses made or sold by a milliner || a milliner's work or business

mil·lion (míljən) 1. *n.* a thousand thousands (*NUMBER TABLE) || the cardinal number representing this (1,000,000, M) **millions of** a very large, indefinite number of 2. *adj.* being a thousand times a thousand

mil·lion·aire (míljənéər) *n.* a person whose possessions are worth a million or more dollars

mil·lionth (míljənθ) 1. *adj.* being number 1,000,000 in a series (*NUMBER TABLE) || being one of the 1,000,000 equal parts of anything 2. *n.* the person or thing next after the 999,999th || one of 1,000,000 equal parts of anything (1/1,000,000)

mill·stone (mílstoun) *n.* one of two large circular channeled slabs of stone, between which grain is ground, the grain being fed into a hole in the middle of the upper one **a millstone around one's neck** some burden (e.g. a moral obligation) that prevents all freedom of action or self-fulfillment

mime (maim) 1. *n.* a form of entertainment in which story and emotion are conveyed by gesture only, without words, but often with music and decor || an entertainment of this kind || an actor in this kind of entertainment 2. *v. pres. part.* **mim·ing** *past and past part.* **mimed** *v.t.* to act (a story etc.) in mime || to mimic || *v.i.* to enact a story without words

mim·e·o·graph (mími:əgræf, mími:əgrɑ:f) 1. *n.* a machine for making many copies of a document written or typed on a stencil || a copy made on such a machine 2. *v.t.* to copy with a mimeograph || to make (copies) on a mimeograph

mim·ic (mímik) 1. *adj.* copying or imitating something 2. *n.* someone who imitates others, often satirically || (*biol.*) something which exhibits mimicry 3. *v.t. pres. part.* **mim·ick·ing** *past and past part.* **mim·icked** to imitate, esp. in order to ridicule || (*biol.*) to exhibit mimicry of **mím·ic·ry** *pl.* **mim·ic·ries** *n.* the act of mimicking || an instance of this || (*biol.*) the superficial resemblance that an organism may show to some other animate or inanimate structure, and which serves as a means of concealment

mi·mo·sa (mimóusə, mimóuzə) *n.* a genus of trees, shrubs and low-growing plants of tropical and warm regions

min·a·ret (minərét, mínəret) *n.* a tall slender tower of a mosque, having one or more balconies, from which Moslems are summoned to prayer

min·a·to·ry (mínətɔ:ri:, mínətɔuri:) *adj.* menacing

mince (mins) 1. *v. pres. part.* **minc·ing** *past and past part.* **minced** *v.t.* to cut up (meat etc.) into very small pieces || to utter (words etc.) with affected refinement || *v.i.* to walk with showy steps and an affected swaying motion || to talk or behave with affected elegance **not to mince matters** (or **one's words**) to speak bluntly 2. *n.* mincemeat || minced meat

mince·meat (mínsmi:t) *n.* a chopped mixture of apples, dried fruits etc., often with suet, used as a filling in pies **to make mincemeat of** to give a thorough beating to || to destroy (an argument etc.)

mind (maind) 1. *n.* the seat of consciousness, thought, feeling and will || the intellect || opinion || desire, purpose || sanity || mentality || (*philos.*) consciousness as an element in reality (contrasted with matter) **on one's mind** occupying one's thoughts, esp. as a source of worry **to bear in mind** to continue to remember **to be in one's right mind** to be sane **to call to mind** to be a reminder of || to recall **to have in mind** to intend || to be thinking of **to keep in mind** to continue to remember **to make up one's mind** to decide **to set one's mind on** to be determined to do or have **to speak one's mind** to say what one thinks **to take (someone's) mind off** to distract (someone's) attention from, help (him) to stop worrying about **2.** *v.t.* to have charge of, take care of ‖ to look out for, be careful of, *mind the step* ‖ to concern oneself with ‖ to pay attention to, heed ‖ to obey ‖ to worry about ‖ *v.i.* to worry ‖ to be vexed or have an objection **never mind** do not worry

mind·ful (máindfəl) *adj.* (with 'of') giving thought or heed to ‖ (with 'of') remembering gratefully, *mindful of her past kindness*

mine (main) *possessive pron.* that or those belong to me, *the fault is mine, friends of mine, that must be your coat because mine is torn*

mine *n.* an excavation in the earth from which minerals are extracted ‖ this excavation with its accompanying buildings, shafts etc. ‖ a deposit of ore etc. ‖ a rich source, *a mine of information* ‖ *(mil.)* an explosive charge in a container, placed on or under the earth or in the sea, or dropped from the air

mine *pres. part.* **min·ing** *past* and *past part.* **mined** *v.i.* to dig a mine ‖ to put explosive mines on or under the earth or in the water ‖ *v.t.* to dig below the surface of (the earth) ‖ to dig (ores etc.) from the earth ‖ *(mil.)* to lay a mine beneath ‖ *(mil.)* to dig a mine beneath ‖ to destroy by mining

mine·field (máinfi:ld) *n.* an area on land or in the sea where mines have been laid

mine·lay·er (máinlẹiər) *n.* a ship used to lay underwater mines

min·er (máinər) *n.* a man who works in a mine ‖ a soldier who lays mines

min·er·al (mínərəl) **1.** *n.* any of various naturally occurring substances (e.g. ores, petroleum, natural gas, sand, clay, coal) of more or less homogeneous composition obtained from the earth for man's use ‖ *(chem.)* a solid, homogeneous crystalline chemical element or compound, formed by natural processes and usually extracted from the earth ‖ *(loosely)* any inorganic substance **2.** *adj.* of, containing or consisting of minerals ‖ *(loosely)* inorganic **min·er·al·ize** *pres. part.* **min·er·al·iz·ing** *past* and *past part.* **min·er·al·ized** *v.t.* to convert into a mineral ‖ to convert (a metal) into an ore ‖ to impregnate with a mineral

min·er·al·o·gy (mínərǽlədʒi:, mínərólədʒi:) *n.* the science of minerals

min·gle (míng'l) *pres. part.* **min·gling** *past* and *past part.* **min·gled** *v.t.* to mix, blend ‖ to bring together, *to mingle guests* ‖ *v.i.* to become part of a mixture, combination, group etc., *their voices mingled in song, to mingle with the crowd*

min·i·a·ture (míni:ətʃər, mínitʃər) **1.** *n.* a very small painting in illuminated manuscripts ‖ a small painting on vellum, ivory etc. ‖ the art of painting miniatures ‖ a small model **in miniature** on a small scale **2.** *adj.* on a small scale, *minature golf* **min·i·a·tur·ist** *n.* an artist specializing in miniatures

min·i·mal (mínəməl) *adj.* pertaining to the least or smallest possible ‖ very small, *minimal requirements* ‖ very small, *a minimal charge*

min·i·mize (mínəmaiz) *pres. part.* **min·i·miz·ing** *past* and *past part.* **min·i·mized** *v.t.* to reduce to the smallest possible degree or amount, *to minimize formalities* ‖ to estimate at the smallest possible degree or amount, *he minimized the inconvenience out of politeness* ‖ to underestimate, *don't minimize the risks*

min·i·mum (mínəməm) **1.** *pl.* **min·i·ma** (mínəmə), **min·i·mums** *n.* the least possible amount, number or

degree, *keep expenses to a minimum* ‖ the lowest amount, number or degree actually reached, *a temperature minimum* **2.** *adj.* least in amount, number or degree

min·ing (máiniŋ) *n.* the act or process of extracting coal, ore etc. from a mine or mines ‖ the industry based on this ‖ the laying of explosive mines

min·is·ter (mínistər) *n.* a person in charge of some high office of state, esp. one responsible for the administration of an autonomous public service department, *minister of health* ‖ a diplomat ranking below an ambassador ‖ a person authorized to conduct worship, administer sacraments etc. in a Christian church, esp. *(Am.)* any Protestant clergyman

minister *v.i.* to give aid or service, *to minister to a person's needs* ‖ to serve as a minister of religion, *to minister to a congregation*

min·is·try (mínistri:) *pl.* **min·is·tries** *n.* (in some countries) a ministerial department of a government, *ministry of labor* ‖ a governing body of ministers ‖ its tenure of office ‖ (in some countries) the building occupied by a ministerial department ‖ the office and duties of a minister of religion ‖ the period during which a minister serves a congregation

mink (miŋk) *pl.* **mink, minks** *n.* the highly valued pelt or fur of one of several small semiaquatic carnivorous mammals of genus *Mustela,* fam. *Mustelidae,* closely related to and resembling the weasel and the ferret ‖ one of these animals

min·now (mínou) *n.* a small freshwater fish about 3 ins long, allied to the carp, native to the northern hemisphere and the East Indies, used as fishing bait ‖ *(loosely)* any of several very small fish

mi·nor (máinər) **1.** *adj.* less in importance, size etc. than something else ‖ not having reached the full legal age ‖ of or designating an academic subject constituting a secondary specialization **2.** *n. (law)* a person under full legal age ‖ a minior subject of study **3.** *v.i.* (with 'in') to study a specified minor subject

mi·nor·i·ty (mainɔ́riti:, mainɔ́riti:, minɔ́riti:, minɔ́riti:) *pl.* **mi·nor·i·ties** *n.* the smaller number, less than half of a total ‖ a group distinguished by its religious, political, racial or other characteristics from a larger group or society of which it forms a part ‖ the state or period of being under legal age

min·strel (mínstrəl) *n. (hist.)* a medieval musician who sang, recited, and accompanied himself on an instrument ‖ a member of a band of public entertainers, usually in blackface, who sing songs and tell jokes

mint (mint) *n.* any of various aromatic plants native to Europe, Asia and Australia and widely cultivated for use as flavoring

mint 1. *n.* a place where official coins are made ‖ (often with 'of money') a vast sum **2.** *adj.* not marred or soiled, as if new, *in mint condition* **3.** *v.t.* to coin (money) ‖ to convert (metal) into money ‖ to invent, fabricate (images, phrases etc.) **mint·age** *n.* the act or process of minting money ‖ money coined in a mint, esp. in a particular mint at a particular time

mi·nus (máinəs) **1.** *prep.* reduced by, *10 minus 3 is 7* ‖ *(pop.)* deficient in, lacking, *he emerged minus his hat* **2.** *adj.* indicating subtraction, *the minus sign* ‖ negative, *a minus number* ‖ (used postpositively) somewhat less than, *a C minus mark* **3.** *n.* a minus sign ‖ a minus quantity

min·ute (mínət) **1.** *n.* a unit of time equal to a sixtieth of an hour ‖ an undefined short time ‖ a unit of angular measure (symbol ′) equal to a sixtieth of a degree ‖ a written record of a decision etc. made at a meeting ‖ a short written communication giving an instruction,

---

making a recommendation or presenting an analysis **2.** *v.t. pres. part.* **min·ut·ing** *past* and *past part.* **min·ut·ed** to make a minute or minutes of

mi·nute (mainú:t, mainjú:t) *adj.* || of small importance, trivial || precise and detailed

mir·a·cle (mírək'l) *n.* a supernatural event regarded as due to divine action || an extremely remarkable achievement or event, e.g. an unexpected piece of luck

mi·rac·u·lous (mirǽkjuləs) *adj.* of, like, involving, or having the nature of a miracle || reputed to work miracles, *a miraculous image*

mi·rage (mirá3) *n.* an optical phenomenon in which remote objects are seen inverted, as if mirrored in water, or suspended in midair || something illusory

mire (máiər) **1.** *n.* an area of swampy land || deep soft mud **2.** *v.t. pres. part.* **mir·ing** *past* and *past part.* **mired** to cause to be stuck fast in mire || to spatter with mud

mir·ror (mírər) **1.** *n.* a polished surface, esp. of glass backed with silver or mercury, which reflects light, and on which images can therefore be seen || any smooth or polished object whose surface reflects light and images || a true portrayal or representation **2.** *v.t.* to reflect in or as if in a mirror

mirth (mə:rθ) *n.* merriment characterized esp. by laughter of the kind that greets ridiculous situations, jokes etc. **mírth·ful, mírth·less** *adjs*

mis- (mis) *prefix* (in combination with verbs) badly or incorrectly || (in combination with nouns) bad, incorrect, wrong

mis·ad·ven·ture (misədvéntʃər) *n.* an unlucky accident **death by misadventure** accidental death, i.e. not involving crime or negligence

mis·an·thrope (mízənθroup, mísənθroup) *n.* a person who hates or distrusts all mankind **mis·an·throp·ic** (mizənθrópik, misənθrópik) *adj.* **mis·an·thróp·i·cal·ly** *adv.* **mis·an·thro·pist** (mizǽnθrəpist, misǽnθrəpist), **mis·án·thro·py** *ns*

mis·ap·pli·ca·tion (misæplikéiʃən) *n.* a misapplying or being misapplied

mis·ap·ply (misəplái) *pres. part.* **mis·ap·ply·ing** *past* and *past part.* **mis·ap·plied** *v.t.* to use badly or mistakenly || to use (money, funds etc.) dishonestly or without proper authorization

mis·ap·pre·hend (misæprihénd) *v.t.* to misunderstand **mis·ap·pre·hen·sion** (misæprihénʃən) *n.*

mis·be·have (misbihéiv) *pres. part.* **mis·be·hav·ing** *past* and *past part.* **mis·be·haved** *v.i.* to behave badly || *v. refl.* to behave (oneself) badly **mis·be·ha·vior** (misbihéivjər) *n.*

mis·cal·cu·late (miskǽlkjuleit) *pres. part.* **mis·cal·cu·lat·ing** *past* and *past part.* **mis·cal·cu·lat·ed** *v.t.* and *i.* to calculate wrongly **mis·cal·cu·lá·tion** *n.*

mis·car·riage (miskǽrid3) *n.* the expulsion of a human fetus from the womb before it is viable || an instance of this || mismanagement || an instance of this

mis·car·ry (miskǽri:) *pres. part.* **mis·car·ry·ing** *past* and *past part.* **mis·car·ried** *v.i.* (of a plan etc.) to go wrong || to undergo a miscarriage of a fetus

mis·ce·ge·na·tion (misid3inéiʃən, mised3inéiʃən) *n.* interbreeding or marriage between members of different races

mis·cel·la·ne·ous (misəléini:əs) *adj.* formed or consisting of things of several kinds

mis·chance (mistʃǽns, mistʃɑ́ns) *n.* bad luck || an instance of this

mis·chief (místʃif) *n.* annoying but not seriously harmful behavior, esp. by children || playful teasing || harm

mis·chie·vous (místʃivəs) *adj.* inclined toward or characterized by playful annoyance or teasing

mis·con·ceive (miskənsí:v) *pres. part.* **mis·con·ceiv·ing** *past* and *past part.* **mis·con·ceived** *v.t.* to misunderstand, interpret mistakenly

mis·con·cep·tion (miskənsépʃən) *n.* the act of misconceiving || an instance of this

mis·con·duct 1. (miskóndəkt, miskóndʌkt) *n.* bad man-

agement || behavior improper according to some code **2.** (miskəndʌ́kt) *v.t.* to mismanage || to conduct (oneself) improperly

mis·con·strue (miskənstrú:) *pres. part.* **mis·con·stru·ing** *past* and *past part.* **mis·con·strued** *v.t.* to interpret mistakenly

mis·cre·ant (mískri:ənt) **1.** *adj.* (*rhet.*) evil **2.** *n.* (*rhet.*) a criminal or villain

mis·deal (misdí:l) **1.** *n.* (*cards*) a mistake made in dealing **2.** *v.t.* and *i.* (*cards*) to deal incorrectly

mis·deed (misdí:d) *n.* an evil or criminal action

mis·de·mean·or (misdimí:nər) *n.* (*law*) an offense technically less than a felony, not punishable by death or long imprisonment || a misdeed

mi·ser (máizər) *n.* an avaricious person, esp. one who lives in discomfort or squalor in order to hoard his wealth

mis·er·a·ble (mízərəb'l) *adj.* extremely unhappy or uncomfortable || causing misery || characterized by wretched discomfort and squalor || extremely inadequate, poor or worthless **mís·er·a·bly** *adv.*

mi·ser·ly (máizərli:) *adj.* characteristic of or relating to a miser

mis·er·y (mízəri:) *pl.* **mis·er·ies** *n.* extreme wretchedness due to poverty, squalor etc. || extreme unhappiness or suffering || a cause of these states || (*pop.*) a doleful, depressing person

mis·fea·sance (misfí:z'ns) *n.* (*law*) the illegal or improper performance of an action in itself lawful || (*law*) an instance of this **mis·féa·sor** *n.*

mis·fire (misfáiər) **1.** *v.i. pres. part.* **mis·fir·ing** *past* and *past part.* **mis·fired** (of a gun or explosive charge) to fail to go off || (of an internal-combustion engine) to fail to ignite properly or at the right time || (of a plan, joke etc.) to fail to have the effect intended **2.** *n.* a misfiring

mis·fit (mísfit) *n.* a person who is unable to adjust himself to society || (mísfít) a garment etc. that does not fit

mis·for·tune (misfɔ́rtʃən) *n.* mischance, bad luck || an instance of this

mis·give (misgív) *pres. part.* **mis·giv·ing** *past* **mis·gave** (misgéiv) *past part.* **mis·giv·en** (misgívən) *v.t.* **mis·gív·ing** *n.* distrust, apprehension, or anticipation of failure || (esp. *pl.*) an instance of these feelings

mis·guide (misgáid) *pres. part.* **mid·guid·ing** *past* and *past part.* **mis·guid·ed** *v.t.* to misdirect **mis·gúid·ed** *adj.* mistaken because of false ideas, poor advice etc.

mis·hap (míshæp) *n.* an unlucky accident

mis·in·form (misinfɔ́rm) *v.t.* to give wrong or misleading information to **mis·in·for·ma·tion** (misinfərméiʃən) *n.*

mis·judge (misd3ʌ́d3) *pres. part.* **mis·judg·ing** *past* and *past part.* **mis·judged** *v.t.* to judge wrongly || to judge unfairly **mis·júdg·ment, mis·júdge·ment** *n.*

mis·lay (misléi) *pres. part.* **mis·lay·ing** *past* and *past part.* **mis·laid** (misléid) *v.t.* to lose (something) temporarily by forgetting where one has put it

mis·lead (mislí:d) *pres. part.* **mis·lead·ing** *past* and *past part.* **mis·led** (misléd) *v.t.* to deceive by causing to infer something not actually true || to lead in a wrong direction **mis·léad·ing** *adj.*

mis·no·mer (misnóumər) *n.* a wrong name or designation || (*law*) the using of a wrong name or title, esp. in a document

mi·sog·a·my (misógəmi:) *n.* hatred of marriage

mi·sog·y·nist (misód3inist) *n.* a man who hates women **mi·sóg·y·nous** *adj.* **mi·sóg·y·ny** *n.*

mis·print 1. (misprínt) *v.t.* to print inaccurately **2.** (mísprint) *n.* a mistake in printing

mis·rep·re·sent (misreprizént) *v.t.* to give a false impression or account of, either deliberately or unintentionally **mis·rep·re·sen·tá·tion** *n.* a false impression or account || the act of misrepresenting

miss (mis) **1.** *v.t.* to fail to hit, reach, meet or make contact with || to allow (an opportunity etc.) to pass by || to fail to perceive || to notice the loss or absence of ‖ to regret the loss or absence of ‖ to escape, avoid ‖ to fail or be unable to attend ‖ *v.i.* (of engines) to fail to fire ‖ to fail to hit something aimed at **to miss the boat** to fail to take advantage of an opportunity **2.** *n.* a failure to hit or catch

mis·sal (mís'l) *n.* (*Roman Catholicism*) a book containing everything said or sung at Mass for the entire year

mis·sile (mís'l) **1.** *n.* a weapon or object that is thrown or fired or designed for this **2.** *adj.* suitable for throwing or being discharged at a distant target

miss·ing (mísiŋ) *adj.* lost or absent

missing link a hypothetical organism intermediate between two known types, esp. between the apes and man

mis·sion (míʃən) *n.* a group of people sent esp. abroad by a Church or other religious organization to make conversions ‖ the area of this group's operations ‖ the buildings acting as its center ‖ a group of people working temporarily in a parish to invigorate its religious life ‖ a body of representatives sent abroad for special diplomatic discussions etc. ‖ the work they are sent to do ‖ any task, esp. of a diplomatic nature, that one is sent to do ‖ a permanent diplomatic delegation abroad ‖ an aim in life, arising from a conviction or sense of calling ‖ an assigned combat operation, e.g. by aircraft

mis·sion·ar·y (míʃənɛri:) **1.** *n. pl.* **mis·sion·ar·ies** a person who undertakes the work of a religious mission **2.** *adj.* of or pertaining to a religious mission ‖ characteristic of or performing the work of a missionary

mis·sive (mísiv) *n.* a formal or official letter, esp. from someone in authority

mis·spell (misspél) *pres. part.* **mis·spell·ing** *past* and *past part.* **mis·spelled, mis·spelt** (misspélt) *v.t.* to spell incorrectly **mis·spéll·ing** *n.* an instance of incorrect spelling

mis·step (mísstep) *n.* a step taken in a wrong or clumsy way ‖ an error or blunder

mist (mist) *n.* a mass of minute particles of water, suspended in the atmosphere or precipitated in particles finer than raindrops ‖ a film or haze before the eyes causing dimness of vision ‖ a thin film of moisture on the surface of something

mist *v.i.* to become misty ‖ *v.t.* to make misty

mis·tak·a·ble (mistéikəb'l) *adj.* that may be mistaken or misunderstood

mis·take (mistéik) **1.** *v.t. pres. part.* **mis·tak·ing** *past* **mis·took** (mistúk) *past. part.* **mis·tak·en** (mistéikən) to misunderstand ‖ to form an incorrect estimate of, have a wrong opinion of ‖ to think wrongly that (someone or something) is another specified person or thing **2.** *n.* a misunderstanding ‖ an instance of incorrectness or of wrong opinion or judgment **mis·ták·en** *adj.* (of persons) committing an error in opinion or judgment ‖ involving error in judgment or behavior

Mis·ter (místər) *n.* (*abbr.* Mr.) a courtesy title for any male adult not styled 'Sir', 'Dr' etc. ‖ a form of address to the holder of any of certain offices, *Mr. Chairman* **mister** (*pop.*, esp. used by beggars and children) sir

mis·tle·toe (mís'ltou) *n.* a Eurasian evergreen semiparasitic shrub growing on esp. deciduous trees, e.g. the apple. It has profuse dichotomous branching, thick, simple leaves, usually dioecious flowers, and bears a white viscous berry ‖ any of several other plants having similar characteristics, esp. any member of *Phoradendron*, a genus of American plants

mis·treat (mistrí:t) *v.t.* to treat wrongly or badly, abuse

mis·tress (místris) *n.* a woman in relation to a man not her husband with whom she frequently has sexual relations ‖ a woman in relation to her servants or pets

mis·tri·al (mistráiəl) *n.* (*law*) a trial declared void because of an error in proceedings ‖ a trial in which the jury cannot agree upon a verdict

mis·trust (mistrʌst) **1.** *v.t.* to regard with suspicion ‖ to feel no confidence in **2.** *n.* suspicion ‖ lack of confidence **mis·trúst·ful** *adj.*

mist·y (místi) *comp.* **mist·i·er** *superl.* **mist·i·est** *adj.* covered in mist ‖ characterized by mist ‖ blurred, indistinct

mis·un·der·stand (misʌndərstǽnd) *pres. part.* **mis·un·der·stand·ing** *past* and *past part.* **mis·un·der·stood** (misʌndərstúd) *v.t.* to interpret incorrectly **mis·un·der·stánd·ing** *n.* a misinterpretation ‖ a quarrel or disagreement **mis·un·der·stóod** *adj.* wrongly interpreted ‖ not getting proper sympathy or appreciation

mis·use 1. (misjú:s) *n.* improper or incorrect use **2.** (misjú:z) *v.t. pres. part.* **mis·us·ing** *past* and *past part.* **mis·used** to use improperly or incorrectly ‖ to treat wrongly or abusively

mis·us·er (misjú:zər) *n.* (*law*) the misuse of a privilege, benefit etc.

mite (mait) *n.* any of several widely distributed, minute, sometimes microscopic arachnids of order *Acarina*, closely related to and resembling ticks, though much smaller

mite *n.* (*hist.*) a coin of very small value ‖ a very small thing, quantity, contribution etc.

mi·ter (máitər) *n.* a tall ornamented liturgical headdress worn by bishops and some abbots as a symbol of office

miter 1. *n.* (*carpentry*) a miter joint ‖ (*carpentry*) either of the surfaces that come together in a miter joint **2.** *v.t. pres. part.* **mi·ter·ing** *past* and *past part.* **mi·tered** to fit together in a miter joint ‖ to shape the ends of (two pieces of wood) for joining them in a miter joint

mit·i·ga·ble (mítigəb'l) *adj.* capable of being mitigated

mit·i·gate (mítigeit) *pres. part.* **mit·i·gat·ing** *past* and *past part.* **mit·i·gat·ed** *v.t.* to make less severe, alleviate, *to mitigate grief* ‖ (*fig.*) to cause to put something in a less harsh light **mit·i·gá·tion** *n.* **mit·i·ga·tive** (mítigeitiv) *adj.* **mít·i·ga·tor** *n.* **mit·i·ga·to·ry** (mítigətɔri, mítigətouri:) *adj.*

mitt (mit) *n.* a glove which leaves the fingers and thumb bare ‖ (*baseball*) a padded glove used to catch the ball ‖ a mitten

mit·ten (mít'n) *n.* a glove which has a single section for the four fingers and a separate division for the thumb ‖ a glove which leaves thumb and fingers bare

mix (miks) **1.** *v.t.* to combine ‖ to bring together into a single uniform mass ‖ to prepare by putting ingredients together ‖ to cause to associate ‖ to crossbreed ‖ *v.i.* to become mixed ‖ to be capable of being mixed ‖ to get along with others socially **2.** *n.* a mixture ‖ a commercial preparation of various ingredients, *a cake mix* **mixed** *adj.* blended ‖ made up of different sorts, types, or qualities ‖ consisting of or including persons of both sexes ‖ for or including people of different races, religions etc. ‖ (*bot.*) combining racemose and cymose formations ‖ (*phon.*, of vowels) central

mixed-up (míkstʌp) *adj.* confused, esp. (*pop.*) emotionally

mix·ture (maikstʃər) *n.* a mixing or being mixed ‖ something made by mixing ‖ (*chem.*) a substance made up of two or more components not in fixed proportion and which are held to retain their separate

---

(a) æ, c*a*t; ɑ, c*a*r; ɔ faw·n; ei, sn*a*ke. **(e)** e, h*e*n; i:, sh*ee*p; iə, d*ee*r; ɛə, b*ea*r. **(i)** i, f*i*sh; ai, t*i*ger; ə:, b*i*rd. **(o)** o, *o*x; au, c*o*w; ou, g*oa*t; u, p*oo*r; ɔi, r*oy*al. **(u)** ʌ, d*u*ck; u, b*u*ll; u:, g*oo*se; ə, bacill*u*s; ju:, c*u*be. x, lo*ch*; θ, *th*ink; ð, bo*th*er; z, *Z*en; ʒ, corsa*g*e; dʒ, sava*g*e; ŋ, oranguta*ng*; j, *y*ak; ʃ, *fi*sh; tʃ, fe*tch*; 'l, rabb*le*; 'n, redd*en*. Complete pronunciation key appears inside front cover.

identities however thoroughly mingled

mix·up (míksʌp) *n.* a state of confusion ‖ an instance of this

mne·mon·ic (ni:mónik, nimónik) **1.** *adj.* meant to help the memory **2.** *n.* an aid (e.g. a rhyme) to prompt the memory **mne·món·ics** *n.* the science or art of improving the memory ‖ a technique or system used to train the memory

moan (moun) **1.** *n.* a low, long sound expressing pain or grief ‖ a sound resembling this **2.** *v.t.* to say with a moan ‖ to lament about, bewail ‖ *v.i.* to utter a moan ‖ (of the wind etc.) to make a sound like a moan ‖ to complain or lament

moat (mout) *n.* a deep, wide trench dug around a fortification, town etc. to prevent invasion, usually filled with water **móat·ed** *adj.* surrounded by a moat

mob (mɒb) **1.** *n.* a large, esp. rough and disorderly crowd ‖ a gang of criminals **the mob** (used contemptuously) the lower classes of society **2.** *v. pres. part.* **mob·bing** *past and past part.* **mobbed** *v.t.* to crowd around and inconvenience or molest ‖ to crowd into ‖ *v.i.* to form a mob

mo·bile (móub'l) **1.** *adj.* capable of moving or being moved ‖ moving or moved with ease ‖ extremely fluid ‖ (of facial expression or features) showing changes of feeling **2.** *n.* a sculpture consisting of an arrangement of carefully balanced and suspended articulated forms kept constantly moving in various planes by air currents

mo·bil·i·ty (moubíliti:) *n.* the state or quality of being mobile

mo·bi·li·za·tion (mɒubəlizéiʃən) *n.* a mobilizing or being mobilized

mo·bi·lize (móubəlaiz) *pres. part.* **mo·bi·liz·ing** *past and past part.* **mo·bi·lized** *v.t.* (*mil.*) to assemble (troops) in readiness for active service ‖ *v.i.* (*mil.*) to be assembled in readiness for active service

moc·ca·sin (mókəsin) *n.* a soft heelless shoe of deerskin, worn by North American Indians ‖ a shoe resembling this ‖ a North American poisonous snake, esp. the water moccasin

mock (mɒk) **1.** *v.t.* to ridicule ‖ to imitate, esp. in order to ridicule ‖ to thwart as if in ridicule ‖ to disappoint, esp. so as to make (someone or something) seem ridiculous ‖ *v.i.* (esp. with 'at') to express ridicule **2.** *adj.* false, sham **3.** *n.* (in the phrase) **to make a mock of** to ridicule

mock·er·y (mókəri:) *pl.* **mock·er·ies** *n.* derision, ridicule ‖ an object of mocking ‖ a travesty

mode (moud) *n.* a way or manner of doing, being etc. ‖ a fashion (esp. style of clothes) ‖ any of various standing waves of which an oscillatory system is capable ‖ any of various simple vibrations that combine to give the overall vibration of an oscillating body or system (e.g. the normal modes of vibration of a molecule) ‖ (*statistics*) the value of the variable occurring most often in a series of data ‖ (*gram.*) mood **the mode** common prevailing style or fashion in behavior, speech etc.

mod·el (mód'l) **1.** *n.* a three-dimensional representation, usually in miniature, of a thing to be constructed, sculptured etc., or of an object etc. that already exists ‖ a design intended for mass production ‖ something made to such a design ‖ a person or thing considered as an object for imitation ‖ a person who poses for an artist or photographer ‖ a person who demonstrates clothes by wearing them in front of customers ‖ (*economics*) a mathematical representation of the facts, factors, and inferences of an entity or situation, e.g., model of the economic condition when certain factors are added **2.** *adj.* serving as or suitable to be a model **3.** *v. pres. part.* **mod·el·ing** *past and past part.* **mod·eled, mod·elled** *v.t.* to make a model (representation) of ‖ to work (clay or other plastic material) ‖ to form in imitation of a model ‖ to wear (clothes) in demonstrations to customers ‖ (*art*) to give the effect of relief to ‖ *v.i.* to make a

model or models ‖ to serve for modeling ‖ to pose as model for an artist or photographer ‖ to act as a mannequin

mod·er·ate (módərit) **1.** *adj.* between extremes in size, quality, degree etc. ‖ avoiding excess in behavior etc., reasonable ‖ not very great or good, limited ‖ not severe or violent ‖ (of political measures or views) not extremist ‖ (of a person) holding nonextremist political views **2.** *n.* a politically moderate person **3.** (módəreit) *v. pres. part.* **mod·er·at·ing** *past and past part.* **mod·er·at·ed** *v.t.* to make less extreme, violent, severe etc. ‖ to preside over (a meeting etc.) ‖ *v.i.* to become less extreme, violent, severe etc.

mod·er·a·tion (mɒdəréiʃən) *n.* the quality or state of being moderate ‖ the act of moderating

mod·er·a·tor (módəreitər) *n.* a mediator ‖ someone who presides at a meeting, e.g. the presiding officer of various Protestant Church assemblies ‖ (*phys.*) a substance (e.g. graphite or deuterium) used to slow down the emissions of neutrons in a nuclear reactor

mod·ern (módərn) **1.** *adj.* of the present day, not ancient ‖ up-to-date **2.** *n.* a person holding progressive opinions in conflict with earlier ideas

mo·dern·i·za·tion (mɒdərnizéiʃən) *n.* a modernizing or being modernized ‖ an instance of this

mod·ern·ize (módərnaiz) *pres. part.* **mod·ern·iz·ing** *past and past part.* **mod·ern·ized** *v.t.* to change, in order to bring into harmony with modern taste and standards

mod·est (módist) *adj.* aware of one's limitations, not vain or conceited ‖ avoiding pretension or display ‖ limited but not negligible ‖ restrained and reasonable ‖ shunning indecency **mód·es·ty** *n.* the quality of being modest

mod·i·fi·a·ble (módifaiəb'l) *adj.* capable of being modified

mod·i·fi·ca·tion (mɒdifikéiʃən) *n.* a modifying or being modified ‖ a partial change produced by modifying

mo·di·fi·er (módifaiər) *n.* someone who or something that modifies

mod·i·fy (módifai) *pres. part.* **mod·i·fy·ing** *past and past part.* **mod·i·fied** *v.t.* to change to some extent but not completely ‖ to make less extreme ‖ (*gram.*) to limit or qualify the general meaning of (a word, phrase, etc.) ‖ (*phon.*) to change the sound of (a vowel) by umlaut

mod·u·lar (módʒulər, módjulər) *adj.* of, relating to or based upon a module or a modulus

mo·du·late (módʒuleit, módjuleit) *pres. part.* **mod·u·lat·ing** *past and past part.* **mod·u·lat·ed** *v.t.* to regulate by a standard measure, esp. to vary the pitch of (a voice or other sound) ‖ (*radio*) to change intermittently the frequency, amplitude etc. of (a wave) ‖ *v.i.* (*mus.*) to lead out of one key into another in the course of a composition, the change itself forming an integral part of the composition ‖ (*radio*) to change intermittently the frequency, amplitude etc. of a wave

mod·u·la·tion (mɒdʒuléiʃən, mɒdjuléiʃən) *n.* a modulating or being modulated ‖ a variation produced by modulating

mod·ule (módʒu:l, módju:l) *n.* a unit used as a standard of measurement, esp. (*archit.*) the size of a certain part of a structure used to determine the proportions of the rest ‖ (*rocketry*) a spacecraft unit that is self-contained and has a limited task or set of tasks to perform ‖ (*electronics*) an independent unit containing electronic components, esp. one that can be incorporated in a computer system ‖ (*architecture*) radius of the lower end of a column

mo·dus   o·pe·ran·di (móudusouperándi:, móudəsɒpərǽndai) *n.* a manner of working or operating

modus vi·ven·di (móudusvivéndi:, móudəsvivéndai) *n.* an agreement establishing a temporary compromise between two groups in conflict

Mo·gul (móug'l) *n.* a Mongolian ‖ someone with conspicuous power and influence in a certain business or some clearly defined sphere, *a movie mogul*

mo·hair (móuhęɚr) *n.* the hair of the Angora goat ‖ a fabric made wholly or partly from this ‖ a fabric of mixed cotton and wool resembling this fabric

moist (mɔist) *adj.* slightly wet ‖ (of a climate) humid, having frequent rain **mois·ten** (mɔ́is'n) *v.t.* to make moist ‖ *v.i.* to become moist

mois·ture (mɔ́istʃɚr) *n.* the diffused or condensed liquid, esp. water, which makes a gas or solid slightly damp

mo·lar (móulɚr) **1.** *n.* one of the posterior teeth in mammals, adapted for grinding **2.** *adj.* (of a tooth) adapted for grinding

mo·las·ses (məlæsiz) *n.* the uncrystallized syrup produced in the process of refining sugar

mold (mould) **1.** *n.* a hollow container into which fluid or plastic material is put and allowed to harden, so that the material takes on the container's interior shape ‖ the shape created in this way ‖ a pudding etc. shaped in such a container ‖ *(archit.)* a molding or group of moldings **2.** *v.t.* to make, form into a certain shape ‖ to form by pouring into a mold ‖ to fit the contours of ‖ to form according to some pattern ‖ to modify the shape or character of ‖ to decorate with moldings ‖ *v.i.* to become covered with mold

mold *n.* a woolly or fluffy growth produced by various fungi on food, leather, clothes etc. that have been left in warm and moist air ‖ a fungus that produces mold

mold·ing (móuldiŋ) *n.* anything formed by, in or as if in a mold, esp. *(archit.)* decorative work in stone, plaster etc. in a continuous band on the cornice of a building, outlining panels, on ceilings of rooms etc. ‖ an ornamental edging for a picture frame

mold·y (móuldi:) *comp.* **mold·i·er** *superl.* **mold·i·est** *adj.* covered with mold ‖ *(pop.)* wretched, miserable

mole (moul) *n.* any of several small burrowing insectivorous mammals, with strong broad forefeet, small eyes and dark velvety fur. Moles are native to temperate regions of Europe, Asia and North America

mole *n.* a congenital mark or small permanent protuberance on the skin, often with hair roots

mole *n.* a wall of masonry constructed in the sea to form a breakwater ‖ a harbor formed by such a wall

mole *n.* an intelligence agent who remains inactive for a long period of time, awaiting a particular order or event to become active

mo·lec·u·lar (məlékjulɚr) *adj.* pertaining to, involving or consisting of molecules

mol·e·cule (mɔ́likju:l) *n.* the smallest amount of a chemical element or compound which can exist while retaining the characteristic properties of the substance ‖ a little bit, a fragment

mo·lest (məlést) *v.t.* to meddle with (someone) in such a way as to harm or annoy him

mo·les·ta·tion (mɔulestéiʃən) *n.* a molesting or being molested

moll (mɔl) *n.* a gangster's girl

mol·li·fi·ca·tion (mɔlifikéiʃən) *n.* a mollifying or being mollified

mol·li·fy (mɔ́lifai) *pres. part.* **mol·li·fy·ing** *past* and *past part.* **mol·li·fied** *v.t.* to lessen the anger of ‖ to soften the effect of

mol·lusk, mol·lusc (mɔ́lask) *n.* a phylum of unsegmented, coelomate, generally shelled and bilaterally symmetrical invertebrates possessing a muscular foot which is variously modified for digging, swimming or creeping. Mollusks include snails, mussels etc.

molt (moult) **1.** *v.i.* (of an animal) to shed feathers, fur, skin etc., which are later replaced by new growth ‖ *v.t.* to shed (feathers etc.) in this way **2.** *n.* the act or process of molting, *in molt* ‖ the feathers, fur etc. that have been molted

mol·ten (móultən) *adj.* melted, esp. by extremely high heat

mo·ment (móumənt) *n.* a small, indefinite period of time ‖ a particular time

mo·men·tar·i·ly (mọumentέərili:) *adv.* for a moment

mo·men·tar·y (móumənteri:) *adj.* lasting only for a moment

mo·men·tous (mouméntəs) *adj.* having great importance, *a momentous occasion*

mo·men·tum (mouméntəm) *pl.* **mo·men·ta** (mouméntə), **mo·men·tums** *n.* a measure of the quantity of motion, defined as the product of the mass and the velocity of a body; and determining the length of time during which constant force must act on a moving body to bring it to rest ‖ *(loosely)* the force built up by a moving body

mon·arch (mɔ́nɚrk) *n.* a person ruling, usually by hereditary right and for his lifetime, over a kingdom or people, and invested with either absolute or constitutional power ‖ *(rhet.)* the chief person or thing of its kind or class ‖ a large orange and black American butterfly **mo·nar·chal** (mənɚrk'l) *adj.*

mo·nar·chic (mənɚrkik) *adj.* of, relating to or having the characteristics of a monarchy or monarch **mo·nár·chi·cal** *adj.*

mon·ar·chism (mɔ́nɚrkizəm) *n.* the monarchical system of government ‖ belief in monarchical principles of government **món·ar·chist** *n.*

mon·ar·chy (mɔ́nɚrki:) *pl.* **mon·ar·chies** *n.* a state ruled by a monarch ‖ rule by a monarch

mon·as·ter·y (mɔ́nəsteri:) *pl.* **mon·as·ter·ies** *n.* the group of buildings housing a community of monks

mo·nas·tic (mənǽstik) **1.** *adj.* pertaining to monks or to a monastery

Mon·day (mʌ́ndi:, mʌ́ndei) *n.* the second day in the week

mon·e·tar·i·ly (mɔnitέərili:, mʌnitέərili:, mɔ́niterili:, mʌ́niterili:) *adv.* with regard to money

mon·e·tar·y (mɔ́niteri:, mʌ́niteri:) *adj.* pertaining to money, esp. to coinage

mon·ey (mʌ́ni:) *pl.* **mon·eys, mon·ies** *n.* anything that serves as a medium of exchange for goods and services, in the form of tokens which have a value established by a commonly recognized authority, e.g. the government of a country, or by custom ‖ personal wealth ‖ *(pl., esp. law)* sums of money **to get one's money's worth** to obtain full value for what one has expended in effort, money or time

mon·grel (mʌ́ŋgrəl, mɔ́ŋgrəl) **1.** *n.* something (esp. a dog) of mixed breed **2.** *adj.* (esp. of a dog) of mixed breed

mon·i·tor (mɔ́nitɚr) **1.** *n.* a pupil appointed to assist in keeping discipline etc. ‖ a person who or an instrument that monitors a broadcast or telephone communication ‖ any of several large tropical lizards related to the iguana, supposed to give warnings of nearby crocodiles ‖ *(computer)* diagnostic program used to respond to questions about a computer program so as to warn of faults or failings ‖ any other device for a similar purpose on other systems **2.** *v.t.* to check (broadcasts) for their information and significance ‖ to check (radio, television or telephonic communication) for quality of transmission ‖ *(phys.)* to test (materials) for radioactivity **mon·i·to·ri·al** (mɔnitɔ́ri:əl, mɔnitóuri:əl) *adj.* **món·i·tor·ship** *n.*

monk (mʌŋk) *n.* a member of a religious community of men, bound by vows of obedience to the rules of the order

---

(a) æ, c*a*t; ɑ, c*a*r; ɔ f*a*wn; ei, sn*a*ke. **(e)** e, h*e*n; i:, sh*ee*p; iə, d*ee*r; ɛə, b*ea*r. **(i)** i, f*i*sh; ai, t*i*ger; ə:, b*i*rd. **(o)** o, *o*x; au, c*o*w; ou, g*oa*t; u, p*oo*r; ɔi, r*o*yal. **(u)** ʌ, d*u*ck; u, b*u*ll; u:, g*oo*se; ə, b*a*cillus; ju:, c*u*be. x, lo*ch*; θ, *th*ink; ð, bo*th*er; z, *Z*en; ʒ, corsa*g*e; dʒ, sava*g*e; ŋ, oranguta*ng*; j, *y*ak; ʃ, *fi*sh; tʃ, fe*tch*; 'l, rabb*le*; 'n, redd*en*. Complete pronunciation key appears inside front cover.

mon·key (mʌ́ŋki:) **1.** *pl.* **mon·keys** *n.* any of certain Old World or New World primates, generally smaller than the anthropoid apes, often arboreal and usually having prehensile hands and feet ‖ the fur of any of these animals ‖ *(loosely)* any of the primates except man, the lemurs and the tarsiers ‖ a playful, mischievous child ‖ *(mach.)* a weight used for driving something by falling on it, e.g. a drop hammer **2.** *v.i.* (with 'with', 'around with') to tamper ‖ (with 'around') to act mischievously or playfully

mono- (mɒ́nou) *prefix* alone, single

mo·nog·a·mist (mənɒ́gəmist) *n.* someone who practices or believes in monogamy

mo·nog·a·mous (mənɒ́gəməs) *adj.* practicing or believing in monogamy ‖ characterized by monogamy, *a monogamous society*

mo·nog·a·my (mənɒ́gəmi:) *n.* marriage to only one husband or wife at a time ‖ *(zool.)* the condition or habit of having only one mate

mon·o·gram (mɒ́nəgræm) *n.* a character composed of two or more interwoven letters, esp. a person's initials **mon·o·gram·mat·ic** (mɒnougrəmǽtik) *adj.*

mon·o·graph (mɒ́nəgræf, mɒ́nəgrɑf) *n.* a treatise about a single subject or aspect of a subject **mo·nog·ra·pher** (mənɒ́grəfər) *n.* **mon·o·graph·ic** (mɒnəgrǽfik) *adj.* **mon·o·gráph·i·cal·ly** *adv.*

mon·o·lith (mɒ́n'liθ) *n.* a very large single block of stone, often one erected as a monument ‖ a large block of concrete etc. used in the construction of a dam or building **mon·o·lith·ic** *adj.* massive, solid

mon·o·logue, mon·o·log (mɒ́n'lɔg, mɒ́n'log) *n.* a long speech by one person ‖ a dramatic speech by one actor ‖ a writing in the form of a soliloquy

mo·nop·o·li·za·tion (mənɒpəlizéiʃən) *n.* a monopolizing or being monopolized

mo·nop·o·lize (mənɒ́pəlaiz) *pres. part.* **mo·nop·o·liz·ing** *past and past part.* **mo·nop·o·lized** *v.t.* to make a monopoly of ‖ to assume exclusive control or use of, *to monopolize a conversation*

mo·nop·o·ly (mənɒ́pəli:) *pl.* **mo·nop·o·lies** *n.* exclusive control of the supply of a product or service in a particular market ‖ an exclusive privilege to engage in a particular business or provide a particular service, granted by a ruler, state etc. ‖ a commodity under exclusive control ‖ a company having exclusive control

mon·o·rail (mɒ́noureil) *n.* a railway consisting of a single rail on which the wheels run ‖ this rail

mon·o·syl·la·ble (mɒ́nəsiləb'l) *n.* a word of one syllable

mon·o·the·ism (mɒ́nəθi:ˌizəm) *n.* belief in only one God **món·o·the·ist** *n.* **mon·o·the·is·tic, mon·o·the·ís·ti·cal** *adjs*

mon·o·tone (mɒ́nətoun) *n.* a succession of sounds of the same pitch ‖ a single tone without variation in pitch ‖ speech of unvarying pitch and stress

mo·not·o·nous (mənɒ́t'nəs) *adj.* tediously repetitious, lacking variety ‖ characterized by a monotone

mo·not·o·ny (mənɒ́t'ni:) *n.* tedious lack of variety ‖ sameness of tone or pitch

Mon·sieur (məsjə́:) *pl.* **Mes·sieurs** (meisjə́:) *n.* the French equivalent of 'Mr', used as a courtesy title for a man and (without the surname) as a term of address to a man

Mon·si·gnor (mɒnsí:njər) *pl.* **Mon·si·gno·ri** (mɒnsi:njɔ́ri:), **Mon·si·gnors** *n.* *(abbr.* Msgr) a title given to certain dignitaries of the Roman Catholic Church ‖ a person with such a title

mon·soon (mɒnsú:n) *n.* a wind system in which there is an almost complete reversal of prevailing direction from season to season, the primary cause being the difference in temperature over land and sea. It is esp. prominent in S.E. Asia ‖ the rainy summer season (Apr.–Sept.) in S.E. Asia

mon·ster (mɒ́nstər) **1.** *n.* a deformed animal or plant ‖ an imaginary beast, usually compounded of incongruous parts ‖ a person who is horrifyingly cruel, brutal, selfish etc. ‖ something of extraordinarily great size **2.** *adj.* of very great size

mon·strance (mɒ́nstrəns) *n.* *(Roman Catholicism)* a vessel of gold or silver in which the consecrated Host is exposed to the congregation for veneration

mon·stros·i·ty (mɒnstrɒ́siti) *pl.* **mon·stros·i·ties** *n.* something monstrous ‖ the quality or state of being monstrous

mon·strous (mɒ́nstrəs) *adj.* having or showing the qualities of a monster

mon·tage (mɒntɑ́ʒ) *n.* *(photog.)* the making of a single picture from several others or pieces of others ‖ a picture formed in this way ‖ *(radio* etc.) the creating of a single composite effect by using music, sound effects, snatches of dialogue etc. in quick succession ‖ the effect so produced ‖ *(movies)* a medley of shots built up into a single unified effect by cutting, dissolving etc. ‖ the technique or process involved in this

month (mʌnθ) *n.* one of 12 periods into which the year is divided in the Gregorian calendar, varying between 28 and 31 days ‖ the period of rotation of the moon around the earth, approx. 29.5 days ‖ *(loosely)* a period of 4 weeks

month·ly (mʌ́nθli:) **1.** *adj.* lasting a month ‖ occurring once each month **2.** *pl.* **month·lies** *n.* a periodical published once a month ‖ *(pl., pop.)* the menses **3.** *adv.* once a month

mon·u·ment (mɒ́njumənt) *n.* something, typically a statue on a plinth or column, errected in memory of a person or event ‖ any structure etc. which acquires a memorial value with the passing of time ‖ a literary or scientific work of lasting value

mon·u·men·tal (mɒnjumént'l) *adj.* of, like or serving as a monument ‖ *(loosely)* very great, *monumental stupidity* ‖ very large, massive

mooch (mu:tʃ) *v.i.* *(pop.)* to wander about idly and aimlessly ‖ *(pop.)* to sponge

mood (mu:d) *n.* an emotional state ‖ *(loosely)* a fit of bad temper

mood·y (mú:di:) *comp.* **mood·i·er** *superl.* **mood·i·est** *adj.* characterized by gloomy moods or by sudden changes of mood ‖ gloomy, depressed

moon (mu:n) **1.** *n.* the only natural satellite of the earth, being responsible (with the sun) for its tidal action ‖ any planetary satellite ‖ *(rhet.)* a month **once in a blue moon** hardly ever, only at very long intervals **2.** *v.i.* (often with 'around', 'about', 'over') to behave in a dreamy abstracted manner ‖ *v.t.* (with 'away') to spend (time) mooning

moon·beam (mú:nbi:m) *n.* a beam of light from the moon

moon·light (mú:nlait) **1.** *n.* light received by reflection from the moon **2.** *v.i.* *(pop.)* to engage in moonlighting

moonlighting working at a job in addition to one's regular one —**moonlight** *v.* —**moonlighter** *n.*

moon·lit (mú:nlit) *adj.* illuminated by moonlight

moor (muər) *n.* *(esp. Br.)* a tract of open uncultivated ground, usually grown over with heather and coarse grasses and having a poor, acid, peaty soil

moor *v.t.* to secure (a vessel, airship etc.) to the land or buoys by means of ropes, chains etc. ‖ *v.i.* to secure a vessel etc. by ropes etc. ‖ (of a vessel etc.) to be secured in this way **móor·age** *n.* a mooring or being moored ‖ a place for mooring ‖ a charge for mooring

moor·ing (múəriŋ) *n.* (usually *pl.)* the cables, ropes etc. by which a vessel is moored ‖ the place where a vessel is moored

moose (mu:s) *pl.* **moose** *n.* a North American deer closely related to the European elk, having enormous branched antlers. Moose are found in the forests of Canada and the northern U.S.A., and weigh up to 1,000 lbs, reaching 7 ft in height at the shoulders

moot (mu:t) *v.t.* to put up (an idea etc.) for discussion

moot 1. *n.* *(law)* a discussion of fictitious cases arranged for practice among law students **2.** *adj.* open to argument, uncertain, *a moot point* ‖ *(law)* no longer a matter of practical importance requiring a decision, *a moot issue*

mop (mɒp) **1.** *n.* an implement for washing or polishing floors etc., made of a bundle of rags or coarse yarn fastened to a stick ‖ something resembling this, e.g. thick, unruly hair **2.** *v.t. pres. part.* **mop·ping** *past and past part.* **mopped** to wipe clean with a mop ‖ to wipe moisture from ‖ (with 'up') to remove (moisture etc.) ‖ *v.i.* (with 'up') to clean a floor etc. with a mop ‖ *(mil.,* with 'up') to destroy the last elements of resistance in an area and complete the occupation of it

mope (moup) **1.** *v. pres. part.* **mop·ing** *past and past part.* **moped** *v.i.* to be listless and gloomy ‖ *v.t.* (with 'away') to spend (time) being listless and gloomy **2.** *n.* (esp. *pl.*) a fit of low spirits **móp·ish** *adj.*

mor·al (mɔ́rəl, mɒ́rəl) **1.** *adj.* concerned with right and wrong and the distinctions between them ‖ virtuous, good ‖ capable of right or wrong action ‖ serving to teach right action ‖ dependent upon moral law ‖ (of a certainty) admitting of no reasonable doubt although not demonstrable ‖ relating to the mind or will, *moral support* **2.** *n.* the moral teaching contained in a fable, story, experience etc. ‖ *(pl.)* moral habits, esp. in sexual matters ‖ *(pl.)* principles of conduct

mo·rale (mɔráel) *n.* psychological state with regard to dependability, confidence, strength of purpose etc.

mor·al·ist (mɔ́rəlist, mɒ́rəlist) *n.* a person who moralizes ‖ a teacher of morals ‖ a student of or writer on human behavior **mor·al·ís·tic** *adj.*

mo·ral·i·ty (mɔráeliti) *pl.* **mo·ral·i·ties** *n.* ethics ‖ upright conduct ‖ conduct or attitude judged from the moral standpoint ‖ a morality play

mor·al·ize (mɔ́rəlaiz, mɒ́rəlaiz) *pres. part.* **mor·al·iz·ing** *past and past part.* **mor·al·ized** *v.i.* to talk or write, esp. boringly or at length, on moral themes etc. ‖ *v.t.* to draw a moral from

mo·rass (mərǽs) *n. (rhet.)* a marsh, swamp

mor·a·to·ri·um (mɔrətɔ́ri:əm, mɒrətɔ́uri:əm, mɒrətɔ́ri:əm, mɒrətɔ́uri:əm) *pl.* **mor·a·to·ri·ums, mor·a·to·ri·a** (mɔrətɔ́ri:ə, mɒrətɔ́uri:ə, mɒrətɔ́ri:ə, mɒrətɔ́uri:ə) *n.* a legally authorized period of delay before debts have to be paid ‖ the authorization for this **mor·a·to·ry** (mɔ́rətɔ:, mɒ́rətɔuri:, mɒ́rətɔ:ri:, mɒ́rətɔuri:) *adj.* of, pertaining to or granting a moratorium

mor·bid (mɔ́rbid) *adj.* (of ideas etc.) not natural or healthy, unwholesome ‖ (of a person) given to unwholesome (esp. gruesome) thoughts or feelings ‖ gruesome ‖ relating to disease **mor·bíd·i·ty** *n.* the quality or state of being morbid ‖ the incidence of disease in a given district

mor·dant (mɔ́rd'nt) **1.** *adj.* (of speech, wit etc.) incisive and caustic ‖ (of acids) corrosive ‖ serving to fix colors in dyeing **2.** *n.* a corroding substance, esp. one used in etching ‖ a substance which serves to fix color in dyeing, by combining with the dye to form an insoluble compound ‖ a substance used to cause gold leaf or paint to adhere **3.** *v.t.* to treat with a mordant

more (mɔr, mour) *superl.* **most** (moust) **1.** *adj.* greater in quantity, amount, number or degree ‖ additional, further **2.** *n.* something additional or further ‖ (construed as *pl.*) a greater number ‖ a greater quantity or portion **3.** *adv.* (often as a comparative with many adjectives and most adverbs) to a greater degree or extent ‖ in addition, further, again **more and more** in a continually increasing degree ‖ an increasing number or quantity **more or less** rather, to some undefined extent

more·o·ver (mɔróuvər, mouróuvər) *adv.* further, besides, in addition to what has been said

mo·res (mɔ́reiz, mɔ́ri:z, móureiz, móuri:z) *pl. n.* customs, esp. the fixed or traditional customs of a society, often acquiring the force of law

morgue (mɔrg) *n.* a place where dead bodies are laid out for identification ‖ a place where photographs, clippings, back numbers etc. are kept for reference by a newspaper or magazine ‖ such a collection

mor·i·bund (mɔ́rəbʌnd, mɒ́rəbʌnd) *adj.* near death ‖ about to collapse

morn·ing (mɔ́rniŋ) **1.** *n.* the early part of the day between midnight or dawn and noon ‖ dawn ‖ the first or early part **2.** *adj.* relating to or occurring in the morning

mo·ron (mɔ́ron, móurɒn) *n.* a mentally deficient person whose mental age in adulthood is about 8–12 years **mo·rón·ic** *adj.*

mo·rose (məróus) *adj.* glum, sour-tempered and unsocial

mor·phine (mɔ́rfi:n) *n.* the principal alkaloid of opium, a bitter white crystalline base, a habit-forming narcotic widely used for the relief of pain and as a sedative **mór·phin·ism** *n.* a diseased condition resulting from addiction to morphine ‖ addiction to morphine

mor·sel (mɔ́rs'l) *n.* a small bite or mouthful of food ‖ a small piece, esp. a choice one

mor·tal (mɔ́rt'l) **1.** *adj.* inevitably subject to death ‖ fatal ‖ ending only with death ‖ implacable ‖ (of pain, fear etc.) extreme ‖ relating to or accompanying death ‖ *(Roman Catholicism,* of a sin) entailing spiritual death ‖ *(pop.)* tedious ‖ *(pop.)* very great, *in a mortal hurry* **2.** *n.* a human being

mor·tal·i·ty (mɔrtǽliti:) *pl.* **mor·tal·i·ties** *n.* the quality or state of being mortal ‖ death on a large scale, e.g. through war ‖ the number of deaths in a given period or place ‖ the death rate

mor·tar (mɔ́rtər) **1.** *n.* a bowl made of strong material, in which substances are pounded and ground to powder with a pestle ‖ a short cannon used to fire shells at high trajectories ‖ a mixture of lime (or cement), sand and water, used for binding stones, bricks etc. in construction **2.** *v.t.* to bind (bricks etc.) with mortar ‖ to bombard with mortar shells

mort·gage (mɔ́rgidʒ) **1.** *n.* a conditional conveyance of land, a house etc. as security for a loan. The property remains in the possession of the borrower but may be claimed by the lender if the loan and interest are not paid according to the agreed terms ‖ the documents making this agreement ‖ the state of property thus conveyed **2.** *v.t. pres. part.* **mort·gag·ing** *past and past part.* **mort·gaged** to make over, grant (a house, land etc.) as security for debt by means of a mortgage ‖ to make (something) liable to future claims **mort·ga·gee** (mɔrgidʒi:) *n.* a creditor who receives a mortgage **mort·ga·gor, mort·gag·er** (mɔ́rgidʒər) *n.* the debtor who gives his property in a mortgage

mor·ti·cian (mɔrtíʃən) *n.* an undertaker

mor·ti·fy (mɔ́rtifai) *pres. part.* **mor·ti·fy·ing** *past and past part.* **mor·ti·fied** *v.t.* to subdue (passions, bodily desires etc.) by discipline ‖ to hurt or wound the feelings of, humiliate ‖ *v.i. (med.)* to become gangrenous

mor·tu·ar·y (mɔ́rtʃu:ɛri:) **1.** *adj.* of or relating to burial of the dead or to death **2.** *pl.* **mor·tu·ar·ies** *n.* a place where dead bodies are kept before burial or cremation

mo·sa·ic (mouzéiik) **1.** *n.* a form of surface decoration made by inlaying small pieces of colored glass, stone etc. ‖ a picture or design so made ‖ a number of aerial photographs placed together to form one continuous view of an area **2.** *adj.* of or relating to mosaic ‖

resembling mosaic in pattern or structure

mo·sey (móuzi:) *v.i.* (*pop.*) to move in a leisurely, sauntering way

mosque (mɒsk) *n.* a Moslem place of worship

mos·qui·to (məskí:tou) *pl.* **mos·qui·toes, mos·qui·tos** *n.* any of many two-winged flies distributed throughout the world, having a narrow abdomen, rigid proboscis and their wings fringed with scales

moss (mɔs, mɒs) *n.* a class of primitive, green land plants in which the gametophyte developing from a protonema is differentiated into a simple vascular stem, rhizoid and leaves ‖ such plants collectively ‖ any of several moss-like plants

most (moust) **1.** *adj.* (*superl.* of MUCH, MANY) greatest in number, quantity, amount, extent or degree **for the most part** in the greater number of instances ‖ as regards the major portion **2.** *n.* the greatest quantity, amount, extent or degree ‖ (construed as *pl.*) the greatest number, the majority **to make the most of** to use to the best advantage **3.** *adv.* (often as a superlative with many adjectives and most adverbs) to the greatest degree or extent ‖ to a great degree, very

-most *suffix* indicating a superlative

most·ly (móustli:) *adv.* in most cases, chiefly ‖ usually

mote (mout) *n.* a small particle, e.g. of dust floating in the air

mo·tel (moutél) a roadside hotel for motorists

moth (mɔθ, mɒθ) *pl.* **moths** (mɔðz, mɒðz, mɔðz, mɒðz) *n.* any of several lepidopterous insects distinguished from butterflies by their tapering antennae and nocturnal habits ‖ (*loosely*) an insect whose larvae feed on fabrics

moth·er (mʌðər) **1.** *n.* a female parent, esp. a woman in relation to her child ‖ (*rhet.*) something regarded as a source ‖ a woman in a position of authority like that of a mother **2.** *adj.* of, relating to or being a mother **3.** *v.t.* to take care of as a mother does

moth·er·hood (mʌðərhud) *n.* the state of being a mother ‖ (*rhet.*) mothers as a class

moth·er-in-law (mʌðərinlɔ) *pl.* **moth·ers-in-law** *n.* a husband's or wife's mother

moth·er·ly (mʌðərli:) *adj.* of or characteristic of a mother ‖ having the qualities suitable in a mother, e.g. tenderness and affectionate solicitude

mo·tif (moutí:f) *n.* a feature or theme, esp. one dominant or recurring in a work of art, music or drama

mo·tile (móut'l) *adj.* (*biol.*) showing, or capable of, spontaneous movement **mo·til·i·ty** (moutíliti:) *n.*

mo·tion (móuʃən) **1.** *n.* the act or process of passing through space or changing position ‖ an act or instance of moving the body or part of the body ‖ a formal proposal made in an assembly, subsequently discussed and voted upon ‖ (*law*) an application to a judge or court for a decision, ruling, order etc. ‖ an evacuation of the bowels ‖ (often *pl.*) the matter evacuated **in motion** moving **to go through the motions of** to perform the superficial gestures of (some action) often insincerely or perfunctorily **2.** *v.t.* to direct by sign or gesture ‖ *v.i.* to make a meaningful gesture **mó·tion·less** *adj.* perfectly still

mo·ti·vate (móutiveit) *pres. part.* **mo·ti·vat·ing** *past* and *past part.* **mo·ti·vat·ed** *v.t.* to be the motive of ‖ to supply a motive to ‖ to make a course of study interesting to (a pupil) **mo·ti·vá·tion** *n.*

mo·tive (móutiv) **1.** *n.* the sense of need, desire, fear etc. that prompts an individual to act ‖ a motif **2.** *v.t. pres. part.* **mo·tiv·ing** *past* and *past part.* **mo·tived** to motivate

motive *adj.* relating to movement ‖ causing movement

mot·ley (mɒtli:) **1.** *adj.* miscellaneous, varied in character, type etc. ‖ (esp. *hist.*, of a jester's clothes) parti-colored **2.** *n.* (*hist.*) the professional dress of a jester, in two colors ‖ an incongruous mixture, e.g. of colors

mo·tor (móutər) **1.** *n.* that which imparts motion, esp. a machine supplying motive power ‖ an internal-combustion engine, oil or gasoline-driven ‖ (*old-fash.*) an automobile ‖ a rotating machine (e.g. a generator) transforming electrical into mechanical energy or sometimes vice versa **2.** *adj.* of any form of movement, *motor activity* ‖ of, pertaining to, or operated by a motor ‖ (*physiol.*, of nerves) transmitting impulses from the central nervous system or a ganglion to a muscle causing movement **3.** *v.i.* to travel by automobile

mo·tor·cy·cle (móutərsaik'l) **1.** *n.* a two-wheeled, gasoline-driven vehicle larger and heavier than a bicycle, which carries its driver and may also carry one passenger on a pillion, and may sometimes have a sidecar **2.** *v.i. pres. part.* **mo·tor·cy·cling** *past* and *past part.* **mo·tor·cy·cled** to drive a motorcycle **mó·tor·cy·clist** *n.*

mo·tor·ist (móutərist) *n.* a person who drives an automobile, esp. regularly

mot·tle (mɒt'l) **1.** *n.* a colored spot or blotch, esp. one of many on a surface ‖ a blotchy surface appearance **2.** *v.t. pres. part.* **mot·tling** *past* and *past part.* **mot·tled** to mark with blotches **mót·tled** *adj.*

mot·to (mɒtou) *pl.* **mot·toes, mot·tos** *n.* a short pithy sentence or phrase inscribed on a coat of arms etc. ‖ a sentence or phrase used as a watchword, maxim or guiding principle ‖ a passage prefixed to a chapter heading of a book or to the book itself

mound (maund) **1.** *n.* a bank of earth, esp. an artificial one, e.g. heaped on a grave or (*hist.*) for defensive purposes ‖ a heap ‖ (*baseball*) a slight rise in the ground where the pitcher stands when pitching **2.** *v.t.* to heap up into a mound ‖ to enclose or fortify with mounds or ramparts

mount (maunt) *n.* (*abbr.* Mt) a mountain (used esp. before a mountain's name) ‖ a high hill ‖ (*palmistry*) one of the fleshy areas on the palm of the hand

mount 1. *v.i.* to ascend ‖ to get up on to something ‖ to increase in quantity, number, degree etc. ‖ *v.t.* to climb ‖ to place oneself in riding position on (a horse, bicycle etc.) ‖ to provide with a horse ‖ to equip with horses ‖ to help (someone) to get on a horse etc. ‖ to put (something) high up ‖ to put in a fixed position ‖ (of a vessel) to carry (guns) in position for use ‖ to put (a picture etc.) inside a raised border, or against a contrasting ground (of paper or material etc.) whose margins serve as a border ‖ to prepare or set up for view, *to mount an exhibition* ‖ to fit into a setting (of gold, silver etc.) ‖ to put (a play, opera etc.) on the stage ‖ (of a male animal) to copulate with **to mount an offensive** (*mil.*) to prepare and make an attack **2.** *n.* the act of mounting ‖ something mounted, esp. a horse ‖ a gun carriage for a cannon etc. ‖ a ground or raised border used in mounting a drawing etc. ‖ a transparent hinge, card etc. for mounting postage stamps in an album ‖ a setting of precious metal for jewels

moun·tain (máuntən) *n.* a conspicuously elevated, steep part of the earth's surface, esp. one rising to more than 1,000 ft above the surrounding land ‖ a high land mass containing a number of such projections ‖ a great quantity

moun·tain·eer (mauntəníər) **1.** *n.* a person skilled in mountain climbing **2.** *v.i.* to climb mountains

moun·tain·ous (máuntənəs) *adj.* containing mountains ‖ huge

moun·te·bank (máuntəbæŋk) *n.* a man who uses showmanship to exploit public credulity unscrupulously ‖ (*hist.*) an itinerant seller of quack medicines who mounted a bench or platform and collected an audience by showmanship etc.

mourn (mɔrn) *v.i.* to express or feel grief esp. because of a death ‖ to show customary tokens of grief for a given period after someone's death, e.g. to wear mourning ‖ *v.t.* to express or feel grief for (a dead person, someone's death etc.)

mourn·er (mɔrnər) *n.* a person who mourns ‖ a person attending a funeral

mourn·ful (mɔrnfəl) *adj.* feeling or showing sadness,

a mournful expression ‖ doleful, causing sadness, *a mournful tune*

mourn·ing (mɔ́rniŋ) *n.* grieving, lamentation ‖ the customary period during which a dead person is mourned ‖ the special clothes or tokens worn by a mourner

mouse (maus) **1.** *pl.* **mice** (mais) *n.* any of a large number of rodents resembling rats but smaller, with hairless tails, esp. one of the smaller members, e.g. *Mus musculus,* the house mouse, a common pest found in most parts of the world ‖ a timid or retiring person **2.** *v.i. pres. part.* **mous·ing** *past* and *past part.* **moused** (esp. of a cat) to hunt and catch mice **móus·er** *n.* an animal, esp. a cat, that is particularly good at catching mice

mous·tache, mus·tache (məstǽʃ, məstάʃ, mʌ́stæʃ) *n.* the hair on the upper lip, esp. of a man ‖ *(zool.)* bristles or hair around an animal's mouth

mouth 1. (mauθ) *pl.* **mouths** (mauðz) *n.* a cavity in the head containing the teeth for mastication, and the tongue, palate etc. for voice production, and bounded by the lips ‖ the external opening of the lips as a facial feature ‖ the opening in an animal's body through which food is taken in, regarded as the beginning of the alimentary canal ‖ a person viewed as something to be fed ‖ the mouth as the source of speech ‖ the part of a river where it empties into the sea **to keep one's mouth shut** to say nothing, remain silent **to put words into someone's mouth** to represent someone as having said something he did not say ‖ to tell someone what to say **to take the words out of someone's mouth** to say just what someone else was about to say **2.** *v.* (mauð) *v.t.* to say, esp. in an affected manner ‖ to shape (words) with the lips without saying them ‖ *v.i.* to speak in an affected manner ‖ to make a grimace **móuth·ful** *n.* the amount of food etc. that will go into the mouth easily **to say a mouthful** *(pop.)* to say something strikingly apt or true

mouth·piece (máuθpiːs) *n.* the part of a wind instrument to which the player's lips are applied ‖ something placed at the mouth, e.g. part of a horse's bit passing between the teeth ‖ the part of a tobacco pipe which is placed in the mouth ‖ the part of a telephone into which one speaks ‖ a spokesman, e.g. a person or newspaper delivering the opinion of others

mov·a·bil·i·ty, move·a·bil·i·ty (muːvəbíliti:) *n.* the state or quality of being movable

mov·a·ble, move·a·ble (múːvəb'l) **1.** *adj.* capable of being moved ‖ (of property) that can be moved from a house, personal ‖ (of a religious feast) changing its date from year to year **2.** *n.* an article, esp. of furniture, that can be moved from a house

move (muːv) **1.** *v. pres. part.* **mov·ing** *past* and *past part.* **moved** *v.t.* to change the location or position of ‖ to cause to become active, stir ‖ to arouse the feelings (esp. of pity, sympathy etc.) of ‖ to influence, impel ‖ to cause (the bowels) to eject feces ‖ to propose formally in an assembly ‖ *v.i.* to be made active, stir ‖ to change location or position ‖ (with 'for') to make an appeal, application etc. in a law court ‖ to change one's residence ‖ (often with 'on') to depart or start to depart ‖ to make progress ‖ *(chess, checkers* etc.) to change the position of a piece as part of the game ‖ to take action ‖ (of the bowels) to eject feces **as the spirit moves one** when one feels inclined to **move out (in)** to remove one's belonging from (take them into) a residence **to move up** to advance, e.g. when standing in line **2.** *n.* a calculated maneuver made to gain some advantage ‖ *(chess, checkers* etc.) the moving of a piece, or the turn of a player to move ‖ a change of place or residence **on the move** moving

from place to place ‖ progressing ‖ departing ‖ to go to a different place ‖ to take action

move·ment (múːvmənt) *n.* the act or process of moving ‖ an instance of this ‖ an impulse ‖ the development of the action in a prose work ‖ the rhythmic quality of a poem ‖ the illusion of motion in a painting, sculpture etc. ‖ the moving parts of a mechanism (esp. of clockwork) ‖ *(mus.)* a usually self-contained structural division of a symphony, sonata etc. ‖ *(mus.)* the character of a composition with regard to rhythm and tempo ‖ a series of acts and events planned towards a definite end by a body of people ‖ a tactical moving of troops as part of a military or naval maneuver ‖ an emptying of the bowels ‖ the matter thus emptied ‖ *(commerce)* a change or trend in the price of some commodity or stock

mov·er (múːvər) *n.* a person who or thing that moves, esp. a person who moves a formal proposal ‖ someone who professionally moves people's belongings from one residence to another

mo·vie (múːviː) *n.* a sequence of pictures projected on a screen from a developed and prepared film, esp. with an accompanying sound track ‖ a theater where such pictures are shown regularly to the public **the movies** such entertainment in general ‖ this entertainment as a branch of industry

mov·ing (múːviŋ) *adj.* changing place, posture etc. ‖ causing movement or action ‖ affecting the feelings, esp. feelings of tenderness, pity, sympathy etc.

moving picture a movie (sequence of pictures)

mow (mou) *past. part.* **mowed, mown** (moun) *v.t.* to cut (grass etc.) with a scythe, sickle, lawn mower etc. ‖ (with 'down') to cause to fall in great numbers ‖ *v.i.* to cut grass etc.

much (mʌtʃ) *comp.* **more** (mɔr) *superl.* **most** (moust) **1.** *adj.* (used esp. after an adverb, e.g. 'not', 'too', 'very') great in quantity, extent or degree ‖ very great, very good **2.** *n.* a great quantity, extent or degree ‖ something great, important, admirable (used esp. in negative constructions) **3.** *adv.* to a great extent or degree ‖ almost

mu·ci·lage (mjúːsəlidʒ) *n.* a sticky gelatinous substance found in seaweeds and in certain other plants ‖ a solution of gum etc. prepared as an adhesive **mu·ci·lag·i·nous** (mjuːsəlǽdʒinəs) *adj.* sticky ‖ containing or producing mucilage

muck (mʌk) **1.** *n.* moist farmyard manure ‖ dark, moist, fertile soil containing decomposing organic matter ‖ dirt, filth ‖ mud ‖ *(pop.)* an untidy state, confusion, *in a muck* **2.** *v.t.* to manure, *to muck a field* ‖ *(pop.)* to make dirty

mu·co·sa (mjuːkóusə) *pl.* **mu·co·sae** (mjuːkóusiː), **mu·co·sa, mu·co·sas** *n. (anat.)* a mucous membrane

mu·cous (mjúːkəs) *adj.* of, covered with or like mucus ‖ containing or secreting mucus

mu·cus (mjúːkəs) *n.* a slippery, slimy substance secreted by mucous glands covering and lubricating the inner surfaces of the respiratory, alimentary and genitourinary tracts etc.

mud (mʌd) *n.* a sticky mixture of water and earth or dust ‖ malicious abuse **to fling** (or **sling, throw**) **mud at** to talk scandal

mud·dle (mʌ́d'l) **1.** *v. pres. part.* **mud·dling** *past* and *past part.* **mud·dled** *v.t.* to mix (things) in a confused manner ‖ to make (speech, words) unclear ‖ to bewilder, esp. with alcohol ‖ to make a mess of, bungle ‖ *v.i.* (with 'about', 'away', 'on' etc.) to act in a confused, disorganized or bungling way **2.** *n.* a state of disorder or messiness ‖ a state of mental confusion

mud·dy (mʌ́di:) **1.** *adj. comp.* **mud·di·er** *superl.*

---

mud·di·est covered with mud ‖ abounding in mud ‖ like mud in color or texture ‖ thick with sediment ‖ confused, muddled ‖ (of light) dull, murky ‖ (of color) lacking brightness or clarity **2.** *v.t. pres. part.* **mud·dy·ing** *past* and *past part.* **mud·died** to make muddy ‖ *v.i.* to become muddy

muff (mʌf) *n.* a covering of fur etc. for protecting the hands from cold, shaped like a tube with open ends into which the hands are put

muff 1. *v.t. (cricket, baseball* etc.) to miss (a catch) ‖ to bungle ‖ *v.i.* to miss a catch in a game ‖ to bungle something **2.** *n. (cricket, baseball* etc.) a fumbled and dropped catch ‖ a bungling performance ‖ a bungler, esp. in games

muf·fin (mʌfin) *n.* a quick bread made of batter containing egg, baked in a cup-shaped mold and eaten hot with butter

muf·fle (mʌfəl) *pres. part.* **muf·fling** *past* and *past part.* **muf·fled** *v.t.* to cover up (the head, throat etc.) for protection against cold, esp. by wrapping oneself in a scarf etc. ‖ to wrap or pad (a drum, oars etc.) to deaden sound ‖ to deaden (sound) by wrapping, padding etc. ‖ to restrict the diffusion of (criticism etc.) **múf·fler** *n.* a scarf for protecting the throat from cold ‖ a device to deaden or muffle noise, esp. the felt pad of a piano hammer or a baffle in the exhaust pipe of an engine

mug (mʌg) **1.** *n.* a drinking vessel, generally cylindrical in shape, with a handle ‖ the amount it holds ‖ (pop.) the face or mouth **2.** *v. pres. part.* **mug·ging** *past* and *past part.* **mugged** *v.i. (pop.)* to grimace ‖ *v.t.* to put a stranglehold on (someone) from behind or strike (him) or otherwise assault (him) in order to commit robbery **múg·ger** *n.* someone who assaults a person in order to rob him

mug·gy (mʌgi) *comp.* **mug·gi·er** *superl.* **mug·gi·est** *adj.* (of weather, climate etc.) warm and damp, oppressive

mug·wump (mʌgwʌmp) *n.* someone who is neutral or undecided, esp. in politics

mul·ber·ry (mʌlbɛri:, mʌlbəri:) *pl.* **mul·ber·ries** *n.* a worldwide genus of trees cultivated for their delicious multiple fruit. The leaves of some species are used for feeding silkworms ‖ the fruit of any of these trees ‖ a rich, dark purple color

mulch (mʌltʃ, mʌlʃ) **1.** *n.* a layer of wet straw, leaves, grass mowings, compost etc. spread over the roots of plants or trees to conserve moisture, protect from frost etc. **2.** *v.t.* to apply mulch to

mulct (mʌlkt) *v.t.* to punish by means of a fine ‖ to get hold of the money of (someone) by swindling or extortion

mulct *n.* a fine ‖ a penalty ‖ a compulsory payment

mule (mju:l) *n.* a slipper made without a back

mule *n.* a usually sterile hybrid produced by crossing a male ass and a mare, used as a pack animal ‖ a stubborn or obstinate person, esp. when also stupid ‖ a sterile plant hybrid ‖ a spinning machine which draws, twists and winds cotton, wool etc.

mul·ish (mju:liʃ) *adj.* obstinate, stubborn

mull (mʌl) *v.t.* (with 'over') to ponder, deliberate mentally over (some question or problem)

multi- (mʌlti:, mʌltai) *prefix* having, containing or consisting of much or many ‖ many times, as in 'multimillionaire'

mul·ti·far·i·ous (mʌltiféəri:əs) *adj.* having great variety or diversity

mul·ti·ple (mʌltipl) **1.** *adj.* having many parts, sections or components ‖ multifarious, manifold **2.** *n. (math.)* a quantity or number which contains another an exact number of times without a remainder, *21 is a multiple of 7*

mul·ti·pli·a·ble (mʌltiplạiəb'l) *adj.* capable of being multiplied

mul·ti·plic·a·ble (mʌltiplíkəb'l) *adj.* multipliable

mul·ti·pli·ca·tion (mʌltiplikéiʃən) *n.* a multiplying or being multiplied ‖ *(math.)* the arithmetical process of multiplying numbers, which abbreviates the process of repeated addition

mul·ti·plic·i·ty (mʌltiplísiti:) *n.* a great number ‖ the quality or state of being many or varied

mul·ti·ply (mʌltiplai) *pres. part.* **mul·ti·ply·ing** *past* and *past part.* **mul·ti·plied** *v.t. (math.)* to increase (a number or quantity) by adding the number or quantity to itself repeatedly in a single arithmetical step, *7 multiplied by 7 makes 49* ‖ to increase in number, quantity or intensity ‖ *v.i.* to increase in number or quantity ‖ to breed

mul·ti·tude (mʌltitu:d, mʌltitju:d) *n.* a great number ‖ a crowd, a large gathering ‖ the quality or state of being numerous

mul·ti·tu·di·nous (mʌltitú:d'nəs, mʌltitjú:d'nəs) *adj.* existing in great numbers

mum·ble (mʌmb'l) **1.** *v. pres. part.* **mum·bling** *past* and *past part.* **mum·bled** *v.i.* to speak in a low indistinct way without proper articulation ‖ *v.t.* to utter inarticulately **2.** *n.* a low indistinct utterance or manner of speaking

mum·mi·fy (mʌmifai) *pres. part.* **mum·mi·fy·ing** *past* and *past part.* **mum·mi·fied** *v.t.* to embalm and dry (a body) so as to preserve it ‖ to preserve, wrap up etc. like a mummy ‖ *v.i.* to shrivel up, dry

mum·my (mʌmi:) *pl.* **mum·mies** *n.* a dead body embalmed for burial by the ancient Egyptians so as to be preserved from decay ‖ any dead body that has been naturally well preserved

mumps (mʌmps) *n.* an acute, contagious, virus disease, most common in children, marked by fever and swelling of the salivary glands of the neck and sometimes of the ovaries or testicles

mun·dane (mʌndéin, mʌndein) *adj.* ordinary, down-to-earth, matter-of-fact, esp. as contrasted with what is ideal

mu·nic·i·pal (mju:nísip'l) *adj.* of, relating to or carried on by local self-government (esp. of a town, city etc.)

mu·nic·i·pal·i·ty (mju:nisəpǽliti:) *pl.* **mu·nic·i·pal·i·ties** *n.* a town, city or district having powers of local self-government ‖ the corporation or council which governs this

mu·nif·i·cence (mju:nífis'ns) *n.* the quality or state of being munificent ‖ an instance of this

mu·nif·i·cent (mju:nífis'nt) *adj.* lavish in giving ‖ characterized by generosity

mu·ni·tion (mju:níʃən) **1.** *n. (pl.)* military stores and equipment of all kinds, esp. ammunition and weapons **2.** *v.t.* to provide with munitions

mu·ral (mjúərəl) **1.** *adj.* of, relating to or like a wall ‖ on a wall **2.** *n.* a fresco or painting made directly on a wall

mur·der (mɔ́:rdər) **1.** *n. (law)* the unlawful killing of a human being with malice aforethought ‖ an instance of this ‖ *(law)* the unlawful killing of a person under certain circumstances, e.g. during the committing of a serious felony, or when accompanied by cruelty, torture etc. ‖ killing that is morally reprehensible and brutal, or an instance of this ‖ *(pop.)* circumstances of great danger or hardship, *it was murder driving over Easter weekend* **2.** *v.t.* to kill (a human being) unlawfully with malice aforethought ‖ to kill brutally ‖ to spoil or ruin by bad performance or interpretation ‖ *v.i.* to commit murder

mur·der·er (mɔ́:rdərər) *n.* a person guilty of murder **múr·der·ess** *n.* a woman guilty of murder

mur·der·ous (mɔ́:rdərəs) *adj.* relating to, like, involving, or having the nature of murder ‖ capable of or intending to commit murder

murk, mirk (mɔ:rk) *n. (rhet.)* thick darkness, intense gloom

murk·i·ly, mirk·i·ly (mɔ́:rkili:) *adv.* in a murky way or manner

murk·y, mirk·y (mɔ́:rki:) *comp.* **murk·i·er, mirk·i·er** *superl.* **murk·i·est, mirk·i·est** *adj.* (of a place, atmosphere, etc.) thickly dark, intensely gloomy ‖ (of air etc.) heavy with mist, smoke etc.

mur·mur (mɔ́:rmər) *v.i.* to utter a murmur ‖ *v.t.* to utter (words) in a soft, low, indistinct voice

murmur *n.* soft, low and indistinct speech ‖ a continuous low, soft sound (e.g. of water in a stream) ‖ a subdued grumble, a half-suppressed expression of complaint or objection ‖ *(med.)* an abnormal sound of the heart as detected by the stethoscope **múr·mur·ous** *adj.*

mus·cle (mʌ́s'l) **1.** *n.* a bundle of fibers (in human and animal bodies) which have the property of contracting and relaxing and which produce motion ‖ that part of the body or flesh which is composed of such fibers ‖ muscular strength **2.** *v.i. pres. part.* **mus·cling** *past* and *past part.* **mus·cled** (esp. in) **to muscle in** *(pop.)* to push one's way in (to some situation) without invitation, esp. so as to take advantage of someone else's efforts

mus·cu·lar (mʌ́skjulər) *adj.* of or affecting the muscles ‖ having well-developed muscles **mus·cu·lár·i·ty** *n.*

muse (mju:z) *n.* *(rhet.)* the source of a poet's or artist's inspiration

muse *pres. part.* **mus·ing** *past* and *past part.* **mused** *v.i.* to meditate, think reflectively

mu·se·um (mju:zí:əm) *n.* a building used for the preservation and exhibition of objects illustrating human or natural history, esp. the arts or sciences

mush (mʌʃ) *n.* any soft pulpy mass ‖ cornmeal boiled in water and eaten hot, as porridge, or when cold, cut in slices and fried ‖ *(pop.)* mawkish sentimentality

mush·room (mʌ́ʃru:m, mʌ́ʃrum) **1.** *n.* the exposed fleshy fruiting body of some fungi that consists of a stem which arises from an underground mycelium, and a pileus whose lower surface is the site of spore development **2.** *adj.* of or made from mushrooms ‖ like a mushroom in shape or in rapidity of growth and decay **3.** *v.i.* to grow with sudden rapidity ‖ to expand or spread out at the end so as to resemble a mushroom (e.g. of atomic explosions in the upper atmosphere) ‖ to pick mushrooms

mush·y (mʌ́ʃi:) *comp.* **mush·i·er** *superl.* **mush·i·est** *adj.* soft and pulpy, like mush ‖ *(pop.)* mawkishly sentimental

mu·sic (mjú:zik) *n.* the art of giving structural form and rhythmic pattern to combinations of sounds produced instrumentally or vocally ‖ instrumental or vocal sounds that have been combined in this way ‖ the written score of a composition of such sounds ‖ such scores collectively ‖ musical compositions collectively ‖ any series or combination of pleasant sounds, e.g. of wind in trees, songs of birds etc. ‖ the quality of being harmonious and pleasant to the ear **to face the music** to meet the consequences (esp. punishment) without shirking **to put** (or **set**) **to music** to compose music for the words of (a poem etc.) so that it can be sung

mu·si·cal (mjú:zik'l) **1.** *adj.* of, relating to or having the nature of music ‖ talented or skilled in music, esp. as a performer or composer ‖ fond of music **2.** *n.* a musical comedy

mu·si·cian (mju:zíʃən) *n.* a person skilled in music, esp. a composer or performer

musk (mʌsk) *n.* a reddish-brown substance with a pungent, lasting odor, secreted in a small sac under the skin near the reproductive organs of the male musk deer, used as a basis for perfumes ‖ the smell of this substance ‖ any of several strong-smelling substances obtained from the muskrat, musk-ox, etc., used in preparing perfume

musk deer a small, sturdy deer of central Asia which secretes musk

musk·rat (mʌ́skræt) *n.* a brown aquatic rodent of North America, about 12 ins long, with webbed hind feet and a hairless tail. It has a strong, musky odor. It burrows in banks of streams ‖ the valuable pelt or fur of this animal

mus·lin (mʌ́zlin) *n.* a woven cotton material ranging from light, soft and fine (used e.g. for dresses, curtains etc.) to coarse (used e.g. in bookbinding). It may be bleached or unbleached

mus·sel (mʌ́s'l) *n.* any of several bivalve marine or freshwater mollusks having dark, more or less oval shells

must (mʌst) **1.** invariable *auxiliary v.*, *infin.* and *parts* lacking, *neg.* **must not, mustn't** (with *infin.*) to be obliged or required or compelled to ‖ to be certain, probable or likely to **2.** *n.* *(pop.)* something that should be done, seen, read etc. without fail

mus·tang (mʌ́stæŋ) *n.* a small, tough, half-wild horse of the southwest U.S. plains

mus·tard (mʌ́stərd) *n.* any of certain plants, having linear beaked pods and yellow flowers. Some species are grown as a fodder crop and as green manure, as well as for the seeds ‖ the powdered seed of these plants, used in preparing a sharp-tasting yellow paste eaten as a condiment ‖ the condiment made from the powdered seeds ‖ the color of the ground seed, a dark yellow

mus·ter (mʌ́stər) *v.t.* to assemble (troops) for inspection, roll call etc. ‖ to gather together ‖ *(fig., often with 'up')* to collect, summon ‖ (with 'out') to discharge from military service ‖ *v.i.* to assemble or gather together

mus·ty (mʌ́sti:) *comp.* **mus·ti·er** *superl.* **mus·ti·est** *adj.* smelling or tasting moldy, stale, e.g. of things kept in a damp place and shut in ‖ old-fashioned, out-of-date

mu·ta·ble (mjú:təb'l) *adj.* liable to change or capable of being changed

mu·tant (mjú:t'nt) **1.** *n.* *(biol.)* an individual organism with transmissible characteristics different from those of the parents, sufficient to form a new variety or even species **2.** *adj.* undergoing or produced by mutation

mu·tate (mjú:teit) *pres. part.* **mu·tat·ing** *past* and *past part.* **mu·tat·ed** *v.i.* to undergo mutation ‖ *v.t.* to cause mutation in

mu·ta·tion (mju:téiʃən) *n.* a changing or being changed ‖ *(biol.)* the hypothetical occurrence of new forms, arising through change in gene construction of the nucleus and differing sufficiently from the parent forms to constitute new varieties ‖ *(biol.)* the process by which such new forms arise ‖ *(biol.)* a mutant so produced ‖ *(linguistics)* umlaut

mute (mju:t) **1.** *adj.* not speaking, not uttering a sound ‖ permanently unable to utter meaningful speech, esp. as a result of being deaf from birth ‖ expressed by nonvocal means ‖ (of a letter) not pronounced though written, e.g. the 'e' in 'late' **2.** *n.* a person who cannot speak, esp. a deaf-mute ‖ a clip clamped on the bridge of a stringed instrument to deaden the resonance of the strings **3.** *v.t. pres. part.* **mut·ing** *past* and *past part.* **mut·ed** to deaden or soften the sound of

mu·ti·late (mjú:t'leit) *pres. part.* **mu·ti·lat·ing** *past* and *past part.* **mu·ti·lat·ed** *v.t.* to hack or tear off a limb or other important part of (a person or animal) ‖ to damage (something) seriously by destroying or removing some essential part of it

mu·ti·la·tion (mju:t'léiʃən) *n.* a mutilating or being mutilated ‖ the resulting injury

mu·ti·ny (mjú:t'ni:) **1.** *pl.* **mu·ti·nies** *n.* open revolt against lawful authority, esp. against naval or mili-

---

tary authority **2.** *v.i. pres. part.* **mu·ti·ny·ing** past and *past part.* **mu·ti·nied** to revolt against lawful authority, esp. naval or military authority

mutt (mʌt) *n. (pop.)* a mongrel dog

mut·ter (mʌ́tər) **1.** *v.i.* to speak in a low, indistinct voice with the lips nearly closed ‖ to murmur in annoyance or complaint ‖ *v.t.* to utter in a low, indistinct voice with the lips nearly closed **2.** *n.* muttered sound or words

mut·ton (mʌ́t'n) *n.* the flesh of a full-grown sheep as food

mu·tu·al (mjúːtʃuːəl) *adj.* given to each other by each of two people ‖ (of two people) having the same relationship to each other ‖ done, shared or experienced in common by all members of a group

muz·zle (mʌ́z'l) **1.** *n.* the part of the head consisting of the projecting jaws and nose in certain animals, e.g. dogs, wolves and bears ‖ a cagelike contrivance of wires or straps put over this part of an animal (esp. a dog) to prevent it from biting or eating ‖ the mouth of a gun, where the bullet or shell comes out when fired **2.** *v.t. pres. part.* **muz·zling** past and *past part.* **muz·zled** to put a muzzle on (an animal, esp. a dog) ‖ to prevent (criticism etc.) from being expressed

my (mai) *possessive adj.* belonging to or relating to me ‖ *(prefixed,* in forms of address) connoting affection, familiarity, condescension etc. ‖ used in interjections expressing surprise, shock, dismay etc.

my·o·pi·a (maióupiːə) *n.* the inability to see distant objects distinctly owing to a condition of the eye in which light from distant objects is brought to a focus before reaching the retina **my·op·ic** (maiópik) *adj.* relating to or affected by this condition

myr·i·ad (míriːəd) **1.** *n.* (usually *pl.* with 'of') a very large number **2.** *adj.* countless, very many

myrrh (məːr) *n.* a gum resin with a sweet smell and a bitter taste, obtained from the bark of trees in E. Africa and Arabia, and used in making perfumes, medicines, dentifrices and incense

myr·tle (mə́ːrt'l) *n.* a genus of fragrant evergreen plants native to W. Asia, long cultivated in Europe as ornamental trees

my·self (maisélf) *pron.* refl. form of 'I', *I knocked myself out* ‖ emphatic form of 'I', *I gave him the money myself*

mys·te·ri·ous (mistíəriːəs) *adj.* of, relating to or characterized by mystery, suggestive of hidden secrets ‖ difficult or impossible to understand or interpret

mys·ter·y (místəriː) *pl.* **mys·ter·ies** *n.* something that cannot be or has not been explained or understood ‖ the quality or state of being incomprehensible or inexplicable, or of being kept a secret ‖ a detective story ‖ *(pl.)* secret religious rites not revealed to the uninitiated, esp. those of ancient religions ‖ a religious tenet which rests on revelation and cannot be understood in terms of human reason

mys·tic (místik) **1.** *adj.* of or relating to mystics or mysticism ‖ of or relating to ancient religious mysteries ‖ having a hidden, secret, esoteric meaning ‖ *(loosely)* mysterious, enigmatic **2.** *n.* a person who believes in mysticism, has mystical experiences or follows a mystical way of life **mys·ti·cal** *adj.* of or relating to mysticism, spiritually true or real in a way which transcends man's reason **mys·ti·cism** (místisizəm) *n.* the doctrine or belief that direct spiritual apprehension of truth or union with God may be obtained through contemplation or insight in ways inaccessible to the senses or reason ‖ the experience of such direct apprehension of truth or union with God

mys·ti·fy (místifai) *pres. part.* **mys·ti·fy·ing** past and *past part.* **mys·ti·fied** *v.t.* to puzzle, bewilder, baffle ‖ to make mysterious, surround with mystery

mys·tique (mistíːk) *n.* a quasi-mystical set of attitudes adopted towards some idea, person, art or skill, investing it with an esoteric significance

myth (miθ) *n.* an old traditional story or legend, esp. one concerning fabulous or supernatural beings, giving expression to the early beliefs, aspirations and perceptions of a people and often serving to explain natural phenomena or the origins of a people etc. ‖ such stories collectively ‖ *(loosely)* any fictitious story or account or unfounded belief ‖ *(loosely)* a person or thing with no real existence

myth·ic (míθik) *adj.* mythical **myth·i·cal** *adj.* of, designating, relating to or existing in myth, *mythical gods* ‖ imaginary, nonexistent, *mythical wealth* **myth·i·cize** *pres. part.* **myth·i·ciz·ing** past and *past part.* **myth·i·cized** *v.t.* to interpret as a myth ‖ to cause to become a myth

my·thol·o·gy (miθólədʒiː) *pl.* **my·thol·o·gies** *n.* a body of myths, esp. those relating to a people's gods and heroes and to their origins, or those connected with a certain subject ‖ myths collectively ‖ the study of myths

N

N, n (en) the 14th letter of the English alphabet

nab (næb) *pres. part.* **nab·bing** past and *past part.* **nabbed** *v.t. (pop.)* to arrest ‖ *(pop.)* to get for oneself, by quick thinking or snatching

na·dir (néidiər, néidər) *n.* the lowest point, *the nadir of despair* ‖ the point of the celestial sphere diametrically opposite to the zenith

nag (næg) **1.** *v. pres. part.* **nag·ging** past and *past part.* **nagged** *v.t.* to scold or find fault with repeatedly ‖ *v.i.* to cause annoyance by scolding or repetition ‖ to cause persistent discomfort **2.** *n.* a person who nags

nag *n.* an inferior or aged horse

nail (neil) *n.* the hard thin covering on the upper surface of the ends of the fingers or toes of men, monkeys etc. ‖ the claw of a bird or animal ‖ a thin, usually

metal, spike, driven into an object (esp. wooden) to join it to another or to fix something to it **a nail in one's coffin** an experience etc. that is thought to shorten life **hard as nails** hardhearted ‖ capable of bearing hardship **to nit the nail on the head** to be or to find just the right words to describe or explain something accurately

nail *v.t.* to fix with a nail ‖ to secure ‖ to prove (a lie) to be false ‖ *(pop.)* to catch **to nail (a person) down** to obtain a definite promise or consent from (a person)

na·ive, na·ïve (nɑːíːv) *adj.* lacking worldly experience or guile ‖ innocently direct but lacking mental power

na·ive·té, na·ïve·té (nɑːíːvtéi) *n.* simplicity, artlessness ‖ a naïve act etc. **na·ive·ty** (nɑːíːvtiː) *n.*

na·ked (néikid) *adj.* without clothes ‖ (of parts of the body) uncovered || without vegetation, leaves etc. || without decoration || undisguised || (of a sword) out of its sheath || without supplementary material **with the naked eye** without the aid of an optical instrument **ná·ked·ness** n.

name (neim) **1.** n. a word or words by which a person, place or thing is known || a word or words by which an object of thought is known || a reputation **by name** with individual mention || by reputation but not by personal acquaintance **in name, in name only** by mere designation but not in reality **in the name of** using the authority of **to call (someone) names** to speak abusively to or of (someone) **to one's name** belonging to one **to put one's name down for** to apply for membership of (a club etc.) || to have one's name put on a list as wishing to receive (publicity etc.) or take advantage of (an offer of some sort) **2.** v.t. pres. part. **nam·ing** past and past part. **named** to give a name to || to identify by name || to appoint **3.** adj. well-known, renowned || bearing, or intended for, a name **náme·a·ble, nám·a·ble** adj.

name·less (néimlis) adj. not known by name || not mentioned by name || having no name || too subtle or mysterious to name

name·ly (néimli:) adv. that is to say

nap (næp) **1.** v.i. pres. part. **nap·ping** past and past part. **napped** to sleep for a short time, esp. by day **to be caught napping** to be caught off guard **2.** n. a short sleep, esp. by day

nap 1. n. the soft, fuzzy surface on cloth or wool material **2.** v.t. pres. part. **nap·ping** past and past part. **napped** to raise such a surface on, by brushing, stroking etc.

na·palm (néipɑm) n. a fuel, made from jellied gasoline, used in incendiary bombs and flamethrowers

nape (neip) n. the back of the neck

nap·kin (næpkin) n. a cloth used at meals for wiping the fingers and lips || a sanitary towel

nar·cis·sism (nɑ́rsisizəm) n. a tendency to erotic self-love || morbid or excessive self-admiration **nár·cis·ist** n. **nar·cis·sís·tic** adj.

nar·co·sis (nɑrkóusis) n. a state of unconsciousness induced by narcotics

nar·cot·ic (nɑrkɔ́tik) **1.** n. a drug which dulls sensibility, relieves pain and induces sleepiness || a drug subject to legal definitions as a narcotic regardless of its chemical features, e.g., LSD, marijuana **2.** adj. pertaining to or having the effects of narcotics **nar·co·tism** (nɑ́rkətizəm) n. narcosis || addiction to narcotics

nar·rate (næreit, næréit) pres. part. **nar·rat·ing** past and past part. **nar·rat·ed** v.t. to tell or write (a story) || to give an account of (events) || v.i. to act as storyteller

nar·ra·tion (næréiʃən) n. the act or process of narrating || an account or story || speaking or writing that narrates

nar·ra·tive (næréitiv) **1.** n. an orderly description of events || the act or art of narrating || that part of a prose work which recounts events (as distinguished from conversation) **2.** adj. of, relating to or having the form of a narrative

nar·ra·tor, nar·ra·ter (næreitər) n. a person who narrates, esp. someone providing connecting explanations or descriptive passages in a theatrical performance

nar·row (nærou) **1.** adj. small in width || restricted in scope || by a small margin, marginal || narrow-minded || thorough, very precise **2.** n. (esp. pl.) a narrow passage in mountains or between two bodies of water **3.** v.t. to make narrower || to fine down, limit further || v.i. to become narrower

nar·row-mind·ed (næroumáindid) adj. lacking tolerance or breadth of ideas, esp. in views of conduct

na·sal (néiz'l) **1.** adj. of or pertaining to the nose || (phon.) sounded with the velum lowered and often with the mouth passage wholly or partly closed so that the breath comes out of the nose || characterized by such sounds **2.** n. a sound so made

nas·ty (næsti:) comp. **nas·ti·er** superl. **nas·ti·est** adj. very unpleasant, repugnant || morally dirty || mean, vicious in a petty way || offensive || very bad || awkward to deal with || dangerous

na·tal (néit'l) adj. of or connected with birth

na·tion (néiʃən) n. a body of people recognized as an entity by virtue of their historical, linguistic or ethnic links || a body of people united under a particular political organization, and usually occupying a defined territory || a federation of American Indian tribes

na·tion·al (næʃən'l) **1.** adj. of or relating to a nation || this in contrast with 'international' || concerning the nation as a whole, nonlocal **2.** n. a member of a nation

na·tion·al·ism (næʃən'lizəm) n. devotion to one's nation || advocacy of national unity or independence

na·tion·al·ist (næʃən'list) **1.** n. a person who believes in or supports nationalism **2.** adj. of nationalism or nationalists **na·tion·al·ís·tic** adj. **na·tion·al·ís·ti·cal·ly** adv.

na·tion·al·i·ty (næʃənǽliti:) pl. **na·tion·al·i·ties** n. membership of a nation || existence as a nation || a nation or ethnic group || national character or quality

na·tion·al·i·za·tion (næʃən'lizéiʃən) n. a nationalizing or being nationalized

na·tive (néitiv) **1.** n. a person born in a given place, country etc., or whose parents are domiciled there at the time of his birth || one of the original inhabitants of a country, esp. at the time of its discovery by Europeans || an inhabitant as opposed to a visitor || a plant or animal which originated in a district or area, i.e. was not imported or introduced **2.** adj. belonging to a person or thing by nature, inherent || belonging to a person by birth || born in a particular place, country etc. || of or relating to the natives of a place || (of plant or animal life) not introduced || (of metals etc.) occurring in a pure state in nature

Na·tiv·i·ty (nətíviti:) n. the birth of Jesus Christ || the festival commemorating this, Christmas || a work of art depicting Christ as a newborn baby **na·tiv·i·ty** pl. **na·tiv·i·ties** birth

nat·ti·ly (nætili:) adv. in a natty way

nat·ti·ness (næti:nis) n. the state or quality of being natty

nat·ty (næti:) comp. **nat·ti·er** superl. **nat·ti·est** adj. very neat and tidy || jauntily smart

nat·u·ral (nætʃərəl, nætʃrəl) **1.** adj. pertaining to, existing in, or produced by nature || not supernatural || not artificial || pertaining to the study of nature || due to the operation of the ordinary course of nature || in accordance with normal human nature || free from self-consciousness, at ease || of food containing no chemical additives || illegitimate || (mus., of a key or scale) having neither sharps nor flats || (chem.) found in the crust of the earth **2.** n. (pop.) a person who takes naturally to an activity || (mus.) a note which is not a sharp or a flat

nat·u·ral·i·za·tion (nætʃərəlizéiʃən, nætʃrəlizéiʃən) n. a naturalizing or being naturalized

nat·u·ral·ize (nætʃərəlaiz) pres. part. **nat·u·ral·iz·ing** past and past part. **nat·u·ral·ized** v.t. to grant citizenship to (an immigrant) || to introduce (a plant or an animal) into a new habitat where it flourishes

nat·u·ral·ly (nætʃərəli:, nætʃrəli:) adv. in a natural or normal way || as one would expect, of course || by

nature ‖ in accordance with the laws of nature

na·ture (néitʃər) *n.* the physical universe and the laws and forces which govern changes within it ‖ the essential character of something ‖ (of a substance) the permanent property or properties ‖ (of persons) inborn character, disposition ‖ sort, type, *other things of that nature* ‖ (of sexual relations) normality, *against nature* ‖ the condition of man prior to civilization **by nature** as a result of inherent quality or temperament **from nature** (of a painting etc.) done in the presence of the subject **in** (or **of**) **the nature of** equivalent to, virtually

naught (nɔt) *n.* (*rhet.*) nothing, nothingness ‖ (*math.*) a zero, nothing (*NUMBER TABLE)

naugh·ti·ly (nɔ́tili) *adv.* in a naughty way

naugh·ti·ness (nɔ́ti:ness) *n.* the state or quality of being naughty

naugh·ty (nɔ́ti:) *comp.* **naugh·ti·er** *superl.* **naugh·ti·est** *adj.* (esp. of children and their behavior) bad, disobedient ‖ mildly indecent

nau·se·a (nɔ́ʒə, nɔ́ʃə, nɔ́zi:ə) *n.* a feeling of sickness with a desire to vomit ‖ strong disgust

nau·se·ate (nɔ́ʒi:eit, nɔ́ʃi:eit, nɔ́zi:eit) *pres. part.* **nau·se·at·ing** *past* and *past part.* **nau·se·at·ed** *v.t.* to cause a feeling of nausea in

nau·seous (nɔ́ʃəs, nɔ́zi:əs) *adj.* causing nausea

nau·ti·cal (nɔ́tik'l) *adj.* of ships, seamen or navigation

na·val (néivəl) *adj.* of, pertaining to or characteristic of a navy

nave (neiv) *n.* the central part of a church, extending from the main door to the choir or chancel

nave *n.* the central block or hub of a wheel, from which the spokes radiate

na·vel (néivəl) *n.* a small hollow in the middle of the belly, marking the point of attachment of the umbilical cord

nav·i·ga·ble (nǽvigəb'l) *adj.* (of rivers) allowing the passage of ships ‖ (of ships, balloons etc.) able to be steered or sailed

nav·i·gate (nǽvigeit) *pres. part.* **nav·i·gat·ing** *past* and *past part.* **nav·i·gat·ed** *v.t.* to direct the course of (a ship or aircraft) ‖ to travel by ship or aircraft across, over, up, down (a sea, river etc.) ‖ to direct (a path etc.) ‖ *v.i.* to direct the course of a ship, aircraft or car

nav·i·ga·tion (nǽvigéiʃən) *n.* the act or practice of navigating ‖ the science by which geometry, astronomy, radar etc. are used to determine the position of a ship or aircraft and to direct its course ‖ maritime traffic, esp. the quantity of ships in passage

nav·i·ga·tor (nǽvigeitər) *n.* a person who navigates or is skilled in navigation

na·vy (néivi:) *pl.* **na·vies** *n.* a state's ships of war ‖ the organization and manpower of a state's force for war at sea ‖ navy blue

navy blue a deep, dark blue

nay (nei) **1.** *adv.* (*rhet.*, for emphasis) and more than that ‖ (*archaic*) no **2.** *n.* a negative vote ‖ someone who votes against ‖ (*archaic*) a refusal or denial

neap (ni:p) *n.* a neap tide

neap tide a tide at the first and third quarters of the moon, in which the high water is lower than at any other time

near (niər) **1.** *adv.* at or within a short distance ‖ (of times and seasons) not far off **near at hand** at a conveniently short distance ‖ not far off in future time **to come** (or sometimes **go**) **near to** to approach, be or do almost **2.** *prep.* within a short distance of ‖ within a short time of ‖ within a small amount or degree of **3.** *adj.* not far distant in space ‖ not far distant in time ‖ not far distant in relationship ‖ only just successful, narrow ‖ (of a guess, estimate etc.) almost correct ‖ (esp. *superl.*, of a route) direct **4.** *v.t.* to approach ‖ *v.i.* to come closer in time

near·by 1. (níərbai) *adj.* near at hand, not far away **2.** (níərbái) *adv.* not far away

near·ly (níərli) *adv.* almost, *it is nearly midnight* ‖

closely, *nearly related* **not nearly** by no means, nothing like

near-sight·ed (níərsaitid) *adj.* myopic

neat (ni:t) *adj.* clean and tidy, orderly ‖ well made, well proportioned ‖ done with dexterity ‖ cleverly appropriate ‖ (of drinks) undiluted

neb·bish (from the Yiddish) (nébiʃ) *n.* (*colloq.*) a meek, ineffectual person

neb·u·la (nébjulə) *pl.* **neb·u·lae** (nébjuli:) *n.* (*astron.*) a diffuse, cloudlike mass of usually luminous gas, glowing under the influence of radiation from nearby stars **néb·u·lar** *adj.*

neb·u·lous (nébjuləs) *adj.* vague, formless ‖ of or like a nebula

nec·es·sar·y (nésisèri:) **1.** *adj.* that is required, that must be ‖ that cannot be done without ‖ (*philos.*) unavoidable, in the nature of things **2. néc·es·sar·ies** *pl. n.* things that one cannot do without, essentials ‖ (*law*) things essential for the support of a dependent or of someone unable through mental deficiency or immaturity to see to his own affairs

ne·ces·si·tate (nəsésiteit) *pres. part.* **ne·ces·si·tat·ing** *past* and *past part.* **ne·ces·si·tat·ed** *v.t.* to make necessary

neck (nek) **1.** *n.* that part of an animal which joins the head to the body, containing, in man, part of the spinal column, the windpipe, the gullet and important nerves and blood vessels ‖ the part of a garment that goes around the neck ‖ the narrowest part of an object, e.g. of a bottle ‖ a narrow stretch of land ‖ a strait ‖ (*archit.*) the lower part of a capital **neck or nothing** with willingness to risk everything **to break one's neck** (*pop.*) to go out of one's way **to risk one's neck** to put one's life in danger **2.** *v.i.* (*pop.*) to hug and kiss

nec·tar (néktər) *n.* (*Gk* and *Rom. mythol.*) the drink of the gods ‖ a sweet substance secreted by the nectaries of plants and collected by bees to make honey

nec·ta·rine (nȩktərí:n) *n.* a smooth-skinned variety of peach

need (ni:d) *n.* a condition necessitating supply or relief ‖ a requirement for subsistence or for carrying out some function or activity ‖ poverty ‖ obligation **at need** as and when needed **if need be** if necessary **to have need of** to need

need *v.i.* to be in want ‖ *v.t.* to be in need of, to require ‖ *verbal auxiliary* (*neg.* **I** (etc.) **need not, needn't** *interrog.* **need I** (etc.)?, *3rd pers. sing.* **one need**) to be under a specified necessity or obligation

nee·dle (ní:d'l) **1.** *n.* a slender pointed piece of steel, bone etc. with an eye for carrying the thread, used in sewing, darning etc. ‖ a similar, larger instrument without an eye, used in knitting etc. ‖ a surgical instrument of similar shape, often with a hollow center ‖ an object of similar shape, e.g. an obelisk ‖ a leaf of similar shape, e.g. of the pine ‖ the pointer of a compass or gauge ‖ a pointed tool used in engraving, etching etc. ‖ a phonograph stylus ‖ a sharp beam of wood used as a support in building **a needle in a haystack** something almost impossible to find **2.** *v.t. pres. part.* **nee·dling** *past* and *past part.* **nee·dled** (*pop.*) to tease or goad (someone) persistently

need·less (ní:dlis) *adj.* unnecessary **needless to say** self-evidently, obviously

need·y (ní:di:) *comp.* **need·i·er** *superl.* **need·i·est** *adj.* poverty-stricken

ne·far·i·ous (niféəri:əs) *adj.* (*rhet.*) wicked, iniquitous

ne·gate (nigéit) *pres. part.* **ne·gat·ing** *past* and *past part.* **ne·gat·ed** *v.t.* to render null and void, as though nonexistent

ne·ga·tion (nigéiʃən) *n.* denial, contradiction

neg·a·tive (négətiv) **1.** *adj.* having the effect of saying 'no', esp. to a question or request ‖ lacking in positive character ‖ not constructive ‖ not affirming the presence of something looked for ‖ (*math.*) of that which is measured by subtracting from zero on some scale of measurement ‖ opposite to a direction regarded as positive ‖ (*elec.*, of a charge) carried by electrons ‖

(*elec.*, of an electrode (cathode)) of a cell or other electric device that is at the lower potential ‖ (*photog.*, of an image) in which the tones or colors of the subject are reversed ‖ (*physiol.*) relating to movement away from a stimulus ‖ (*logic*, of a statement) disagreeing with a premise or earlier statement **2.** *n.* a proposition which denies or contradicts ‖ a reply which has the effect of saying 'no' ‖ (*math.*) a quantity less than zero ‖ (*photog.*) a developed negative image, usually on a transparent base from which positive prints may be made ‖ (*elec.*) a negative plate or element in a voltaic cell **3.** *v.t. pres. part.* **neg·a·tiv·ing** *past* and *past part.* **neg·a·tived** to reply 'no' to (a proposal) ‖ to contradict ‖ to prove false ‖ to neutralize

neg·a·tiv·ism (négətivĭzəm) *n.* an attitude of resistance to other people's suggestions ‖ a negative philosophy (skepticism, agnosticism etc.) **nég·a·tiv·ist** *n.* and *adj.*

ne·glect (niglékt) **1.** *v.t.* to fail to perform (an act, duty etc.), esp. through carelessness ‖ to fail to attend to, fail to care for ‖ to fail to attend to, disregard **2.** *n.* a neglecting ‖ negligence ‖ the state of being neglected **ne·gléct·ful** *adj.*

neg·li·gee, nég·li·gée (négliʒéi) *n.* a woman's light dressing gown, usually loose and flowing

neg·li·gence (néglidʒəns) *n.* want of attention or care ‖ an instance of this **nég·li·gent** *adj.*

neg·li·gi·ble (néglidʒəb'l) *adj.* so small or unimportant that it may be neglected, disregarded or omitted

ne·go·tia·ble (nigóuʃəb'l, nigóuʃiːəb'l) *adj.* which can be negotiated ‖ (*commerce*, of checks, bills of exchange, securities etc.) which can be transferred from one person to another, with or without endorsement

ne·go·ti·ate (nigóuʃiːeit) *pres. part.* **ne·go·ti·at·ing** *past* and *past part.* **ne·go·ti·at·ed** *v.i.* to discuss something in order to reach an agreement, confer ‖ *v.t.* to carry through (a transaction) by a process of discussion ‖ to transfer or cash (a check, securities etc.) ‖ (*pop.*) to succeed in accomplishing, crossing, climbing etc.

ne·go·ti·a·tion (nigouʃiːéiʃən) *n.* a negotiating ‖ (esp. *pl.*) discussion to bring about some result, esp. involving bargaining

ne·go·ti·a·tor (nigóuʃiːeitər) *n.* a person who negotiates

ne·gri·tude (negritu:d) *n.* **1.** the state and pride of being black **2.** pride in the cultural heritage of black people —**negritudinous** *adj.*

neigh (nei) **1.** *v.i.* to make the cry of a horse **2.** *n.* this cry

neigh·bor (néibər) **1.** *n.* a person living next door or relatively close to another ‖ a person or thing situated near or relatively near to another **2.** *v.t.* to be situated near to, adjoin ‖ *v.i.* (with 'on' or 'upon') to abut

neigh·bor·hood (néibərhud) *n.* a district ‖ the people in a district, *the whole neighborhood came* **in the neighborhood of** close to (a place) ‖ approximately

neigh·bor·ing *adj.* situated in the neighborhood

neigh·bor·ly (néibərliː) *adj.* friendly, sociable

nei·ther (níːðər, náiðər) **1.** *adj.* not either of two **2.** *pron.* not either of two (usually with a singular verb) **3.** *conj.* (negative correlative with 'nor' to connect two or more alternatives) ‖ nor yet **neither here nor there** irrelevant

nem·a·tode (némətoud) **1.** *n.* unsegmented worms including the hookworm. They are found free-living in soil and water, and are parasites of most animals and plants **2.** *adj.* of or relating to these worms

nem·e·sis (némisis) *pl.* **nem·e·ses** (némisi:z) *n.* retribution and punishment, esp. for evil on a vast scale ‖ an act of retributive justice

neo- (níːou) *prefix* now, recent ‖ a later revival of ‖ recently discovered or developed ‖ (of hydrocarbons)

recently classified

ne·o·lith (níːəliθ) *n.* a polished stone implement of the last period of the Stone Age

ne·on (níːɒn) *n.* an inert gaseous element found in the atmosphere and used at low pressure in a tube to convey an electronic discharge, which causes it to emit an intense orange-red light ‖ this light, esp. as used in illuminating advertisements

neph·ew (néfjuː) *n.* a son of a person's brother or sister

nep·o·tism (népətizəm) *n.* favoritism shown in the advancement of relatives, esp. by appointing them to offices for reasons other than personal worth **nép·o·tist** *n.*

nerve (nəːrv) **1.** *n.* any of the cordlike fibers or bundles of fibers of neural tissue that connect the nervous system with other organs of the body for the purpose of conducting nervous impulses to or away from these organs ‖ nervous fiber ‖ the vein of an insect wing ‖ the midrib or vein of a leaf ‖ courage ‖ (*pop.*) impudence ‖ (*pl.*) emotional upset, resulting in fright, excitement or irritability **to get on one's nerves** to annoy one **to have the nerve to do something** to be brave enough to do something ‖ (*pop.*) to be impudent enough to do something **to lose one's nerve** to lose self-confidence or courage **2.** *v.t. pres. part.* **nerv·ing** *past* and *past part.* **nerved** to invigorate or give courage to

ner·vous (nɔ́ːrvəs) *adj.* of or relating to the nerves or the nervous system ‖ originating in or affected by the nerves ‖ timid, apprehensive ‖ made up of nerves ‖ excitable, easily agitated ‖ self-conscious and without confidence

nerv·y (nɔ́ːrviː) *comp.* **nerv·i·er** *superl.* **nerv·i·est** *adj.* (*pop.*) impudent, brazen

nest (nest) **1.** *n.* the structure built or place chosen and prepared by a bird for holding its eggs during incubation and for rearing its young ‖ a place built or prepared by certain mammals (e.g. mice, moles, squirrels, rabbits) and by certain fish, reptiles, crustaceans and insects to rear their young in ‖ a brood or swarm ‖ a place of retreat, esp. snug and cozy ‖ a haunt of criminals etc., a den ‖ a collection of similar objects, esp. ones that fit into one another ‖ a gun emplacement **2.** *v.t.* to place in protective packing ‖ *v.i.* to build and occupy a nest ‖ to bird's-nest ‖ (esp. of pieces of furniture) to stack compactly together

nes·tle (nés'l) *pres. part.* **nes·tling** *past* and *past part.* **nes·tled** *v.i.* to settle oneself down comfortably and snugly ‖ to press snugly (against) ‖ to lie protected ‖ *v.t.* to press snugly (the head etc.) ‖ to make snug, settle protectively

net (net) **1.** *n.* an open-meshed fabric of cord, hair, nylon etc. ‖ a piece of such fabric used for catching fish, birds, insects or animals ‖ a piece of such fabric used for carrying, protecting, confining or dividing ‖ (*fig.*) a snare, trap ‖ a network ‖ (tennis etc.) a ball which hits the net **2.** *v. pres. part.* **net·ting** *past* and *past part.* **net·ted** *v.t.* to catch or enclose with a net ‖ to make (an article) in network ‖ to mark or cover with a network pattern ‖ (*tennis* etc.) to drive (the ball) into the net ‖ *v.i.* to make nets or netting

net (net) **1.** *adj.* clear of all charges and deductions ‖ clear of tare **2.** *v.t. pres. part.* **net·ting, nett·ing** *past* and *past part.* **net·ted, nett·ed** to gain as a clear profit **3.** *n.* clear profit

net·ting (nétiŋ) *n.* the act or process of making nets ‖ the act or process of fishing with a net ‖ netted wire, thread or string ‖ a piece of such material

net·tle (nét'l) **1.** *n.* a plant, esp. the stinging nettle and

---

the small nettle, with stinging hairs on the leaves. The young shoots are edible ‖ any of several unrelated plants, e.g. the dead nettle 2. *v.t. pres. part.* **net·tling** *past* and *past part.* **net·tled** to irritate or provoke (someone) by small wounds to his pride

net·work (nétwə:rk) *n.* a fabric of crossed threads knotted at the intersections ‖ any set of interlinking lines resembling a net ‖ an interconnected system ‖ a chain of radio or television stations

neu·ral·gia (nurǽldʒə, njurǽldʒə) *n.* a severe intermittent pain in a nerve or nerves, usually without change in the nerve structure **neu·rál·gic** *adj.*

neu·ri·tis (nuráitis, njuráitis) *n.* a chronic condition of a nerve involving inflammation and degeneration, and causing pain and loss of nerve functions in the affected region

neu·ro·sis (nuróusis, njuróusis) *pl.* **neu·ro·ses** (nuróusi:z, njuróusi:z) *n.* a nervous disorder not accompanied by structural change in the nervous system, and often with the symptoms of hysteria, anxiety, obsessions and compulsions **neu·rot·ic** (nurótik, njurótik) 1. *adj.* of or relating to the nerves ‖ of or affected by a neurosis 2. *n.* a person suffering from a neurosis **neu·rót·i·cism** *n.*

neu·ter (nú:tər, njú:tər) 1. *adj.* *(gram.)* of the third gender, neither masculine nor feminine, which exists in some highly inflected languages ‖ *(gram., of verbs)* neither active nor passive, intransitive ‖ *(bot., of flowers)* sexless, without stamens or pistils ‖ *(biol.)* sexually sterile or underdeveloped 2. *n.* *(gram.)* a word or form of neuter gender ‖ the neuter gender ‖ a castrated animal ‖ a sexually underdeveloped female insect, e.g. the worker bee

neu·tral (nú:trəl, njú:trəl) 1. *adj.* assisting or siding with neither of two opposing sides in a war, dispute, controversy etc. ‖ of, relating to or characteristic of a nation having declared a policy of neutrality ‖ having no distinctive color or other quality ‖ *(chem.)* neither alkaline nor acid ‖ *(phys.)* uncharged ‖ *(biol.)* neuter ‖ *(phon., of a vowel)* reduced in quality, esp. through lack of stress, so as to become a mid-central vowel (ə) 2. *n.* someone who, or something which, is neutral ‖ *(mech.)* a disengaged position of gears

neu·tral·i·ty (nu:trǽliti:, nju:trǽliti:) *n.* the quality or state of being neutral ‖ neutral status, e.g. of a seaport ‖ *(internat. law)* the status of a State committed to a declared policy of nonparticipation in a war between other States ‖ the status of any nation which remains neutral while hostilities between other nations are going on

neu·tral·i·za·tion (nu:trəlizéiʃən, nju:trəlizéiʃən) *n.* a neutralizing or being neutralized ‖ *(chem.)* the act or process of forming a salt from the reaction of an acid with a base

neu·tral·ize (nú:trəlaiz, njú:trəlaiz) *pres. part.* **neu·tral·iz·ing** *past* and *past part.* **neu·tral·ized** *v.t.* to render ineffective by counterbalancing ‖ *(internat. law)* to make (a country etc.) neutral ‖ *(chem.)* to modify or destroy the peculiar properties of (a substance), e.g. to destroy the acidity of a substance by allowing it to react with a base ‖ *(phys.)* to make electrically inert by combining equal positive and negative charges ‖ to make (a color) neutral, setting it off against or blending it with its complementary

neu·tron (nú:tron, njú:tron) *n.* a constituent of all atomic nuclei except that of the lightest hydrogen isotope

nev·er (névər) *adv.* not at any time, not on any occasion ‖ *(rhet.,* in emphatic negation) not at all **never mind** it doesn't matter, don't worry **never a. . .** not a

nev·er·the·less (nevərðəlés) *adv.* in spite of that

new (nu:, nju:) *adj.* made, discovered, known, heard or seen for the first time ‖ recently made, produced or arrived ‖ already in existence but discovered or known for the first time ‖ replacing the former ‖ different ‖ poorly adapted through inexperience ‖ freshly attempted ‖ additional, further ‖ renewed, *new strength* ‖ regenerated ‖ never before used, esp. not

previously worn ‖ (of land) about to be cultivated for the first time

new·el (nú:əl, njú:əl) *n.* the central pillar of a winding staircase ‖ the top or bottom post of a handrail on a staircase

new·fan·gled (nú:fǽŋg'ld, njú:fǽŋg'ld) *adj.* *(contemptuous)* modern and inferior

new·ly (nú:li:, njú:li:) *adv.* in a new way ‖ recently

new·ly·wed (nú:li:wed, njú:li:wed) *n.* a person recently married

news (nu:z, nju:z) *n.* recent information ‖ recent events, esp. as reported in newspapers, on the radio or on television

next (nekst) 1. *adj.* nearest in space ‖ following in time without anything similar intervening ‖ ranking second **next best** second best **next to** almost amounting to ‖ virtually **next to nothing** hardly anything 2. *adv.* in the place, time or order immediately following ‖ on the first occasion to come 3. *prep.* closest to

nib·ble (níb'l) 1. *v. pres. part.* **nib·bling** *past* and *past part.* **nib·bled** *v.t.* to take small, quick bites of ‖ *v.i.* (often with 'at') to take small, usually cautious, bites to show signs of interest (in a proposition etc.) 2. *n.* the act of nibbling ‖ an instance of this ‖ a small bite

nice (nais) *adj.* (used as a loose term of general approval) pleasant, kind, attractive, delightful, fine ‖ minutely subtle, evincing discrimination or fine judgment ‖ delicate, precise ‖ sensitive, alert ‖ *(ironical)* poor, unsatisfactory, *a nice mess we're in now* **nice and** *(pop., intensive)* agreeably, *nice and warm*

ni·ce·ty (náisiti:) *pl.* **ni·ce·ties** *n.* delicacy and precision ‖ the quality of requiring delicate treatment ‖ *(pl.)* fine details

niche (nitʃ) 1. *n.* a recess in a wall, esp. for a statue, vase etc. ‖ a place or position precisely suited to a person's talents 2. *v.t. pres. part.* **nich·ing** *past* and *past part.* **niched** to place in, or as if in, a niche

nick (nik) 1. *n.* a notch serving as a guide ‖ a shallow, usually unintentional, cut or chip **in the nick of time** just before it is too late 2. *v.t.* to make a nick in

nick·el (ník'l) 1. *n.* a metallic element which is hard and rust-resisting and takes a fine polish ‖ a five-cent coin in the U.S.A. and Canada 2. *v.t. pres. part.* **nick·el·ing** *past* and *past part.* **nick·eled** to plate with nickel

nick·name (níkneim) 1. *n.* a name by which a person is called familiarly, other than his real name 2. *v.t. pres. part.* **nick·nam·ing** *past* and *past part.* **nick·named** to dub with a nickname

nic·o·tine (níkəti:n) *n.* a very poisonous volatile alkaloid. It is the most active constituent of tobacco, from which it is obtained for use as an insecticide. It is responsible for the narcotic properties of tobacco

niece (ni:s) *n.* a daughter of a person's brother or sister

nig·gard (nígərd) *n.* a stingy person

nig·gard·ly (nígərdli:) 1. *adj.* stingy 2. *adv.* in a stingy way

nigh (nai) *adv.* *(archaic)* near **nigh on** *(archaic)* almost

night (nait) *n.* the time during which the sun is below the horizon ‖ darkness ‖ mental or moral darkness ‖ a night or evening as a point of time ‖ an evening performance of a play etc. **a night off** a night or evening taken off from work **a night out** a night or evening spent in entertainment outside the home **all night, all night long** throughout the night **at night** during the hours of darkness **by night** during the night as opposed to the day **night and day** continually **to have a good (bad) night** to sleep well (badly) **to make a night of it** to spend a night or evening in festivity

night·in·gale (náitiŋgeil) *n.* any of several European thrushes noted for the song of the male, usually heard at night, in the breeding season

night·ly (náitli:) 1. *adj.* happening every night or every evening 2. *adv.* every night

night·mare (náitmɛər) *n.* a terrifying dream ‖ a frightening experience or persistent fear **night·mar·ish** *adj.*

night·time (náittẹim) *n.* the period between dusk and dawn

nil (nil) *n.* nothing

nim·ble (nímb'l) *adj.* light and quick in motion, agile ‖ alert, quick-witted **ním·bly** *adv.*

nine (nain) **1.** *adj.* being one more than eight (*NUMBER TABLE) **2.** *n.* three times three ‖ the cardinal number representing this (9, IX) ‖ nine o'clock ‖ a playing card marked with nine symbols ‖ a team of nine members, esp. in baseball **dressed to** (or **up to**) **the nines** very elaborately dressed in an eye-catching way

nine·teen (náintí:n) **1.** *adj.* being one more than 18 (*NUMBER TABLE) **2.** *n.* ten plus nine ‖ the cardinal number representing this (19, XIX) **to talk nineteen to the dozen** to talk continually

nine·teenth (náintí:nθ) **1.** *adj.* being number 19 in a series (*NUMBER TABLE) ‖ being one of the 19 equal parts of anything **2.** *n.* the person or thing next after the 18th ‖ one of 19 equal parts of anything (1/19) ‖ the 19th day of a month

nine·ti·eth (náintí:iθ) **1.** *adj.* being number 90 in a series (*NUMBER TABLE) ‖ being one of the 90 equal parts of anything **2.** *n.* the person or thing next after the 89th ‖ one of 90 equal parts of anything (1/90)

nine·ty (náinti:) **1.** *adj.* being ten more than 80 (*NUM-BER TABLE) **2.** *pl.* **nine·ties** *n.* nine times ten ‖ the cardinal number representing this (90, XC) **the nineties** (of temperature, a person's age, a century etc.) the span 90–9 **the Nineties** the last decade of the 19th c.

nin·ny (níni:) *pl.* **nin·nies** *n.* a person who behaves stupidly

ninth (nainθ) **1.** *adj.* being number nine in a series (*NUMBER TABLE) ‖ being one of the nine equal parts of anything **2.** *n.* the person or thing next after the eighth ‖ one of nine equal parts of anything (1/9) ‖ the ninth day of a month **3.** *adv.* in the ninth place ‖ (followed by a superlative) except eight, *she is ninth biggest*

nip (nip) *n.* a small measure or drink of liquor

nip 1. *v. pres. part.* **nip·ping** *past and past part.* **nipped** *v.t.* to pinch, squeeze sharply ‖ (with 'off') to pinch off, remove by pinching ‖ (of frost) to damage (plants etc.) ‖ to benumb by cold **to nip in the bud** to stop (something) before it has time to develop **2.** *n.* a sharp pinch or bite ‖ a mildly stinging coldness

nip·per (nípər) *n.* (*pl.*) small pincers for gripping or pulling, e.g. forceps, pliers etc. ‖ the claw of a crustacean ‖ the incisor tooth of a horse, esp. one of the middle four

nip·ple (níp'l) *n.* a protuberance marking the opening of the mammary duct in mammals, e.g. of a woman's breast ‖ a teat on an infant's feeding bottle ‖ a protuberance shaped like this, e.g. on skin, metal, glass etc. ‖ a mechanical device for regulating the flow of a liquid

ni·tro·gen (náitrədʒən) *n.* a colorless, tasteless, gaseous element, the principal constituent of the atmosphere and an essential constituent of living matter

ni·tro·glyc·er·in, ni·tro·glyc·er·ine (naitrouglísərin) *n.* glyceryl trinitrate, an unstable oily liquid obtained by nitration from glycerol. It explodes, esp. on percussion, and is used in making dynamite and other explosives and as a vasodilator in certain heart ailments

nit·ty-grit·ty (níti:gríti:) *n.* the basic issues; the essential, practical point —**nitty-gritty** *adj.*

nit·wit (nítwịt) *n.* (*pop.*) an ignorant, stupid person

no (nou) **1.** *adv.* used to express negation, refusal, denial etc. ‖ (with a comparative adjective or adverb) not at all, not in any degree ‖ (expressing surprise or disbelief) surely not **2.** *pl.* **noes, nos** *n.* the word 'no' ‖ (*pl.*) those who vote against a motion

no *adj.* not any, *he has no money* ‖ not a, quite other than a, *he is no genius* ‖ hardly any, *it's no distance* ‖ (preceded by 'to be' and followed by a gerund) not any possibility of, *there's no accounting for tastes*

no·bil·i·ty (noubíliti:) *n.* the quality or state of being noble

no·ble (nóub'l) **1.** *adj.* illustrious by rank or birth ‖ of high character, lofty ideals etc. ‖ magnanimous, generous ‖ impressive, splendid, grand in appearance **2.** *n.* a nobleman or noblewoman

no·ble·man (nóub'lmən) *pl.* **no·ble·men** (nóub'lmən) *n.* a man of noble rank, a peer

no·ble·wom·an (nóub'lwụmən) *pl.* **no·ble·wom·en** (nóub'lwimən) *n.* a woman of noble rank, a peer

no·bly (nóubli:) *adv.* in a noble way ‖ of noble ancestry, *nobly born*

no·bod·y (nóubɒdi:, nóubʌdi:, nóubədi:) **1.** *pron.* not anybody **2.** *pl.* **no·bod·ies** *n.* a person of no importance

noc·tur·nal (nɒktə́:r'l) *adj.* of or relating to the night ‖ happening at night ‖ (*zool.*) active mainly at night

nod (nɒd) **1.** *v. pres. part.* **nod·ding** *past and past part.* **nod·ded** *v.i.* to bow the head forward quickly in greeting, agreement or command ‖ to bow the head involuntarily because of sleepiness ‖ to sway lightly ‖ to make an error through momentary inattention ‖ *v.t.* to bow (the head) ‖ to indicate (assent, agreement etc.) by bowing the head **2.** *n.* a quick forward nodding movement of the head

nod·u·lar (nɒ́dʒulər) *adj.* of, pertaining to or having nodules

nod·ule (nɒ́dʒu:l) *n.* a small rounded mass ‖ (*bot.*) a root nodule ‖ a small protuberance, e.g. a tumor or ganglion **nod·u·lose** (nɒ́dʒulous), **nod·u·lous** (nɒ́dʒuləs) *adjs*

no-fault insurance (nóufɔltinʃúərəns) *n.* legal provision in some states that motorists be reimbursed for medical expenses by their own insurance companies (sometimes with other provisions), no matter which party is at fault in an accident

noise (nɔiz) **1.** *n.* sound due to irregular vibration ‖ any sound which causes discomfort to the hearer ‖ (*loosely*) any sound ‖ a loud outcry, shouting, clamorous outbursts etc. ‖ irrelevant background sounds in a recording or film ‖ (*electr.*) radiation at several changing frequencies or amplitudes **2.** *v.t. pres. part.* **nois·ing** *past and past part.* **noised** (*rhet.,* with 'about', 'abroad') to spread by rumor ‖ to make noise ‖ to bring a group's attention to a subject **nóise·less** *adj.* silent

nois·i·ly (nɔ́izili:) *adv.* in a noisy way

nois·y (nɔ́izi:) *comp.* **nois·i·er** *superl.* **nois·i·est** *adj.* making or usually making noise ‖ full of noise ‖ (of color, costume, style) violent, loud

no·mad (nóumæd) *n.* a member of a people, tribe etc. without a fixed location, wandering from place to place in search of pastureland for thier flocks or herds, cultivable land or hunting grounds etc. ‖ a person who chooses to roam **no·mád·ic** *adj.* **nó·mad·ism** *n.*

no-man's-land (nóumænzlænd) *n.* an unowned area, esp. an extraterritorial strip between facing frontiers ‖ a belt of debated ground between entrenched enemies

nom de plume (nɒmdəplú:m) *pl.* **nom de plumes** (nɒmdəplú:mz) *n.* a pen name

no·men·cla·ture (nóumənklẹitʃər, nouménklətʃər) *n.* the names used in a particular branch of knowledge, esp. names which classify things ‖ systematic naming

nom·i·nal (naómin'l) *adj.* existing only in name or form, not real or actual ‖ very small, hardly worth the name

---

|| of or consisting of a name or names || normal; without unexpected deviation || (of shares etc.) bearing the name of a person || giving or listing names || (of an adjective or adverb used as a noun) substantival || (of wages) measured in money rather than actual purchasing power

nom·i·nate (nómineit) *pres. part.* **nom·i·nat·ing** *past and past part.* **nom·i·nat·ed** *v.t.* to name as a candidate || to appoint to office

nom·i·na·tion (nɒminéiʃən) *n.* a nominating or being nominated || the right of nominating || an instance of nominating

nom·i·na·tive (nóminətiv, nómnətiv) **1.** *n. (gram.)* the case of the subject of a verb, or of a word in agreement with it || *(gram.)* a word in this case **2.** *adj. (gram.)* describing or pertaining to the nominative || chosen or appointed by nomination

nom·i·na·tor (nómineitər) *n.* a person who nominates

nom·i·nee (nɒminí:) *n.* a person nominated for a position or office

non·cha·lance (nɒnʃəláns, nónʃələns) *n.* the quality of being nonchalant

non·cha·lant (nɒnʃəlánt, nónʃələnt) *adj.* casual || offhand, without enthusiasm || unperturbed

non·com·bat·ant (nɒnkómbətənt, nɒnkəmbǽtənt) **1.** *n.* a person in or attached to the armed forces whose duties do not include fighting || a civilian **2.** *adj.* not involving combats || of noncombatants

non·com·mit·tal (nɒnkəmít'l) *adj.* not committing the speaker to either side in a dispute or to any particular attitude or course

non·con·form·ist (nɒnkənfórmist) **1.** *n.* a person who does not conform to the beliefs or ritual of an established Church || a person who does not conform to rule or convention **2.** *adj.* of or relating to a nonconformist

non·con·form·i·ty (nɒnkənfórmiti) *n.* the beliefs or practices of nonconformists || lack of correspondence between things, e.g. between words and actions

non·de·script (nɒndiskrípt) **1.** *adj.* lacking distinctive characteristics || not easily classified or described **2.** *n.* a nondescript person or thing

none (nʌn) **1.** *pron.* not any, not one || *(rhet.)* nobody || not any such thing or person || no part, nothing **2.** *adv.* not at all, to no extent, by no amount

non·en·ti·ty (nɒnéntiti) *pl.* **non·en·ti·ties** *n.* a person or thing of no importance or distinction || nonexistence || something existing only in the imagination

non·fea·sance (nɒnfí:z'ns) *n. (law)* failure to do something, esp. something that should have been done

non·ob·jec·tive (nɒnəbdʒéktiv) *adj.* of a work of art which does not represent recognizable objects or natural appearances

non·pa·reil (nɒnpərél) **1.** *n.* a person or thing of matchless excellence || *(pl.)* very small pellets of colored sugar, used for decorating cakes **2.** *adj.* matchless

non·par·ti·san (nɒnpártizən) **1.** *adj.* not involved in political party ties || objective **2.** *n.* someone who is nonpartisan

non·plus (nɒnplʌs) *pres. part.* **non·plus·ing** *past and past part.* **non·plused** *v.t.* to perplex completely, baffle

non·prof·it (nɒnprófit) *adj.* not maintained or organized for profit

non·sense (nóns'ens, nóns'ns) **1.** *n.* senseless or meaningless talk, language or ideas || behavior that is foolish or not straightforward **2.** *interj.* I don't believe a word of it!

non·sen·si·cal (nɒnsénsik'l) *adj.* foolish, full of nonsense

non se·qui·tur (nɒnsékwitər) *pl.* **non·se·qui·turs** *n. (logic)* a conclusion that does not follow from the stated premise or premises

non·vi·o·lence (nɒnváiələns) *n.* the policy or practice of refusing to use violence, esp. as a way of meeting oppression

noo·dle (nú:d'l) *n.* a strip of pasta, served in quantity e.g. with meat or in soup

nook (nuk) *n.* a sheltered, hidden or quiet corner || a recess in a room, esp. beside a fireplace

noon (nu:n) *n.* 12 o'clock in the daytime

noon·time (nú:ntaim) *n.* midday

noose (nu:s) **1.** *n.* a loop in a rope etc. with a running knot which draws tighter as the rope is pulled, e.g. in a snare, lasso or halter || *(fig.)* a snare **2.** *v.t. pres. part.* **noos·ing** *past and past part.* **noosed** to entrap by a noose || to arrange (cord) in a noose

nor (nɔr) *conj.* used as a negative correlative with 'neither' to connect two or more alternatives || (often with inversion of subject and verb) and not

norm (nɔrm) *n.* an average, esp. one taken as a measure or standard of attainment || that which is normal

nor·mal (nórməl) **1.** *adj.* conforming to a norm, standard, regular || *(psychol.)* conforming to the standard or average for a particular type or group || *(loosely)* mentally or emotionally sound || approximating a statistical norm or average **2.** *n.* the usual or average state, level etc. **nor·mal·i·ty** (nɔrmǽliti) *n.* the state or quality of being normal

nor·mal·ly (nórməli) *adv.* in a normal way || in normal circumstances, under normal conditions

north (nɔrθ) **1.** *adv.* towards the north **2.** *n.* (usually with 'the') one of the four cardinal points of the compass || the direction to the left of a person facing east **the North** the northern part of a country **3.** *adj.* of, belonging to or situated towards the north || facing north || (of winds) blowing from the north

north·ern (nórðərn) *adj.* situated, facing or moving towards the north **North·ern** of or relating to the North

northern lights the aurora borealis

north·ward (nórθwərd, nórðərd) **1.** *adv. and adj.* towards the north **2.** *n.* the northward direction or part **north·wards** *adv.*

nose (nouz) **1.** *n.* the facial prominence above the mouth of man and other mammals, containing the nostrils and the nasal cavity, and serving as a respiratory and olfactory organ || the corresponding part of the head of other animals || a sense of smell, *the dog has a very good nose* || an ability to detect what is hidden, *a nose for scandal* || a forward or projecting part **on the nose** *(pop.)* exactly **to cut off one's nose to spite one's face** to do something hurtful to someone else knowing that it is also to one's own detriment **to follow one's nose** to go straight on || to do as instinct suggests **to lead someone by the nose** to make someone foolishly do whatever one wants him to **to look down one's nose at** to show disdain for **to pay through the nose** to pay an exorbitant price **to thumb one's nose** to make a rude, derisive gesture by holding one's thumb to one's nose, with the fingers of the hand outstretched **to turn up one's nose at** to scorn **under someone's nose** immediately in front of someone **2.** *v. pres. part.* **nos·ing** *past and past part.* **nosed** *v.t.* (with 'out') to detect by or as if by smelling || to work (one's way) forward || *v.i.* **to nose about** (or **around**) to investigate, esp. inquisitively **to nose forward** (of a boat, motor vehicle etc.) to advance slowly and as if with great care **to nose into** to pry into

nos·tal·gia (nɒstǽldʒə) *n.* a longing, usually sentimental, to experience again some real or imagined former pleasure **nos·tál·gic** *adj.*

nos·tril (nóstrəl) *n.* one of the external apertures of the nose

nos·y, nos·ey (nóuzi) *comp.* **nos·i·er** *superl.* **nos·i·est** *adj. (pop.)* offensively inquisitive

not (nɒt) *adv.* (with auxiliary verbs and 'to be', often suffixed in the contracted form *n't*) used to express a negative || (without a verb) used to introduce a clause, *not that it matters* || used as an emphatic denial, *not him!* || *(rhet.)* used to emphasize the opposite, *not a few, not often* || (with 'to say') used to introduce a stronger word or expression than one already used, *he is unkind, not to say cruel* || (with 'to mention', 'to speak of') used to introduce a further, usually negative, consideration **not half** very much

no·ta·ble (nóutəb'l) 1. *adj.* worthy of note 2. *n.* a prominent person, esp. of high social position **nó·ta·bly** *adv.* in a notable way ‖ especially, particularly

no·ta·rize (nóutəraiz) *pres. part.* **no·ta·riz·ing** *past* and *past part.* **no·ta·rized** *v.t.* to validate (a legal document) as a notary

no·ta·ry (nóutəri:) *pl.* **no·ta·ries** *n.* (in some countries) a public officer appointed to administer oaths, draw up and attest documents etc.

notary public *pl.* **notaries public** a notary

no·ta·tion (noutéiʃən) *n.* the representation of numbers, quantities or other things by a set or scale of symbols ‖ a system of symbols used for this purpose, e.g. 0 to 9 in the decimal scale of notation ‖ *(mus.)* the system of writing down a piece of music by means of symbols ‖ *(mus.)* the symbols themselves

notch (nɒtʃ) 1. *n.* a V-shaped cut or indentation, esp. one made to record ‖ a narrow pass or gap between mountains 2. *v.t.* to cut notches in ‖ (often with 'up') to record (a score etc.) by or as if by notches

note (nout) 1. *n.* (often *pl.*) a brief written record made to assist the memory ‖ a brief, informal, written communication ‖ a formal diplomatic communication, esp. one addressed personally, and usually in the first person ‖ a promissory note ‖ a bank note ‖ *(mus.)* a sound of definite pitch ‖ *(mus.)* a symbol denoting the pitch and duration of a musical sound ‖ *(mus.)* a key of a piano or similar instrument ‖ an indication of an underlying attitude or opinion **to compare notes** to exchange opinions and ideas about something **to strike a false note** to be unsuitable to the occasion ‖ to strike one as false **to strike the right note** to be, do or say what is exactly appropriate to the occasion **to take note** to pay attention ‖ (with 'of') to note mentally 2. *v.t. pres. part.* **not·ing** *past* and *past part.* **not·ed** to fix in the mind ‖ to pay special attention to ‖ (often with 'down') to make a written note of ‖ to take official notice of ‖ to call attention to

not·ed (nóutid) *adj.* eminent, well-known

note·wor·thy (nóutwȩ:rði:) *adj.* worthy of being noted, remarkable

noth·ing (nʌ́θiŋ) 1. *n.* no thing, not anything at all ‖ *(loosely)* not anything of importance or interest ‖ *(math.)* naught, zero ‖ *(pl.)* trifling remarks, *secret nothings* **for nothing** for no payment ‖ for no reward ‖ for no reason **nothing but** no less than **nothing doing** no activity or success **nothing doing!** *(pop.)* no I won't! **there is nothing for it but** there is no alternative but **there is nothing in it** it is untrue ‖ *(pop.)* there is no profit to be gained from it **to have nothing to do with** to leave entirely alone, have no dealings with **to make nothing of (something)** to be unable to understand ‖ to treat as unimportant ‖ to make little or no use of **to make nothing of (doing something)** to treat (the doing of something) as no hardship **to say nothing of** not to mention **to think nothing of** not to hesitate to, to do readily 2. *adv.* not in any way **nóth·ing·ness** *n.* the state of nonexistence ‖ the absence of any thing whatsoever ‖ total insignificance

no·tice (nóutis) 1. *n.* mental awareness, attention ‖ a printed or written announcement displayed publicly or inserted in a newspaper etc. ‖ a review (of a book, exhibition etc.) in a newspaper etc. ‖ previous warning ‖ a warning that a contract is to terminate ‖ a warning that something must be done within a certain time **at short notice** with very little advance warning **on notice, under notice** in the condition of having been warned 2. *v.t. pres. part.* **no·tic·ing** *past* and

past part. **no·ticed** to be or become aware of ‖ to write a notice of (a play etc.) **nó·tice·a·ble** *adj.* conspicuous ‖ capable of being noticed **nó·tice·a·bly** *adv.*

no·ti·fi·ca·tion (nóutifikéiʃən) *n.* a notifying or being notified ‖ a written or printed communication which formally gives notice

no·ti·fy (nóutifai) *v.t.* to inform (someone) of a fact

no·tion (nóuʃən) *n.* a conception, idea ‖ a general concept, *the notion of late* ‖ a theory or idea lacking precision or certainty ‖ an understanding, *she had no notion what he meant* ‖ a whim or fancy ‖ *(pl.)* inexpensive small useful articles (hairpins, needles, thread, combs etc.) sold in a store

no·to·ri·e·ty (noutəráiiti:) *pl.* **no·to·ri·e·ties** *n.* the quality or state of being notorious ‖ a notorious person

no·to·ri·ous (noutɔ́ri:əs, noutóuri:əs) *adj. (pejorative)* widely known ‖ widely known to someone's or something's discredit

not·with·stand·ing (nɒtwiθstǽndiŋ) 1. *prep.* in spite of 2. *adv.* nevertheless 3. *conj.* although

nou·gat (nú:gət, nú:gɑ) *n.* a confection of sugar, with almonds or other nuts or candied fruit or honey

nought (nɔt) *n.* *(math.)* a naught ‖ *(rhet.)* naught

noun (naun) *n. (gram.)* a word used to name a person, place, thing, state or quality

nour·ish (nʌ́riʃ, nɔ́:riʃ) *v.t.* to supply or sustain with food ‖ to foster or keep alive in the mind **nóur·ish·ment** *n.* food

nou·veau riche (nú:vourí:ʃ) *pl.* **nou·veaux riches** (nú:vourí:ʃ) *n.* someone newly rich who lacks social standing, culture etc.

nov·el (nɒ́vəl) *n.* an imaginative prose narrative of some length, usually concerned with human experience and social behavior, and normally cast in the form of a connected story **the novel** this genre of literature

novel *adj.* new in one's experience and having an element of the unexpected ‖ new and ingenious

nov·el·ist (nɒ́vəlist) *n.* a person who writes novels

nov·el·ty (nɒ́vəlti:) *pl.* **nov·el·ties** *n.* a novel thing or event ‖ the quality or state of being novel ‖ *(commerce)* a small manufactured article, esp. for personal or household adornment, usually without intrinsic value or merit

No·vem·ber (nouvémbər) *n. (abbr.* Nov.) the 11th month of the year, having 30 days

nov·ice (nɒ́vis) *n.* a beginner in some pursuit which demands skill ‖ *(eccles.)* a person received on probation in a religious order, prior to taking vows

now (nau) 1. *adv.* at the present time ‖ without delay ‖ used to introduce and emphasize a command, warning, reproof etc. ‖ used to introduce or emphasize a further development or transition in a narrative ‖ *(rhet.,* with following 'now') sometimes, *the countryside swept past, now mountains, now plains* ‖ at a certain time under consideration ‖ reckoning to the present moment **now and again, now and then** sometimes, occasionally **now now!** used to pacify, reprove etc. **now or never** used to affirm the necessity of grasping an opportunity which will not recur 2. *conj.* (often with 'that') because 3. *n.* (after 'by', 'for', 'from', 'up to', 'till', 'until' etc.) the present time

no·where (nóuhwȩər, nóuwȩər) 1. *adv.* not anywhere **nowhere near** at a considerable distance from ‖ not nearly **to get nowhere** *(pop.)* to make no progress towards being successful 2. *n.* a state of not existing or seeming not to exist ‖ a place that does not exist

nox·ious (nɒ́kʃəs) *adj.* harmful ‖ corrupting

noz·zle (nɒ́z'l) *n.* a projecting aperture at the end of a tube, pipe etc. serving as an outlet for a fluid etc.

nu·ance (nú:ɑns, njú:ɑns) *n.* a slight difference in color or in tone ‖ a slight difference in meaning, emotion

---

(**a**) æ, c*a*t; ɑ, c*a*r; ɔ f*aw*n; ei, sn*a*ke. (**e**) e, h*e*n; i:, sh*ee*p; iə, d*ee*r; ɛə, b*ea*r. (**i**) i, f*i*sh; ai, t*i*ger; ə:, b*i*rd. (**o**) o, *o*x; au, c*ow*; ou, g*oa*t; u, p*oo*r; ɔi, r*oy*al. (**u**) ʌ, d*u*ck; u, b*u*ll; u:, g*oo*se; ə, b*a*cillus; ju:, c*u*be. x, lo*ch*; θ, *th*ink; ð, bo*th*er; z, *Z*en; ʒ, corsa*g*e; dʒ, sava*g*e; ŋ, oranguta*ng*; j, *y*ak; ʃ, *fi*sh; tʃ, fe*tch*; 'l, rabb*le*; 'n, redd*en*. Complete pronunciation key appears inside front cover.

etc.

nu·bile (nú:bail, njú:bail, nú:bil, njú:bil) *adj.* (of women) of an age or condition to marry **nu·bíl·i·ty** (nu:bíliti:, nju:bíliti:) *n.*

nu·cle·ar (nú:kli:ər, njú:kli:ər) *adj.* pertaining to a nucleus ‖ of or relating to atomic energy

nu·cle·us (nú:kli:əs, njú:kli:əs) *pl.* **nu·cle·i** (nú:kli:ai, njú:kli:ai) *n.* the central part of a whole, having its own identity, about which the rest of the whole gathers or grows ‖ a center of activity, influence etc. ‖ *(anat.)* a mass of gray matter or nerve cells in the central nervous system ‖ *(astron.)* the brightest and densest part of the head of a comet, galaxy or other celestial body ‖ *(biol.)* the inner spheroid protoplasmic mass of a cell, essential to the life of most cells and to the transmission of hereditary character ‖ *(chem.)* a stable formation of atoms, e.g. the benzene ring ‖ *(chem., phys.)* the positively charged dense mass at the center of an atom

nude (nu:d, nju:d) **1.** *adj.* (of the body) naked ‖ (of representations of the body) undraped **2.** *n.* an undraped figure in painting, sculpture etc. ‖ such a figure in striptease etc. ‖ (with 'the') the state of being nude

nudge (nʌdʒ) **1.** *v.t. pres. part.* **nudg·ing** *past* and *past part.* **nudged** to push gently, esp. with the elbow ‖ to draw the attention of, or give a hint to (someone) with, or as if with, such a push **2.** *n.* such push

nud·ism (nú:dizəm, njú:dizəm) *n.* the belief in, and practice of, living naked, as being physically and psychologically beneficial

nud·ist (nú:dist, njú:dist) **1.** *n.* a person who accepts or practices nudism **2.** *adj.* of or pertaining to nudism or nudists

nu·di·ty (nú:diti:, njú:diti:) *n.* the state or quality of being nude

nug·get (nʌ́git) *n.* a small lump of native precious metal, esp. gold

nui·sance (nú:s'ns, njú:s'ns) *n.* a person or thing causing annoyance or trouble, or preventing one from the full enjoyment of a pleasure (freedom, quiet etc.) ‖ *(law)* an act or circumstance which causes annoyance or offense to another person or to the community at large

null (nʌl) *adj.* *(law)* having no force in law ‖ of, relating to or amounting to zero

nul·li·fy (nʌ́lifai) *pres. part.* **nul·li·fy·ing** *past* and *past part.* **nul·li·fied** *v.t.* to make null (esp. a contract etc.)

numb (nʌm) **1.** *adj.* lacking sensation, esp. as a result of exposure to cold ‖ lacking the ability to feel any emotion, eps. as a result of shock, fatigue etc. ‖ so possessed by a specified strong emotion as to be incapable of action ‖ characterized by lack of sensation **2.** *v.t.* to make numb

num·ber (nʌ́mbər) *n.* a word or symbol used to express how many or what place in a sequence ‖ a figure used to denote one thing in particular ‖ a total ‖ the property of being countable ‖ an item (e.g. of singing or dancing) performed on the stage, television etc. ‖ *(gram.)* a difference of form showing whether only one person or thing is meant, or more than one ‖ such a form itself ‖ *(pl.)* a large collection of persons or things ‖ numerical superiority **the numbers** an illegal lottery in which betting depends on a selected multidigit number turning up in some prearranged published context (e.g. stock market figures) **a number of** several **beyond** (or **without**) **number** too many to be counted **number one** the first of a series ‖ the best of many ‖ *(pop.)* oneself **one's number is up** *(pop.)* one is to die, through an ordeal etc. shortly **in number** in all, in total **to have some one's number** *(pop.)* to have penetrated someone's character or intentions

number *v.t.* to denote by a number ‖ to include within a collection ‖ to be equal to (a number) ‖ *v.i. (mil.,* esp. with 'off') to call one's number at a roll call

etc. **one's days are numbered** one has not much longer to live

num·ber·less (nʌ́mbərlis) *adj.* too many to be counted

nu·mer·al (nú:mərəl, njú:mərəl) **1.** *n.* the symbol, or group of symbols, of a number **2.** *adj.* pertaining to, having or denoting number

nu·mer·ate (nú:məreit, njú:məreit) *pres. part.* **nu·mer·at·ing** *past* and *past part.* **nu·mer·at·ed** *v.t.* to enumerate

nu·mer·a·tor (nú:məreitər, njú:məreitər) *n. (math.)* that part of a fraction, written above the denominator and separated from it by a horizontal or oblique line, which denotes the number of parts, specified by the denominator, that are taken of the whole, e.g. 2 in 2/3

nu·mer·i·cal (nu:mérik'l, nju:mérik'l) *adj.* pertaining to or denoting number

nu·mer·ous (nú:mərəs, njú:mərəs) *adj.* of large number, composed of many

nu·mis·mat·ic (nu:mizmǽtik, nju:mizmǽtic) *adj.* of or relating to the study of coins or currency **nu·mis·mát·ics, nu·mis·ma·tist** (nu:mízmətist, nju:mízmətist), **nu·mis·ma·tol·o·gy** (nu:mizmətɔ́ləʤi:, nju:mizmətɔ́ləʤi:) *n.*

num·skull, numb·skull (nʌ́mskʌl) *n.* a stupid person

nun (nʌn) *n.* a woman belonging to a religious order, esp. one under vows of poverty, chastity and obedience and living in a convent

nun·ner·y (nʌ́nəri:) *pl.* **nun·ner·ies** *n.* a communal residence of nuns

nup·tial (nʌ́pʃəl) **1.** *adj.* pertaining to marriage **2.** *n.* *(pl., rhet.)* a wedding, marriage

nurse (nə:rs) *n.* a person, usually a woman, trained to care for the sick or the infirm under the direction of a doctor ‖ a woman employed to look after young children ‖ a dry nurse ‖ a wet nurse ‖ an individual member of a species (of ant, bee etc.) whose function is to protect or care for the young of the species ‖ a tree planted to protect others during their growth

nurse *pres. part.* **nurs·ing** *past* and *past part.* **nursed** *v.t.* to take care of, be a nurse to (children, the sick, infirm etc.) ‖ to suckle (an infant) ‖ to hold protectively in the arms or lap ‖ to take special care of in order to promote growth or development ‖ to try to cure, esp. by taking care, *to nurse a cold* ‖ to take care of or consume slowly or sparingly in order to maintain a reserve ‖ to keep (a feeling etc.) alive in one's mind ‖ *(billiards)* to keep (balls) close together for a series of caroms ‖ *v.i.* to be a nurse ‖ (of a woman) to suckle a child ‖ (of a child) to feed at the breast

nurs·er·y (nə́:rsəri:) *pl.* **nurs·er·ies** *n.* a room set apart for children in a house ‖ a nursery school ‖ a place where young plants or trees are grown for subsequent transplanting ‖ a place where young animals, esp. fish, are raised ‖ a place or set of circumstances in which people acquire a certain training

nur·ture (nə́:rtʃər) **1.** *n. (rhet.)* food, or whatever nourishes figuratively ‖ *(rhet.)* upbringing, training **2.** *v.t. pres. part.* **nur·tur·ing** *past* and *past part.* **nur·tured** to provide for (growing things, e.g. children, plants etc.) those conditions which are favorable to their healthy growth

nut (nʌt) **1.** *n.* a dry, dehiscent or indehiscent one-celled fruit or seed consisting of a fleshy kernel (often edible) enclosed in a hard or tough shell or pericarp ‖ the kernel itself ‖ a piece of metal, usually polygonal, whose central hole has a screw thread which engages on a screw or bolt, to hold one thing to another ‖ *(mus.)* the piece located at the lower end of a bow by means of which the hairs are tightened ‖ *(pop.)* a person behaving in a crazy way **a hard nut to crack** a difficult problem to solve ‖ a difficult person to deal with in the way one would wish **2.** *v.i. pres. part.* **nut·ting** *past* and *past part.* **nut·ted** to gather edible nuts

nut·meg (nʌ́tmeg) *n.* a hard seed, used as a spice,

obtained from an evergreen tropical tree cultivated in the Moluccas and the West Indies ‖ the tree itself

nu·tri·ent (nú:tri:ənt, njú:tri:ənt) **1.** *n.* a substance serving as food, esp. for plants **2.** *adj.* nourishing

nu·tri·tion (nu:tríʃən, nju:tríʃən) *n.* a nourishing or being nourished, esp. the process of feeding

nu·tri·tious (nu:tríʃəs, nju:tríʃəs) *adj.* nourishing

nut·ty (nʌ́ti) *comp.* **nut·ti·er** *superl.* **nut·ti·est** *adj.* tasting like nuts ‖ producing nuts ‖ silly

nuz·zle (nʌ́z'l) *pres. part.* **nuz·zling** *past* and *past part.* **nuz·zled** *v.t.* to make pushing movements with the nose against, or into ‖ *v.i.* to thrust or press the nose against something or someone ‖ to snuggle or nestle

ny·lon (náiɒn) *n.* any of several polymeric thermoplastic amides formed into strong elastic thread by forcing a melt through fine jets ‖ the fabric made from this thread ‖ (*pl.*) stockings made of this

nymph (nimf) *n.* (*Gk* and *Rom. mythol.*) one of the lesser goddesses, portrayed as beautiful girls, inhabiting fountains, trees, rivers, mountains ‖ an insect in the stage between larva and imago in a species displaying complete metamorphosis

nym·pho·ma·ni·a (nimfəméini:ə) *n.* excessive sexual desire in a woman or female animal **nym·pho·ma·ni·ac** (nimfəméini:æk) *n.* a woman with nymphomania

O

O, o (ou) the 15th letter of the English alphabet

oaf (ouf) *pl.* **oafs, oaves** (ouvz) *n.* a stupid lout **óaf·ish** *adj.*

oak (ouk) *n.* evergreen tree and shrub native to the northern hemisphere and including some 500 species. Oaks yield some tannin and hard, durable wood ‖ this wood, used esp. in shipbuilding and furniture

oak·en (óukən) *adj.* (*rhet.*) made of oak

oar (ɔr, our) **1.** *n.* a long, usually wooden shaft with a flattened blade at one end, used as a lever in propelling a boat, the oarlock being the fulcrum ‖ an oarsmen **to rest** (or **lie, lay) on one's oars** to sit back and do nothing after a period of activity, out of contentment with what has already been achieved **2.** *v.t.* and *i.* to row

oar·lock (ɔ́rlɒk, óurlɒk) *n.* a device, usually U-shaped, fastened to the side or gunwale of a boat so as to hold the oar and provide leverage for its action

oars·man (ɔ́rzmən, óurzmən) *pl.* **oars·men** (ɔ́rzmən, óurzmən) *n.* a rower, esp. a proficient rower

o·a·sis (ouéisis) *pl.* **o·a·ses** (ouéisi:z) *n.* an area in a desert made fertile by the presence of water ‖ a quiet, peaceful place in the midst of turbulent surroundings

oat (out) *n.* (usually *pl.*) a genus of wild and cultivated grasses of temperate regions having a much-branched, panicle inflorescence ‖ (*pl.*) the crop or its yield **to feel one's oats** to feel important and powerful ‖ to feel frisky

oath (ouθ) *pl.* **oaths** (ouðz, ouθs) *n.* the invoking of God or some sacred or revered person or thing as witness of the truth of a statement or the binding nature of a promise ‖ the statement or promise itself ‖ a prescribed form used in making such a statement or promise ‖ a profane use of a sacred name or phrase

ob·du·rate (óbdərit, óbdjərit) *adj.* unyielding, in opinion or feeling, to influences seeking to effect a change

o·be·di·ence (oubí:di:əns) *n.* submission of one's own will to the will, expressed or otherwise, of another or to an impersonal embodiment of authority ‖ an instance of acting in such a way as to display this submission **in obedience to** according to the instructions or ruling of

o·be·di·ent (oubí:di:ənt) *adj.* submitting one's will ‖ (*rhet.*) not resisting

o·bei·sance (oubéisəns, oubí:səns) *n.* (*rhet.*) a movement of the body towards the ground, e.g. a curtsy, salaam etc., expressing very great respect for, or submission to, someone **to do** (or **make, pay) obeisance to** (*rhet.*) to perform an act of homage to

o·bese (oubí:s) *adj.* (of a person) very fat

o·bes·i·ty (oubí:siti:) *n.* (*med.*) the state of being obese

o·bey (oubéi) *v.t.* to be obedient to (a person, a principle etc.) ‖ (*phys., econ., chem.,* etc.) to act in conformity with ‖ *v.i.* to be obedient

o·bit·u·ar·y (oubítʃu:eri:) **1.** *adj.* relating to or recording the death of someone **2.** *pl.* **o·bit·u·ar·ies** *n.* a notice announcing a person's death, or an article about someone who has just died, esp. in a newspaper or journal

ob·ject (óbdʒikt) *n.* a perceptible body or thing ‖ a thing or conception towards which the action of the thinking mind, considered as subject, is directed ‖ (*phys.*) a source of light waves, of which an image may be formed by reflection or refraction ‖ an aim or purpose ‖ a person or thing exciting attention or emotion **price (money** etc.) **is no object** price (money etc.) need not be considered as a limiting factor

ob·ject (əbdʒékt) *v.i.* (usually with 'to') to be opposed, have an aversion ‖ (with 'to') to express opposition ‖ *v.t.* to present or put forth as an objection to a statement, proposal etc.

ob·jec·tion (əbdʒékʃən) *n.* an act of objecting ‖ a feeling of opposition, dislike ‖ a reason for objecting or statement of such reasons **ob·jec·tion·a·ble** *adj.* unpleasant, causing offense ‖ open to objection **ob·jec·tion·a·bly** *adv.*

ob·jec·tive (əbdʒéktiv) **1.** *adj.* of or pertaining to an object ‖ having a real, substantial existence external to an observer ‖ pertaining to an external object or event quite independent of the observer's emotions or imagination ‖ unbiased ‖ (*gram.*) of the case of an object governed by transitive verbs or prepositions **2.** *n.* an aim or goal ‖ (*mil.*) a place to be captured, destroyed etc. ‖ (*gram.*) the objective case ‖ something having an existence external to an observer ‖ (*optics*) the principal image-forming device in an optical instrument

ob·jec·tiv·i·ty (ɒbdʒektíviti:) *n.* the state or quality of

(**a**) æ, cat; ɑ, car; ɔ fawn; ei, snake. (**e**) e, hen; i:, sheep; iə, deer; ɛə, bear. (**i**) i, fish; ai, tiger; ə:, bird. (**o**) o, ox; au, cow; ou, goat; u, poor; ɔi, royal. (**u**) ʌ, duck; u, bull; u:, goose; ə, bacillus; ju:, cube. x, loch; θ, think; ð, bother; z, Zen; ʒ, corsage; dʒ, savage; ŋ, orangutang; j, yak; ʃ, fish; tʃ, fetch; 'l, rabble; 'n, redden. Complete pronunciation key appears inside front cover.

ob·jur·gate (óbdʒərgeit) *pres. part.* **ob·jur·gat·ing** *past and past part.* **ob·jur·gat·ed** *v.t. (rhet.)* to reprove strongly **ob·jur·gá·tion** *n.* **ob·jur·ga·to·ry** (obdʒɔ́:rgətɔri:, obdʒɔ́:rgətouri) *adj.*

ob·li·gate 1. (óbligeit) *v.t. pres. part.* **ob·li·gat·ing** *past and past part.* **ob·li·gat·ed** to place (someone) under a moral or legal obligation ‖ to cause (someone) to be indebted by rendering him a service **2.** (óbligit, óbligeit) *adj. (biol.,* e.g. of certain parasites) restricted to a particular condition

ob·li·ga·tion (obligéiʃən) *n.* an obligating or being obligated ‖ a binding legal agreement or a moral responsibility ‖ something which a person is bound to do or not do as a result of such an agreement or responsibility ‖ the restricting power inherent in such an agreement or responsibility

ob·lig·a·to·ry (əblígətɔri:, əblígətouri:) *adj.* which must be done, as required by civil or moral law ‖ required by authority ‖ of or being an obligation

o·blige (əbláidʒ) *pres. part.* **o·blig·ing** *past and past part.* **o·bliged** *v.t.* to cause (someone) by physical or moral means to do something ‖ to cause (someone) to be indebted by rendering him a service, favor etc. ‖ to render a service or favor to ‖ *(law)* to bind (someone) by contract or promise ‖ *(law,* of a contract etc.) to bind (someone) ‖ (with 'to') to be bound by feelings of indebtedness ‖ *v.i. (pop.)* to contribute entertainment

o·blig·ing (əbláidʒiŋ) *adj.* helpful and accommodating to others

ob·lique (əblí:k) *adj. (geom.,* of a line or plane surface) having a direction which makes an angle less or greater than a right angle with a specified line or surface of reference ‖ *(geom.)* (of a solid figure) having an axis not perpendicular to the plane of the base ‖ slanting, diverging ‖ *(anat.)* neither parallel nor vertical to the longer axis of the body or limb ‖ *(bot.,* of a leaf) having unequal sides ‖ indirect, implied but not specified ‖ *(gram.)* of other cases than the nominative and vocative

ob·lit·er·ate (əblítəreit) *pres. part.* **ob·lit·er·at·ing** *past and past part.* **ob·lit·er·at·ed** *v.t.* to remove all trace of, destroy ‖ to make illigible ‖ to blot out from memory, knowledge etc. **ob·lit·er·á·tion** *n.*

ob·liv·i·on (əblívi:ən) *n.* the state of being completely forgotten ‖ utter forgetfulness ‖ unconsciousness

ob·liv·i·ous (əblívi:əs) *adj.* totally unaware ‖ *(rhet.)* forgetful, neglectful

ob·long (óblɔŋ, óblɒŋ) **1.** *adj.* of a rectangular or oval figure or body with greater length than breadth or of greater breadth than height **2.** *adj.* of such a figure or body

ob·nox·ious (əbnókʃəs) *adj.* unpleasant, offensive

o·boe (óubou) *n. (mus.)* a woodwind instrument with a long, thin double reed and a range of two octaves up from B flat below middle C ‖ an organ stop producing a similar reedy quality **o·bo·ist** *n.* someone who plays the oboe

ob·scene (əbsí:n) *adj.* of that which depraves, esp. of that which offends or wounds the imagination in sexual matters ‖ offensive, revolting

ob·scen·i·ty (əbséniti:, əbsí:niti) *pl.* **ob·scen·i·ties** *n.* the state or quality of being obscene ‖ (usually *pl.*) an instance of this, esp. an obscene utterance

ob·scure (əbskjúər) *comp.* **ob·scur·er** *superl.* **ob·scur·est** *adj.* dim, insufficiently lit ‖ difficult to see, e.g. through insufficient light or because partially covered by mist, fog etc. ‖ difficult to understand through insufficient information or abstruse expression etc. ‖ (of places) remote, out-of-the-way ‖ (of people) not attracting attention, not known to people at large ‖ indistinctly heard

ob·scure *pres. part.* **ob·scur·ing** *past and past part.* **ob·scured** *v.t.* to make obscure ‖ to hide from view ‖ to dim the importance or glory of

ob·scu·ri·ty (əbskjúəriti:) *pl.* **ob·scu·ri·ties** *n.* the state or quality of being obscure ‖ something that is obscure

ob·se·qui·ous (əbsí:kwi:əs) *adj.* (of behavior or attitude) so self-abasing as to lack a proper degree of personal dignity

ob·serv·ance (əbzɔ́:rvəns) *n.* the act of obeying a command, law, rule etc. ‖ the keeping of a custom, day of obligation etc. ‖ a ceremonial keeping ‖ *(pl.)* the ceremonies or rites performed in keeping a religious feast, custom etc.

ob·serv·an·cy (əbzɔ́:rvənsi:) *n.* the quality of being observant

ob·serv·ant (əbzɔ́:rvənt) *adj.* giving careful attention ‖ quick to observe ‖ strict in observance

ob·ser·va·tion (obzərvéiʃən) *n.* an observing or being observed ‖ the faculty of observing something observed or learned from observing ‖ an act of scientifically observing and recording e.g. a natural phenomenon, often using precision instruments ‖ a record so made ‖ an expression of an opinion **ob·ser·vá·tion·al** *adj.* of or based on scientific observation

ob·serv·a·to·ry (əbzɔ́:rvətɔri:, əbzɔ́:rvətouri:) *pl.* **ob·serv·a·to·ries** *n.* a room or building sheltering instruments (telescopes, chronometers etc.) used by observers studying heavenly bodies ‖ a room or building for the study of other (e.g. meteorological) natural phenomena ‖ a structure which by its position commands an extensive view

ob·serve (əbzɔ́:rv) *pres. part.* **ob·serv·ing** *past and past part.* **ob·served** *v.t.* to look at with attention ‖ to comply with (a command, custom, law etc.) ‖ to celebrate ceremonially ‖ to watch or make a scientific measurement of with instruments ‖ to perceive, notice, come to know by seeing ‖ to comment ‖ *v.i.* to note attentively ‖ (with 'on' or 'upon') to comment ‖ to make observations with a precision instrument

ob·sess (əbsés) *v.t.* to occupy or engage the mind of (someone) to an inordinate degree

ob·ses·sion (əbséʃən) *n.* the state of being obsessed ‖ something or someone that obsesses **ob·sés·sion·al, ob·sés·sive** *adjs* of, being or causing an obsession

ob·so·les·cence (obsəlés'ns) *n.* the state of being virtually obsolete or the process of becoming obsolete ‖ *(biol.)* the process of becoming obsolescent or the state of being obsolescent

ob·so·les·cent (obsəlés'nt) *adj.* becoming obsolete ‖ *(biol.,* of an organ, feature, characteristic, species etc.) slowly vanishing, vestigial

ob·so·lete (óbsəli:t, obsəlí:t) *adj.* no longer in use, practice or favor, out-of-date ‖ *(biol.,* of a plant or animal organ) rudimentary or vestigial as compared with corresponding organs in related species

ob·sta·cle (óbstək'l) *n.* an obstruction, esp. one which prevents a forward movement or course of action

ob·stet·rics (obstétriks) *n.* the branch of medical practice which is concerned with the care of mothers before, during and immediately after childbirth

ob·sti·na·cy (óbstinəsi:) *n.* the quality or state of being obstinate

ob·sti·nate (óbstinit) *adj.* (of people) stubbornly adhering to an opinion or purpose ‖ (of people) stubbornly refusing to concede to reasonable arguments ‖ (of animals or things) stubbornly resisting attempts at controlling or manipulating ‖ *(med.)* stubbornly unresponsive to treatment

ob·strep·er·ous (əbstrépərəs) *adj.* noisily resisting control or defying commands

ob·struct (əbstrʌ́kt) *v.t.* to prevent or greatly impede (something) by placing an obstacle in its path ‖ to block from sight ‖ to close or practically close (a passage) ‖ to hinder (a person or his action or purpose) by creating difficulty or opposition ‖ to practice obstruction, esp. in parliamentary or legislative procedure ‖ *v.i.* to hinder, impede

ob·struc·tion (əbstrʌ́kʃən) *n.* an obstructing or being obstructed ‖ something which obstructs ‖ prevention of legislative enactment by filibuster **ob·strúc·tion·ism, ob·strúc·tion·ist** *ns*

ob·struc·tive (əbstrÁktiv) *adj.* of, being or producing an obstruction

ob·tain (əbtéin) *v.t.* to become the possessor of, secure for oneself or another **ob·táin·a·ble** *adj.* which can be obtained

ob·tuse (əbtú:s, əbtjú:s) *adj.* (*math.*) of an angle greater than 90° but less than 180° ‖ not keenly perceptive or sensitive ‖ not acutely perceived ‖ (*biol.*, of a plant or animal part) blunt-ended

ob·verse (ɒ́bvəːrs, ɒbvə́ːrs) **1.** *adj.* being a counterpart ‖ turned towards the spectator ‖ (*biol.*) having a base narrower than the apex **2.** *n.* the principal surface of a coin, medal etc. ‖ the other side of a question or statement ‖ (*logic*) an inference made by denying the opposite of an affirmation

ob·vi·ate (ɒ́bvi:eit) *pres. part.* **ob·vi·at·ing** *past and past part.* **ob·vi·at·ed** *v.t.* to remove, get rid of (a difficulty etc.)

ob·vi·ous (ɒ́bvi:əs) *adj.* not requiring proof or demonstration, self-evident ‖ easily seen, attracting immediate attention ‖ (*pop.*) undesirably prominent

oc·ca·sion (əkéiʒən) **1.** *n.* a set of circumstances associated with a point in time ‖ such a set of circumstances viewed as having special importance **on occasion** from time to time, when the circumstances require **to rise to the occasion** to act with the degree of skill, generosity etc. required by the special circumstances in which someone is placed **2.** *v.t.* to cause, directly or indirectly **oc·ca·sion·al** *adj.* occurring at irregular intervals of some length ‖ directly related to a special occasion ‖ designed for, and used, only on particular occasions

oc·ca·sion·al·ly (əkéiʒən'li:) *adv.* at irregular intervals of some length

oc·clude (əklú:d) *pres. part.* **oc·clud·ing** *past and past part.* **oc·clud·ed** *v.t.* to close up (a passage) ‖ to keep (something) from passing through a passage ‖ (*chem.*) to adsorb and retain (esp. gases)

oc·clu·sion (əklú:ʒən) *n.* an occluding or being occluded ‖ (*chem.*) the act or process by which some solid surfaces build up a local high concentration of the molecules of a gas or solute with which they are in contact ‖ (*meteorol.*) a front, wind, storm etc. that has been occluded

oc·cult (əkÁlt, ɒ́kʌlt) **1.** *adj.* beyond the range of normal perception ‖ secret, mysterious, esoteric ‖ dealing with magic, alchemy, astrology etc., *the occult sciences* **2.** *n.* (with 'the') that which is occult, the supernatural

oc·cult·ism (əkÁltizəm) *n.* occult beliefs or practices

oc·cu·pan·cy (ɒ́kjupənsi:) *pl.* **oc·cu·pan·cies** *n.* a taking or retaining possession by settling in or on something ‖ a residing or being resided in ‖ the act of becoming an occupant ‖ (*law*) the establishing of a right of ownership by taking possession of something which has no owner

oc·cu·pant (ɒ́kjupənt) *n.* someone holding temporary or permanent rights of ownership or tenancy over a place or building which he occupies ‖ someone who occupies a particular space, position etc. ‖ (*law*) a person who has established his right by taking possession of ownerless land or property

oc·cu·pa·tion (ɒkjupéiʃən) *n.* an occupying or being occupied, esp. by a military force ‖ a holding in one's possession, esp. as a resident or tenant ‖ an activity by which one earns one's living or fills one's time, or an instance of this **oc·cu·pá·tion·al** *adj.* arising from or pertaining to one's occupation or an occupation

oc·cu·py (ɒ́kjupai) *pres. part.* **oc·cu·py·ing** *past and past part.* **oc·cu·pied** *v.t.* to take, or have, possession of by setting in or on, esp. as resident or tenant ‖ to reside in ‖ to take or retain possession of by military force ‖ to fill (a space or period of time) ‖ (of someone) to fill (a position) ‖ to keep (one's mind) busy ‖ to keep employed

oc·cur (əkə́:r) *pres. part.* **oc·cur·ring** *past and past part.* **oc·curred** *v.i.* to happen, to be at a point in time or during a period of time ‖ to be found at a place or within a region ‖ (of an idea) to come into the conscious mind

oc·cur·rence (əkə́:rəns, əkÁrəns) *n.* the fact, act or process of occurring ‖ something which occurs

o·cean (óuʃən) *n.* the part (seven tenths) of the earth's surface which consists of salt water ‖ one of its chief expanses, *the Atlantic Ocean* ‖ any great expanse, *an ocean of sand*

o·ce·an·ic (ouʃi:ǽnik) *adj.* of, relating to or found in the ocean **O·ce·an·ic** *adj.*

o·cher, o·chre (óukər) *n.* a yellow or red form of hydrated ferric oxide occurring naturally and used as a pigment ‖ the color of yellow ocher

oc·ta·gon (ɒ́ktəgɒn) *n.* (*geom.*) a plane figure having eight sides ‖ an object or building having eight sides

oc·tave (ɒ́ktiv, ɒ́kteiv) **1.** *n.* (*mus.*) the note having twice or one half the frequency of a given note ‖ an organ stop sounding a note eight steps above the note played ‖ (*poetry*) a stanza of eight lines, e.g. ottava rima ‖ the first eight lines of a sonnet **2.** *adj.* consisting of eight parts or an octave ‖ (*mus.*) producing tones an octave higher, *an octavo stop*

oc·ta·vo (ɒktéivou, ɒktávou) (*abbr.* 8vo) *n.* the size of a book leaf formed by folding a sheet three times, giving eight leaves or 16 pages ‖ paper of this size ‖ a book having pages of this size

oc·tet, oc·tette (ɒktét) *n.* a musical composition written for eight players or singers ‖ a group of eight players or singers performing together ‖ a group of eight lines of verse

Oc·to·ber (ɒktóubər) *n.* (*abbr.* Oct.) the tenth month of the year, having 31 days

oc·to·pus (ɒ́ktəpəs) *pl.* **oc·to·pus·es, oc·to·pi** (ɒ́ktəpai) *n.* a marine cephalopod mollusk of fam. *Octopodidae*. Octopuses have eight arms equipped with suckers, and a large head including highly developed eyes and a strong beak ‖ something thought of as like an octopus, esp. a business organization having many branches and tending to get control of small local businesses

oc·u·lar (ɒ́kjulər) **1.** *adj.* of, by, with or pertaining to the eye **2.** *n.* the eyepiece of an optical instrument

odd (ɒd) *adj.* of a number which is not a multiple of 2 ‖ numbered, signified, known by such a number ‖ (placed after the noun) of a number or quantity which would only be accurate if an unspecified small addition were made, *200–odd people attended* ‖ lacking a mate to make a pair ‖ unusual, not fitting in to the accepted pattern ‖ miscellaneous, random ‖ occasional ‖ out-of-the-way

odd·i·ty (ɒ́diti:) *pl.* **odd·i·ties** *n.* something which or someone who does not conform to the accepted standard of normality ‖ the quality of being odd

odds (ɒdz) *pl. n.* the measure or ratio of inequality ‖ the chances of success or failure ‖ probability ‖ the advantage given by a bettor who appears to have the greater chance of winning a wager ‖ the ratio supposed to exist between the chances of winning or losing a wager and which is used as a basis for reckoning bets ‖ material difference **at odds with** in conflict with

o·di·ous (óudi:əs) *adj.* offensive, hateful

---

o·di·um (óudi:əm) n. hatred or condemnation of the community ‖ the state or quality of being subjected to such hatred ‖ the hatefulness of some act or stigma involved in some situation

o·dom·e·ter (oudómitər) n. an instrument used to measure distance traveled

o·dor (óudər) n. something which stimulates the sense of smell ‖ the characteristic smell of something

o·dor·if·er·ous (oudərífərəs) adj. diffusing an odor, either pleasant or obnoxious

o·dor·ous (óudərəs) adj. (rhet.) odoriferous

of (ʌv, ɒv) prep. in a direction from ‖ during ‖ expressing cause ‖ derived from ‖ originating or coming from ‖ produced by ‖ expressing deprivation, separation ‖ constituted by ‖ made from ‖ with respect to ‖ indicating the object of an action implied by the preceding agent noun, a reader of mysteries, a reader of ghost stories ‖ (in telling time) before, 5 of 1 ‖ set aside for, the hour of prayer ‖ indicating simple apposition, a terror of a child

off (ɔf, ɒf) 1. adv. at a distance in time or space ‖ so as to be at a distance ‖ so as to be separated in some way ‖ so as to deviate from a course, turn off into the lane ‖ so as to be no longer in operation etc., turn the light off ‖ so as to be smaller, fewer etc., the population is dying off ‖ away from one's usual activity etc., he took a year off ‖ into a state of unconsciousness, he dozed off ‖ (naut.) away from the wind ‖ (theater) offstage **off and on, on and off** from time to time, at frequent intervals **off with!** put off! remove! 2. prep. at a distance from, my house is off the main road ‖ in a direction diverging from, the street leads off the main road ‖ from the substance of, they lived off the garden ‖ so as to be separated from in some way, it fell off the table, off the point ‖ not up to a usual standard etc. in, off his game ‖ (pop.) abstaining from, she is off pastries ‖ (naut.) away from (shore) 3. adj. far, further away, the off side of the road ‖ in error, his answer is 30 points off ‖ not functioning, the light is off ‖ canceled, the match is off ‖ less, fewer, subscriptions are off this week ‖ free of the obligations of one's usual activity, she is always off on Saturday and Sunday ‖ not up to standard, an off day ‖ remote, an off chance ‖ circumstanced, well off ‖ wrong, his aim was badly off ‖ (pop.) odd, eccentric 4. n. the fact or condition of being off, offs and ons 5. interj. go away 6. v. (slang) to kill

off·beat (ɔfbí:t, ɒfbí:t) 1. adj. (pop.) of or having a style which departs from the ordinary or conventional 2. n. (mus.) the unaccented beat in a measure

of·fend (əfénd) v.t. to affront, hurt the feelings of (someone) ‖ to arouse feelings of disgust in ‖ v.i. (often with 'against') to act contrary to law, moral principle etc. ‖ to cause resentment or disgust **of·fend·er** n.

of·fense, of·fence (əféns, ɔfens, ɒfens) n. an act against the law ‖ a sin ‖ the act of offending someone ‖ the state of being offended ‖ something which causes someone to be offended ‖ the act of attacking ‖ (sports) a team in possession of the ball **to take offense** to consider oneself affronted ‖ to be scandalized

of·fen·sive (əfénsiv, ɔfensiv, ɒfensiv) 1. adj. insulting, intended to give offense ‖ revolting to the senses ‖ aggressive, ready or serving for attack 2. n. a large-scale attack ‖ an attitude of intended aggression

of·fer (ɔfər, ɒfər) n. something offered for acceptance, rejection or consideration ‖ an expression of willingness to give or do something ‖ a sum named by a would be purchaser in bargaining

offer v.t. to put forward for acceptance, rejection or consideration ‖ to hold out in the hand or present ‖ to present in order to meet a specific requirement ‖ (followed by an infinitive) to state one's inclination or preparedness (to do something), to offer to drive ‖ to make or give ‖ to present to notice or view ‖ to present for sale ‖ to bid, propose as a price ‖ to afford,

make available ‖ (often with 'up') to present (a sacrifice or prayer)

of·fer·ing (ɔfəriŋ, ɒfəriŋ) n. the act of offering ‖ something offered, esp. a gift to propitiate or appease ‖ a contribution to a church to help support it or its various activities

off·hand (ɔfhǽnd, ɒfhǽnd) 1. adv. without preparation or reference 2. adj. done without preparation or reference ‖ curt or casual to the point of rudeness **óff·hánd·ed** adj.

of·fice (ɔfis, ɒfis) n. a room or premises for administrative or clerical work, or for transacting business ‖ the personnel working in such an office ‖ a doctor's consulting room ‖ a position of authority in administration ‖ the fact or state of holding a public position of authority ‖ any religious rite, the office of the Mass ‖ an administrative division below a department

of·fi·cer (ɔfisər, ɒfisər) 1. n. a person holding a public appointment ‖ a policeman ‖ a person holding a position of responsibility and trust, in a company, club etc., e.g. a president, secretary or treasurer ‖ a person holding a commission to command others in the army, navy, air force etc. or merchant marine 2. v.t. to command as officer ‖ to provide with officers

of·fi·cial (əfíʃəl) n. a person who holds a public office or is employed on authorized duties

official adj. of or relating to an office or the administering of an office ‖ (of persons) holding an office ‖ vouched for by authority or an authority, an official report **of·fi·cial·dom** n.

of·fi·cious (əfíʃəs) adj. too zealously exercising authority ‖ offering unwanted services or intruding with unsought advice ‖ (diplomacy) unofficial

off·set (ɔfset, ɒfset) 1. n. a short lateral branch from a stem or root which is a source of propagation ‖ an offshoot (branch of a family) ‖ a spur from a range of hills ‖ a compensation or counterbalance ‖ (mech.) a bend made in a pipe to circumvent an obstacle ‖ (printing) setoff ‖ a method of printing in which the impression is first transferred from a flat plate to a rubber-surfaced cylinder and thence to paper 2. v.t. pres. part. **off·set·ting** past and past part. **off·set** to balance (one thing) against another, to compensate for ‖ to make an offset in (a wall, pipe etc.) 3. adj. of or printed by offset

off·shoot (ɔfʃu:t, ɒfʃu:t) n. a shoot, or branch from a main stem ‖ a subsidiary activity, by-product ‖ a collateral branch of a family etc.

off·spring (ɔfspriŋ, ɒfspriŋ) n. a child or children, progeny

of·ten (ɔfən, ɒfən) adv. frequently, repeatedly at short intervals ‖ in a number of instances

o·gle (óug'l) 1. v. pres. part. **o·gling** past and past part. **o·gled** v.i. to cast amorous glances ‖ v.t. to try to attract by giving enticing looks 2. n. an amorous or provocative glance

o·gre (óugər) n. a fairy-tale monster or giant who eats humans ‖ a hideous or cruel man **ó·gre·ish, o·grish** (óugriʃ) adjs

oil (ɔil) 1. n. one of a large group of substances which are typically viscous liquids or easily liquefiable solids. They are insoluble in water, and may have animal, vegetable (sometimes called fatty oils), mineral or synthetic origin. Their uses vary, according to their type: thus essential oils (e.g. petroleum) are used as fuels and lubricants, and others are used for their medicinal or food value ‖ petroleum ‖ a toilet preparation, hair oil ‖ (pl., painting) oil color ‖ a painting worked in oil colors **to pour oil on the flames** to intensify the violence of a quarrel **to pour oil on troubled waters** to exert a soothing influence 2. v.t. to lubricate with oil ‖ to treat with oil, e.g. so as to make flexible or watertight ‖ to convert into oil, e.g. by melting ‖ v.i. to become an oil, or become oily ‖ (naut.) to take oil aboard as fuel

oil·y (ɔili:) comp. **oil·i·er** superl. **oil·i·est** adj. containing, saturated with, or covered with oil ‖ having the characteristics of oil ‖ (of human behavior) heavily ingratiating, using suave hypocrisy, *an oily smile*

oint·ment (óintmən) *n.* an unguent used externally for healing or cleansing the skin, or for ritual anointing

OK, o·kay (oukéi, óukei) **1.** *adj.* all right, agreed **2.** *v.t. pres. part.* **OK'ing, o·kay·ing** *past* and *past part.* **OK'd, o·kayed** to approve, endorse **3.** *pl.* **OK's, o·kays** *n.* an endorsement or authorization

old (ould) **1.** *adj.* advanced in years ‖ having a specified age or duration ‖ of or pertaining to advanced age or to persons advanced in years ‖ having characteristics or manners of an elderly person ‖ no longer new ‖ stale ‖ inveterate ‖ former ‖ of, belonging to or done in the past ‖ antique ‖ of long standing ‖ familiar, accustomed, *the same old faces* ‖ out-of-date, *an old timetable* ‖ *(pop.,* often with 'good') used to convey either familiar regard or contempt, *good old Joe, a dirty old man* **2.** *n.* (only in the phrases) **the old** old people **of old** in the old days, from olden times

old·en (óuldən) *adj.* (only in the phrases) **in olden days, in olden times** belonging to a time long past

old-fash·ioned (ouldfǽʃənd) *adj.* of or belonging to former times ‖ out-of-date ‖ retaining the ideas, standards etc. of a past age

old fo·gy, old fo·gey (fóugi:) *pl.* **old fo·gies, old fo·geys** *n.* a bore with old-fashioned, ridiculously conservative ideas

o·le·o (óuli:ou) *n.* margarine

o·live (óliv) **1.** *n.* a small evergreen tree, with silvery green leaves, native to the Mediterranean region and now also cultivated in North and South America and Australia ‖ its small, oval, edible fruit (a drupe), which yields olive oil **2.** *adj.* of or pertaining to the olive tree or its fruit ‖ of the color olive ‖ (of a complexion) of a light brownish-yellow color

om·buds·man (ómbudzmən) *pl.* **om·buds·men** (ómbudzmən) *n.* a person appointed by a legislative body to receive, investigate and report on complaints by private individuals against government officials

om·e·let, om·e·lette (ómlit, óməlit) *n.* eggs beaten lightly together and cooked in a frying pan, often with cheese, ham, herbs etc.

o·men (óumən) **1.** *n.* a phenomenon or occurrence interpreted as a sign of good or evil to come ‖ *(rhet.)* presage or foreboding **2.** *v.t. (rhet.)* to portend

om·i·nous (óminəs) *adj.* threatening, foreboding

o·mis·sion (oumíʃən) *n.* an omitting or being omitted ‖ something which is left undone or left out

o·mit (oumít) *pres. part.* **o·mit·ting** *past* and *past part.* **o·mit·ted** *v.t.* to leave out either deliberately or through forgetfulness or neglect ‖ to neglect or fail (to do something)

om·ni·bus (ómnəbəs) **1.** *pl.* **om·ni·bus·es** *n.* a book collecting together several different but related works ‖ *(old-fash.)* a bus **2.** *adj.* relating to or containing several miscellaneous items, *an omnibus clause in a bill*

om·nip·o·tence (ɒmnípətəns) *n.* the state or quality of being omnipotent

om·nip·o·tent (ɒmnípətənt) **1.** *adj.* all-powerful, having unlimited authority **2.** *n.* **the Om·nip·o·tent** God

om·nis·cience (ɒmníʃəns) *n.* infinite knowledge or wisdom

om·nis·cient (ɒmníʃənt) *adj.* all-knowing, infinitely wise

om·ni·vore (ómnivɔr, ómnivour) *n.* an animal (e.g. a man, a pig) adapted to eat a wide variety of food, both animal and vegetable

om·ni·vor·ous (ɒmnívərəs) *adj.* feeding on animal and vegetable substances ‖ taking in everything, not selective, *an omnivorous reader*

on (ɒn, ɒn) **1.** *prep.* supported or suspended by ‖ occupying part of and supported by ‖ attached to ‖ located at, *a house on Madison Avenue* ‖ immediately beside, near by, *castles on the Rhine* ‖ concerning, about, *a book on magic* ‖ used to indicate membership, *on the advisory board* ‖ in a condition or state of, *on fire* ‖ deriving from, yielded by, *profit on a book* ‖ by, with or through the means of ‖ *(pop.)* at the expense of, *have a drink on me* ‖ having as a basis, *on whose authority?* ‖ added to, *brick on brick* **on time** punctual **to have something on someone** to be in possession of damaging information about someone **2.** *adv.* expressing forward movement or progress in space ‖ in a situation of covering or contacting, *put the lid on* ‖ by way of clothing, *what did she have on?* ‖ as a planned activity, *have we anything on tonight?* ‖ working, *he's on one Sunday in three* **and so on** and more of the same sort **on and off** intermittently **on and on** relentlessly continuing **to look on** to be an observer taking no active part **3.** *adj.* functioning, in action, *the light is on*

once (wʌns) **1.** *adv.* on one occasion only ‖ a single time ‖ at any time, ever, *if the news is once printed* ‖ formerly, at some time **more than once** several times **not once** never **once and** (or **once**) **for all** finally **once in a while** occasionally **one or twice** occasionally, a few times **2.** *conj.* whenever, *once it goes, it goes well* ‖ if ever, *once he realized what was meant, he would be furious* ‖ as soon as, *once they arrive, we can leave* **3.** *n.* one time, *once is enough* **all at once** at one and the same time ‖ suddenly **at once** immediately ‖ simultaneously, *you can't do two things at once* ‖ both, *she is at once clever and modest* **for once** on this particular occasion, for a change **this once** just on this particular occasion

on-com·ing (ɔ́nkʌmiŋ, ɔ́nkʌmiŋ) **1.** *adj.* approaching **2.** *n.* the approaching

one (wʌn) **1.** *adj.* being a single unit (*NUMBER TABLE) ‖ being a particular unit, creature or thing as compared with another or others ‖ so closely identified as to be virtually a single unit, *horse and rider were one* ‖ on an unspecified (occasion) ‖ a certain (person), *one John Brown telephoned* **for one thing** for one reason **one and the same** exactly the same **one or two** a few **taking one thing with another** on balance **the one** the only ‖ the (person, thing etc.) above all others **2.** *pron.* a certain person or thing, usually of a specified kind ‖ any person whatever ‖ *(rhet.)* someone, *like one possessed* ‖ *(pop.)* a blow, *he gave him one on the jaw* ‖ *(pop.)* a joke (at someone's expense), *that's one on you* **all in one** combined **for one** at least **one after another** successively **one and all** everyone without exception **one by one** one at a time **3.** *n.* the lowest of the cardinal numbers, denoting unity and represented by the figure 1 or the letter I ‖ a single unit, being or thing as compared with another or others ‖ one o'clock **at one** in agreement

on·er·ous (ɔ́nərəs, óunərəs) *adj.* burdensome, troublesome

one·self (wʌnsélf) *pron. refl.* form of ONE, *one owes it to oneself* ‖ emphatic form of ONE, *one would not choose it oneself* **by oneself** unaided ‖ alone, without a companion or companions **in oneself** at heart, basically

one-sid·ed (wʌnsáidid) *adj.* limited to one side ‖ partial, unfair ‖ having only one side

one·time (wʌntáim) *adj.* former ‖ occurring only once

one-track (wʌntræk) *adj.* obsessed by or dwelling boringly on one thing only

on·ion (ʌ́njən) *n.* a Middle Eastern plant widely culti-

(a) æ, c*a*t; ɑ, c*a*r; ɔ f*aw*n; ei, sn*a*ke. **(e)** e, h*e*n; i:, sh*ee*p; iə, d*ee*r; ɛə, b*ea*r. **(i)** i, f*i*sh; ai, t*i*ger; ə:, b*i*rd. **(o)** o, *o*x; au, c*ow*; ou, g*oa*t; u, p*oo*r; ɔi, r*oy*al. **(u)** ʌ, d*u*ck; u, b*u*ll; u:, g*oo*se; ə, b*a*cillus; ju:, c*u*be. x, lo*ch*; θ, *th*ink; ð, bo*th*er; z, *Z*en; ʒ, cor*s*age; dʒ, sava*g*e; ŋ, oranguta*ng*; j, *y*ak; ʃ, *fi*sh; tʃ, fe*tch*; 'l, rabb*le*; 'n, redd*en*. Complete pronunciation key appears inside front cover.

vated for its sharp-tasting edible bulb, consisting of layers arranged concentrically || this bulb, cooked or pickled or raw, served as food

on·look·er (ɔ́nlʊkər, ɔ́nlʊkər) *n.* a passive spectator

on·ly (óunli:) *adj.* single, sole || belonging to a unique class || alone worthy of consideration

only 1. *adv.* solely || merely, just || as little as || as the sole consequence, *it will only upset you* **if only** used to express a wish or regret **only just** by a very small margin, *he only just missed the train* || very shortly before or just recently **only too (pleased, true** etc.) very (pleased, true etc.) **2.** *conj.* but, except that, *he'd like to go only he promised not to*

on·set (ɔ́nset, ɔ́nset) *n.* an attack || the beginning of something thought of as an attack

on·slaught (ɔ́nslɔt, ɔ́nslɔt) *n.* a fierce attack

on·to (ɔ́ntu:, ɔ́ntu:) *prep.* to a position on or upon || on the trail or track of

o·nus (óunəs) *n.* responsibility, burden

on·ward (ɔ́nwərd, ɔ́nwərd) **1.** *adj.* advancing, directed forward **2.** *adv.* further forward, towards the front **ón·wards** *adv.* onward

ooze (u:z) **1.** *n.* an infusion of bark used in tanning leather || an oozing or that which oozes **2.** *v. pres. part.* **ooz·ing** *past* and *past part.* **oozed** *v.i.* to flow slowly and viscously, esp. through small bodily apertures || (of substances) to exude moisture etc. || *(fig.)* to escape or leak out gradually and imperceptibly || *v.t.* to exude (moisture etc.)

ooze *n.* mud saturated with water, esp. in a riverbed || a deposit of shells (e.g. of foraminifers), volcanic dust etc. deposited on the bed of a deep ocean **ooz·y** *comp.* **ooz·i·er** *superl.* **ooz·i·est** *adj.* containing, consisting of or like ooze || exuding moisture etc.

o·pac·i·ty (oupǽsiti) *pl.* **o·pac·i·ties** the quality or state of being opaque || the degree of being opaque || obscurity of meaning

o·pal (óup'l) *n.* an amorphous form of hydrous silica cut and used as a gem. Opals vary widely in color, and are usually iridescent

o·paque (oupéik) **1.** *adj.* of a medium whose molecular aggregation is such that radiant energy (usually light) cannot pass through it || obscure || obtuse, slow-witted || *(bot.)* not shining, dull **2.** *n. (photog.)* an opaque paint used for blocking out sections of a negative

o·pen (óupən) *adj.* not shut || admitting customers, visitors etc. || expanded, unfolded, outspread || free and unoccupied, not engaged, *he keeps Saturday mornings open for his students* || allowing passage, unblocked || exposed, unfenced, unobstructed, *open country* || not closed or covered || receptive || vacant || available || not definite, decided or concluded, *an open question* || undisguised, unconcealed || frank, concealing nothing in the mind || not restricted || widely spaced, *open ranks* || loose-textured, *an open weave* || (of water) free from ice or other water hazards || *(naut.)* not foggy || offering legal hunting or fishing, *the open season* || (of an account) not closed, still operative

open *v.t.* to make open || to unwrap, unfasten || to unfold || to begin, start (something), esp. functioning on a regular basis, *to open a bank account, to open a restaurant* || to declare formally open || to unblock, to make clear or passable || to loosen, to spread out, *to open ranks* || to free (bodily passages) of obstructions || to enlighten || to make more responsive or sympathetic || to make an incision in, to cut into || to start (a card game) by bidding or betting first || *v.i.* to become open || to expand, unfold || to break open, come apart || to begin, *the book opens with a quotation* || to become receptive to ideas, to become aware || (often with 'on' or 'into') to give access, *the house opens onto the moor* || (often with 'on' or 'into') to have an opening or outlet **to open fire** to begin shooting **to open one's heart** (or **mind**) **to** to confide one's feelings (or thoughts) to **to open the door to** to offer opportunity for **to open up** to prepare (a house) for

habitation || to make accessible, to develop || to become active || to speak without reticence, talk freely and readily

open *n.* (with 'the') the open air || (with 'the') open country || (with 'the') open water, water well out from shore || (with 'the') public knowledge, *why drag his secrets into the open?* **to come into the open** to come out of hiding or cover

o·pen·er (óupənər) *n.* someone or something that opens, esp. a gadget for opening cans || the first game in a series e.g. in baseball or bridge tournaments

o·pen·hand·ed (óupənhǽndid) *adj.* generous

o·pen·ing (óupəniŋ) **1.** *n.* a making or becoming open or an instance of this || an act of initiating or beginning something || a gap, an aperture || a beginning || a counsel's initial statement of his case in court || *(stock exchange)* the start of trading for the day || a vacancy in any kind of employment, esp. one thought of as an opportunity || the occasion or ceremony when an exhibition, production of a play etc. becomes available to the public || *(chess)* a recognized series of moves at the beginning of a game || a forest clearing **2.** *adj.* first, introductory, *opening remarks*

o·pen·ly (óupənli:) *adv.* frankly || without concealment, publicly

o·pen-mind·ed (óupənmáindid) *adj.* unprejudiced, ready to consider any suggestions or ideas

op·er·a (ɔ́pərə, ɔ́prə) *n.* a stage drama with orchestral accompaniment, in which music is the dominant element, the performers singing all or most of their lines || the score or libretto for such a drama || a company that performs such dramas, or a theater designed for the performances of these || such drama as an art form

op·er·a·ble (ɔ́pərəb'l) *adj.* admitting of a surgical operation || capable of being operated

op·er·ate (ɔ́pəreit) *pres. part.* **op·er·at·ing** *past* and *past part.* **op·er·at·ed** *v.i.* to be in action, function || to take effect || to perform an operation, esp. a surgical one || to carry out military movements || (of a stockbroker) to buy and sell || *v.t.* to put into action, cause to work || to manage, run

op·er·at·ic (ɒpərǽtik) *adj.* of, relating to, or resembling opera **op·er·át·i·cal·ly** *adv.*

op·er·a·tion (ɒpəréiʃən) *n.* the act of operating, or an instance of this || the way in which a thing works || *(pl.)* work, activity || an instance of the work done by a surgeon || a financial transaction, esp. a complex speculative one || one of the specific processes or actions in a sequence || *(computer)* the action indicated by a single instruction || a military action on a large scale **in operation** functioning or in working condition **op·er·á·tion·al** *adj.* of or connected with an operation, esp. a military one || (e.g. of an aircraft) fit for action

op·er·a·tive (ɔ́pərətiv, ɔ́pɒrətiv, ɔ́pəreitiv) **1.** *adj.* working, in operation || effective || relating to a surgical operation || having to do with physical or mechanical operations **2.** *n.* a hand (workman), e.g. in a factory || a private detective

op·er·a·tor (ɔ́pəreitər) *n.* someone who operates a machine or instrument, esp. a telephone switchboard || someone habitually engaged in large financial dealings || *(pop.)* a shrewd individual capable of evading legal restrictions

o·pi·ate (óupi:it, óupi:eit) **1.** *n.* a drug containing opium, used to induce sleep or deaden pain || anything that soothes or quiets **2.** *adj.* containing opium || having the effect of an opiate

o·pin·ion (əpínjən) *n.* a mental estimate || a belief or conviction, based on what seems probable or true but not on demonstrable fact || a formal expression by an expert of what he judges to be the case or the right course of action

o·pin·ion·at·ed (əpínjəneitid) *adj.* stubbornly affirming one's own opinions, esp. through complacency or arrogance

o·pi·um (óupi:əm) *n.* a habit-forming, narcotic drug

consisting of dried latex extracted from unripe capsules of the opium poppy

o·pos·sum (əpósəm) *pl.* **o·pos·sums, o·pos·sum** *n.* an American family of nocturnal, largely arboreal marsupial mammals native to the eastern U.S.A., about 15 ins in length not including the long, prehensile tail. When threatened with danger or caught, they pretend to be dead

op·po·nent (əpóunənt) *n.* a person who or group that opposes another in a fight, game, debate, contest etc. ‖ someone who opposes some idea, practice etc.

op·por·tune (ɒpərtú:n, ɒpərtjú:n) *adj.* suitable, well chosen ‖ timely **op·por·tún·ism** *n.* the practice of grasping at opportunities without regard for moral considerations ‖ the practice of adjusting one's policy in the light of each new situation as it arises, not according to principle or a plan **op·por·tún·ist 1.** *n.* someone who practices opportunism **2.** *adj.* characterized by opportunism **op·por·tu·nís·tic** *adj.*

op·por·tu·ni·ty (ɒpərtú:niti:, ɒpərtjú:niti:) *pl.* **op·por·tu·ni·ties** *n.* a set of circumstances providing a chance or possibility ‖ a stroke of good fortune which presents itself and can either be grasped or lost

op·pose (əpóuz) *pres.* **op·pos·ing** *past and past part.* **op·posed** *v.t.* to express disagreement with or dislike of, or make an effort to stop or prevent the activity, efficacy or success of ‖ to cause (something or someone) to be or act against something or someone

op·po·site (ɒpəzit, ɒpəsit) **1.** *adj.* in such a condition as to be pointing, looking, going etc. directly toward or away from someone or something ‖ utterly different ‖ (*bot.*, of leaves) placed in pairs, one on either side of the stem ‖ (*bot.*, of floral parts) so placed that one part is before the other **2.** *n.* something opposite **3.** *adv.* on opposite sides, in an opposite position or direction **4.** *prep.* in an opposite direction to or across from ‖ in a leading theatrical role complementary to, *he has played opposite her in many productions*

op·po·si·tion (ɒpəzíʃən) *n.* disagreement, hostility or resistance ‖ the political group or groups in a democracy opposing the party in power and working to take its place by constitutional methods ‖ any group opposing authority, or those opposing some proposal etc. ‖ the act of setting opposite, or the state of being placed opposite ‖ an opposite position ‖ (*astron.*) the position of a heavenly body when it is directly opposite another one, esp. the sun, as seen from the earth ‖ an opposite, a contrast ‖ (*logic*) a difference in quality and/or quantity between two propositions with the same subject and predicate **op·po·sí·tion·al** *adj.*

op·press (əprés) *v.t.* to treat with unjust harshness, esp. to rule over tyrannically ‖ to cause to feel mentally or spiritually burdened or physically as though suffocating

op·pres·sion (əpréʃən) *n.* an oppressing or being oppressed ‖ something that oppresses

op·pres·sive (əprésiv) *adj.* burdensome, unjustly harsh ‖ heavy, overpowering

op·pres·sor (əprésər) *n.* someone who oppresses

opt (ɒpt) *v.i.* to make a choice

op·tic (ɒptik) **1.** *adj.* relating to the eye or to vision **2.** *n.* an optical system or part of one (lens, mirror etc.) **óp·ti·cal** *adj.* optic ‖ designed to aid sight ‖ acting on or actuated by light ‖ relating to the science of optics

op·ti·cian (ɒptíʃən) *n.* a person who makes or sells optical instruments, esp. glasses to correct vision

op·tics (ɒptiks) *n.* the science of the origin, nature and laws of light

op·ti·mal (ɒptəməl) *adj.* most favorable, best

op·ti·mism (ɒptəmi̱zəm) *n.* the inclination to take a

hopeful view, the tendency to think that all will be for the best ‖ (*philos.*) the doctrine that this world is the best of all possible worlds **óp·ti·mist** *n.* **op·ti·mís·tic** *adj.* **op·ti·mís·ti·cal·ly** *adv.*

op·ti·mum (ɒptəməm) **1.** *pl.* **op·ti·mums, op·ti·ma** (ɒptəmə) *n.* the most favorable or best quality, number etc. ‖ (*biol.*) the most favorable condition (e.g. of moisture, temperature) in which an organism will flourish **2.** *adj.* most favorable or best possible for a certain purpose, or under certain conditions

op·tion (ɒpʃən) *n.* a choosing ‖ that which is chosen ‖ freedom of choice ‖ (*commerce*) the right, usually purchased, of buying or selling something at a certain rate and in a certain time **óp·tion·al** *adj.* not compulsory ‖ left to a person's discretion or choice

op·tom·e·ter (ɒptómitər) *n.* an instrument for measuring the refractive power of the eye **op·tóm·e·trist** *n.* someone who specializes in optometry **op·tóm·e·try** *n.* the profession of examining people's eyes for faults in refraction and prescribing corrective lenses and exercises

op·u·lence (ɒpjuləns) *n.* great wealth, riches ‖ profuse abundance

op·u·lent (ɒpjulənt) *adj.* extremely rich ‖ profuse, luxuriant

or *conj.* introducing an alternative, *clean or dirty* ‖ introducing something that explains or is a synonym for the preceding, *the egg should be hard-boiled, or cooked until the inside is firm* ‖ indicating vagueness or uncertainty, *nine or ten people were there*

or·a·cle (ɒrək'l, ɒrək'l) *n.* the place where the ancient Greeks and Romans went to ask the advice of their gods about the future ‖ a person regarded as an infallibly wise prophet, judge or adviser ‖ the advice, judgment etc. given by such a person

or·ac·u·lar (ɒrǽkjulər, ourǽkjulər) *adj.* of, relating to or being an oracle ‖ like an oracle, esp. in authority, obscurity or ambiguity

o·ral (ɔ́rəl, óurəl) **1.** *adj.* using speech rather than writing, spoken ‖ of or relating to the mouth ‖ done or taken by the mouth **2.** *n.* an oral examination

or·ange (ɒrindʒ, órindʒ) **1.** *n.* the reddish-yellow, globose or nearly globose fruit (a large berry) of any of certain trees of genus *Citrus* which are native to China and Indochina but widely cultivated in tropical and subtropical climates ‖ any evergreen tree of genus *Citrus* which bears oranges ‖ the color of the fruit, a reddish yellow **2.** *adj.* having the color orange

o·rang·u·tan (ɒrǽŋutæn, ourǽŋutæn) *n.* a large heavy reddish-brown anthropoid ape found in Borneo and Sumatra. It is well developed for arboreal life, having long, powerful arms, with hooking hands. Adult males may exceed 4 ft in height and 160 lbs in weight

o·rate (ɔréit, ouréit) *pres. part.* **o·rat·ing** *past and past part.* **o·rat·ed** *v.i.* to hold forth in a bombastic style

o·ra·tion (ɔréiʃən, ouréiʃən) *n.* a formal speech or discourse, esp. one given on a ceremonial occasion

or·a·tor (ɔrətər, órətər) *n.* a person who speaks in public, esp. one distinguished by his eloquence

or·a·tor·i·cal (ɔrətórik'l, ɒrətórik'l) *adj.* of or relating to an orator or to oratory ‖ given to using oratory

or·a·to·ry (ɔrətɔ́ri:, óurətɔ́ri:, óurətɔ́uri:, ɒrətɔ́uri:) *n.* the art of public speaking ‖ rhetorical speech or language

orb (ɔrb) **1.** *n.* a sphere ‖ a heavenly body, e.g. the sun, moon etc.; dv a round ball surmounted by a cross, as part of judicial or royal regalia in Christian countries, symbolizing the domination by Christ of secular power **2.** *v.t.* to form into a circle or sphere ‖ *v.i.* to move in an orbit ‖ to form an orb

or·bit (ɔrbit) **1.** *n.* the closed path, usually elliptical, in which a planet moves around the sun, or a satellite

---

(a) æ, c*a*t; ɑ, c*a*r; ɔ f*aw*n; ei, sn*a*ke. **(e)** e, h*e*n; i:, sh*ee*p; iə, d*ee*r; ɛə, b*ea*r. **(i)** i, f*i*sh; ai, t*i*ger; ə:, b*i*rd. **(o)** o, *o*x; au, c*ow*; ou, g*oa*t; u, p*oo*r; ɔi, r*oy*al. **(u)** ʌ, d*u*ck; u, b*u*ll; u:, g*oo*se; ə, b*a*cillus; ju:, c*u*be. x, lo*ch*; θ, *th*ink; ð, bo*th*er; z, *Z*en; ʒ, cor*s*age; dʒ, sava*ge*; ŋ, oranguta*ng*; j, *y*ak; ʃ, fi*sh*; tʃ, fe*tch*; 'l, rabb*le*; 'n, redd*en*. Complete pronunciation key appears inside front cover.

around the parent body || the path of a body (e.g. a particle) in a force field || a sphere of influence or region of activity || the bony socket of the eye **2.** *v.i.* to move in an orbit || *v.t.* to revolve in an orbit around || to cause to revolve in an orbit

or·bit·al (ɔ́rbit'l) *adj.* of, relating to or describing an orbit

or·chard (ɔ́rtʃərd) *n.* a stretch of land with cultivated fruit trees || the trees collectively

or·ches·tra (ɔ́rkistrə, ɔ́rkestrə) *n.* a large body of instrumental musicians who perform symphonies etc., or a smaller group of musicians who play dinner music or dance music || the instruments of either of such a group || the orchestra pit in a theater || the section of seats on the main floor of a theater, esp. the section nearest the stage || the main floor of a theater **or·ches·tral** (ɔrkéstrəl) *adj.*

or·chid (ɔ́rkid) *n.* a family of perennial monocotyledonous terrestrial plants, epiphytes or saprophytes. They are cosmopolitan, and very abundant in the Tropics. The flowers differ from the normal monocotyledonous type, being more varied and complicated, with specialized pollinia and a twisted ovary || (*pl.*) compliments, praise **or·chi·da·ceous** (ɔrkidéiʃəs) *adj.* of, like or being a member of *Orchidaceae*

or·dain (ɔrdéin) *v.t.* to consecrate (someone) a Christian deacon, priest etc. || to qualify as a rabbi || to appoint, decree, establish

or·deal (ɔrdíːl, ɔ́rdiːl, ərdíːəl) *n.* a severe or exacting experience that tests character or powers of endurance

or·der (ɔ́rdər) *n.* a sequence, arrangement, the way one thing follows another || the condition in which everything is controlled as it should be, is in its right place, performing its correct function etc. || the proper working of the law, peaceful regularity of public life, *the police restored order after the riots* || the rules, laws and structures which constitute a society, *the social order* || (*philos.*) the natural, moral or spiritual system governing things in the universe || an authoritative instruction, command || (*commerce*) an instruction to a tradesman or manufacturer to supply goods || the goods supplied || something ordered, e.g. in a restaurant || (*archit.*) one of the orders of architecture || a military or monastic brotherhood under discipline || a secret fraternity united by common interest or for social purposes, *the Masonic order* || (*pl., eccles.*) ordination, *to take holy orders* || (*eccles.*) a prescribed form of service || (*eccles.*) one of the grades in the Christian ministry || (*biol.*, in plant and animal classification) a category of closely allied organisms between family and class || (*pl., mil.*) commands issued by an officer in command or by the competent authority, *standing orders* || (*law*) a decision by a court or judge, usually not a final judgment || (*finance*) a written direction to pay money or surrender goods || (*math.*) degree of complexity, *an equation of the first order* **in order** in sequence || in good condition || according to the rules, e.g. of a meeting etc. **in order that** with the intention that **in order to** (+ infin.) for the purpose of (+ pres. part.) **in short order** with no delay **of the order of** about as many as or as large as **on order** (of goods) requested but not yet delivered **on the order of** similar to, roughly like in style **out of order** out of proper sequence || not according to the rules || not in working condition || inappropriate **to order** according to the specific requirements of the buyer, *a suit made to order*

order *v.t.* to put in order || to give authoritative instruction to (someone) to do something or for (something) to be done || (of fate) to ordain || to request (goods etc.) to be supplied || to prescribe as a remedy, *the doctor ordered complete rest* **to order arms** (*mil.*) to bring the rifle to an upright position with its butt against one's right foot, and remain at attention

or·der·li·ness (ɔ́rdərliːnis) *n.* the quality or state of being orderly

or·der·ly (ɔ́rdərliː) **1.** *adj.* in good order, well arranged || disciplined and peaceable || (*mil.*) of, relating to or charged with the execution or sending out of orders **2.** *pl.* **or·der·lies** *n.* a soldier attendant on an officer to carry messages, orders, etc. || an attendant in charge of cleaning etc. in a hospital, often in a military hospital

or·di·nance (ɔ́rd'nəns) *n.* a decree or authoritative order, e.g. of a council or municipal government || a religious ceremony or rite that is not a sacrament

or·di·nar·i·ly (ɔrd'néərili:, ɔ́rd'nɛrili:) *adv.* generally, in the usual course of events

or·di·nar·y (ɔ́rdinɛri:) *adj.* usual || not exceptional or unusual, undistinguished

ord·nance (ɔ́rdnəns) *n.* heavy guns, artillery || military stores and materials (ammunition, small arms etc.) || the branch of the U.S. army concerned with the supply of essential stores and the maintenance of arsenals and depots

ore (ɔr, our) *n.* a naturally occurring metallic compound from which the metal can be extracted

or·gan (ɔ́rgən) *n.* a musical wind instrument, in its modern forms the largest, most versatile, and most powerful of instruments || any of several similar keyboard instruments without pipes, e.g. the reed organ and the electric organ || any of certain simple wind instruments of a specified kind, e.g. a barrel organ || a structure of an animal (e.g. lung, stomach) or of a plant (e.g. pistil, leaf) adapted for some specific and usually essential function || a means or instrument of action, *parliament is the chief organ of government in England* || a medium of communication of opinion or information, esp. a publication attached to some group, party etc.

or·gan·ic (ɔrgǽnik) *adj.* of or relating to an organ of the body || (*med.*) affecting the structure of the organism or an organ || (*biol.*) having the physical structure characteristic of living organisms || (*chem.*) of or relating to the compounds of carbon (other than some of its simpler compounds) || inherent, structural || organized, systematic, esp. having parts that work together in a way that recalls the complex interactions of bodily organs || (*law*) pertaining to the fundamental and constitutional laws by which countries or states are governed **or·gán·i·cal·ly** *adv.*

or·gan·ism (ɔ́rgənizəm) *n.* (*biol.*) a living being or entity adapted for living by means of organs separate in function but dependent on one another || any living being or its material structure || any complete whole which by the integration, interaction and mutual dependence of its parts is comparable to a living being

or·gan·ist (ɔ́rgənist) *n.* a person who plays the organ

or·gan·i·za·tion (ɔrgənizéiʃən) *n.* an organizing or being organized || the way in which something is organized || an association or society of people working together to some end, e.g. a business firm or a political party **or·gan·i·zá·tion·al** *adj.*

or·gan·ize (ɔ́rgənaiz) *pres. part.* **or·gan·iz·ing** *past* and *past part.* **or·gan·ized** *v.t.* to give an orderly or organic structure to, arrrange the parts of (something) so that it works as a whole || to make arrangements for, prepare || to unionize (workers or an industry) || *v.i.* to become organic or systematized **ór·gan·iz·er** *n.* someone who or something that organizes || (*biol.*) a substance that acts as an inductor in embryonic development

or·gy (ɔ́rdʒiː) *pl.* **or·gies** *n.* a bout of debauchery || a display of excessive indulgence, *an orgy of self-pity*

or·i·ent (ɔ́riːent, óuriːent) *v.t.* to determine the position of (someone or something) with reference to the points of the compass || to place with regard to points of the compass || to adjust (someone or something) to the surroundings or a situation || to turn or guide in a specified direction || to cause to face eastward, esp. to build (a church) with its altar at the eastern end, or bury (a body) with the feet pointing east

Or·i·en·tal (ɔriːént'l, ouriːént'l) **1.** *adj.* of, relating to, characteristic of or coming from the Orient **2.** *n.* a native or inhabitant of the Orient, esp. of the Far East

or·i·en·tate (ɔ́ri:enteit, óuri:enteit) *pres. part.* **or·i·en·tat·ing** *past* and *past part.* **or·i·en·tat·ed** *v.t.* to orient

or·i·en·ta·tion (ɔ̀ri:entéiʃən, òuri:entéiʃən) *n.* an orienting or being oriented ‖ position with relation to the points of the compass ‖ situation of a church on an east-west axis so that the altar is at the east end ‖ *(chem.)* the relative position of atoms or groups about a nucleus or existing configuration ‖ the ordering of chemical groups, molecules or crystals in a particular or desired sense

or·i·fice (ɔ́rifis, órifis) *n.* a mouthlike opening

o·ri·ga·mi (ɔ̀rəgáːmi:) *n.* the art or process of folding paper into representational or decorative forms

or·i·gin (ɔ́ridʒin, óridʒin) *n.* the point in time or space at which a thing first exists ‖ the first existence of something ‖ a source or cause ‖ (esp. *pl.*) a person's parentage or ancestry ‖ *(anat.)* the point of attachment of a muscle that is most firmly fixed

o·rig·i·nal (ərídʒin'l) **1.** *adj.* of, relating to or belonging to an origin or beginning ‖ firsthand, not copied or derivative ‖ inventive, creative ‖ designating something from which a copy, translation, summary etc. has been made **2.** *n.* a model or archetype that has been copied, translated etc. ‖ *(old-fash.)* a person who is eccentric in behavior or character

o·rig·i·nal·i·ty (ərìdʒinǽliti:) *n.* the quality or state of being original, esp. creative or novel

o·rig·i·nate (ərídʒineit) *pres. part.* **o·rig·i·nat·ing** *past* and *past part.* **o·rig·i·nat·ed** *v.i.* (with 'in', 'from', 'with') to have its source or beginning ‖ *v.t.* to cause to begin, be the source of **o·rig·i·ná·tion** *n.* origin, an originating or being originated

or·na·ment 1. (ɔ́rnəmənt) *n.* an object, detail etc. meant to add beauty to something to which it is attached or applied or of which it is a part ‖ such objects, details etc. collectively ‖ *(mus.)* a grace note or group of them, e.g. a turn or trill ‖ *(rhet.)* a person who enhances or does credit to his society, milieu, profession etc. ‖ *(eccles.)* an accessory used in worship or church furnishing **2.** (ɔ́rnəment) *v.t.* to add or apply an ornament or ornaments to **or·na·men·tal** (ɔ̀rnəmént'l) *adj.* **or·na·men·ta·tion** (ɔ̀rnəmentéiʃən) *n.* an ornamenting or being ornamented ‖ ornaments collectively

or·nate (ɔrnéit) *adj.* elaborately adorned ‖ (of literary style) making use of elaborate rhetorical devices

or·ner·y (ɔ́rnəri:) *adj. (pop.)* inclined to be stubborn and not cooperative

or·ni·tho·log·i·cal (ɔ̀rnəθəlɔ́dʒik'l) *adj.* of or pertaining to ornithology

or·ni·thol·o·gist (ɔ̀rnəθɔ́lədʒist) *n.* a specialist in ornithology

or·ni·thol·o·gy (ɔ̀rnəθɔ́lədʒi:) *n.* the branch of zoology which deals with birds

or·phan (ɔ́rfən) **1.** *n.* a child whose parents are dead ‖ a child one of whose parents is dead **2.** adj. designating an orphan, *an orphan child* **3.** *v.t.* to bereave (a child) of his parents by death **ór·phan·age** *n.* an institution for the care and education of orphans

or·tho·don·tia (ɔ̀rθədɔ́nʃi:ə, ɔ̀rθədɔ́nʃə) *n.* orthodontics **or·tho·dón·tic** *adj.* of or pertaining to orthodontics **or·tho·dón·tics** *n.* the branch of dentistry concerned with the prevention and correction of displacement or overcrowding of the teeth **or·tho·dón·tist** *n.*

or·tho·dox (ɔ́rθədɒks) *adj.* of, conforming to or holding the official, accepted or standard opinions, not heretical or independent ‖ standardized, conventional

or·tho·dox·y (ɔ́rθədɒksi:) *pl.* **or·tho·dox·ies** *n.* the quality or state of being orthodox ‖ an orthodox opinion

or practice

or·tho·pe·dic, or·tho·pae·dic (ɔ̀rθəpíːdik) *adj.* of, relating to or used in orthopedics

or·tho·pe·dics, or·tho·pae·dics (ɔ̀rθəpíːdiks) *n.* the prevention or curing of deformities of bones, joints, ligaments, muscles and tendons, esp. in children **or·tho·pé·dist, or·tho·páe·dist** *n.*

os·cil·late (ɔ́səleit) *pres. part.* **os·cil·lat·ing** *past* and *past part.* **os·cil·lat·ed** *v.i.* (of a rigid body pivoted on an axle) to swing to and fro ‖ to vibrate ‖ to waver, vacillate ‖ to vary in condition or degree, fluctuate ‖ *v.t.* to cause to oscillate

os·cil·la·tion (ɔ̀səléiʃən) *n.* an oscillating ‖ fluctuation ‖ *(elec.)* a current fluctuation in a circuit from positive to negative or from maxima to minima ‖ *(phys.)* a single swing of an oscillating body, e.g. of a pendulum from one extreme to another ‖ *(math.)* the variation between highest and lowest values of a function **ós·cil·la·tor** *n.* something which oscillates ‖ *(elec.)* a device for the production of oscillations ‖ a device for measuring rigidity by means of the vibrations of a loaded wire

os·cil·la·to·ry (ɔ́sələtɔri:, ɔ́sələtɔuri:) *adj.* characterized or marked by oscillation

os·cu·late (ɔ́skjuleit) *pres. part.* **os·cu·lat·ing** *past* and *past part.* **os·cu·lat·ed** *v.t.* (math., of a curve, surface etc.) to coincide in three or more points with ‖ *v.i.* (biol.) to have characters intermediate between two groups, genera, species etc.

os·cu·la·tion (ɔ̀skjuléiʃən) *n.* (rhet.) the act of kissing ‖ (math.) of a curve, surface etc.) the fact of coinciding in three or more points

os·mo·sis (ɒzmóusis, ɒsmóusis) *n.* the passage of a solvent, but not its solute, through a semipermeable membrane into a more concentrated solution, tending to equalize the concentrations on either side of the membrane **os·mot·ic** (ɒzmɔ́tik, ɒsmɔ́tik) *adj.*

os·si·fi·ca·tion (ɒsifikéiʃən) *n.* the process of becoming bone or an instance of this process ‖ the changing of body tissue into an osseous substance

os·si·fy (ɔ́sifai) *pres. part.* **os·si·fy·ing** *past* and *past part.* **os·si·fied** *v.i.* to change into bone ‖ (of ideas, behavior etc.) to make or become hardened, set or rigid ‖ *v.t.* to cause to change into bone ‖ to cause (ideas, behavior etc.) to become hardened, set or rigid

os·ten·si·ble (ɒsténsəb'l) *adj.* apparent, pretended, avowed **os·tén·si·bly** *adv.*

os·ten·ta·tion (ɒstentéiʃən) *n.* unnecessary show or display of wealth, luxury, skill, learning etc. **os·ten·tá·tious** *adj.* fond of display, showy ‖ intended to attract attention

os·te·op·a·thy (ɒsti:ɔ́pəθi:) *n.* a form of medical treatment purporting to cure a wide variety of diseases primarily by manipulation of the joints of the body

os·tra·cism (ɔ́strəsizəm) *n.* an ostracizing or being ostracized

os·tra·cize (ɔ́strəsaiz) *pres. part.* **os·tra·ciz·ing** *past* and *past part.* **os·tra·cized** *v.t.* to refrain deliberately and ostentatiously from having any sociable dealings at all with, esp. in order to punish by humiliating

os·trich (ɔ́stritʃ, óstritʃ) *n.* a cursorial flightless bird inhabiting the sandy plains of Africa and formerly Arabia. It is the largest living bird, attaining a height of 6–8 ft and a weight of 300 lbs., and capable of running at 40 miles an hour

oth·er (ʌ́ðər) **1.** *adj.* different, not the same ‖ alternative, *he has no other place to go* ‖ further or additional, *give some other examples* ‖ former, *the youth of other days* **every other** alternate, *skip every other line* **on the other hand** used to introduce an argument or fact in contrast with a previous one **other things**

---

being equal if the conditions were the same in everything but the point under discussion **the other day** recently, a few days ago **the other world** life after death **2.** *n.* or *pron.* other person or thing **among others** with others, *my life was there among others* **one after the other** in succession **one from the other** apart, *it is hard to tell the twins one from the other* **someone or other** some unknown person **some time or other** someday **3.** *adv.* **other than** in any other way ‖ besides, *is anyone other than yourself coming?*

oth·er·wise (ʌðərwaiz) **1.** *adv.* in another or different way ‖ in other respects, apart from that ‖ under other circumstances **2.** *adj.* in a different state, *he does not wish it otherwise* ‖ different, *if circumstances were otherwise*

o·ti·ose (óuʃi:ous, óuti:ous) *adj. (rhet.)* idle, lazy ‖ superfluous

ot·to·man (ótəmən) *n.* an upholstered or cushioned seat, stool or sofa without a back

ought (ɔt) *(infin.* and *parts.* lacking, used only as present) *auxiliary v.* expressing duty or obligation, *we ought to tell them, it ought not to be allowed, he ought to have known better* ‖ expressing necessity or expedience, *the grass ought to be cut* ‖ expressing desirability, *you ought to have been with us yesterday* ‖ expressing strong likelihood, *he ought to win the race easily*

oui·ja (wí:dʒə, wí:dʒi:) *n.* a board marked with the alphabet and various signs, fitted with a planchette, and used to obtain messages in spiritualist practice

ounce (auns) *n. (abbr.* oz.) a unit of weight equal to 1/16 of a pound avoirdupois (28.35 gms) or 1/12 of a pound troy (31.1 gms) ‖ a very little, *not an ounce of sympathy*

our (auər) *possessive adj.* of, pertaining to or belonging to us ‖ experienced, done or made by us ‖ (used formally, esp. by a sovereign, author or judge) my, *this is a mistake in our opinion*

ours (auərz) *possessive pron.* that or those belonging to us

our·self (auərsélf, ɑrsélf) *pl.* **our·selves** (auərsélvz, ɑrsélvz) *pron. refl.* form of WE, *we blame ourselves for the accident* ‖ emphatic form of WE, *we did it ourselves*

oust (aust) *v.t. (law)* to dispossess of property or an inheritance ‖ *(law)* to take away (a privilege, right etc.) ‖ to force or drive out, eject

oust·er (áustər) *n. (law)* an illegal or wrongful dispossession from property or an inheritance

out (aut) **1.** *adv.* away from a place, situation etc. ‖ on the outside ‖ away from home, place of work etc. ‖ not in office, *his party is out* ‖ outside, out-of-doors ‖ into violent or sudden activity, *a fire broke out* ‖ so as to be no longer functioning, burning etc., *put out the light* ‖ expressing finality, *my shirt is worn out, tired out* ‖ expressing projection, *his chin jutted out* ‖ into sight, *the sun came out* ‖ into or in circulation, *his book has just come out* ‖ in or into public knowledge ‖ openly, without reticence, *tell him right out* ‖ expressing extension or prolongation, *stretch out your arm* ‖ away from the center, interior etc., *spread out* ‖ expressing discord, *they fell out* ‖ into or in disuse, *long skirts have gone out* ‖ expressing selection, *pick out the winners* ‖ in the condition of having lost money on a transaction ‖ *(pop.)* into or in a state of unconsciousness, *he passed out* ‖ *(baseball)* in a manner producing an out, *to strike out* **all out** with one's whole effort **out and away** by far **out from under** *(pop.)* away from difficulty or danger **2.** *adj.* (of sizes of clothing) irregular, esp. very large ‖ *(baseball,* of a player) failing to get on a base or complete a successful play **3.** *prep.* forth from, *jump out the window* ‖ on the outside of, *hang it out the window* **4.** *n. (pop.)* a way out, an excuse **5.** *interj.* get out! go away! **6.** *v.i. (rhet.)* to be revealed, *the truth will out*

out- *prefix* beyond ‖ in excess of ‖ excelling

out·break (áutbreik) *n.* a sudden, violent bursting out ‖ an epidemic or near epidemic ‖ a revolt, an insurrection

out·burst (áutbe:rst) *n.* a violent emotional fit ‖ an eruption, *sudden outbursts of flame*

out·cast (áutkæst, áutkɑst) **1.** *adj.* cast out from home, friends etc. or by society, *an outcast waif* **2.** *n.* someone who has been so treated

out·class (autklǽs, autklɑ́s) *v.t.* to surpass by so much as to seem to belong to a higher class

out·come (áutkʌm) *n.* a result or consequence

out·cry (áutkrai) *pl.* **out·cries** *n.* a public expression of anger or disapproval

out·date (autdéit) *pres. part.* **out·dat·ing** *past* and *past part.* **out·dat·ed** *v.t.* to make out of date or obsolete

out·dis·tance (autdístəns) *pres. part.* **out·dis·tanc·ing** *past* and *past part.* **out·dis·tanced** *v.t.* to leave far behind in a race, competition etc.

out·do (autdú:) *pres. part.* **out·do·ing** *past* **out·did** (autdíd) *past part.* **out·done** (autdʌ́n) *v.t.* to do better than, surpass **not to be outdone** refusing defeat or loss of advantage **to outdo oneself** to excel oneself

out·doors (autdɔ́rz, autdóurz) **1.** *adv.* out of the house ‖ in the open air **2.** *n.* the out-of-doors

out·er (áutər) **1.** *adj.* farther out or outside, *outer space* ‖ away from the center ‖ of or pertaining to the outside ‖ objective, external **2.** *n.* the outside ring of a target ‖ a shot striking in this ring

out·er·most (áutərmoust) *adj.* furthest out from the inside or the center

out·face (autféis) *pres. part.* **out·fac·ing** *past* and *past part.* **out·faced** *v.t.* to stare down ‖ to resist by bravery

out·fit (áutfit) **1.** *n.* articles or instruments required to equip or fit out ‖ the act of equipping ‖ clothing etc. for a special purpose ‖ *(pop.)* persons making up an organization, institution, regiment etc., *the whole outfit was against him* **2.** *v.t. pres. part.* **out·fit·ting** *past* and *past part.* **out·fit·ted** *v.t.* to supply with an outfit ‖ to furnish, supply **óut·fit·ter** *n. (commerce)* a retail dealer in readymade clothing, sports material etc.

out·flank (autflǽŋk) *v.t. (mil.)* to extend one's own flank beyond the flank of (the enemy) ‖ to circumvent the plans of (an opponent) and retain the advantage

out·flow (áutflou) *n.* a flowing out ‖ the amount of such a flowing out

out·go 1. (áutgou) *pl.* **out·goes** *n.* outflow ‖ expenditure (opp. INCOME) **2.** (autgóu) *pres. part.* **out·go·ing** *past* **out·went** (autwént) *past part.* **out·gone** (autgɔ́n, autgón) *v.t.* to go one better than, with an advantage over

out·go·ing (áutgouiŋ) **1.** *adj.* going out ‖ leaving, *outgoing ships* ‖ retiring, *the outgoing government* ‖ willing to be sociable **2.** *n. (pl.)* outlay, expenditure

out·grow (autgróu) *pres. part.* **out·grow·ing** *past* **out·grew** (autgrú:) *past part.* **out·grown** (autgróun) *v.t.* to grow too big for ‖ to grow away from, become too old for ‖ to grow faster than

out·growth (áutgrouθ) *n.* that which grows out from something ‖ a result, product or by-product

out·ing (áutiŋ) *n.* a pleasure trip or excursion, sometimes organized for a large number of people ‖ a walk outdoors ‖ an athletic contest

out·land·ish (autlǽndiʃ) *adj.* bizarre-looking ‖ uncouth ‖ very remote and without amenities

out·last (autlǽst, autlɑ́st) *v.t.* to last longer than, outlive

out·law (áutlɔ) *n. (hist.)* a person deprived of the protection of the law

outlaw *v.t.* to place beyond or deprive of the benefit of the law ‖ to cause, esp. by the force of public opinion, to be no longer tolerated ‖ *(law)* to void the legal force of (an act, contract, claim etc.)

out·lay 1. (áutlei) *n.* expenditure ‖ an instance of this **2.** (autléi) *v.t. pres. part.* **out·lay·ing** *past* and *past part.* **out·laid** to expend (money)

out·let (áutlet, áutlit) *n.* an opening which provides a way to the outside ‖ a means of channeling ‖ a stream flowing from a lake or larger stream etc. ‖ *(commerce)* a market for goods ‖ a pair of terminals in an electric wiring system at which current may be taken for use

out·line (áutlain) **1.** *n.* a line or lines bounding the outer limits of a figure ‖ the shape defined by such bounding lines ‖ a sketch showing only the outer bounding lines ‖ a rough draft of a plan, scheme of work etc. ‖ a short summary, often in note form and omitting detail ‖ a compendious presentation of general features, *an outline of history* ‖ (pl.) general principles or chief elements of a subject **in outline** drawn etc. so as to show only the outer bounding lines ‖ indicating only the most significant matters **2.** *v.t. pres. part.* **out·lin·ing** *past* and *past part.* **out·lined** to draw or mark the outline of ‖ to give the main points of

out·live (autlív) *pres. part.* **out·liv·ing** *past* and *past part.* **out·lived** *v.t.* to live longer than, survive ‖ to live down, *to outlive a disgrace*

out·look (áutluk) *n.* a prospect or view ‖ a prospect for the future ‖ a way of looking at things

out·mod·ed (autmóudid) *adj.* left behind by changes or developments ‖ no longer widely accepted ‖ not fashionable

out·num·ber (autnÁmbər) *v.t.* to be greater than in number

out-of-date (áutəvdéit) *adj.* old-fashioned ‖ not current, defective in regard to the present situation

out·post (áutpoust) *n.* (mil.) a position held by a detachment in front of the main body of troops to prevent surprise action ‖ (mil.) the soldiers holding this position ‖ a military base established by agreement in another country ‖ a settlement on a frontier or in a remote area

out·put (áutput) *n.* the total product of a factory, mill etc. ‖ the amount produced of a specified product ‖ the amount produced by an individual or by one machine ‖ the amount of energy delivered by a machine ‖ the creative work of an artist

out·rage (áutreidʒ) **1.** *n.* a violent attack, esp. on people's rights or feelings or property ‖ a flagrant offense against order or dignity or against principles ‖ a feeling of angry resentment provoked by great injustice or offense to one's dignity **2.** *v.t. pres. part.* **out·rag·ing** *past* and *past part.* **out·raged** to subject to an outrage ‖ to make furious or angrily resentful

out·ra·geous (autréidʒəs) *adj.* constituting an outrage ‖ (pop.) extravagant, outré

out·rank (autræŋk) *v.t.* to have a higher rank or greater importance than

out·right 1. (autráit, áutrait) *adv.* not by installments or degrees, once for all ‖ openly, straightforwardly **2.** *adj.* (áutrait) thorough, downright, *outright denial* ‖ complete

out·set (áutset) *n.* the first stage, the beginning

out·shine (autʃáin) *pres. part.* **out·shin·ing** *past* and *past part.* **out·shone** (autʃóun), **out·shined** *v.t.* to shine brighter than ‖ to surpass

out·side (áutsáid, áutsaid) **1.** *n.* the surface, exterior, outer parts ‖ the space or region situated beyond a boundary, or other limit ‖ external appearance ‖ superficial aspect **at the outside** (or **very outside**) at the most **2.** *adj.* on, of or nearer the outside ‖ of, pertaining to or being the outer side of a curve, circle etc. ‖ from a source other than some specified or understood group ‖ involving an extreme limit, *an outside estimate* ‖ not connected with one's main work or preoccupation, *outside interests* ‖ (of a chance) just within the limit of possibility **3.** *adv.* on or to the outside ‖ out-of-doors **4.** *prep.* on or to the outer side of, *wait outside the office* ‖ beyond the limits of ‖ apart from, other than

out·sid·er (autsáidər) *n.* a person not included in some particular group, party, clique etc. ‖ a competitor (horse, athlete etc.) believed to have only an outside chance in a race

out·skirts (áutskə:rts) *pl. n.* outlying parts remote from the center

out·smart (autsmárt) *v.t.* to outwit

out·spo·ken (autspóukən) *adj.* said without fear of the consequences ‖ not conventionally or prudently reticent

out·stand·ing (autstǽndiŋ) *adj.* conspicuous, standing out ‖ remarkable ‖ not yet settled or completed, *outstanding debts*

out·strip (autstríp) *pres. part.* **out·strip·ping** *past* and *past part.* **out·stripped** *v.t.* to go at a quicker rate than and leave behind

out·ward (áutwərd) **1.** *adj.* moving or directed toward the outside ‖ exterior **2.** *adv.* towards the outside and away from the inside

out·ward·ly (áutwərdli:) *adv.* externally ‖ on the surface, *outwardly calm*

out·wards (áutwərdz) *adv.* outward

out·wear (autwέər) *pres. part.* **out·wear·ing** *past* **out·wore** (autwɔ́r, autwóur) *past part.* **out·worn** (autwɔ́rn, autwóurn) *v.t.* to last longer in use than

out·wit (autwít) *pres. part.* **out·wit·ting** *past* and *past part.* **out·wit·ted** *v.t.* to defeat by cleverness or cunning

o·val (óuvəl) **1.** *adj.* having the form of an ellipse ‖ egg-shaped **2.** *n.* an oval figure or shape

o·va·ry (óuvəri:) *pl.* **o·va·ries** *n.* one of a pair of female reproductive organs that produce eggs and (in vertebrates) female sex hormones

o·va·tion (ouvéiʃən) *n.* an enthusiastic public welcome, esp. a spontaneous outburst of applause expressing this

ov·en (Ávən) *n.* an enclosed cavity of stone, brick, metal etc. for baking, roasting, heating or drying

o·ver (óuvər) **1.** *prep.* above ‖ so as to cover, *ink spilled over the book* ‖ so as to close, *stretched over the neck of the bottle* ‖ in excess of ‖ near, *he dozed over the fire* ‖ so as to dominate, influence, change the opinion of etc., *a mood has come over him* ‖ in authority with respect to ‖ in a relationship of superiority ‖ along, *drive over the new route* ‖ by means of, *over the telephone* ‖ throughout, in every part of, *she traveled over the whole Commonwealth* ‖ during, *over several days* ‖ more than ‖ covered or submerged up to ‖ up to and including ‖ in preference to, *he chose the cheaper model over the more expensive one* ‖ across and down from ‖ against and across the top of, *she stumbled over the mat* **2.** *adv.* across ‖ across and down from an edge, height etc. ‖ expressing upward and outward motion from a container ‖ so as to turn the upper surface forward and down, *fold it over* ‖ from one side to the other, *to turn over* ‖ expressing movement away from the perpendicular, *to fall over* ‖ across a space or distance, *over in Ireland* ‖ (pop.) to one's or someone's house, *come over tonight* ‖ more, *it weighs two pounds and over* ‖ at the end or finish ‖ with thorough, precise and concentrated effort or attention, *talk the case over* ‖ afresh, *do it over again* ‖ from one person to another, *hand over the keys* **3.** *adj.* in excess, *the total was five dollars over* **4.** *n.* (mil.) a shot that falls beyond the target

o·ver·age (óuvəréidʒ) *adj.* beyond a specified or usual age

o·ver·all (óuvərɔl) *n.* (pl.) loose trousers of durable material, with apron and shoulder straps, worn when doing heavy or dirty jobs

overall *adj.* including everything, total ‖ from end to end

o·ver·bear (ouvərbéər) *pres. part.* **o·ver·bear·ing** *past* **o·ver·bore** (ouvərbɔ́r, ouvərbóur) *past part.*

---

o·ver·borne (ouvərbɔ́rn, ouvərbóurn) v.t. to bear down by greater force, weight, determination etc. ‖ v.i. to bear excessively (e.g. of a fruit tree) **o·ver·béar·ing** adj. aggressively masterful

o·ver·blown (ouvərblóun) adj. (of flowers) just past full bloom

overblown adj. blowzy ‖ (of style) pretentious, windy

o·ver·board (óuvərbɔrd, óuvərbɔ́urd) adv. over the side of a ship etc., to fall overboard **to go overboard** to go to extremes

o·ver·cast 1. (ouvərkǽst, ouvərkάst) v.t. pres. part. **o·ver·cast·ing** past and past part. **o·ver·cast** (sewing) to stitch (raw edges) to prevent unraveling **2.** (óuvərkæst, óuvərkάst) adj. cloudy, covered with clouds

o·ver·charge 1. (ouvərtʃάrdʒ) v. pres. part. **o·ver·charg·ing** past and past part. **o·ver·charged** v.t. to charge (someone) too high a price ‖ to charge (an amount) in excess of a specified price ‖ to load too highly with electricity, explosive etc., or as if with these ‖ v.i. to charge excessively **2.** (óuvərtʃάrdʒ) n. an excessive charge

o·ver·coat (óuvərkout) n. a warm coat worn over ordinary clothes in cold weather

o·ver·come (ouvərkʌ́m) pres. part. **o·ver·com·ing** past **o·ver·came** (ouvərkéim) past part. **o·ver·come** v.t. (rhet.) to conquer ‖ to get the better of ‖ to overpower or overwhelm (a person) physically or emotionally

o·ver·do (ouvərdú:) pres. part. **o·ver·do·ing** past **over·did** (ouvərdíd) past part. **o·ver·done** (ouvərdʌ́n) v.t. to exaggerate, carry too far ‖ (esp. past part.) to cook too long **to overdo it** to overtax one's strength ‖ to make too great a display

o·ver·dose 1. (ouvərdóus) v.t. pres. part. **o·ver·dos·ing** past and past part. **o·ver·dosed** to give an excessive dose to **2.** (óuvərdous) n. an excessive dose

o·ver·due (ouvərdú:, ouvərdjú:) adj. not paid by the time it was due ‖ behind the scheduled time of arrival ‖ more than ready

o·ver·es·ti·mate 1. (ouvəréstəmeit) v. pres. part. **o·ver·es·ti·mat·ing** past and past part. **o·ver·es·ti·mat·ed** v.t. to put the value, amount etc. of (something) too high ‖ v.i. to make too high an estimate **2.** (óuvəréstəmit) n. an estimate that is too high

o·ver·flow (ouvərflóu) v.t. (of liquids) to flow over the brim of ‖ to flood ‖ v.i. to flood, spill over ‖ to be abundant

o·ver·flow (óuvərflou) n. a flowing over ‖ something which flows over ‖ an outlet or receptacle for excess fluids

o·ver·grown (óuvərgroun) adj. grown over with rank weeds etc. ‖ grown to an excessive size

o·ver·growth (óuvərgrouθ) n. excessive growth ‖ dense vegetation, esp. of weeds

o·ver·haul 1. (ouvərhɔ́l) v.t. to examine thoroughly and repair or correct defects in ‖ (esp. naut.) to overtake ‖ (naut.) to loosen (a rope) by hauling it through the block in the opposite direction to that in which it was hoisted **2.** (óuvərhɔl) n. a thorough examination followed by the necessary repairs, renovations etc.

o·ver·head (óuvərhed) **1.** adj. located, working etc. above one's head ‖ (of expenses) due to charges necessary to the carrying on of a business **2.** n. (collect.) expenses which are a general charge to a business and cannot be allotted to a particular job or process (e.g. rent, light, depreciation, administration, insurance, as opposed to materials, wages etc.) **3.** adv. (óuvərhéd) above one's head

o·ver·hear (ouvərhíər) pres. part. **o·ver·hear·ing** past and past part. **o·ver·heard** (ouvərhə́:rd) v.t. to hear (conversation etc.) accidentally or by eavesdropping

o·ver·joyed (ouvərdʒɔ́id) adj. exceedingly delighted

o·ver·kill (óuvərkil) **1.** n. national capacity in nuclear armament over and above what would be needed to destroy an enemy ‖ an instance of destruction using this capacity **2.** v. to exert more force than necessary,

e.g., having the effect of extirpating several times over

o·ver·lap 1. (ouvərlǽp) v. pres. part. **o·ver·lap·ping** past and past part. **o·ver·lapped** v.t. to cover partly ‖ to cover and extend beyond ‖ v.i. to coincide partly **2.** (óuvərlæp) n. an instance or place of overlapping ‖ the extent of overlapping ‖ the part that overlaps

o·ver·lie (ouvərlái) pres. part. **o·ver·ly·ing** past **o·ver·lay** (ouvərléi) past part. **o·ver·lain** (ouvərléin) v.t. to lie over or on

o·ver·look (ouvərlúk) v.t. to look over from above ‖ to fail to notice **o·ver·lóok·er** n. an overseer

o·ver·ly (óuvərli:) adv. excessively

o·ver·night 1. (óuvərnáit) adv. during or for the night ‖ during the night just past **2.** (óuvərnait) adj. during the evening or night ‖ lasting or staying one night ‖ used for a single night ‖ happening etc. in the space of one night, overnight success

o·ver·pass 1. (ouvərpǽs, óuvərpæs) n. a raised crossing, e.g. of a road over a railroad **2.** (ouvərpǽs, ouvərpǽs) pres. part. **o·ver·pass·ing** past **o·ver·passed** past part. **o·ver·passed, o·ver·past** v.t. to pass over, travel over, go beyond (e.g. an area) ‖ to get through, surmount (e.g. a difficulty) ‖ to go beyond, surpass in amount, value etc. ‖ to overlook, omit

o·ver·pow·er (ouvərpáuər) v.t. to overcome physically ‖ to supply with more power than is desirable or necessary

o·ver·print 1. (ouvərprínt) v.t. (printing) to print (matter) on top of something already printed ‖ (photog.) to print too long or with excess of light ‖ to print too many copies of ‖ (philately) to make an overprint on (a stamp) **2.** (óuvərprint) n. (philately) a word, device, figure etc. printed across the surface of a stamp to alter its value or use ‖ a stamp bearing such a print ‖ something printed over other printed matter

o·ver·rate (ouvərréit) pres. part. **o·ver·rat·ing** past and past part. **o·ver·rat·ed** v.t. to value or prize too highly

o·ver·ride (ouvərráid) pres. part. **o·ver·rid·ing** past **o·ver·rode** (ouvərróud) past part. **o·ver·rid·den** (ouvərríd'n) v.t. to decide to disregard or go against ‖ to dominate

o·ver·rule (ouvərrú:l) pres. part. **o·ver·rul·ing** past and past part. **o·ver·ruled** v.t. to give a legal decision or ruling about something which goes against (the decision or ruling of a lower authority)

o·ver·run 1. (ouvərrʌ́n) v.t. pres. part. **o·ver·run·ning** past **o·ver·ran** (ouvərrǽn) past part. **o·ver·run** (esp. mil.) to attack and obtain complete mastery over by weight of numbers ‖ to infest, rats overran the house ‖ to extend or go beyond (in space or time) **2.** (óuvərrʌn) n. an overrunning ‖ the amount of this ‖ a clear area beyond a runway used in case of emergency in landing an aircraft

o·ver·seas 1. (óuvərsí:z) adv. beyond the sea **2.** (óuvərsi̩:z) adj. of or pertaining to countries or people or things beyond the sea

o·ver·see (ouvərsí:) pres. part. **o·ver·see·ing** past **o·ver·saw** (ouvərsɔ́) past part. **o·ver·seen** (ouvərsí:n) v.t. to supervise, direct **ó·ver·se·er** n. a person in charge of work, a foreman or supervisor

o·ver·sha·dow (ouvərʃǽdou) v.t. to cast a shade over ‖ to cause to seem to have less than full merit, because of detrimental comparisons

o·ver·sight (óuvərsait) n. failure to notice something or an instance of this ‖ supervision

o·ver·sleep (ouvərslí:p) pres. part. **o·ver·sleep·ing** past and past part. **o·ver·slept** (ouvərslépt) v.i. to sleep beyond the time for getting up

o·ver·state (ouvərstéit) pres. part. **o·ver·stat·ing** past and past part. **o·ver·stat·ed** v.t. to express in stronger terms than the truth warrants **ó·ver·státe·ment** n.

o·ver·step (óuvərstép) pres. part. **o·ver·step·ping** past and past part. **o·ver·stepped** v.t. to go beyond (what is prudent or acceptable)

o·vert (óuvə:rt, ouvɔ́:rt) adj. unconcealed, public, an overt attack on authority

o·ver·take (ouvərtéik) *pres. part.* **o·ver·tak·ing** *past* **o·ver·took** (ouvərtúk) *past part.* **o·ver·tak·en** (ouvərtéikən) *v.t.* to catch up with ‖ to happen to or come upon suddenly and usually disagreeably, *a storm overtook them two hours later* ‖ to catch up with and do better than (in competition), *experts have already overtaken last year's figure*

o·ver·tax (ouvərtǽks) *v.t.* to strain by making excessive demands on ‖ to tax excessively

o·ver·throw 1. (ouvərθróu) *v.t. pres. part.* **o·ver·throw·ing** *past* **o·ver·threw** (ouvərθrú:) *past past.* **o·ver·thrown** (óuvərθroun) to cause to fall from power, *to overthrow a government* ‖ *(games)* to throw (a ball) beyond the point intended ‖ *(rhet.)* to upset, overturn **2.** (óuvərθrou) *n.* an overthrowing or being overthrown

o·ver·time (óuvərtaim) **1.** *n.* extra time worked, beyond regular hours ‖ money paid for such work ‖ *(sports)* extra playing time beyond the usual fixed limits of the game when the score is a tie **2.** *adv.* beyond the usual hours ‖ *(sports)* beyond the usual playing time **3.** *adj.* for overtime, *overtime pay* **4.** (óuvərtáim) *v.t. pres. part.* **o·ver·tim·ing** *past* and *past part.* **o·ver·timed** to give more than the proper time to

o·ver·ture (óuvərtʃuər, óuvərtʃər) *n.* a preliminary proposal or a formal offer intended to assess the state of mind of the person or group addressed ‖ *(mus.)* an orchestral piece preceding the rise of the curtain in an opera, musical comedy etc.

o·ver·turn 1. (ouvərtɔ́:rn) *v.t.* to turn over, upset ‖ to overthrow (e.g. a government) ‖ *v.i.* to turn over, upset **2.** (óuvərtɔ́:rn) *n.* an overturning or being overturned

o·ver·view (óuvərvju:) *n.* a general survey

o·ver·weight 1. (óuvərweit) *n.* weight over that usual or required ‖ bodily weight that is higher than is compatible with good health **2.** (óuvərwéit) *adj.* beyond the allowed weights ‖ suffering from bodily overweight **3.** (ouvərwéit) *v.t.* to emphasize to excess ‖ to overburden

o·ver·whelm (ouvərhwélm, ouvərwélm) *v.t.* to submerge suddenly by irresistible force ‖ to overpower ‖ to leave emotionally too moved for speech or expression

o·ver·work (ouvərwɔ́:rk) **1.** *v.t.* to work excessively ‖ to weary or exhaust with too much work ‖ *v.i.* to work too hard **2.** *n.* work in such quantity that mental or physical health is endangered or affected

o·ver·wrought (ouvərrɔ́t) *adj.* worked up, under great nervous tension ‖ much too elaborate

o·vi·form (óuvifɔrm) *adj.* ovoid

o·void (óuvɔid) **1.** *adj.* egg-shaped **2.** *n.* an egg-shaped body or surface

o·vu·late (óuvjuleit) *pres. part.* **o·vu·lat·ing** *past* and *past part.* **o·vu·lat·ed** *v.i.* to produce an egg or eggs, or to discharge them from the ovary

o·vum (óuvəm) *pl.* **o·va** (óuvə) *n.* *(biol.)* the usually nonmotile female haploid gamete ‖ a mature egg or egg cell, esp. of mammals, fish or insects

owe (ou) *pres. part.* **ow·ing** *past* and *past part.* **owed** *v.t.* to have an obligation to pay or repay (money etc.) in return for money etc. that one has received ‖ to have or bear (a specified feeling) toward someone, *to owe someone gratitude* ‖ to be or feel obliged to render (something) ‖ to have, enjoy etc. (something) as a result of the action, existence etc. of a specified person, cause etc. ‖ *v.i.* to be in debt

owl (aul) *n.* a large cosmopolitan family of nocturnal birds of prey. They have flattened faces and forward-facing eyes, hooked bills and powerful claws, and their soft, fluffy plumage allows them to fly noiselessly ‖ a solemn-appearing person, usually stupid

owl·ish (áuliʃ) *adj* (of a person, or his appearance) having characteristics suggestive of those of an owl

own (oun) **1.** *adj.* (usually following a possessive adj.) belonging to oneself or itself (often used to denote exclusive or particular possession or agency), *he brought his own lunch* **to be one's own man** to be independent of the control or influence of others **2.** *n.* that which belongs to one **of one's own** belonging to one **on one's own** independent ‖ independently or without the help etc. of others **to come into one's own** to get what rightly belongs to one (esp. recognition or prosperity) **to hold one's own** to maintain one's position or strength

own *v.t.* to have, possess, be the proprietor of ‖ *v.i.* (with 'to') to make an admission, *he owned to a sense of shame* **to own up** *(pop.)* to confess, admit guilt ‖ *(pop.,* with 'to') to confess frankly that one has committed a crime etc. **ówn·er, ówn·er·ship** *ns*

ox (ɒks) *pl.* **ox·en** (ɒ́ksən) *n.* the adult castrated male of *Bos taurus* kept as a draft animal or raised as food ‖ any of several animals of *Bos* and related genera, e.g. the bison, buffalo, yak

ox·y·gen (ɒ́ksidʒən) *n.* a colorless, tasteless, normally gaseous element

oys·ter (ɔ́istər) *n.* an edible marine bivalve lamellibranch mollusk having a rough irregular shell and living free on the sea floor or attached to submerged rocks, usually in temperate or tropical coastal waters or estuaries ‖ any of several mollusks resembling this, e.g. a pearl oyster ‖ a choice morsel of meat contained in a hollow of the pelvic bone on each side of the back of a chicken ‖ a color between light gray and white

o·zone (óuzoun, ouzóun) *n.* an allotropic form of oxygen in which three atoms form one molecule. It has a pungent smell, is produced by a silent discharge of electricity, and is present in the air after a thunderstorm **o·zon·ic** (ouzɒ́nik, ouzóunik) *adj.* **o·zo·nif·er·ous** (ouzounífərəs) *adj.* **o·zon·ize** (óuzounaiz) *pres. part.* **o·zon·iz·ing** *past* and *past part.* **o·zon·ized** *v.t.* to convert into ozone ‖ to treat or combine with ozone **o·zon·iz·er** (óuzounaizər) *n.* an apparatus that converts oxygen into ozone by passing a silent electrical discharge through it

---

P

P, p (pi:) the 16th letter of the English alphabet **to mind one's P's and Q's** to be careful to avoid language or behavior that could offend

pab·u·lum (pǽbjuləm) *(rhet.)* nourishment

pace (peis) **1.** *n.* rate of traveling or progressing ‖ manner of walking or running ‖ a step made in walking ‖ the distance covered by a single step in walking, often taken as 30 ins ‖ any of the gaits of a horse **to keep pace with** to move or develop at the same speed as **to put (someone or an animal) through his** (or **its**) **paces** to test or rehearse the abilities of (someone or an animal) **2.** *v. pres. part.* **pac·ing** *past* and *past part.* **paced** *v.i.* to walk with regular steps

pace·mak·er (péismeikər) *n.* a person who sets the pace, e.g. for a race ‖ *(med.)* a part of the body serving to establish and maintain a rhythmic activity ‖ *(med.)* a device for stimulating the heart to resume a steady beat, or to restore the rhythm of an arrested heart

pac·er (péisər) *n.* a horse with a pacing gait, used esp. in harness racing

pach·y·derm (pǽkidə:rm) *n. (zool.)* any of certain thickskinned, hoofed mammals, esp. the rhinoceros and elephant **pach·y·der·ma·tous** *adj.*

pa·cif·ic (pəsífik) *adj.* peaceful, seeking, making or tending toward peace ‖ unaggressive in disposition **Pa·cif·ic** of the Pacific Ocean or the regions bordering it **pa·cif·i·cal·ly** *adv.*

pac·i·fism (pǽsifizəm) *n.* the belief that war is morally wrong and, in the long run, ineffective, and that disputes should be settled by negotiation **pác·i·fist** *n.* a person who subscribes to this

pac·i·fy (pǽsifai) *pres. part.* **pac·i·fy·ing** *past* and *past part.* **pac·i·fied** *v.t.* to cause (someone) to be calm, satisfied or no longer angry ‖ to establish peace in (a country etc.)

pack (pæk) **1.** *n.* a bundle or parcel of things, esp. one carried on the shoulders or back ‖ a company of animals, esp. of wolves or hounds ‖ a company or gang of people ‖ a great quantity, *a pack of lies* ‖ a packet or container ‖ a complete set of playing cards ‖ a piece of wet or dry cloth, applied hot or cold as a medical or cosmetic treatment ‖ a treatment in which such a cloth is applied **2.** *v.t.* (often with 'up') to put in a container with other things, esp. for carrying on a trip ‖ (often with 'up') to fill (a container) with things ‖ to fill tightly, cram, *a train packed with people* ‖ (with 'off') to send (someone) away, esp. summarily ‖ *v.i.* to put things together for a trip ‖ to settle into a solid or compact mass ‖ to assemble, crowd together **to send (someone) packing** to dismiss (someone) unceremoniously

pack *v.t.* to select members of (a committee etc.) so as to secure an unfair advantage

pack·age (pǽkidʒ) **1.** *n.* a parcel or wrapped bundle ‖ a box or wrapper in which something is packed **2.** *v.t. pres. part.* **pack·ag·ing** *past* and *past part.* **pack·aged** to make into a parcel

pack·et (pǽkit) *n.* a small package or parcel ‖ a packet boat

packet boat a boat sailing a regular route, carrying passengers, mail and packages

pact (pækt) *n.* an agreement between two persons, or a treaty between states

pad (pæd) **1.** *n.* something soft, e.g. a flat cushion or thick mat, used as a shock absorber ‖ a piece of soft material used to fill or distend ‖ *(sports)* a protective guard worn on the front of the legs etc. ‖ *(colloq.)* person's apartment or residence ‖ graft for a group ‖ a small absorbent cushion soaked in ink, for inking a rubber stamp ‖ the fleshy cushion forming the sole of the paw of a dog, cat etc. ‖ a tool handle into which different tools may be inserted **2.** *v.t. pres. part.* **pad·ding** *past* and *past part.* **pad·ded** to fill or line with soft material ‖ to lengthen (a piece of writing, speech etc.) by adding superfluous material

pad **1.** *v.i. pres. part.* **pad·ding** *past* and *past part.* **pad·ded** to walk steadily and unhurriedly ‖ to walk with muffled steps **2.** *n.* the dull sound of a footfall

pad·ding (pǽdiŋ) *n.* the act of someone who pads ‖ the material used to pad something

pad·dle (pǽd'l) **1.** *v.i. pres. part.* **pad·dling** *past* and *past part.* **pad·dled** to wade or play in shallow water ‖ to toddle **2.** *n.* the act or a period of paddling

paddle **1.** *n.* a wooden pole with a broad blade at one end, used singly without an oarlock to propel and guide a canoe or other small craft ‖ the act or period of using this or of using an oar in this way ‖ any of several implements resembling a canoe paddle, for stirring, mixing, beating etc. ‖ one of the projecting boards of a paddle wheel ‖ a seal's flipper ‖ a tabletennis racket **2.** *v. pres. part.* **pad·dling** *past* and *past part.* **pad·dled** *v.t.* to propel (a canoe etc.) by using a paddle ‖ *(pop.)* to spank ‖ *v.i.* to propel a canoe etc. by a paddle ‖ to row gently ‖ (of a bird) to move in water as if by means of paddles

pad·dock (pǽdək) *n.* a small grassy enclosed area in which a horse can graze and exercise ‖ a racecourse enclosure in which the horses are walked for inspection and are saddled and unsaddled

pad·lock (pǽdlɒk) **1.** *n.* a small, portable lock, with a curved bar hinged to it at one end **2.** *v.t.* to fasten with a padlock

pa·dre (pádrei, pádri:) *n. (armed services, pop.)* a chaplain

pa·gan (péigən) **1.** *n.* a heathen, esp. one who worshipped the gods of ancient Greece and Rome **2.** *adj.* pertaining to or characteristic of a pagan

pa·gan·ism (péigənizəm) *n.* the state of being pagan ‖ pagan beliefs and practices

page (peidʒ) **1.** *n.* one side of a piece of paper or leaf of a book ‖ *(loosely)* a leaf of a book ‖ a fixed block or number of blocks of data or instructions **2.** *v.t. pres. part.* **pag·ing** *past* and *past part.* **paged** to make up (printed matter) into pages ‖ to number the pages of (a manuscript or printed text)

page **1.** *n.* a boy employed in a hotel to carry messages or otherwise be of personal service to guests ‖ a boy attendant upon the bride at a wedding ‖ a boy attendant in a legislative body, esp. Congress **2.** *v.t. pres. part.* **pag·ing** *past* and *past part.* **paged** to attend as a page ‖ to summon (a person, e.g. in a hotel) by calling his name repeatedly

pag·eant (pǽdʒənt) *n.* a colorful spectacle, either on a fixed stage or site or taking the form of a procession of tableaux representing esp. historical events ‖ a sequence of things or events resembling such a spectacle ‖ pageantry **pág·eant·ry** *n.* pageants collectively ‖ spectacular, colorful display

pag·i·nate (pǽdʒineit) *pres. part.* **pag·i·nat·ing** *past* and *past part.* **pag·i·nat·ed** *v.t.* to divide (a printed text) into pages ‖ to number the pages of (a manuscript or printed text) **pag·i·ná·tion** *n.* a paginating or being paginated ‖ the numbers etc. distinguishing the pages of a book etc.

pa·go·da (pəgóudə) *n.* an elaborately decorated Far Eastern sacred building, usually a tower with many stories that taper toward the top, with an unwardcurling, projecting roof over each story

pail (peil) *n.* an open container, esp. of metal, usually almost cylindrical and wider at the top than at the bottom, having an arched handle at the top and used esp. for carrying liquids ‖ a pailful

pain (pein) **1.** *n.* an unpleasant sensation caused by the stimulation of certain nerves, esp. as a result of injury or sickness ‖ a distressing emotion ‖ *(pl.)* specially concentrated effort ‖ *(pl.)* the labor of childbirth **on**

(or **upon** or **under**) **pain of** with the certainty of incurring (some punishment) unless a specified command or condition is fulfilled **to take pains** to make a special, concentrated effort **2.** *v.t.* to inflict esp. mental pain upon

pain·ful (péinfəl) *adj.* causing or characterized by pain ‖ requiring or showing laborious care or effort

pain·less (péinlis) *adj.* not causing pain ‖ not requiring trouble or hard work

pains·tak·ing (péinztɛikiŋ) *adj.* showing or using great care and effort

paint (peint) **1.** *v.t.* to apply paint to (a surface) ‖ to create (a picture, design etc.) on a surface, using paint ‖ to represent in paint ‖ to make a vivid written or spoken description of ‖ to apply cosmetics to ‖ to apply medicine etc. to (a throat etc.) as if applying paint ‖ (with 'out') to efface by covering with paint ‖ *v.i.* to practice the art of creating pictures with paint **to paint the town red** to go out and celebrate on a grand scale **2.** *n.* a liquid or paste consisting of a suspension of a pigment in oil or water etc.

paint·er (péintər) *n.* an artist who paints pictures ‖ an artisan who applies paint to walls etc. as a profession

paint·ing (péintiŋ) *n.* a picture produced by applying paint to a surface ‖ the act or art of making such pictures

pair (pɛər) **1.** *pl.* **pairs, pair** *n.* a set of two things of the same kind ‖ a single unit made up of two corresponding parts ‖ two persons associated together, e.g. a husband and wife, two friends, partners or dancers ‖ two playing cards of the same denomination ‖ two horses in harness **2.** *v.t.* to join (two people or things) in a pair ‖ to divide or arrange into groups of two ‖ *v.i.* to form a pair **to pair off** to divide (members of a group) into pairs ‖ to join (two people or things) in a pair

pa·ja·mas (pədʒáməz) *pl. n.* a loose-fitting sleeping garment consisting of jacket and trousers, the latter suspended by a cord or elastic around the waist ‖ loose silk or cotton trousers worn by men and women Moslems in Eastern countries

pal·ace (pǽlis) *n.* a large, often ornate residence of an emperor, king, pope etc. ‖ a large mansion ‖ a large, often ornate place of public entertainment

pal·at·a·bil·i·ty (pælətəbíliti:) *n.* the quality or state of being palatable

pal·at·a·ble (pǽlətəb'l) *adj.* pleasant to taste ‖ pleasant or acceptable to the mind **pál·at·a·bly** *adv.*

pal·ate (pǽlit) *n.* the roof of the mouth, separating the mouth cavity from the nasal cavity ‖ the sense of taste, *pleasing to the palate*

pa·la·tial (pəléiʃəl) *adj.* having the size, magnificence etc. of a palace

pa·lav·er (pəlǽvər, pəlávər) **1.** *n.* a long-drawn-out conferring or bargaining, esp. in tribal custom ‖ *(pop.)* any wordy discussion ‖ flowery, ingratiating language **2.** *v.i.* to engage in palaver or a palaver

pale (peil) *n.* a length of wood driven into the ground, with a pointed upper end, used with others in a fence ‖ an enclosed district or territory ‖ *(heraldry)* a vertical stripe dividing the shield into two halves

pale *adj.* lacking intensity of color or of illumination ‖ (of complexion) of a whitish color

pale *pres. part.* **pal·ing** *past* and *past part.* **paled** *v.i.* to become pale ‖ to lose importance or quality, esp. by contrast ‖ *v.t.* to make pale

pa·le·on·to·log·ic, pa·lae·on·to·log·ic (péili:ɒntəlɒ́dʒik, pǽli:ɒntəlɒ́dʒik) *adj.* pertaining to paleontology **pá·le·on·to·lóg·i·cal, pá·lae·on·to·lóg·i·cal**

pa·le·on·tol·o·gist, pa·lae·on·tol·o·gist (pɛili:əntɒ́lədʒist, pæli:ɒntɒ́lədʒist) *n.* a specialist in paleontology

pa·le·on·tol·o·gy, pa·lae·on·tol·o·gy (pɛili:ɒntɒ́lədʒi:, pæli:ɒntɒ́lədʒi:) *n.* the branch of geology concerned with the study of the fossil remains of animal and plant life of past geological periods

pal·ette (pǽlit) *n.* a small board on which a painter mixes his colors ‖ the range of colors used by a particular artist or for a particular picture

pal·i·sade (pæliséid) **1.** *n.* a fence of wooden or iron pales ‖ *(mil. hist.)* a strong, sharply pointed wooden stake set with many others in a row, upright or oblique, as a defense work ‖ a fence made of such stakes **2.** *v.t. pres. part.* **pal·i·sad·ing** *past* and *past part.* **pal·i·sad·ed** to enclose or fortify with palisades

pall (pɔl) *v.i.* to cease to be interesting or attractive

pall·bear·er (pɔ́lbɛərər) *n.* one of the little group of men who carry the coffin at a funeral or who are its closest attendants

pal·let (pǽlit) *n.* a narrow, hard bed ‖ a mattress stuffed with straw

pal·li·ate (pǽli:eit) *pres. part.* **pal·li·at·ing** *past* and *past part.* **pal·li·at·ed** *v.t.* to cause (an evil) to seem less than it is, or disguise the gravity of (a fault) with excuses etc. ‖ to relieve (pain or disease) but not cure it

pal·lid (pǽlid) *adj.* (e.g. of complexion) abnormally pale ‖ lacking brightness or warmth of color

pal·lor (pǽlər) *n.* unusual paleness of the skin

palm (pɑm) **1.** *n.* the inner part of the hand, between wrist and fingers ‖ the corresponding part of a glove ‖ a flat extension of an implement, e.g. the blade of a paddle **to have an itching palm** to have a greedy desire for money **to hold** (or **have**) **someone in the palm of one's hand** to have someone at one's mercy **2.** *v.t.* to conceal in the palm, esp. for the purpose of cheating **to palm something off** (often with 'on') to get rid of something by inducing someone to take it

palm *n.* a family of monocotyledonous, largely tropical trees and shrubs, generally having a tall trunk with no branches and a crown of large leaves ‖ the leaf of one of these trees ‖ one of these leaves or a substitute carried on Palm Sunday ‖ *(rhet.)* victory or success, or a token symbolizing this

palm·ist (pɑ́mist) *n.* a person who practices palmistry

palm·is·try (pɑ́mistri:) *n.* the practice or profession of foretelling a person's future or reading his character by interpreting the crease lines in the palm and other aspects of his hand

pal·o·mi·no (pæləmí:nou) *pl.* **pal·o·mi·nos** *n.* a horse of a light tan or golden color with a whitish mane and tail

pal·pa·bil·i·ty (pælpəbíliti:) *n.* the quality or state of being palpable ‖ something palpable

pal·pa·ble (pǽlpəb'l) *adj.* tangible, perceptible to the touch ‖ easily perceptible to the mind, obvious, *a palpable falsehood* **pál·pa·bly** *adv.*

pal·pate (pǽlpeit) *pres. part.* **pal·pat·ing** *past* and *past part.* **pal·pat·ed** *v.t.* to examine by feeling, esp. in medical examination **pal·pá·tion** *n.*

pal·pi·tate (pǽlpiteit) *pres. part.* **pal·pi·tat·ing** *past* and *past part.* **pal·pi·tat·ed** *v.i.* to tremble ‖ (of the heart) to throb rapidly and strongly

pal·pi·ta·tion (pælpitéiʃən) *n.* an irregular and violent heartbeat resulting from malfunction or from physical or emotional stress ‖ a trembling

pal·sy (pɔ́lzi:) *pl.* **pal·sies** *n.* (not used technically) paralysis, sometimes with shaking tremors

pal·tri·ness (pɔ́ltri:nis) *n.* the quality of being paltry

pal·try (pɔ́ltri:) *comp.* **pal·tri·er** *superl.* **pal·tri·est** *adj.*

---

trivial, petty ‖ mean, despicable

pam·pas (pǽmpəs) *pl. n.* treeless plains in South America, south of the Amazon, esp. the cattle-raising grasslands of E. central Argentina

pam·per (pǽmpər) *v.t.* to overindulge (someone), coddle

pam·phlet (pǽmflit) *n.* a small printed publication sewn or stitched as a paper-covered booklet, comprising an essay or treatise of a controversial, topical nature ‖ a small printed publication, often just a folder, containing informative literature **pam·phlet·éer 1.** *n.* a person who writes controversial pamphlets **2.** *v.i.* to write such pamphlets

pan (pæn) **1.** *n.* any of a number of metal containers of different shapes, used in cooking and baking ‖ any shallow, open receptacle of metal, earthenware or plastic, used for any of a variety of domestic purposes ‖ any container like this in shape, e.g. a vessel in which gold etc. is separated from gravel by washing ‖ a vessel for heating or evaporating ‖ one of the receptacles in a beam balance etc. ‖ a salt pan **2.** *v. pres. part.* **pan·ning** *past and past part.* **panned** *v.t.* to wash (gravel or sand bearing gold etc.) in a pan to separate the valuable particles from the rest ‖ to separate (gold etc.) from gravel or sand in this way ‖ *(pop.)* to criticize harshly (a play, concert etc.) ‖ (with 'out') to turn out (in some specified way), *it panned out poorly for him* ‖ (with 'out') to turn out well, *the project didn't pan out*

pan *pres. part.* **pan·ning** *past and past part.* **panned** *v.i.* to move a cinema or television camera to get a panoramic effect or to follow a moving object ‖ (of the camera) to be moved in this way ‖ *v.t.* to move (the camera) in this way

pan- *prefix* all ‖ completely

pan·a·ce·a (pænəsí:ə) *n.* a cure for all ills, a universal remedy

pa·nache (pənǽʃ) *n.* a tuft of feathers, esp. on the headdress or helmet ‖ bravura, swagger

pan·a·ma (pǽnəmɑ) *n.* a hat of fine material plaited from the dried young leaves of the jipijapa ‖ a machine-made imitation of this

pan·cake (pǽnkeik) **1.** *n.* a thin, flat cake made of batter cooked on a griddle, or in a pan **2.** *v. pres. part.* **pan·cak·ing** *past and past part.* **pan·caked** *v.i. (aviation)* to drop or land almost vertically though with the aircraft horizontal ‖ *v.t.* to cause (an aircraft) to do this

pan·chro·mat·ic (pænkroumǽtik) *adj.* (of a photographic film) sensitive to all the wavelengths of the visible spectrum ‖ (of a lens) transmitting the whole of the visible spectrum

pan·cre·as (pǽŋkri:əs) *n.* a large gland that in man lies behind the stomach. It consists of two portions, one secreting digestive juices which pass into the duodenum, the other secreting insulin which passes into the bloodstream **pan·cre·at·ic** (pæŋkri:ǽtik) *adj.*

pan·dem·ic (pændémik) *adj.* (of a disease) affecting a whole country, or the whole world

pan·de·mo·ni·um (pændəmóuni:əm) *n.* a state of utter confusion and uproar

pan·der (pǽndər) **1.** *v.i.* (with 'to') to give active encouragement (to someone or something that should not be encouraged) or provide gratification (for someone or something that should not be gratified) **2.** *n.* a procurer for prostitutes ‖ someone who encourages the vices or weaknesses of another

pane (pein) *n.* a single sheet of glass in a window, greenhouse etc. ‖ a division of a window etc. containing such a sheet of glass in a frame ‖ a flat side or edge of a many-sided object

pan·e·gyr·ic (pænidʒírik) **1.** *n.* a speech or writing eulogizing someone or something **2.** *adj.* having the nature of a panegyric **pan·e·gýr·i·cal** *adj.* **pan·e·gýr·ist** *n.*

pan·el (pǽn'l) **1.** *n.* a flat, rectangular piece of wood etc. forming part of a wall, door etc. but distinguished from the rest by being recessed, framed etc. ‖ a vertical strip of material let into or partially attached to a dress, skirt etc. as a structural or decorative element ‖ a thin board sometimes used instead of a canvas in oil painting ‖ a picture or photograph of much greater height than width ‖ a board etc. in which the controls or instruments of a machine etc. are set ‖ a group of persons, usually experts, required to judge or give an answer **2.** *v.t. pres. part.* **pan·el·ing** *past and past part.* **pan·eled** to furnish with panels ‖ *(law)* to empanel **pán·el·ing** *n.* panels of wood applied to a wall or ceiling **pán·el·ist** *n.* a member of a panel (group of persons)

pang (pæŋ) *n.* a brief, keen spasm of pain ‖ a sudden mental or emotional pain

pan·han·dle (pǽnhænd'l) **1.** *n.* a narrow, protruding strip of land or political territory, esp. the northern part of Texas between Oklahoma and New Mexico **2.** *v. pres. part.* **pan·han·dling** *past and past part.* **pan·han·dled** *v.i. (pop.)* to beg, esp. on the street

pan·ic (pǽnik) **1.** *n.* intense, contagious fear affecting a body of people ‖ an instance of this fear, e.g. a widespread hysterical anxiety over the prevailing financial situation, resulting in hasty sale or protection of securities etc. ‖ intense, irrational fear felt by an individual **2.** *v. pres. part.* **pan·ick·ing** *past and past part.* **pan·icked** *v.i.* to lose rational control of one's behavior out of sudden intense fear ‖ *v.t.* to affect with panic **3.** *adj.* of, relating to or showing panic, *panic haste*

pan·o·ram·a (pænərǽmə, pænərámə) *n.* a wide uninterrupted view over a scene ‖ a picture, unrolled so as to give the impression of such a wide, continuous view ‖ a comprehensive survey of a series of events **pan·o·rám·i·cal·ly** *adv.*

pan·sy (pǽnzi:) *pl.* **pan·sies** *n.* a wild or cultivated plant with richly and variously colored flowers ‖ *(pop.)* an effeminate or homosexual man

pant (pænt) **1.** *v.i.* to breathe quickly and in spasms, esp. after exertion, exposure to heat etc. ‖ *(rhet., with 'for', 'after')* to yearn ‖ (of the heart) to throb rapidly ‖ *v.i.* to utter gaspingly **2.** *n.* one of a series of spasms in labored breathing ‖ one of a series of throbs or gasps made by escaping steam

pan·ther (pǽnθər) *n.* a leopard, esp. a large fierce one or a black one ‖ a cougar ‖ a jaguar

pant·ie, pant·y (pǽnti:) *pl.* **pant·ies** *n.* (esp. *pl.*) underpants for a woman or a child

pan·to·mime (pǽntəmaim) **1.** *n.* a form of entertainment in which story and emotion are conveyed by gesture only, without words, but often with music and decor ‖ dumb show **2.** *v. pres. part.* **pan·to·mim·ing** *past and past part.* **pan·to·mimed** *v.t.* to represent by pantomime ‖ *v.i.* to express oneself by pantomime

pan·try (pǽntri:) *pl.* **pan·tries** *n.* a larder ‖ a room where the silver, glass etc. under the care of a butler are kept

pants (pænts) *pl. n.* trousers

pan·ty·hose or **pan·ti·hose** (pǽnti:houz) *n.* woman's garment consisting of panties and stockings as a single unit

pap (pæp) *n.* soft, mashed or semi-liquid food for babies or invalids ‖ political patronage ‖ vapid literature etc. with no intellectual content

pa·pa (pɑ́pə, pəpɑ́) *n.* (a child's word for) father

pa·pa·cy (péipəsi:) *pl.* **pa·pa·cies** *n.* the office of the pope ‖ a pope's term of office ‖ the organization of the Roman Catholic Church

pa·pal (péipəl) *adj.* of the pope, his office, jurisdiction, acts etc.

pa·per (péipər) **1.** *n.* a substance consisting of a felted thin sheet of compactly interlaced fibers of cellulose etc. obtained from wood, rags, straw etc. and used for writing, printing or drawing on, wrapping parcels, covering the walls of a room etc. ‖ a piece of this substance ‖ an essay, esp. on a scholarly subject ‖ an official document ‖ a set of examination questions or a student's written answers ‖ an essay which a student is required to write ‖ a newspaper ‖ *(pl.)* documents carried to prove identity, nationality etc. ‖ money (banknotes, bills etc.) in the form of written promises to pay ‖ *(pl.)* the collective letters, writings, documents etc. belonging or pertaining to a person **on paper** in writing **2.** *adj.* made of paper ‖ hypothetical, not having any real substance, *paper promises* **3.** *v.t.* to cover (a wall etc.) with paper

pa·per·back (péipərbæk) *n.* a book bound in paper

pa·pier-mâ·ché, pa·per-mâ·ché (peipərməʃéi) *n.* a light, tough material made of paper pulp mixed with a liquid adhesive, shaped or molded, and allowed to dry

pa·poose (pæpú:s, pəpú:s) *n.* a North American Indian baby

pap·ri·ka (pæprí:kə, pæprikə) *n.* a mildly pungent, red spice ground from the dried ripe fruit of sweet pepper ‖ the fruit itself

Pap smear or **Papanicolaou smear** diagnostic test to detect uterine or cervical cancer

pa·py·rus (pəpáirəs) *pl.* **pa·py·ri** (pəpáirai), **pa·py·rus·es** *n.* an aquatic plant indigenous to the Nile Valley. The pith, shredded and pressed into sheets, was used to write on, chiefly by the ancient Egyptians, Greeks and Romans ‖ this material ‖ a document written on papyrus

par (pɑr) **1.** *n.* equality of value, status or condition ‖ average or normal state, quality, physical condition etc. ‖ *(commerce)* nominal value ‖ *(golf)* the ideal number of strokes in which a hole, or the course, should be played by a scratch golfer **2.** *adj. (commerce)* at par ‖ average, normal

par·a·ble (pǽrəb'l) *n.* a story designed to teach a moral or religious principle by suggesting a parallel

par·a·chute (pǽrəʃu:t) **1.** *n.* a collapsible umbrella-shaped contrivance of nylon or silk fabric used esp. in aeronautics **2.** *v. pres. part.* **par·a·chut·ing** *past* and *past part.* **par·a·chut·ed** *v.t.* to land (a person or thing) by parachute ‖ *v.i.* to descend by parachute

par·a·chut·ist (pǽrəʃu:tist) *n.* a person, esp. a soldier, who makes descents from aircraft by parachute

pa·rade (pəréid) **1.** *n.* an assembly of troops in strict order for inspection or drill ‖ a ceremonial procession, esp. of troops ‖ an area where troops assemble for inspection or drill ‖ a passing in review for appraisal ‖ a place where people stroll for amusement, a promenade **on parade** exhibited for inspection **2.** *v. pres. part.* **pa·rad·ing** *past* and *past part.* **pa·rad·ed** *v.t.* to make a display of ‖ to cause (soldiers) to be drawn up for inspection or drill ‖ *v.i.* to assemble for the purpose of, and take part in, a parade ‖ to stroll, promenade, in order to attract attention

par·a·digm (pǽrədim, pǽrədaim) *n.* an example serving as a pattern ‖ *(gram.)* a conjugation or declension serving to demonstrate the inflections of a word **par·a·dig·mat·ic** (pærədigmǽtik) *adj.* **par·a·dig·mát·i·cal·ly** *adv.*

par·a·di·sa·ic (pærədiséiik) *adj.* paradisiacal **par·a·di·sá·i·cal** *adj.*

par·a·dise (pǽrədais) *n.* a place or state in which spiritual bliss is enjoyed after death, the Christian or Moslem heaven ‖ *(Bible)* an intermediate place or state in which, after death, the souls of the righteous await judgment ‖ any place of or offering perfect happiness, *a swimmer's paradise* **Par·a·dise** the garden of Eden

par·a·dox (pǽrədɒks) *n.* a statement which, though true, seems false and self-contradictory ‖ a statement which is self-contradictory and false, though it may seem true or clever ‖ a person or thing displaying contradictory qualities **par·a·dóx·i·cal** *adj.*

par·a·gon (pǽrəgɒn, pǽrəgən) *n.* a model or pattern of something good

par·a·graph (pǽrəgræf, pǽrəgrɑf) **1.** *n.* a distinct unit of writing (generally containing more than one sentence, but shorter than a chapter), usually a subsection dealing with a particular point. It is always begun on a new line and usually indented (symbol ¶) ‖ a brief article or item in a newspaper or magazine **2.** *v.t.* to divide or arrange into paragraphs ‖ *(journalism)* to write paragraphs in a newspaper or magazine **pár·a·graph·er** *n.* **par·a·graph·ic** (pærəgrǽfik), **par·a·gráph·i·cal** *adjs*

par·a·le·gal (pærəli:g'l) *n.* a paraprofessional legal assistant; one trained to assist an attorney —**par·a·le·gal** *adj.*

par·al·lel (pǽrəlel) **1.** *adj.* (of lines, curves or planes) equidistant from each other at all points and having the same direction or curvature **2.** *n.* a line, curve or plane which is parallel to another ‖ a situation, event, narrative etc. which is similar to another ‖ similarity between situations etc. ‖ a comparison, *to draw a parallel between two circumstances* ‖ the arrangement of electrical devices in a parallel circuit ‖ *(geog.)* a parallel of latitude **3.** *v.t. pres. part.* **par·al·lel·ing** *past* and *past part.* **par·al·leled** to be parallel to ‖ to find or quote a fact, event, thing or circumstance that is similar to (another)

pa·ral·y·sis (pərǽlisiz) *pl.* **pa·ral·y·ses** (pərǽlisi:z) *n.* inability to move a muscle or group of muscles, often coupled with lack of sensation in the affected area ‖ inability to act or move

par·a·lyt·ic (pærəlítik) **1.** *adj.* of, characterized by or affected with paralysis **2.** *n.* a person affected with paralysis **par·a·lýt·i·cal·ly** *adv.*

par·a·lyze, par·a·lyse (pǽrəlaiz) *pres. part.* **par·a·lyz·ing, par·a·lys·ing** *past* and *past part.* **par·a·lyzed, par·a·lysed** *v.t.* to affect with paralysis

par·a·med·ic (pærəmédik) *n.* **1.** trained medical worker (usu. with 2 yrs of training) capable of performing basic emergency medical functions **2.** *(mil.)* parachuting member of the medical corps —**paramedical** *adj.*

pa·ram·e·ter (pərǽmitər) *n. (math.)* a variable which is kept constant while others are being investigated ‖ *(math.)* a variable of which other variables are taken to be functions **par·a·met·ric** (pærəmétrik) *adj.*

par·a·mount (pǽrəmaunt) *adj.* supreme in rank, importance etc.

par·a·mour (pǽrəmuər) *n. (old-fash., rhet.)* a married man's mistress or married woman's lover

par·a·noi·a (pærənɔ́iə) *n.* a mental disorder in which the sufferer believes that other people suspect, despise or persecute him or, less commonly, in which the sufferer has delusions of grandeur **par·a·noi·ac** (pærənɔ́iæk) *n.* and *adj.* **pár·a·noid** *n.* and *adj.*

par·a·pet (pǽrəpit, pǽrəpet) *n.* a low wall at the edge of a bridge, flat roof, balcony etc. to prevent people from falling off

par·a·pher·nal·ia (pærəfərnéiljə, pærəfənéiljə) *pl. n.* (sometimes construed as singular) miscellaneous personal belongings or equipment ‖ *(law)* a wife's personal possessions as distinct from her dowry

par·a·phrase (pǽrəfreiz) *n.* a restatement in different words or free rendering of a text, passage etc. **paraphrase** *pres. part.* **par·a·phras·ing** *past* and *past part.* **par·a·phrased** *v.t.* to make a paraphrase of ‖ *v.i.* to make a paraphrase

par·a·site (pǽrəsait) *n.* an organism living in or on another living organism and deriving its nutriment partly or wholly from it, usually exhibiting some special adaptation, and often causing death or damage to its host ‖ someone who associates with a person or organization for the purpose of living at the expense of that person or group, without contributing anything to their or its well-being

par·a·sit·ic (pӕrəsítik) adj. of, relating to, having the nature of or characteristic of a parasite **par·a·sít·i·cal** adj.

par·a·sol (pӕrəsɒl, pӕrəsɒl) n. an umbrella to give shade from the sun

par·boil (párbɔil) v.t. to boil until partially cooked, usually as a preparation for roasting etc.

par·cel (párs'l) 1. n. one or more things secured by a string or wrapping to make a single object for handling and transport ‖ a number of things dealt with as a single unit ‖ a portion, esp. of land forming part of a property 2. v.t. pres. part. **par·cel·ing** past and past part. **par·celed** (with 'out') to distribute in portions ‖ (esp. with 'up') to make a parcel of ‖ (naut.) to wrap or cover with parceling **pár·cel·ing** n. the act of making a parcel ‖ (naut.) a strip of canvas, usually covered with pitch, used to cover a caulked seam or to bind around a rope so as to keep moisture out

parch (partʃ) v.t. to make dry by heating, esp. to excess ‖ to make very thirsty ‖ to dry (beans, grain etc.) by exposure to steady, intensive heat ‖ v.i. to become hot and dry

parch·ment (pártʃmənt) n. (esp. hist.) the skin of a calf, kid or sheep prepared for writing on ‖ a sheet of such prepared skin ‖ paper made to resemble this ‖ a document written or printed on this material

par·don (párd'n) n. a pardoning or being pardoned ‖ (law) an official release from a penalty, or the document granting this ‖ (pl., Roman Catholicism) indulgences **to beg someone's pardon** to ask someone to excuse one, e.g. for some minor breach of manners

pardon v.t. to choose to let (a person) be unpunished or no longer punished for wrongful acts they have committed ‖ to require no punishment for (a fault) ‖ to excuse or forgive

par·don·a·ble (párd'nəb'l) adj. (of a crime, fault etc.) capable of being pardoned

pare (pɛər) pres. part. **par·ing** past and past part. **pared** v.t. to cut off (the outer surface, skin or edge) from something

par·e·gor·ic (pӕrəgɔ́rik, pӕrəgɒ́rik) n. camphorated tincture of opium, used to relieve pain, e.g. of diarrhea

par·ent (pɛ́ərənt, pӕ́rənt) n. someone who begets or gives birth to offspring ‖ an organism, thing or organization which is the source of a new one

pa·ren·tal (pərént'l) adj. pertaining to, characteristic of, or like a parent

pa·ren·the·sis (pərénθisis) pl. **pa·ren·the·ses** (pərénθisi:z) n. a word, phrase or sentence, usually having its own complete meaning, inserted into a sentence which is grammatically complete without this insertion, and marked off from it by punctuation ‖ either of the punctuation marks (or) used to contain such a word, phrase etc. **pa·rén·the·size** pres. part. **pa·ren·the·siz·ing** past and past part. **pa·ren·the·sized** v.t. to insert parentheses in (a speech etc.) ‖ to insert (a word etc.) in a sentence as a parenthesis ‖ to place parentheses around (a written word etc.)

pa·ri·ah (pəráiə, pӕ́ri:ə) n. a social outcast ‖ a member of a low caste in parts of S. India and Burma, usually employed as a servant or common laborer

par·i·mu·tu·el (pӕri:mjú:tʃu:əl) n. a betting system by which all bets are recorded, the sums wagered on each eventuality are totaled, and the total sum wagered (minus a percentage for running costs and tax) is divided, in proportion to the stake, among those who placed bets on the winner ‖ the machine that totalizes the bets

par·ish (pӕ́riʃ) n. an administrative district of some churches, esp. a part of a diocese in the charge of a priest or minister ‖ (often construed as pl.) the residents of such a district ‖ the members of the congregation of a Protestant church ‖ a civil division in Louisiana, corresponding to a county

pa·rish·ion·er (pəríʃənər) n. someone who belongs to a parish

par·i·ty (pӕ́riti) n. equality in status, values etc. ‖ equality of purchasing power at a legally fixed ratio, between two convertible currencies at par

park (park) 1. n. a very large area of land belonging to the government preserved in its natural state and accessible to the public ‖ an enclosed area that is used for games or sports 2. v.t. to put or leave (a vehicle) temporarily by the roadside or in a space set aside for this purpose ‖ (pop.) to deposit for the time being in a certain place, park your baggage in the hall

par·ka (párkə) n. a long fur jacket with an attached hood, worn by Eskimos ‖ a similar garment of windproof fabric worn by campers, mountaineers etc.

park·way (párkwei) n. a broad highway lined with trees and grass, sometimes landscaped in the middle and usually closed to heavy vehicles, usually having an imposed speed limit

par·lay (párlei, párli) 1. n. a bet or series of bets made by parlaying 2. v.t. to lay (a former bet and its winnings) on a later race, contest etc. ‖ to make use of (some asset) to gain some greater advantage

par·ley (párli:) 1. v.i. to confer, esp. to talk peace terms with an enemy 2. pl. **par·leys** n. an official conference, esp. for settling a dispute, e.g. one held under truce arrangements with an enemy

par·lia·ment (párləmənt) n. the supreme legislative body of certain countries

par·lia·men·tar·i·an (parləməntɛ́əri:ən) n. a person well versed in parliamentary procedure **par·lia·men·tár·i·an·ism** n. the doctrine of government by a parliament

par·lia·men·ta·ry (parləméntəri:) adj. of or relating to parliament ‖ in accordance with the uses and practices of parliament ‖ (of language) permitted to be used in parliament

par·lor (párlər) n. (old-fash.) the best reception room of a house, not usually used as a living room ‖ a shop or business establishment specially equipped to perform some specified service, a funeral parlor

pa·ro·chi·al (pəróuki:əl) adj. relating to a parish ‖ (of opinions, ideas) narrowly limited in scope, provincial **pa·ró·chi·al·ism** n. narrowness of opinions or ideas

par·o·dy (pӕ́rədi:) 1. pl. **par·o·dies** n. an imitation of the characteristic style of a writer, composer etc. or of a literary, artistic or musical work, designed to ridicule ‖ a poor imitation, travesty 2. v.t. pres. part. **par·o·dy·ing** past and past part. **par·o·died** to make (someone or something) the subject of parody

pa·role (pəróul) 1. n. a promise given by a prisoner of war that in return for liberty or a degree of liberty he will respect certain conditions ‖ the conditional release of a civil prisoner ‖ liberation gained by parole 2. v.t. pres. part. **pa·rol·ing** past and past part. **pa·roled** to release on parole

par·ox·ysm (pӕ́rəksizəm) n. a sudden and violent muscular contraction and relaxation ‖ periodic intensification of an illness ‖ a sudden explosive burst of laughter, rage etc. **pár·ox·ys·mal** adj.

par·quet (parkéi, parkét) 1. n. flooring consisting of pieces of wood arranged in a pattern, e.g. of parquetry ‖ the lower floor of some theaters, or the front section of this, i.e. excluding the part beneath the balcony 2. v.t. to provide (a room) with parquet flooring ‖ to make (a floor) of parquet

par·quet·ry (párkitri:) n. woodwork of small, thin inlaid pieces arranged in esp. geometric patterns, used for flooring etc.

par·ra·keet, par·a·keet (pӕ́rəki:t) n. any of various small, slender, long-tailed parrots

par·ri·cid·al (pӕrisáid'l) adj. of, relating to or guilty of parricide

par·ri·cide (pӕ́risaid) n. someone who murders his father ‖ (rhet.) someone who murders his mother or another close relative ‖ any of these crimes

par·rot (pǽrət) **1.** *n.* any of a great number of tropical birds with a strong, curved, hooked bill, and usually brilliant plumage. Many can be trained to imitate human speech and other sounds ‖ someone who repeats words or actions mechanically without using the intelligence **2.** *v.t.* to repeat mechanically, without using the intelligence

par·ry (pǽri:) **1.** *v. pres. part.* **par·ry·ing** *past and past part.* **par·ried** *v.t.* to stop (a blow, weapon etc.) from striking by putting something in its path to change its direction ‖ to avert by interposing something ‖ *v.i.* to ward off a blow, weapon, unwelcome question etc. in that way **2.** *pl.* **par·ries** *n.* the act of parrying esp. in boxing, fencing etc. ‖ an instance of this

par·si·mo·ni·ous (pɑrsəmóuni:əs) *adj.* too careful and sparing with money or assets ‖ scanty, meager, *a parsimonious contribution*

pars·ley (pɑ́rsli:) *n.* a European aromatic herb with divided, curly or smooth leaves, native to the Mediterranean. It is widely cultivated for use as a garnish and for flavoring

pars·nip (pɑ́rsnip) *n.* a European biennial plant. Its long whitish taproot, consisting mainly of phloem cells filled with starch, in cultivated varieties develops a sweet flavor after exposure to cold, and is used as a vegetable ‖ the root itself

par·son (pɑ́rs'n) *n.* a Protestant clergyman

par·son·age (pɑ́rs'nidʒ) *n.* the house of a parish parson ‖ the house of any minister of religion

part (pɑrt) **1.** *n.* that which is less than all ‖ one of several equal amounts, numbers, quantities etc. which, when combined, constitute a whole ‖ any activity, function, duty etc. allotted to or performed by an individual and regarded as contributing to some enterprise, event etc. ‖ the lines and actions assigned to a performer in a play, opera etc. ‖ one of the parties in a transaction, contest, dispute etc. ‖ an individual thing, organ, member etc. that constitutes an essential element in something ‖ one of the units of a serial publication ‖ a dividing line formed where the hair is combed in opposite directions ‖ *(pl.)* regions, *foreign parts* ‖ *(pl., rhet.)* abilities **for my part** as far as I am concerned **in part** partly **on my (his,** etc.) **part** for which I am (he is etc.) responsible **part and parcel** an essential element **to play a part in** to contribute something towards the total effect or result or activity of **to take part in** to participate in **to take someone's part** to side with (someone) in a dispute etc. **2.** *adv.* partly

part *v.t.* to divide into parts ‖ to separate ‖ to comb (the hair) so as to make a part ‖ *v.i.* (with 'from', 'with') to go away, take one's leave ‖ (with 'with') to let go of the possession of something ‖ to separate into two or more pieces **to part company** to cease to associate

par·take (pɑrtéik) *pres. part.* **par·tak·ing** *past* **par·took** (pɑrtúk) *past. part.* **par·tak·en** (pɑrtéik'n) *v.i.* (with 'in' or 'of') to take or receive a share in ‖ *(rhet.,* with 'of') to eat (a meal)

par·tial (pɑ́rʃəl) **1.** *adj.* of, affecting or involving only a part ‖ having or showing a bias in favor of one of several disputants, contestants etc., *a partial judgment* ‖ *(pop.,* with 'to') fond of, *he is very partial to claret* **2.** *n.* *(mus.)* any note in the harmonic series

par·ti·al·i·ty (pɑrʃi:ǽliti:, pɑrʃǽliti:) *n.* bias ‖ *(pop.)* liking, fondness, *a partiality for sweets*

par·tic·i·pant (pɑrtísəpənt) **1.** *n.* someone who participates **2.** *adj.* participating

par·tic·i·pate (pɑrtísəpeit) *v.i. pres. part.* **par·tic·i·pat·ing** *past and past part.* **par·tic·i·pat·ed** (often with 'in') to be active or have a share in some activity, enter-

prise etc.

par·tic·i·pa·tion (pɑrtisəpéiʃən) *n.* the act of participating

par·ti·ci·ple (pɑ́rtisip'l, pɑ́rtisəpəl) *n.* *(gram.)* a derivative of a verb which shows tense and voice and which functions in various verb forms or as an adjective or in absolute constructions

par·ti·cle (pɑ́rtik'l) *n.* a small portion ‖ *(phys.)* an idealization in physics whereby a body is considered as having finite mass but infinitesimal size

par·tic·u·lar (pərtíkjulər) **1.** *adj.* of, relating to or designating one thing singled out among many ‖ unusual, special, *take particular care not to offend him* ‖ *(oldfash.)* concerned with details, minute ‖ fussy, fastidious ‖ *(logic)* applicable to only some members of a class **2.** *n.* *(pl.)* details of information ‖ *(logic)* a particular proposition **in particular** specifically, specially, by contrast with others

par·tic·u·lar·i·ty (pərtikjulǽriti:) *pl.* **par·tic·u·lar·i·ties** *n.* the quality or state of being particular ‖ a particular feature or detail

par·tic·u·lar·ly (pərtíkjulərli:) *adv.* in a particular manner ‖ in particular

part·ing (pɑ́rtiŋ) *n.* separation or division ‖ a place where separation or division occurs

par·ti·san, par·ti·zan (pɑ́rtiz'n) **1.** *n.* someone who actively supports (a party, cause or principle) ‖ someone not in a regular army who engages in guerrilla warfare **2.** *adj.* of, relating to or characteristic of a partisan ‖ one-sided, biased **pár·ti·san·ship, pár·ti·zan·ship** *n.*

par·ti·tion (pɑrtíʃən) **1.** *n.* a dividing into parts ‖ something that divides a room etc. into parts, esp. a thin wall ‖ one of the parts so separated ‖ *(law)* the sale of jointly owned property and distribution of the proceeds among the co-owners ‖ *(math.)* in set theory, the division of the members of the set into subsets such that each member belongs to one and only one of the subsets **2.** *v.i.* to divide into parts ‖ (esp. with 'off') to separate (one area from another) by erecting a partition

part·ly (pɑ́rtli:) *adv.* in part, not completely

part·ner (pɑ́rtnər) **1.** *n.* someone associated with another in a common undertaking ‖ one of two or more persons who are associated in a business or other joint venture and share risks and profits **2.** *v.t.* to be the partner of

part·ner·ship (pɑ́rtnərʃip) *n.* the state of being a partner or partners ‖ the relationship between partners ‖ an association of persons who share risks and profits in a business or other joint venture ‖ the legal contract binding such persons

par·tridge (pɑ́rtridʒ) *n.* any of certain plump gallinaceous game birds native to Europe, Asia and N. Africa, having short wings and tail, variegated grayish-brown plumage and unfeathered legs ‖ any of several somewhat similar gallinaceous game birds of North America, e.g. the bobwhite, the ruffed grouse ‖ the tinamou

part-time (pɑ́rttaim) *adj.* entailing less than the full number of hours of work, attendance etc. ‖ working, operating etc. for less than a full number of hours

par·tu·ri·ent (pɑrtúəri:ənt, pɑrtjúəri:ənt) *adj.* giving birth or about to give birth ‖ of or relating to parturition

par·tu·ri·tion (pɑrturíʃən, pɑrtjuríʃən, pɑrtʃuríʃən) *n.* the act of giving birth

par·ty (pɑ́rti:) *pl.* **par·ties** *n.* a group of people united by some common interest or for some common purpose ‖ a group of people united in support of a common cause, esp. a national political organization ‖ a gathering to which guests are invited in order to enjoy one another's company, *a cocktail party* ‖ one of the

(**a**) æ, cat; ɑ, car; ɔ fawn; ei, snake. (**e**) e, hen; i:, sheep; iə, deer; ɛə, bear. (**i**) i, fish; ai, tiger; ə:, bird. (**o**) o, ox; au, cow; ou, goat; u, poor; ɔi, royal. (**u**) ʌ, duck; u, bull; u:, goose; ə, bacillus; ju:, cube. x, loch; θ, think; ð, bother; z, Zen; ʒ, corsage; dʒ, savage; ŋ, orangutang; j, yak; ʃ, fish; tʃ, fetch; 'l, rabble; 'n, redden. Complete pronunciation key appears inside front cover.

persons or groups of persons engaged in a dispute or legal action ‖ *(pop.)* a person

par·ve·nu (párvənu:, párvənju:) **1.** *n.* a person who has suddenly risen from comparative poverty or obscurity to wealth, power etc., esp. one who makes a vulgar, ostentatious display **2.** *adj.* like or characteristic of such a person

pass (pæs, pɑs) *v.i.* to move along, proceed ‖ to go by something in the course of moving, *keep to the left as you pass* ‖ to go from one place, quality, state etc. to another ‖ to cease ‖ *(rhet.)* to occur ‖ (of time) to be spent, elapse ‖ to circulate or be transferred among people or places ‖ to be interchanged, *angry letters passed between them* ‖ to be just barely acceptable ‖ to be judged satisfactory in an examination, inspection, course of study etc. ‖ (of a proposed bill etc.) to be approved by a legislative body ‖ (with 'for' or 'as') to be accepted (as something else) ‖ *(law,* of a jury, the court etc., with 'on', 'upon') to pronounce the verdict or judgment ‖ *(law,* of a judgment etc., with 'for' or 'against') to be pronounced ‖ *(ball games)* to throw, kick etc. the ball to a teammate ‖ *(cards)* to decline one's turn to play, bid, take cards etc. ‖ *v.t.* to go by, beyond, over, through etc. and leave behind ‖ to meet successfully the requirements of (an examination etc.) ‖ to judge as satisfactory (someone being examined, their performacne etc.) ‖ to spend (time etc.) ‖ (of a committee, legislative body etc.) to approve (a motion, bill etc.) ‖ to convey, esp. by handing ‖ to cause to move past, *the general passed the troops in review* ‖ to pronounce (a sentence or judgment) ‖ to use (counterfeit money, invalid checks etc.) as if valid ‖ to expel (feces, urine etc.) from the body ‖ *(ball games)* to convey (the ball) to a teammate ‖ *(baseball,* of the pitcher) to walk (a batter) **to pass away** to come to an end, cease **to pass out** *(pop.)* to faint ‖ *(pop.)* to lose consciousness through drinking too much alcohol **to pass over** to consider and reject **to pass through** to undergo, experience, *to pass through a crisis* **to pass up** *(pop.)* to decline (an offer) or decide not to take advantage of (an opportunity)

pass *n.* a mark sufficient for passing an examination or test ‖ a document which gives the holder permission to do what would otherwise be forbidden, or to enjoy a special privilege ‖ a free ticket ‖ *(baseball)* a walk ‖ *(cards)* a declining of one's turn to play, bid etc. **to make a pass at** to try to attract sexually

pass *n.* a narrow way by which one can cross over or between mountains

pas·sage (pǽsidʒ) *n.* a corridor in a building ‖ an alley, lane, channel, path or other way providing communication ‖ a passage from one place, state or thing to another ‖ a moving along, progressing ‖ the passing of a measure by a legislative body ‖ the right or opportunity to pass ‖ a journey by sea or air ‖ a passenger's accommodation on board ship ‖ the charge made for this ‖ an esp. brief extract from a literary or musical work

pas·sé (pæséi, pǽsei) *adj.* no longer in style, out-of-date

pas·sen·ger (pǽsindʒər) *n.* a person who travels in a vehicle, ship, boat, aircraft etc. but is not the driver, nor one of the crew

pass·ing (pǽsiŋ, pɑ́siŋ) **1.** *adj.* going past ‖ transitory, *a passing whim* ‖ incidental ‖ (of a mark) indicating that one has passed an examination, course of study etc. **2.** *n.* the act of someone who or something that passes ‖ *(rhet.)* death **in passing** by the way, incidentally

pas·sion (pǽʃən) *n.* intense or violent emotion, esp. sexual desire or love ‖ intense anger ‖ a great liking or enthusiasm ‖ a violent emotional outburst

pas·sion·ate (pǽʃənit) *adj.* easily moved to strong emotion ‖ showing or inspired by strong emotion ‖ (of emotion) intense ‖ *(old-fash.)* easily angered

pas·sion·less (pǽʃənlis) *adj.* without passion, not moved by or showing emotion

pas·sive (pǽsiv) **1.** *adj.* acted upon by someone or something else ‖ not reacting to an external influence, inert ‖ offering no resistance ‖ (of a person) lacking initiative or drive ‖ *(gram.)* designating or expressed in a voice which denotes that the subject is also the object of the verb ‖ *(phys.)* of an instrument designed to reflect, but not record or amplify, energy impulses, e.g., transducer, filter **2.** *n.* *(gram.)* the passive voice

Pass·o·ver (pǽsouvər, pɑ́souvər) *n.* a Jewish feast commemorating the release of the Israelites from slavery in Egypt

pass·port (pǽsport, pǽspourt, pɑ́sport, pɑ́spourt) *n.* a document certifying nationality, issued by the government of a country, to a citizen intending to travel abroad ‖ something that enables a person to achieve a desired end, *a passport to success*

pass·word (pǽswə:rd, pɑ́swə:rd) *n.* a word or phrase used to show that one is authorized to enter, pass a barrier etc. ‖ a word used by members of a secret society etc. in recognition of one another

past (pæst, pɑst) **1.** *adj.* (of a period of time) just ended ‖ relating to an earlier time, *one's past life* ‖ (of a period of time, used post-positively) gone by, elapsed ‖ (of the holder of an office, position etc.) former, no longer in office, *a past president* ‖ *(gram.)* of or designating a tense that expresses an action or state in time that has gone by **2.** *n.* time that has gone by ‖ the earlier part of a person's life or the earlier history of a community, country, institution etc. ‖ *(pop.)* a wild or discreditable earlier life, *a woman with a past* ‖ *(gram.)* the past tense **3.** *prep.* beyond or further than (in time or place) ‖ (in time expressions) used to indicate the period after the hour, *10 past 8* ‖ beyond the scope, capacities or limit of **4.** *adv.* in such a way as to pass by, *the car drove past*

pas·ta (pɑ́stə) *n.* an alimentary paste of wheat flour used in processed form (noodles, macaroni, spaghetti etc.) or as fresh dough (ravioli)

paste (peist) **1.** *n.* a moist, fairly stiff mixture of liquid and a powdery substance ‖ a soft, creamy foodstuff made by pounding, grinding etc. ‖ a hard, brilliant lead and glass substance used to make imitation jewels ‖ dampened clay used in making earthenware or porcelain ‖ an adhesive made typically from flour and water **2.** *v.t. pres. part.* **past·ing** *past* and *past part.* **past·ed** to make (something) stick, using paste ‖ to cover with paste ‖ *(pop.)* to deal a hard blow or blows to

paste·board (péistbord, péistbourd) **1.** *n.* a stiff material made by pasting together two or more sheets of paper **2.** *adj.* made of pasteboard ‖ *(fig.)* unsubstantial, being merely a facade

pas·tel (pæstél, pǽstel) *n.* a powdered pigment mixed with very little gum, compressed into small, colored sticks for drawing ‖ a stick of this material ‖ the art of drawing with such sticks ‖ a drawing made with these ‖ (of color) light in tone **pas·tél·ist** *n.*

pas·teur·i·za·tion (pæstʃərizéiʃən, pæstərizéiʃən) *n.* a process which renders milk free of disease-producing bacteria and helps to prevent it from spoiling without destroying the vitamins or changing the taste

pas·teur·ize (pǽstʃəraiz, pǽstəraiz) *pres. part.* **pas·teur·iz·ing** *past* and *past part.* **pas·teur·ized** *v.t.* to sterilize by pasteurization

past·ies (péisti:z) *n.* small adhesive covering for a woman's nipples, esp. to avoid laws against indecent exposure

pas·tille (pæstí:l) *n.* a flavored or medicated lozenge

pas·time (pǽstaim, pɑ́staim) *n.* anything that serves as agreeable recreation

pas·tor (pǽstər, pɑ́stər) *n.* a priest or minister in charge of a parish or congregation

pas·to·ral (pǽstərəl, pɑ́stərəl) **1.** *adj.* of, relating to or characterized by the care of grazing animals, esp. sheep and goats ‖ (of land) used for grazing ‖ dealing with idealized country life ‖ relating to the office and work of a minister of religion **2.** *n.* a pastoral poem, play, opera etc. ‖ a circular letter sent by a bishop to his clergy, often to be read in all churches

pas·try (péistri:) *pl.* **pas·tries** *n.* dough consisting of flour, water or milk and a high proportion of butter etc., used baked as piecrust etc. ‖ baked goods consisting of this ‖ an individual tart, pie etc. made with this

pas·tur·age (pǽstʃəridʒ, pάstʃəridʒ) *n.* grazing land, or grass for grazing ‖ the pasturing of cattle e.g. on common land

pas·ture (pǽstʃər, pάstʃər) *n.* grass or other vegetation that provides food for cattle, sheep, horses, goats etc. or for wild animals ‖ land which produces such vegetation ‖ a particular piece of such land

pasture *pres. part.* **pas·tur·ing** *past* and *past part.* **pas·tured** *v.t.* to cause (an animal) to feed on pasture ‖ *v.i.* (of an animal) to feed on pasture

past·y (péisti:) *comp.* **past·i·er** *superl.* **past·i·est** *adj.* like paste in color or consistency ‖ pale, flabby, or unhealthy in appearance

pat (pæt) **1.** *n.* a gentle stroke or blow made with something flat (esp. with the hand) ‖ the sound of a gentle blow ‖ a small, neat piece of some soft substance, esp. butter **to give someone a pat on the back** to praise or congratulate someone **2.** *v.t. pres. part.* **pat·ting** *past* and *past part.* **pat·ted** to give a pat to, often as a sign of affection or sympathy ‖ to shape with blows of the hands or of some flat implement **to pat on the back** to praise or congratulate

pat 1. *adv.* in exactly the right way or at exactly the right time, *his answer came pat* **2.** *adj.* glib **to stand pat** *(poker)* to play the hand as dealt without drawing further cards ‖ to stand firmly by what one has said, or the position one has taken

patch (pætʃ) **1.** *n.* a piece of material sewed on, let into, or otherwise attached to something in order to mend it ‖ any of the bits of cloth which, when sewn together, form patchwork ‖ a small piece of ground, esp. under a specified crop ‖ *(mil.)* an emblem sewn on the sleeve of a soldier's uniform to indicate the unit to which he belongs ‖ a piece of cloth worn over an injured eye **2.** *v.t.* to mend by putting a patch on or over ‖ to make by sewing bits of cloth together **to patch up** to put together ‖ to put together out of odds and ends ‖ to become reconciled after (a quarrel etc.)

patch·y (pǽtʃi:) *comp.* **patch·i·er** *superl.* **patch·i·est** *adj.* consisting of or containing patches ‖ uneven in quality

pate (peit) *n.* *(pop., old-fash.)* the head, *his bald pate was glinting in the sun* **pát·ed** *adj.* *(pop.,* in combinations) having a specified kind of head or mind, *bald-pated, addlepated*

pâ·té (pɑteí) *n.* an edible paste of finely minced meat or fish ‖ a small meat pie or patty

pat·ent 1. (pǽt'nt) *n.* an official paper conferring a right, privilege etc., esp. one issued by a government, guaranteeing an inventor and his heirs exclusive rights over an invention, process etc. for a given length of time ‖ this invention or process **2.** (pǽt'nt, péit'nt) *adj.* (of an invention) protected by a patent ‖ made or sold under a registered trademark or trade name ‖ of or relating to the granting of patents ‖ original and individual as if protected by a patent ‖ evident, obvious **3.** *v.t.* to obtain a patent for (an invention) **pat·ent·ée** *n.* the person to whom a patent has been granted

pat·ent·ly (pǽt'ntli:, péit'ntli:) *adv.* obviously, evidently

pa·ter·nal (pətə́:rn'l) *adj.* of or relating to a father ‖ having or showing fatherly qualities ‖ related through the father **pa·ter·nal·ís·tic** *adj.* **pa·ter·nal·ís·ti·cal·ly** *adv.*

pa·ter·ni·ty (pətə́:rniti:) *n.* the state of being a father ‖ descent from a father, male parentage ‖ authorship or origin

path (pæθ, pɑθ) *pl.* **paths** (pæðz, pɑðz, pæθs, pɑθs) *n.* a narrow way or trail, esp. one formed by the frequent passage of people or animals ‖ *(computer)* the proper sequence for executing a routine ‖ any way or space by which people may pass ‖ the course of a moving person or thing

pa·thet·ic (pəθétik) *adj.* arousing pity or sympathetic sorrow ‖ arousing pitying contempt **pa·thét·i·cal·ly** *adv.*

path·o·log·ic (pæθəlɒ́dʒik) *adj.* pertaining to pathology **path·o·lóg·i·cal** *adj.* pathologic ‖ involving or resulting from disease ‖ morbid

pa·thol·o·gist (pəθɒ́lədʒist) *n.* a specialist in pathology

pa·thol·o·gy (pəθɒ́lədʒi:) *n.* the study of disease and all its manifestations, esp. of the functional and structural changes caused by it ‖ all the manifestations of a disease

pa·thos (péiθɒs) *n.* a quality in an experience, narrative, literary work etc. which arouses profound feelings of compassion or sorrow

pa·tience (péiʃəns) *n.* the capacity to put up with pain, troubles, difficulties, hardship etc. without complaint or ill temper ‖ the ability to wait or persevere without losing heart or becoming bored **to have no patience with** to feel nothing but irritation with or contempt for, to be unable to put up with

pa·tient (péiʃənt) **1.** *adj.* showing or having patience **2.** *n.* a person receiving medical attention ‖ a client of a doctor, dentist etc., whether sick or not

pat·i·na (pǽt'nə) *n.* a surface formed on metal (esp. bronze) by long exposure to the air, or produced artificially by an acid ‖ a surface formed on wood by age or constant care and handling

pa·ti·o (pǽti:ou) *pl.* **pa·ti·os** *n.* an open courtyard enclosed by the walls of a house, characteristic of Spanish and Spanish-American houses ‖ an area, usually paved, adjoining a house, used esp. for outdoor cooking or dining

pat·ois (pǽtwɑ) *n.* the speech or dialect peculiar to one part of a country, differing from the standard written or spoken language

pa·tri·arch (péitri:ɑrk) *n.* the father or head of a family or tribe ‖ *(rhet.)* any venerable head of a large family or tribe ‖ *(rhet.)* any very old and dignified man

pa·tri·ar·chy (péitri:ɑrki:) *pl.* **pa·tri·ar·chies** *n.* a social system in which the chief authority is the father or eldest male member of the family or clan ‖ a community characterized by this system

pa·tri·cian (pətríʃən) **1.** *n.* *(hist.)* a member of one of the privileged families of ancient Rome, who alone until the 4th c. B.C. had the right to hold office **2.** *adj.* noble, aristocratic ‖ having or exemplifying qualities and standards associated with the aristocracy

pat·ri·mo·ny (pǽtrimouni:) *pl.* **pat·ri·mo·nies** *n.* property, money etc. inherited from one's father or an ancestor ‖ anything valuable handed down by earlier generations and looked on as a trust ‖ an endowment of an institution, e.g. a church or college

pa·tri·ot (péitri:ət, péitri:ɒt) *n.* a person who loves his native country and will do all he can for it

pa·tri·ot·ic (peitri:ɒ́tik) *adj.* inspired by, showing or aimed at arousing love of one's country **pa·tri·ót·i·cal·ly** *adv.*

pa·tri·ot·ism (péitri:ətịzəm) *n.* zealous love of one's country

pa·trol (pətróul) *pres. part.* **pa·trol·ling** *past* and *past part.* **pa·trolled** *v.t.* to go the rounds of (an army camp, town etc.) for the purpose of guarding, in-

---

(a) æ, c*a*t; ɑ, c*a*r; ɔ f*a*wn; ei, sn*a*ke. (e) e, h*e*n; i:, sh*ee*p; iə, d*ee*r; ɛə, b*ea*r. (i) i, f*i*sh; ai, t*i*ger; ə:, b*i*rd. (o) o, *o*x; au, c*o*w; ou, g*oa*t; u, p*oo*r; ɔi, r*oy*al. (u) ʌ, d*u*ck; u, b*u*ll; u:, g*oo*se; ə, b*a*cillus; ju:, c*u*be. x, lo*ch*; θ, *th*ink; ð, bo*th*er; z, *Z*en; ʒ, cor*s*age; dʒ, sava*g*e; ŋ, oranguta*ng*; j, *y*ak; ʃ, *fish*; tʃ, fe*tch*; 'l, rabb*le*; 'n, redd*en*. Complete pronunciation key appears inside front cover.

specting etc. ‖ *v.i.* to go the rounds of a place in order to guard it etc.

patrol *n.* a patrolling ‖ an instance of this ‖ the men, aircraft, ships etc. engaged in patrolling ‖ a subdivison of a troop of boy scouts or girl scouts, usually having six to eight members

pa·tron (péitrən) *n.* a person or institution that gives practical (e.g. financial) support to a cause, individual or group regarded as deserving it ‖ a person who lends his name to a deserving institution or cause as an indication of his approval and support ‖ a patron saint of a specified person, place, group etc. ‖ a customer, esp. a regular one, in a shop, restaurant etc.

pat·ter (pætər) 1. *n.* the quick talk or chatter of a comedian or entertainer, salesman etc. ‖ the slang or private language used by a particular group or class ‖ mechanically repeated words 2. *v.t.* to repeat (words, prayers, a formula etc.) mechanically without considering the meaning ‖ *v.i.* to talk volubly but without much sense

patter 1. *v.t.* to make a series of short, light, rapid taps ‖ to run or move making a series of light tapping sounds 2. *n.* the noise made by pattering

pat·tern (pætərn) 1. *n.* an orderly sequence consisting of a number of repeated or complementary elements, decorative motifs etc. ‖ a style of design or applied decoration ‖ a model from which a copy can be made ‖ a sample of cloth, paper etc. showing the design or color 2. *v.t.* to make or form in imitation of another person or thing, *pattern yourself on him* ‖ to decorate with a pattern

pat·ty (pæti:) *pl.* **pat·ties** *n.* a little pie, generally with a savory filling ‖ a small, flat, esp. fried cake of minced meat etc.

pau·ci·ty (pɔ́siti:) *n.* smallness, esp. insufficiency, in number or amount

paunch (pɔntʃ) *n.* a fat, protruding belly, esp. a man's ‖ *(zool.)* the rumen

pau·per (pɔ́pər) *n.* a completely destitute person, esp. one entirely dependent on public charity **páu·per·ism, pau·per·i·zá·tion** *ns* **páu·per·ize** *pres. part.* **pau·per·iz·ing** *past* and *past part.* **pau·per·ized** *v.t.* to reduce to the condition of a pauper

pause (pɔz) *n.* a short period of time when sound, motion or activity stops before starting again **to give (someone) pause** to cause (someone) to hesitate or think again before taking action

pause *pres. part.* **paus·ing** *past* and *past part.* **paused** *v.i.* to make a pause ‖ to hesitate, stop to reflect

pave (peiv) *pres. part.* **pav·ing** *past* and *past part.* **paved** *v.t.* to cover (a road, path etc.) with a surface to walk or travel on **to pave the way for** (or **to**) to provide an easy road for (or to)

pave·ment (péivmənt) *n.* a paved street or road ‖ any paved surface ‖ the material used in paving

pa·vil·ion (pəvíljən) *n.* a large tent, often open on one side ‖ a light, elegant building or shelter in a garden, park etc. ‖ one of several buildings into which a large institution, esp. a hospital is sometimes divided ‖ *(anat.)* the auricle of the ear

paw (pɔ) 1. *n.* the foot of a four-footed animal having claws ‖ *(pop.)* a hand, esp. a clumsy or dirty one 2. *v.t.* (of an animal) to strike, scrape or scratch with the hoof or paw ‖ (of a person) to feel, touch or handle with the hands in a rude or clumsy way

pawn (pɔn) 1. *n.* the state of being pawned ‖ something pawned 2. *v.t.* to hand over as a pledge or security for a loan of money

pawn *n.* *(chess)* one of the men of least size and value, each player having eight ‖ a person whom others use for their own ends

pawn·bro·ker (pɔ́nbroukər) *n.* a person licensed to lend money on articles pawned

pay (pei) 1. *v. pres. part.* **pay·ing** *past* and *past part.* **paid** (peid) *v.t.* to give (someone) money in return for goods, work or services ‖ to give (someone) money owed or due ‖ to discharge (a debt) ‖ to be rewarding to ‖ to make return for, repay ‖ to give or render (a service, visit, compliment etc.) ‖ *v.i.* to give money in return for goods, work or services ‖ to be profitable, *it pays to buy good quality* **to pay for** to meet the cost of ‖ to suffer the consequences of, *make him pay for his rudeness* **to pay in** to deposit (money etc.) in an account **to pay off** to finish paying ‖ to give (someone) his wages and dismiss him ‖ to recompense for good or evil ‖ to turn out profitably **to pay one's way** to pay one's share of costs or expenses ‖ to remain solvent **to pay out** to distribute (money etc.) ‖ *(past* and *past part.* **payed**) to pass along the slack of a rope **to pay up** to pay in full or on time 2. *adj.* (of earth) yielding oil or valuable metals ‖ made available for use by the insertion of a coin or coins in a slot, *a pay toilet*

pay *n.* money received as wages or salary for work or services (always used instead of 'wage' or 'salary' in the armed services) **in the pay of** receiving money from, in return for work or services (often with the suggestion of being bribed)

pay·a·ble (péiəb'l) *adj.* that must, can, should or may be paid

pay·ment (péimənt) *n.* a paying for work, services, goods bought, charges incurred, debts etc. ‖ the money etc. paid for work or services ‖ something given in return, or as a reward, punishment or revenge

peace (pi:s) *n.* the condition that exists when nations or other groups are not fighting ‖ the ending of a state of war ‖ the treaty that marks the end of war ‖ friendly relations between individuals, untroubled by disputes ‖ freedom from noise, worries, troubles, fears etc., *peace of mind* **at peace** in a state of peace, friendliness or calm **to hold** (or **keep**) **one's peace** *(rhet.)* to be silent **to keep the peace** to prevent or avoid strife **to make (one's) peace** to put an end to a quarrel, become friendly again

peace·a·ble (pí:səb'l) *adj.* not given to fighting or quarreling ‖ in a state of peace **péace·a·bly** *adv.*

peace·ful (pí:sfəl) *adj.* calm, quiet, untroubled, undisturbed by noise, worries, fears etc. ‖ not warlike or violent ‖ not given to fighting or quarreling

peach (pi:tʃ) 1. *n.* a small tree of the temperate zone, native to China, having lanceolate leaves. The fruit is a sweet, juicy, yellow or white drupe occurring in clingstone and freestone varieties and having a thin, downy skin ‖ the fruit of this tree ‖ *(pop.)* any particularly excellent person or thing, *a peach of a house* ‖ a color resembling that of the fruit, a soft, pale, yellowish red 2. *adj.* of the color peach

pea·cock (pí:kɒk) *n.* a male member of a genus of large gallinaceous birds, native to India and Asia but widely kept for their ornamental value

pea jacket a short, double-breasted black or navy blue overcoat worn esp. by seamen

peak (pi:k) *n.* a pointed top or projection ‖ the pointed top of a mountain ‖ a high mountain, esp. one that stands alone ‖ the projecting brim at the front of a cap ‖ the highest point, maximum ‖ *(elec.)* the maximum value of a varying quantity during a specified period

peak *v.t.* *(naut.)* to raise (a yard, a gaff, oars) to or towards the vertical

peaked (pí:kt) *adj.* having a peak or point ‖ (pí:kid) looking sickly and thin

peal (pí:l) 1. *n.* a loud ringing of a bell or bells ‖ a set of bells tuned to the notes of the major scale for ringing changes ‖ a complete set or part of a set of changes, rung on these ‖ a sudden burst of noise 2. *v.i.* (of bells, thunder, laughter etc.) to ring out, burst into sudden noise ‖ *v.t.* (often with 'out') to sound vigorously in a peal

pea·nut (pí:nʌt) *n.* a branched, trailing annual plant, probably indigenous to Brazil, but cultivated widely in warm regions for its oily, nutritious seeds ‖ its nutlike seed

pear (pεǝr) *n.* a tree native to W. Asia and E. Europe. Many strains and hybrids are cultivated in all temperate regions ‖ its fruit, a fleshy, juicy, sweet pome, varying in color between yellow-green and russet, and usually tapering at the stem from a bulbous base

pearl (pǝːrl) **1.** *n.* a secretion, chiefly of calcium carbonate, produced by some mollusks ‖ a hard, lustrous, usually white, almost spherical deposit of this around a small solid irritant ‖ something rare and precious, *his words are pearls of wisdom* ‖ a very pale gray color with bluish overtones **to cast pearls before swine** to say wise or witty things to people unable to appreciate them **2.** *adj.* made of or resembling pearl

pearl·y (pǝːrliː) *comp.* **pearl·i·er** *superl.* **pearl·i·est** *adj.* of or like a pearl or mother-of-pearl ‖ decorated with mother-of-pearl or pearls ‖ abounding in pearls

peas·ant (pézʾnt) *n.* a hired farm laborer or the owner or tenant of a small farm or holding **péas·ant·ry** *n.* a body of peasants ‖ peasants collectively

peat (piːt) *n.* a dense accumulation of water-saturated, partially decayed vegetable tissue. The first stage in the formation of coal, it is itself, after drying, used as a fuel

peat·y (píːtiː) *comp.* **peat·i·er** *superl.* **peat·i·est** *adj.* of, like or consisting of peat

peb·ble (pébʾl) **1.** *n.* a small stone, naturally rounded and worn smooth by the action of water ‖ transparent rock crystal, used instead of glass in spectacles ‖ a lens of this ‖ pebbled leather or its surface **2.** *v.t. pres. part.* **peb·bling** *past and past part.* **peb·bled** to pave or cover with pebbles set in cement, plaster etc. ‖ to give a roughly indented surface to (leather etc.) **péb·bly** *adj.*

pe·can (pikén, pikán, píːkæn) *n.* an edible, smooth-shelled, olive-shaped nut, a species of hickory often of great size, with rough bark and hard wood, found wild and cultivated in the southern U.S.A. and N. Mexico ‖ this tree ‖ the wood of this tree

pec·ca·dil·lo (pεkǝdílou) *pl.* **pec·ca·dil·los, pec·ca·dil·loes** *n.* a trifling fault or transgression

pec·cant (pékǝnt) *adj. (rhet.)* sinful ‖ *(rhet.)* offending against accepted rules or conventions ‖ *(med.)* diseased or causing disease

peck 1. *v.t.* (of a bird) to strike or make holes in with the beak ‖ to make (a hole) by striking with a rapid movement ‖ to kiss perfunctorily ‖ *v.i.* (esp. with 'at') to make striking movements or holes in something with the beak or as if with the beak ‖ (with 'at') to nibble food without appetite **2.** *n.* an instance of pecking ‖ a quick perfunctory kiss ‖ a little mark or hole made by or as if by pecking

pec·tin (péktin) *n.* any of a group of polysaccharides occurring in plant tissues esp. in fruits, solutions of which readily form a gel. Added to jams or fruit juices, they induce setting into a jelly

pec·to·ral (péktǝrǝl) **1.** *adj.* of or relating to the chest or breast ‖ used in treating diseases of the chest or lungs ‖ worn on the chest or breast **2.** *n.* a pectoral muscle or fin ‖ a pectoral cross ‖ the decorated breastplate worn by the Jewish high priest ‖ a pectoral medicine

pec·u·late (pékjuleit) *pres. part.* **pec·u·lat·ing** *past and past part.* **pec·u·lat·ed** *v.i.* to embezzle ‖ *v.t.* to embezzle money **pec·u·lá·tion, péc·u·la·tor** *ns*

pe·cu·liar (pikjúːljǝr) *adj.* odd, unusual, strange ‖ (often with 'to') belonging to or associated with a particular person, place, time, thing etc. **pe·cu·li·ar·i·ty** (pikjuːliːéritiː) *pl.* **pe·cu·li·ar·i·ties** *n.* a distinctive characteristic, a feature peculiar to a particular per-

son, place, thing etc. ‖ oddness, unusualness ‖ an odd, unusual characteristic

pe·cu·ni·ar·y (pikjúːniːεriː) *adj.* consisting of money ‖ of or relating to money ‖ (of an offense) having a fine as penalty

ped·a·gog·ic (pεdǝgɔ́dʒik, pεdǝgóudʒik) *adj.* of, characteristic or or like a pedagogue ‖ having to do with teaching **ped·a·góg·i·cal** *adj.* **ped·a·góg·ics** *n.* the science of teaching

ped·a·gogue, ped·a·gog (pédǝgɔg, pédǝgɒg) *n.* a teacher, esp. a narrowminded pedant

ped·al (pédʾl) **1.** *n.* a lever operated by the foot, e.g. to sound, sustain or dampen notes on a piano etc., work the brake etc. of a car, propel a bicycle etc. **2.** *v. pres. part.* **ped·al·ing** *past and past part.* **ped·aled** *v.t.* to operate by a pedal or pedals ‖ *v.i.* to operate a pedal or pedals

ped·al (píːdʾl) *adj. (zool.)* of or relating to a foot, esp. of a mollusk ‖ (of) of, relating to or involving the use of a pedal or pedals

ped·ant (pédʾnt) *n.* a person who makes a tedious show of dull learning ‖ an overprecise person who is unimaginative about using rules or knowledge **pe·dan·tic** (pǝdéntik) *adj.* **pe·dán·ti·cal·ly** *adv.*

ped·ant·ry (pédʾntriː) *pl.* **ped·ant·ries** *n.* the pedantic show or use of learning or knowledge ‖ an instance of this ‖ the quality or state of being pedantic

ped·dle (pédʾl) *pres. part.* **ped·dling** *past and past part.* **ped·dled** *v.t.* to sell (goods) as one travels from place to place ‖ *v.i.* to travel around with goods to sell

ped·dler (pédlǝr) *n.* someone who travels about peddling goods

ped·es·tal (pédistǝl) *n.* a separate base supporting a column, statue, large vase etc. **to place (someone) on a pedestal** to attribute ideal qualities to (someone)

pe·des·tri·an (pidéstriːǝn) **1.** *n.* a person going about on foot **2.** *adj.* of, for or relating to pedestrians ‖ dull, commonplace, lacking imagination, *a pedestrian performance*

pe·di·at·ric, pae·di·at·ric (piːdiǽtrik) *adj.* of or relating to the medical care of children **pe·di·a·tri·cian, pae·di·a·tri·cian** (piːdiːǝtríʃǝn) *n.* a specialist in pediatrics **pe·di·at·rics, pae·di·at·rics** (piːdiǽtriks) *n.* the branch of medicine concerned with the health and illnesses of children

ped·i·cure (pédikjuǝr) *n.* chiropody ‖ a chiropodist ‖ *(loosely)* a cleaning, cutting and polishing of the toenails

ped·i·gree (pédigriː) *n.* a chart or table showing how and from whom a person or family is descended, a genealogical or family tree ‖ a table of descent of purebred animals ‖ ancestry **péd·i·greed** *adj.* (of domestic animals) having a recorded pedigree

pe·dom·e·ter (pidɔ́mitǝr) *n.* an instrument which counts the number of steps taken by a person walking and measures the approximate distance covered

peek (piːk) **1.** *v.i.* to peep, look, esp. in such a way as not to be seen **2.** *n.* a quick or furtive look

peel (piːl) **1.** *v.t.* to remove the outer covering, skin, rind etc. from ‖ (with 'off') to remove (an outer covering, skin, rind etc.) ‖ *v.i.* (of an outer covering, skin etc.) to come off, flake off ‖ to shed an outer covering or skin **2.** *n.* the rind or outer skin of a fruit or of some vegetables

peen (piːn) **1.** *n.* the thin end of the head of a hammer **2.** *v.t.* to strike or work with a peen

peep (piːp) **1.** *v.i.* to take a look through a small hole, around a corner, over a wall etc., esp. in such a way as not to be seen ‖ to take a quick look ‖ (with 'out') to be visible briefly, incompletely or from a distance

‖ to come into view, as if from hiding ‖ *v.t.* (with 'out') to cause to protrude a bit **2.** *n.* the act of peeping ‖ a surreptitious, furtive glance ‖ *(rhet.)* the first sign, *at peep of dawn*

peep 1. *n.* the high, weak noise made by very young birds **2.** *v.i.* to utter a peep ‖ *v.t.* to utter in a high, weak voice

peep·er (píːpər) *n.* a person who looks furtively

peer (piər) *n.* a member of one of the British degrees of nobility: a duke, marquis, earl, viscount, or baron ‖ a nobleman of any country ‖ someone having the same status in rank, age, ability etc. as another, *to be judged by one's peers* **péer·age** *n.* **péer·less** *adj.* so excellent as to have no equal

peeve (piːv) **1.** *v.t. pres. part.* **peev·ing** *past* and *past part.* **peeved** to make peevish **2.** *n.* *(pop.)* a peevish mood **a pet peeve** some trivial, frequent source of annoyance

peev·ish (píːviʃ) *adj.* irritable, apt to complain, grumble and be ill-tempered ‖ showing such crossness, *peevish gesture*

peg (peg) **1.** *n.* a small piece of wood, metal, plastic etc., generally cylindrical and slightly tapered, used to hold together two parts of a construction, to secure a joint, bung a hole, hang things on, mark the score in cribbage or darts, fasten ropes to etc. ‖ a step or degree, *to move up a peg in an organization* **a square peg in a round hole** (or **a round peg in a square hole**) a person who is out of place in the circumstances in which he finds himself **2.** *v. pres. part.* **peg·ging** *past* and *past part.* **pegged** *v.t.* to fasten, secure or attach with a peg or pegs ‖ *v.i.* (with 'away', 'at' etc.) to work hard and steadily **to peg out** to mark out with pegs

peign·oir (penwár, pénwɑr) *n.* a negligee

pel·i·can (pélikən) *n.* a genus of large, web-footed, gregarious birds with a large wingspread. They are widely distributed in temperate and tropical zones

pel·let (pélit) *n.* a little ball, e.g. of rolled-up paper ‖ a small piece of shot, fired singly from an air gun, or in groups packed into the cartridge of a shotgun

pell-mell (pélmél) **1.** *adv.* in great haste and confusion **2.** *adj.* confused, disorderly, *pell-mell haste* **3.** *n.* hurry and confusion

pelt (pelt) **1.** *v.t.* to strike by throwing things at continuously and in great quantity ‖ to throw (objects) continuously ‖ *v.i.* (e.g. of rain) to pour or beat down continually with force ‖ *(pop.)* to run as fast as possible **2.** *n.* a hard blow ‖ a pelting **at full pelt** at full speed

pelt *n.* the skin of an animal with the hair or wool on ‖ a raw hide after the hair or wool has been removed

pel·vic (pélvik) *adj.* related to or situated at or near the pelvis

pel·vis (pélvis) *pl.* **pel·vis·es, pel·ves** (pélviːs) *n.* *(anat., zool.)* a bony cavity in vertebrates, formed in man by the pelvic girdle together with the coccyx and sacrum ‖ the bones that form this cavity, collectively

pen (pen) **1.** *n.* an instrument for writing in ink ‖ the nib of such a writing instrument ‖ a bird's feather, sharpened at the broad end and split to form a nib, formerly used for writing ‖ *(rhet.)* style or manner of writing ‖ professional writing, *a journalist lives by his pen* **2.** *v.t. pres. part.* **pen·ning** *past* and *past part.* **penned** *(rhet.)* to write

pen *pres. part.* **pen·ning** *past* and *past part.* **penned** (with 'in', 'up') *v.t.* to shut up in a pen or other confined space

pe·nal (píːn'l) *adj.* concerned with esp. legal punishment of crime ‖ constituting an esp. legal punishment for crime ‖ (of an offense) legally punishable **pé·nal·ize** *pres. part.* **pe·nal·iz·ing** *past* and *past part.* **pe·nal·ized** *v.t.* to inflict a penalty upon ‖ to subject to a disadvantage **pe·nal·i·zá·tion** *n.* a penalizing or being penalized

pen·al·ty (pén'lti:) *pl.* **pen·al·ties** *n.* a punishment for breaking a law or otherwise committing an offense

against established authority ‖ a disagreeable consequence suffered as a result of one's own folly or wrongdoing ‖ *(games)* a disadvantage imposed as punishment for breaking the rules **on** (or **upon** or **under**) **penalty of** with the certainty of incurring (some penalty) if a specified command or condition is not fulfilled

pen·ance (pénəns) *n.* punishment or suffering undergone voluntarily to atone for sin or wrongdoing ‖ the acts which a priest requires of a penitent **to do penance** *(Roman Catholic and Orthodox Churches)* to perform the acts required for absolution after confession ‖ to perform some act as atonement for sin or wrongdoing

pen·chant (péntʃənt, pãʃã) *n.* an inclination towards, a liking for, *a penchant for ice cream*

pen·cil (pénsəl) **1.** *n.* an instrument for writing or drawing, consisting of a slim cylinder esp. of wood, with a core of graphite or black lead which can be sharpened to a point and which is sometimes mechanically retractable ‖ anything like such an instrument in shape or function ‖ a long, converging, narrow beam of light **2.** *v.t. pres. part.* **pen·cil·ing** *past* and *past part.* **pen·ciled** to write, draw or mark in pencil

pen·dant (péndənt) **1.** *n.* something suspended ‖ a piece of jewelry hanging from a brooch, necklace, chain etc. ‖ a companion piece, e.g. a picture meant to be seen in conjunction with another ‖ *(naut.)* a short line hanging from a masthead, with an eye for attaching gear or tackle ‖ *(archit.)* a decorative finial or spiked ornament projecting downward from a ceiling or roof **2.** *adj.* pendent

pen·dent (péndənt) *adj.* *(rhet.)* hanging ‖ *(rhet.)* overhanging ‖ undetermined, pending

pend·ing (péndiŋ) **1.** *adj.* in process of being decided, settled, arranged etc. ‖ about to happen **2.** *prep.* during the wait for, until, *a temporary arrangement pending a final settlement*

pen·du·lum (péndʒuləm, péndjuləm, pénduləm) *n.* a body suspended from a pivot and able to swing to and fro as a result of gravitational force, when displaced from its position of rest

pen·e·tra·ble (pénitrəb'l) *adj.* capable of being penetrated **pén·e·tra·bly** *adv.*

pen·e·trate (pénitreit) *pres. part.* **pen·e·trat·ing** *past* and *past part.* **pen·e·trat·ed** *v.t.* to go into by piercing ‖ to make or force a way through ‖ to spread through ‖ to discern ‖ *v.i.* to go into something by piercing it ‖ to make or force a way ‖ (with 'into', 'through' or 'to') to discern the truth or meaning of something obscure **pén·e·trat·ing** *adj.*

pen·e·tra·tion (penitréiʃən) *n.* the act of penetrating ‖ keenness of mind, insight ‖ *(mil.)* the depth to which a projectile penetrates into a target

pen·e·tra·tive (pénitreitiv) *adj.* penetrating

pen·guin (péŋgwin, péngwin) *n.* aquatic, flightless bird of Antarctic and subantarctic regions

pen·i·cil·lin (penisílin) *n.* a mixture of antibiotic substances produced by molds of the genus *Penicillium*, preparations of which are widely used for their potent bacteriostatic action against a variety of pathogenic bacteria

pen·in·su·la (pənínsulə, pənínsjulə) *n.* a piece of land that is almost an island, either connected to the mainland by a narrow neck or projecting into the sea, with the sea on three sides **pen·ín·su·lar** *adj.*

pe·nis (píːnis) *pl.* **pe·nes** (píːniːz), **pe·nis·es** *n.* the male organ of copulation in mammals

pen·i·tence (pénitəns) *n.* the quality or state of being penitent

pen·i·tent (pénitənt) **1.** *adj.* feeling or showing sorrow for having sinned or done wrong **2.** *n.* a penitent person ‖ *(Roman Catholic and Orthodox Churches)* a person receiving the sacrament of penance

pen·i·ten·tia·ry (peniténʃəri) **1.** *pl.* **pen·i·ten·tia·ries** *n.* a prison for criminals ‖ such a prison, esp. a state or federal prison, in which the inmates are required to do labor **2.** *adj.* relating to civil prisons ‖ of or relating to penance

pen·nant (pénənt) *n.* a long, narrow, triangular or tapering flag used esp. on ships for signaling etc. ‖ a similar flag as a symbol of sports championship

pen·ni·less (péni:lis) *adj.* having no money or virtually none

pen·ny (péni:) *pl.* **pen·nies** *n.* (symbol [¢]) a U.S. or Canadian coin worth one cent **a penny for your thoughts** what are you thinking about so abstractedly? **a pretty penny** a large sum of money spent or gained

pe·nol·o·gist (pi:nólədʒist) *n.* a specialist in penology

pe·nol·o·gy (pi:nólədʒi:) *n.* the study of how to treat criminals and of how prisons or other establishments for their reform should be organized

pen·sion (pénʃən) **1.** *n.* a sum of money paid regularly to a person who no longer works because of age, disablement etc., or to his widow or dependent children, by the state, by his former employers, or from funds to which he and his employers have both contributed ‖ a similar sum paid, either by the state or by a firm or a private individual, to enable e.g. a research scientist or poet to live and carry on his work **2.** *v.t.* to pay a pension to ‖ (with 'off') to dismiss and pay a pension to **pén·sion·a·ble** *adj.* entitled to a pension ‖ entitling to a pension

pen·sion·er (pénʃənər) *n.* a person who receives a pension

pen·sive (pénsiv) *adj.* deep in serious thought ‖ showing this state, *a pensive look*

pent (pent) *adj.* (usually with 'up' or 'in') shut in, confined, *pent up in school*

pen·ta·gon (péntəgɒn) *n.* a plane figure with five angles and five sides **the Pentagon** a pentagonal building in Arlington, Virginia, headquarters of the U.S. Department of Defense **pen·tag·o·nal** (pentǽgən'l) *adj.*

pen·tath·lon (pentǽθlɒn) *n.* an athletic competition in which each competitor has to take part in five events

pent·house (pénthaus) *pl.* **pent·hous·es** (pénthauziz) *n.* a shed or other structure built against a main building with its roof sloping away from the larger building's wall ‖ a sloping roof projecting from the wall of a building to form a shelter ‖ a rooftop apartment or other structure

pe·num·bra (pinʌ́mbrə) *pl.* **pe·num·bras, pe·num·brae** (pinʌ́mbri:) *n.* the partial shadow cast by a body where light from a given source is not wholly excluded, e.g. in an eclipse ‖ the outer shaded part of a sunspot **pe·num·bral** *adj.*

pe·nu·ri·ous (pənúari:əs, pənjúari:əs) *adj.* poor or showing extreme poverty

pen·u·ry (pénjəri:) *n.* poverty ‖ lack, scarcity

pe·on (pí:ən, pí:ɒn) *n.* (in Latin America) a laborer, esp. formerly one compelled to work for a master in order to work off a debt ‖ any laborer **pe·on·age** (pí:ənidʒ) *n.* the condition of a peon ‖ (loosely) servitude of any kind

pe·o·ny (pí:əni:) *pl.* **pe·o·nies** *n.* a genus of usually herbaceous plants native to Europe and Asia, widely cultivated for their large, showy single or double red, pink, yellow or white flowers

peo·ple (pí:p'l) **1.** *pl. n.* human beings, *you can't treat people like cattle* ‖ other persons in general, *what will people say?* ‖ a collective group of persons ‖ one's family or parents **a people** the members of a particular race or nation **the people** the working classes as contrasted with the privileged ‖ the electorate **2.** *v.t. pres. part.* **peo·pling** *past* and *past part.* **peo·pled** to populate ‖ to fill as if with people, *his memoirs are peopled with imaginary creatures*

pep (pep) **1.** *n.* (pop.) energy, liveliness **2.** *v.t. pres. part.* **pep·ping** *past* and *past part.* **pepped** to put new life into, *to pep up a dull party*

pep·per (pépər) **1.** *n.* a product consisting of the dried, usually ground fruit of *Piper nigrum,* fam. *Piperaceae,* a plant native to the East Indies and cultivated in the Tropics. It is used universally as a culinary seasoning ‖ this plant ‖ any of several similar condiments, e.g. cayenne pepper **2.** *v.t.* to season with the ground fruit of *Piper nigrum* ‖ to sprinkle or pelt as if with this

pep·per·mint (pépərmint) *n.* a small, perennial, aromatic plant with toothed leaves and pale purple flowers, native to Europe, but now found wild and cultivated in most temperate zones ‖ an oil with an aromatic taste, distilled from its leaves, stems and flowers, used in confectionery etc. ‖ a candy flavored with this ‖ any of several related plants

pep·tic (péptik) *adj.* helping digestion, esp. by the action of pepsin ‖ of, like or involving pepsin ‖ relating to digestion or to gastric juice

per- *prefix* through, throughout ‖ thoroughly, completely ‖ (chem.) containing a large or the largest possible proportion of a specified element or radical

per (pə:r, pər) *prep.* for each ‖ by means of, *send it per diplomatic agent*

per·am·bu·late (pərǽmbjuleit) *pres. part.* **per·am·bu·lat·ing** *past* and *past part.* **per·am·bu·lat·ed** *v.t.* (rhet.) to walk through ‖ *v.i.* (rhet.) to walk about, stroll

per·am·bu·la·tor (pərǽmbjuleitər) *n.* (Br.) a baby carriage ‖ a wheeled odometer used by surveyors

per an·num (pərǽnəm) *adv.* (abbr. per an.) yearly, *he is paid $15,000 per annum*

per·cale (pərkéil) *n.* a smooth, closely woven cotton material

per cap·i·ta (pərkǽpitə) *adv.* and *adj.* (abbr. per cap.) per head of population for each person

per·ceive (pərsí:v) *pres. part.* **per·ceiv·ing** *past* and *past part.* **per·ceived** *v.t.* to become aware of through the senses, e.g. by hearing or seeing ‖ to become aware of by understanding, discern

per·cent (pərsént) (abbr. p.c., pct, per ct. *symbol* %) **1.** *adv.* in a hundred, for each hundred **2.** *pl.* **per·cent, per·cents** *n.* a hundredth part ‖ percentage, the amount or rate per hundred **per·cent·age** *n.* rate or proportion per hundred ‖ (loosely) a proportion **per·cen·tile** (pərséntail, pərséntil) *n.* (statistics) one of a hundred parts, each containing an equal number of members, into which a series of individual things, persons etc. has been divided **per·cents** *pl. n.* securities yielding a specified rate of interest

per·cept (pə́:rsept) *n.* (philos.) a product of perception, a recognizable mental impression of something perceived

per·cep·ti·ble (pərséptəb'l) *adj.* capable of being perceived **per·cep·ti·bly** *adv.*

per·cep·tion (pərsépʃən) *n.* the act of perceiving ‖ the ability to perceive, esp. to understand ‖ (philos.) the action of the mind in referring sensations to the object which caused them ‖ (psychol.) awareness through the senses of an external object ‖ (psychol.) a percept ‖ (law) the collection of rents etc. **per·cep·tion·al** *adj.* of or having the nature of perception

per·cep·tive (pərséptiv) *adj.* capable of perceiving ‖ having or showing keen understanding or insight **per·cep·tiv·i·ty** (pərsəptíviti:) *n.*

perch (pə:rtʃ) *n.* a small, edible European freshwater fish with a broad, laterally flattened body and spiny fins ‖ a related North American food fish

---

(**a**) æ, c*a*t; ɑ, c*a*r; ɔ f*a*wn; ei, sn*a*ke. (**e**) e, h*e*n; i:, sh*ee*p; iə, d*ee*r; ɛə, b*ea*r. (**i**) i, f*i*sh; ai, t*i*ger; ə:, b*i*rd. (**o**) o, *o*x; au, c*ow*; ou, g*oa*t; u, p*oo*r; ɔi, r*oy*al. (**u**) ʌ, d*u*ck; u, b*u*ll; u:, g*oo*se; ə, b*a*cillus; ju:, c*u*be. x, lo*ch*; θ, *th*ink; ð, bo*th*er; z, *Z*en; ʒ, corsa*g*e; dʒ, sava*g*e; ŋ, oranguta*ng*; j, *y*ak; ʃ, *fi*sh; tʃ, fe*tch*; 'l, rabb*l*e; 'n, redd*e*n. Complete pronunciation key appears inside front cover.

perch *n.* anything on which a bird alights or rests, e.g. a horizontal bar in a cage ‖ any resting place, esp. an elevated or temporary one

perch *v.i.* (of a bird) to alight or sit ‖ to sit or settle on or as if on a perch ‖ *v.t.* to place on or as if on a perch

per·chance (pərtʃǽns, pərtʃáns) *adv.* (*rhet.*) perhaps, maybe

per·co·late (pɔ́:rkəleit) *pres. part.* **per·co·lat·ing** *past* and *past part.* **per·co·lat·ed** *v.i.* to seep through a porous substance ‖ to become diffused ‖ (of coffee) to be brewed in a percolator ‖ *v.t.* to cause to filter gradually through a porous substance ‖ (of a liquid) to permeate (a substance) in this way ‖ to prepare (coffee) in a percolator

per·co·la·tor (pɔ́:rkəleitər) *n.* a machine for percolating, esp. one for preparing coffee as a drink by passing boiling water repeatedly through the ground beans

per·cus·sion (pərkʌ́ʃən) *n.* the act of causing one body to make a sudden impact on another ‖ such an impact ‖ the sound produced by this ‖ (*med.*) the percussing of a body part ‖ (*mus.*) percussion instruments collectively, esp. as a section of an orchestra or band

per di·em (pərdí:əm, pərdáiəm) **1.** *adv.* daily, by the day **2.** *adj.* daily, *a per diem allowance* **3.** *n.* the money allotted to someone, e.g. a salesman, for expenses incurred in connection with work

per·di·tion (pərdíʃən) *n.* damnation, eternal death

per·emp·to·ry (pərémptəri:, pérəmptɔ̀ri:, pérəmptɔ́uri:) *adj.* imperious, curtly authoritative ‖ (*law*, pérəmptɔ̀ri:) final, absolute

per·en·ni·al (pəréni:əl) **1.** *adj.* perpetual, long-lasting ‖ (*bot.*) living more than two years **2.** *n.* perennial plant

per·fect (pɔ́:rfikt) **1.** *adj.* complete or correct in every way, conforming to a standard or ideal with no omissions, errors, flaws or extraneous elements ‖ utter, absolute ‖ (*gram.*, of a tense) expressing the completion of an action at the time of speaking or at the time indicated **2.** *n.* (*gram.*) the perfect tense **3.** (pərfékt) *v.t.* to put the finishing touches to, make as good as possible

per·fec·tion (pərfékʃən) *n.* the quality or state of being perfect ‖ an instance of this ‖ a perfecting or being perfected **to perfection** perfectly **per·féc·tion·ism** *n.* the theory of the moral perfectibility of man **per·féc·tion·ist** *n.* a person who is not content with anything less than the very best

per·fi·dy (pɔ́:rfidi:) *pl.* **per·fi·dies** *n.* treachery, faithlessness ‖ an instance of this

per·fo·rate (pɔ́:rfəreit) *pres. part.* **per·fo·rat·ing** *past* and *past part.* **per·fo·rat·ed** *v.t.* to make a hole through, pierce ‖ to make a row of holes through (paper etc.) so that it can easily be pulled into parts ‖ *v.i.* to make a perforation

per·fo·ra·tion (pə̀:rfəréiʃən) *n.* a perforating or being perforated ‖ a small hole cut or punched into something ‖ a series of holes made in paper etc. to facilitate division ‖ (*philately*) one of such a series of holes on a sheet of postage stamps ‖ (*philately*) one of the teeth left on a stamp after it has been torn off the sheet

per·fo·ra·tor (pɔ́:rfəreitər) *n.* a machine for making perforations

per·force (pərfɔ́rs, pərfóurs) *adv.* (*rhet.*) through necessity

per·form (pərfɔ́rm) *v.t.* to do, fulfill, carry out, accomplish (an action, obligation etc.) ‖ to render, execute (a stage role, play, piece of music, dance etc.), esp. before an audience ‖ *v.i.* to execute a stage role, play, piece of music etc., esp. in public ‖ to carry out, accomplish an action, function etc. **per·fór·mance** *n.* the act of performing ‖ an instance of this ‖ the quality or manner of performing ‖ something performed, a deed, feat etc.

per·form·ance (pərfɔ́rməns) *n.* what is accomplished, contrasted with capability

per·fume (pɔ́:rfju:m, pərfjú:m) *n.* a sweet smell ‖ a sweet-smelling liquid for personal use prepared from

essential oils from flowers or aromatic chemicals and fixed, e.g. with musk

per·fume (pərfjú:m) *pres. part.* **per·fum·ing** *past* and *past part.* **per·fumed** *v.t.* to give a sweet smell to ‖ to apply perfume to **per·fúm·er** *n.* a person who or firm that makes or sells perfumes **per·fúm·er·y** *pl.* **per·fum·er·ies** *n.* a place where perfumes are manufactured ‖ the technique or business of making perfume ‖ perfumes collectively

per·func·to·ry (pərfʌ́ŋktəri:) *adj.* behaving or performing in an offhand manner without any show of interest or concern ‖ done, given etc. in this way

per·haps (pərhǽps) *adv.* possibly, maybe

per·i·gee (péridʒi:) *n.* (*astron.*) the point in the orbit of the moon or another satellite of the earth when it is nearest the earth

per·i·he·li·on (pèrihí:li:ən, pèrihí:ljən) *pl.* **per·i·he·li·a** (pèrihí:li:ə, pèrihí:ljə) *n.* (*astron.*) the point of a comet's or planet's orbit when it is nearest the sun

per·il (pérəl) *n.* risk of serious injury, destruction, disaster, etc. ‖ the state of being exposed to such risk **at** (or **to**) **one's peril** taking the risk and assuming the responsibility for the ill effects that are likely to result from it **in peril of** (*rhet.*) in danger of losing, *in peril of one's life*

per·il·ous (pérələs) *adj.* involving or exposing one to peril

pe·rim·e·ter (pərímitər) *n.* the line bounding a closed plane figure or an area on the ground ‖ the length of this line ‖ an optical instrument for testing a person's field of vision **per·i·met·ric** (pèrimétrik) *adj.*

pe·ri·od (píəri:əd) **1.** *n.* a portion of time forming a division in a development, life, chronology, timetable ‖ (*phys.*) the interval of time required for the completion of a single complete cycle of some periodic or cyclical phenomenon (e.g. the period of a planetary orbit) ‖ (*gram.*) a complete, esp. a complex, sentence ‖ a pause marking the completion of a sentence ‖ the symbol (.) denoting this pause, or following an abbreviation, or marking a decimal ‖ a single menstruation ‖ (*geol.*) a division of geological time, part of an era ‖ (*pl.*) rhetorical language **2.** *adj.* having the characteristics of a particular historical period

pe·ri·od·ic (pìəri:ɔ́dik) *adj.* occurring again and again, at constant intervals ‖ recurring intermittently ‖ characterized by regularly recurring stages or processes **pe·ri·ód·i·cal 1.** *adj.* periodic ‖ (of a magazine etc.) published at regular intervals ‖ characteristic of or pertaining to such publications **2.** *n.* a periodical publication

per·i·pa·tet·ic (pèrəpətétik) *adj.* moving about from place to place **per·i·pa·tét·i·cal·ly** *adv.*

pe·riph·er·y (pərífəri:) *pl.* **pe·riph·er·ies** *n.* the line bounding a figure, esp. a rounded one ‖ the outermost part of something thought of as ringed or circled ‖ the boundary or outer surface of a space or body ‖ (*anat.*) the areas in which the nerves terminate

per·i·scope (périskoup) *n.* a tubular optical device used in submarines etc. and in scientific observation, by which light received by an oblique mirror or prism at one end of the tube is reflected by another at the other end **per·i·scop·ic** (pèriskópik) *adj.*

per·ish (périʃ) *v.i.* to suffer utter ruin or destruction, or die a violent death ‖ to suffer spiritual death **perish the thought!** don't even consider the possibility of such a thing! **pér·ish·a·ble** *adj.* liable to decay or deterioration **pér·ish·a·bles** *pl. n.* perishable goods **pér·ish·ing** *adj.* (of cold, pain etc.) extreme ‖ (*pop.*) damned, blasted

per·i·to·ne·um, per·i·to·nae·um (pèritəní:əm) *pl.* **per·i·to·ne·a, per·i·to·nae·a** (pèritəní:ə) *n.* (*anat.*) the membrane lining the abdominal viscera and the interior of the abdominal wall

per·jure (pɔ́:rdʒər) *pres. part.* **per·jur·ing** *past* and *past part.* **per·jured** *v. refl.* to make (oneself) guilty of perjury

per·jur·er (pɔ́:rdʒərər) *n.* a person guilty of perjury

per·ju·ry (pə́:rdʒəri:) *pl.* **per·ju·ries** *n. (law)* the crime of swearing on oath that something is true which one knows is false, or of telling a lie when under oath to tell the truth ‖ failure to do what one has sworn on oath to do

perk (pə:rk) *v.t.* (with 'up') to restore good spirits or courage to ‖ (with 'up') to make bright or gay in appearance ‖ *v.i.* (with 'up') to recover one's health, energy or good spirits after sickness, depression etc.

per·ma·nent (pə́:rmənənt) **1.** *adj.* continuing and enduring without change **2.** *n. (pop.)* a permanent wave

per·me·a·ble (pə́:rmi:əb'l) *adj.* able to be permeated

per·me·ate (pə́:rmi:eit) *pres. part.* **per·me·at·ing** *past and past part.* **per·me·at·ed** *v.t.* to penetrate wholly, pervade, soak through ‖ *v.i.* to diffuse or spread through something **per·me·a·tion** *n.*

per·mis·si·ble (pərmísəb'l) *adj.* that may be permitted **per·mis·si·bly** *adv.*

per·mis·sion (pərmíʃən) *n.* freedom, power, privilege etc. which one person or authority grants to another ‖ a permitting, or being permitted

permit 1. (pərmít) *v. pres. part.* **per·mit·ting** *past and past part.* **per·mit·ted** *v.t.* to give voluntarily or officially to (someone or something) some right, opportunity, power etc. ‖ to accept or agree to (something) ‖ to make possible ‖ *v.i* to provide opportunity **2.** (pə́:rmit, pərmít) *n.* a written license issued by an authority

per·mu·ta·tion (pə:rmju:téiʃən) *n. (math.)* any of the different arrangements in linear order that can be made of a given set of objects ‖ *(math.)* the act or process of making such variations ‖ a change or the process of changing

per·mute (pərmjú:t) *pres. part.* **per·mut·ing** *past and past part.* **per·mut·ed** *v.t.* to change the order of (esp. things in a series)

per·ni·cious (pərníʃəs) *adj.* destructive, extremely injurious, or deadly, *a pernicious pest*

per·o·ra·tion (perəréiʃən) *n.* a protracted tedious speech, often pompously delivered ‖ the concluding portion of a speech, rhetorical composition etc.

per·pen·dic·u·lar (pə:rpəndíkjulər) **1.** *adj.* (of a line, plane or surface) forming an angle of 90° with another line, plane or surface ‖ (of two lines, planes or surfaces) forming a 90° angle ‖ at right angles to the horizontal at any point on the earth's surface **2.** *n.* a direction which is perpendicular, esp. as represented by a straight line ‖ an instrument, e.g. a plumb line, for determining the perpendicular line from any point **per·pen·dic·u·lar·i·ty** (pərpəndikjuláeriti:) *n.*

per·pe·trate (pə́:rpitreit) *pres. part.* **per·pe·trat·ing** *past and past part.* **per·pe·trat·ed** *v.t.* to commit, perform (something bad), *to perpetrate a crime* **per·pe·tra·tion**, **pér·pe·tra·tor** *ns*

per·pet·u·al (pərpétʃu:əl) **1.** *adj.* eternal, everlasting ‖ constant, continual ‖ *(bot.)* flowering throughout the season **2.** *n.* a hybrid perpetual rose

per·pet·u·ate (pərpétʃu:eit) *pres. part.* **per·pet·u·at·ing** *past and past part.* **per·pet·u·at·ed** *v.t.* to make perpetual ‖ to cause to continue ‖ to save from oblivion **per·pet·u·a·tion, per·pet·u·a·tor** *ns*

per·plex (pərpléks) *v.t.* to make (someone) uncertain about the nature of, or the reason for or answer to, something difficult to understand ‖ to complicate (a situation etc.)

per·qui·site (pə́:rkwizit) *n.* an extra profit or item received over and above one's agreed wage ‖ a tip, gratuity

per se (pərséi) *adv.* intrinsically, considered independently of other things

per·se·cute (pə́:rsikju:t) *pres. part.* **per·se·cut·ing** *past*

and *past part.* **per·se·cut·ed** *v.t.* to suffer, esp. for religious or political reasons ‖ to vex, harass

per·se·cu·tion (pə:rsikjú:ʃən) *n.* a persecuting or being persecuted

per·se·ver·ance (pə:rsivíərəns) *n.* the quality of being persistent and persevering ‖ the act of persevering

per·se·vere (pə:rsivíər) *pres. part.* **per·se·ver·ing** *past and past part.* **per·se·vered** *v.i.* to try hard and continuously in spite of obstacles and difficulties

per·si·flage (pə́:rsiflɑʒ) *n.* light-hearted and bantering speech, writing etc.

per·sist (pərsist) *v.i.* to continue, esp. in spite of opposition or difficulties ‖ to continue to exist

per·sist·ence (pərsístəns) *n.* the quality or state of being persistent ‖ the act of persisting

per·sist·ent (pərsístənt) *adj.* continuing in spite of opposition ‖ enduring, lasting or recurrent ‖ *(zool.,* of horns, hair etc.) permanent, not disappearing or falling off ‖ *(chem.,* of toxic chemicals) nondegradable or slowly degradable ‖ *(med.,* of a disorder) not readily cured

per·snick·et·y (pərsníkiti:) *adj.* fastidious, finicky, fussy ‖ complex, requiring careful, precise handling

per·son (pə́:rs'n) *n.* a man, woman or child, regarded as having a distinct individuality or personality, or as distinguished from an animal or thing ‖ *(gram.)* one of the three referents for pronouns and the corresponding verb forms in many languages ‖ *(law)* a human being or a collection of human beings considered as having rights and duties **in person** being physically present, *apply in person*

per·son·a·ble (pə́:rs'nəb'l) *adj. (old-fash.,* of people) good-looking

per·son·al (pə́:rs'n'l) **1.** *adj.* belonging or particular to one person, private ‖ done by oneself, in person ‖ of or concerning the body ‖ referring to a person without proper respect for his privacy ‖ considered as a person with human faculties of reason etc., *a personal God* ‖ *(gram.,* of a verb ending or pronoun) denoting the first, second or third person **2.** *n.* (esp. *pl.*) newspaper paragraphs about individual persons, or containing paid personal messages to individuals

per·son·al·i·ty (pə:rs'næliti:) *pl.* **per·son·al·i·ties** *n.* the total of the psychological, intellectual, emotional and physical characteristics that make up the individual, esp. as others see him ‖ an eminent or famous person ‖ the quality, state or fact of being a person ‖ pronounced individuality ‖ *(pl.)* reference, esp. critical, to a person or people

per·son·al·ly (pə́:rs'n'li:) *adv.* in a personal way ‖ in person, not using an agent ‖ for one's part, so far as one is oneself concerned

per·son·i·fi·ca·tion (pə:rsɒnifikéiʃən) *n.* the treating of an abstract quality or thing as if it had human qualities ‖ an instance of this ‖ a person regarded as the embodiment of a quality, *she is the personification of generosity*

per·son·i·fy (pərsɒ́nifai) *pres. part.* **per·son·i·fy·ing** *past and past part.* **per·son·i·fied** *v.t.* to treat (an abstraction, thing or inanimate object) as a person

per·son·nel (pə:rs'nél) *n.* the body of employees in a service, business, factory etc.

per·spec·tive (pərspéktiv) *n.* the art of representing solid objects on a flat surface so that they seem to be in relation to one another in space just as the eye would see them ‖ a picture made using this technique ‖ the appearance of objects with reference to distance, relative position etc. ‖ relative importance ‖ evaluation of events according to a particular way of looking at them ‖ a view or prospect

per·spi·ca·cious (pə:rspikéiʃəs) *adj.* having clear insight, *a perspicacious judge of people*

per·spic·u·ous (pərspíkju:əs) *adj.* clearly expressed so as to be easily understood ‖ (of a person) clearly intelligible in speech or writing

per·spi·ra·tion (pə̣:rspəréiʃən) *n.* sweat ‖ the act of sweating

per·spire (pərspáiər) *pres. part.* **per·spir·ing** *past* and *past part.* **per·spired** *v.i.* and *t.* to sweat

per·suade (pərswéid) *pres. part.* **per·suad·ing** *past* and *past part.* **per·suad·ed** *v.t.* to cause (someone) to do something by reasoning ‖ to cause (someone) to believe something by reasoning etc.

per·sua·sion (pərswéiʒən) *n.* a persuading or being persuaded ‖ capacity or power to persuade ‖ a strongly held conviction, esp. a sectarian belief

pert (pə:rt) *adj.* forward and self-confident, and not entirely respectful ‖ jaunty ‖ in good spirits, lively

per·tain (pə:rtéin) *v.i.* (with 'to') to be a natural part ‖ (with 'to') to be suitable ‖ (with 'to') to have reference

per·ti·nent (pɔ́:rt'nənt) *adj.* (often with 'to') referring centrally to the matter being discussed or considered

per·turb (pərtɔ́:rb) *v.t.* to cause to be anxious

pe·ruse (pərú:z) *pres. part.* **pe·rus·ing** *past* and *past part.* **pe·rused** *v.t.* to read through carefully or critically

per·vade (pərvéid) *pres. part.* **per·vad·ing** *past* and *past part.* **per·vad·ed** *v.t.* to spread throughout and into every part of **per·va·sion** (pərvéiʒən) *n.* **per·va·sive** (pərvéisiv) *adj.* pervading or tending to pervade

per·verse (pərvɔ́:rs) *adj.* willfully doing what is wrong or unreasonable ‖ indicating such willfulness ‖ obstinate, intractable ‖ (*law*, of a verdict) contrary to the evidence or to judicial direction

per·ver·sion (pərvɔ́:rʒən) *n.* a perverting or being perverted ‖ a deviation from usual behavior, esp. from normal sexual behavior

per·vert 1. (pərvɔ́:rt) *v.t.* to damage the mind or will of (a person) so that he thinks or acts in an immoral way ‖ to cause to be misused, falsified, wrongly understood etc. **2.** (pɔ́:rvərt) *n.* a person who is perverted, esp. someone given to homosexuality or other abnormal sexual practices

per·vi·ous (pɔ́:rvi:əs) *adj.* capable of being permeated or passed through, e.g. by heat ‖ (with 'to') willing to be influenced (by something stipulated, e.g. reason)

pes·ky (péski:) *comp.* **pes·ki·er** *superl.* **pes·ki·est** *adj.* (*pop.*) annoyingly troublesome

pes·si·mism (pésəmjzəm) *n.* the tendency to expect the worst or to stress the worst aspect of things ‖ the belief that the world is fundamentally evil **pes·si·mist** *n.* someone who persistently takes the worst view of things **pes·si·mís·tic** *adj.* **pes·si·mís·ti·cal·ly** *adv.*

pest (pest) *n.* an animal (e.g. an insect or rodent) which is destructive to crops, stored food etc. ‖ a tiresome, annoying person ‖ (*hist.*) the plague

pes·ter (péstər) *v.t.* to annoy with persistent requests, questions etc.

pest·i·cide (péstisaid) *n.* a susbtance, e.g. an insecticide, used for destroying pests

pes·ti·lence (péstələns) *n.* a deadly epidemic disease, esp. (*hist.*) the bubonic plague ‖ something morally or socially pernicious

pes·tle (pés'l, péstəl) *n.* a blunt-ended implement for reducing hard substances to powder by pounding them in a mortar ‖ any of several instruments used for pounding or stamping

pet (pet) **1.** *n.* a tame animal kept as a companion or for fun, and affectionately cared for ‖ someone who is treated as a favorite **2.** *adj.* kept as a pet ‖ favorite **3.** *v. pres. part.* **pet·ting** *past* and *past part.* **pet·ted** *v.t.* to pat or caress (e.g. a pet animal) ‖ to pamper ‖ *v.i.* (*pop.*) to caress someone of the opposite sex in sexual play

pet·al (pét'l) *n.* one of the colored, modified leaves forming part of the corolla of a flower **pét·aled,** **pét·alled** *adj.*

pe·tite (pətí:t) *adj.* (of a person) small and neat in figure

pe·ti·tion (pətíʃən) **1.** *n.* a formal request, esp. to a sovereign, a governing body etc., often a written one signed by a large number of people ‖ a formal written request to a court of law ‖ that which is requested **2.** *v.t.* to make a petition to (someone) for something to be done ‖ to make a request for (something) ‖ *v.i.* to make a petition

pet·ri·fy (pétrifai) *pres. part.* **pet·ri·fy·ing** *past* and *past part.* **pet·ri·fied** *v.t.* to turn (an organic structure) into stone, or a substance hard as stone, through the replacement of organic tissues by deposited silica, agate or calcium carbonate in solution ‖ to render (a person) rigid or numb with fear or horror ‖ *v.i.* to be turned into stone or a stony substance

pe·trog·ra·phy (pətrógrəfi:) *n.* the scientific description and classification of rocks

pe·tro·le·um (pətróuli:əm) *n.* an oily liquid mixture of complex hydrocarbons occurring naturally in the pores and fissures of sedimentary rock, usually in association with its gaseous form, natural gas

pet·ti·coat (péti:kout) *n.* an undergarment hanging from the waist, esp. one bedecked with lace, ruffles etc. to be worn under a skirt

pet·ty (péti:) *comp.* **pet·ti·er** *superl.* **pet·ti·est** *adj.* minor, trivial ‖ (of a person) giving minor matters, esp. minor faults or grievances, unwarranted importance ‖ characteristic of such a person

pet·u·lance (pétʃuləns) *n.* the quality or state of being petulant

pet·u·lant (pétʃulənt) *adj.* discontented and irritable over trifles

pew (pju:) *n.* a long bench with a back used as church furniture

pew·ter (pjú:tər) **1.** *n.* any of several gray alloys of tin, usually with lead ‖ utensils made of this alloy **2.** *adj.* made of this alloy

pe·yo·te (peióuti:) *n.* any of several cacti growing in the southwest U.S.A. and Mexico, esp. mescal ‖ a stimulant from mescal buttons used in some esp. Mexican Indian religious rituals

phal·lic (fǽlik) *adj.* of or relating to a phallus or phallicism ‖ like a phallus **phal·li·cism** (fǽlisizəm) *n.* worship of the phallus as symbol of the generating force in nature

phal·lus (fǽləs) *pl.* **phal·li** (fǽlai) *n.* a symbol of the penis

phan·tasm (fǽntæzəm) *n.* an illusion ‖ a ghostly apparition, esp. of a person, dead or alive ‖ (*philos.*) the mental image of a person or an object

phan·tom (fǽntəm) **1.** *n.* something, esp. a ghost, that appears to be seen but that has no real physical existence ‖ someone who or something which is only apparently what they or it purports to be **2.** *adj.* illusory

phar·aoh (fɛ́ərou, fǽrou) *n.* the title of ancient Egyptian kings **phar·a·on·ic** (fɛəreiónik) *adj.*

phar·ma·ceu·tic (fɑrməsú:tik) *adj.* of or relating to pharmacy **phar·ma·céu·ti·cal** *adj.* **phar·ma·céu·tics** *n.* the science of the preparation and use of medicines **phar·ma·céu·tist** *n.* a pharmacist

phar·ma·cist (fɑ́rməsist) *n.* a person skilled or engaged in pharmacy

phar·ma·col·o·gy (fɑrməkólədʒi:) *n.* the study of the preparation, properties, use and effects of drugs

phar·ma·cy (fɑ́rməsi:) *pl.* **phar·ma·cies** *n.* the art or profession of preparing and dispensing medicinal drugs ‖ a pharmacist's shop ‖ a drugstore

phase (feiz) **1.** *n.* each of the successive aspects or stages in any course of change or development ‖ (*astron.*) an aspect in the cycle of changing form or quantity of illumination of the moon or of a planet ‖ in a synchronized manner **2.** *v.t. pres. part.* **phas·ing** *past* and *past part.* **phased** to cause to be in phase **to phase in** to bring in in phases or as a phase **to phase out** to stop using or cause to cease by phases ‖ to cease by phases **phá·sic** *adj.*

pheas·ant (féz'nt) *n.* a genus of large, long-tailed gallinaceous game birds

phe·no·bar·bi·tal (fį:noubárbitəl, fį:noubárbitɔl) *n.* a white crystalline powder, phenylethylbarbituric acid, used medicinally as a hypnotic and sedative

phe·nom·e·nal (finómən'l) *adj. (philos.)* recognized by or experienced by the senses rather than through thought or intuition || concerned with or constituting a phenomenon or phenomena || extraordinary, unusual

phe·nom·e·non (finómənɒn) *pl.* **phe·nom·e·na** (finómənə) *n. (philos.)* something known by sense perception rather than by thought or intuition || any fact or event which can be described and explained in scientific terms || an extraordinary or remarkable event, thing, person etc.

phi·lan·der (filǽndər) *v.i.* (of a man) to flirt || (of a man) to have many but casual love affairs **phi·lan·der·er** *n.*

phil·an·throp·ic (fįlənθrópik) *adj.* doing good works, actively benevolent || showing philanthropy **phil·an·thróp·i·cal** *adj.*

phil·an·thro·pist (filǽnθrəpist) *n.* a humanitarian, esp. one who disinterestedly gives large gifts of money for particular causes

phi·lan·thro·py (filǽnθrəpi:) *pl.* **phi·lan·thro·pies** *n.* generous help or benevolence toward one's fellow men || an instance of this

phil·a·tel·ic (fįlətélik) *adj.* relating to philately

phi·lat·el·ist (filǽt'list) *n.* an expert in philately || a stamp collector

phi·lat·e·ly (filǽt'li:) *n.* the collection and study of postage stamps, envelopes bearing postmarks etc., usually as a hobby

phil·har·mon·ic (fįlhɑrmónik, fįlɑrmónik) *adj.* loving music (only used in titles of orchestras, musical societies etc.)

phi·lol·o·gist (filólədʒist) *n.* a specialist in philology

phi·lol·o·gy (filólədʒi:) *n.* the study of language from the written texts by which it is known || the study of texts and their transmission

phi·los·o·pher (filósəfər) *n.* a person who engages in the study of philosophy || *(pop.)* a person who accepts misfortune with stoic calm

phil·o·soph·ic (fįləsófik) *adj.* of or relating to philosophy || *(pop.)* resigned in the face of troubles, wisely unemotional about what cannot be altered **phil·o·sóph·i·cal** *adj.*

phi·los·o·phize (filósəfaiz) *pres. part.* **phi·los·o·phiz·ing** *past* and *past part.* **phi·los·o·phized** *v.i.* to theorize || *(pop.)* to moralize

phi·los·o·phy (filósəfi:) *pl.* **phi·los·o·phies** *n.* the love or pursuit of wisdom, i.e. the search for basic principles || systematized principles of any subject or branch of knowledge || an attitude towards life || *(pop.)* calm resignation

phlegm (flem) *n.* mucus esp. when it occurs in excessive quantity in the respiratory passages || *(hist.)* one of the four humors || stoic self-possession, imperturbability **phleg·mat·ic** (flegmǽtik) *adj.* having or showing stoic self-possession, imperturbable **phleg·mát·i·cal** *adj.*

pho·bia (fóubi:ə) *n.* morbid and often irrational dread of some specific thing

phoe·nix, phe·nix (fí:niks) *n. (Egypt. mythol.)* a bird of gorgeous plumage, sacred to the sun, reborn from the ashes of the funeral pyre which it made for itself when each life span of 500 or 600 years was over || something or someone seen as resembling this bird, esp. with respect to its power of self-regeneration

pho·net·ic (fənétik, founétik) *adj.* of or relating to vocal sounds and speech || consistently representing sounds by the same symbols || relating to phonetics

pho·nét·i·cal·ly *adv.* **pho·ne·ti·cian** (founitíʃən) *n.* a specialist in phonetics **pho·nét·i·cist** *n.* a phonetist

pho·nét·ics *n.* the branch of language study concerned with the production of speech sounds, alone or in combination, and their representation in writing || the phonetic system of a given language

phon·ics (fóniks) *n.* the use of sound-symbol (phoneme-grapheme) relationships in the teaching of reading

pho·no·graph (fóunəgræf, fóunəgrɑf) *n.* a machine for reproducing sounds recorded on a disk or cylinder **pho·no·graph·ic** (founəgrǽfik) *adj.* **pho·no·gráph·i·cal·ly** *adv.*

pho·nog·ra·phy (founógrəfi:) *n.* a phonetic spelling or writing || a phonetic shorthand system

pho·ny, pho·ney (fóuni:) *comp.* **pho·ni·er** *superl.* **pho·ni·est** 1. *adj. (pop.)* not genuine, counterfeit 2. *pl.* **pho·nies** *n. (pop.)* a person who is not what he pretends to be

phos·pho·resce (fɒsfərés) *pres. part.* **phos·pho·resc·ing** *past* and *past part.* **phos·pho·resced** *v.i.* to exhibit phosphorescence

phos·pho·res·cence (fɒsfərés'ns) *n.* a luminescence characterized by a temperature-dependent time rate of decay after the stimulation has been removed

phos·pho·res·cent (fɒsfərés'nt) *adj.* exhibiting phosphorescence

pho·to·cop·y (fóutoukɒpi:) 1. *pl.* **pho·to·cop·ies** *n.* a photographic reproduction of a document, illustration, etc. 2. *v.t. pres. part.* **pho·to·cop·y·ing** *past* and *past part.* **pho·to·cop·ied** to make a photocopy of

pho·to·e·lec·tric (foutouiléktrik) *adj.* of any of the factors involved in the effect of electromagnetic radiation on the electrical behavior of matter

pho·to·en·grav·ing (foutouingréiviŋ) *n. (printing)* a process by which a printing block is made from a photograph || a print taken from such a block

photo finish the finish of a race so close that a photograph at the finish line is required to identify the winner || the end of any very close contest

pho·to·gen·ic (foutədʒénik) *adj.* photographing to advantage || causing or producing light

pho·to·graph (fóutəgræf, fóutəgrɑf) 1. *n.* a reproduction, usually on photographic paper, made by photography 2. *v.t.* to take a picture of by photography || *v.i.* to practice photography || to appear (in a specified way) in a photograph **pho·tog·ra·pher** (fətógrəfər) *n.* a person who practices photography

pho·to·graph·ic (foutəgrǽfik) *adj.* pertaining to photography || resembling the process of photography, *a photographic memory* **pho·to·gráph·i·cal·ly** *adv.*

pho·tog·ra·phy (fətógrəfi:) *n.* the art, process or occupation of producing photographs

pho·to·sen·si·tive (foutousénsitiv) *adj.* affected by the incidence of radiant energy, esp. light **pho·to·sen·si·tív·i·ty** *n.*

pho·to·stat (fóutəstæt) 1. *n.* a machine used to make photographs of documents etc. to any desired scale || a photograph thus made 2. *v.t. pres. part.* **pho·to·stat·ing** *past* and *past part.* **pho·to·stat·ed** to make a photostatic copy of **pho·to·stát·ic** *adj.*

pho·to·syn·the·sis (foutəsínθisis) *n.* the synthesis of chemical substances with the aid of light, esp. the formation of carbohydrates (e.g. in green plants) from carbon dioxide and water with the liberation of oxygen, in the presence of chlorophyll

phrase (freiz) 1. *n.* a sequence of words expressing a single idea, esp. *(gram.)* a group of words without a subject and predicate, functioning together within a sentence || an expression that is pithy or idiomatic 2. *v.t. pres. part.* **phras·ing** *past* and *past part.*

---

phrased to express in words

phra·se·ol·o·gy (freizi:ɔ́ləʒi:) *n.* manner of using and arranging words

phy·lum (fáiləm) *pl.* **phy·la** (fáilə) *n.* (*biol.*) the primary division of classification in the plant or animal kingdom, based on common characteristics and assumed common ancestry

phys·i·cal (fízik'l) *adj.* of or pertaining to matter or nature || pertaining to the body (in contrast to the mind) || of or pertaining to the science of physics

phy·si·cian (fizíʃən) *n.* a doctor of medicine, licensed to diagnose and treat diseases

phys·i·cist (fízisist) *n.* a specialist in physics

phys·ics (fíziks) *n.* the science of matter and energy, and their interactions || physical properties or processes

phys·i·og·no·my (fizi:ɔ́gnəmi:, fizi:ɔ́nəmi:) *pl.* **phys·i·og·no·mies** *n.* the facial features as indicative of character || the art of assessing character by studying the features of the face

phys·i·ol·o·gy (fizi:ɔ́ləʒi:) *n.* the branch of biology concerned with the functions of living organisms || the functions, collectively, of an organism or its parts

phy·sique (fizí:k) *n.* the form, structure, organization or constitution of a person's body

pi·a·nis·si·mo (pi:ənísəmou, pjɑní:ssi:mɔ) (*mus., abbr.* pp.) **1.** *adj.* very soft **2.** *adv.* very softly **3.** *pl.* **pi·a·nis·si·mos** *n.* a pianissimo passage

pi·an·ist (pi:ǽnist, pjǽnist, pí:ənist) *n.* a person who plays the piano, esp. professionally **pi·a·nis·tic** (pi:ənístik) *adj.* relating to or suitable for performance on the piano **pi·a·nis·ti·cal·ly** *adv.*

pi·a·no (pi:ɑ́nou) (*abbr.* p.) **1.** *adv.* (*mus.*) softly **2.** *adj.* (*mus.*) soft **3.** *pl.* **pi·a·ni** (pi:ɑ́ni:), **pi·a·nos** *n.* (*mus.*) a passage rendered softly

pi·an·o (pi:ǽnou, pjǽnou) *pl.* **pi·an·os** *n.* a musical stringed percussion instrument before which the player sits (as if at a table), playing on a horizontal keyboard

pi·ca (páikə) *n.* (*printing*) a size of type equal to 12 point || a typewriter face of 10 characters to the inch, 6 lines to the vertical inch

pic·a·yune (pìki:jú:n) **1.** *n.* anything of little value **2.** *adj.* of very small value || picayunish **pic·a·yún·ish** *adj.* trivial || too concerned with petty detail

pic·ca·lil·li (píkəlili:) *pl.* **pic·ca·lil·lis** *n.* a relish of chopped vegetables and pungent spices

pic·co·lo (píkəlou) *pl.* **pic·co·los** *n.* a small flute pitched an octave higher than the standard flute

pick (pik) **1.** *v.t.* to gather (a flower, fruit etc.) by severing it from the rest of the plant or tree || to choose or select carefully || to probe or scratch with an instrument or with one's fingers in order to remove extraneous matter from || to steal from (the pockets of the clothes which someone is wearing) || to pluck (the strings of a banjo, guitar etc.) || to open (a lock) with a wire etc. instead of with a key, esp. for purposes of robbery || to find an opportunity or pretext for, and begin (a quarrel, fight etc.) || *v.i.* to work with a pick || to eat sparingly or with small bites || (of a bird, esp. a chicken) to tap at the ground or take bits of food up with the bill **to pick and choose** to be fastidious about making a choice **to pick apart** to separate or rip into parts || to find defects in (an argument etc.) **to pick at** to eat (one's food) in small bites and without appetite **to pick on** to choose, select || to single out in order to attack, criticize or tease **to pick out** to select **to pick up** to lift or take up || to get or acquire, esp. by chance or casually || to meet casually and get to know (someone, esp. of the opposite sex) || to increase (speed) || to accelerate || to improve in health, spirits or performance **2.** *n.* the act of selecting || the right or privilege of selecting, *to have one's pick of the items* || the person or thing selected || someone or something selected as the best || the amount of a crop that is picked at one time

pick *n.* a pickaxe || any of several tools used for picking, e.g. an ice pick || a plectrum

pick·et (píkit) **1.** *n.* a small group of soldiers posted against surprise attack or sent out to counter enemy reconnoitering parties || a group of workers posted to dissuade other workers or clients from entering their place of work during a strike || a member of such a group || a group of demonstrators, or a member of such a group, carrying placards to advocate a cause or register a protest || a pointed stake used e.g. as part of a fence or to mark positions in surveying **2.** *v.t.* to protect by means of a picket fence || to act as a picket at (a place of business etc.) || to post (men) as a picket || *v.i.* to act as a picket || to set or place a picket

pick·le (pík'l) **1.** *n.* a liquid (brine, vinegar etc.) in which food is preserved || food or a piece of food (e.g. a cucumber) so preserved || an acid solution for cleaning metal articles || (*pop.*) an awkward situation, sorry plight **2.** *v.t. pres. part.* **pick·ling** *past* and *past part.* **pick·led** to preserve in, or treat with, a pickle

pick·pock·et (píkpɒkit) *n.* a person who picks people's pockets

pick·up (píkʌp) *n.* a picking up, e.g. of a ball from the ground, esp. just after its impact || (*pop.*) recovery || a device in a phonograph which converts the vibration of the needle into electrical impulses || (*radio, television*) the reception of sound (or light) by the transmitter || the apparatus used for this || (*pop.*) a person whose acquaintance one makes casually, esp. for purposes of love-making || acceleration, esp. of a car || a light truck used esp. for deliveries

pick·y (píki:) *comp.* **pick·i·er** *superl.* **pick·i·est** *adj.* (*pop.*) choosy, finical, *a picky eater*

pic·nic (píknik) **1.** *n.* an outing in which the people involved eat a meal outdoors, brought along for the occasion || the food prepared for this || (*pop.*) something easy or pleasant to do or experience **2.** *v.i. pres. part.* **pic·nick·ing** *past* and *past part.* **pic·nicked** to have or participate in a picnic **pic·nick·er** *n.*

pic·to·ri·al (piktɔ́ri:əl, piktóuri:əl) **1.** *adj.* of, containing, expressing or illustrating by pictures **2.** *n.* an illustrated periodical or newspaper

pic·ture (píktʃər) **1.** *n.* a representation or image on a surface, e.g. a painting, drawing, print or photograph, esp. as a work of art || a perfect likeness || a type, symbol || a mental image, idea || a film, movie || a situation as a combination of circumstances || a picturesque sight **in the picture** (of actions, events or persons) forming part of the circumstances under consideration **to take a picture** to record on film the image of an object by means of a camera **2.** *v.t. pres. part.* **pic·tur·ing** *past* and *past part.* **pic·tured** to imagine || to depict, esp. in writing

pic·tur·esque (pìktʃərésk) *adj.* (of scenery, landscapes etc.) full of charm, esp. through having an irregular prettiness or quaintness or antique quality, rather than classical beauty || (of language etc.) strikingly vivid

pid·dle (píd'l) *pres. part.* **pid·dling** *past* and *past part.* **pid·dled** *v.i.* to trifle, waste time || to urinate || *v.t.* (with 'away') to pass (time etc.) wastefully **pid·dling** *adj.* trivial

pie (pai) *n.* a dish of fruit, meat etc., baked with a pastry crust

pie·bald (páibɔld) **1.** *adj.* marked in patches of two different colors, esp. black and white **2.** *n.* a piebald animal, esp. a horse

piece (pi:s) **1.** *n.* a distinct part, separated or broken off from a whole || a single example or unit of a class of things || a single unit || belonging to a set || a coin of a specified kind, *a 50-cent piece* || a musical or literary composition, esp. a short one **in one piece** integral, not being in nor consisting of separate pieces || not broken **in pieces** broken in pieces or otherwise destroyed **of a piece** consistent **to come to pieces** to be able to be disassembled into its component parts **to give (someone) a piece of one's mind** to rebuke (someone) severely and bluntly **to go to pieces** to lose control of oneself or suffer a nervous or emotional collapse **2.** *v.t. pres. part.* **piec·ing** *past* and *past part.* **pieced** to mend or patch by adding a piece ‖ (with 'together') to join (things) so that they make a whole ‖ (often with 'out' or 'together') to make by joining parts or pieces

pièce de ré·sis·tance (pjesdəreizi:stãs) *n.* the choice item in a collection or series, esp. the chief dish in a meal

piece·meal (pí:smi:l) **1.** *adv.* by degrees, one part after another **2.** *adj.* done bit by bit

piece·work (pí:swə:rk) *n.* work paid for by the amount done, not by the time taken

pied (paid) *adj.* parti-colored

pier (piər) *n.* a breakwater of masonry ‖ a wooden-decked structure, supported on piles and built to extend for some distance into the sea or other body of water, used to give passengers access to vessels ‖ *(archit.)* a pillar or other structure supporting an arch or lintel or the span of ridge ‖ a buttress of masonry or brick ‖ a section of wall between two doors or other openings

pierce (piərs) *pres. part.* **pierc·ing** *past* and *past part.* **pierced** *v.t.* to make a hole in or through (something) using a sharp implement ‖ to affect (the senses, esp. the sense of hearing, or the emotions) intensely ‖ to make a way into or through ‖ to understand or see through, *to pierce a mystery* **pierc·ing** *adj.* penetrating sharply or deeply

pi·e·ty (páiiti:) *pl.* **pi·e·ties** *n.* devotion and reverence for God ‖ an act which shows this quality

pig (pig) **1.** *n.* a young hog less than 120 lbs in weight ‖ a greedy, dirty or selfish person ‖ an oblong mass of iron, lead etc. obtained when the molten metal from a furnace cools in a trough ‖ pig iron **a pig in a poke** something which one buys or accepts without seeing it first, taking a chance on its being satisfactory **to make a pig of oneself** to eat too much **2.** *v.i. pres. part.* **pig·ging** *past* and *past part.* **pigged** (of a sow) to bring forth young ‖ (with 'out') to gorge oneself

pi·geon (pídʒən) *n.* a large family of birds of worldwide distribution having stout bodies, short legs, smooth plumage and small heads and beaks ‖ a clay pigeon

pi·geon·hole (pídʒənhǫul) **1.** *n.* a recess in a desk, cabinet etc. for keeping letters, papers etc. **2.** *v.t. pres. part.* **pi·geon·hol·ing** *past* and *past part.* **pi·geon·holed** to put away for future attention or indefinitely ‖ to classify mentally

pi·geon-toed (pídʒəntǫud) *adj.* having the toes turned inwards

pig·gy·back (pígi:bæk) **1.** *adj.* of a transport system by which road-haulage loads in their vehicles are carried by rail ‖ of something carried along with another more important package **2.** *adv.* carried in this way ‖ on the back and shoulders **3.** *n.* a ride made piggyback ‖ a piggyback transport system

pig·head·ed (píghędid) *adj.* stupidly obstinate

pig iron the impure iron, with a large content of combined carbon, obtained directly from a blast furnace

pig·ment (pígmənt) *n.* a coloring matter, esp. in dry powdered form, used in paints etc. ‖ the coloring matter in the cells and tissues of an animal or plant

pig·men·ta·tion (pigməntéiʃən) *n.* (esp. *biol.*) coloring or discoloring, esp. in tissues, as a result of pigment

pig·skin (pígskin) *n.* leather made from a hog's skin ‖ *(pop.)* a football

pig·tail (pígteil) *n.* a braid of hair

pike (paik) *pl.* **pike, pikes** *n.* a genus of voracious freshwater fishes of the northern hemisphere, with narrow, elongated snout and sharp teeth

pike *n.* a gate or bar across a road where a toll is paid ‖ a road, esp. one on which a toll is levied ‖ a toll

pi·laf, pi·laff, pi·lau (pí:lɑf, pilɑ́f) *n.* an Oriental dish of rice boiled with fish, meat or chicken and spices

pile (pail) **1.** *n.* a stout beam of wood or steel driven vertically into unfirm ground or the bed of a lake, river or sea, as a support for a superstructure, e.g. a house or causeway **2.** *v.t. pres. part.* **pil·ing** *past* and *past part.* **piled** to support with or furnish with piles ‖ to drive piles into

pile 1. *n.* a number of things lying one upon another, or a quantity of material placed in or as if in layers forming an elevated mass ‖ *(pop.)* a large amount of **2.** *v. pres. part.* **pil·ing** *past* and *past part.* **piled** *v.t.* to place in a pile ‖ (esp. with 'together' or 'up') to gather, accumulate ‖ to cover with a pile or piles ‖ *v.i.* to crowd together ‖ (esp. with 'up') to come together in or as if in a pile

pile *n.* a soft, furry or velvety raised surface consisting of threads standing out from the surface of a fabric or carpet, either singly or as loops ‖ soft down, fur, hair or wool

pile driver a machine used to drive piles into the ground with a drop hammer ‖ a person who operates this machine

piles (pailz) *pl. n.* hemorrhoids

pil·fer (pílfər) *v.t.* to steal in small quantities ‖ *v.i.* to commit petty thefts

pil·grim (pílgrim) *n.* a person who makes a journey to some sacred place as an act of religious devotion

pill (pil) *n.* a small ball or pellet of medicine usually coated with sugar, which is swallowed whole ‖ (with 'the') an oral contraceptive ‖ something unpleasant that must be accepted ‖ *(pop., old-fash.)* a disagreeable person

pil·lage (pílidʒ) **1.** *n.* the act of taking goods by force, esp. by armed force in war **2.** *v. pres. part.* **pil·lag·ing** *past* and *past part.* **pil·laged** *v.t.* to plunder (persons or places), esp. in wartime ‖ *v.i.* to make plundering raids

pil·lar (pílər) **1.** *n.* *(archit.)* a vertical structure of masonry, metal etc., of much greater height than thickness, used as a support for a superstructure or as an ornament ‖ anything like this in shape or function ‖ a chief supporter of a cause or institution **from pillar to post** from one place of refuge, resource etc. to another **2.** *v.t.* to support or ornament with pillars

pil·lo·ry (píləri:) **1.** *pl.* **pil·lo·ries** *n.* *(hist.)* a wooden framework with three holes into which the head and hands of an offender were locked, exposing him to public abuse and ridicule **2.** *v.t. pres. part.* **pil·lo·ry·ing** *past* and *past part.* **pil·lo·ried** *(hist.)* to set in a pillory ‖ to expose to public scorn

pil·low (pílou) **1.** *n.* a rest and support for the neck or head of a recumbent person ‖ *(engin.)* a block, e.g. of wood, used as a cushioning support **2.** *v.t.* to lay (the head etc.) on a pillow or on something serving as a pillow

pil·low·case (píloukęis) *n.* a loose, removable cover of cotton or linen for a pillow

pi·lot (páilət) **1.** *n.* a person qualified to direct a vessel on its course into or out of a port, river mouth, canal etc., or along a coast, and taking over navigational control from the master of the vessel while so employed ‖ a person qualified to operate the flying controls of an aircraft ‖ someone who acts as a guide ‖ *(engin.)* a machine part which guides another part in its movement ‖ a pilot light **2.** *adj.* serving as an experimental model for others to follow, *a pilot factory plant* ‖ *(engin.)* serving as a device to direct the operation of a larger device ‖ serving as a guide

pilot *v.t.* to act as the pilot of (a ship, aircraft etc.) ‖ to guide (someone)

(**a**) æ, *cat*; ɑ, *car*; ɔ *fawn*; ei, *snake*. (**e**) e, *hen*; i:, *sheep*; iə, *deer*; ɛə, *bear*. (**i**) i, *fish*; ai, *tiger*; ə:, *bird*. (**o**) o, *ox*; au, *cow*; ou, *goat*; u, *poor*; ɔi, *royal*. (**u**) ʌ, *duck*; u, *bull*; u:, *goose*; ə, *bacillus*; ju:, *cube*. x, *loch*; θ, *think*; ð, *bother*; z, *Zen*; ʒ, *corsage*; dʒ, *savage*; ŋ, *orangutang*; j, *yak*; ʃ, *fish*; tʃ, *fetch*; 'l, *rabble*; 'n, *redden*. Complete pronunciation key appears inside front cover.

pi·men·to (piméntou) *pl.* **pi·men·tos** *n.* allspice ‖ the pimiento

pi·mien·to (pimjéntou) *pl.* **pi·mien·tos** *n.* any of certain red sweet peppers used for stuffing olives, as a source of paprika etc.

pimp (pimp) **1.** *n.* a male procurer of clients for a prostitute **2.** *v.i.* to act as a pimp

pim·ple (pímp'l) *n.* a small, solid, rounded, raised area on the skin, caused by inflammation etc. **pím·pled, pím·ply** *adjs*

pin (pin) **1.** *n.* a short, very thin, sharp-pointed length of metal, with a small, flat or round head at one end, used to fasten textiles, paper etc., or one without a head, mounted on a badge or brooch to fasten it to clothing ‖ any of several other fastening devices, e.g. a hairpin or safety pin, or a wooden peg used in carpentry ‖ a brooch ‖ *(carpentry)* the tenon of a dovetail ‖ a bottle-shaped piece of wood bowled at in ninepins or tenpins ‖ a linchpin ‖ *(golf)* the flagpole marking a hole ‖ *(pl., pop.)* the legs, *to knock someone off his pins* **2.** *v.t. pres. part.* **pin·ning** *past* and *past part.* **pinned** to fasten with or as if with a pin **to pin (someone) down** to hold (someone) down by force ‖ to cause (someone) to commit himself or to be specific **to pin (something) on someone** to put the blame for (something) on someone

pin·a·fore (pínəfɔr, pínəfour) *n.* a sleeveless, apronlike garment fastened at the back and worn over good clothing, esp. by little girls

pin·ball (pínbɔl) *n.* a game played on a pinball machine

pinball machine a glass-covered slot machine used for amusement or gambling

pin·cers (pínsərz) *pl. n.* (sometimes construed as *sing.*) a tool consisting of two arms, hinged together not far from their curved gripping ends and serving as a pair of levers, used to crush, extract nails, grip etc. ‖ *(zool.)* an appendage for grasping, e.g. the chela of certain crustaceans

pinch (pintʃ) **1.** *v.t.* to grip between the forefinger and thumb with a sudden, strong pressure ‖ to grip a portion of the flesh of (someone) in this way ‖ to squeeze ‖ to cause to become thin, worn, haggard etc., *pinched by poverty* ‖ (often passive and with 'for') to restrict to a narrow space or range of activity, spending etc. ‖ *(pop.)* to steal ‖ *(pop.)* to arrest ‖ *v.i.* to exert painful pressure by squeezing ‖ to overeconomize, be stingy **2.** *n.* the act or an instance of pinching between forefinger and thumb ‖ an amount which can be taken up between the forefinger and thumb ‖ suffering caused by the pressure of poverty etc. **in a pinch** if absolutely necessary

pinch-hit (píntʃhit) *pres. part.* **pinch-hit·ting** *past* and *past part.* **pinch-hit** *v.i.* (baseball) to bat for the regular player ‖ *(pop.)* to act as substitute in an emergency

pinch hitter (baseball) a player who pinch-hits for another ‖ *(pop.)* someone who acts as a substitute for another person

pine (pain) *n.* a genus of chiefly north temperate, coniferous, resinous trees with needlelike evergreen leaves, usually in clusters ‖ the wood of any of these trees

pine *pres. part.* **pin·ing** *past* and *past part.* **pined** *v.i.* (often with 'away') to lose vitality gradually through hunger, unhappiness etc. ‖ (with 'for') to long for, often so intensely as to suffer

pine·ap·ple (páinæp'l) *n.* a perennial tropical plant with spiny, recurved leaves and a short, thick stem, native to South America and widely cultivated for its fruit ‖ the edible fruit of this plant, which has juicy, yellowish flesh and a covering of floral bracts topped with short, stiff leaves

ping (piŋ) **1.** *n.* a sharp ringing sound, e.g. of a pebble hitting a rock, a bullet flying through the air etc. **2.** *v.t.* to make this sound

pin·hole (pínhoul) *n.* a hole in paper etc., made by or as if by a pin ‖ a hole into which a pin or peg fits

pin·ion (pínjən) *n.* the smallest and smallest-toothed of two or more gear wheels forming a train or set of gear wheels

pinion 1. *n.* a flight feather of a bird's wing ‖ the end joint of a bird's wing **2.** *v.t.* to cut off or bind the pinions or wings of (a bird) to prevent flight ‖ to bind (the arms) of a person so as to make him powerless ‖ to make (someone) powerless by binding his arms

pink 1. *n.* a genus of plants native to E. Europe, widely cultivated in temperate zones for their fragrant, white, pale red or crimson flowers ‖ a pale, bluish-red color ‖ a pigment, fabric etc. of this color **in the pink of health** (or **condition**) in perfect health (or condition) **2.** *adj.* having the color pink ‖ *(pop.)* tending towards communism

pink·eye (pínkai) *n.* a highly contagious form of conjunctivitis

pin·na·cle (pínək'l) **1.** *n.* a slender, usually pointed, turret ornamenting a gable, tower etc. ‖ a slender peak of rock ‖ *(fig.)* the highest point, climax **2.** *v.t. pres. part.* **pin·na·cling** *past* and *past part.* **pin·na·cled** to ornament with a pinnacle or pinnacles ‖ to place on or as if on a pinnacle ‖ to be the pinnacle of

pin·point (pínpɔint) **1.** *n.* the pointed end of a pin **2.** *v.t.* to locate (e.g. a target) precisely ‖ to direct (an attack, bomb etc.) on a small objective with great accuracy **3.** *adj.* (of a bombing target) requiring extreme accuracy of aim ‖ extremely precise, *pinpoint accuracy*

pint (paint) *n.* any of various liquid or dry units of capacity equal to 1/8 gallon, a unit equal to 28.875 cu. ins ‖ a dry measure equal to 33.600 cu. ins

pin·to (píntou) *pl.* **pin·tos** *n.* a pony or horse that is mottled, esp. with blotches of two or more colors ‖ a pinto bean

pi·o·neer (paiəníər) **1.** *n.* a person who experiments and originates, or plays a leading part in the early development of something ‖ an early settler ‖ a member of a military unit which clears the way in advance of the main body of troops, building bridges, roads, trenches etc. **2.** *v.t.* to prepare, initiate and champion ‖ to explore and be among the first to develop (a region etc.) ‖ *v.i.* to be a pioneer

pi·ous (páiəs) *adj.* devout or showing religious devotion ‖ designating or making a hypocritical show or pretense of virtue, propriety etc.

pipe (paip) *pres. part.* **pip·ing** *past* and *past part.* **piped** *v.t.* to convey through pipes ‖ to utter in a squeaky or shrill voice ‖ *(naut.)* to summon (a crew) by sounding a boatswain's whistle ‖ to play (a tune) on a pipe ‖ to furnish with pipes ‖ to ornament with piping ‖ *v.i.* to play a pipe, esp. the bagpipes ‖ to make squeaky or shrill sounds ‖ *(metall.*, e.g. of steel castings) to develop longitudinal cavities ‖ *(naut.)* to summon a ship's crew by sounding a boatswain's whistle **to pipe down** *(pop.)* to stop talking, or become quiet and subdued

pipe *n.* a long hollow cylinder, used chiefly to convey fluids, gas etc. ‖ a musical wind instrument consisting of a hollow cylinder in which the air is made to vibrate, producing a note ‖ one of the hollow tubes in an organ, in which the note is produced in this way ‖ a tubular organ, vessel etc. in the body ‖ a device for smoking tobacco, opium etc. ‖ a quantity of tobacco etc. contained in the bowl of this device ‖ a session of smoking such a device ‖ *(naut.)* a boatswain's whistle or the sounding of it ‖ the shrill sound of a bird ‖ *(pl.)* bagpipes

pipe·line (páiplain) *n.* a long line of pipes jointed together, with pumping stations at intervals, used to convey liquids or gases, esp. to convey the crude product from an oil field to a port or refinery ‖ a channel of communication or transport

pi·quant (pí:kənt) *adj.* sharply stimulating the sense of taste ‖ stimulating the curiosity or interest

pique (pi:k) *pres. part.* **piqu·ing** *past* and *past part.* **piqued** *v.t.* to cause resentment in, esp. by wounding the pride of ‖ to stimulate, arouse

pique *n.* resentment caused by injured self-esteem

pi·qué (pikéi, pi:kéi) *n.* a rather stiff fabric of esp. cotton with a ribbed surface

pi·ra·cy (páirəsi:) *pl.* **pi·ra·cies** *n.* robbery of ships at sea ‖ robbery on land by a descent from the sea by persons not acting under the authority of a state ‖ unauthorized use of a patented or copyrighted work ‖ an instance of any of these

pi·rate (páirət) **1.** *n.* someone who commits piracy **2.** *v. pres. part.* **pi·rat·ing** *past* and *past part.* **pi·rat·ed** *v.t.* to use (another's copyright material) for one's own profit without permission or without paying fees ‖ *v.i.* to practice piracy **pi·rat·ic** (pairǽtik), **pi·rát·i·cal** *adjs*

pi·rogue (piróug) *n.* a dugout canoe

pir·ou·ette (piru:ét) **1.** *n.* a rapid spin or whirl of the body on the point of the toe or ball of the foot, esp. in ballet **2.** *v.i. pres. part.* **pir·ou·et·ting** *past* and *past part.* **pir·ou·et·ted** *v.i.* to execute a pirouette

pis·ta·chi·o (pistǽʃi:ou, pistáʃi:ou) *pl.* **pis·ta·chios** *n.* a small dioecious tree native to W. Asia. Its fruit, a drupe, contains an edible seed, the pistachio nut, used as a flavoring in ice cream, confectionery etc. ‖ this nut ‖ the yellowish-green color of the nut

pis·til (pístil) *n.* (*bot.*) the female seedbearing organ of a flower, including the ovary, stigma and style **pis·til·late** (pístilit, pístileit) *adj.* having or bearing a pistil, esp. without a stamen

pis·tol (pístəl) *n.* a small firearm held and fired with one hand

pis·ton (pístən) *n.* a disk or short cylinder attached centrally to a rod and fitted closely inside a hollow cylinder, within which it can be driven up and down by fluid pressure (in engines) or create a partial vacuum on one side of it as the piston rod is moved up and down (in pumps or compressors) ‖ (*mus.*) a sliding valve in a brass wind instrument

pit (pit) **1.** *n.* a deep hole in the ground, either natural or made by digging ‖ a covered hole in the ground used as a trap for animals ‖ a coal mine, including the shaft and all the workings ‖ a hole made in the floor of a garage or workshop enabling a car or machine to be examined or repaired from below ‖ an enclosed, often sunken area for fights between animals, esp. cocks ‖ (*bot.*) a specialized depressed region of the secondary wall of plant cells that plays a role in the intercellular transport of fluids ‖ the space, often depressed, in front of the stage in a theater, where the orchestra sits ‖ (*commerce*) an area of an exchange devoted to a particular commodity, *wheat pit* **2.** *v. pres. part.* **pit·ting** *past* and *past part.* **pit·ted** *v.t.* (with 'against') to match (one's strength, courage, willpower) against another's or against some natural force ‖ to make a pit in (the skin etc.), *a face pitted by smallpox* ‖ to set (one animal) to fight against another ‖ to put into a pit, usually for storage ‖ *v.i.* to become marked with pits

pit **1.** *n.* the stone of a peach, cherry, plum etc. **2.** *v.t. pres. part.* **pit·ting** *past* and *past part.* **pit·ted** to remove the pit from

pitch (pitʃ) **1.** *n.* a dark-colored, sticky, resinous substance, liquid when heated, hard when cold, which is a residue from distillation of tars, turpentine or fatty oils etc. and occurs naturally as asphalt ‖ this substance as a criterion of blackness or obscurity ‖ a resin derived from certain conifers, sometimes considered to have medicinal properties **2.** *v.t.* to coat or smear with pitch

pitch **1.** *v.t.* to fix and set up, *to pitch a tent* ‖ to set or place in a definite position ‖ (*baseball, cricket*) to

throw or deliver (the ball) to the batter or batsman ‖ (*mus.*) to set (a part, note etc.) in a scale or key or at a particular pitch ‖ to set in a particular style, degree, manner, mood, feeling etc. ‖ *v.i.* to encamp ‖ (of a ship) to plunge or toss with bow and stern alternately rising and falling ‖ to plunge headlong ‖ to dip, slope **to pitch in** to get down to work vigorously **to pitch into** (*pop.*) to attack violently **2.** *n.* the act of pitching or an instance of this ‖ a place claimed for doing business in an open market, for street performance or for camping ‖ (*baseball*) the act of pitching or manner in which the ball is pitched ‖ the quality of a sound with respect to the frequency of vibration of the sound waves ‖ degree of intensity ‖ the degree of slope of something, e.g. of a roof ‖ (*geol., mining*) the dip of a vein or bed ‖ the pitching motion of a ship ‖ (*pop.*) a line of talk, e.g. of a salesman

pitch·er (pítʃər) *n.* a jug for holding liquids, esp. one with a wide lip and a handle or ears

pitcher *n.* a person who pitches, esp. (*baseball*) the player who pitches the ball to the batter ‖ (*golf*) an iron with a blade lofted more than a mashie niblick but less than a niblick, used for short approach shots to the green

pitch·fork (pítʃfɔrk) **1.** *n.* a longhandled fork with sharp, curved prongs for lifting and turning hay, straw etc. **2.** *v.t.* to shift with a pitchfork ‖ to thrust (someone) suddenly or forcibly or without preparation (into some job or position)

pit·e·ous (píti:əs) *adj.* arousing pity

pit·fall (pitfɔl) *n.* a hidden danger or difficulty

pith (piθ) *n.* the medulla or central region of parenchymatous cells in the stem of a vascular plant ‖ the soft white lining of e.g. orange peel ‖ the substance or gist of a matter ‖ forceful relevance, *comments full of pith*

pith·y (píθi:) *comp.* **pith·i·er** *superl.* **pith·i·est** *adj.* forcefully concise, tersely cogent ‖ of, like or containing pith

pit·i·a·ble (píti:əb'l) *adj.* arousing or deserving pity ‖ arousing or deserving pitying contempt **pit·i·a·bly** *adv.*

pit·i·ful (píti:fəl) *adj.* calling forth pity or compassion ‖ contemptible

pit·i·less (píti:lis, pítilis) *adj.* showing or feeling no pity

pit·tance (pít'ns) *n.* a very small income wage or allowance

pi·tu·i·tar·y gland (pitú:iteri:glænd, pitjú:iteri:glænd) a small vascular endocrine gland located at the base of the brain and found in most vertebrates

pit·y (píti:) **1.** *pl.* **pit·ies** *n.* a feeling of sympathy for the sufferings or privations of others ‖ a cause of sorrow or regret **to have** (or **take**) **pity on** to act with compassion toward **2.** *v.t. pres. part.* **pit·y·ing** *past* and *past part.* **pit·ied** to feel pity for

piv·ot (pívət) *n.* a fixed shaft or pin having a pointed end which acts as the point of balance upon which a plate or bar can turn or oscillate ‖ the pointed end of such a shaft or pin ‖ the turning or oscillating movement of something mounted on such a shaft or pin ‖ a person, thing or factor on which a set of circumstances etc. depends, *this point is the pivot of the argument*

pivot *v.t.* to supply with or balance on a pivot ‖ *v.i.* to turn or oscillate on or as if on a pivot

pivot *n.* (*sports*) the key participant in an action —**pi·votman** (*basketball*) the center

pix·ie, pix·y (píksi:) *pl.* **pix·ies** *n.* a small, mischievous elf or fairy

pix·i·lat·ed, pix·il·lat·ed (píksəleitid) (*pop.*) slightly crazy ‖ (*pop.*) rather drunk

pi·zazz (pizǽz) *n.* (*slang*) a provocative vitality

(**a**) æ, c*a*t; ɑ, c*a*r; ɔ f*a*wn; ei, sn*a*ke. (**e**) e, h*e*n; i:, sh*ee*p; iə, d*ee*r; ɛə, b*ea*r. (**i**) i, f*i*sh; ai, t*i*ger; ə:, b*i*rd. (**o**) o, *o*x; au, c*ow*; ou, g*oa*t; u, p*oo*r; ɔi, r*oy*al. (**u**) ʌ, d*u*ck; u, b*u*ll; u:, g*oo*se; ə, b*a*cillus; ju:, c*u*be. x, lo*ch*; θ, *th*ink; ð, bo*th*er; z, *Z*en; ʒ, corsa*g*e; dʒ, sava*g*e; ŋ, oranguta*ng*; j, *y*ak; ʃ, fi*sh*; tʃ, fe*tch*; 'l, rabb*le*; 'n, redd*en*. Complete pronunciation key appears inside front cover.

piz·za (pí:tsə) *n.* a large, round, flat, breadlike crust spread with tomatoes, cheese and sometimes other ingredients, e.g. shreds of meat, anchovies and herbs, and baked

piz·zi·ca·to (pǐtsikátou) **1.** *adj. (mus.,* of a note) played on a stringed instrument by plucking the strings with the finger instead of using the bow **2.** *adv. (mus.)* in a pizzicato manner **3.** *pl.* **piz·zi·ca·ti** (pǐtsikáti:), **piz·zi·ca·tos** *n. (mus.)* a note or passage played pizzicato

plac·a·ble (plǽkəb'l, pléikəb'l) *adj.* capable of being placated, or easily placated ‖ showing tolerance or forgiveness, *in a placable mood*

plac·ard (plǽkɑrd, plǽkərd) **1.** *n.* a notice for advertising or display purposes **2.** *v.t.* to set up placards in or on ‖ to advertise by such means ‖ to display as a placard

pla·cate (pléikeit, plǽkeit) *pres. part.* **pla·cat·ing** *past* and *past part.* **pla·cat·ed** *v.t.* to pacify, esp. by making concessions **pla·ca·tion** (pleikéiʃən) *n.* **pla·ca·to·ry** (pléikətɔri:, plǽkətɔri:, pléikətɔuri:, plǽkətɔuri:) *adj.*

place (pleis) **1.** *n.* a particular part of space ‖ a particular spot or area on a surface ‖ a particular city, town, village, district etc. ‖ position in space, or in some hierarchy, scale, orderly arrangement etc. ‖ proper function that goes with status, *it's not your place to criticize* ‖ a building or area appointed for a specified purpose ‖ (in names) a square in a city ‖ (in street names) a short street ‖ (in names) a country mansion ‖ home, dwelling ‖ a particular passage in a book etc. ‖ *(racing)* a position among the winners, esp. second or third ‖ a stage or step in an argument or sequence, *in the first place we must define our terms* **in place** in the usual or correct place ‖ proper, appropriate **in place of** as a substitute for, rather than **out of place** inappropriate, unsuitable ‖ not in keeping with the surroundings etc. **to go places** *(pop.)* to achieve worldly success or distinction **to know one's place** *(old-fash.)* to act humbly and respectfully in accordance with one's relatively low rank or standing **to take place** to occur, happen **to take the place of** to be a substitute for **2.** *v. pres. part.* **plac·ing** *past* and *past part.* **placed** *v.t.* to put in a particular place, position, rank, office, condition etc. ‖ to identify by recalling the context or circumstances connected ‖ to invest (money) ‖ to give (an order for goods etc.) ‖ (followed by 'in', 'on' or 'upon') to bestow (confidence, trust etc.) upon something or someone ‖ to pitch (the voice) in singing or speech ‖ *v.i. (racing)* to be among the first three contestants to finish, esp. to finish second in a horse or dog race

pla·ce·bo (pləsí:bou) *pl.* **pla·ce·bos, pla·ce·boes** *n.* an inactive but harmless preparation given to humor a patient

pla·cen·ta (pləséntə) *pl.* **pla·cen·tas, pla·cen·tae** (pləsénti:) *n.* the vascular organ in most mammals which joins the fetus to the maternal uterus and acts as the site of metabolic exchange between them ‖ any of various functionally similar organs in other animals ‖ *(bot.)* the part of the carpel bearing ovules

plac·er (pléisər) *n.* a deposit of sand or gravel e.g. in the bed of a stream, where gold or other valuable minerals can be obtained in particles

plac·id (plǽsid) *adj.* (of temperament) not easily roused ‖ (of a person) having such a temperament **plac·id·i·ty** (pləsíditi:) *n.*

pla·gia·rism (pléidʒərizəm, pléidʒi:ərizəm) *n.* the act of plagiarizing or an instnace of this ‖ a plagiarized idea etc. **plá·gia·rist** *n.* someone who plagiarizes

pla·gia·rize (pléidʒəraiz, pléidʒi:əraiz) *pres. part.* **pla·gia·riz·ing** *past* and *past part.* **pla·gia·rized** *v.t.* to use and pass off (someone else's ideas, inventions, writings etc.) as one's own ‖ *v.i.* to take another's writings etc. and pass them off as one's own

pla·gia·ry (pléidʒəri:, pléidʒi:əri:) *pl.* **pla·gia·ries** *n.* plagiarism ‖ a plagiarist

plague (pleig) **1.** *n.* an epidemic, often fatal disease occurring in various forms, e.g. as bubonic plague ‖ a social scourge, *a plague of petty thieving* ‖ a nuisance, annoyance **2.** *v.t. pres. part.* **pla·guing** *past* and *past part.* **plagued** to pester or harass **plá·guey, plá·guy 1.** *adj. (pop.)* annoying, bothersome **2.** *adv. (pop.)* plaguily **plá·gui·ly** *adv.*

plaid (plæd) **1.** *n.* a long piece of woolen cloth of tartan pattern worn esp. over the shoulder and breast by Scottish Highlanders ‖ cloth having a tartan pattern **2.** *adj.* made of cloth with a tartan pattern ‖ having a tartan pattern **pláid·ed** *adj.* wearing a plaid ‖ made of or wearing plaid

plain (plein) **1.** *adj.* easy to see or understand ‖ simple, not embellished or complicated ‖ absolute, complete ‖ (of food) unelaborate, not having unusual or spicy ingredients ‖ bluntly frank ‖ unsophisticated ‖ lacking physical beauty, but not ugly **2.** *n.* a large expanse of level, open country **3.** *adv.* manifestly ‖ clearly, candidly

plain·tiff (pléintif) *n. (law)* a person who brings a lawsuit against another

plain·tive (pléintiv) *adj.* quietly mournful ‖ weakly complaining

plait (pleit, plæt) **1.** *n.* a length of hair, straw, ribbon etc. consisting of at least three interlaced strands **2.** *v.t.* to interlace at least three strands of (hair, ribbon etc.) to form a plait ‖ to make (a basket, mat etc.) by interlacing strands together

plan (plæn) **1.** *n.* a design for a construction, layout, system etc. ‖ a drawing representing a horizontal section of a solid object ‖ a detailed diagram ‖ a formulated scheme setting out stages of procedure ‖ (often *pl.*) a proposed or intended course of action **2.** *v. pres. part.* **plan·ning** *past* and *past part.* **planned** *v.t.* to make a design for (a building, garden, city etc.) ‖ to devise a program of action for ‖ *v.i.* to make plans

plane (plein) **1.** *n.* a carpenter's tool used for producing a smooth surface on wood by paring away irregularities. It consists of an adjustable blade fixed at an angle in a wooden or metal stock **2.** *v. pres. part.* **plan·ing** *past* and *past part.* **planed** *v.t.* to work (wood) with this tool ‖ *v.i.* to work with this tool

plane 1. *adj.* flat, level ‖ *(math.)* lying on a surface which is a plane ‖ of such surfaces **2.** *n.* a level surface such that if any two points on it are joined by a straight line, every part of that line will lie in that surface ‖ an imaginary plane surface in which points or lines are regarded as lying, e.g., in perspective ‖ a level of development, existence, accomplishment, thought, value etc. ‖ an aircraft ‖ one of the main supporting surfaces of an aircraft or hydroplane, for controlling balance and elevation in flight ‖ one of the natural faces of a crystal ‖ a main road in a mine

plane *pres. part.* **plan·ing** *past* and *past part.* **planed** *v.t.* to glide ‖ to travel in an aircraft ‖ (of a boat or seaplane) to skim the surface of the water

plan·et (plǽnit) *n.* one of the bodies in space, other than a comet, meteor or satellite, which revolve around the sun of the earth's solar system, shining by reflected light from the sun ‖ any similar body revolving about a star

plan·e·tar·i·um (plǽnitéəri:əm) *pl.* **plan·e·tar·i·ums, plan·e·tar·i·a** (plǽnitéəri:ə) *n.* a complex system of optical projectors by means of which the positions and relative motions of the planets and visible stars are displayed on the inner surface of a large dome within which observers are situated ‖ the building containing this

plan·e·tar·y (plǽniteri:) *adj.* of or pertaining to a planet or the planets ‖ of or pertaining to the earth ‖ *(phys.)* moving like a planet

plan·et·oid (plǽnitɔid) *n.* an asteroid

plank (plæŋk) **1.** *n.* a long, heavy board, usually at least 2 ins thick and at least 8 or 9 ins wide ‖ a miain idea, principle etc. in an argument, political program etc. ‖ planking **to walk the plank** *(hist.)* to be made to walk blindfold along and off a plank projecting from a ship over the sea (a method of killing used by pirates) **2.** *v.t.* to cover or provide with planks ‖ to cook and serve on a wooden board ‖ *(pop.,* esp. with 'down') to put (something) on a counter, table etc. with force ‖ to put down (money) in payment on the spot **plánk·ing** *n.* planks collectively

plank·ton (plǽŋktən) *n.* minute plants (chiefly algae) and animals which float in great quantities near the surface of fresh or salt water. They provide the only source of food for many kinds of fish **plank·ton·ic** (plæŋktónik) *adj.*

plant (plænt, plɑnt) *v.t.* to put the roots of (a plant) in the ground to enable it to grow, or to sow (seed) ‖ to stock with plants ‖ to introduce (living things) in the hope that they will settle and multiply ‖ to instill (ideas, principles etc.) in the mind ‖ to put firmly in position ‖ *(pop.)* to place as a trap ‖ *(pop.)* to deliver (a blow) ‖ (with 'out') to transplant (young plants) to the ground where they are to mature

plant *n.* any organism belonging to the kingdom *Plantae,* characterized usually by lack of independent locomotion, absence of a central nervous system, cell walls composed of cellulose, and a nutritive system based on photosynthesis ‖ the assemblage of buildings, tools etc. used to manufacture some kind of goods or power ‖ mechanical equipment for a particular operation ‖ *(pop.)* a carefully planned swindle ‖ *(pop.)* a carefully planned trap laid to catch a wrongdoer

plan·tain (plǽntin, plǽntein) *n.* a member of *Plantago,* fam. *Plantaginaceae,* genus of plants with a radical, ribbed rosette of leaves. They are cosmopolitan weeds. The inflorescence is a spike or head

plantain *n.* a species of banana plant native to India ‖ its fruit, starchy and green-skinned, a basic food in the Tropics, commonly baked, boiled or fried

plan·ta·tion (plæntéiʃən) *n.* a group of growing plants or trees ‖ an estate, esp. in a tropical or warm region, on which a crop such as sugarcane, cotton, tea etc. is cultivated ‖ *(hist.)* the settling of a colony or new country ‖ *(hist.)* a colony or settlement

plant·er (plǽntər, plɑntər) *n.* a person who plants ‖ a machine used to plant ‖ a person who manages a plantation ‖ a container for potted or unpotted house plants ‖ *(hist.)* a colonist

plaque (plæk) *n.* a flat piece of metal, ivory etc. attached to a wall or inset in wood, either as an ornament or to record a fact of historical interest ‖ *(virology)* in a culture, an area destroyed by a virus

plas·ma (plǽzmə) *n. (biol.)* the viscous living matter of a cell surrounding the nucleus, the protoplasm ‖ the blood plasma **plas·mat·ic** (plæzmǽtik), **plás·mic** *adjs*

plas·ter (plǽstər, plástər) *n.* a mixture of slaked lime, sand and water, sometimes with hair or fibers added as binding material, applied wet to an interior wall or ceiling and hardening to a smooth surface when dry ‖ plaster of paris ‖ a medicinal preparation spread on a cloth and applied to the body, *a mustard plaster*

plaster *v.t.* to cover (a wall etc.) with wet plaster ‖ to put (something adhesive) on a surface, esp. in great quantity or with force ‖ to apply a medicinal plaster to ‖ to treat (wine) with plaster of paris to neutralize acidity ‖ to bomb or shell heavily

plas·ter·board (plǽstərbɔrd, plástərbɔrd, plǽstərbourd, plástərbourd) *n.* a board made by compressing sheets of fiber separated by a layer of partly set plaster of paris and used esp. as a surface to be plastered

plaster of paris a white or pinkish powder, essentially the hemihydrate of calcium sulfate, obtained by cal-

cining gypsum. With water it forms a quick-setting paste, drying to form a tough, hard solid. It is used for casts and molds and building materials

plas·tic (plǽstik) **1.** *adj.* of material which changes shape when pressure is applied and retains its new shape when the pressure is removed ‖ of the processes involved in using such materials to fashion things ‖ of an object fashioned from such a material ‖ *(art)* of, relating to or characterized by three-dimensional movement, form and space ‖ pliable, easily influenced ‖ *(biol.)* capable of undergoing variation, growth, repair etc. ‖ *(colloq.)* unnatural, synthetic ‖ so changeable as to be phony **2.** *n.* a plastic material **plás·ti·cal·ly** *adv.*

plate (pleit) **1.** *n.* a flat, shallow dish (usually circular, and typically of porcelain or earthenware) from which food is eaten ‖ the food served on such a dish ‖ the main course of a meal (meat, vegetables, salad etc.) all served on one plate ‖ a thin flat piece of metal for engraving on or bearing an inscription ‖ a full-page illustration (usually on coated paper or some paper other than what is used for the text) bound in a book ‖ *(collect.)* domestic utensils (esp. tableware) made of gold, silver etc., or plated ‖ a thin coating of precious metal put on base metal by electrolysis ‖ *(photog.)* a rectangular piece of metal or glass, coated with a sensitized emulsion, on which a photograph is taken ‖ *(dentistry)* that part of a denture which fits against the mouth and holds the artificial teeth in position ‖ *(pop.)* a set of false teeth ‖ a metal or wooden dish used for taking up the collection in church ‖ *(baseball)* home plate ‖ *(baseball)* a piece of rubber upon which the pitcher stands when delivering the ball to the batter ‖ *(elec.)* the anode or positive element of an electron tube toward which the stream of electrons flows **2.** *v.t. pres. part.* **plat·ing** *past* and *past part.* **plat·ed** to cover with metal plates ‖ to cover with a thin layer (e.g. of metal) mechanically, chemically or electrically ‖ to make a solid plate of (type) for printing

pla·teau (plætóu) *pl.* **pla·teaus, pla·teaux** (plætóuz) *n.* a level, horizontal region at a considerable height above sea level or surrounding regions ‖ a roughly level section in a graph (e.g. of progress in production, showing little or no advance)

plat·form (plǽtfɔrm) *n.* a raised structure of planks on which a speaker or a performer stands, acts etc. so that he can be seen by an audience ‖ a raised structure next to the track, by which passengers enter or leave a train in a station ‖ the open area at the end of a railroad passenger car, trolley car etc. ‖ a ledge, e.g. on a cliff face ‖ a flat structure on which a gun is mounted ‖ a flat, esp. raised, piece of ground ‖ a statement of aims and policies in the program of a person or party seeking electoral support

plat·ing (pléitiŋ) *n.* the process or result of covering with a plate or plates, esp. with a thin layer of metal ‖ the plates of a vessel, tank or other armored vehicle

plat·i·num (plǽt'nəm, plǽtnəm) *n.* a very heavy, ductile, malleable, silvery white metallic element

plat·i·tude (plǽtitu:d, plǽtitju:d) *n.* a flat, stale or commonplace remark or statement uttered as if it were informative and important ‖ (in speech, writing, thinking) the quality of being dull or commonplace **plat·i·tu·di·nize** *pres. part.* **plat·i·tu·di·niz·ing** *past* and *past part.* **plat·i·tu·di·nized** *v.i.* to utter platitudes **plat·i·tu·di·nous** *adj.*

pla·ton·ic (plətónik) *adj.* of or designating love for a person, usually of the opposite sex, that is free of carnal desire **pla·tón·i·cal·ly** *adv.*

pla·toon (plətú:n) *n. (mil.)* a tactical infantry unit, smaller than a company, and under the command of a lieutenant

plat·ter (plǽtər) *n.* a shallow, usually oval serving dish

plat·y·pus (plǽtipəs) *n.* a small, primitive aquatic Australian mammal, about 18 ins long. It has thick blackish-brown fur, a flat, leathery bill like that of a duck, no lips, a long, flat tail and webbed feet. It lays eggs, but nurses its young

plau·dits (plɔ́dits) *pl. n.* (*rhet.*) praise or approval

plau·si·ble (plɔ́zəb'l) *adj.* (of a statement, argument etc.) apparently true or reasonable, winning assent ‖ (of a person) genuine, trustworthy etc. in appearance, but probably not to be trusted **pláu·si·bly** *adv.*

play (plei) *n.* movement or activity, esp. quick or unconstrained ‖ activity or exercise performed for amusement ‖ freedom of movement, scope ‖ (*games*) manner of playing, *defensive play* ‖ a maneuver in a game etc. ‖ a turn to play, in a game ‖ a dramatic stage performance ‖ the written or printed text for this ‖ gambling **in play** (*games,* of the ball) available for kicking etc. in accordance with the rules **out of play** (*games,* of the ball) not available for kicking etc. **to make a play for** to use various wiles in an effort to win the love, admiration, interest etc. of (someone)

play *v.t.* to take part in games or a game of ‖ to make music on (a musical instrument) ‖ to perform (a piece of music) ‖ to act (a part) in a theatrical performance ‖ to give a theatrical performance of ‖ to perform in (a city etc.) ‖ to perform (a trick, joke etc.) ‖ to move, use, place etc. (a card, piece etc.) in a game ‖ to place a bet on (something), *to play the horses* ‖ to fill (a position) in a game ‖ to imitate or pretend to be, for fun ‖ *v.i.* to engage in activity for amusement ‖ to trifle, toy, *stop playing with your food* ‖ to flutter, flit, in a light, erratic manner, *shadows played on the ceiling* ‖ to frolic, gambol ‖ to gamble ‖ to be serious in appearance but not in fact ‖ (of a play, film etc.) to be performed or be showing ‖ (*mach.*) to show loose movement, *the steering plays badly* **to be played out** to be exhausted ‖ to be no longer effective ‖ to hold no more interest **to play around** to be active without doing anything useful ‖ (*pop.*) to engage in flirtation or illicit or promiscuous lovemaking **to play at** to take part in (some activity) in the spirit of make-believe or without being in earnest **to play back** to play and listen to (a recording which one has just made) **to play ball** to be cooperative **to play both ends against the middle** to set rivals or opposing interests against each other, to one's own advantage **to play by ear** to play a musical instrument without being able to read music or without reading the music ‖ to act in (a situation) as seems best while it is developing, rather than in accordance with some plan **to play down** to make (something) appear less important, worthy etc. than it really is **to play fair** to obey the rules ‖ to behave toward another person without cheating or deception **to play (someone) false** (*rhet.*) to deceive (someone) **to play for time** (*games*) to play out a game defensively, without risking real attack ‖ to seek to postpone an undesired event by dodges and delaying tactics **to play into someone's hand** to do something that gives one's opponent a sudden and overwhelming advantage **to play off one person against another** to set one person against another for one's own advantage **to play on** to take advantage of, exploit **to play the field** to have dates or romantic involvements with many people, not confining one's interests to one person ‖ to operate over a broad area or range **to play the fool** to behave or act as if one were a fool **to play to the gallery** to seek to win admiration in a way that is beneath one, by appealing to those who will respond most easily **to play up to** to insinuate oneself into the favor of by flattery

play·back (pléibæk) *n.* a playing back of a recording ‖ the part of a tape recorder etc. which serves to play back transcriptions

play·bill (pléibil) *n.* a poster or handbill advertising a theatrical performance ‖ a theater program

play·boy (pléibɔi) *n.* a rich young man who cares chiefly about having a good time

play·er (pléiər) *n.* a person who plays in a game ‖ a person who performs on a specified musical instrument ‖ a device for operating a piano mechanically ‖ (*old-fash.*) an actor

play·ful (pléifəl) *adj.* tending or liking to play ‖ lighthearted and humorous

play·ground (pléigraund) *n.* a piece of ground set apart for children to play on, often attached to a school ‖ a favorite district for recreation, esp. as giving scope for some particular activity

play·house (pléihaus) *pl.* **play·hous·es** (pléihauziz) *n.* (usually in titles) a theater ‖ a little house for children to play in

play·mate (pléimeit) *n.* a child's friend with whom he plays

play·off (pléiɔf, pléiɒf) *n.* (*games*) a match played to decide a tie or where a previous game has given an inconclusive result

play·thing (pléiθiŋ) *n.* something designed to be played with ‖ (*rhet.*) a person treated as a toy by another or by fate etc.

play·wright (pléirait) *n.* a writer of theatrical plays

pla·za (plázə, plǽzə) *n.* a public square in a town or city

plea (pli:) *n.* (*rhet.*) an appeal ‖ (*rhet.*) a request ‖ an argument used to excuse ‖ (*law*) a statement made in court by either party in argument of his case

plea bargaining negotiation between defense attorney in a criminal action and the prosecutor for a reduced charge in exchange for a plea of guilty

plead (pli:d) *pres. part.* **plead·ing** *past* and *past part.* **plead·ed, pled** (pled) *v.i.* to beg with emotion and at length, implore ‖ (*law*) to state a plea ‖ (*law*) to argue in court ‖ *v.t.* (*law*) to cite (something) in legal defense ‖ (*law*) to argue (a case) in court **to plead (not) guilty** (*law*) to admit (deny) guilt, as a method of procedure

pleas·ant (pléz'nt) *adj.* agreeable, pleasing

pleas·ant·ry (pléz'ntri) *pl.* **pleas·ant·ries** *n.* (in conversation) pleasant, goodhumored joking back and forth ‖ an instance of this

please (pli:z) *pres. part.* **pleas·ing** *past* and *past part.* **pleased** *v.t.* to gratify, satisfy, give pleasure to ‖ *v.i.* to desire and intend ‖ to make oneself pleasant, agreeable ‖ (in requests or commands) be good enough to, *please come along* **if you please** if you wish **please God** if it is God's wish ‖ may it be God's wish **to please oneself** to do as one wishes **pléased, pléas·ing** *adjs*

pleas·ur·a·ble (pléʒərəb'l) *adj.* giving or capable of giving pleasure **pléas·ur·a·bly** *adv.*

pleas·ure (pléʒər) *n.* a general feeling of satisfaction, enjoyment ‖ something which causes this feeling ‖ self-gratification

pleat (pli:t) **1.** *n.* a fold, esp. one made by doubling cloth etc. upon itself and pressing or stitching it in place or allowing it to hang free **2.** *v.t.* to make a pleat or pleats in

ple·bei·an, ple·bi·an (pləbí:ən) **1.** *n.* a member of the common people **2.** *adj.* of or characteristic of the common people, uncultured, vulgar

pleb·i·scite (plébisait, plébisit) *n.* a vote of the entire electorate on a national issue (e.g. constitutional change)

pledge (pledʒ) **1.** *n.* something of value left as security for a loan or as a guarantee that an obligation will be met ‖ a solemn promise ‖ the state of being pledged, *in pledge* ‖ a person who has agreed to become a member of a club, fraternity etc. but who has not yet been initiated **2.** *v.t. pres. part.* **pledg·ing** *past* and *past part.* **pledged** to hand over as security for a loan ‖ to commit (oneself, one's reputation etc.) ‖ to promise ‖ to agree to become a member of (a club, fraternity etc.)

ple·na·ry (plí:nəri:, plénəri:) *adj.* complete, absolute ‖ (of a legislative body) attended by all members

plen·i·po·ten·ti·ar·y (plɛnipəténʃi:ɛri:, plɛnipəténʃəri:) **1.** *adj.* invested with unlimited power ‖ of or relating to a plenipotentiary **2.** *pl.* **plen·i·po·ten·ti·ar·ies** *n.* an ambassador or envoy with full powers of decision

plen·i·tude (plénitu:d, plénitju:d) *n.* completeness ‖ (*rhet.*) abundance

plen·te·ous (plénti:əs) *adj.* (*rhet.*) plentiful

plen·ti·ful (pléntifəl) *adj.* abundant ‖ producing or yielding abundantly

plen·ty (plénti:) **1.** *n.* prosperity, abundance ‖ more than enough ‖ a great quantity ‖ (esp. with 'in') the quality or state of being plentiful **2.** *adj.* abundant **3.** *adv.* (*pop.*) more than adequately

ple·num (plí:nəm) *pl.* **ple·nums, ple·na** (plí:nə) *n.* the entirety of a space regarded as being filled with matter ‖ (esp. of a legislative body) a full assembly

ple·o·nasm (plí:ənæzəm) *n.* the using of more words than necessary in expressing an idea, with redundancy ‖ an instance of this or a redundant word or expression, e.g. 'falsely fraudulent' **ple·o·nás·tic** *adj.* **ple·o·nás·ti·cal·ly** *adv.*

pleth·o·ra (pléθərə) *n.* a great quantity, esp. more than desirable ‖ an unhealthy physical condition caused by an excess of blood and characterized by a highly flushed complexion **pleth·or·ic** (pleθɔ́rik, pleθɔ́rik) *adj.* (esp. of speech, writing etc.) pretentious ‖ having an excess of blood

pleu·ra (plúərə) *pl.* **pleu·rae** (plúəri:), **pleu·ras** *n.* a thin serous membrane lining the chest cavity and surrounding each lung in most air-breathing mammals

pleu·ri·sy (plúərisi:) *n.* inflammation of the pleura, resulting in fever and sharp pain in the chest or side

plex·us (pléksəs) *n.* (*anat.*) a network of intertwining nerves or blood vessels ‖ an exceedingly complex organization or network

pli·a·ble (pláiəb'l) *adj.* readily bent, pliant ‖ readily influenced **plái·a·bly** *adv.*

pli·ant (pláiənt) *adj.* (of materials) pliable ‖ (of people) readily yielding to influence

pli·ers (pláiərz) *pl. n.* small pincers with long jaws, used for handling small objects, for bending or cutting wire etc.

plight (plait) *n.* a state of distress, predicament

plod (plɒd) **1.** *v.i. pres. part.* **plod·ding** *past* and *past part.* **plod·ded** to walk heavily and slowly ‖ to make slow, laborious progress when working **2.** *n.* a laborious tread or the sound of this **plód·der** *n.* someone who works diligently and learns by hard work rather than by natural aptitude

plop (plɒp) **1.** *n.* the sound made when an object or body drops into a liquid **2.** *v.i. pres. part.* **plop·ping** *past* and *past part.* **plopped** to make this sound ‖ to fall with a plop ‖ to let one's body fall wearily, *to plop into a chair*

plot (plɒt) **1.** *n.* a small piece of ground, esp. one used or to be used for a particular purpose ‖ a ground plan ‖ a secret, usually evil, plan or conspiracy ‖ the plan of events in a novel, play etc. **2.** *v. pres. part.* **plot·ting** *past* and *past part.* **plot·ted** *v.t.* to plan secretly (esp. something evil) ‖ to make a plan or map of ‖ to mark (a position, course etc.) on a chart ‖ to construct the plan of (events in a novel, play etc.) ‖ to determine and mark (a point) e.g. on a graph, by working from coordinates ‖ *v.i.* to conspire

plow (plau) **1.** *n.* an agricultural implement drawn by a tractor, oxen, horses etc., used for cutting through and turning over soil, esp. in a field to be planted ‖ any implement or device resembling this ‖ (*carpentry*) a plane for making a groove etc. **2.** *v.t.* to turn over, break up etc. (soil) with a plow ‖ to furrow as if with a plow ‖ (of ships) to cut through the surface of (water) ‖ (*carpentry*) to cut a groove etc. in with a plow ‖ *v.i.* to work with a plow ‖ (of a field etc.) to admit of plowing ‖ (with 'through', 'along' etc.) to cut a way as a plow does ‖ to proceed slowly and laboriously **to plow into** to begin (work) with vigor and enthusiasm

plow·share, esp. *Br.* **plough·share** (pláuʃɛr) *n.* the cutting and turning blade of a plow

ploy (plɔi) *n.* a cunning tactic or gambit, e.g. in a game

pluck (plʌk) **1.** *v.t.* to pull off or out with sudden sharp force ‖ to pull the feathers from ‖ to pull quickly at, *to pluck a harp string* ‖ to pick ‖ (*pop.*) to dwindle ‖ *v.i.* (with 'at') to give a quick little pull **to pluck up one's courage** to overcome nervousness or timidity **2.** *n.* an act of plucking ‖ courage **plúck·i·ly** *adv.* **plúck·y** *comp.* **pluck·i·er** *superl.* **pluck·i·est** *adj.* courageous

plug (plʌg) **1.** *n.* a piece of wood etc. used to fill a gap or hole ‖ smoking or chewing tobacco compressed into a solid cake ‖ a fireplug ‖ any electrical connection, esp. the male part ‖ a spark plug ‖ (*pop.*) the favorable mention of a product etc., esp. on a radio or television program ‖ (*pop.*) an old, worn-out horse ‖ (*angling*) a lure that darts and dives, usu. used for catching pike **2.** *v. pres. part.* **plug·ging** *past* and *past part.* **plugged** *v.t.* to insert a plug in ‖ (*pop.*) to publicize (something) frequently, esp. on a radio or television program ‖ *v.i.* (with 'up') to become obstructed ‖ (*pop.*, with 'away') to persevere laboriously **to plug in** to connect (an electrical device) to an outlet

plum (plʌm) *n.* a small tree widely cultivated in temperate regions ‖ the edible fleshy fruit of the tree, or of other trees of the same genus ‖ the bluish-red color of many varieties of this fruit ‖ (*pop.*) an opportunity, appointment etc. offering exceptional advantages

plum·age (plú:midʒ) *n.* the feathers of a bird

plumb (plʌm) **1.** *n.* a small, heavy piece of metal, usually lead, attached to a line and used to indicate the vertical ‖ a similar contrivance for ascertaining the depth of water in a well etc. **out of plumb** not vertical **2.** *adj.* vertical **3.** *adv.* vertically **4.** *v.t.* to ascertain the depth of (water etc.) by sounding ‖ to test for verticality, *to plumb a well* ‖ to do the work of a plumber on (something)

plumb·er (plʌ́mər) *n.* a skilled worker who fits, repairs and maintains pipes, bathroom fixtures, cisterns, drains etc.

plumb·ing (plʌ́miŋ) *n.* the craft of a plumber ‖ the entire water-supply and drainage system of a building ‖ the act of using a plumb

plume (plu:m) *n.* a feather, esp. a large feather ‖ a cluster or tuft of feathers worn as an ornament or as a symbol of office, rank etc. ‖ (*envir.*) visible emission from a chimney flue or volcano ‖ anything having the lightness and form of a feather

plum·met (plʌ́mit) **1.** *n.* the weight attached to a plumb line, a sounding line or a fishing line ‖ the line and bob together ‖ a clock weight **2.** *v.i.* to drop vertically downwards

plump (plʌmp) **1.** *v.i.* to fall heavily ‖ (with 'for') to decide on (one of several courses of action, choices etc.) ‖ to come or go suddenly with determination or in a huff ‖ *v.t.* to drop, place, put down etc. heavily or with abrupt unconcern **2.** *adv.* suddenly and heavily downwards **3.** *n.* the act of falling heavily or the sound of this

plump 1. *adj.* (of people) pleasantly rounded, without

---

being fat ‖ (of animals) fleshy **2.** *v.t.* (with 'up') to knead (a pillow, cushion etc.) so as to shake up the feathers etc. in it ‖ *v.i.* (with 'out', e.g. of sails) to become rounded or distended

plun·der (plʌ́ndər) **1.** *v.t.* to strip (a person or place) of goods by force, esp. in wartime ‖ *v.i.* to commit robbery **2.** *n.* the act of plundering ‖ the goods obtained by plundering

plunge (plʌndʒ) **1.** *v. pres. part.* **plung·ing** *past* and *past part.* **plunged** *v.t.* to thrust (something) forcefully into something else, *to plunge a knife into someone's heart* ‖ to force (something or someone) into a new set of circumstances ‖ *v.i.* to throw oneself into water, esp. headfirst ‖ to go headlong, make one's way swiftly and resolutely ‖ (esp. of a ship) to pitch **2.** *n.* the act of plunging ‖ a leap into or as if into water **to take the plunge** to decide to take a risk despite the possible consequences **plúng·er** *n.* *(mech.)* a moving machine part serving as a ram in a hydraulic press, a piston in a force pump etc. ‖ a pistonlike part in a tire valve unit ‖ a rubber suction cup attached to the end of a wooden rod and used to clear a blockage in a water pipe, drain etc.

plunk (plʌŋk) **1.** *n.* the dull, short sound made by the forceful impact of inelastic bodies ‖ a twang ‖ *(pop.)* a forceful blow **2.** *v.t.* to put (something) down suddenly and heavily ‖ to pluck the strings of (e.g. a banjo) ‖ *v.i.* to make a twanging sound ‖ to fall or sink heavily **3.** *adv.* with the sound of a plunk

plu·ral (plúərəl) **1.** *adj.* of or including more than one ‖ *(gram.)* of or designating more than one of the things referred to **2.** *n.* *(gram.)* the plural number ‖ the plural form of a word ‖ a word in the plural form

plu·ral·i·ty (plurǽliti:) *pl.* **plu·ral·i·ties** *n.* the state of being plural ‖ a great number ‖ the holding of more than one office by one person ‖ *(eccles.)* the holding of two or more benefices by one person ‖ (in a political election involving three or more candidates) a number of votes obtained by one candidate exceeding that of any other candidate but not constituting an absolute majority

plus (plʌs) **1.** *prep.* added to, *4 plus 2 is 6* ‖ *(pop.)* in addition to **2.** *adj.* indicating addition, *the plus sign* ‖ positive ‖ (used postpositively) somewhat more than ‖ *(pop.,* used predicately) having as an addition, *he was plus $10 on the sale* ‖ *(bookkeeping)* credit ‖ *(elec.)* positive **3.** *pl.* **plus·es, plus·ses** *n.* a plus sign ‖ a plus quantity ‖ an additional quantity

plush (plʌʃ) **1.** *n.* a fabric resembling velvet, but having a longer, softer pile **2.** *adj.* luxurious and expensive

plu·toc·ra·cy (plu:tɔ́krəsi:) *pl.* **plu·toc·ra·cies** *n.* rule by the rich ‖ a ruling class of rich people **plu·to·crat** (plú:tɔkræt) *n.* a member of a plutocracy **plu·to·crát·ic** *adj.*

plu·to·ni·um (plu:tóuni:əm) *n.* an artificial metallic element

ply (plai) *pres. part.* **ply·ing** *past* and *past part.* **plied** *v.t.* to use with vigor and diligence ‖ to work busily at, *to ply a trade* ‖ to supply (someone) persistently ‖ to keep at (someone) constantly, *to ply someone with questions* ‖ (of boats) to sail or row across (a river etc.) and back more or less regularly ‖ *v.i.* to sail or go, usually regularly, between two places ‖ (e.g. of a taxi driver) to have a regular stand where one waits for customers ‖ *(naut.)* to make progress to windward by tacking

ply *pl.* **plies** *n.* one of the lengths of spun fiber which are twisted together to make rope, cord etc. ‖ one of the thin wooden layers in plywood ‖ one of several layers of fabric sewn or stuck together

ply·wood (pláiwud) *n.* a material used in light construction composed of thin layers of wood glued or cemented together, usually having the grain of one layer at right angles to that of the next

pneu·mat·ic (numǽtik, njumǽtik) *adj.* of, pertaining to, or using air, wind or gas ‖ operated by pressure of air ‖ filled with air ‖ *(zool.,* of bones) characterized

by air-filled cavities ‖ *(zool.)* of the duct between the swim bladder and the alimentary tract in some fish **pneu·mát·i·cal·ly** *adv.* **pneu·mát·ics** *n.* the branch of physics dealing with the mechanical properties of gases, esp. air, and certain elastic fluids

pneu·mo·nia (numóunjə, njumóunjə, nju·móuni:ə, njumóuni:ə) *n.* any of several diseases of the respiratory tract characterized by inflammation of the lungs and caused by bacteria, viruses or chemical irritants **pneu·mon·ic** (numɔ́nik, njumɔ́nik) *adj.*

poach (poutʃ) *v.t.* to cook (fish, chicken etc.) in a liquid that is never allowed to boil ‖ to drop (an egg removed from its shell) into simmering water and let it cook until the white coagulates, or steam it in a special pan

poach *v.t.* to take (game or fish) illegally from another person's property ‖ to soften or make holes in (ground) by trampling ‖ *v.i.* (with 'on') to trespass (on another person's property) ‖ to take game or fish illegally from another person's property ‖ *(racket games)* to play a ball that should be played by one's partner ‖ (of ground) to become soggy or full of holes when trampled **póach·er** *n.* someone who trespasses in order to steal or kill game ‖ someone who takes or kills game illegally

pock·et (pɔ́kit) **1.** *n.* a small, baglike receptacle of fabric, leather etc., having the top or side open, inserted in or served on a garment, for carrying a handkerchief, small change etc. ‖ a hollow place in which something has collected or could collect ‖ a deposit of material (e.g. gold, oil) found on or in the earth ‖ an air pocket ‖ any of the pouches, usually of netting, at the sides or corners of a billiard table ‖ the external pouch of some animals **in one's pocket** under one's influence ‖ virtually secured **2.** *v.t.* to put into a pocket ‖ to take (money etc.) dishonestly ‖ *(billiards)* to drive (a ball) into a pocket ‖ to suppress (pride, anger, scruples etc.) ‖ to accept submissively **3.** *adj.* suitable for or adapted for carrying in a pocket ‖ small

pock·et·book (pɔ́kitbʊk) *n.* a wallet for carrying paper money, papers etc. ‖ a woman's purse or handbag

pock·et·knife (pɔ́kitnaif) *pl.* **pock·et·knives** (pɔ́kitnaivz) *n.* a small knife having a blade or blades folding into the handle

pock·mark (pɔ́kmɑrk) *n.* the pitlike scar left in the skin by the pustule of esp. smallpox **póck·marked** *adj.* having or as if having pockmarks

pod (pɔd) **1.** *n.* a dry dehiscent fruit that is either monocarpellary, e.g. legume, or consists of two or more carpels, e.g. the poppy ‖ a protective envelope, e.g. a cocoon **2.** *v.t.* to split and empty the pods of (peas etc.)

po·di·a·trist (poudáiətrist) *n.* a chiropodist

po·di·a·try (poudáiətri:) *n.* chiropody

po·di·um (póudi:əm) *pl.* **po·di·a** (póudi:ə), **po·di·ums** *n.* *(archit.)* a low wall supporting a row of columns or serving as a foundation for the wall of a building ‖ a dais, e.g. for an orchestra conductor ‖ *(zool.)* the foot of an echinoderm

po·em (póuəm) *n.* a piece of poetry

po·et (póuit) *n.* a person who writes poetry

po·et·ic (pouétik) *adj.* of, pertaining to or characteristic of poets or poetry ‖ of the language or meaning of a poem or of poetry ‖ composed in verse ‖ having qualities associated with poetry

po·et·i·cal (pouétik'l) *adj.* poetic

po·et·ry (póuitri:) *n.* a type of discourse which achieves its effects by rhythm, sound patterns and imagery ‖ poems ‖ the quality of a poem

po·grom (pəgrɔ́m, pəgróm, póugrəm) *n.* an organized massacre, esp. of Jews in Russia (1881, 1903, 1905)

poign·an·cy (pɔ́injənsi:) *n.* the quality or state of being poignant

poign·ant (pɔ́injənt) *adj.* causing or marked by feelings of sadness ‖ (of grief) deeply felt ‖ stimulating, *of poignant interest*

point (pɔint) *n.* a specific place having a definite position in space but no definite size or shape ‖ a measurable position in a scale, *boiling point* ‖ a definite, often decisive, moment in time ‖ (of something spoken or written) the most prominent or important idea, *the point of a story* ‖ the climax of a joke ‖ a particular item in a speech, argument, exposition etc. ‖ a distinguishing characteristic, *generosity is not one of her strong points* ‖ purpose, *is there any point in going on?* ‖ the sharp end of something ‖ something having such a sharp end ‖ a particular place, e.g. on a route ‖ a period (punctuation mark) ‖ a decimal point ‖ *(games)* a unit of counting in scoring ‖ a unit of academic credit ‖ *(printing)* a unit for measuring size of type (1/72 in.) ‖ a unit for assessing performance in boxing etc. ‖ *(fencing)* a lunge ‖ *(boxing)* the tip of the chin ‖ *(ballet)* the tip of the toe ‖ any of a number of types of lace worked with a needle, esp. needlepoint lace ‖ (of certain gundogs) the act of pointing ‖ a tine of an antler ‖ a physical feature of an animal used esp. as a standard in judging its quality ‖ *(naut.)* any of the 32 marks around the circumference of a compass ‖ *(elec.)* either of the two contacts serving to make or break the circuit in a distributor ‖ a useful suggestion **at all points** in every respect **beside the point** not relevant **in point of fact** in reality **to carry one's point** to establish an argument, proposition etc. by persuasion **to come to the point** to discard irrelevancies and get to the heart of the matter **to make a point of** (with pres. infin.) to do with marked deliberateness **on the point of** just about to **to stretch a point** to be indulgent in interpreting or applying a rule **to the point** relevant **to win on points** *(boxing)* to win by performance over the rounds fought, not by knockout

point *v.t.* to give a point to ‖ (often with 'up') to give force or emphasis to ‖ to cause (something) to be turned towards a particular person or object, or in a particular direction ‖ *v.i.* (with 'at', 'to', 'towards' etc.) to indicate position or direction with or as if with a finger ‖ to be turned in a particular direction ‖ to explain, *he pointed out that it was not his fault* **to point to** (or **towards**) to be an indication of a specified probability, *everything points to his guilt*

point-blank (pɔintblǽŋk) **1.** *adv.* with level aim ‖ directly **2.** *adj.* (of a shot) fired at a very close target ‖ (of a shooting range) so close that one takes level aim ‖ direct

point·ed (pɔintid) *adj.* having, or being given, a sharp point ‖ (of a remark) sharply, though obliquely, critical ‖ made deliberately obvious ‖ lively, piquant, *pointed wit*

point·er (pɔintər) *n.* a person or thing that points ‖ a rod used for pointing, e.g. by a lecturer ‖ a gundog of a breed having a smooth, usually white coat with brown or black spots, used for pointing game ‖ a useful indication or suggestion

poise (pɔiz) *n.* balance ‖ carriage, bearing ‖ emotional stability, self-possession

poise *pres. part.* **pois·ing** *past* and *past part.* **poised** *v.t.* to balance ‖ to hold suspended for a moment ‖ to hold (the head) in a particular way ‖ to put (esp. oneself) in a state of readiness ‖ *v.i.* to be balanced ‖ to hang suspended or as if suspended

poi·son (pɔiz'n) **1.** *n.* a substance which, by its direct action on tissues, a mucous membrane etc., or after absorption into the circulatory system, can seriously injure an organism or destroy life completely ‖ anything having a pernicious effect on the mind or character of an individual or individuals **2.** *adj.* poisonous

poison *v.t.* to injure or destroy by using a poison ‖ to

make poisonous ‖ to exert a pernicious influence on (the mind or character of an individual or individuals)

poi·son·ing (pɔiz'niŋ) *n.* the condition produced by the application or absorption of a poison

poi·son·ous (pɔiz'nəs) *adj.* having the properties or effects of a poison ‖ impregnated with, or containing poison ‖ as pernicious or deadly as a poison ‖ *(pop.)* hateful, *a poisonous fellow*

poke (pouk) **1.** *v. pres. part.* **pok·ing** *past* and *past part.* **poked** *v.t.* to thrust quickly the tip of some object, e.g. a finger, into (someone or something) ‖ to thrust (something) forward, or into or through an aperture ‖ to stir up (a fire in a grate etc.) with a poker ‖ *(pop.)* to hit with a short, jabbing blow of the fist ‖ *v.i.* to make little digs or thrusts with a stick, finger etc. ‖ to be thrust forward through an aperture ‖ to go slowly, dawdle **to poke around** to examine things in a nosy or desultory way ‖ to busy oneself without any apparent purpose **to poke fun at** to make the object of ridicule **2.** *n.* the act of poking ‖ *(pop.)* a short, jabbing blow with the fist ‖ a slow-moving person, slow coach

po·ker (póukər) *n.* a gambling game played with 52 cards (each player being dealt 5 or 7 cards), and based on the relative value of certain combinations of cards

poker *n.* a heavy, usually iron, rod used to poke a fire

po·lar (póulər) **1.** *adj.* of or pertaining to the regions of the earth, or of the celestial sphere, located near the poles ‖ of or pertaining to the pole of a magnet ‖ of or pertaining to positive and negative electric charges ‖ *(chem.)* electrovalent ‖ *(chem., phys.)* having a dipole ‖ *(math.)* of a relationship to a fixed point (pole) ‖ opposite in nature, character etc., *polar views* **2.** *n.* *(math.)* a polar curve ‖ *(math.)* a line joining the intersections of tangents drawn from a pole to a conic section

po·lar·i·ty (poulǽriti:) *n.* the quality of having poles ‖ the state of having one or other of two opposite polar conditions ‖ the tendency of bodies having magnetic poles to align them with the earth's poles

po·lar·i·za·tion (poulərizéiʃən) *n.* the act of polarizing ‖ the state of being polarized, used esp. of light and other transverse wave radiation to signify a special relation between the direction of propagation and the plane of vibration of the waves

po·lar·ize (póuləraiz) *pres. part.* **po·lar·iz·ing** *past* and *past part.* **po·lar·ized** *v.t.* to produce polarization in or give polarity to ‖ to determine the relative importance of, or to fix the relative direction of ‖ *v.i.* to become concentrated around two opposites or extremes ‖ to serve as a point around which concentration takes place

pole (poul) *n.* *(biol.)* either of two differentiated areas that lie at opposite ends of an axis ‖ either of the terminals of a battery, cell or dynamo etc. between which a current will flow when connected by an external conductor (i.e. between which a potential difference exists) ‖ one of the two or more points in a magnet where most of the magnetic flux is concentrated ‖ one of two extremes ‖ a point of attraction **Pole** either end of the axis of a sphere, e.g. the North Pole or South Pole of the earth or the celestial sphere

pole 1. *n.* a long, usually rounded piece of wood or other material, *tent pole, telegraph pole* ‖ the wooden shaft of a wagon or carriage attached to the front axle and extending between the wheelhorses ‖ a unit of length, esp. one measuring 16½ ft ‖ a unit of area measuring 30¼ square yards ‖ *(naut.)* a mast, esp. the upper end **2.** *v.t. pres. part.* **pol·ing** *past* and *past part.* **poled** to propel (a punt etc.) by using a pole

po·lem·ic (pəlémik, poulémik) **1.** *adj.* of or pertaining

---

to controversy **2.** *n.* a disputation ‖ a person who takes part in a controversy, esp. a theological controversy **po·lém·i·cal** *adj.* **po·lém·i·cist** *n.* a person who engages in polemics **po·lém·ics** *n.* (construed as *sing.* or *pl.*) the art or practice of theological disputation

po·lice (pəlí:s) *pl.* **po·lice** *n.* a department of government responsible for the preservation of public order, detection of crime and enforcement of civil law ‖ the police force ‖ *(pl.)* members of the police force ‖ any body of people whose job is to keep order and enforce regulations ‖ *(mil.)* the act or process of putting and keeping in order (e.g. the grounds of an army camp) ‖ *(mil.)* enlisted men assigned to perform a specific function

police *pres. part.* **po·lic·ing** *past* and *past part.* **po·liced** *v.t.* to control, or maintain law and order in, by means of police ‖ to provide with police ‖ to exercise police control over (an area etc.) ‖ to control, regulate etc. as if by means of police ‖ *(mil., esp. with 'up')* to clean and put in order (a camp, garrison etc.)

pol·i·cy (pólisi) *pl.* **pol·i·cies** *n.* a selected, planned line of conduct in the light of which individual decisions are made and coordination achieved ‖ shrewdness in support of an aim, *would it be good policy to accept the invitation?*

policy *pl.* **policies** *n.* a document containing the contract made between an individual and an insurance company

po·li·o·my·e·li·tis (póuli:oumaiəláitis) *n.* *(pop., abbr.* polio) a serious infectious virus disease, esp. of children, caused by inflammation of the gray matter of the spinal cord, and characterized by fever, motor paralysis and muscular atrophy, often resulting in permanent deformity

pol·ish (póliʃ) **1.** *v.t.* to make smooth and lustrous by rubbing, esp. by exerting a back-and-forth pressure on the waxed surface of ‖ to cause (a person, his speech, behavior etc.) to become more refined or cultivated ‖ to bring (a style, sentence etc.) nearer perfection ‖ *v.i.* to take a polish **to polish off** to consume quickly ‖ to dispose of completely **to polish up** to make brighter by rubbing ‖ to revise and improve **2.** *n.* a polishing or being polished ‖ the lustrous surface of something polished ‖ a preparation used in polishing ‖ personal refinement or cultivation

po·lite (pəláit, pouláit) *adj.* having good social manners ‖ characterized by refinement

pol·i·tic (pólitik) *adj.* shrewdly judicious in support of an aim

po·lit·i·cal (pəlítik'l) *adj.* of or pertaining to politics ‖ engaged in politics, *a political figure*

pol·i·ti·cian (pplitíʃən) *n.* a person engaged in politics and in the techniques of civil government ‖ (in a derogatory sense) a person engaged in politics merely for personal gain

pol·i·tics (pólitiks) *n.* the art and science of the government of a state ‖ public affairs or public life as they relate to this ‖ the opinions, principles or policies by which a person orders his participation in such affairs ‖ scheming and maneuvering within a group, *college politics*

pol·ka (póulkə, póukə) **1.** *n.* a lively dance in duple time for couples, originating in Bohemia ‖ the music for this type of dance **2.** *v.i.* to dance the polka

poll (poul) **1.** *n.* the number of votes cast in an election ‖ the casting of votes ‖ (esp. *pl.*) the place where votes are cast and recorded ‖ the period of time during which votes may be cast ‖ a poll tax ‖ a canvassing of persons chosen at random or from a sample group in order to discover trends of public opinion ‖ the blunt end of a hammer, miner's pick etc. **2.** *v.t.* to receive (a number of votes) ‖ to record the votes of ‖ to canvass (people) in order to discover their opinions ‖ to cut off the horns of (cattle etc.) ‖ to pollard (a tree) ‖ *v.i.* to cast a vote

pol·len (pólən) *n.* the male reproductive cells or microspores produced by and discharged from the anther of a seed plant

pol·lute (pəlú:t) *pres. part.* **pol·lut·ing** *past* and *past part.* **pol·lut·ed** *v.t.* to make unhealthily impure ‖ to corrupt ‖ to make ritually unclean

pol·lu·tion (pəlú:ʃən) *n.* a polluting or being polluted

po·lo (póulou) *n.* a game played on horseback by two teams of three or four players on a ground 300 yds by 160 or 200 yds

po·lo·ni·um (pəlóuni:əm) *n.* a radioactive element appearing during the disintegration of radium

pol·y·chrome (póli:kroum) *adj.* painted or printed in many colors

po·lyg·a·mist (pəlígəmist) *n.* a person who practices polygamy

po·lyg·a·mous (pəlígəməs) *adj.* having more than one wife or husband ‖ *(zool.)* having more than one mate at the same time ‖ *(bot.)* bearing male, female or hermaphrodite flowers on the same plant

po·lyg·a·my (pəlígəmi:) *n.* the state or practice of being polygamous

pol·y·gon (póli:gɒn) *n.* a plane figure enclosed by five or more straight lines **po·lyg·o·nal** (pəlígən'l) *adj.*

polygraph *LIE DETECTOR

pol·y·he·dron (pɒli:hí:drən) *pl.* **pol·y·he·dra** (pɒli:hí:drə), **pol·y·he·drons** *n.* (geom.) a figure or solid formed usually by seven or more plane faces

pol·y·no·mi·al (pɒlinóumi:əl) **1.** *adj.* (math., of an algebraic expression) having two or more terms **2.** *n.* an expression of this kind

pol·yp (pólip) *n.* any of various coelenterates, such as those building coral reefs, having tubular, hollow bodies and an anterior mouth surrounded by tentacles ‖ a projecting growth of hypertrophied mucous membrane, e.g. in the nasal passages

pol·y·syl·lab·ic (pɒli:siláebik) *adj.* having more than three syllables **pol·y·syl·láb·i·cal** *adj.*

pol·y·tech·nic (pɒli:téknik) **1.** *adj.* of or pertaining to instruction in a number of technical subjects **2.** *n.* a school giving instruction of this kind **pol·y·téch·ni·cal** *adj.* **pol·y·tech·ní·cian** *n.*

pol·y·the·ism (póliθi:izəm, pɒliθí:izəm) *n.* belief in or worship of more than one god **pól·y·the·ist** *n.* **pol·y·the·ís·tic** *adj.*

pom·ace (pámis) *n.* a mass of apple pulp crushed for cider-making ‖ some other crushed or pulpy substance, e.g. seeds for oil

pome·gran·ate (pómgrænit, pómigrænit) *n.* a small shrubby tree, native to Asia and Africa ‖ its edible, orange-sized fruit, consisting of a succulent crimson pulp containing many seeds and enclosed in a tough golden red rind

pom·mel (páməl) **1.** *n.* a knob on a sword hilt ‖ a knoblike projection on the front of a saddle **2.** *v.t.* *pres. part.* **pom·mel·ing** *past* and *past part.* **pom·meled** to pummel

pomp (pɒmp) *n.* splendor in display, esp. ceremonial magnificence

pom·pa·dour (pómpədr, pómpədour, pómpəduər) *n.* a woman's hairstyle in which the hair is drawn in a high roll up over the forehead ‖ a man's hairstyle in which the hair is brushed straight up and back from the forehead

pom·pon (pómpɒn, pɔ̃pɔ̃) *n.* a small, brightly colored ball usually of yarn used for ornamenting women's and children's hats, sailors' caps etc. ‖ a dwarf cabbage rose ‖ any of several varieties of chrysanthemum or dahlia bearing small round flowers

pom·pos·i·ty (pɒmpósiti:) *pl.* **pom·pos·i·ties** *n.* the quality of being full of self-importance ‖ an instance of behavior revealing this

pom·pous (pómpəs) *adj.* (of people) full of ridiculous self-importance ‖ (of language) inflated, pretentious

pon·cho (póntʃou) *pl.* **pon·chos** *n.* a Spanish-American cloak like a blanket with a central slit for the head ‖ a waterproof garment made like this

pond (pɒnd) *n.* a small area of still water, in a natural or contrived hollow ‖ an area of water smaller than a lake

pon·der (póndər) *v.i.* (often with 'on' or 'over') to meditate, be absorbed in thought ‖ *v.t.* to consider carefully, *to ponder a problem*

pon·der·a·bil·i·ty (póndərəbíliti:) *n.* the state or quality of being ponderable

pon·der·a·ble (póndərəb'l) *adj.* able to be weighed ‖ able to be assessed

pon·der·ous (póndərəs) *adj.* (of style or manner) lacking ease and a light touch ‖ (of movement) slow, lumbering ‖ (*rhet.*, of weights) very heavy

pon·tiff (póntif) *n.* the pope ‖ a bishop

pon·tif·i·cal (pɒntífik'l) **1.** *adj.* of or relating to a pontiff ‖ celebrated by a bishop, *pontifical mass* ‖ absurdly dogmatic or pretentious **2.** *n.* a book setting out the forms for sacraments and rites performed by a bishop ‖ (*pl.*) vestments and insignia worn by a bishop when he celebrates a pontifical mass

pon·toon (pɒntú:n) *n.* a flat-bottomed boat or a metal cylinder used in quantity to support a temporary bridge ‖ in a low, flat boat carrying equipment for sinking shafts at sea, raising sunken ships etc. ‖ a float of an aircraft

po·ny (póuni:) *pl.* **po·nies** *n.* a small, sturdy horse of any of several breeds measuring up to 14 to $14^1/_2$ hands in height, in the case of polo ponies, 15 hands ‖ (*pop.*) a literal translation used by students, a crib ‖ (*pop.*) a small liqueur glass, or the amount it holds

pool (pu:l) *n.* a small body of fresh water ‖ a small body of standing water or other liquid ‖ a deep, cool, quiet spot in a stream or river ‖ a swimming pool

pool 1. *n.* (*gambling*) the total of sums staked and (sometimes) of fines paid in, all to be taken by the winner, or divided among several winners ‖ pocket billiards ‖ (*commerce*) a combination of resources for some common enterprise or for removing competition, manipulating prices etc. ‖ (*commerce*) a fund common to various undertakings on a basis of shared profits and liabilities ‖ a source of supply to which members of a group or organization have access **2.** *v.t.* to contribute (something) to a common fund

poop (pu:p) **1.** *n.* a raised, sometimes enclosed deck at the stern of a ship ‖ the stern of a ship **2.** *v.t.* (of a wave) to break over the stern of (a ship) ‖ to ship (a wave) over the stern

poor (puər) **1.** *adj.* having little money, few possessions and no luxuries ‖ of, relating to, or characterized by poverty ‖ meager ‖ showing small yield ‖ (of soil) unproductive ‖ inferior ‖ (of a person) failing to arouse respect ‖ in bad condition through underfeeding **2.** *n.* **the poor** poor people collectively

poor·ly (púərli:) **1.** *adv.* inadequately **to think poorly of** to have a low opinion of **2.** *adj.* not in good health but not seriously ill

pop (pɒp) **1.** *n.* a small, sharp, explosive sound ‖ an effervescent nonalcoholic drink **2.** *v. pres. part.* **pop·ping** *past* and *past part.* **popped** *v.t.* to cause to make a sharp explosive sound ‖ to cause to burst open with a sharp explosive sound ‖ to place quickly, *to pop a peanut into one's mouth* ‖ *v.i.* to move, come, enter etc., suddenly or unexpectedly or for a short time ‖ (of the eyes) to protrude, or seem to protrude, from the sockets ‖ to explode with a sharp sound **to pop the question** (*pop.*) to propose marriage **3.** *adv.* with a pop ‖ like a pop

pop·corn (pópkɔrn) *n.* a variety of corn, the kernels of which burst open with a pop when heated in butter or oil ‖ these popped kernels

pope (poup) *n.* the head of the Roman Catholic Church ‖ (*Orthodox Eastern Church*) a parish priest

pop·eyed (pópaid) *adj.* having protruding eyes

pop·lin (póplin) *n.* a tightly woven fabric, frequently of mercerized cotton, used for shirts, pajamas etc.

pop·o·ver (pópouvər) *n.* a puffy, light muffin having a hollow center caused by the intense heat of baking [it pops up from the rim of the baking tin]

pop·py (pópi:) *pl.* **pop·pies** *n.* a genus of annual, biennial and perennial plants usually containing white latex ‖ the flower of any of these plants ‖ an extract made from poppy juice, used in pharmacy ‖ the color of a red poppy

pop·py·cock (pópi:kɒk) *n.* (*pop.*) nonsense, foolish talk

pop·u·lace (pópjuləs) *n.* (*rhet.*) the common people, the masses

pop·u·lar (pópjulər) *adj.* liked or admired by people in general or by a particular group or section ‖ adapted to the tastes, understanding or needs of people in general, *popular science* ‖ (*commerce*) cheap, *popular prices* ‖ of, relating to or carried on by the people in general, *a popular election* ‖ commonly held, prevalent, *popular opinions*

pop·u·lar·i·ty (pɒpjulǽriti:) *n.* the state or quality of being popular

pop·u·lar·ize (pópjuləraiz) *pres. part.* **pop·u·lar·iz·ing** *past* and *past part.* **pop·u·lar·ized** *v.t.* to cause (a commercial product) to become widely known and adopted ‖ to cause (a resort etc.) to become popular ‖ to present (e.g. a technical subject) in a form easily understood by people in general

pop·u·late (pópjuleit) *pres. part.* **pop·u·lat·ing** *past* and *past part.* **pop·u·lat·ed** *v.t.* to provide with inhabitants

pop·u·la·tion (pɒpjuléiʃən) *n.* the inhabitants of a country, town etc. ‖ the total number of these ‖ a specified group of people of a country or area ‖ the act or process of supplying with inhabitants ‖ (*statistics*) a group of individuals or items ‖ (*biol.*) all the organisms living in a particular area

pop·u·lous (pópjuləs) *adj.* densely populated

por·ce·lain (pórslin, póurslin) **1.** *n.* fine, translucent nonporous ceramic ware made of quartz, feldspar and kaolin, and used esp. for tableware ‖ (*pl.*) articles made of this **2.** *adj.* made of porcelain

porch (pɔrtʃ) *n.* the covered entrance of a building jutting out from the main wall ‖ an open, roofed gallery extending along a side of a house, used for sitting out on, or giving access to rooms

por·cine (pórsain, pórsin) *adj.* of, relating to, or resembling a pig

por·cu·pine (pórkjupain) *n.* any of several vegetarian rodents constituting the Old World terrestrial fam. *Hystricidae* and the New World arboreal fam. *Erthizontidae*, measuring about 2 ft in length, and having the body covered with brown or black barbed spines intermixed with stiff hairs

pore (pɔr, pour) *pres. part.* **por·ing** *past* and *past part.* **pored** *v.i.* (only in **to pore over** to study intently ‖ to think deeply about, *to pore over a problem*

pore *n.* a minute opening or interstice, esp. in mammalian skin, through which fluids, e.g. sweat, pass ‖ a similar opening in plant tissue through which respiration etc. takes place

pork (pɔrk, pourk) *n.* hog's flesh (fresh or cured) as food

por·nog·ra·pher (pɔrnógrəfər) *n.* a person who writes etc. pornography

por·no·graph·ic (pɔrnəgrǽfik) *adj.* of, relating to, or characterized by pornography

por·nog·ra·phy (pɔrnógrəfi:) *n.* obscene literature, photographs, paintings etc., intended to cause sexual excitement ‖ the treating of obscene subjects in art, literature etc.

po·rous (pórəs, póurəs) *adj.* full of pores, permeable

por·poise (pórpəs) *n.* a genus of toothed whales, 5–8

---

ft in length, having a blunt snout. *P. phocaena,* inhabiting the N. Atlantic and Pacific, is the most commonly known

por·ridge (pɔ́ridʒ, pɒ́ridʒ) *n.* a soft food made by boiling oatmeal or other cereal substance in water or milk

port (pɔrt, pourt) *n.* a harbor ‖ a town or place with a harbor ‖ a port of entry

port 1. *n.* the side of a ship or aircraft that is on the left of someone aboard facing the bow **2.** *v.t.* to turn (the helm) to the left

port *n.* a fortified, sweet, rich red or white wine from Portugal ‖ an imitation of this

port·a·bil·i·ty (pɔrtəbíliti:, pourtəbíliti:) *n.* the condition or quality of being portable

port·a·ble (pɔ́rtəb'l, póurtəb'l) **1.** *adj.* easily carried or transported ‖ that can be carried or transported **2.** *n.* anything easily carried

por·tage (pɔ́rtidʒ, póurtidʒ) **1.** *n.* the carrying of boats or goods by land from one river etc. to another, around falls or rapids etc., or the place or route over which this is done **2.** *v.t. pres. part.* **por·tag·ing** *past* and *past part.* **por·taged** to carry (boats or goods)

por·tal (pɔ́rt'l, póurt'l) *n.* a door, gateway or other entrance, esp. when large and imposing ‖ a portal vein

por·tend (pɔrténd, pourténd) *v.t.* to give signs of (impending evil or catastrophe) ‖ to indicate broadly (some coming change)

por·tent (pɔ́rtent, póurtent) *n.* an inexplicable event taken as an omen, esp. as an evil omen ‖ a sign of some coming change for good or bad

por·ten·tous (pɔrténtəs, pourténtəs) *adj.* of the nature of a portent ‖ *(rhet.)* highly significant

por·ter (pɔ́rtər, póurtər) *n.* a person employed in railroad stations, hotels, markets etc. to carry baggage or other loads ‖ a man who cleans or does errands in a store etc. ‖ an attendant in a parlor car or sleeping car

port·fo·li·o (pɔrtfóuli:ou, pourtfóuli:ou) *pl.* **port·fo·li·os** *n.* a case for keeping loose papers, drawings, prints etc. ‖ such a case for carrying state documents ‖ the office and functions of a government minister ‖ the securities etc. held by a bank, investment trust etc.

port·hole (pɔ́rthoul, póurthoul) *n.* an opening in a ship's side to admit light and air ‖ an opening in a tank, fortification etc. to shoot through

por·ti·co (pɔ́rtikou, póurtikou) *pl.* **por·ti·coes, por·ti·cos** *n.* a colonnade or covered passageway in classical architecture

por·tion (pɔ́rʃən, póurʃən) **1.** *n.* a part of a whole ‖ a helping of food ‖ *(hist.)* a share of an estate received by inheritance or gift ‖ *(rhet.)* one's lot in life

portion *v.t.* to divide into portions ‖ (with 'out') to share

port·li·ness (pɔ́rtli:nis, póurtli:nis) *n.* the state or quality of being portly

port·ly (pɔ́rtli:, póurtli:) *comp.* **port·li·er** *superl.* **port·li·est** *adj.* (of adults) stout, corpulent

por·trait (pɔ́rtrit, póurtrit) *n.* a painting, photograph, drawing etc. of a person, esp. of his face, usually made from life ‖ a vivid verbal description of someone or something **pór·trait·ist** *n.* a person who makes portraits

por·tray (pɔrtréi, pourtréi) *v.t.* to paint etc. a portrait of ‖ to describe vividly in words, so as to bring out the character of ‖ to represent (a character) on the stage **por·tráy·al** *n.*

pose (pouz) *n.* a way of standing or sitting, esp. the position held by a model etc. in posing ‖ an attitude of mind, or manner of behavior assumed for its effect on others

pose *pres. part.* **pos·ing** *past* and *past part.* **posed** *v.t.* to place (an artist's model, a person being photographed etc.) in a certain position for artistic effect ‖ to state or present (a problem etc.) ‖ *v.i.* to assume a certain position, e.g. in having one's portrait made ‖ to represent oneself falsely

po·seur (pouzɔ́:r) *n.* a person who pretends to be what he is not, out of affectation, insincerity, guile or silliness

posh (pɒʃ) *adj. (pop.)* very smart ‖ *(pop.)* high-class

po·si·tion (pəzíʃən) **1.** *n.* the place occupied by a person or object in relation to another person or object ‖ *(mil., chess)* strategical advantage, *to maneuver for position* ‖ a way of looking at things, mental attitude ‖ a person's relative rank or standing in the social or business world ‖ exalted rank or standing, *a man of position* ‖ financial circumstances ‖ office or employment ‖ physical posture ‖ any of the formal postures of the feet and arms upon which all movements in ballet are based ‖ *(sports)* a place in a team or on the playing field **in a (in no) position to** (not) enabled by circumstances to **in position** normally placed **out of position** abnormally placed **2.** *v.t.* to place in position **po·si·tion·al** *adj.*

pos·i·tive (pɒ́zitiv) **1.** *adj.* leaving no doubt or question ‖ (of people) given to significant action ‖ (of people) apt to be dogmatic ‖ indicating affirmation ‖ *(philos.)* constructive as opposed to skeptical ‖ *(photog.)* of a photographic print or transparency in which the distribution of light and dark areas corresponds to that of the original optical image ‖ *(bacteriol.)* showing the presence of a specific condition, disease etc. ‖ downright, *he is a positive nuisance* ‖ *(gram.)* designating an adjective or adverb in its simple uncompared degree, e.g. 'good' in contrast to 'better' or 'best' ‖ of this degree ‖ *(math.,* symbol +) greater than zero ‖ *(elec.)* of an electrode (anode) of a cell or other electric device that is at the higher potential ‖ of a magnetic pole attracted towards the magnetic north ‖ of a counterclockwise movement or rotation ‖ acting or moving in a direction conventionally or arbitrarily taken as that of increase, progress or superiority **2.** *n.* that which is positive ‖ *(photog.)* a positive print or transparency ‖ *(gram.)* the positive degree ‖ *(elec.)* the plate of a cell at the higher potential (the anode)

pos·se (pɒ́si:) *n.* a force of men having legal authority, *a posse of police*

pos·sess (pəzés) *v.t.* to have as property, own ‖ to have as a faculty, quality etc. ‖ to get control over ‖ (of an evil spirit) to enter into in order to control ‖ to command (a language other than one's own) **pos·séssed** *adj.* crazy ‖ controlled by an evil spirit

pos·ses·sion (pəzéʃən) *n.* a possessing or being possessed ‖ that which is possessed ‖ *(pl.)* property ‖ a territory under the political and economic control of another country ‖ *(law)* actual enjoyment of property not founded on any title of ownership **to take possession of** to begin to occupy as owner ‖ to affect so as to dominate

pos·ses·sive (pəzésiv) **1.** *adj. (gram.,* of a case, form, or construction) expressing possession or a comparable relationship ‖ tending to want to concentrate all another's affections on oneself ‖ jealously assertive of one's rights over something **2.** *n. (gram.)* a possessive case or form

pos·ses·sor (pəzésər) *n.* a person who owns or controls ‖ a person who holds property without title of ownership

pos·si·bil·i·ty (pɒsəbíliti:) *pl.* **pos·si·bil·i·ties** *n.* the fact or state of being possible ‖ something that is possible

pos·si·ble (pɒ́səb'l) **1.** *adj.* that may exist, happen, be done etc. ‖ potential, *a possible enemy* ‖ reasonable, *the only possible explanation* **2.** *n.* the highest attainable score, esp. in target shooting ‖ a person whom it is reasonable to consider seriously for some position etc. **pós·si·bly** *adv.* by any possible means ‖ perhaps

post (poust) **1.** *n.* a strong, usually square or cylindrical piece of wood, metal etc., fixed or meant to be fixed in an upright position, and serving as a support ‖ something resembling this, e.g. one of the stakes in a fence ‖ *(horse racing)* a pole marking the starting point or finishing point **2.** *v.t.* to affix (a public notice, placard etc.) to a post, wall etc. ‖ to put (a list of names etc.) on a bulletin board etc. ‖ to warn trespassers to stay off (esp. private property) by placing notices around the boundaries ‖ to publish (a name) in a public notice, *posted missing* ‖ to advertise (a show, speaker etc.) by poster

post 1. *n.* the position a soldier occupies, or the area he patrols when he is on duty ‖ the place at which a soldier or body of troops is stationed ‖ the body of troops occupying this place ‖ a position being held by troops, *advance post*, or the troops themselves ‖ a position to which a person is assigned ‖ a position to which a person is appointed ‖ a trading post ‖ a local branch of an army veterans' organization 2. *v.t.* to station in a specific place ‖ *(mil.)* to assign (e.g. a sentry) to a specific station

post- *prefix* after ‖ behind

post·age (póustidʒ) *n.* the charge for conveying a letter or parcel by mail

post·date (poustdéit) *pres. part.* **post·dat·ing** *past* and *past part.* **post·dat·ed** *v.t.* to assign a later than actual date to (e.g. a check, event etc.) ‖ to be later in time than (a certain date, event etc.)

post·er (póustər) *n.* a placard displayed in public

pos·te·ri·or (postíəriːər) 1. *adj.* located behind ‖ *(anat.)* away from the head ‖ *(human anat.)* dorsal ‖ *(bot.)* facing or on the same side as the axis ‖ *(bot.)* on the side next to the main stem ‖ later in time 2. *n.* the buttocks

pos·te·ri·ty (postériti) *n.* the successive descendants of a person ‖ generations not yet born

pos·tern (póustərn) 1. *n.* (*hist.,* esp. of castles) a back or side door or gate ‖ (*hist., fortification*) an escape tunnel leading to the ditch and outworks 2. *adj.* (*hist.,* of a door or gate) at the back or side

post·grad·u·ate (poustgrædʒuːit) 1. *adj.* of or relating to studies that go beyond the first degree ‖ of or relating to a student engaged in such studies 2. *n.* a student who continues his studies beyond a first degree

post·haste (póusthéist) *adj.* with the greatest possible speed

post·hu·mous (póstʃuməs) *adj.* published after the death of the author ‖ (of a child) born after the death of the father ‖ occurring after death, *a posthumous award* **póst·hu·mous·ly** *adv.*

post·mark (póustmɑrk) 1. *n.* an official post-office mark stamped on a piece of mail, recording the date, place and usually time of mailing, and serving to cancel the stamp 2. *v.i.* to stamp with a postmark

post·me·rid·i·an (poustmərídiːən) *adj.* of or relating to the afternoon

post me·rid·i·em (poustmərídiːəm) *adv.* (*abbr.* p.m., P.M.) after noon and before midnight

post·mor·tem (poustmɔ́rtəm) 1. *adj.* of or relating to the period after death ‖ after an event, *a postmortem analysis of a campaign* 2. *n.* a postmortem examination

post·na·tal (poustnéit'l) *adj.* after birth

post·pone (poustpóun, pouspóun) *pres. part.* **post·pon·ing** *past* and *past part.* **post·poned** *v.t.* to put off, defer, *to postpone a holiday* **post·póne·ment** *n.*

post·script (póustskript) *n.* (*abbr.* P.S.) a brief afterthought, or series of these, added to a letter below the signature ‖ a short section at the end of a book, often a commentary on what has gone before

pos·tu·late (póstʃulit) *n.* an assumption ‖ a hypothesis ‖ an essential condition for something

pos·tu·late (póstʃuleit) *pres. part.* **pos·tu·lat·ing** *past* and *past part.* **pos·tu·lat·ed** *v.t.* to demand, to require as an essential condition ‖ to assume without need to prove ‖ (*eccles. law*) to elect or nominate (a person) subject to acceptance by an ecclesiastical superior

pos·tu·la·tion *n.* **pós·tu·la·tor** *n.*

pos·ture (póstʃər) 1. *n.* the way a person holds himself ‖ the position held by a model in posing 2. *v.i. pres. part.* **pos·tur·ing** *past* and *past part.* **pos·tured** to assume a physical posture, esp. for effect ‖ to pretend to be something one isn't

post·war (póustwɔr) *adj.* of or relating to the period after a war

po·sy (póuzi) *pl.* **po·sies** *n.* a flower

pot (pɒt) 1. *n.* a container of earthenware, glass, metal etc. used for holding liquids or solids, for cooking, boiling etc. ‖ such a container with its contents ‖ a lobster pot ‖ a chamber pot ‖ (*card games,* esp. poker) the total of bets ‖ a large prize or sum to be won, e.g. in a contest ‖ (*pl., pop.*) a lot of, *pots of money* ‖ (*pop.*) marijuana **to go to pot** to go to ruin 2. *v. pres. part.* **pot·ting** *past* and *past part.* **pot·ted** *v.t.* to set (e.g. a plant) in a flowerpot ‖ to preserve (meat, fish etc.) and pack it in pots ‖ to kill (an animal) by a potshot ‖ (of a potter) to make or shape (earthenware) ‖ *v.i.* to take potshots

po·ta·ble (póutəb'l) *adj.* suitable for drinking

po·tas·si·um (pətǽsiːəm) *n.* a silver-white univalent metallic element that oxidizes rapidly in the air

po·ta·to (pətéitou) *pl.* **po·ta·toes** *n.* a plant grown in most temperate regions for its edible tubers ‖ the starchy tuber eaten cooked as a vegetable, and used for stock feed and to produce alcohol

pot·bel·ly (pótbeli) *pl.* **pot·bel·lies** *n.* a protuberant belly ‖ a person having a protuberant belly ‖ a heating stove having a rounded body

po·ten·cy (póut'nsi) *pl.* **po·ten·cies** *n.* the state or quality of being potent ‖ degree of being potent ‖ capability

po·tent (póut'nt) *adj.* strong, powerful ‖ convincing ‖ (of a male) able to perform the act of sexual intercourse

po·ten·tate (póut'nteit) *n.* a powerful monarch, ruler

po·ten·tial (pəténʃəl) 1. *adj.* existing but not fully developed, exploited etc. ‖ having the capacity to be ‖ (*gram.*) expressing possibility 2. *n.* that which is potential ‖ potentiality ‖ (*gram.*) the mood of a verb which expresses possibility ‖ (*gram.*) a potential construction ‖ (*math.*) a potential function ‖ (*phys.*) electric potential **po·ten·tial·iz·ing** *pres. part.* **po·ten·tial·ized** *v.t.*

po·tion (póuʃən) *n.* a dose of medicine or poison or drug in liquid form

pot·luck (pótlʌk) *n.* what can be produced in the way of a meal for an unexpected guest or guests

pot·pour·ri (poupuríː) *n.* dried flower petals and flavoring herbs stored in jars or displayed in bowls to scent a room ‖ a musical medley ‖ a literary anthology

pot·tage (pótidʒ) *n.* a thick soup made from vegetables or vegetables and meat

pot·ter (pótər) *n.* a person who makes pottery

pot·ter·y (pótəri) *pl.* **pot·ter·ies** *n.* clay vessels, esp. earthenware ‖ the potter's craft ‖ the workshop of a potter

pouch (pautʃ) 1. *n.* a small bag, esp. for carrying tobacco or ammunition ‖ an abdominal receptacle for the young of a marsupial ‖ a baglike dilatation of the cheeks of some monkeys and rodents for storing food ‖ any baglike fold of skin, e.g. under the eyes ‖ a bag equipped with a lock for holding first-class mail or diplomatic papers ‖ a baglike plant part, e.g. the seed vessel of certain plants 2. *v.t.* to put into a pouch, esp. to put (first-class mail etc.) into a locked bag ‖ to store or carry in a cheek pouch ‖ to cause (skin) to form baglike folds, esp. under the eyes ‖ *v.i.* to form a pouch

poul·tice (póultis) 1. *n.* a warm, soft, moistened mass, e.g. of bread, bran, linseed etc., spread on cloth and applied to a sore or inflamed part of the body to draw pus, act as a counterirritant etc. **2.** *v.t. pres. part.* **poul·tic·ing** *past* and *past part.* **poul·ticed** to apply a poultice to

poul·try (póultri:) *n.* chickens, ducks, geese, turkeys and other domesticated birds raised for food

pounce (pauns) **1.** *n.* the act of pouncing ‖ the swooping, grabbing or springing motion made in pouncing **2.** *v.i. pres. part.* **pounc·ing** *past* and *past part.* **pounced** (with 'at', 'on' or 'upon') to make a sudden swoop, spring or grasp ‖ (with 'on' or 'upon') to seem to swoop, spring or grab

pound (paund) *n.* an enclosure where stray or unlicensed animals are kept until they are claimed or disposed of ‖ an enclosure for trapping animals ‖ an enclosure for fish, esp. the inner compartment of a pound net ‖ a pound net ‖ a place where personal property is held until redeemed by the owner, *a car pound*

pound 1. *v.t.* to thump with or as if with repeated blows ‖ to reduce to small particles by crushing, grinding etc. ‖ (with 'out') to produce with or as if with vigorous thumps ‖ *v.i.* to strike heavy, thumping blows ‖ to make a thumping noise ‖ (of a ship) to hit the water heavily and repeatedly ‖ (of the heart, an engine etc.) to throb violently ‖ to move quickly but heavily or with force or effort and a dull thudding sound **to pound away** to persevere in work calling for effort **2.** *n.* a pounding ‖ a thud or blow or the sound of a thud or blow

pound *pl.* **pounds, pound** *n.* *(abbr.* lb.*)* the unit of mass equal to 16 oz. avoirdupois or to 12 oz. troy ‖ (symbol £) the pound sterling, the British monetary unit equal to 100 pence ‖ the monetary unit of various countries, e.g. Egypt, Ireland, Syria, Turkey

pour (pɔr, pour) **1.** *v.t.* to send out in a stream ‖ to discharge profusely ‖ (esp. with 'out') to send forth (words, music etc.) as if in a stream ‖ *v.i.* to flow in copious streams ‖ to flow out as if in a stream, *the crowd poured out of the theater* ‖ to rain heavily ‖ to preside at a tea table **2.** *n.* the act of pouring ‖ a downpour ‖ *(founding)* a quantity of molten metal poured at one time

pout (paut) **1.** *v.i.* to express displeasure, resentment, bad humor etc. by thrusting out the lower lip and looking sulky ‖ to sulk ‖ *v.t.* to thrust out (the lips) ‖ to utter with a pout **2.** *n.* a sulky thrusting out of the lips ‖ *(pl.)* a fit of sulking

pov·er·ty (póvərti:) *n.* the condition or quality of being poor ‖ (of soil) unproductiveness ‖ deficiency in or inadequate supply of something, *poverty of ideas* ‖ monastic renunciation of the right to own, *a vow of poverty*

pow·der (páudər) **1.** *n.* a dry substance composed of fine particles ‖ a medicine in powdered form ‖ a scented cosmetic for the face or body ‖ gunpowder **2.** *v.t.* to cover, sprinkle or dust with or as if with powder ‖ to convert to powder ‖ to apply cosmetic powder to (the face etc.) ‖ to decorate (a surface) with dots, small figures etc. ‖ *v.i.* to use cosmetic powder ‖ to become powder

pow·der·y (páudəri:) *adj.* resembling powder ‖ covered with powder ‖ apt to become powder

pow·er (páuər) **1.** *n.* an ability or faculty ‖ physical strength ‖ military strength ‖ controlling influence ‖ authority, authorization, *the power to sign a document* ‖ a person of great influence or authority ‖ a country having international influence or authority ‖ mechanical or electrical energy ‖ *(phys.)* the rate at which work is done or energy transmitted ‖ *(math.)* the number of times a quantity is multiplied by itself, or the index denoting this, *10 to the power of 3 is 1,000* ‖ the magnifying capacity of a lens measured as the ratio between the dimensions of the image and the object ‖ the reciprocal of the focal length of a lens **in power** in authority or control **2.** *v.t.* to supply with a source of power

pow·er·ful (páuərfəl) *adj.* having great power ‖ physically strong ‖ (of drugs, medicine etc.) potent

pow·er·less (páuərlis) *adj.* without power ‖ (followed by an infinitive) unable

pox (pɒks) *n.* any of various specified diseases characterized by pustules, e.g. chicken pox

prac·ti·ca·bil·i·ty (præktikəbíliti:) *n.* the quality or condition of being practicable

prac·ti·ca·ble (præktikəb'l) *adj.* capable of being done, feasible ‖ capable of being used

prac·ti·cal (præktik'l) *adj.* of, relating to, or obtained through practice or action ‖ that can be put into practice ‖ able to apply theory, esp. in constructing, repairing etc., *a practical man* **prac·ti·cál·i·ty** *n.*

prac·ti·cal·ly (præktik'li:) *adv.* in a practical way ‖ virtually, *she is practically deaf now*

prac·tice (præktis) **1.** *v.* (also **practise**) *pres. part.* **prac·tic·ing** *past* and *past part.* **prac·ticed** *v.t.* to make a practice of ‖ to follow or work at as a profession, *to practice medicine* ‖ to study, exercise one's skill in regularly or frequently so as to win greater command ‖ to drill ‖ *v.i.* to perform an act or exercise a skill repeatedly in order to achieve greater command ‖ to be active in a profession, *does he still practice?* **2.** *n.* (also **practise**) a customary action or customary code of behavior ‖ a way of behavior, *evil practices* ‖ repeated performance or systematic exercise for the purpose of learning or acquiring proficiency ‖ the exercise of a profession, esp. law or medicine ‖ a professional business, *to sell one's practice* ‖ *(law)* the established method of conducting and carrying on suits and prosecutions **in practice** in a condition to be able to perform with skill as a result of exercise and repeated performance **out of practice** not in this condition **to put into practice** to apply (theory etc.) in action **prác·ticed, prác·tised** *adj.* expert through long experience

prac·ti·cian (præktíʃən) *n.* a person who practices a skill, art etc. ‖ a practitioner

prac·ti·tion·er (præktíʃənər) *n.* a person who practices a profession, esp. a doctor

prag·mat·ic (prægmátik) *adj.* of or relating to pragmatism ‖ dealing with events in the light of practical lessons or applications ‖ of or relating to state affairs **prag·mát·i·cal** *adj.*

prag·ma·tism (prǽgmətizəm) *n.* a doctrine which tests truth by its practical consequences. Truth is therefore held to be relative and not attainable by metaphysical speculation

prai·rie (prέəri:) *n.* a wide tract of treeless and gently undulating grassland in North America, esp. in the Mississippi valley

praise (preiz) **1.** *v.t. pres. part.* **prais·ing** *past* and *past part.* **praised** to speak of with approval or admiration ‖ to glorify (God or a deity) **2.** *n.* a praising or being praised ‖ the act of glorifying God or a deity

pra·line (práli:n, préili:n) *n.* a confection of almonds or other nuts browned in boiling sugar

prance (præns, prɑns) **1.** *v. pres. part.* **pranc·ing** *past* and *past part.* **pranced** *v.i.* (of a mettlesome horse) to leap up on the hind legs in a rearing motion, or to move forward by so doing ‖ to ride or drive a horse leaping in this way ‖ (of a person) to move in a gleeful or arrogant way ‖ *v.t.* to cause (a horse) to prance **2.** *n.* a prancing movement

prank (præŋk) *v.t.* *(rhet.)* to deck, adorn

prank *n.* a piece of mischief **pránk·ish** *adj.*

prate (preit) **1.** *v.i. pres. part.* **prat·ing** *past* and *past part.* **prat·ed** *(rhet.)* to babble or chatter idly or nonsensically ‖ *v.t.* *(rhet.)* to utter (nonsensical chatter) **2.** *n.* *(rhet.)* foolish talk

prat·tle (prǽt'l) **1.** *v. pres. part.* **prat·tling** *past* and *past part.* **prat·tled** *v.i.* to talk incessantly, esp. to gossip ‖ to chatter ‖ *v.t.* to babble (gossip, nonsense etc.) **2.** *n.* chatter, esp. childish chatter

prawn (prɔn) *n.* any of several decapod crustaceans related to the shrimp and the lobster, having thin legs and long antennae

pray (prei) *v.i.* to enter into spiritual communion with God or an object of worship ‖ to implore God or an object of worship ‖ *v.t.* (*archaic*) to implore (God or an object of worship) ‖ (*rhet.*, contr. of 'I pray you') you must tell me, *what, pray, is the meaning of this behavior?*

prayer (prɛər) *n.* a humble communication in thought or speech to God or to an object of worship expressing supplication, thanksgiving, praise, confession etc. ‖ that which is prayed for ‖ the liturgical formulation of a communication to God or to an object of worship, *the Lord's Prayer* ‖ (esp. *pl.*) a public or private religious service consisting mainly of such formulations ‖ the act or practice of praying ‖ (*rhet.*) an entreaty made to someone, *a prayer to the king for mercy*

pre- (pri:) *prefix* earlier than, preceding ‖ beforehand ‖ preparatory to ‖ before, in front of (in location, order of importance or degree etc.)

preach (pri:tʃ) *v.i.* to deliver a religious address publicly, esp. to expound the gospel ‖ to offer moral advice in a tiresome manner ‖ *v.t.* to deliver (a sermon) ‖ to expound (the gospel) ‖ to advocate (a course or principle) **preach·er** *n.* someone who preaches, esp. a minister

pre·am·ble (prí:æmb'l) *n.* an introductory part of a speech or piece of writing, esp. the introductory part of a statute, ordinance etc. stating the reasons and purpose of the text that follows

pre·car·i·ous (prikɛ́əri:əs) *adj.* uncertain ‖ dangerous ‖ not firmly founded

pre·cau·tion (prikɔ́ʃən) *n.* care with respect to the foreseeable future ‖ a measure taken against some possible future evil or calamity or undesirable happening, *fire precautions* **pre·cáu·tion·ar·y, pre·cáu·tious** *adjs*

pre·cede (prisí:d) *pres. part.* **pre·céd·ing** *past and past part.* **pre·céd·ed** *v.t.* to go before in rank, importance etc. ‖ to come before in time ‖ to go or come before or in front of ‖ (with 'by' or 'with') to preface ‖ *v.i.* to go or come before

prec·e·dence (présidəns, prisí:d'ns) *n.* the act, fact, right or privilege of preceding another or others, usually according to rank, esp. on ceremonial or highly formal social occasions

prec·e·dent 1. (présidənt) *n.* a previous instance or case that may serve to justify a subsequent act, procedure etc. of a similar kind ‖ (*law*) a previous judicial decision, proceeding etc., taken as a rule in dealing with subsequent similar cases **2.** (prisí:dənt) *adj.* (*rhet.*) coming before in order, time etc. **préc·e·dent·ed** *adj.* having an established precedent

pre·cept (prí:sept) *n.* a commandment or instruction intended as a rule of action or conduct ‖ a technical instruction

pre·cep·tor (priséptər) *n.* (*archaic*) a teacher

pre·cinct (pri:síŋkt) *n.* the space within the boundaries of a church, school or other building or place ‖ the boundary itself ‖ (*pl.*) the immediate surroundings of a place ‖ a subdivision of a county, city or city ward for police and election purposes

pre·ci·os·i·ty (preʃi:ɔ́siti:) *n.* excessive refinement

pre·cious (préʃəs) **1.** *adj.* of great material value ‖ of great nonmaterial value ‖ exhibiting preciosity ‖ (used as a term of endearment) beloved ‖ (*pop.*) complete **2.** *adv.* (*pop.*) extremely

prec·i·pice (présəpis) *n.* the very steep or overhanging part of the face of a cliff, side of a mountain etc.

pre·cip·i·tant (prisípitənt) **1.** *adj.* precipitate **2.** *n.* (*chem.*) that which causes precipitation to occur

pre·cip·i·tate 1. (prisípiteit) *v. pres. part.* **pre·cip·i·tat·ing**

past and past part. **pre·cip·i·tat·ed** *v.t.* (*rhet.*) to hurl downward, throw violently ‖ to hasten ‖ (*chem.*) to cause (a soluble substance) to become insoluble and separate from a solution ‖ (*meteorol.*) to cause (vapor) to condense and fall as rain, snow etc. ‖ *v.i.* (*chem.*) to separate from a solution ‖ (*meteorol.*) to condense from a vapor and fall as rain, snow etc. **2.** (prisípitit) *adj.* sudden, hasty ‖ rushing violently ‖ rash, headstrong **3.** (prisípitit) *n.* (*chem.*) a solid substance separated from a solution as the result of a chemical reaction, esp. a crystalline solid that can be separated from the solution by filtration

pre·cip·i·ta·tion (prisipitéiʃən) *n.* a precipitating or being precipitated ‖ excessive or reckless haste ‖ (*meteorol.*) a deposit of water in either liquid or solid form, e.g. rain, snow, which reaches the earth from the atmosphere ‖ (*meteorol.*) the quantity deposited ‖ (*chem.*) a precipitate

pre·cip·i·tous (prisípitəs) *adj.* resembling a precipice ‖ containing precipices ‖ hasty

pre·cise (prisáis) *adj.* accurate in every detail ‖ exact ‖ excessively attentive to detail, punctilious ‖ very, *at that precise moment he came in* **pre·císe·ly** *adv.*

pre·ci·sion (prisíʒən) *n.* the quality of being precise ‖ (*computer*) the exactness of a quantity, sometimes expressed in the number of significant digits in the solution

pre·clude (priklú:d) *pres. part.* **pre·clud·ing** *past and past part.* **pre·clud·ed** *v.t.* to prevent ‖ to make practically impossible, esp. by anticipatory action

pre·clu·sion (priklú:ʒən) *n.* a precluding or being precluded

pre·clu·sive (priklú:siv) *adj.* tending to preclude

pre·co·cious (prikóuʃəs) *adj.* displaying highly developed mental or physical characteristics at an early age ‖ done or made by someone having these characteristics, *a precocious work* ‖ (*bot.*) fruiting or flowering earlier than usual

pre·coc·i·ty (prikɔ́siti:) *n.* the condition or quality of being precocious

pre·con·ceive (pri̩kənsí:v) *pres. part.* **pre·con·ceiv·ing** *past and past part.* **pre·con·ceived** *v.t.* to form (an idea or opinion) beforehand

pre·cur·sor (prikə́:rsər) *n.* someone who prepares the way for another or who precedes him in office ‖ something which precedes something else

pre·da·cious, pre·da·ceous (pridéiʃəs) *adj.* preying upon other animals **pre·dac·i·ty** (pridǽsiti:) *n.* the quality or condition of being predacious

pred·a·tor (prédətər) *n.* a predatory animal

pred·a·to·ry (prédətɔri:, prédətouri:) *adj.* (of persons) given to preying upon others ‖ predacious

pre·de·cease (pri̩disí:s) *pres. part.* **pre·de·ceas·ing** *past and past part.* **pre·de·ceased** *v.t.* to die before (another person)

pred·e·ces·sor (prédisesər, predisésər) *n.* a person preceding another in an office, position etc. ‖ something which has been succeeded by something else

pre·des·ti·nate 1. (pri:déstineit) *v.t. pres. part.* **pre·des·ti·nat·ing** *past and past part.* **pre·des·ti·nat·ed** to predestine **2.** (pri:déstinit) *adj.* determined beforehand

pre·des·ti·na·tion (pri:destinéiʃən) *n.* the act of predestinating ‖ (*theol.*) the doctrine that everything was determined by God from the beginning, esp. with reference to the play of divine omnipotence and human free will in determining the fate of the soul

pre·de·ter·mi·na·tion (pri̩ditə:rminéiʃən) *n.* a predetermining or being predetermined

pre·de·ter·mine (pri̩ditə́:rmin) *pres. part.* **pre·de·ter·min·ing** *past and past part.*

---

pre·de·ter·mined *v.t.* to calculate or determine in advance ‖ to predestine ‖ to give a mental bias to

pre·dic·a·ment (pridíkəmənt) *n.* a situation involving a hard or unpleasant choice

pred·i·cate 1. (prédikeit) *v. pres. part.* **pred·i·cat·ing** *past* and *past part.* **pred·i·cat·ed** *v.t.* to state as an assumed attribute, quality or property ‖ to imply, connote ‖ *(logic)* to affirm or deny (something) about the subject of a proposition ‖ to base (a thesis, statement, attitude etc.) on ‖ *v.i.* to make a statement **2.** (prédikit) *n. (logic)* that which is affirmed or denied about the subject of a proposition ‖ *(gram.)* the words (verb with object or adverbial modifier, or copula with noun or adjective) which express what is stated of the subject of a clause or sentence

pred·i·ca·tion (prędikéiʃən) *n.* a predicating or being predicated

pre·dict (pridíkt) *v.t.* to make known beforehand, foretell ‖ *v.i.* to foretell the future **pre·díct·a·ble** *adj.*

pre·dic·tion (pridíkʃən) *n.* the action of predicting ‖ that which is predicted

pre·di·lec·tion (prį:d'lékʃən, pręd'lékʃən) *n.* a special taste or liking

pre·dis·pose (prį:dispóuz) *pres. part.* **pre·dis·pos·ing** *past* and *past part.* **pre·dis·posed** *v.i.* to make (someone) tend to act, feel, suffer etc. in a particular way or be prone

pre·dis·po·si·tion (prį:dispəzíʃən) *n.* the condition of being predisposed ‖ a tendency, susceptibility, *a predisposition to quarrelsomeness*

pre·dom·i·nance (pridómınəns) *n.* the quality or state of being predominant

pre·dom·i·nant (pridómınənt) *adj.* most frequent, prevailing

pre·dom·i·nate (pridómineit) *pres. part.* **pre·dom·i·nat·ing** *past* and *past part.* **pre·dom·i·nat·ed** *v.i.* to be most frequent, or lead in quality

pre·em·i·nence (pri:émınəns) *n.* the quality or state of being preeminent

pre·em·i·nent (pri:émınənt) *adj.* superior to others, esp. in some specified quality or sphere

pre·empt (pri:émpt) *v.t.* to purchase before others have the opportunity to purchase ‖ *(Am. hist.)* to settle on (public land) in order to establish the right of preemption ‖ to acquire beforehand ‖ *v.i. (bridge)* to make a preemptive bid

pre·emp·tion (pri:émpʃən) *n.* the act or right of purchasing before others have a chance to purchase ‖ *(Am. hist.)* the preempting of public land ‖ a taking possession before others **pre·emp·tive** (pri:émptiv) *adj. (bridge)* of, relating to, or constituting a bid that is higher than necessary, in order to discourage one's partner or opponents from bidding

pre·emp·tive *adj.* occurring before, and in anticipation of, a situation developing, e.g., preemptive attack, preemptive seizure

preen (pri:n) *v.t.* (of a bird) to trim (the feathers) with the beak ‖ (of a person) to make (oneself) trim in appearance ‖ to congratulate (oneself) mildly

pre·fab·ri·cate (pri:fǽbrikeit) *pres. part.* **pre·fab·ri·cat·ing** *past* and *past part.* **pre·fab·ri·cat·ed** *v.t.* to construct sections of (e.g. a house) in a factory for assembly on a site elsewhere **pre·fab·ri·cá·tion** *n.*

pref·ace (préfis) **1.** *n.* a written introduction to a book or the opening remarks of a speaker intended to elucidate the text or speech to follow ‖ a leading up to something ‖ *(eccles.)* the part of the Mass before the canon **2.** *v.t. pres. part.* **pref·ac·ing** *past* and *past part.* **pref·aced** to introduce by or furnish with a preface ‖ to lead up to

pre·fer (prifə́:r) *pres. part.* **pre·fer·ring** *past* and *past part.* **pre·ferred** *v.t.* to like better ‖ to choose rather ‖ *(law)* to place (a charge, complaint etc. against a person) before someone in authority ‖ *(law)* to give priority to (a creditor) **pref·er·a·ble** (préfərəb'l) *adj.* **préf·er·a·bly** *adv.*

pref·er·ence (préfərəns) *n.* a preferring or being preferred ‖ the person or thing preferred ‖ the right to choose ‖ a system whereby lower import duties are levied on goods from certain countries ‖ *(law)* priority in the right to demand payment of a debt

pref·er·en·tial (prefərénʃəl) *adj.* relating to, or constituting preference

pre·fix 1. (pri:fíks, prí:fiks) *v.t. (gram.)* to place or put (a syllable, group of syllables or word) in front of a word to modify its meaning or form a new word **2.** (prí:fiks) *n. (gram.)* that which is placed in front in this way, e.g. 'un' in 'unable'

preg·nan·cy (prégnənsi:) *pl.* **preg·nan·cies** *n.* the condition of being pregnant

preg·nant (prégnənt) *adj.* (of a female) carrying an unborn child or unborn young within the body ‖ deeply significant, *pregnant remarks*, or full of implication, *a pregnant silence* ‖ full of ideas, imaginative

pre·hen·sile (prihénsil, prihénsail) *adj. (zool.)* able to grasp and hold, *a prehensile tail* **pre·hen·sil·i·ty** (pri:hensíliti:) *n.*

pre·his·tor·ic (prį:histórik, prį:histórik) *adj.* of or relating to the period before recorded history ‖ existing during this period **pre·his·tór·i·cal·ly** *adv.*

pre·his·to·ry (prį:hístəri:) *n.* the study of the period of history before there were written records, esp. the study of prehistoric man ‖ the period of history before there were written records

prej·u·dice (prédʒudis) *pres. part.* **prej·u·dic·ing** *past* and *past part.* **prej·u·diced** *v.t.* to cause (someone) to have a prejudice ‖ to cause injury to ‖ *(law)* to impair the validity of (a right)

prejudice *n.* a preconceived opinion, usually unfavorable ‖ the holding of such an opinion ‖ an unjustified and unreasonable bias ‖ *(law)* injury due to some judgment or action of another, e.g. the disregard of a person's rights **without prejudice** *(law)* without detriment to a person's claims or rights

prej·u·di·cial (prędʒudíʃəl) *adj.* injuring, or likely to injure

prel·ate (prélit) *n. (eccles.)* a high-ranking Church dignitary, e.g. an archbishop, bishop pr patriarch **pre·lat·ic** (prilǽtik) *adj.*

pre·lim·i·nar·y (prilímineri:) **1.** *adj.* introductory or preparatory **2.** *pl.* **pre·lim·i·nar·ies** *n.* a preliminary step, procedure etc. ‖ a preliminary examination

prel·ude (prélju:d) **1.** *n.* something serving to introduce, or set the mood for, some event, performance, action etc. to follow ‖ a piece of music serving as an introduction to the theme of a fugue, an act of an opera etc. ‖ the title used by some composers for some self-contained pieces for piano and orchestra **2.** *v.t. pres. part.* **prel·ud·ing** *past* and *past part.* **prel·ud·ed** to serve as a prelude to

pre·ma·ture (prį:mətúər, prį:mətjúər, prį:mətʃúər) *adj.* occurring, done, existing etc. before the proper time ‖ (of an infant) born before the 37th week of pregnancy or weighing less than $5^{1}/_{2}$ lbs **pre·ma·túre·ly** *adv.*

pre·med·i·tate (priméditeit) *v.t. pres. part.* **pre·med·i·tat·ing** *past* and *past part.* **pre·med·i·tat·ed** to think about and plan beforehand

pre·mier (primíər, primjíər, prí:mjər) **1.** *adj.* first in position, importance etc. **2.** *n.* prime minister

pre·miere, pre·mière (primíər, primjíər, primjéər) *n.* the first public performance of a play or showing of a film ‖ the female star of a theatrical production

prem·ise, prem·iss 1. (prémis) *n.* a fact, statement or assumption on which an argument is based or from which conclusions are drawn ‖ (esp. **premiss,** *logic*) one of the two propositions (major and minor) of a syllogism from which the conclusion is drawn ‖ *(pl., law)* the section of a deed stating the names of the parties involved and giving an explanation of the transaction ‖ *(pl.)* a piece of land and the house and buildings on it **2. prem·ise** (primáiz) *v.t. pres. part.* **prem·is·ing** *past* and *past part.* **prem·ised** to state or assume as a premise

pre·mi·um (príːmiːəm) *n.* a prize or reward, esp. a sum paid in addition to wages or salary ‖ a sum paid, either all at once or periodically, for an insurance contract ‖ the rate above nominal value at which something sells ‖ a fee paid for instruction or training in a trade etc. ‖ a sum given for a loan in addition to interest at a premium worth more than the nominal value ‖ very hard to get and therefore valuable **to put a premium on** to stress the importance of, put a high value on, *to put a premium on honesty*

pre·mo·ni·tion (priːməníʃən, prɛməníʃən) *n.* a forewarning ‖ a presentiment

pre·na·tal (priːnéitˈl) *adj.* occurring or existing before birth

pre·oc·cu·pa·tion (priːɒkjupéiʃən) *n.* a preoccupying or being preoccupied

pre·oc·cu·pied (priːɔ́kjupaid) *adj.* completely engrossed, esp. in thought ‖ *(biol.,* of a generic or specific name) not available as a designation because already in use

pre·oc·cu·py (priːɔ́kjupai) *pres. part.* **pre·oc·cu·py·ing** *past* and *past part.* **pre·oc·cu·pied** *v.t.* to engage the attention or interest of (someone) almost completely

prep·a·ra·tion (prɛpəréiʃən) *n.* a preparing or being prepared ‖ that which is prepared, esp. a chemical substance or medicine, for subsequent use ‖ *(pl.)* preparatory measures ‖ the work done in preparing school lessons

pre·par·a·to·ry (pripǽrətɔri:, pripɛ́ərətɔri:, pripǽrətɔuri:, pripɛ́ərətɔuri:) *adj.* of that which prepares or introduces ‖ undergoing preliminary instruction, *a preparatory student*

pre·pare (pripɛ́ər) *v.t. pres. part.* **pre·par·ing** *past* and *past part.* **pre·pared** to make the necessary preparations for ‖ to get ready for by study, work, practice etc. ‖ to get (someone) ready ‖ to put (someone) in a receptive state of mind ‖ to make (e.g. a chemical preparation), *to prepare a vaccine* ‖ *v.i.* to take necessary previous measures, *to prepare for a journey* ‖ to make oneself ready in one's mind, *to prepare for the worst* **to be prepared** to be willing to **pre·par·ed·ly** (pripɛ́əridli:) *adv.* **pre·pár·ed·ness** *n.* the state of being prepared, esp. of being prepared for war

pre·pay (priːpéi) *pres. part.* **pre·pay·ing** *past* and *past part.* **pre·paid** *v.t.* to pay for in advance **pre·páy·ment** *n.*

pre·pon·der·ance (pripɔ́ndərəns) *n.* the condition of being preponderant

pre·pon·der·ant (pripɔ́ndərənt) *adj.* superior in weight, number, influence, power, importance

prep·o·si·tion (prɛpəzíʃən) *n. (gram.)* a word (in some languages) expressing the relationship between a noun, pronoun or noun phrase (which usually follows the preposition and is called the 'object' of the preposition) and another element of the sentence, e.g. a verb ('down' in 'he walked down the street'), a noun ('of' in 'the mother of twins') or an adjective ('for' in 'grateful for favors') ‖ a compound construction which functions as a preposition (e.g. 'on top of') **prep·o·sí·tion·al** *adj.*

pre·pos·ter·ous (pripɔ́stərəs) *adj.* grotesquely or comically ridiculous ‖ unreasonable, unlikely

pre·puce (príːpjuːs) *n.* the foreskin, or a similar fold of skin over the clitoris

pre·req·ui·site (prirékwizit) **1.** *adj.* requisite in an antecedent condition **2.** *n.* that which is prerequisite

pre·rog·a·tive (prirɔ́gətiv) **1.** *n.* an exclusive right or privilege possessed by a person or body of persons ‖ a right attached to an office or rank, *the royal*

prerogative **2.** *adj.* pertaining to a prerogative, arising from special privilege

pres·age 1. (présidʒ) *n.* that which foretells a future event ‖ a presentiment **2.** (présidʒ, priséidʒ) *v.t. pres. part.* **pres·ag·ing** *past* and *past part.* **pres·aged** to foretell (a future event)

pre·scribe (priskráib) *pres. part.* **pre·scrib·ing** *past* and *past part.* **pre·scribed** *v.t.* to order with the force of authority ‖ to order the use of (a medicine or treatment) ‖ *(law)* to state (a prescriptive right or title) ‖ *v.i.* to lay down a rule ‖ to write a medical prescription ‖ *(law)* to claim a title etc. by a prescription

pre·scrip·tion (priskrípʃən) *n.* the act of prescribing ‖ that which is prescribed, esp. *(med.)* a written statement, giving directions for making and using a medicine ‖ *(law)* negative prescription ‖ *(law)* positive prescription ‖ ancient custom, esp. when regarded as authoritative

pres·ence (préz'ns) *n.* the state or fact of being in a certain place ‖ the space immediately surrounding a person ‖ distinction of bearing and demeanor ‖ the quality which marks a dominating personality, esp. the quality which enables a performer to dominate his audience ‖ an intangible spirit or mysterious influence felt to be present

pres·ent (préz'nt) *n.* a gift

present 1. *adj.* being in a specified place ‖ existing, being done, or occurring at this time ‖ used as a form of reference to oneself, *the present writer* ‖ *(gram.)* of or designating a tense that expresses action now taking place, or state in time now existing **2.** *n.* this time ‖ *(gram.)* the present tense ‖ *(gram.)* a verb in the present tense **at present** at this time, *I cannot receive him at present* **for the present** at this time and for some little time to come

pre·sent (prizént) **1.** *v.t.* to bring (someone) to the notice of or into the presence of someone else, esp. a superior ‖ to introduce (someone) formally at court ‖ to offer as a gift ‖ (with 'with') to make a gift to ‖ (with 'with') to cause to face, *to present with a problem* ‖ to exhibit or offer to view or notice, *to present a fine appearance* ‖ to offer as a public entertainment ‖ to submit for consideration or action, *to present an argument, to present a bill* ‖ *(law)* to bring a formal charge against ‖ *(law)* to lay (e.g. a charge) before a court etc. ‖ *v.i.* (of a fetus) to be directed towards the opening of the womb ‖ *(med.)* to come forward as a patient **to present arms** *(mil.)* to display the rifle perpendicularly in front of the center of the body as a salute while at the position of attention **2.** *n.* the position of presenting arms **pre·sent·a·bíl·i·ty** *n.* the condition or quality of being presentable **pre·sént·a·ble** *adj.* fit to be presented, shown, or offered **pre·sént·a·bly** *adv.*

pres·en·ta·tion (prɛzəntéiʃən, priːzəntéiʃən) *n.* a presenting or being presented ‖ that which is presented, e.g. a theatrical performance ‖ a formal introduction, esp. an introduction at Court ‖ a formal presenting of a gift, usually before a gathering of people ‖ *(med.)* the position of the fetus at birth **pres·en·tá·tion·al** *adj.* **pres·en·tá·tion·ism** *n. (philos.)* the doctrine that the mind has immediate cognition of the objects of perception

pres·ent·ly (préz'ntli:) *adv.* in a short time from now ‖ in a short time from then

pre·serv·a·tive (prizə́ːrvətiv) **1.** *adj.* having the ability to preserve **2.** *n.* a substance added to preserve, esp. a chemical added to prevent food from decomposition

pre·serve (prizə́ːrv) **1.** *v. pres. part.* **pre·serv·ing** *past* and *past part.* **pre·served** *v.t.* to prepare (fruit, vegetables, meat or fish) by boiling, salting, pickling

---

(**a**) æ, c*a*t; ɑ, c*a*r; ɔ f*aw*n; ei, sn*a*ke. (**e**) e, h*e*n; iː, sh*ee*p; iə, d*ee*r; ɛə, b*ea*r. (**i**) i, f*i*sh; ai, t*i*ger; əː, b*i*rd. (**o**) o, *o*x; au, c*ow*; ou, g*oa*t; u, p*oo*r; ɔi, r*oy*al. (**u**) ʌ, d*u*ck; u, b*u*ll; uː, g*oo*se; ə, b*a*cillus; juː, c*u*be. x, lo*ch*; θ, *th*ink; ð, bo*th*er; z, *Z*en; ʒ, corsa*g*e; dʒ, sava*g*e; ŋ, oranguta*ng*; j, *y*ak; ʃ, *fish*; tʃ, fe*tch*; 'l, rabb*le*; 'n, redd*en*. Complete pronunciation key appears inside front cover.

etc. and packing into containers for future use ‖ to keep up, maintain, prevent from ruin or decay ‖ to keep from decomposition by freezing, treating with chemicals etc. ‖ to retain (e.g. a quality) ‖ to maintain and protect (fish or game) for private use ‖ *v.i.* to be suitable for preserving ‖ to make preserves **2.** *n.* a large area of land or body of water where game or fish is protected ‖ something, e.g. an occupation, place etc., regarded exclusively as one's own ‖ (esp. *pl.*) jam

pre·side (prizáid) *pres. part.* **pre·sid·ing** *past* and *past part.* **pre·sid·ed** *v.i.* to be in a position of control or authority, *to preside over a meeting*

pres·i·den·cy (prézidənsi:) *pl.* **pres·i·den·cies** *n.* the office or function of president ‖ the term of office of a president ‖ the region under the control of a president

pres·i·dent (prézidənt) *n.* the elected head of government in the U.S.A. and many other republics ‖ a person elected to preside over an organization ‖ the chief officer of a bank, company, corporation etc. ‖ the head of a college or university

press (pres) *v.t.* to exert a steady force upon (something) by applying pressure ‖ to make flat by exerting such pressure ‖ to make smooth by applying pressure, *to press clothes* ‖ to try to force or persuade, *to press someone to stay* ‖ to put forward (a claim) with energy ‖ to squeeze (fruit etc.) in order to extract juice ‖ to make more forceful by insistence ‖ to cause distress to (the mind or spirits) ‖ to clasp or hold in an affectionate embrace ‖ to make (a phonograph record) ‖ *v.i.* to throng about someone or something ‖ to force one's way ‖ to require immediate action ‖ (of time) to suffice barely for what must be done ‖ (with 'for') to make an insistent demand or recommendation, *to press for higher wages* **pressed for** desperately short of (money, time, space etc.) **to press on** to advance with grim resolution

press *n.* a pressing or being pressed ‖ an instance of pressing ‖ an instrument or machine by which a substance or material is shaped, smoothed, stamped, compressed etc. by the force of pressure ‖ a printing press ‖ an establishment for printing and publishing books etc. ‖ the personnel of such an establishment ‖ newspapers and periodicals collectively ‖ journalists collectively ‖ critical notice in newspapers etc. ‖ a cupboard in which linen, clothes etc. are kept ‖ a device for holding a tennis racket etc., in order to keep it from warping **in press** in the process of being printed **off the press** just printed **to go to press** to print off the edition of a newspaper etc.

press·ing (présiŋ) *adj.* requiring immediate attention ‖ (of a request, invitation etc.) very earnest ‖ very persistent

pres·sure (préʃər) **1.** *n.* the action of pressing ‖ *(phys.)* the force acting per unit area ‖ *(elec.)* electromotive force ‖ atmospheric pressure ‖ interference, by an interested party, with someone's freedom in making a decision ‖ *(fig.)* a burden, *pressure of work* **2.** *pres. part.* **pres·sur·ing** *past* and *past part.* **pres·sured** to influence or force by using psychological pressure ‖ to pressurize

pres·sur·ize (préʃəraiz) *pres. part.* **pres·sur·iz·ing** *past* and *past part.* **pres·sur·ized** *v.t.* to cause the air pressure within (an aircraft cabin etc.) to remain equal to atmospheric pressure at ground level whatever the external air pressure may actually be

pres·ti·dig·i·ta·tion (prẹstididʒitéiʃən) *n.* sleight of hand

pres·ti·dig·i·ta·tor (prẹstidídʒiteitər) *n.* someone skilled in sleight of hand

pres·tige (prestí:ʒ) *n.* widely acknowledged high reputation, as a source of power, credit or influence

pres·tig·ious (prestídʒəs, prestídʒi:əs, prestí:dʒəs, prestí:dʒi:əs) *adj.* held in high esteem

pre·sum·a·ble (prizú:məb'l) *adj.* that may be presumed **pre·súm·a·bly** *adv.*

pre·sume (prizú:m) *pres. part.* **pre·sum·ing** *past* and *past part.* **pre·sumed** *v.t.* to assume as true, take for

granted ‖ (with *infin.*) to take upon oneself boldly or rashly, venture ‖ to imply, presuppose ‖ *v.i.* (with 'on', 'upon') to take advantage of or rely on something or someone more than is warranted

pre·sump·tion (prizÁmpʃən) *n.* the act of presuming ‖ something presumed, a supposition ‖ unwarranted taking for granted of someone's approval, acquiescence etc. ‖ a too high opinion of oneself ‖ *(law)* a deduction made from known facts but lacking direct evidence

pre·sump·tu·ous (prizÁmptʃu:əs) *adj.* displaying excessive self-confidence and taking liberties

pre·tend (priténd) *v.t.* to allege falsely, make deliberately (a false impression) ‖ to claim ‖ to imagine in play or go through motions representing (an imaginary situation) ‖ *v.i.* to make a pretense **to pretend to (something)** to lay claim to (some honor, quality etc.)

pre·tend·er (priténdər) *n.* a claimant to a throne without just title ‖ someone who pretends

pre·tense (priténs, prí:tens) *n.* the deliberate creating of a false impression ‖ something pretended ‖ pretentiousness ‖ a claim, *no pretense to originality*

pre·ten·sion (priténʃən) *n.* a claim, whether true or false ‖ the putting forth of a claim ‖ pretentiousness

pre·ten·tious (priténʃəs) *adj.* claiming to possess superior qualities or great importance, esp. without justification

pre·text 1. (prí:tekst) *n.* a false reason given to conceal the real reason for an action etc. **2.** (pritékst) *v.t.* to advance (a pretext) for one's actions etc.

pret·ti·ly (prítili:) *adv.* in a way that is charming to see or hear, *she curtsied prettily*

pret·ty (príti:) *comp.* **pret·ti·er** *superl.* **pret·ti·est 1.** *adj.* pleasing to see or hear, esp. on account of grace, delicacy or charm, but less than beautiful ‖ excellent, fine, good (used ironically), *a pretty mess* **2.** *adv.* (used as a mild intensive before another adv. or an adj.) rather **sitting pretty** *(pop.)* well placed for taking advantage of a situation

pret·zel (prétsəl) *n.* a cracker shaped like an open knot, glazed and salted

pre·vail (privéil) *v.i.* (often with 'against', 'over') to be victorious ‖ to be the chief characteristic ‖ to be widespread or current ‖ (with 'on', 'upon') to persuade **pre·váil·ing** *adj.*

prev·a·lent (prévələnt) *adj.* widespread, generally used, followed, circulated etc.

pre·var·i·cate (privǽrikeit) *pres. part.* **pre·var·i·cat·ing** *past* and *past part.* **pre·var·i·cat·ed** *v.i.* to speak or act evasively, hiding the truth

pre·vent (privént) *v.t.* to cause not to do something ‖ to cause not to happen, or not to be made or done

pre·vent·a·ble, pre·vent·i·ble (privéntəb'l) *adj.* capable of being prevented

pre·ven·tion (privénʃən) *n.* the act of preventing ‖ something that serves as a preventive

pre·ven·tive (privéntiv) **1.** *adj.* preventing or intended to prevent something ‖ *(med.)* intended to prevent disease **2.** *n.* something that prevents or is intended to prevent something ‖ a medicament etc. used for preventing disease

pre·view (prí:vju:) **1.** *n.* a presentation of a film, book etc. to critics, press reporters etc. before it is presented to the general public ‖ a brief view or foretaste of something that is to come ‖ (also **prevue**) short extracts from a new film exhibited as advance publicity **2.** *v.t.* to see or show a preview of

pre·vi·ous (prí:vi:əs) **1.** *adj.* occurring or done earlier ‖ *(pop.)* before the right time **2.** *adv.* (with 'to') before

prey (prei) *(sing.* and *collect.) n.* an animal or animals seized as food by another animal ‖ a victim or victims

prey *v.i.* (of an animal, esp. with 'on', 'upon') to seek for or seize prey ‖ (with 'on', 'upon') to make raids in order to take booty ‖ (with 'on', 'upon') to have a destructively wearing effect

price (prais) *n.* that which is given or demanded in

return for a thing, service etc. offered for sale or for barter ‖ *(rhet.)* that which must be done, sacrificed, suffered etc. in return for something **a price on someone's head** a reward offered for the capture or killing of someone **at a price** at an unusually high cost ‖ with great sacrifice **beyond** (or **without**) **price** of so great a value that no buyer could pay for it **to have one's price** to be willing to be bribed if the bribe is big enough **what price (something)?** what is the use or value of (something)?

price *pres. part.* **pric·ing** *past and past part.* **priced** *v.t.* to state or ascertain the price or market value of ‖ to set the price of (something one is selling)

price·less (práislis) *adj.* too valuable to carry any price ‖ very valuable ‖ *(pop.)* very funny, ridiculous, *a priceless story*

prick (prik) *v.t.* to make a very small hole in with a sharp point ‖ to make (a hole) in something with a sharp point ‖ to deflate (a balloon etc.) by piercing its surface ‖ to wound by piercing with a sharp implement ‖ to pain mentally, esp. to goad as if with spurs ‖ to mark (a surface) with little punctures or dots, esp. in tracing ‖ to form (a pattern etc.) on a surface with little punctures or dots ‖ (with 'off') to mark (a name or item) on a list by putting a dot etc. next to it ‖ (with 'up') to cause (esp. the ears) to point upward or forward as a sign of sudden attention or interest ‖ (esp. with 'out') to transplant (seedlings) ‖ *v.i.* (with 'up') to point upward or forward ‖ to have or cause a feeling of being pierced

prick *n.* the act or an instance of pricking ‖ a small puncture made by pricking ‖ the pain caused by pricking

prick·le (prík'l) **1.** *n.* *(bot.)* a pointed process arising from epidermal tissue, e.g. of a bramble, rose etc., and which can be peeled off with the outer skin ‖ a tingling or prickling sensation **2.** *v. pres. part.* **prick·ling** *past and past part.* **prick·led** *v.i.* to feel a tingling or prickling sensation ‖ *v.t.* to pierce with or as if with a prickle ‖ to cause to feel a tingling or prickling sensation

prick·ly (príkli:) *comp.* **prick·li·er** *superl.* **prick·li·est** *adj.* armed with prickles ‖ feeling as if pricked by prickles ‖ causing such a feeling ‖ quick to take offense, very touchy

pride (praid) **1.** *n.* excessive self-esteem ‖ behavior that shows this ‖ proper self-respect ‖ a sense of satisfaction with one's achievements etc. ‖ the best ‖ (of a bird) the state of having the tail fully displayed, *a peacock in his pride* ‖ (of lions) a group, often a family, in the wild state **to take pride in** to set oneself a high standard in (one's work etc.) for the satisfaction it brings ‖ to be proud of (some achievement etc.) **2.** *v. refl. pres. part.* **prid·ing** *past and past part.* **prid·ed** to feel pride in some achievement or prowess

priest (pri:st) *n.* *(Christian churches)* an ordained person trained and authorized by a bishop to be an intermediary between the people and God by conducting sacred rites, administering the sacraments, making intercession, pronouncing absolution and safeguarding sacred buildings and treasures ‖ any member of the clergy ‖ a minister of a non-Christian religion

prig (prig) *n.* a narrow-minded person who makes an annoying parade of being morally or culturally superior to others **prig·gish** *adj.*

prim (prim) **1.** *adj. comp.* **prim·mer** *superl.* **prim·mest** (of a person) stiff in manner, too clipped or precise in speech, too formal in dress, or narrow and intolerant in opinion ‖ (of manners or expression) stiff and formal **2.** *v.t. pres. part.* **prim·ming** *past and past part.* **primmed** to shape (the face or lips) into

a prim expression

pri·ma·cy (práiməsi:) *n.* the state of being first in rank, importance etc. ‖ *(eccles.)* the office or dignity of a primate

pri·ma don·na (pri:mədónə, prɪmədónə) *pl.* **pri·ma don·nas** *n.* the chief woman singer in an opera

pri·ma fa·cie (práiməféiʃi) *adj.* *(law,* of evidence) having every appearance of proving a fact though it may not constitute certain proof

pri·mal (práiməl) *adj.* primitive or earliest in history ‖ first in importance

pri·ma·ri·ly (praiméərili:, práimerili:, práimərili:) *adv.* principally ‖ originally

pri·ma·ry (práiməri:) **1.** *adj.* first in time of origin or order of development ‖ basic, fundamental ‖ first in a succession or series ‖ first in importance ‖ not derived ‖ first in order of production, *gas, coke and tar are primary products of the coal-gas industry* **2.** *pl.* **pri·ma·ries** *n.* something which is primary ‖ a primary color ‖ (esp. *pl.*) a primary election ‖ a primary feather ‖ *(astron.)* a primary planet ‖ *(chem.)* a primary compound or product ‖ *(elec.)* a primary cell

pri·mate (práimeit) *n.* *(eccles.)* an archbishop ‖ *(eccles.)* a bishop having authority over other bishops ‖ *(zool.)* a member of the order *Primates,* the highest order of mammals, including man, apes, monkeys, lemurs etc.

prime (praim) **1.** *adj.* first in time, importance, quality or rank ‖ fundamental ‖ *(math.,* of a number) divisible only by itself and by 1, not by any other integer **2.** *n.* a minute of angle or the symbol (′) for this ‖ *(math.)* a prime number ‖ a symbol (′) used after a character to distinguish it from another, e.g. to distinguish A′ from A ‖ *(mus.)* the tonic ‖ *(mus.)* a unison ‖ *(mus.)* the fundamental note in a harmonic series

prime *n.* *(eccles.)* the first service of the day ‖ the time or hour of this service ‖ the best, most flourishing stage or state ‖ *(rhet.)* the earliest state ‖ *(rhet.)* the best or chief part or member

prime *pres. part.* **prim·ing** *past and past part.* **primed** *v.t.* to fill (a pump) with water to initiate action ‖ to inject gasoline into the carburetor of (an engine) ‖ to fill pores of (wood etc.) with a first coat of paint etc. ‖ to provide (someone) with information etc. beforehand ‖ to ply (someone) with liquor ‖ *(hist.)* to put the charge in (a gun) ‖ *v.i.* (of a steam cylinder) to carry over water with the steam

prime meridian the meridian at 0° longitude, passing through Greenwich, England, from which longitude is measured

prim·er (práimər) *n.* something that primes ‖ a cap, cylinder etc. containing an explosive compound used to fire the charge of a gun

pri·me·val, pri·mae·val (praimí:vəl) *adj.* belonging to the earliest era of life on the earth

prim·i·tive (prímitiv) **1.** *adj.* of, pertaining to or characteristic of the earliest period of origin of something ‖ having the characteristics of the earliest stages of civilization ‖ roughly constructed, crude and simple ‖ without civilized accretions ‖ (of a work of art or artist) of the period just before the Renaissance ‖ of modern (often deliberately) unsophisticated works of art, or artists painting in such a style ‖ *(math.)* of a figure, line etc. from which another is derived ‖ *(biol.)* of or pertaining to an early stage of development ‖ *(biol.)* showing little change from an early ancestral type ‖ *(geol.)* primary ‖ *(gram.)* of a root form in contrast to a derived word **2.** *n.* a primitive person ‖ a primitive work of art or artist ‖ *(math.)* a primitive line, figure etc. ‖ *(gram.)* a primitive form **prim·i·tiv·ism** *n.* primitivity ‖ primitive practices, customs etc. ‖ a belief in the superiority of a primitive way of life or of things primitive ‖ the style of a primitive (deliberately unsophisticated) artist **prim·i·tiv·i·ty** *n.* the quality or state of being primitive

pri·mor·di·al (praimɔ́rdi:əl) *adj.* existing from the beginning, of that which was the first to be created ‖ fundamental, underived ‖ (*biol.*, of a species, organ, cell etc.) earliest developed

primp (primp) *v.i.* to busy oneself fussily about one's dress or appearance ‖ *v.t.* to fuss over (one's hair, clothes etc.) so as to impress ‖ to put in order (a room etc.), esp. for visitors' eyes

prince (prins) *n.* a son or son's son of a ruling sovereign ‖ any male member in certain royal families ‖ the ruler of a principality ‖ a courtesy title in some countries, accorded to certain members of noble families ‖ a ruler ‖ a distinguished and powerful person in some walk of life, *a merchant prince* ‖ (*Roman Catholicism*) a cardinal

prince·ly (prínsli:) *comp.* **prince·li·er** *superl.* **prince·li·est** *adj.* worthy of a prince, splendid ‖ of or relating to a prince

prin·ci·pal (prínsəp'l) **1.** *adj.* first in importance **2.** *n.* a person having the chief authority or responsibility ‖ a person employing another as his agent ‖ (*law*) a person actually committing or directly aiding in a crime ‖ the sum of money on which interest is earned ‖ a person playing a chief role in a play, film, ballet etc. ‖ (*mus.*) the first player of any division of orchestral instruments except first violins ‖ (*law*) someone who is primarily liable, as distinct from someone who stands surety or endorses ‖ (*building*) a roof truss ‖ one of the combatants in a duel

prin·ci·ple (prínsəp'l) *n.* a law of nature as formulated and accepted by the mind ‖ an essential truth upon which other truths are based ‖ the acceptance of moral law as a guide to behavior ‖ a rule by which a person chooses to govern his conduct, often forming part of a code ‖ a fundamental implication, *he objects to the principle of the thing, not to the method* **in principle** as regards essentials **on principle** by virtue of the principles one accepts, *to agree on principle*

print (print) **1.** *n.* a picture or design made by an inked impression of a block, engraved plate etc. ‖ a mark made on something by pressure ‖ a photograph made from a negative ‖ printed matter ‖ handwritten letters imitating typographical forms ‖ an object for making a mark by impression, a stamp, seal ‖ a textile made with an applied colored or black and white pattern ‖ a dress made of this **in print** printed in a publication etc. ‖ still available from the publisher **out of print** no longer available from the publisher

print *v.t.* to make a mark on (a surface) by pressure or stamping ‖ to make (a mark) on a surface by pressing or stamping ‖ to make an impression on the surface of (paper, fabric etc.) by pressing inked blocks etc. on it ‖ to reproduce (a text, news etc.) by this process ‖ to write or draw (letters) in imitation of type forms ‖ to make (a photograph) from a negative ‖ to fix firmly (a memory, idea etc.) on the mind ‖ *v.i.* to practice the art of making inked impressions on paper etc. ‖ to write in characters resembling type forms **to print off** to go to press with (the edition) after proofing is finished **print·a·ble** *adj.* good enough or proper enough to be printed and published **print·er** *n.* someone who prints, esp. as a profession

print·ing (príntiŋ) *n.* the action of someone who or something that prints ‖ the art or business of a printer ‖ the style or quality of that which is printed ‖ the total number of printed copies of a book etc. made at one time

print·out (príntaut) *n.* (*computer*) the printed record of the solution to the program or of the contents of the computer memory —**print out** *v.*

pri·or (práiər) **1.** *adj.* earlier ‖ preceding in order or importance **2.** *adv.* (with 'to') earlier than

pri·or·i·ty (praiɔ́riti:, praiɔ́riti:) *pl.* **pri·or·i·ties** *n.* the

quality or state of coming first in time ‖ something that comes first or among the first in importance ‖ the right or privilege of precedence over others

prism (prízəm) *n.* (*geom.*) a solid figure having two parallel polygonal faces, the other faces being parallelograms ‖ (*crystall.*) a crystal form having three or more faces parallel to one axis ‖ (*optics*) a device used to disperse light or change its direction, consisting of a transparent solid with two nonparallel plane faces ‖ an electric or magnetic field used to deviate or disperse a beam of charged particles

pris·on (príz'n) *n.* a building used to confine offenders or suspects awaiting trial, or enemy captives ‖ imprisonment

pris·on·er (príz'nər) *n.* a person who is confined in a prison ‖ a person who is in custody or under restraint ‖ a person who is captured or held captive

pris·sy (prísi:) *comp.* **pris·si·er** *superl.* **pris·si·est** *adj.* (*pop.*) primly precise about little details of dress, behavior etc. ‖ prudish

pris·tine (prísti:n, prístain, pristí:n) *adj.* unspoiled, still in an uncorrupted state ‖ of or in ancient or original condition

pri·va·cy (práivəsi:) *n.* the quality or state of being hidden from, or undisturbed by, the observation or activities of other persons ‖ freedom from undesirable intrusions

pri·vate (práivit) **1.** *adj.* belonging to a particular person or group and not shared with others in any way ‖ not holding public office ‖ secret, hidden from others ‖ not available to or not supported by the general public **2.** *n.* a soldier in the U.S. army one grade above a new or recent recruit **in private** not openly, without witnesses

pri·va·tion (praivéiʃən) *n.* complete or serious lack of the usual necessities of life (food, shelter, warmth etc.) ‖ an instance of this

priv·i·lege (prívəlidʒ) *n.* a benefit or advantage possessed by one person only or by a minority of the community ‖ any of the fundamental rights common to all persons under a modern constitutional government ‖ (*law*) a right or power conferred by a special law

priv·i·leged (prívəlidʒd) *adj.* enjoying a privilege

priv·y (prívi:) **1.** *adj.* (in the phrase) **privy to** (*rhet.*) having private knowledge of, taken into the secret of ‖ (*law*) having a personal interest or part in **2.** *pl.* **priv·ies** *n.* (*pop.*) an outdoor toilet with no flushing mechanism

prize (praiz) **1.** *n.* something of value or satisfaction received in recognition of distinction ‖ such a thing offered to the winner of a competition, to the drawer of a lucky lottery ticket etc. ‖ something of value or satisfaction that is gained or worth gaining by an effort **2.** *adj.* awarded or worthy of receiving a prize, *a prize bull* ‖ awarded as a prize, *prize money*

prize *pres. part.* **priz·ing** *past* and *past part.* **prized** *v.t.* to value highly

prize 1. *n.* (also **prise**) leverage, *to get a prize on a weight to be lifted* ‖ a vessel or property captured at sea in wartime **2.** *v.t. pres. part.* **priz·ing** *past* and *past part.* **prized** to capture (a ship) as prize ‖ (also **prise** *pres. part.* **pris·ing** *past* and *past part.* **prised**) to leverage, to pry, force open or lift with or as if with a lever

pro (prou) *n.* (*pop.*) a professional, esp. a professional athlete or coach

pro- *prefix* favoring or advocating ‖ taking the place of ‖ forward, to the front of ‖ before, in advance

pro and con *adv.* for and against **pros and cons** *pl. n.* the arguments for and against ‖ those persons who are, respectively, in favor of or opposed to a proposal or proposition ‖ their respective affirmative and negative votes

prob·a·bil·i·ty (prɔbəbíliti:) *pl.* **prob·a·bil·i·ties** *n.* the state or quality of being probable ‖ (*math.*) the likelihood of an event, based on the ratio between its occurrence and the average number of cases favorable to its occurrence, taken over an indefinitely extended series of such cases || something regarded as probable, based on the experience that of two or more possible effects one tends to predominate **in all probability** quite probably

prob·a·ble (próbəb'l) **1.** *adj.* likely though not certain to occur or to be true **2.** *n.* a person, horse etc. likely to participate in a race || a person likely to be selected as a member of a team, or to participate in a competition, or to be a candidate in an election or examination

prob·a·bly (próbəbli:) *adv.* very likely, with probability

pro·bate (próubeit) **1.** *n.* (*law*) the official establishing of the legal validity of a will || (*law*) a copy of a will certified to be legally valid **2.** *v.t. pres. part.* **pro·bat·ing** *past* and *past part.* **pro·bat·ed** (*law*) to prove (a will) || to put on probation

pro·ba·tion (proubéiʃən) *n.* a critical testing, esp. to discover a person's suitability for a job, membership of an organization or institution etc. || a period of such testing || the suspension of the sentence of a convicted offender, allowing him his freedom subject to regular supervision by a probation officer || a period of such supervision **on probation** in the condition of being a probationer **pro·ba·tion·ar·y** *adj.* of or relating to probation || undergoing probation **pro·ba·tion·er** *n.* a person undergoing probation

probe (proub) **1.** *n.* a blunt surgical instrument used to explore and examine wounds or cavities in the body || a device, e.g. a space satellite, used for scientific exploration and investigation || an investigation **2.** *v. pres. part.* **prob·ing** *past* and *past part.* **probed** *v.t.* to investigate thoroughly || to examine with a surgical probe || *v.i.* to make a thorough investigation || to make an examination with a surgical probe

pro·bi·ty (próubiti:, próbiti:) *n.* scrupulous honesty

prob·lem (próbləm) **1.** *n.* a question whose answer is doubtful or difficult to find || a question for discussion or consideration || a matter that causes worry or perplexity || (*math.*) a statement of what has to be done **2.** *adj.* (of a play, novel etc.) presenting or dealing with a human or social problem || that constitutes a problem or is difficult to deal with

prob·lem·at·ic (prɒbləmǽtik) *adj.* constituting a problem || open to question || uncertain, *his success is very problematic* **prob·lem·át·i·cal** *adj.*

pro·bos·cis (proubósis) *pl.* **pro·bos·cis·es, pro·bos·ci·des** (proubósidi:z) *n.* a trunklike process of the head e.g. in many insects and annelids, and in elephants

pro·ce·dure (prəsí:dʒər) *n.* an act or manner of proceeding || a prescribed way of doing something || rules of parliamentary practice || a particular course of action

pro·ceed (prəsí:d) *v.i.* to move forward, to go further || to continue || to begin some action and persist in it || to come forth, arise || (*law,* with 'against') to begin action or take legal measures **pro·ceed·ing** *n.* the act of someone who or something which proceeds || a course of action, *an illegal proceeding* || (*pl.*) transactions or negotiations || (*pl.*) a record of the activities of a body or organization || (*pl.*) a legal action || (*pl.*) legal measures **pro·ceeds** (próusi:dz) *pl. n.* the sum yielded by a sale or other money-raising transaction

proc·ess (próses) **1.** *n.* a series of acts or changes, proceedings from one to the next || a method of manufacturing or conditioning something || a moving forward, esp. as part of a progression or development || (*biol.*) an outgrowth or extension of an organ or an organism || (*law*) legal proceedings, or the writ or summons beginning them **in process** in progress **in process of, in the process of** during the course of

2. *v.t.* to submit (something) to a treatment, preparation or process, *to process milk* || to submit (something) to a routine handling procedure || to submit (data etc.) to analysis || (*printing*) to produce by a photomechanical process

process *v.t.* (*law*) to take legal action against by serving a writ

pro·ces·sion (prəséʃən) *n.* an orderly line of persons, animals or things, singly or in rows, moving together in the same direction || the act of moving thus || (*theol.*) a divine issuing forth, *the procession of the Holy Ghost*

pro·claim (proukléim) *v.t.* to announce publicly or officially || to declare (someone or something) officially to be || to declare (war, peace) || to announce the accession to the throne of || to reveal as

proc·la·ma·tion (prɒkləméiʃən) *n.* a proclaiming or being proclaimed || an announcement, esp. an official one

pro·cliv·i·ty (prouklíviti:) *pl.* **pro·cliv·i·ties** *n.* a tendency or inclination towards some habit, attitude of mind etc., esp. an undesirable one

pro·cras·ti·nate (proukrǽstineit) *pres. part.* **pro·cras·ti·nat·ing** *past* and *past part.* **pro·cras·ti·nat·ed** *v.i.* to keep delaying and putting things off **pro·crás·ti·na·tor** *n.*

pro·cras·ti·na·tion (proukræstinéiʃən) *n.* the act or habit of procrastinating

pro·cre·ate (próukri:eit) *pres. part.* **pro·cre·at·ing** *past* and *past part.* **pro·cre·at·ed** *v.t.* to produce (offspring) || *v.i.* to bear offspring **pró·cre·a·tive** *adj.*

pro·cre·a·tion (proukri:éiʃən) *n.* a procreating or being procreated

proc·tor (próktər) **1.** *n.* someone who supervises students at a written examination || a person who manages another's cause in a court of canon or civil law or admiralty law **2.** *v.t.* to supervise students at (a written examination) **proc·tó·ri·al** *adj.*

proc·u·ra·tor (prókjəreitər) *n.* someone who manages another's legal affairs || a proctor in a court of civil or canon law || (*hist.*) a financial administrator in a province of the Roman Empire **proc·u·ra·tó·ri·al** *adj.*

pro·cure (proukjúər) *pres. part.* **pro·cur·ing** *past* and *past part.* **pro·cured** *v.t.* to obtain, esp. as a result of some degree of effort || to bring about, contrive || to obtain (women) for prostitution || *v.i.* to obtain women for prostitution **pro·cúre·ment** *n.*

pro·cur·er (proukjúərər) *n.* someone who procures (esp. women for prostitution) **pro·cúr·ess** *n.* a female procurer

prod (prɒd) **1.** *v. pres. part.* **prod·ding** *past* and *past part.* **prod·ded** *v.t.* to poke with a finger, stick or pointed instrument || to goad, rouse || *v.i.* (with 'at') to poke **2.** *n.* a poke or sharp dig || an urge to activity, a sharp reminder || a pointed instrument for prodding with

prod·i·gal (pródig'l) **1.** *adj.* given to reckless spending, wasteful || (*rhet.*) lavishly generous **2.** *n.* (*rhet.*) a spendthrift

pro·di·gious (prədídʒəs) *adj.* amazing, esp. marvelously great, *a prodigious memory*

prod·i·gy (pródidʒi:) *pl.* **prod·i·gies** *n.* a person, esp. a child, with extraordinary talents || an exceptional instance (of some quality)

pro·duce 1. (prədú:s, prədjú:s) *v. pres. part.* **pro·duc·ing** *past* and *past part.* **pro·duced** *v.t.* to bring forward, present for inspection, *to produce one's ticket* || to bring forth, cause to appear || to create (a work of art), write (books etc.) || (of land, plants etc.) to bear, yield || to give birth to || to yield as an exportable product || to manufacture || to bring (a play) before the public, arranging financial backing etc. || to su-

---

pervise the presentation of (a play), directing the actors etc. at rehearsals ‖ to assume overall responsibility for the making of (a film) ‖ to cause to accrue, *money invested produces interest* ‖ *v.i.* to yield or manufacture economically valuable products **2.** (pródu:s, pródju:s, próudu:s, próudju:s) *n.* agricultural or horticultural products ‖ a result (of efforts etc.) ‖ an amount produced **pro·dúc·er** *n.* a person who or a thing which produces ‖ a furnace for making producer gas

prod·uct (pródəkt, pródʌkt) *n.* something produced, esp. something grown or manufactured ‖ an outcome, result ‖ *(math.)* the number obtained by multiplying numbers together ‖ *(chem.)* a new compound formed as a result of chemical change

pro·duc·tion (prədʌ́kʃən) *n.* a producing or being produced ‖ something produced, esp. a literary, artistic or dramatic work

pro·duc·tive (prədʌ́ktiv) *adj.* able to produce or producing in abundance ‖ (with 'of') being the direct or indirect cause ‖ yielding results or profit ‖ *(econ.)* producing goods which have economic value **pro·duc·tiv·i·ty** (prɒudʌktíviti:, prɒdəktíviti:) *n.* ability to produce ‖ productive yield

pro·fane (prəféin) *adj.* blasphemous, irreverent ‖ heathen ‖ not connected with things sacred or biblical ‖ *(rhet.)* not initiated into sacred mysteries, *the profane multitude* ‖ *(rhet.)* not possessing esoteric knowledge or tastes

profane *pres. part.* **pro·fan·ing** *past* and *past part.* **pro·faned** *v.t.* to treat (something sacred) with irreverence, desecrate ‖ *(rhet.)* to treat disrespectfully,

pro·fan·i·ty (prəfǽniti:) *pl.* **pro·fan·i·ties** *n.* irreverence ‖ an irreverent act or utterance

pro·fess (prəfés) *v.t.* to claim ‖ to claim or declare falsely ‖ to declare one's faith in by observances and practices ‖ to follow as one's profession ‖ to accept into a religious order ‖ *v.i.* to make a profession, esp. of religious vows **pro·féssed** *adj.* openly declared, self-acknowledged ‖ pretended, claiming to be ‖ having taken religious vows, *a professed nun* **pro·fess·ed·ly** (prəfésidli:) *adv.* according to a person's own claims, *he is professedly an authority on the subject*

pro·fes·sion (prəféʃən) *n.* one of a limited number of occupations or vocations involving special learning and carrying a certain social prestige, esp. the learned professions: law, medicine and the Church ‖ any vocation or occupation ‖ the people engaged in such an occupation ‖ open declaration, avowal ‖ a declaration of religious belief ‖ a taking of religious vows **pro·fés·sion·al 1.** *adj.* of or relating to a profession ‖ showing a sound workman's command ‖ engaging in some activity as a remunerated occupation ‖ following some line of conduct as if it were one's profession ‖ of or done by professionals **2.** *n.* someone who engages in an activity, esp. a sport, to earn money ‖ someone engaged in one of the learned or salaried professions **pro·fés·sion·al·ism** *n.*

pro·fes·sor (prəfésər) *n.* a university teacher of the highest rank in a faculty ‖ someone who declares or confesses views, a faith etc. **pro·fés·sor·ate** *n.* the office or term of office of a professor **pro·fes·so·ri·al** (prɒufəsɔ́ri:əl, prɒfəsɔ́ri:əl, prɒufəsóuri:əl, prɒfəsóuri:əl) *adj.* **pro·fes·só·ri·ate** *n.* a body of professors **pro·fés·sor·ship** *n.*

prof·fer (prófər) *n.* an offer, *a proffer of help*

proffer *v.t.* to offer, tender, *to proffer a bribe*

pro·fi·cien·cy (prəfíʃənsi:) *n.* the state or quality of being proficient

pro·fi·cient (prəfíʃənt) *adj.* having or showing effective command in an art, skill, study etc.

pro·file (próufail) **1.** *n.* the shape of something, esp. the face, as seen from a side view ‖ a drawing of the side view of something, esp. the face ‖ a concise biographical description ‖ any short historical, geographical or other descriptive sketch in writing ‖ a flat, cutout piece of stage scenery ‖ *(archit., engin.* etc.) a side elevation or a section **2.** *v.t. pres. part.* **pro·fil·ing** *past* and *past part.* **pro·filed** to draw or write a profile of

prof·it (prófit) *n.* advantage, benefit ‖ financial gain ‖ *(sing.* or *pl.)* an excess of income over expenditure, esp. in a particular transaction or over a period of time ‖ the ratio of this annual excess to the amount of capital invested ‖ *(econ.)* net income

profit *v.i.* (with 'by' or 'from') to obtain financial gain or other benefit

prof·it·a·ble (prófitəb'l) *adj.* yielding profit or a profit **próf·it·a·bly** *adv.*

prof·li·ga·cy (prófligəsi:) *n.* the state or quality of being profligate

prof·li·gate (prófligit) **1.** *adj.* dissolute ‖ wildly extravagant **2.** *n.* a profligate person

pro·found (prəfáund) *adj.* searching into the deepest and most subtle problems or truths ‖ possessing particular wisdom and shrewdness ‖ requiring deep thought ‖ very great, intense ‖ coming as if from a great depth

pro·fun·di·ty (prəfʌ́nditi:) *pl.* **pro·fun·di·ties** *n.* depth, intensity ‖ something profound

pro·fuse (prəfjú:s) *adj.* (of persons) lavish, very generous ‖ (of things) very abundant

pro·fu·sion (prəfjú:ʒən) *n.* the quality or state of being profuse ‖ great abundance

pro·gen·i·tor (proudʒénitər) *n.* an ancestor of a person, animal or plant ‖ an originator of an idea, theory etc.

prog·e·ny (pródʒəni:) *pl.* **prog·e·nies** *n.* offspring

prog·no·sis (prɒgnóusis) *pl.* **prog·no·ses** (prɒgnóusi:z) *n.* a doctor's assessment of the probable course of an illness and the prospects of recovery ‖ the act of making such an assessment ‖ a forecast

prog·nos·ti·cate (prɒgnóstikeit) *pres. part.* **prog·nos·ti·cat·ing** *past* and *past part.* **prog·nos·ti·cat·ed** *v.t.* to foretell, predict ‖ *v.i.* to make a prediction

pro·gram, esp. *Br.* **pro·gramme** (próugræm, próugrəm) **1.** *n.* a plan or sequence of things to be done, *a research program* ‖ a list of items planned to constitute a concert, dramatic performance, athletic meet etc., esp. a printed list giving the names of the participants etc. ‖ the performance itself ‖ a complete item broadcast on radio or television ‖ a plan of the operations to be executed by a computer **2.** *v.t. pres. part.* **pro·gram·ing** *past* and *past part.* **pro·grammed** to work out a plan of the operations to be executed by (a computer) ‖ to plan the details of, esp. with respect to timing **pró·gram·mer** *n.* someone who programs a computer

prog·ress 1. (prógres) *n.* forward movement ‖ *(fig.)* movement nearer to some aim ‖ a forward course of development ‖ improvement, advancement ‖ a supposed gradual advancement or improvement in the condition of mankind, esp. seen from a scientific or material standpoint ‖ *(esp. hist.)* an official or ceremonial journey **in progress** going on now or at the time in question **2. pro·gress** (prəgrés) *v.i.* to go forward or onward ‖ to go on, continue ‖ to develop, show improvement ‖ *(fig.)* to advance, move nearer to some aim

pro·gres·sive (prəgrésiv) **1.** *adj.* moving forward or onward ‖ increasing in severity, intensity etc. ‖ increasing or advancing in stages or in series ‖ having to do with, or favoring, political and social progress or reform ‖ of or favoring modern educational ideas which stress informal teaching methods and the encouragement of self-expression ‖ *(gram.)* of or being a verbal form designating action going on (e.g. 'he is running') **2.** *n.* someone who is progressive ‖ *(printing, pl.)* progressive proofs

pro·hib·it (prouhíbit) *v.t.* to forbid with authority, esp. by law ‖ to prevent or make impossible

pro·hi·bi·tion (prouəbíʃən) *n.* a prohibiting by authority ‖ a law that prohibits ‖ the forbidding by law of the manufacture or sale of liquor, or the law itself ‖ *(law)* a high-court writ prohibiting a lower court from proceeding in a case beyond its jurisdiction **Pro·hi·bi·tion** *(Am. hist.)* the forbidding, under the 18th amendment to the constitution, of the manufacture, sale, import or export of liquor throughout the U.S.A. **pro·hi·bi·tion·ist** *n.* an advocate of prohibition of the sale of liquor

pro·hib·i·tive (prouhíbitiv) *adj.* serving to prohibit, *prohibitive laws* || (of prices or tax) so high as to discourage purchase or use

proj·ect (pródʒekt) *n.* a course of action intended or considered possible || a systematic planned undertaking || a set task for a class of schoolchildren in which, for a given period of time, subjects are taught with special reference to some chosen topic, and pupils are encouraged to make independent inquiries to supplement formal teaching

pro·ject (prədʒékt) *v.t.* to throw by mechanical means || to cause (light, an image etc.) to fall on a certain surface || to have in mind as an intention or possibility || to direct (the mind etc.) || to cause (oneself) to enter imaginatively || to externalize (one's own hopes, ideas, frustrations etc.) in something outside oneself or in some other person || *(geom.)* to represent on a given plane or surface a point, line, surface or solid, as viewed from a particular direction or in accordance with a fixed correspondence || to represent (e.g. a map of the earth or heavens) in this way || *v.i.* to stick out, protrude || (of an actor etc.) to establish effective sympathy with the audience

pro·jec·tile (prədʒéktil, prədʒéktail) **1.** *n.* a body projected, esp. a missile projected from a gun etc. **2.** *adj.* suddenly thrusting forward, *projectile force* || capable of being projected with force

pro·jec·tion (prədʒékʃən) *n.* a projecting or being projected || a system by which lines of longitude and latitude are translated onto a plane surface so as to represent the curved surface of the earth or the celestial sphere || the result of projecting a geometrical figure || *(psych.)* accusation of, or unconscious attribution to another of, one's own thoughts, feelings, or actions

pro·jec·tor (prədʒéktər) *n.* an instrument for projecting a beam of light or for throwing an image or a series of images onto a screen

pro·le·tar·i·an (proulitéəri:ən) **1.** *n.* a member of the proletariat **2.** *adj.* of or relating to the proletariat

pro·le·tar·i·at (proulitéəri:ət) *n.* the lowest class in a modern society, esp. (in Marxist theory) industrial wage earners possessing neither property nor capital and living by the sale of their labor || *(Rom. hist.)* the lowest class in ancient Rome

pro·lif·er·ate (proulífəreit) *pres. part.* **pro·lif·er·at·ing** *past* and *past part.* **pro·lif·er·at·ed** *v.i. (biol.)* to grow or reproduce rapidly by cell division, budding etc. || to multiply fast, grow by multiplying || *v.t.* to cause to increase greatly in number

pro·lif·er·a·tion (proulífəréiʃən) *n.* a proliferating or being proliferated

pro·lif·er·ous (proulífərəs) *adj. (bot.)* developing buds from a normally terminal organ (e.g. a leaf or flower) || *(biol.)* reproducing by budding

pro·lif·ic (proulífik) *adj.* reproducing rapidly and in large numbers || producing abundantly || abundant, *a prolific output* || *(rhet.)* (with 'in' or 'of') very productive **pro·líf·i·ca·cy** *n.* **pro·líf·i·cal·ly** *adv.*

pro·logue, pro·log (próulɔg, próulɒg) *n.* an introduction or preface, often in verse, to a literary work, esp. a play

pro·long (prəlɔ́ŋ, prəlɒ́ŋ) *v.t.* to make longer, extend, draw out (usually in time) || to lengthen the pronunciation of (a syllable etc.)

prom·e·nade (prɒmənéid, prɒmənád) **1.** *n.* a slow walk or ride taken for pleasure, esp. for display or as a social custom || a place suitable for this, esp. a paved walk along the seafront at a resort || a series of walking steps in a square dance || the opening of a formal ball in which all the guests particpate in a stately march || *(Am. hist.)* a competitive walk or strut to music by couples **2.** *v. pres. part* **prom·e·nad·ing** *past* and *past part.* **prom·e·nad·ed** *v.i.* to take a stroll || to go on a promenade || to perform a promenade in a dance || *v.t.* to take a stroll through || to take for a stroll or ride so as to display

prom·i·nence (prɒ́minəns) *n.* the state or quality of being prominent || a hill, elevation etc. **próm·i·nen·cy** *n.*

prom·i·nent (prɒ́minənt) *adj.* conspicuous || jutting out, projecting || distinguished, eminent || leading

prom·is·cu·i·ty (prɒmiskjú:iti:) *pl.* **prom·is·cu·i·ties** *n.* the fact or an instance of being promiscuous

pro·mis·cu·ous (prəmískju:əs) *adj.* having sexual relations with many || indiscriminate || made up of various kinds indiscriminately mixed together

prom·ise (prɒ́mis) **1.** *n.* an assurance that one will do or refrain from doing a specified thing || a firm prospect || potential greatness or distinction **2.** *v. pres. part.* **prom·is·ing** *past* and *past part.* **prom·ised** *v.t.* to make a promise (to do something, that something will be done etc.) || to assure (someone) that he will receive || to give cause for expectation of || *v.i.* to make a promise || (with 'well') to show potential good quality

prom·is·ing (prɒ́misiŋ) *adj.* giving hope of achievement or success in the future, likely to turn out well, *a promising pupil*

prom·is·so·ry (prɒ́misɔri:, prɒ́misɔuri:) *adj.* containing a promise

prom·on·to·ry (prɒ́məntɔri:, prɒ́məntɔuri:) *pl.* **prom·on·to·ries** *n.* a point of high land jutting out into an area of water || *(anat.)* any one of certain protuberances

pro·mote (prəmóut) *pres. part.* **pro·mot·ing** *past* and *past part.* **pro·mot·ed** *v.t.* to raise in rank or status || to help forward, further || to push the sales of by intensive advertising etc. || to encourage || to organize, present and secure financial backing for || to support actively, devote energy and influence to securing the passage of

pro·mo·tion (prəmóuʃən) *n.* a promoting or being promoted || advancement to higher rank or status || a striving to secure greater sales by intensive advertising etc. || the organization or setting up of an enterprise **pro·mó·tion·al, pro·mó·tive** *adjs*

prompt (prɒmpt) **1.** *adj.* quick to respond and act without delay || immediate, instant **2.** *n. (commerce)* a time limit given for payment of the account for goods bought

prompt 1. *v.t.* to move or rouse to action || to give rise to, inspire || to whisper to (an actor) words which he has forgotten || to suggest words to (a hesitating speaker) **2.** *n.* the prompting of an actor or speaker || the words said in prompting **prómpt·er** *n.*

prom·ul·gate (prɒ́məlgeit, proumʌ́lgeit) *pres. part.* **prom·ul·gat·ing** *past* and *past part.* **prom·ul·gat·ed** *v.t.* to proclaim, make publicly known (a statute, decree, dogma etc.) || **prom·ul·gá·tion, prɒ́m·ul·ga·tor** *ns*

prone (proun) *adj.* lying face down || flat on the ground, prostrate || (with 'to') inclined, liable, disposed

prong (prɔŋ, prɒŋ) **1.** *n.* a tine of a fork || a fork for lifting hay etc. || any thin pointed object, e.g. the point of an antler **2.** *v.t.* to pierce or lift (soil etc.)

---

with a fork or prong

pro·noun (próunạun) *n.* a word used to replace noun. It functions as a noun and represents a person or thing previously mentioned or known, or being asked about

pro·nounce (prənáuns) *pres. part.* **pro·nounc·ing** *past and past part.* **pro·nounced** *v.t.* to make the sounds of, utter, articulate || to utter or declare formally || to declare authoritatively || *v.i.* to produce speech sounds || to give one's considered or authoritative opinion **pro·nóunced** *adj.* strongly marked, very noticeable **pro·nóunce·ment** *n.* an official statement or announcement || an opinion, decision etc. announced in a formal way

proof (pru:f) **1.** *n.* a proving or being proved || convincing evidence || *(law)* a document receivable as evidence || *(law)* a written version of the evidence a witness is willing to give on oath in court || the alcoholic content of a beverage compared with the standard for proof spirit || *(printing)* an impression of composed type to verify correctness || *(engraving)* an impression carefully taken, for approval before general printing proceeds || *(photog.)* a test print || *(geom.)* the operations which demonstrate and verify a proposition **2.** *adj.* (with 'against') able to resist || (in compounds) impenetrable by, *bulletproof* || (of gold and silver) pure and serving as a standard for comparison (in a mint etc.) || of a standard alcoholic strength **3.** *v.t.* to make (something) impervious (esp. to water) || *(printing, engraving* etc.) to take a trial impression of || to proofread

proof·read (prú:fri:d) *pres. part.* **proof·read·ing** *past and past part.* **proof·read** (prú:fred) *v.t.* to read and correct (a printer's proof) || *v.i.* to read and correct a printer's proof

prop (prɒp) *n.* *(theater)* a property

prop *n.* a propeller

prop 1. *n.* a support placed under or against something to hold it up || any person or thing serving as a support **2.** *v.t. pres. part.* **prop·ping** *past* and *past part.* **propped** (often with 'up') to support with or as if with a prop, keep upright || to make to stand or stay in a specified condition

prop·a·gan·da (prɒpəgǽndə) *n.* information and opinions (esp. prejudiced ones) spread to influence people in favor of or against some doctrine or idea || the spreading of such information and opinions **prop·a·gán·dist** *n.* someone who uses or spreads propaganda **prop·a·gán·dize** *pres. part.* **prop·a·gan·diz·ing** *past* and *past part.* **prop·a·gan·dized** *v.t.* to spread (ideas etc.) through propaganda || to expose (a person or people) to propaganda || *v.i.* to spread propaganda

prop·a·gate (prɒpəgeit) *pres. part.* **prop·a·gat·ing** *past and past part.* **prop·a·gat·ed** *v.t.* to cause to multiply by natural reproduction || to transmit from one generation to another || to spread, disseminate, make widely known || to transmit (heat, light, sound etc.) || *v.i.* to multiply by natural reproduction

prop·a·ga·tion (prɒpəgéiʃən) *n.* a propagating or being propagated

pro·pel (prəpél) *pres. part.* **pro·pel·ling** *past* and *past part.* **pro·pelled** *v.t.* to push or drive forward or onward **pro·pél·lant, pro·pél·lent 1.** *adj.* able or serving to propel **2.** *n.* a propelling agent, esp. a rocket fuel or an explosive which propels a bullet or shell from a gun **pro·pél·ler** *n.* something that propels, esp. a screw propeller

pro·pen·si·ty (prəpénsiti:) *pl.* **pro·pen·si·ties** *n.* a natural disposition, tendency

prop·er (prɒpər) **1.** *adj.* decent, seemly || fitting, suitable || accurate, *in the proper sense of the word* || (usually following the noun) strictly so-called, *excluding adjuncts etc.* || (with 'to') belonging particularly or exclusively || *(eccles.)* appointed for a certain day || *(heraldry)* represented in its natural colors **2.** *n. (eccles.)* a special office, or part of one, appointed for a certain day

prop·er·ty (prɒpərti:) *pl.* **prop·er·ties** *n.* a thing or things owned || real estate || a piece of real estate || abundant wealth, *a man of property* || ownership, the exclusive right to possess and use something || an attribute, characteristic || virtue, quality || *(logic)* an attribute common to a whole class but not necessary to distinguish it from others || *(theater, movie)* any piece of furniture or accessory used on the stage or set (excluding only fixed scenery and clothes actually worn by actors)

proph·e·cy (prɒfisi:) *pl.* **proph·e·cies** *n.* a prediction or foretelling of what is to come || the power to speak as a prophet || something said by a prophet

proph·e·sy (prɒfisai) *pres. part.* **proph·e·sy·ing** *past and past part.* **proph·e·sied** *v.t.* to foretell by divine inspiration || to predict || *v.i.* to act as a prophet || to make a prediction or predictions

proph·et (prɒfit) *n.* a person who, by divine inspiration, declares to the world the divine will, judgments etc. || a person who foretells the course or nature of future events || a leader, founder or spokesman of a cause or party, *an early prophet of socialism* **Proph·et** one of the Old Testament writers of the prophetic books **the Prophet** Mohammed **próph·et·ess** *n.* a woman prophet

pro·phy·lac·tic (proufəlǽktik, prɒfəlǽktik) **1.** *adj.* guarding against disease || preventive, protective **2.** *n.* a prophylactic medicine || anything which guards against disease

pro·phy·lax·is (proufəlǽksis, prɒfəlǽksis) *pl.* **pro·phy·lax·es** (proufəlǽksi:z, prɒfəlǽksi:z) *n.* measures aiming to prevent disease || the prevention of disease

pro·pin·qui·ty (prəpíŋkwiti:) *pl.* **pro·pin·qui·ties** *n.* nearness in place or time || nearness of kinship

pro·pi·ti·ate (prəpíʃi:eit) *pres. part.* **pro·pi·ti·at·ing** *past and past part.* **pro·pi·ti·at·ed** *v.t.* to gain the favor of by appeasement or conciliation

pro·pi·tious (prəpíʃəs) *adj.* favorable disposed || favorable, giving promise of success || advantageous

pro·po·nent (prəpóunənt) *n.* a person who advocates or supports a proposal or idea || *(law)* someone who propounds a will etc.

pro·por·tion (prəpɔ́rʃən, prəpóurʃən) *n.* a part, share (in relation to the whole) || relative size or number, ratio, comparative relation || satisfactory relation between things or parts as regards size, symmetry, balance || *(pl.)* dimensions || *(math.)* an equality of ratios between two pairs of numbers, as in the statement 2 is to 4 as 3 is to 6

pro·por·tion·al (prəpɔ́rʃən'l, prəpóurʃən'l) **1.** *adj.* in proportion || *(math.)* having the same or a constant ratio **2.** *n. (math.)* any number in a proportion **pro·por·tion·ál·i·ty** *n.*

pro·por·tion·ate 1. (prəpɔ́rʃənit, prəpóurʃənit) *adj.* being in proportion, proportionally adjusted **2.** (prəpɔ́rʃəneit, prəpóurʃəneit) *v.t. pres. part.* **pro·por·tion·at·ing** *past and past part.* **pro·por·tion·at·ed** to proportion

pro·po·sal (prəpóuz'l) *n.* a course of action put forward for consideration || an offer of marriage || the act of proposing

pro·pose (prəpóuz) *pres. part.* **pro·pos·ing** *past* and *past part.* **pro·posed** *v.t.* to offer for consideration || to intend || to put forward for approval (a person for office or as a new member of a society) || to offer as a toast || to expound the arguments in favor of || *v.i.* to offer marriage

prop·o·si·tion (prɒpəzíʃən) **1.** *n.* a proposal || *(logic)* an expression or statement of which the subject can be affirmed or denied || the point to be discussed in formal disputation, usually framed in a single sentence || *(math.)* the statement of a theorem or problem to be demonstrated or solved || a scheme, offer, usually commercial || an invitation to sexual intercourse || *(pop.)* any project, thing or person considered to be difficult to handle, *a tough proposition* **2.** *v.t.* to make a business proposal to || to suggest sexual intercourse to **prop·o·si·tion·al** adj.

pro·pound (prəpáund) v.t. to set forth (a problem, plan, interpretation etc.) for consideration ‖ (law) to produce (a will or other testamentary document) before the probate authority so as to establish its legality

pro·pri·e·tar·y (prəpráiiteri:) 1. adj. relating to ownership ‖ owning property ‖ legally made or distributed only by those holding patents or special rights 2. pl. **pro·pri·e·tar·ies** n. a body of owners ‖ right of ownership ‖ (Am. hist.) the owner of a proprietary colony

pro·pri·e·tor (prəpráiitər) n. a person who has legal rights of possession of land, an object, or a process of manufacture or distribution, an owner ‖ a person who has the temporary but not the absolute control and use of property ‖ (Am. hist.) a proprietary **pro·pri·e·tress** n. a woman proprietor

pro·pri·e·ty (prəpráiiti:) pl. **pro·pri·e·ties** n. suitability, correctness ‖ accepted conventions of behavior or morals ‖ (pl.) details of correct conduct in polite society

pro·pul·sion (prəpʌ́lʃən) n. a propelling or being propelled ‖ a driving force

pro ra·ta (prouréitə, prourátə) 1. adv. at a proportionate rate 2. adj. calculated at a proportionate rate

pro·sa·ic (prouzéiik) adj. commonplace, without great imaginative gifts ‖ dull, ordinary **pro·sá·i·cal·ly** adv.

pro·scribe (prouskráib) pres. part. **pro·scrib·ing** past and past part. **pro·scribed** v.t. to outlaw (a person) ‖ to condemn or forbid (a practice)

prose (prouz) 1. n. the language of ordinary speech ‖ this language artificially heightened for literary effect, in nonmetrical rhythms (cf. POETRYA) ‖ dull, commonplace discourse or writing ‖ (rhet.) humdrum commonplace quality, the prose of everyday life ‖ (eccles.) a sequence 2. v.i. pres. part. **pros·ing** past and past part. **prosed** to talk or write boringly and tediously

pros·e·cute (prósikju:t) pres. part. **pros·e·cut·ing** past and past part. **pros·e·cut·ed** v.t. to start legal proceedings against ‖ to start legal proceedings with reference to (a claim etc.) ‖ (rhet.) to carry on ‖ v.i. to start and continue legal proceedings ‖ to act as prosecutor

pros·e·cu·tion (prɒsikjú:ʃən) n. a prosecuting or being prosecuted ‖ (law) the prosecuting party or his legal representatives ‖ (law) the bringing of formal criminal charges against an offender in court

pros·e·cu·tor (prósikjuːtər) n. a person who starts legal proceedings against another or others ‖ a prosecuting attorney

pros·pect 1. (próspekt) n. a wide or distant scenic view ‖ the scene itself ‖ the assumed course of the future ‖ a view of some specified eventuality ‖ reasonable expectation ‖ a potential client or customer ‖ (pl.) social or financial expectations ‖ (mining) property on which signs of mineral deposit are found ‖ (mining) a partly developed mine ‖ (mining) mineral extracted from a test sample **in propsect** likely to materialize 2. (próspekt, prəspékt) v.i. to explore a region in search of oil, gold, minerals etc. ‖ v.t. to explore (an area, mine) for minerals

pro·spec·tive (prəspéktiv) adj. (of payments etc.) relating to the future ‖ destined or expected to be

pros·pec·tor (próspektər, prəspéktər) n. someone who prospects for oil, gold, minerals etc.

pros·pec·tus (prəspéktəs) n. a circular containing information or plans of enterprise, literary work, issue of securities etc., designed to win support

pros·per (próspər) v.i. to thrive ‖ to achieve financial success

pros·per·i·ty (prɒspériti:) n. the condition of being prosperous, the condition of high economic activity

pros·per·ous (próspərəs) adj. financially successful

pros·tate (prósteit) 1. adj. of the partially muscular gland at the neck of the bladder surrounding the beginning of the urethra in male mammals 2. n. this gland **pro·stat·ic** (proustǽtik) adj.

pros·the·sis (prósθisis) pl. **pros·the·ses** (prósθisi:z) n. (gram.) the prefixing of a letter or syllable to a word, e.g. 'be' in 'bemoan' ‖ (med.) an artificial device to replace a missing part of the body (e.g. false teeth, an artificial limb)

pros·thet·ic (prɒsθétik) adj. of or relating to prosthesis or prosthetics **pros·thet·ics** n. the branch of surgery or dentistry which deals with artificial limbs, teeth etc.

pros·ti·tute (próstitu:t, próstitju:t) 1. n. a woman who has promiscuous sexual intercourse for payment ‖ (hist.) a woman who has sexual intercourse as part of a religious cult ‖ a person who degrades his talents for money 2. v.t. pres. part. **pros·ti·tut·ing** past and past part. **pros·ti·tut·ed** to degrade (a science, talents etc.), esp. for money

pros·ti·tu·tion (prɒstitú:ʃən, prɒstitjú:ʃən) n. the act, practice, or profession of offering the body for sexual relations for money ‖ the degradation of some science, talent etc. for money

pros·trate 1. (próstreit) v.t. pres. part. **pros·trat·ing** past and past part. **pros·trat·ed** to cast to the ground face downwards ‖ to abase (oneself) in submission, worship etc. ‖ (rhet.) to reduce to utter submission ‖ to exhaust bodily, wear out ‖ to overcome with shock, grief etc. 2. adj. lying full-length face downwards ‖ overcome with shock, grief etc. ‖ physically exhausted ‖ (rhet.) utterly defeated ‖ (bot.) lying loosely along the surface of the ground

pro·te·an (próuti:ən, prouti:ən) adj. versatile ‖ extremely variable, often changing ‖ able to take on different shapes

pro·tect (prətékt) v.t. to shield or defend against danger, injury etc. ‖ (econ.) to guard (home producers) from foreign competition in the home market by imposing protective tariffs on imported goods ‖ (commerce) to guarantee the availability of funds to meet (a draft, note etc.) when it matures

pro·tec·tion (prətékʃən) n. a protecting or being protected ‖ a person who or a thing which protects ‖ (econ.) the theory, policy or system of helping home producers to face foreign competition by putting protective tariffs on imported goods ‖ money paid to gangsters under threat of damage to property etc. **pro·téc·tion·ism, pro·téc·tion·ist** ns

pro·tec·tive (prətéktiv) adj. giving or intended to give protection ‖ seeking to guard

pro·tec·tor (prətéktər) n. a person who or thing which protects **pro·téc·tor·al** adj. **pro·téc·tor·ate** n. government by a protector ‖ the office of protector ‖ authority assumed by a strong state over a weak or underdeveloped one, without direct annexation, for the defense of the latter from external enemies ‖ a state so governed, esp. a territory ruled in foreign and domestic affairs but not having the legal status of a colony ‖ the period of such government

pro·té·gé (próutəʒei) n. someone who is under the patronage, care or guidance of another, esp. for help in his career **pro·té·gée** (próutəʒei) n. a female protégé

pro·tein (próuti:n) n. (chem.) any of a class of naturally occurring, usually colloidal, complex combinations of amino acids (containing carbon, hydrogen, oxygen, nitrogen, usually sulfur, occasionally phosphorus) which are essential constituents of all living cells, being responsible for growth and maintenance of all tissue, and the essential nitrogenous constituent of the food of animals. They can be synthesized from inorganic nitrogenous material by plants, but apparently not by animals **pro·tein·a·ceous, pro·téin·ic, pro·téin·ous** adjs

pro tem·po·re (proutémpəri:) adv. and adj. (abbr. pro tem.) for the time being

pro·test (próutest) n. a strong affirmation of, dissent from or disapproval of something done or some policy adopted ‖ a written declaration by a notary of an unpaid or unaccepted bill ‖ a written declaration by the master of a ship giving details of disaster, accident or injury at sea ‖ (in diplomacy etc.) a solemn declaration of disapproval **to do (something) under protest** to do (something) having first stated one's disapproval

pro·test (prətést) v.i. to express strong dissent or objection ‖ v.t. to affirm emphatically ‖ to write a declaration of nonpayment or nonacceptance of (a bill) ‖ to make a protest against

Prot·es·tant (prótistənt) n. a member of any Christian body which separated from the Roman Catholic Church at the Reformation, or of any later offshoot of such a body **prot·es·tant 1.** n. someone who protests **2.** adj. protesting

pro·to·col (próutəkɔl) **1.** n. a code of precedence in rank and status and correct procedure in diplomatic exchange and state ceremonies ‖ a preliminary draft or memorandum of a diplomatic document, e.g. of resolutions arrived at in negotiation to be incorporated in a formal treaty, and signed by the negotiators ‖ official formulas at the beginning and end of a charter, papal bull etc. **2.** v. pres. part. **pro·to·col·ling, pro·to·col·ing** past and past part. **pro·to·colled, pro·to·coled** v.t. to record (something) in a protocol ‖ v.i. to draw up a protocol

pro·ton (próutɒn) n. (phys.) a baryon of mass and net electric charge + 1 that is a constituent of all atomic nuclei (the proton is the nucleus of the lightest hydrogen isotope) ‖ a hydrogen ion of at. mass 1

pro·to·plasm (próutəplæzəm) n. a viscous, translucent, colloidal substance constituting all living cells. It consists of compounds of oxygen, hydrogen, carbon and nitrogen and is usually differentiated into cytoplasm and nucleoplasm **pro·to·plás·mic** adj.

pro·to·type (próutətaip) n. an original model or pattern from which subsequent copies are made, or improved specimens developed ‖ (biol.) an ancestral form or archetype **pro·to·typ·i·cal** (proutətípik'l) adj.

pro·to·zo·an (proutəzóuən) n. a member of Protozoa, a phylum of small (often microscopic) single-celled or colonial organisms. They are of worldwide distribution and are usually restricted to water **pro·to·zó·ic** adj.

pro·tract (proutrǽkt) v.t. to draw out in time, prolong ‖ (surveying) to plot to scale **pro·tráct·ed·ly** adv. **pro·trac·tile** (proutrǽktil) adj. (zool., of an organ etc.) capable of being pushed out, extended or lengthened

pro·trac·tor (proutrǽktər) n. an instrument for measuring or drawing angles on a flat surface, often in the form of a semicircle graduated in 180 degrees ‖ (zool.) a muscle whose function extends a limb or part of the body

pro·trude (proutrú:d) pres. part. **pro·trud·ing** past and past part. **pro·trud·ed** v.t. to thrust forward or outward ‖ v.i. to stick out or project

pro·tru·sion (proutrú:ʒən) n. a protruding or being protruded ‖ something which protrudes

pro·tu·ber·ance (proutú:bərəns, proutjú:bərəns) n. something that is protuberant ‖ the condition of being protuberant

pro·tu·ber·ant (proutú:bərənt, proutjú:bərənt) adj. bulging, swelling out

proud (praud) adj. manifesting inordinate self-esteem ‖ feeling proper satisfaction ‖ arousing or marked by feelings of great satisfaction ‖ having a proper sense of self-esteem ‖ (rhet.) splendid, glorious, a proud heritage ‖ (rhet., of a horse) mettlesome **to do oneself proud** to indulge oneself lavishly **to do someone proud** to honor someone with lavish hospitality or attentions

prove (pru:v) pres. part. **prov·ing** past and past part. **proved,** (old-fash. and legal) **prov·en** (prú:vən) v.t. to establish the truth of by evidence ‖ to show to be true by reasoning ‖ (math.) to test (a calculation) ‖ to test for conformity to standard ‖ to test the alcoholic content of ‖ to establish the authenticity of (a legal document) ‖ to obtain probate of (a will) ‖ to test experimentally ‖ (printing) to proof, take proofs of (a block etc.) ‖ v.i. (sometimes with 'to be') to be shown by later knowledge to be

pro·verb (próvə:rb) n. a brief familiar maxim of folk wisdom, usually compressed in form, often involving a bold image and frequently a jingle that catches the memory

pro·vide (prəváid) pres. part. **pro·vid·ing** past and past part. **pro·vid·ed** v.t. to supply ‖ to equip ‖ (law) to stipulate ‖ v.i. to make advance preparations (for, against some eventuality) ‖ to ensure a supply of the necessities of life **pro·vid·ed** conj. (sometimes with 'that') on condition that, on the understanding that

prov·i·dence (próvidəns) n. prudent looking ahead, forethought ‖ thrift **Prov·i·dence** God as prescient guide and guardian of human beings ‖ divine care and guidance

prov·ince (próvins) n. (Rom. hist.) a territory outside Italy ruled by a Roman governor ‖ an administrative division, sometimes overseas, of certain countries ‖ (eccles.) an area under the charge of an archbishop or metropolitan ‖ (eccles.) an administrative area of a religious order ‖ proper scope of professional or business action ‖ a particular sphere of learning ‖ (pl., with 'the') the parts of a country beyond the capital

pro·vin·cial (prəvínʃəl) **1.** adj. of or relating to a province ‖ characteristic of the provinces in manner, mode or speech ‖ taking or characterized by a limited view **2.** n. a native or inhabitant of a province or of the provinces ‖ (eccles.) a superintendent of the daughter houses of a religious order in a province, responsible to the general of the order **pro·vin·cial·ism** n. the narrow attitude of mind or the unpolished behavior held to be characteristic of the provinces ‖ a word, pronunciation, custom etc. peculiar to a province ‖ love of one's own region not enlarged into patriotism **pro·vin·ci·al·i·ty** (prəvinʃi:ǽliti:) n.

pro·vi·sion (prəvíʒən) **1.** n. a providing or being provided ‖ preparation ‖ a clause in a legal document, esp. a proviso ‖ a supply or stock ‖ (pl.) food supplies **2.** v.t. to supply with provisions **pro·ví·sion·al** adj. temporary, filling an interval until a definite decision is made ‖ requiring later confirmation

prov·o·ca·tion (prɒvəkéiʃən) n. a provoking or being provoked ‖ something which provokes

pro·voc·a·tive (prəvókətiv) adj. tending to provoke ‖ arousing annoyance deliberately ‖ involved in the planning stage of a crime; provocative of a crime

pro·voke (prəvóuk) pres. part. **pro·vok·ing** past and past part. **pro·voked** v.t. to rouse to anger ‖ to incite, instigate, esp. deliberately ‖ to excite, call forth

prow (prau) n. the forepart of a boat or ship, the bow

prow·ess (práuis) n. dexterity and daring ‖ great ability

prowl (praul) **1.** v.i. to roam stealthily in search of prey, or as if in search of prey ‖ v.t. to roam over (a place) in search of prey or as if searching for prey **2.** n. a prowling **on the prowl** prowling

prowl·er (práulər) n. someone who prowls, esp. a sneak thief

prox·i·mate (próksəmit) adj. (in space, time or kinship, or in a series of events) nearest, next ‖ approximate ‖ (of a cause) direct, immediate

prox·im·i·ty (prɒksímiti:) n. the state or quality of being near in space, time or kinship

prox·y (próksi:) **1.** pl. **prox·ies** n. authority given by one person to another to act for him ‖ the person thus authorized ‖ a document empowering a person to act for another **to stand proxy for** to act as proxy for **2.** *adj.* of an act done by a proxy, *a proxy vote*

prude (pru:d) *n.* a person who affects an excessively rigid attitude in matters of personal modesty and proper conduct

pru·dence (prú:d'ns) *n.* foresight leading a person to avoid error or danger ‖ the virtue by which the practical reason distinguishes the things useful for salvation ‖ practical discretion

pru·dent (prú:d'nt) *adj.* (of a person) exercising prudence ‖ (of behavior) guided by prudence

prune (pru:n) *n.* a plum that has been dried without allowing fermentation to take place and that has a dark, wrinkled, pruinose skin

prune (pres. part. **prun·ing** *past* and *past part.* **pruned** *v.t.* to cut off from (a tree or bush) branches, twigs etc. which are diseased or not desired, so as to encourage fruiting or flowering, and to shape ‖ to reduce, cut down ‖ *v.i.* to prune trees or bushes

pru·ri·ent (prúari:ənt) *adj.* (of people) excessively interested in or curious about sexuality ‖ (of ideas, books etc.) tending to excite such interest or curiosity

pry (prai) *pres. part.* **pry·ing** *past* and *past part.* **pried** *v.i.* to look closely into something which is not one's own concern merely to satisfy one's curiosity, *to pry into someone's affairs*

pry 1. *v.t. pres. part.* **pry·ing** *past* and *past part.* **pried** to force open or lift with or as if with a lever ‖ *(fig.)* to extract with difficulty **2.** *pl.* **pries** *n.* a lever used in prying

Psalm (sɑm) *n.* any of the sacred songs in the Book of Psalms ‖ a metrical version of any of these, for chanting **psalm** *(rhet.)* a song to God

pseudo- (sú:dou) *prefix* sham ‖ spurious ‖ unreal ‖ showing a superficial resemblance to ‖ being an abnormal form of

pseu·do·nym (sú:d'nim) *n.* a name other than one's own, assumed for some purpose **pseu·do·nym·i·ty** *n.* **pseu·don·y·mous** (su:dónəməs) *adj.* having or bearing a pseudonym

pshaw (ʃɔ) **1.** *interj. (old-fash.)* used as a mild expression of irritation, disbelief etc. **2.** *n. (old-fash.)* an exclamation of 'pshaw!'

psy·che (sáiki:) *n.* the soul ‖ *(psychol.)* the mind, both conscious and unconscious

psych·e·del·ic (saikidélik) *adj.* of a mental condition induced by certain drugs and characterized by an impression of greatly heightened sensory perception. It may be accompanied by feelings of elation or misery, by hallucinations, or by sharp perceptual distortion ‖ of a drug inducing this state ‖ of patterns, images etc. characteristic of this state

psy·chi·a·trist (sikáiətrist, saikáiətrist) *n.* a doctor who specializes in psychiatry

psy·chi·a·try (sikáiətri:, saikáiətri:) *n.* the branch of medicine concerned with the treatment and study of mental and emotional disorders

psy·chic (sáikik) **1.** *adj.* nonphysical, *psychic forces* ‖ of or pertaining to the mind or spirit ‖ apparently able to respond to nonphysical influences, *a psychic medium* **2.** *n.* a person seemingly sensitive to nonphysical influences ‖ a person able to act as a medium **psy·chi·cal** (sáikik'l) *adj.*

psy·cho·a·nal·y·sis (saikouənǽlisis) *n.* a technique of psychotherapy which renders conscious the contents of the unconscious mind through a dialogue between analyst and analysand ‖ the psychological system or doctrine elaborated from the results of this technique **psy·cho·an·a·lyst** (saikouǽnəlist) *n.* a person who practices psychoanalysis **psy·cho·an·a·lýt·ic,**

psy·cho·an·a·lýt·i·cal *adjs* **psy·cho·an·a·lýt·i·cal·ly** *adv.* **psy·cho·an·a·lyze, psy·cho·an·a·lyse** (saikouǽnəlaiz) *pres. part.* **psy·cho·an·a·lyz·ing, psy·cho·an·a·lys·ing** *past* and *past part.* **psy·cho·an·a·lyzed, psy·cho·an·a·lysed** *v.t.* to subject (someone) to psychoanalytic treatment

psy·cho·gen·ic (saikoudʒénik) *adj.* belonging to or originating in the mind, mental

psy·cho·log·i·cal (saikəlódʒik'l) *adj.* of or pertaining to psychology ‖ of or relating to the mind

psy·chol·o·gy (saikólədʒi:) *n.* the scientific study of human or animal behavior ‖ the mental and behavioral characteristics of a person or group ‖ the mental characteristics associated with a particular kind of behavior

psy·cho·path (sáikəpæθ) *n.* a person suffering from a mental disorder

psy·cho·sis (saikóusis) *pl.* **psy·cho·ses** (saikóusi:z) *n.* serious mental derangement

psy·cho·so·mat·ic (saikousəmǽtik) *adj.* of, pertaining to or resulting from the interaction between mind and body

psy·cho·ther·a·pist (saikouθérəpist) *n.* a person who practices psychotherapy

psy·cho·ther·a·py (saikouθérəpi:) *n.* the treatment of mental illness by psychological methods, esp. psychoanalysis

pto·maine (tóumein, touméin) *n.* any of a number of alkaloids, some highly poisonous, formed by the action of bacteria on putrefying proteins

ptomaine poisoning poisoning by ptomaines ‖ *(pop.)* any food poisoning

pu·ber·ty (pjú:bərti:) *n.* the period of life when the reproductive glands begin to function ‖ the condition of becoming able to reproduce

pu·bes·cence (pju:bésn's) *n.* the reaching of puberty ‖ *(biol.,* of some plants and certain insects) a downy or hairy covering **pu·bés·cent** *adj.*

pu·bic (pjú:bik) *adj.* of or pertaining to the pubis ‖ of or pertaining to the pubes

pu·bis (pjú:bis) *pl.* **pu·bes** (pjú:bi:z) *n.* the foremost of the three sections of the hipbone

pub·lic (pʌ́blik) **1.** *adj.* of or pertaining to the community as a whole ‖ for the use of the community at large and maintained at the community's expense ‖ that is or can be known by all members of the community ‖ acting for the people ‖ of or relating to the service of the community ‖ often receiving publicity **2.** *n.* (usually with 'the') the members of a community in general ‖ a group or section of a community characterized by some common interest etc. **in public** in the state of being visible or accessible to the public

pub·li·ca·tion (pʌblikéiʃən) *n.* a publishing or being published ‖ the issue of printed matter for public sale or free distribution ‖ a printed and published book, magazine, pamphlet etc.

pub·lic·i·ty (pʌblísiti:) *n.* the whole of the methods and materials used in making an enterprise, product etc. known to the public with a view to increasing business ‖ the methods and materials used in making some noncommercial matter similarly known ‖ the disseminating of advertising or informative matter ‖ the condition of being exposed to the knowledge of the general public, esp. through newspaper reports

pub·li·cize (pʌ́blisaiz) *pres. part.* **pub·li·ciz·ing** *past* and *past part.* **pub·li·cized** *v.t.* to bring to public notice

pub·lish (pʌ́bliʃ) *v.t.* to arrange the printing and distribution of (books, newspapers etc.) for sale to the public ‖ *(loosely)* to be the author of (a work thus offered to the public) ‖ to make known to the public ‖ to announce publicly **púb·lish·er** *n.* someone who arranges for the multiplication of copies of a work

---

(a) æ, cat; ɑ, car; ɔ fawn; ei, snake. **(e)** e, hen; i:, sheep; iə, deer; ɛə, bear. **(i)** i, fish; ai, tiger; ə:, bird. **(o)** o, ox; au, cow; ou, goat; u, poor; ɔi, royal. **(u)** ʌ, duck; u, bull; u:, goose; ə, bacillus; ju:, cube. x, loch; θ, think; ð, bother; z, Zen; ʒ, corsage; dʒ, savage; ŋ, orangutang; j, yak; ʃ, fish; tʃ, fetch; 'l, rabble; 'n, redden. Complete pronunciation key appears inside front cover.

(a book, record, sheet music etc.) and for their handling by distributive agencies. He remunerates, or is remunerated by, the author (or performer etc.) according to the terms of the contract made between them

puck (pʌk) *n.* a hard rubber disk used in ice hockey as the object to be shot into the goal

puck·er (pʌ́kər) **1.** *v.t.* (often with 'up') to gather into narrow folds or wrinkles ‖ *v.i.* to become gathered into narrow folds or wrinkles **2.** *n.* a narrow fold or wrinkle, or a number of them together

pud·ding (púdiŋ) *n.* a sweet dessert, thick and soft, typically composed of flour and milk and eggs and sometimes fruit ‖ *(naut.)* a pad of rope etc. used as a fender

pud·dle (pʌ́d'l) **1.** *n.* a small pool of liquid, esp. rainwater ‖ clay and sand kneaded together with water and used to construct a watertight lining for the bank of a canal, the bottom of a pond etc. **2.** *v. pres. part.* **pud·dling** *past and past part.* **pud·dled** *v.t.* to knead (clay, sand and water or concrete etc.) into an impervious mass ‖ to stir (molten iron) in order to reduce its carbon content ‖ to make (water etc.) dirty ‖ *v.i.* to dabble in mud etc. ‖ to play about messily with paints, clay etc. **púd·dly** *adj.* having many puddles, *a puddly road*

pudge (pʌdʒ) *n.* *(pop.)* a short, fat person **púdg·i·ness** *n.* the quality of being pudgy **púdg·y** *comp.* **pudg·i·er** *superl.* **pudg·i·est** *adj.* short and fat

pueb·lo (pwéblou) **1.** *pl.* **pueb·los** *n.* a type of Indian village in the southwest U.S.A. and some parts of Latin America built as communal dwelling houses of adobe or stone **Pueb·lo** a member of certain Indian tribes of Arizona and New Mexico, e.g. the Zuñi and the Hopi, inhabiting such a village ‖ their languages **2. Pueb·lo** *adj.* of the Pueblo Indians or their culture

pu·er·ile (pjú:əril, pjú:ərail) *adj.* (of an adult's ideas, behavior) not befitting an adult, childish **pu·er·il·i·ty** (pju:əríliti:) *n.*

puff (pʌf) **1.** *v.i.* to breathe quickly, esp. after exertion ‖ to emit steam, smoke etc. in a series of whiffs or puffs ‖ to blow in rapid gusts, whiffs or puffs ‖ (with 'up' or 'out') to swell, become inflated ‖ (with 'at' or 'on') to draw (on a pipe etc.) ‖ *v.t.* to blow or emit in whiffs or puffs ‖ to draw on (a pipe, cigar, or cigarette), emitting puffs of smoke ‖ (with 'out') to extinguish (a candle etc.) by blowing on it ‖ (with 'up' or 'out') to cause to swell, inflate ‖ (with 'out') to arrange (hair etc.) in a loose, fluffy mass ‖ (sometimes with 'up') to praise excessively ‖ (with 'up') to make conceited **2.** *n.* a short, light gust of air, steam, smoke etc. ‖ a small cloud, emission of smoke etc. ‖ a draw on a cigarette etc. ‖ a shell of soft light pastry etc. ‖ a fluffy mass ‖ a powder puff ‖ a quilt ‖ a laudatory critical notice written to publicize a work ‖ publisher's blurb ‖ *(genetics)* an intensely active portion of an enlarged chromosome

pug (pʌg) *n.* a dog of a small, short-haired breed having a broad, flat nose and short, tightly curled tail

pu·gil·ism (pjú:dʒəlizəm) *n.* boxing **pú·gil·ist** *n.* a boxer **pu·gil·ís·tic** *adj.*

pug·na·cious (pʌgnéiʃəs) *adj.* fond of fighting, aggressive

puke (pju:k) **1.** *v. pres. part.* **puk·ing** *past and past part.* **puked** *v.i.* *(pop.)* to vomit ‖ *v.t.* *(pop.)* to vomit **2.** *n.* *(pop.)* vomit

pul·chri·tude (pʌ́lkritu:d, pʌ́lkritju:d) *n.* *(rhet.)* physical beauty

pull (pul) **1.** *v.t.* to apply a force to (something) in order to make it move towards the person or thing applying the force ‖ to extract, *to pull a tooth* ‖ to strain (a muscle etc.) ‖ (sometimes with 'up') to uproot (vegetables etc.) ‖ to draw out (a knife, gun etc.) ready for use ‖ to draw off (beer) from a container ‖ *(pop.)* to accomplish with daring, *to pull a coup* ‖ *(pop.)* to assert (superiority) in order to obtain an advantage over someone ‖ *v.i.* to apply a force to something in

order to make it move towards the person or thing applying the force ‖ to be capable of being so moved ‖ (often with 'away', 'ahead', 'into', 'out' etc.) to move by means of physical or mechanical energy ‖ (with 'at') to draw (on a pipe) ‖ (with 'at') to take a drink (from a bottle) ‖ to row a boat **to pull around** to handle (a person) roughly **to pull a fast one** to play an unfair trick **to pull apart, to pull to pieces** to tear apart ‖ to find great fault with (a piece of work etc.) **to pull down** to demolish (a building) ‖ to weaken in health **to pull for** *(pop.)* to encourage by shouting or cheering **to pull off** to be finally successful in (something difficult or chancy) **to pull oneself together** to regain control of one's emotions or behavior **to pull one's punches** (of a boxer) to abstain from hitting as hard as one can ‖ to criticize or accuse less forcibly than would be justifiable **to pull one's weight** to take one's full share of work or responsibility **to pull out** (of a vehicle) to move out from the side of the road or from the line of traffic ‖ *(pop.)* to leave, esp. to abandon some group effort **to pull over** (of a vehicle) to move suddenly across the road or move to the edge of the road **to pull through** to survive illness, danger etc. ‖ to enable (someone) to survive illness, danger etc. **to pull together** to cooperate in a task **to pull up** (of a moving vehicle, horse etc.) to come to a stop ‖ to improve one's position relative to other competitors in a race **2.** *n.* the act of pulling ‖ an instance of this ‖ a force which pulls or attracts ‖ an effort necessary for forward or upward movement ‖ a draw on a cigarette, drink etc. ‖ *(golf, baseball, cricket* etc.) a stroke which pulls the ball ‖ the force needed to pull a bow or the trigger of a firearm ‖ an advantage due to influence, relationship etc. ‖ influence exerted to obtain a privilege or advantage ‖ a knob, handle etc. by which a drawer, bell etc. may be pulled ‖ *(printing)* a proof ‖ the checking of a horse by pulling on the bridle, esp. to prevent it from winning a race ‖ a row (in a boat etc.) ‖ a distance or period of time spent in rowing

pul·let (púlit) *n.* a hen before the first moult

pul·ley (púli:) *pl.* **pul·leys** *n.* a wheel with a grooved rim, used to raise or lower a load attached to one end of a rope, chain etc. passing around the groove and pulled from the other end ‖ a wheel on a fixed shaft used to transmit power by means of a belt, chain etc. passing over its circumference

pul·mo·nar·y (púlmənəri:) *adj.* of, like or affecting the lungs ‖ pulmonate ‖ of the artery conveying blood from the heart to the lungs ‖ of the vein conveying blood from the lungs to the heart

pulp (pʌlp) **1.** *n.* a soft, moist mass of animal or vegetable matter ‖ such a part of a fruit (e.g. of an orange) or of an animal body (e.g. of a tooth) ‖ soft pithy matter found in plant stems ‖ a mixture, made by mechanical or chemical treatment of wood, consisting of water and cellulose fibers, and used as the raw material in papermaking **2.** *v.t.* to make into a pulp ‖ *v.i.* to become a pulp **púlp·i·ness** *n.* the quality or state of being pulpy

pul·pit (púlpit, pʌ́lpit) *n.* a small stone or wooden structure reached by a short flight of stairs and from which a preacher preaches, in a church or chapel

pul·sate (pʌ́lseit) *pres. part.* **pul·sat·ing** *past and past part.* **pul·sat·ed** *v.i.* to move rhythmically to and fro, esp. to expand and contract in a regular way (e.g. of the heart) ‖ to be as if throbbing or vibrating

pulse (pʌls) **1.** *n.* the regular expansion and contraction of the arteries due to the rhythmical action of the heart in forcing blood through them ‖ the frequency with which the resultant throbs occur ‖ a single one of these throbs ‖ the magnitude of the arterial expansions and contractions ‖ the best in music or verse ‖ any rhythmical beat ‖ a disturbance of brief duration transmitted through a medium ‖ a transitory disturbance of voltage, current, pressure or some other normally constant quantity ‖ a generalized group sentiment divined rather than known by direct experience **2.** *v. pres. part.* **puls·ing** *past* and *past part.* **pulsed** *v.i.* to pulsate ‖ *v.t.* to emit in a regular succession of pulses or waves

pul·ver·ize (pʌ́lvəraiz) *pres. part.* **pul·ver·iz·ing** *past* and *past part.* **pul·ver·ized** *v.t.* to reduce to a fine powder ‖ to defeat with devastating effect ‖ *v.i.* to become powder **púl·ver·iz·er** *n.* someone who or something which pulverizes ‖ a harrow for breaking soil into a fine tilth

pu·ma (pjú:mə) *pl.* **pu·mas, pu·ma** *n.* a cougar ‖ the fur of the cougar

pum·ice (pʌ́mis) **1.** *n.* a light, porous volcanic stone formed by the escape of steam or gas from cooling lava, used as an abrasive in cleaning, smoothing and polishing ‖ a piece of this **2.** *v.t. pres. part.* **pum·ic·ing** *past* and *past part.* **pum·iced** to clean, smooth or polish with pumice

pump (pʌmp) **1.** *n.* a device for raising or moving a liquid or gas by decreasing or increasing the pressure on it ‖ an act or the process of pumping **2.** *v.t.* to raise, move or eject by using a pump or as if with a pump (sometimes with 'out') to remove a liquid or gas from ‖ to supply with air by means of a pump or bellows ‖ (usually with 'up') to inflate by means of a pump ‖ to inject (someone) with a stream of something ‖ to extract information from (a person) by subtle questions ‖ to move (something) energetically up and down as if working a pump handle ‖ to invest (capital) heavily in a business, industry etc. ‖ *v.i.* to work a pump

pump *n. (old-fash.)* a man's light shoe fitting without laces or other fastening, esp. one of patent leather worn with evening dress ‖ a lady's high-heeled shoe without fastenings

pum·per·nick·el (pʌ́mpərnik'l) *n.* a very dark, close-textured German wholemeal rye bread

pump·kin (pʌ́mpkin) *n.* a genus of vines bearing a large, edible, globular fruit with a firm yellowish-orange rind ‖ the fruit of such a plant

pun (pʌn) **1.** *n.* a witticism involving the playful use of a word in different senses or of words which differ in meaning but sound alike **2.** *v.i. pres. part.* **pun·ning** *past* and *past part.* **punned** to make a pun

punch (pʌntʃ) **1.** *v.t.* to indent or make a hole in (metal, paper etc.) using a punch ‖ to make (this indentation or hole) ‖ to strike with the closed fist ‖ to herd (cattle) **2.** *n.* the action of punching ‖ a blow with the closed fist ‖ forcefulness

punch *n.* a tool, usually cylindrical but tapered at one end, used to emboss or make holes in metal, paper etc. ‖ a tool for forcing a bolt from a hole ‖ a tool for driving the head of a nail beneath a surface ‖ a tool used to stamp a die or impress a design

punch *n.* a drink composed of sugar, spice and fruit, usually mixed with wine or liquor, and drunk hot or cold

punc·til·i·ous (pʌŋktíli:əs) *adj.* paying scrupulous attention to points of detail in behavior, ceremony or matters touching one's honor

punc·tu·al (pʌ́ŋktʃu:əl) *adj.* occurring, arriving etc. at the agreed, right or stated time ‖ of or pertaining to a point ‖ having the nature of a point **punc·tu·ál·i·ty** *n.* the quality of being punctual

punc·tu·ate (pʌ́ŋktʃu:eit) *pres. part.* **punc·tu·at·ing** *past* and *past part.* **punc·tu·at·ed** *v.t.* to mark the divisions of (written matter) into sentences, clauses etc. or to indicate exclamation, interrogation, direct speech etc. by inserting punctuation marks ‖ to interrupt by, or intersperse with, sound or gesture ‖ *v.i.* to use punctuation

punc·tu·a·tion (pʌŋktʃu:éiʃən) *n.* a punctuating or being punctuated ‖ the act, practice or system of inserting the correct marks to punctuate written matter ‖ punctuation marks

punc·ture (pʌ́ŋktʃər) **1.** *n.* the act of making a hole in something by pricking ‖ a small hole made thus, esp. one made accidentally in a tire **2.** *v. pres. part.* **punc·tur·ing** *past* and *past part.* **punc·tured** *v.t.* to make a small hole in by pricking ‖ to make (a hole, perforation etc.) by pricking ‖ to sustain a puncture in ‖ to destroy as if by pricking and deflating ‖ *v.i.* (of a tire etc.) to sustain a puncture

pun·gent (pʌ́ndʒənt) *adj.* pricking or stinging to the taste or smell ‖ (of speech or writing) sharply biting ‖ (of remarks, a speech etc.) forthright and very much to the point

pun·ish (pʌ́niʃ) *v.t.* to cause to suffer for some offense committed ‖ to prescribe a form of suffering in penalty for (an offense) ‖ *(pop.)* to treat harshly, *to punish an engine* ‖ *(pop.)* to deal (someone) hard blows ‖ *v.i.* to inflict punishment **to take a punishing** to be subjected to rough treatment **pún·ish·a·ble** *adj.* deserving or capable of being, or liable to be, punished **pún·ish·ment** *n.* a punishing or being punished ‖ the suffering given or received

punk (pʌŋk) **1.** *n.* a person, esp. a young one, regarded as inferior **2.** *adj. (pop.)* worthless, of poor quality

punt (pʌnt) **1.** *n.* a long, shallow, square-ended, flat-bottomed boat, usually propelled by thrusting a long pole with a two-pronged iron end on the riverbed **2.** *v.t.* to propel (someone or something) in this way ‖ *v.i.* to go by punt

pu·ny (pjú:ni:) *comp.* **pu·ni·er** *superl.* **pu·ni·est** *adj.* much below normal in development, size or strength

pup (pʌp) **1.** *n.* a puppy ‖ a young seal **2.** *v.i. pres. part.* **pup·ping** *past* and *past part.* **pupped** (of a bitch) to bring forth young **to sell someone a pup** to sell someone something which proves to be worthless

pu·pa (pjú:pə) *pl.* **pu·pae** (pjú:pi:), **pu·pas** *n.* the stage in the metamorphosis of an insect between the larva and the imago, in which the insect is enclosed in a hardened case ‖ an insect in this stage **pú·pal** *adj.*

pu·pate (pjú:peit) *pres. part.* **pu·pat·ing** *past* and *past part.* **pu·pat·ed** *v.i.* to pass into or through the pupal stage **pu·pá·tion** *n.*

pu·pil (pjú:p'l) *n.* a person, esp. a child, receiving tuition ‖ *(Rom. and Scot. civil law)* a child under the age of puberty in the care of a guardian

pupil *n.* the aperture in the iris of the eye, contracted or dilated by the muscles of the iris to control the amount of light entering the eye

pup·pet (pʌ́pit) *n.* a small model of a human being or an animal with mobile limbs controlled by strings or wires, or made in the form of a glove and operated by a hand inserted in it ‖ a person whose actions are initiated nad controlled by the will of another **pup·pet·eer** (pʌpitíər) *n.* a person who operates puppets **púp·pet·ry** *n.* the art of making or operating puppets

pur·chase (pə́:rtʃəs) **1.** *v.t. pres. part.* **pur·chas·ing** *past* and *past part.* **pur·chased** to acquire by paying money ‖ to acquire at the cost of sacrifice, work, exposure to danger etc. ‖ *(law)* to become the owner of (real estate) otherwise than by inheritance ‖ to move or raise by means of a lever, pulley etc. **2.** *n.* the act of purchasing ‖ a thing purchased ‖ (in assessing value) annual yield in rent ‖ mechanical advantage gained by the use of a pulley, lever etc. ‖ a device, e.g. a lever or pulley, by which this may be gained ‖ a hold or position in which leverage may be applied

---

pure (pjuər) *comp.* **pur·er** *superl.* **pur·est** *adj.* (of a substance) free from the presence of any other substance ‖ free from contamination or admixture ‖ free from moral guilt ‖ (*fig.*) unalloyed ‖ chaste, *a pure girl* ‖ not lascivious ‖ not turned or related to practical use, *pure mathematics* ‖ (of an animal) with an unmixed ancestry ‖ (*phon.*, of a vowel) not diphthongized ‖ (of a language) free from foreign elements ‖ (*philos.*) a priori ‖ (*phys.*, of a note) due to one simple periodic vibration, unmixed with any overtones

pu·rée (pjuréi, pjurí:) 1. *n.* a thick liquid prepared by forcing cooked fruit or vegetables through a sieve ‖ a thick soup prepared in this way 2. *v.i.* to make a purée of (fruits or vegetables)

pur·ga·tive (pɔ́:rgətiv) 1. *adj.* having the quality of purging (esp. the bowels) 2. *n.* a medicine which has this quality

pur·ga·to·ry (pɔ́:rgətɔri, pɔ́:rgətouri) *pl.* **pur·ga·to·ries** *n.* a condition or place of purification, esp. (*Roman Catholicism*) the state or place where the souls of the departed, though in a condition of grace, are purified by suffering before they enter paradise ‖ a condition of suffering

purge (pɔ:rdʒ) 1. *v. pres. part.* **purg·ing** *past* and *past part.* **purged** *v.t.* to cause (the bowels) to be evacuated by administering or taking a purgative ‖ to remove undesirable elements from, *to purge a political party* ‖ to make expiation for, *to purge a sin* ‖ to clear (oneself or another) of a charge or suspicion 2. *n.* a purging or being purged ‖ a purgative

pu·ri·fy (pjúərifai) *pres. part.* **pu·ri·fy·ing** *past* and *past part.* **pu·ri·fied** *v.t.* to make pure by removing impurities ‖ to free from guilt or sin ‖ to free from corrupting elements

pur·ism (pjúərizəm) *n.* strict emphasis on purity, esp. in language ‖ an instance of this

pur·ist (pjúərist) *n.* a person who places great emphasis or overemphasis on linguistic purity (freedom from foreign words or bastard forms etc.) ‖ a person, who will admit no departures from some chosen method, technique or ideal of perfection

Pu·ri·tan (pjúəritən) *n.* (*hist.*) a member of a Protestant movement in England (16th and 17th cc.) which sought to purify worship in the Church of England by excluding everything for which authority could not be found in the Bible **pu·ri·tan** 1. *n.* a person who seeks to regulate his own way of life and that of the community by a narrow moral code, esp. someone who intolerantly denounces many usual pleasures as sinful or corrupting 2. *adj.* of or relating to the Puritans **pu·ri·tán·ic, pu·ri·tán·i·cal** *adjs* **Pú·ri·tan·ism, pú·ri·tan·ism** *ns*

pu·ri·ty (pjúəriti:) *n.* the state or quality of being pure

purl (pə:rl) 1. *n.* a stitch in knitting in which the yarn is held in front of the work and the right needle is inserted into a stitch in front of the left needle to form a new stitch 2. *v.t.* to invert (stitches) in knitting ‖ to make (a garment) in purl stitches ‖ to border or decorate with purl ‖ *v.i.* to do purl stitches

purl 1. *v.i.* (of little streams) to flow in eddies, making pleasing soft sounds 2. *n.* the sound or movement of purling

pur·loin (pə:rlɔ́in, pɔ́:rlɔin) *v.t.* to steal

pur·ple (pɔ́:rp'l) 1. *n.* a composite deep color of red and blue ‖ a pigment, fabric etc. of this color ‖ Tyrian purple **the purple** royal or very noble rank 2. *adj.* of the color purple 3. *v. pres. part.* **pur·pling** *past* and *past part.* **pur·pled** *v.i.* to assume a purple color ‖ *v.t.* to make purple

pur·port (pə:rpɔ́rt, pə:rpóurt) *v.t.* (*rhet.*) to have as meaning or purpose ‖ (with 'to be') to be meant to appear 2. (pɔ́:rpɔrt, pɔ́:rpourt) *n.* the meaning of a document, speech etc.

pur·pose (pɔ́:rpəs) *n.* a result which it is desired to obtain and which is kept in mind in performing an action ‖ (*old-fash.*) willpower **on purpose** deliberately, intentionally ‖ with a specific intention **to no**

(little, good) purpose with no (little, good) effect **to the purpose** relevant **púr·pose·ful** *adj.* serving or having a purpose **púr·pose·less** *adj.* **púr·pose·ly** *adv.* on purpose **púr·pos·ive** *adj.* purposeful

purr (pə:r) 1. *n.* the soft, intermittent vibratory sound made by a contented cat ‖ a similar sound 2. *v.i.* to make this sound

purse (pə:rs) 1. *n.* a small container for coins etc., carried in a pocket or handbag ‖ a handbag ‖ a sum of money collected for a charity, or offered as a gift or prize ‖ (*rhet.*) financial resources ‖ a baglike receptacle **to hold the purse strings** to control the money in a household etc. 2. *v.t. pres. part.* **purs·ing** *past* and *past part.* **pursed** (sometimes with 'up') to pucker

purs·er (pɔ́:rsər) *n.* a ship's officer responsible for accounts etc. and for the welfare of passengers on a passenger boat

pur·su·ant (pərsú:ənt) 1. *adj.* (*rhet.*) pursuing 2. *adv.* (with 'to') in accordance with

pur·sue (pərsú:) *pres. part.* **pur·su·ing** *past* and *past part.* **pur·sued** *v.t.* to follow in order to capture, overtake etc. ‖ to harass (someone) persistently ‖ to inflict persistent attentions on (someone) ‖ to continue with ‖ to engage in ‖ to go on talking about ‖ *v.i.* to go in pursuit ‖ to resume an argument or narrative after interruption

pur·suit (pərsú:t) *n.* the act of pursuing ‖ the act of proceeding with or towards an aim ‖ an occupation, *an aimless pursuit*

pu·ru·lent (pjúərulənt, pjúərjulənt) *adj.* consisting of, or exuding pus

pur·vey (pə:rvéi) *v.t.* (*old-fash.*) to supply (groceries) as a commercial activity ‖ to provide (information)

pur·view (pɔ́:rvju:) *n.* the extent of the meaning of a document ‖ the extent of the knowledge, authority or responsibility etc. of a person, group etc. ‖ (*law*) that part of a statute which includes the enacting clauses

pus (pʌs) *n.* yellowish-white fluid matter, produced by infected body tissue, and composed of bacteria and disintegrated tissue

push (puʃ) 1. *v.t.* to apply a force to (something) in order to make it move away from the person or thing applying the force ‖ to move (something) away or forward by applying such a force ‖ to make (a way) by forcing obstacles aside ‖ (with 'up', 'down', 'along' etc.) to cause to move by exerting pressure ‖ (with 'up') to cause (something) to increase as if under pressure ‖ to exert influence upon (someone) so that he acts in a desired way ‖ *v.i.* to apply a force to something in order to make it move away from the person or thing applying the force ‖ to move by the application of such force ‖ to make a steady effort towards some end ‖ to advance, esp. with persistence or energy **to push off** (*pop.*) to leave **to push on** to proceed, esp. with determination **to push one's luck** to act rashly, take a dangerous risk 2. *n.* the act of pushing ‖ an instance of this ‖ a force which pushes ‖ (*mil.*) an offensive ‖ influence, *to use push* ‖ self-assertion, aggressive drive

push·o·ver (púʃouvər) *n.* (*pop.*) something very easy to accomplish, or very easily accomplished ‖ (*pop.*) a person easily persuaded, tricked etc.

pu·sil·lan·i·mous (pjuːsəlænəməs) *adj.* showing a lack of moral courage

puss·y (púsi:) *pl.* **puss·ies** *n.* (pet name for) a cat

puss·y·foot (púsi:fut) *v.i.* (*pop.*) to avoid committing oneself

pus·tule (pʌ́stʃuːl) *n.* a tiny abscess on the skin surface ‖ (*zool.*) a warty excrescence on the skin, e.g. in toads ‖ (*bot.*) a small wart or swelling on a leaf, either natural or caused by parasitic influence

put (put) 1. *v. pres. part.* **put·ting** *past* and *past part.* **put** *v.t.* to cause to be in a specified place, position etc. ‖ to cause to be in a specified condition, situation, relationship etc. ‖ to submit for attention or consideration ‖ to cause to be voted on ‖ (usually followed by 'in' or 'into') to formulate, *put it in writing* ‖ (followed by 'on', 'upon') to impose, *to put a tax on beer* ‖ (followed by 'to' or 'into') to apply, bring to bear, *to put one's mind to a problem* ‖ (followed by 'on') to lay (blame, responsibility etc.) ‖ (followed by 'in or 'into') to invest, *to put one's money in' copper shares* ‖ (followed by 'on') to gamble (money), *he put his last penny on that horse* ‖ to fix (a limit etc.), *to put an end to something* ‖ *v.i.* (of a ship) to take a specified course **to put across** to convey effectively the meaning, dramatic effect etc. of **to put aside** to place to one side, esp. as of no immediate use or importance ‖ to save (money etc.) for later use **to put away** to place (something) where it should be when not in use ‖ to have (an animal) killed painlessly **to put back** to restore (something) to its former place ‖ to move the hands of (a clock) backwards **to put down** to stop (a rebellion etc.) by force ‖ to commit to writing ‖ to pay as deposit **to put forward** to submit (a proposal etc.) for attention or consideration ‖ to propose (someone or oneself) as a candidate **to put in** to present (a claim) ‖ to do (a specified amount of a specified activity) ‖ (of a boat) to enter a port **to put it on** to pretend **to put it over** (someone) *(pop.)* to deceive (someone) **to put it past (someone) to do (something)** *(neg. and interrog.)* to consider (someone) morally incapable of doing (something) **to put off** to postpone (something planned) ‖ to postpone an engagement made with (someone) ‖ to cause (someone) to cease to like something ‖ to cause (someone) to be unable to concentrate on something ‖ to avoid giving a direct answer to (someone) or undertaking (something) **to put on** to clothe oneself with ‖ to assume (an attitude, expression etc.) deceptively ‖ to apply (a brake etc.) ‖ to cause (a light etc.) to work ‖ to increase (speed) ‖ **to put out** to extinguish (a flame, light or fire) ‖ to publish **to put over** to convey effectively the meaning, dramatic effect etc. of ‖ to postpone ‖ to succeed in doing (something) by craft or against odds **to put through** to cause to undergo ‖ to negotiate (a business deal) **to put together** to assemble **to put up** to offer (resistance, a fight etc.) ‖ to offer (someone) as candidate ‖ to offer oneself as candidate ‖ to provide (someone) with lodging ‖ to be provided with lodging at a hotel etc. ‖ to provide (financial backing) ‖ to stake (money) ‖ to construct ‖ to offer (for sale, auction etc.) ‖ (with 'to') to incite (a person) to some action, esp. to some mischief or crime **to put upon** to impose on **to put up with** to endure, esp. without resentment or complaint **2.** *n.* a throw of the weight or shot **3.** *adj.* (in the phrase) **to stay put** to remain in the same position, condition, situation etc.

pu·ta·tive (pjú:tətiv) *adj.* commonly thought to be, reputed

pu·tre·fac·tion (pjụ:trifǽkʃən) *n.* the chemical decomposition of animal or vegetable tissue, esp. proteins, caused by bacteria, fungi etc.

pu·tre·fy (pjú:trifai) *v. pres. part.* **pu·tre·fy·ing** *past and past part.* **pu·tre·fied** *v.i.* to become putrid ‖ *v.t.* to cause to become putrid

pu·trid (pjú:trid) *adj.* rotten, decayed ‖ of, relating to or caused by decay **pu·trid·i·ty** *n.*

putt (pʌt) **1.** *v.t.* *(golf)* to strike (the ball) gently so that it rolls across the green towards the hole ‖ *v.i.* *(golf)* to play the ball in this way **2.** *n.* *(golf)* a stroke made in this way

putt·er (pʌtər) *n.* *(golf)* a short-shafted wood or iron with an almost vertical face, used for putting

put·ter (pʌtər) *v.i.* to busy oneself in an agreeable though somewhat aimless way ‖ to loiter, dawdle

put·ty (pʌti:) **1.** *n.* powdered chalk mixed with linseed oil to form a highly malleable mass which hardens when the oil oxidizes, used e.g. to hold window glass in its frame ‖ any of several other malleable cements made with linseed oil ‖ impure tin oxide used for polishing by jewelers **2.** *v.t. pres. part.* **put·ty·ing** *past and past part.* **put·tied** to fix, fill or cover with putty

puz·zle (pʌz'l) **1.** *v. pres. part.* **puz·zling** *past and past part.* **puz·zled** *v.t.* to perplex (someone) ‖ *v.i.* to make a great mental effort to find a solution or meaning **to puzzle out** to find (a solution or meaning) by means of great mental effort **2.** *n.* a question or device which sets a problem to be worked out by ingenuity ‖ something which puzzles ‖ the state of being puzzled

pyg·my, pig·my (pígmi:) **1.** *pl.* **pyg·mies, pig·mies** *n.* a person of very small stature **Pyg·my, Pig·my** *pl.* **Pyg·mies, Pig·mies** a member of a Negrillo people of very small stature of equatorial Africa **2.** *adj.* of or relating to a person of very small stature **Pyg·my, Pig·my** of or relating to the Pygmies

py·lon (páilɒn) *n.* a lofty structure, typically of open steelwork, used esp. to carry electric cables etc. over a long span ‖ *(archit.)* a large monumental gateway having two truncated pyramidal towers, esp. on an ancient Egyptian temple

py·or·rhe·a, py·or·rhoe·a (pạiərí:ə) *n.* *(med.)* a discharge of pus, esp. from the gums

pyr·a·mid (pírəmid) **1.** *n.* *(geom.)* a solid figure of which the base is a polygon and the other faces are triangles with a common vertex ‖ any of the very large square-based stone monuments of this form, constructed by the ancient Egyptians as royal burial places and by the Aztecs and Mayas as centers of ritual worship ‖ anything shaped thus ‖ a group of things piled up or arranged in this form ‖ *(anat.)* any of various parts resembling this form **2.** *v.t.* to build up in the form of a pyramid **py·ra·mi·dal** (pirǽmid'l) *adj.*

pyre (páiər) *n.* a heaped mass of material for the burning of a corpse

py·ro·ma·ni·a (pạirouméini:ə) *n.* an irrational compulsion to destroy by fire **py·ro·ma·ni·ac** (pạirouméini:æk) *n.* **py·ro·ma·ni·a·cal** (pạiroumənáiək'l) *adj.*

py·rom·e·ter (pairómitər) *n.* an instrument used to measure temperatures too high for ordinary thermometers **py·ro·met·ric** (pạiroumétrik), **py·ro·mét·ri·cal** *adjs* **py·róm·e·try** *n.*

py·ro·tech·nics (pạiroutékniks) *n.* the art of making or displaying fireworks ‖ *(pl.)* a brilliant or witty display **py·ro·tech·nist, pý·ro·tech·ny** *ns*

py·thon (páiθɒn, páiθən) *n.* a genus of nonvenomous snakes up to 30 ft long, which kill their prey by constriction, native to the Old World tropics ‖ any of several large snakes which kill by constriction